TO THE STUDENT: A Study Guide for the textbook is available through your college bookstore under the title Study Guide to accompany **CHILD DEVEL-OPMENT: A TOPICAL APPROACH** by **Alison Clarke-Stewart, Susan Friedman, and Joanne Koch.** The Study Guide can help you with course material by acting as a tutorial, review and study aid. If the Study Guide is not in stock, ask the bookstore manager to order a copy for you.

CHILD DEVELOPMENT
A Topical Approach

CHILD DEVELOPMENT
A Topical Approach

ALISON CLARKE-STEWART
University of California at Irvine

SUSAN FRIEDMAN

JOANNE KOCH

JOHN WILEY & SONS
New York
Chichester
Brisbane
Toronto
Singapore

COVER PHOTO: Marion Bernstein
COVER AND BOOK DESIGNER: Joan A. Willens
PHOTO EDITOR: Linda Gutierrez
PRODUCTION SUPERVISOR: Maryellen Costa
COPY EDITOR: Andrew Yockers

Library of Congress Cataloging in Publication Data:

ISBN 0-471-81347-8

Printed in the United States of America

10 9 8 7 6 5 4 3 2

To Christopher and to Andrew David

PREFACE

To write a comprehensive and engrossing book about the early years of human development has been our goal from the very moment, one rainy winter morning, that we first sat around the conference table in the Wiley library and sketched out the bare bones of a plan. For Alison, this would be the book that she, as a developmental psychologist, teacher, and mother of a young boy, had always wanted to write. Here would be a chance to cull work from the best and the brightest in every corner of developmental psychology and to organize the topics into broad conceptual chunks—an organization that made most sense to her for teaching capable undergraduates. For Susan, as a writer and mother of an even younger boy, this would be a chance to present the data clearly, cogently, and understandably. And so, halfway through their first cups of coffee, the plan of attack was clear to both of them: Alison would dig and delve through the literature on human development, and Susan would translate into English. Because Alison had written a chronologically organized text on children's development, *Children, Development through Adolescence,* we made arrangements with her coauthor, Joanne Koch, to borrow some sections from that text. The present book would expand the previous one in areas that had boomed since the latter had appeared in 1981 (such as information processing and the development of emotions), and it would be pitched at a somewhat more advanced and technical level. It would give more detail about what studies in developmental psychology are actually like, by describing individual exemplary studies. It would, as the earlier text had, reflect the latest thoughts in the field without neglecting the classics. Its focus would be on the normal development of most children in our own culture, but exceptions to the course of normal development would also be discussed: hyperactivity, autism, obesity, anorexia, Down's syndrome, childhood diseases, sudden infant death syndrome, and so on. Development in other cultures would be mentioned when it would illustrate important points about the diversity and range of environments that support human development. Equal stress would be given to norms and milestones of development and to individual differences in the rate and outcomes of development. Considerable attention would be paid to the social milieu as a context for development and a source of concern in discussions of day care, divorce, child abuse and neglect, television, gender-role socialization, and so on.

A handshake, a thousand phone calls, and a trillion pages later, we hopefully present you with our results. To the extent that this book illuminates for you the complex processes of human development, we have met our goals. To the extent that it does not, we would like to hear from you, our readers, about how we might clarify and improve it.

We have organized the book to cover the major topics in developmental psychology:

- Foundations—the history of the field plus the seminal topics of heredity and environment.

- Beginnings—which includes prenatal and infant development.

- Physical Bases—physical growth and emotions.

- Cognition—not only its structure, but how people process information, the nature of intelligence, and human language.

- Social Relations and Understanding—including what psychologists know about family life and friendships.

- Personality—moral development and becoming an individual.

We have included a number of features that we believe will supplement this organization and make the text useful for teachers and students alike.

- The nature-nurture issue, which is central in developmental psychology, is explored at the outset of the text, where a separate chapter is devoted to each.

- Each chapter also contains both relevant theory and research findings.

- Research Focus boxes in each chapter describe particular studies in detail, to give a glimpse of relevant research methods.

- Key glossary terms are highlighted.

- Annotated suggested readings and summaries appear after each chapter.

- Supplementary materials include a Study Guide, Test File, and Microtest.

ACKNOWLEDGMENTS

We have had support of several indispensable friends during the labor that has produced this book. These include the editorial staff at Wiley—Mark Mochary, editor, Carol Luitjens, publisher, and Susan Goodall, tireless assistant, and the production staff as well—Susan Winick, Joan Willens, Maryellen Costa, and Linda Gutierrez. Beth Ferrant checked and double-checked the hundreds of references and somehow kept her sanity. Fergus Craik read parts of the manuscript and offered valuable suggestions for its improvement.

We owe double thanks to Harris, Andrew, and Christopher for putting up with us when we got bleary-eyed, for their perpetual good nature, and for being, in the final analysis, what makes it all worthwhile.

Alison Clarke-Stewart
Susan Friedman

CONTENTS

RESEARCH FOCUS BOXES

CHILD DEVELOPMENT
A Topical Approach

PART I

FOUNDATIONS

CHAPTER 1

History, Theories, and Methods

THE CHILD BEFORE THE SCIENCE OF CHILD PSYCHOLOGY

Today a child is regarded as someone to be cherished, a tender and precious human being who must be nurtured and protected. A child's development is worthy of careful attention and scientific study. This view of the child, which our society tends to take for granted, is distinctly modern. Popular views of childhood in the 16th and 17th centuries were radically different from those we hold dear. Specific child-rearing practices in England and the American colonies during this period were, to our present way of thinking, cruel and inhumane.

Rules for child behavior were not adapted to the special needs and limitations of children, and children were frequently beaten for any infraction. Children were to stand when adults entered a room and to remain standing and silent until they were given permission to sit or speak. In dire circumstances, they might even be given the death penalty were they chronically disobedient to their parents.

In the sixteenth and seventeenth centuries parents dressed their children like little adults and expected them to behave like grown-ups. This portrait of Mrs. Freake and her baby Mary, painted in 1674, even gave mother and daughter similar somber expressions.

Infants were tightly swaddled and hung like bundles on the wall while parents went about their tasks. If infants or children were noisy, they were given alcohol or opiates. Advances made by infants and children, which we today await patiently and herald as important phases of their development, were scorned. Crawling, for example, was regarded by many parents as animal-like. From the moment they could stand, children were made to wear special clothes that were reinforced with iron and whalebone and that held them in adult postures. Many children were sent away from home to work as servants when they were as young as 6 or 7 years old. At the age when a child of the 1980s would be entering first grade, children of the 1600s were starting their first full-time jobs; at their workplaces they were treated even more harshly than at home. A child's will had to be broken, it was believed, or society would be thrown into chaos. From 1500 until the mid-1700s, such views and practices went unquestioned.

The goal for child rearing at that time was salvation. Puritans in particular, because of their fundamentalist religion, considered it necessary to stamp out sin in children. There was no choice but to defeat the child, to bend the child's initially satanic will by hard work and constant, even severe, punishment. It was less important to raise a healthy or happy child than a saved child. Happiness could well be the mark of the devil, playfulness and cheeriness signs of damnation.

As for health, accurate information on the ways to make children—and adults—thrive was totally lacking. Before 1750 only one out of four children survived to the age of 5 in the city of London. Although conditions were somewhat more favorable in the country and in small villages, there, too, children's lives were very often short and not so sweet.

The health of the poor was more endangered than that of the rich, but ignorance was rampant at every level of society. Breast feeding was considered vulgar; those who could afford servants passed their infants to wet nurses. These women were poor and were already nursing their own children and sometimes others as well. They therefore lacked an adequate diet for themselves and an adequate supply of milk for the babies. Because people knew nothing about germs, let alone inoculations or the need for antiseptic conditions, and because medical treatment was primitive, diseases raged unchecked. There were no effective methods of birth control; adults simply abandoned unwanted children or killed them (Piers, 1978). In Paris, for every three births registered, one child was abandoned. Abandonment was tantamount to infanticide. In foundling homes, unwanted children faced nearly certain death. Records for Dublin during the 18th century indicate that of 10,272 infants admitted to one such home, only 45 survived (Kessen, 1965). The strong possibility that a child would die may have kept parents emotionally detached, thereby adding psychological burdens to the physical dangers children endured.

The notion that development is a gradual physical and mental progress, with crawling preceding walking and impulsiveness preceding self-control was not popular centuries ago. Parents generally expected adult behavior from children. Children were regarded much like dogs or horses: they needed training in adult behavior. The 16th- and 17th-century emphasis on child training foreshadowed the recognition in the 18th century that childhood is a unique and crucial period of human life.

THE CHILD AS FATHER OF THE MAN: LOCKE AND ROUSSEAU

Child development as a field of study belongs to the 20th century. Yet the field has a "family tree," with its own influential forebears, the first of whom were philosophers of the 18th century. During that time, children first were recognized as proper subjects of inquiry and concern.

The idea that early experience could have a profound effect on adult life was expressed forcefully in the writings of physician and philosopher John Locke (1632–1704). In his *Essay Concerning Human Understanding* and *Some Thoughts Concerning Education,* first published in the 1690s, Locke (1794) opposed the idea that children are innately sinful. He proposed that the newborn child was like a blank slate or *tabula rasa* upon which experience would write its story. Contact with adults and the outside world would establish the character and mental ability that would be the child's unique gift or curse throughout life. Locke believed that because childhood shaped later behavior and was

the period during which lifelong habits are formed, it deserved a great deal of attention. If parents took the time to guide children into the path of reason, to teach them socially desirable habits, to help them to control their appetites and impulses, they would surely see the fruits of their labor as their children grew into rational and responsible members of society.

Parents were also to encourage children's curiosity. In Locke's view, children could become rational only if they learned to express their curiosity. Parents could provide encouragement by answering their children's questions with previously unheard-of attentiveness and respect. If parents behaved in the eminently rational fashion Locke described, they would automatically command the child's respect, attention, and affection. Punishment would not be necessary. Although Locke admitted to some innate differences in children's intelligence and temperament, his emphasis on learning and his depiction of the parent as a rational tutor shaping a virtually empty but infinitely receptive student made him the forerunner of modern psychologists who believe that children develop through the influence of the external environment. Locke rejected the idea of innate knowlege, which had been much discussed in the 17th century. In contemporary terms, Locke would be regarded as the first significant champion of **nurture** as the force behind development rather than **nature**.

Jean-Jacques Rousseau (1712–1778), writing some 50 years after Locke's death, further revolutionized human thought about the child. With the publication in 1762 of *Émile, or a Treatise on Education,* Rousseau offered a view of childhood that laid the basis for educational reform in his time and that is still debated today. If Locke was the first champion of nurture as the force behind development, Rousseau was the first outspoken proponent of nature. Even more than Locke, Rousseau believed in the importance and uniqueness of childhood. He regarded children as qualitatively different from adults, not merely as incomplete adults or uninformed students. Children must be understood and valued for what they are rather than for what they will become. They are born as physical and psychological individuals, and adults need to respond to this individuality rather than leveling it in the name of reason or social good. Rousseau saw the child as a busy, testing, motivated explorer of the world, using it to suit his or her individual interests. Adults do not have a monopoly on knowledge. Theirs is knowledge of only one, limited variety. It cannot be poured into a child as into a vessel, for children construct knowledge naturally, as they live and grow. They are capable of discovering for themselves how the world operates. With Rousseau, the nature-nurture controversy, a debate that has been central to developmental psychology, was first joined.

Children should be allowed to grow as nature dictates, asserted Rousseau, with little guidance or pressure from parents. Only through a natural unfolding of ability and a self-motivated exploration of the world would children eventually arrive at an ability to understand and use logic. Only at this point, reached late in childhood, should an adult reason with children and teach them. In Rousseau's writings, the term "development" as applied to children begins to take on its modern usage. Rousseau introduced the concept of developmental stages, a concept that would figure significantly in subsequent studies of children. It was Rousseau who insisted that the needs of children change as they pass through certain developmental stages and that these stages are not created by, or imposed by, adults but are present as potentialities and emerge without adult intervention.

THE SCIENTIFIC FOREFATHER: DARWIN

The scientific basis for the concept of developmental stages in human life was provided nearly 100 years after Rousseau, when Charles Darwin (1809–1882) shook the world with his theory of evolution. Development was a central theme of his *Origin of Species*, published in 1859. Species develop; societies develop; human beings develop. The development of a child offers a microcosm of the development of *homo sapiens*. From the publication of *Origin of Species* to the end of the 19th century, many thinkers were intrigued with drawing parallels between animal and child, between primitive human and child, between early human history and child development. The developing human being was seen as a natural museum of human **phylogeny** and history. Thus the child's development was believed to reveal the unfolding

of the species. By careful observation of the infant and child, the descent of the human species could be traced. The search for phylogenetic and societal clues in the child's development marked the beginning of a science of child behavior. Thus Darwin was truly the scientific forefather of child psychology.

Darwin also brought scientific respectability to a method for studying children that remains vitally important today. Like the developmentalists who came after him, Darwin believed that as the human being develops and grows in the first years, it is useful to record the visible changes. Darwin kept a "baby journal," a systematic record of observations, in this case of his firstborn child, William Erasmus or "Doddy" (Kessen, 1965). The baby journal became the first major tool, the first systematic method of collecting information in developmental psychology.

THE EARLY 20TH CENTURY: CHILD PSYCHOLOGY BECOMES A SCIENCE

G. Stanley Hall (1844–1924) brought Darwin's wide-ranging curiosity and naturalist's outlook to the new study of human behavior known as psychology. Hall believed that to understand human development would be to unlock the secrets of human life. Towards this end, he wrote prodigiously on a wide range of subjects. Hall produced more than 400 books and papers: psychological investigations of Jesus Christ, sex, old age, morality, music, physical education, and many others. It was Hall who founded the *American Journal of Psychology*, and it was he who taught men like Thomas Dewey, Arnold Gesell, and Lewis Terman, men who would lead the next generation of psychologists.

Hall's contributions to psychology, and specifically child and adolescent psychology, derived from his dedication to developing the questionnaire as an investigative tool and his enduring interest in the evolution of the young. Hall made the study of children's behavior a legitimate pursuit for psychologists. He wrote many papers on children, including "The Contents of Children's Minds," "The Story of a Sand Pile," and "A Study of Dolls." These were enthusiastic, spirited, if scientifically undisciplined attempts to fathom children's development. Hall oversaw more than 100 questionnaire studies on many topics, yet he is criticized for having neglected the rigors of the **scientific method.**

Before the 1880s the concept of adolescence, as we commonly understand it today, did not exist (Demos and Demos, 1969). Although people had been concerned about the "irreverent and unruly spirit [that] has come to be prevalent, an outrageous evil among the young people of our land" (Burton, 1863), adolescence as a distinct and distinctive period did not enter into popular consciousness until the end of the nineteenth century. The change accompanied the movement of many families from a rural to an urban culture, a shift that fractured family life into age-defined units. A continuity of work and attitude had characterized rural families, "a continuum between the generations" (Demos and Demos, 1969, p. 636), in which children were essentially miniature adults. But by the end of the century, popular and scientific literature began to regard children and adolescents as special groups whose behavior, if sometimes unusual, was appropriate to their particular stage.

In 1904, Hall virtually created adolescence as a subject of scientific inquiry with the publication of his monumental, two-volume *Adolescence*. There he integrated the previous century's scientific, literary, and anthropological works. As a staunch Darwinist, Hall believed that adolescence would prove the bridge between humans in their present state and the "super anthropoids" into which they would evolve. Correctly identifying idealism as a peculiarly adolescent trait, Hall mistakenly assumed that idealistic beliefs would be translated automatically into idealistic acts. He also believed that sexuality first appeared in adolescence and that sexuality and physical growth were more important then than cognitive growth. Hall depicted adolescence as a period of *Sturm und Drang*—**storm and stress**— and this stereotype of adolescence as a period of disruptions and extremism lives on today.

Certain of Hall's views were controversial. He came to champion the psychoanalytic work of the ambitious young doctor from Vienna, Sigmund Freud; and at Clark University in Worcester, Massachusetts, where he taught psychology and became president, Hall hosted Freud's only American visit. For his interests in psychoanalysis and sex, his

In 1909 G. Stanley Hall convened a historic gathering of psychoanalysts at Clark University, of which he was president. He is shown here (bottom center) with Sigmund Freud (bottom left), Carl Jung (bottom right) and, in the back row A.A. Brill (a translator of Freud's work), Sandor Ferenzi, and Ernest Jones (a well known American psychoanalyst). This meeting marked the beginning of Freud's enormous influence on American psychology and culture.

more conservative peers never forgave him. Hall rarely confined himself to a single theory or method—for which he also has been criticized. In fact, the very breadth of his interests at a time when psychology was forming itself into firmly identifiable schools of thought ultimately limited Hall's influence. Hall was a generalist at a time when specialists took all the laurels, an intuitive, passionate enthusiast at a time when dispassionate, precise measurement and observation were the rule.

Thus, at the turn of the century, the study of children, or "child study," was established as an independent discipline. Societies and Hall's journal for the communication of information about research on children had been launched, and a series of biographical studies focusing on the childhood years appeared. Yet the field had no tools by which to gather the objective and quantifiable data necessary to science. Its only methods of study were observational accounts, which regarded children rather like trees or botanical plants, and Hall's questionnaires, which were meant to call forth retrospective recollections of childhood from adults.

It was in France, early in this century, that child study became a science. Alfred Binet (1857–1911) and Théophile Simon (1873–1961) developed the first objective and standardized intelligence test, in response to a practical problem confronting the French school administration. Was it possible to measure individual differences in mental ability so

The four Research Focus boxes in this chapter illustrate the evolution of research methods and questions starting with G. Stanley Hall's 1896 "A Study of Dolls" and continuing all the way to Jay Belsky and colleagues' "Maternal Stimulation and Infant Exploratory Competence: Cross-sectional, Correlational, and Experimental Analyses," published in 1980. As the very language of these two articles' titles implies, the attitudes and investigative methods of developmentalists have changed profoundly in the course of nearly a century of research. Hall's first attempts at working with questionnaires as research tools and his (as you will see) rather quaint, subjective approach have given way increasingly to detachment, objectivity, and scientific rigor. In Hall's study of children and their dolls, we see little that can be considered theoretical influence. In contrast, the 1950 study of infants' drinking from cups by Robert Sears and George Wise, is rife with theoretical considerations, and the 1973 study of the effects of television by Lynette Friedrich and Aletha Huston Stein has strong theoretical underpinnings.

For our purposes in this chapter, these four studies are important as illustrations of varied *methods* of research. Hall's questionnaire, Sears's interviews, Belsky's combination of methods, and Friedrich and Huston Stein's experiment illustrate techniques that remain useful to developmentalists today.

RESEARCH FOCUS

A STUDY OF DOLLS

G. Stanley Hall believed that because dolls were so popular among children, "so nearly universal among both savage and civilized peoples," and because playing with dolls showed children's instincts at work, a study of dolls would be exceptionally important to the young and growing field of child psychology. He therefore designed a series of questions about children's experiences with their dolls and circulated them among some 800 teachers and parents. He received 648 completed questionnaires—a good return by any standard. Hall remarked that the quality and authorship of the completed questionnaires varied. Some consisted of long reminiscences by adults about their own experiences with dolls, some were mothers' observations of their children's doll play, and some were children's own reports of their doll play. Hall wrote:

There were also school compositions by pupils of high and normal schools; 94 boys were reported on, the rest were girls; 96 were reminiscences, and the majority were written by females between 14 and 24. . . . It was decided that, intractable, and lacking in uniformity as it was, it merited as careful a statistical treatment as could be given it, and this laborious task was finally undertaken (Ellis and Hall, 1896, cited in Kessen, 1965, p. 153).

Hall began to codify and categorize the thousands of pages of manuscript returned by his subjects. There were no computers in 1896, no courses in statistics. Hall was charting new territory as he worked with the returned questionnaires. He first described:

"Material of Which Dolls Are Made, Substitutes, and Proxies"

Of 845 children, with 989 preferences, between the ages of three and twelve, 191 preferred wax dolls; 163, paper dolls; 153, china dolls; 144, rag dolls; 116, bisque dolls; 83, china and cloth dolls; 69, rubber dolls; 12, china and kid [leather] dolls; 11, pasteboard dolls; 7, plaster of Paris dolls; 6, wood dolls; 3, knit dolls; while a few each preferred papier-maché, clay, glass, cotton, tin, celluloid, French, Japanese, brownie, Chinese, sailor, negro, Eskimo dolls, etc. (Kessen, 1965, p. 153).

Hall believed that nothing illustrated the "doll instinct" and the "vigor of the animistic fancy" so well as the kinds of doll substitutes children made. He presented a list of these substitutes, which gives a charming example of the flavor of his research:

Pillows were treated as dolls by 39 children, who often tied strings around the middle of the pillow, using a shawl for the skirt; sticks, sometimes dressed in flowers, leaves and twisted grass were used by 29; bottles, filled with different-colored water and called different people, some with doll-head corks, by 24; cob or ear of corn (red ears favored, corn silk for the hair, a daisy perhaps serving for a hat) by 19; dogs by 18; cats and kittens by 15 (Kessen, 1965, p. 154).

Rudimentary as his methods were, out of Hall's "statistical" descriptions emerge a detailed picture of children's play late in the Victorian era. Children,

that "mentally defective" children could be identified and specially educated? Binet and Simon were charged with developing a series of tests to measure mental ability. They were the first to bring to the study of children a quantitive yardstick, a way of comparing one individual to another on the basis of certain identifiable and measurable characteristics.

The intelligence tests developed by Binet and Simon consisted of a set of questions, starting with the least difficult, ending with the most difficult, and covering a range of intellectual abilities from visual perception to verbal definitions. The tests were given in a standard manner to all children, and their scores were then compared to **norms,** which

Binet and Simon established by determining how many questions a large number of children of the same chronological age could answer correctly. No longer did school administrators have to rely on loose categories of "moron," "imbecile," and "idiot" as assigned by unreliable judges and unscientific procedures. The actual tests were later widely accepted in the United States and elsewhere, but even more significant was the fact that Binet and Simon had established a method with the virtues of objectivity, quantification, and standardization.

Arnold Lucius Gesell (1880–1961) also relied on systematic observations of many different children at different ages, but he, unlike Binet and Simon, developed his methods to prove a theoret-

---

then as now, were treating the household cat and dog as dolls and, in imaginative leaps, saw dolls in bottles of colored water, clothespins, vegetables, and pillows.

Hall was interested in when and how children learned that dolls are not real. Later psychologists would similarly be interested in the relationshp between fantasy and reality. Hall wrote that children continued to *feel* that their dolls were flesh and blood long after they *knew* that they were wood, wax, or china. He describes how the child, finding a doll's head to be hollow or filled with sawdust, may grow so disenchanted as to give up playing with dolls forever. "It seems," he wrote, "to be at about the age of six, three years before the culmination of the doll passion, that the conflict between fancy and reality becomes clearly manifest." One little girl had tried hard to keep her doll from knowing that she (the doll) was not alive.

Hall's questionnaire responses convey the real affection children have for their dolls and the degree to which the psychic life of child and doll are intertwined. Thus deaf girls teach their dolls "the finger alphabet," and dolls share "every secret and confidence in solitude . . . so that the child's psychic life seems entirely bound up with it." The features his respondents loved in their dolls describe a Victorian standard of beauty:

In our returns curly hair is preferred to straight; red cheeks are a special point of beauty, as are red knees in fewer cases. Boy dolls are only about one-twelfth of all,

and it is remarkable how few dolls are babies rather than little adults . . .

Out of 579 answers . . . 88 mentioned preference for blue eyes; 27, for brown eyes; and 8, for black eyes. As to hair preferences 118 mention light hair; 62, curly hair, 27, dark hair; 8, real hair; and 5, red hair, while 15 mention love for red cheeks; 7, nice teeth; 8, pretty hands or feet; 3, red lips (Kessen, 1965, p. 157).

The doll study included sections on feeding and disciplining dolls, on doll's sleep, illnesses, names, hygiene, families, and accessories. Hall noted that there seemed to be no "law of relationship"—what today's researcher might term a correlation—between the size of a doll and the size or age of its child-owner. He took up the question of sex differences, too, and whether boys did or should play with dolls. Boys, he found, "are naturally fond of and should play with dolls." Hall believed it was unfortunate that doll play was considered right for girls rather than boys. Although one must beware of making boys effeminate, Hall said, he was nevertheless convinced that "on the whole, more play with girl dolls by boys would tend to make them more sympathetic with girls as children, if not more tender with their wives and with women later." (Kessen, 1965, p. 160).

Hall believed that the study of doll play was supremely well suited to opening up the "juvenile soul to the student of childhood." He understood that children often hide things, knowingly or not, from adult inquisitors—a problem that all researchers into child development must still contend with.

ical point. Some of his methods (e.g., the photographic dome, a room within a room for observing children's activities without disturbing them[1]), have held up better than his theory. The information he collected with his observational methods also has held up well. Schedules of ages at which most children reach developmental milestones are still available in such works as *An Atlas of Infant Behavior* (1934) and *Infant and Child in the Culture of Today* (1943), written with Louise Ames and Frances Ilg, and are used by parents to measure the progress of their own children today. But these detailed schedules of development were all designed to demonstrate Gesell's pet theory, that development is, to use his word, **maturational,** and rooted in anatomy and physiology. For example, when the bodies of children are sufficiently developed, they will learn to walk. Gesell obtained a medical degree to help him understand physical development.

In Gesell we hear echoes of Rousseau. To his mind, development was a process of "unfolding" or "blooming." Environment was merely the setting for this unfolding, contributing only a slight variation or modification of development.

The tempo and trend of development in each infant appear to be constitutional characteristics, for the most part hereditary in nature. . . . [The child] benefits liberally from what is good in our practice, and suffers less than he logically should from our unenlightenment (Gesell, 1928, p. 116).

But even while Gesell was making his early systematic observations at his clinic, his hereditarian views were being overshadowed by those of his contemporary, John Watson.

Between 1913 and 1920 John Broadus Watson (1878–1958) "shook the house of psychology to its foundations" (Kessen, 1965, p. 228). At that time, consciousness and the contents of the mind were considered primary subjects of psychology, and introspection was the method of studying them. Psychology asked questions of adults about their subjective experiences of specific stimuli. Watson regarded introspective reports as unverifiable

and the procedure inapplicable to his special interests, which were the study of animals and young children. He sought to establish a single discipline of psychology that would use one method consistently. His solution was to reduce all of psychology to the "least common denominator," the observation of behavior. The approach known as **behaviorism** was born.

"Psychology as the behaviorist views it," wrote Watson in 1913, "is a purely objective experimental branch of natural science. Its theoretical goal is the prediction and control of behavior" (p. 158). Following Watson's 1913 manifesto, the field of psychology changed in the United States from the science of mind to the science of behavior, to the study of explicit stimuli and observable responses. Watson soon associated his notion that behavior was predictable and controllable with the work of Ivan Pavlov (1849–1936) on the conditioning of reflexes in dogs. In 1918, he began experimentation with children and used the techniques of **classical conditioning** in an attempt to prove that they could be taught or conditioned to fear previously neutral objects, just as Pavlov's dogs were conditioned to salivate at the sound of a bell. Here

John Broadus Watson sought to make psychology an objective natural science by giving it one direction and one method, the observation of behavior.

---

[1] The opening photograph for this chapter shows Gesell in his photographic dome.

is an excerpt from Watson's *Psychological Care of Infant and Child* (1928).

Fear of all [things other than loud sounds or sudden loss of support] is home-made. Now to prove it. Again I put in front of you the nine month old infant. I have my assistant take his old playmate, the rabbit, out of its pasteboard box and hand it to him. He starts to reach for it. But just as his hands touch it I bang the steel bar behind his head. He whimpers and cries and shows fear. Then I wait awhile. I give him his blocks to play with. He quiets down and soon becomes busy with them. Again my assistant shows him the rabbit. This time he reacts to it quite slowly. He doesn't plunge his hands out as quickly and eagerly as before. Finally he does touch it gingerly. Again I strike the steel bar behind his head. Again I get a pronounced fear response. Then I let him quiet down. He plays with his blocks. Again the assistant brings in the rabbit. This time something new develops. No longer do I have to rap the steel bar behind his head to bring out fear. He shows fear at the sight of the rabbit. *He makes the same reaction to it that he makes to the sound of the steel bar. He begins to cry and turn away the moment he sees it (p. 52–53).*

In such writings, Watson comes across as almost ghoulishly dispassionate. Through his work, experimental manipulation of behavior and systematic observation of its effects became a hallmark of experimental child psychology.

As a result of their success at modifying children's behavior in such experiments, Watson and his followers took a strong stand in claiming that development is environmentally determined. Learning and development, they asserted, are brought about through external means, through the kind of progressive conditioning that could be demonstrated on a small scale in the laboratory. While Gesell was reassuring parents that children with problems would outgrow their temporary disequilibrium, Watson was charging parents with complete and total responsibility for any fear, misbehavior, or other negative conditioning they might perpetrate:

All we have to start with in building a human being is a lively squirming bit of flesh, capable of making a few simple responses such as movements of the hands and arms and fingers and toes, crying and smiling, making certain sounds with its throat. . . . Parents take this raw material and begin to fashion it in ways to suit themselves. This means that parents, whether they know it or not, start intensive training of the child at birth (Watson, 1928, pp. 45–46).

Watson may have left parents with an unreasonable view of their responsibilities, but he endowed child study with something valuable, an experimental method.

Earlier, while Watson was still working out his behaviorist manifesto and Gesell was still collecting material for his doctoral dissertation in psychology, Sigmund Freud (1856–1939) was preparing *Three Contributions to the Sexual Theory,* first published in Vienna in 1905, then translated and published in America in 1910. This work exploded previous conceptions of children by ascribing to them a sexual life, a sexual drive right from the beginning. Freud's patients had revealed childhood thoughts and feelings that suggested sexuality was present from birth. "The newborn child," he wrote, "brings with it germs of sexual feelings." To a society that was still repressive in its public attitudes, the notion of sexuality in an innocent child was anathema. Freud was undaunted by the shock he aroused. He would later write:

Childhood was looked upon as "innocent" and free from the lusts of sex, and the fight with the "demon of sensuality" was not thought to begin until the troubled age of puberty. Such occasional sexual activities as it had been impossible to overlook in children were put down as signs of degeneracy and premature depravity or as a curious freak of nature. Few of the findings of psychoanalysis met with such universal contradictions or have aroused such an outburst of indignation as the assertion that the sexual function starts at the beginning of life and reveals its presence by important signs even in childhood. And yet no other finding of analysis can be demonstrated so easily and so completely (Freud, 1935, pp. 58–59).

A child, as depicted by Freud, was dramatic and complicated. Conflict was present at every stage of development. Even though we "forget," or repress, these conflicts, they determine our entire development. Not only did Freud draw parallels between early physical pleasure and later sexual satisfaction, he also insisted that early sexual experiences influence adult behavior. Thus the pleasure of an infant nursing at its mother's breast foreshadowed adult pleasure in kissing, sucking, or licking, and the events connected with early oral pleasure (or its absence) determined whether the adult would eat too much or drink or smoke heavily. This linking of childhood and adult behavior related events that once had seemed totally unrelated.

Freud's analytical and far-ranging mind theorized a common course in the emotional development of individuals. This theory embraced human behavior throughout the lifespan. Early erotic pleasures, Freud stated, leave behind the profoundest unconscious impressions in the person's memory; if the individual remains healthy they determine his character and if he becomes sick they determine the symptomatology of his neurosis. Instead of positing a sharp break between innocence and experience, Freud said that the drive for pleasure is present in everyone from the beginning. According to Freud, criminals, saints, and ordinary folk alike all have dealt with the same impulses and lived through universal stages in the ongoing drive for gratification.

For Freud, human behavior is not, as Gesell had insisted, directed by heredity. Although driven by biological urges, individuals are deeply affected by the environment and the people in that environment. Freud believed that the influence of the mother is profound. How infants and children come through each stage of development depends on how their mother handles their sexual impulses and behavior. In earliest infancy, during the **oral stage,** the mouth is foremost as a source of sustenance and pleasure, and the mother must not frustrate the baby's impulse to suck and mouth objects. In the second year of life, the child is occupied with pleasures of the anal zone and the conflict between letting go and holding back, between defecating impulsively and conforming to an imposed schedule. In this **anal stage,** the mother's management of toilet training is central. After toilet training is settled, the pleasures of the genitals occupy the child and with them desire for the opposite-sex parent and a wish to displace father as mother's

prime love object (in boys) or mother as father's (in girls). How both parents respond to this **Oedipal** conflict in their son, and **Electra** conflict in their daughters in the **phallic stage** of psychosexual development also profoundly affects children's development.

Freud had what Jerome Bruner calls "the eye of the tragic dramatist." He expressed his unified theory of human behavior in dramatic terms that are well suited to his view of the child as a conflicted character. Freud believed that within each child and adult are three potentially warring mental structures. The blind, energetic, pleasure-seeking **id** represents impulse and is governed by the pleasure principle, which means that it wants whatever satisfies and gratifies—and wants it immediately. The battling **ego** represents "enlightened self-interest" and is governed by the reality principle. Dealing with life as it is, the ego controls impulses and determines which thoughts will rise to the level of consciousness; it is also responsible for logical thinking and the selection of appropriate goals. The moralistic and punitive **superego** represents the imposition of civilization or culture as filtered through parents—rules and regulations of adult society. The superego is synonymous with what we call a "conscience," and it allows the child to exercise some self-control instead of being controlled at all times by parents.

In addition to his theory of psychosexual development, Freud established a method of treating psychiatric patients called **psychoanalysis.** In this method, the therapist helps an individual bring to awareness unconscious thoughts and conflicts. Critics of Freud's theory of development have argued that the lives of the bourgeois European patients from which he drew his information are of little help in charting "normal" development in childhood. Yet Freud changed child psychology with his compelling conception of development. We are all post-Freudians: we agree that children have motivations that are neither rational nor obvious, that they possess at least the beginnings of the sexual and emotional attributes that adults express, that their drive for pleasure often conflicts with the society's need for order and predictability, and that the degree to which children resolve their earlier internal and external conflicts will affect the course of their adult lives.

THE MIDDLE 20TH CENTURY: THEORIES OF CHILD DEVELOPMENT

Between 1930 and 1960 a new wave of significant thinkers appeared. John Dollard, Neal Miller, and Robert Sears were the major figures in the first generation of social-learning theorists (Dollard and Miller, 1950; Sears, Rau, and Alpert, 1965). During this period, all American psychology was dominated by learning theory. After Watson, experiments conducted by Clark Hull and B. F. Skinner went beyond the mechanism of learning offered by classical conditioning. They introduced notions of **drive, reinforcement,** and **operant conditioning,** which became the major mechanisms for explaining behavior change. According to the principles of operant conditioning, individuals act in ways that bring either good or bad consequences. Rewarded by good consequences or punished by bad, they are likely either to repeat or to cease these actions.

Robert Sears used principles of learning theory to explore hypotheses from Freud's psychosexual theory in studies of child rearing and development.

Dollard, Miller, and Sears were students of Clark Hull at Yale University's Institute of Human Relations, founded in 1930. Under Hull they began to apply principles of learning to the issues of child development. One principle of particular interest to them was that of the **learned drive.** The human being has a number of basic biological needs, or **primary drives,** such as hunger and thirst, that are necessary to survival. When other stimuli are regularly associated with the satisfaction of these drives, a person develops a secondary or learned drive for these stimuli.

Because these first social-learning theorists were influenced by Freud as well as by learning theory, they tried to fit Freud's concepts into a stimulus-response framework. For example, they attempted to explain children's deeply emotional and dependent relationship with their mother, a relationship central in Freud's account of development and which he considered an outgrowth of the drive for pleasure, in terms of Hull's learned drives. They proposed that the drive for maternal attention and affection was secondary and learned, stemming from the mother's satisfaction of the infant's primary drive for food. By feeding her infant, soothing it, and relieving pain, a mother creates a bond with her child. How intensely children are attached to their parents depends on the mother's feeding and training practices and the degree to which both parents are reinforcing and nurturant. Thus social-learning theorists focused on mother-child relations, the basis of much current information on child development. They also devised new methods of child study. They conducted in-depth interviews with mothers about their rearing practices. They systematically observed and recorded children's behavior—such as their aggressive acts and what they say—as the children played with a standard set of dolls representing family members. These methods are still used today.

An *émigré* from Europe, a Danish Jew who reached the United States by way of Vienna, Erik Erikson integrated an unconventional and varied background in teaching, psychoanalysis, and anthropology into a theory of human development. In Vienna, Erikson had worked with Anna Freud, Sigmund Freud's daughter, at her school for children being psychoanalyzed or whose parents were being psychoanalyzed. Under her influence, Erikson developed an interpretive approach to children's play, using dolls and other toys for diagnosing children's characters and problems. In America, Erikson observed groups as diverse as Pacific Northwest Indians, Harvard students, soldiers discharged during World War II, and civil rights workers. His varied experience prompted him to adapt and expand psychoanalytic theory.

By 1950, Erikson had incorporated the sequence of changes he had observed in children and adults into a conception of personality development spanning the entire life cycle. Erikson proposed that human development is eased or hindered by the nature and degree of adjustment to social experiences. Erikson adapted Freud's oral, anal, and phallic stages; the vague stretch of **latency;** and the explosive period following puberty, the **genital stage,** to a new framework in which the individual faces a succession of eight crises (Table 1.1). These crises are periods of great vulnerability but also of great potential. Erikson stressed the effects on development of social feelings, such as trust, shame, industry, and intimacy, and the effects of social and cultural events. He also emphasized the possibilities for change throughout the life cycle and the need to study children and adults over time. He stressed adolescence as a period when all previous conflicts are refocused in a youth's comprehensive conflict of establishing a personal identity (Erikson, 1963).

Erikson considered *each* of the eight crises in his life-cycle conception of personality development "a crucial period of increased vulnerability and heightened potential . . . the source of both generational strength and maladjustment" (1968, p. 96). But he regarded adolescence as a turning point among turning points, requiring a resolution of all past crises. Although a person's identity is continuously modified throughout the life cycle, it is during adolescence that the bits and pieces of past crises and resolutions are shaken into a new configuration. Over a period of six or seven years, various aspects of the individual's identity come into focus: the sexual self; a sense of confidence or doubt; work or career goals; personal, ideological values; and feelings of recognition or isolation.

It is as though the self were shifting its design within a kaleidoscope. At adolescence the person is outside the kaleidoscope, looking in at the pieces and recognizing the particular pattern of selfhood,

Erik Erikson adapted, refined and extended Freud's stages of psychosexual development, incorporating into them more of the child's and adult's social experiences.

of inner, maturing identity. The radical change of perspective that initiates this awareness, the double take of self-recognition, is the beginning of the **identity crisis.** The very act of becoming aware of an inner, maturing self is such a profound step in development that people need a period of time to assimilate the pieces and to find the role, the work, the attitude, and the sense of social connectedness that will allow them to assume a place in adult society. Erikson calls this period of experimentation with roles and finding a niche a **psychosocial moratorium.** Erikson did not overemphasize the finality of choices made during this moratorium, for he believed that people have other opportunities for growth after adolescence. But he recognized that a "lasting pattern of 'inner identity' is scheduled for relative completion" during adolescence.

TABLE 1.1
DEVELOPMENTAL PROGRESSION

Age	Freud's stages	Erikson's crises
1st year	*Oral Stage* Infants obtain gratification through stimulation of the mouth, as they suck and bite.	*Trust versus Mistrust* Infants learn to trust, or mistrust, that their needs will be met by the world, especially by the mother.
2nd year	*Anal Stage* Children obtain gratification through exercise of the anal musculature during elimination or retention.	*Autonomy versus Shame, Doubt* Children learn to exercise will, to make choices, to control themselves; or they become uncertain and doubt that they can do things by themselves.
3rd to 5th year	*Phallic (Oedipal) Stage* Children develop sexual curiosity and obtain gratification through masturbation. They have sexual fantasies about the parent of the opposite sex and guilt about their fantasies.	*Initiative versus Guilt* Children learn to initiate activities and enjoy their accomplishments, acquiring direction and purpose. If they are not allowed initiative, they feel guilty for their attempts at independence.
6th year through puberty	*Latency Period* Children's sexual urges are submerged; they put their energies into acquiring cultural skills.	*Industry versus Inferiority* Children develop a sense of industry and curiosity and are eager to learn; or they feel inferior and lose interest in the tasks before them.
Adolescence	*Genital Stage* Adolescents have adult heterosexual desires and seek to satisfy them.	*Identity versus Role Confusion* Adolescents come to see themselves as unique and integrated persons with an ideology; or they become confused about what they want out of life.
Early adulthood		*Intimacy versus Isolation* Young people become able to commit themselves to another person; or they develop a sense of isolation and feel they have no one in the world but themselves.
Middle age		*Generativity versus Stagnation* Adults are willing to have and care for children, to devote themselves to their work and the common good; or they become self-centered and inactive.
Old age		*Integrity versus Despair* Older people enter a period of reflection, becoming assured that their lives have been meaningful, and they grow ready to face death with acceptance and dignity; or they despair for their unaccomplished goals, failures, and ill-spent lives.

Although the so-called "inner laws of development" create what Erikson described as a "succession of potentialities," this ground plan is constantly shaped, enhanced, or, in some cases, distorted by the people who tend and respond to the individual. Institutions, too, can either recognize or ignore a person's special needs. The "widening radius of significant individuals" (1968, p. 93) who interact with the developing child include mother, father, siblings, peers, teachers, mentors, leaders, mates, colleagues, bosses, employees, and grandchildren. As this radius widens, so does the individual's contact with institutions of religious guidance, education, and political action. At each stage of the life cycle, a particular component of personality "comes to its ascendance, meets its crisis, and finds its solution," but each individual's life cycle unfolds in a particular community. Although the ascendance of a particular component of personality may

be predetermined, the crisis and resolution of each phase of personality development must be worked out within specific social and cultural situations. Social interaction, Erikson believed, always influences human development.

As Erikson's theory of identity and life-cycle development was taking hold, a new wave of social-learning theorists was coming to the fore. This second generation of social-learning theorists can be divided into two groups; members of the first, Jacob Gewirtz, Sidney Bijou, Donald Baer, and others, were disciples of the behaviorist B. F. Skinner and stressed operant conditioning. Unlike the disciples of Clark Hull, the Skinnerians disregarded both learned and unlearned drives altogether. Theirs was the most mechanistic learning theory to be applied to social behavior since child study had emerged as a field of investigation. An individual's social behavior, as they viewed it, was completely

RESEARCH FOCUS

A STUDY OF FEEDING AND THUMB SUCKING IN INFANTS

In Robert Sears and George Wise's (1950) study of how weaning from bottle or breast to cup—and therefore from sucking to drinking—affects infants, the theoretical basis of the research is clear and explicit. Their aim was to test empirically a hypothesis of Sigmund Freud. This hypothesis was that an infant's lips and mouth produce pleasurable sensations when they are stimulated by activities like sucking a nipple or a thumb because sucking is associated with feeding. To test this hypothesis however, Sears and Wise, influenced by contemporary American learning theory, restated it thus:

Sucking is an almost universal instrumental act in infant feeding. It is closely followed on nearly every occasion by the goal response of eating. Sucking therefore becomes a secondary goal response, and children may be said to possess an oral drive that instigates sucking and other related oral manipulatory actions (Sears and Wise, 1950, p. 124).

Accordingly, these researchers stated their intention to investigate how much and what kind of influences "infant feeding experiences" exerted.

If Freud's restated hypothesis was correct, Sears and Wise predicted that they would find several

relationships among the strength of the oral drive, the age of weaning, and the frequency with which thumb sucking and other behaviors occurred in reaction to weaning. To test their hunch, Sears and Wise contacted the families of 80 children who were private patients of a Kansas City, Kansas, pediatrician. At the time of the study, which was spring of 1946, the 80 children ranged in age from 2 to 3 and 7 to 10 years old. They came from 75 different families, of which the majority were middle class, Protestant, and headed by a working father and a mother who stayed at home to care for her children. The fathers' median age was 34; the mothers' median age, 31. Sears and Wise believed that all the children studied were normal and healthy members of stable, functioning families. They were selected for the variety of feeding experiences they represented, and "there is no way of knowing how random a sample of the total population" of pediatric patients the group represented.

The study consisted of a series of interviews of mothers who had been asked in a preliminary letter to participate in a study of normal child development. Proceeding from an eight-page mimeographed questionnaire, the interviewer, a man, spent roughly an hour asking about the children's general health and development, sleeping and eating habits, toilet training, social relationships, level

shaped by his or her reinforcement history, by the accumulation of **reinforcement contingencies** over time. They believed that the individual will continue to do what he or she has been rewarded for in the past. The Skinnerians focused on the occasions of stimulus and response in an individual's early life and sought to demonstrate that when desired behavior (response) was followed by reinforcement (stimulus), its repetition was encouraged. For example, Gewirtz (Gewirtz and Boyd, 1977b) applied reinforcement contingency analysis to interaction and attachment between mother and child. He demonstrated that a mother's smiles and playful and encouraging remarks to her child are contingent on the infant's pleased behavior. The infant's smiles, gurgles, and movements toward the mother are in turn strengthened by the contingent responses of the mother. Operant theory has the virtue of being demonstrable, especially in a tightly controlled setting. The effectiveness of simple reinforcement has been amply proved in numerous laboratory experiments.

The natural relations between parents and children appear to involve more than a series of observable stimulus-response events, however. Learning often seems to occur without any obvious reinforcement. Why do children imitate parents and, later, other people, even when others do not appear to be rewarding them for the imitation? A second group of social-learning psychologists, Albert Bandura, Richard Walters, and Walter Mischel, addressed this question and evolved observational-learning theory (Bandura, 1977; Bandura and Walters, 1963; Mischel, 1968). They proposed that children learn social behavior through their eyes and ears merely by observing people and events, which they subsequently imitate. For example, a child may kick a big rubber Bobo doll or donate a

of activity, nervous habits, temperament, and sexual development. The interviewer was careful not to stress feeding habits over other aspects of the children's histories, and he "adopted an objective but interested and sympathetic attitude." Sears and Wise were aware of the limitations inherent in such a plan. First, the interviewer could not record the mothers' comments verbatim, so, the language of the answers was sometimes that of the interviewer. Psychologists did not use tape recorders in 1946. Second, the researchers had to depend on the mothers' inevitably subjective interpretations of their children's behavior. Third, they had to rely on mothers' memories of events, and human memory is never infallible. Despite these acknowledged problems, Sears and Wise believed that the information they gleaned from the interviews provided grounds for testing their original hypothesis.

Sears and Wise broke their data down into several subsets and used it to verify or disprove several different but related questions. First, did the data confirm their hunch that the longer a child feeds by means of sucking, the stronger the child's oral drive will be? To answer the question, they divided the 80 children according to how long they had fed by sucking. A group of 10, they reported, were weaned to the cup by the age of 2 weeks. A middle group of 18 were weaned between 2 weeks and 3 months. The "late" group of 52 children were weaned after 4 months of age. By establishing a scale that assigned a numerical value to the degree of frustration each child demonstrated in reaction to weaning, Sears and Wise quantified their data. The answer was, as they predicted, that the longer a child is fed by sucking, the more disturbed the child is at being weaned.

Sears and Wise then wanted to test whether thumb sucking was related to the strength of the child's oral drive. Here they found only a weak correlation. One could *not* conclude that early weaning produced thumb sucking. They asked another question after dividing the children into groups according to the suddenness of their weaning and assigning a numerical value to each. "If our reasoning is correct," Sears and Wise wrote, "there should be greatest vigor of frustration reactions in the suddenly weaned group and least vigor in the very gradually weaned." Did the data bear them out? Yes. "All differences are in the predicted direction."

How did the data square with the original hypothesis? Sears and Wise believed that they supported it, that infants who fed by sucking had a stronger oral drive than infants fed by drinking from a cup. Despite their limitations, the interviews had been productive.

Albert Bandura maintains that children will imitate the behavior of people they perceive as important, with or without receiving rewards from them.

Konrad Lorenz (1957) showed that a built-in set of biases predisposed animals to learn particular behavior during **sensitive periods** of their existence. For example, for a brief period after hatching, ducklings will follow or **imprint** upon the closest large moving object. Imprinting is meant to be the mechanism by which the duckling "attaches" itself to the mother, but events during this sensitive period can conspire to alter this pattern. Could the same thing happen to human beings?

John Bowlby (1969), originally trained as a psychoanalyst, adopted the ethological perspective in explaining the way in which children form deep and affectionate relationships with their mothers. The infant's goal, like the duckling's, is to stay close to its mother. In the evolutionary past, proximity served the important function of protection. Behavior that the infant is born with, like crying, smiling, and, later, following, allows the child to achieve this closeness to mother, on which the child's so-called **attachment** to her is based. But she may not always be there. Bowlby drew attention to the dangers of maternal deprivation in orphanages and asylums.

All the theorists we have talked about have been important in their own ways, but if we had to single out the individual who had the greatest impact on modern developmental psychology, it would be Jean Piaget. Piaget (1896–1980) was unique in

penny to a charity box after observing an adult do so, without receiving any obvious reward for such behavior.

Bandura set up an innovative program of research into varying conditions under which imitation occurred. He found that, in the laboratory, children are most likely to imitate adults who are nurturant and powerful, who act affectionate and control resources that the children want. In that children receive most of what they want from their parents—from material goods, such as toys, food, and clothing, to psychological benefits, such as love or "fun"—Bandura has suggested that children at home are likely to imitate their parents. Thus parents need not give their little boy a toy to teach him to hold his fork or to act friendly. Their warmth and power guarantee that observed behavior will be imitated.

In the 1950s and 1960s, **ethology,** the study of animal behavior in natural surroundings, became influential. Ethologists Niko Tinbergen (1951) and

Konrad Lorenz demonstrated that goslings will imprint on the closest large, moving object—the mother goose or a white-haired ethologist.

John Bowlby focused the attention of researchers and policy makers on the essential importance for health development of having a strong relationship with mother in the first years of life.

developmental psychology. Rarely does one person's theory so dominate investigation in a particular field. Working virtually alone for many years, Piaget elaborated and tested the most comprehensive and systematic explanation to date of how human thought and knowledge develop from infancy to adulthood. Although Piaget's works were published in French in the 1920s and 1930s, the influence of this Swiss psychologist was not really felt in the United States until the 1960s.

According to Piaget's (1970) **interactionist, structuralist** model of development, knowledge is gained as the individual's mental predisposition to find order in things interacts with information from the environment. For Watson and Skinner, knowledge consisted of an accumulation of discrete bits of information about the outside world over time. For Piaget, the notion of knowledge independent of an internal conceptual context was unthinkable. Knowledge is always put in some order, he insisted; acquiring knowledge is not a matter of simply adding or subtracting discrete units. As chil-

dren actively manipulate and explore their surroundings, Piaget wrote, they are guided by their thoughts, their mental representation of things. Over time these mental representations change qualitatively. Ways of representing and organizing knowledge about the world, which Piaget called "mental structures," are constructed as the child interacts with the environment. Furthermore, these organizing mental structures appear in a particular order. The sequence of cognitive stages is invariant; the order cannot be shuffled or rearranged, no matter what the environmental circumstances may be.

Children have an inborn tendency both to adapt to, and to learn from, the outside world: they interact with their surroundings much as an explorer would approach a new land. If the environment provides adequate "food for thought," children learn on their own, requiring little direct guidance or tangible reinforcement from parents or teachers. Just as children do not have to be taught deliberately to walk, so they do not have to be taught about time and space and the fact that objects have categorical dimensions and physical properties. They actively construct this knowledge of the physical world through their interactions with objects.

Recall that earlier thinkers about child development like Locke, Watson, and the learning theorists suggested that knowledge was imposed on the child from without, whereas Rousseau and Gesell stressed the innate abilities of children. Piaget brought these two sides into relative balance for the first time. He saw human thought as a creative translation of reality, as information from the environment is organized by the individual's mental processes. Piaget's theory has continued to dominate cognitive research and has also influenced theories of social development. Through his influence, developmental psychologists take into consideration the interactive nature of human experience.

SOCIAL INFLUENCES ON THE STUDY OF CHILD DEVELOPMENT

Theories do not exist in a vacuum. As a field of inquiry, child development grew not just from a progression of theoretical positions and increasingly

Through observing children in their ordinary activities and asking them probing questions, Swiss psychologist Jean Piaget was able to construct a theory of how children's minds develop.

refined empirical methods but from social concerns about the health, education, and welfare of children as well as the general tendency for government to become involved in their destinies.

In the first two decades of the 20th century, services for children expanded rapidly in schools, hospitals, clinics, and social agencies. School enrollment is one index of this expansion. The proportion of children in elementary school during 1870 was 57 percent; by 1910 the figure had risen to 75 percent. "Normal schools" were established to keep pace with the growing need for instruction, and universities added departments of education. In 1912, a federal Children's Bureau was created, concerning itself with the welfare of children and the monitoring of their working conditions. During the 1920s, children's nutrition, physical growth, and dental development became areas of special interest. X-rays, discovered at the end of the nineteenth century, were in wide clinical use by this time, making studies of skeletal growth possible. The Child Guidance Movement concerned itself with problem children and delinquents; workers in the

movement gained insights into the development of delinquency and in 1927 formed their own professional organization, the American Orthopsychiatric Association.

Child Welfare Research Stations, established by the Laura Spelman Rockefeller Memorial Fund at several universities—Iowa, Minnesota, Yale, Berkeley, and Columbia—undertook systematic programs of empirical investigation. The first of these stations began operating in 1917 at the University of Iowa, through the persistent efforts of Mrs. Cora Bussey Hillis. In 1906, she had come to the conclusion that if research could help improve corn and hogs, it could help with the rearing of children (Sears, 1975). It was at these Child Welfare Research Stations that important and invaluable longitudinal studies, including the Berkeley Growth Study and the Berkeley Guidance Study, were begun.

World War II had temporarily interrupted the study of child development, but a new generation of young scientists resumed with renewed enthusiasm. Grants to support research were made available through the National Institute of Mental Health. Carmichael's *Manual of Child Psychology,* first published in 1946, outlined the field: its 1000 pages of information showed norms, averages, and developmental milestones in memory, perception, intelligence, emotions, and personality.

Questions of social relevance have continued to affect the course of child development research. In the 1960s, the influence of the War on Poverty showed up in the formation of Project Head Start, in research on children's early experiences in rich and poor families, and in studies comparing minority groups of various ethnic backgrounds to the white majority. Researchers became conscious of sex differences, too. They paid more attention to adolescents, to the possibility that there may be a separate youth culture, and to discrepancies in the values of the old and young. Researchers began to note **cohort** effects. A cohort is a group of individuals born at the same time. People growing up during a depression, a war, a period of political upheaval, or a time of sex-role reevaluation may develop differently from those born before or after such historical periods. Researchers began to take note of the social influence of television on growing children. Finally, with so many mothers working in jobs outside the home, developmental psycholo-

(a)

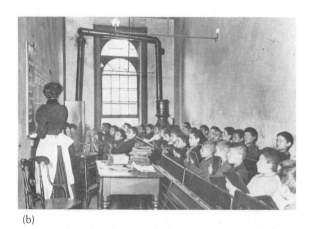
(b)

(c)

(d)

(e)

(a) In the nineteenth century children provided society with useful labor. Huddled over coal, in dust-laden air, these "breaker-boys" spent the long working day picking out slate. (b) In the early 1900s children were taken out of the factories, the mines and the sweatshops and brought into the classroom for education and edification. (c) By the middle of the twentieth century, attention was given to the developing psyches and social adjustment of preschool-aged children. Nursery schools proliferated. (d) The cognitive development of poor children was a major focus of policy efforts and research in the 1960s. Here children in a Head Start class hear a story from their teacher. (e) And in the 1980s a major concern is the provision and quality of day care for infants of working mothers.

gists became more aware of the roles fathers, siblings, grandparents, and baby-sitters play in the development of the child.

STUDY OF CHILD DEVELOPMENT IN THE 1970s

In the 1970s, the field of child development responded to a number of new trends. The first conceptual shift was a "retreat to infancy." Through increasingly sophisticated methods of research and the help of film, videotape, and computers, research frontiers were pushed back farther and farther. Investigators began looking for the origins of development in earliest infancy and, even beyond that, in prenatal events and conditions.

A second, related shift was to view the infant as an initiator. Once considered a helpless, unresponsive creature, buffeted by random stimuli, the infant achieved new status in the 1970s. Infants are now recognized as active, capable of initiating contact and influencing their surroundings from birth. Infants cry and look, vocalize and smile; they manipulate objects, engage the attention of their parents, and place their own stamp on interactions. One result of seeing infants as active participants has been an interest in infants' temperaments and how differences in temperament affect parents and others in the infants' environment. Interactions between infants and adults also have been scrutinized in attempts to document how infants contribute to relationships. The assumption underlying all this work is that infants have and use real skills.

In the 1970s as well, psychologists began to question whether early experience inexorably determines what a child becomes. New or reinterpreted evidence suggested that early experience did not always affect development either irreversibly or permanently—as psychologists had believed.

RESEARCH FOCUS

A STUDY OF TELEVISION'S EFFECTS ON CHILDREN'S BEHAVIOR

By 1973, the science of studying children was no longer itself a child. In that year, Lynette Friedrich and Aletha Huston Stein of Pennsylvania State University published a study of how young children reacted to films in which the content was either aggressive or prosocial, that is, helpful and cooperative.

Their study was one in a long tradition of investigations into the effects of television on children. In a society in which the average child is a veteran TV watcher, developmentalists, parents, government officials, teachers, and others have wanted to learn all they could about the effects of television programs on young, impressionable viewers. Several studies, the authors noted, had investigated the effects of televised violence on children's aggressive behavior, but they were interested in the possible positive influences of television as well.

Friedrich and Stein took pains to describe the theoretical antecedents to their work. They mention, for example, their debt to the influential work of Albert Bandura (1969), in which he theorizes that children can learn to imitate behavior simply by observing it. But imitation does not inevitably follow observation, and it was precisely this that Friedrich and Stein used as their point of departure. As they noted, imitation depends on

the reinforcement consequences that [a child] has experienced or . . . has seen the model experience. Imitative behavior is also more likely when the model has high status, when the model is perceived as similar to the child, when the model is warm and nurturant, and when the environmental conditions for the child are similar to those [the child] has observed (Bandura, 1969, p. 199).

It was their intent to study imitation in a "naturalistic" rather than in a "contrived" setting. Their method is called an observational experiment. The study would consist of experimental manipulations "in order that inferences about causal relations could be made." They would take into account "several intervening variables" that would be expected to influence the effects of television programs on children, variables that included the children's level of intellectual development, how thoroughly the children learned the programs' content, and the children's TV-watching habits at home. They classified the children according to sex,

Some psychologists still advocated continuity of development and continued to search for long-term stabilities. Others began to see discontinuity. The issue still is not settled, and many research studies reflect a bias toward one view or the other. However, gradually psychologists have tended to abandon extreme either-or thinking. They now want to learn how reversible early experiences are, under what circumstances discontinuity is likely, and whether reversibility is likelier for some children than for others.

Similarly, thinking about nature *or* nurture as the force behind development has been modulated. In recent years, developmental psychologists have tried to patch up the nature-nurture split, integrating in any study or explanation the contribution of each. Now they are more likely to talk about *interactions* between nature and nurture—between the child's biologically based (innate) characteristics and abilities and the child's family, school, neigh-

borhood, and culture—or to distinguish between aspects of development that are relatively resistant to the environment and those that are relatively responsive or vulnerable.

Ever since American psychologists "discovered" Piaget in the early 1960s, the field of child development had felt a "cognitive revolution." Thus there was an abundance of studies on the perception of form and depth and the establishment of perceptual constancies, and studies on how children assemble words into sentences and learn grammar. In the 1970s, investigators of social and emotional development sought to integrate into their work the methods, findings, and theoretical explanations from studies of cognitive development. A new field of developmental study, social cognition, was created. The increasing sophistication of research in the 1970s allowed for the integration of findings and theories from different fields of developmental psychology.

social class, and initial levels of aggressive and prosocial behavior.

The subjects were 97 children—52 boys, 45 girls—between the ages of 3 and 5 years. They were all attending a summer nursery school; none had gone to school before. For the first 3 weeks, the psychologists established baseline measures of children's behavior and verified the reliability of their observations. The middle 4 weeks were devoted to showing groups of children aggressive, prosocial, or neutral television programs. The last 2 weeks were used for evaluating any extended effects from the television viewing. The psychologists also gave intelligence tests, rated the children's attention to the shows, interviewed mothers about the children's patterns of television watching at home, and tested the children's knowledge of the programs' content.

Within each of two classrooms, children were divided into an Aggressive Condition, in which they saw aggressive "Batman" and "Superman" cartoons; a Prosocial Condition, in which they saw episodes of "Mr. Rogers," a program emphasizing sharing, friendship, accepting rules, controlling aggression, and the like; and a Neutral Condition, in which they saw films that were neither aggressive nor prosocial. The effects of the programs were in accord with the researchers' initial hypotheses.

Children in the Aggressive Condition were found to be less able to tolerate delay than they had been before seeing the aggressive films. Also, if they were children who were already relatively aggressive— "half of a sample of normal boys and girls"—they acted even more aggressive toward others after viewing aggressive cartoons. The behavior of children in the Prosocial Condition changed too. They persisted longer at tasks, obeyed rules, and tolerated delay better. Bright children, especially, persisted at tasks, perhaps, the authors suggested, because they are more successful at tasks and therefore receive more reinforcement. Children from lower socioeconomic groups played more cooperatively, were more nurturant, and verbalized their feelings more than they had before seeing the prosocial films. Much to their surprise (because earlier studies had shown boys reacting more aggressively to aggressive, often male models), the psychologists found no sex differences in the effects of the programs. The children's behavior was found to have been affected at home as well as at nursery school, and the changes persisted for the most part during the 2-week follow-up period.

The authors of this elaborate, carefully controlled, and complex experiment concluded that their findings had "shed some light on the usefulness of observational learning theory."

THEORIES OF DEVELOPMENT FOR THE 1980S

New perspectives in research and theory emerge during each decade, as the field of child development itself continually develops. Our family tree is still a sapling, but it is strong and growing fast. The Society for Research in Child Development, the professional organization of researchers in developmental psychology, has 4000 members and continues to expand. The number of journals, articles, and books on children grows every year as well. Carmichael's *Manual of Child Psychology* (renamed the *Handbook of Child Psychology*) was recently updated in four volumes containing about 4000 pages (Mussen, 1983). Keeping up with the latest findings from these studies and the evolving theories they reflect is a real challenge. The theories that we discussed in the preceding sections still influence researchers in child development, but several new theoretical views have been articulated. Researchers in the 1980's will be strongly influenced by these recent theoretical perspectives as well.

Perhaps the most prominent of the emerging theories is **information processing.** A perspective that has grown exceedingly rapidly since the early 1970s, information processing dominates in the field of cognitive psychology because it has the virtues of both flexibility and precision. Information processing has come to psychology from the fields of linguistics, computer science, and communications theory. From linguistics have come intriguing questions about how grammar and syntax are built and understood and about how people can understand—as they constantly do—remarks that they have never heard before. From computer science has come the recognition that the computer and the human being are both manipulators of symbols. From communications theory have come the notions of coding and channel capacity. Psychologists apply principles of information processing when they ask how the human brain adds and deletes knowledge, where and how it stores and processes information, how memory works, and under what conditions the brain receives clear or confused signals (Siegler, 1983).

It is in studying the flow of information in and out of memory that developmental psychologists have most often applied information-processing theory. Younger children and older children are considered to have similar mental equipment; both have "computers" that process information. To remember things, children of all ages focus attention on the sensory input from their senses, perceive or recognize patterns, and retain and store information (Figure 1.1). In the course of committing things to memory, children must first try to take in as much as they can of sensory impressions. These are held in sensory memory as brief and fleeting afterimages for less than a second. The impressions that the mind notices pass into short-term memory. In short-term memory, which lasts less than a minute, most impressions are used briefly and then lost. The mind does pick out a few outstanding impressions for remembering, however. These it must classify and link to information already in long-term memory or they, too, will be lost. A few impressions go directly into long-term memory, but most that are retained must be prepared for filing, as it were. The filing system of long-term memory puts information into organized storage so that later it can be retrieved.

The information-processing view recognizes that young children do not think as well as older ones. But the young child's limitations are not attributed to differences in mental processes. Whereas Piaget explained cognitive development as progress through a set of stages, each with its own qualitatively different mental processes and strategies, information-processing theory sees it as the accumulation of quantities of knowledge and the expansion of memory.

Another theoretical view that has begun relatively recently to influence North American developmental psychologists is the **dialectical view.** The modern dialectical analysis of events, be those events psychological, social, or political in nature, derives from the theoretical writings of the German philosopher Georg Hegel (1770–1831). Hegel proposed that one event, or thesis, always produces an opposite reaction, or antithesis.. As these react together, they produce a new event, a synthesis. Esssentially, the dialectical view conceives of human development—and specifically such processes as the development of communication, language, or problem solving—as a constantly changing process of thesis, antithesis, and synthesis. The dialectical view focuses more on the inevitable flux and change in human development than on the periods of stability, or equilibrium. It also focuses on the

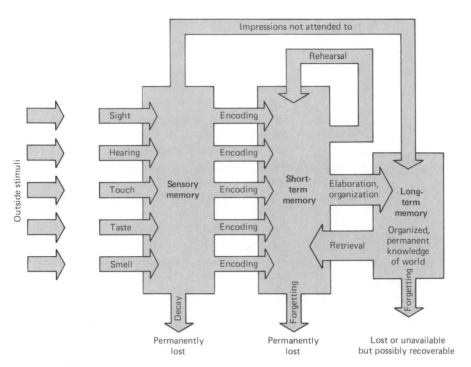

FIGURE 1.1

Information-processing theorists conceive of memory as a succession of stores. The senses send sensory impressions in to sensory memory; from these the mind selects what to notice and pass on to short-term memory. Through rehearsal, or repeating them over in the mind, these impressions are retained, used, and then forgotten, all in less than a minute. To remember impressions longer, the individual must elaborate on and organize them, classifying them and linking them to material already in long-term memory.

social origins of learning rather than on innate or biological predispositions. Originally rejected by Western psychologists as ideologically oppressive, the dialectical view is now considered a useful analytical tool by many in the West.

One of the most influential psychologists within the dialectical school was Lev Semenovich Vygotsky (1896–1934). Prominent in the Soviet Union soon after the Revolution, Vygotsky held that humans learn as they interact with others. Knowledge, he believed, derives from human culture. Just as some developmentalists asserted that advanced psychological processes, such as remembering, perceiving, solving problems, or paying attention, emerged in a series of universal stages, Vygotsky asserted the opposite. Thinking is determined by the social and historical assumptions of those who populate a child's world. Vygotsky did not altogether ignore the contribution of "nature," or biological predispositions, and believed that before children developed speech, most of their responses derived from basic, biological givens. Culture, he

said, "creates nothing; it simply modifies the natural environment to conform to human goals" (Vygotsky, 1979, p. 166).

Vygotsky chose to study social actions to understand individual behavior. He did not believe that people were merely passive recipients of knowledge and insisted that children learn *actively*. Children are influenced by their environments, he believed, even as they in turn influence that environment. In Vygotsky's dialectic, children are affected by, and themselves affect, the adults and peers around them. Specifically, as the child communicates with these significant figures, the child develops cognitively. Knowledge that is shared by people in the child's world—knowledge about how to speak, solve problems, remember, or pay attention—is transmitted to the actively seeking child. Adults do not teach knowledge or skills so much as they gradually guide and help children to function independently. To Vygotsky, development could be described by the Russian word *obuchnie*, which means teaching *and* learning: children de-

Lev Semenovich Vygotsky presented a dialectic alternative to the dominant American and European views of intellectual development.

velop even as they are developed.

The process of learning or developing advanced psychological functions is a process in which children first participate with others and then internalize social interactions, Vygotsky believed. Children are first exposed to the shared speech and actions of others. They are guided and regulated by adults or children who are more experienced members of their culture. Children then take over this shared knowledge and skills, especially speech, as they learn to guide and regulate their own actions. Children begin their functioning at a social (interpsychological) level and move to an independent (intrapsychological) level when they have internalized certain psychological functions.

Vygotsky believed that the distance between these two levels of functioning, which he called the *zone of proximal development,* was the area within which the child's learning takes place. A child's

actual level of functioning is described by the mental processes that he or she already can regulate, the situations in which he or she can act independently and autonomously. The same child's potential level of functioning is described by the psychological functions that he or she is just beginning to master. At this level of potential functioning, a child still needs someone else's help. The zone of proximal development represents the area between a child's actual and potential levels of functioning, an area of readiness or sensitivity. As an adult makes demands on a child that are just beyond the child's grasp—perhaps by asking probing questions or setting up intriguing problems—the child has to stretch mentally to solve or make sense of the problem. The child actively struggles for a solution and eventually internalizes the route to the solution. Of course, if the adult makes the task too easy or too hard, the child does not struggle after the solution and makes no progress. A child will be flushed with excitement as his teacher gives him addition and subtraction problems that are just at the edge of his comprehension, but he will be crestfallen when the problems are too simple or too advanced.

A German emigrant to Canada, Klaus Riegel (1925–1977) put his own stamp on dialectical psychology. It has been suggested (Birren, 1978) that Riegel, who grew up in Nazi Germany, was reacting against a society that demanded rigid adherence to received truths in his belief that contradictions, flux, and change lie at the very heart of human development. Riegel reacted to the rigidities of his childhood with a sense of the injustice that they do to human beings. It was with some passion that he would later write:

I reject . . . the preference for equilibrium, balance, or stability. Instead of directing our attention toward the question of how tranquility of the mind or of the social situation is achieved, for example, of how problems are solved and answers are found, at least equal emphasis should be devoted to the issue of how problems are created and questions are raised (Riegel, 1976, p. 689).

Riegel believed that in the wake of Piaget's enormously influential work, the behavioral sciences erroneously had adopted an equilibrium model of development. For a dialectician like Riegel, all development necessarily evolves out of a state of imbalance, not balance. Upheaval and disequilibrium are utterly necessary. Stability and calm—synthesis—are merely temporary stepping-stones in the turbulent stream of human development. Riegel criticized Piaget's bias:

He [Piaget] investigates how children resolve conflicting situations, contradictory evidence, or inconsistent impressions, but rarely does he report how children come to question their earlier judgments and how they create their own problems (Riegel, 1976, p. 691).

Riegel believed that Piaget did not go far enough, that the logical extension of Piaget's ideas about cognition was a closed mind. He proposed that there is a cognitive stage beyond the resolution of contradictions. At such a stage, the human mind not only tolerates, but manipulates contradictions and works them through into further contradictions. This dynamic stage, to Riegel, is truly dialectical, in that it embodies developmental transformation. Consistent with this view, he insisted that crises should not always be interpreted negatively; a crisis can just as well provide a positive basis for individual and social development.

Riegel wanted students of human behavior to study the concrete actions of people in concrete social situations. Like Vygotsky, he emphasized the social rather than the abstract basis of human life. Riegel believed that dialogues between two people, a mother and child, for example, provided prototypes for developmentalists to analyze. Dialogues are grist for the dialectician's mill, said Riegel, because they exist in time and bridge the gap between two human beings. Dialogues require that the participants coordinate their remarks, lest they degenerate into mere alternating monologues. As children develop, their dialogues with their mothers proceed from exchanges of looks, sounds, and facial expressions to exchanges of privately shared signs and, finally, to signs—language itself—that are generally shared by members of society. In his "Manifesto for Dialectical Psychology" (1976), Riegel sets forth two guiding principles for Western psychology: the first, "Dialectical psychology is committed to the study of actions and changes;" the second, "Dialectical psychology is concerned with short-term situational changes as well as with long-term individual and cultural developments."

Riegel ended his dialectical manifesto by urging psychologists to reject the traditional developmentalists' emphasis on childhood in favor of an emphasis on the whole lifespan. His recommendation has found increasing support in recent years. Under the tutelage of such developmentalists as Paul Baltes and Warner Schaie (1973), the lifespan school of human development made a strong showing during the 1970s and continues to influence theorists in the 1980s. In addition to psychologists, the lifespan approach has affected biologists, economists, sociologists, and others (Baltes, 1978). The lifespan approach attempts, in its methods and its ideology, to correct for certain biases in traditional developmental psychology. Thus, for example, the traditional position has been to use a biological model of maturation for psychological development. In such a model, bones and muscles mature at certain rates and in a certain direction—longer, bigger, heavier—along with cognition, perception, memory, and the like. Traditional developmentalists have portrayed childhood and adolescence as periods of growth and developmental gain, adulthood as an essentially static period of quantitative rather than qualitative change, and old age as a period of loss and decline. The traditional model of child development has been criticized for equating development with gain rather than loss, for viewing development as cumulative, and for assuming that an individual's development is not affected by the social-historical era in which he or she grows up.

Lifespan developmentalists want to shift the traditional emphasis and consider all human change from the very beginning to the very end of life. They focus on change throughout the human life cycle and stress that such changes may have many different starting and end points and may lead in several directions at once. Although the traditional, biologically based view is to depict change as leading in a single direction, toward a single end point at a given period of life, the lifespan view explodes that conception. Intelligence, for example, traditionally has been considered to increase during childhood and adolescence, to remain stable in adulthood, and to grow rusty with old age. According to the lifespan perspective, intelligence is an amalgam of many qualities, some of which appear early in life and weaken later, some of which appear most strongly in middle or late adulthood and little, if at all, during childhood. In its stress on the potentials for growth during adulthood and old age (and, conversely, for decline during childhood or adolescence), the lifespan view rather sharply departs from more traditional approaches.

Those who work within the lifespan approach share with other contemporary approaches a commitment to analyzing the social and historical contexts within which psychological events unfold. But they place particular emphasis on the effects of social relationships, individual life histories, and historical change on psychosocial development. Thus in their research, lifespan developmentalists are likely to follow a particular cohort, or group of agemates, to assess the role of historical events on development. In one study of the development of adolescent personality, 1800 male and female adolescents between 12 and 17 years old were given a battery of personality tests in 1970, 1971, and again in 1972 (Nesselroade and Baltes, 1974). The researchers found effects of cohort, time, age, and sex on many of these dimensions. For example, not only did achievement scores of different cohorts drop from 1970 to 1972, but 14-year-olds in 1972 scored lower in achievement than 14-year-olds in 1970. The researchers speculated that "change in personality traits occurred from 1970 to 1972 because the socialization context for adolescents changed during this period" (Nesselroade and Baltes, 1974, p. 59).

Lifespan developmentalists are concerned with isolating those early traits that are greatly affected by later experience as well as the traits that are especially unstable. In searching for these evanescent traits, the lifespan developmentalists echo Klaus Riegel's exhortation to consider change rather than equilibrium as the heart of human development.

In its emphasis on studying how people interact within their environments and on studying people at every age, the **ecological approach** is first cousin to both the dialectical and lifespan views. As proposed by Cornell University's Urie Bronfenbrenner, an ecological view of human behavior would consider how people accommodate throughout their lives to the changing environments in which they grow and live. Bronfenbrenner has criticized what he perceives as narrowness and artificiality in traditional research designs:

Much of contemporary developmental psychology is the science of the strange behavior of

children in strange situations with strange adults for the briefest possible periods of time *(Bronfenbrenner, 1977, p. 513)*.

Although he does not want to dispense with the rigor of the traditional laboratory experiment in favor only of the immediacy and relevance of naturalistic observation of subjects, Bronfenbrenner does want to adapt the virtues of each to a new approach: the "ecology of human development."

Central to an ecology of human development is the examination of "multiperson systems of interaction not limited to a single setting" that takes "into account aspects of the environment beyond the immediate situation containing the subject" (Bronfenbrenner, 1977, p. 514). It is Bronfenbrenner's belief that human development is best illuminated when psychologists systematically compare at least two environmental systems within which the growing human being adapts and accommodates. "Systems," furthermore, exist simultaneously at various levels. A *microsystem* is com-

An ecological model of development has been proposed by Urie Bronfenbrenner, which suggests that a child's development is influenced by factors at many different levels, from immediate interaction with mother to broad social and economic conditions.

posed of the network of ties between a person and an immediate setting, such as a school or an office. A *mesosystem* is composed of the network of ties among the major settings in a person's life. For example, the mesosystem for an American 12-year-old might include ties among family, school, friends, church, and camp. Finally, a *macrosystem* is composed not of settings that impinge directly on a person, but of broad, general, institutional patterns in the person's culture, such as the legal, political, social, educational, and economic systems. Macrosystems are important in analyses of children's development:

> [They are] carriers of information and ideology that, both explicitly and implicitly, endow meaning and motivation to particular agencies, social networks, roles, activities, and their interrelations. What place or priority children and those responsible for their care have in such macrosystems is of special importance in determining how a child and his or her caretakers are treated and interact with each other in different types of settings (Bronfenbrenner, 1977, p. 515).

Bronfenbrenner has proposed that developmentalists analyze environmental structures as independent systems. Consistent with this systems approach, he has proposed that the ecological experiment:

1. Allow for the reciprocal effects among variables. The traditional experiment examines the effect of *A* on *B*; the ecological model examines the effect of *B* on *A* as well.

2. Recognize the entire social system operating within the research setting—not only all of the participants present, but the experimenter, too.

3. Assess large systems (those that include more than two people) and all of their subsystems. For example, an investigation of mother-child interaction might also account for the interaction of mother and father and the interaction of father and child.

4. Recognize how the physical environment might indirectly affect the social processes within the setting.

5. Recognize the combined effects of, and the interaction between, settings.

In the ecological view, the most important findings from any piece of research are likely to be the interactions. Whereas the classical experimenter labors to isolate a single variable of behavior and to "control out" all other variables, the design of ecological research will "control in" as many relevant variables as possible or practical. Like the ecologist in the natural sciences who investigates the life and times of the porpoise by studying all of the nearby sea creatures and the human boaters and hunters and water polluters who impinge on the porpoise's world, the ecologist in the behavioral sciences examines many different factors, or systems, in the human environment. For instance, suggests Bronfenbrenner, the developmentalist studying children's socialization might, as is traditional, control for the social class of the children under study. But the research design might also include family structure and type of child care (e.g., home or day care). An ecological approach would tend to show complex patterns of interactions between children and several of their environments.

Developmental psychologists of every stripe are interested in the relationship between biology and behavior, but nowhere has the trend taken a more controversial form than in the field of **sociobiology**. Essentially, sociobiologists propose that social behavior has a genetic basis—a radical twist on the old nature-nurture debate. Theorists like Harvard's Edward Wilson, an entomologist, and Robert Trivers, a biologist, have theorized that human behavior is the direct product of evolution and, furthermore, that behavior that improves the chances of survival will be passed on genetically to the next generation.

> Sociobiology has emerged from the recognition that behavior, even complex social behavior, has evolved and is adaptive. Its excitement derives from the further recognition that evolution has a great deal to say about behavior; it is the underlying thread that unifies all living things, not only in terms of genealogical relatedness and, therefore, ultimate unity but also as the primary mechanism to which all life is subject. Correctly used, evolutionary theory is a predictive and analytic tool of enormous power. The strength of sociobiology derives from its grounding in the universalities of evolutionary biology. Its promise for the study of behavior lies in the hope of a good paradigm (Barash, 1977, p. 8).

Sociobiologists have attempted to solve, among others, one puzzle that perplexed even Darwin: Why do some individuals help others, at great personal risk, if the survival of the fittest predisposes each individual to fight selfishly for one's own reproductive advantage? The sociobiologist's answer is that helping behavior really does promote genetic survival, but of *other* members of the altruist's species. Thus the soldier ant and the soldier human who die to protect their home territories effectively promote the survival of members of their species who, of course, share their genes. (Brothers and sisters, parents and children, share ½ of their genes; first cousins, ¼; etc.)

In addition to providing this explanation of altruism, sociobiologists have offered analyses of a number of other human qualities. They suggest, for instance, that people who refuse to help others and people who take without giving are in the long term selected against; that if natural selection has made humans good at cheating, it has also made them good at detecting cheating; that human evolution has favored self-deception because people who can lie to themselves as well as others are actually more convincing deceivers.

Certain developmental psychologists have found the sociobiological perspective useful for understanding important questions about child development, such as why there are inborn differences between the sexes, how children's social groups are organized into dominance hierarchies, what the bases of the attachment between parents and children are, and how and why parents invest their time and energy in caring for their offspring (comparing parents' investment in sons versus daughters and biological versus stepchildren).

The sociobiologists' camp has internal divisions; some, like the University of Chicago's Daniel Freedman (1979), a developmental psychologist who advocates a sociobiological approach, believe that the proper focus is on groups rather than the individuals or individual genes that Wilson and Trivers discuss. But the internal divisions are nowhere near as passionate as the debate between believers and nonbelievers. To its critics, sociobiology is dangerous and benighted, a political credo masquerading in scientific clothing. Critics believe that sociobiology is a new brand of social Darwinism, the disreputable nineteenth-century offshoot of Darwinism that attempted to ascribe, for example, racial "traits" to genetic heritage. Its critics point out that sociobiology can be used to justify racism or male dominance as "natural." To them, it is a political tool by which the powerful can justify themselves and prevent social change. How useful sociobiology will prove for understanding human development is still an open question.

In sum, the perspectives we have described are very different from each other and very different from more traditional developmental theories. In small and large ways, they seem to be changing the flavor of developmental psychology. The changes that these approaches—information processing, dialecticism, sociobiology, and the lifespan and ecological perspectives—bring to the study of human development during the 1980s will in turn shape the work of future generations of developmental psychologists.

METHODS OF CHILD STUDY

As the theoretical explanations of child development have changed and multiplied, so, too, have ways of studying children. Today the child development researcher can choose from a wide range of diverse methods, measures, and procedures. Designing and conducting a study is a series of choices. There is no one right way, no guaranteed method. Although each choice has its own advantages and limitations, psychologists have found a great deal of room for innovation and individuality.

The first choice is to select a research design. There are two major ways of comparing children at different ages in order to study development. One is **longitudinal;** the same population of children is followed over an extended period of time to see how it changes with age. The other is **cross-sectional;** the investigators choose as subjects groups of children who are similar in important ways—educational level, socioeconomic status, proportion of males to females—but who are of different ages, and they determine how the groups compare. From cross-sectional studies, results are gathered more quickly and provide at least a rough outline of development. Most of the extant research in many areas of development is cross-sectional, comparing, for example, first graders, fourth graders, and sixth graders, rather than following the same sample of children from first through sixth grades. Longitudinal research, as William Kessen notes, "is laborious and time consuming, but it exerts a calming influence on the tendency to make simple what is very complicated in child development" (Kessen, 1960, p. 50). Only longitudinal studies can show actual growth curves and progressive changes with age. Only longitudinal studies can corroborate continuities and discontinuities in development.

If the researcher wishes to determine how a particular condition affects children's behavior, there are several methods from which to select. First, the researcher may choose to do an **experiment.** In an experiment, one group of children, the experimental group, is treated in a special way; another, the control group, is not. Children are assigned to one group or the other at random. For example, many social-learning experiments expose one group of children to a particular kind of model, an aggressive model or a prosocial one, whereas another group does not see a model.

When a controlled experiment with randomly assigned subjects is not possible, the investigator may be able to find a **natural experiment.** One group of subjects who are in real life exposed to a particular condition are compared with another group of subjects, similar in every other way, who are not exposed to such a condition. It is not ethical to assign children randomly to experimental conditions of deprivation, for example, but children in orphanages may be thought of as the experimental group in a natural experiment and compared to children raised at home. Children in one culture may be compared to children in another, children who are identical twins to children who are siblings, children who are adopted to children raised by their biological parents.

Observational research is another option. When using this method, the researcher does not manipulate or select a situation for the behavior in which he or she is interested, but instead systematically observes its occurrence in different children. The children may be observed in the natural setting of home or school or in a standard or structured play situation in the laboratory. The researcher may also choose to use standard tests, such as those of intelligence, or to conduct interviews with children, parents, and teachers.

Of course, there are certain general guidelines concerning what makes better or worse research.

Researchers seldom undertake a study of only two or three children. They are very cautious about using only a brief interview. Having more subjects, more measures, and reliable instruments is better. But to a large extent, all these decisions are controlled not so much by rules for the best of all possible experiments but by the taste, stamina, interests, and practical considerations of the individual researcher.

To illustrate, suppose investigators are interested in language development. To study how children acquire language, they may call on any or all of the following research strategies. They might compare the vocabularies of identical twins and of other siblings to see what influence heredity has on language ability (natural experiment). They might give a group of children repeated tests of comprehension every year from the time they begin to talk to see how their understanding of language increases with age (longitudinal testing). They might observe these same children in conversations with their mothers to see whether tested language comprehension is related to spontaneous speech production or to see whether either is related to the mothers' verbal "input" (naturalistic observation). They might study the communication of children who have been deprived of the usual language models and opportunities—children whose parents are deaf or who are deaf themselves, for example—to see how language is retarded under these circumstances (natural experiment). They might offer a group of children language "enrichment" by having mothers talk more to their children or by having an experimenter elaborate on what the children say to see whether their language improves (experiment). Each of these strategies has its own merits and limitations, but, most important, each is useful for answering a somewhat different research question (see Table 1.2). Designs, methods, strategies, and measures in research are simply tools; most important are the guiding idea or question and the appropriateness of the tools chosen for answering the question.

Ethics is another factor limiting the choice of research methods. Researchers should not deliberately impose cruel or inhuman treatment on their subjects in the interests of scientific discovery. But just how much should researchers intervene in the lives of their subjects? Should a child be exposed to a violent movie and then put in a threatening situation? Should an adolescent be interviewed about her secret fears of rape? Is it permissible to train a baby to turn his or her head every time someone hums "Yankee Doodle"? Researchers should not lie outright to subjects about the research or the possible negative effects it may have.

But how much deception should the researcher be allowed? Is it all right to record a mother's interactions with her child and not tell her that she as well as the child is being observed? Should a child be allowed to think that the research is about his views on sports when actually the researcher is

RESEARCH FOCUS

HOW MOTHERS AFFECT THEIR INFANTS' PLAY

Because they felt that most research into the relationship of mothers and children suffered from serious shortcomings, a team of researchers from Pennsylvania State University, Jay Belsky, Mary Kay Goode, and Robert Most, designed their own study. Published in 1980, this two-part investigation was designed to overcome two criticisms that the researchers leveled at other studies in the field. First, they criticized other researchers in the field for describing correlations rather than causes. Second, they criticized the lack of theoretical statements in which researchers predict, from the outset, which of the parents' actions they expect will influence infants. Therefore the Belsky study attempted to show quite specifically how mothers influence their children's play. In an elegant and unusual design, the research began by charting (cross-sectional) observations of *natural* behaviors by mothers and their infants. It then tested *experimentally* the relationships uncovered—that is, the correlations traced—between mothers' stimulation and infants' exploratory play.

Defining "maternal stimulation" as a mother's verbal or physical attempts to focus her baby's attention on objects or events in the immediate environment, the researchers hypothesized that

by directing the child's attention to objects and events in the home, the mother (or other adult) teaches the infant how to gain control over and focus his or her own attention. In essence, we propose that infants learn from their mothers how to stimulate themselves. Since such skill is considered essential for initiating and maintaining self-directed exploration, infant play is the hypothesized product of maternal stimulation that we examine (Belsky et al., 1980 p. 1169).

In the first phase, eight infants at each of the ages of 9, 12, 15, and 18 months were studied as they interacted with their mothers. All of the mothers were their infant's primary caregiver; all but four were middle class. A researcher made two, 45-minute visits to the family's house at a time when the baby was expected to be awake and alert and when the father was at work. Mothers were told to go about their usual household routine.

The researchers carefully and elaborately broke down "maternal stimulation" into several categories, each of which was coded at 15-second intervals by the observer. Mothers were coded for six kinds of attention-focusing acts:

1. Point/reposition: when the mother pointed to an object or moved something so the child could get to it.
2. Demonstrate: when the mother showed the child how to do something.
3. Move: when the mother physically moved the child's hands through the motions of an activity.
4. Instruct/question.
5. Highlight: when a mother described an object's unique property.
6. Name object.

The child's play and exploration were also coded:

1. Manipulative exploration: when the child looked at and manipulated objects.
2. Juxtaposing: when the child put together two or more unrelated objects.
3. Functional play: when the child exploited the unique quality of an object.
4. Pretend play: when the child played imaginatively with an object.
5. Extended exploration: when a child explored for more than one, 15-second interval.
6. Attending to mother: when the child paid attention to the mother's attempts to focus his or her attention.
7. Imitating/complying: when the child imitated the mother's actions or followed her attention-focusing cues.

systematically reinforcing his use of the pronoun "I"? Is it all right to tell the child that the noises she hears in the next room are the cries of another child in distress, when they are really a tape recording?

These issues have been given more and more attention in recent years, and more stringent standards for research on human subjects have been set. To do any research involving children, researchers must now have their research plans approved by a university committee for the protection of the rights of human subjects. They must con-

---

The findings were much as the research team had predicted. Mothers increasingly prompt their infants verbally and physically during the last quarter of their first year of life. During the second year of life, mothers use increasingly more verbal than physical promptings. Infants grow more attentive and compliant as they get older, and their play grows more competent as well. Older children spend more time manipulating and juxtaposing objects and engaging in functional play and extended explorations. The correlational analysis showed, also as predicted, that "infants who display the greatest competence while exploring have mothers who frequently focus their attention on objects and events in the environment" (Belsky et al., 1980, p. 1173). The researchers further analyzed their results to conclude that physical, as opposed to spoken, promptings were more effective overall in focusing infants' attention and in shaping their more competent play.

The second half of the study was experimental in nature and set out to test the hypothesis that mothers' attention focusing teaches children how to find stimulation themselves. The 16 subjects here were 1-year-olds who were randomly assigned to either the experimental or the control group. The groups were equated for the child's sex and birth order and for the parents' education. Mothers and babies from each group were observed several times in their own homes. They were told that these visits were to give an observer a chance "to take some notes on babies' experiences in home settings which might be of assistance in designing an infant day-care program."

During three consecutive weekly visits, when the observers were ostensibly making notes for a day-care program, the experimental group was not told that it was part of an experiment for fear of biasing their behavior. The mothers were told that the observer would stop writing from time to time to "share his observations" with the mother. In fact, the observer tried to influence the mother's behavior by making her conscious of when she stimulated her baby. The observer might remark how interesting it was that the mother was pointing to an object or highlighting it for the baby. Each of the eight mothers in the experimental condition received between 37 and 49 such pointed interventions in the three visits. Mothers in the control condition did not receive any such interventions. The visits were structured so that the child felt at ease, and the observers' notes on the infants' behavior were later coded by someone who did not know the purpose of the study or even the infants' age or sex. The coders scored the notes for the same kinds of play and exploration as had been coded in the naturalistic part of the study.

The experimenters found, as they had predicted, that compared to those in the control group the mothers in the experimental condition more often stimulated their toddlers one week after the first treatment had been administered. The "treatment" had met its stated—but covert—goal. Furthermore, the infants in the experimental condition engaged in more competent play than their control-group counterparts at a follow-up visit 2 months later. Rather proudly, the team concluded:

While the control infants were significantly more likely to engage in the least cognitively sophisticated kind of play coded (simple play), the experimental infants engaged in functional play significantly more frequently, scored significantly higher on the composite exploratory competence score, and were significantly less likely to be unfocused during the play sessions (Belsky et al., 1980, p. 1176).

The four Research Focus Boxes in this chapter illustrate not only the increasing sophistication of research in developmental psychology, but also the very wide range of research methods and underlying theoretical perspectives among developmentalists then and now.

TABLE 1.2
PROS AND CONS OF RESEARCH DESIGNS AND METHODS

Designs and methods	Pros	Cons
Longitudinal Design: Same sample observed at different ages.	Shows developmental curves for individuals or groups. Shows temporal (causal) sequences of events.	Expensive, time consuming. Subjects may drop out during course of study.
Cross-sectional Design: Different samples observed at different ages.	Gives view of average developmental changes with age.	Does not indicate individual growth curves. Does not indicate temporal (causal) relations.
Experiment: Controlled treatment given to subjects selected at random.	Subjects in different groups can be compared. Known, specified, controlled treatment.	Questionable whether findings apply to situations outside the often artificial one of the experiment. Treatment is usually short term.
Test: Standardized assessment given to all subjects.	Data from different subjects can be compared. Individual's performance can be compared to norms.	Data limited to preestablished responses.
Interview: Questions posed to children, parents, teachers.	Quick way to get information. Only way to assess conscious intentions and attitudes.	Interviewees are biased, not accurate reporters of past events or their own behavior.
Natural Experiment: Groups chosen for the differences in their treatment in the real world.	Gives group (average) differences related to conditions that occur naturally, such as socioeconomic status.	Subjects may be different in ways besides the condition of interest; these differences are not controlled.
Structured Observation: Behavior observed in a standard situation.	Data from different subjects can be compared. Data not restricted to preestablished test responses.	Does not get at underlying attitudes. Not known whether observations can be generalized to other situations.
Naturalistic Observation: Spontaneous behavior observed in familiar environment.	Provides information about behavior in the real world. Offers description of activities, behavior, interactions.	Settings for different subjects are not comparable. Does not assess maximum performance possible. Some kinds of abilities may not be observable.

vince the committee that their procedures will be totally harmless to the child, that they do not constitute treatment in any way unlike that a child might encounter in his or her everyday life, that the potential benefit of the research for science or society justifies the procedures, and that the child or parent will know in advance what the research entails and will have given his or her "informed consent" for participation in the study.

After the research has been done, investigators must analyze the data obtained. They can look for **correlations** or associations between variables. For example, they can see whether children who are highly intelligent also have considerable athletic ability; if they do, the two variables of intelligence and athletic ability are positively correlated. They can find out whether children who are highly intelligent have mothers who are seldom punitive; if they do, the two variables of intelligence and punitiveness are negatively correlated.

Other statistical analyses indicate whether differences observed in experiments—that boys are taller than girls, that children living in two-story houses are more outgoing than children living in apartments, or that children in an exercise group run faster than a control group of children—are **statis-**

tically significant. A difference is significant if it is unlikely to have occurred by chance. The more children in the study and the larger the difference between groups, the more likely that the difference will be significant.

After all the decisions have been made and the tedious work has been done, after all the data have been analyzed, the investigator still faces the challenge of interpreting the results, of saying what they mean. This may not be as easy as it sounds because there may be a variety of indices pointing in different directions or the relation between age and behavior may be confusing. Moreover, investigators sometimes give in to the temptation to overinterpret their results—to claim that one variable caused another, for example, that maternal punitiveness

caused children's low intelligence when only a simple correlation has been documented or to generalize to *all* children when they have studied only 9-year-old white boys from upstate New York. After you have read this textbook, you will not be familiar with all the methodological fine points of child development research, but you should be able to spot unjustified or illogical interpretations.

This first chapter has provided just a brief glance at the theories illuminating the study of development. In later chapters, the theories relevant to particular topics will be discussed in greater detail. Other research methods and paradigms are also illustrated in greater detail in the Research Focus reports that punctuate each chapter.

SUMMARY

1. The study of child development as we know it today is a product of the 20th century. Although its philosophical roots reach back to John Locke and Jean Jacques Rousseau's ideas about human nature, it was really Darwin who made the method for studying children scientifically respectable. G. Stanley Hall founded the study of child and adolescent development in the United States. Early in this century in France, the first objective, standardized test of children's intelligence was devised. Later, the study of norms of children's development, the school of behaviorism, and psychoanalytic theory dominated much of the young field of psychology.

2. During the middle of the 20th century, American psychology was dominated by learning theory. Some social-learning theorists tried to fit Freud's concepts into the model of stimulus and response, and their methods of study are still in use today. Erik Erikson introduced his theory of human development as a succession of crises over the whole lifespan. The Skinnerians applied a mechanistic learning theory to the study of social behavior, proposing that it is a series of observable stimuli and responses. Other social-learning psychologists proposed that children learn social behavior by observing and imitating others. Perhaps the most influential modern developmental theorist was Jean Piaget. He elaborated an interactionist, structuralist

theory of children's cognitive development that remains influential today.

3. Recent trends in the study of child development have included the study of *ever* younger infants, the introduction of the belief that infants initiate interchanges with others, and a new questioning of the belief that early experience invariably affects development both irreversibly and permanently. In the 1980s, approaches that have influenced the study of child development include information processing; dialecticism, especially as proposed by the Russian psychologist Vygotsky and the North American Klaus Riegel; lifespan psychology; Urie Bronfenbrenner's ecological view; and sociobiology.

4. Psychologists use several different methods for studying children's behavior. First, they must choose a research design that is either longitudinal or cross-sectional (or both). For some purposes, an experiment is the best approach. Some experiments occur naturally and offer psychologists the chance to study forms of behavior that it would be unethical for them to try to create artificially. In their data, researchers often look for correlations between variables, although cause and effect cannot always be inferred from correlations alone. When meaningful patterns show up in data, researchers say that they have found something that is statistically significant.

KEY TERMS

Nurture	Electra conflict	Identity crisis	Dialectical view
Nature	Phallic stage	Psychosocial	Zone of proximal
Phylogeny	Id	moratorium	development
Scientific method	Ego	Reinforcement	Ecological approach
Storm and stress	Superego	contingencies	Microsystem
(Sturm und Drang)	Psychoanalysis	Ethology	Mesosystem
Norm	Drive	Sensitive period	Macrosystem
Maturational	Reinforcement	Imprint	Sociobiology
Behaviorism	Operant conditioning	Attachment	Longitudinal
Classical conditioning	Learned drive	Interactionist	Cross-sectional
Oral stage	Primary drive	Structuralist	Experiment
Anal stage	Latency	Cohort	Natural experiment
Oedipal conflict	Genital stage	Information processing	Correlation
			Statistical significance

SUGGESTED READINGS

Aries, Philippe. *Centuries of Childhood.* New York: Random House (Vintage Books), 1962. The metamorphosis of the concept of childhood from the Middle Ages to the present view of childhood as a distinct phase of life, traced through paintings, diaries, school curricula, and the history of games.

Hall, Calvin S. *A Primer of Freudian Psychology.* New York: New American Library, 1979. Delivers what it promises, an overview of Freud's prodigious output, in digestible prose for those who are starting to examine his ideas.

Kessen, William. *The Child.* New York: Wiley, 1965. Readings selected from 1200 years of Western writing about children, connected by comments tracing the history of child study.

These are the major 20th-century figures in the field of child development, introducing their theories in their own words.

Bandura, Albert. *Social Learning Theory.* Englewood Cliffs, N.J.: Prentice-Hall, 1977.

Erikson, Erik. *Childhood and Society.* New York: W. W. Norton, 1963 (first edition, 1950).

Freud, Sigmund. "Three Contributions to the Theory of Sex," in *The Basic Writings of Sigmund Freud,* translated and edited, with an introduction by Dr. A. A. Brill. New York: Random House (Modern Library), 1938.

Piaget, Jean, and Inhelder, Bärbel. *The Psychology of the Child,* translated by Helen Weaver. New York: Basic Books, 1969.

Skinner, B.F. *About Behaviorism.* New York: Knopf, 1974.

The "new theories" are represented in the following books:

Baltes, Paul B., and Schaie, K. Warner (Eds). *Lifespan Developmental Psychology: Personality and Socialization.* New York: Academic Press, 1973.

Bronfenbrenner, Urie. *The Ecology of Human Development: Experiments by Nature and Design.* Cambridge: Harvard University Press, 1979.

Freedman, Daniel G. *Human Sociobiology: a Holistic Approach.* New York: The Free Press, 1979.

Wilkening, Friedrich, Becker, Judith, and Trabasso, Thomas (Eds). *Information Integration by Children.* Hillsdale, N.J.: Lawrence Erlbaum Associates, 1980.

CHAPTER 2

Heredity

THE NATURE-NURTURE INTERACTION

THE BASIC FORMULA

As we have learned, in times past individuals concerned with child development usually considered it to be directed either by nature (heredity) or by nurture (environment). Today, although behavioral scientists may lean toward explanations on one side or the other, most accept these two forces as interacting continually and inseparably. They attempt to *integrate* the distinctive contributions of heredity and environment, of nature and nurture, not to separate them.

From the very beginning, the interaction between **genes,** the smallest units that carry information about heredity, and the environment is complex. In the first place, most human characteristics, even physical characteristics, are determined by a *number* of genes, not just one. Most traits are **polygenic.** But the fact that individuals are born with genes for a certain trait does not mean that they will necessarily exhibit that trait. The expression of a genetic trait depends on interaction with other genes and with factors in the environment.

A basic, deceptively simple, formula expresses the relation between an individual's genetic inheritance and the environment: phenotype = genotype + environment. The **genotype** is the individual's genetic code, the totality of the genes inherited. The genetic code is present in each cell of the developing individual, beginning with the fertilized egg. But the expression of the genotype in the individual's visible characteristics and behavior, called the **phenotype,** depends on all the environmental influences that impinge upon that individual from the moment of conception. Were we able to decipher the genetic code in its entirety, we still would not be able to predict the phenotype. From the moment of conception, a number of possibilities are open to each unique potential being.

Skin color illustrates the complex interactions of genes with one another and with the environment. The coloration of the skin is decided by a number of genes, including genes producing melanin pigment, which, depending on its amount, makes skin dark or fair. These genes in turn may be blocked from expressing themselves fully by other genes,

notably the gene for albinism, which blocks production of the melanin pigment. The amount of sunlight in the environment also affects the **expression** of skin-color genes. In less sunny climes far from the Equator, the person born with a dark-skin genotype will have a lighter phenotype; the genotype will not be fully expressed. But individuals who have inherited a genotype for dark skin and who live in the tropics, where they are continuously exposed to sunlight, will have a phenotype of very dark skin. The environment will be conducive for full expression of their genetic endowment.

To give another example, the effect of social interaction on intelligence may be compared to the effect of sunlight on the expression of skin color. Intelligence that would have seen expression in a normal or enriched environment can be blocked in an impoverished environment. Differences in stimulation may even have a physiological effect and alter brain chemistry (Vandenberg, 1968). When there is little touching and other forms of loving interest and little stimulation of the mind, intelligence is less than it might be.

As these examples illustrate, the expression of genes is complicated by the patterns in which they operate and by numerous environmental factors. Other genes and the environment shape and limit the expression of their potential. It is very difficult therefore to trace the path of development for any individual child or for any particular trait, especially for complex qualities, like sociability and intelligence, which interest developmental psychologists. But even though the details cannot yet be filled in, psychologists have proposed hypothetical models of the nature-nurture interaction. They make analogies in hopes of giving us a clearer picture of the way genes interact with environment.

REACTION RANGE

The **reaction range** model (Figure 2.1) was introduced by Irving Gottesman (1963) to explain the range of phenotypes that develop from the same genotype under varying environmental conditions. To illustrate how this model works, let us assume that Jennifer (child *A*) and Cindy (child *B*) are sisters and have very similar genotypes but were treated very differently by their parents. The par-

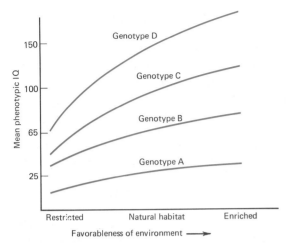

FIGURE 2.1

Several genotypes for intellectual development—*A, B, C,* and *D*—may vary in expression in more and less favorable surroundings. Depending on the environment, a person with genotype *C*, for example, may have an IQ phenotype of anywhere from 50 to 120, a person with genotype *D*, one anywhere from 70 to 170. The range of possible scores for any genotype is its *reaction range* (Gottesman, 1963).

ents doted on Jennifer, showered her with attention, gave her books and lessons, and sent her to private schools. Cindy, the Cinderella figure, was ignored, punished, and kept from school. Because Jennifer and Cindy were raised so differently, they

are very likely to have dissimilar behavior patterns and abilities despite the fact that they have one-half of their genes in common. Similar genotypes can produce different phenotypes when environments vary. In contrast, the environment can diminish genetic differences, creating similar phenotypes from a variety of genotypes. Thus in any sample of children from suburban America, many will have IQ scores of 100, even though they have different genotypic potentials for intelligence. As Figure 2.1 also indicates, if child *A* has a genotype for low intelligence and child *B* has one for high intelligence, but child *A* is given particularly favorable treatment—special attention, lessons, private school—whereas child *B* is reared in a rather ordinary manner, both may end up with an IQ of 100.

THE "LANDSCAPE"

A second model of nature-nurture interaction, the "landscape" model proposed by Conrad Waddington (1957), is three-dimensional and applies to the development of particular traits. The contour of the landscape is determined by the genotype. The ball on the landscape represents an individual trait, such as intelligence, as it is expressed in the phenotype. As the child grows older, the ball rolls forward down

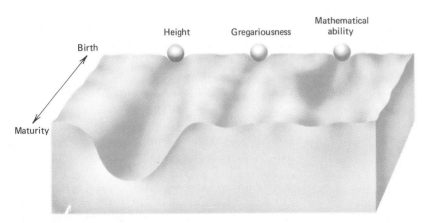

FIGURE 2.2

This adaptation of Waddington's (1962) epigenetic "landscape" shows the hypothetical development of three different kinds of characteristics. Physical appearance, here height, is highly canalized, that is, under strict genetic control. Social behavior, here gregariousness, is much less canalized and more susceptible to environmental influences. Intellectual development, here mathematical ability, is highly canalized in the early years but less so later.

the landscape, which has slopes and valleys. If the valley floor is wide and its slopes are shallow, the phenotype will be less protected from adverse environmental forces. The ball can be thrown off course, pushed off the normal developmental path, by an extreme environmental condition. But when the valleys are deep and have narrow floors, and the walls around them are steep, the "winds" of the environment are less likely to blow the ball off course. Even if the phenotype is displaced by an extremely strong force, it has a good chance of returning to its place. The deep-valleyed pathway is highly **canalized** and protected from environmental impact. A shallow pathway is less canalized and more vulnerable. At some periods in development and for some traits, paths are highly canalized and traits resilient, but at other times or for other traits, the environment strongly influences development.

Waddington's landscape has been expanded in Figure 2.2 to illustrate pathways for three different kinds of traits: physical (height); social (gregariousness); and intellectual (mathematical ability).

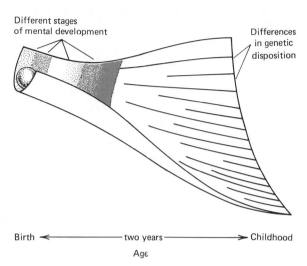

FIGURE 2.3

Robert McCall conceptualizes the minds of individuals as developing while they roll down their own genetic grooves in the scoop of human development, hastened or slowed in their progress or put off course by changes in the surroundings (McCall, 1981).

THE "SCOOP"

A third model specifies the course of mental development; Robert McCall (1981) pictures it as occurring on a "scoop" (Figure 2.3). In this model, a person rolls down the scoop as he or she becomes older. The scoop represents the developmental pathway for the human species, the ball the individual, and the force that moves the ball the environment. The grooves in the scoop are individual variations in genotype. In McCall's model, variation from what is normally expected in the environment, like a strong wind, can propel individuals more or less quickly from one developmental stage to another. A strong enough force could throw a ball considerably off course.

Like Waddington's landscape, McCall's scoop for intellectual development incorporates the notion of canalization. During the early years, the slope of the sides of the scoop is greater and development is more highly canalized than later. Infants stay on the general pathway along which the human species has followed for thousands of years. Divergence through either genetic differences (the grooves), or environmental differences (the winds),

is unlikely. But as a person rolls down the scoop, canalization is reduced. Differences in the environment or individual genetic differences are then more likely to be expressed. As any given individual develops, the timing of events can change the expression of a trait. McCall offers the example of a child of 8 who is taken to Cape Kennedy during a period when he is studying airplanes and space; he also has a teacher who pilots his own plane. The experience for this child at this particular time may be formative, influencing the future course of his mental development. But for the teenager absorbed in rock music and wanting to be alone with his girlfriend, a trip with the family to Cape Kennedy may be little more than a nuisance. McCall's model suggests that we might restate the basic formula this way: phenotype = genotype + environment *at a specific time*.

These three models have substantial similarities. They are not mutually exclusive approaches but rather variations on a theme. There is no one "right" nature-nurture model. All three illustrate the complex relation of heredity and environment in determining the development of any individual.

GENETIC BUILDING BLOCKS

THE RAW MATERIAL: DNA

A single fertilized cell is the beginning of an enormously complex human being. How does development proceed from such humble origins? This question has preoccupied philosophers and scientists for thousands of years. In the 4th century B.C., Aristotle inferred from examining a chick embryo that the human embryo must be a mixture of male seminal fluid and female menstrual blood. The female must provide the basic embryo substance, and the male semen must stimulate its growth. The Greek physician Galen, 500 years later, proposed a theory that dominated thinking about prenatal life for the next 16 centuries. According to Galen, a minute prefabricated embryo was encapsulated in the "female semen." The preformed baby was set free to increase in size by contact with the male's ejaculate.

Even after development of the microscope in 1677, Galen's theory of **emboitement,** or encasement, prevailed. The debate in the 17th and 18th centuries concerned which parent carried the preformed child. The "ovists" said the baby was contained in the ovary; the "homunculists" claimed that the infant was preformed in the head of the sperm and that the womb served merely as an incubator in which the already assembled child flourished. Finally, in 1759, a medical student named Caspar Friedrich Wolff replaced these misconceptions with two sound concepts: (1) the body is not preformed but assembled out of small structures (Wolff called them "globules"), and (2) male and female make equal contributions to their offspring. Wolff's first premise was the beginning of the field of study called **embryology.**

With the aid of the microscope, the field of embryology grew to higher levels of sophistication between the 18th and 20th centuries. Technological advances in the 20th century brought the picture of prenatal development into even sharper focus. Until Wolff, scientists had resorted to theories of preformed babies because, in that pretechnological age, miniaturization seemed the only possible way of transferring information from parent to offspring. Once scientists could observe directly the union of parent cells and the first 6 days of life under the microscope, they realized that a "code" is transferred from parents to offspring, not a tiny being.

In the late 19th century and in the 20th, embryologists have worked to crack this code. They have identified chromosomes and genes, and they have demonstrated the duplicating powers of **deoxyribonucleic acid (DNA),** the fundamental genetic ingredient. Each human cell was found to contain 23 pairs of chromosomes, 46 altogether, each very long and thin chromosome being made up of more than 1000 genes strung out like a chain. The two chromosomes of each pair, one having come from the male parent and from the female parent, are similar in size and shape and are called **homologous.**

Each gene, which occupies a specific location on the chromosome, is either a whole DNA molecule or a part of one. DNA had been recognized for some time as a constituent of genes; in the 1940s, Oswald Avery proved it responsible for the transmission of hereditary traits in bacteria. Then in 1953, scientists James D. Watson and Francis Crick at Cambridge University figured out the unique construction of the molecule and demonstrated the synthesizing powers that make it the chief architect of human and all other development.

The very long DNA molecule (Figure 2.4) consists of two strands twisted about each other and connected by cross steps to form a laddered spiral called a "double helix." These strands, made up of alternating sugar and phosphate molecules, are not joined together at random. They are formed from specific combinations of molecules: A (adenine), C (cytosine), G (guanine), and T (thymine) pair in particular combinations. T will pair only with A, G only with C. Adenine, cytosine, guanine, and thymine are nitrogen bases. One of the pair of nitrogen bases making up a rung therefore determines what the other will be. Each nitrogen base plus the sugar and phosphate molecules to which it is attached constitute a nucleotide. Thus one strand of nucleotides is a **template** for the other.

The DNA making up a gene and, in turn, part of a chromosome, which is normally packed tightly into the cell nucleus, "unzips" during cell division, or **mitosis,** to form two single strands. Each strand of the helix synthesizes the complementary strand, an old T + sugar + phosphate picking up a new A + sugar + phosphate from the substances in the cell nucleus, an old A picking up a new T, and

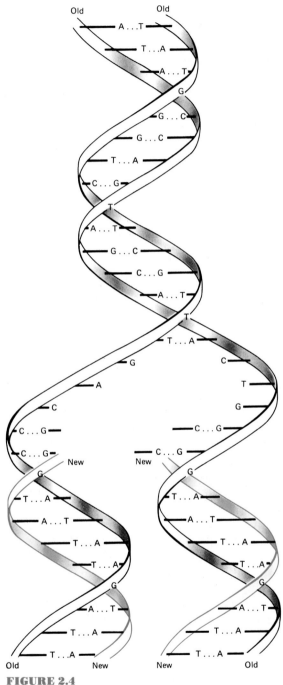

Old   Old

A...T

T...A

A...T

G

G...C

G...C

T...A

C...G

T

A...T

G...C

C...G

A...T

T

T...A

G   C

A   T

C   G

C...G   C...G

C...G   New   New

New   G

G

T...A   T...A

A...T   A...T

T...A   T...A

T...A   T...A

G   G

A...T   A...T

T...A   T...A

T...A   T...A

Old   New   New   Old

FIGURE 2.4

Two polynucleotide chains intertwine to form a double helix, which is the structure of the DNA molecule. When a parent DNA molecule replicates to form two identical daughter molecules, the two strands of the double helix separate. Each serves as the template for the synthesis of a complementary strand. Individual nucleotides are incorporated at the correct positions according to the base-pairing rules, adenine (A) picking up thymine (T), guanine (G) picking up cytosine (C), and so on.

so on. Thus two new and identical helixes are formed in place of the unzipped one. In this way all 46 chromosomes of the cell duplicate themselves; then they draw apart. Each of the two sets of 46 chromosomes moves to a far side of the cell. A wall forms between the sets, and the cell begins to divide. The remarkable ability of DNA to duplicate itself and transmit the blueprint of the human being from one cell to the next allows development to proceed from the one-cell zygote to the multi-million-celled fetus.

TRANSMITTING THE GENETIC BLUEPRINT: RNA

Although each cell of the human being carries the blueprint for the whole structure via DNA, it is impossible for cells to become specialized and form different body parts without additional building specification. The specification is provided by **ribonucleic acid (RNA).** Once the genes are partitioned into newer progeny cells, the blueprint is broken down into **transcripts of RNA.** These guide the synthesis of any one of the thousands of proteins needed to create and sustain life in a cell or organ.

The information coded in DNA molecules is transcribed into RNA molecules, and from RNA the information is translated into protein molecules. Enzyme or catalytic protein molecules participate in almost all chemical reactions within living cells. Structural proteins are the building blocks of the cells. The developing human being is formed from these proteins and ends up as a complex system of interdependent functioning parts.

MEIOSIS

How is it possible for two cells, sperm and ovum, to combine during conception, yet *not* produce a fertilized egg with double the right number of chromosomes? How does the fertilized cell get 46 chromosomes instead of 92? The answer is **meiosis.** The germ cells of the testes and ovaries, from which the **gametes,** the sperm and ova, are formed, divide by meiosis, a process of chromosome division unique to these cells. Each sperm or ovum has only one-half the chromosomes of its parent cell; it carries 23 chromosomes (Figure 2.5).

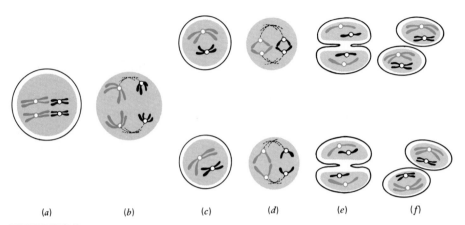

FIGURE 2.5
(a) Meiosis begins when the homologous chromosomes pair together and double. (b) Then the membrane of the nucleus dissolves, a spindle forms, and the members of each pair separate and move toward opposite ends of the cell. (c) The cell divides. (d) In the next phase a spindle forms in each of the two cells, and each set of doubled chromosomes lines up along the equator of the spindle. Each doubled chromosome splits into two daughter chromosomes, which move to opposite poles. (e) The daughter chromosomes are completely separate, and the cells begin to divide. (f) Four gametes, each with half the chromosomes of the parent cell, have formed.

The chromosomes of a germ cell line up side by side in homologous pairs. As indicated earlier, one chromosome of each pair is paternal in origin, the other maternal. While aligned thus, the **homologues** of each pair double. At this stage any of the four strands lying together may break and the broken segments rejoin. If two strands from different chromosomes break at the same level, **crossover** may occur and portions of the strands rejoin in new combinations. Crossing-over increases the many possible gene combinations from one set of parents from 144 billion possibilities to an almost infinite number. After this exchange of genetic material, the paired and doubled chromosomes separate and separate again as their cells divide and divide again, leaving the eventual sperm and ovum with only half the chromosomes that body cells contain. Because the first separation, that of the paired homologues, is random, each gamete is a random combination of maternal and paternal chromosomes. Thus when the 23 chromosomes from the sperm and the 23 chromosomes from the ovum line up in that fateful half hour of nucleic combination, at conception, they both restore the double number of chromosomes and create a brand new cell or zygote. From every such union a human being with genetic endowment unlike any other is created.

THE SEX CHROMOSOMES

The chromosomes in that human being determine, among other things, whether the individual is male of female. Of the 23 chromosome pairs in the zygote, one consists of the 2 sex chromosomes. If 2 large X chromosomes constitute the pair, the zygote will develop into a female. If the pair consists of a large X and a small Y chromosome, a male will develop.

Because females are XX, when a female's germ cells divide to form eggs, every egg contains an X sex chromosome. In contrast, when a male's germ cells divide to form sperm, some sperm contain an X and some a Y sex chromosome. Whether a baby turns out to be male or female depends on which **sperm** unites with the egg, not which egg is available.

The desire to control the sex of one's children has been channeled into the "great sperm race." Examining the contestants, scientists have found a number of differences between the X-carrying **gynosperm** and the Y-carrying **androsperm.** The X-carrying sperm is fatter, a bit slower, and somewhat harder than the Y-carrying sperm. The Y-carrying sperm is sleeker, swifter, and shorter lived. These differences suggest that the timing of conception and the chemical state of the vagina during conception are relevant factors for determining or predicting a baby's sex. Ovulation, female orgasm, and a baking soda douche all increase the alkalinity of the vagina, a condition favorable for all sperm, but especially so for the Y-carrying sperm, which are more likely to be killed by the normal acidity of the vagina. The likelihood of conceiving a boy has been found to increase from 53 percent to between 60 and 68 percent if a woman douches with baking soda, has intercourse at the time of ovulation, and has an orgasm. The likelihood of conceiving a girl has been increased from 47 to 54 percent if a woman uses a vinegar douche, has intercourse the day before ovulation, and does not have an orgasm (Annis, 1978; Whelan, 1975).

The most recent efforts to control sex of offspring involve separating gynosperm and androsperm before artificial insemination. W. Paul Dmowski and his colleagues (1979) at Michael Reese Hospital in Chicago use a separating technique that causes the most active, Y-carrying, sperm to swim to the bottom of a test tube filled with blood protein. This bottom layer, with its greater concentration of Y-carrying sperm, is then used to inseminate the woman. The majority of conceptions in Dmowski's research have been male. An electrophoresis process being developed by Rafael Tejada of the Tyler Clinic in California depends on the fact that X- and Y-carrying sperm have different surface electric charges. Sperm are injected at the top of a specifically designed machine that draws 65 percent of the Y-carrying sperm to a positively charged pole (Fleming, 1980).

A perfect formula for determining a child's sex may never be found. But with couples having fewer children, the pursuit of sex-predicting or sex-determining techniques is likely to become more intense than ever.

THE AUTOSOMAL CHROMOSOMES

The sex chromosomes are only 1 pair in 23. The other 22 are **autosomes.** These carry most of the genetic code for development—for intelligence, for physical size, for eye color, and so on.

Patterns of Genetic Inheritance

There are two simple patterns of genetic inheritance for the 22 pairs of autosomes. The first pattern is that of **autosomal recessive** inheritance. It works this way. The gene for a characteristic must be inherited from both parents for the trait to appear in the offspring. When both parents pass on the gene for the characteristic, giving the zygote a double dose, the zygote will be **homozygous** for this trait. Persons with blue eyes are homozygous for eye color: they inherited two recessive light-pigmentation genes from their two parents. If they had only one of these recessive genes, they would have brown eyes. In that case, they would have a single dose of the recessive gene, and would be **heterozygous** for eye color. Their recessive gene for light pigmentation would very likely remain unexpressed, and they would be a carrier for that trait. The light-pigmentation gene might be passed on unexpressed for generations, until one of their descendants carrying the trait married another carrier and produced a blue-eyed child. If only one gene causes a particular characteristic to appear, the pattern of inheritance is **autosomal dominant.** This means simply that a person needs only a single dose to show the trait.

Physical Appearance

Pathways for inheriting physical features are relatively simple and direct. Brown eye color can be attributed to genes for heavy pigmentation. Such genes are dominant over those for light pigmentation, which give the illusion of blue color. Skin color can be attributed to the same pigment that causes eye color plus a related pigment, the effects of blood pigment shining up through the skin, and the bluish tinge from the opaque underlying layers of the skin (Scheinfeld, 1965). Curly hair grows out curved from hair follicles with a flat, oval construction. Genes for curly hair are dominant over genes for straight hair, except in children with Down's syndrome. Prominent noses are dominant over moderate-sized noses, thick lips over thin, cleft chins over smooth, shortness over tallness. Nevertheless, although a given physical trait of an individual may be traceable to a particular gene or combination of genes, extreme differences in environment, including diet, health, and living conditions, can still play a role in determining how fully these traits are expressed. Skin color, as we have noted, is an inherited characteristic that may be modified by the amount of available sunlight. Body weight is another aspect of physical appearance that has a hereditary basis but is vulnerable to environmental influences, particularly in females.

Until scientists can decode the genetic combination for every single human being, no one can predict another being's physical appearance. True, we may know from observing the parents that a zygote probably has inherited straight hair, a high forehead, brown eyes, a cleft chin, and tallness. We may even know with certainty that a fetus is male or female and carrying a gene or chromosome for a specific condition like Down's syndrome. But we still cannot read all of the signals in the genetic code, and there is always an element of chance in sexual reproduction. Embryologists are working hard to decode the signals, to read the chemical pieces that comprise human beings. But we are all still far more than the known sum of our chemical parts.

INHERITANCE OF BEHAVIORAL TRAITS

Research into human genetics is extremely complex. A single facial feature, such as the nose, is affected by genes for nostrils, bridge, size and rate of development, skin tone, blood type, and so on. When we go beyond physical features into the realm of social behavior, the situation becomes infinitely more complicated because all human behavior and perception are influenced to some degree by environment and because the behavior of human beings cannot easily be divided into discrete units controlled by identifiable genes on particular chromosomes (Rosenthal, 1970). The best psychologists can do is to tease apart the characteristics that are caused primarily by genes and that resist environmental influence from those that are more vulnerable to the environment.

Genetic research is one of the most exciting fields in science today, and new discoveries about how genes operate roll off the presses with remarkable speed. Geneticists now know, for example, that genes are not static in their regulation of behavior. Genes themselves may "jump" or "split," thereby generating complex organizational changes in systems of genes. They may turn on and off at different points in development. Therefore, genetically influenced characteristics may change over time and, conversely, characteristics that seem stable over long periods of time, in fact, may not have a hereditary basis. Although most developmental psychology textbooks—including this one—have a chapter on heredity before a chapter on environmental effects, that arrangement of topics may be inadvertently misleading. Genetic influences are not programmed in and then locked on course, at the moment of conception. Genetic effects do not always precede environmental effects, and "genetic" is not a synonym for "unchanging" (Plomin, 1983).

Yet even as geneticists learn more and more about how genes work, their findings are not always immediately applicable to the study of human behavior and development. Several obstacles stand in the way of easy cross-fertilization of ideas. For one thing, within the field of developmental psychology, much work focuses on group processes and norms prevailing among large numbers of people. Developmentalists may ask, for example, about differences between males and females or about how humans come to use language. But behavior genetics focuses almost entirely on the inheritance of differences between individuals. A second reason that findings about the genetics of behavior have been slow to infiltrate the field of child development is that behavior geneticists most often have studied complex clusters of genetic variations rather than simple single-gene variations. Developmentalists have wanted simple answers to their questions about whether traits are inherited or not. Geneticists have not yet discovered a single gene that produces variations in the sorts of complex behaviors that interest these psychologists. They do not even know of a complex behavior that is entirely under genetic influence. Rarely can more than half of the variability of an observed trait be traced to genetic influence (Plomin, 1983). At present, therefore, although the principles and findings of geneticists are extremely important to students of human development, it will be some time before we understand specifically how human chemistry affects complex human behavior. In the meantime, we can continue our efforts to chart the hereditary basis of behavior by means of various indirect methods.

BEHAVIOR GENETICS: METHODS

Studies of Twins

Sir Francis Galton, a cousin of Charles Darwin, led scientists to one of the most effective strategies for identifying characteristics with a strong inherited basis. Galton realized that two children born with exactly the same genotype, that is, identical twins, would provide scientists with a unique opportunity for observing the contributions of heredity and environment. Since the turn of the century, studies of twins have been a major source of information about the relative power of heredity and environment over human behavior. Advances in our understanding of how twinning occurs have given this strategy additional scientific merit.

There are two types of twins, commonly called "identical" and "fraternal," but more accurately referred to as **monozygotic (MZ),** or single-egg twins, and **dizygotic (DZ),** or double-egg twins. Monozygotic twins originate from the same fertilized egg and thus have the same genotype. In an early stage of development, the single egg divides to form two embryos. In the uterus, these two individuals usually share a single fetal bag, or chorion, and one placenta, but in about one out of

four cases, the two identical embryos move into the womb separately and become implanted at different points (Scheinfeld, 1965). Dizygotic twins develop when the hormone that triggers ovulation is elevated and two ova are released at the same time and are fertilized by two sperm. The two zygotes have genotypes that are as different as those of any two siblings. Monozygotic twins are the same in every way, including sex, but DZ twins may receive the same or different sex chromosomes. They may be completely different in appearance or look very much alike, just as other brothers and sisters do.

The basic method of studying twins is to compare the similarity or **concordance** of MZ twins with that of DZ twins. Differences in MZ twins can be attributed solely to differences in the environment. Differences in DZ twins can be attributed to environment plus heredity. Comparing the two types of twins helps show which traits are inherited. Comparing MZ twins reared together and MZ twins reared apart is an even surer means of studying how environmental factors affect development. Adoption agencies usually place MZ twins in similar circumstances, however.

Although they are very useful to the behavior geneticist, twin studies have a number of limitations. First, these studies cannot totally separate

Monozygotic twins (front) are identical in appearance and abilities; dizygotic twins (back) can be as unalike as any two brothers or sisters.

environment and heredity. For instance, identical twins, because they look so much alike, may be treated more nearly alike than fraternal twins are (Nichols, 1969; Scarr, 1969a). They may also spend more time together. Thus their environments may be more nearly similar than those of fraternal twins. Although in the womb they may occupy the same chorion, one identical twin may occupy a more favorable spot than the other, perhaps receiving a little more oxygen or nutrients. Even so slight an advantage can bolster one twin's physical development. Abnormalities in chromosomes and resulting disorders (for example, leukemia) also have been found to occur in one identical twin and not in the other (Levitan and Montagu, 1971), suggesting that even identical twins are not always identical. Finally, twin studies cannot usually tell researchers exactly which genes are in question, even for traits that are demonstrated to be inherited.

Analysis of Pedigrees or Family Trees

In another method of studying heritability, a researcher may find an individual with a particular trait or disorder, the **index case,** and examine each relative on the family tree for the same trait

or disorder. Sir Francis Galton's *Hereditary Genius,* published in 1869, applied the **pedigree** technique to a number of outstanding judges, statesmen, men of literature and science, poets, painters, and musicians. But perhaps the most famous applications of the pedigree technique, although by no means the most scientific, were the studies of the "Jukes," by Richard Dugdale (1877), a New York prison inspector, and of the "Kallikaks," by Henry Goddard (1912), director of a New Jersey school for the mentally retarded. The study of the family Dugdale called the "Jukes" covered seven generations, 540 blood relatives and 169 related by marriage and cohabitation. Through the generations, Dugdale found "crime, pauperism, disease, and insanity" rampant in this family. He identified more than 500 of its members as social degenerates.

"Kallikak" is also a dubbed name, from the Greek *kalos,* "good," and *kakos,* "bad." As a young Revolutionary War soldier, Martin Kallikak sired an illegitimate son by a retarded tavern maid. Later he married a woman of "good stock." The testimony of townsfolk was the basis for evaluating each Kallikak (Figure 2.6). In five generations, some 480 people descended from the maid. There were a number of drunkards, harlots, paupers, convicts, and horse thieves as well as many illegitimate children and 143 descendents reported to be fee-

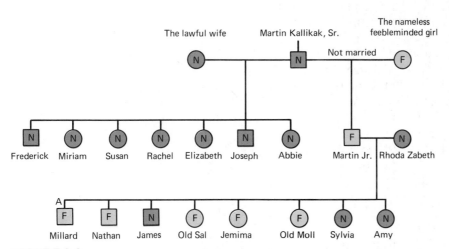

FIGURE 2.6

Henry Goddard's study of the notorious "Kallikaks"—good and bad—was an early use of the pedigree technique for tracing genetic influences on development. This family tree indicates that, in the judgment of their townsfolk, Martin's legitimate sons and daughters were all normal (N), but illegitimate Martin Jr., was feebleminded (F) like his mother and so were a number of the grandchildren (Goddard, 1912).

bleminded. Among the 496 descendants of Martin's marriage, all judged to be at least normal in intelligence, were one who was "sexually loose" and two with an "appetite for strong drink." The others became landholders, traders, and educators and married well. Goddard ignored the differences in rearing and background of these two lines of descent and attributed all to heredity. Although these two examples of the pedigree method are more interesting than they may be accurate, pedigree studies, if done systematically and authentically, can yield useful information about heritability.

Consanguinity Studies

Consanguinity studies examine the degree of relationship between family members who have an identical trait or disorder. They are like a cross-sectional pedigree study. If the incidence among first-degree relatives—mothers, fathers, offspring, siblings—is higher than among second-degree relatives—aunts, uncles, nieces, nephews, cousins—some genetic basis for the characteristic can be inferred (Rosenthal, 1970).

Observation of Adopted Children

If an adopted child in some way resembles his or her adopted parents more than the biological parents, the resemblance is assumed to come from environmental influences. Researchers have compared the IQ scores of adopted children with IQ scores of their biological mothers and adoptive mothers. Adoptive families are said to provide **cross-fostering** when they have characteristics that differ markedly from those of the natural parents. The rearing of children of retarded parents in families of normal IQ is an example. Comparisons can be made between the adopted children and children reared by their natural, in this case retarded, parents. In a classic work, Marie Skodak and Harold Skeels (1949) studied children of retarded mothers with a mean IQ of 63 who had been adopted by parents with normal IQs. The mean IQ of the children was 104. This was higher than the IQ of children who stayed with their retarded mothers, but lower than that of children of nonretarded mothers adopted into the same kinds of families. This study illustrates how one charac-

Like father, like son. Similarities between parents and their children suggest the importance of heredity in determining the child's nature and development as well as appearance. But they do not prove it, because how the parent acts with the child also is likely to influence his or her development. The relative contributions to development of heredity and environment cannot be established by examining parent-child similarities.

TRANSRACIAL ADOPTIONS

Sandra Scarr and Richard Weinberg (1983) put a new wrinkle on adoption studies when they decided to follow black children who had been adopted into white families. One question they hoped their study might help to answer was why black children, as a group, score lower than white children on standard IQ tests. Was the reason, as some have asserted, because blacks inherit lower intelligence? Was the reason, as others have asserted, because environments within which many black children are reared poorly prepare them for performing on IQ tests—indeed, as poorly as children of any color might perform under the same circumstances? The relationship between race and intelligence is a politically touchy issue, but knowing the truth of the matter would help psychologists plan strategies of intervention. Accordingly, in 1974, Scarr and Weinberg launched two large adoption studies. The Transracial Adoption Study, conducted in Minnesota between 1974 and 1976, was to test the hypothesis that black children raised in white families would score on IQ and school-achievement tests as well as other adopted children. The second, the Adolescent Adoption Study, was to measure the cumulative effects of differences in family environments on children's development when they reached late adolescence and the end of child rearing.

Participants in the Transracial Adoption Study were 101 families with 176 adopted children, of whom 130 were classified as black. Of the adopted children, 111 had been adopted before they turned 1 year old, and 65 were adopted after that age. Another 143 biological children of the adoptive parents were also included in the study. Tests given when the children averaged 7 to 10 years of age showed that adoptive parents and their biological children scored somewhat above average on intelligence tests appropriate to their ages. The black adoptees were also found to score above average. Black children adopted before they turned 1 year old scored 110 on IQ tests, some 20 points higher than comparable children from the black community. What did these scores mean? Scarr and Weinberg interpreted them to mean that (1) genetic differences between blacks and whites do *not* ac-

count for most of the demonstrated differences in IQ scores between the racial groups and (2) black children reared and schooled in the white culture that produces the IQ tests perform as well as other adoptees in white families.

But environment was not all-powerful. Correlations of the IQ scores of children and their biological and adoptive parents showed that intelligence was related to both genetic and environmental variation. Statistical analyses showed an average correlation with the adoptive parents' scores of .29 and with the biological parents' scores of .43. When they were corrected for the restricted variance in the sample (a product of the adoptive parents' above-average brightness), these correlations were .37 and .66 respectively. Either way, the correlation between biological relatives was significantly higher than that between adoptive relatives. Scarr and Weinberg conclude that, after correcting for selective placement, 40 to 70 percent of the IQ variation they found derived from genetic differences in the children.

The correlations of IQ test scores among siblings showed a different picture, however. All young siblings living together—adopted or biological—scored similarly. In fact, the correlations among their scores (.43) were *too* high to fit comfortably into any psychologist's model of the genesis of intelligence. Should not one expect biological siblings' scores to correlate more highly than adoptive siblings' scores? After all, such was the case between parents and children.

To solve the puzzle, Scarr and Weinberg turned to the findings from their Adolescent Adoption Study. In this study, both children and their adoptive families were white; 194 adoptive children had spent an average of 18 years in 115 different adoptive families. All of the children had been adopted before they turned 1 year old. At the time of the study, 1975 to 1977, the adoptees were all between 16 and 22 years old. All of the parents in the study were of working- or middle-class status and scored similarly—about 115, slightly above average—on the IQ tests. The adoptees scored an average of 106 on IQ tests. In this study, the correlation of .52 between biological parents' and their adolescent children's scores was reasonably close to that from the Transracial Adoption Study and, as in that study, was higher than the correlation between

Studies of transracial adoptions can help tease apart the relative influences of heredity and environment.

adoptive parents' and children's scores (.14). The correlation between biological siblings' scores was also close to that of siblings in the Transracial Adoption Study (.35). So far, no major surprises. *But the IQ correlation of adopted children reared together in the same family was absolutely zero!* Here is a set of figures that seems too *low* to fit comfortably into any model of intelligence.

But on second glance, that utter lack of correlation in the scores of adoptees reared as brothers and sisters makes good sense. Scarr and Weinberg speculated that older adolescents are essentially free of their families' influences. They have made important choices on their own, choices that are in keeping with their own talents and inclinations. They have chosen their own niches and in so doing have grown to resemble their siblings less and less. When data from both studies are combined, the picture is consistent. Young children, whether they are related genetically or not, resemble each other intellectually because they share one family environment. But as unrelated children grow up and find their own places in the world, as they "graduate" from their families' influence, they resemble each other less and less. Adolescents choose niches that are related to their genotypes, and for adopted individuals, these genotypes can be very different from those of their adoptive "brothers" and "sisters."

What do these findings tell us about the development of intelligence, about racial differences, and about the possibilities for change? First, say Scarr and Weinberg, black adoptees respond, like any adoptee, to the environment in which they are raised. The IQ scores of both samples of adoptees in these studies, white and black, were higher than the norm because their environments were more advantageous than the norm. Second, white and black adoptees will respond to the advantages in their environment consistently with their biological inheritance. Those with higher intellectual abilities will flourish in their adoptive families and will outperform those with lower intellectual abilities. Third, individual differences in young and adolescent adoptees are related to variations in intellect among **both** adoptive and biological parents, even though most adoptees' IQ scores were higher than those of their biological parents. Ultimately, people have only so much potential for a favorable environment to draw out. Finally, when psychologists understand which environmental factors make a difference in development and which do not, and when they can realistically predict which sorts of interventions will most affect which individuals, they can best serve the interests of all children.

teristic—intelligence—is affected by both genetic endowment, the natural parents' IQ, and by environment, that is, the adoptive parents' IQ.

BEHAVIOR PATTERNS

Even though many aspects of behavior cannot be traced directly to specific single genes, the studies of twins and the other methods just described have allowed those interested in children's psychological development to survey the contributions of heredity and environment to particular temperaments, abilities, and behavior problems. Some behavior patterns seem to have a definite genetic basis (see Figure 2.7).

Personality refers to the unique and consistent way an individual behaves and approaches the world—outgoing, cheerful, determined; quiet, shy, passive; boisterous, greedy, aggressive, blundering. **Temperament,** the natural disposition of the infant—active or quiet, irritable or calm, and so on—is a developmental forerunner of personality. Alexander Thomas, Stella Chess, and Herbert Birch

When these triplets, who had been separated in infancy, discovered one another as young men, they found that they shared more than physical appearance. They smiled and talked in the same way, had similar food preferences, and listened to the same kind of music. They had identical IQs, smoked too much, and held their cigarettes the same way.

(1968) did a longitudinal study on temperament, following a number of children from infancy to adolescence.[1] They found that parents' perceptions of their children's temperaments had a high degree of stability throughout infancy and childhood, suggesting that there is indeed some hereditary basis for temperamental traits. Their findings also indicated that individuals of similar temperament may develop differently, however, depending on the ways in which they interact with their parents and the ways parents respond to their children's particular traits. For example, two of the infants in the study were MZ twins adopted into separate families of similar socioeconomic level. The baby girls had similar temperamental traits as newborns. Their sleep patterns were highly irregular, and they cried a great deal when they were awake. Thomas, Chess, and Birch identified them as "difficult infants;" a mother might call them, at this stage, "cranky babies." One set of parents handled their adopted daughter's night awakening by affectionately checking her for physical discomfort, then consistently ignoring the crying. The night awak-

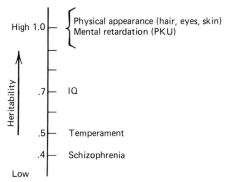

FIGURE 2.7

Some aspects of human development are fully under the control of genetic information. Eye and hair color are two physical traits with essentially total genetic bases. They are relatively unaffected by environmental factors. But IQ is more vulnerable to environmental effects, and temperament may be equally a product of environment and heredity. Schizophrenia may have only a 40 percent inherited basis and may owe its expression more to environmental than genetic causes. Thus although environment and heredity are always potentially present in their effects on human development, their relative influence on particular traits varies widely.

---

[1] We will have more to say about temperament and the particular findings of these researchers in Chapter 14.

ening gradually disappeared, and no behavior problem developed. The other set of parents reinforced night crying by picking up the child every time she cried and soothing and feeding her. At age 27 months, this child had become so difficult to handle that the parents came in for counseling.

Activity level is another aspect of infant temperament that seems to be genetically influenced. Some babies may kick a great deal in the uterus before they are born and then move around in their cribs and flail their arms and legs. Others remain rather still. Later behavior related to activity, such as the speed of reaction, the variety of activities engaged in, and the anxiety or impatience felt concerning a particular action have been shown by Scarr (1966) to be more concordant in MZ twins than in DZ twins.

Sociability is part of an individual's personality. There are many shadings from moderate to extreme, but studies of MZ and DZ twins as well as

RESEARCH FOCUS

A QUESTIONNAIRE STUDY OF TWINS' TEMPERAMENTS

When Arnold Buss and Robert Plomin (1975) set out to learn the degree of heritability of temperament styles, they turned naturally to twins. By comparing the concordances among identical and fraternal twins, they could infer whether and to what extent temperament styles are inherited. They therefore made up a list of 20 questions, five for each of the following characteristics: emotionality, activity, sociability, and impulsivity. They chose these characteristics because earlier twin studies had shown that these probably are inherited. Emotionality describes whether a child is upset, angered, frightened, or cries easily or, conversely, whether a child is easygoing. Activity describes whether a child is always on the go or fidgety or, conversely, whether a child is quiet and sedentary. Sociability describes whether a child is outgoing and friendly or shy and solitary. Impulsivity describes whether a child can resist temptation, has self-control, bores easily, or flits from toy to toy.

The sample consisted of mothers of twins, drawn from a Mothers of Twins Club, who answered the 20 questions. Among the twins, 81 pairs were identical and 57 were fraternal. Of the identical twins, 38 pairs were boys and 43 were girls. Of the fraternal twins, 33 were boys and 24 were girls. The twins' average age was 55 months, and they ranged in age from 1 to 9 years. Most were of white, Anglo stock and middle class.

When Buss and Plomin compared the correlations for the four scales, they found, as expected, higher correlations for identical than fraternal twins. Correlations differed so much that on all measures,

except for impulsivity in girls, the authors considered the findings significant. They concluded that this similarity among identical twins suggests an inherited basis for three of the characteristics measured: emotionality, sociability, and activity. They could not draw a firm conclusion about the heritability of impulsivity. Buss and Plomin noted something peculiar in their data, however. As they explain:

When a trait is partly determined by genetic factors, the fraternal twin correlation should be roughly half the identical twin correlation regardless of the environmental input. Major departures from this expectation suggest environmental biases that differentially influence identical and fraternal twins, and this is the case for the correlations [in the present study]. . . . Our fraternal twin correlations are too low. So there must be nongenetic influences making identical twins more alike or fraternal twins less alike, or both. Buss and Plomin, 1975, (p. 20).

The data, in other words, showed correlations for fraternal twins that were suspiciously low. But what was causing the discrepancy? Was it that identical twins had more similar environments than fraternal twins? Or perhaps the problem lay in the way that they had solicited information. Buss and Plomin had used *ratings* of young twins made by their mothers. Maternal-rating studies might be likelier to minimize differences between MZ twins and maximize differences between DZ twins because mothers would use the other twin as the frame of reference for their ratings of each child.

The investigators concluded that temperaments have a strong inherited component. But they also concluded that the issue of bias and the question of the heritability of impulsiveness must be tested further. In real studies of real people, it seems, investigators cannot always tie up every loose end.

Studies of similarities between identical twins suggest that there is a genetic basis for abilities, intelligence, temperament, sociability, interests, and mental illness.

of groups of individuals followed from birth to maturity suggest that the inclinations to be friendly, uninhibited, and outgoing, or **extroverted,** and to be shy, anxious, and withdrawn, or **introverted,** are inherited (Gottesman, 1963, 1965; Shields 1962; Thomas and Chess, 1977). In her study of the sociability of 6- to 10-year-old MZ and DZ twin girls, Scarr (1969b) stresses the fact that people inherit not specific traits, but general ways of reacting to the environment. These predispositions can be reinforced, modified, or changed. A moderately withdrawn infant whose parents are stimulating and responsive is more likely to become less withdrawn than a similarly predisposed infant who receives little support and stimulation.

There is evidence that heredity has a bearing on a variety of other personality characteristics—adaptability (Klissouras, 1971; Matheny and Dolan, 1975) and dominance, assertion, self-confidence, conformity, motivation, and depression (Vandenberg, 1968). Intriguing studies of identical twins and triplets reared apart since infancy suggest that inheritance governs very fine, even idiosyncratic, traits (e.g., Shields, 1962). When one set of triplets

was reunited recently at the age of 19, for example, it was found that they not only looked like the proverbial peas in a pod, but they also smiled, talked, and laughed alike. They liked the same foods, even held their cigarettes identically (*New York Times,* September 19 and 23, 1981). A pair of identical twins, reunited at age 47, discovered mystifying similarities. Both excelled at sports but not at math, spoke at the same rapid rate, had quick tempers, and flushed the toilet *before* using it (Chen, 1979).

In brief, we have strong evidence for the influence of genetic factors on personality. The evidence is weakest in three separate areas: (1) for very early ages, such as the first 6 months of life; (2) for personality traits that verge on social attitudes; and (3) for very specific behaviors (like the twins' toilet flushing, noted above). In contrast, evidence is strongest for personality "traits," or characteristics, like sociability, emotionality, and physical activity. Further investigation of people's fears, anxieties, angers, and even their fidgeting styles may well show that these aspects of personality, too, have biological foundations (Goldsmith, 1983).

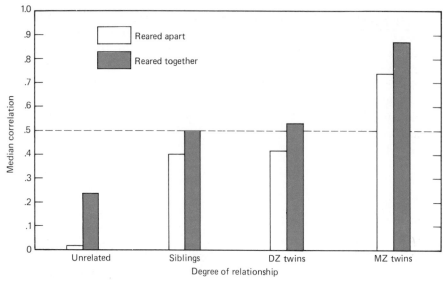

FIGURE 2.8

The contributions to intellectual development of heredity and environment are indicated by the mean values for correlations of IQ scores of unrelated individuals, brothers and sisters, DZ (fraternal) twins, and MZ (identical) twins raised in the same homes or in different homes. The correlations were gathered from many studies (Erlenmeyer-Kimling and Jarvik, 1963).

INTELLIGENCE

The abilities that constitute intelligence—verbal comprehension and fluency, numerical ability, spatial perception, reasoning, memory—are also, in part, genetically determined; a number of genes are involved. Numerous studies of twins and family trees have supported the view that intelligence is related to genetic inheritance. From a review of the literature extending back 50 years and drawing on 52 studies and 30,000 correlations between parents and children, brothers and sisters, Loise Erlenmeyer-Kimling and Lissy Jarvik (1963) concluded that individuals who are genetically related resemble one another in intellectual abilities and that the resemblance increases in proportion to the degree of relationship (Figure 2.8). In this review, the correlation, or degree of association or concordance, between IQ scores averaged .49 for siblings, .53 for DZ twins raised together, and .87 for MZ twins raised together—demonstrating statistically that genetic factors make a strong contribution to IQ.

But environmental effects on intelligence were also clearly in evidence. When MZ twins were raised apart, the correlation between their IQ scores dropped to .75. In fact, even the IQ scores of *unrelated* children raised together, in orphanages or foster homes, had a correlation average of .23.

A correlation of their scores would not necessarily be expected, unless somewhat similar children were sent to the orphanages or selected for the foster homes. Environmental influences on the development of intelligence, too, are clearly at work.

How much does the environment affect the phenotype for intelligence? That depends on a number of factors. One is the depth of canalization, the degree to which particular aspects of intelligence are protected from the environment. Overall intelligence and the pattern of an individual's intellectual development seem to be rather deeply canalized, within about 25 IQ points, according to one estimate (Scarr-Salapatek, 1975). Specific abilities may be more responsive to circumstances, but we cannot say which ones at present. A second factor that affects expression of the phenotype for intelligence is how extreme the environmental conditions actually are. Never talking to a baby, for instance, would far more dramatically impair the baby's intellectual development than, say, not teaching it nursery rhymes. Furthermore, never talking to an infant during the period when speech ordinarily develops would be far more harmful to the infant's intellectual development than not talking to a teenager. For *when* an environmental factor is encountered is crucial, too.

INHERITANCE OF DISORDERS

Zygotes that have abnormal genes or chromosomes are usually aborted spontaneously, before pregnancy even becomes apparent. It is estimated that only 31 babies are born for every 100 natural conceptions (Fleming, 1980). A defective fetus may be miscarried later in the pregnancy or be stillborn. The majority of pregnancies carried to term result in normal babies. Yet approximately 1 in 16 babies are born with a problem at birth (Apgar and Beck, 1974). These so-called **congenital** problems may show up as soon as the baby is delivered, but half such problems do not appear until later in life. Professionals can counsel families and children who are affected by these handicaps. Some congenital problems can be treated; others may be detected early in the pregnancy and prepared for.

RESEARCH FOCUS

SIMILARITIES OF MENTAL DEVELOPMENT IN TWINS

Because we know that genetic influences are manifested throughout life, and not just at conception or birth, developmental behavior geneticists have devised various ways of tracking such genetic manifestations. One longitudinal study of twins has provided excellent data on the development of intelligence. By comparing the mental development of MZ and DZ twins, Ronald S. Wilson (1983) of the University of Louisville has demonstrated important facts about the nature and extent of the genetic basis of intelligence. Wilson's work is part of the Louisville Twin Study, begun in the 1950s and still under way, in which 494 pairs of twins regularly visit for testing of all kinds. The twins range in age from 3 months to 15 years and are recruited from birth records in the Louisville, Kentucky, area. Twins are tested at various time points: 3, 6, 9, and 12 months; 18, 24, and 36 months; 4, 5, 6 years; 7 and 8 years; 15 years. The tests that they take include the Bayley Scales of Infant Development, the Wechsler Preschool and Primary Scales of Intelligence (WPPSI), the McCarthy Scales of Children's Abilities, and the Wechsler Intelligence Scale for Children (WISC). From such tests, Wilson has been able to chart the course of intellectual development in MZ and DZ twins. The twin study uses blood tests to identify which same-sex twins are MZ and which are DZ. Monozygotic twins, who are always the same sex, share all of their genes. Dizygotic twins, who may or may not be of the same sex, share roughly 50 percent of their genes, the same proportion as any two siblings.

The successive intelligence tests show conclusively that bursts and pauses in intellectual development are closely synchronized in twins and especially in MZ twins (see Figure 2.9). As the curves show, test scores shifted considerably for infant twins. In the early months, twins' scores bobbed up and down but stabilized later in childhood. During their first year, the concordance among MZ and DZ twins was essentially comparable. But from the age of 18 months onward, the concordance between MZ twins' scores was significantly higher than that between DZ twins. The concordance for MZ twins was .82 at 18 months and .88 at 15 years. So strong were these concordances that each MZ twin was a better predictor of the co-twin's score than of his or her own score at the following age. Concordances between DZ twins, in contrast, peaked at 36 months and declined steadily until the concordance at age 15 was only .54. These trends were mirrored in the scores within pairs of twins. Differences between scores of MZ twins were much smaller than those of DZ twins at nearly every age after the first year.

To round out the study of twins' mental development, Wilson also studied their home environments. Psychologists have long believed that a child's home and relationship to his or her parents significantly affect mental development. Interviewers made home visits and noted 200 different factors, some by direct observation, some by asking questions. Four broad categories of factors were rated in these home visits. The first factor, "adequacy of home environment," described how well the physical and emotional environment appeared likely to promote intellectual and social development. The other factors characterized the mother: her temperament; her intellectual, verbal, and housewifely skill; and her warmth, sociability, and talkativeness. These four factors were combined with measures of the parents' level of education and socioeconomic status (SES). When all of these

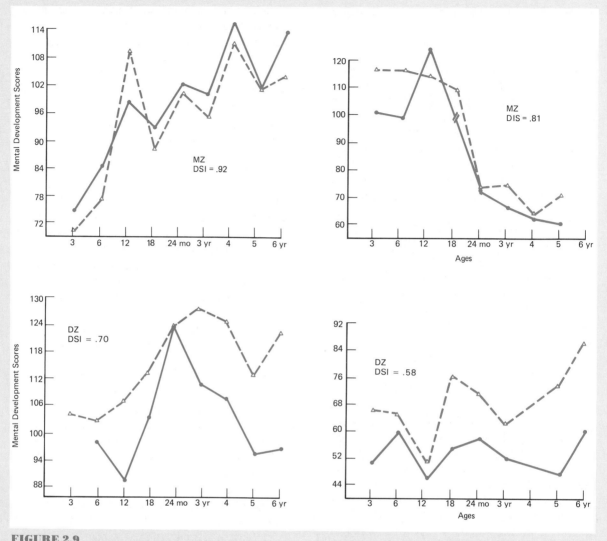

FIGURE 2.9
Trends in IQ scores during early childhood for two MZ pairs and two DZ pairs, showing the greater similarity of developmental patterns in MZ twins (Wilson, 1978).

measures were taken into account and related to the twins' intellectual development, a pattern emerged. At 6 months of age, any relations between mental development and home environment were quite weak. But by 24 months, the relations were stronger, and from the age of 3 onwards, the relations were highly significant. The quality of the twins' home environments thus was implicated in their mental development. It appeared that the atmosphere that prevailed in the family multiplied the effects of parents' capabilities on their children, that environment augmented the effects of heredity.

As Wilson noted, it is always difficult to separate the effects of the environment from heredity in family studies because the parents furnish not only the genetic material, but the home environment as well. But analysis of the data led Wilson to conclude, nevertheless, that the *principal* link between parents' and children's intelligence is a genetic one. Thus intelligence exhibits a strong developmental pattern between very early childhood and adolescence, a pattern with firm genetic roots, but a pattern that is susceptible also to environmental influences.

PROBLEMS RELATED TO SEX CHROMOSOMES

Chromosomal abnormalities that are apparent in the phenotype are estimated to occur only once in every 200 births (Reed, 1975). Normally, meiosis results in the separation of the sex chromosomes into a single X and a single Y or a second X. But sometimes the split is uneven, and sperm and ova have too many or no sex chromosomes. If the sex chromosomes fail to separate at the first meiotic division, the male may wind up with either of two aberrant types of sperm, those with both sex chromosomes (XY) or those with none (O). If the XY sperm fertilizes a normal ovum, the chromosomal composition of the zygote will be XXY. This zygote develops into a male with what is called **Klinefelter's syndrome.** The individual is typically sterile, lacks functional testes, and is likely to develop small breasts. A quarter of the males with Klinefelter's syndrome are also of limited intelligence.

If the sex chromosomes fail to separate at the second meiotic stage, the resulting sperm can be XX, YY, or O. A YY sperm fertilizing a normal ovum produces an individual with XYY sex chromosomes. This genotype, the **XYY syndrome,** has been associated with a high degree of antisocial behavior, unusual tallness, facial acne at adolescence, mental dullness, and a high incidence of abnormal genitalia. Studies in this country have revealed a high percentage of XYY males to be prison inmates (McClearn, 1970). Some scientists interested in human development have suggested that children with this chromosomal makeup are at risk for psychosocial problems and should receive therapy. But not every XYY individual will break the law. In fact, one recent study suggests that the reason there are disproportionately more XYY individuals in prison is not that they are more likely to break the law but that they are more likely to get caught (Witkin et al., 1976). The expectation by parents and others that XYY individuals will have behavior problems, however, may foster them. The XYY dilemma underlines the difference between genes and their phenotypic expression in particular individuals and points to the distinction between prediction and prevention.

If the sperm with no sex chromosomes fertilizes a normal egg, the single X condition causes **Turner's syndrome.** The individual is female but suffers from sexual infantilism. She has a small stature, a broad neck, no secondary sex characteristics, and undeveloped gonads. In some cases, this syndrome may result from the loss of the other sex chromosome shortly after fertilization. Women with Turner's syndrome, in addition to being sterile, also have perceptual-cognitive deficiencies, as proved by their poor performance on tests measuring spatial ability (Levitan and Montagu, 1971; McClearn, 1970).

In the usual meiosis, whether the zygote has one X chromosome and one Y and becomes a boy or two X chromosomes and becomes a girl may also determine whether the infant inherits certain characteristics or disorders that are "sex linked." The large X chromosome carries many genes; the smaller Y chromosome carries fewer genes, and those it carries are primarily involved with initiating male sexual development. The combination of the large X and small Y makes the male zygote more vulnerable to certain genetic disorders. If a female inherits a deleterious gene on one of her X chromosomes from one parent, it is counteracted by a parallel gene on the other X, with a great likelihood that a normal gene will dominate or disguise the effect of the defective gene. But males have no second X and thus no second chance at a normal gene. They are therefore vulnerable to any disorders caused by genes on their single X. For this reason, certain defects occur almost exclusively in males (Reed, 1975).

Hemophilia, the lack of blood-clotting chemicals, for example, appears only in males. We do not find hemophiliac women because male hemophiliacs rarely reproduce. For a female to be born hemophilic, she would have to have both a mother who carries the gene for the disease and a father who has the disease. Half the daughters of mothers who carry the gene for hemophilia will become carriers; half the sons will have the disease. Baldness and color blindness are other X-linked conditions occurring almost exclusively in males (Reed, 1975).

PROBLEMS RELATED TO AUTOSOMAL CHROMOSOMES

When something goes awry during meiosis and the zygote ends up with more or fewer than the required 22 pairs of autosomal chromosomes, there can also be problems. If chromosome pair 21 does not separate, the individual will have 47 instead of 46 chromosomes and suffer from **Down's syndrome.** The extra chromosome brings disturbances in fetal development that are revealed in a number of distinctive physical signs. The child may have retarded motor development; a broad, flat face; oval, upward-slanted eyes and the epicanthic eyefold (a prolongation of the fold of the upper eyelid over the inner corner of the eye); sparse, fine, straight hair; stubby hands and feet; and heart defects (Reed, 1975). Down's syndrome is the most prevalent single-factor cause of mental retardation. Despite the complex problems related to Down's syndrome, a combination of loving care, education, and medical treatment can help those affected to live longer and more self-sufficient lives.

The risk of having a Down's syndrome child increases sharply when the mother is over 30. Only 1 in 3000 children born to mothers under 30 have Down's syndrome. Between ages 30 and 34, the

risk increases to 1 in 600. Mothers in the 35 to 39 age range run a 1 in 280 risk. But 1 child in *every* 80 born to mothers aged 40 to 44 suffers from Down's syndrome. With mothers over 44 years of age, the risk is 1 Down's syndrome child born for 40 normal births (Apgar and Beck, 1974). One explanation for this increasing risk relates to female sex cells. The germ cells that undergo meiosis to become ova or spermatozoa are not affected by aging in the way that body cells are. But they may be vulnerable to certain environmental forces, such as X-rays, viral infections, and possibly even emotional stress (Sameroff and Chandler, 1975; Stott, 1971). This is particularly true of the germ cells of females, which are already partially formed before birth and ripen into ova after puberty. The gametes of older females, then, have been exposed to environmental forces for a long time. This exposure seems to increase the likelihood that pairs of chromosomes will not separate during female meiosis. Recent research, however, indicates that in as many as 25 percent of Down's syndrome cases, sperm carry the extra chromosome (Magenis, Overton, Chamberlin, Brady, and Louvrien, 1977).

OTHER INHERITED PHYSICAL DISORDERS

A number of physical disorders are caused by the pairing of recessive genes. One such condition, **sickle cell anemia,** alters the shape of an individual's blood cells. People with this disorder have hemoglobin molecules that crystallize and stick together to form elongated bundles of rods when the oxygen level is low. Red blood cells, which are normally disk-shaped, assume a sickle shape when their hemoglobin molecules crystallize and form these bundles. Sickled blood cells can clump together and block small blood vessels, causing severe pain. If an essential blood vessel leading to the brain or lung is blocked, the affected person may die (Reed, 1975).

In Africa, where malaria was a common, life-threatening disease, carriers of the recessive gene for the sickled cells were likelier to survive than their relatives with the gene for normal hemoglobin. The sickle cell characteristic thus was adaptive, and its carriers reproduced. The population came to have a high frequency of the gene. In the United

Down's syndrome is the major single-factor cause of mental retardation. These children are today living longer and more productive lives, thanks to better physical care and a better understanding of their capacity to learn.

States, Afro-Americans do not face malaria, but they do face a higher risk of this serious form of anemia. The gene for sickle cell anemia is carried by about 10 percent of American blacks. Thus in one marriage in 100, the two spouses are carriers and may give their children a double dose of this gene. Those who inherit the disorder must be protected from infections and kept from strenuous exercise and high altitudes, any of which may deoxygenate hemoglobin, sickle their red blood cells, and threaten them with pain, debilitation of parts of the body—because they are not receiving enough blood and oxygen through their capillaries—and death. Life-threatening crises are treated with bed rest, pain relief, and transfusions. A vaccine for sickle cell anemia is currently being investigated.

Phenylketonuria (PKU) is a disorder of amino acid metabolism. When infants have received the genes for this recessive trait from both mother and father, they are unable to produce phenylalanine hydroxylase, an important enzyme that converts a basic amino acid, phenylalanine, to tyrosine. If these infants eat normally, they are unable to digest the phenylalanine found in many foods, including milk. This amino acid and its derivative, phenylpyruvic acid, which eventually gives the urine a musty odor, accumulate and prevent normal brain development. Infants are irritable and hyperactive, and one-third of them have seizures; in childhood they will be retarded (Reed, 1975). Once the newborn has consumed milk for several days, however, an excess of the unconverted phenylalanine may be detected in the blood; 8 days after birth seems to be a peak time for detection (Cedarbaum, 1976). The affected infant is given a milk substitute and, later, a special diet containing only the minimum essential amount of phenylalanine. The child must be kept on this special diet for at least the first 6 years of life, until brain development is relatively complete.

Although early diet control limits the abnormalities associated with phenylalanine buildup, treated PKU children seem to have certain residual effects. They are more prone to emotional disturbances in infancy and early childhood, and they may have learning problems in school (Steinhausen, 1974) and IQs lower than those of siblings without PKU (Berman and Ford, 1970; Dodson, Kushida, Williamson, and Friedman, 1976). Claire Kopp and

Arthur Parmelee (1979) suggest that parents' reactions to a child with PKU may be a contributing cause. Parents of PKU children tend to be extremely anxious, for their children are in danger of retardation or poor physical growth if the prescribed diet is not suitable. Their anxiety and guilt may make them overprotective or rejecting toward the affected child.

GENETICALLY TRANSMITTED BEHAVIOR DISORDERS

Childhood behavior problems were examined extensively by Harry Bakwin (1970, 1971a, 1971b, 1971c, 1971d) in a series of studies comparing MZ and DZ twins. For some of these problems, such as sleepwalking, car sickness, bed wetting, constipation, and nail biting, Bakwin found much greater concordance in MZ twins than in DZ twins, suggesting that there may be a genetic component underlying these behavior problems. For other traits, such as thumb sucking, no such concordance of MZ twins was found.

Other studies have focused on more severe behavior disorders. For example, in the last 40 years, many researchers have tried to determine what causes **schizophrenia.** People with schizophrenia, the most common psychosis, have the awesome jumbling of thoughts and speech, hallucinations, and delusions that are usually thought of as madness. The disorder may become evident in adolescence. Twin, consanguinity, and adoption studies all suggest that schizophrenia has a genetic base. The offspring of a schizophrenic parent is 15 times more likely to have schizophrenia than a member of the population at large. Monozygotic twins were found to be concordant for schizophrenia four times as often as DZ twins. Even individuals born of schizophrenic mothers and then reared in adopted homes have a greater likelihood of developing schizophrenia. Foster children reared in the same homes as the children born of schizophrenic parents did not develop schizophrenia, but a large proportion of those with schizophrenic parents did (Rosenthal, 1970). In studies of twins conducted by a number of researchers, relatively few twins of schizophrenics were found to be normal. Most of the twins who did not have schizophrenia behaved in a manner that bordered on it. These so-called "schizoid" individuals were suspicious and rigid in their thinking, had attacks of panic, or became afraid in the face of ordinary challenges.

Findings of this kind, significantly those of Franz Kallman in the United States and Eliot Slater in England, have suggested three principal explanations of the disorder: (1) the polygenic explanation attributes schizophrenia to a number of genes (Gottesman and Shields, 1966); (2) the single-gene theory makes a case for one principal gene modified by multiple factors, such as intelligence (Heston, 1970); and (3) the environmental explanation suggests that genes for schizophrenia are brought to full expression by a stressful environment. This last view is based on research indicating that both MZ twins develop schizophrenia after stressful childhoods. Sociologists have found a higher incidence of schizophrenia in lower socioeconomic classes (Hollingshead and Redlich, 1958). Poverty, inadequate education, and low status may bring on schizophrenia or stress the schizoid to deteriorate. Finally, a number of studies suggest a link between obstetrical complications and schizophrenia (Mednick, 1970; Sameroff and Zax, 1973). In a study of MZ twins who did not both have schizophrenia, the births of the twins who did become schizophrenic had had more obstetrical complications, such as **anoxia,** or oxygen deprivation, and low birth weight (Pollin and Stabenau, 1968).

Another disorder that developmentalists have studied is **dyslexia,** a difficulty in reading and spelling. Dyslexia is an "unexpected" difficulty because those it affects are of normal intelligence, they are people without emotional disturbances, known neurological problems, or other sensory handicaps. Dyslexia is estimated to affect as many as 10 percent of school-age children, and three to four times as many males as females are affected. Late in the 19th century, dyslexia was called "congenital word blindness." Since that time, studies of twins and other relatives have shown dyslexia to have a strong hereditary base. Among MZ twins, the concordance rate for dyslexia is a full 91 percent. Among DZ twins, the concordance is 31 percent. Family studies also show strong evidence for the genetic influence of dyslexia. Siblings and parents of dyslectics test lower for reading than do relatives of unaffected children. Family studies also show that there are several subtypes of dyslexia, some of which appear consistently within families, some of which do not. In one study of 125 dyslectic

Some reading disabilities appear to be inherited.

children (Decker and DeFries, 1981), evidence for the heritability of the "pure" reading disability, which affected 41 percent of the sample, was strongest. Other studies of dyslexia indicate that it is transmitted by more than one gene. Although there are differences between males and females in incidence and type, there is no evidence to date that dyslexia is a sex-linked disorder (Pennington and Smith, 1983).

To correct for the lack of longitudinal data, roughly 5 years after the Colorado Family Reading Study had been completed, John DeFries and Laura Baker (1983) invited the dyslectic control subjects who had not yet turned 17 to take part in a follow-up study. They recruited 102 (51 matched pairs) subjects and tested them and their family members. The investigators wanted to know whether family members' scores resembled each other more over time. They found that parents' and children's reading scores *were* indeed more highly correlated at the later age for the reading-disabled children. DeFries and Baker concluded that children's reading disability seems likely to be the inherited effect of a "major gene." They also

THE GENETICS OF DYSLEXIA

Dyslexia, which afflicts otherwise normal children and adults, makes it difficult for them to read or spell. Letters on a page may seem backwards: one dyslectic boy named Fred called himself "Derf" because of the way his name looked to him. Although investigators have for years tried to locate the precise neurological basis for dyslexia, they have not yet succeeded. The evidence is strong, however, that dyslexia has at least some genetic basis. Twin and family studies show dyslexia as inherited; only adoption studies are missing, because of the difficulty investigators face in trying to locate enough biological parents who gave their dyslectic children up for adoption.

The Colorado Family Reading Study has provided psychologists with their best evidence on the heritability of dyslexia. The study consisted of 125 reading-disabled children with their parents and siblings and 125 matched comparison children with their parents and siblings, for a total of 1044 subjects. Children were admitted to the study if they met the following requirements: (1) reading at least one-half grade lower than expected; (2) age between 7½ and 12 years; (3) IQ of at least 90; (4) living with both biological parents; (5) emotionally and neurologically healthy; and (6) suffering no uncorrected eye or ear problems (Decker and DeFries, 1981). Comparison children were matched for age, grade, sex, school, and home neighborhood. The comparison children's reading levels, however, were at, or higher than, expected for their grade level. All subjects were given an extensive battery of psychometric tests; these measured achievement, mathematical ability, word recognition, reading comprehension, spelling, abstract and spatial reasoning, coding (the ability to transcribe numbers into abstract symbols), and perception.

After wading through a mass of statistical analyses, the investigators, University of Colorado's Sadie Decker and J. C. DeFries, reduced the test results to three comprehensive categories. The first was reading ability; the second was called coding/speed, that is, the speed at which subjects could encode symbols—an ability considered important for reading fluently; the third was spatial visualization and abstract reasoning, which was dubbed spatial/reasoning. Of the dyslectic group, 90 percent fell into one of four subtypes. Each subtype differed significantly from the matched control group. The first subtype, which represented 23 percent of the reading-disabled sample, had low reading and spatial/reasoning scores. The second subtype, which represented 18 percent of the sample, had low reading and coding/speed scores. The third subtype, which represented a full 41 percent of the dyslectic sample, had low reading scores but normal spatial/reasoning and coding/speed scores. The fourth subtype, which represented 9 percent of the sample, scored low on all three clusters of abilities tested.

Next, Decker and DeFries classified the siblings and parents of the reading-disabled sample into these subtypes: 41 percent of the siblings fell into one of the four subtypes. Statistical analysis revealed that the number of siblings who fell into subtype 3—low reading scores but normal spatial/reasoning and coding/speed—was greater than one might expect by chance. Of the parents, 38 percent could be classified into one of the four subtypes, but the numbers of parents in each subtype were *not* greater than might be expected on the basis of chance alone. In short, there was a significant concordance between family members—siblings—only for reading disability (subtype 3). Therefore the evidence for a genetic cause is greatest for this subtype. Why there was no significant concordance between parents' and reading-disabled children's scores is puzzling. One possible explanation was that the method Decker and DeFries used did not chart any changes over time in the reading abilities of family members.

found a marked difference in the degree of correlation with parental scores for reading-disabled versus comparison children. In families of reading-disabled children, over 60 percent of the stability in the children's reading scores over this 5-year period could be attributed to parental factors, whereas less than 1 percent of the stability of reading scores of "normal" children was related to parental factors.

GENETIC COUNSELING

Couples who are planning a family and suspect themselves to be at risk of transmitting a genetic disorder may want the advice of experts. Genetic counseling may someday be an automatic part of family planning, but today certain circumstances should alert prospective parents to their need for it. These include:

1. The couple have at least one child with a condition that might have a genetic base.

2. The prospective mother has had several earlier pregnancies that ended in spontaneous abortion.

3. The couple have relatives who have a genetic problem.

4. The couple are from the same genetic stock or are actually related. In the Old Order Amish religious group, founded two centuries ago by three couples, members are required to marry within the order. They carry a gene for dwarfism, a rare condition that has affected 61 members of this small sect. The recessive gene for **Tay-Sachs disease** has been traced back to a section of Poland originally inhabited by Jews, many of whom dispersed to eastern Europe and America. The disease, not apparent at birth, eventually debilitates and kills its victims in early childhood.

Testing the blood of parents will reveal whether they carry the recessive genes for Tay-Sachs disease, sickle cell anemia, hemophilia, or PKU. When a particular illness is more common in a given ethnic group, all members of that group may be advised to have their blood analyzed. Many Jews of eastern European origin are now tested for Tay-Sachs disease, many blacks for sickle cell anemia. If both parents have the recessive gene, there is

one chance in four that each child will inherit the disorder.

Many gene-based disorders can now be detected prenatally. Couples at risk for passing on recessive-gene and other disorders or for having gametes with an extra chromosome 21 can now proceed to pregnancy with considerable assurance that defects will be identified early. The mother's blood can be tested between the 14th and 20th weeks of pregnancy for an excessive amount of a particular protein. Two very serious conditions of the fetus—spina bifida (a cleft of the vertebral column) and anencephaly (parts of the brain and skull are missing)—can be detected in this way. The principal technique for prenatal detection of genetic abnormalities is **amniocentesis.** In this procedure, the doctor first locates the precise position of the fetus by means of **ultrasound.** High-frequency sound waves directed toward the fetus bounce off its contours and are then transformed into a fairly detailed picture. The doctor is then able to insert a long, hollow needle through the mother's abdomen, through the uterine wall, and into the amniotic sac surrounding the fetus without touching it or piercing the placenta or the umbilical cord (Fig-

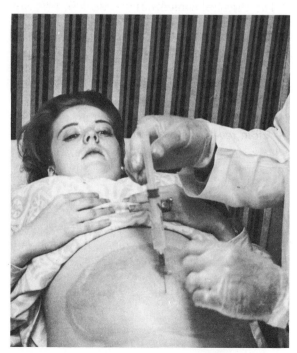

A syringe of amniotic fluid is removed during amniocentesis during the woman's fourth month of pregnancy.

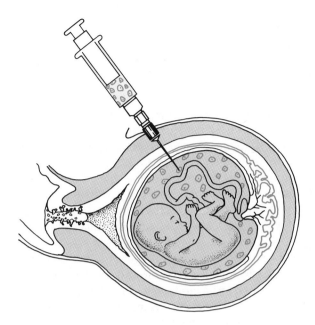

FIGURE 2.10
In amniocentesis a small amount of amniotic fluid is withdrawn through the mother's abdomen by means of a long-needled syringe. The fluid contains cells sloughed off by the growing fetus. The chemical contents of the fluid can be studied directly for evidence of some diseases; skin tissue cells will reveal others. And cells can be cultured and later studied for chromosome irregularities.

ure 2.10). The procedure is usually done in the 14th to 16th week of pregnancy, because earlier the volume of amniotic fluid is insufficient. The fluid withdrawn contains loose cells and other substances from the fetus.

The chemical contents of the amniotic fluid are analyzed directly for any abnormal substances or the absence of enzymes that would reveal the presence of recessive-gene disorders. Approximately 100 of these disorders and other abnormalities can be detected in this way. The loose fetal cells in the fluid have the same genotype as all cells throughout the baby's body. Cultures grown from these cells therefore reveal the presence of an extra chromosome 21 as well as other chromosomal abnormalities. They also indicate the sex of the fetus by identifying chromosome pair 23 as either XX or XY. Thus sex-linked disorders, such as hemophilia, can be predicted.

A new technique, **chorionic villi biopsy,** may soon replace amniocentesis as the most popular method for detecting defects in the fetus. In this procedure, which can be performed as early as the 10th week of pregnancy, a sample of fetal tissue is taken directly through the mother's cervix. The tissue sample is larger and the results faster than with amniocentesis. Chorionic villi, which are taken either by suction or clipped off, are tiny protrusions on the chorion, the membrane that surrounds the fetus and eventually forms part of the placenta. In combination with tests of DNA, chorionic villi biopsies may eventually make it possible for scientists to detect, early in pregnancy, virtually any of the 3800 different genetic problems for which faulty genes may be responsible (Schmeck, 1983).

If tests reveal a genetic disorder, parents may choose to have the fetus aborted, or they may decide that the mother should carry the pregnancy to term. This decision may be influenced by the availability of treatment for the disorder. Some disorders are not presently treatable; others can be controlled. The family's knowledge of the disorder and their psychological readiness for it may be a form of early therapy that improves the outcome. Advances in detection and prediction of genetic disorders place a great burden on prospective parents. But parents who have had affected children without such forewarning advise other couples to take advantage of the knowledge now available.

Couples at risk for bearing infants with disorders eventually may have their eggs and sperm meet in petri dishes. After about 6 days, a few cells would be "microbiopsied," removed from the embryo, without harming it, and studied for normality. Then if all is well, the embryo would be inserted in the uterus. By this method, defective embryos could **be discarded approximately 3 months before amniocentesis is possible** (Fleming, 1980).

SUMMARY

1. An individual is the product of a continual interaction of inheritance and environment. The environment acts on the individual's genotype, the total of his or her inherited genes, to produce a particular phenotype, the individual's visible characteristics and behavior. Most human characteristics are determined by a number of genes.

2. Before initiating a new life, a man and woman may deliberate. One out of 10 couples in this country is childless, because the couple has chosen to delay childbearing or not to have children at all or because the couple has not been able to conceive. Of couples who decide to have children, 1 in 5 has difficulty with conception. Advances in artificial insemination, fertility drugs, surgery to repair fallopian tubes, and the advent of external fertilization have increased the chances of conception.

3. Deoxyribonucleic acid (DNA) is the agent for transmitting heredity; each of the thousands of genes on the individual's 46 chromosomes consists of a whole or part of a DNA molecule. The double-helix structure of this molecule and its unique synthesizing powers allow DNA to transfer genetic information from parents to fertilized egg and from the one-celled fertilized egg to what will eventually be a multicelled human being.

4. Meiosis, the process of chromosome division when gametes form, leaves each ovum or each sperm with one-half the chromosomes of the parent cell. Thus the union of ovum and sperm brings together 46 chromosomes.

5. The so-called 23rd pair of chromosomes determine the sex of the individual. A zygote receiving an X chromosome from each parent will become a girl; a zygote receiving an X from the mother and a Y from the father will be a boy. The other chromosomes, or autosomes, carry most of the genetic code for physical appearance. Inheritance of physical traits is relatively simple, although the expression of these traits varies with the environment.

6. Inheritance of behavioral traits is much more complicated and indirect. Researchers have tried to discover which traits are heritable by determining whether identical twins share them more often than do fraternal twins. Family trees are examined for relatives with the same trait. Adopted children are observed to see whether they have the traits of their biological parents. Although activity levels, sociability, and intelligence cannot be attributed to specific genes, they do appear to be at least partially inherited.

7. Genetic counseling, tests of the blood of prospective parents, and tests of fetal cells taken during pregnancy allow some inherited disorders to be detected in time for parents to prevent, or prepare for, the birth of a handicapped child.

KEY TERMS

Gene	Ribonucleic acid (RNA)	Monozygotic (MZ)	XYY syndrome
Polygenic	Transcript of RNA	Dizygotic (DZ)	Turner's syndrome
Genotype	Meiosis	Concordance	Hemophilia
Phenotype	Gamete	Index case	Down's syndrome
Expression	Homologue	Pedigree	Sickle cell anemia
Reaction range	Crossing-over	Consanguinity	Phenylketonuria (PKU)
Canalized	Gynosperm (X)	Cross-fostering	Schizophrenia
Emboitement	Androsperm (Y)	Personality	Anoxia
Embryology	Autosome	Temperament	Dyslexia
Deoxyribonucleic acid (DNA)	Autosomal recessive	Extroverted	Tay-Sachs disease
Homologous	Homozygous	Introverted	Amniocentesis
Template	Heterozygous	Congenital	Ultrasound
Mitosis	Autosomal dominant	Klinefelter's syndrome	Chorionic villi biopsy

SUGGESTED READINGS

Apgar, Virginia, and Beck, Joan. *Is My Baby All Right?* New York: Pocket Books, 1974. The major congenital problems carefully explained, with personal accounts to humanize the complex medical and psychological impact of birth defects.

Goodfield, June. *Playing God.* New York: Random House, 1977. Cloning, test tube fertilization, and the rest of the brave new world of genetic engineering and the manipulation of life explored by an outstanding science writer.

Guttmacher, Alan F. *Pregnancy, Birth, and Family Planning: A Guide for Expectant Parents.* New York: Viking Press, 1973. Information on conception and family planning as well as a detailed account of pregnancy by an established medical authority.

Lewontin, Richard. *Human Diversity.* New York: W. H. Freeman, 1982. A scholarly treatment of human variety and its basis in evolution, heredity, and environment, including an up-to-date overview of the nature of genetic mechanisms.

Watson, James D. *The Double Helix.* New York: New American Library, 1968. A thrilling suspense story of the competition to unlock the secret of life by discovering the structure of DNA. One of the few lively descriptions of the scientific community.

CHAPTER 3

Environment

A person does not need to be trained as a developmental psychologist to distinguish a child who is flourishing from one who is stagnating. The child who is flourishing will seem curious, alert, and tuned in to the sights, the sounds, and the people of the environment. The child who is stagnating will seem not curious but slow, foggy rather than alert, perhaps dull and inarticulate. But what makes one child flourish and another stagnate? Could it be the amount or kind of stimulation a child receives? How much of the child's development derives from hereditary and biological variables, and how much derives from the environment? Can the effects of heredity be reversed, even partially, in an exceptionally stimulating or exceptionally depriving environment? Can the effects of early environmental deficits be reversed later in life? Psychologists have long been interested in answering questions like these. To do so, they study children's various environments and the people within them to see whether and how they might affect development. In this chapter, we shift now from a focus on heredity to considering the environment as it contributes to children's behavior and development.

STUDYING THE EFFECTS OF ENVIRONMENT

Essentially, psychologists have taken three major approaches to studying the effects of environment on early development. First, they have studied children or the young of other species growing up in poor, deprived environments and have watched for the effects of that deprivation on development. Second, they have observed the development of children in a range of naturally occurring environments—from rich to poor. Third, they have directly intervened in, or enriched, the environments of some children. In this chapter, you will read about the findings, strengths, and weaknesses of each of these three broad approaches to studying the effects of environment on children's development.

DEPRIVATION

The only ethical way that researchers can deliberately deprive young and growing beings of stimulation considered necessary to normal development

Comparing the development of children who live under conditions of severe deprivation with those in adequate circumstances is one way of finding out about environmental effects.

is by experimenting on animals other than humans. They therefore turn to cats, rats, and primates. There is always a danger in applying research findings on animals to human beings, but in carefully constructed experiments, cause and effect can be ascertained precisely enough to justify tentative generalizations to human behavior. Animal research is valuable because it allows for extreme, varied, and well-controlled manipulations of environment. Thus one common starting point for discussions about the effects of environment on development has been animal studies. In 1949, Donald Hebb published a now classic piece of work, *The Organization of Behavior*, in which he theorized about the importance of early experience on intellectual growth. In his wake, many researchers tested the effects of early sensory deprivations on later performance. They found that among rats (Nyman, 1967), dogs (Thompson and Heron,

1954), cats (Riesen, 1965), and chimpanzees (Rogers and Davenport, 1971), early sensory deprivation impairs intellectual development and, conversely, that enriched environments enhance the intellectual development of many species. These studies tell us that the link between sensory experience and intellectual development is a solid one—in laboratory animals.

What about the effects of early deprivation on animals' social and emotional development? Here the work of Harry and Margaret Harlow and their associates at the University of Wisconsin (e.g., Harlow and Griffin, 1965; Harlow and Zimmerman, 1959) provides the classic example. They performed many different sorts of laboratory experiments with rhesus monkeys, depriving infants of social contacts for various lengths of time, watching to see how mothers and infants respond when they are separated, and many other kinds of manipulation. That such separations are painful is apparent to anyone who sees a picture of the animals: they are abject, pitiful creatures. So miserable do separated mothers and infants seem after even brief separation that some researchers have terminated their experiment after just a few minutes, concluding that even brief separations can have dire consequences for development (Hinde and Spencer-Booth, 1971). But Stephen Suomi and his col-

leagues, Susan Mineka and Roberta DeLizio, at the University of Wisconsin carried out a study of the short- and long-term effects of repeated separations of mother and infant rhesus monkeys (1983). Each pair of monkey mothers and infants was separated 16 times, for 4 days each time, when the infants were between 3 and 9 months old. At first, the infants protested being separated, but as the separations were repeated, the infants protested less. Toward the end of the first year, the infants were separated permanently from their mothers and placed together in a group. When these youngsters were observed playing together, their behavior seemed normal, but when 30 weeks later they finally were reunited with their mothers, they avoided them. Monkeys who had not had the early, brief separations, in contrast, actively sought their mothers when they were reunited. This experiment clearly demonstrates the effects of early separations on the mother-child relationship in monkeys, but it is only suggestive as far as human mothers and babies are concerned.

When psychologists study the effects of deprivation on human infants' development, they look for those whose environments lack a particular kind of experience and then compare them with others whose environments are not so lacking. They cannot ethically impose deprivation on human subjects. Studies of children in orphanages and other institutions have been a relatively common way of investigating the effects of deprivation on human development. There, psychologists have found children whose environments lack everyday sights and sounds: the talk of parents and siblings, music from toys or the television set, the sun and tree branches through a window, spoons banging on the kitchen table, the ringing of the telephone or doorbell. In the normal environment, the variety and complexity of everyday experience are sufficient to stimulate children's physical and intellectual growth. But although children in orphanages may be kept clean and dry and well fed, in many of these institutions they receive no continuous care from a single attendant of whom they might grow fond. They receive minimal educational stimulation. They may lie in white-sheeted cribs where they see and hear almost nothing and where the hurried ministrations of an attendant are their only regular contact with others. Many studies have found that institutionalized children develop less

Experimenters cannot deliberately impose deprivation on human infants, so they have used animal subjects to explore the effects of extremes in rearing conditions. This monkey has been reared in isolation, and its effects are evident in his pathetic posture.

quickly and less fully than other children (e.g., Dennis, 1973; Goldfarb, 1945; Spitz, 1946).

Early investigators saw the pale and retarded children in institutions and asserted that the children were suffering from a lack of mother love. Soon the investigators realized that the institutionalized children were deprived of perceptual stimulation as well. They wanted for more than a mother's love. Toys were scarce, the children rarely moved about, and no one played with them or engaged them in conversation. The early comparisons of children in such institutions with groups of children reared at home failed to control for such variables as diet, health, and heredity, and they did not specify which of the depriving conditions accounted for the observed developmental delays. But these early studies did show clearly that environment profoundly affects children's development.

More recent studies have explored variations in the institutional environment. Wayne Dennis (1960, 1973) examined children between birth and 3 years of age confined in institutions in Iran. In two of these institutions, children were given little attention. The attendant-child ratio was 1 adult to 8 children in one institution and 1 adult to 20 children in the other. The children were not put on their stomachs or held in a sitting position when fed, and they had no chance to play with toys, caretakers, or other children. They were very slow in developing basic motor skills. In one orphanage, most of the 1-year-olds could not sit up, and most of the 3-year-olds could not walk. In another, the motor development of the institutionalized infants was from 2 to 12 months behind that of infants in Lebanese and American homes. In a third institution, however, there was 1 attendant for every 3 children. Here attendants often put the infants on their stomachs, held them for feedings, and encouraged them to play actively. These children walked at the usual age.

Dennis and others (see reviews by Clarke-Stewart and Apfel, 1979; Rutter, 1974) have shown that several factors modify the degree of developmental deficit caused by deprivation. The length of a child's stay, the age of the child, and the institution's quality of care all modify the effects of institutionalization. An infant will progress normally for its first 3 months in an institution that meets its basic physical needs for food, warmth, and comfort. But by 3 to 6 months, the first developmental deficiencies may show up. In an impoverished environment, an infant's smiling, vocalizing, and motor development may all be delayed. By the time the child is 1 or 2 years old, intellectual development may be impaired by as much as 50 IQ points. Of course, not all institutions are barren. Where they offer field trips, books, and films and have caretakers who are interested in fostering their charges' development, the children's intellectual growth is much less retarded than it is in other, bleaker environments. Studies show that stimulation and exercise are sufficient to promote children's normal cognitive and motor development, but for social, emotional, and language development, regular and close contact with an adult is necessary.

In the past, institutions have provided naturally occurring environments for psychologists to study. But because psychologists have demonstrated that impoverished institutional environments deprive children of essentials for normal, healthy development, many such institutions now have been closed down or improved. Researchers therefore must study children in other diminished environments that occur naturally. Besides residential institutions, another "natural" form of environmental deprivation occurs among "wild" or **"lost-and-found" children.** Fortunately, cases of lost-and-found children are relatively rare. These are children whose environments are almost unimaginably bleak. Their parents or other caretakers, whether out of ignorance, fear, or prejudice, isolate and deprive the children of virtually all normal social contact. When they are found and released by others, the children are severely retarded in development. Twin boys, for example, were banished to the cellar by their stepmother (Koluchova, 1972, 1976). Other children have been found who were reared in isolation by retarded, mute, or deaf relatives.

Susan Curtiss (1977) has written about the case of a girl she dubbed Genie after the mythical creatures who spend long periods confined in small spaces and then emerge to create miracles. Genie was locked in a room by her father when she was 20 months old. During the day, she was strapped naked onto a potty-chair. During the night, she was strapped into a crib. She almost never saw anyone; she could only overhear her father and brother. Any noise she made was met with a beating. At the age of 13, she was rescued and rehabilitation begun. After 5 years of living in foster care, Genie had progressed remarkably. She could put together utterances several words long, but she could not count. Her language was deficient in important ways; she could not, for example, use pronouns or verb tenses. Curtiss provides evidence to show that Genie was not retarded when her father isolated her, a fact that often cannot be known in other cases of "wild" children. The developmental progress that Genie did make is a tribute to human resiliency. Like many children released from severely deprived environments, Genie began to develop certain skills when she began receiving care and attention. But her developmental deficiencies, notably her language, probably can never recover from the effects of such severe environmental deprivation.

OBSERVATION

Another good way for psychologists to find out about the effects of the environment is to study children in a wide range of natural, or existing, environments rather than in a laboratory or institution, and then to relate differences in these environments to differences in the children's development. Some such studies focus on children from different groups. One kind of group is racial or cultural. In a **cross-cultural study**, a psychologist might observe the ages at which Nigerian and American babies first sit up, crawl, and walk, for example. Another kind of group is socioeconomic. Harvard's Jerome Kagan and Steven Tulkin (1971) conducted a study of the differences in child rearing among a sample of babies and their mothers from two different socioeconomic groups. The design of their study provides a good example of observational research. The 60 subjects studied were 10-month-old, white baby girls from the Boston-Cambridge area. Half of the sample was lower class; the other half was middle class. Class status was assigned according to the amount of formal education and the jobs of the babies' parents: lower class meant one or both parents were high-school dropouts or that the father worked at a semiskilled or unskilled job; middle class meant one or both parents had graduated from college and that the father worked at a professional job. About one-third of the sample was Catholic, and about two-thirds was Protestant. A trained observer visited each home twice, for about 2 hours. He coded behavior at 5-second intervals for 20 minutes, rested for 10 minutes, and then resumed coding for 20-minute segments. The maternal behaviors that were coded included: kissing, initiating physical contact, holding, tickling and bouncing, and talking. The babies' behaviors that were coded included: playing, inspecting, positive vocalization, and negative vocalization. Then followed laboratory assessments in which children listened to tape recordings of meaningful and nonmeaningful speech and to tape recordings of their mother's voice. Children were also observed playing with their mothers in a small room. Kagan and Tulkin found meaningful differences in mothers' behavior and somewhat less marked differences in infants' behavior that were related to social class. Middle-class mothers were more likely to talk to and entertain their infants; their infants were more likely to quiet when their mothers talked and to vocalize after they stopped.

By contrast, sometimes researchers start out with a single, diverse group rather than two social classes, races, or cultures, and they look for correlations between variations in the environment and variations in development. One such study was conducted by Diana Baumrind and Allen Black (1967). The sample consisted of 103 children who were 3 and 4 years old and enrolled at a nursery school affiliated with the University of California at Berkeley. Over a period of at least 3 months, four trained psychologists observed and recorded behavior as the children went through the nursery-school day.

The children were rated on continua of traits such as:

1. Submits to group consensus versus takes independent stand.

2. Suggestible versus has mind of his or her own.

3. Provokes versus avoids conflict with adults.

4. Permits self to be dominated versus will not submit.

Parents' behavior was also measured and a system developed by which an observer recorded the details of parent-child interactions in which one person tried overtly to influence the behavior of another. Every parent was interviewed about child rearing, and the transcripts of the interviews were rated for 56 items, including tolerance of verbal protest, strictness, demand for obedience, consistency, empathy, approval, and others. When all of the data were tallied, the researchers found significant correlations between children's behavior and parents' child rearing—correlations that, it turned out, were affected by the child's sex. For instance, maternal warmth correlated positively with boys' autonomy but correlated not at all with that of girls.

This method yields valuable information about child rearing and development. But the observational method, too, has its drawbacks. One drawback is the difficulty a researcher has in controlling all of the variables in the environment under study. It is far more difficult to exert control in the complex, real world than in a laboratory with animals. Even more serious, it is almost impossible to establish cause and effect in natural settings. How is a psychologist to know, for example, whether parents are influencing child or child influencing parents?

A significant correlation only proves that the behavior of each is related to that of the other. To solve this problem, researchers often try to intervene directly in children's environments, providing "causes," of which they then measure "effects."

INTERVENTION

Intervention is the most direct way of studying environmental effects and the only reliable way of proving cause and effect. A good example of an intervention study is provided by Burton White's (1966) work with infants. He divided institutionalized infants into several different groups. The environment of one group of 10 infants was only slightly enriched. This group received from the nurses 20 extra minutes of attention a day for 30 days. The infants were touched, held, and talked to. The only difference this extra handling seemed to make in the development of the 10 infants, compared to a control group that received no extra

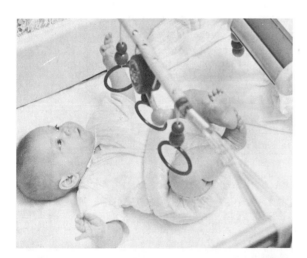

In which bed would you like to spend 20 hours a day? Moderate stimulation arouses interest; overstimulation causes confusion; understimulation provokes boredom.

attention, was an increase in their visual attention. But when White took a second group of infants and added to the 30 days of extra attention a bigger "dose" of enrichment, the results were more powerful. For another 87 days, these infants were placed in a prone position for 15 minutes after each of three daily feedings. Their surroundings were made colorful and interesting. Over each crib was placed a stabile made of mirrors, rattles, and shiny objects, and the crib sheets and bumpers were brightly colored. The infants were observed and assessed weekly. At first, the stimulated infants did not look about at their surroundings very much. But well before the end of the experimental period and a full 45 days before the infants in the control group, they were moving around and reaching for the stabile and the colorful crib accessories. A third group of infants got still a different set of enriching experiences. For the first couple of months, two large nipples on red and white backgrounds were attached to the sides of the cribs. Then they, too, had the colorful stabile placed above their heads. Compared to the more thoroughly stimulated group, this moderately and progressively stimulated group began reaching at an even earlier age and never went through a depression in visual exploration. White's study demonstrates some of the effects of environmental stimulation on early visual and motor development.

When intervention occurs in the laboratory, it is difficult to generalize from the artificial situation to the real one. Nevertheless, researchers have collected useful information about potential environmental effects on development by measuring the immediate effects of adults' behavior on children in the controlled laboratory setting. In this vein, Albert Bandura and his associates (e.g., Bandura, Ross, and Ross, 1961) have tested whether children imitate the aggressive behavior of people they see modeling it. Children between the ages of 3 and 5 watched an adult kick, punch, and throw a rubber Bobo doll. Other children watched a film of a cartoon character hitting the doll. A control group of children saw an adult paying no attention to the doll. The children who had watched aggression against the doll later acted aggressively toward it themselves. This study proved that children will imitate aggressive actions of an adult in the laboratory. It suggests, but does not prove, that children imitate their parents' aggressive acts at home.

To test this suggestion, it is necessary to intervene in parent-child interactions themselves. Although it has not been considered ethical to train parents to be more hostile or punitive toward their children, the opposite strategy—training them to be less punitive—can be, and has been, tried. Parent-training programs have been established to change this and many other aspects of child-rearing practices and attitudes. It has proved difficult to alter parents' deeply held attitudes and well practiced behavior patterns. But through a combination of modifying some of the parents' specific child-rearing techniques (e.g., teaching or talking to the child) and direct stimulation of the child by the trainer, these programs have had considerable success in improving children's development.

All three of these approaches to the study of environmental effects—deprivation, observation, and intervention—have their strengths and limitations, their pros and their cons. The most compelling evidence that an environmental effect exists would come from consensus among researchers using all of these methods. But this, of course, is seldom possible. In the following sections of this chapter, we have tried to distill the most solid generalizations about environmental effects from the many methods that have been used in their investigations.

THE PHYSICAL ENVIRONMENT

The physical environment profoundly affects human development. The spaces they inhabit, the nutrients they ingest, the sounds that surround them, and the objects with which they play and explore are some of the components of the physical environment with direct effects on how children develop.

THE PRENATAL ENVIRONMENT

Some of the clearest and most dramatic effects of the physical environment on development occur before the child is even born, in that very first environment, the uterus of the child's mother. Although the uterus protects the developing infant by

PARENT-CHILD DEVELOPMENT CENTERS

A comprehensive program designed to enrich the early development of poor children was started in 1970, the New Orleans Parent Child Development Center (PCDC). The general plan consisted of : (1) a curriculum that provided mothers with information on child development and child rearing, home management, and nutrition and health, as well as information on their own personal development and community and government resources; (2) a program for the children; and (3) broad support services. Mothers and their 2-month-old infants were assigned randomly either to the program or to a control group. They stayed in the program until the children were 3 years old. Control-group participants received health services and a stipend for meeting test appointments. The program group consisted of 67 inner-city black mothers and their children; the control group consisted of 59 pairs of comparable mothers and children. The average age of the mothers was 23; all were below the poverty level.

First, the researchers, Susan Andrews, Janet Blumenthal and their colleagues (Andrews et al., 1982), wanted to know whether the mothers' behavior changed as a result of being in the program. Trained observers coded the behavior of the mothers toward their children when the children were 2, 12, 24, and 36 months old. The observation sessions took place in a room furnished with an armchair, a table covered with magazines, a child's table and chair, a toy chest, and shelves full of toys. Two kinds of behavior were coded: interactions and language. Interactions consisted of teaching, showing affection, talking, restricting, punishing, or ignoring the child. Language was coded as elaboration, praise, general conversation, questioning, suggesting, teasing, warning, or criticizing. Following the observation, the mother's sensitivity to her child's communications and actions was rated. When the children were 36 months old, they and their mothers were observed, videotaped, and rated on a teaching task.

To learn about the program's effects on children,

the infants were tested repeatedly. (They took so many tests in fact that the researchers wisely controlled for the effects of repeated testing in their analyses.) They took the Bayley, Stanford-Binet, and the Ammons Picture Vocabulary tests of intellectual development. They were tested for sensorimotor development and for perceptual and abstraction abilities.

Clear results began to show up when the children were 2 years old. After 2 years in the program, the mothers were more sensitive, accepting, and cooperative than control mothers. But neither their language nor their techniques in interacting with their children was significantly more positive than that of the controls. After 3 years in the program, mothers were more sensitive, accepting, and were using more positive techniques toward their children (e.g., playing, helping, and showing interest and affection). Their language was now significantly more positive than that of the control mothers. Whereas the program mothers were giving information, explaining, labeling, asking questions, or giving praise 70 percent of the time, the program mothers were doing so only 48 percent of the time. The program mothers' interactions with their children started out as quite positive but grew more negative toward the end of the first year and remained negative until the children were 3; then, as the "terrible twos" passed, they suddenly grew more positive. The control mothers' interactions and language continued to be more negative. On the teaching task as well, program mothers were significantly more effective than control mothers.

As for the program's effects on the children, almost no differences between the program and control groups were apparent until the children were 2 to 3 years old. At graduation, however, when the children were 36 months old, the program children scored significantly higher on several tests of mental development. The program had intervened successfully in the early development of poor, black, inner-city children. Their intellectual skills and patterns of interaction with their mothers were significantly more positive and promising than they might otherwise have been. This study clearly demonstrates the effect of environment on development.

warm fluid and layers of membrane and abdominal muscle, it is far from impervious to the external environment. Connected to its mother's bloodstream through a remarkable organ, the **placenta,** the developing embryo is affected by whatever the pregnant mother does (or does not) eat, drink, smoke, or breathe. Not only does a mother's diet during pregnancy affect the health of the embryo, but her whole medical and nutritional history before her pregnancy can affect it as well. At the very end of her pregnancy, the medication she accepts to ease the pain of childbirth can cause her infant problems that will impede further development. Analgesic medication can depress the infant's breathing so that its brain lacks essential oxygen. This condition, called **anoxia,** is responsible for certain kinds of cerebral palsy and other serious problems.

Although scientists have long known about the ability of certain substances to cross the placenta and to enter the embryo's bloodstream, in the past quarter century this knowledge has expanded remarkably. So many substances are known to cross the placenta, in fact, that most women who even suspect that they *might* be pregnant are advised to stop all medication until they have talked to a specialist in prenatal care. Even recreational habits, like smoking cigarettes and drinking liquor, can impair development before and after birth. Evidence on the adverse effects of cigarette smoking during pregnancy continues to mount. The carbon monoxide and nicotine in smoke, which enter the mother's bloodstream through her lungs, quickly pass into the fetus's bloodstream. Carbon monoxide is known to cut down the amount of oxygen available to the fetus, and oxygen is essential to life. Smokers have 28 percent more miscarriages, stillbirths, and deaths soon after birth than nonsmoking mothers (Frazier, Davis, Goldstein, and Goldberg, 1961). Their babies are smaller at birth, more irritable and less regular in their feeding and sleeping patterns, and may suffer impaired mental development in early childhood. Even a pregnant mother's social drinking can harm the developing fetus. Although no one yet knows exactly what dose of alcohol is too high, pregnant women are advised to forego all drinking to avoid producing a child with mental retardation or physical deformities.

The list of drugs that are known to affect fetal development is long and growing. Many of these effects are harmful, or **teratogenic,** a word that derives from the Greek root for "monster." The **thalidomide** scare in Europe in the early 1960s alerted the medical community to the possible dangers of presumably safe drugs. Mothers who took thalidomide for relief of nausea and stress early in pregnancy, during the period of rapid embryonic development, produced infants with just the buds of arms and legs. Many other tranquilizers, antibiotics, hormones, painkillers, and other classes of drugs have been shown to harm the physical development of the embryo or fetus. The effects on the unborn child are especially pronounced because its liver is still quite inefficient at breaking down and ridding the body of harmful substances.

Certain illnesses also can harm the fetus. Physicians know, for example, that viral infections during the first third of pregnancy, when the embryo is rapidly developing specialized cells, can cause severe birth defects or even death. German measles (rubella), mumps, hepatitis, and the high fever sometimes associated with them can seriously afflict the hearing, the heart, and the brain of the embryo. X-rays used for medical and dental diagnosis must be avoided during pregnancy, because radiation is known to cause genetic mutations of the embryo or fetus, as well as cancerous tumors and leukemia. Exposure to radiation can stunt growth, and it may be associated with elevated levels of miscarriage, stillbirth, and severe birth defects.

NUTRITION

Both before and after birth, human development depends on the quantity and quality of available nutrients. A good deal of prenatal care is devoted to the expectant mother's diet, because it is amply documented that a good and balanced diet can make the difference between health and illness in both mother and child. Infants who lack necessary proteins and calories may suffer a form of starvation called **marasmus.** Marasmus usually strikes those infants in their first year whose mothers' breast milk is inadequate. These infants barely grow at all. Their muscles soon atrophy. If they live, they are unresponsive and never catch up to children of normal weight. They learn less and later perform poorly in intelligence and psychological tests (Pollitt, 1973). Children between 2 and 4 may suffer from severe protein deficiency, a kind of starvation called **kwashiorkor.** With bloated bellies, thin and colorless hair, skin lesions, these children are apathetic, withdrawn, and irritable. Their motor skills are poor, and their intelligence is often impaired, although somewhat less severely than in cases of marasmus (Thomson and Pollitt, 1977). If there is to be growth, there must be calories for fuel and protein for building.

Malnutrition also lowers children's resistance to disease. They are less able to resist viruses, bacteria, and fungi than other children (Edelman, 1977; Edelman, Suskind, Sirisinha, and Olson, 1973). Susceptible to diarrhea, malnourished children's bodies may not be able to use what little food they take in. In a longitudinal study of the effects of nutrition on infants' social, physical, and mental development, conducted in a poor Mexican community, investigators supplemented the diets of mothers and children. During pregnancy, mothers got an extra 205 calories and 15 grams of protein a day. During breast feeding, mothers got an extra 305 calories and 15 grams of protein. Babies began to receive whole cow's milk and prepared baby food when they were 3 to 4 months old. A control group of mothers and babies received no supplementary food. Tests of the supplemented children showed clear effects of adequate nutrition. The IQ scores of the supplemented babies were substantially higher than the controls' scores. Their physical development was also better. They walked and talked earlier, slept less, refused to be carried on their mothers' backs, acted more independent, spent more time outside, and were talked to more by both parents than the babies in the control group (Martinez and Chavez, 1971).

Mexico is not the only country in which malnutrition is a problem. Much of the world's population subsists on too few calories and far too little protein. A survey of 190,000 Asian, African, and South American children found 80 percent of them to be suffering from moderate to severe malnutrition. Extrapolations from this survey produced an estimate of 100 million children under 5 as suffering from malnutrition (Suskind, 1977). Many studies, in many different countries, attest to the effect of malnutrition on intellectual functioning (see Brozek, 1978). In Indonesia, the IQ scores of children classified as "poorly" or only "fairly" nourished were significantly below those of a group labeled "ac-

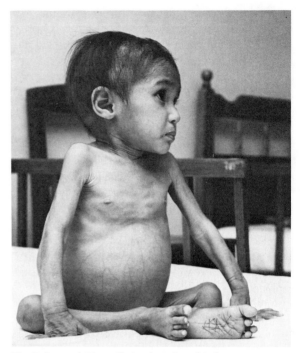

This Bolivian child is suffering from kwashiorkor, the result of severe protein deficiency.

ceptably" nourished (Soewondo, Abednego, Pekerti, and Karjadi, 1971). A Colombian study of 400 boys and girls showed that the average scores on a test of mental abilities were 98 for "well nourished children" and 83 for "less adequately nourished" children (Mora et al., 1974). In Delhi, India, a study of children's IQ scores showed that they decreased in direct proportion to the degree of malnutrition, measured by how much the child was underweight (Guptâ, Dhingra, Singh, and Anand, 1975). The effects of malnutrition on mental function often persist beyond the period of malnutrition itself. A review of 11 studies of severe malnutrition showed that even after children under 5 began receiving more food, their behavioral development was retarded (Brozek, 1978).

At the physical level, malnutrition may work by causing damage to the central nervous system or the brain. Animal studies have shown that chronic malnutrition before birth and in the early months before weaning actually diminishes the total number of brain cells. Neurological evidence of malnutrition in children is harder to find, however (Klein, Habicht, and Yarbrough, 1971). Several factors complicate the study of malnutrition in children. In particular, it can be difficult or impossible for an investigator to know with certainty when a child first became malnourished or to separate the effects of malnutrition from the knot of social and economic problems typical of the environment of poverty that produces inadequate nutrition. A review of studies of malnutrition on several continents found that mothers of malnourished children tended to be less educated, in poorer health, and less responsive than mothers of children who were poor but adequately nourished (Thomson and Pollitt, 1977).

Malnutrition is an ecological problem that does not occur alone. Its consorts are poverty, chaotic family structure, poor housing, ignorance, and despair. Although the need for dietary supplements is critical, the problem of malnutrition is larger than diet alone. Malnutrition is so often found enmeshed in the circumstances of poverty that it is impossible to eradicate without substantial social and economic reform. In this country, a study of children

between the ages of 6 and 11, conducted by the National Center for Health Statistics, showed that children from wealthy families were 1.2 inches taller than children from poor families (Goldstein, 1971). In contrast, a study of city children in Sweden showed no connection between children's height and family income (Lindgren, 1976). Why not? Presumably because in a society like Sweden, in which both poor and rich have access to food and social services, the link between income and malnutrition has been broken.

NOISE

Life in the complex physical environments that most of us inhabit today is noisy indeed. Televisions blare in the living room or bedroom, records and radios play in the car and the supermarket, traffic noises filter into buildings, and the sound of airplanes overhead interrupts conversation and con-

RESEARCH FOCUS

MOTHERS' NUTRITION AND INFANTS' DEVELOPMENT

For purposes of investigating the effects of nutrition—unconfounded by other factors, like poverty—on children's development, experimental studies are preferable to observational studies. Experimental studies like the one reported by Sandra Joos and her associates at the University of Texas at Houston (Joos, Pollitt, Mueller, and Albright, 1983) offer the advantage of controlling subjects' diets and of monitoring the consequences over time. In this study, the researchers chose to study rural Taiwanese mothers whose diets were moderately deficient. They wanted to learn whether supplementing the women's diet immediately after pregnancy, when they were breast feeding their infants, would benefit their children's growth and development.

Out of a total of about 300 lactating women, half were randomly assigned to receive a high-calorie and protein supplement that also contained vitamins and minerals. The others received a **placebo,** which provided just a few extra calories a day, as well as a vitamin and mineral pill. The mothers in the treatment group started taking the liquid supplement 3 weeks after childbirth. Their usual diet consisted of rice, sweet potatoes and other vegetables but little animal protein, and they were considered at risk because they ate so little protein (less than 40 grams a day). Nurses in the villages where the mothers lived gave out and watched the mothers drink the cans of liquid. Neither nurse nor mother in this **double-blind study** knew whether the can contained protein. To assess the effect of the nutrition supplement, the babies were tested for motor and intellectual abilities.

Results of the tests showed that overall mental scores of infants in the treatment group were not significantly higher than those of infants in the control group, but overall motor scores were higher. The difference was particularly marked for the ages at which the infant was able to sit, stand, and bring two objects together in front of him or her (an indicator of neurological maturity). These results demonstrate that nutrition does have a measurable, though modest effect on development—even when that nutrition takes a somewhat indirect route through the mother's system to the infant's.

centration. To learn whether noise impairs functioning and to guide public policy on noise control, psychologists have embarked on studies of how noise affects the performance of children. Not surprisingly, they have found in general that children whose schools or homes are noisy perform less well and feel more helpless than other children. They have also documented hearing loss among people subjected to prolonged intense noise. Also worrisome are the findings that brief exposure to loud noise can raise a person's stress level.

The harmful effects of noise may be felt early in life. When the noise level was measured in the homes of infants at five different ages, it was found that at every age noisiness and confusion correlated with impaired mental functioning (Wachs, Uzgiris, and Hunt, 1971). In other studies, living in a noisy and chaotic home has been shown to be related to impaired intellectual development of children up to 5 years old. Boys, fussy babies, and babies otherwise at risk are most severely affected (Wachs and Gruen, 1982).

In one study of the relation between children's hearing, verbal skills, and the noisiness of their homes, investigators concentrated on a 32-story apartment building in Manhattan (Cohen, Glass, and Singer, 1973). The building was actually built on an overpass spanning an interstate highway, and the noise from the heavy traffic was funneled upwards into the building. The noise, it was found, was more pronounced on the lower floors of the building than on the higher floors. The researchers tested the hearing of 29 grade-school boys and 25 grade-school girls living in the building by asking them to discriminate between pairs of words like "gear" and "beer" or "cope" and "coke." They were also tested on their reading vocabulary and comprehension. The results showed that the floor on which a child lived and the amount of traffic noise to which he or she was subjected correlated with the child's ability to hear the difference between the similar-sounding words. Furthermore, this ability to hear differences in words was related to reading ability. Only children who had lived in the noisy building for less than 3 years were free of these impairments. After that, the longer a child had lived in the building, the more severely performance was affected.

In a pair of studies of the effects of noise on children at school, Sheldon Cohen and his associates (Cohen, Evans, Krantz, and Stokols, 1980, 1981) observed children in a different noise-filled environment. Their first study compiled data on children whose elementary schools were in the flight paths of the Los Angeles Airport. Planes flew overhead every few minutes, and the noise at times grew very loud (95 dB). Comparison groups matched on social class and ethnicity were drawn from quiet schools. The children from the noisy schools did poorer on tests of cognitive ability than children from quiet schools. They had higher blood pressure. They were more likely to give up working on a problem before the allotted testing time. They felt more helpless. They were more easily distracted. Living in a quiet home seemed to make no difference in the performance of these children from noisy schools. One year later, in the second study, the children were tested again. There was little evidence that they had adapted to the noise. Even when the noise diminished, the affected children did not score much better than before on tests of cognitive ability, hearing, or school achievement. Various studies show that the effects of noise on performance are usually cumulative and long lasting (Cohen and Weinstein, 1982).

PLAY MATERIALS

All children grow up within a physical environment that contains inanimate objects. Be they bright or dull, colorful or drab, familiar or novel, accessible or forbidden, natural or synthetic, these inanimate objects stimulate children's vision, exploration, and play. Children may grow interested in common household objects, like cooking pots, the telephone, old clothes, and packing crates, or in specially designed toys, like rocking horses, crayons, and board games.

Evidence from observational, institutional, and intervention studies all suggest that children's early cognitive growth depends on the availability of stimulating objects. When 2½-month-old, institutionalized infants were placed near decorative mobiles and distinctive sounds, they did not show the intellectual decline often found in institutionalized babies (Brossard and Decarie, 1971). When hospitalized infants were stimulated by colored stabiles and bedding, they responded by actively engaging with their physical environments (White, 1966).

When 5-month-old black infants from various socioeconomic groups were observed at home, it was found that the variety of objects available to the babies was related to their scores on tests of intelligence, problem solving, object permanence, and exploration (Yarrow, Rubenstein, and Pedersen, 1975). Young children's mental abilities are stimulated when they can play with a variety of interesting materials, when they are allowed to explore their surroundings, and when they receive encouragement from their parents to do both (Wachs and Gruen, 1982).

Although objects cannot provide children with the wide range of spontaneous social interactions that another person can provide, some objects do react and change as they are acted on by a child. Jack-in-the-boxes pop open, squeeze toys squeak, and bath toys float and bob. Several studies of children up to the age of 2 confirm the importance to intellectual development of responsive inanimate objects. It is also possible that infants in an unresponsive environment eventually tune out, thereby reducing their exposure to stimulation. Their lack of responsiveness may also in turn make the people around them unresponsive—a vicious cycle (Wachs and Gruen, 1982).

In contrast, infants may tune out when stimuli are *too* stimulating. The babies in the study we described by Burton White, for example, who received "too much" visual stimulation reacted by looking less at the stimuli. With a more moderate amount of stimulation, infants developed more steadily and rapidly. Children seem to develop best when the objects available for play are matched to their level of development. Objects that force them to reach a bit but are not too stimulating seem best.

Play materials not only affect children's intellectual development, but they have immediate effects on their activities. Reviews of studies that have explored the effects of various play materials on children's behavior (e.g., Clarke-Stewart, 1982; Minuchin and Shapiro, 1983) suggest the following: playground equipment elicits large motor skills, like running, climbing, and rough-and-tumble play. When children play outdoors, they are less aggressive, more mature and cooperative. Their games can be long and complex. Indoors, play materials encourage more talkative and elaborate social interactions. Building materials, like blocks and boards, dolls and dress-up materials, all promote rich and complex play. Sand, clay, buttons, and other materials for "messing around" encourage

Play materials have an immediate impact on children's activities and a long-term effect on their development. Dress-up props promote rich and complex play.

creative, experimental, but somewhat less complex play. Small toys, like guns or checkers, microscopes or gyroscopes, encourage still less complex play, as children do what the materials suggest. Art, sandboxes, and books hold children's attention longer than other activities do. Group activities that involve music and movement most readily produce contagious glee. Blocks, climbing, and playing house provoke conflict most readily. But conflict may occur whenever children must share play space and materials or when one group can exclude another. When materials are scarce or fixed and inflexible, children do less playing than watching, waiting, or cruising around. Their play is neither complex nor intellectually challenging (Clarke-Stewart, 1982).

SPACE

Just as the objects within the environment affect children's activities and development, so do the size and spaciousness of their environment. Cultures vary quite dramatically in the amount and type of space allotted to children or others. Mothers in some cultures, for example, tightly swaddle their infants, whereas mothers elsewhere wrap them loosely or not at all. The distance people are expected to keep between themselves and others varies as well by culture. What is pleasantly close in one culture may seem uncomfortable and intrusive in another. Most of the studies psychologists have conducted into the effects of space on children's behavior focus on schools and preschools. Space generally affects children in combination with other factors of their physical and social environments, like the number and distribution of people, the arrangement of furniture, and the accessibility of play or study materials.

Many observational studies of preschoolers focus on how crowding—or the number of children occupying a space—affects children's behavior. In a series of carefully controlled experiments in an English preschool, Peter Smith and Kevin Connolly (1981) found that 3 and 4-year-old boys and girls from a mixture of class backgrounds played together well under a wide variety of conditions. The incidence of desirable or undesirable sorts of play varied little with changes in the number of children present, the size of their classroom, or the richness of equipment. But under two conditions, aggres-

sion did increase. One condition was extreme crowding (fewer than 15 square feet per child); the other condition was a combination of extreme crowding and other forms of stress, such as limiting the number of available toys. Other studies (reviewed by Clarke-Stewart, 1982) bear out the finding that when space is limited (less than 25 square feet per child), children act more physically and aggressively with others and more destructively with their toys. They also spend more time doing nothing and less time running, jumping, chasing, and interacting. When nursery-schoolers are crowded, the amount of hitting, laughing, anxious behavior (finger sucking, hand holding, etc.) and physical contact increases; large body movements decrease (McGrew, 1972). Older children, too, feel the effects of crowding. One experimental study of 4th, 8th, and 11th-graders (Aiello, Nicosia, and Thompson, 1979) showed that students who were subjected to crowding felt significantly more tense, annoyed, uncomfortable, and more competitive during a game.

Other investigators interested in the effects of space on behavior have focused on the spatial arrangement of the preschool room. Many preschools are divided into separate areas of open and sheltered space, for noisy and quiet play. When rooms are organized into open pathways and clear play areas, children talk more and are less physical, and their physical behavior is less disruptive and more productive (Rogers, 1976). Clear spatial boundaries between activity areas have been found to foster cooperation, especially under crowded conditions (Rohe and Nuffer, 1977).

Studies of elementary schools also focus on the classroom space that students inhabit. Some of these studies are observational; some rely on the self-reports of students. Several investigators have reported problems with "open" classrooms—rooms with open areas, movable furniture, room dividers, and activity stations rather than traditional rows of desks. These problems include noisiness, lack of privacy, and overstimulation. In some open classrooms, students tend to cluster around the teacher, and this tendency may contribute to students' and teachers' feelings of being crowded (Rivlin and Rothenberg, 1976). When classrooms have open spaces around their edges and when ceilings are high, teachers say they feel less crowded (Ahrentzen, 1981). Other investigators have found productive distributions of students around the open

Extreme crowding in children's spaces has been found to lead to more aggressive and destructive behavior, less constructive activity, and feelings of tension and anxiety.

classroom even without these qualifications. What this demonstrates once again is the difficulty of separating the effects of the physical environment from those of other, related factors, in this case the rules and programs instituted by teachers.

By high-school age, when students move from classroom to classroom throughout the day, studies show no consistent relation between students' behavior and physical aspects of the classroom. However, the size of a school is related to high-school students' behavior. Students in smaller schools tend to be more prosocial and less antisocial than those in large schools (although the findings on antisocial behavior are the more equivocal). Smaller schools offer students more chances to participate in various school activities, both curricular and extracurricular, and more students at small schools do participate and actively identify with school activities than do students at large schools. It is much easier for students at large schools to get lost in the crowd, to feel little sense of responsibility to the school, to feel alienated or in conflict (Minuchin and Shapiro, 1983).

Thus we see again how the effects of the physical environment are mediated by elements of the social environment. It begins *in utero*. The effect of the physical environment on the developing embryo and fetus is made through the mother's bloodstream and buffered by the mother's body. It continues when the baby receives its nutrition from the mother's breast or takes in food provided by another human caregiver. The finest preschool, grade school, or high school in the world, chock full of the latest equipment, comes alive only when teachers and students fill its spaces. In the following section, we discuss how the social environment affects children's development directly.

THE SOCIAL ENVIRONMENT

Common sense tells us, and empirical studies confirm it, that the people in a child's environment deeply affect that child's development. The tiniest baby is part of a social world. Tended at first by parents, watched warily by brothers and sisters, admired by grandparents, the baby's social world soon expands outward from the immediate family. Neighbors and classmates in day care, babysitters and teachers, familiar faces on the television, people at church or synagogue, the family pets, and even the folks who chat on the supermarket checkout line all form part of a young child's social world.

PARENTS AND EARLY STIMULATION

Most babies in the United States remain at home with their mother or other caretaker until they enter a formal day-care program, nursery school, or kindergarten. Psychologists have studied the development of infants to learn more about how their parents affect them. One recent observational study was undertaken by Susan Crockenberg (1983) of the University of California at Davis. Its subjects were 25 pairs of mothers and their infants, nearly all of them white, who were tested and observed to ascertain whether there were any correlations between the mothers' behavior and the infants' scores on the Bayley Scales of Infant Development, a test of mental development. When the babies were 3 months old, mother and baby were observed at home for 3½ hours. Crockenberg coded these observations of mothers' behavior into variables describing caretaking, smiling and eye contact, responsiveness to the baby's crying, and the like. When the babies were about 21 months old, they were given the Bayley test. The results were clear-cut: the babies' mental development correlated significantly and positively with the level of their mothers' education, responsiveness, smiling and eye contact, but negatively with the frequency of routine caretaking (such as feeding and diapering). In short, there was a clear connection between the quality and quantity of mothers' stimulation of their children and the children's mental development. Other studies (reviewed by Appleton, Clifton, and Goldberg, 1975; Clarke-Stewart, 1977; Yarrow et al. 1975) have found that mothers' education and stimulation of their infants are related to how the infants develop. Mothers with more education talk more to their babies. They respond to their babies' babblings by talking. They provide more interesting toys for their children, and they are more effective teachers, giving explicit instruc-

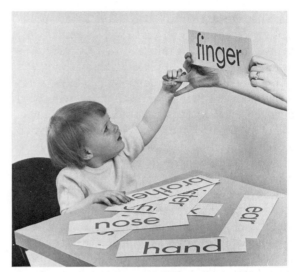

Many American mothers today implement deliberate stimulation programs with their infants and toddlers in an effort to speed up their verbal and intellectual development.

tions, offering help, and using praise—the carrot—rather than criticism or disapproval—the stick—when teaching their children new skills. Better educated mothers are also more likely than less educated mothers to have a husband living at home, more money, fewer children, and quieter households, factors that make it easier for mothers to provide this kind of attention and stimulation to their infants and young children.

A mother's education is a good predictor, but not a guarantee, of stimulating interaction. What matters most is the amount and kind of time children and mothers spend together. Babies seem to thrive on jiggling, rocking, being looked at, talked to, and played with. Just being in the same room with the mother or being cared for in routine fashion does not benefit the infant's mental development. But mothers, fathers, or other caretakers all may foster intellectual growth when they respond to and stimulate children on a level appropriate to their development. Responsiveness is the key here. Babies love toys that react—pots and pans that spin or make loud noises when hammered on; bells that ring; toys that squeak (McCall, 1977). But people make the best playthings of all. The father who goes "honk" when his nose is squeezed, the mother who pretends to sleep when the baby says "night-night," and the babysitter who chats through make-believe phone calls are all responsive teachers. They are teaching the baby that its actions have real consequences. From responsive teachers, the baby learns that the world is a place of predictable actions and reactions, a place worth exploring and learning about. Children respond to attention and encouragement. Adults who share children's daily discoveries and feelings, who are ingenious in their use of speech and praise, can more than make up for any lack of special toys, books, or trips.

A program designed to allow poor mothers to work together under the guidance of trained leaders underscores this point. In this study, directed by Merle Karnes (Karnes, Teska, and Hodgins, 1968), mothers of preschool children met for 11 weekly 2-hour sessions. They put together educational toys out of inexpensive materials: sock puppets, counting books out of magazine pictures, matching games out of colored chips and gummed seals. The teachers showed the mothers finger games and songs. After the work sessions, the mothers and teachers talked about how to use the toys at home. The mothers were paid for their time and made to understand that they were participating in an educational project. By the end of the program, mothers talked more to their children, taught them more, and were more responsive and supportive. When their children were tested, they were found to have made significant gains in IQ and other test scores over children whose mothers had not participated.

In general, what sort of early home environment best promotes children's development? After reading exhaustively through the available literature, Bettye Caldwell and her associates (e.g., Bradley, Caldwell, and Elardo, 1977) created a set of scales to assess the quality of stimulation in a home. In a substantial number of studies since then, these scales consistently have been found to correlate with young children's mental development.

1. The mother should be emotionally and verbally responsive. For instance, she might respond in words to a child's babblings.

2. The mother should avoid restricting and punishing the child; she should not always interfere with the child's movements.

3. The physical environment should be organized, safe, and free from hazards.

4. The child should have appropriate materials for play. Ball and tricycle are available for muscle ac-

tivity, stacking and fit-together toys for eye-hand coordination. Toys should be appropriate to the child's age.

5. The mother should be involved with the child, keep the child in sight, and look at him or her often.

6. The child should have variety of daily stimulation. The mother or another person should read stories to the child at least three times a week. The child should eat at least one meal a day with the family, and the child should be taken on several outings a week.

Although children's intellectual development has a strong genetic underpinning, as we saw in Chapter 2, studies that find consistent correlations between parental stimulation and responsiveness and infants' development suggest that the social environment, too, plays some part in how well and how fast an individual advances. The best researchers take the genetic contribution into account when they interpret correlations between parents' behavior and infants' development. (See for example Research Focus: Effects of Mother's IQ and Home Environment on Children's IQ, p. 110.) When this is done, it appears that parental stimulation does still make a modest contribution to early intellectual development.

SOCIALIZATION AND DISCIPLINE

As children take on the habits, skills, and standards that adults consider important, they are said to be socialized. Parents and older brothers and sisters, teachers and relatives, books and television figures all show the child of what acceptable behavior consists and teach the child the accumulated knowledge of the culture. Many such **socialization agents** try to influence the child to become mature, productive, and responsible. But parents are pivotal. Some parents may especially want their children to grow up to be highly moral. Other parents may hope that their children will acquire wealth and prestige. Still others value intellectual achievement, social success, or personal fulfillment. Their values determine the particular goals and methods of their socialization efforts. Parents' values also reflect their times and their subculture.

In this country, parents with lower levels of education, income, and social status are more likely to value conformity to rules and to authority for their children (see Clarke-Stewart, 1977; Walters and Stinnett, 1971; Wandersman, 1973). In their socialization, they are usually more restrictive, coercive, authoritarian, and physically assertive; they are less warm and talk less to their children. Parents with more education, better incomes, and higher social status are more likely to value self-direction for their children, to have a more egalitarian relation with them, to make requests and give explanations, to emphasize reasoning and reciprocity. Although there is a great deal of overlap in the ways the two classes socialize their children, their particular emphases, it has been suggested, are rooted in the living conditions of the two groups (Kohn, 1977). "Advantaged" individuals need to be able to decide for themselves how to act even in childhood and to a greater extent in adolescence and adulthood. Less privileged, less affluent people are more likely to have to follow someone else's orders. They are more likely to be employees than employers, for example.

As for the social pressures and mores of the particular era in which parents rear their children, a survey of 1230 parents in the 1970s (Yankelovich, Skelly, and White, 1977) claimed to find a "new breed" of parents. These people rejected marriage, religion, patriotism, thriftiness, and the "Protestant ethic," translated as hard work for its own sake. Interestingly, though, they rejected these institutions and values only for *themselves*. They intended to pass on traditional values to their children, because the children would have to live in a society that still operates by the old rules. One thing the new breed did insist on, they said, was giving boys and girls the same goals. Yet even on this point, most parents may not be as "modern" in teaching their children as they are in demanding equality for men and women. Jeanne Block (1973) summarized old and new research on parents of different socioeconomic groups and on children of different ages. Parents, particularly fathers, still consistently emphasized achievement, competition, and control of feelings for boys but they emphasized close interpersonal relations, showing their feelings and reflecting on them for girls. Boys and girls were *not* given the same goals. Although any issue of *Ms* testifies that the rules for adult **gender**

roles are clearly changing and although there does seem to be less emphasis on teaching such rules to children (Barnett, 1978), basic child-rearing goals alter slowly. But individual parents who hold nontraditional ideas about gender roles may, whatever their social class and era, teach their children goals that are not gender typed.

Researchers have since the 1920s attempted to study how the ways in which parents socialize and discipline their children affect the children's behavior, development, and mental health. One early study began in Yellow Springs, Ohio, in 1929. Over the next two decades, 300 children and parents in white, middle-class families were observed at home twice a year by a trained observer-interviewer from the Fels Institute; 89 of the children were studied from 6 months to adulthood, others for shorter periods. At the end of each visit, the observer rated the parents' behavior and the home atmosphere as accepting, hostile, controlling, protective, or arbitrary. The results of this longitudinal study, published in the 1940s (Baldwin, 1949; Baldwin, Kalhorn, and Brese, 1945), indicated that there were three major ways of rearing children. Democratic parents valued their children as individuals and allowed them freedom to explore and test their skills. They justified their disciplinary decisions to their children and were emotionally warm. Casual and indulgent parents also allowed their children freedom and were warm, but they babied their children and did not encourage independence and maturity. Rejecting parents were autocratic, restrictive, and cold.

Another early study, dating from 1928, the Berkeley Growth Study, also collected longitudinal data on white middle-class families, but in this study, maternal and child behavior were observed during mental and physical testing of the child rather than at home. Despite this difference in the source of data, similar patterns of parental behavior were found (Schaefer, 1960; Schaefer and Bayley, 1963). Parents were loving or hostile, permissive or authoritarian (Figure 3.1). The loving parent was warm and accepting, supportive, rewarding, gave praise and comfort, and was interested in the child; the hostile parent was critical, dissatisfied, derogatory, insensitive to the child, did not state or enforce rules or consequences, and always gave in to the child's demands. The authoritarian parent imposed strict and often arbitrary demands on the child and

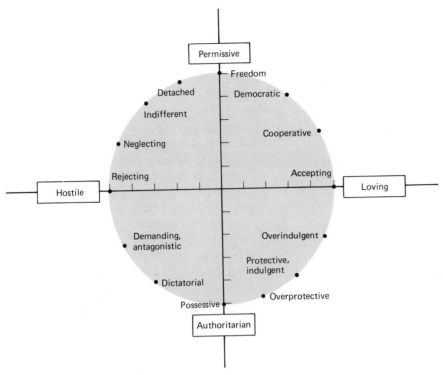

FIGURE 3.1

In studies of parental child-rearing practices, two dimensions were consistently found: *affection*, which ranges from hostile to loving, and *control*, which ranges from permissive to authoritarian. This circle shows the relations between them in parents' behavior (Schaefer, 1959).

made certain the child obeyed the rules.

The most recent major study of disciplinary styles, by Diana Baumrind (1971), revealed three distinct patterns of discipline, which parallel earlier findings.

Authoritarian parents are those she found to be firm, punitive, unaffectionate, and unsympathetic. They value obedience from their children and authority for themselves. They try to shape their children's behavior according to a set standard of conduct and to curb their children's will. They do not encourage independence. They are detached and seldom praise their youngsters. Children in these families have few rights, but they are expected to assume as much responsibility as adults.

In contrast, **permissive parents** do not feel in control and do not exert control. They give the child as much freedom as possible. Mother is loving, father lax. Children in these families have few responsibilities but the same rights as adults.

Again, decisions are unilateral. Whereas authoritarian parents make all the decisions, permissive parents allow their children to make them all.

Authoritative parents view the rights and duties of parents and children as complementary. As their children mature, they gradually allow them responsibility for their own behavior. They reason with their children, encourage give and take, and listen to objections. These parents are firm, but they are also loving and understanding. Their demands are reasonable as well as rational and consistent. They set limits, but they also encourage independence. They give their children a sense of being loved and clear ideas about what is expected of them.

Baumrind found that these three styles were consistently related to children's social behavior, at home, in nursery school, and in the laboratory. Authoritarian parents had unfriendly, discontented, distrustful, and withdrawn children. The children of permissive parents were immature, dependent, unhappy, and were the least self-reliant and the least self-controlled. Children raised by authoritative parents were friendly, cooperative, self-reliant, independent, happy, and socially responsible—an ideal combination of social skills.

Baumrind's study, along with a variety of others (reviewed by Becker, 1964), suggest that discipline can have long-lasting effects on a child's social and emotional development. Strict, heavy-handed discipline, although fostering well controlled, socialized behavior, tends also to make children fearful, dependent, and submissive, to dull their exploration and intellectual striving. Children who have many restrictions put on them are not "spontaneous" and not friendly. If children are strictly disciplined early, before the age of 3, they are conforming, dependent, and hostile, but they inhibit their hostility. If heavy discipline begins later, children do not inhibit their hostility and express it in aggressiveness. Permissiveness, on the other hand, fosters outgoing, sociable behavior and intellectual striving, but it may make children less persistent and more aggressive.

In his review, Becker concluded that the amount of love parents express for their children has much to do with the effects of their disciplinary practices. A parent who is restrictive but affectionate is more likely to raise a child who is polite, obedient, dependent, and nonaggressive, a child who follows the rules. A restrictive parent who is also hostile may raise a socially withdrawn, immature, neurotic, and quarrelsome child who directs aggression inward. A warm, permissive parent encourages active, independent, socially outgoing, creative, mature behavior; but a hostile, permissive parent is likely to have an uncompliant and aggressive child.

Thus there is some suggestion that broad disciplinary styles have long-term consequences. It is unlikely, however, that this is a simple, one-way effect. As Catherine Lewis (1981) pointed out in her critique of these studies, it is equally plausible that parents of more mature and competent children are able to follow their regimen of moderate, authoritative, or democratic discipline and to feel affectionate toward their children *because* those children are "naturally" compliant and cooperative. Children's individual temperaments are an inextricable aspect of the *effectiveness* of parents' disciplinary styles.

But what about the immediate effects of parents'

attempts to control their children's behavior? What kinds of requests, commands, incentives, and rewards are most effective in eliciting children's immediate compliance? Here we are on firmer ground regarding the direction of causes.

In 1959, Edward Clifford described disciplinary practices during the preschool period. He found that 3-year-olds were given more physical forms of discipline, such as spankings and being sent to their rooms, and that they were disciplined more often than 6-year-old children. Parents used some reasoning in discipline at all ages, but they did a great deal more explaining when disciplining older children. Florence Goodenough (1931) also had found that children received fewer spankings as their verbal ability increased. Discipline was administered most often by the mother, in brief bouts, which increased in frequency as the day progressed. Discipline usually concerned daily routines, relations with siblings, and inappropriate behavior.

Recently, when Barry McLaughlin (1983) observed mothers and fathers controlling their children, he also found that as children got older, parents changed their control techniques, and children changed their willingness to comply. Attempts at controlling the children's actions diminished and children's compliance increased overall from 1½ to 3½ years. Moreover, 3½-year-olds were more likely to comply with a request that was indirect—"Why don't you open the box?"—than one that was direct—"Put the box down."

Some of the most painstaking detail about discipline and compliance comes from Hugh Lytton's (1976, 1979) observations of parents actually trying to control the behavior of their young boys at home. Here, for example, a mother tries to teach her 2-year-old son table manners (Lytton, 1976, p. 301):

C My nose is dirty.

M What do you say?

C My dirty nose.

M What do you say?

C Clean it off.

M Say "please."

C Clean it off.

M What do you say?

C (Demands again.)

M Is that how you ask nice?

C (Demands again, then whines, then demands

again with a yell.)

M Where's "please"?

C (Demands again.)

M Where's "please"?

C (Demands again.)

M Say "please."

C (Still does not comply. M feeds him.)

M Don't spill this milk.

C My nose is dirty.

M What do you say?

C Please.

M (Shows her approval and cleans his nose.) You can say "sorry."

C Sorry.

M Just bad boys say bad words. Don't say bad words.

C (Says something in compliance with M's wishes, and M shows her approval.)

Lytton also found the mother to be the principal disciplinarian. She was likely to forbid messing, romping, hitting, crying, talking out of turn, or playing with an unsuitable object, and to use commands and prohibitions to control her son. Adding physical control to a simple command *detracted* from its effectiveness. However, hugging the child as she asked him to do something increased the likelihood of compliance, and making a suggestion rather than stating a command was also more effective. Parents tend to be somewhat erratic in trying to control their sons, however. Whether the child *did* or *did not* comply with a request or command, the parent usually just ignored it. The occasions when the parent praised the child for complying or spanked him for not doing so were rare indeed. The boy who complied was more likely to be faced with another request or suggestion than with a respite or a word of praise. It is not surprising that controlling the behavior of children is an irritant to both parents and children.

On the basis of a synthesis of laboratory and naturalistic studies, Ross Parke (1977) has suggested that *effective discipline meets five criteria.* First, it is prompt. The less time that elapses between a child's misbehavior and an adult's discipline, the more effective the discipline is likely to be. Best of all is to stop a child in the act of misbehaving. Second, punishment must be neither too severe—for a child may become anxious and with-

drawn—nor too lenient. Moderate punishment is best. Third, discipline from a person who is on good terms with the child is effective, because the child loses more if a scolding comes from someone who is usually warm and affectionate. Fourth, an explanation should accompany the discipline. This criterion may be the most important of all. The explanation must be appropriate to the child's level of understanding: "You don't hit other children" may be sufficient explanation for a young child. Anything more elaborate could be confusing. Finally, consistent punishment is effective; inconsistent punishment may be worse than no punishment at all. Children can be quite cagey about pleading with or defying their parents not to discipline them. The best rule is for parents to discipline on the few, simple, realistic issues that matter most.

SIBLINGS

Not only do parents affect children's behavior and development, but others in the family do, too. A child's development is to some extent influenced by whether he or she has older or younger siblings, by the amount of time between siblings' births, and by the sex of those siblings. A number of studies suggest that firstborns tend to have a distinctive personality, to number prominently among the high achievers on intelligence tests, and to go to college and graduate school (Altus, 1966). Their reading and verbal abilities, grades, motivation, and willingness to buckle down to work make firstborns' school achievement somewhat higher than that of laterborns (Adams and Phillips, 1972; Altus, 1966; Breland, 1972).

The advantages (and disadvantages) enjoyed by firstborns can explain these achievements. The birth of many a firstborn is greeted by its parents with great enthusiasm. For a while, firstborns share their parents' attention and affection with no competitors. Their parents talk to them and spend time with them. Help and comfort are quickly forthcoming. Their parents also stimulate them, train them to be independent, and surround them with high aspirations for achievement. In turn, firstborns identify with their parents and adopt their values, holding high standards for themselves. Firstborns have been called "adult-civilized" because their parents are likely to have attended to every detail of their rearing. When a brother or sister appears on the scene, the firstborn must struggle to regain the parents' attention and approval. As other babies arrive, parents spend less time on each individual child. The developmental milestones of subsequent children are greeted with less attention by the more experienced, more relaxed, but more harried parents.

Psychologists have offered several different theories to explain the effects of birth order on development. The most salient of these at present is the **confluence theory** proposed by Robert Zajonc and Gregory Markus (1975). This theory suggests that intellectual ability varies according to the combined intellectual levels of all the family members. As more children arrive, available intellectual resources diminish, and each subsequent child has a lower IQ score. Long intervals between children raise the family's intellectual level, and later children can benefit by being taught by more advanced siblings. The confluence theory gives rise to a number of hypotheses about intellectual development and birth order that can be tested empirically. One study to attempt this was carried out by Yvonne Brackbill and Paul Nichols (1982) on data collected in the National Institute of Neurological and Communicative Disorders Collaborative Perinatal Project. These data included intelligence and achievement tests of 53,000 youngsters at 4 and 7 years of age. Brackbill and Nichols tested the hypothesis derived from confluence theory that when only one twin of a pair survives, that twin will have a higher intellectual score than will twins in which both of the pair survive. This hypothesis of the "single twin" was not, in fact, borne out by data on ability and achievement tests, that had been collected in the Perinatal Project. Another hypothesis they tested was that as the interval between births increases, the effects of family size on intellectual ability decrease. This hypothesis was supported to some extent (for one of the groups included in the Perinatal Project), but both socioeconomic status and birth order were more important in influencing intellectual development than was the interval between childrens' births. A third hypothesis tested was that only-children would test lower in achievement and ability than firstborn children because "onlies" do not have as much experience teaching younger siblings. The data bore out half of this prediction: achievement scores were higher for firstborns; ability scores did not vary in accordance with the hypothesis. Thus support from this sample for the confluence theory model of birth-order effects is quite weak. Other studies also have failed to support the model (e.g., Cicirelli, 1976; Marjoribanks, 1976). At the present time therefore, there is no *simple* theory of birth order or sibling effects that adequately explains the differences in achievement and ability that have been observed.

Birth order and spacing between siblings are not the only sibling variables that have been suggested to affect children's development. The sex of the siblings also has been studied. Helen Koch (1955, 1956) studied 384 children who were 5 and 6 years old from families with two children each. In these families, the possible combinations of siblings (older brother–younger sister, older sister–younger brother, two brothers, two sisters) were represented equally. The children were observed and rated on several characteristics by their teachers. Children with brothers were rated by the teachers as more competitive, ambitious, enthusiastic, and decisive than children with sisters. Having a brother seemed to motivate children, especially girls, to be ambi-

Having an older brother makes it more likely that a girl will be competitive, enthusiastic, decisive, and nonconformist.

tious and assertive. Boys with younger brothers tended to learn leadership, responsibility, and to be less aggressive than boys with younger sisters. Boys with younger sisters were likely to get along with girls their age and to be friendlier to adults. Girls with older brothers tended to be nonconformists, often tomboys. Girls with older sisters tended to be traditionally feminine: sociable, conforming, and dependent.

There is nothing simple about the family constellation that includes more than one child. Siblings add substantial complexity to a child's social environment. Suggestive correlations between a child's achievement and social style and the order, number, sex, and spacing of his or her siblings hint at the complicated and subtle social influences of brothers and sisters. It should be stressed, however, that these influences are but one small part of the complex family package we have unwrapped a bit here—a package that includes the parents' education and income, affection and stimulation, socialization and discipline.

EARLY EDUCATION PROGRAMS

By the time they are 4 years old, most children in the United States are attending some form of early childhood education program, be it a nursery school, a Head Start program, or a day-care program. With each passing year, more and more 3-year-olds, 2-year-olds, and even 1-year-olds are attending early childhood programs in day-care centers. This trend has aroused deep feelings and controversies. A central issue is whether day care is harmful to children's social, emotional, and intellectual development. Many people consider day care a poor substitute for care at home by a parent. Selma Fraiberg (1977) and Burton White (1975) are two prominent psychologists who have expressed the view that children need to be taken care of at home by their parents until they are at least 3 years old. In contrast, other experts have suggested that day care can offer a decided advantage for early social and intellectual development (e.g., Caldwell, 1970; Caldwell, Wright, Honig, and Tannebaum, 1970). But many parents have little choice, no matter which view they hold. Economic realities are such that they *must* put their children in day care. In an age when approximately 50 percent of mothers of young children hold jobs and when certain other traditional child-care arrangements are unavailable, many parents simply must rely on day care of some sort. The traditional extended family, for instance, in which a near relative could be counted on to mind the youngsters, has become uncommon, and the two-parent family is becoming rarer as well. Many single parents of young children must find affordable, convenient, and (they hope) high-quality day care. More and more parents are expected to place their children—infants and toddlers as well as older preschoolers—in day care over the next decade. At present, most children—87 percent—whose mothers work outside the home are taken care of in their own homes or someone else's; only 13 percent go to a day-care center or nursery school.

Nursery school, which we distinguish from day care, traditionally has helped to prepare children in the United States for kindergarten and grade school. **Day-care centers** ordinarily are open all day, five days a week. Nursery schools have a shorter day, perhaps half a day three to five times a week. Day-care centers may offer programs indistinguishable from those of nursery schools. But the term **day care** ordinarily implies a substitute custodial arrangement made because parents are working or otherwise unavailable.

In the traditional nursery school, short periods of group activities make up the day: singing sessions; snack time; show and tell; group discussion of important events such as a holiday or the birth of a new sister; brief trips; story time; and so on. Children have access to a variety of activities and materials at a nursery school: blocks, clothes for dress-up, paints, scissors, and playground equipment, to name a few.

Montessori nursery schools are devoted to a philosophy of education in which children are believed to have natural curiosity, a desire to grow, and a wish to work on activities that systematically train their muscles and senses. Montessori schools teach children about everyday tasks, like washing, buttoning and folding their own clothes, opening and closing drawers. Children work with blocks of various sizes and shapes, graduated series of colors or musical tones, ranked weights that fit into holes in a board, and similar objects that develop the ability to make sensory discriminations. They handle sandpaper-covered alphabets as they say and hear the letters. They watch other children work and learn from them. As each child works on a project he or she has chosen, the school is relatively quiet.

The **Head Start** program attempts to give poor children the advantages available to middle-class preschoolers. For years educators had realized that children raised in impoverished homes and communities enter school at a considerable disadvantage. In the 1960s, with the growing concern about poverty, their predicament received more searching attention. It was suggested that providing poor 4-year-olds with the experiences they were missing at home—being read to, learning rhymes, playing dress-up, drawing, coloring with crayons, cutting with scissors, playing with blocks and puzzles, riding tricycles, becoming acquainted with fish, birds, and animals—would allow them to catch up and be better prepared for school. In 1965, a federally funded project, Head Start, began as an 8-week summer program for children who were about to enter school. It was soon realized that 8 weeks was much too brief a period. Head Start became a year-round program for preschool children. In 1980, about 350,000 children attended Head Start, and it appears likely that this program will continue.

Head Start centers provide medical and dental examinations and immunizations for children, a hot meal and a snack, and one teacher and two aides for every 15 children. Parents are invited to participate on a volunteer or paid basis. Some centers provide classes for them in home economics, food purchase and preparation, and child care. Furthermore, the staffs of the centers work closely with community agencies to solve the problems of the child and family. Now Head Start centers no longer uniformly offer the traditional nursery-school activities, such as coloring and dressing up. Some centers have adopted a strictly scheduled and highly didactic approach. In the Distar curriculum designed by Carl Bereiter and Siegfried Engelmann (1966), children in groups of 5 are drilled by a teacher in a fast-paced sequence of academic exercises to learn language, reading, or arithmetic skills.

Teacher (showing picture of a car) This is a vehicle.
Children This is a vehicle.
Teacher What is this?
Children This is a vehicle.
Teacher What is this? Say it louder.
Children THIS IS A VEHICLE.

Other centers, by contrast, have adopted a low-key "discovery" approach to education. Children are free to explore and learn from a smorgasbord of materials—wooden blocks, sand, water, weights, science materials, geometric forms, books—laid out for them by the teacher. The teacher responds with a "mini-lesson" only when specifically requested by a child. In between these extremes are programs that stress language and communication skills, others that emphasize emotional expressiveness and creativity, and still others that focus on social interaction and adjustment. These programs also vary in the teaching methods they employ, ranging from large group discussions to individual "tutorials," from highly structured lessons to unstructured learning experiences.

Many evaluative studies have been conducted to measure the impact of Head Start on preschool children. One of the first, the Westinghouse Learning Corporation and Ohio University study (1973), indicated that Head Start may have a significant effect on children's IQ scores, raising them 10 points, but that the gains made were not persistent once the children entered school. Other studies revealed that Head Start children, compared to neighborhood children not in the program, were more attentive and less impulsive, were more receptive to language, and had greater curiosity and motivation (Brink, Ellis, and Sarason, 1968; Lesser and Fox, 1968; Miller and Dyer, 1970).

Recently, a consortium of investigators has documented long-term differences between impoverished children who had attended preschool programs, like the best Head Start programs, and neighborhood children who had not. Although the differences in IQ observed at the end of the programs had faded, children who had attended were less likely to be held back from passing to the next grade or to be put in special classes. These differences persisted up through high school (Lazar, Darlington, Murray, Royce, and Snipper, 1982). It seems that early childhood education programs not only provide a different initial experience for children, but also and more important, they set in motion a series of experiences and motivations more conducive to achievement in school. The children have an ongoing experience of greater success.

At day-care centers, in nursery schools, and in Head Start programs, preschool children do crafts, learn academic skills, are read wonderful stories from books, and practice everything from measuring height to tying shoes. Attentive teachers and the company of their peers make it fun.

The Effects of Day Care

Day-care and nursery school programs also have been extensively evaluated. In a review of these evaluations, Alison Clarke-Stewart and Greta Fein (1983) drew several conclusions about the effects of these programs. First, day care and nursery school do not appear to diminish the child's relationship with his or her mother. Day-care children, like home-reared children, are attached to their mothers. Their relationships with day-care providers do not replace their attachment to their mother. Although infants in day care may become fond of, and feel comfort and security with, a day-care provider, they still prefer their mothers. They go to their mothers for help when they are distressed or bored, go to her more often, stay closer to her, and greet her return with more joy than they show in greeting the day-care provider.

But are children in day care as *securely* attached as children cared for at home? Most studies show that day care causes no ill effects on the security of children's attachment, but a few studies have found that day-care children, and boys in particular, maintain a greater physical distance between themselves and their mothers in a laboratory assessment than

home-care children do. This effect is especially likely to be true if day care begins in the first year, before a strong and stable attachment to the mother has formed. Day-care children are not more likely than home-care children to be anxious or angry or to protest their mother's leaving, however. What can explain the observed tendency for day-care children to distance themselves more from their mothers? Is it because their mothers spend less time with them than do home-care mothers? This seems unlikely. Working mothers may have less time at home, but they spend just about as much time as homebound mothers do in actual child care. A likelier explanation is that working mothers are less emotionally and psychologically accessible to their children than home-care mothers are. Working mothers tend to feel overworked and overtired. Although working improves their self-image and even their health, they may feel guilty about taking time from their children and feel that their mothering is rushed and harried. Many have stormy relationships with their husbands as well. Could this account for the physical distance between day-care children and their mothers? *Home-reared* children who maintain more distance from

RESEARCH FOCUS

EARLY CHILDHOOD EDUCATION

In a unique collaboration, headed by Irving Lazar at Cornell University, developmental psychologists who had independently conducted 11 studies of the effects of early childhood education programs on disadvantaged children's intellectual development and achievement pooled their results to answer several broad and important questions (Lazar et al., 1982). In part the psychologists wanted to refute statements that early childhood education programs were ineffective and wasteful of public funds. The investigators also wanted to learn whether early childhood education programs had long-term effects, and they wanted to know whether such programs are more effective for some children rather than others. By aggregating their results, they could answer these questions more definitively than could any investigator alone.

The programs studied had been located in cities and towns in the Northeast, Southeast, and Mid-

west. Some had been center-based; the children attended nursery schools or day-care centers. Some had been home-based; toys, play materials, and ideas about education were brought to the child's home. For example, in Phyllis Levenstein's Verbal Interaction Project on Long Island, New York, a toy demonstrator brought commercially available books and toys to the homes of 2- and 3-year-old children every week. She showed the mother how to use the materials with her child. Over the course of two school years, the toys and books grew increasingly—and appropriately—complex in cognitive and conceptual content. Other programs in the collaboration combined both home visits and center-based education. In David Weikart's program for 3- and 4-year olds, for example (Weikart, Deloria, Lawser, and Wiegerink, 1970), the children attended half-day sessions at a center 5 days a week for 2 years and were also visited by teachers at home for 90 minutes every week. The program, based on principles derived from Jean Piaget's theory of development, aimed at stimulating children's cognitive development.

their mothers have been observed to have mothers who are rejecting and angry, who do not reciprocate their children's initiation of physical contact. Yet the few studies that bear on this issue suggest that day-care mothers do not, as a group, differ from home-care mothers on measures of rejection or reciprocity toward their children. Is it then simply that day-care children get used to being with many different people outside of their families and become more independent of their mothers? Is it that their distance from their mother just reflects generally advanced development? There is some evidence to support these explanations. It does seem that for *most* children, the pattern of greater distance from mother probably reflects an adaptive reaction to a realistic appraisal of the situation rather than an emotional disturbance. Nevertheless, this issue bears continuing scrutiny and evaluation as more and more infants are sent to day-care homes and centers.

How does day care affect the development of children's social skills with other children and adults? Day-care offers many opportunities for interaction with peers and caregivers, opportunities that most home-reared children do not have. Does this affect these children's social development? Several studies suggest that day care, indeed, does increase children's social competence and maturity and that children attending day care or nursery school are more self-confident, more outgoing, and less timid than home-care children. Day care seems to decrease children's dependence on adults at the same time that it increases their cooperativeness when the situation so requires. Day-care children know more about aspects of the social world— gender roles, perspective taking, labels for feelings, how to solve social problems—earlier, are less stereotyped and more mature in their play, and more realistic about their achievements. The advanced social competence of day-care children cuts two ways however. Not only are they more independent, they may also be less polite and agreeable, less obedient, louder, more aggressive, bossy, and rebellious than home-care children.

When psychologists sift the evidence to find out why children in day-care differ socially from their home-reared counterparts, they must answer the question indirectly. It is unlikely, first of all, that these independent, assertive, rebellious day-care children simply reject adults' standards. For they

---

For all the programs included in the collaborative study, success was measured in the following ways: by standard IQ and achievement tests at the end of the program and again later; by whether graduates of the program—who by this time were 8 to 18 years old—needed special education or stayed back any grades (measures of school competence); by tests of children's achievement-orientation and self-esteem in elementary or high school; and by changes in the families.

Analyses of the combined data from all projects showed that early childhood education programs for poor children had lasting effects in three areas: school competence, attitudes and values, and family attitudes. Children who had participated in these programs were about half as likely as their peers who had not been included to need special education, with its expense and stigma, and they were less likely to be held back a grade (25 percent versus 31 percent). This result held true for all children, regardless of their sex, ethnic group, ability on entering the program, or family background. Children in the programs also scored higher on intelligence tests at the conclusion of the programs and for several years after the programs had ended: IQ scores averaged 7 points higher at the programs' end, 4 points after 1 to 2 years, and 3 points after 2 to 4 years. By the time program graduates were 10 to 17 years old, however, there was no significant difference between their IQ scores and those of controls. After attending an early education program, children were more likely to say that they did well in school and were proud of themselves for their accomplishments. Mothers of these children were more satisfied with their children's performance in school and had higher occupational goals for their children.

The investigators took it as a mark of the value of early education that so many different program designs produced positive results, for no one program seemed clearly superior to all others. They strongly urged that public policy provide good education for disadvantaged children. As they put it, they found themselves in the position of asserting "the commonsense notion that children will benefit from good experiences" (Lazar et al., 1982, p. 65).

remain quite responsive to adults' needs, quite sympathetic and cooperative under certain circumstances, and quite sensitive to which situations require cooperation. Although the question cannot yet be settled with certainty, it is likely that the difference between home- and day-care children is a result of a temporary acceleration in the willingness and ability of day-care children to interact with other people and an earlier exposure to social rules, norms, conflicts, and knowledge in day-care programs. Day-care children may develop social competence sooner because they learn and practice social skills as they interact with other children and with adults who encourage independence and self-direction. These qualities, at the same time, may be encouraged and reinforced at home by the parents who send their children to early childhood programs.

Early childhood programs that have an educational component temporarily accelerate children's intellectual development as well. Mothers of day-care children report that their children learn more about concepts, practical matters, and counting than they would have learned at home. (Mothers report that children learn more bad language, too!) Day-care children are more advanced than home-care children on both verbal and nonverbal skills: language comprehension and fluency, eye-hand coordination, and drawing. This acceleration has been documented consistently in many studies of day-care centers and nursery schools. In one study, for example, day-care children were 6 to 9 months ahead of home-care children in their scores on tests of intellectual development (Clarke-Stewart, 1984). Research suggests that this intellectual advancement may derive from the teaching that is done in these programs, the availability of a variety of materials and equipment, and the more systematically educational environment of the early childhood program compared to that of a home. Although the evidence on the intellectual advantage of children in early childhood programs seems quite straightforward, there is one complication. It is difficult to know just how much of the observed acceleration is a direct result of the program, because researchers also have found that the children who attend these educational programs come from families with higher levels of education. The only research that has experimentally assigned children to stay home or to attend a program (e.g., Ramey

and Mills, 1977) has been done with very poor children. The direct effect of early education on middle-class children is undoubtedly less pronounced than on these disadvantaged children. However, even though parents' selection of day-care settings mediates the direct effects of these programs, one thing is clear: many of the worries parents once expressed about day care can be laid to rest. Attendance in decent day-care programs does not appear to cause intellectual retardation, emotional disturbance, or overdependence on other children, and it does not disturb the relationship between parents and children. Like the advantages in mental development that children get from Head Start, day-care children's social and intellectual acceleration relative to home-care children diminishes by the time that kindergarten or first grade rolls around.

SCHOOL

In the years between kindergarten and the end of high school, children are influenced in their social, intellectual, and emotional development by the school environment. For some children, school is the first taste of the world beyond home and mother. For others, it is a continuation of experiences familiar from an early childhood program. Classmates and teachers shape children's school experience, their self-perceptions, and opinions of themselves and others.

Open and Structured Classes

We have already described differences in openness and "closedness" in the physical space of the classroom. In the last two decades, many school classes have also become more open in their curriculum and scheduling. In the **open class,** scheduling is flexible. An interesting and changing buffet of materials is available for children to explore and manipulate, at their own pace, much of the time. But the teacher also plans group and individual activities, which can be initiated as the appropriate moment arrives. A visitor to the class is likely to see children, often of different ages, scattered around the room and working either individually or in small groups. Older children may help to teach the younger ones, and the teacher studies with the children, discussing subject matter rather than lecturing to them. The warm atmosphere and the rich store of educational materials are meant to make learning exciting. Children are more likely to be judged by what they make and by their individual progress than by group tests.

In the traditional **structured class,** children spend most of their time on lessons, usually in the basics, the three R's. The teacher gives them the facts and maintains order. Subject matter is from a set curriculum established for the class as a whole. Tests are also given to the whole class, and promotion depends on children's grades.

Barbara Day and Richard Brice (1977) compared the academic achievement of 100 6-year-olds from four first-grade classes that varied in openness. There were an equal number of boys and girls, whites and nonwhites in the study. No significant differences related to openness of the class were found in the achievement test given to the children at the end of the school year.

In a study of third-grade open and structured classes, Ann Lukasevitch and Roland Gray (1978) examined their effects on achievement and also attempted to separate those of an open style of teaching from those of an architecturally open classroom. Lukasevitch and Gray had a greater chance to detect differences, because the children in their study had been attending the same schools for 3 years instead of just 1 year, as in the Day and Brice study. It is possible that the effects of the different teaching styles and classrooms may require several years to become obvious. The chil-

Elementary classes may be "open" or "structured." Creative and original work may be fostered in an open environment; the 3 R's are more likely to be mastered in a structured one.

dren's vocabularies, reading comprehension, math concepts, and problem-solving abilities were tested. Scores indicated that a self-contained, architecturally closed classroom was better for teaching math concepts, that a structured teaching style was better for both math concepts and reading comprehension. Children whose classrooms were closed and teaching structured did especially well on math concepts. Research by Jere Brophy and Carolyn Evertson (1974) also suggested that teachers whose second- and third-grade students made learning gains tended to be direct in most of their methods.

The results of these studies done in the United States are supported by those of a major study of 871 primary schools in England. Neville Bennett (1976) found that the more structured style was superior for teaching math, reading, and English, especially to anxious children who need to know what is expected of them. Bennett also reported that less actual work was accomplished in an open classroom. On the other hand, creative work and children with less need for structure seemed to benefit from indirect teaching. But moderation of either extreme seemed the most beneficial, even for creative work, in this and other studies (Soar and Soar, 1976). An upper limit to the amount of freedom allowed children is apparently better for any kind of achievement or growth. Leaving students too much on their own is likely to hinder their creativity as well as their academic achievement.

The benefits of open education may be social rather than academic. But do the social benefits of open classes offset their possible academic drawbacks? Bennett (1976) concludes that they do not, stating that formal teaching fulfills its academic aims without detriment to the social and emotional de-

RESEARCH FOCUS

12 LONDON SCHOOLS

In an ambitious comparative study of children in 12 London secondary schools, Michael Rutter and his colleagues (Rutter, Maughan, Mortimore and Ouston, 1979) assessed many different features of the schools' physical and social environments. They were particularly interested to learn what, if anything, might be singled out as causing one school to be better than another—better in terms of students' achievement and behavior in and out of school. The families of many students in these schools suffered from various psychological, economic, and social problems; some were immigrant families from Cyprus and the West Indies; some were poor; some had only one parent living at home. Yet most of the children came from "ordinary happy homes which were fairly unexceptionable" (p. 34). The schools tended to be homogeneous to the extent that all maintained fairly formal relations between students and staff, and all offered similar curricula. School size varied from 450 to 2000 pupils, and the space available per pupil ranged from 80 to 200 square feet. The prevailing philosophies of the schools were diverse. Some of the educators considered preparing students to pass examinations their highest goal, whereas others considered it to be developing students' personalities.

The investigators used five measures to assess students' performance: the students' behavior in school; school attendance; success in passing standardized examinations; employment; and delinquency. They gathered information in several ways: from interviews with teachers, department heads, principals, and other staff; from confidential questionnaires collected by students in class when no teachers were present; and from systematic observations of both teachers and students in class and out.

Rutter and his colleagues found many interesting associations between school "processes" and students' performance. Among these associations, they found that schools in which homework was assigned often and in which the assignments were checked had better behaved students and students who did better academically. Schools in which students' work was hung on the walls (a form of praise) also had better academic achievement— and fewer graffiti. The amount of actual teaching time students were exposed to each week was positively related to student attendance. Attendance and academic performance both related positively to the number of students who reported using the school library.

In the areas of teachers' planning and actual teaching of lessons, the schools with the best attendance and least delinquency required teachers to

velopment of pupils, whereas informal teaching is of only limited help to children socially and emotionally and can be harmful to them academically.

In contrast, some studies have found that children who are in open classes have more positive attitudes toward school than do children in traditional classes, although this difference does not always appear (Minuchin and Shapiro, 1983). Open classrooms also may affect how children feel about themselves. In that they are designed to provide children with support and opportunities for mastery, open classrooms may be expected to make children feel better about themselves. But a review of the research in this area (Horwitz, 1979) shows that in a majority of cases, no differences in self-esteem appear between children in open versus traditional classes. When differences do crop up, though, children in open classes have greater self-confidence.

The structure of the class correlates with another aspect of self-concept: children's perceptions of themselves as masculine or feminine. In open classes, children's sense of their individuality is heightened and their sense of gender roles—girls' especially—is less conventional and stereotyped. They play in less sex-typed fashion and tend to make more friends of the other sex (Minuchin, 1965; Minuchin, Biber, Shapiro, and Zimiles, 1969). In general, open settings foster less stereotyped play, more play between boys and girls, and less stereotyped ideas about present and future gender roles.

But this is not the only way that patterns of social interaction vary in open and traditional classes. Open classes generally foster a wider variety of interactions, greater cooperation on projects, and more ways for children to make friends and to be

coordinate lesson planning within their departments. In less successful schools, teachers worked more independently. Other measures of academic emphasis did not relate to any student outcomes: the number of students who consulted teachers about a problem; the hours of preparation teachers spent; whether teachers' records were checked by other staff. Students behaved better in schools where teachers spent most of class time actually teaching rather than setting up and also where the class was taught as a whole. (Rutter made clear that individualized teaching was not detrimental but that he had observed so little of it as not to be able to judge its effects. But when a class *was* arranged for group teaching, it was important that the teacher kept the whole group involved.) In general, schools that stressed academic matters produced children who did better both academically and behaviorally. Interestingly enough, there seemed to be no disadvantages associated with higher teacher turnover. In general, too, all forms of reward and praise were associated with better outcomes; associations between punishment and outcomes were not statistically significant (although the students reported receiving three times as much punishment as reward).

When students were given the chance to take responsibility for, and participate in, running the school—acting as the equivalent of class president,

for example, or as monitors—they were also likely to do well. Schools in which many of the students had stayed in the same peer groups over time and also those in which students associated with many friends from outside of their class showed lower levels of delinquency. Overall, there were many significant associations between the schools' social environment and student performance. But the cumulative effect of the social factors was far greater than that of any individual factor. Each school had its own set of values, or ethos, which was a product of combined social factors. In contrast, there were few meaningful associations between performance and physical factors or aspects of administrative organization.

Of course, the school environment did not eliminate all individual differences in students' abilities or families. Schools whose students tested at average or better intellectual ability on admission had more students who succeeded at examinations. Schools that admitted students with lower than average ability had higher rates of delinquency. The kind of students did not affect school functioning, however. Rutter suggests that it is likely that the associations between school environment and student performance were not merely correlational but also causal. School experiences, especially the ethos of a school, shaped children's behavior and beliefs.

popular. Among children in open classrooms, dominance and popularity hierarchies are less pointed: there are fewer stars but fewer isolates and scapegoats either. Children are more self-reliant and autonomous in open settings. One study of 11-year-olds in Ontario found that those in open classes began projects and adhered to their own values more often than those in traditional classes did (Traub, Weiss, and Fisher, 1974).

When studies compare high-school students in traditional and open, or alternative, schools, findings similar to those on younger children appear, although the research is scantier. Generally speaking, students in open high schools have been found to have more positive attitudes toward school and higher self-confidence. They are less likely to drop out of school or to get into fights. Like their younger counterparts, they have more varied friendships than students in traditional schools (Minuchin and Shapiro, 1983).

Self-fulfilling Prophecies

Regardless of the openness of the class schedule and the flexibility of activities, teachers' beliefs and expectations about their students' abilities can become self-fulfilling prophecies. In this way, too, the social environment of the school can influence children's development. Children in elementary school are still forming their academic self-concepts. They are creating an image of themselves as students, an image that will influence the effort they put into mastering various subjects and their attitudes and enthusiasm for school and learning in general. How does it affect a child's achievement in school if he or she is considered a slow learner? Do teachers who believe girls are better than boys in reading but worse in math somehow teach in a way that confirms their beliefs? Disturbingly, the answers to these questions appear to be yes.

Robert Rosenthal and Lenore Jacobson (1966, 1968) conducted a landmark study of teacher expectations. Intelligence tests were administered to students in the first to the sixth grades of a school in California. The names of 20 percent of the students were randomly chosen, and teachers of these students were told that the tests had identified them as "bloomers" who could be expected to show unusual intellectual gains in the coming year. The IQ test was given again 8 months later. The randomly selected "bloomers," in particular those in

the first and second grades, had made unusual gains. The younger children improved more for several possible reasons. First, having less formulated academic self-images, they may have been more susceptible to differential treatment, whether intentional or unintentional, on the part of the teachers. Second, less background information had accumulated about them, and their teachers may have found their promised blooming more credible.

The Rosenthal and Jacobson study has been criticized on several methodological grounds. Nevertheless, after a rigorous and comprehensive reanalysis of it, Janet Elashoff and Richard Snow (1970), although recommending further study, concluded that teachers' expectancies had probably affected at least the first- and second-grade "bloomers." In a review of the other studies done on this subject since Rosenthal and Jacobson did theirs, Jere Brophy and Thomas Good (1974) concluded that the weight of the evidence supports expectancy effects but that teachers' expectations and their interactions with students are influenced by many factors. The teacher's own attitudes; the children's appearance, race, social class, abilities, interests; and personal, academic, and family histories all impinge on the message transmitted and the one received.

A number of related studies have indicated the wide-ranging influence of expectancies. First-grade boys whose teachers believed that boys do not learn to read as well as girls, read less well than first-grade boys whose teachers were unhampered by such notions (Palardy, 1969). Students with little ability who were taught French by teachers with a positive attitude toward them learned much more of the language than did poor students whose teachers had a negative attitude (Durstall, 1975). The reading achievement of students whose teachers overestimated their IQ scores was significantly higher than that of students whose teachers underestimated their IQ scores (Doyle, Hancock, and Kifer, 1971). Finally, future teachers were found to have different expectancies of children based on the children's race and social class (Cooper, Baron, and Lowe, 1975). They expected blacks and poor children to be less successful and less internally responsible for failure, whites and middle-class children to succeed academically and to feel personally responsible if they failed. Educators may never be able to eliminate the bias of teacher expectancy, but being aware of this bias as a possible factor in the schoolroom may prevent us from placing too great an emphasis on any one school grade.

Behavior Modification in the Classroom

Because research evidence indicates the value to children of receiving approval from their teachers, as well as the generally unequal distribution of that approval, efforts have been made to reward children more methodically and thereby modify their behavior. Although teaching itself is in many ways an art, one that cannot be taught, children's behavior in the classroom can be improved by behavior modification techniques.

In a typical behavior modification treatment, baseline observations are first made, class periods are broken down into brief intervals, and a record is kept of the percent of intervals in which children behave as desired. The teacher then increases the

frequency of his or her positive comments to students for appropriate behavior, and observations are made of the effects on children's classroom behavior. To check that the manipulation is really responsible for greater frequency of desired behavior, the teacher may discontinue systematic reinforcement and see whether good behavior returns to the baseline frequency. She or he then increases reinforcement once more, and this time continues it (Figure 3.2). Periodic checks ensure that the desired behavior is still being reinforced and that the children are still behaving well.

This kind of treatment has been used effectively in many classrooms to increase decorum (Sherman and Bushell, 1975). Many teachers use contingent rewards: if the students are quiet, their recess or playtime is increased. Deals and contracts made between children and parents, whereby parents promise a suitable reward such as a record album if children's school behavior improves, have been

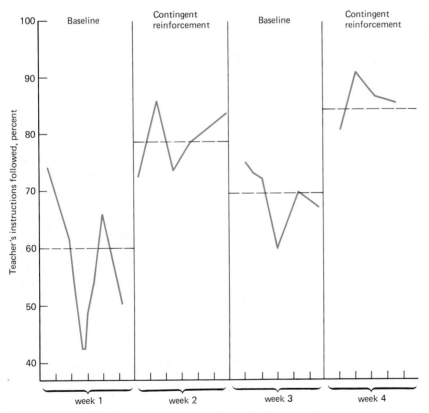

FIGURE 3.2
Children's behavior improves when the teacher consistently praises the class for following instructions. The broken lines indicate the mean percent of good behavior in the classroom for each week.

effective. Daily report cards, which determine whether children gain or lose home privileges, have also worked. Systems in which children earn points and tokens that can be exchanged for candy, money, toys, and privileges have decreased disruptive behaviors, even when other methods—rules, praise, ignoring disruptions—have had little effect. As James Sherman and Don Bushell point out, however, token systems have a problem; when tokens are no longer given, improvements in behavior disappear. It seems that decorum bought by tokens does not generalize to other situations and is not itself maintained unless the special token system is kept in place. Sherman and Bushell suggest that reinforcements be built into the classroom program and that more research be done on training students to respond to long-term consequences rather than immediate rewards.

School Organization

School systems in the United States vary in how they organize school grades into units. Some offer kindergartens, some do not. Some school systems group their elementary schools into the grades up to sixth, some go only to third or fourth grade; some have middle schools of fourth to sixth or seventh grade, followed by high school. In other school systems, elementary school goes up to sixth grade, junior high school from seventh to ninth grade, and high school thereafter. The organization of the school also can affect children's development, psychologists have found. It makes intuitive sense that children who are the oldest and most experienced in their grade school will feel more self-confident and will have different social relations from children of the same age who are the youngest and least experienced in their middle or junior high school. The same set of factors operates for the students at the boundaries of high school. One study of sixth-graders in a middle school—where they were bottom dogs—and sixth-graders in an elementary school—where they were top dogs—showed substantial differences between them (Shovlin, 1967). The girls in elementary school were less interested in boys than were the girls in middle school, no doubt because they had no exposure to postpubescent boys and girls in the lower grades. The boys in elementary school were also less mature socially, but these boys were higher in self-esteem than their middle-school counterparts,

probably because they were the biggest and strongest boys in their school—a source of self-esteem for boys.

Desegregation

Schools reflect the society they serve and the social problems of that society. Attempts in the United States to root out racial inequality have deeply affected the schools. Desegregation, ordered by the courts and enacted by individual school systems, has aimed to improve the ratio of whites to minority-group members, to improve the quality of education for those formerly discriminated against, and to improve race relations generally through contact and interaction. Have schools met these goals? Yes and no. Although busing may integrate a school system in theory, in fact, black children bused into a white district may be segregated in their classrooms. When students are actually assigned to work together, however, race relations have been found to improve. A large study by Garlie Forehand, Majorie Ragosta, and Donald Rock (1976) of more than 5000 5th-graders from over 90 grade schools and 400 10th-graders from 72 high schools showed that when students were encouraged and assigned to work on projects about racial issues, when their school work encompassed people of various races and ethnic groups, when curricula promoted concepts of equal racial status, and when they worked in class or on sports teams with students of other races and backgrounds, race relations improved. When school principals, teachers, or guidance counselors did not encourage integrated work or play, however, desegregation and race relations faltered.

Although desegregation tends to improve students' cooperation and relations between races, it does not inevitably enhance the self-esteem of black students (Minuchin and Shapiro, 1983)—contrary to the hopes and expectations of many people. To the minority-group child, desegregation can offer the first exposure to the values of the dominant white group, an exposure that may prove alienating. Desegregation can intensify hostility and harden differences. It can expose students to racial prejudice, academic competition, and conflicting demands from peers and teachers (Rosenberg and Simmons, 1971). To succeed in a desegregated school, some black students may have to "act white" and court rejection from other blacks. Findings on self-concept have not been strong and consistent across studies. Further research that looks at how desegregation affects children's actual social experiences would help us to predict the effects of this environmental variation.

TELEVISION

In many households the television set is on as long as anyone is at home, and it is often the child who is intently perched in front of it waiting for the next scene. With approximately 97 percent of American homes equipped with at least one television set, it is little wonder that many children devote more time to watching it than to any other single activity, except sleep (Keye, 1974). On the average, children spend 3 hours a day watching television, and by the age of 16 most children in this country will have spent more time watching television than going to school (Liebert and Poulos, 1975). For many children of school age, television becomes the primary source of information about other peo-

ple—about other races and ethnic groups, other social classes, the outside world, our culture. In one study, 40 percent of a group of 300 elementary school students from urban, suburban, and rural areas learned from television most of what they knew about blacks in terms of looks, manner of speaking, and dress (Greenberg, 1972). Children probably also learn more about occupational groups from television than from personal contact or from the community (De Fleur and De Fleur, 1967). In this sense, "All television is educational television," as former federal communications commissioner Nicholas Johnson has stated (Liebert and Poulos, 1975).

Viewing Habits

Whether children watch a great deal of television or just a daily hour will depend on their parents' viewing habits and on their own sociability. The children of parents who are light viewers and have considerable education are likely to be light viewers themselves. Children who are passive and with-

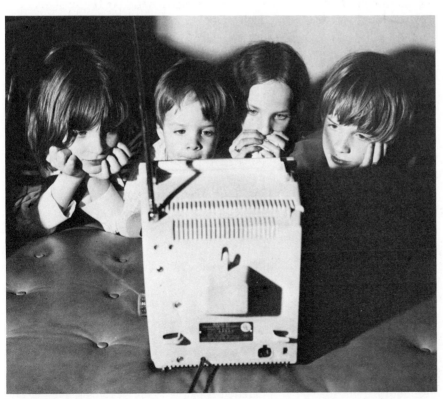

Television absorbs children for hours of every day. Its impact on their development has been investigated and argued over.

drawn may use television as an electronic peer. Parke (1978) suggests that watching a great deal of television may be a symptom of social-adjustment problems, not a cause of the passive, bashful, and distractible behavior often associated with excessive viewing.

Researchers have learned that children benefit little from the programs they most often see on television (Liebert and Poulos, 1975), that children who are avid watchers of television lag developmentally behind their peers (Carew, 1980). They have even found that though children can imitate what they see on television, they usually do not learn problem solving strategies from watching "educational" programs (Hodapp, 1977). Other researchers have suggested that the limited positive effect of even "good" television programs on children's development may depend on an adult's being present during the viewing (Singer and Singer, 1974). Children appear to benefit from the guidance and explanations the older person provides as they watch together.

Viewing varies over the course of childhood and adolescence, increasing from age 3 until the beginning of adolescence and then declining among high-school students. Thus middle childhood is a period for considerable television viewing and influence. Lower-class children tend to watch more television and more violence than do middle-class children. Ethnic studies suggest that blacks generally watch more television than whites (Stein and Friedrich, 1975).

Various studies of the programs families watch together suggest that most children are finished with their television viewing by 9:00 P.M. But studies reviewed by Robert Liebert and Rita Poulos (1975) indicate that millions of children between the ages of 7 and 12 are still watching television from 9:00 P.M. to midnight. For preschoolers, television may have been an electronic babysitter, but parents of school-age children are more likely to use television as a way of keeping their sons and daughters out of trouble and avoiding the need to teach or supervise them. Parents seem to put few restrictions on their children's television viewing until preadolescence or adolescence, after they have been watching excessively for years (Stein and Friedrich, 1975). Because parents now spend more time away from home, because both parents may work, and because many families are headed by one parent, there is what Aletha Huston Stein and Lynette Friedrich (1975) call a "socialization void." Parents provide little guidance, and children acquire much of their socialization from television.

What's on Television?

What are children likely to see on television? The content of television programs reflects—and probably accelerates—current social trends. Families on television today have problems—divorce, adolescent upheavals, brushes with drugs and alcohol. There are blacks on television and at least a few representatives of the working class. Women are seen at work as well as at home. Nevertheless, the proportions of violence and stereotyped sex roles remain high.

George Gerbner (1972) found 30 percent of the prime-time and Saturday programs saturated with violence and 58 percent of them featuring a good deal of violence, with violence defined as an actual act of physical force or one causing pain. On these programs, socially disapproved means, such as force and illegal escape, succeeded more frequently than legal and socially approved means. This was especially true of children's programs. Foreigners were more likely to be involved in causing violence and more likely to pay a price for it.

Reviews of sex stereotyping on television have indicated that women are more likely to be victims. In the 1980s, the "dumb blond" is more popular than ever. Moreover, even if new programs reflect recent shifts in attitudes, reruns are common in the afternoon; the stereotyped characters in these programs are popular with children long after they have disappeared from prime time. Television constantly bombards children with images of people in traditional sex roles. This is even the case on educational programs, like "Sesame Street," where Big Bird is told he is "a boy bird and will have to help with men's work, important work, heavy work," and he "should get a girl bird to help Susan with her work of flower arranging" (Gardner, 1970). In one analysis of popular children's programs (Sternglanz and Serbin, 1974), men and boys outnumbered women and girls two to one. Males were aggressive, constructive, and rewarded for action; females, passive, deferential, and rewarded for reaction.

Elderly people, who are becoming a larger proportion of the population, and Asians, Hispanics, and Indians are still rarely seen on television.

Clearly then, television, as Stein and Friedrich have commented, is not a mirror reflecting the whole of society but a prism refracting its pluralism and projecting only the facets of the dominant culture.

Parents and educators have long been concerned about the content of the programs children watch and have sought to channel the educational potential of television to good purpose. "Sesame Street," "Mr. Rogers' Neighborhood," and "The Electric Company" are excellent examples of the kinds of programs needed for preschool children. In 1969, "Sesame Street" made its debut on national public television as a direct attempt to combine entertainment, attention-holding techniques, and educational content, specifically for the disadvantaged preschool viewer. Through moving letters, numbers, and other symbols; amusing, clear and uncomplicated animation; and the verbal and active Muppets who have personalities of their own, children are given an exciting presentation of A,B,C's and 1,2,3's, of problem solving and reasoning, of classification and ordering, and develop a greater awareness of the surrounding world.

What Are the Effects of Watching Television?

During the first 2 years that the program was broadcast, a nationwide study by the Educational Testing Service evaluated the educational impact of "Sesame Street." It was found that 3-year-olds gained more than 5-year-olds and frequent viewers more than infrequent; that after the first year, children learned little more, despite consistent viewing; and that after entering school, children who had frequently watched "Sesame Street" enjoyed school more than did infrequent viewers (Bogatz and Ball, 1971).

But another study (Sprigle, 1971, 1972) found that "Sesame Street" did not prepare poor children for first grade, nor did it substantially narrow the achievement gap that exists between poor and middle-class children. Judith Minton (1972) found that only on an alphabet subtest did scores of poor children improve from watching "Sesame Street." Other analyses (Cook et al., 1975) suggest that the popularity of the program has encouraged adults in middle-class homes to watch it with their children and use it as an educational resource, accounting for the positive results reported. Moreover, the animation and rapid pace of the program are sus-

pected of inducing impulsiveness in children and making it difficult for them to be attentive in school (Clark, 1970; Wright, 1974). Yet over the many years of its existence "Sesame Street" has proved to be a viable, temporary means of increasing children's knowledge.

The effect of television violence has been a special concern in recent years, for it is estimated that by graduation from high school, the average American child has seen 18,000 televised murders (Brody, 1975). Experiments have indicated that exposure to television violence increases children's subsequent aggression in the laboratory. Children who had watched television violence were more likely to hit a Bobo doll and to strike the doll more frequently than those who had not (Bandura, 1969). But it is difficult to generalize from the laboratory situation to real life; children in these studies may just have been trying to do what they thought was expected of them.

In a more naturalistic study (Friedrich and Stein, 1973—see p. 22) groups of preschoolers watched one of three types of television program daily for 4 weeks at their own nursery school: cartoons showing aggression, "Batman" and "Superman"; episodes of the prosocial "Mr. Rogers' Neighborhood"; or neutral programs, such as children visiting a farm. The children's behavior was observed beginning 3 weeks before the viewing sessions and continuing until 2 weeks after. At that point, children in the first group were less willing to exert self-control, less able to tolerate delays in obtaining their desires, and less likely to obey the rules of the nursery school. If they had been aggressive before the 4 weeks of special viewing, they were more so afterward; but children who were not aggressive did not become so. Children who watched "Mr. Rogers' Neighborhood" became more self-controlled, more persistent at tasks, and more obedient. The differences were not very large, and we do not know how long they lasted beyond the 2 weeks. Given the extensiveness of most children's television viewing, however, we should not dismiss the possibility that the effects of actual television consumption are profound and persistent.

In another naturalistic study (Singer, Singer, and Sherrod, 1979), 3- to 4-year-old children were observed repeatedly in nursery school. Their behavior during free play—their imaginativeness, emotionality, aggression, cooperation, interaction, and mood—was related to their parents' reports of all the television watched by their child. A strong relation was found between frequent physical aggression and frequent viewing of all but educational children's programs. Watching educational programs, on the other hand, which were usually followed more intently and were viewed more often by girls than boys, was related to prosocial behavior and using mature language in nursery school. These relations held up even when the education of the parents and the child's IQ were controlled for. The study did not, however, establish whether aggressive children choose to watch a great deal of violent television or watching violent television makes children more aggressive. Probably both are true. Whatever the causal direction, this study joins a substantial number of others in suggesting that there is some link between frequent viewing of violent television and aggression in children.

In a 10-year longitudinal study of school children in Columbia County, New York (Lefkowitz, Eron, Walder, and Huesmann, 1977), the preference of third-grade boys for violent television related strongly to aggressive behavior during adolescence. In fact, the preference for violent television programs in the third grade was a better predictor of aggression at age 19 than social class, IQ, age, parental aggression or punitiveness, or watching violent programs at 19. This study does suggest that liking and watching violence on television contribute to, and are not merely correlated with, aggressiveness.

A unique study of a Canadian town before and after television became available to residents makes the suggestion even more strongly. Tanis Williams (1977) found that a 2-year exposure to television significantly increased children's verbal and physical aggression. Children also tended to have rigid sex stereotypes, and their creativity and fluency with words decreased significantly. Children who were in grades four and five at the time television was introduced maintained reading skills above those of children in other towns who had grown up with television. The reading skills of children who were in lower grades when television was introduced declined.

If television can have such potent negative effects on children's socialization, can it increase prosocial behavior? Aimee Dorr (1979) used the self-reports of children, from kindergarten through fifth grade, before and after they viewed television programs. These reports revealed that the prosocial

and moral content of programs became more salient with age. The younger children were more likely to remember violent episodes and characters. Facts and physical skills were remembered at all ages. The growth in social understanding during middle childhood makes it an ideal period in which to expose children to prosocial material. The programs should include considerable physical action, show characters in a familiar setting, and present several characters behaving in the desirable way (Liebert and Poulos, 1975).

Television has indirect effects as well. By reducing social interaction, television may serve as a means of controlling tension, especially in crowded households. In such homes, television may reduce fighting and diminish the potential for family violence and family breakup (Rosenblatt and Cunningham, 1976). But in less crowded homes, television is more likely to increase tensions by causing arguments about meals and bedtime. Even in the crowded home, less tension and family fighting may be bought at the price of too little social interaction in the family (Parke, 1978). Addiction to television also keeps the family home and disinclines members from visiting other families or serving the community.

CLASS AND CULTURE

Widening concentric circles bring us finally to a consideration of the macro level of the environment—social class and culture—a level that includes both social and physical features. Comparison of children's experiences and behavior in different cultures or social classes is another source of valuable information about environmental effects on development. One recent example of such research is a study by Harold Stevenson (1983). He studied the reading and mathematical abilities of 1440 first- and fifth-graders in Minneapolis, Minnesota, in Taipei, Taiwan, and in Sendai, Japan. He found that the American children were included among the very best and very worst readers, but disproportionately more of them did poorly. Results of the mathematics test were even less favorable for American children. Among the 100 students from the three cities who received the lowest scores in each grade, there were 58 American children at the first-grade level and 67 at fifth-grade. (By chance, there should have been 33.) Among the 100 top first-graders in mathematics, there were only 15 American children. Only 1 American child appeared among the top 100 fifth-graders. Among the 20 American fifth-grade classrooms, in not one was the average score on the mathematics test equivalent to that of children in the worst performing Japanese classroom.

Testing of children's cognitive abilities and interviews with their mothers and teachers help explain why American children do so poorly. The reason apparently is not the children's level of intelligence—they did just as well on the cognitive tests—not the parents' educational status, and not the level of training of the children's teachers. But American children spend less time in school (1000 fewer hours every year), receive proportionately less instruction in mathematics, and spend more classroom time engaged in inappropriate activities like talking to friends or staring into space than Chinese or Japanese children do. American children also do less homework and spend more time playing. They sleep slightly longer at night and do more household chores. When mothers were asked to evaluate their children's abilities, American mothers had high esteem for their children's cognitive abilities, their school performance, and the quality of their education. In contrast, few Japanese or Chinese mothers said that they were "very satisfied" with their children's school performance. American mothers were more likely than Japanese or Chinese mothers to believe that their children's success in school is determined by ability and less likely to believe that it is the result of exerting more effort. All of these factors, and perhaps others besides, are likely to be responsible for the observed differences in children's reading and mathematics achievement in the United States, Taiwan, and Japan. They serve to illustrate the complex web of factors that constitute culture. These factors include overt behavior, underlying beliefs and values, and social institutions.

Social class subsumes a host of factors, too— income, education, social status, occupation, residence, values, child rearing practices, disciplinary styles. The 1971 study of 10-month-old girls conducted by Jerome Kagan and Steven Tulkin (see p. 73) is an example of research that documents social-class differences in parents' behavior and development. As you recall, it showed that middle-class mothers spent more time talking to their babies and entertaining them and were more likely to respond to their fussing and crying with a kind

word. No class differences were found in the mothers' amounts of kissing, holding, tickling and bouncing, other nonverbal interaction, or spoken prohibitions. As for the infants themselves, although they did not differ in mobility, length of play, or nearness to their mothers, middle-class infants were more likely to stop crying at the sound of their mother's voice. Studies of older children and their mothers (reviewed by Clarke-Stewart and Apfel, 1979) document differences that are extensions of these observed in infants. Middle-class mothers are more accepting and affectionate, impose fewer restrictions, talk and play more with their children, and discipline by explaining or asking rather than punishing or threatening. The way they speak to their children is likely to be more complex, abstract, and varied, and their responses are likely to be more rewarding and prompter than those of lower-class mothers. Middle-class children in turn score higher on IQ tests and tests of problem solving, cognitive tasks, and do better in school.

The inference has repeatedly been drawn that these differences along social-class lines for both parents and children demonstrate the effect of environment, specifically social class, on development. Unfortunately, this inference is oversimplified at best. Many studies have confounded social class with race, ethnicity, religion, or family structure. Many have used, without acknowledging the fact, tests that reflect a middle-class bias and have administered them in a middle-class, university setting, thereby penalizing lower-class children unfairly. Many have failed to discuss important variations *within* social classes, presenting differences in group averages as if behavior patterns in different social classes did not overlap. Inevitably, there is substantial overlap in the distribution of behaviors (e.g., see Figure 3.3). Finally, many have ignored the fact that the very gene pools of people from different classes and cultures can and do vary. Thus class and cultural differences reflect heredity as well as environmental effects.

EARLY VERSUS LATER EXPERIENCE

Since the 1960s, developmental psychologists have argued about the relative importance of early and later experience for children's development. Early

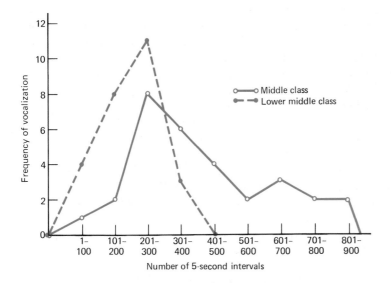

FIGURE 3.3

Frequency with which mothers vocalize to their infants in two social-class groups, showing that there is both a *difference* between the groups in the *average* amount of vocalization and a *similarity* between the groups in the *typical* amount of vocalization (Kagan and Tulkin, 1971).

education programs begun in the 1960s, like Head Start, were predicated on the ideas that early experience is critical and its effects permanent. But a substantial number of studies has called these assumptions into question. These studies have demonstrated that the effects of early experience are at least partly reversible. Most developmental psychologists now believe that psychological development in children is not characterized by the strict **critical periods** that characterize physical development before birth. Some of them use the less restrictive **sensitive period** to describe periods when specific forms of development occur most quickly and easily. Most forms of development, they believe, can be acquired later, if with more difficulty, once the sensitive period is past. The case of Genie (described earlier, p. 72) suggests the possibility that there may be a sensitive period for language acquisition. Genie was forbidden speech as a child, but after she was rescued in adolescence, she did develop rudimentary language—minus pronouns and important inflections. Today the prevalent view is a balanced one: it is not that early experience is critical, unique, and its effects irreversible, *nor* that later experience is identical in effect to early experience. There are continuities in development, but what happens at age 1 does not totally determine the way a person will be at 17. Lack of early stimulation can be compensated for by later opportunities. The benefits of early enrichment can fade away—almost completely—if the environment becomes barren or threatening.

Children from deprived early environments who were later adopted into middle-class families provide one source of evidence about the **reversibility** of early experience. Studies (reviewed by Clarke and Clarke, 1976; Clarke-Stewart and Apfel, 1979) show, for example, that institutionalized infants who are adopted recover from their early deprivation completely by the time they are 4 years old. But children who are over 2 when they are adopted may not recover. When retarded children from a Lebanese orphanage were adopted by American or Lebanese families, the deficits in mental age that they showed on intelligence tests corresponded to the number of years beyond the age of 2 at which they had been adopted (Dennis, 1973). We do not know whether those adolescents might yet catch up as they get older nor whether special, remedial education of the older children might repair their deficits in intelligence. But the evidence is clear that early experience is different from later, although both affect development. Another source of evidence about the reversibility of early experience comes from children who go in the opposite direction. Children from poor families have been given individualized care, intellectual stimulation, and social opportunities in the preschool years (e.g., see Lazar et al., 1982). In these early childhood programs, they flourish. Once out of the program and into a regular grade school, their intellectual gains drop off radically. Reversibility clearly goes both ways.

A third source of evidence about reversibility

comes from laboratory experiments in which monkeys, cats, rats, and other species are subjected to dramatic changes in their environment. In one of Harry Harlow's studies (Novak and Harlow, 1975), for example, monkeys first were isolated for a year—emerging from the experience utterly ravaged. They were emotionally disturbed, fearful, and withdrawn. They bit themselves and could not play or interact socially with other monkeys. They explored little and seemed to try to comfort themselves by rocking and clasping themselves. But then they were placed together with 3-month-old female monkeys, who had been raised normally, and the formerly isolated monkeys interacted appropriately and gently with them. With the "therapist" monkeys' help, the isolates learned to play and explore, and their "autistic" behavior decreased markedly. By the time they had reached adolescence, the former isolates interacted socially and sexually with the other monkeys. The effects of their early isolation had been substantially reversed by their later, therapeutic experience.

Finally, evidence about reversibility comes from human studies in which the environments of young children are substantially altered by the normal course of child rearing. Field studies of the development of children in Guatemala, by Jerome Kagan and his associates (Kagan and Klein, 1973; Kagan, Klein, Finley, Rogoff, and Nolan, 1979) provide one example. Infants in the western Guatemalan village of San Marcos spend most of their first year inside a dark hut. No one talks or plays with them much, and they look depressed and withdrawn. As 1- to 2-year olds, they are retarded in the development of speech, concepts of objects and people, and other forms of behavior. Once they venture outside of the hut, in their second year, however, they begin to meet the variety that the world offers, and their lives become substantially more stimulating. Compared to children from the nearby village of San Pedros, in which infants are not so severely restricted, the San Marcos children under 10 or 11 years old do poorly on **culture fair** tests of memory and reasoning. But by adolescence (age 15 to 18), the San Marcos children seem to have caught up to their San Pedros peers and to children raised in the United States. They just have taken longer. Although these results have been interpreted by Kagan as supporting the view that early experience is not important to later development (because the San Marcos children

eventually caught up to the others), they provide better support for the more moderate or balanced view that although early experience may not be critical, it is of profound importance to later development. The San Marcos children were 3 to 9 years delayed before they reached the level of children from San Pedros and the United States. A further difficulty in interpreting the results of this study is that although the environment of the 5-year-old child in San Marcos was substantially better than that of the 1-year-old, it was never quite as stimulating as the environment of the San Pedros or American children. These later environments could have contributed to the San Marcos children's delay, too. In brief, all available evidence points toward the position that development can be affected by both early and later experience.

INTERACTION WITH GENETICS

We have now discussed both components in the equation: heredity and environment. It should be clear that development is determined by both. Evidence supports the contributions of each—in varying degree—to every aspect of human performance. The ecology of environments, the composition of chromosomes, and the assessment of development each is inordinately complex. Yet identifying specific links between genes, environments, and behavior is a challenge that has fascinated investigators in the past and will continue to propel research in the future. Meanwhile, we are building theories of the interaction of heredity and environment. Some of these theories were discussed in Chapter 2. Here, to conclude our presentation of the effects of environment and heredity, and to bring the two together once again, we will describe one more variation on the theme that genotype (heredity) + environment produce phenotype (development).

Sandra Scarr and Kathleen McCartney (1983) have proposed that people, in essence, make their own environments. They suggest that genetic differences predispose people to experience and to be influenced by various environments in different ways. The genotype, in other words, is largely responsible for the individual's responsiveness to environments, and some genotypes are more likely to receive and select certain environments than others. Scarr and McCartney have argued that the old nature-nurture dichotomy implies falsely that these two constructs are parallel. Although both genes and environment can and do produce differences among individuals, they do so not in parallel fashion but in an order whereby genotype precedes environment and determines a person's responsiveness to the environment.

In their theory of the process of children's development there are three kinds of relations between genes and environment:

1. A *passive* relation between genes and environment exists when, in biological families, parents provide both genes (for example, for intelligence) and environment (for example, books) to their children.

2. An *evocative* relation exists when a particular genotype evokes a particular response from the environment. For example, active, happy babies probably evoke more social reactions than expressionless, passive babies.

3. An active, *niche-picking* relation exists when an individual actively seeks out the environment that he or she finds stimulating and compatible. Examples are everywhere: the child who loves music and learns to play an instrument; the girl gifted at languages who becomes an anthropologist or world traveler; the boy with high visual-spatial ability who becomes a pilot.

As individuals develop, the relative importance of each of these gene-environment relations changes. Young children, for example, can do less active niche-building than adolescents. The passive relation between genotype and environment is therefore more important in early life than later. We see the effects of early, passive environments waning during the course of development and being overshadowed by later, active effects of genotype on environment, in the observation that pairs of children who are fraternal twins or adopted siblings (compared to the trends for identical twins and natural siblings) grow progressively more dissimilar as they grow older.

RESEARCH FOCUS

EFFECTS OF MOTHERS' IQ AND HOME ENVIRONMENT ON CHILDREN'S IQ

A group of developmental psychologists at the University of North Carolina wanted to examine not only how genes and environment contribute to intellectual development in children, but also how those contributions change with age (Yeates, MacPhee, Campbell, and Ramey, 1983). For subjects, they chose 112 children who had been studied longitudinally from birth to the age of 4. These children had been chosen because they were at high risk for developing mental retardation on the basis of their mothers' being single, poor, uneducated, and of low IQ. The children were given IQ tests at 6, 18, 24, and 48 months of age.

When the researchers tabulated the results of these tests, they found that as the children got older, their IQ scores grew increasingly stable (correlated from age to age) and more highly predicted by both their mothers' IQs—genetics—and observers' ratings of children's homes—environment. When the children were 2 years old, 11 percent of the variation in their IQ scores could be explained by the combination of their mothers' IQs and their home environments; when they were 3 years old, this figure rose to 17 percent; at 4 years, it was 29 percent. But although the overall predictability of children's IQs increased over this age range, the relative contributions of genetic and environmental factors changed markedly. At 2 years, the principal predictor of children's IQ was maternal IQ—genetics. After the variation in children's IQ owing to maternal IQ was predicted, home environment added nothing further. By 4 years of age, the principal predictors were maternal behavior and home stimulation. Maternal IQ added nothing to the prediction.

The study supports the view (e.g., McCall, 1981; Scarr and McCartney, 1983) that an important shift in the relative contributions of genes and environment occurs at the end of infancy, as the 2-year-old begins actively to meet the world. By the time a child is 4, home environment is at least equal in importance to mother's IQ in determining or predicting the child's intellectual development.

SUMMARY

1. In studying the effects of the physical and social environments on human development, psychologists may focus on individuals from deprived environments, such as an institution or an isolated laboratory cage. They may observe naturally occurring environments, or they may intervene in an environment.

2. The first physical environment that a human being encounters is the prenatal, uterine environment. Through the placenta and umbilical cord, substances ingested by the mother reach the embryo or fetus and affect its development.

3. Both before and after birth, the nutrients available to a child influence the quality and rate of its development. Severe deficiencies of calories and protein can retard physical and mental development, although these effects are reversible in cases where adequate nutrition is available early enough in a child's life.

4. When the environment is noisy, children's physical and mental development suffer. They may lose part of their hearing, do poorly on tests of reading, and show signs of stress and helplessness in the face of problems. Noise particularly impairs the functioning of children with low aptitudes.

5. Play materials offer necessary stimulation for children's cognitive growth. Infants who lack play materials lag behind in sensorimotor development. Objects that respond to children's actions teach them that the world is a predictably responsive place over which they have some control. According to the nature of the play materials, they may help children to develop large or fine motor skills, simple or complex social interaction, imaginative or realistic play.

6. The arrangement and amount of space within which children live, learn, and play influence their perceptual and intellectual development. Observational studies show that children play and learn less well when they are crowded and when play or work space is not well demarcated. The size and arrangement of play areas and classrooms also influence the sorts of social interactions in which children engage.

7. The amount and type of early stimulation that infants receive, especially from their parents, is related to their cognitive development. Babies thrive on active engagement with others, and responsive parents foster their children's development.

8. Socialization is the process by which children learn the habits, skills, and standards that adults consider important. Parents seem to adopt one of three major styles of socializing their children. Some parents are democratic but authoritative, allowing their children freedom to explore and test their skills, but disciplining when appropriate and explaining their reasons for doing so. Other parents are permissive, casual, and indulgent, not encouraging independence. They rarely exert control. A third group of parents is rejecting, restrictive, and cold. They tend to be authoritarian and demand obedience from their children. Children of the first group of parents tend to be the most mature and competent.

9. Siblings and birth order can influence some of the course of children's development. Firstborns tend to be high achievers and to hold high standards for themselves. They are "adult-civilized." To account for differences in intelligence or achievement, the confluence theory suggests that as more children arrive, the available intellectual resources in a family diminish.

10. Attendance in an early childhood education or day-care program, necessary to so many children in the United States, does not appear to disturb or dilute the emotional relationship of children with their mothers, although in laboratory assessments some of these children stay farther away from their mothers than home-reared children do. Children in these programs are also socially more adept and cognitively more advanced than home-reared children—at least until they all get to school.

11. Open and structured, or traditional, classrooms have different physical arrangements and create different social environments as well. The open classroom can foster a greater variety of social interaction, reduce dominance hierarchies, and increase children's autonomy and freedom from stereotyped play. Few differences in self-esteem between children in the two kinds of classroom have been noted.

12. The organization of schools into clusters of grades influences how students feel about themselves and interact with others. Not surprisingly, being the youngest and smallest in a school has different effects on behavior and self-image from being the oldest and biggest.

13. Schools reflect the societies they serve, and schools in the United States reflect race relations and attempts to equalize educational opportunities for all. Busing may improve numerical ratios, but it may not succeed in improving relations between racial or ethnic groups or, equally important, the self-image of minority group members. Desegregation can cast minority group children into a hostile environment where they must violate the standards of their own group to succeed socially or academically.

14. Television is a socializing force for many children, because they watch it for so many hours as they grow up. Of particular concern is the violence and stereotyping to which children are exposed. Studies have shown that watching televised violence increases children's own aggression.

15. Studies that compare the development of par-ents and children from different cultures and classes can shed light on complex environmental effects. They can help explain observed differences in school achievement or the age at which children acquire sensorimotor and other cognitive skills. But it is exceedingly difficult to separate the effects of culture and biology, and results from such studies must be interpreted with great caution.

16. Most developmental psychologists now believe that the effects of experience on human development are not characterized by strict critical periods but that most forms of development can be acquired more easily and quickly during a sensitive period and later with more difficulty. Early learning is not irreversible, and later learning is not irrelevant. There are continuities in development but changes as well.

17. Sandra Scarr and Kathleen McCartney have proposed a theory of gene-environment interaction in which heredity influences how an individual responds to the various environments he or she encounters. The basic genetic predisposition interacts either passively or actively or evocatively with the environment.

KEY TERMS

Cross-cultural study	Kwashiorkor	Nursery school	Structured class
Placenta	Placebo	Day-care center	Critical period
Anoxia	Double-blind study	Day care	Sensitive period
Teratogenic	Socialization agents	Montessori nursery	Reversibility
Thalidomide	Gender roles	schools	Culture fair
Marasmus	Authoritarian parents	Head Start	
	Permissive parents	Open class	
	Authoritative parents		
	Confluence theory		

SUGGESTED READINGS

Barth, Roland. *Open Education and the American School.* New York: Agathon Press, 1972. One of many books explaining and criticizing the theory and practice of open education. This one was written by an elementary school principal who actually instituted open instruction in his school.

Brophy, Jere and Good, Thomas. *Teacher-Student Relationship: Causes and Consequences.* New York: Holt, Rinehart & Winston, 1974. A good book for understanding the social interaction of teachers with children. Provides excellent examples of teacher-student interactions and teaching strategies used to modify student behavior.

Clarke, Ann M., and Clarke, A. D. B. (Eds.) *Early Experience: Myth and Evidence,* New York: The Free Press, 1976. A collection of articles demonstrating the remarkable resiliency of children to recover from extremely depriving and depressing early experiences. This book takes the position that early childhood is *not* a critical period for intellectual and social development.

Clarke-Stewart, Alison. *Daycare.* Cambridge: Harvard University Press, 1982. All about day care—its history, politics, ecology, effects—with some practical suggestions for parents on how to find and select a good day-care arrangement.

Cole, Michael, and Scribner, Sylvia. *Culture and Thought: A Psychological Introduction.* New York: Wiley, 1974. The question whether there are important cultural differences in thought processes examined by reviewing research on culture and cognition, perception, language, memory, and problem solving.

Liebert, Robert M., Neale, John M., and Davidson, Emily S. *The Early Window: Effects of Television on Children and Youth.* Elmsford, N.Y.: Pergamon Press, 1973. A comprehensive overview of the effects of television on youth. Includes research on the psychological processes underlying the influence of television and a critical analysis of the positive or negative influence of television on youth.

Rosenthal, Robert, and Jacobson, Lenore. *Pygmalion in the Classroom: Teacher Expectation and Pupils' Intellectual Development.* New York: Holt, Rinehart & Winston, 1968. The original research that alerted the educational community to the possible effects of teachers' positive and negative expectations about their students' achievement.

BEGINNINGS

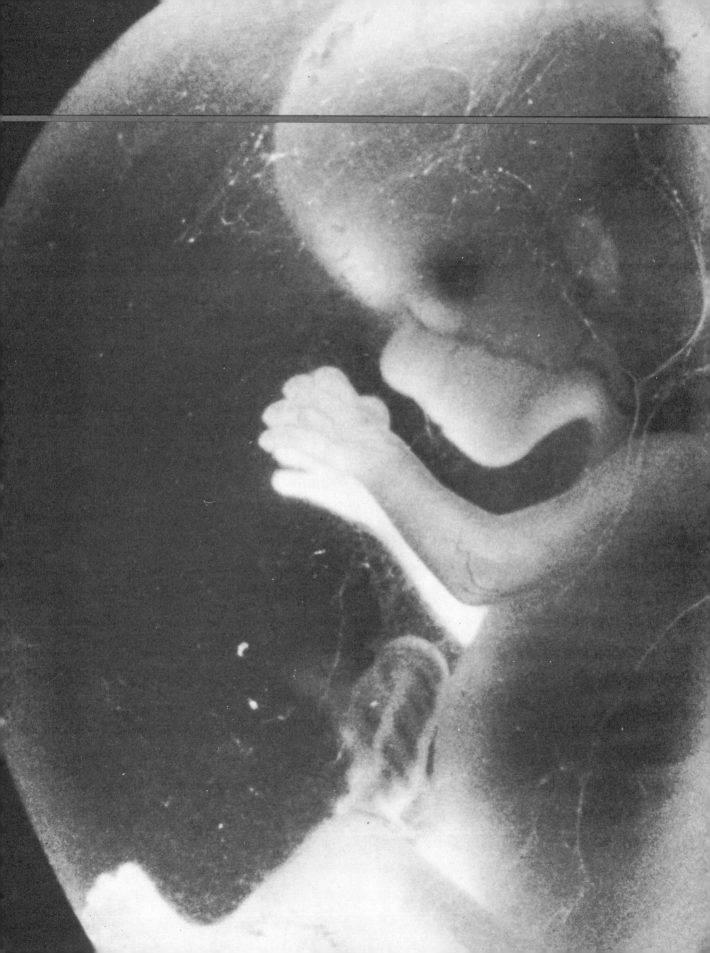

CHAPTER 4

PRENATAL DEVELOPMENT

BEGINNING NEW LIFE

THE PARENTS' CHOICE

It is a sign of modern times that in our culture the initiation of a new life has become, for many, a matter of choice. The decision not to have a child used to be so rare that until 1968 major reference books listed "childlessness" under "sterility." Why else would anyone decide against parenthood? In 1967, only one couple in 100 wanted no children. In 1972 however, four couples in 100 did not want to have children (Whelan, 1975). Now there are ten couples in 100 who are childless, some by choice, some because they have been unable to conceive, and some because they have decided to postpone having children (U.S. Bureau of the Census, 1979; Veevers, 1979). A national organization for nonparents has been formed to promote the child-free marriage; it proposes that women and men have been brainwashed from their first primer to their last rerun of "Happy Days" into believing that marriage with children is the one and only good life. Even couples who delayed childbearing in the 1970s and are now deciding to have children are having fewer of them (Glick and Norton, 1977).

Means of preventing conception had been available for some time. Earlier attempts of parents to limit the number of their children—dating back to at least 1850 B.C. and relying on such substances as cabbage, pitch, oxgall, animal earwax, and elephant dung (Himes, 1936)—had been replaced by more reliable and appealing measures: the condom, the diaphragm, birth control pills, and a variety of intrauterine devices (IUDs). But not until the 1960s did large numbers of people openly and deliberately ponder the question of having children.

The number of children a couple has is now, for many couples, a matter of deliberate decision.

There were, and still are, pressures to have children. Leaders of religious movements striving toward perpetuation instruct their flocks to be fruitful and multiply; others declare it a sin to prevent conception or abort the fetus. The family picture on an employee's desk stands for stability, and until recently family men were favored for political office and management positions. Peers who are parents want to know what the couple without a child is waiting for. And the older generation insistently pushes for grandchildren.

But social attitudes in this country have changed somewhat in the last 20 years. New possibilities for women's careers have brought a strong element of choice into parenting. For many young people parenthood appears to be an obstacle to the satisfaction of self rather than a means to completion and fulfillment. Others are seriously concerned about the population explosion. In the professional community of psychologists, influential theories, such as those of Freud and Erikson, that insisted on an ''instinct'' for parenthood and a female drive for completion through motherhood have been modified. Psychologists now recognize that parenting is not the only way of contributing to the next generation.

Many couples now discuss rationally the decision whether to have a baby. But this decision is inevitably affected by nonrational elements, by biological and psychological pressures, and by conscious and unconscious thoughts about the desirability of having children. Men and women may choose to have children to manipulate spouse or parents, to save a shaky marriage, to resolve nagging doubts about masculinity or femininity, to possess or control someone completely, to go along with friends and family, or to ward off fears of a lonely old age and a meaningless death. Even after rational calculations or extensive discussions, many women leave the ''decision'' up to fate.

WHEN TO HAVE A CHILD

When is the right time to have a child? Is there a best time? Should a couple wait until they are established in their work and their marriage? Should they plunge right in while they are young and energetic? How does the timing of children affect the parents' own relationship? These were some of the questions that two psychologists at Wellesley College, Pamela Daniels and Kathy Weingarten (1982), wanted to answer. They wondered how married couples go about deciding when and whether to have children and how these decisions affect their lives. Daniels and Weingarten worked within Erik Erikson's theory of development, according to which the most important psychological tasks facing young adults in their 20s and 30s—ages when many become parents—are to find their own identity and sense of themselves, to create an intimate relationship with another person, and to care for a person of the younger generation. Failure to consolidate one's personal identity means that one risks feeling confused about who one is. Failure to create an intimate relationship means that one risks isolation. Failure to create a generative relationship means that one risks self-absorption and stagnation.

Daniels and Weingarten interviewed 86 white couples living in the northeastern United States who had had their first child together and had remained married. The couples were selected according to the wife's age when she had their first child: 36 had had a child when the wife was 22 or younger, 36 when the wife was 28 or older, and 14 when the wife was 37 or older. The researchers interviewed parents of grown as well as of younger children to learn about the long-term effects of timing decisions. They found that the most notable change in family timing during the 1970s was a postponement of childbearing. More women were waiting until their late 20s or their 30s to conceive, a trend with far-reaching consequences for all family members.

Daniels and Weingarten found that nearly all couples had a scenario of when they would have children, even if nature had conspired against that scenario in the form of an unplanned pregnancy, infertility, or illness. They classified and labeled these family-timing scenarios.

In the scenario of the *natural ideal,* couples believe that nature should be allowed to take its course, that children will appear naturally. These couples tend not to plan or to space their children and to treat intercourse and procreation as closely tied. (Many—34 out of 58 ''natural ideal'' individuals—were Roman Catholics.) As one said:

We never made a decision to have or not to have a baby. After we were married it never occurred to us to wait to have a family. It was a very natural kind of thing (Daniels and Weingarten, 1982, p. 16).

In the scenario of the *brief wait,* couples postpone their first child for 2 or 3 years after they are married. The couples interviewed tended to have a short courtship, early marriage, and to use contraception. As one couple said, they were,

conservative New Englanders who wanted to get their feet on the ground, get out of the service, get a job, travel a little, or buy a house first (p. 20).

The scenario of *programmatic postponement* allows couples time to reach certain professional or personal goals before having a child. For some, the postponement is time to find their own identity. For others, it is time to build a strong, intimate marriage. For nearly all, it is a time for husband and wife to meet career goals. As one such father said,

We didn't want a situation in which one of us was the "ready one" and the other went along. I mean, one of us wasn't going to do it for the other. . . . We wanted to raise our children together, and we knew that. We wanted it to be something that we would both be involved in— which meant to us that we both had to be ready (p. 24).

Many, but not all, of these couples know that they want children eventually; others weigh parenthood as one option among others; for still others, the parenthood question is a "gripping dilemma whose resolution signals a shift that is both a developmental moment in itself and the setting for subsequent growth and change" (p. 38).

Finally, in the scenario of the *mixed script,* husband and wife disagree about when or whether to have children, and in the *unformed scenario,* they do not really think at all about the issue. Each timing pattern sets in motion very different currents in a couple's life. The couple whose first child appears when they are 20-year-old students, newcomers to marriage, and perhaps near strangers to each other, may stagger them. But as still energetic 40-year-olds, these parents launch that child into the world and face their own middle age relatively unencumbered by child care. In contrast, the cou-

ple whose first child arrives as they approach 35 or 40, faces a middle age of active child care, diapers, babysitters, and adolescent crises. But they have had perhaps two decades as adults to weave a marriage and career that will embrace that much-wanted child.

CONCEPTION

Regardless of whether the pregnancy was planned or unplanned, the biological details of sexual intercourse and conception, the real beginnings of life, are the same. A woman may become pregnant when sexual intercourse occurs about 14 days before her menstrual period begins, at the time when she is **ovulating.** One of the egg cells—present in the human female even before birth—has developed in the **ovary** into an **ovum,** and it is swept into one of the **fallopian tubes** and moved along by millions of tiny beating cilia (Figure 4.1). As a baby girl, the woman was born with as many as 2 million immature egg cells, called **oocytes.** By age 20, some 300,000 remain; approximately 400 of the oocytes ripen into ova during the woman's childbearing years (Rugh and Shettles, 1971). The male is, after adolescence, continually producing much smaller and more active reproductive cells called **spermatozoa** in his **testes,** about 200 million a day. Every time he ejaculates, millions of these spermatozoa travel from testes through the two **vasa deferentia** to the **seminal vesicles.** There they mix with a whitish lubricating fluid to form semen, which is then expelled through the penis. A single sperm, out of the millions expelled into the woman's vagina and swimming up through the **cervix** into the **uterus,** may join with the "ovum of the month" in the fallopian tube. When sperm and ovum combine, fertilization occurs. This first step in the development of a new human being is called **conception.**

Though the design is grand, the basic elements of conception are minute. The tiny round ovum is even smaller than the period at the end of this sentence. But the ovum is gigantic compared to the other actor in the drama, the spermatozoon, which consists of tiny oval head, connecting middle piece, and tail and that measures all of $1/500$ *of an inch.* It has been estimated that the ova that produced all the people in the world would fit into a shoebox

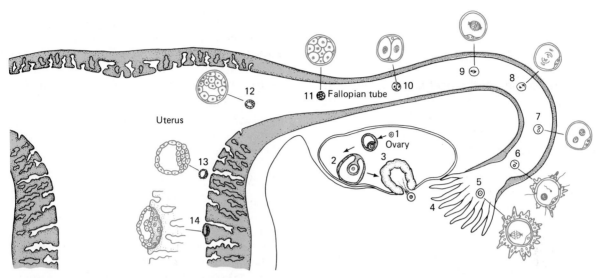

FIGURE 4.1

Preparing the human ovum for the main event, fertilization, is a complex process. It begins when the primary follicle of the month (1) develops and becomes a mature follicle. (2) The follicle rises above the surface of the ovary and ruptures (3), releasing the ovum into the abdominal cavity. The movements of millions of cilia on the feathery flaps projecting from the fallopian tube draw the ovum toward its funnel (4). The ovum, in which the first stage of meiotic division (see Figure 2.5) had started but been suspended, completes this first stage at ovulation and extrudes a polar body from its surface. Now it begins the second stage of meiosis (5). When the sperm penetrates the cell membrane and then the cytoplasm of the egg, it stimulates the egg to complete meiosis, extrude to a second polar body, and form the female pronucleus (6). Then the sperm head swells to form a male pronucleus (7). The two pronuclei fuse; male and female chromosomes mingle (8). The chromosomes go through mitosis (9) (see Figure 2.4), and the fertilized egg, or zygote, has its first cleavage (10). Successive cleavages as the zygote moves along the fallopian tube form the morula (11), the blastula (12), and the blastocyst (13), which has an inner cell mass that will become the embryo. On the 7th day the blastocyst is implanted in the uterine wall (14) (Grobstein, 1979).

and the spermatozoa would fit into a thimble. The main event of the drama takes place in the fallopian tube, which is about 4 inches long and no wider than a hair.

In each cubic centimeter of semen that the male ejaculates there are 300 million active spermatozoa. Why so many to greet one ovum? Millions of sperm are necessary, because nearly all die or go astray in the vagina and uterus. The ovum can live for only 12 to 24 hours after it is expelled from the ovary, and sperm can live for only about 48 hours after ejaculation. Thus conception can occur only within a period of 72 hours each menstrual cycle. If sexual intercourse takes place during, or shortly before, the ripe ovum is swept into the fallopian tube, sperm find a particularly hospitable environment. At the time of ovulation, the vagina, cervix, uterus, and fallopian tube are more alkaline and the usually thick, viscous mucous plug at the en-

trance to the cervix is transformed into a transparent, half-liquid egg-white state. The molecules of this mucus are arranged so the sperm can swim through it easily.

The spermatozoon, with its small rounded head and long tail for propulsion, swims a number of inches from the cervix to that part of the fallopian tube where the ovum awaits. Meanwhile, cilia and undulations of the fallopian tube move the ovum toward the sperm. Of the hundreds of millions of spermatozoa deposited in the vagina, a few hundred manage to travel upstream into the correct fallopian tube and arrive in the vicinity of the ripe ovum. As one sperm merges with the ovum, its tail and the protective covering of its head erode, and its head alone penetrates the ovum. No other sperm will enter.

The head of the sperm contains its long, thin chromosomes, the bearers of its genes. The sperm

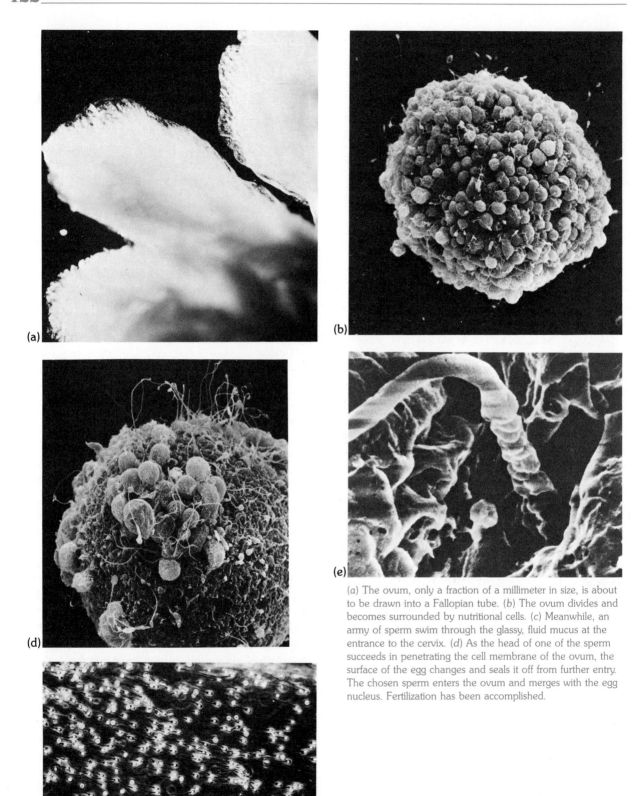

(a) The ovum, only a fraction of a millimeter in size, is about to be drawn into a Fallopian tube. (b) The ovum divides and becomes surrounded by nutritional cells. (c) Meanwhile, an army of sperm swim through the glassy, fluid mucus at the entrance to the cervix. (d) As the head of one of the sperm succeeds in penetrating the cell membrane of the ovum, the surface of the egg changes and seals it off from further entry. The chosen sperm enters the ovum and merges with the egg nucleus. Fertilization has been accomplished.

head galvanizes the genetic material in the ovum. The chromosomes from the female's ovum and the chromosomes of the male's sperm line up side by side. Within a half hour the merger has taken place. The now-fertilized ovum contains pairs of chromosomes, one member of each pair from the mother, one from the father. It is now officially a **zygote,** the first stage in the prenatal growth process, which will proceed with amazing rapidity. The life of a new individual has begun.

FERTILITY

Not every couple who wants a child conceives a child, and few do on their first try. Even when a couple is trying, only about one third conceive in the 1st month, something over half by the 3rd month, and three-quarters within 6 months. Conception is not automatic, even after several months of regular intercourse. Because ovulation brings about a temporary increase in temperature, one of the first steps a couple having difficulties may take is daily monitoring of the woman's temperature. Couples are also often counseled to relax. Anxiety about fertility may cause infertility. One in five couples has true **fertility** problems. The male's semen may not contain enough sperm to ensure fertilization, or the sperm may not be viable. Women may not be able to release ova, fallopian tubes may be blocked, or there may be difficulty in maintaining the ovum after it has been fertilized and before it has implanted in the uterus. Female fertility is reported to drop off sharply between ages 31 and 35, according to a medical study of over 2000 women who received **artificial insemination,** a simple procedure in which either the husband's sperm or a donor's are introduced into the vagina via syringe. Despite repeated inseminations at peak periods of fertility, only 61 percent of the women aged 31 to 35 and only 53 percent of those over 35 conceived (Federation CECOS, Schwartz and Mayaux, 1982).

In 60 percent of infertility cases, the problem resides with the woman. Physicians may recommend drugs that stimulate ovulation. Unless very carefully measured these drugs cause superovulation, with the woman's ovaries releasing several ova rather than just one. This accounts for the multiple births among women taking fertility drugs that were quite common until recently (Grobstein,

1979). Surgery, often delicate microsurgery requiring a microscopic viewer, is necessary for dilating or repairing blocked fallopian tubes and is successful less than half the time. Since 1978 it has become possible to bypass a woman's damaged tubes with dramatic fertilization outside her body.

In 40 percent of infertility cases, the problem resides with the man. Medical procedures can help men with certain fertility problems, including a low sperm count or poor quality sperm. Some infertile men choose artificial insemination. Artificial insemination of women has been practiced for over 80 years and now accounts for approximately 20,000 babies a year (Fleming, 1980). If the husband's sperm count is low, his sperm may be collected and concentrated until the level is high enough for potential fertilization. Sperm can be frozen at temperatures of less than $-300°F$ and remain viable for years. Men planning to undergo **vasectomy,** which severs the vasa deferentia and prevents the transfer of sperm to the seminal vesicle, men undergoing chemotherapy, which is likely to damage the genetic content of sperm, or men who for other reasons wish to donate sperm, may have their sperm stored for later insemination. If a man is sterile, his physician may select a sperm donor who is physically similar and suitable to supplement the man's sperm. The man has the psychological comfort of knowing that because fertilization takes only one sperm, perhaps his arrived first at the ovum.

On the frontiers of conception are other procedures that may become more common. In **surrogate mothering,** a fertile woman is hired by a couple and artificially inseminated with the husband's sperm. She carries the baby to term for the infertile mother, having agreed to give the couple the baby after delivery. The first baby born of surrogate mothering was delivered in 1978. A **test tube baby** is conceived outside the mother's fallopian tube. Since Louise Joy Brown was delivered on July 25, 1978, in England, more than 700 other test tube babies have been born. The term "test tube baby" is misleading. It is only fertilization and the initial cell divisions that take place *in vitro,* literally "in glass" or in a glass Petri dish. Dr. Patrick Steptoe, together with Dr. Robert Edwards, carried out the successful work that allowed Louise to be born, but to develop the procedure, they used extensive research on human fertility and on external fertilization by marine animals dating back to 1893.

Since Louise was born in 1978, more than 700 other "test tube babies" have been born.

cervix is held open with a speculum, and the cell mass is inserted with a nylon catheter. The process has bypassed the obstructed or damaged fallopian tubes, so now the tiny mass of cells, carefully brought along to this stage, may implant themselves and grow. If they do, all prenatal development, from implantation onward, occurs not in the Petri dish but inside the mother's uterus (Fleming, 1980; Grobstein, 1979).

The most recent advance in treating infertility is **ovum transfer.** Doctors have been working to perfect the techniques involved in this procedure, which entails removing a fertilized egg from another woman's uterus and transferring the donor's egg to the uterus of an infertile woman. Donors are given thorough physical and psychological examinations, and even their genes are checked for abnormalities. Couples suited to ovum transfer are those in which the husband is fertile but the wife is not, her fallopian tubes being irreversibly damaged. In such cases, if a fertilized egg can be implanted in the woman's uterus, a pregnancy has an excellent chance of proceeding normally. After locating donors who are physically and psychologically suitable, doctors synchronize the donors' menstrual cycles with those of the eventual recipients. When hormone readings tell doctors that the donor is releasing an ovum, she is artificially inseminated with sperm from the husband of the infertile woman. Within 5 days, time for the fertilized egg

The woman is first given hormones that ripen her ova. Doctors hope to retrieve several to improve the chances of obtaining a viable ovum. Ova are recovered from the ovary by **laparoscopy.** After general anesthesia is administered, very small incisions are made in the woman's navel and at the base of her abdomen. A tiny telescope and a fibre-optic illuminator called a "laparoscope" are introduced through the incisions. The ovary and mature follicles are examined, and the ripe ova are removed from the follicles by a tiny vacuum aspirator.

After the ova are removed, they are allowed to mature in an incubator for about 3 hours. Then a few drops of concentrated sperm are combined with the ova in a Petri dish. Within 36 hours after fertilization, the zygote begins to divide. When the zygote reaches the eight-cell stage, it is ready for implantation in the woman's uterus. The woman's

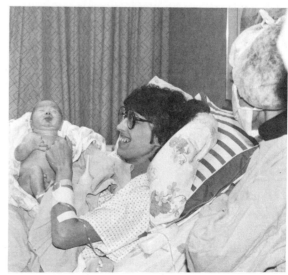

Moments after the birth, surrogate mother Elizabeth Kane holds her baby for the first and only time as his adoptive mother looks on.

to migrate through the donor's fallopian tubes and into her uterus, doctors remove it from the donor's uterus and transfer it into the uterus of the recipient. Because her body is at a point in the menstrual cycle when it might sustain a pregnancy, the fertilized egg implants in her uterus. If all goes well, a normal pregnancy begins (Buster, 1983). In February 1984, the first American child born from an ovum transfer was born in Long Beach, California. Ovum transfer is likely to gain popularity among fertile couples in situations where the wife's fallopian tubes have been damaged by disease or earlier tubal pregnancies.

PRENATAL DEVELOPMENT

The prenatal period extends from conception to birth. During these 9 months, the transformation of a single microscopic fertilized cell into a recognizable baby seems nothing short of miraculous. Yet for each baby the transformation proceeds according to a master plan; various parts and functions develop at approximately the same time and in the same sequence for all individuals.

It is readily apparent in the prenatal period that a new function can begin only after prerequisite structures have been laid down. The sequence and precise timing with which these structures and functions appear are crucial in prenatal growth. In the early stages of development, the embryo is highly vulnerable; adverse forces invading the uterus during this crucial period can do irreparable damage. But the fact that the vast majority of infants are born normal indicates that the ongoing transaction between the embryo and the womb is remarkably conducive to health. The biological needs of the developing embryo, and later the fetus, for protection, warmth, and specific nutrients, are admirably met by the environment the womb provides.

STAGES OF PRENATAL DEVELOPMENT

The 9 months of pregnancy during which the fertilized cell becomes a fully developed infant are divided into three phases. The first, the **germinal stage,** sometimes called the period of the ovum, lasts from fertilization until about 14 days later, when the many-celled zygote implants in the wall of the uterus. The second, the **embryonic stage,** during which all the organs of the body are differentiated, extends from the 2nd to 8th week. The last period, from the 8th week until delivery, is called the **fetal stage.** The fetus grows large in these months, and its organs and muscles begin to function.

Germinal Stage: Days 1 Through 14

During the germinal phase, the fertilized egg, or zygote, divides by mitosis into 2 daughter cells, then 4, then 8, and so on into many cells. The first division begins within 36 hours after sperm and ovum have combined. Thereafter, the pace of cell division speeds up. By 60 hours after fertilization, there are 12 to 16 cells. They form a mulberrylike sphere called a **morula.** Up to this point, the cells are **totipotent.** Each one of them has the potential to develop into a complete person if separated from the zygote. But the cells lose their independence and uniformity as they multiply; after they have formed a morula, they are no longer totipotent, even though their genetic material is the same as that of the zygote on the first day. The inner cells are larger, the outer ones smaller, and they are destined for different functions.

The mass of cells moves slowly down the fallopian tube to the uterine cavity, dividing all the while. When the mass arrives there, some 4 days after fertilization, it is composed of more than 100 cells and has become a hollow, fluid-filled sphere called a **blastula.** Its wall is one cell thick, with the larger cells at one side. They multiply there to form an inner cell mass. Within another few days, organization and differentiation of cells have become more apparent; the sphere of cells is called a **blastocyst.** The heap of larger cells at one side have formed the **embryonic disk,** which will become the embryo and subsequently the **fetus.** The rest of the cells will become, or help to form, the support tissues for the embryo and fetus: the **chorion,** or outer covering, the multipurpose placenta, the **amnion,** or "bag of waters," and the yolk sac.

The blastocyst floats freely in the uterus for one or two days and then, on the 7th day, begins to **implant** itself into the lining of the uterine wall. It has arrived at the time in the mother's menstrual cycle when the lining is engorged with blood. The outer layer, the **trophoblast,** sends out rootlike extensions, or **villi,** that rupture the small blood

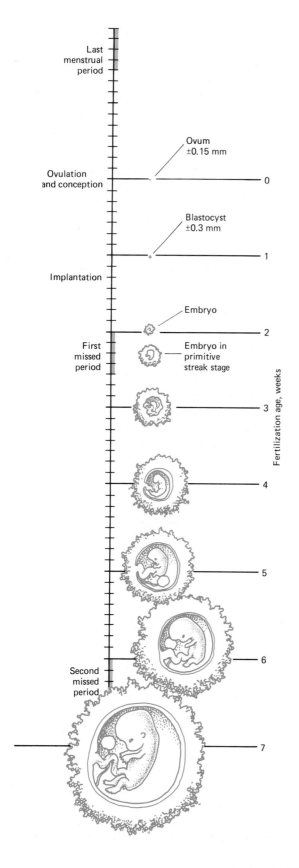

Last menstrual period

Ovulation and conception

Ovum ±0.15 mm — 0

Blastocyst ±0.3 mm — 1

Implantation

Embryo — 2

First missed period

Embryo in primitive streak stage

3

Fertilization age, weeks

4

5

Second missed period

6

7

vessels they meet and glut themselves on the nourishment provided by the blood. In the process, the trophoblast implants itself deeper into the uterine wall, which is spongy and receptive. A selection process is already at work; abnormal blastocysts, as many as half of those formed after conception, fail to implant (Roberts and Lowe, 1975). After about one week, the uterine epithelium heals over the breach through which the blastocyst passed, and the process of implantation is complete (Figure. 4.2).

By this time, some 13 days after fertilization, the cells of the embryonic disk have folded over to form definite layers and are known as the **embryo.** The embryo has an outer layer called the **ectoderm.** This layer develops a bulge called the **primitive streak,** which will ultimately give rise to the brain, the spinal cord, all the nerves and sensory organs, and the skin. The inner layer, or **endoderm,** will become the lining of the digestive tract, the salivary glands, pancreas, liver, and the respiratory system. A later intermediate layer called the **mesoderm** will become the skeleton, muscles, blood vessels, and the heart and kidneys.

By the time implantation is complete, the amnion has also formed and begins to fill with secreted amniotic fluid, which will serve as a cushioning device and prevent a fall or blow to the mother from injuring the developing embryo and fetus. The yolk sac is producing blood cells and forming the germ cells, which will ensure the future reproductive capacity of the developing individual. And the placenta is beginning to function.

The placenta is truly the prenatal tree of life. The blood vessels of the mother and the capillaries of the embryo, which soon extend into the villi, connect intimately in this remarkable organ. It will breathe, digest, and excrete for the multiplying cells as they form into a functioning fetus. The bloodstreams of the mother and embryo do not mix but are separated by the thin walls of the embryo's capillaries. Oxygen, nutrients, and waste products pass freely through these walls, though blood cells do not. The placenta is connected to the embryo by the umbilical cord, which remains untangled, like a water-filled garden hose, by the flow of blood

FIGURE 4.2

The ovum, blastocyst, and then the embryo and its membranes are shown in their actual sizes during the first 7 weeks of life (Patten, 1968).

within it. A single vein in the umbilical cord carries oxygen and carbohydrates, fats, some protein elements, and mineral salts to the embryo, and two arteries remove carbon dioxide and urea, to be disposed of eventually by the mother's lungs and kidneys. The placenta is somewhat selective, allowing in beneficial nutrients and antibodies and screening out some harmful substances, including most bacteria. But gases, viruses, and many drugs can pass through the placenta.

Embryonic Stage: 2 weeks to 2 months

The basic plan of the body emerges in the embryonic stage. This is a **critical period** when insults to the embryo can bring permanent, irreversible damage. Critical periods are times when certain developmental events must occur if the organism is to progress along its normal developmental pathway. Heart, eyes, and ears must appear during the embryonic stage; hands and feet must change from buds to human form. If these events do not happen, they cannot be compensated for later on. During the critical embryonic stage the emerging person is particularly susceptible to the environment.

This environment must provide certain protections and the nutrients necessary for growth. If instead there is radiation or if toxic substances pass through the placental wall, structures may be permanently impaired. But susceptibility at this stage represents an enoromous biological advantage. Susceptible cells may be vulnerable to infection, but they are also exceedingly responsive to instructions from the genes and other cells. At every stage of embryonic development, structures already present act as "organizers," inducing the emergence of whatever structures are next on the timetable. Thus both the genetic code, contained in the molecules of deoxyribonucleic acid (DNA) of each cell, and the interaction between cells cause organs and systems of the body to develop and function. In the chick embryo, for example, skin cells cannot be induced to become feather cells until nerve cells are present. In the human embryo, interaction between two types of cells is necessary for kidney tubules to form. By the end of the embryonic stage of development, the cells have become specialized. If the basic structures have not emerged by then, the embryo has no way to go back and produce them. The embryo has been compared to

a little workshop started by one man of all-around talents. His first employees learn the business from him and as the factory grows they become department heads, each organizing his own part of the work until all sorts of specialized workers [have been trained], capable in their turn of [training] new employees but only in their own narrow fields (Corner, 1944, p. 105).

3rd and 4th Weeks. The word embryo comes from the Greek *embryein,* meaning to swell or teem. The embryo does indeed teem as its cells multiply at an astonishing rate. This period is also one of great organization; the basis for all human functions is laid down, beginning with the nervous system and the primitive heart. The shallow groove forming along the primitive streak rapidly becomes a tube and then, by the 20th day, the foundations for the child's brain, spinal cord, nervous system, and eyes. By the end of the first month, a tubular, then chambered, heart is pumping blood; a system for digesting and assimilating food has begun to form; and the first of a series of kidneylike structures has appeared. All of this is happening within an insubstantial creature half the size of a pea! Development proceeds in a **cephaiocaudal,** or head-to-tail, direction, beginning in the head area and following down the trunk as the various cells organize into rudimentary nervous, circulatory, muscular, digestive, and skeletal systems. Development also proceeds in a **proximodistal** direction, from near to far, from the center of the body or spine to the extremities.

2nd Month. During the 2nd month major structures spring up almost daily from the rudiments laid down in the first month. Within one period of 3 days for example—days 27, 28, and 29—protruding buds emerge that will, before the month is up, become arms and legs, and the optic stalk, at the end of which eyes will soon develop, appears. In close succession, the stomach and the food tube, or esophagus, form. The heart moves from the mouth region to the chest, and the valve separating its upper and lower parts appears. The germ cells from the yolk sac migrate to the later site of the ovaries or testes. Before the 10th week is over, gonads differentiate into ovaries or testes, and a high-powered microscope will reveal the sex of the embryo.

During the 2nd month, the "telephone system" of nerve cells has reached out from its central head-

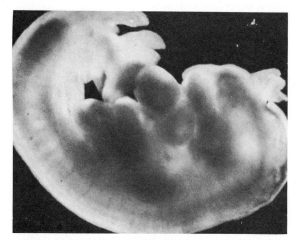

Almost 30 days old and about 4 millimeters in length, this embryo already has the buds that will become arms and legs.

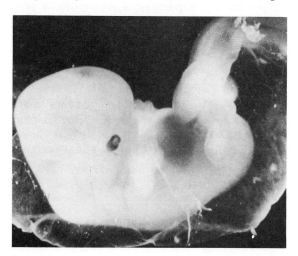

At 6 weeks the embryo has a definite head, and the retinas of the eyes have formed. The embryo looks much less like a tadpole and much more like a human being.

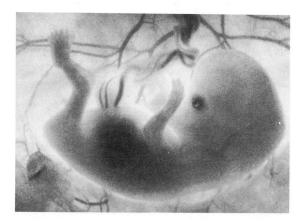

At 3 months the muscles go into action and the fetus actually moves. The greatest dangers are now past.

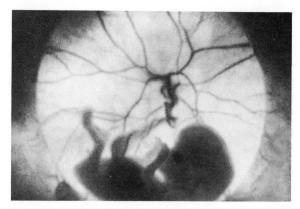

Face, nose, and mouth are distinguishable by eleven weeks and the muscles have formed.

Nourishing blood flows to this 4-month-old fetus at the rate of 0.25 liter each minute.

quarters and is beginning to receive messages. The groundwork for a sense of smell is laid as nerve fibers from the olfactory lobe of the brain connect with sensory nerve fibers from the nose. Connection from the brain to the retina is made. There are, however, no known nervous connections between the mother and the embryo, either in the umbilical cord or in the placenta. The mother's sensations or thoughts cannot be directly transmitted to the embryo.

By the end of the 2nd month, the translucent embryo is beginning to look decidedly human. Its eyes, ears, and nose have assumed their proper position on the face, and its jaws have formed a mouth and lips. The tiny arms have elbows, hands, stubby fingers, and thumbs; the legs have knees, ankles, and toes. Up until this point the skeleton has been formed of flexible cartilage, a material similar to that at the tip of the adult nose. Now bone cells begin to replace the cartilage cells in the centers of the structures that will eventually be the long bones of the arms and legs. These bone cells appear when the body is basically completed; the replacement of cartilage with bone, called **ossification,** signals another phase of prenatal development.

Fetal Stage: 2 to 9 months

In the fetal stage, lasting from the end of the 2nd month to birth, the systems already laid down become integrated, and the various organs grow and function more efficiently. Advances in technology, such as the scanning electron microscope, miniature cameras, and film that can be viewed in slow motion, have allowed embryologists to study every stage of prenatal development. Lennart Nilsson's (1977) photographs, taken by a magnifying lens, have allowed us to see development within the womb more vividly than ever before. Aborted fetuses have been observed within their amniotic sacs or in a fluid bath that is kept at normal body temperature and thus simulates the intrauterine environment. These direct observations reveal that the fetus begins to respond to its environment early in prenatal development. These findings, combined with the ongoing observations of prenatal development in birds, reptiles, and a variety of mammals, give us a fairly accurate picture of the elegant process by which the fetus prepares for independent existence.

3rd Month. Approximately 1 inch long, less than $1/10$ of an ounce in weight, and certainly small enough to hold in the human hand, the fetus resembles a large-headed miniature doll. Eyelids form and seal the eyes shut during the 9th week. The roof of the mouth closes over in the 10th week. If the fetus is male, the genital tubercle becomes a penis. The eye meshes with the optic nerves, and other nerves connect with the proliferating muscles, making it possible for the fetus to move. Although movements are at first mechanical and reflexive, they become more fluid in this period.

By the end of the 3rd month, the fetus is able to kick its legs, curl its toes, turn its feet, make a fist, move its thumb in opposition to the fingers, bend its wrist, turn its head, frown, open its mouth, press its lips together, and swallow. Responses that began as a total pattern, with the whole body re-

acting, gradually become localized. If the newly formed eyelid is stroked, the baby, instead of shifting its entire body, merely squints (Humphrey, 1970). The fetus is now able to move spontaneously and already has its own particular overall level of activity. The organ systems begin rehearsing in the 3rd month. The fetus swallows its first gulps of amniotic fluid, moves amniotic fluid in and out of the developing lungs in practice breaths, and excretes its first few drops of urine.

4th Month. The 4th month is an important period for growing, strengthening, and toughening. During the 4th month the little 3½ inch, 1-ounce manikin grows to 6 inches and 4 ounces; no other month shows a comparable rate of growth. At this time the mother will experience the **quickening;** she will perceive for the first time the movements of the now larger and stronger fetus as it turns and kicks against her abdominal wall. The placenta is keeping pace with the baby's growth and has also become the principal source of the hormones that will prepare the mother's breasts for lactation as well as supplying infection-fighting globulins to the fetus. The neck muscles and the ossifying skeleton are able to hold the fetus's head up, and further refinements in the face make that head look even more human. Touch pads have formed on the palms, soles, and toes, revealing the pattern of ridges, whorls, and lines that render its fingerprints and footprints unique. Female sexual structures develop; fallopian tubes merge to form uterus and vagina, and the genital tubercle becomes the clitoris. The eyes are sensitive to light, even though they are sealed.

5th month. In the 5th month, the fetus grows to be 1 foot long and 1 pound in weight. The fetus must still rely on the amniotic fluid to control its temperature, yet its preparations for independence proceed. Sweat glands form, coarse eyebrows and eyelashes grow, and a bit of fine hair appears on the head. During the 5th and 6th months a soft, fine hair called **lanugo,** a Latin word for "down," grows and covers the body. Most of it will be shed by birth. The movement of the fetus at this stage has been compared to that of an astronaut. Liberated from gravity, it kicks and turns freely and gracefully. Its life is now divided into periods of sleep and wakefulness, and it has a favorite position in the uterus. During this month, the fetus begins to exchange new cells for old, a process that will continue throughout life. The loosened dead skin the fetus sheds mix with a fatty substance from the oil glands to form the pasty **vernix.** This substance serves as a protective coating for the fetus, preventing its skin from hardening in the mineral-laden amniotic fluid.

6th month. In the 6th month, the intestines of the fetus descend into their proper place and no longer bulge. The skin is still wrinkled and covered with vernix. Important replacement of cartilage cells by bone cells is still taking place. Necessary immunities have yet to be transferred. The eyelids, which have been sealed, can now open, and the fetus can look up and down as well as sideways.

The fetus has a well developed grasping reflex now, abundant taste buds, and can make slight, irregular breathing movements. Some fetuses even hiccough. Knowing the fetus can swallow and taste, one obstetrician (reported in Montagu, 1962) injected a sweetener directly into the amniotic fluid of a pregnant woman who had too much fluid. The fetus began to swallow the fluid, it was absorbed into the fetus's circulation, returned to the mother through the placenta, and passed from the mother's body through urination—an ingenious cure.

The fetus's ability to breathe regularly for as long as 24 hours gives it at this age some chance of surviving in an incubator if born prematurely. In a few rare instances, fetuses born between 23 and 25 weeks and weighing about 1 pound have survived in incubators (McCleary, 1974), but they have no fatty deposits under the skin for insulation, and their lungs and digestive system are immature, making their chances of survival slim. A new specialization in medicine called **neonatology,** devoted to medical care in the newborn period, is helping to improve the survival chances of fetuses, however. The finding that the brains of some fetuses with low birth weight had been damaged in the nursery rather than during birth or through genetic defects originally led to improved prenatal care. Now younger and younger preterm neonates are surviving, and more and more of them have chances for normal functioning. Another new area of medicine, called **fetology,** treats fetal problems before birth. Blood transfers and surgical repairs have been performed on fetuses *in utero.* Now that ultrasound and prenatal monitoring have become more sophisticated, techniques for treating the hu-

man fetus are rapidly being perfected (Kotulak, 1981).

Doctors at the University of California, San Francisco, inserted a catheter into the bladder of a fetus to correct a potentially fatal blockage. In another case they removed the fetus from the womb, performed surgery on its urinary tract, and returned it to the womb; its development then progressed normally. Surgeons at the University of Colorado successfully drained excess fluid from the brain of a fetus that otherwise would have resulted in **hydrocephaly.** Harvard researchers treated another case of fetal hydrocephalus by puncturing the brain to relieve pressure from the excess fluid. When the baby was born, it showed no signs of the punctures. Virginia doctors drained the fluid from a fetus's collapsed lung. Yale doctors drained excess fluid from the chest and abdomen of a fetus. At New York's Mount Sinai School of Medicine, a fetus known to be afflicted with Down's syndrome was aborted, whereas its normal twin was allowed to develop to term. Fetology is likely to offer treatment for many other problems in the future, and as many as 1 in 400 to 500 fetuses may be candidates for surgery before birth.

7th month. Finally, late in the 7th month, when the fetus weighs about 2 pounds and its organs are sufficiently formed and their functions sufficiently rehearsed, the fetus has an even chance of surviving if kept in a heated incubator and protected from infection. The brain has developed enough cells to direct breathing, control swallowing, and regulate body temperature.

In the male fetus, the testes descend into the scrotum, which much later will provide a cooling system for the spermatozoa, for they cannot survive at the normal body temperature of 98.6°F. Ova, unaffected by body heat, are already present in a rudimentary form. Areas of the brain are being given over to specific functions: hearing, sight, smell, vocalization, and limb movements. All the telephone cables of the world would comprise only a small fraction of the trillions of connections of the brain and spinal cord already present in the fetus, connections assuring that each newborn will be able to respond to its surroundings (Figure 4.3). Nervous system connections will continue to develop through learning and experience that take place after birth. But numerous reflexes, including

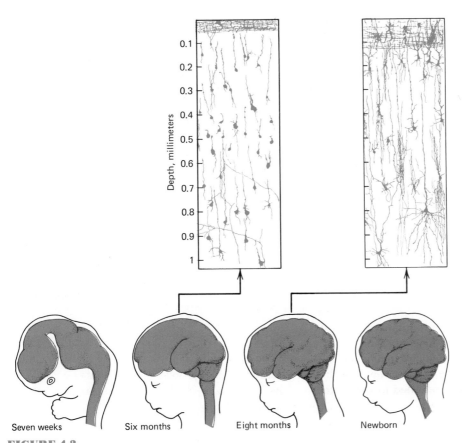

FIGURE 4.3
The tubelike early brain begins to achieve its mature form through a series of bends. Areas of the brain enlarge, and the cerebral hemispheres overgrow the cerebellum and other regions. Although the main outlines of the brain are established by the 6th month, the convolutions of the surface, which enormously increase the area and volume of the cortex, do not appear until the 8th month. Meanwhile, inside, as the sections from the visual cortex show, the dendrites, the shorter structures that allow the transmission of nerve impulses between neurons, are increasing in number and length (Grobstein, 1979).

sucking and grasping, are already apparent. Some mothers even report hearing the fetus cry.

8th month. In the 8th and 9th months, a padding of fat is deposited under the skin, making it smoother and the limbs chubbier, but most of all providing insulation against the day when the fetus will encounter the varying temperatures of the outside world. The tiny air pockets of the lung, called **alveoli,** are not yet ready to exchange oxygen for carbon dioxide, however. The digestive tract is still immature and more vulnerable to infection than it will be at birth. The chances of survival if the fetus is born prematurely are good, however, more than 85 percent when it weighs over 3 pounds. The

fetus is sensitive to a variety of outside sounds; the mother may feel the fetus respond with vigorous movements to a piano, a voice, or a dishwasher. Her own heartbeat and the rhythmic movements of her walking soothe the fetus. The responsive fetus reacts in a characteristic pattern if it is startled, and it responds also to light and touch. It can lift its head and can even learn. Two studies that inquired into prenatal learning were done in the 1940s. In one study (Sontag and Newbery, 1940), the fetus was subjected to loud noise from outside the mother's uterus. At first the noise increased the fetus's heartrate, but over time the noise caused no apparent response. The fetus had learned to adapt to the sound. In the second study (Spelt, 1948), a loud noise was paired with vibrations from a doorbell. At first the doorbell did not cause any reaction from the fetus, but after 15 to 20 repetitions of the vibration with the loud noise, the vibration alone caused the fetus to startle. Apparently, no further studies of prenatal learning were done. But recently, Lewis Lipsitt (1984) of Brown University has been trying to condition fetuses to adapt to a sound, and then he tests the effectiveness of the conditioning after birth. This procedure allows him to separate the reactions of the mother from those of the baby, something that was not done in the Spelt or Sontag experiments and that makes their results difficult to interpret. Ongoing research using animal fetuses (see Kolata, 1984) does clearly demonstrate the existence of prenatal learning.

9th month. Near the end of the 9th month, the average fetus is almost 20 inches tall and weighs 6 to 8 pounds, too large to have room in the uterus for much activity. Growth must slow down now or the child by its first birthday would weigh 200 pounds and by adulthood would be an unwieldy dinosaur of a person. This slowdown, probably brought about by the aging of the placenta, which is turning from spongy to tough and fibrous, usually occurs on day 260, about a week before birth. During these final days, the fetus continues to receive antibodies from the mother's blood that will protect it from measles, mumps, whooping cough, and other illnesses to which the mother is immune. In 266 days the unique fertilized cell has become a unique individual ready for life outside the womb.

Although some fetuses remain upright and are later born feet first, the weight of the baby's head usually causes it to become the presenting part to be delivered. The shift of the fetus's head to a downward position is felt by the mother as a "lightening." Pressure on her diaphragm and lungs lightens. The baby's head becomes wedged in the circle of pelvic bones, pinned here until the placenta releases the hormone **oxytocin,** which initiates the birth process. When physicians want to induce labor, they administer synthetic oxytocin. The hormones that the placenta is already releasing to prepare the mother for lactation temporarily cause the breasts of the fetus, whether male or female, to protrude.

EFFECTS OF PREGNANCY ON PARENTS

During the prenatal period, the environment for the developing infant is the mother. But she in turn is subject to profound psychological and physiological changes brought on by her pregnancy. The course of pregnancy is not the same for all women. Some seem to have more physical difficulties. For others the changes of pregnancy bring anxieties and reactivate past fears and doubts. Even for the woman who has few adverse reactions to pregnancy, this is a period of emotional flux, of swings from high spirits to low and back again. For most women, pregnancy becomes a period of growth and further human development. In fact, pregnancy has sometimes been called a "maturational crisis" (Ballou, 1978; Bibring, Dwyer, Huntington, and Valenstein, 1961). Fathers are also affected by the prospect of becoming parents. Their reaction to this prospect and to wives as pregnant women will have an indirect but nevertheless important effect on their wives and thereby on the developing offspring.

Emotional Strains

Most pregnant women have mood swings and fear for the fetus and themselves, but they do not develop severe emotional problems. Several detailed studies of psychological reactions during pregnancy give a picture of the normal adjustments to mothering. Myra Leifer (1977) studied a group of 27 women and found that from the first **trimester** (the first 3 months) to 2 months after birth, all had some mood swings, or ups and downs, but those who had stable personalities before the pregnancy had fewer symptoms and fewer anxieties about themselves. When these women did express anxieties, their concern tended to be more for the developing fetus and less for themselves. As the pregnancy progressed, they gained confidence and self-esteem. Only the women judged poorly adjusted *before* pregnancy, many of whom had not planned their pregnancies and had unsatisfying relationships, lost self-esteem. Leifer found that the pregnant woman's fears during the first trimester centered on the fetus. "Is it alive? Will I miscarry?" During the second trimester, most women were intensely relieved by the first signs of fetal activity. Concerns during this period had to do with whether

Pregnancy is a time when moodiness and anxiety are common and the mother-to-be feels fear and concern for herself and the developing fetus.

the developing child would be normal. During the third trimester, many women were distressed about the changes in their appearance. But as they neared the delivery date, they were anxious about themselves and the fetus. They feared losing their husbands or being abandoned by them. They feared death. They worried whether the fetus would be deformed.

In another longitudinal study, Pauline Shereshefsky and Leon Yarrow (1973) followed 57 women through a first pregnancy. They agreed with Leifer and others (Davids and Holden, 1970) that how women adapt to pregnancy predicts how they will adapt to parenthood. They also found a number of factors that affect the woman's adaptation to pregnancy and parenting. Adaptation is easiest for women who are nurturant and have strong egos; who can visualize themselves as mothers early in their pregnancy; who remember their own mothers as being warm, empathic, close, and happy; who have harmonious relationships with their husbands; and who have an interest in children even before they become pregnant.

The feelings of the pregnant woman shift often, and she becomes more sensitive. She must be given attention and support. Her marital relationship will have a powerful bearing on how she reacts to her pregnancy. Through empathy, affection, and cooperation in making decisions, a couple can better withstand the transition to parenthood and any temporary sexual difficulties. Sexual activity of the couples in the Shereshefsky and Yarrow study decreased long before the standard last-month moratorium on sexual intercourse. Many men were afraid of harming the baby and abstained from sexual activity as soon as the fetus began to move at the beginning of the 4th month. Women in both the Leifer study and this one were also anxious about sexual activity after the quickening, some in Leifer's group reporting that they refrained from reaching orgasm because it evoked fantasies for them of harming the fetus.

In addition to sexual strain, the wife's pregnancy may make the husband remember earlier parent-child conflicts, threatening his stability. The stress may sometimes cause physical symptoms. Many of the men indicated envy of the pregnant woman, either through empathic reactions known as the **couvade syndrome** or by denying the significance of the pregnancy.

Expectant fathers suffering from the couvade syndrome are affected by symptoms that bear a resemblance to those that their wives experience during pregnancy and labor. The name comes from the French verb *couver*, meaning to brood or hatch. In 1865 Sir Edward Burnett Tylor, the father of modern cultural anthropology, applied the term *couvade* to the ritual of some cultures in which the father is expected to take to his bed when his child is born and complain that he himself has suffered the pains of childbirth. He may submit himself to fasting and to purification rites and generally behaves like a woman in confinement.

The couvade ritual has been practiced all over the world in ancient and in modern times. Fathers took to their beds on the island of Corsica in the 1st century A.D.; this also occurred on Cyprus and in Spain. Marco Polo observed the custom in

Chinese Turkistan. The Maiotzu tribe of southern China practiced couvade in the 18th century, the Ainu of Japan and peoples in India in the 19th. Of North American Indians, only the California tribes had such a ritual, but it was found in the West Indies and among the South American Indians east of the Andes and as far south as Paraguay. Couvade was reported in Africa in the Congo in recent times, on the Balearic Islands in the 19th century, in the Baltic states, and in Holland in the early 20th century (*Encyclopaedia Britannica,* 1973).

Expectant fathers in industrial nations that accord them no special status and observe no rituals encouraging paternal birth pains may have physical problems. The couvade syndrome, unlike the ritual, is an unintentional acquisition of symptoms. A major study of 327 expectant fathers conducted by W. H. Trethowan and M. F. Conlon (1965) revealed that significantly more men whose wives were pregnant lost their appetites and suffered toothache, nausea, and sickness than those whose wives were not. Approximately 1 out of 4 expectant fathers had symptoms that were intense and frequent enough to be identified as part of the couvade syndrome. In the Shereshefsky and Yarrow study (1973), 65 percent of the expectant fathers developed nausea, backache, or other physical complaints similar to symptoms of pregnancy.

Now that the psychological stress—for both men and women—brought on by pregnancy is better appreciated, prenatal psychological assessments and preventive counseling are offered. In Soviet Russia, this type of screening is already a standard part of prenatal care. In England, Professor Richard Cohen has tested an assessment procedure that alerts the obstetrician to the pregnant woman's need for extra support in managing the long 9 months (Horsley, 1972). Shereshefsky and Yarrow (1973) found that casework counseling helps couples adapt to the new family configuration.

Physical Distress

The physical difficulties of the pregnant woman may depend to some degree on how she adapts to maternity. Biochemical changes taking place at the beginning of a pregnancy do lower a woman's threshold to nausea and vomiting (MacFarlane, 1977). But women who suffer from morning sickness also seem to be more anxious about their pregnancies. No conclusive causal relationship has been established between vomiting and an emotional attitude, such as ambivalence toward the pregnancy. As with the chicken and egg, we cannot be sure which comes first. It does seem likely, though, that the relatively minor physical disturbances of pregnancy may be seriously aggravated by psychological reactions to it. Many psychological causes have also been suggested for the more serious **toxemias** of pregnancy, in which there are severe and persistent nausea and vomiting, hypertension, sudden and rapid increase in weight, retention of fluid in the tissues, albumin in the urine, and even seizures, coma, and death if the condition is not treated (McDonald, 1968).

Physical changes accentuated by psychological reactions may also explain cravings for particular foods. Taste is dulled during pregnancy, which may partially account for the preference of pregnant women for sharp, sour, salty, spicy, and otherwise strong tasting substances (Trethowan and Dickens, 1972). Psychological stress may intensify these cravings. Between one-third and two-thirds of pregnant women are said to suffer to some degree from cravings for or aversions to certain foods.

Despite the upheaval of pregnancy, most women are able to bring themselves into harmony with the physiological processes by becoming increasingly involved with the child they will bear and the role they will play. "It is this harmony . . . that makes discomfort and pain bearable and robs childbirth of a sense of threat or terror, freeing the woman's energies for moving into the role of mother" (Shereshefsky and Yarrow, 1973, p. 250).

Adjustment to Pregnancy

Pregnancy can be looked at as a period of development during which a woman responds to a series of unfolding demands. These demands are biological, social, and psychological. In her process model of pregnancy, Gabriele Gloger-Tippelt (1983) of the University of Heidelberg, West Germany, divides the 9 months of pregnancy into four phases. During the first, *disruption phase,* a woman experiences sudden and dramatic disruptions in her accustomed ways of feeling and acting. The disruption phase lasts from conception until about the 12th week of pregnancy, at which time the chances of miscarriage decrease and many of the early discomforts diminish. The first biological disruptions of a woman's stable physical systems are hormonal and physiological. Hormonal disruptions account for the absence of menstruation and the fluctuation of certain hormones that, in combination with physiological disruptions, can cause a woman fatigue, nausea, sensitive breasts, a growing uterus, and the need to urinate often. During the early weeks of pregnancy, a woman also may find elements of her identity threatened. She may face psychological disruptions in her sense of age ("I'm a woman now, not a girl"), her sense of responsibility ("I will have to be a good mother,"), her sexual identity ("How do I balance being a lover with being a mother?"), her work identity ("Should I leave my job to stay home with the baby?"), and her sense of creativity and power ("I have created life"). During this stage, many women worry about how to cope with their diminished personal independence, the strains on their economic resources, and the changes in their physical appearance. Social disruptions include the changes in a pregnant woman's relationship with her partner, friends, relatives, and employer. Her partner's own altered sense of identity can create stress both for him and for her.

If the first phase of pregnancy has an atmosphere of crisis, the second, or *adaptation phase*, is the calmer period, when pregnant women try to reduce the effect of earlier disruptions. On a biological level, many of the unpleasant symptoms like nausea and fatigue give way to relief and satisfaction. The body begins to look pregnant. Obstetrical devices make it possible now to hear the fetus's heartbeat or to see it by means of ultrasound, and these signs reaffirm the psychological adjustment of the pregnant woman and her partner. Many women have by now committed themselves to, and feel familiar with, their pregnancy. Anxiety and depression, if they were present, may well diminish during this phase. The important people in the pregnant woman's life are also coming to terms with her pregnancy. If they do not, the adaptation phase may be prolonged or may break down altogether.

Once through the adaptation phase, a woman enters the *centering phase*. Focused largely on the rapidly developing fetus, the pregnant woman is very conscious of her body, is introspective, and concentrates her energies on the developing child. The child now gives clear signals of its presence in its movements and kicking, and the changes in the mother's body are ordinarily not uncomfortable. Psychologically, the mother finds the child's movements deeply meaningful, for now the child is a concrete, living presence rather than the symptom or abstraction it had been earlier in the pregnancy. Anxieties tend to be at a low ebb now, and the pregnant woman tends to start thinking of her child as an independent being. At the same time, she makes the practical arrangements in her education, work, and relationships that ready her for active motherhood. She may suspend some tasks, finish, or break off others. Socially, now that she looks pregnant, she evokes certain stereotypical responses from others. As people respond to her increasingly as pregnant and decreasingly as an independent, complex woman, the centering process is enhanced. If she violates social ideals for a pregnant woman's behavior, she may run into negative reactions. Employers and obstetricians may also impose routines and regimens during this phase. The public and private spheres of the pregnant woman's life have begun to overlap.

At around the 8th month of pregnancy, a woman enters the phase of *anticipation and preparation*. Now she casts her mind ahead to the future: to the baby soon to be born, the preparations that will be necessary, and to her own role as mother. Most woman adjust in preparation for delivery. On the biological level, her large abdomen, the heavy baby settled in her pelvis, and the increased demands on her circulation and digestion can make a pregnant woman uncomfortable during sleep, eating, and moving around in general. Psychologically, a woman faces birth and motherhood. She may worry about pain, helplessness, losing self-control, or about bearing a deformed child. Her anxieties may cause her to gather information, to enroll in prepared childbirth classes, and to engage with her partner in relaxation exercises. She may also rehearse meeting and interacting with her child and actively prepare for its arrival by buying clothes and equipment, by learning about feeding, furniture, and the like. Socially, the woman anticipates and prepares for the birth with others in her life. She may leave her job and increase her visits to doctors or hospitals. With the beginning of labor and the birth of her child, pregnancy ends—and a vastly new developmental phase, parenthood, begins.

EFFECTS OF THE PRENATAL ENVIRONMENT ON THE DEVELOPING FETUS

The prenatal environment is more than just the mother's uterus. It consists of all the influences, direct and indirect, that impinge on the human organism as it moves from fertilized egg to embryo to fetus and finally through the birth canal to independent existence. Anything that can be translated into a physiological change in the mother, any substance that can pass through the placenta and travel via the umbilical cord into the bloodstream of the fetus, may affect the individual's development. Intense or long-lasting emotional turmoil upsets the balance of chemical substances in the mother's brain (Scarf, 1977); the physiological consequences may be transmitted to the fetus. Thus an extremely stressful marriage or an earlier negative mother-daughter relationship, which makes the woman anxious at the thought of becoming a mother, may affect the intrauterine environment and prenatal development. The mother's general physical condition; her intake of vitamins and nutritional history; her age; the drugs she inhales or swallows, such as nicotine, alcohol, and barbiturates; radiation; and harmful substances to which she may be exposed may all have even more powerful effects. The interplay of these environmental influences with genetic endowment can tilt the course of development even before the baby has taken its first breath. Figure 4.4 illustrates some of the multitude of environmental factors that may eventually affect the newborn infant. In this section and the next we discuss some of the more important of these factors.

MATERNAL EMOTION

Hippocrates is said to have saved the life of a princess who had borne a black child by explaining that a picture of a Moor located near the bed of the princess had so impressed itself on her mind that the baby's skin had turned black (Clegg, 1971). The notion that the mother's imagination affects the fetus was subscribed to by many thoughtful people in earlier times, when viruses and other harmful agents were unknown. "We know by experience," wrote the French philosopher Montaigne, "that women impart the marks of their

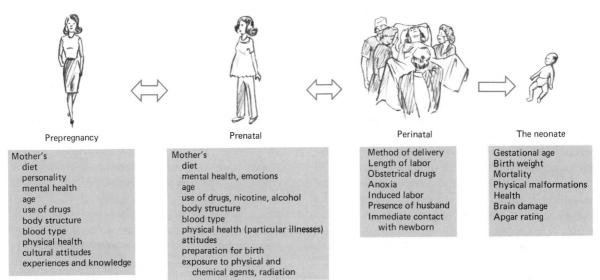

Prepregnancy

Mother's
  diet
  personality
  mental health
  age
  use of drugs
  body structure
  blood type
  physical health
  cultural attitudes
  experiences and knowledge

Prenatal

Mother's
  diet
  mental health, emotions
  age
  use of drugs, nicotine, alcohol
  body structure
  blood type
  physical health (particular illnesses)
  attitudes
  preparation for birth
  exposure to physical and
    chemical agents, radiation

Perinatal

Method of delivery
Length of labor
Obstetrical drugs
Anoxia
Induced labor
Presence of husband
Immediate contact
  with newborn

The neonate

Gestational age
Birth weight
Mortality
Physical malformations
Health
Brain damage
Apgar rating

FIGURE 4.4
Here are some of the many factors that influence an infant's earliest development, beginning even before conception with the mother's health, age, nature, and attitudes, continuing through the critical 9 months spent in her womb, then through the conditions and manner of the delivery and birth, and ending with the condition of the neonate at birth. Development gets off to a complicated start—and then increases in complexity.

fancy to the bodies of the children they carry in the womb'' (Clegg, 1971). For centuries, fright to the mother was said to cause birthmarks on the child or more serious defects.

But in the 20th century, the belief in the magical transmission of maternal feelings to the fetus has been replaced, for scientists at least, by the discovery of possible chemical pathways for transmitting stress and trauma from mother to child. Extreme degrees of fear, grief, or anxiety can produce profound physiological changes. These changes are expressed through the part of the nervous system that controls involuntary functions, such as heart rate, respiration, and glandular secretions—the so-called *autonomic nervous system*. A state of fear, for example, may cause the pregnant woman's brain to trigger the secretion of a hormone; the hormone causes the adrenal glands to produce cortisone; cortisone enters the mother's blood and can be transmitted to the fetus. The production of adrenaline in response to fear can cause maternal blood flow to be diverted from the uterus to other organs in her body. A drop in circulating blood to the placenta may result in a deficient supply of oxygen to the fetus. Emotions, then, can affect the chemistry of the mother's blood, but it is difficult to assess accurately the extent to which they alter the behavior of the newborn (Joffe, 1969). Stress has different effects on different genotypes, and the influence of an adverse emotional state on the fetus is a complex one. It depends on the severity of the stress, the mother's constitution, the genotype of the fetus, the timing of the stress, and whether there are other physiological complications. An experiment in which pregnant women are deliberately subjected to stress cannot be justified. Even though prenatal stress has been shown to affect later behavior in rats (Ward, 1972), animal studies do not provide conclusive proof of what happens in human beings.

One way to examine the problem in human beings is to do longitudinal studies and follow the course of many pregnancies and births, assuming that some may be stressful. Between 1930 and 1950, Dr. Lester Sontag and his colleagues at the Fels Research Institute followed the pregnancies of a number of women. Eight of them happened to undergo severe emotional stress during pregnancy. The fetuses of these women tended to become much more active, in many cases increasing their

movements by several hundred percent. At birth, these more active fetuses weighed less in relation to length and also had gastrointestinal and feeding difficulties (Sontag, 1940, 1944). In their first year, the infants were more advanced in motor development. They were also more likely to be restless, irritable, highly sensitive to sounds and to vomit, cry, and have diarrhea more often.

More recently, investigators have found a connection between mothers' emotional stress and infants born with a narrowed stomach opening, called **pyloric stenosis** (Revill and Dodge, 1978). Mothers of infants with pyloric stenosis, which is treated surgically, scored significantly higher on an index of stressful life events during their pregnancies than did mothers with normal children and mothers of children with spina bifida. In another study, which tried to disentangle prenatal and postnatal effects of stress, Finnish researchers (Huttunen and Niskanen, 1978) compared families in which a husband died during his wife's pregnancy with families in which the husband died during the child's first year of life. Children whose fathers died before they were born had significantly more psychiatric and behavior problems than the other group.

The researchers found no difference between the groups in incidence of complications of pregnancy or birth in this study. However, other investigations of women who have repeated spontaneous abortions suggest another way in which the mother's emotional state may affect the fetus. In one of these studies (Grimm, 1962), 61 pregnant women who had previously had three or more successive spontaneous abortions were compared with 35 pregnant women who had had none. A battery of psychological tests administered to these women revealed marked differences in anxiety and tension in the two groups. Then 18 of the repeated aborters were given psychotherapy during their pregnancies. Their anxieties and tensions were supposedly to some extent dispelled, for they were able to complete their pregnancies. Was there something in the constitution of these mothers that might have explained both the tendency to abort and their anxiety and tension? Were the anxious states triggered by physiological complications, or were the emotions of these mothers causing the spontaneous abortions? As yet we do not know. We cannot separate cause and effect. There are pathways by which maternal emotions influence prenatal development, but they are not well marked, and any one can be called into question.

MATERNAL ILLNESS

Maternal illnesses may also influence the fetus in a number of ways. Of all the chronic illnesses, disorders, and conditions that a mother may have two that seem the most potentially dangerous for the developing fetus or newborn are diabetes and **Rh incompatibility.** In diabetes, the high blood sugar levels of the mother, the insulin of her treatment, or both, increase the risk that the fetus will spontaneously abort or be stillborn, or, if it survives, that the infant will be abnormally large in size and have physical and neurological abnormalities. With suitable medical care, exercise, and diet for the mother, the risks can be reduced.

The Rh factor is a protein substance in the red blood cells of about 85 percent of the population. This inherited blood trait is genetically dominant and is named for the rhesus monkey, an animal that is always positive for this trait. Rh incompatibility is a threat only when an Rh-positive man and an Rh-negative woman conceive an Rh-positive child. Yet only 10 percent of the Rh-positive children born to Rh-negative mothers have Rh disease. When the mother and fetus are Rh incompatible, the first child may sensitize the mother. It is subsequent children who are in danger. The process is as follows. Although the fetal and maternal blood systems are separate, some mixing of the blood may occur as a result of hemorrhaging, often during the birth process. This will cause the mother's immunogenic system to develop antibodies to the Rh factor soon after the birth of her first child. These antibodies will cross the placenta and destroy red blood cells of her second Rh-positive fetus. The baby may be born anemic and also have a yellowish cast to its skin, called *jaundice,* from the toxic substances released by the destroyed red blood cells. Stillbirth, brain damage, or a birth before the infant is able to survive outside the uterus are other possible outcomes of Rh incompatibility. An injection of Rh immune globulin (RhoGam) given to the Rh-negative mother immediately after each pregnancy and after every abortion and miscarriage will prevent her system from building up Rh antibodies. If a baby has Rh disease, it can be given blood

transfusions immediately after birth or even months before, while still in the uterus.

In addition to her chronic health problems, the acute infectious diseases that the mother contracts may damage the fetus. Even influenza causes a 3 percent increase in malformations. German measles, or **rubella,** is particularly damaging to the embryo. While the organs are forming—a process called **organogenesis,** which takes place between days 18 and 60—the embryo is, as we have mentioned, especially vulnerable. Rubella does not have a detrimental effect before the blastocyst forms, in the first 2 weeks of prenatal development, but if mothers are infected in the next 2 weeks, approximately 50 percent of their infants will have congenital defects. Infection occurring during the 2nd month causes defects in only 22 percent of births; during the 3rd month the risk is 6 to 8 percent. In the wake of the severe rubella epidemic in the winter of 1964–1965, there were in the United States 30,000 fetal and neonatal deaths and 20,000 babies born blind, deaf, mentally retarded, or with heart malformations. Today, women who contemplate having children can take a blood test to determine whether they are immune to rubella; nearly 85 percent of American women are. A woman who is not immune should be vaccinated at least 6 months before becoming pregnant. The vaccine is routinely given to preschool children.

MATERNAL NUTRITION

How well nourished a woman is before, during, and after pregnancy can affect her child's development. Because pregnancy itself places so many demands on her system, a woman ideally should be well nourished as she begins her pregnancy. It is very difficult for a pregnant woman to overcome previously existing nutritional deficiencies. During pregnancy, her caloric needs increase by about 20 percent; a pregnant woman must eat about 2000 calories daily in carefully chosen foods. Her needs for protein and riboflavin increase by 45 percent, and her needs for calcium and vitamin C increase 100 percent. So important is nutrition to fetal development that children conceived during the cool weather of autumn and winter seem to be heavier, healthier, more likely to go to college and to appear in *Who's Who in America* than children who are conceived in the warmer months. Mentally retarded children are more often conceived during the spring and summer than in the colder months. In the 8th to 12th weeks of development, the embryo's brain is developing rapidly. Embryos in this stage of development during the hottest months were found to be the most severely mentally retarded in a sample of retarded patients in Columbus, Ohio (Knobloch and Pasamanick, 1966). It was also found that the hotter the summer, the more defective children were born the following spring. When summers were cool, no increase in defective children occurred. Why would weather affect development? In cool weather, mothers are likelier to eat the heavier foods that contain protein vital to fetal development, especially brain development.

But in hot weather, mothers are likely to skip heavy meals in favor of fruit and salads.

Early in the 20th century, a rare piece of clear-cut evidence revealed the connection between diet deficiency and human fetal development. In several cantons in Switzerland, an alarming number of infants were born with the severe mental deficiency called **cretinism.** The soil of the regions where these infants were born was found to be deficient in iodine, depriving its plants and animals and, ultimately, its childbearing women of this substance crucial to thyroid functioning. The thyroid disturbances of the mother caused severe thyroid distur-

RESEARCH FOCUS

NEWBORN INFANTS OF DIABETIC MOTHERS

The medical people who care for pregnant diabetic women and who later care for their babies know to be alert for problems. Babies of diabetic mothers are at greater risk than normal for birth defects and for other problems of development. Their uterine environment is usually too high in blood sugar, and in response they secrete high levels of the hormone insulin. After birth, their bodies must readjust. A team of researchers at Boston Children's Hospital, headed by Michael Yogman (Yogman, Cole, Als, and Lester, 1982), wanted to find out whether infants of diabetic mothers acted differently from normal infants in the period right after birth. They therefore chose a group of 10 infants of diabetic mothers who had been delivered by **cesarean section.** These babies were considered healthy and full-term and were due to be discharged from the hospital. Their mothers' diabetes had been well controlled throughout their pregnancies. A comparison group of 10 healthy infants of nondiabetic mothers was chosen; they also had been delivered by cesarean section and were comparable to the other group in type of anesthesia used and in length, weight, and head circumference.

The infants were observed on the 3rd, 5th, and 7th days after delivery, and the Brazelton Neonatal Behavioral Assessment Scale was used to check

their behavior and reflexes. The results of the tests showed that babies of diabetic mothers differed significantly in several areas from the babies in the comparison group. The diabetic mothers' babies oriented less readily to stimuli and were less alert. Their eye movements were jerky, and they had trouble looking at a human face. They had trouble remaining alert for any extended periods. On the motor items, they had poor head control when pulled into a sitting position. They trembled, and their skin color changed rapidly to a deep red or mottling. The test scores of the control group improved on successive days, but those of the diabetic group fell.

Although the babies were all considered healthy, the babies of diabetic mothers were clearly different from the comparison group. It is possible that the degree of difference corresponded to the severity of the mother's diabetes. Three of the babies had abnormally low levels of calcium; this might also account for the differences in behavior. The researchers hypothesized that the uterine exposure to high levels of insulin continued to affect the babies of diabetic mothers even after birth. But no matter the cause, one implication of the differences in behavior is that the two groups of babies would react to their caretakers in different ways. The less responsive, less alert, more tremulous babies of diabetic mothers would be more difficult babies to care for. As many of their parents said, the babies were "difficult to get to know" or "very difficult to get started." Only further studies will tell how long lasting and far reaching these effects are.

bances in the fetus. As infants they suffered mental deficiency and deafness as well as distinctively heavy faces and stunted growth. When the connection was made, iodine was added to the diet of the citizens of these areas, and the endemic cretinism was eradicated within one generation (Montagu, 1962).

Severe prenatal malnutrition of a more general nature appears to lower the intellectual performance of children. Those conceived during a famine, when the mother's intake of nutrients is less, do not score as well on tests of intelligence (Montagu, 1962). Newborn babies of malnourished mothers show clear deficiencies in neuromotor functioning compared to normal babies (Bhatia, Katiyar, and Agarwal, 1979). These babies are themselves malnourished; they weigh less, the placenta weighs less, and the protein content of the placenta is lower than among normal babies.

What happens when diet is improved for pregnant women? A study of enduring value (Ebbs, Brown, Tisdall, Moyle, and Bell, 1942) was conducted at a prenatal clinic in Toronto with women who had had inadequate diets for the first 4 or 5 months of their pregnancies. A total of 120 women continued on their deficient diets, while 90 women were given an enriched diet that increased the protein, calcium, iron, and number of calories they received each day. Mothers eating the enriched diet and their offspring as well had much better health records compared to mothers and infants in the poor-diet group. The women eating poor diets lost 14 of their babies and had 9 premature births. Those on good diets had no miscarriages, no stillbirths, and only 2 premature births and were 5 hours less in labor than the women on poor diets. Their babies for the first 6 months had fewer major illnesses and minor diseases.

Physicians, 20 years ago, rather routinely cautioned women not to gain more than 2 pounds a month during pregnancy. Gaining too much weight was then a suspected cause of toxemia. Now obstetricians are aware that too much curtailment of weight in pregnant women may contribute to high infant mortality rates in the United States. The Committee on Maternal Nutrition of the National Research Council has warned against limiting the weight of pregnant women too severely; an average gain of 24 pounds is now considered not only

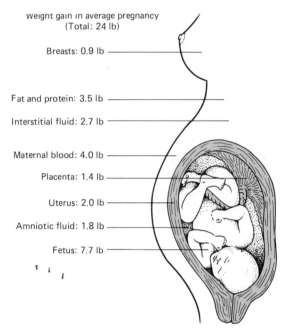

weight gain in average pregnancy
(Total: 24 lb)

Breasts: 0.9 lb

Fat and protein: 3.5 lb

Interstitial fluid: 2.7 lb

Maternal blood: 4.0 lb

Placenta: 1.4 lb

Uterus: 2.0 lb

Amniotic fluid: 1.8 lb

Fetus: 7.7 lb

FIGURE 4.5

Of the 24 lb recommended as the weight gain during a normal pregnancy, only about 3 1/2 lb is stored as fat and protein. This extra weight acts as a buffer against the stresses of the postnatal period (Newton and Modahl, 1978).

acceptable but advisable (Figure 4.5). It is even better for a baby if its mother comes from a family that has had good nutrition for several generations. Samuel Kirkwood's (1955) 20-year longitudinal study showed the significance of diet going back to the grandmother of a baby about to be born.

AGE

Lina Medina of Lima, Peru, gave birth to a healthy baby boy when she was only 5 years and 8 months old (Montagu, 1962). This is the youngest age on record for what doctors term a **primapara,** the mother of a firstborn. Most girls do not begin to menstruate until they are 12 or 13. An additional period of time is usually necessary until they develop full reproductive capacity, or *nubility.* They continue to have this capacity until menopause, which usually occurs between the ages of 45 and 50. But this reproductive span of 35 to 40 years contains a stretch of prime time for having babies. The optimum ages of the mother for childbearing, when she and the baby are most likely to survive, avoid complications, and thrive, appear to be from her 23rd to 28th year (Montagu, 1962).

Recent social trends, however, are causing increases in births at both ends of the age spectrum, before and after "prime time." A greater number of teenagers are having babies, and a greater number of women delay having their first child until their late 20s or 30s (Glick, 1977). We have mentioned the risk to older women of bearing children with Down's syndrome and the greater difficulty of becoming pregnant; delivery may also be more complicated. Teenage pregnancy, too, is a high-risk venture. Many pregnant teenage girls are unmarried and tend to fall outside of the health network, receiving little if any prenatal care. Young teenagers are not physiologically or psychologically prepared for childbearing. Their labor is more difficult. Larger numbers of premature and low-birth-weight babies are born, and more mothers and infants die in pregnancies of these early teen years.

Just as genetic and environmental factors work together to ensure health, a number of factors are usually necessary to divert the developing fetus from its normal, healthy pathway. The immature womb of a very young woman plus inadequate nutrition and medical care may be sufficient to cause such a perilous detour. This combination of physical and psychosocial disadvantage makes having babies extremely early as dangerous to mother and baby as having them late.

There seems to be less correlation between the age of the father and deficiencies in his children, but some instances suggest that paternal age should be given more consideration. As indicated earlier, the sperm of older men may carry the extra chromosome 21 that causes Down's syndrome. A disorder of cartilage growth called **achondroplasia,** the most common type of congenital abnormal bone development, has also been linked to the age of the father. Achondroplastic individuals have unusually large heads, long trunks, and short limbs. L. S. Penrose found that 80 percent of achondroplastic individuals have no family history of this disorder. In these nonfamilial cases of achondroplasia and in a few other rare conditions, a mutation is strongly suspected. Penrose found older paternal age to be a significant factor in many of these nonfamilial cases (Evans and Hall, 1975). Although

the risk of a man's fathering a child with a mutation increases between the ages of 30 and 60, the danger should not be overestimated. Even in very old men, the overall risk of a mutation is under 1 percent.

PARITY

Parity, or the number of previous pregnancies a woman has had, will also affect the course of prenatal development, birth, and infancy. When parity is separated from maternal age, it seems that the prenatal environment favors later-born infants. Circulation between uterus and placenta tends to be slower in the woman carrying her first child than in the woman who has had at least one child. Later-born children have had greater growth as fetuses than firstborns, and certain birth complications and malformations are more common in the firstborn. The mother's body seems to handle pregnancy and birth better with at least one practice session. But if the births are too widely spaced or occur after too short an interval, this "practice" benefit is lost or offset by other difficulties. Some recent evidence (Maccoby, Doering, Jacklin, and Kraemer, 1979) suggests that without an interval of at least 4 years, second children may be at a disadvantage because the mother's endocrine system will not have fully recovered from the first pregnancy.

EXTERNAL FACTORS

Deformed babies have fascinated artists, philosophers, and scientists for centuries. The Greek word *teras,* meaning "monster" or "marvel," was adapted and given to the biological study of structural and functional abnormalities. Nineteenth-century **teratology** consisted for the most part of cataloguing abnormal births. But 20th-century advances in embryology have taken the study of teratology much farther. Its goal now is to understand causes of abnormalities and to anticipate risks in prenatal development. Thus teratology informs us about normal prenatal development by pointing out its critical periods as well as identifying the external agents or **teratogens** that may cross the barrier of the placenta and interfere with it.

When this 7-year-old's mother was pregnant, she took an antinausea drug for morning sickness. Her son was born without hands or arms, and his legs are short because he has no thighs. Yet he feeds himself, colors, draws, writes, and plays several instruments with his feet.

DRUGS

Until 1961 biomedical scientists did not fully appreciate the possibility that outside chemical agents could actually penetrate the protective mechanisms of the mother and damage the conceptus (Wilson, 1977). A presumably harmless drug called thalidomide had come on the market in England, Canada, West Germany, and Scandinavia. In the United States, thanks to Dr. Frances Kelsey of the Food and Drug Administration, thalidomide was not allowed to be sold pending additional testing. Because thalidomide was particularly effective at relieving the nausea and vomiting of morning sickness, pregnant women took the drug during the critical embryonic period. In 1960 several hundred children were born with stunted limbs. Their arms and legs resembled the buds that precede limb

development in the human embryo. From 1949 to 1959 only 15 cases of this condition, called **phocomelia,** had been seen in West Germany. By 1961 cases numbered in the thousands (Annis, 1978). The mothers of these newborns, who were normal in other respects, all had taken thalidomide when they were pregnant. By the time this connection was made (Lenz, 1961; McBride, 1961), 10,000 babies had been born with phocomelia; 5,000 would survive into adulthood. The drug had no toxic effect on the mother, only on the embryo developing within. The thalidomide catastrophe tended to raise the consciousness of biomedical researchers. They became aware as never before of the vulnerability of the "intrauterine occupant" to a variety of substances (Wilson and Fraser, 1977). In the period since the catastrophe, work in teratology has increased significantly. We now know of, and are on the lookout for, many chemicals and drugs that can harm the embryo or fetus. Moreover, we understand more about environmental influences throughout the course of prenatal development.

Even after the thalidomide catastrophe came to light, however, pregnant women in one study were taking an average of three different drugs every day (Peckham and King, 1963). In a more recent study in Texas (Hill, 1973), 156 pregnant women were found to ingest an average of 10 different drugs during the course of their pregnancy, not counting vitamins, iron, caffeine, nicotine, and alcohol. More than half the women took aspirin or other analgesics, diuretics, and antihistamines. One-third took sedatives and one-fifth continued to take hormones. Yet most hormones as well as sedatives and tranquilizers, such as bromides, Thorazine, and Valium, have proven harmful effects on the human fetus; so, too, have commonly prescribed antibiotics, such as tetracycline and streptomycin, and anticoagulants (O'Brien and McManus, 1978). The best policy for pregnant women appears to be no drugs unless absolutely necessary and prescribed by a knowledgeable obstetrician.

Before and after the effects of thalidomide were discovered, the hormone **diethylstilbestrol (DES)** was prescribed to prevent miscarriages. At least 500,000 and perhaps as many as 2 million pregnant women took DES between 1948 and 1969. Then tests showed that it was ineffective. Cases of vaginal cancer in the teenage daughters of these women were first discovered in 1965. So far, about 1 in 500 of the DES daughters has developed cancer of the genital tract; as many as 59 percent have abnormalities of vaginal tissue and structures and of the cervix (Elliott, 1979). A number of DES sons, first thought to be unaffected, have testicular abnormalities, which sometimes cause sterility (Cosgrove and Henderson, 1977). The anxious children of women who took DES have formed self-help groups. In 1982, DES daughters won their lawsuit against the University of Chicago for having given this experimental drug to their mothers without sufficient testing.

When a woman who is addicted to either heroin or methadone becomes pregnant, her offspring will become addicted inside the uterus because the drug passes through the placenta. After birth, these babies must receive the drug immediately or they will die of severe withdrawal symptoms. Thereafter they can gradually be cured of their addiction. The babies of addicts are likely to be preterm, underweight, and irritable; they are not alert, cry a great deal, do not cuddle when held, and are irregular in their sleep habits for a year or more. At 1 year of age, they are likely to be delayed in their cognitive and motor development (Householder, Hatcher, and Burns, 1982; Ostrea and Chavez, 1979; Strauss, Lessen-Firestone, Starr, and Ostrea, 1975).

The reason that drugs have such profound effects on the developing baby is that enzymes in the liver, which break down drugs, do not develop until after birth. The fetus is therefore incapable of getting rid of the drugs. Although women may discontinue taking drugs once they learn of their pregnancy, they may not become aware of it until the end of the crucial embryonic stage, when the damage has probably already been done. Drugs, such as tranquilizers, birth-control pills, heroin, and lysergic acid diethylamide (LSD) may cause deafness, heart and joint defects, cleft palate, and malformed limbs as well as behavioral disorders and neurological deficits, which may not be apparent at birth. The effects of taking more than one drug at a time may be more devastating than taking drugs separately (Wilson and Fraser, 1977).

SMOKING

Smoking mothers have 28 percent more miscar-

riages, stillbirths, and babies who die soon after birth (Frazier, Goldstein, and Goldberg, 1961). A mother's smoking appears to have its most obvious effect on the fetus during the last trimester, especially in the final 2 to 4 weeks when it is supposed to gain weight (Tanner, 1974). The birth weight of babies whose mothers smoke during pregnancy is significantly lower, by 6 ounces, than that of babies born to mothers who do not smoke. In fact, women who smoke heavily (over 30 cigarettes a day) are twice as likely to deliver a low-birth-weight baby as nonsmoking mothers, regardless of the length of pregnancy (Frazier et al., 1961; Niswander and Gordon, 1972), suggesting that the carbon monoxide and nicotine in the mother's blood impair fetal development rather than initiate early labor. Small head size and low birth weight correlate with such serious problems as lower IQ at age 4 and increases in deaths among newborns (Broman, Nichols, and Kennedy, 1975). A questionnaire study of 27,000 nurses and anesthetists turned up the fact that smoking mothers of all ages had higher rates of miscarriages than nonsmokers (Himmelberger, Brown, and Cohen, 1978).

One investigation showed how smoking deprives fetuses of oxygen. Eight pregnant women smoked two cigarettes for 10 minutes each, while their blood was sampled every $2\frac{1}{2}$ minutes (Quigley, Sheehan, Wilkes and Yen, 1979). Cigarette smoking quickly raised the women's blood pressure, pulse rate, and blood carboxyhemoglobin (a blood gas from the carbon monoxide in cigarette smoke). The carboxyhemoglobin in the bloodstream replaces oxygen, causing the fetuses long-term oxygen shortage. Within $2\frac{1}{2}$ minutes after starting to smoke, the mothers' blood levels of norepinephrine and epinephrine also rose significantly. These chemicals cause the blood vessels between the mother's uterus and the placenta to narrow, and the effect is temporarily to deprive a fetus of oxygen (and nutrients). The effects on the fetus of oxygen deprivation include brain abnormalities (Evans, Newcombe, and Campbell, 1979; Naeye, 1978), small skull size, cleft lip and palate (Ericson, Kallen, and Westerholm, 1979), and low birth weight. After $7\frac{1}{2}$ minutes of maternal smoking in the Quigley experiment, it was observed that the fetuses' heartrates rose and continued rising to an **average of 23 beats per minute.**

Could the psychological state of the smoker as well as the chemical substances account for some of the effects on the fetus? Jacob Yerushalmy (1971, 1972) is one researcher who has raised this possibility. The mother's anxious state, which causes her to smoke, or indirect stress from an anxious husband, may contribute to the adverse effects of smoking. The high mortality rates of low-birth-weight infants with nonsmoking mothers and smoking fathers may be blamed on the psychological stress imposed on mothers by their mates, on the simple fact that tobacco smoke can be taken in through the mouth and throat of a nonsmoker, or on both.

In an English study of 17,000 pregnancies (Butler, Goldstein, and Ross, 1972)—those of every baby born between March 3 and March 8, 1958 in England, Scotland, and Wales—mothers who had stopped or at least cut down to four or five cigarettes a day by the fourth month of pregnancy bore babies who weighed almost as much as babies born to nonsmoking mothers. The babies of mothers who had continued to smoke, besides being light in weight, were more likely to have impaired brain development and heart abnormalities. Infants of nonsmokers stood the best chance of being normal.

Researchers disagree about the long-term effects on children of the pregnant mother's smoking. Some point to the shortness of the children and their poor academic functioning at ages 7 and 11 (Butler and Goldstein, 1973; Fogelman, 1980). Other studies found no significant physical or intellectual differences at ages 4 and 7 (Hardy and Mellits, 1972) and age 10 (Lefkowitz, 1981). If the babies of smokers survive the immediate prenatal period, they may not suffer significant problems in childhood.

ALCOHOL

Women who continue to drink heavily during their pregnancies have a 17 percent chance of delivering a stillborn child. They also have a 44 percent chance of giving birth to a deformed infant. Doctors have long been concerned about the effects of alcohol on the human fetus. It is known to cross the placenta rapidly and to remain a long time, because the immature liver is only half as effective as the adult's in breaking down alcohol. In 1973, the **fetal alcohol syndrome** was identified in in-

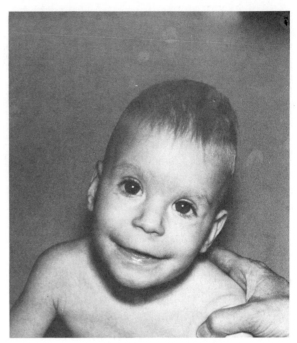

When a pregnant woman drinks 12 ounces of beer or 1 1/2 ounces of liquor, the fetus receives a full and debilitating adult dose of alcohol. Continued drinking during pregnancy can affect a baby's intelligence and facial structure.

fants of women who drink excessively during pregnancy (Jones, Smith, Ulleland, and Streissguth, 1973). The children are born quite short for their weight, and they do not catch up afterward. They lag in motor development and are mentally retarded. Their heads may be small, and they have distinctive facial features: widely spaced eyes, flat noses, and underdeveloped upper jaws. They may also be born with eye, heart, limb, and joint defects. A 1982 study (Rawat, 1982) of how alcohol affects laboratory rats led to speculation that alcohol consumption by pregnant and nursing mothers may interfere with the formation of brain proteins and ribonucleic acids, which may explain the retardation of their children. Biochemist Dr. Anun Rawat believes that about 20 percent of children in mental retardation centers may be victims of fetal alcohol syndrome.

Alcohol affects the fetus directly. In a study of pregnant women who drank occasionally, one group got an ounce of 80-proof vodka in diet ginger ale, and one group got only ginger ale. The women were all between 37 and 39 weeks pregnant. In all of the women who drank the vodka, the fetus stopped breathing at some point between 3 and 30 minutes after the alcohol was ingested. Many of the fetuses did not breathe for over half an hour. As mothers' blood alcohol levels dropped, the fetuses' breathing picked up again (Fox et al., 1978). Because fetuses are so sensitive to alcohol, even small amounts may cause abnormalities in development. During the last trimester of pregnancy, when the fetus's brain is developing, alcohol may be extremely dangerous. One study of almost 3500 embryos aborted during the first trimester showed that mothers who drank had embryos with no more abnormalities than mothers who did not drink (Matsunaga and Shiota, 1981). The effects of alcohol, in other words, are most severe later in pregnancy. Mothers who drink heavily but who can cut down their alcohol intake during the last trimester bear significantly fewer babies who are below the 10th percentile in weight, length, and head circumference (Rosett, Weiner, Zuckerman, Mc-Kinlay, and Edelin, 1980). Fully 27 percent of the babies born to heavy drinkers had a head circumference below the 10th percentile, but only 4 percent did when mothers cut down on their drinking at the last trimester of pregnancy. Similarly, 45 percent of babies born to heavy drinkers were low in birth weight, compared to 8 percent born to mothers who cut down in the last trimester. For women who drink alcohol or smoke cigarettes, the chances of bearing a baby whose growth is retarded double. For women who smoke and drink, the chances quadruple (Sokol, Miller, and Reed, 1980). Psychologists suspect that children of drinking mothers suffer from problems like hyperactivity and learning deficits, but these effects are not yet well documented.

When fetal alcohol syndrome was first described, doctors believed that pregnant women could drink moderately without harming the fetus. But they have since come to revise this idea. There may be no safe level of alcohol during pregnancy. A study of 74 moderate drinkers, women who drank an average of 2 ounces of 100-proof alcohol a day, showed that 12 percent of their babies showed one or more signs of fetal alcohol syndrome. Only two of the babies born to a control group of 90 women who drank little or no alcohol showed these signs (Hanson, 1977). The amount of alcohol pregnant women consumed seemed to correspond roughly with the rate of abnormalities in their babies—up

to 50 to 74 percent in heavy drinkers. Doctors therefore now advise pregnant women to exercise great caution towards alcohol in any amounts at all.

RADIATION

Radiation can have detrimental effects even before conception, by altering the chromosomes of the father's or mother's germ cells. This means that X-ray examinations of the lower abdomen and pelvis for women, particularly those of childbearing age, should be avoided unless absolutely necessary. Radiation after conception, before implantation, is very likely to destroy the zygote, but if the zygote survives, it has a good chance of normal development and growth. Exposure to radiation after implantation is likely to retard growth or cause malformations. Malformations of the baby's central nervous system stemming from the embryonic period often cause death soon after birth. Children exposed to radiation in utero are at risk for malignant tumors and leukemia and do not grow as much throughout childhood and into adulthood (Table 4.1). Experiments on animals indicate that irradiation destroys the fetus's germ cells. Human beings seem more resistant, or, as Brent (1977) suggests, the dosage necessary to sterilize a human organism in utero may also be lethal.

The large doses of radiation that have been used in radiation therapy can cause **microcephaly,** or small head size, and mental retardation of the treated mother's unborn child. Growth retardation was the most common adversity of victims exposed in utero to the atomic bomb explosions in Japan in World War II, but the grisly list also includes microcephaly, hydrocephalus, mental deficiency and Down's syndrome, head ossification defects, and skull malformations as well as death (Joffe, 1969). There is also some cause for concern about fallout radiation from the air and ground. One report connects higher levels of radioactivity of natural materials, such as rocks, with greater incidence of malformations (Joffe, 1969), but other authorities believe that current levels of exposure for the fetus do not seem sufficient to cause spontaneous abortions or malformations or to retard growth (Brent, 1977). Leakage of atomic wastes buried underground or under oceans or other waterways as well as accidents at nuclear power plants are other potential threats to the unborn child.

TABLE 4.1
SOME MATERNAL CONDITIONS ENDANGERING THE CHILD

Mother's condition or behavior	Possible effect on embryo, fetus, or newborn
Incompatibility of maternal and fetal blood	Jaundice, anemia, death
Any viral infection: rubella, mumps, hepatitis, influenza, etc.	Malformations, fetal death, prematurity, retarded fetal growth, disorders and infection in the newborn
Malnutrition	Retarded fetal growth, malformations, less developed brain, greater vulnerability to disease
Use of thalidomide	Hearing defects, deformed limbs, death
Excessive use of vitamin A	Cleft palate, congenital anomalies
Use of analgesics	Respiratory depression
Use of aspirin in large doses	Respiratory depression, bleeding
Use of anesthetics or barbiturates	Respiratory depression
Use of tetracycline	Inhibition of bone growth, discolored teeth
Use of streptomycin	Hearing loss
Narcotic addiction	Growth deficiency, withdrawal syndrome, respiratory depression, death
Heavy smoking	Retarded fetal growth, increased fetal heartrate, prematurity
Daily use of alcohol	Growth deficiency, developmental lag
Exposure to X-ray	Malformations, cancer

Source: Adapted from Carole Lotito Blair and Elizabeth Meehan Salerno. *The Expanding Family: Childbearing,* Boston: Little, Brown & Co., 1976, Table 12.2. Copyright 1976, by Carole L. Blair and Elizabeth M. Salerno.

OCCUPATIONAL AND ENVIRONMENTAL HAZARDS

Two trends increase the hazards to which the developing individual may be exposed, the greater number of women who work outside the home and the tendency for pregnant women to continue working. For example, textile workers are exposed to dust, dyes, moth proofers, flame retardants; laboratory technicians to radiation, carcinogenic chemicals, solvents, and bacteria. Certain pesticides and pollutants are present in the air we breathe and in the waters we drink. Benzene, carbon monoxide, carbon disulfide, hydrocarbons, lead, mercury, and vinyl chloride are substances known to have harmful effects on the fetus and on parents' reproductive functioning. Agent Orange, a defoliant used in Vietnam, and the dumping of toxic chemical wastes in places like Love Canal in Niagara Falls, New York, are also suspected of causing such damage.

BEING SAFE

Physical checkups during pregnancy are the best way to ensure the health of mother and child. Many potential complications can be prevented or minimized by regular visits to a doctor. Early knowledge of pregnancy alerts women to be particularly cautious about taking medication and exposing themselves to other agents that may be harmful to their babies. The buildup of fluid in the fetal brain and blockage of the fetus's urinary tract are among the conditions that can be detected early by ultrasound and treated before birth.

The expectant mother's health and nutrition are monitored during prenatal visits, with vitamins and iron often recommended to supplement her diet. Checking for high blood pressure, sudden weight gain, and protein in the urine can be useful in detecting toxemia, a condition that affects 6 percent of all pregnancies in the last trimester (Pritchard and MacDonald, 1980). Pregnant teenagers have higher rates of toxemia, because they do not see doctors for medical care and checkups (Alan Guttmacher Institute, 1976, 1981).

If obstetricians have reasons for concern, new methods of fetal monitoring allow them to determine whether labor should be induced or special procedures applied before or during delivery. Late in pregnancy amniotic fluid can be withdrawn by amniocentesis and analyzed to tell the physician whether the fetus is sensitive to the mother's blood type or has spina bifida. We have already noted that ultrasound will locate the exact position of the fetus before amniocentesis. The sound wave picture, or **sonogram,** is also useful to obstetricians in deciding whether the delivery will require a cesarean section or the use of forceps to ease the passage of the head through the birth canal.

PRENATAL VULNERABILITY

Teratogens, like more benign influences on development, operate along a number of pathways. They may damage chromosomes, cause mutations, interfere with cell division, and disrupt or distort growth through biochemical changes. The effects of teratogens vary from slight defects to death. Three factors determine the seriousness of the effect: the constitution of the developing individual and the timing and dosage of the teratogen (Wilson, 1977). Constitutional dissimilarities of fraternal triplets, for example, would account for their differing reactions to the same teratogen. One of the triplets might die, another suffer a severe malformation, and the third have only a moderate defect. As for timing, before cells are differentiated into specific functions, an insult to one causes damage to all and is likely to bring immediate death. Then during the embryonic period and differentiation the baby is susceptible to malformations; each organ has its own period of greatest vulnerability (Figure 4.6). Studies of pregnant women exposed to atomic bomb explosions in Hiroshima and Nagasaki reveal the effects of different dosages of a teratogen. Not one of those who were within a mile of the center and survived gave birth to a live baby. Three-fourths of those who were from 1 to 4 miles from the center lost their children through spontaneous abortions and stillbirths or bore infants with severe physical malformations (Wilson, 1977). For women farther away, the most common effects on the developing fetus were retardation of physical growth and mental development and abnormal head size (Joffe, 1969). The combination of these three factors, constitution, timing, and dosage, ul-

timately determines the outcome of any individual's exposure to a teratogen.

Despite the fact that the most damaging external agents rather regularly cause severe malformation, even death, there is a **self-righting** tendency in prenatal development. Evolution appears to have built into the human organism regulative mechanisms for normal development under all but the most adverse circumstances. Most children because of this self-righting tendency move toward normality, even in the face of pressures toward deviation. A reasonable estimate of malformations from all the various causes—genetic anomalies, viral infections, nutrient deficiencies, drugs, nicotine, alcohol, radiation, and chemicals—is only 3 to 6 percent (Heinomen, Slone, and Shapiro, 1976; Warkany and Kalter, 1964). Severely deformed embryos and fetuses are likely to be eliminated through spontaneous abortions during the first 3 months of pregnancy (Queenan, 1979). In addition to the self-righting tendency of prenatal development, which fosters normality, there is also, then, a "self-cleansing" tendency, which eliminates abnormality.

DELIVERY AND BIRTH

LABOR

The first stage of childbirth, or labor, averages 14 hours for a firstborn child, 8 hours for later-born children (Flanagan, 1962). It often begins during the night. The mother may awaken feeling forceful and regular involuntary tightenings of the muscles of her uterus or simply waves of dull discomfort. The muscle contractions, which in the beginning come 15 to 20 minutes apart and last from 15 to 60 seconds, cause the cervix to stretch. Later the contractions come every 2 to 5 minutes and are more intense. The dilation of the cervix from its usual 0.2-inch opening to 4 inches will allow the baby to pass out of the uterus into the birth canal, or vagina. The baby's head has some flexibility because of the soft spots, the fontanels, where the bones have not fused. When the long hours and effort of the dilation are over, the head starts to push through the cervix, which acts as though it were a tight bathing cap. The second stage of labor, which will last from 30 minutes to 2 hours, has

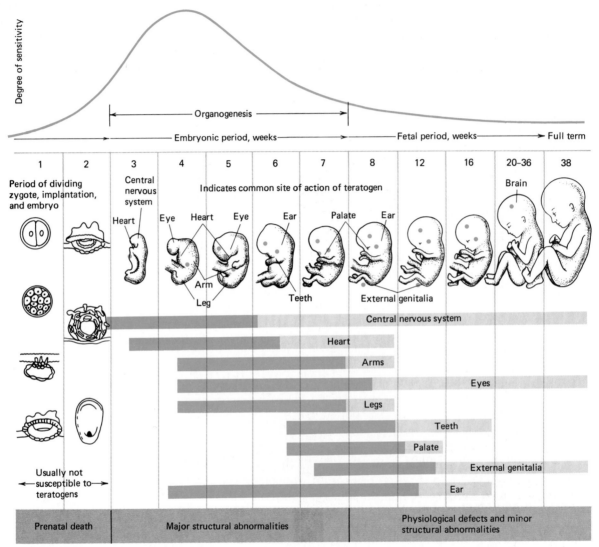

FIGURE 4.6
Critical periods in the prenatal development of the body organs are shown in this graph. Sensitivity to teratogens peaks at around 4 weeks after conception. Early on in the embryonic period the likelihood of a structural defect in an organ is greatest (dark color), for they are being formed at this time. After organogenesis is complete, susceptibility to anatomical defects diminishes (light color). Exposure to teratogens during the later fetal period is more likely to stunt growth or cause functional problems, for the fetus is now growing and using its organs (Moore, 1977).

begun. Now the uterine contractions come every 1 to 2 minutes and are about 1 minute in length. With each batch of them, the mother may have a powerful urge to bear down—to take a deep breath, contract her abdominal muscles, and push the baby out. The first appearance of the head,

usually with the face toward the mother's back, is called **crowning.** In most hospital deliveries, the obstetrician makes a small incision to control tearing of the vagina, called an **episiotomy.** The doctor may also use forceps to help bring the baby's head out. Once the head has cleared the vaginal opening, the baby rotates to the side, and the shoulders and body quickly slide forth (Figure 4.7). As soon as the umbilical cord is exposed to the air, a jellylike substance in the cord swells up and compresses the vessels like a tourniquet. A nurse quickly suctions fluid and mucus from the infant's mouth and nose with a small rubber bulb. Very soon after the baby has emerged, contractions force the parts of the placenta and other membranes not already separated from the uterus to detach. They are delivered within minutes as the **afterbirth** in the third and final stage of labor.

The first stage of labor

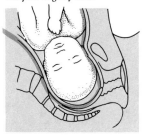 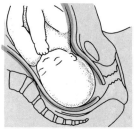 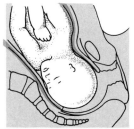

In early labor, where effacement, or thinning, has occurred and the cervix is starting to dilate.

The continuation of dilation of the cervix.

Approaching full dilation of the cervix.

The second stage of labor

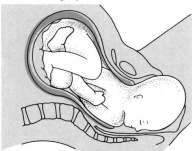 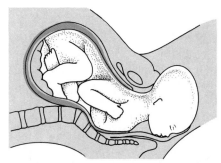

Face down, the baby's head is pressed against the perineum, which gradually stretches, widening the vaginal opening.

The baby's skull extends as it sweeps up over the perineum. The top of the skull and then the brow emerge first.

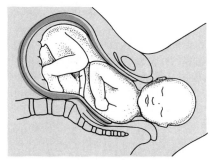 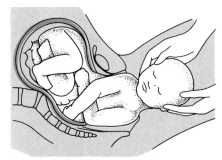

Once the head is born, the shoulders rotate in the pelvis, turning the head to left or right.

The top shoulder is born first, after which the rest of the body slides out easily.

FIGURE 4.7
The first stage of childbirth begins with effacement and continues through long hours of labor to full dilation of the cervix. During the second stage of labor, the fetus pushes through the cervix, the vagina, and its opening, and is born.

CHANGING ATTITUDES TOWARD CHILDBIRTH

There in no one "right" way to have a baby. Different cultures hold different attitudes toward birth (Mead and Newton, 1967). In non-Western cultures these attitudes run the gamut. The Cuna Indians of Panama view birth as an illness, requiring frequent visits to the medicine man and continual medication. The Janara of South America treat birth casually, as a normal occurrence that can take place in any passageway or shelter in full view of siblings or any onlookers who happen to be there. In the Chagga culture, on the southern slopes of Kilimanjaro, birth is cloaked in secrecy. The Laotians stress the sexuality of birth, diverting the woman in labor with licentious remarks. The Siriono of eastern Bolivia practice breast manipulation during birth, recognizing the connection between breast stimulation and the onset and heightening of labor. In some cultures, only females may be present at a delivery. In others, birth is a communal event, a celebration embracing the whole family as well as relatives and neighbors.

American patterns of childbirth have undergone radical shifts in this century. Birth first was moved outside the home and into the hospital delivery room. Now attempts are being made to restore birth to the family, if not by bringing deliveries back inside the home, then at least by making fathers and sometimes even children welcome in hospital labor and delivery rooms. To understand these cultural shifts, we must go back to the nineteenth century, when modern obstetrics really began, and even earlier.

Until the 16th century, all babies were born at home, and midwives delivered them. Physicians attended births only when deliveries had to be made by cesarean section. Gradually, however, information about anatomy and physiology involved physicians in childbirth. In the 18th century, the teaching and practice of obstetrics became an important part of medicine itself. Large cities established maternity hospitals to train midwives and medical students and to care for poor mothers, unmarried mothers, and those whose deliveries were expected to be complicated. Physicians more often attended childbirths in the home.

Then a serious problem became apparent. Nearly a quarter of the women who delivered in maternity hospitals were dying of **childbed fever.** In the early 1840s, Dr. Ignaz Semmelweis, who worked in an obstetrical clinic in Vienna, realized that medical students went directly from dissecting patients who had died to assisting healthy women in labor. Two decades before Louis Pasteur established the germ theory of disease and Dr. Joseph Lister, borrowing from him, introduced **antiseptic** procedures into surgery. Dr. Semmelweis began the practice of thorough hand washing before touching a woman in labor. Deaths from childbed fever declined sharply in the clinic, but the profession was slow to accept Dr. Semmelweis's advice for training of midwives and students attending confinements.

During the same decade, **anesthesia** was introduced into surgical practice; in 1846 Dr. William T. Morton administered ether to a patient at Massachusetts General Hospital while another doctor painlessly removed a tumor from his neck. The next year, Scottish physician James Young Simpson became the first doctor to use anesthesia to reduce the pains of childbirth. He soon found chloroform to be better suited for delivery than ether. Anesthesia was considered a step forward in humanizing the process of childbirth, but clergymen resisted the use of chloroform at first, claiming that it interfered with the intent of God as set forth in the Bible. Eve had eaten forbidden fruit. Therefore she was told, "In sorrow thou shalt bring forth children" (Genesis 3:16). To reduce her sorrow, they argued, was to side with the devil. But the argument that chloroform was "a decoy of Satan" was silenced in 1853 when Queen Victoria gave birth to her eighth child, Prince Leopold, under chloroform, announced her satisfaction, and later requested it for the delivery of her next child.

By the end of World War I, medicine had progressed. Hospitals had become more numerous and advanced in procedures. **Asepsis,** denying germs access to tissues by sterilizing the instruments and gowns, was their *sine qua non.* The techniques of blood transfusion had been perfected. Childbirth actually appeared to be safer and, with anesthesia, less painful in hospitals. The automobile could transport mothers in labor quickly. So doctors began to deliver babies regularly in hospitals. Mothers were routinely anesthetized, and banished fathers paced the floors of waiting rooms. The choice and administration of **anesthetics** became more complicated, and because a drug that brings unconsciousness can stop labor, mothers were given other drugs, often in combination—**analgesics** to reduce pain, stimulants to induce or strengthen contractions, local anesthesia for the lower birth tract.

An English obstetrician, Dr. Grantly Dick-Read, was soon asking new questions. Was excessive pain inevitable in childbirth? Might not fear and helplessness cause physical tensions and intensify the pain experienced during labor? In 1933 he published his *Childbirth Without Pain,* putting forth the revolutionary notion that reduction of fear would lessen the pain of labor. Understanding and the ability to relax were crucial to this task. He prescribed for the expectant mother not a new and more sophisticated regimen of drugs but a course of instruction on the mechanics of labor and birth and a series of exercises to strengthen the abdominal musculature and to encourage proper breathing. With this preparation the mother would have a much calmer and less painful delivery, what Dick-Read called **natural childbirth.** Small quantities of anesthetic could be given to the mother when she needed them. Even with natural childbirth, pain might be present. The mother's physical activity during labor, however, would help her transcend discomfort.

In 1951, at an obstetrical conference in Leningrad, a French physician, Fernand Lamaze, saw women who had not taken medication participate actively in labor. He learned that the Russians had developed the **psychoprophylactic method** of childbirth, based on Ivan Pavlov's theory of conditioned reflexes. Through intensive training the expectant mother prepares herself to concentrate on control of her breathing and relaxation of her muscles so that they will not act against the natural muscular contractions of labor. When Lamaze took this method back to France, he decided to train other women to assist the mother during childbirth, to coach and monitor her breathing and relaxation, and to help her concentrate on the work to be done. The method attracted attention in France and was soon imported to the United States. Here, in the six weekly classes beginning in the mother's 7th month, husbands are trained to coach and monitor their wives and to support them physically during childbirth. In 1977, an estimated 325,000 couples went through the Lamaze training course, usually run by physiotherapists or trained nurses. And the numbers are increasing every year.

In the last 5 years, there has been a marked move away from the use of general anesthesia during delivery and toward participation of fathers in the birth process. New approaches to childbirth, one of them French obstetrician Frederick Leboyer's "birth without violence," have made hospital deliveries less impersonal. Leboyer had delivered 9000 babies in the conventional manner, that is, in a brightly lit, cold delivery room. The first sound the newborn hears is the clank of metal instruments. The baby is immediately held upside down to drain any remaining fluids from its windpipe. A slap on the buttocks startles the baby to draw air into its lungs. Once breathing has started, the umbilical cord is tied off and cut. Leboyer began to look at birth from the infant's point of view and found it to be a violent, terrifying experience. From muffled womb, where the infant hears the reassuring beat of the mother's heart and feels peristaltic waves and an enveloping liquid warmth, the baby is thrust into a cold world and assaulted by bright lights and harsh noises. The sensitive spine, accustomed to a curved position, is suddenly forced to straighten when the body is brusquely turned upside down. With the umbilical cord cut, the baby is abruptly dependent on air and has no time to adjust gradually to breathing on its own instead of getting oxygen from the placenta.

Leboyer decided to try to make the transition from the womb easier and less startling. For the next 1000 babies Leboyer delivered, birth was a different experience. The delivery room was warm, lights were dimmed, sounds muffled. The newborn was eased from the mother's body and placed immediately on her abdomen, where its back was gently massaged in movements approximating the body's internal rhythms. Leboyer found that in this position and with this help, the infant readily expels amniotic fluid from the windpipe. The thorax, relieved of pressure, allows air to rush in. The baby utters a small cry or two. Only when the umbilical cord has stopped pulsing is it cut. Gradually then the baby is raised upright. Physicians and attendants transfer it not to a metal scale but to a warm bath like the amniotic waters that have carried and caressed it for the past 9 months. The hands that touch the infant move slowly and comfortingly, easing it out of the bath to a warm diaper. Leboyer found that newborns welcomed in this way radiate peace and contentment (Leboyer, 1975). Leboyer's method of **gentle birth** represents two important trends in childbirth: a new awareness of the newborn's potential for sensation from the first moment of life and an appreciation of birth as the first opportunity for the formation of family bonds.

Systematic studies on the effects of the Leboyer method of delivery are still few. Dr. Danielle Rapoport, a clinical psychologist who studied a sample of 120 Leboyer-delivered babies when they were 8 months to 4 years old, found that these children had been "spared nearly all of the major and minor psychopathologies—of eating, sleeping, maternal relations, and so on—of infancy. They showed a markedly greater precocity of interest in the world and in people. They used their intelligence in more positive and socially adaptive ways than . . . other babies" (Salter, 1978, pp. 85–86). When she gave the older children a French version of the Gesell

RESEARCH FOCUS

GENTLE BIRTH

Leboyer's gentle birth method is supposed to benefit babies in many ways. Advocates believe that gentle birth makes babies more quietly alert, socially responsive, and less irritable than other babies, and that it improves mothers' reactions to their babies and their experience of childbirth in general. Jean Sorrells-Jones at the University of Chicago (1983) decided to test these beliefs. She chose a group of 40 mothers and babies and randomly assigned half to a Leboyer gentle birth group and half to a control group that experienced the usual hospital delivery. Most of the mothers were poor, black, and single. None had participated in prepared childbirth training, none received spinal or general anesthesia, and all of the babies were healthy firstborns. The mothers were told late in labor which type of delivery they would receive; as it turned out, they were so thoroughly engaged in laboring that none perceived anything unusual about her delivery. None had heard about the philosophy of gentle birth beforehand. The hypothesis that mothers who experienced gentle birth would describe their labor and delivery more positively than the mothers in the control group was not borne out.

Sorrells-Jones collected six separate sets of data from the two groups of mothers and babies. In the delivery room, she observed for 17 minutes after each birth. Then she assessed each baby 2 and 3 days after birth for reflexes and behavior. She interviewed each mother 2 and 3 days after delivery for her reactions to her experience and for her perceptions of her baby. She observed each mother feeding her baby between 2 and 3 days after delivery. At 6 weeks, psychologists—who did not know to which group any baby belonged—administered tests of infant development.

The results showed that newborns in the gentle birth group did, as advocates had claimed, have more periods of quiet alertness than the other babies. But, contrary to their claims, the gentle birth babies were not less irritable or more sociable. Mothers of the gentle birth group did not perceive their babies more positively than the other mothers, and they did not engage in more looking or touching with their babies. At 6 and 12 weeks, the babies did not differ appreciably on tests of intellectual and motor development. Sorrells-Jones concluded that any differences between the two groups did not last beyond the period immediately following delivery. Of course, as she said, any method of childbirth that produces quiet and alert babies is worthy of support.

This newborn infant is being gently lowered into a warm bath similar to the amniotic waters he has just left. French obstetrician Frederick Leboyer recommends this practice to ease transition from womb to room.

baby test, which measures adaptivity, they scored significantly higher than average. Being born without violence, she concluded, seemed to provide these children with conditions particularly favorable to their development. But there was no control group of infants born the traditional way in this study.

In another study (Oliver and Oliver, 1978), 20 infants delivered by the Leboyer method were compared with 17 infants delivered by routine hospital procedure. There were significant differences during their first 15 minutes. Newborns in the control group had more body tensions and blinked, cried, sucked, trembled, and shuddered more than those in the Leboyer group. Leboyer babies appeared more relaxed and were more likely to open their eyes, grunt, sigh, and make other soft sounds than the other newborns. In the water bath, their muscles slackened, they opened their eyes, and they made exploratory movements. They did not cry. These are only two studies, one of them of only the first few minutes of life. Whether Leboyer's gentle birth makes a significant difference in the long run is not yet known for sure, but a recently completed study suggests that permanent differences in the children are unlikely (Sorrells-Jones, 1983).

One Chicago obstetrician who now routinely performs Leboyer deliveries finds the most significant benefit accruing to the family (Merrick, 1978). "It seems to be one more step that brings the family closer together from the beginning, and starts them off on a sounder emotional footing. For that reason alone, it is well worth doing." Now in most hospitals participation by both parents is the rule, not the exception. Some hospitals have converted space into birthing rooms. Labor, delivery, and recovery all take place in the same homelike room, an arrangement that allows the laboring mother and the assisting father some privacy and comfort.

MEDICATED VERSUS NATURAL CHILDBIRTH

Approximately 95 percent of hospital deliveries in the United States are estimated to take place under

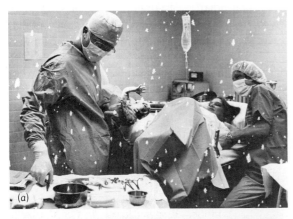

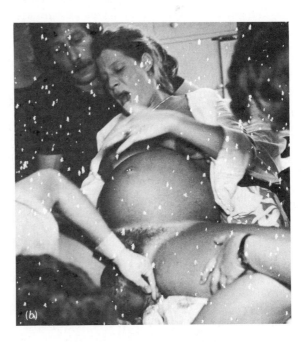

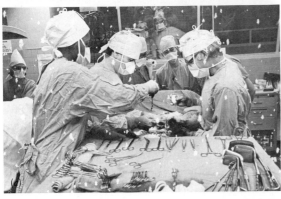

The birth itself can be a very different experience depending on the type of delivery that is elected or required: (a) the traditional delivery in a sterile hospital delivery room. (b) A natural childbirth in a hospital birthing room or at home. (c) A surgical caesarian section.

some form of anesthetic (Brackbill, 1979). Anesthetics and analgesics used during delivery pass into the fetal bloodstream from the placenta within minutes. As these drugs are administered, the mother's blood pressure and oxygen intake are reduced. This tends to reduce the supply of oxygen to the fetal bloodstream. Consequently, once born, the baby may not have the strength to start breathing promptly and vigorously and may suffer anoxia, a deprivation of oxygen. The vigor of the newborn's sucking and the baby's attentiveness are also affected by maternal medication (Brazelton, 1961). The kind and number of drugs and the proximity of drug intake to the time of delivery all make a difference. The babies of mothers who had received a depressant (such as Demerol) within 90 minutes of delivery, for example, were less attentive to pictures shown them at 2 to 4 days of age than were babies whose mothers had received no drugs (Stechler, 1964). Administering the sedative Secobarb during labor made babies suck less hard and fast and eat less than babies of mothers who went through labor without drugs (Kron, Stein, and Goddard, 1966).

Not all these effects disappear right away. Newborn babies tend to retain drugs in the bloodstream and in the midbrain area, which is responsible for much of their behavior. Before birth the baby might have been able to rid its system of some of the drugs through the placenta. But the drug level in the baby's blood at the time the cord is cut is 70 percent that in the mother's blood; and as we have

RESEARCH FOCUS

ANESTHESIA AND NEWBORNS' BEHAVIOR

Because some researchers had tentatively concluded that low doses of painkillers administered during childbirth do not affect newborns' behavior, Barry Lester, Heidelise Als, and T. Berry Brazelton (1982) decided to test this suggestion empirically. They hypothesized that even small amounts of painkillers might *in combination with other factors* affect newborns' behavior. Accordingly, they assessed the obstetrical medication given to 54 white women who delivered their infants vaginally. First they assessed the type of drug given:

1. None
2. Lidocaine just before delivery only
3. Lidocaine spinal within 1 hour of delivery only
4. Alphaprodine and/or promazine
5. Alphaprodine and/or promazine plus lidocaine spinal
6. Alphaprodine and/or promazine plus lidocaine local
7. Mepivicaine or lidocaine epidural within 4 hours of delivery
8. Mepivicaine or lidocaine epidural within 4 hours of delivery and/or promazine

Then they assessed the timing and dosage of the drugs given:

1. Time from first administration of drug to delivery
2. Time from last administration of drug to delivery
3. Total number of different drugs administered during labor
4. Total number of administrations of drugs during labor

They also recorded the length of labor, number of previous pregnancies, and the baby's weight and length. Finally, they tested the babies on the Brazelton Neonatal Behavioral Assessment Scale every day for 1 week and then at 10 days of age.

When all of these factors were analyzed, the researchers found that how well infants did on the Brazelton scales was not significantly related to any of the drug measures taken separately. But when they were all combined into a measure that included the amount, timing, and type of drug administered, and when this measure was combined with length of labor, parity, and size of infant, there were significant relations. Babies did worse when their mothers were given more and stronger drugs after a long labor, and when the baby was skinny and firstborn. The researchers concluded that even low doses of painkillers during childbirth have subtle but significant effects on newborn babies' behavior and reflexes for at least the first 10 days of life, and that obstetrical medications work synergistically (i.e., their effects are multiplied or diminished in the presence of other factors).

noted, the newborn's immature organs are not capable of eliminating drugs quickly. The babies of mothers subjected to anesthesia and analgesia tend to have poorer vision and to lag behind in muscular and neural development, compared to babies whose mothers receive no medication. These retarding effects continue for at least 4 weeks after birth (Brackbill, 1979).

Epidural anesthesia, which numbs the mother's body between the chest and knees, slows down the newborn's motor abilities, especially its ability to control its head when it is pulled into a sitting position (Scanlon, Brown, Weiss, and Alper, 1974). Although these newborns were tested in their first 8 hours after birth, some investigators believe that the effects of medication last longer (Aleksandrowicz and Aleksandrowicz, 1974; Brackbill, 1977). It is difficult for investigators to isolate specific causes of long-lasting effects because so many factors contribute to the development of the newborn. In general, however, newborns who are irritable and unresponsive interact differently with their mothers or other people from newborns who are alert and responsive. One study found that 3-day-old babies whose mothers had been more heavily medicated during childbirth opened their eyes during feeding significantly less than other babies and responded less to sounds (Brown et al, 1975). It is likely that early effects can persist if they become the bases for patterns of interaction between babies and parents.

Medication also appears to make birth a greater physical risk for the mother. Anesthesia is the decisive factor in 5 percent of maternal deaths and a contributing cause in another 5 percent (Hellman and Pritchard, 1971). Women in labor, unlike patients prepared for surgery, may have food in their stomachs, which increases the danger of anesthetic deaths (Journal of the American Medical Association, 1957). But maternal death is extremely rare, fewer than 20 in every 100,000 (Queenan, 1979). An anesthetic more often affects the mother psychologically. Fortunately, recent advances in pharmacology and medicine are greatly improving mothers' and babies' chances for a safe and harmless delivery.

To compare the psychological impact of natural childbirth with that of medicated delivery without psychological preparation, Deborah Tanzer and Jean Block (1976) interviewed 36 women three times: at the 7th month of pregnancy, 2 weeks

before their due date, and 1 month after delivery. Expectant mothers who did not take a course in natural childbirth were no more anxious overall than those who did. Those who took the course had a better attitude toward their pregnancy, however, and their experiences during the birth process were dramatically different. They generally required less medication and afterward recollected less pain during their labor. Their self-image was also enhanced. For some women, birth is a "peak experience"—transcendent, ecstatic, a blissful state beyond happiness. All the women of this group who experienced feelings of "rapture or near-mystical bliss" had taken the natural childbirth course *and* had had their husbands present during the birth.

A much larger study, undertaken at Evanston Hospital in 1975–1976 (Hughey, McElin, and Young, 1978), revealed that pregnant women who used the Lamaze method of prepared childbirth fared much better than those who did not. In the study, 500 Lamaze-trained pregnant women were compared to a group of 500 pregnant women not prepared by this method. Expectant mothers in the two groups were matched for age, race, number of previous pregnancies, and educational level. Lamaze-prepared women had only one-fourth the number of cesarean sections and one-fifth the amount of fetal distress. Only one-fourth as many of their fetuses and newborns died as did those of the control mothers. Postpartum infection in the Lamaze-prepared mothers was one-third less. The Lamaze group had fewer perineal lacerations, and those that occurred were less serious than in the control group. Three times as many women in the control group had toxemia of pregnancy, and they had twice as many premature infants. This study did not establish that Lamaze training *alone* was responsible for these differences, for the parents in the Lamaze classes were a self-selected group who might have had other physiological and psychological advantages that were not controlled. Another study, however, has established that women who maintained control over the birth situation were better able to cope than were women whose pain was reduced (Entwisle and Doering, 1981). Control, in other words, was even more important than pain relief in helping women to manage the stress of childbirth.

Engaging the father is another great psychological benefit of natural childbirth. Witnessing the birth process can be a "peak experience" for the father, as birth can be for the mother. One father, a syndicated columnist, allowed in the delivery room to participate in the birth of his third child, wrote these words a few years later:

The memory of Joshua's birth is always with me—when I change his diapers, when I muss his curly hair, or just watch him as he sleeps. It will be with me when he goes to school for the first time, when he goes out on his first date, when he goes off to college or work, when he gets married. I hope, when the time comes, he will ask me if he should watch the birth of his child. I would take such pleasure in describing how I watched his birth. I would tell him it was the most exhilarating, the most awesome experience I have ever had (Koch, 1973).

BIRTH COMPLICATIONS

If labor does not begin spontaneously at around 40 weeks of pregnancy, or if it does not proceed quickly and smoothly enough once it does begin, labor may be **induced** by one of several different methods. One way to induce labor is to break open the membranes that hold the fetus and placenta. This quick, painless procedure, performed through the vagina and cervix, often causes uterine contractions to begin or to pick up strength. Another way to induce labor is to give the pregnant woman one or more drugs. Oxytocin is a hormone that stimulates uterine contractions; prostaglandins cause both contractions and dilation of the cervix. Unless the cervix is softened and "ripe," a condition normally found at the very end of pregnancy, labor may be especially painful and difficult. Some drugs are taken by mouth, some by injection, and some are administered right into the uterus. In many cases, doctors administer drugs through an intravenous drip, because this method has the advantage of allowing for close coordination between dosage and the rate of contractions. Although induction technically refers to medical intervention that begins labor, the intervention may continue so that it produces a **speeded labor.**

Except in certain clearcut instances—when induction will save the life of mother or child—when and why to induce labor are matters of judgment for the obstetrician. Some obstetricians induce the majority of their patients; some induce very few.

The "gray area" is large, and the pros and cons of induced labor always must be weighed. In favor of induction, of course, is its use to save the life or reduce the risk of damage to mother or child. Medication can speed along contractions and dilation when a woman and fetus are in danger of exhaustion from a protracted labor. Some people also argue in favor of induction because a mother can be well rested, well prepared for birth, and her stomach empty of food. Others argue against it, noting that babies of oxytocin-induced mothers run an elevated risk of jaundice, that induced labor requires more painkillers than normal labor, that more babies need special medical care and separation from their mother after an induced labor (Macfarlane, 1977). Although there is little question that induction changes the experience of labor for the pregnant woman and may affect her baby, studies on the effects of induced labor offer sometimes conflicting results. This is an area that requires further empirical study.

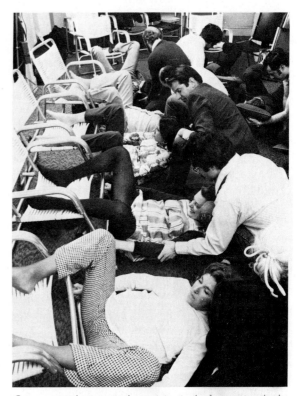

Some research suggests that training in the Lamaze method leads to fewer birth stresses and complications. In this Lamaze class pregnant women and their partners practice for labor and delivery.

Another birth complication that affects the course of labor and delivery is the baby's position in the uterus. Normally, the crown of the baby's skull presents first through the vagina. Shoulders, trunk, and legs follow. This position offers the baby the best chances for navigating the anatomical obstacles of the birth passage. A small percentage of babies present head first, but with the face toward the vaginal opening. Some of these "sunnyside up" babies turn spontaneously during labor; others must be turned with forceps. Still other babies present in a **breech position,** with their buttocks first. Breech babies are in danger because they may begin to breathe when their bottom is delivered but when their head remains in the uterus. In such a case, they may breathe in fluid and either suffocate or contract serious respiratory infection. In other cases, the breech baby cannot pass through the birth opening and must be delivered by cesarean section.

The number of cesarean deliveries increased from 5 percent in 1968 to 16 percent in 1978 (Donovan, 1977; Hausknecht and Heilman, 1978). Breech babies, twins, exceptionally large babies, and those showing unusual distress during pregnancy or delivery all may require this procedure. But some cesareans are performed because physicians desire a convenient schedule or are being cautious about the possibility of malpractice suits. Prospective parents should inquire about any unusual procedures that are suggested.

During the actual labor and delivery, as soon as the amniotic sac is broken, electronic devices can be attached to the fetus to record movements and heartrate and signal any need for hurrying up the birth. Excessive movements of the baby and ab-

RESEARCH FOCUS

CESAREAN BIRTH

The differences are dramatic between an uncomplicated vaginal delivery during which little or no medication is used and the complicated cesarean delivery that requires anesthesia. The vaginal delivery takes place in a delivery or birthing room in the presence of a relatively alert mother and, in many cases, a joyous father; the cesarean delivery takes place in an operating room when the mother is groggy or unconscious and the father usually is absent. Do these different types of delivery have long-term effects on the behavior of parents and babies? A research team from the National Institute of Child Health and Human Development, headed by Frank Pedersen (Pedersen, Zaslow, Cain, and Anderson, 1981), suggests that they do.

After weeding out differences in family background to form a homogeneous sample, the researchers observed parents who had experienced either a vaginal or a cesarean delivery. Their sample consisted of 41 white, two-parent families recruited from childbirth preparation groups in Washington, D.C., who were having their first child. Six of the babies were delivered by cesarean section; four of these required general anesthesia. No fathers were present during the cesarean deliveries. Mothers who delivered vaginally stayed in the hospital for shorter periods and were separated for shorter periods from their infants. Over 80 percent of the fathers were present during the vaginal deliveries, and some of them described the birth of their child as a peak emotional experience.

When the families were observed at home 5 months after childbirth, the researchers found two significant differences in the behavior of mothers related to their delivery experience. The first was that during the observations, which occurred during the early evening when fathers were present, the mothers who had delivered by cesarean played less robustly and vigorously with their babies than did the mothers who had delivered vaginally. The second finding was that these same mothers and babies in the cesarean group interacted less positively than the others. As for differences in fathers' behavior, the researchers found the fathers of cesarean-delivered babies showed a marked degree of concern and apprehensiveness for their baby's well-being. They not only reported taking more care of their babies than the other group of fathers, but were observed to share equally in caregiving with their wives and to respond more to the fussing or crying of their babies. Why? Perhaps, the researchers hypothesized, this group of fathers felt they had to compensate for their wives' diminished capacity as a result of surgery. The consequences of perinatal events, like the method of delivery, may be more far reaching than we had suspected.

normal changes in heartbeats indicate unusual pressure on the head—the baby may have been thrust forward too fast, the mother's pelvic bones may be too narrow, or dilation of the cervix may have been insufficient. The placenta also may be separating early, or the umbilical cord may be wrapped around the infant's neck, depriving it of oxygen. The electronic apparatus, however, may make the mother tense, which will slow down contractions. The procedure has also occasionally caused injury to mother or child and is now recommended only for high-risk deliveries.

PREMATURITY

Although the average pregnancy lasts 40 weeks, or 280 days, as measured from the first day of the mother's last menstrual period, a range of 259 to 293 days is considered normal (Tanner, 1974). Babies born within these limits are **full-term babies.** Babies born earlier are called *preterm babies,* and those born later are called *postterm babies* (Tanner, 1974).

Prematurity is the most common birth abnormality in the United States, accounting for 5 to 7 percent of all births. Most preterms weigh less than normal full-term infants because they have had a shorter gestation period, but their weight is appropriate for their gestational age. Recent studies reviewed by Claire Kopp (1983) and Susan Goldberg and Barbara DiVitto (1983) indicate that preterm births have few serious consequences if the infants receive good hospital care. Hospitals now carefully monitor the physiological functions of preterm infants, keeping track of their heartrates and breathing rates, blood pressure and blood sugar, and their urine. The sterile **incubator** is equipped to control their body temperatures and provide proper amounts of humidity and oxygen. Preterm infants may have problems breathing because their systems do not produce enough surfactin, a substance coating the lungs. Ventilators help infants to breathe, and infusion pumps supply their nutrition and fluids at controlled rates. The outlook for preterm babies has improved enough that now only 5 to 15 percent, usually those born with the lowest birth weights, are likely to have serious intellectual or neurological impairments. They may, however, have some developmental delays. Even calculating the age of these children from conception rather

than from birth, prematurely born infants compared with their full-term agemates are delayed in early motor development. This delay may be the result of the relative inactivity imposed on them by life in an incubator compared to the uterus. As for intellectual development, 85 percent of prematurely born infants are in the normal range for infants of their conceptual age, but on the average their IQ scores are somewhat lower (99 versus 109 in a study by Goldberg, in Goldberg and DiVitto, 1983) by the time they are 1 year old.

A number of studies suggest that males are more vulnerable to the stresses of being born preterm, particularly when the mother has had a toxemia of pregnancy or anemia. In one study, 351 preterm poor, black babies who had weighed 4½ pounds or less at birth were tested at 13½ months and compared with 50 full-term babies from the same community (Braine, Heimer, Wortis, and Freedman, 1966). All male preterm babies and the females in the lowest birth weight group scored significantly lower in gross motor development and on infant mental tests. At 13½ months, male prematures were significantly inferior to female prematures of the same birth weight on mental and motor tests, but there was no such comparable sex difference in the full-term infants. The slight lag that the male has in neurological development may be magnified by the stress of a preterm birth. The conjunction of two separate factors, being male and preterm—neither of which might have caused any serious difficulty separately—for these babies did to produce a problem.

Births are premature for a number of reasons, many of which have already been mentioned as affecting prenatal development. Mothers who are very young and in poor health and who are undernourished before pregnancy are more likely to have preterm babies. So are those who smoke or use drugs during pregnancy, who have uterine problems and do not receive prenatal care (Kopp and Parmelee, 1979). For half of the premature births in the United States, there is no apparent cause (Annis, 1978). Many of the known conditions precipitating prematurity are related to adverse socioeconomic circumstances. Malnutrition, excessive drug use, poor medical care, teenage pregnancies, toxemias of pregnancy, placental disorders, as well as maternal fatigue and most acute and chronic infections, are all more common in the lowest socioeconomic strata of a population (Pasamanick and Knoblock, 1966). Thus disadvantaged mothers have a higher rate of preterm births. In Aberdeen, Scotland, in the 1960s, for example, a high level of obstetrical care was available to both upper- and lower-class members of the population; the majority of mothers gave birth in the same large teaching hospital. A study of deliveries in the hospital revealed that the prematurity rate was significantly higher for the lower-class mothers. The less affluent group of mothers had babies with lower birth weights at all gestational ages. Good obstetrical care was not enough to compensate for lifelong disadvantages. The weight of a baby born to an upper-class mother tended to fall below the 5½-pound level only if the placenta and umbilical cord had functioned inadequately (Baird, 1964; Illsley, 1967).

The numbers of premature babies who survive and the severity of the problems they are left with have declined dramatically in this century and continue to do so. Now at the best hospitals, fully 80 to 85 percent of preterm infants weighing between 2½ and 3½ pounds survive, and 50 to 60 percent of those weighing 1½ to 2¼ pounds survive. About 11 percent of these babies are left with serious problems, like blindness, mental retardation, or cerebral palsy. Another 15 percent have moderately severe problems, and 74 percent—the majority—are minimally handicapped or normal.

The hospital incubators in which premature babies are placed to control their body temperatures are descendants of those designed in Paris early in this century and publicized at American fairs and expositions. (At the 1932 Chicago World's Fair, these "child hatcheries" attracted more admissions than any exhibit other than Sally Rand, the fan dancer!) Today, incubators mean the difference between life and death for premature infants. The first American hospital to care for preterms was opened in Chicago in 1923. Babies born at home were brought to the hospital and fed by **wet nurses.** Doctors then believed that overfeeding would kill these little babies and prescribed a regimen of starvation for the first day or two and then:

13th hour: 1 teaspoon boiled water
15th hour: 1½ teaspoons boiled water
17th hour: 1 teaspoon breast milk
19th hour: 2 teaspoons water
21st hour: 1½ teaspoons milk
23rd hour: 2½ teaspoons water

As we now know, this regimen does not meet the infant's nutritional needs for quantity or quality of food. The breast milk of mothers bearing preterm babies is higher than that of term mothers, such as the wet nurses were likely to be, in concentrations of nitrogen, protein nitrogen, sodium chloride,

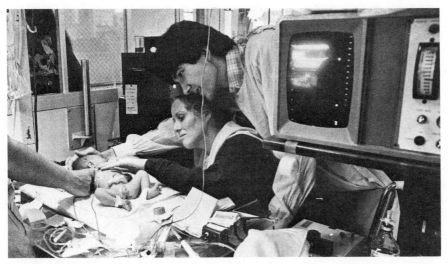

The complicated equipment that ensures the physical survival of the premature infant can be very intimidating to new parents, but many hospitals now are implementing programs to help parents overcome their fears and begin interacting with the infant while it is still in the newborn intensive care unit.

magnesium, and iron (Lemons, Moye, Hall, and Simmons, 1982). The next 40 years or so saw few changes in the treatment of preterm infants. In the 1960s, however, better equipment for detecting physical problems, tubes for feeding, new drugs, new surgical techniques, and finer needles for injections were developed. Regional centers came to specialize in neonatal intensive care for preterms. In the 1970s, neonatologists refined their methods. They learned that an excess of oxygen given to preterm babies on ventilators, for example, causes blindness.

Today neonatologists are concerned not only with the physical survival of the preterm infant, but also with the quality of later development. They are concerned that preterm babies not develop problems from their treatment in the intensive care unit. There, the tiny, scrawny babies lie attached to tubes and wires in their incubators. Without fat beneath the skin, they do not look like the plump, cute creatures to which parents or nurses are accustomed. The head may be covered with a cotton stocking cap to conserve heat; the eyes may be blindfolded. Equipment monitors heartrate, respiration, temperature, blood gases, and helps the baby to breathe, feed, fight infection or jaundice. The intensive care unit is noisy: 60 to 88 decibels (the typical business office is 54 decibels). Fluorescent lights are never turned off. The babies are handled often for tests and medical care, but most of the contacts are brief and unpleasant for the baby. It is hard for parents to feel at home in such a stressful environment, even if they live nearby. Many live far away. All of these factors mean that the hospitalized preterm infant rarely gets the same kind of loving care that the term infant does. When the treatment of infants in the intensive care unit is made more humane, these infants gain weight faster and do better on tests of motor and visual responses to stimulation. It has been shown to benefit them if the hospital nursery is made more like the womb—with recorded maternal heartbeats; a rocking hammock lined with warm, soft sheepskin; a waterbed—or like home—with lots of loving handling and bright, attractive objects, such as mobiles, over the incubators. When parents are drawn into discussion groups, they visit more, feel more confident, and better understand the problems that their tiny preterm babies face (Goldberg and DiVitto, 1983).

SUMMARY

1. About 1 couple in 10 does not have children, whether out of choice or infertility. When in the course of their relationship a couple has children profoundly affects their experiences of parenthood and their own adult development.

2. Humans reproduce sexually. When an ovum from a female is released from one of her ovaries and unites with a sperm cell from a male, conception occurs. Sperm enter the vagina during sexual intercourse and travel from there into the uterus and fallopian tubes, where most conceptions occur. Ovum and sperm carry the complete chemical instructions for forming a human baby. Half of the fertilized egg's chromosomes come from the father, half from the mother.

3. Some couples who want to conceive suffer from fertility problems. In slightly fewer than half of these cases, the problem lies in the quantity or quality of the man's sperm. In slightly more than half the cases, the problem lies in the woman's failure to ovulate or the failure of the fallopian tubes to transport ova and sperm, or in problems with other organs that make conception or pregnancy impossible. Many infertile couples can be treated successfully with drugs or surgery, artificial insemination, test tube fertilization, ovum transfers, or some combination of these methods.

4. Prenatal development begins with conception and ends with birth. It can be divided into three stages: the earliest, the germinal stage, is when the zygote divides, multiplies, and implants in the wall of the uterus; the embryonic stage is when basic organ systems form; and the fetal stage is from the 13th week of pregnancy onwards, when the organ systems grow and the fetus rehearses many physical functions.

5. Pregnancy is a time of change and development for mothers and fathers. Both may feel emotional strains and physical discomforts. As pregnancy progresses, a woman and the people with whom she is intimate can be said to proceed through successive stages of social, physical, and psychological adjustment: from disruption in the earliest weeks to adaptation, centering, and finally anticipation and active preparation for childbirth and parenthood.

6. The prenatal environment affects the course of fetal development in many different and interrelated ways. Not only does the mother's level of stress during pregnancy influence her blood chemistry and, thereby, affect her fetus, but so do her illnesses, the food and drugs she takes, her age, her previous pregnancies (if any), whether she smokes or drinks, and whether she is exposed to radiation or other environmental hazards.

7. Environmental factors affect the developing fetus in several different ways: by causing genetic mutations, by interfering with cell division, and by delaying or distorting growth. Teratogenic effects may be mild or severe enough to kill. Their severity depends on: the constitution of the developing individual, the dosage of the teratogen, and the timing of the exposure.

8. Biology provides humans with a self-righting tendency, which assures normal development under any but the most harmful conditions, and a self-cleansing tendency, which causes the most severely abnormal embryos and fetuses to be miscarried early in pregnancy.

9. Labor begins spontaneously at around the 40th week of pregnancy. During the first stage of labor, the cervix thins and then dilates as a result of powerful uterine contractions. During the second stage, the baby is pushed out of the uterus and born. During the brief third stage of labor, the placenta and membranes separate from the uterus and are delivered. If labor does not begin spontaneously, or proceeds too slowly for the safety of mother and child, a medical practitioner may choose to induce labor with drugs.

10. Each culture and subculture has its own attitudes toward childbirth. In Western cultures today, many people favor preparing pregnant women for birth with breathing and relaxation exercises that help her to cope with the stresses of labor and delivery. Some people also prefer the gentle birth method: in a warm, dimly lit room where the newborn is handled calmly and gently rather than with the brisk dispatch of the usual hospital delivery room. Although the effects of gentle versus traditional hospital births do not seem to last beyond a few hours, the effects of mothers' medication do seem to affect newborns.

11. Complications of childbirth arise when labor is late in starting or protracted, when the baby is lying in an unusual position in the uterus, or when the pelvis is too narrow for the baby to pass through. To treat the latter two conditions, cesarean sections may be necessary.

12. Prematurity is the most common birth abnormality in the United States. The majority of preterm infants can be saved with advanced medical technology. As more and smaller babies can be saved, doctors turn their concerns to the effects of prematurity or its treatment on later development. The neonatal intensive care unit is a noisy, stressful place, but attempts to humanize treatment there are increasing.

KEY TERMS

Ovulating	Zygote	Blastocyst	Critical period
Ovary	Artificial insemination	Embryonic disk	Cephalocaudal
Ovum	Vasectomy	Fetus	Proximodistal
Fallopian tubes	Surrogate mothering	Chorion	Ossification
Oocytes	Laparoscopy	Amnion	Quickening
Spermatozoa	Ovum transfer	Implant	Lanugo
Testes	Germinal stage	Trophoblast	Vernix
Vas deferens	Embryonic stage	Villi	Neonatology
Seminal vesicles	Fetal stage	Ectoderm	Fetology
Cervix	Morula	Primitive streak	Hydrocephaly
Conception	Totipotent	Endoderm	Alveoli
Uterus	Blastula	Mesoderm	Oxytocin

Trimester
Couvade syndrome
Toxemias
Ultrasound
Pyloric stenosis
Rh incompatibility
Rubella
Organogenesis
Cesarean section
Cretinism
Primipara

Achondroplasia
Parity
Teratology
Teratogens
Phocomelia
Diethylstilbestrol
  (DES)
Fetal alcohol syndrome
Microcephaly
Sonogram
Cesarean section

Self-righting
Crowning
Episiotomy
Afterbirth
Childbed fever
Antiseptic
Anesthesia
Asepsis
Analgesics
Natural childbirth

Psychoprophylactic
  method
Gentle birth
Epidural anesthesia
Induced labor
Speeded labor
Breech position
Full-term babies
Preterm babies
Postterm babies
Incubator
Wet nurses

SUGGESTED READINGS

Annis, Linda F. *The Child Before Birth*. Ithaca, N.Y.: Cornell University Press, 1978. A thorough and clearly written presentation of the prenatal physical development of the child, with explanations of Rh disease and other possible prenatal complications.

Goldberg, Susan, and DiVitto, Barbara A. *Born Too Soon: Preterm Birth and Early Development.* San Francisco: W. H. Freeman, 1983. An up-to-date consideration of significant aspects of preterm infants' development, including methods of caring for them and aiding their development.

Kitzinger, Sheila. *Giving Birth: The Parents' Emotions in Childbirth.* New York: Taplinger, 1971. Highly individual and often poetic descriptions of pregnancy, labor, and delivery from mothers and fathers.

Macfarlane, Aidan. *The Psychology of Childbirth.* Cambridge: Harvard University Press, 1977. A warm and revealing account of the feelings of expectant parents before and during childbirth.

Nilsson, Lennart. *A Child Is Born: The Drama of Life Before Birth,* with text by A. Ingelman-Sundberg and C. Wirsen. New York: Dell, 1981. Remarkable photographs taken in the womb between conception and birth.

Tanzer, Deborah, and Block, Jean Libman. *Why Natural Childbirth? A Psychologist's Report on the Benefits to Mother, Fathers, and Babies.* New York: Schocken Books, 1976. Based on Tanzer's study comparing the experiences of parents whose babies were born by conventional, medicated methods and those of parents who chose prepared, unmedicated natural childbirth.

CHAPTER 5

Infancy

During the first month of life, an infant is exceptionally vulnerable. The infant is still so young that its ability to adapt is quite limited. More individuals die during this first month of life than at any other time before 55 years of age. In the United States, 12 out of every 1000 infants born do not survive this first month. Those who are born after at least 30 weeks of pregnancy and who weigh at least 5 pounds have a better chance of surviving than lighter, less mature infants. Baby girls have a better chance of surviving than baby boys do, and black newborns have a better chance of surviving than white newborns of comparable weight and maturity.

Because the change from uterine environment to the outside world places such enormous stresses on an infant's system, doctors use a quick and simple test to assess the newborn's condition. The **Apgar test,** developed by Dr. Virginia Apgar of Columbia University in 1953, is widely used in the United States and abroad. Dr. Apgar's test is given to the newborn 1 minute and again at 5 minutes after birth (see Table 5.1). The test consists of five categories: heart rate, respiration, muscle tone, reflex irritability, and color. A baby receives 0, 1, or 2 points for each of the categories. The healthiest babies, whose scores are between 7 and 10, have strong heart rates of over 100 beats a minute, their cry is strong, and their muscle tone is good. Tickled on the soles of their feet, these babies quickly and reflexively cough, sneeze, or cry. Their skin tone is pinkish rather than blue or gray. Of the babies born in this country, 90 percent receive a score of 7 or better, but the newborns who score 4 or below need immediate medical attention if they are to survive.

TASKS FOR THE NEWBORN

In the first hours after birth, the newborn must accomplish four physical tasks critical to life: breathing, circulating blood in a new pattern, controlling body temperature, and ingesting food (Lowrey, 1973).

In a few moments each newborn must abandon one respiratory system—the placenta and its circulation—and make functional another, which is not only untried but also solid and full of fluid. Until that sudden indrawing of air occurs, the baby's life is in doubt, even though the heart is beating. . . . Other problems may be put off for hours, days, or weeks, but, if the baby is to live, it must begin moving air into and out of its lungs within minutes after emerging from the birth canal (Smith, 1963, p. 27).

Taking that first breath requires removing amniotic fluid and mucus from the lungs. Much of the fluid is expelled through the nose and mouth by the pressure of the vaginal delivery on the baby's thorax. More fluid is lost by gravity when, after delivery, as usually happens, the infant is suspended by the feet and slapped on the back. The

TABLE 5.1
THE APGAR SCORING SYSTEM

Sign	Score		
	0	1	2
Heart rate	Absent	Slow (<100)	>100
Respiratory effort	Absent	Weak cry; hyperventilation	Good; strong cry
Muscle tone	Limp	Some flexion of extremities	Good flexion
Reflex irritability (response to skin stimulation to feet)	No response	Grimace	Coughing, sneezing, crying
Color	Entire body blue or pale	Body pink, extremities blue	Entire body pink

rest of the fluid evaporates or is absorbed into the blood. After the infant is freed from the birth canal, the thorax is no longer squeezed. It can expand and take in air to replace the fluid that has been expelled. Even before they are severed from the placenta, newborns begin to snuffle, snort, and sneeze to clear their passages and then expend the enormous effort necessary to fill the thousands of uninflated air sacs of the lungs with air.

In addition to getting fluid out and air in, taking that first breath also requires the flow of blood through the lungs so that oxygen and carbon dioxide can be exchanged. This brings the circulatory system into the picture.

As soon as the infant is born, the umbilical cord is exposed to cooler air, sponging, and handling, all of which cause it to constrict. The cord is then usually cut by the doctor. This stops the flow of blood from the placenta that has supported the infant during fetal life. Separation from the placenta, together with the first breath, has marked effects on circulation. Blood flows now for the first time to the baby's lungs. This alters the pressure in the chambers of the heart; pressure becomes greater in the left atrium. This pressure shift causes circulation to change in direction from its prenatal right-to-left movement to its postnatal left-to-right movement. The neonate's blood pressure may drop as it makes the transition from fetal to the customary circulatory patterns, and its irregular heartbeat continues to be very rapid, averaging 140 beats per minute. Blood pressure does not stabilize until about the 10th day after birth.

Once outside the steady 98.6°F of its womb bath, the newborn, with only a thin layer of fat beneath its delicate skin, must adjust to fluctuating temperatures. The cooling effect of emerging from the uterus into the outside world will be felt by the baby within 15 minutes of birth. Its temperature drops as much as 5°, returning to normal within about 8 hours. Because the neonate is not well insulated, it is generally wrapped to help keep it warm.

Finally, as the neonate ends its parasitic existence, it must also ingest food through its mouth, digest it, and excrete metabolic wastes. Newborns can suck and swallow and have most of the stomach and intestinal secretions necessary for digestion. At first they consume only 1 to 2 ounces of fluid at each of about a dozen feedings a day and excrete a stringy greenish-black waste of the fetal intestines.

The transition from womb to delivery room is also a transition from a sterile environment to a germ-filled one. The newborn may indeed seem to undergo a setback (Eichorn, 1970). Its white-cell count declines after birth as its system is assaulted by germs. The fetus may have acquired antibodies from its mother, which render it immune to such illnesses as measles, mumps, polio, diphtheria, and tetanus. These immunities last from 6 to 12 months after delivery. But when the newborn first emerges from the womb, a flood of other bacteria and viruses compete for the production of antibodies by an underdeveloped, relatively unpracticed immune system.

NEWBORN REFLEXES

More than 20 **reflexes**, swift and finely coordinated responses to certain external stimuli, have been described in newborns (see Table 5.2). Two of these reflexes are clearly useful for feeding. In the **rooting reflex**, the newborn turns its mouth toward the finger or nipple that touches its cheek. In the **sucking reflex**, the newborn sucks on anything that touches its lips. Sucking is part of an intricate pattern of behavior in which the infant must synchronize sucking with swallowing and breathing. The infant forms a seal around the nipple with its lips, and it creates a vacuum in its mouth by moving its jaw. This vacuum helps to draw milk from the nipple. At the same time, the newborn uses its tongue to express milk from the nipple and to draw it toward the back of its mouth. Infants can suck and inhale simultaneously, swallowing between breaths at a rate three times that of adults. After a week or two of earnest tries, most infants have mastered the complex procedure of feeding.

One of the most interesting of the newborn's reflexes is the **palmar grasp**, also called the "automatic hand grasp." When a finger or thin object is pressed into the newborn's palm, the infant grasps it so tightly with the fingers that muscles in the upper arm and forearm as well as those in the hand are flexed. The infant does not apply the opposable thumb in this effort. Nevertheless, newborn infants can suspend their entire weight for a brief period while grasping an adult's hand. This

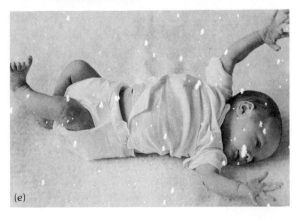

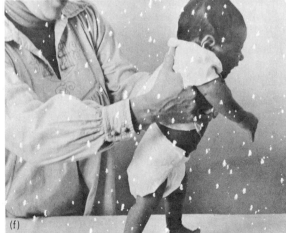

These reflexes of the newborn—(a) the rooting and (b) sucking reflexes, (c) the palmar grasp, (d) the tonic neck reflex, (e) the Moro and (f) the stepping reflexes—are present at birth but are modified or disappear soon after. They help ensure the physical survival of the not-so-helpless baby.

TABLE 5.2
NEWBORN REFLEXES

Name	Testing Method	Response	Developmental Course	Significance
Blink	Flash a light in infant's eyes	Closes both eyes	Permanent	Protects eyes from strong stimuli
Biceps reflex	Tap on the tendon of the biceps muscle	Contracts the biceps muscle	Brisker in the first few days than later	Absent in depressed infants or those with congenital muscular disease
Knee jerk or patellar tendon reflex	Tap on the tendon below the patella, or kneecap	Quickly extends or kicks the knee	More pronounced in the first 2 days than later	Absent or difficult to obtain in depressed infants or infants with muscular disease; exaggerated in hyperexcitable infants
Babinski	Gently stroke the side of the infant's foot from heel to toes	Flexes the big toe dorsally; fans out the other toes; twists foot inward	Usually appears near the end of the 1st year, replaced by plantar flexion of big toe in the normal adult	Absent in infants with defects of the lower spine; retention important in diagnosing poor myelination of motor tracts of the brainstem in older children and adults
Withdrawal reflex	Prick the sole of the infant's foot with a pin	Flexes leg	Constantly present during the first 10 days; present but less intense later	Absent with sciatic nerve damage
Plantar or toe grasp	Press finger against the ball of the infant's foot	Curls all toes under	Disappears between 8 and 12 months	Absent in infants with defects of the lower spinal cord
Tonic neck reflex	Lay baby down on back	Turns head to one side; baby assumes fencing position, extending arm and leg on this side, bending opposite limbs, and arching body away from direction faced	Found as early as 28th prenatal week; frequently present in first weeks, disappears by 3 or 4 months	Paves way for eye-hand coordination
Palmar or hand grasp	Press rod or finger against the infant's palm	Grasps the object with fingers; can suspend own weight for brief period of time	Increases during the first month and then gradually declines and is gone by 3 or 4 months	Weak or absent in depressed babies

TABLE 5.2
(continued)

Name	Testing method	Response	Developmental Course	Significance
Moro reflex (embracing reflex)	Make a sudden loud sound; let the baby's head drop back a few inches; or suspend baby horizontally, and then lower hands rapidly about 6 inches and stop abruptly	Extends arms and legs and then brings arms toward each other in a convulsive manner; fans hands out at first, then clenches them tightly	Begins to decline in 3rd month, generally gone by 5th month	Absent or constantly weak Moro reflex indicates serious disturbance of cental nervous system; may have originated with primate clinging
Stepping or automatic walking reflex	Support baby in upright position with bare feet on flat surface; move the infant forward and tilt the infant slightly from side to side	Makes rhythmic stepping movements	Disappears in 2 to 3 months	Absent in depressed infants
Swimming reflex	Hold baby horizontally on stomach in water	Alternates arm and leg movements, exhaling through the mouth	Disappears at 6 months	Demonstrates coordination of arms and legs
Rooting reflex	Stroke cheek of infant lightly with finger or nipple	Turns head toward finger, opens mouth, and tries to suck finger	Disappears at approximately 3 to 4 months	Absent in depressed infants; appears in adults with severe cerebral palsy
Sucking response	Insert finger about 1 to 1½ inches into the baby's mouth	Sucks rhythmically	Sucking often less intense and less regular during the first 3 to 4 days	Poor sucking (weak, slow, and in short bursts) found in apathetic babies; depressed by maternal medication during childbirth
Babkin, or palmar-mental reflex	Apply pressure on both the baby's palms when lying on back	Opens mouth, closes eyes, and turns head to midline	Disappears in 3 to 4 months	Inhibited by general depression of central nervous system

ability becomes more pronounced in the first few weeks of life, then gradually declines and vanishes after 3 or 4 months. By 6 months of age, babies are able voluntarily to grasp objects and to use their thumbs. Not until infants are 5 years of age, however, will they again have the grasping capacity that was theirs as newborns (McGraw, 1940).

The **Moro**, or embracing, **reflex** is an early startle reflex to an abrupt loud sound or to the sensation of falling. Newborns quickly fling their arms and legs to the sides, their hands open, and their fingers spread. They then bring their arms in toward their body in a hugging manner, with hands now fisted; the back is arched, and the legs are fully extended. Newborns also let out a loud and lusty cry and open their eyes wide. The failure of the Moro reflex to disappear is an early indication of deficiency in the central nervous sytem.

Most of the reflexes disappear in a relatively short period of time. What is the purpose of behavior so short lived? The rooting and sucking reflexes clearly help babies take in milk until they have voluntary control over sucking. The grasping reflex is believed to have evolved in primates to help infants maintain contact with their mobile mothers. Reflexes are controlled by centers in the brainstem. As the infant's cerebral cortex develops, however, it is soon able to modulate these reflexes. It then inhibits reflexes that are of no use to the developing child and replaces them with voluntary and deliberate behavior.

Several of the reflexes closely resemble later skills that are acquired by the infant only through great perseverance and effort. The complex skills of walking and swimming, for example, seem to be anticipated in early infancy in the form of reflexes. Infants, when held under their arms with their feet on a flat surface, will move their legs as though walking. Held on their stomachs in water, they will move their arms and legs as though swimming. The possible connections between reflexes and the later voluntary skills they resemble is currently being explored by researchers.

It is essential that at birth most of these motor reflexes be present. Absence of a reflex—or worse, of a number of reflexes—may indicate a medical problem. Later, after the cerebral cortex has taken over and controlled movements are possible, the persistence of these reflexes signals problems. In cerebral palsy, for example, which is caused by damage to the motor centers of the brain, poor myelination, or a stroke, early reflexes may persist.

Because many early reflexes indicate the ability of the infant to survive, physicians routinely test the reflexes of newborns to determine their developmental level and whether they require special care. The Brazelton Neonatal Behavioral Assessment Scale has 20 items testing the integrity and strength of the reflexes, 26 testing other reactions of infants to their surroundings and people. Throughout the assessment a great deal of attention is paid to the infant's state of arousal, for it can greatly influence performance. There has thus been a great deal of interest in defining the states of the newborn.

NEWBORN STATES

It is usually quite obvious whether an infant is in a state of sleep or waking. But there are subtle differences in these two states. To explore these dif-

ferences, researchers monitor eye movements beneath the lids when the baby is asleep, heartrate with the **electrocardiograph (EKG)**, respiration rate, electrical activity in the brain through scalp recordings with the **electroencephalograph (EEG)**, and the electric conductance of the skin, or the **galvanic skin response (GSR)**. Continu-

(a)

(b)

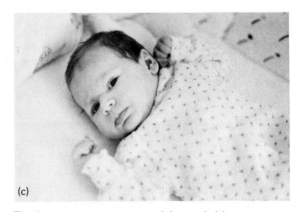

(c)

The three most common states of sleep-wakefulness are shown here: (a) quiet regular and restful sleep, (b) active sleep, during which the baby moves, smiles, grimaces, and has rapid eye movements, and (c) alert inactivity, the best state for learning.

ous recording of these factors show increases or decreases that indicate changes in the baby's state.

Two physiologically different forms of sleep have been distinguished: active, irregular sleep with **rapid eye movements (REM)** and quiet, regular sleep with no rapid eye movements (NREM). During active sleep there are, in addition to rapid eye movements, brain waves of greater frequency than in quiet sleep; increases and irregularities in heartrate, blood pressure, and respiration; and an increase in skin conductance similar to that found in waking levels. Infants also occasionally smile, grimace, pucker their mouths, and move their limbs during active sleep. At birth newborns spend 50 percent of their sleep time in the active or REM stage, by one year only 25 percent (Figure 5.1).

For adults the REM stage signifies not only greater cortical activity and eye movements but dreaming as well, according to the self-reports of adults awakened from REM sleep. Researchers explain the high proportion of REM sleep in newborns as a mechanism for exercising higher parts of the brain, which allow the infant to handle the stimulation it must process during waking time. As the brain becomes better able to coordinate and integrate internal and external sensory information, less "exercise" time is needed. This notion that REM sleep provides practice or exercise for the brain is called the **autostimulation** theory (Roffwarg, Muzio, and Dement, 1966).

In addition to active and quiet sleep, the infant may be in a state of drowsiness, awake activity, alert inactivity, or crying. Putting an infant to the shoulder is the most effective way of shifting him or her from crying or sleeping to alert inactivity (Korner and Thoman, 1970). Alert inactivity has been judged the optimal state for early learning. Babies who are crying or absorbed in physical activity are less likely to be listening to, and looking at, the world around them. Anneliese Korner (1970, 1972) found that infants who spend a good part of their time alert and inactive fixate on and follow visual stimuli more readily. She suggests that newborns' visual exploration may be one of their

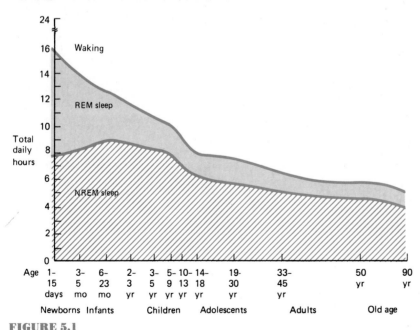

FIGURE 5.1

The daily amounts of quiet and REM sleep change during the lifespan, but the percentage of REM sleep drops dramatically during early childhood. Newborns spend 50 percent of their sleep time in REM sleep and 50 percent in quiet sleep; they are more difficult to awaken from the latter. The sleep of 2- to 3-year-olds is only 25 percent REM sleep, but they get about the same hours of quiet sleep as newborns (Roffwarg, Muzio, and Dement, 1966).

main avenues for becoming acquainted with their surroundings and for early learning.

During the early weeks of life, newborns sleep about 70 percent of their days and nights. Their sleep is divided into seven or eight segments. With time these segments become longer and fewer. When infants are 6 or 7 months old, they can sleep through the night without waking; from then on until they are 1, they require only two or three naps a day, and after that even fewer.

MOTOR DEVELOPMENT

Motor abilities after birth are acquired in the same cephalocaudal-proximodistal manner in which the body grew physically before birth. Myelination of the nervous system spreads out and down from the brain. The myelin sheath covers, first, nerve fibers in the head, then in the shoulders, down the arms and to the hands, those in the upper chest, and

Major milestones of motor development in the first year are (a) crawling, (b) standing, and (c) walking. It's up, up, and away, as the infant hails each new skill with great satisfaction.

then the abdomen, and finally reaches the fibers in the legs and feet. Thus infants first lift the head and neck. Then they are able to control their shoulders before their elbows, their elbows before their fingers, their knees before their toes. Motor abilities also proceed from mass acts to specific acts. Infants swipe at objects before they are able to grasp them. And only later do they become engrossed in the demands of plucking a penny or a bit of dust from the floor.

POSTURE AND LOCOMOTION

1 to 3 Months

At birth many infants can voluntarily turn their heads from side to side and lift their chins while lying supine on their backs. They can also lift their head enough to turn it while lying prone on their stomachs. They soon try, while prone, to lift their head up farther by using their arms; at 2 months they succeed in lifting their shoulders and chest too. At this age they can also lift their heads off the mattress while supine. When babies are held in a sitting position at 2 months, the head will sag or bob; at 3 months it will balance slightly forward but remain erect. When lying on their stomachs, infants rest on their knees, abdomen, chest, and the side of the head. They make no active attempt at locomotion. Their legs will not support their weight at this time, but they can offer some resistance when pushed upon with the hand or when the infant is placed in a standing position. The **tonic neck reflex** is the principal supine posture.

4 to 6 Months

Infants gain a freer range of postures. The tonic neck reflex disappears, and babies have enough control over the neck so that when they pull up to a sitting position, they can maintain the head erect. The trunk of the body is less flaccid and has more muscle control. At 4 months infants can sit up for 1 or 2 minutes if propped or supported, at 6 to 7 months for a short period without support. Babies at 4 months can roll to their sides from their stomachs, at 5 months all the way over to their backs. Infants of 6 months can touch their hands together in front of them, and they can move their hands up and down and from side to side at will.

7 to 9 Months

At 7 months babies can easily roll from their backs to their stomachs and are often quite interested in repeating this exercise. They can stand holding onto furniture and are 2 months later pulling themselves to a standing position. They can now play for periods by themselves. At 9 months infants can rise up on their toes. When on their backs at this age, they begin to grasp their toes. They can sit alone for 10 minutes or longer and can pull themselves into a sitting position when they begin to fall forward. They may also, with some difficulty, push themselves into a sitting from a prone position.

Between 7 and 9 months babies begin to have some mobility. From a prone position they wriggle forward on their stomachs, pulling themselves with their forearms and elbows and pushing a bit with their feet. Or instead of crawling, they may hitch or scoot from a sitting position, propelling themselves along with their arms and legs. Then infants lift their stomachs up off the floor and support themselves and move on their hands and knees. Creeping is a much faster means of travel, and so is the bear walk on all fours.

10 to 12 Months

At 10 months lying on the back is the least preferred position if infants are awake and alert. They would rather sit and can do so for long periods of time. They easily pivot from side to side and change from a sitting to a prone position. Infants will also walk when led by their hands or on their own by holding onto one piece of furniture after another. At 11 months they can stand alone. About a month later they take their first step—and quickly plop or tumble to the floor.

13 Months Onward

By about 13 months babies can walk alone, rather unbalanced and toppling frequently. But they keep at it with great excitement. Very soon thereafter walking ceases to be the focus of their activity, and they can employ their new skill as a means of reaching a location. With practice, walking and balance become more refined; by the end of the second year, the baby, now a toddler, can also run (Bayley, 1971a; Watson and Lowrey, 1967).

VARIATIONS

Norms are useful as a means of detecting a developmental disorder. When a child lags far behind norms for his or her age group, such as not walking until the age of 2, the child may have a physical or mental disorder. Yet the age at which motor milestones are achieved vary 1 to 3 months from one generation to the next, from one culture to another, and even in different samples within the same country. Two American studies conducted in the 1930s and compared by Nancy Bayley (1971a) indicated differences of nearly 2 months for age of first walking alone. Half the babies in one California study walked at 13 months. In the other study, done in Minnesota, half the babies were not walking until nearly 15 months. A study of 1036 children in Denver, Colorado, in the 1960s (Frankenberg and Dodds, 1967) showed that half of them walked at 12 months (Figure 5.2). Whether the infant is a boy or girl and whether the father is a plumber or a professor do not seem to have much effect on the age at which the child will be able to walk and achieve other milestones of motor development. But place of birth is related to motor mastery.

A number of explanations for wide variations in individual and group timetables have been suggested. Nutrition, training, encouragement, and opportunities to move freely—unrestricted by a crib or playpen—account for some of the variations in motor skill development. A unique study conducted by Myrtle McGraw (1935) indicated how differences in early experience led to lifelong differences in physical ability. One boy, Jimmy, was allowed the usual opportunities and given only modest encouragement for motor development. Johnny, his fraternal twin brother, was given more freedom of movement, more encouragement, and deliberate physical exercise and training.

As soon as Johnny began to show definite attempts at creeping he was given daily practice on the floor . . . . whereas Jimmy was kept in a crib. During the time spent at the clinic Jimmy was allowed on the floor only at the time of the weekly examination periods given to test his developmental behavior (McGraw, 1935, p. 71).

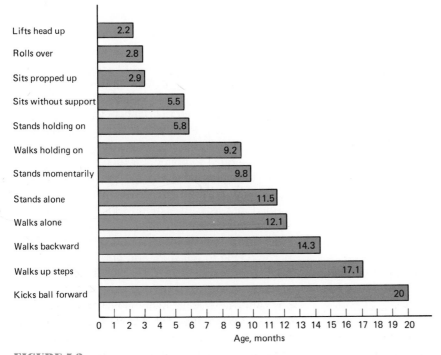

FIGURE 5.2
Of the 1036 normal Denver babies tested in the 1960s for motor skills in the Denver Developmental Screening Test, 50 percent had mastered them at the ages indicated (Frankenberg and Dodds, 1967).

Differences in the motor abilities of these two boys soon appeared and persisted into adulthood. Johnny was clearly more athletic and physically coordinated than his twin. In another study, researchers found that active exercise of infants in their reflexive stepping movements, for four 3-minute sessions each day between 2 and 8 weeks of age, significantly lowered the age at which they took their first voluntary steps (Zelazo, Zelazo, and Kolb, 197).

The training of infants may vary from one family to another. In Kenya babies of poor families in rural areas are given practice and encouragement for sitting and walking. They are more advanced in these skills than babies of more affluent families in cities, who receive less practice (Super, 1976). Training may also vary from one country to another. In the United States, cognitive training of children usually has been stressed more than physical training in the first few years of life. In the Soviet Union, where physical training begins early, precocious motor achievements are common.

Differences in the age at which motor milestones are reached may also derive from genetic factors. Identical twins are more likely to have the same motor development timetable than fraternal twins (Wilson and Harpring, 1972). American babies of African ancestry tend to inherit a different body type and are likely to walk 2 months earlier than American babies of European ancestry, even though they are reared similarly (Tanner, 1970). Finally, activity level and other temperamental traits that have a basis in heredity seem significant in creating an adventurous or a cautious child, and this can affect the age at which children achieve particular motor skills. Of the twins Jimmy and Johnny, Jimmy at first was actually slightly younger than Johnny in reaching physical milestones, but he tended to be much more cautious than his brother. His gingerliness may have added to his lack of training in slowing down his long-term motor progress.

Three infants' accomplishments at 6 months of age have been described by Brazelton (1969) to indicate individual variations in motor development. At 6 months Louis sits and plays in his bounce chair, happily dropping toys over the side and having them retrieved, leaning forward to reach his feet and over the side to explore the ground. His ability to stand, at first using his chair tray for support, later by just stiffening his legs while in the chair, is a source of great delight to him. At the same age another infant, Daniel, develops a method of crawling by pushing with his feet and steering with his arms, first going backward like a crab, then finding the forward thrust speedier. He demands to be walked along with his parents holding his hands, not content, as is Louis, to stand for periods in a stationary chair or playpen. A third baby, Laura, is determined to progress at her own pace. At 6 months she is excellent at manipulating toys but is limp to pick up, sags when she is sat up, and resists being pulled up to a standing position. Unlike Daniel, who doggedly persists when on his stomach until he can go backward then forward, Laura makes no attempt to move when placed on her stomach. Although she seems reluctant to crawl, she plays peekaboo better than her fast-moving infant confreres. Individual variations are clear and complex.

HAND SKILLS

Much finer control of smaller muscles is needed for grasping and manipulating objects than for the gross motor activities of sitting and walking. At birth infants have no control over arm movements, even gross ones. Then during the first few weeks of life the forearm, hand, and fingers behave as one limb, like a flipper. When infants are 1 month old, they will stare at an attractive suspended object but make no directed attempt to grab it. In the second month infants clench their fingers to the palm and grasp an object placed in their hand. But they hold it only briefly and nonchalantly drop it, as though they have quite forgotten it is there.

At 3 months infants swipe at dangling objects but rarely grasp them. Their hands are often formed into fists. At 4 months they are fascinated by the movements of their own fingers as they reach for a toy. Between 4 and 6 months infants become able to reach for and grasp an object and hold it for some time. They can now coordinate posture, seeing, and arm and hand movements for this purpose. Initially, their movements may take much concentration and a great deal of glancing back and forth between hand and object, and they may succeed only in touching it. During this period they may use both hands at once to trap the object, if all else fails.

During the first year, infants acquire fine hand skills and coordinate them with looking. They progress from (a) an interest in their own tiny fingers to (b) grasping a toy to (c) manipulating and making a toy work.

When babies begin to pick up small objects, they hold them in the palm with the fourth and fifth fingers, then with the middle fingers. By 7 months they oppose the thumb to several fingers and the next month are able to transfer an object from one hand to the other if they want to. At 9 months the thumb will probably begin to oppose the forefinger, giving infants immense control. They take to picking up all the tiniest objects in sight, in celebration of their mastery. Much of children's activity and experience during early infancy have to do with hand skills. Grasping and manipulation give them notions about objects, actions, three-dimensional space, and causal relations between events.

SENSORY AND PERCEPTUAL CAPACITIES

In the last 15 years or so, researchers have been keenly interested in the range of infants' sensory and perceptual capacities and have devised rather ingenious ways of testing them. But infants are hard to study for many reasons. If they are lying on their backs, they are likely to fall asleep; if they manage to stay awake, they usually need to move their arms and heads to maintain balance. Infants who are tightly swaddled doze off, but infants who are undressed start to cry. If the room is too warm, infants fall asleep; if it is too cool, they fuss. If the lights are too bright, infants shut their eyes and grimace; if the lights are too dim, back to sleep they go. It can be hard indeed to enlist the cooperation of subjects so young. What is more, infants spend most of their time asleep; 6 minutes of wakefulness at a stretch is the best anyone can expect from a newborn. On top of all these problems is the fact that infants cannot speak; everything must be inferred from their behavior. And what is the researcher to make of the infant's *lack* of response? Does it mean that the baby is ignoring the stimulus, uninterested in it, or perhaps that she or he cannot even see or hear it?

Nevertheless, researchers persevere. Monitoring infants' attention to specific visual stimuli is one procedure they follow. Apparently, infants can make visual distinctions. Like older people, they orient more toward, and look longer at, certain stimuli. Researchers use a technique whereby light reflected from the infant's cornea is filmed to show where the infant is looking. This technique is more precise than simple notations of the general orientation of an infant's head or eyes.

Rate of sucking also serves as an index of discrimination of sights and sounds. The infant is given a pacifier inside which is a device that allows the rate of sucking to be accurately monitored. A baseline sucking rate is recorded before a stimulus is presented. When the infant is first confronted with the stimulus, he or she usually sucks noticeably faster or slower. After a short time the baby **habituates** to the stimulus, that is, becomes used to it or bored, and the rate of sucking returns to baseline. The researcher then changes the stimulus in some way. If the sucking rate remains the same, the researcher assumes that the infant cannot distinguish the difference. If it again increases or decreases, the researcher concludes that the infant does perceive the difference. The infant can also be given a pacifier that, when sucked on, will turn on a recording, bring a screened image into better focus, or provide other treats. In other measurement procedures, the heart rate of infants can be monitored; a decrease indicates that something has caught their attention. Infants' movements can be measured if they are placed on a **stabilimeter** and their breathing rate measured if a **pneumograph** is put around the abdomen. Infants' reaching and head turning also can be used as indicators

of their attention and perception. All these techniques have provided researchers with important information about what infants see and hear from the first days of life.

VISION

The last 10 years have seen significant advances in understanding of the anatomy and physiology of infants' vision, although our knowledge is still not complete. The infant's **retina** (the part of the eye that transforms light into nerve signals to the brain) resembles that of the adult in its components— rods, cones, and synapses—but it has no distinct **fovea**. In the adult retina, it is on the fovea that central visual images are formed. Without this retinal structure, the central retina's handling of spatial resolution is poor, and therefore we have to infer that the newborn's sight is not sharp. The retina matures fairly quickly, and by 11 months or earlier, its major structures are formed and adultlike. During this period of maturation the **lateral geniculate nucleus (LGN)**, which relays visual impressions between the retina and the cortex of the brain, also operates with increasing efficiency, speed, and endurance until it becomes comparable to the adult's. In the visual cortex itself, **dendrites** at the ends of the nerve cells form more branches, and the myelin sheaths that insulate the nerve cells continue to form.

Not only does the anatomy of the infant's vision change, but its eye movements change as well. In infants the **saccadic eye movements**, which are the rapid movements between one point of visual fixation and another, are slower than those of

One month

Two months

Three months

Adult

These photographs stimulate what mother looks like to her infant at 1 month, 2 months, and 3 months, at which time the child has sufficient spatial resolution to recognize many faces.

adults. Saccadic movements are used to line up targets of sight from the field of peripheral vision to the fovea for fine analysis. In an adult a saccade moves the eye 90 percent of the distance required to line up the target. But in infants several saccades are necessary to move the eyes to their targets.

The infant's eyes also do not move as smoothly as an adult's in tracking a moving target. Although they actually seem to prefer looking at moving objects to those that are still (Haith, 1966), infants trying to track a passing stimulus refixate their eyes often, first gazing at one spot and then another. This jerkiness may be necessary because convergence, the focusing of both eyes on the same point so that only one stimulus is seen, is difficult for newborns. By 48 hours after birth most infants can track a slowly moving object (Haith, 1966). But only at 6 weeks of age do infants track a moving object smoothly (Dayton et al., 1964)—see Figure 5.3. The investigation of infants' temporal vision, that is, their perception of movement, has just begun. But observations suggest that temporal resolution, unlike spatial resolution, is mature by 2 to 3 months of age.

The degree of curvature, the thickness of the cornea and lens, and the distance between cornea and lens are also important in determining the quality of vision. Because the newborn's eyeball is short and the distance between retina and lens is reduced (Mann, 1964; Spears and Hohle, 1967), most infants are quite far-sighted. Many also have an **astigmatism** during their first year, a difficulty in focusing that arises because the cornea is not symmetrical. Because of weak ciliary muscles, newborns are unable to change the curvature of the lens of the eye to **accommodate** to the shifting plane of focus for visual targets. Until they are 1 month old, babies can make adjustments in their focus only for targets that are between 5 and 10 inches away. The median length of their "fixed" focus is about 8 inches. Although it seems logical to expect that infants at this age could therefore see objects more clearly at a distance of 8 inches, this is not the case. Apparently the infant's **depth of focus**, the distance that an object can be moved without a perceptible change in sharpness, is so large because of other inadequacies in the visual system that even substantial focusing errors do not cause a noticea-

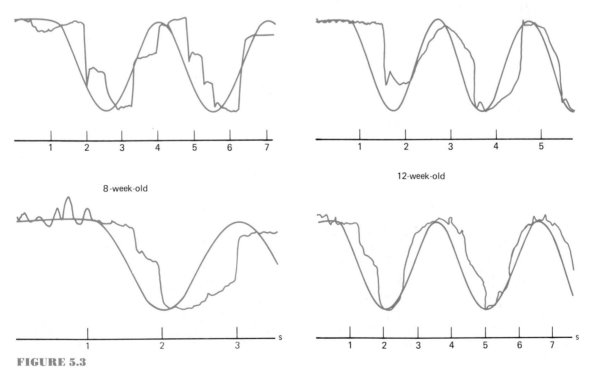

8-week-old

12-week-old

FIGURE 5.3

Records of tracking eye movements by infants of different ages. The infants were presented a target that moved sinusoidally. This target motion is represented by the smooth lines. The eye movements are represented by the other lines. (Aslin, 1981.)

ble increase in blurring. By 4 months of age, infants can accommodate to shifting planes of focus as well as adults can.

Visual acuity, which is the smallest distance between two lines or repeated stripes that a person can detect, is poor early in infancy and improves dramatically in the first year. In one investigation of infants' visual acuity (Allen, 1978), infants between 2 weeks and 6 months old were shown two slides at the same time that were equal in size, brightness, and color. One had no pattern on it, and the other had high-contrast stripes. The experimenter progressively increased the width of these stripes from narrow to wide. By recording the point at which infants first discriminated between the unpatterned and the striped slides, the experimenter measured the infants' visual acuity and demonstrated that it increased with the infants' age. At 2 weeks infants could discriminate stripes that were ⅛-inch wide; at 6 months they could make out ¹⁄₄₀-inch wide stripes. In another study, newborns' visual acuity was shown to range from about 20/150 to 20/800 (Fantz, 1961). A person with 20/150 visual acuity sees an object 20 feet away as if it were 150 feet away. By the second half of their first year, infants have 20/20 vision. A third demonstration of the increase in visual acuity in the first year of life is the observation that newborns attend to large objects, older infants to small objects or features that even their parents have trouble seeing.

Another measure of visual perception is **contrast sensitivity**, the smallest degree of contrast between light and dark that a person can detect. Contrast sensitivity is also quite limited at birth and increases after that. These limitations in visual acuity and contrast sensitivity at birth and in the early weeks may be due to any of the inadequacies in the visual system that we have discussed. But the current view of psychologists is that the major deficiency is neural rather than optical or motor. It is most likely the lack of a retinal fovea and the lack of spatial tuning of neurons in the retina, LGN, and visual cortex that impose such severe limitations on infant vision.

But the infant is far from blind. Martin Banks and Philip Salapatek (1981) have suggested a useful way of thinking about the perceptual limitations of infants. They refer to the amount of information in a pattern that an infant can perceive as his or her visual "window." Early in life, an infant's visual window is quite limited, but the contours of many common objects are well within this "window." The contrast between hair and skin on the mother's face, for example, is readily detectable by young infants. Although infants cannot see objects on the other side of the room, they can see large objects close up—at the distance at which much of the interaction between the young infant and its caretakers takes place.

Pattern Preference

Psychologists have been interested not only in finding out how *well* infants can see, but in finding out what they like to look at. Infants show clear preferences for looking at certain kinds of stimuli. They look longer at a pattern than at a plain surface (Fantz, 1965; Stirnimann, 1944). But too much pattern can make them tune out. Newborns look longer at a pattern made up of a 4-square checkerboard than at a checkerboard of 144 squares (Hershenson, 1964). Infants 3 weeks old also look longer at 4-square patterns than at more complex patterns (Brennan, Ames, and Moore, 1965). But as they get older, they prefer increasingly complex checkerboards (Greenberg, 1971).

When infants are shown a picture of a face, newsprint, a bull's-eye target, and plain red, white, and yellow disks, newborns look longest at the black-and-white face, next longest at the bull's-eye target, and third longest at the newsprint. They look

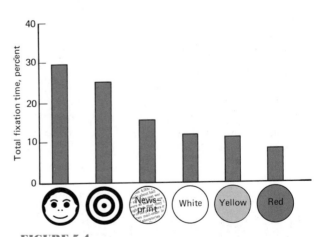

FIGURE 5.4
Robert Fantz (1963) selected 18 infants from 10 hrs. to 5 days old who kept their eyes open long enough to see a stimulus. Of the six circular patterns varying in complexity, they preferred the most complex, that showing a human face.

least of all at the plain red disk (Fantz, 1963)—see Figure 5.4. Is there something about faces that attracts infants, or was this study reflecting infants' preference for moderately complex patterns?

In one study to explore this question, Carolyn Goren and her associates (Goren, Sarty, and Wu, 1975) found that newborns were more likely to turn their heads to follow a picture of a face than an equally complex picture of facial features scrambled into inappropriate positions (see Figure 5.5). This finding suggested that the configuration of the human face was particularly interesting to a newborn. But the finding of the Goren study was not replicated in a subsequent study, with better controls, by Daphne Maurer and Rosemary Young (1983). When these researchers showed newborns normal and scrambled faces, they found no difference in how far infants turned their heads or their eyes to follow the pictures. They suggested that Goren had biased her results by holding the babies on her lap and supporting their heads while she showed them the visual stimuli. Other studies support Maurer and Young's results, showing that infants younger than 2 months do *not* fixate on normal-looking faces in preference to scrambled faces (Fantz, 1961, 1967; Maurer and Barrera, 1981). It is now generally thought that faces have no innate attractiveness but contain attractive elements—like curved contours, a moderate amount of complexity, and movement (Olson, 1983).

Why *do* infants apparently prefer patterns with these characteristics? One suggestion has been that infants prefer a bull's-eye target to a field of stripes because the target includes curved and concentric lines (Fantz and Nevis, 1967). But this does not explain their preference for a 4-square checker-board over a 144-square checkerboard. To account for the checkerboard preferences, psychologists have used the concept of complexity, suggesting that in the early months, infants prefer moderately simple patterns and, as they get older, prefer increasing complexity. But complexity is hard to define. Therefore, some psychologists have suggested simply that infants prefer increasing numbers and decreasing sizes of elements rather than increasing complexity. Unfortunately, this does not explain infants' preference for certain configurations or arrangements of elements. Infants are known to prefer asymmetrical, irregular configurations for example, Another suggestion (Karmel, 1969) has been that infants are attracted to patterns for their "contour density," that is, the number of inches of black-white contrast. But this explanation is limited to patterns that contain contours. None of these explanations satisfies the quest for a single generalization that would describe the entire range of infants' visual preferences. The most recent and comprehensive suggestion to date, made by Banks and Salapatek (1983), is that infants' pattern preferences can be predicted by **linear systems analysis**. In this kind of analysis, the contours and contrasts of elements in a pattern are analyzed into sine waves. Any two-dimensional pattern can be analyzed into a set of sine-wave grating patterns called an "amplitude spectrum." Perception of a pattern is determined both by this amplitude spectrum and by the perceiver's visual acuity and sensitivity to that spectrum (see Figure 5.6).

In an attempt to predict by linear systems analysis the patterns infants prefer, Ilse Gayle and her colleagues at the University of Colorado (Gayl, Roberts, and Werner, 1983) calculated the amplitude spectra for four checkerboard and four randomly checkered patterns. They predicted and found that infants preferred the most salient, or visible, patterns, those with the largest discernible elements and the highest total amplitude that fit their visual "window" and matched their peak of sensitivity to contrast. Linear systems analysis now has been shown to predict the pattern preferences of infants up to 3 months old (Banks and Salapatek, 1983). (After that age, infants' preferences are based on memory and familiarity with objects as well as these perceptual factors.)

Visual Scanning

A second way of finding out what infants like to look at is to photograph their eye movements as they scan their surroundings. Newborns, it has been found, scan in an organized and systematic fashion and do so even when no object or picture is visible. They spend from 5 to 10 percent of their

FIGURE 5.5
Faces used by Goren, Sarty, and Wu, 1975, in testing looking preferences of newborn infants.

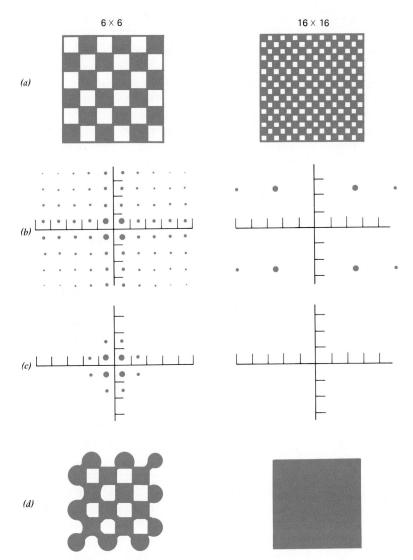

FIGURE 5.6

An example of the application of linear systems analysis. The left column depicts
the technique for a 6 × 6 checkerboard. The right column depicts the technique
for a 16 × 16 checkerboard. The rows depict in sequence, from top to bottom,
how linear systems analysis can be used to predict the outputs for the two checkerboards when processed by a visual system similar to the infant's. (a) The 6 × 6
and 16 × 16 checkerboards. (b) The so-called amplitude spectra of the two checkerboards. The spectra show the spatial frequency, orientation, and amplitude of
the checkerboards' sine-wave components. Each dot represents one component.
Spatial frequency is represented by the distance of the dot from the origin. Orientation is represented by the angle of a vector running from the origin to the dot.
Contrast or amplitude is represented by the area of the dot. (c) The amplitude
spectra of the two checkerboards, once filtered by a visual system sensitive to
frequencies between 0 and 2c/deg only. (d) The resultant appearance of the checkerboards themselves to the infant. Note that the patterning of the 16 × 16 checkerboard is lost but that of the 6 × 6 remains.

waking hours scanning their surroundings (White, 1971), and they scan faces an average of 21 percent of the time they are awake and a person is in view (Bergman, Haith, and Mann, 1971). During their scanning, infants tend to look at contours and corners, their eyes making small movements back and forth across the lines. Marshall Haith (1980) suggests that newborns' visual scanning can be summed up in a few simple rules:

If awake and alert and if the light is not too bright, open eyes.

Look for edges in broad, jerky sweeps of the visual field.

If an edge is found, keep looking in its general vicinity.

Try to look back and forth across the edge.

If this is impossible, search for other edges.

Continue to scan close to the edge.

As babies get older, they scan more extensively. Infants 1 month old fix their gaze on external, outer elements in a stimulus. They might gaze at their mother's hairline, for example. Infants 2 months old are likely to gaze at internal elements as well, so that they are more likely to gaze at their mother's

eyes and mouth (Haith, Bergman, and Moore, 1977; Salapatek, 1975)—see Figure 5.7. This issue seems to be not simple "external" or "internal" per se, however, but the salience of elements. When 1-month-olds were shown patterns in which the internal elements were a bull's-eye target or a checkerboard—highly visible and preferred patterns—they readily distinguished changes in these patterns (Ganon and Swartz, 1980). Because infants have only a limited ability to encode complex patterns, they tend to look at the most salient aspect of a pattern, which is the part that is moving, or largest, or of greatest contrast—and it happens that this is most often the outside contour. Why do infants scan for contrast or salience or, in other terms, prefer patterns with the greatest amplitude spectrum? Haith has suggested that they do so to keep the neurons of the visual cortex firing at a high level. This firing seems to prod the development of the visual cortex. Psychologists know from research with cats, for example, that exposure to patterns and not just to light is necessary for normal development of the visual cortex.

Color

A newborn can see color, brightness, and darkness (Barnet, Lodge, and Armington, 1965). The rods

LOOKING AT MOTHER AND STRANGER

Can 1-month-old infants recognize their own mother by sight? Edward Melhuish (1982), an English psychologist, set out to explore this question. He tested 31 infants between 24 and 35 days old. Each was seated in an observation chamber with cloth sides facing a screen. Through an opening in the screen that was 10 inches in front of the infant, the mother's and a female stranger's face were presented. For each face, the infant saw the following five conditions: (1) face alone, no voice; (2) face and neutral voice; (3) face and affectionate voice; (4) face averted 45°, no voice; and (5) face averted 45°, affectionate voice.

When naive observers tried to tell from videotapes of the infants' visual reactions which faces the infants had recognized, they could not guess be-

yond a chance level. Melhuish concluded that 1-month-olds did not recognize their mothers by sight. But Melhuish had presented his own dark-haired, dark-bearded, pale-skinned face to the infants as a way of checking the observers' accuracy at judging where an infant was looking. As he scored these accuracy tests, he noticed that the infants usually had paid greater attention to his face than to either of the women's faces. He went back and reclassified his data according to the hair color of the mother and the female stranger. (All of the adults were white-skinned.)

This time, Melhuish found that the infants looked significantly longer at dark-haired adults. He concluded that contrast between light and dark is most important in 1-month-olds' visual attention to faces. In any study of infants' attention to mothers or strangers, he went on to suggest, several strangers should be used to avoid contamination of the results by infants' attention to some individual characteristic of the stranger.

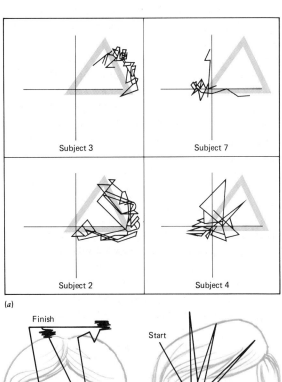

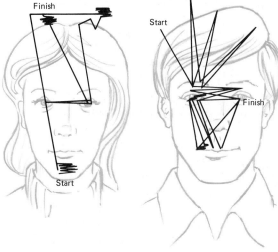

FIGURE 5.7
Infrared marker lights placed behind a stimulus reflect off babies' eyes, permitting the movements of their pupils to be photographed and their visual scanning patterns to be traced. (a) The focus of four newborn babies, looking at a large black triangle, hovered near a vertex and sometimes on the sides forming it (Kessen, 1967). (b) Babies 1 month old when looking at faces concentrated on areas of contrast, the eyes and the edges of the face. Babies 2 months old scanned features, especially the eyes and the mouth (Maurer and Salapatek, 1975).

and cones in the retina, which perceive light, function at, or just after, birth. By 2 to 3 months, infants can discriminate between two patterns on the basis of their color alone. By 3 to 4 months, infants notice the difference between red, blue, green, and yellow. At this age also, the time infants spend looking at these different colors matches adults' ratings of the "pleasantness" of the same colors. These preferences tend to be high for red and blue, low for yellow and green (Bornstein, 1975). Psychologists do not know, however, how acutely infants perceive color differences. If stimuli are presented at one time, infants can discriminate differences in brightness of as little as 5 percent. Adults can discriminate differences of 1 percent in brightness (Bornstein, 1976).

Depth and Distance

Psychologists have long been concerned with whether the ability to judge an object's distance, or depth, from the viewer is innate, that is, present at birth. Because newborn infants have had no experience with objects and have lived in the confining uterus, how can they know about visual cues to distance? Although most studies have failed to find evidence of depth or distance perception in newborns, studies by Thomas Bower (Bower, 1970; Bower, Broughton, and Moore, 1970) suggested that in life-threatening situations, newborns do perceive depth. In these studies, infants were put at the end of a table, and a large box was moved toward them. As the box approached, the infants pulled in their heads, raised their arms protectively, put their hands in front of their faces, and widened their eyes or grew distressed. Bower inferred that when babies saw the box getting larger, they understood that it was getting closer and might harm them. Bower's interpretation remains speculative, however. Another interpretation that has been suggested is that infants were reacting not to an impending collision but were simply moving their arms or heads to parallel the rising or falling contours of the visual stimulus as it got closer (Yonas and Pettersen, 1979).

Other researchers have tested infants' defensive reactions to objects that seem to be coming toward them on a collision course and that then veer away, using blinking to indicate a defensive reaction to an impending collision. Linda Pettersen, Albert

This young fellow is clearly aware of depth and does not want to venture from the "safe" runway of the "visual cliff."

Yonas, and Robert Fisch (1980) tested two groups of 6-week-old infants for their reactions to a triangle that loomed toward them. One group of infants had been born at full term, and one group had been born 3 to 4 weeks after term. It was found that full-term infants blinked on only 16 percent of the approaches but that the postterm infants blinked at 75 percent of the approaches. The researchers believe that their results argue strongly that defensive reactions to impending collisions develop according to an inborn maturational plan and are not learned forms of behavior.

In other studies of infants' depth perception, a **visual cliff** has been used (see photo). Infants old enough to crawl are put on a slightly raised runway in the center of a large glass table several feet high. On one side of the runway, a checkerboard pattern is fixed to the underside of the glass. On the other side, the checkerboard extends from the runway toward the floor, creating the illusion of a steep drop. Infants are beckoned by their mothers to cross the glass over what looks to be a cliff. In one study with 6- to 14-month-olds, the infants would not cross the cliff, but they would cross the glass on the other side of the runway (Gibson and Walk, 1960).

But what about younger infants? In a study of 2- to 4-month-olds by Joseph Campos and his associates (Campos, Langer, and Krowitz, 1970), infants were placed on their stomachs on the cliff side. Their heart rates slowed noticeably, they cried less, and they were more attentive to what lay below them—all signs that they may have perceived the drop-off beneath them, although they were not frightened by it. Some research scientists remain skeptical, however, that these findings prove that infants so young have depth perception. An alternative explanation for the slowed heart rate and other signs is that the infants were responding to a perceived difference in the patterns' contour density or salience rather than to depth or distance. Alternative explanations for older infants' hesitation to cross the visual cliff also have been raised. John Richards and Nancy Rader (1981) tested 7- to 13-month-old infants on a visual cliff. All of the infants crossed the shallow side, but the longer an infant had been crawling, the more likely he or she was to cross the cliff side. The researchers speculated that infants who had developed the ability to crawl very early (before 6½ months) were guided by their sense of touch and that they were therefore more likely to follow the tactile cues from the glass surface and to continue crawling over the visual cliff. They did not look at the surface they were crawling on. But less experienced crawlers were guided by visual rather than tactile cues, and they refused to cross the visual cliff.

Yet another approach to exploring the origins of depth perception uses tests of **stereopsis,** the ability of the two eyes to perceive depth when two pictures of an object are presented to the two eyes at slight distances from each other. Adults have stereoscopic vision and are known to perceive such pictures as three-dimensional or as having depth. Researchers have looked for depth-appropriate responses to stereoscopic displays in infants. Bower (Bower, 1971, 1972; Bower et al., 1970) has found that infants as young as 1 week old reach for a stereoscopically presented object and seem distressed when their sense of touch tells them there is nothing there. But these results have not been replicated in other studies (Dodwell, Muir, and DiFranco, 1976; Ruff and Halton, 1977) and may not be reliable.

Another way to test when infants begin to perceive depth is to investigate their monocular (single eye) sensitivity to depth cues, such as linear perspective. Linear perspective cues are those used by artists to render three-dimensional perspective to a two-dimensional drawing. After putting a patch over one eye for each subject, one group of researchers tested where infants would reach for a

FIGURE 5.8
Infant reaching for the side of a "trapezoidal window" that appears to be closer to her.

trapezoidal "window," a two-dimensional cutout of a window that looked as if the long end of the window was closer than the short end (see Figure 5.8). Adults viewing the trapezoidal window with one eye think that its longer end is nearer; so apparently do 7-month-olds. However, 5-month-olds did not use linear perspective cues when viewing with one eye. In a second study, Ruth Kaufman, Joan Maland, and Albert Yonas (1981) used the same trapezoidal window, but now the window was presented to the infants at a 45° angle. Adults had reported that when the window was at an angle like this, its long (farther) end looked closer than the short (nearer) end. By measuring which end infants reached for, the researchers found that 5-month-olds reached consistently toward the near end of the display and showed no significant differences in reaching for the trapezoid and a control display that gave no illusion of depth. Infants 7 months old reached more often toward the nearer side of the control display, but they reached toward the near side of the trapezoid only about half of the time. On the basis of these and other studies (see Research Focus: Familiar Size as a Cue to Distance), these researchers concluded that sensitivity to monocular depth cues develops between 5 and 7 months of age.

In trying to sum up what psychologists know about depth perception in general, the welter of conflicting and ambiguous results is a problem. It seems unlikely that infants are born with depth perception as adults have it, however. More likely,

they develop the separate abilities (like accommodation, binocular resolution of disparate images, and sensitivity to linear perspective cues) that make depth perception possible during the first 6 months of life, as their visual and motor systems mature.

HEARING

We know from studies of infants born prematurely that the auditory system can function a few weeks before birth, but we still have only inklings of what is heard in the uterus. Recordings of fetal heartbeats 2 months before birth show that they increase when a sound is presented (Bernard and Sontag, 1947). Newborns clearly are physiologically equipped to hear; their ears have a nearly adult-sized **tympanum** and a well-formed **cochlea** (Northern and Downs, 1974). By placing a small microphone in the uterus early in a mother's labor, after the membranes surrounding the fetus have broken, researchers have been able to learn more about what the unborn baby hears. From experiments in which a loud noise is made at the mother's abdominal wall and the infant's heart rate recorded, it has been concluded that "patterned" sounds elicit a larger response than pure tones do and that the most stimulating sounds are those with the frequencies of the human voice (Macfarlane, 1977).

Although data from various investigations are not completely consistent, after birth it seems that newborns' hearing thresholds are at least 10 to 25 dB higher than those of adults. (A threshold is the lowest level at which a response occurs.) The reasons for this auditory deficiency may be a lack of neural organization, attention, motivation, or sensation. First, the amniotic fluid that remains in the outer ear plus the fluid and residual connective tissue left in the middle ear after birth may impair the newborn's hearing. In the first few days after birth, the outer ear drains and the middle ear absorbs nearly all the fluid and tissue. At that point, researchers can investigate infants' hearing by recording changes in their heartrates or sucking rates or brain-wave patterns when a sound is presented. Studies using these techniques show that newborns can discriminate differences in both loudness and pitch. When **auditory evoked responses (AERs)** from the brainstem of sleeping infants are measured, newborns are found to respond to clicks of 10 to 20 dB loudness. Adults respond to clicks of

5 dB. Brainstem AERs first appear in premature babies at about 28 weeks after conception and approach adult levels as the infants approach full term (Schulman-Galambos and Galambos, 1979; Starr, Amlie, Martin, and Saunders, 1977). When heart rate is the measure, newborns' hearing thresholds range from 48 to 55 dB. The median threshold of measured AERs and heart rates for newborns is 20 to 30 dB, although there are significant differences among individuals (Acredolo and Hake, 1982). Newborns are quite sensitive to changes in pitch. They can detect the difference between tones of 200 to 250 cycles per second (or about one note apart on a musical scale) (Weir, 1976). Over the first year or two of life, the infant's hearing continues to improve.

RESEARCH FOCUS

FAMILIAR SIZE AS A CUE TO DISTANCE

When do infants develop depth perception? What cues do they use to judge depth? Albert Yonas and his colleagues at the University of Minnesota (Yonas, Pettersen, and Granrud, 1982) set about answering those questions by testing infants' sensitivity to pictures of familiar and unfamiliar objects. But first, they asked adult subjects to judge how far away the photographs looked to them. In front of each adult, who had closed his or her eyes, a yardstick was placed across the table for reference. When the adult opened one eye, the display was uncovered, and the adult was asked to judge how far away the picture looked. One group of adults saw pictures of faces (familiar objects); a second group saw pictures of checkerboard patterns (unfamiliar objects). The checkerboards and faces were actually the same sizes; all were 12¾ inches from the viewer.

Adults clearly based their judgment of distance on familiar size. On average, they thought that a picture of a large face was 8.9 inches away and a picture of a small face was 20.6 inches away, whereas the same-sized and same-shaped checkerboards were judged to be 8.5 inches and 11.5 inches away. Thus they judged the large face to be within an infant's reaching distance and the small face to be out of reach. If the infants saw the objects as the adults did, they could be expected to reach more to the large than the small face. The investigators expected no differences in the infants' reaching for the large and small checkerboards, because they were not familiar objects. They expected no differences in infants' reaching for the faces, viewed with two eyes, because stereoscopic vision would show the large and small faces as equally far away.

To test these expectations, Yonas presented 78 infants of 5 months and 78 infants of 7 months with the same pictures as the adults had seen. Only infants whose parents said that they had begun reaching were used as subjects. Each infant was presented with a randomly selected set of pictures portraying a large and a small photograph of the same face. One group of infants viewed one face picture at a time, with only one eye. A second group viewed the large and small face photographs with both eyes. A third group saw photographs of large and small checkerboards with one eye only.

Infants were seated in a canvas infant seat that was placed on a table. The photographs were presented on the tabletop, and a videotape camera recorded the infants' responses. Infants in the monocular conditions wore an eye patch over their left eye. Every time the infant looked at the photograph, the experimenter pushed a button. If an infant's attention wandered, the experimenter tried to redirect it by tapping on the back of the photo. Infants who fussed were taken out of the infant seat and soothed. All of the infants viewed the large and small photographs alternately until they grew too fussy or bored to go on. A baby was considered to have reached for a picture if, while looking at it, he or she moved one or both hands forward with a grasping or swiping motion that crossed a line 4 inches in front of him.

Like the adults, 7-month-olds who had viewed the faces monocularly reached significantly more often and longer for the larger face, suggesting that they perceived the large faces but not the small faces to be within their reach. Younger infants in the binocular and checkerboard comparison groups did not differentiate between the large and small photographs. This study shows that sensitivity to familiar size is one more way of judging depth or distance that develops between 5 and 7 months of age.

Speech Perception

Of special interest to developmental psychologists has been the infant's ability to perceive not just clicks and tones but the sounds of speech. Newborns have lower thresholds for sounds in the range of speech (1000 to 3000 Hz) (Eisenberg, 1965, 1979; Hoversten and Moncur, 1969). Although they show large body movements and a speeded up heartbeat when listening to single tones and noises, when they hear patterned sounds, like speech or sequences of tones, newborns show fine movements, such as grimaces, crying (or stopping crying), dilation of the pupils, and searching with their eyes for the source of the sound (Eisenberg, 1976, 1979). By 2 weeks of age, infants notice the difference between a human voice and other sounds, such as the sound of a bell. At 4 weeks, they can discriminate between **phonemes**—the smallest meaningful units of a language—as similar as /b/ and /p/. In a study by Peter Eimas and his colleagues (Eimas, Siqueland, Jusczyk, and Vigorito, 1971), babies at first sucked diligently on a nipple that turned on a recording of the /bah/ sounds. But after they had heard the sound repeatedly, they grew accustomed to it and sucked less. Gradually the recording changed to a /pah/ sound. When the sound was clearly /pah/ and not something intermediate, the babies sucked harder again. The study showed that infants can process sounds into categories.

Infants 5 months old have demonstrated their ability to discriminate between a naturally and a synthetically produced /baba/ (Trehub and Curran, 1979). They paid attention longer to the natural sound. By the age of 1 year, infants can discriminate all phonemic contrasts. The evidence suggests that infants actually process speech and nonspeech sounds differently, not simply that they have extremely sharp hearing. In one experiment, for example, the ability of 1½-month-olds to distinguish between /ba/ and /ga/ depended on whether the sounds they heard were spoken or simulated (Morse, 1972).

Within the first month, the basic sensory mechanisms are present for discriminating categories of sounds. This sensory ability seems to be innate rather than learned; it exists prior to the infant's exposure to much language. Cross-language studies (e.g., Lasky, Syrdal-Lasky, and Klein, 1975; Trehub, 1973) show that infants from many different linguistic backgrounds can discriminate between certain highly distinctive phonemes. The effects of learned abilities to discriminate do not show up for several months after birth. The fact that young infants can discriminate foreign-speech contrasts to which adult speakers are less sensitive suggests that adults have had long practice at learning not to hear many sounds that are insignificant in their native language.

Although scientists still do not know exactly which innate mechanisms govern infants' ability to discriminate categories of sounds, empirical evidence from humans and animals suggests that they do not discriminate according to phonetics. The reason infants discriminate among categories of sounds seems to be that some acoustical attributes are more salient than others rather than that humans have some specialized "speech processor." First, human infants discriminate among categories of nonspeech sounds as well as speech sounds (Jusczyk, Rosner, Cutting, Foard, and Smith, 1977, 1980). Second, animal subjects such as chinchillas as well as humans discriminate among speech categories (Kuhl, 1981).

Even though infants *can* discriminate between speech sounds like /pah/ and /bah/ psychologists still do not have the answer to how babies actually segment the speech they hear. Do they segment it into phonemes, syllables, words, all of these or none of them? Although they have demonstrated that infants *can* discriminate between syllables like /bah/ and /pah/, phonemes like /b/ and /p/, and words like *ball* and *Paul*, they have not yet demonstrated whether infants *do* divide the speech stream they hear in these ways. At some point, we know, infants must begin to segment speech in some meaningful way, or they would never learn to talk. But they may not begin until they have communication as their goal and have received feedback about the meaning of their utterances. It seems plausible that syllables or single-syllable words may be the first divisions infants make (Bertoncini and Mehler, 1981). Finer distinctions, like the categorization into phonemes, may not happen until children are learning to read (Jusczyk, 1977; Liberman, Shankweiler, Fischer, and Carter, 1974).

Infants do seem to show "perceptual constancy" for speech sounds. Evidence for this comes from a study of 1- to 4-month-old infants who learned to discriminate between the phonetically contrasting /a/ and /i/ sounds and then were observed to "sort" sounds into these two categories even when they were uttered by different speakers or with different intonations (Kuhl, 1979). The same ability to categorize sounds has been observed for differences in consonants and pitch contour (Kuhl, 1980; Kuhl and Hillenbrand, 1979).

RESEARCH FOCUS

CATEGORIZATION OF VOWEL SOUNDS

Patricia Kuhl (1983) of the University of Washington wanted to find out whether preverbal infants could categorize sounds as either /a/ as in "cot" or /ɔ/ as in "caught," one of the most difficult vowel contrasts in English. She reasoned that if infants could categorize sounds as being one or the other of these two vowels, it could be reasonably inferred that they could categorize sounds into other vowel contrasts also. Her subjects were four infants between 5½ and 6 months old. With a computer, she synthesized the two vowel sounds. For each she synthesized a falling pitch, such as occurs in declarative sentences, and a rising pitch, such as occurs in questions, and each vowel was synthesized to sound like a child's, a woman's, and a man's voice. Her goal was to find out whether infants would perceive the same vowel (e.g., /a/) as equivalent when it was spoken in these different ways and as different from the other vowel (i.e., /ɔ/).

Each infant was held by his or her parent and faced Kuhl's assistant. The assistant held the infant's attention straight ahead by shaking a silent toy. At 90° to the assistant was a loudspeaker, in front of which was a mechanical toy—a monkey clapping cymbals, a bear banging a drum, or a dog wagging its tail. The mechanical toy was in a dark plastic box at the infant's eye level, and only when lights went on and the toy was activated could the infant see it. First, the infants were trained to turn their head whenever a vowel sound, spoken in the simulated man's voice and repeated every 2 seconds changed to the other vowel sound also spoken in the simulated man's voice. If both the experimenter and the assistant judged that the infant's head had turned during a 6-second trial, the mechanical toy was activated for 3 seconds to reinforce the head turning. To rule out inadvertent cues from the adults, assistant and parent both wore earphones that played music.

After the infants had learned to turn their heads when they heard a change in the vowel sound, they were presented with variations in pitch contour, from rising to falling, or vice versa, and with variations in speaker: male, female, and child.

To demonstrate that they could hear the difference between /a/ and /ɔ/, despite changes in speaker or pitch contour, the infants had to get 9 out of 10 consecutive trials correct. It took them an average of 5½ sessions to complete the whole test. But infants did indeed learn to turn their heads when /a/ changed to /ɔ/, regardless of the distractors of speaker and pitch, suggesting that infants perceive categorical equivalents for vowel sounds.

In a second part of the study, Kuhl analyzed the performance of eight new infants on recognizing each vowel the first time it was presented after the initial training. With this more stringent test of equivalence, there were marked individual differences: half the infants did well; half did not. The latter infants generalized across speakers but not across changes in pitch contour.

This study suggests that 6-month-old infants can perceive equivalent as categories that conform to vowel categories. They demonstrate vowel constancy across changes in speaker and, to a lesser extent, pitch contour, and they can probably do so for all vowels in English. Although infants do seem to categorize vowels, psychologists still have to learn the acoustical rule on which they proceed. Furthermore, as the vowels presented to an infant sound more alike and therefore are more difficult to distinguish, individual differences in infants' abilities to distinguish them grow larger. In this study, with a very different contrast, half of the infants did very well (91 percent correct during training); half did poorly (40 percent correct). Psychologists do not yet know whether these individual differences arise from differences in general intelligence, language skills, or perceptual abilities.

COORDINATION OF LOOKING AND LISTENING

We have described the abilities of infants in the two separate domains: vision and hearing. But in real life, seeing and hearing occur simultaneously, and people integrate the information from both domains to make sense of their world. One way they do this is by looking to locate the source of a sound. Even newborn infants do this in a rudimentary way. In one study of 2- to 4-day-old infants, conducted by Darwin Muir and Jeffery Field (1979), a tape-recorded rattle sounded from one of two loudspeakers on either side of the infant. Three-quarters of the time, infants turned toward the source of the sound, although it took them about 2½ seconds to begin responding and nearly 6 seconds to turn their heads fully. This study was important for several reasons. It measured not only how infants turned their eyes but also their heads; it allowed them the long response time they apparently required for locating a sound; and it kept the infants alert while they listened to the sound. Oddly enough, during the second and third months of life, infants less often turned their head toward a sound, although in the fourth month the response reappeared strongly (Muir, Abraham, Forbes, and Harris, 1979).

Infants coordinate their visual and auditory systems in other ways as well. One series of studies by Elizabeth Spelke (1976, 1978, 1979a, 1979b) has shown that 4-month-olds synchronize a sound track with the more appropriate of two films. When they were shown a film of a bouncing toy donkey on one screen and a bouncing toy kangaroo on the other, 4-months-olds preferred to watch the film of the animal that was bouncing in time to a projected sound track. In tests to determine whether the infants were attracted by the similar rates of bouncing and sound or the fact that sight and sound were synchronized, it was found that the infants were responding to the synchronization. Thus infants can link sight and sound. Another demonstration of this ability is research showing that infants 15 weeks and older link a parent's voice to the correct parent (Spelke and Owsley, 1979).

TASTE AND SMELL

Newborns can distinguish water, sugar, and salt

Almost everyone responds to baby cuteness, the round face, chubby cheeks, and snub nose of the young infant.

solutions from milk, and they show different responses to different concentrations of sweet, salty, and bitter solutions (Ganchrow, Steiner, and Daher, 1983; Jensen, 1932). Lewis Lipsitt and his associates (Lipsitt, Reilly, Butcher, and Greenwood, 1976) found that newborns sucked longer and paused for shorter periods when they were given a sweet solution. They also sucked more slowly, as if they were savoring the sweetness. In addition to sucking, newborns smile and lick their upper lip when given a sweet solution (Ganchrow et al., 1983).

Newborns are also equipped with a good sense of smell, although their levels of discrimination are not as fine as they will be later. Infants will turn away from a noxious odor, such as ammonia. They have also been observed to distinguish other odors. They breathe faster and move around more when they smell asafetida, which has a garlic-like odor, than when an odorless solution is put under their noses (Lipsitt, Engen, and Kaye, 1963). They turn their faces toward a sweet smell, and their heart rates and respiration slow down (Brazelton, 1969).

TABLE 5.3
PERCEPTUAL-COGNITIVE MILESTONES OF INFANTS

0 to 1 week:

- see patterns, light, dark
- are sensitive to the location of sounds
- can distinguish volume and pitch
- prefer high voices
- will grasp object if they touch it accidentally
- stop sucking to look at a person momentarily

1-4 weeks:

- become excited at sight of person or toy
- look at objects only if in their line of vision and for short periods
- prefer patterns to any color, brightness, or size
- coordinate eyes sideways, up and down
- can follow a toy from side to center of body

4-8 weeks:

- prefer people to objects
- stare at human face, become quiet to human voice
- link particular behavior with particular people— meals with caregiver, etc.
- startle at sounds and make a facial response
- reach out voluntarily instead of grasping reflexively
- can focus on large or moving objects at several feet
- can perceive depth
- can coordinate eye movements in a circle when looking at light or an object
- discriminate voices, people, tastes, and objects

9-12 weeks:

- follow moving object with eye for at least 10 seconds
- glance from one object to another
- distinguish near objects from those distant
- stop sucking to listen
- search with eyes for sound
- become aware of self through exploration of face, eyes, mouth
- show signs of memory in waiting for expected rewards (like feeding), in recognizing and differentiating family members

4 to 7 months:

- see world in color and with near-adult vision, with lens of eye adjusting to objects at varying distances
- can pull dangling objects toward them, bring object to mouth
- follow dangling or moving objects
- are alert 1 or 2 hours at a time
- turn to follow sound, vanishing object
- visually search out fast-moving or fallen objects, familiar objects
- become aware of and compare size differences of similar objects
- begin to anticipate a whole object by seeing only part
- deliberately imitate sounds and movements
- remember a segment representative of an entire situation
- can recall short series of actions if series includes their own and is in immediate past
- show interest in consequences of their own actions
- look briefly for a toy that disappears

8 to 12 months:

- put small objects into and out of containers
- search behind screen for an object if they see it hidden
- can hold and manipulate one object while looking at a second
- recognize dimensions of objects
- recognize regions of differing depth
- can reach behind themselves for a toy without seeing it

By 1 year of age:

- group objects by shape and color
- have a clear perception of objects as detached and separate
- can relate objects in time and space
- search for object even if they have not seen it hidden
- remember only where object was last seen
- imitate more deliberately, even absent models
- may begin to process actions mentally before acting them out
- solve simple problems

Within days, breast-fed newborns distinguish and prefer the odor of their mother's milk to that of another mother's milk (Russell, 1976).

LEARNING: CLASSICAL AND OPERANT CONDITIONING

Motor skills and perceptual information provide the basis for early mental activity. Learning moves development ahead. Two kinds of learning that have been investigated experimentally in infants are classical conditioning and operant conditioning. In classical conditioning, the subject makes a response to a stimulus that did not originally cause it, because the stimulus has been repeatedly paired with, actually closely preceded by, another stimulus to which the subject innately makes the response. In Pavlov's classic experiment, food caused a dog to salivate, an innate response; but then for a number of feedings a bell was rung before the dog was fed. The dog eventually salivated at the sound of the bell. The conditioned response resembles, in less intense form, the original innate, unconditioned response.

In the second kind of learning, operant conditioning, the subject makes a response more frequently because it brings or has brought a reward. In this manner, pigeons have been trained to peck at red keys in bombers and chimps to push the right buttons in space capsules, to get to their favorite foods.

Conditioning experiments have been done with infants in an attempt to determine what kinds of infant behavior can be learned and how early. A substantial number of these experiments with very young infants have failed to produce conditioning. As Arnold Sameroff and Patrick Cavanaugh (1979) point out, working with newborns in such experiments is at best difficult and at worst frustrating. Whenever a researcher has reported some interesting result, a second researcher has been unable to obtain the same result. Often experiments have been done with small samples, with fewer than 10 babies in a group, or without taking each infant's state of wakefulness into consideration. The infant must be in an awake, alert, and active state—not drowsy, crying, or even quiet—for conditioning to occur. After reviewing all the studies of newborn

conditioning, Sameroff and Cavanaugh conclude that it is questionable whether classical conditioning can occur with newborns at all. Operant conditioning is more successful.

Sameroff (1968) himself found that the operant response of sucking, on a nipple that the experimenter controlled, could be made more frequent or stronger if only fast or strong sucking was rewarded with milk. He also found that infants could learn to change their sucking strategy from biting to negative pressure, and vice versa, to keep the milk flowing. In another example of successful infant operant conditioning, Einar Siqueland and Lewis Lipsitt (1966) were able, after half an hour, to make newborns turn their heads to one side or the other 75 percent of the time by brushing their cheeks and giving them a bottle with sugar water to suck for 2 seconds every time they turned their head. Earlier, the rooting reflex had been weak, as it usually is right after birth, occurring only about 25 percent of the time. The success of these experiments depended on two reflexes, sucking and rooting. Successful newborn operant conditioning apparently always involves as responses existing behavior that is connected with the survival of the infant.

The reflexes of the newborn may be conditionable, Sameroff and Cavanaugh suggest, because through them the newborn is physiologically "prepared" to be affected by environmental stimulation and reinforcement. In fact the operant learning that is apparent in the newborn in these experiments may not be the same as the conditioning that occurs with adults. It may be a more fundamental developmental adaptation of the reflexes.

The behavior of infants 3 months and older consists of more than just reflexes and therefore is more modifiable. Consequently, more of their behavior can be conditioned. The frequency of vocalizing, smiling, looking, reaching, pressing, touching, for example, have all been modified in conditioning experiments. But even at this age the infant has apparently been prepared by past experience or predisposition to give the response that is to be conditioned.

In one experiment (Cavanaugh and Davidson, 1977) 6-month-old infants were seated before a clear plexiglass panel on which they could press; they were on occasion able to see a multicolored light display and hear a bell ring. There were three groups in the experiment. Infants in Group 1 saw a light display behind the plexiglass panel and heard a bell *every* time they pressed the panel; those in Group 2 saw the light display behind the panel and heard the bell as often as those in Group 1, but lights and sound were not related to when they pressed; infants in Group 3 saw a light display *every* 20 seconds, but it was not behind the plexiglass panel. Infants in *all three* groups increased their panel pressing, whether or not lights and sound followed their pressing. They had already pressed buttons, busy boxes, and buzzers countless

---

REINFORCEMENT OF INFANTS' VOCALIZATION

Many researchers have investigated operant conditioning in infants. Often they have contrasted what happens when a behavior is contingently reinforced with what happens when it is no longer reinforced. But this experimental design raises problems. The first problem is that infants tend to cry a great deal during extinction, or nonreinforcement, phases of an experiment. The second is that the design does not separate the effects of elicitation of a response from the effects of reinforcement of a response. In experiments on infant vocalization, for instance, the social stimulation used as a *reinforcer* is also an *elicitor* of infant vocalization, and in the extinction phase lack of elicitation as well as lack of reinforcement might cause decreased vocalization. Claire Poulson (1983) wanted to demonstrate that reinforcement would increase the frequency of infants' vocalization. She reasoned that she could do so by showing that vocalization rate increased during continuous reinforcement of vocalization and decreased when a behavior other than vocalization was contingently reinforced.

The subjects in Poulson's study were four infants between 2½ and 3 months old who were seen once a day for 21 to 27 sessions. The sessions were conducted two to four times a week for 37 to 77 days. Infants were placed in a carseat facing a playhouse with a window that opened and closed. Mothers were asked to do what they normally did to get their infant to "talk" to them whenever the window was open. Experimental sessions were 12 minutes long. They were interrupted if the infant fussed or cried for a minute or fell asleep.

The rates of infants' vocalization were recorded under two conditions of social reinforcement. During the continuous reinforcement-of-vocalizations condition, the window opened as soon as the baby vocalized, and the parent stimulated the baby socially for 8 seconds by making eye contact, talking, touching, or showing toys to the baby. During the reinforcement of other-than-vocalizations condition, the window opened every 2 seconds for 8 seconds of social stimulation from the mother, so long as the baby did *not* vocalize. If the baby vocalized, the window did not open until there had been at least 4 seconds of silence. During both conditions, if the baby vocalized during the social reinforcement, there were no differential consequences. Fussing or crying were treated as vocalizations but were not counted as vocalizations during data analysis. Distinct voiced sounds, excluding fussing, crying, sneezing, belching, or hiccoughing were considered vocalizations for the analyses.

Infants served as their own controls and were subject to both experimental conditions. Each condition remained in effect until the data showed a stable pattern and then shifted to the other condition. The dependent measure was the infant's rate of vocalizations per minute while the playhouse window was closed. (Because parents could vary the time that the window was open, the experimenter could not include the vocalizations when the window was open.) Graphs of the infants' vocalization rates per minute showed that all of them vocalized significantly more during the reinforcement-of-vocalization condition than the reinforcement-of-other-than-vocalization condition.

In sum, mothers' social stimulation of their infants' vocalizations had controlled them through reinforcement rather than simple elicitation. Each infant vocalized significantly more when vocalization was being reinforced, even though amount of social stimulation during the reinforcement-of-other condition was equal to, or higher than, that in the reinforcement condition. This study clearly demonstrates that the frequency of infants' vocalization can be affected directly by contingent social reinforcement.

times; thus when faced with an interesting stimulus in front of them, they responded by reaching out and pressing. But there was some learning in the experiment. When the lights and bell sound were discontinued in the extinction phase of the study, the infants in Group 1, who had seen the lights and heard the bell after pressing the panel, did less pressing than they had before the experiment. Their original level of response had been modified by the experiment.

MEMORY

The fact that very young infants can be operantly conditioned to turn their heads towards an interesting display of lights suggests that they remember the consequences of their actions. To find out how much and how long infants remember, researchers have used several different methods. In the **paired comparison** procedure, infants repeatedly see two stimulus patterns, one on the left and one on the right. They then see, in the testing sessions, a novel stimulus, either to the left or to the right, and the familiar stimulus on the other side. The side on which the novel stimulus appears must be carefully varied, for infants tend generally to look longer and more frequently to the right. A difference in the amounts of time that infants look at the new stimulus and at the old—they will look alternately at both—indicates that they remember the old.

By delaying the testing sessions for a period of time, experimenters can assess how long an infant can remember the stimulus. The paired-comparison procedure has indicated that 1-month-old infants remember nursery mobiles for up to 24 hours (Weizmann, Cohen, and Pratt, 1971) and that 5-month-old infants recognize visual patterns after 48 hours and photographs of faces after 2 weeks (Fagan, 1973).

With the **habituation** method, infants are repeatedly shown one visual stimulus until they spend little time looking at it, and it has become boring. Then a new stimulus is presented alternately with this familiar one. The speed with which habituation occurs and the difference in the amounts of time infants spend looking at the stimuli are the measures of memory. Using this method, researchers have found that the older infants are, the more rapidly they habituate. The speed of habituation has been found to

be related to indicators or predictors of adequate development. Fast habituation is related to a high Apgar score, absence of medication at birth, good central nervous system function, good performance on learning tasks, high socioeconomic status, and high IQ (Lewis, 1971).

A third method of testing infants' memory focuses on their retention of a learned response. Studies have shown that in their first and second months of life infants can remember a learned response from one day to the next (Papousek, 1959, 1961, 1967; Weizmann et al., 1971). Infants 3 months old can remember even longer. Carolyn Rovee-Collier and her associates (Rovee-Collier, Sullivan, Enright, and Lucas, 1980) placed 3-month-olds in their own crib at home with a ribbon tying one of their feet to a lever that activated a mobile. Getting the mobile to move reinforced the infants' efforts. The infants spent two sessions, a day apart, learning to operate the mobile. During each session, 9 minutes of reinforcement were followed by 3 minutes of nonreinforcement, when the mobile was in view but detached from the lever and therefore stationary. Hypothesizing that infants' memories of this learning experience could be **reactivated** if they later were exposed to stimuli from the original training sessions, Rovee-Collier gave the infants another brief (3 minute) session with the mobile after an interval of 2 or 4 weeks. As predicted, when the infants were tested 24 hours after the brief reactivation treatment, they clearly remembered how to operate the mobile. These studies all suggest that by the age of 3 months, if not earlier, infants can remember what they have learned over several weeks, and their memories can be jogged by reminders of the learning experience.

With older infants, several studies have demonstrated excellent long-term memories even without reminders. In a study that used the habituation model, Joseph Fagan (1973) presented various stimuli—photographs of faces, three-dimensional face masks, small patterns, and others—to infants between 21 and 25 weeks old. When the infants were tested for their memory of these stimuli over intervals of up to 2 weeks, they had excellent retention for most of the stimuli. Only the face mask seemed hard to remember. Studies that have tested shorter intervals of retention generally confirm the finding that infants between 3 and 6 months remember well over this period (Cornell, 1979; Martin, 1975).

Is the information infants remember after 1 or 2 weeks the same as what they remember right away? Infants 5 months old were brought to a laboratory and shown a three-dimensional figure made of styrofoam (Strauss and Cohen, 1978). They were tested for their memory of the figure right away, again after 10 minutes, and again after 24 hours by comparing it with another figure that was different in shape, size, color, and orientation. Immediately after seeing the styrofoam figure, all the infants remembered all four of these elements. But after 10 minutes, they remembered only the color and form of the figure. After 24 hours, they remembered only its form. It is possible that these results represent a hierarchical ordering in memory for objects. Form may be more salient and therefore more memorable than color, and both may be more salient than shape or orientation.

IMITATION

The important question of whether infants can imitate behavior that they see modeled has sparked a lively debate among researchers. Kenneth Kaye and Janet Marcus (1978) studied imitation in 6-month-old babies. When the babies were allowed to control when and how many times the adult model made particular mouth movements, they imitated these movements selectively and systematically. The babies controlled the model's behavior, in that the model only made the mouth movements when the babies looked at her eyes. The researchers divided the mouth movements into five elements. Mouth movements consisted of a burst of five openings and closings of the mouth, each opening preceded by a popping sound. The five elements analyzed were: (1) the rhythm of the sequence, (2) the number of movements, (3) the open-and-close movement, (4) movement of the mouth, and (5) the popping sound. Imitation of

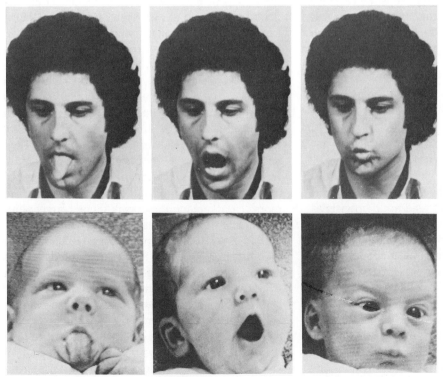

These photographs, well selected by Andrew Meltzoff and Keith Moore, show a 2-week-old apparently imitating an adult experimenter's tongue protrusion, open mouth, and lip protrusion.

any *one* of these elements, the researchers suggested, could be reflexive. But a systematic adaptation by the infant to the whole complex pattern would indicate true imitation. They found that during the course of a session, they could observe progressive phases of the babies' responses to the model. Babies first grew less active as they oriented to the model. Then they imitated single elements of the mouth movements, at first moving their mouths just a bit. Then they tried combinations of elements, until finally they opened and closed their mouths several times, complete with noise and rhythm.

So imitation does seem to occur by 6 months of age. But the question in this area has been at what age infants *first* imitate. In one controversial study, Andrew Meltzoff and Keith Moore (1977) got babies in their first 2 weeks of life to imitate various facial gestures shown to them by an adult: sticking out the tongue, protruding the lips, and opening the mouth. Meltzoff and Moore argued that this early imitation showed that babies have innate sensorimotor coordination that allows them to match their movements with those of another person and that they have some knowledge of this matching. Kaye and Marcus argued back that the early mouth imitations were more like reflexes:

While it may be important that such a response in the first few months of life should have evolved in a species for which the mouth later plays several crucial social roles, it is no more remarkable than other neonatal reflexes or, for example, the pecking responses of a herring gull chick to a red spot on its mother's beak (Kaye and Marcus, 1978, p. 142).

They state that the photographs Meltzoff and Moore presented (see p. 195) did not demonstrate "systematic accommodation" of the baby's mouth to the mouth movements of the model. Only that kind of demonstration, they argued, would prove that the newborn's response was imitative rather than reflexive.

Meltzoff and Moore (1983b) came back with another investigation of newborns' abilities to imitate an adult's facial gestures. Babies less than 3 days old were tested for their ability to imitate a model who opened his mouth or stuck out his tongue. This time, the reactions were videotaped, and an observer who did not know which gesture

the babies had seen rated the expressions of the babies. Again Meltzoff and Moore concluded that infants match the gestures shown to them. Similarly, an investigation by Tiffany Field and her associates (Field, Woodson, Greenberg, and Cohen, 1982) of 74 infants whose average age was 36 hours suggested that they can imitate facial expressions of happiness, sadness, and surprise. Naive observers rated the infants' responses from a videotape of the sessions. These observers correctly guessed that infants were imitating surprise on 76 percent of the trials, happiness on 58 percent, and sadness on 59 percent. Field and her associates conclude that their findings support those of Meltzoff and Moore: that newborns have an innate ability to compare and match behavior that they have seen.

Unfortunately, neither of these studies takes Kaye and Marcus's comments into account, and what is more problematical, several other investigators have not been able to replicate the results. Beryl McKenzie and Ray Over (1983b) tested 14 babies between 9 and 30 days old. They modeled facial and arm gestures, such as mouth opening, tongue protrusion, bringing hand to face, moving hand to and from the midline of the body. When 16 judges tried to identify which gesture the model had demonstrated, they found only weak and statistically insignificant relationships between the modeled behavior and that of the infants. McKenzie and Over concluded that their results were not consistent with claims that newborns can imitate gestures of the face and hands. Similarly, Jean Koepke and her associates (Koepke, Hamm, Legerstee, and Russell, 1983b) tried to replicate Meltzoff and Moore's findings. In one experiment they modeled sticking out lips and tongue, opening the mouth, and moving the fingers. They corrected for an effect of experimenter bias in this procedure, which they felt had contaminated Meltzoff and Moore's findings. Their subjects were six 2-week-old babies. Naive judges rated the infants' responses from videotapes of the sessions. In a second experiment with 14 babies between 17 and 21 days old, mouth opening and tongue protrusion were modeled. These researchers found no evidence of imitation by the infants they studied.

In the next round, Meltzoff and Moore (1983a) shot back that procedures like McKenzie and Over's, which failed to replicate the earlier findings of newborn imitation, in fact failed to demonstrate that the infants were watching or reacting to the adult model, much less imitating that model. In reply, McKenzie and Over (1983a) argued that Meltzoff and Moore's criticisms of their method were unfounded and that the infants did indeed attend to the model. Jean Koepke (Koepke et al., 1983a) fired back at Meltzoff and Moore that they had failed to reply to charges of experimenter bias in their work. Perhaps the infants had been influenced by the model in subtle ways, and these explained why Meltzoff and Moore's findings could not be replicated in other settings. Meltzoff and Moore argued that their second experiment, in which an adult had modeled only two forms of behavior and had kept his face impassive between times, corrected for any experimeter bias that might have crept into their first procedure. The question of what facial expressions newborn infants can even see—given the serious limitations of their visual acuity that we have discussed—does tend to undermine the believability of Meltzoff and Moore's claims of newborn imitation, however. The debate continues, and the question of whether newborn babies can imitate remains open. It is unlikely to be settled soon—but try sticking out your tongue at the next new baby you see.

SOCIAL RELATIONS

The human infant appears to be a helpless creature. Yet babies come into the world with formidable capacities to establish social relations. These capacities ensure their physical survival and their social nurturance. From the moment of birth, the infant is an active participant in a world prepared to support and foster social inclinations. By means of his or her sociability, the infant constructs a social world and is formed as an individual.

In the first minutes of life the newborn sees, hears, and moves, and these behaviors of the newborn are linked with those of the mother. The increasingly coordinated interactions of the two can be viewed as a "dance." Their behavior is synchronized so that each response strengthens their relationship and stimulates the baby's development. At first the mother is like Fred Astaire dancing with a hat rack—she must take the lead. The baby affects the mother and participates in the dance,

but the newborn's behavior is social only because the mother responds to it as such. Soon, each is influencing the other in a series of "feedback loops." In a few short months the infant is initiating as well as following.

THE FIRST MEETING

Look at his little face. His little nails. Oh. His little squashed-up nose like your nose. He has red hair.

Little baby got big feet—he has got big feet, hasn't he?

He's blowing bubbles. His little hands are all wrinkled—looks like he's done the washing up, doesn't he?
Yes (laughs). *Oh dear!*

Oh, he's opened his eyes, there—look.
Hello (as baby opens his eyes for the first time)!

(Macfarlane, 1977, pp. 91, 94, 95)

Mother and infant, when they first see each other, are not truly strangers meeting for the first time; their history of prenatal connectedness only intensifies the moment for the mother. The behavior of most mothers who have been observed in their first meeting with their infant follows a common pattern. The mother starts to get acquainted by tentatively touching the infant's fingertips, then its arms and legs. Within a few minutes she makes palm contact with the baby's trunk and proceeds to massage and stroke the baby's body (Klaus, Kennell, Plumb, and Zuehlke, 1970). She looks at her infant and establishes eye-to-eye contact. Even immediately after birth the infant will follow her face. Mothers of blind infants report feeling "lost" because they cannot satisfy the urge to have their babies look back at them (Fraiberg, 1974). What is so special about that first meeting right after birth? The infant remains in a quiet, alert state with open eyes for close to an hour after birth. Then however the baby goes into a deep sleep, usually for 3 or 4 hours. So the first hour, when the baby is alert, awake, and capable of following the mother visually, can be an important time.

It is also a time of heightened receptivity for the mother. Because of elevated hormone levels and other physiological factors, she is on the qui vive for cues from her infant, alert to the baby's signals. The mother talks to her infant, and some observers claim that the newborn moves in time with her words. Seeing her infant moving and looking at her face, the mother is encouraged to continue to engage her baby. If labor has been relaxed and the mother is able to hold her baby immediately, her feelings of satisfaction with the first sight of her baby are enhanced; and later she is more likely to continue breast feeding (Klaus and Kennell, 1976; Newton and Newton, 1972). If during initial contact the infant's attentiveness is temporarily depressed by medication, seeds of doubt may be planted in the mother's mind and color her attitude toward her child. But if the baby is attentive and the mother is able to welcome and encourage the first eye movements and attempts to suckle, their relationship is off to a very good start.

THE MOTHER-CHILD BOND

Even before the moment of birth, the mother has a unique feeling for her infant, a feeling that usually develops into a deep bond as the baby becomes older. For most mothers this bond is so great that it enables her to make unusual sacrifices necessary for the care of the infant, day after day, night after night. As an old Russian proverb puts it, "You cannot pay anyone to do what a mother will do for free."

This bond has been acknowledged in literature and art, but it has been scientifically observed and explored only in the last decade. Two pediatricians, Marshall Klaus and John Kennell, are primarily responsible for initiating these observations. The explorations began in their own clinical practice when they noticed that the course of mother-infant relationships was affected by contact between the two in the first few hours or days after birth. When mothers were separated from their newborns immediately after birth, usually because their babies were premature or ill or because they themselves were ill, mothers were more likely to mistreat their infants and the babies were less likely to thrive after the pair went home from the hospital. Separation had apparently interfered with the formation of the bond that commits the mother to the nurture of the infant. Klaus and Kennell observed these mothers to be fearful and tentative about their infants' destinies. One mother, after she was finally reunited with her infant, looked at the child with trepidation,

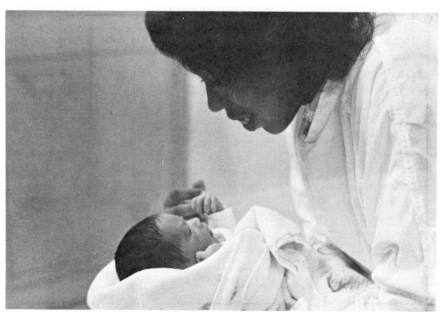

The mother-infant bond has its earliest expression in mutual gazing that begins in the first hours after birth, as the mother holds, touches, and explores her newborn. John Kennell and Marshall Klaus suggest that this period is critical for establishing a strong and continuing maternal bond.

asking: "Are you mine? Are you really mine? Are you alive? Are you really alive?" (Klaus and Kennell, 1976, p. 10).

On the basis of their clinical observations, Klaus and Kennell were alerted to the possibility that for human beings the period immediately after birth may be critical in the formation of the maternal bond. They conducted a number of subsequent studies, and other researchers too began to investigate the **bonding** process. Of course, mothers and infants could not be separated for experimental purposes. But in most hospitals during the 1960s and early 1970s infants were separated from their mothers routinely. Except for visits for feeding, infants were kept in newborn nurseries from the first postpartum moments until their mothers took them home. These separations were certainly not as extreme or as worrisome as the separations of premature or sick babies from their mothers that had first alerted Klaus and Kennell to the dire effects of separation. Because the early contact in most hospital births amounted to little more than the mother glimpsing her newborn however, the bonding phenomenon could be studied easily and ethically by increasing the amount of this early contact.

Studies were done to explore the effects of rooming in, of keeping the baby in the mother's room during the hospital stay (Greenberg, Rosenberg, and Lind, 1973); of early contact, of giving the baby to the mother for a few hours immediately after birth (Hales, Lozoff, Sosa, and Kennell, 1977); and of extended contact, of allowing the mother to keep her infant with her an extra 5 hours each day of her hospital stay (Kennell et al., 1974). Compared to mothers who went through the usual hospital procedure of separation from their infants, the mothers given this additional contact with their babies claimed to feel more competent and were more reluctant to leave their infants with someone else. They stayed closer to their infants, often looking into their eyes, touched and soothed them more often, and fondled and kissed them more frequently. They acted this way immediately after leaving the hospital and continued to do for a year or possibly longer.

Unlike mothers of many animal species, however, human mothers can form bonds of attachment to their babies even if the circumstances of their first meeting are not ideal. Mothers who are anesthetized during delivery and do not see their infants for several hours do not reject them (Klaus and Kennell, 1976; Williams, 1979). Mothers who cannot see or hear their infants, mothers of infants in incubators who cannot be touched for several weeks, adoptive parents, fathers who have not been present at their baby's birth, and others intimately concerned with the well-being of the newborn all can form bonds of attachment. The bond of those who have early contact with their infant may be stronger—*all other things being equal*—but all other things seldom are equal, and later experience can readily compensate for this early, missed opportunity.

Not all studies have documented the effects that Kennell and Klaus observed. The mothers originally studied by Kennell and Klaus were young and poor. Studies of middle-class mothers have not shown that they benefit so clearly from additional early contact with their babies. In one such investigation of the short-term effects of contact between parents and infants, 30 lower-middle-class parents were randomly assigned to one of two groups at the delivery of their firstborn child (Svejda, Pannabecker, and Emde, 1982). Those in the early contact group had 15 minutes of skin contact between mother and newborn in the delivery room, 45 minutes together with their baby in the recovery room, and 1½ hour at each of the next seven feedings. Those in the routine contact group had 5 minutes of contact with their newborn as the mother was wheeled to the recovery room, where there was no further contact, and then 20 to 30 minutes of contact at each feeding. The investigators found no differences in the maternal bond between the two groups. The investigators concluded that the bonding model does not generalize to middle-class families and does not take into account the dynamics of the developing affectional system between mother and infant. They also speculated that other factors—perhaps the presence of the father, for example—may be more important in the development of a maternal bond than simply the experience of early contact.

Especially controversial is the issue of whether the relationship between mother and child is affected beyond infancy (Whiten, 1977; Taylor, Carrysbell, Maloni and Dickey, 1979). In a methodologically careful study in Germany (Grossmann, Thane, and Grossmann, 1981), investigators found weak but positive effects of early contact that weakened further over time. Mothers delivering their firstborn child were randomly divided into one of four groups. The early contact group had at least 30 minutes of contact between mother and infant in the first hour after delivery. The extended contact group had 5 hours of rooming in per day. The early and extended contact group had both of the above conditions. Mothers in a control group had a brief look at the baby right after delivery, medical care, and then the clothed baby was placed next to the mother's bed in a bassinet. Films of feedings during the first 10 days showed that on days 2 and 3, mothers in the early contact group touched their babies more tenderly and cuddled them more than the mothers in the extended contact and control groups. However these differences were apparent only in the mothers whose pregnancies had been planned, and the differences disappeared by the fourth day after delivery.

One further study of the long-term effects of early and extended contact (Siegel, Bauman, Schaefer, Saunders, and Ingram, 1980) also showed weak effects. Two hundred mothers, most of whom were black and single, were interviewed and observed for their acceptance of the infant, stimulation, and consoling at 4 and 12 months. The investigators found that differences in early contact accounted for only about 3 percent of the differences in mothers' acceptance and consoling, and slightly over 3 percent of the differences in infants' positive and negative behavior.

In sum, extra early contact has been shown—in some studies—to affect mothers' affectionateness during feedings, protectiveness during a newborn's physical examination, feelings about separating from the child, patterns of speaking to the child, affection when playing, and length of breastfeeding (Trause, 1981). But these effects are far from universal, inevitable, reliable, or permanent.

Whether the mother is awake during delivery or asleep, whether she is continually with her newborn or they are separated immediately after birth, the period of assuming full responsibility for a baby when she gets home seems to be a difficult one for many women. A majority of new mothers, from 50 to 80 percent of those studied, have mood swings and crying spells for at least 10 days after childbirth (Davidson, 1972; Pitt, 1973; Yalom, Lunde, Moos, and Hamburg, 1968). Birth itself may be an ecstatic experience, but the mother has many moments of frustration, resentment, and fatigue, especially in the first 4 to 6 weeks.

Kenneth Robson and Howard Moss (1970), studying the development of maternal attachment of 54 new mothers, found that these bonds developed slowly and did not become strong until about 3 months after birth. Many women felt both a lack of personal connection to their infants and guilt and inadequacy for this feeling. As one new mother put it:

My euphoria from the actual birth continued until I actually began to care for our helpless baby. Suddenly I felt completely overwhelmed and started crying constantly. I was struck with the realization that I had become responsible for the well-being of another human being (Robson and Moss, 1970, p. 13).

Her state of acute sensitivity, enhanced by the physiological changes occurring after birth, renders a new mother extremely vulnerable. In her review of the literature on postpartum experiences, Elizabeth Magnus (1978) points out that the new mother needs rest and a support network of husband and other family members during this period of adjustment. A study of new mothers found that those who became psychiatric patients had not received the emotional support and practical assistance from husband, friends, and relatives that the other mothers had (Gordon and Gordon, 1960). And a later study found that expectant mothers who were alerted to the need for setting up a support network and given other instructions on reducing stress had fewer emotional problems during pregnancy and in the postpartum period (Gordon, Kapostins, and Gordon, 1965).

The infant's responsiveness also plays a part in the postpartum adjustment period. Fred Astaire may dance with a hat rack for a time, but he prefers a responsive Ginger Rogers. Mothers look for infant responsiveness at this time. In the Robson and Moss (1970) study 72 percent of the mothers who had strong and clearly articulated feelings of attachment during the first 4 to 6 weeks gave the responsive behavior of their infants—smiling, laughing, eye contact, and the tendency to follow with their eyes—as the reason. In subsequent weeks the feeling that their babies actually recognized them was rewarding for mothers.

THE INFANT "SPEAKS"

Most babies are immensely appealing creatures. Mothers, fathers, grandparents, adolescents and adults who are not parents, young boys and girls— all respond to the cuteness of babies and act in special ways when with them (Stern, 1977). They are responding, according to Konrad Lorenz (1971) and others (Eibl-Eibesfeldt, 1970; Fullard and Reiling, 1976) to the infant's appearance, its "babyness"—the tininess, large head and small body, prominent forehead, small face, large eyes, chubby cheeks, and small mouth of a very young animal. People are touched by the infant's thrashings and its helpless, uncoordinated movements, and they delight in the baby's smiles and eye brightenings, its open mouth and pink tongue, its sighs and gurgles (Bell and Harper, 1977).

Thus, through its sounds, facial expressions, and movements, the infant has powerful sources of appeal and is capable of attracting its parents. In the ethological view (e.g., Bowlby, 1969; Lorenz, 1971) these physical and behavioral "signals" serve the adaptive function of ensuring survival of the infant, and of the species, by keeping its parents near, involved, and interested in the infant. Parents provide for the infant's physical needs by giving food and warmth and for the infant's psychological needs by acting in ways to which the infant is particularly receptive. They exaggerate their faces by opening their eyes wide and raising their eyebrows, and they baby-talk in high voices. These responses appear to be largely instinctual, for all people, regardless of age, sex, or experience with children, behave in this way to human and animal babies (Stern, 1977). Parents so greet their newborns even when they think their babies cannot see (Papousek and Papousek, 1978). Learning, however, heightens the caretaker's responsiveness to an infant. Nurses are more attracted to a baby after caring for it in the newborn nursery and doctors after examining a newborn (Corter et al., 1978; Klaus and Kennell, 1976).

GAZING

As we have already described, infants can see— fuzzily—as soon as they are born, and they see objects better that are close up. Feeding times are when infants are most alert during their first few weeks, and during feedings, most mothers spend about 70 percent of their time facing and gazing at their infants. The contrast, brightness, and movements of the mother's face and eyes make them attractive to the infant. Infants find the outline of the mother's face and the sharp angles provided by the corners of her eyes especially fascinating. This meshing between the mother's face and what attracts the infant is one indication of how the infant is naturally adapted to social encounters. The position the mother assumes when she is feeding or playing with her infant makes these situations the ideal starting point for the development of social relatedness (Stern, 1977; Walters and Parke, 1965).

At some time around the sixth week of life, the infant's visual-motor system reaches a developmental landmark, catapulting the infant onto a new level of social interaction. The infant becomes capable of visually fixating the mother's eyes and then holding the fixation while it widens and brightens its own eyes (Wolff, 1963). The mother feels for the first time that her infant is looking *at her.* Even though she does not necessarily identify what is causing the change, she becomes markedly more interactive with her infant.

The infant's responsiveness is most important in engaging parents. Mothers of blind babies have difficulty in forming attachments to them (Fraiberg, 1974). In the Robson and Moss (1970) study of maternal attachment, the mothers who felt little or no attachment to their infants had originally not wished to have babies or found theirs to be unresponsive or exceedingly difficult to console. Most infants do have the resources for responding to their mothers, and in responding they encourage further contacts.

Mothers and infants have been videotaped during these early face-to-face contacts, and the nature and sequences of their behavior have been analyzed. The mother's exaggerated facial expressions include frowns, smiles, and looks of great concern, such as the "oh you poor dear" face. She frequently shows "mock surprise"—her eyes open very wide, her eyebrows go up, her mouth opens wide, and her head is raised and tilted up slightly. At the same time she usually says something like "Ooooh" or "Aaaah." Sometimes her face becomes quite active and animated; sometimes she makes her expressions in slow motion. She changes her pace from moment to moment.

The mother uses these relatively few and somewhat stereotyped signals to regulate interactions with the infant. She invites the infant to play with her mock-surprise expression whenever the infant looks at her, which may be every 10 or 15 seconds while they are together. With her smile she signals that the interaction is going well. An expression of concern appears when the interaction is running down, and the mother then attempts to reengage the infant's attention. To terminate the interaction, even briefly, the mother frowns, averts her gaze, or assumes a neutral expression. The mother's exaggerated expressions serve not only to regulate interaction, but to help the infant recognize and discriminate salient social expressions (Stern, 1977).

By the end of the third month of their developing relationship, infant and mother engage in prolonged, mutual gazing—for 20 seconds in play and 12 seconds during feeding (Peery and Stern, 1976; Schaffer, Collis, and Parsons, 1977), longer than any gazing except that between lovers. When they are interacting, the mother spends three-quarters of her time gazing at her infant. But when the infant turns away, the interaction stops; the mother interprets this behavior to mean that the baby does not like something and does not want to continue. As soon as the infant is able to maintain his or her gaze at the mother in their eye-to-eye contacts, the mother's feelings of attachment take another leap. They are now so strong that her infant's absence is unpleasant and the imagined loss of her child intolerable (Robson and Moss, 1970). These mother-infant interactions, observed in front of a video camera, are intense and exciting. But in the baby's daily life they are probably not very frequent. Even in the most sociable families they are likely to account for only a few minutes of the baby's time each day. And in families in which the mother is depressed, under financial strain, or burdened by the demanding pressure of other small children, they are likely to be rare indeed.

SMILING

Newborn infants are capable of a surprising range of facial expressions. Those that in adults signify pleasure, displeasure, anger, fear, joy, sorrow, or disgust are all present at birth or within the first few months (Charlesworth and Kreutzer, 1973). One of the most important of these, for mother and psychologist, is the smile. Smiling has been systematically observed, manipulated, and studied in the

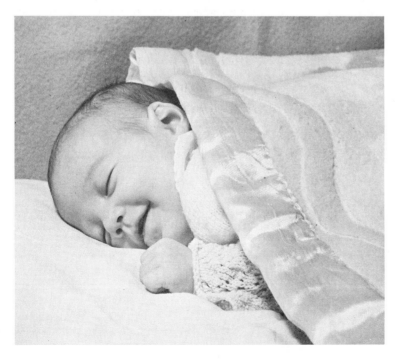

Spontaneous smiles suffuse the infant's face in sleep.

laboratory. Investigators have done everything but stand on their heads to to get babies to smile in their efforts to chart the course and causes of smiling.

During the first 2 weeks of life, smiles are seen during light sleep and drowsiness, rarely when the baby is awake and alert. These are called **endogenous** (spontaneous) **smiles** (Sroufe, 1979) because they bear no relation to the external world. They are triggered by an internal event, by neurophysiological arousal and discharge in the brain. When the baby is aroused and then relaxes below his or her threshold of arousal, the smile muscles relax too and the baby appears to smile (Figure 5.9). During light sleep, excitation in the nervous system is hovering near this critical threshold; bursts of these tiny smiles are seen for short periods of time. If the infant is startled while he or she is sleeping, as by a loud noise, the level of excitation is raised and no smiles are seen until the infant has settled down. Although these smiles may be associated with a pleasant, relaxed state, they cannot be thought of as signifying pleasure in any conscious sense. They are related to later smiles, not because they signify pleasure but because later smiles also involve excitation and relaxation. Soon after birth these endogenous smiles can be encouraged by gentle stimulation. When the infant is asleep or drowsy, a light touch or soothing word may evoke a smile within 6 to 8 seconds. Later, during the first month of life, gently stimulating the infant when awake, still later, at the end of the first month, more intense stimulation, such as bouncing, may bring on the smiles. In all these situations it seems that the stimulation raises the infant's arousal level above threshold; when arousal decreases, 6 to 8 seconds later, the infant smiles.

Month-old infants will also smile at a nodding head speaking with a high voice, and 2-month-olds will respond with smiles to blinking lights, to silent noddings, and to anything rhythmic or repeated. These smiles, triggered by something in the external world, are called **exogenous smiles**.

Beginning about the third month, the infant smiles in response to static visual stimuli—human faces seen full and in profile, dolls, and other familiar objects. At this age the smile takes on even more significance. It becomes *social*. Not only can it be caused by external stimuli, such as Mother's face, but it may also, for the first time, be instrumental—produced to get Mother to smile back. As well as being instrumental, the smile may also reflect pleasure. Jerome Kagan (1971) suggests that the smile signals a new awareness, such as recognition of an object seen many times before. The cognitive effort involved in recognizing the object seems to cause tension or arousal, and success at matching the stimulus to a familiar internal picture brings relaxation, which begins to carry with it the new element of satisfaction or pleasure

At 3 to 4 months of age, the infant's smiling apparently continues to reflect new levels of cognitive mastery. The immobile face, now easily recognized, no longer brings a smile, perhaps because it no longer creates tension. But a mobile face, which takes additional effort to master, will. By the age of 5 months or even earlier, the infant smiles with pleasure after doing something (Piaget, 1952). He or she will smile after moving a ball or a mobile and then repeat the pleasurable cause-effect sequence (Watson, 1972).

The smile not only indicates mastery and expresses pleasure; it is also a means of communication. The infant's smile draws others into inter-

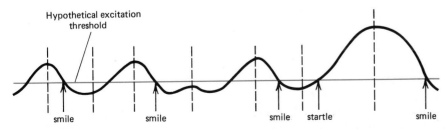

FIGURE 5.9
This schematic drawing of the excitation-relaxation cycle shows the baby's behavior in relation to a hypothetical threshold of arousal. When babies are aroused and then relax just below the threshold, they give a tiny, endogenous (spontaneous) smile (Sroufe, 1979).

action and rewards them for doing "something right." The more the infant smiles, the more the mother or other caregiver stays nearby and responds to these smiles, usually with a return smile (Clarke-Stewart, 1973; Etzel and Gewirtz, 1967). This responsiveness to the infant has a spiraling effect; the infant smiles repeatedly, and so does his or her companion (Brackbill, 1958).

CRYING

The sound a mother hears from her infant in the first 6 months is more often a loud and unpleasant cry than a delighted chuckle. This cry is usually the end point in a sequence of expressions of increasing displeasure. The face sobers. A frown forms. The eyes partly close. The upper cheeks rise and become flushed. The lower lip quivers. The lips are pulled back as the mouth opens. The breath catches. The corners of the mouth turn down. Finally, the cry bursts forth.

This cry, or even the first steps in the sequence leading up to it, is a strong expression of emotion and a potent form of communication with the mother. A baby's cry exerts an immediate effect on anyone within eyeshot or earshot. A mother's heart rate increases when she watches a silent videotape of an infant the same age as hers crying (Donovan, Leavitt, and Balling, 1978). Her heart races even faster when sound is added or when the videotape is of her own infant (Wiesenfeld and Klorman, 1978). Listeners report feelings of anger and irritation, as well as physiological arousal (Frodi, Lamb, Leavitt, and Donovan, 1978), whichever their sex or whatever their prior experience with babies (Freudenberg, Driscoll, and Stein, 1978). A study of parents who admitted to being child abusers, however, showed that abusing mothers were more aroused, annoyed, and less sympathetic when shown the videotape than other mothers. They were also angered and aroused by a videotape of a smiling baby, which ordinarily brings pleasant emotion and decreases arousal (Frodi and Lamb, 1978).

Arousal at the sight or sound of a crying baby may be virtually automatic, but effective soothing of the infant is not. In the first place, some listeners are less willing to respond to the cry, believing it not good to "spoil" the baby by rewarding him or her for crying. In the second place, even though the mother may be willing and primed to provide the comfort required, she may not know what to do. Is the baby in pain? Hungry? Bored? Tired? Sick? Certain kinds of cries are distinguishable. The birth cry, pain cry, hunger cry, mad cry, and other types can supposedly be discriminated by listeners, especially experienced listeners, such as midwives, children's nurses, and mothers. Graphs of the sound waves of cries indicate differences (Wasz-Hoeckert, Lind, Vuorenkoski, Partanen, and Valanné, 1968; Wolff, 1969). But cries are not necessarily identifiable in real life (Mueller, Hollien, and Murry, 1974). The hunger cry, for example, has a basic rhythmic pattern to which infants sooner or later revert, no matter the initial type of cry (Wolff, 1969). What is more, on any day much of an infant's crying may not lend itself to a simple analysis of cause and effect. A baby girl attempts to reach a toy and falls in the effort, bumping her head. Mother comes over and kisses the hurt place, saying "Boo-boo all better now." The infant stops crying. If mother had not seen the fall, she might still have offered comfort and stopped the crying, even though she did not know its cause.

Peter Wolff (1969) made the most systematic attempt to observe and analyze infants' cries. As a participant–observer in babies' homes, Wolff watched infants for 15 to 30 hours a week over the first 6 months of life, supplementing these observations with observations of infants in a hospital. He was then able to suggest the principal causes of crying.

For the newborn, he found, crying has physical and physiological causes. Hunger of course causes considerable crying, but feeding is a complex experience. Wolff studied a group of infants being fed through tubes to their stomachs and other infants who were doing their own sucking and swallowing. He found the full stomach, not the sucking, more effective in stopping crying.

Babies in rooms kept at 88 to 90°F cried less than those kept in rooms at 78°F. But babies in warmer places also slept more; deeper sleep may protect infants from distress in addition to coldness. Being naked also causes babies to cry. Nearly half of those observed by Wolff, from the third day on, began to cry when they were undressed, even when temperature was controlled.

Violent or sudden stimulation of eye or ear or balance startles babies and may make them cry

(Wolff, 1969). The very young infant may also begin to cry when he or she gets "locked into" a stimulus after prolonged gazing (Sroufe, 1979; Tennes, Kisley, and Metcalf, 1972). This is true of any stimulus that causes excess arousal. The musical toy or bright mobile that fascinates and then makes infants cry, presumably because it overexcites them, will in a few short weeks, when they have a higher threshold for arousal, bring smiles and cooing. Even at this early age infants seem to be especially sensitive to the sound of newborns' crying. A tape recording of the baby's own cries or those of another has been found to make him or her cry (Simner, 1971).

During the first 1 or 2 weeks, rhythmic stimulation and reducing the sensations caused by the baby's own movements will comfort the newborn. Wrapping the baby securely and picking up and holding the infant upright are two of the effective ways to stop his crying (Korner and Thoman, 1972). Gentle, continuous rocking can be effective (Ambrose, 1961; Korner and Thoman, 1972). Certain sounds—such as white noise, a blend of all audible frequencies of sound; tape recordings of sounds heard *in utero;* the noise of an air conditioner; or Beethoven played at high volume—can also calm the infant (Brackbill, 1958; Rosner and

Doherty, 1979). Sucking, too, for example, on a pacifier, is regular and rhythmic and can release the infant's tension, reduce thrasing, and stop tears.

As infants get past the newborn period, they have new reasons to cry. Soon, within the first few weeks, the infant cries when feeding is interrupted (Bernal, 1972; Wolff, 1969). At 2 to 3 months removing something the infant is holding, approaching him or her suddenly, mother's "still face," as well as loud noises will make the infant cry. Daniel Stern (1974) asked mothers to keep their faces unexpressive instead of greeting their babies in their usual way. The infants sobered, attempted to interact with their mothers, then looked away, fussed, and either cried or avoided looking at them. But when the mother looked at and talked to her infant, she could stop the infant's fussing and make the baby watch her. The baby sometimes even cried briefly when she left. The face and voice of anyone, not just mothers', soothe an infant (Wolff, 1969). The baby may cry when any person departs, but because he or she calms down after a minute or so, the crying is clearly not intended to make the person come back. But an important change has taken place between the newborn period and 3 months: now the infant can be soothed by social interaction as well as physical comforting.

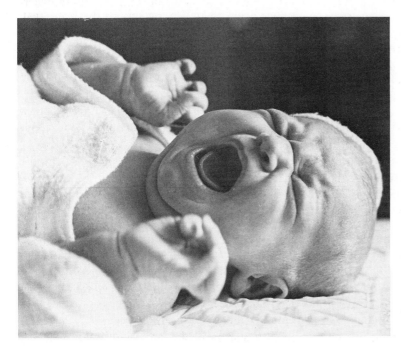

The infant cry: a frowning, screwed-up face; eyes closed and mouth open; a lusty wail.

When is it appropriate to respond to the infant's cries? Controversy over this question continues to rage, leaving many new mothers confused and perplexed about what to do. Everyone agrees that the caregiver should respond immediately to a pain cry and at least eventually to a hunger cry, but that leaves every other cry. Some suggest that responding to these other cries will reinforce crying and "spoil" the baby, turning the infant into a tiny tyrant. Researchers have studied the evidence for this opinion, but they, too, are divided (Ainsworth and Bell, 1977; Gewirtz and Boyd, 1977a). Under controlled, laboratory-like conditions it has been demonstrated that the duration of crying can be decreased by not rewarding it and by reinforcing incompatible behavior, like smiling (Etzel and Gewirtz, 1967). But at home, over the long run, crying may become more frequent if ignored (Bell and Ainsworth, 1972).

The situations in which babies cry and their mothers' possible responses are too many and too complex to allow for a simple "Yes, it's good to respond" or "No, don't respond." Many factors must be taken into account: the overall level of irritation; whether the baby is really distressed or is just crying to get attention; which cries and what else such as vocalizations, the mother responds to; and the effectiveness and consistency of the mother's responses. At present, these are our best guesses. If the mother responds promptly, she may be reinforcing a short cry rather than a long one so the amount of crying will decrease. If she responds consistently, the infant will come to expect her to respond again; crying will become shorter, controlled, with a pause as the baby waits for a response—what is known as a "request" cry. Only if the response is not forthcoming will the infant go to a long "demand" cry (Bruner, 1978). If the mother responds positively to other forms of communication, such as frowns, frets, and vocalizations, the baby will probably choose these signals more often and have less need to cry.

VOCALIZING

One of the most important channels of human communication is vocalization. During the first year of life, the infant develops the ability to communicate vocally and to convey effectively considerable meaning. The baby's first sounds other than cries are usually coos or gurgles made after food and sleep, usually in the mother's arms. Soon babies make such sounds when they hear Mother's voice or see her approaching face. Vowel-like and consonant-like sounds are made at first. Sounds are relaxed and undifferentiated and do not have the pure tone qualities heard in adult speech. Vocalization at this age is reflexive; deaf infants and those with normal hearing make the same sounds (Lennenberg, Rebelsky, and Nichols, 1965). The rate and variety of vowellike sounds and, to a somewhat lesser extent, consonantlike sounds, increase rapidly through this period.

From 4 to 12 months, more vowellike and consonant-like sounds are discovered or invented by the baby. The infant also begins to alternate vowels and consonants repetitively, forming "Babababa" or "Mamamama," which delights the parents. **Babbling** is vocal play, not an attempt at communication. At first the infant discovers the sounds when in a fussy state. Later, a baby babbles more often when playing alone, contentedly (Jones and Moss, 1971; Wolff, 1969). During this period infants vocalize a wealth of sounds, even sounds that do not appear in their native language. They combine these sounds in ever more complex ways, often using the intonation rhythm and stress patterns of adult speech. Their babbling often sounds like a string of real sentences. Near the end of this period, infants begin to imitate the sounds that they hear. They become quiet while someone nearby speaks and then babble excitedly. Then they listen again. At first the baby just imitates the pitch of sounds but does not copy the precise sound (Wolff, 1969). Gradually, the playful and inexact babbling decreases and real language begins. Although deaf infants and children in all cultures have similar patterns of babbling, there are some variations. At the same time that infants are discovering and producing their own sound systems, they are hearing sounds. This world of sounds in which they are embedded has certain universal regularities.

Baby talk, or **motherese,** is a far-reaching change at all levels of adults' speech: pitch, loudness, intonation, rhythm, syntax, phonetics. Nearly all adults use a special register when talking to babies and young children. The voice is usually high but has an exaggerated range of pitch, from bass to squeaks and squeals, and radical swings in loudness, from whispering to shouts (Figure 5.10).

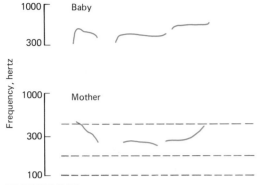

FIGURE 5.10

A sequence of babbling by a 4-week-old baby is matched by his mother within the constraints of adult English, as indicated by these voice frequency contours. The broken lines show the range and the mode of the mother's usual expressive speaking voice. Her first response to her infant, a fall, starts at the very top of her range. In her normal speech a high-to-middle-range fall is not heard (Fourcin, 1978).

Nonsense sounds are often stressed, and the rhythm is singsong. The tempo is exaggerated, too, either speeded up or slowed down, and words and phrases are repeated with the vowels elongated (Slobin, 1975; Snow, 1972).

Jacqueline Sachs (1977) argues that baby talk to prelinguistic infants is not just a culturally transmitted play ritual. Rather, it is adaptive, for its patterns are geared to the sensory capacities of infants and their requirements for the development of normal communication with their social world. Sachs presents evidence that higher pitch, special intonation patterns, special rhythm and temporal patternings, and the use of certain sounds are characteristic of baby talk in all cultures and that infants are perceptually sensitive to each and use them in their own vocalizations. Higher pitch, for example, has been consistently observed in languages from Arabic to Latvian (Ferguson, 1964; Ruke-Dravina, 1977) and in speakers from grandfathers to older sisters (Fourcin, 1978). One language researcher transcribing a tape of an adult speaking to a Thai baby thought the speaker was a woman because of the high-pitched voice—until the speaker spoke to the baby's grandmother at his normal pitch (Tuaycharoen, 1978). Infants apparently prefer high-pitched tones (Kearsley, 1973). When they hear a high-pitched voice, they tend to raise their own pitch (Webster, Steinhardt, and Senter, 1972); the pitch of the infant's voice reflects that of the

voice heard the most recently (Lieberman, 1967).

The baby talk of adults includes an unusually large proportion of syllables beginning with initial-stop consonants, such as "bababa" (Sachs, 1977). These are the sounds that infants use in their earliest babblings (Pierce, 1974). When an infant begins to use real speech sounds, baby talk from the partner changes too. Playing less with sounds, partners speak in concrete words and short, simple phrases, sentences, and questions, which they repeat. They transform many sounds in words to a more "primitive" form. "Tum on," for "come on," "pwitty wabbit," and "big puddy tat," for example, use consonants that appear early in infant speech.

RECOGNIZING VOICES

Not only do infants hear talk in a special register, but they soon recognize the voices of different speakers talking it. Most research demonstrating this has focused on infants' ability to distinguish between familiar and unfamiliar voices. In a study by Anthony DeCasper and William Fifer (1980), 3-day-old infants with as little as 12 hours of contact with their mothers preferred to listen to their mother's rather than a stranger's voice. A second study (Spence and DeCasper, 1982) showed that newborns preferred hearing the mother read a passage she had read aloud while she was pregnant to one that she had never read before. Preferences for mother's voice so soon after birth lead one to speculate that the fetus hears the mother's voice while it is still in the uterus. In one study to explore this speculation (Armitage, Baldwin, and Vince, 1980), hydrophones implanted in the uteri of two pregnant ewes revealed that normal conversational tones from outside the uterus were somewhat dulled but that louder sounds (above 65 decibels) could be heard. Sounds from inside the ewes, of drinking, eating, swallowing, and heavy breathing were also audible, although heartbeats were not. The researchers concluded that in the fluid environment of the uterus, fetal sheep could hear various low-frequency sounds from both inside and outside the mother. When hydrophones were placed in the amniotic sac of human mothers (Querleu and Renard, 1981), sounds of 1000 Hz or lower were picked up clearly, but sounds at higher frequencies—like speech—were very muffled. These studies demonstrate that sounds do penetrate the uterus, and we have already discussed the studies of infants born prematurely showing that the infant ear is capable of hearing some weeks before birth. The question of what the fetus actually hears in utero—with its ears full of amniotic fluid—has not been settled yet, however. These studies using hydrophones suggest that what the fetus hears of the mother's voice is muffled at best.

In another study of infants, 4- to 6-week-olds heard 20-second speeches by their mothers and by another woman; some of the speeches were monotonous and some highly intonated (Mehler, Bertoncini, Barriere, and Jassik-Gerschenfeld, 1978). As in the study of newborns by DeCasper and Fifer (1980), the infants preferred their mother's voice—

but only when it was highly intonated. Although scientists have known that infants can distinguish between specific spoken sounds, they only recently have begun to investigate what infants prefer to listen to in speech. Now certain patterns are becoming clear. One study has found that babies will choose to listen to a rising tone rather than a falling tone (Sullivan and Horowitz, 1983). Other studies have shown that babies prefer to listen to speech that is friendly, female, high pitched, exaggerated, and expressive (Lieberman, 1967; Turnure, 1971). Mother's voice probably sounds best to a baby because it contains all of these attractive elements. When 4-month-olds who were allowed to grow familiar with both normal adult speech and baby

RESEARCH FOCUS

NEWBORNS PREFER MOTHER'S VOICE

How early in life can infants recognize their own mother's voice? Anthony DeCasper and William Fifer (1980) provide some provocative data. In their study, 10 white newborns and their mothers were subjects. Soon after delivery, DeCasper and Fifer taped the mothers reading from Dr. Seuss's *To Think That I Saw It on Mulberry Street*. Testing began within 24 hours. The newborns were coaxed into a quietly alert state, placed in a bassinet, and given earphones and nipple. A naive assistant held the nipple in the infant's mouth. Through the nipple, the infants' rates of sucking could be recorded, and the investigators determined a baseline sucking rate. By sucking at or faster than baseline, one group of infants could activate a recording of their mother's voice reading. By sucking more slowly, they heard a different mother reading. Conditions were reversed for a second group of infants. The experimenters also controlled for characteristics of the infants' responses, such as long or short intervals between bursts of sucking, and the acoustic qualities of particular voices that might make them particularly effective feedback.

Of the 10 infants, 8 produced rates of sucking that activated the recording of their own mother's voice more than half the time. The experimenters then changed the requirements for the rate of suck-

ing that would elicit the mother's voice. The babies adjusted to the change and again produced the sound of their own mother reading. When the experiment was repeated with 16 newborn girls and a different discrimination procedure (sucking or not sucking as a tone sounded or during a period of silence), the results were the same. The infants preferred their mother's voice. Although during the first third of the test, the infants were just as likely to suck during a stimulus period that activated another mother's voice as their own, during the last third of the test, they sucked some 24 percent more during periods that activated their own mother's voice. During the 20-minute test session, they had produced clear evidence of auditory discrimination and a preference for their mother's voice.

One interesting fact about these infants was that they had had at most 12 hours of contact with their mothers since birth. All had been cared for in the general nursery of the hospital where they were born, and none roomed in with his or her mother. Yet within the first 3 days of life, these newborns showed a preference for a human voice over a tone or silence, could discriminate between speakers, and preferred their own mother's voice. DeCasper and Fifer concluded that the rapid development of these abilities is made possible because newborns are sensitive to rhythm, intonation, variations in frequency, phonetic components of speech, and perhaps are affected as well by what they hear before birth.

talk could choose to listen to one or the other, they clearly preferred (turned their heads toward) the baby-talking voice (Fernald, 1981). Similar findings have been reported for British babies of 9 and 18 months (Glenn and Cunningham, 1983). These babies could choose between listening to a children's rhyme from "Sesame Street" or a pure spoken tone, or they could choose between listening to their mother talking about their favorite game in baby talk or talking to an adult. Babies at both ages significantly preferred the rhyme to the tone. The 18-month-olds liked to listen to the baby talk even more than the younger babies did, and they listened to it longer than they listened to the rhyme.

TAKING TURNS

From the beginning, parents respond to their infant's babblings as though they are meaningful. Immediately after or while the infant vocalizes, the mother is likely to speak and vice versa (Jones and Moss, 1971; Lewis and Freedle, 1973). The speech of one stimulates that of the other (Figure 5.11). Every social communication is a complex affair extending through time, involving voice, face, gestures, gazing, and other aspects and actions of the person. Its temporal patterns have been examined in detail only recently through **microanalytic** techniques, such as stop-frame or slow-motion analysis of films and videotapes. These techniques demonstrate vividly the turn-taking nature of human communication.

Perhaps the earliest turn taking of babies takes place during feeding. From the moment of birth, the baby's sucking is temporally organized into burst-pause patterns regulated by the brain—suck, suck, suck, suck—pause—suck, suck, suck (Sameroff, 1967). There is no apparent physiological reason for the pauses; infants breathe and swallow as they suck, and the number of pauses does not increase when they are becoming tired at the end of a feeding. But what happens? The mother, during the feeding, interacts in synchrony with the pattern. During the bursts of sucking she is quiet and inactive, but she fills in the pauses with jiggles, strokes, and talk, behavior that has no physiological rationale. It does not make the feeding proceed more smoothly or quickly. If the mother does nothing, the baby will still suck and pause. But the mother's behavior during the infant's pauses makes

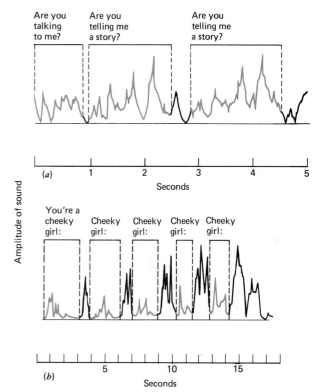

FIGURE 5.11

In these illustrations of vocal turn taking, the mother's words are indicated with light-color lines, the baby's sounds with dark-color lines. (a) A 9-week-old baby boy makes small cooing sounds in answer to his mother's rhythmic and repeated baby-talk questions. (b) A 22-week-old girl chuckles, giggles, and laughs loudly as her mother calls her a "cheeky girl," each time making the words more compacted and emphatic and bringing her face toward her daughter (Trevarthen, 1977).

the feeding into an interaction. It is as if she wanted to convey this notion: "I'm not just passively sitting here. I'm *feeding* this baby." Treating the pause in sucking as though it were the baby's way of saying, "Now my turn is over; you take yours," she gives the infant a jiggle or says, "Hi, sweetie" (Kaye, 1977).

The mother may also interpret the baby's mouth movements as attempts to talk and respond in alternation to them (Trevarthen, 1977). What the listener hears is not really a dialogue then, but a maternal monologue in the form of an imaginary dialogue.

Mother	"Aren't you my cutie?" (1.42 seconds)
Pause	(0.60 seconds)
Imagined response from baby	"Yes" (0.43 seconds)
Pause	(0.60 seconds)
Mother	"You sure are!"

Even more clearly, as soon as the infant begins babbling, the mother fills in between his or her vocal bouts, creating sequences that have the appearance of conversation or dialogue (Schaffer, 1978). Daniel Stern (1977) speculates that, after speaking, the mother waits the average length of a pause in an adult conversation. Then she remains silent for the duration of an imagined verbal response, during which time the infant may babble. Finally, the mother waits the average length of an adult pause again before speaking. As a result, her pauses, compared to those in her speech to an adult, are elongated. The mother unconsciously and without thinking is teaching her infant the speaking turns that normal conversation requires. The exchange has been observed with infants as young as 3 months (Stern, 1977).

But the smoothness of this **pseudodialogue** depends, at this age, on the mother. Remember Fred Astaire and the hat rack. The infant is preadapted to learn social interaction by having biological rhythms, cycles that allow for alternation of turns. But it is up to mother to "fill in the blanks" (Schaffer, 1978). Sometimes she does not wait, and that can be fun too. Then mother-infant play becomes especially lively and engaging. Mother may vocalize in unison with the infant in a duet or "chorus" (Stern, Jaffe, Beebe, and Bennett, 1975).

By the end of the first year, the infant is beginning to hold up his or her end of the turn-taking conversation, vocalizing when Mother pauses, and real dialogues emerge. J. L. Newson (1977) documents a typical "conversation" with an infant.

Baby	(Looks at a toy top.)
Mother	"Do you like that?"
Baby	"Da!"
Mother	"Yes, it's a nice toy, isn't it?"
Baby	"Da! Da!"

Very few clashes in turns are observed in most mother-child "dialogues" (Schaffer, 1978). When they occur, it is as likely to be mother as baby who interrupts, and these clashes do not disrupt the flow of interaction. The vocalizations of Down's syndrome children are as many and varied as those of normal children, but they do not learn to take turns. Because they do not leave pauses, their mothers' vocalizations are more likely to clash with theirs (Jones, 1977). Normal children of 1 year are beginning to realize that dialogue needs to be sustained by *both* partners, that they are equally responsible, and that roles are interchangeable (Schaffer, 1978).

GESTURING

We have discussed pseudodialogues in terms of the *vocal* channel. Babies learn to participate in the other aspects of conversation from a very early age too. When Sarah, a baby videotaped by Ben Sylvester-Bradley and Colwyn Trevarthen (1978), was supposedly "chatting" with her mother, behavior that characterizes adult chatting was observed: smiling, frowning, surprise, patterned eye contact, spontaneous and reciprocal eyebrow flashing, tongue protrusion, gesturelike arm movements, imitation, **synchrony** of her body positions with those of her mother. Sarah used few facial expressions and gestured much less in other, nonsocial situations, for example, when she reached for a ball or played with an object.

Mothers capitalize on such behavior and see it as communicative. Sarah's mother, for example, says when Sarah shakes her head, "You're looking very pensive, aren't you? You don't want to smile." Mothers scarcely ever refer to themselves in these conversations. Only 9 percent of Sarah's mother's pronominal subjects were "I"; 77 percent were "you." Only 2 percent of her sentences referred to her own feelings or intentions, and these were often playful: "I'll bite your little hand off." Only 3 percent were directive, and these also were playful: "You let me go!" when Sarah was holding onto her hair. Most of the mother's talk was about Sarah's psychological state; she was continually interpreting her moods.

Another infant, at 6 months, differentiated his vocalizations toward objects and to mother by his pitch, using a lower pitch for mother. When his voice dropped, his mother would check to see whether he had redirected his attention to her. A third baby vocalized more sharply when he wanted an out-of-reach object; hearing this cue, mother would look for the object and give it to him (Bruner, 1978).

Jerome Bruner describes one vignette in a mother-child communication attempt observed in his lab (1978). Jon often made the gesture of reaching out with both his hands. His mother usually interpreted this as a signal that Jon wanted some familiar, hand-sized object beyond his reach, and she generally provided it. One day, at 8 months, Jon used the signal. His mother interpreted it as calling for her hand, because there was no object close by, and she performed her "walking hand" game—walking her fingers up Jon's front to his chin. Jon tolerated this, unenthusiastically, then reached again. Mother interpreted his gesture as a request for repetition. Jon participated even more reluctantly. Mother, on completion, repeated the game, even though Jon made no signal. He averted his gaze and whimpered a little. She repeated it once more and Jon was completely disgusted. There was a pause. Then, 27 seconds after Jon first reached out, he reached again, this time pulling the mother's hand to a position where he could hold on and raise himself to standing—achieving the goal he had been after in the first place.

These brief interactions clearly illustrate step and counterstep, match and mismatch in mother's and infant's effort to "dance"—to communicate. For Sarah, Jon, and the other children, learning that someone will try to interpret their actions, learning what interpretations their actions evoke, and learning how these may be modified are just as essential to the development of communication as the later mastery of grammar.

PLAYING

Something mothers and babies do best together and enjoy most is play. Play becomes more frequent during the first year though it never becomes very frequent—on the average less than half an hour a day in one study (Clarke-Stewart, 1973). Play need not be a formal game, just an animated little episode filled with joy and laughter, excitement, even hilarity for mother and infant. It usually includes meaningless words repeated rhythmically, such as changing rhymes, and some physical activity, such as dancing or tickling, patting or jiggling.

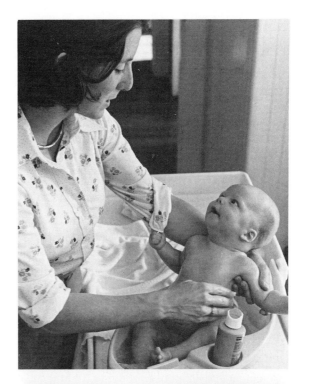

Mother–infant play makes an enjoyable break from the bath for the young infant, causes gales of giggles for the older infant. Either way, the behavior of mother and baby is finely meshed and in tune.

When a mother is playing she is emotionally alive. In this state she provides stimulation within the range of what the infant is constitutionally ready to receive. Exciting, stimulating play sessions are interspersed with periods of quiet and rest.

Stern (1974) and Alan Fogel (1977) have analyzed mother-infant play through detailed examinations of films and videotape. The play period is subdivided into episodes of engagement and time out. An engagement episode is a discrete burst of active, structured play that engages and maintains the infant's attention or gets him or her to play a game. Time out is a pause that lasts at least 3 seconds; Mother stops playing and may look away, a pause that refreshes. This brief moment gives her time to assess the level of the infant's excitement, judge whether their play ended on a high note or a low one, to formulate a goal, and correct strategies to "reset" the interaction. She uses a calming-down strategy if the engagement was too exciting, a speed-up strategy if it was not exciting enough. The infant can also regulate the stimulation. These engagement and time-out episodes occur at regular intervals throughout the play period, with a predictable tempo that allows the infant to form an expectation about the interactions.

The analogy of the dance seems particularly apt for mother-infant play. At the end of a measure, the leading partner must indicate to the following partner which way they will turn. Once the signal is transmitted, the two partners can follow the known dance steps and move in synchrony for a short period (1,2,3; 1,2,3; . . .). The longer they have danced together, the longer the sequences of patterns partners can string together without requiring a new decision. So it is with mother and baby. Together they evolve some exquisitely intricate dyadic patterns.

But not all couples achieve the same smooth skill as Fred Astaire and Ginger Rogers. And sometimes mother or baby or both misstep in their dance. The infant may resist being held or be "rejecting" or less alert while held (Thoman, Korner, and Beason-Williams, 1977). The mother may be depressed or overstimulating, or her abilities to play may be limited.

Stern (1971) describes a pair of twins, Fred and Mark, whose mother had somehow developed different feelings toward them even while they were in the womb. One baby kicked more and, because the mother thought of herself as a lively and en-

ergetic person, she identified with this active and yet unseen presence. After delivery she assumed that Mark, who was the more active, was the one who had been kicking inside. Her feelings toward him were more positive. Toward Fred, the quiet one, who was "more like his father," her feelings were much less positive. These twins were filmed in face-to-face play when they were 3½ months old. The meshing of the behavior of Mark and his mother was normal. He moved synchronously with her when they were facing and looking at each other but did not pay attention to her when they were not so engaged. When Mother approached Fred, however, he turned away; when she withdrew, he turned toward her. Fred and his mother were never really together and never fully apart.

If, during a lively play session, the infant suddenly becomes sober-faced or grimaces, yawns, or looks away, the mother should take this as a signal to ease off. The intrusive mother will react with greater intensity, complexity, and richness, which will further distress her young son or daughter. The baby will have lost a valuable opportunity to learn that he or she can, through emotional communication, regulate the external world. If such experiences are repeated, the infant may learn that his or her facial expressions are not relevant communications or that they only make matters worse. If the mother is insensitive not only to facial cues but to all her baby's efforts at communicating, the infant may learn that the world is totally beyond his or her control.

Other mothers cannot muster the energy for play sessions. They may be preoccupied with other responsibilities or under psychological strain. A mother may resent her caretaking role and thus resent the baby. If she is insecure, she may be oversensitive to the infant's averted gaze, interpreting it as a personal rejection. If she is inhibited or suffers from obsessive fears or phobias, she may avoid playing with her child. The mother-infant "fit" may also be awry. An infant with an extremely high threshold for stimulation and a mother with few capabilities for providing it are likely to have boring, unsatisfactory play sessions. Reciprocity is perhaps the key to the infant's early social development. The newborn enters the world with a full set of competencies, characteristics, and behaviors. These qualities strongly influence parents right from the beginning, just as those of parents influence the infant.

SUMMARY

1. More infants die in the first month of life than at any other time before old age. An Apgar test is a quick appraisal of the newborn's condition that alerts medical attendants to those infants who need immediate, life-saving attention. In the first hours of life, newborns must begin to breathe on their own, control their body temperature, and ingest food, and their blood circulation must change from that of the uterine state as well.

2. An infant acquires motor abilities in the same cephalocaudal and proximodistal directions that it developed physically before birth. At birth, infants can move only in uncoordinated fashion, but they do have finely tuned and highly specific reflexes. These reflexes include sucking, rooting for a nipple when the cheek is brushed, the palmar grasp, and the Moro startle reflex. Absence of several reflexes at birth may indicate a neurological problem.

3. The *sequence* of motor milestones varies little among infants. But the wide variation in *rates* of motor development among both individuals and cultural groups may be ascribed to several factors. Early experience, training, and genetic factors all play a role.

4. Investigators continue to learn about infants' perceptual and sensory capacities, although infants raise obstacles for any investigator. Investigators use infants' head turning, eye movements, heart rates, and sucking rates to find out what they can see, hear, smell, taste, and remember.

5. Reseach on infants' vision shows that the anatomy and functioning of the eye are immature at birth but develop rapidly during the first year of life. They are quite farsighted, and their vision is fuzzy. Visual acuity is poor at the start of life—20/150 to 20/800—but improves to 20/20 in the first year.

6. Infants prefer looking at stimuli that are large, moving, and moderately complex; that have contours, curves, and high light-dark contrast; and that fit their visual capacity, or "window." The human face is particularly interesting. Infants scan visual stimuli in an organized and systematic fashion. They can see color, and their depth perception seems to develop between 5 and 7 months after birth.

7. Infants in utero can hear several weeks before birth. They have lower thresholds for sounds in the range of the human voice and react differently to patterned sounds (like voices) and clicks or tones. At 1 month, infants can discriminate between some phonemes, although it takes until 12 months for discrimination of the most subtle phonemic contrasts. Newborns turn their eyes and heads toward a sound; older infants may reach for it.

8. Newborns can taste the differences among water, milk, sweet, and salty solutions. They can distinguish pleasant and unpleasant odors, and soon after birth they can pick out the smell of their own mother's breast pad.

9. It is unlikely that the behavior of young infants can be classically conditioned. But operant conditioning has been shown to strengthen newborns' reflexes and older babies' customary behaviors.

10. Researchers have used paired comparisons, habituation, and reactivation to investigate the capacities of infant memory. Several studies suggest that infants between 3 and 6 months old have memories lasting at least 2 weeks for salient experiences or qualities.

11. The question of whether newborns can imitate behavior they see modeled has sparked a lively debate among psychologists. Some investigators have claimed to find evidence that newborns can imitate an adult's facial gestures; others have not been able to replicate these results. The question therefore is still open.

12. Despite their apparent helplessness, newborns are equipped to establish powerful social relations with those around them. The newborn's appearance, vocalization, facial expression, and movements elicit from parents and others social reactions that assure continuing care. A bond of affection from mother to baby is perhaps the most powerful of these reactions. Extra contact between mother and infant immediately after birth has been suggested as one way of fostering that bond. Extra contact has been shown to increase mothers' affectionateness toward their young infants and to affect the length of time they breastfeed, but long-term effects are unlikely. Many factors influence the mother-child bond.

13. Mothers and infants have been likened to dancers whose movements grow increasingly well coordinated with experience. The infant's repertoire of gazing and crying gradually expands to include smiling and laughing. When the infant can recognize its mother, the pair engage in a new level of reciprocity. Responsive babies reinforce bonds with their parents, but unresponsive or irritable babies may undermine those bonds.

14. Vocalizing and babbling are important means of communication between babies and others. Adults use a special "baby talk" register when talking to infants, and infants come to prefer and, later, to imitate these sounds. They find the mother's voice especially attractive, presumably because it is familiar, friendly, high pitched, and often expressive and exaggerated.

KEY TERMS

Apgar test
Reflex
Rooting reflex
Sucking reflex
Palmar grasp
Moro reflex
Electrocardiograph (EKG)
Electroencephalograph (EEG)
Galvanic skin response (GSR)

Rapid eye movements (REM)
Autostimulation
Tonic neck reflex
Habituate
Stabilimeter
Pneumograph
Retina
Fovea
Lateral geniculate nucleus (LGN)
Dendrites

Saccadic eye movements
Astigmatism
Accommodate
Depth of focus
Visual acuity
Contrast sensitivity
Linear systems analysis
Visual cliff
Stereopsis
Tympanum
Cochlea

Auditory evoked response (AER)
Phoneme
Paired comparison
Reactivation
Bonding
Endogenous smiles
Exogenous smiles
Babbling
Motherese
Microanalytic
Pseudodialogue
Synchrony

SUGGESTED READINGS

Belsky, Jay. *In the Beginning: Readings on Infancy.* New York: Columbia University Press, 1982. A collection of articles illustrating research on social, emotional, and cognitive development in infancy, with emphasis on the transactional nature of early development.

Kaye, Kenneth. *The Mental and Social Life of Babies: How Parents Create Persons.* Chicago: University of Chicago Press, 1982. An original theory of the roles of mothers and infants, respectively, in their early face-to-face interactions.

Klaus, Marshall H., and Kennell, John H. *Parent-Infant Bonding.* St. Louis: C. V. Mosby, 1982. Support for the critical period explanation of maternal bonding, gathered by its chief proponents from animal and human studies.

McCall, Robert C. *Infants.* Cambridge: Harvard University Press, 1979. Developmental milestones of the infant's cognitive and social progress, clearly explained for parents.

Schaffer, H. Rudolph. *Mothering.* Cambridge: Harvard University Press, 1977. A lucidly written review of psychological research on the different roles that an infant's mother fills and how they relate to the infant's development.

Stern, Daniel. *The First Relationship.* Cambridge: Harvard University Press, 1977. A most readable account of what we have learned through close analysis of videotapes of early mother-infant interactions.

PART III

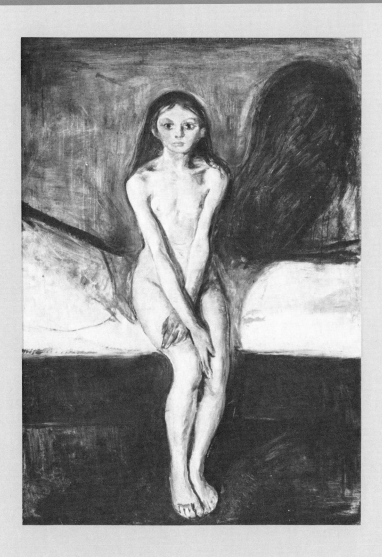

PHYSICAL
BASES

CHAPTER 6

Growth and Health

If we look down a row of newborn babies in a hospital nursery, all of them born on schedule, we find considerable differences in weight, shape, size, and physical maturity. One baby may be less than 6 pounds, another over 10 pounds. Variability in birth weight is normal. It is caused by a number of factors, genetic and environmental.

Hereditary factors actually have surprisingly little effect in controlling size before birth, but they are largely responsible for **catch-up growth** during the first year (Tanner, 1974). Characteristics of the mother control the size of the fetus before birth, enabling a child who has a big father and is genetically programmed to be large to develop in the uterus of a small mother. The maternal **restraining effect** keeps the fetus to a size that will usually allow for a successful delivery at the proper time. The baby is born smaller, but after birth its genes controlling adult size quickly express themselves (Tanner, 1974). The classic example of the maternal restraining effect is seen in the crossing of shire horses with much smaller Shetland ponies. The shire mother gives birth to a large foal and the Shetland mother to a small foal, but both foals reach the same size after a few months.

The sex of the baby and its order of birth also affect its weight and maturity. Boys generally weigh ½ ounce more at birth, have larger heads and faces, have a greater proportion of muscle tissue, and are longer, whereas girls tend to have skeletons and nervous systems that are more mature by approximately 2 weeks. Firstborns are usually lighter, but they grow faster once they are out of the uterus, typically making up the initial weight deficit (Tanner, 1974). Twins are usually premature and have lower birth weights. When the mother gives birth to more than two babies, they are almost always premature and underweight.

POSTNATAL GROWTH

Birth appears to be a dramatic break with prenatal life. To those in the delivery room, the climactic entry of the newborn seems to be a conclusion of the growth process that has unfolded covertly within the womb. Yet birth, in terms of physical growth, is more a comma than a period. Postnatal growth is primarily a continuing expansion of tissues and organs already established, a period of development and enlargement of existing cells, not a time for new parts and functions to appear (Tanner, 1978).

The nervous system shows the most striking continuities from prenatal to postnatal development. The **electroencephalogram (EEG)**—brain wave records—of 6-week-old infants born at 28 weeks after conception were almost identical to those of infants born at 34 weeks after conception and tested immediately, although the first group had been exposed to extrauterine life for 6 weeks, whereas the second group had been in the uterus during that time (Dreyfus-Brisac, 1975). Thus the time of the actual birth does not seem to affect brain maturation as measured by brain waves.

Certain physical and physiological changes do, of course, occur at birth. Very small babies gain weight even more rapidly than babies of average weight. The catch-up growth of an infant whose size was restricted by a small womb or by maternal smoking or by malnutrition takes place largely during the first 5 months of life. A baby weighing 4 pounds at birth may have doubled its weight in 2 or 3 months and weigh five times the birth weight at 1 year (Tanner, 1974).

CELLS AND GROWTH OF TISSUES

Growth is not uniform. At any given moment during infancy, one body part or organ may be growing ahead of, or at a different rate from, that of another. This **asynchrony** is a characteristic of human growth throughout prenatal and postnatal life (Figure 6.1). Different rates of growth of vital organs are based on differing patterns of cell division and growth. The physical changes that parents witness in their infants and children are all based on activity at the microscopic, cellular level. There are three patterns of cellular growth. Cells of one type, such as those lining the gut and comprising the skin and blood, are continuously dying and being replaced. Glands and parts of the liver and kidney are made up of long-lived cells, which constitute a second category. Cells in these body parts tend to be stable, though they can regenerate when damaged. The cells of a third category cannot form after their growth period is over. Nerve, fat, and muscle cells are in this category. At birth the newborn has all the muscle fibers it will ever have. Fat cells appar-

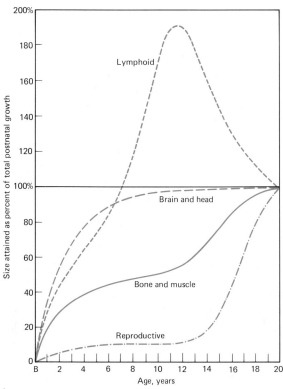

FIGURE 6.1
These growth curves for parts and tissues of the body illustrate the asynchrony of human growth after birth (Harrison, Weiner, Tanner, and Bernicot, 1964).

later in life (Hirsch, 1975; Winick, 1971). Later, when cells are simply increasing in size, malnutrition or an excess of nutrients is not likely to have a permanent effect (Tanner 1978).

GROWTH CURVES

Internally, growth proceeds in a tumultuous manner. The body is in a constant state of flux. Nutrients are continually being ingested and metabolized. Some cells are dividing, whereas others have stopped dividing but are changing in consistency, and still others remain fairly stable. But externally, to the pediatrician who weighs and measures the infant and then the child, the process of growth proceeds gradually and regularly.

The average North American newborn weighs 7½ pounds and measures 20 inches. During the first few days of life, the baby loses as much as 10 percent of its body weight because its digestive system is not working properly. By about the fifth day, it begins to gain again and is expected to increase its weight by 1 ounce a day for the next few months. Babies double their birth weight in 4 months and nearly triple it in 1 year. During the second year, the body lengthens and less weight is added. At 24 months babies weigh four times their birth weight and measure about 34½ inches.

A **growth curve** is a record that shows the pattern of physical change over successive ages. If we view birth to maturity as a journey, one kind of growth curve, the upper curve in Figure 6.2, shows us how far the individual or the group has traveled. The lower curve indicates how fast they have traveled. The two parts of Figure 6.2 are actually the earliest known individual growth curves. They plot the growth in height of an 18th-century French nobleman's son from 6 months to 18 years. The upper curve increases gradually, as De Montbeillard's son grew taller and taller. The lower curve decreases through infancy and childhood, as the boy's rate of growth slowed down; then it increases sharply as growth accelerated at adolescence. If the boy's rate of growth could have been plotted from conception, the decrease would have been shown to begin even earlier, in the fourth month of prenatal development (Tanner, 1978).

The graphs of the growth of De Montbeillard's son are typical of curves of normal physical development. Although children reach particular heights

ently increase in numbers only at certain times: before birth, during the first 2 years, and in early adolescence (Hirsch, 1975).

Most of the division of nerve cells making up the central nervous system is finished by 18 weeks, though other supporting cells called **neuroglia** continue to multiply until 1 or 2 years after birth (Tanner, 1978). If the nutrients necessary for cell division and growth are not present during this early critical period, a smaller number of nerve cells or **neurons** may actually form (Winick, Brasel, and Rosso, 1972). It is not yet fully understood what effect fewer brain cells have on psychological development. Because malnutrition is usually only one of a number of deprivations, behavioral deficits that show up later on in malnourished children cannot be attributed solely to the smaller number of brain cells. As for fat cells, some recent research suggests that excessive intake of nutrients in infancy may cause too many of them or too many precursors of fat cells to form; this abundance of cells may mean that the child is at risk of becoming obese

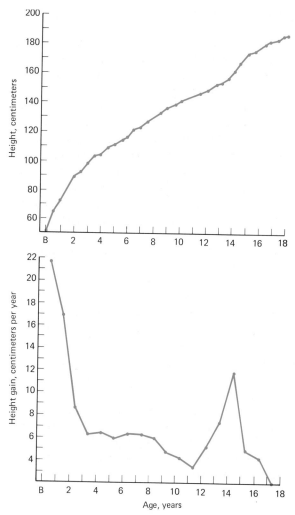

FIGURE 6.2

The growth curve at the top traces the increasing height of De Montbeillard's son, who grew to be 18 back in the years 1759 to 1777. The bottom growth curve shows that his rate of growth decreased, except for a spurt in adolescence (Tanner, 1978). (10 centimeters = 3.9 inches)

cross section of the population. If a population is made up of an ethnic mosaic, like that of the United States, separate growth standards for the groups of different origins are needed (Eichorn, 1979). Should the growth of a child from a genetically tall subgroup be measured against standards set for a population that includes many genetically small persons, the individual may be judged normal when his or her development is actually retarded by malnutrition or illness. Genetically small children measured against national norms might be singled out as abnormally short when they are growing normally. On the other hand, an entire subgroup may be suffering from a dietary deficiency. It will not be evident if standards are set for the subgroup. The deficiency will be revealed only when their growth is measured against a national or international sampling (Figure 6.4).

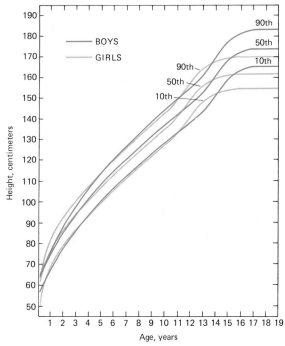

FIGURE 6.3

The dark-colored lines trace the norms of height from birth to 19 years of age for tall American boys, those in the 90th percentile and taller than 90 percent of their contemporaries; average American boys (50th percentile); and short American boys, those in the 10th percentile and shorter than 90 percent of their contemporaries. The light-colored lines indicate the norms of height for tall, average, and short American girls from birth to 19 years of age. (10 centimeters = 3.9 inches.)

or other markers of growth at somewhat different ages, average curves for all children in a population are helpful for alerting us to individual abnormalities of growth (Figure 6.3). Radical departure from the norm suggests physical problems or poor care. "Abnormality" is a word reserved for the far extremes of the typical curve for any age group. A child below the third percentile, for example, would be regarded as pathologically small. If such an assessment is to be meaningful, the standards themselves must represent an adequate and up-to-date

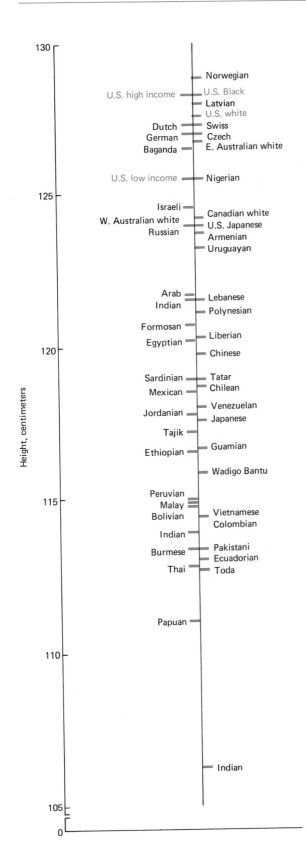

Height, centimeters

MEASURES OF MATURITY

Although inches and pounds increase as children grow up, they are not the best indicators of physical maturity. The length, thickness, and hardness of bones are the most accurate measures of maturing. Bone age, or skeletal maturity, can be determined by X-raying the child's hand (Tanner, 1970). As we have mentioned, during fetal life, the cartilage of the individual's frame begins to be replaced by bone cells. For each bone in the body, cartilage cells in the center of the limb break down and bone cells appear (Tanner, 1978). This area is the primary center of ossification. Secondary centers, called **epiphyses,** appear later, shortly before birth. For the most part these are at each end of the bone. By the end of their first year, most children have finished the ossification of 3 of the 28 hand and wrist bones. By the time they are 2 years old, ossification of the skull is complete, and its six **fontanels** (soft spots) have disappeared. The epiphyses at the ends of a bone do not fuse with the bone's main body until puberty, when the individual has reached his or her full height.

The first baby tooth, a front one of the lower jaw, is another milestone of physical maturity. It will appear between 6 and 9 months, and the rest of the baby teeth will appear by the infant's second birthday. These teeth are replaced by permanent teeth from about ages 6 to 13.

CHANGING SIZE AND PROPORTIONS

The proportions of the infant's body change in the two related directions of growth so evident in prenatal development: cephalocaudal and proximodistal. Because of the prenatal growth of the head, that of the newborn is large compared to the rest of its body. The head of the newborn infant is a full fourth of its body length. Its legs, however, are very short, only a little longer than its head. The top of the baby's head and its enormous eyes have grown much more than the chin, which is tiny. The

FIGURE 6.4

The heights of 8-year-old boys from around the world are compared to those of 8-year-old boys from white and black, high- and low-income families in the United States (Meredith, 1978). (10 centimeters = 3.9 inches)

feet, which will be five times larger in adulthood, are proportionately the smallest parts of the infant's body. This combination of parts that are very large and very small, judged by the proportions of older people, engages and fascinates most of those who look at the baby.

After birth it is the baby's head that continues to grow the most rapidly. The quick weight gain in the first year is mainly body fat, which gives many infants their round, dimpled appearance. Although infants require some of this padding for warmth and as a food reserve during their teething, they do not need to be fat. Overfeeding may give them weight problems later. Toward the end of the first year, the infant's weight gain slows, and growth of muscle and bone accelerates. The baby's trunk becomes its fastest growing portion.

After 1 year, the baby's extremities grow more rapidly than the body (Bayer and Bayley, 1959). Longer legs allow the baby greater mobility. By the age of 2 or 3 the child is losing much of his or her baby fat. The chubby infant thins down to the slimmer and more active toddler, who may have a much smaller appetite and very definite ideas about what is good to eat. From ages 6 to 9, accelerating leg growth may give the child a wiry appearance. By age 9 boys and girls are so similar in build and body proportions that from the back we cannot tell them apart.

The most accurate predictions of adult stature would be based on an individual's bone age. Because most children do not have regular X-rays to determine the development of their bones, however, predictions of adult stature generally rely on predictive formulas based on the child's present height. George Lowery (1973) gives this simple rule of thumb: at age 2 a boy is half his adult stature, a girl slightly more than that. Girls 6 years old are approximately 70 percent of their final size, 11-year-old girls are 90 percent of it. The older the child, the more accurate predictions are likely to be (Garn, 1966). Many children, however, particularly those whose parents are extremely different in size, will not fall neatly into their predicted slot.

OBESITY

Fat babies may turn into fat adults, or so the findings from some research suggest. Jules Hirsch (1975) has found that the number of fat cells, or **adipocytes**, is influenced by an infant's diet. According to the **adipocyte hypothesis**, the first year or two of life may be a critical period during which diet affects how many fat cells actually form. If an excess of fat cells forms during this early period, it may permanently predispose the individual toward obesity (Harding, 1971). Although dieting may reduce the size of the fat cells, their absolute number remains so high as to thwart attempts to remove weight and keep it off. Some

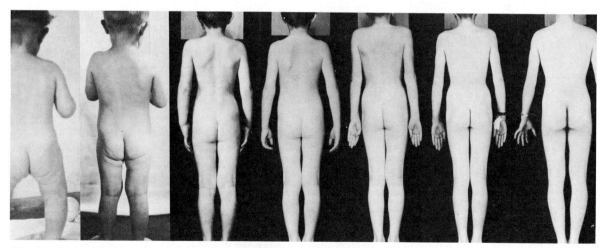

The photographs of this boy, taken at successive ages, show the typical changes in proportions from infancy to maturity. His head, which was half of his body at 2 months after conception, makes up less and less of his body size. The ages, left to right, are 15 months, 30 months, and 6, 11, 14, and 18 years.

Will the fat infant become a fat adult? Overfeeding a chubby infant may weight the balance on the side of obesity. What is cute in a young child may bring loneliness and rejection later.

evidence, on the other hand, suggests that fat babies are not necessarily doomed to be fat adults. Alex Roche (1981) has challenged the adipocyte theory with data from animal experiments that suggest the number of fat cells is not fixed in the early years. Furthermore, in humans, measures of obesity in infancy and in adulthood show no significant correlations. Correlations between early and later obesity do increase as children grow older, and they are significant by the time the children are 6 years old. Obesity that begins in childhood, in short, does tend to persist into adulthood, and it is more difficult to treat than obesity that begins later in life. But this tendency is as likely to depend on social and psychological pressures as on the number of fat cells. By the time children are 6, overeating has become a habit that is hard to break. A child needs eat only an extra 100 calories a day—a cookie or two, a bag of potato chips, a glass of soda pop— to gain 3000 calories in a month. Only 3500 extra calories make a weight gain of 1 pound.

The extra few pounds on the child turn into extra tens of pounds on the adolescent. Overweight children tend to feel rejected by others and to feel that people always react to their fatness. Jean Mayer (1975) showed to a number of both thin and fat girls a picture of a girl a short distance away from a group of other girls. All the thin girls interpreted the picture to mean that the girl was walking *toward* the group; all the fat girls interpreted the picture to mean that the girl had been *excluded* from the group. In fact, overweight young people, especially girls, may be rejected from social activities. One study of college admissions showed that, if applicants were interviewed, obese girls had only one-third the chance of acceptance to their chosen college as thin girls (Canning and Mayer, 1966). Whether the problem is fat cells or eating patterns, therefore, overfeeding a child is one cause of obesity that parents can—and should—control.

But other factors influence weight gain as well. Kelly Brownell at the University of Pennsylvania has found that the size of fat cells influences how much a person weighs (Turkington, 1984). He suggests that when the size of fat cells is normal for an individual, the risks associated with obesity, such as diabetes or high blood pressure, diminish. When people try to lose weight and shrink their fat cells below their normal size, however, their bodies feel starved. Even with 20 or 30 extra pounds on them, these people feel obsessed with food. Brownell also has found from animal studies that seesaw cycles of weight loss and gain are counterproductive. Each successive attempt to lose weight takes longer, and weight is gained again ever more readily. Furthermore, although people may lose muscle as well as fat, they tend to put back only fat. Although the scale may read the same number of pounds after each diet, the proportion of body fat actually has increased.

Another factor that contributes to leanness or obesity, according to the **thermogenesis theory**, is a person's general body **metabolism**, the rate at which calories are burned. This theory, which is well supported by research on rodents, suggests that how efficiently people burn calories is more important in determining obesity than the number of calories they consume. Proponents of yet another theory, the **set-point theory**, maintain that everyone's weight settles around a given point and does not vary much from that point (Bennett and Gurin, 1982). Some mechanism in the brain, as yet undiscovered, regulates calorie burning so that the body remains at or near the set point. Lean people, according to this theory, burn the extra calories they take in without turning them into deposits of fat. The governing mechanism in their brain, in effect, makes their body "waste" extra calories. But the metabolism of fat people makes their bodies economical about burning extra calories; they store those calories as extra fat. For that reason, diets that attempt to change a set point almost invariably fail.

Finally, taste preferences and levels of activity may contribute to obesity. From the very beginning, it has been found, some infants prefer sweet flavors; later, these individuals ignore internal cues that they are full (Milstein, 1978). Such infants are thought to be likely candidates for later overweight; so, too, are inactive babies. Fatter babies, who eat only moderately, tend to be quiet and placid. The biggest eaters are thin, tense babies who cry often (Mayer, 1975).

BRAIN GROWTH

Major developmental changes in the human brain have been discovered by scientists in the last few decades. Present knowledge comes from several different sources. Animal studies have shown that stages of brain development are similar among young mammals of various species—including human beings. Microscope studies of the structure of the human brain are rarer, but they have contributed their share of important information. Scientists also rely on tracings of the brain's electrical responses to stimuli such as the EEG.

At any stage of human development, these sources of evidence suggest, the brain's functioning depends on several factors. One of these factors is the location and arrangement of brain cells in relation to one another. Scientists know that certain types of neurons are organized in clusters in the brain. Genetic instructions are responsible for orderly patterns of brain growth and development.

In the human fetus's brain, the earliest neurons form the lower layers of the **cerebral cortex**—that region of the brain responsible for complex and conscious thought. The cortex thus develops from the inside out, as related columns of cells move together (Sidman and Rakic, 1973). The cortex ultimately consists of horizontal layers of clusters of neurons interspersed with vertical columns of cells. The six layers of cells in the cortex are in place in fetuses of 7 months of age. But the development of the **cerebellum**—the region of the brain that coordinates movement and sensory input—is not completed until well into the first year after birth. Thus the cerebellum is especially susceptible to toxic substances late in fetal development and in the months just after birth (Conel, 1939–1967; Sidman and Rakic, 1973; Takashima, Chan, Becker, and Armstrong, 1980). Connections between the cerebellum and the cerebral cortex mature in the first 4 years after birth, and **myelination**—the deposit of a white, fatty substance that improves the transmission of impulses—in these areas continues into adulthood.

At birth, the infant's brain contains all of the neurons it will have but weighs only about one-quarter of its adult weight. If the brain were any larger, the skull would have trouble passing through the birth canal. The brain is immature at birth in several ways. **Glial cells**, which help nourish the neurons and provide their myelin sheaths, form and grow after birth; myelination increases the size and weight of the brain; connecting fibers between the neurons also grow in number and length. By 2 years of age, a child's brain has reached about three-quarters of adult size and weight.

Because the cortex of the newborn is immature, reflexes govern much of its behavior. In painstaking studies of a few children at birth, 1 month, 3 months, 6 months, 15 months, 2 and 4 years old, Jesse Conel (1939–1967) demonstrated that as various areas of the cortex develop, the infant gains voluntary control over movement. The brain develops according to the cephalocaudal and proximodistal principles that also govern physical development before and after birth. The first cells to function are those in the primary motor area controlling the arms and trunk, allowing babies to control head and trunk before legs and arms, and these before hands and fingers (see Chapter 5). By about 4 months of age, the infant's cortex has enough mature cells to direct voluntary arm movements. Cortical control of legs and fingers does not occur for several months. Meanwhile, the primary sensory (touch) area of the cortex develops, followed by development of the primary visual and then the primary auditory areas. A study by Robert Hoffman (1978), in which he recorded changes in brain responses when infants were shown visual stimuli, showed that control of such sights shifted to the visual cortex at about 2 months. The auditory cortex is not involved in processing sounds until somewhat later. Finally, cortical association areas develop, and the 2-year-old can integrate sight, sound, and voluntary movement. She or he can reach for a ball, put a peg in a hole, and walk on stepping stones.

What is happening inside the nerve cell as all of these changes take place in the cortex? The neuron includes a cell nucleus and, surrounding it, **Nissl substance**, which often appears just as evidence of some new function appears, and **ribosomes**, which contain ribonucleic acid (RNA) and produce proteins necessary for the functioning and survival of the neuron. Microscope studies show that these and other structures of the neurons develop grad-

ually. Energy for brain-cell processes comes mainly from glucose, a simple sugar, which the cells metabolize. Computerized studies of radioactive glucose in the brain have shown that the metabolic activity of neurons increases markedly when specific areas of the brain are stimulated. The cells of the visual cortex, for example, metabolize more actively when people are presented with visual stimuli. Studies of human fetuses' and children's brain cells have demonstrated that signs of glucose metabolism are absent or scant at 22 weeks gestational age, show clearly throughout the deep layers of the cortex at 36 to 38 weeks gestational age, have expanded noticeably in infants 4½ months of age, and continue to increase until children are 11 years old (Farkas-Bargeton, 1978).

The brain matures in functional units. Neurons that carry impulses to a certain area of the cortex are myelinated at the same time as those carrying impulses away from it. Individual neurons transmit impulses along **dendrites**, which usually receive the impulses, and **axons**, which usually send the impulses (Figure 6.5). Axons and dendrites begin to develop soon after the neurons have migrated to their final destination within the brain and ner-

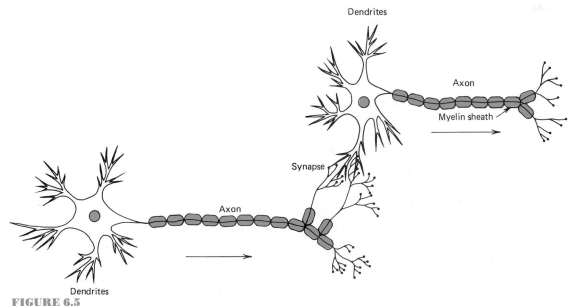

FIGURE 6.5

A schematic drawing of two neurons (neurons differ considerably in size and shape and may have many more branchings than are shown here). Impulses always travel in the same direction (arrows) down the axon. When an impulse reaches the knobs at the end of the axon, small amounts of certain chemicals are released from inside the knobs, cross the synapse to the dendrite of the receiving neuron and cause it to fire. An electrically insulating sheath of myelin forms on many neurons as the nervous system develops after birth.

vous system. Dendrites begin branching out between 34 and 36 weeks gestational age. From birth through childhood, the signs of neuron maturation are increases in the length and branching of the dendrites and increases in the length and width of axons. There are individual variations in the rate at which these developments occur, and some evidence suggests that stimulation from the environment can increase the growth of dendrites. In one study, 4- to 6-week-old kittens were trained to pull back one of their front paws to avoid a mild electric shock (Spinelli, Jensen, and Viana Di Prisco, 1980). Microscopic analysis of cells showed that in the corresponding area of the brain, the dendrites had developed more branches. This kind of branching of dendrites is the most important clue to the functional capacity of the brain. The more connections, the wider the range of behavior (Tanner, 1978).

Neurons transmit impulses from axons to dendrites by releasing chemical **neurotransmitters** that carry or inhibit an electrical charge across **synapses** between neurons. Points of synaptic contact usually occur between axons and dendrites, but they also occur between neuron cell bodies and between dendrites. In human fetuses and infants, the development of synapses follows the same sequence as the branching of dendrites. Microscopic analyses show immature synapses in fetuses of 15 weeks. The synapses continue to mature throughout prenatal life, and mature synapses appear at 35 weeks (Purpura, 1975). About 30 neurotransmitters have been identified so far; some excite and others inhibit the individual's response. The neurotransmitters include: norepinephrine, involved in arousal, dreaming, and moods; serotonin, involved in temperature regulation, sensation, and sleep; and dopamine, involved in emotional response and complex movement. During the course of development, the types of neurotransmitters present at various sites in the brain and the strength of their deactivating substances change (Axelrod, 1974; Iverson, 1979).

These chemical processes are directed by the genes and are therefore responsible for the extremely precise "wiring" by which various regions of the brain progressively interconnect and begin to function (Wilson, 1983). Genetic instructions also govern successive phases of cell death. It seems that various brain regions originally develop an excess of cells. In the course of normal development, the extra cells die off. But if some cells develop abnormally, the extras can be used as replacements for normal development. Research has shown that, in infants whose brains are damaged, central brain pathways can regenerate and reconnect (Kalil and Reh, 1979). Once the extra cells have died off, extra connections between cells are reduced as well. After the first 2 years of life, unnecessary branches are discarded and replaced by more efficient ones (Huttenlocher, 1979; Mark, 1974). Today, researchers (Goldman, 1976; Tanner, 1970) believe that maturation should be viewed as a system of closely coordinated developments at every level of the nervous system. In this view, brain functioning depends on growth and formation of brain cells, myelination, complexity of dendrites, growth of connections among cells, and elimination of redundant or inefficient pathways.

Brain Lateralization

The brain is divided into two halves (hemispheres) connected by a band of myelinated tissue called the *corpus callosum*. Each brain hemisphere has its own special functions, a characteristic called *lateralization*. For example, muscles on one side of the body are controlled by areas of the brain in the opposite hemisphere. Although the hemispheres seem physically symmetrical, closer analysis reveals that the symmetry is only an illusion (Geschwind, 1979). The area that governs language is larger in one hemisphere than in the other, for example. For most people, even as infants, electrical activity is greater in the left hemisphere than in the right when they listen to spoken sounds, and it is greater in the right cortex when they listen to music (Molfese, Freeman, and Palermo, 1975). This division is related to later processing and production of language and music. In right-handed people, language is governed by the left hemisphere; the opposite holds for left-handed people. The muscles for speech are primarily controlled by **Broca's area** in the motor cortex. Neurons connect Broca's area to **Wernicke's area**, which coordinates vision and hearing (Geschwind, 1979—see Figure 6.6). As these areas of the cortex mature, infants acquire language. Thought processes unique to human beings probably develop from the top three of the six cortical layers of cells; myelination of the third

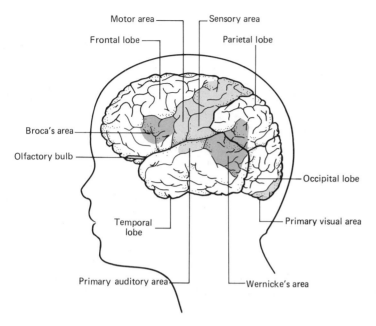

FIGURE 6.6

Language, attention, memory, spatial under-standing, and motor skills are located in the cor-tex, which is immature at birth. This drawing shows the left hemisphere of the mature cortex, where for most people speech production is controlled by Broca's area and speech comprehension by Wernicke's area.

such layer occurs when infants first speak in words (Milner, 1976). As children develop from one-word to two-word utterances, the number of neural con-nections multiplies extremely rapidly. Finally, as children expand their speech skills, that is, until they are about 4 years old, the myelination and the branching of neurons in Broca's area continue.

Research also suggests that in most people the right hemisphere processes music and nonspeech sounds, emotions, and spatial abilities (Figure 6.7). In one study by L. Saxby and M. P. Bryden (1984), for example, children were tested for which ear—and thus the opposite hemisphere of the brain—was favored for processing sentences with emo-tional content and sentences with just verbal con-tent. It was found that in even the youngest children (kindergartners), the right hemisphere was favored for processing emotional material and the left hem-isphere for processing verbal material. Other stud-ies have shown that people whose right hemisphere has been damaged show inappropriate emotional responses, misperceive others' emotions (Gesch-wind, 1979), and cannot draw or build a model from a plan (Kimura, 1975). Spatial abilities, like map reading and figure drawing, are lateralized at some later time in childhood, although the exact age is not known for certain (Carter and Kins-bourne, 1979; Flanery and Balling, 1979). It has

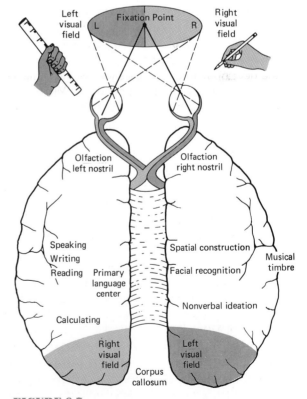

FIGURE 6.7

Each side of the brain controls half of the visual field; in addi-tion, each hemisphere performs some tasks better than the other.

been suggested that the two hemispheres process inputs differently, with the left being more efficient at logic, sequential tasks, and processing of rapidly changing stimuli and with the right being more efficient at spatial processing, emotion, and intuition (Ornstein, 1978).

PUBERTY

The physical transformation from child to adult gets under way with a still somewhat mysterious signal from the brain. The signal, which comes from the region called the *hypothalamus*, stimulates the pituitary gland to step up the release of the growth hormone, which then acts on all body tissues to stimulate their rate of growth. Both boys and girls have produced the male androgens and the female estrogens in about equal small amounts throughout childhood, although both have produced more androgens than estrogens. Now the hypothalamus directs the pituitary to begin producing these hormones as they are found in adult men and women. So the pituitary in turn directs the adrenals and the testes of boys and the ovaries of girls to secrete into the bloodstream androgens and estrogens in such quantities that boys will have larger amounts of androgens, girls larger amounts of estrogens.

THE GROWTH SPURT

The most dramatic and most visible signal to society at large that adolescence has begun is a spurt in growth unprecedented in the individual's development since the age of 2 (Tanner, 1970). Growth in height has been continuous so that boys often have already attained about 78 percent and girls 84 percent of their adult height (Katchadourian, 1976). But then the growth rate doubles in speed so that boys in their peak year, usually the 14th, grow an average of 3 to 5 inches. Although growth does not stop until approximately 18 years for women and 20 years for men, girls of 14 and boys of 16 have reached 98 percent of their ultimate adult height (Figure 6.8).

The **growth spurt**, of course, affects more than just skeletal growth. Muscular growth along with changes in the amount and distribution of fat alter the adolescent's body composition. The lungs grow in size and capacity, and the heart doubles in

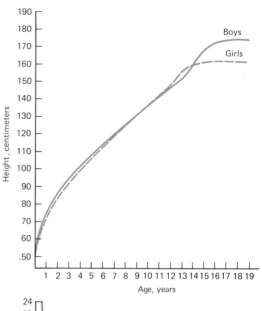

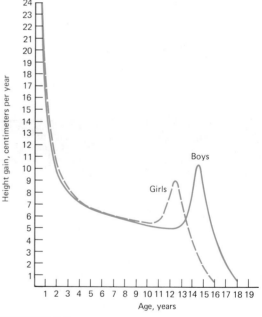

FIGURE 6.8

At about age 10½, girls begin their growth spurt (top) and are temporarily taller than their male peers. When boys, at about age 12, begin their growth spurt (bottom), they usually grow faster and for a longer period of time than girls (Tanner, Whitehouse, and Takaishi, 1966). (1 centimeter = 3.9 inches.)

weight. Stomach, kidneys, and blood volume all attain final adult size and level of functioning during the growth spurt. Strength, endurance, and stamina increase, particularly for boys (Marshall and Tan-

The age at which the adolescent growth spurt begins varies widely, at anywhere from 7 years to 13 for girls. These two girls are both 13 years old.

the age of 5. Now the nose, lips, and ears gain their full size before the upper part of the head does its final bit of growing. Growth in the adolescent is distoproximal rather than proximodistal as it was in the fetus and infant.

The complexions of adolescents coarsen, and their pores become larger. Much to their consternation, adolescents' sebaceous and sweat glands become more active. Eyes also grow and change in shape, making many adolescents near-sighted.

DEVELOPMENT OF REPRODUCTIVE AND SEXUAL CHARACTERISTICS

In the course of physical development through infancy and childhood, there is little need to make continual distinctions between boy baby and girl baby, between schoolgirl and schoolboy. Puberty, however, not only separates the men from the boys, but also the young men from the young women. Other systems of the body may change during puberty, but the reproductive system alters the most dramatically, making it possible for young people to reproduce. During puberty all the primary sexual organs enlarge, and adolescents develop **secondary sex characteristics,** the bodily signs that help to distinguish males from females and indicate physiological maturity (Figure 6.9).

About 1 year before the growth spurt begins for boys, their testes begin to enlarge and the skin of the scrotum reddens and coarsens. Downy, unpigmented pubic hair may appear at this time; it will gradually become darker and coarser and spread. About 1 year later the penis begins to grow and continues to do so for the next 2 years. The internal seminal vesicles are also developing. After the penis has grown for 1 year, boys become able to ejaculate seminal fluid containing sperm. The concentration of sperm does not become great enough for them to be considered fertile, however, until months or even a year or more later.

Downy facial hair and underarm hair appear. As the larynx grows and vocal cords double in length, the voice register of boys lowers an octave in pitch. Facial hair becomes coarse and pigmented. Chest hair tends to appear rather late in the sequence of changes. Midway through adolescence boys may have some breast enlargement; it disappears about a year later. During all this time, boys' general body

ner, 1974), whose blood also acquires a greater capacity for carrying oxygen. Boys also gain a greater ability to neutralize the chemical by-products of muscular exercise, such as lactic acid, which make muscles sore and fatigued. Some parts of the body do not take part in the growth spurt. Until early adolescence the tonsils and adenoids, the lymph nodes, and the lymph masses of the intestines have all gradually increased in size; thereafter, they shrink.

As we have seen, growth is not synchronous, and adolescents may look and feel gawky. First legs grow, then body, then shoulders. Even the forearm develops before the upper arm. The head and brain had attained 90 percent of their adult size by

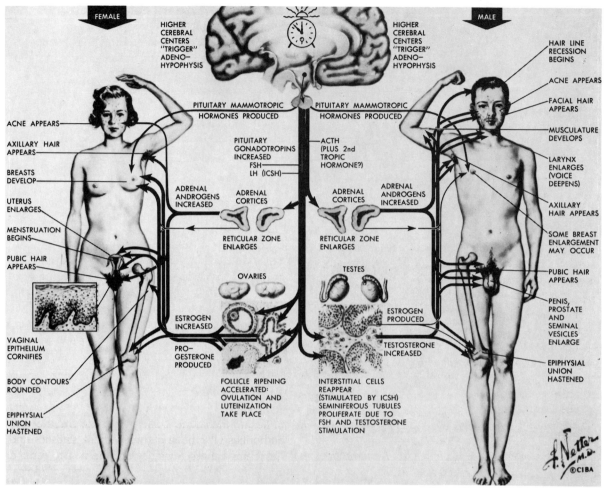

FIGURE 6.9

The effects of hormones on development at puberty are extremely complex, stimulating a number of physical changes and affecting many bodily tissues and functions. Copyright © 1965, by CIBA Pharmaceutical Company, Division of CIBA-GEIGY Corporation. Reprinted with permission from *The CIBA Collection of Medical Illustrations*, illustrated by Frank. H. Netter, M.D. All rights reserved.

configuration has been changing. They tend to be plump before adolescence, with half of them looking noticeably fat. The padding of adolescent boys decreases, even though they weigh more than girls. Their faces gradually reveal more muscle and bone. Moreover, androgens are stimulating the cells in their shoulder bones. By the end of puberty their widened shoulders, enlarged rib cage, and long legs give them an angular look.

In girls, the uterus begins to grow and the vaginal lining thickens, even before there are outward bodily signs of puberty. Then small accumulations of fatty and connective tissues and proliferating glandular cells cause a small rise around their nipples. These are the breast buds; they and downy pubic

hair appear shortly before the growth spurt starts. The breasts continue to grow in size for several years, and the pigmented area around the nipples becomes larger and darker in color. During these years external genitalia enlarge, pubic hair becomes pigmented and covers a greater area, and underarm hair appears.

Some 18 months after their growth spurt has reached its peak, girls have their first menstruation, called **menarche** (Figure 6.10). Estrogen production has become intense and cyclical in the preceding year and a half. Early menstrual periods are often irregular, however, and girls are usually not yet fertile. Ovulation, the release of a mature ovum, generally begins 10 to 12 months later.

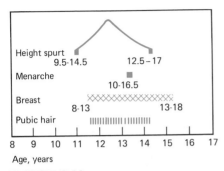
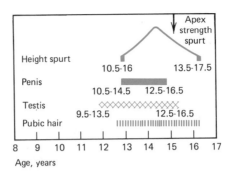

FIGURE 6.10

The lines and bars of these diagrams give the sequence and duration of physical events at puberty for the average girl (left) and boy (right). The range of ages at which each change may begin and conclude is indicated by the figures directly below the average start and finish points (Marshall and Tanner, 1970).

Girls' voices deepen somewhat, and girls generally develop some facial hair, a sign of sexual maturity. Throughout puberty the body configuration of adolescent girls also changes. Estrogens stimulate the cells in the hipbones; the pelvis becomes larger to facilitate childbearing. Layers of fat are also laid down just under the skin. This subcutaneous fat gives the curves of face and body a soft and rounded look.

THE TIMING OF PUBERTY

When does the growth spurt begin? A number of studies on physical changes during adolescence—

most notably those of James Tanner (1970), the Stolzes (1951), Leona Bayer and Nancy Bayley (1976), and Margaret Faust (1977)—allow us to chart average chronological ages for such events as increase in height, development of breasts and pubic hair, and age of menarche. The height or growth spurts begins, on the average, at 10½ for girls, peaks at 12, and is over at 14. The growth spurt for boys usually begins at 12 or 13, peaks at 14, and ends at 16. Shortly after girls reach their peak in height, menarche is likely to occur. But the very authorities who have garnered these statistics and determined these averages are the first to remind us of the wide range of variation among adoles-

On the average, girls start to grow tall two years before boys do.

cents. Faust (1977), in her longitudinal study of 94 girls from childhood to maturity, noted wide variations in the age at which any given physical change happened. The youngest girl to begin her growth spurt was 7 years, 5 months old, and the oldest was 13 years, 3 months. Some girls had completed their growth spurt before others had even begun. Girls vary more than boys in the age at which the growth spurt starts, and most girls begin their growth spurt before most boys, but the duration of puberty is approximately the same for both sexes: 2.81 years for boys, 2.82 years for girls (Faust, 1977).

THE SECULAR TREND IN AGE AT PUBERTY

We know that the age at which puberty begins has, over past generations, been decreasing. The trend has been documented in Canada, Sweden, Japan, Great Britain—in fact, in most places for which there are adequate growth statistics (Moore, 1970). In the United States, girls now begin menstruating at 11, 12, and 13 instead of at 13, 14, and 15, as they did 100 years ago (Bullough, 1981; Tanner, 1962), and the same **secular trend** is seen in boys, although they mature roughly 2 years later (Blizzard et al., 1974; Hamburg, 1974). The secular trend also applies to the growth spurt, now several years earlier than it was 100 years ago. People today are also generally heavier and taller than they were centuries ago (See Figure 6.11). In the United States, in this century, the average increase in the height of white adults from 1915 to 1940 was ½ inch each decade, from 1940 to 1960 ¼ inch each decade (Espenschade and Meleney, 1961).

A number of factors have caused puberty to happen earlier. Improved nutrition and health care are two important ones. Poverty, malnutrition, and disease can deflect individuals from their genetically programmed schedule of physical development; nutritious diet and control of disease can accelerate maturation. For instance, in Hong Kong, daughters of the rich have menarche at a mean age of 12.5, but daughters of the poor have menarche at 13.3 years (Tanner, 1962). Rose Frisch and Roger Revelle (1970) have noted that the adolescent growth spurt and menarche correlate with a mean body weight. They have proposed that when a girl reaches a **critical body weight,** of about 100

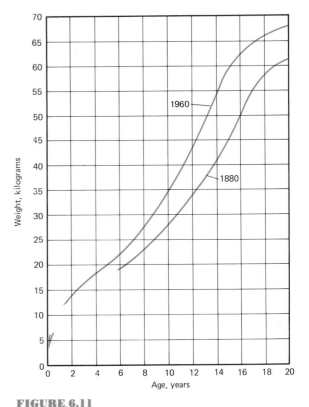

FIGURE 6.11
The secular trend in body weight is indicated by these schematic curves of mean body weight of children and adolescents in North America in 1880 and 1960. (1 kilogram = 2.2 pounds)

pounds, her metabolism initiates the changes of adolescence. At her critical weight, she begins producing more estrogens, whether because of some chemical signal from the body tissues to the hypothalamus, a change in the hypothalamus, or both, and she begins to mature sexually.

We still do not know whether reaching the critical weight triggers menarche or whether the timing is merely coincidental. Researchers have found that height, which has increased as racial and ethnic groups have moved from their places of origin to other parts of the world, also correlates with menarche. Faust (1977) has noted that menarche usually occurs close to, and most often after, girls reach their maximum height. But here, too, we do not know whether we are looking at correlation or cause and effect.

More recently, James Adams (1981) has speculated that a comprehensive **stimulation-stress factor** can account for the decreasing age of menarche. In stimulation and stress, he includes everything received through the senses—crowding, handling, noise, light, smells, temperature, humidity, altitude, socioeconomic class, race, body structure, and child-rearing practices. Adams notes that the decreasing age of menarche in the last 100 years parallels the Industrial Revolution, a faster tempo of life, and crowding into cities. He points out that many researchers have found that girls from many different cultures who live in cities reach menarche earlier than rural girls. Even one's position in the family may make a difference, for the later a girl is born into her family, the earlier she tends to reach menarche. Why? Adams believes that birth order contributes because laterborns receive more stimulation and stress from their siblings than earlier born children do. Adams's hypothesis is a speculative, but intriguing, one that needs further exploration.

A question of interest has been whether this secular trend toward earlier puberty would continue indefinitely. Twenty years ago Tanner (1965) suggested that there must be a threshold for sexual development and that some populations had already reached it. Over the last 30 years the average age at which girls first menstruate, 12.6 years, has not changed (McAnarney and Greydanus, 1979). Poverty or malnutrition may be able to delay sexual development, and good health and stimulation may be able to accelerate it, but only up to a point.

FACTORS AFFECTING GROWTH

GENETIC FACTORS

Physical growth is primarily under genetic control. The pituitary gland receives genetic instructions for size and produces growth hormone and other hormones that influence growth. There seems to be a hereditary core of parent-child similarities in physical characteristics (Bayley, 1971b). The Berkeley Growth Study indicates a similar pattern in rate of growth for parents and their children and for siblings but differences in final size (Tanner, 1970); this is one of the many pieces of evidence suggesting that final size and rate of growth are controlled by separate genes. Bone age and the age at which teeth erupt are other aspects of physical development that demonstrate that growth is under genetic control.

NUTRITION

The major means by which the surroundings affect individual growth is nutrition. In this country, the principal concerns about nutrition have to do with whether children are getting their minimum daily requirements of specific vitamins and minerals. Although infants receiving breast milk or the suggested amount of infant formula generally have their nutritional needs met, children between 1 and 5 often do not get enough iron, and nearly half of the children in this age group receive less vitamins A and C than is recommended (National Center for Health Statistics, 1975). With more and more prepared foods being consumed, parents must check the additives in baby food and later monitor their children's intake of additives, sugar, and salt. Some hyperactive children, in particular, may benefit from additive-free diets (Trites, Ferguson, and Tryphonas, 1978).

Over the course of evolution, human milk has been specialized to meet human physical needs. The cleanliness of breast milk, its digestibility, and the special immunities it confers have not been duplicated in 75 years of milk science (Gartner, 1978). The breast-fed baby has better protection against allergies, infantile diarrhea, respiratory infections, and other diseases. Human milk has been called "nature's vaccine."

For a few days before the baby's birth and for 2 to 4 days after, only **colostrum,** a yellowish, protein-rich fluid, is secreted from the breasts. By the end of 3 weeks it has been completely replaced by breast milk. From colostrum infants receive maternal white cells, which destroy bacteria and viruses directly and also produce antibodies, and a carbohydrate that promotes the growth of harmless bacteria in the intestine. They in turn inhibit the growth of dangerous organisms. In countries where food is scarce and disease prevalent, even a short period of breast feeding can mean the difference between life and death.

Breast-fed babies gain weight at a faster rate during the first month of life, but they are less likely to become obese (Newman and Alpaugh, 1976). There are a number of possible reasons why breast-fed babies do not become obese. Mothers who bottle feed often feel that they must keep after the babies to empty the bottle. Breast feeding is more likely to allow the infant to take in only as much milk as it wishes. The mother's lactation is attuned to the baby's vigorous sucking; the more the baby sucks and empties the breast, the more milk is produced. Breast-fed babies are also more active (Bernal and Richards, 1969). Moreover, the women who choose to breast feed may have attitudes about nutrition and child rearing that put them on guard against allowing their babies to become obese (Weil, 1975).

Mothers who are breast feeding must take in the proper nourishment. Recently, they have been warned to avoid freshwater fish, whitefish and trout, for example, which may carry industrial pollutants, such as polychlorinated biphenyls (PCBs). Chemicals, alcohol, and nicotine will make their way to breast milk. Evidence collected from laboratory rats suggests that there may be a newborn alcohol syndrome transmitted by alcoholic nursing mothers. Because the baby's brain continues to develop, especially in the first few days of life, nursing mothers who consume alcohol may jeopardize their newborns (Rawat, 1982).

Despite the advantages of breast feeding, only about half the mothers of newborn babies in the United States are nursing their infants at the time they are discharged from the hospital (Nutrition Committee, 1978). Many working women find breast feeding incompatible with their jobs. Only a few workplaces have experimental nurseries. Inconvenience, anxieties about insufficient milk supply, and concerns over the cosmetic effects of nursing are other reasons women give for not nursing. The American Academy of Pediatrics, to celebrate the International Year of the Child in 1979, urged strongly that breast feeding be promoted because of its nutritional and immunizing advantages and because it brings mother and child into close and frequent physical contact.

Public health experts Derrick Jelliffe and Patrice Jelliffe (1982) consider breast feeding to be always desirable, but they regard it as vital for the baby's survival in poor families. Even in America, infants and children in families living at or near the poverty level may suffer from malnutrition of protein and calories. In 1982, 40 percent of the people at poverty level—11.4 million—were children (Reese et al., 1982). Nutrition is one of the most significant reasons why the growth of individuals varies by social class, with children of higher socioeconomic status attaining larger average body size (Tanner, 1962; Gaffar and Corbier, 1966). A study of American children between the ages of 6 and 11 conducted by the National Center for Health Statistics showed children of rich families to be 1.2 inches taller than children of the poor. Half of these height differences in childhood persist into adulthood (Goldstein, 1971). A study of urban children in Sweden, however, showed no relationship between the height of the children, aged 7 to 17, and the occupation of their fathers (Lindgren, 1976). The link between lower social class and failure to grow may be broken when, as happens in Sweden, rich and poor have equal access to food and social services.

Malnutrition in relatively affluent societies, such as the United States, may figure as a secondary cause of renal, liver, and cardiopulmonary diseases; but we must look to Asia, Africa, and South America to see malnutrition as a direct cause of disease and death. In a survey of 190,000 children living in Asia, Africa, and South America, 80 percent of them were found to be suffering from moderate to severe forms of malnutrition. From these figures it is estimated that on these continents 100 million children under 5 years of age are severely or moderately malnourished (Suskind, 1977). In Latin America, over one-third of the deaths of children under 5 years of age are directly or indirectly related to malnutrition.

Very young children who are severely deprived of necessary proteins and calories may suffer a form of starvation called **marasmus.** Marasmus usually develops in infants under 1 year of age when the quantity of mother's breast milk is not sufficient and supplements are inadequate. Marasmic infants gain no weight and hardly grow. Their muscles waste away, and they become emaciated. If they survive, they remain unresponsive and never do catch up to the children who as infants had normal weight. They learn less and later do very poorly on psychological and intelligence tests (Pollitt, 1973). Children of 2 to 4 whose diet consists mostly of carbohydrates and very little protein may suffer from **kwashiorkor.** They retain water so that their stomachs swell, but they have little body fat and lose most of their muscle tone. Their hair thins and loses color, and they have skin lesions. These children are withdrawn, apathetic, and irritable, with poorly developed motor skills and other neurological deficits. Their intelligence may be impaired, but not as severely as that of children who have suffered marasmus (Thomson and Pollitt, 1977).

Malnutrition also seriously impairs children's immune response. Malnourished children are less able to resist viruses, bacteria, and fungi (Edelman, 1977; Edelman, Suskind, Sirisinha, and Olson, 1973). They become subject to diarrhea, which dehydrates them and prevents even their meager intake of food from benefiting them.

In countries where malnutrition is prevalent, why are some children malnourished and others not? One significant study of a Mexican farming village found the mother's health to be the single most significant determinant of the infant's growth in the first month (Cravioto, Birch, DeLicardie, Rosales, and Vega, 1969). The size of the family was also important. In this poor village, the fact that there were other sibling mouths to feed was detrimental to the infant's growth, but the presence of other adults in the household enhanced its chances. Reviewing numerous studies on malnutrition in South America, Asia, and Africa, Carol Thomson and Ernesto Pollitt (1977) concluded that the families of malnourished children lived in crowded conditions, in more intense poverty, and with greater instability. Mothers of malnourished children tended to be less educated, in poorer health, and less responsive than mothers of children who were poor but adequately nourished. For a number of physical, economic, and social reasons, these mothers were unable to give adequate care to their children.

CLIMATE AND ALTITUDE

Unless the physical climate, hot or cold, is linked to a difference in nutrition, temperature seems to have little effect on growth. Contrary to some popular beliefs, children living in hotter climates do not mature much earlier than those living in more temperate zones (Tanner, 1970). Altitude appears to slow up growth, but people in mountainous areas also tend to be undernourished. High altitude does induce larger chest circumference and bigger lungs, as proved by a study comparing coastal and mountain children in Peru (Tanner, 1978). Similar adaptations aeons ago are probably responsible for the different body types of Africans, Asians, and Caucasians.

DISEASE

Congenital defects in the heart, lungs, liver, kidneys, or any of the endocrine glands also affect normal physical growth. The growth of children born with heart disease, for example, is often 2 years behind that of their peers. But after corrective heart surgery, these patients have shown remarkable catch-up growth, one youngster gaining as much as 4 years of bone age within 6 months. In almost all cases in which an underlying illness has retarded growth, the stunted child self-rights and acquires almost magical powers of compensatory growth once the illness has been treated (*How Children Grow,* 1972). Minor diseases caused by viruses and bacteria—measles, flu, even pneumonia—usually have little if any effect on growth (Lowrey, 1973). Advances in medicine have reduced their threat to children. They can, however, be serious and even fatal if the child is malnourished.

NEGLECT

Children born today have a better chance of surviving and growing to healthy maturity than children born only a generation ago. But even the enormous medical advances made in this century and the wide dissemination of child-care information cannot protect children from all risks. Some babies suffer **failure to thrive.** They do not attain expected height and weight for their age, even though no organic cause is evident, because their mothers are not able to give them the necessary attention (Newberger, Newberger, and Harper, 1976). At later ages, too, very severe emotional stress and insufficient affection can apparently cause the pituitary gland to malfunction so that it does not produce enough growth hormone for normal physical development. In the 1960s, the National Institutes of Health received reports on children who had been admitted to hospitals with all the symptoms of **hypopituitary dwarfism.** These children were short, had low levels of growth hormone, and their bones and sexual development were immature; 6-year-olds had a bone age of 3½. The youngsters were also shy and lethargic. All these children came from strife-torn homes where they were neglected by one or both parents. Some of them showed signs of physical abuse. They had been admitted to the hospitals to receive growth hormone therapy. But the therapy they needed turned out to be separation from their parents. In the new surroundings, without any hormone ther-

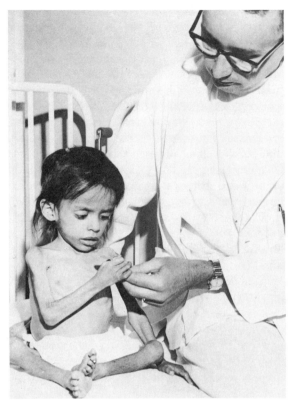

This 5-year-old, 13-pound girl failed to thrive because her parents were unable to give her the attention and nutrition she needed.

apy and with an ordinary diet, they started to develop and became more social and lively. Children who had grown at the rate of 1.4 inches per year were now growing at the rate of 6.3 inches per year. The children in the group who were placed in foster care continued to become larger in this catch-up fashion. But others who returned to their own homes slowed down in growth and gave signs of returning to their earlier depression (*How Children Grow*, 1972; Powell, Brasel, Raiti, and Blizzard, 1967).

One small, emaciated 8-month-old infant was brought to a Boston hospital. She could not sit up, and she did not respond when spoken to. In the hospital the infant gained weight and began to play and smile. She was then discharged, only to be brought back 2 months later, underweight, dirty, smelly, restless, and apathetic. This time the hospital treated the mother as well as the child. The mother had no husband, four children, little money, and few friends or relatives. She was given dental care for her badly neglected teeth, medication for

a chronic urinary infection, and regular counseling with a social worker. The older two children were placed in a nursery school. Daily visits by a homemaker and a public health nurse helped relieve the mother's depression and afforded her the time and energy for nurturing her infant. This time the child continued to gain weight at home, and when seen 4 years later, at the age of 5, her physical and psychological growth were in the normal range (Newberger et al., 1976).

HEALTH AND HEALTH HAZARDS

INFANT RISKS

In the broadest sense, the news about infant mortality is encouraging. Following a plateau in the 1950s and 1960s, the survival rates for infants of all races are increasing. However, black infants long have suffered higher mortality rates than white infants; in 1979, 22 black infants died per 1000 live births, compared with 11 white infants. The mortality rate in the first year of life is 80 percent higher for black than white infants. In general, why are more babies surviving every year? The reasons are several: better nutrition and prenatal care for pregnant women, improvements in socioeconomic conditions (these especially affect infants' chances of survival after birth), and medical advances in saving low-birth-weight babies.

Low Birth Weight

In Chapter 4, we discussed the risks associated with premature births. Here we will focus on full-term babies who are born **small for gestational age** or **small for dates.** Low birth weight is one example of a risk factor that may combine with other risk factors—low socioeconomic class, poor functioning of the central nervous system, oxygen starvation before or during birth (to name just a few possibilities)—to produce developmental deficits.

Infants of low birth weight constitute a population at risk. At one end of the continuum of risk, the consequences are lethal: stillbirth or death soon after birth; in the middle there are severe but nonlethal consequences: cerebral palsy, epilepsy, and mental deficiency; and at the better end of the continuum, children are normal or have minor school problems, learning difficulties, or slight intellectual deficits, which may disappear over time. Studies of twins highlight the impact of weight. In one sample of twins born with widely disparate weights but no physiological disorders, the IQ of the smaller twin was uniformly lower than that of the larger twin (Babson and Benson, 1971). In his review of 18 studies of prematurity, Gerald Weiner (1962) found the majority of the investigators reporting some IQ deficit; most of the deficits were associated with low birth weights.

Poor caretaking in the home compounds risks for the underweight baby. The IQ scores of poor infants born underweight are more likely to decline with age, whereas those of low birth-weight infants

RESEARCH FOCUS

INFANTS WHO SURVIVE SEVERE HEART PROBLEMS

Why do some infants born with a serious heart defect develop quite well after they have had open heart surgery but others, born with the same defect, do poorly? Margaret O'Dougherty and her colleagues (O'Dougherty, Wright, Garmezy, Loewenson, and Torres, 1983) wanted to answer this question. In doing so, they considered several different kinds of stress that affect the development of infants born with a heart defect called transposition of the great arteries. The research team believed that only by considering multiple (rather than single) stress factors would they be able to identify accurately which infants were at greatest risk for later problems in development. They knew that this heart condition can subject infants to many physical and psychological problems—heart failure, failure to grow, chronically low oxygen, seizures, stroke, brain infection, mental retardation, and others.

The subjects were 31 children who had survived open heart surgery for transposition of the great arteries at the University of Minnesota Hospital. Their mean age was 9 years. All but one subject were white; most came from working-class families. The researchers presumed that the following factors placed children at risk for developmental problems: other heart defects; more than one heart operation; congestive heart failure in the first month of life; child's height and weight before open heart surgery; child's age before open heart surgery, as an index of how long the child had suffered chronically low oxygen; seizures; central nervous system (CNS) infection; stroke; duration of heart surgery; duration of hospital stay following surgery. They also measured the children's families' SES and current levels of stress. The children were assigned a cumulative risk score that accounted for the relative severity of each risk factor. For analytical purposes,

the children then were assigned to categories of low, moderate, and high risk. They were also examined for brain-wave patterns, anatomical abnormalities, motor skills, and IQ.

Results showed that overall, more of the sample than might be expected by chance scored in the mental retardation range of IQ; 10 of the subjects had abnormal EEGs; and 4 had abnormal visual-evoked potentials. But how did these findings relate to the factors the investigators had designated as risks?

1. Children who had undergone surgery at younger ages had higher IQ scores, academic achievement, and perceptual-motor scores, and they were less likely to have anatomical abnormalities.

2. Children who were larger at the time of surgery had higher IQ and academic achievement scores.

3. Children who had not had congestive heart failure had higher IQ scores.

4. Children who had undergone only one operation were less likely to have neurological abnormalities or behavior problems.

5. Children who did not have reduced blood oxygen levels were less likely to have neurological abnormalities.

6. Children who had not had strokes showed higher school performance and IQ.

More important than these individual findings, however, was the finding that children who experienced more than one of these risks developed the most severe neurological and psychological problems. The child born with transposition of the great arteries who was at greatest risk had open heart surgery later (after the age of 2), had more than one operation, and had congestive heart failure. The researchers concluded that although infants can rebound from a limited period of great physical stress, if the period of stress is prolonged, the harmful effects intensify and detrimental long-term effects are inevitable.

from more advantaged homes rise (Weiner, 1962). In one study of small-for-dates babies in Oxford, England, where the standard of living was high and the population healthy, of 55 small-for-dates babies, 53 developed normally during their first 7 years and had no particular problems in school (Ounsted, Moar, and Scott, 1982). Only two babies remained small and had other developmental problems. One, a boy, had been born to parents who were short themselves and of the lowest social class. He did below-average schoolwork and scored quite poorly on tests of gross and fine motor skills. The other, a girl, had two older brothers who had been of low birth weight. Her parents were young, of average height, but below-average intelligence. Her physical development was slow, and she was moderately retarded in all developmental areas. Like the small-for-dates boy, she showed no major neurological abnormalities and was classified as having "minimal cerebral dysfunction." Thus, in this well functioning population, low birth weight did not generally lead to negative long-term effects.

The effects of low birth weight combined with other risk factors were demonstrated in a study conducted by David Harvey and his associates in London (Harvey, Prince, Bunton, Parkinson, and Campbell, 1982; Parkinson, Wallis, and Harvey, 1981). One marker of risk that the researchers used was a smaller than normal fetal skull size (skull size giving some indication of fetal and infant brain development). By following 60 small-for-dates infants who also had small heads (as measured by ultrasound before birth), these researchers found that children whose skull growth slowed before 34 weeks gestation were likely to be short at 4 years of age. Those whose skull growth had slowed before 26 weeks gestation had delayed development at age 4 or 5 and problems in balancing and coordinating their movements at age 6. They also scored significantly lower than children born of normal size on tests of cognitive skills—verbal, reading, drawing, reasoning, handwriting, number, perception, motor, and memory. Perceptual performance and motor skills were found to be particularly affected. When the children's teachers were asked to rate the children's behavior and school performance, low birth-weight children whose skull growth had slowed before 34 weeks scored lower than low birth-weight children whose skull growth had slowed after 34 weeks gestation and a group of normal birth-weight children. Teachers were most likely to mention as common for these children such problems as frequent absences from school, problems in communicating with teachers and peers, problems related to the children's physical smallness, and problems with schoolwork.

Another marker of risk used in this study was SES. Low birth-weight children from lower social classes scored significantly lower than those from higher social classes. Three girls from the small-skull group whose families were of high SES were doing very well at school, leading the researchers to suggest that social class may override the influence of low birth weight. A third risk marker was sex. Boys were judged to have the most severe problems.

Sudden Infant Death Syndrome (SIDS)

Some babies are born with vulnerabilities that may not at first be obvious, although they manifest themselves early and with tragic consequences. In the United States, some 7000 to 10,000 babies die suddenly and unexpectedly each year after suffering few, if any, symptoms. These babies go to sleep and are later found dead, victims of **sudden infant death syndrome (SIDS),** or crib death. Found mostly in 2- to 6-month-olds, SIDS may strike as early as 2 weeks but rarely occurs after 1 year. It seems to peak in the winter and spring (Figure 6.12) and, in about 60 percent of cases, afflicts infants who have mild upper respiratory infections (Duffty and Bryan, 1982), especially those who have been given phenothiazine for their colds (Kahn and Blum, 1982). Some evidence suggests that SIDS is associated with the infant's having had a low Apgar score or low birth weight. Often the mothers of SIDS infants are found to have suffered anemia or flu or to have smoked during pregnancy, to have had little prenatal care, to be of low SES status, or to have experienced a rapid second stage of labor (Lipsitt, McCullagh, Reilly, Smith, and Sturner, 1981). Some SIDS infants have been found to have grown slowly after birth or to have suffered from jaundice. It also has been found that SIDS occurs more often in babies who are relatively slow to develop long periods of quiet sleep (Haddad, Walsh, Leistner, Grodin, and Mellins, 1981) and that it is more common at high altitudes (Getts and Hill, 1982).

Early detection and prevention certainly are major goals in investigations of SIDS. But what causes

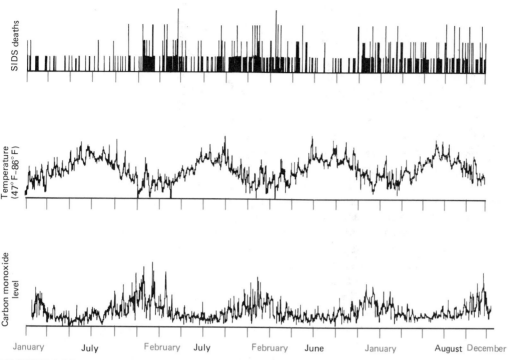

FIGURE 6.12
Daily incidence of SIDS in Los Angeles County between January 1974 and December 1977.
The number of SIDS per day ranges between 0 and 4. Notice that low temperature and high
level of carbon monoxide during the winter months tended to coincide with an increase in SIDS.
(Hoppenbrouwers et al 1981).

SIDS? One theory links SIDS with an imbalance of the hormone triodothyronine (T-3). Researchers at the University of Maryland found high levels of T-3 in 45 out of 50 infants who had died from SIDS (Tilden and Chacon, 1981). They are trying to develop a test to screen for this imbalance so that the condition can be controlled with drugs. Another suggestion is that infants at risk for SIDS have blocked airways and constricted vocal tracts, which can be detected in a characteristic cry (Colton and Steinschneider, 1981; Golub and Corwin, 1982). Breathing abnormalities during sleep are by far the most common characteristic associated with SIDS. Normally, a respiratory control center in the brain regulates breathing during sleep. As the amount of carbon dioxide in the blood rises, a person breathes in more oxygen in response. Several researchers suggest that SIDS may be related to faulty chemical regulation of breathing (Shannon, Kelly, and O'Connell, 1977). Dr. Carl Hunt (1982) has found that the respiratory control center operates improperly in SIDS infants. Their blood levels of carbon

dioxide rise, but they do not compensate by breathing in more oxygen. Eventually, they stop breathing. Dr. Hunt advocates early detection of abnormal breathing patterns during sleep and administration of the drug theophylline. This drug, which resembles caffeine, stimulates the breathing reflex and is often prescribed for asthma. Some parents are taught how to monitor their infant's breathing at home with apparatus that sounds an alarm when the infant experiences an **apnea** (interruption of breathing). Everyone commonly experiences apneas, both asleep and awake, but infants at risk for SIDS may not spontaneously begin breathing again. The monitor alerts parents, who can take measures to help the baby start breathing again.

CHILDHOOD DISEASES AND DISORDERS

Children are born with immunity to only a few diseases, and because they lack immunity, they contract more of these diseases than older people do. Measles and mumps, for example, can strike people of any age, but usually people get them in childhood and thus acquire immunity to them, preventing later occurrences. Other "childhood" diseases are those that attack the most vulnerable group in the population, and that group often—but not always—consists of children (Lewis and Craft, 1982).

Just as "childhood" diseases can strike vulnerable people of any age, diseases that usually strike adults often show their first traces in childhood. Risk factors for cardiovascular disease, cancer, and stroke—the causes of two-thirds of deaths among adults in the United States—are common in children. These risk factors include excess weight, high levels of cholesterol in the blood, hypertension, poor physical fitness, and diabetes (Williams, Arnold, and Wynder, 1977). In a sample of 8- to 12-year-old boys from California, 46 percent had one risk factor associated with heart disease, and 14 percent had two risk factors (Wilmore and McNamara, 1974). In another sample of 3000 11- to 14-year-old public school children, 40 percent had one or more of the risk factors associated with heart disease. Many researchers believe that prevention of heart disease, cancer, and stroke should begin in childhood. One of the few such preventive screening and education programs, the "Know Your Body" program, has been instituted in New York City and suburban Westchester County to determine whether certain risk factors for chronic disease can be reduced in a population of middle-school children (Williams et al., 1977). Preliminary results show that 43 percent of the students had abnormally high blood cholesterol levels; 10 percent smoked cigarettes; 17 percent of the students from inner-city schools and 10 percent from middle-class schools were obese; 3 percent of inner-city students and 1.5 percent of middle-class students had high blood pressure. Results over the long term will tell the research team whether the program has motivated the students to modify their behavior enough to reduce their risk and, ultimately, their incidence of fatal disease.

In the first year of life, disease and health problems are the leading cause of death, affecting 1 percent of white and 2 percent of black infants. In preschoolers over 1 year old, accidents are the leading cause of death, followed by congenital abnormalities, flu and pneumonia, cancer, and meningitis. At any given time, 10 to 20 percent of children under 18 have chronic physical disorders (Pless and Satterwhite, 1975). If sensory impairments, mental retardation, and behavior disorders are included, then 30 to 40 percent of children under 18 suffer from one or more chronic disorders (Mattson, 1972). The most common chronic disorders of childhood are asthma (2 percent), heart problems (0.5 percent), cerebral palsy (0.5 percent), orthopedic problems (0.5 percent), and diabetes (0.1 percent) (Mattson, 1972). Children with chronic illnesses are also more likely than other children to suffer problems of social or psychological adjustment (Sperling, 1978); such problems afflict 30 percent of chronically ill children by the time they turn 15 (Pless and Roghmann, 1971). In part, these problems reflect the negative reactions of other children and teachers. In one study, both handicapped and nonhandicapped children, told to rank pictures from most to least attractive, ranked them in the following order: (1) a nonhandicapped child; (2) a child on crutches with a leg brace; (3) a child in a wheelchair, both legs covered by a blanket; (4) a child missing a hand; (5) a child with a minor facial disfigurement; and (6) an obese child (Richardson, Goodman, and Hastorf, 1961). But it would be wrong to conclude that the most severely physically handicapped children are the most psychologically and socially troubled (McAnarney, Pless, and Satterwhite, 1974). In fact, the most severely handicapped children often are better adjusted than moderately handicapped children, perhaps because the most severe handicaps limit children's own and others' expectations about what they can or should do (Richman and Harper, 1978).

Among preschoolers the most common health problems are acute infectious diseases, of which fully 80 percent are respiratory infections. The next most common health problems among preschoolers are accidents, emotional disorders, tooth decay, sensory impairments, and iron deficiency. Surveys have found chronically poor nutrition in 20 percent of children under 6; the figure increases to 30 percent among children from poor families (Ten State Nutrition Survey, 1972). The emotional disorders most prevalent among preschoolers include poor adjustment to school, speech problems, and problems of bowel and bladder control (Schroeder, Teplin, and Schroeder, 1982).

Immunization has wiped out or dramatically reduced the incidence of many previously common childhood diseases—measles, rubella (German measles), pertussis (whooping cough), and mumps (Figure 6.13). Most children are immunized by the time they enter school. In the United States, polio vaccine reduced the number of cases from 29,000 in 1955 to 8 in 1975. Chicken pox is still common, however. Epidemiologists are concerned because the numbers of children being immunized against measles, rubella, DPT (diphtheria, pertussis, and tetanus), and polio have leveled off or actually declined since 1975. In consequence, these illnesses are growing more common again. For example, the number of measles cases was 385,000 in 1963 when the vaccine first became available. In 1968, there were 22,000 cases of measles, but in 1971, the number had climbed to 75,000. The children who are not immunized tend to occur in clusters according to race and place of residence. The story on mumps immunization, in contrast, is brighter;

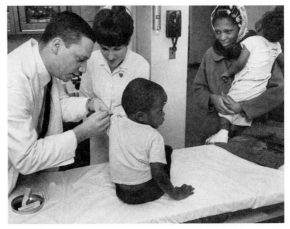

Inoculation has dramatically reduced the incidence of many childhood diseases.

FIGURE 6.13

Reported cases of selected diseases before and after immunization was available in the United States. (*Source:* Centers for Disease Control.)

the number of immunizations has continued to rise. Smallpox, too, has been virtually eliminated throughout the world. Of the infectious diseases that affect children, the common cold is the best known. Children between 1 and 2 average eight or nine colds a year, and until age 15, children average four colds a year (Ray, 1977). Although most are self-limiting, colds may produce complications, such as ear infections. As with other viral infections, antibiotics are useless, and treatment—bed rest, increased fluids, medication to reduce fever and congestion—is directed at the symptoms. Middle-ear infections, **otitis media,** strike one-half to two-thirds of all children by the time they are 2 (Krugman, Ward, and Katz, 1977). Viral throat infections are more common among 4- to 7-year-olds.

The elementary-school years are for many children the healthiest of their lives. Generally, elementary schoolers' incidence of infectious diseases is lower than it is among preschoolers. But during the school years, sensory impairments and other health problems are likely to be diagnosed. About 25 percent of elementary-school children have vision problems, 10 to 20 percent have reading problems, 3 percent have hearing problems, 3 percent are mentally retarded, 1 percent have epilepsy, and 1 percent have a major speech disorder. In many cases, parents are the first to suspect that a child has a hearing problem, although newborns at high risk for such problems increasingly are being identified and screened. Improved methods of testing have made it easier for specialists to diagnose early sensory impairments. Hearing losses that occur before a child learns to speak interfere with development far more severely than those that occur later, and unless children with these early hearing losses are diagnosed and treated early, they are at high risk for developing long-lasting emotional and academic problems (Schlesinger and Meadow, 1972).

Another common and preventable problem in school-age children is tooth decay, which results from the interaction of normal bacteria, sugars, and inherited or acquired factors that predispose teeth to decay. By the age of 12, fully 90 percent of all children have at least one cavity (Nizel, 1977). **Scoliosis** (lateral curvature of the spine), juvenile rheumatoid arthritis, malnutrition, obesity, poor posture, and sexual abnormalities are less prevalent but still serious problems among children in ele-

mentary school. Many children who suffer from hunger appear nervous or listless, conditions that indirectly affect their performance in school. Between 5 and 14 percent of preschoolers are obese (Neumann, 1977), most of them from higher socioeconomic groups. But by adolescence, the trend has reversed, and more children from lower socioeconomic groups are obese (Schroeder et al., 1982).

Sleep Disorders

Sleep disorders of various kinds are common among children. The **parasomnias,** which include sleepwalking, sleep terrors, nightmares, head banging, tooth grinding, and bed wetting, are probably the most common of all. The parasomnias rarely signify more serious underlying problems; at one time or another, they afflict roughly 20 percent of all children, especially boys (Ware and Orr, 1983). Most parasomnias have no clear cause and eventually disappear. Sleepwalking usually occurs in the first third of the night's sleep, during very deep sleep (Kales, Jacobson, Paulson, Kales, and Walter, 1966b). A loud noise or standing a child on his or her feet can start a boy or girl sleepwalking (Broughton, 1968; Kales et al., 1966a).

Sleep terrors, like sleepwalking, usually strike during the first 2 hours of sleep and during very deep sleep. The child sits up in bed, screams loudly, and cries excitedly for several minutes. Typically, the child's pulse rate soars to over 100 beats a minute, but after the episode passes, the child remembers nothing about it. Sleep terrors, like sleepwalking, may set in after a child has had a fever (Kales, Kales, Soldatos, Chamberlin, and Martin, 1979) and seem not to be related to any other forms of pathology. The best treatment for sleep terrors ordinarily is reassurance and education. In some cases, parents have found it effective to wake their child and have him or her urinate just before the parents retire for the night, for a distended bladder has been thought to trigger sleep terrors.

Sleep enuresis (bed wetting) is found among an estimated 5 to 17 percent of children between the ages of 3 and 15 (Lovibond, 1964). It is more common in boys than in girls (Rutter, Yule, and Graham, 1973). Enuresis may be primary, in children who have never had bladder control during sleep, or secondary, in children who have lost their bladder control. Although secondary enuresis often is ascribed to psychological causes, it may actually have an organic basis (Guilleminault and Anders, 1976). Sleep enuresis is not related to any stage of sleep (Broughton and Gaustaut, 1975), but bed wetters have been found to sleep exceptionally deeply (Hallgren 1957). One treatment for bed wetting is to use an apparatus that rings a bell and wakes the child as soon as he or she wets the bed. Another kind of treatment is to train a child to increase his or her bladder capacity.

Insomnia is another kind of sleep disorder that afflicts certain children. Insomnia may be a symptom of many different psychological and organic problems. When insomnia is associated with an organic problem, like an ear infection, the cause is usually easy for a physician to detect. But when the insomnia is associated with a psychological problem, the cause may be harder to find. For instance, children who are depressed may also complain of insomnia, and the two may aggravate each other. Treating the depression can often alleviate the insomnia. Other causes of insomnia include neurological problems and food allergies (Salzman, 1976). Finally, some children sleep badly because they have poor sleep hygiene. Elements of their bedtime routine or other habits may subtly interfere with their ability to sleep. Generally, regular bed and awakening times help children to fall asleep promptly and to stay asleep. Light snacks can improve sleep, but heavy meals can interfere with it. Milk and cereals promote sleep, but chocolate and caffeinated drinks interfere with it. Regular exercise is likely to improve sleep, but children need a calming transition between periods of exercise and sleep. Environmental disturbances, like noise, lights, temperature, or pets (which often are overlooked) can also interfere with children's sleep (Ware and Orr, 1983).

Hyperactivity

Adults have found overactive children a problem for centuries (Aries, 1962). Thomas Edison's teachers continually complained about and berated the boy's unrestrainable activity until his mother had to withdraw him from school and teach him herself. Winston Churchill's very active behavior was appraised by his school as a decided detriment; fortunately for young Winston, his English nanny had another opinion. Impossible and incorrigible was the judgment made of many children who later turned out to be eminent men and women (Goertzel and Goertzel, 1962). Before World War II, highly active schoolchildren were often paddled, whipped, and expelled from school. After the war, the same type of school behavior began to be regarded as a behavior disorder to be treated by psychotherapy, psychoactive drugs, and special educational programs (Ross and Ross, 1982). And parents of the 1970s and 1980s have continued to deplore the overactivity of their children.

When does activity reach an "abnormal" level? A few children are so active, distractible, and excitable that no one would quarrel about their being called disturbed or abnormal, but many children are brought into treatment who are overly active but probably not "abnormally" so. Some critics of current diagnosing and drug treatment of **hyperactivity** believe the condition to be a myth created by a culture that has grown intolerant of deviance (Schrag and Divoky, 1975). England, for example, reports only 1 hyperactive child in 1000, whereas the United States reports 50 times that number (Stewart, 1976).

In the United States, hyperactivity is the single most common behavior disorder seen by child psychiatrists, affecting an estimated 1 to 6 percent of America's schoolchildren (Ross and Ross, 1982). It is five to nine times more common in boys than in girls. The first exposé of the use of drugs to control children's behavior revealed that 5 to 10 percent of the 62,000 grade-school children in Omaha, Nebraska, were being given dextroamphetamine (Dexedrine) or **Ritalin.** Their teachers had identified them as hyperactive and unmanageable (Maynard, 1970). **Amphetamines** and Ritalin, stimulants that have the seemingly paradoxical effect of calming hyperactive children, are still being prescribed. These drugs actually help many hyperactive children to concentrate, although they do not improve their ability to learn. (See Research Focus: A Teacher Responds to Medicated and Unmedicated Hyperactive Boys.) But serious questions have been raised about their side effects—they initially cause insomnia and diminish appetite and may temporarily suppress growth—and about their use as a solution to what is at least in part a social problem (Safer, 1971; Sroufe and Stewart, 1973). There is considerable controversy about the definition, cause, and treatment of hyperactivity.

Hyperactive children are persistently restless and inattentive in situations in which they should be still, and they are unable to control their activity when asked to be quiet. Distractibility, impulsiveness, readily aroused emotions, little tolerance for frustration, aggressiveness, destructiveness, poor schoolwork, and poor relations with peers are other symptoms (Ross and Ross, 1982). Minimal brain dysfunction, brain damage, and learning disability are alternate diagnoses.

Hyperactivity may take different forms and meet with different reactions during childhood. In infancy hyperactivity may show up in thrashing legs and flailing arms. The hyperactive toddler may never sit still but incessantly struggle to be walking, then running and climbing. At preschool the hyperactive child dashes from one free-play activity to another. In elementary school the child's inability to remain seated and his or her high distractibility as well as an unpredictability that makes the child "a disor-

RESEARCH FOCUS

A TEACHER RESPONDS TO MEDICATED AND UNMEDICATED HYPERACTIVE BOYS

Many children diagnosed as hyperactive are treated successfully with medication. In most cases, drugs, such as Ritalin, have been found to improve hyperactive children's ability to concentrate and to pay attention. Carol Whalen, Barbara Henker, and Sharon Dotemoto (1981) wanted to find out whether Ritalin also affects hyperactive children's social interactions. They assumed that children whose behavior improves so dramatically would also generate changes in the people with whom they interact, and they decided to test this assumption with a group of 22 hyperactive boys who were enrolled in a summer-school program. Half of the hyperactive boys were randomly assigned to take a placebo and half to take Ritalin for 4 days. Then 4 days were allowed for the effects of the drugs to wash out. Finally, the two groups of boys were reversed, and the first group got Ritalin and the second the placebo for 4 more days. Thirty-nine normal boys were chosen as a comparison group. An elementary-school teacher taught classes that contained a mixture of normal boys and medicated and unmedicated hyperactive boys. The teacher was not told that any of the boys were considered hyperactive or were medicated. The project was explained to her as one that would assess "social and academic behaviors under various environmental conditions."

The researchers isolated and varied six factors in the classroom: (1) supervision or no supervision by teacher; (2) crowding or no crowding; (3) sufficient or insufficient supplies; (4) activities paced by self or others; (5) noisy or normal level of sound;

and (6) easy or difficult activities. Four raters who did not know the purpose of the study observed and coded the frequency and kind of contact—primarily attempts at control versus ordinary small talk and information giving—between teacher and each student. The latter were called "regular" contacts. They also coded the intensity of contacts, whether they were spoken or physical, whether they were initiated by the student or the teacher, and whether they explicitly included calling the boy's name.

How had the teacher reacted to the three different groups of children? The research team found that, overall, slightly fewer than half of the teacher's contacts were attempts at control; slightly more than half were "regular" contacts. The majority of contacts were spoken rather than physical, and three-quarters of the time they were initiated by the teacher. But there were significant differences in the teacher's behavior toward the three groups. In each classroom situation, the teacher did more intense controlling, guiding, and disciplining of the hyperactive boys who were on the placebo than of the other boys. She also spoke more often to these boys and called them by name in her attempts to control them. They, in turn, were less attentive to class tasks and showed more bursts of energy, movement, talking, and disruptiveness. They initiated more contacts with the teacher. There were no differences between the hyperactive boys on medication and the normal boys. As expected, both the teacher's behavior and the students' reflected the effect of medication. The research team concluded that even though the teacher had not been aware that many of the students were hyperactive, she had behaved in ways that could be predicted by knowing that fact.

ganized tornado'' one minute and an obedient and industrious student the next (Ross and Ross, 1982) will alarm the teacher. The child may then for the first time be referred to a doctor or psychiatrist. In middle childhood, psychiatric problems frequently surface for the hyperactive child (Ament, 1974).

Cultural prejudices and fears seem to account for the bias of parents and teachers against hyperactive boys. According to a study based on information gathered in the Fels Longitudinal Study (Battle and Lacey, 1972), mothers of 31 hyperactive girls remained involved with, and affectionate toward, their daughters as they followed a pattern of being daring in infancy, striving for achievement in the preschool period, and being sociable and aggressive toward peers in the school years. The mothers tried to encourage their daughters. Mothers of hyperactive boys, however, were critical and disapproving of them in infancy. When the 43 boys in this sample attended preschool and school, they failed to receive the affection and protectiveness shown the hyperactive girls. Their acts of disobedience tended to be severely punished, and their

mothers tended to underestimate the level of their sons' intelligence. The physical disruptiveness of these boys in early childhood and their attempts to control peers in middle childhood cost them not only the affection and support of parents, then teachers, and eventually peers, but also their self-esteem. Their excessive activity, physical boldness, and aggression apparently presented more of a threat, and age increased this threat. Intimidated parents and teachers want to control or contain these boys with discipline or drugs. It appears from this limited sample that the "downward spiral of performance" (Douglas, 1972) of hyperactive boys may be greatly accelerated by how parents and then teachers treat them.

Specific situations seem to affect hyperactive children in different ways. Some children are hyperactive when they are in groups but not when they are with just one other person; for others, just the reverse pattern holds true; still others are hyperactive only in unfamiliar situations. In the classroom, hyperactive children show more gross motor activity than other children do, and they act up at

Having a hyperactive master is a trial for stuffed animals.

inappropriate times (Abikoff, Gittelman-Klein, and Klein, 1980). Compared to normal children, hyperactive children make more mistakes in tasks that require sustained attention, and they also test poorly in experimental situations that require impulse control (Douglas, 1980). Some hyperactive children have been found to show poor judgment (Kinsbourne, 1973). It has been suggested (Routh, Schroeder, and O'Tuama, 1974) that many of the traits associated with hyperactivity signal delays in maturation; hyperactive children's behavior is normal for children 3 to 4 years younger. Because they are often in conflict with others—the result of their impulsiveness, poor judgment, inattention, and so on—many hyperactive children develop poor self-images. They tend to think of themselves as "bad" children who have few friends; others tend to rate them negatively as well (Campbell and Paulaukas, 1979). When hyperactive children are also aggressive and hostile, they tend to develop more and more problems as they get older (Loney, Langhorne, and Paternite, 1978). Aggression and hostility, in short, make the prognosis poor for the hyperactive child's later development. Although social class itself is not useful as a predictor of hyperactivity, hyperactive children from families of lower SES tend to suffer more from low self-esteem, aggression, and delinquency than hyperactive children from families of higher SES (Paternite, Loney, and Langhorne, 1976).

Research on hyperactive infants has shown that they are irritable and sleep little (Ross and Ross, 1976). As they grow older, they continue to have sleep problems. Many have trouble settling down to sleep; many awaken during the night. Although studies of young hyperactive children have failed to find significant differences in their IQs compared to those of normal children, studies of older children do show that hyperactive children score lower on IQ tests (Loney, 1974). Their achievement is also poor. In one study of children diagnosed as hyperactive, for example, only 25 percent scored above their grade level in mathematics, only 18 percent in reading recognition, and only 26 percent in reading comprehension (Lambert and Sandoval, 1980).

What causes hyperactivity? It is possible that hyperactivity stems at least in part from genetic factors. Natural parents of hyperactive children tend to have more psychiatric problems, including hyperactivity as children, than parents of normal children (Morrison and Stewart, 1971, 1973). Environmental variables also may help explain the occurrence of hyperactivity. In this vein, some people have suggested that hyperactivity is associated with a child's blood sugar level. They recommend eliminating refined sugars from the hyperactive child's diet. This suggestion is based on personal testimonial rather than objective data, however. Another school of thought is that food additives set off hyperactivity (Feingold, 1975). Many investigators have not found evidence to support this hypothesis (e.g., Conners, 1980). But others have suggested that food dyes and preservatives may have an effect on some hyperactive children (see Research Focus: Food Dyes Affect Hyperactive Children). Still other environmentalists have suggested that food allergies relate to hyperactivity. The research-based view at present is that dietary factors are likely to be the cause of hyperactivity in at most only a fraction of children (Henker and Whalen, 1980; Kerasotes and Walker, 1983). Other environmental factors that have been blamed for hyperactivity include exposure to radiation, heavy drinking by the mother during pregnancy, stressful child rearing, stressful experiences in school, chronic low levels of lead in the body, and fluorescent lighting (Henker and Whalen, 1980; Ross and Ross, 1982). Research to establish these links is still continuing.

Autism

One childhood disorder that is rare but devastating is **autism.** Autism is a form of psychosis that strikes 4 or 5 out of every 10,000 children (Brask, 1967), usually before they are 2½ (Rutter, 1978). In about 70 percent of cases, the autistic person is also seriously mentally retarded (DeMyer, et al., 1974). Although the diagnostic criteria have been debated, generally autism is characterized by a child's profound aloneness and inability to communicate or to form social relationships (Eisenberg and Kanner, 1956; Rutter, 1978). Unlike normal children their age, autistic children do not imitate others' social behavior, use objects appropriately, or play simple games. They do not form emotional attachments to their parents or other people, express empathy, or exhibit cooperation. They do not make friends, and they tend to stare at other people's eyes with an unusual gaze. Their behavior is rigid, ritualistic, and compulsive (Rutter, 1978). Parents of autistic children long were thought to be cold and obsessive (Eisenberg, 1957; Kanner, 1949), but most psychologists now reject this explanation of autism's cause. Instead they look for an organic explanation for autism. The role of several neurotransmitters, particularly serotonin, has been investigated, as has the role of zinc deficiency (Coleman, 1978). But to date autism has not been related conclusively to any one biochemical agent. In one study of 21 same-sex pairs of twins, in which at least one twin was autistic, Susan Folstein and Michael Rutter (1977) found that 4 of 11 monozygotic (MZ) pairs but none of the 10 dizygotic (DZ) pairs were concordant for autism. In 12 of 17 pairs of twins that were discordant for autism, the autistic twin had had a brain injury. But among the twins concordant for autism there were no histories of brain injury. The researchers concluded that autism probably derives from several causes, including both brain damage and a genetic abnormality. Several investigators have pointed out that the language and cognitive problems typical of autism are problems in left hemisphere functions. The right

Autistic children avoid social interaction and eye contact. They may also have other sensory handicaps, as this child does.

RESEARCH FOCUS

FOOD DYES AFFECT HYPERACTIVE CHILDREN

Is the controversial "Feingold diet" (Feingold, 1975) fact or fiction? Do food dyes, additives, and artificial flavorings cause a significant number of children to act hyperactively? In a study of how food dyes affect behavior, two researchers, James Swanson and Marcel Kinsbourne (1980), chose a group of 18 boys and 2 girls who had been diagnosed as hyperactive. The children's average age was 12; all were tested in the hospital. All of the children had responded well to medication for control of hyperactive symptoms.

A day before the study was to begin, all of the children were taken off medication. The experimental period lasted 1 week, during which time the children ate a diet without any artificial colors or flavors, the preservatives BHT and BHA, and "natural salicylates." For the first 3 days, the children grew accustomed to the learning tasks that required

pairing pictures of animals and numbers between 1 and 10. On the fourth and fifth days of the experiment, at 10:00 A.M., the children took either a capsule containing food dyes or a placebo. On the sixth day, the children received whichever of the capsules they had not taken the day before. Then the children were tested on the learning task at 9:30 A.M., 10:30 A.M., 11:30 A.M. On the first two tests, no differences appeared between the two treatment groups. But by 11:30 A.M., children who had ingested food dyes performed significantly worse than the children who had taken placebos. The difference persisted at the 1:30 P.M. testing. Fully 17 of the 20 subjects made more mistakes after taking the food dyes.

The investigators concluded that artificial food coloring can interfere with cognitive performance. They also suggested that children who respond to drugs for the control of hyperactivity are likely to show sensitivity to food coloring, for a group of 20 subjects who did not respond to drugs for hyperactivity did not respond adversely to food coloring either.

hemisphere functions—such as musical, visual, and spatial skills—of many autistic children are normal or even superior (Blackstock, 1978; Lockyer and Rutter, 1970). In fact, many autistic children show signs of early damage to the left hemisphere (Dawson, 1982). Anatomical studies have shown specific forms of brain pathology and abnormal patterns of asymmetry in autistic children (Hier, LeMay, and Rosenberger, 1979; Rutter, 1974).

ACCIDENTS AND POISONS

In the United States every year, accidents kill more children than any other cause. Accidents kill 16,000 and permanently injure 40,000 to 50,000 children every year (U.S. Department of Health and Human Services, 1982). The types of accidents that befall young children include poisoning, drowning, falls, fires and explosions, and inhaling and ingesting substances. Deaths from accidental poisonings have declined markedly in the past few decades. It has been estimated that of the half-million children who ingest poison every year, only 2000 die. A large study in the late 1960s of children admitted to a large city hospital for treatment of poisoning showed that aspirin was the culprit in 35 percent of the cases and hydrocarbon distillates in 18 percent (Deeths and Breeden, 1971). Most of the accidental deaths among children result from fires and car accidents (Figure 6.14). Children are killed when they ride as passengers in cars, when they fall from cars, and when the passenger compartment overheats (King, Negus, and Vance, 1981;

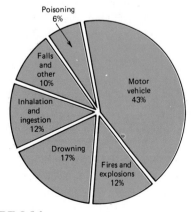

FIGURE 6.14
Deaths from accidents among children aged 1 to 14 years (1982).

Scherz, 1981; Williams, 1981). An analysis of the deaths of children in car accidents showed that 36 percent had been passengers (Baker, 1979). The highest mortality rate was among infants younger than 6 months old, presumably because they were traveling on other passengers' laps or on the front seat of the car. The mandatory use of infant safety seats now being enforced in some states should reduce the number of such deaths.

Frederick Rivara (1982) analyzed data from hospital emergency room records of 197,000 cases of injury to children between birth and 19 years. He found that for girls, 1- and 2-year-olds are most likely to have accidents. For boys, the most dangerous years are those between 1 and 2 and between 13 and 18, but at every age boys have more accidents than girls do. The vast majority of injuries result from household accidents: children are injured falling down stairs; they are cut by broken windows; they hurt themselves on the sharp corners of coffee tables; they fall in the bathtub. For children between birth and 4 years old, household items like tables, chairs, sofas, beds, stairs, and play equipment cause the most accidents. Bicycles cause the most accidents among children between 5 and 14; these are followed by other sports-related injuries (NEISS, 1980). Drowning peaks in incidence among infants 1 year old; one-half of all drowning victims in the United States are children under 10, and of these, three-fourths are boys (Iskrant and Joliet, 1968). The incidence of deadly burns follows that of car accidents and drownings for children in most developed countries (Smith, 1969).

Because accidents kill and injure so many children, many researchers have investigated environmental and social factors that lead to accidents. They have found that hunger, fatigue, illness, or death in a family or the presence of a new caretaker are factors associated with the occurrence of accidents to children (Mofenson and Greensher, 1978). Marie McCormick and her associates (McCormick, Shapiro, and Starfield, 1981) investigated a random sample of 5000 infants 1 year old. They found that infants who had learned to walk were more likely to be injured than those who had not begun walking, but few other factors—SES, sex of the infant, weight at birth—could be clearly identified as correlates of injury. As for the personal characteristics of young accident victims, it has been found

Some children can be characterized as accident prone. . . perhaps because they take so many physical risks.

that about 30 percent have had previous accidents, leading some investigators to posit the existence of an accident prone syndrome. Accident-prone children have been characterized as being physically active but immature in their neurological control of movement. They are also believed to have trouble anticipating, judging, and accommodating to the consequences of their behavior (Wright, Schaefer, and Solomons, 1979). Studies have not yet empirically documented these suggestions, but they have identified certain traits in such accident-prone groups as adolescent boys. As a group, adolescent boys are quite likely to take great risks, to deny pain, and to avoid medical care (U.S. Department of Health and Human Services, 1982; Mechanic, 1964).

Death and the injuries that result from accidents are disturbingly obvious, but are there more subtle health hazards in the environment? Yes, say the results of many different investigations: in the water we drink, the air we breathe, the places where we live. Because mercury, lead, the PCBs,

and many other toxins have no taste, color, or odor, parents and children may not realize when they are being exposed to them. Lead, for example, may be present in food, car exhaust, old paint chips or dust, plumbing lines and fixtures, soil, air, and water. People who live in cities have higher blood levels of lead than people who live in rural areas. In a 7-year study of children living in Omaha, Nebraska, the highest levels of lead were found in those who lived in a commercial area of the city near a small factory that produced batteries; the next highest levels were in those who lived in a residential area of the city; the lowest levels were in suburban children (Angle and McIntire, 1979; McIntire and Angle, 1973). Children who lived within 500 feet of a major road had higher lead levels than children who lived farther away (Angle, McIntire, and Vest, 1975). A study of preschool children in 14 Illinois cities revealed that nearly 20 percent had elevated levels of lead in their blood (Fine, Thomas, Subs, Cohnberg, and Flashner, 1972; Fine and Dobin, 1974). Because it is often difficult to separate the effects of lead from those of stress, poverty, and other pollutants, there is some debate about whether exposure to lead directly causes children intellectual and behavioral problems. But it does seem likely that for poor, inner-city children, exposure to lead in combination with other factors interferes with intellectual development. One careful retrospective study by Herbert Needleman and his associates (Needleman et al., 1979), in which lead levels in the baby teeth of first- and second-graders were used as a cumulative index of exposure to lead, showed that among children without any overt symptoms of lead poisoning, those with high lead levels were more likely to have IQs below 80 and less likely to have IQs above 125.

Greta Fein and her associates (Fein, Schwartz, Jacobson, and Jacobson, 1983) studied the effects of chemical toxins on development. They found that in many cases of prenatal and postnatal exposure, gross abnormalities are absent. Low levels of exposure may produce quite subtle effects: slightly lower than normal size at birth, slightly increased susceptibility to infections, or subtle behavioral changes. Different people react differently to any given dose of toxin, and the effects of toxic substances vary according to genetic predisposition, point of exposure during development, type of toxin, and length of exposure. Although high levels of exposure are likely to manifest themselves as recognizable clinical signs, low levels of exposure may produce symptoms like fatigue, apathy, irritability, distractibility, and tremors. It may be only in subtle changes of behavior and in emotional or sensorimotor problems that symptoms of exposure show themselves.

CHILD ABUSE

Sometimes the physical well-being of children is directly threatened by their parents. Each day in this country abusive parents are responsible for the deaths of one or two children. The number of children under 5 killed each year by their own parents may be greater than the number of those who die from disease (Kempe and Helfer, 1972). An estimated 500,000 children are beaten, burned, thrown, kicked, and battered without losing their lives. Exact figures are not known. Since 1967 all 50 states have had laws requiring that suspected cases of **child abuse** be reported; most require doctors, clinic and hospital personnel, teachers, social workers, psychologists, lawyers, police officers, and coroners to do so (Mnookin, 1978). In 1974, the U.S. Congress passed the Child Abuse Preven-

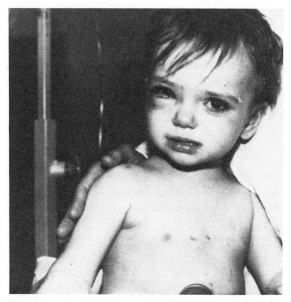

This 15 month-old child is one of the 500,000 who are abused by their own parents every year in the United States.

tion and Treatment Act. The numbers of cases reported jumped by tens of thousands after these laws were enacted.

Most abusive parents claim that they love their children, and studies show that only a few of them can be judged mentally ill by any specific psychiatric diagnosis. Psychological research does allow us to put together a profile of abusive parents and their ideas about rearing children. Henry Kempe and Ray Helfer (1972) found that those who mistreat their children have often themselves been treated harshly by abusive and uninformed parents. Abusive parents have never learned to be patient. They often believe that their children should behave in a manner to gratify them. They expect their children to be aware of their problems, all the time ignoring the children's needs. They depend on their children for emotional support, expecting love and affection from them to fill up their own emptiness and to make up for intolerable conditions of their own lives. Abusive parents have unrealistic expectations about what babies and children can do. They do not want their babies to cry. They often think that toddlers can hold a glass of milk or manage a spoon without spills long before their hands and fingers are able. They expect their energetic children to sit quietly through a long adult discussion. In fact, a recent study by Viki McCabe (1984) reveals that abused children have typically old-looking faces, compared to their nonabused agemates. This, she suggests, may lead to caregivers' unrealistic expectations of these particular youngsters. According to Kempe and Helfer (1972), abusive parents also regard ordinary infant behavior as intentional wrongdoing, and they attribute children's failure to obey instructions to deliberate stubbornness, willful disobedience, or malice. They deem severe physical punishment necessary to ensure "proper" behavior. Abusive parents are themselves vulnerable to mistreatment by their spouse—to criticism, neglect, and abandonment. Moreover, they have a sense of personal inadequacy and little self-esteem, a feeling that they have failed in all their undertakings.

Sociologists have found that parents are much more likely to abuse children when they have a prior belief that hitting is acceptable and when they have a violent spouse. Both fathers and mothers are much more likely to abuse their children if their partners also use physical punishment (Dibble and

Straus, 1980). Parents who abuse are frequently dismissed from jobs and often move to other communities. They are not members of extended families and do not establish ties by joining community groups or by being neighborly. They often keep their children socially isolated, too, not allowing them to go to a birthday party or to play in the yard next door. They have no relatives, close friends, or neighbors to call on for help in times of stress (Elmer, 1967; Young, 1964). Poor parents who are abusive are not able to afford baby-sitters or recreation that might give them respite from the 24-hour-a-day responsibility of parenthood (Galdston, 1971). Chronic stress, an unwanted pregnancy, or the expectation that a child will secure a parent's identity and social role are factors sometimes associated with child abuse (Steele and Pollack, 1968; Walsh, 1977). Some parents are actively abusive; others—passive abusers—fail to protect a child from violence or covertly comply with active abuse.

Overburdened parents are more likely to abuse a particularly troublesome child. Nearly half the children who are harmed have been found to indicate some symptom of mental retardation or hyperactivity before the abusive incident (Elmer and Gregg, 1967; Morse, Sahler, and Friedman, 1970). Low birth-weight babies, with their thin faces, frequent crying, and needs for special care, are more likely to be abused than those with normal weight (Spinetta and Rigler, 1972). Infants and children who demand greater amounts of attention and unusual sensitivity on the part of their mothers and fathers may have the tragic and sometimes fatal misfortune of being born to parents who lack even the ordinary social and psychological resources.

How is the vicious cycle—abusive parents misrearing children who then, if they survive, become abusive parents themselves—to be broken? Kempe and Helfer (1972) suggest that these parents receive therapy to raise their low self-esteem and to improve their self-image and, at the same time, instruction in parenting skills, which they did not receive from their own parents. These specialists believe that, with proper training, the majority of abusive parents can learn gentler means of discipline and what to expect of their children and can break their pattern of social isolation. Parents Anonymous, a self-help organization with chapters in major cities, allows child abusers to admit what

they have done, to receive support, and to find out from those who have had the same problem how they can stop abusing their children.

Fortunately, most parents are able to handle the demands of their children, especially when their efforts are supported by caring members of the family and the community. Parents want to do what is right for their babies. When they themselves have the necessary physical, psychological, and social resources, they are able to rear healthy children.

ADOLESCENT ILLS

Adolescence brings with it a new set of health problems and hazards. Not only do adolescents face problems of social and physical adjustment, but they may have to contend with pregnancy and sexually transmitted diseases; they may turn to cigarette smoking or to drug or alcohol abuse. Difficult as any chronic illness or handicap can be during childhood, the sense of being different from others that these conditions bring can be acutely uncomfortable for adolescents (Magrab and Calcagno, 1978). In a period of preoccupation with appearance, 15 percent of adolescent girls and 7 to 9 percent of adolescent boys are obese (Schroeder et al., 1982). In adolescence, violence and suicide are the second and third most common causes of death (Schroeder et al., 1982).

Alcohol and Drugs

Most adolescents begin drinking at home. Parents who are excessive drinkers foster excessive drinking in their children; moderate drinkers or abstainers foster similar moderate drinking habits or abstinence in their children (U.S. Public Health Service, 1974). After the tenth grade, however, teenagers are more likely to drink with their friends, and 90 percent of them have some contact with drinking. The heaviest drinking among young men occurs at ages 18 to 20, among young women at 21 to 24. At least half a million young people have a serious drinking problem (Chafetz, 1974); in some cases, the problem is aggravated by the mixing of alcohol with drugs.

For some boys drinking may be a sign of conflict about their sex role, which takes the misguided form of exaggerated masculinity and bravado (Zucker, 1967). In one longitudinal study, boys who were overly dependent in junior high school, rebellious, and generally unable to maintain adequate relations with others were more likely than their peers to drink excessively later on (Jones, 1968).

In this country, marijuana is the most widely used drug other than alcohol. An estimated 1 out of 10 people gets high every day, and 6 out of 10 have tried marijuana at least once (Johnston and Bachman, 1981). After testing 1704 affluent suburban boys and girls between the ages of 15 and 18, Nechama Tec (1972) decided that two factors were significantly related to their use of marijuana: lack of involvement in conventional educational pursuits and dislike of school. Students who had aspirations to be "the best" at something—athletics, studies, a profession, or just popularity—were not likely to use marijuana. Reports on lower-class, urban teenagers indicate that they probably smoke marijuana as an easy escape from their everyday lives.

Teenagers who use pot regularly tend to become unresponsive and even unaware of their surroundings. In high-school jargon, they are "vegged out," "space cadets," or "burnouts" (Coates, 1980). As one physician put it, "Marijuana is the great alienator" (Brynner, 1980, p. 45). Although marijuana may be a personal threat to an adolescent, it is not as much of a social threat as alcohol or other drugs, such as heroin. Because marijuana often makes people passive rather than aggressive, it is not closely linked to crime. One study has found that as marijuana smoking increases, delinquency decreases (Gold and Reimer, 1975).

The most significant reason for smoking marijuana, especially for younger adolescents, is that their friends do so (Brynner, 1980). Adolescents often begin to use drugs when they are 11 to 13 years old, the period when they are the most susceptible to peer pressures (Figure 6.15).

Appearance

A preoccupation with complexion is part of the adolescent's heightened reaction to old and new aspects of the physical body. Even moles and birthmarks provoke intense concern. In a study reported by Peter Blos (1974), Betty suddenly became concerned about a mole on her face that had always been there. As Betty put it, "When I came into

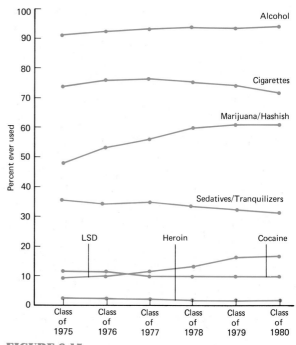

FIGURE 6.15

Percentages of adolescents graduating from high school who had used the drugs indicated, without a doctor's order, at least once (Johnston and Bachman, 1981).

about the seventh grade, I didn't think about it, and then I became very, very conscious of it. . . . I never looked at myself before" (Blos, 1974, p. 234).

In a highly sympathetic article on adolescent skin conditions, William Zeller (1970) calls the skin "a canvas on which the psyche reveals its emotions," a canvas that becomes a particular cause of concern to the adolescent. The young person believes the appearance of the surface of the skin makes him or her acceptable or unacceptable. Believing this, the adolescent can allow skin problems to affect self-esteem.

Although emotional factors play a part in one-quarter to one-half of all skin diseases, there is a physical basis for adolescent skin worries. The androgens secreted by the adrenal glands at this time cause sebaceous glands to become more active and produce excess oil. The ducts carrying the oil to the hair follicles and skin do not grow enough to keep pace with this increase in production, another asynchrony of adolescence. If the oil in a pilosebaceous duct is exposed to the air, it will oxidize and become a blackhead. If the oil is not exposed to air, if a layer of skin covers the duct, it becomes a whitehead. But it is the irritation of surrounding tissue by these overloaded oil sacs that brings the skin eruptions known as acne.

Cleaning the face and eating a balanced diet may be sufficient to take care of oily skin. Acne, especially the severe cases, requires treatment by a dermatologist. But Zeller makes it clear that such treatment is not only a question of checking endocrine deviations and prescribing appropriate salves or ointments. Most adolescent patients are equally in need of "sympathy, reassurance and understanding of their personal problems and concerns" (Zeller, 1970, p. 119).

Of more serious concern than acne, eating disorders may also result from adolescents' preoccupation with their appearance. Some adolescent girls who are abnormally concerned about their weight and make repeated attempts to control it by dieting engage in occasional eating binges, secretly stuffing themselves. They usually plan their binges and choose food sweet in taste, high in calories, and of a texture that can be gobbled down without much chewing. Once they start on their binge of eating, they feel that they cannot stop, and they keep eating until they fall asleep or have abdominal distension and pain, which they relieve by vomiting. This pattern of abnormal behavior is called **bulimia.** Usually after indulging in a binge, bulimics eat normally for a time or alternate between normal eating and fasting. Their weight remains within a normal range but has frequent fluctuations of 10 pounds or more. Michael Thompson (1979) found that one-quarter of the young women in introductory psychology and sociology classes at a small liberal arts college in the Midwest reported controlling their weight by vomiting or by alternating fasting and binge eating. Many bulimics are deeply depressed; some have tried to kill themselves (Cunningham, 1984).

An especially severe eating disorder, which affects about 1 out of every 300 teenage girls, is **anorexia nervosa.** Those suffering from this syndrome lose 25 percent or more of their weight within a few months by denying the body its physiological needs for nutrition and rest. Being a little plump, or perhaps obese, they decide to diet. But then their dieting knows no bounds. Moreover, they

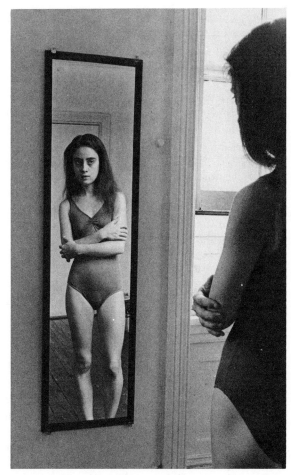

Anorexic girls become thinner and thinner and eat less and less in a misguided effort to win approval.

expend great amounts of energy on physical exercise as long as they are able. Almost half of them are bulimics. Anorexics tend to be girls who have been good students and compliant daughters. As children they have put up a façade of adequate functioning; at adolescence the demands of maturing and becoming independent from parents cause the façade of health to crumble (Bruch, 1969). Fear of growing up combined with a yearning for parents' attention causes them to reduce their bodies to an emaciated, childlike form. In a fictionalized case study written by psychotherapist Steven Levenkron (1978), who has treated many anorexic girls, "Kessa" expresses her fears of growing up as she attempts to deny the signs of puberty.

Somehow it seemed very important that her mother not know. If she did, if she knew that Kessa had stopped being a dependent little girl who needed her desperately, her mother would stop loving her. Kessa was sure of that. It had been the same when her breasts had begun to develop. Kessa had not let her mother see her without clothes for almost a year after that. If she had seen her body, had seen her become a woman, her mother would not have wanted to take care of her anymore. So she'd been delighted when her breasts had begun to shrink and her period had ceased to appear (Levenkron, 1978, p. 26).

Anorexics spend many moments before mirrors, scrutinizing their bone-knobby, broomstick figures, which they see as either too fat or finally at an attractive weight. They also develop a preoccupation with food, even while they limit themselves to minuscule, low-calorie amounts. They become interested in its preparation, collect recipes, plan and cook elaborate meals for others. Anorexics may eventually realize that they are starving, but this realization is not enough to make them eat. Marlene Boskind-Lodahl (1976), who has treated a number of anorexic young women, found them to have no confidence in their ability to control their own behavior. They had never gained a sense of self-mastery. The high academic achievement of all these young women was not an effort at self-fulfillment but in every case an attempt to please parents. These girls had become totally "other directed," to use a term coined by sociologist David Riesman. First they had handed control over to families, then to the young men they began to date. The predictable, occasional male rejection at adolescence led these young women to assume that their bodies were the cause of the failure to please. The anorexic syndrome was set in motion.

Because eating disorders quickly become deep-seated, they often require extensive therapy, which includes work with the girl's family. In severe cases, hospitalization is necessary to give the anorexic the strength to cope with the needed therapy. Without proper treatment, up to 20 percent of anorexics die of their self-inflicted, chronic starvation (Brody, 1982). Although anorexia probably begins for psychological reasons, it can create hormonal abnormalities associated with dehydration (Turkington, 1984).

Pregnancy

Sexual behavior in adolescence has far outpaced sex education and the use of contraception. Despite the substantial increases in sexual activity of teenagers that Zelnik and Kantner (1977) reported for the 1970s, they did not find a comparable increase in awareness of the risk of pregnancy. Only two out of five unmarried women between 15 and 19 years of age generally understood the time during the menstrual cycle at which they were at greatest risk of conception. Regardless of adolescents' sexual experience or age, many of them do not have a clear comprehension of the processes of human reproduction.

Adults seem to deny that adolescents are sexually active, and they deny them information about sex. A research effort called the Project on Human Sexual Development, sampling a cross section of

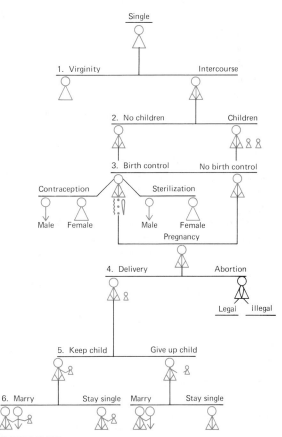

FIGURE 6.16
This tree of sexual decision making indicates the complex implications and ramifications of any sexual act (McCreary-Juhasz, 1975).

1400 parents, found that they discussed only elementary anatomical differences between male and female and a few facts about pregnancy and birth with their 11-year-old children. Most parents do not mention intercourse, contraception, abortion, menstruation, or wet dreams (Cory, 1979). In 1980, the majority of American high schools still were not offering sex education courses, although most states permitted them. Of those that did offer courses, only one-third discussed contraception. This discussion typically occurred in the junior year, when one-third of the girls were already sexually active. Even when sexual facts are offered as part of the curriculum, teachers are prevented from teaching values. Such a depersonalized approach is particularly ineffective with young adolescents.

Although sex education improves understanding to some extent, it does not necessarily have a dramatic effect. According to an Alan Guttmacher Institute report, *Teenage Pregnancy: The Problem That Hasn't Gone Away* (1981), only 43 percent of girls who had a sex education course were aware of the high-risk period for conception compared to 33 percent of those who had not taken a course. Moreover, adolescents, especially young adolescents, are not skilled in applying what they do know about sex to their actual behavior. Even if they are aware of the ovulation cycle and understand the need for contraception, they rarely use their knowledge to plan for birth control. Considering all the possible consequences of sexual activity constitutes a very complicated "decision tree" indeed (Figure 6.16). Many young people do not even consider pregnancy a possible outcome of their lovemaking. It might happen to others, but they simply do not believe that anything bad can ever happen to them.

In 1971, only 45 percent of teenagers had used any method of contraception at last intercourse, and just 16 percent used an oral contraceptive or an intrauterine device (IUD). By 1976, 63 percent had used a method of contraception at last intercourse, and one-third used the pill or an IUD. In 1979, 70 percent had used some form of contraception at last intercourse (Figure 6.17). Even so, the majority of teenagers do not use contraception when they first have intercourse, and many adolescent girls wait until after they have been pregnant once. "Delayed contraceptors" are about three times as likely to become pregnant as those who begin to use contraception right away (Zelnik and Kantner, 1977).

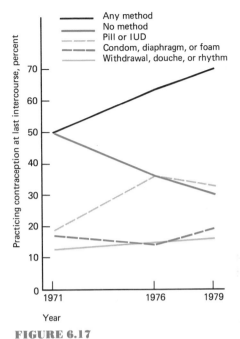

FIGURE 6.17

The percentage of never-married, sexually active young women, ages 15 through 19, who practiced contraception at last intercourse increased during the 1970s, and they chose more effective methods (Alan Guttmacher Institute, 1981).

Many girls who experience powerful sexual feelings must act, for the sake of their self-image, as though sex is never consciously chosen, but is always utterly spontaneous. Girls who cannot predict when they are going to have intercourse and girls who see birth control as conflicting with ideals of romantic, spontaneous love are the two groups most likely to have intercourse without protection, according to a report on 2500 sexually active girls in the Los Angeles area (Lindemann, 1974)—see Figure 6.18.

The family also plays a role in teenage pregnancy. Dennis Hogan (1982) together with Evelyn Kitagawa has found that if a teenage girl's parents are not currently married, if she comes from a large family, or if her parents are lax in monitoring her dating behavior, her chances of becoming pregnant during her teens are several times greater than they would otherwise be. For whatever reasons—not using contraception when teenagers first start having intercourse, the girl's wish to preserve the ideals of romantic love, or inattention on the part of the girl's parents—there are over 1 million teenage pregnancies a year in this country, ending in some 400,000 abortions and more than half a million new teenage mothers.

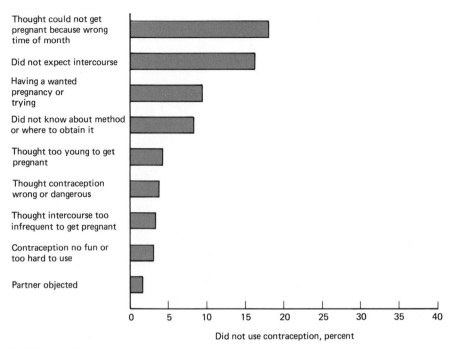

FIGURE 6.18

These percentages of teenage girls had premarital intercourse more than once, at some time did not use a contraceptive, and gave these reasons for their last nonuse (Alan Guttmacher Institute, 1981).

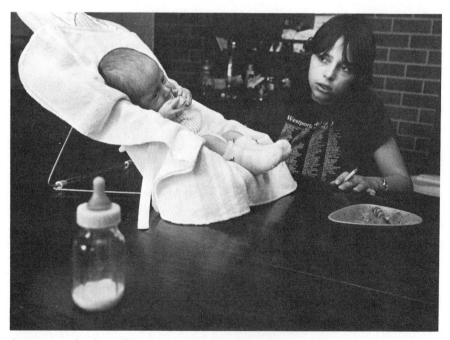

A teenage mother faces all the pressures of adolescence at the same time as those of new motherhood. The burden can be overwhelming as the two grow up together.

When teenagers marry because the girl is pregnant, the marriage is likely to break up within 6 years (Alan Guttmacher Institute, 1976). Especially among blacks, fewer teenagers who are soon to become parents have married in the last decade, and out-of-wedlock births have increased (Alan Guttmacher Institute, 1981). The decision to go ahead and have the baby is often based on storybook notions of becoming a parent and living happily ever after. In the short run, having the baby may satisfy the adolescent's longing for a sense of adult worth. In the long run, when teenagers have babies, both teenage father and mother end up with less education, poorer economic opportunities, and, usually, more children than they want or can afford to support (Card and Wise, 1978). They feel sadder and more tense than those who wait to have their children (Brown, Adams, and Kellam, 1981)—see Figure 6.19.

Adoption is an alternative that very few teenagers are choosing; 94 percent of the teenagers who give birth keep their babies. The frustration of lives prematurely harnessed to the care and feeding of other utterly dependent human beings soon catches up with these young mothers and their children. Teenage parents have a high incidence of child abuse; their children in turn develop behavioral problems and add to the numbers of those who will themselves later have difficulty being self-sufficient people and loving parents.

Sexually Transmitted Diseases

Sexually transmitted diseases are now epidemic, and they are a particular danger to sexually active adolescents. Of reported cases, three out of four are those of young people between the ages of 15 and 24 (U.S. Department of Health and Human Services, 1980). A new strain of the microbe gonococcus, which causes gonorrhea, resists all forms of penicillin treatment. The condom, which is partially effective in preventing sexually transmitted disease, has been largely replaced by the oral contraceptive. And now an estimated 20,000,000 Americans have genital herpes (*Concerns,* 1980). Although untreated syphillis and gonorrhea can do more damage than herpes simplex virus, type 2, herpes does not go away. "It won't kill you, but you won't kill it either" (*Time,* August 2, 1982, p. 63).

Facilities for teenagers that give them thorough care are still quite few. Sexually transmitted disease often goes undetected in its early stages. The fact that teenagers may have more than one partner heightens their vulnerability to disease. The spread of herpes at the rate of half a million cases per year has caused some to speculate that such a threat will change sexual behavior, but there is no indication yet among teenagers or adults that sexual activity is abating.

PROMOTING HEALTH, PREVENTING INJURY

Serious injuries, accidents, and illnesses are not inevitable aspects of growing up, and parents are not helpless to prevent or alleviate them. Many different forms of prevention and treatment have significantly improved the outlook for children today. Not surprisingly, several studies have shown an association between parents' attitudes toward children's health and their child-rearing practices. One such study showed that among 250 poor mothers, use of well-child clinics was more common among mothers who were interested in preventing illness, who tended to agree with doctors' diagnoses, and who saw their children as basically healthy (Becker, Nathanson, Drachman, and

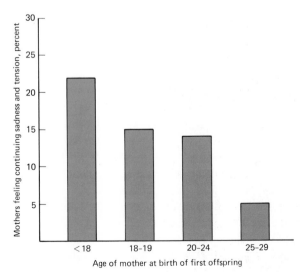

FIGURE 6.19
The likelihood of a mother's claiming to feel recurrently sad and tense depends on the age she was when she had her first baby (Brown, Adams, and Kellam, 1980).

Kirscht, 1977). In another study, children were found to have good health habits, such as exercising or brushing teeth, when their parents encouraged such self-reliance (Pratt, 1973). How parents feel about health and illness determines if and when they seek medical care for their child. More educated parents are more likely to believe that illness is preventable and to use a physician (Mechanic, 1964). How they feel about the seriousness of their child's illness, about the benefits and effectiveness of treatment, about the diagnosis itself, and about the quality of medical care also influence whether parents comply with physicians' instructions on such issues as giving medication (Becker, 1974; Becker, Drachman, and Kirscht, 1972). Two strategies can induce parents to cooperate with medical care: informing them of the negative consequences of not complying and making their health care accessible, affordable, responsive, and of good quality (Rosenstock and Kirscht, 1974).

Attitudes are not alone in determining the like-

lihood and quality of health services to children. Specific remedies for specific injuries and hazards also contribute in important ways. Both laws and education have been helpful in preventing certain childhood injuries. To prevent injuries to infants in cars, seat restraints and specially padded and constructed car seats are now legally required by many states. Deaths from poisonings have declined in response to the growth of poison control centers, better treatments, protective packaging of medicine and dangerous household products, and health education. Falls from high windows have been prevented by such laws as that passed by the New York City Board of Health requiring apartment landlords to install window guards in apartments where there are children under 10. As a society, we have become more concerned about the health and safety of our children, and the future should see further advances in promoting health and preventing injury to young Americans.

SUMMARY

1. Growth during infancy is not uniform, but growth curves chart the rate and degree of physical development. Over time not only do height and weight increase, but the proportions of the body change markedly as well.

2. At any stage of development, brain functioning depends on, among other things, the location and arrangement of brain cells and brain lateralization. Neurons are nerve cells, which develop in clusters, and they communicate by means of various neurotransmitters across gaps called synapses. As the cerebral cortex of the infant matures, noticeable changes in function appear. Brain development normally follows a genetically programmed sequence as the brain matures in functional units.

3. Two asymmetrical hemispheres of the brain govern separate functions. In right-handed people, language, logic, and sequential tasks are left hemisphere functions. Music, emotional material, and drawing are processed in the right hemisphere.

4. Puberty is characterized by a growth spurt and the development of secondary sex characteristics. Girls generally enter puberty earlier than boys

do, and various explanations have been offered as to why the age of girls' first menstrual period has declined gradually over the course of the last 100 years.

5. A child's growth is affected by genetic factors, by nutrition, disease, climate and altitude, and by the quality of parents' care.

6. Risks to an infant's growth include low birth weight, a condition that in some cases is related to later developmental problems. Children with small head circumference—a measure of brain growth—are more likely than other low birth-weight children to develop later school and social problems.

7. SIDS, which kills apparently healthy infants under 1 year old, has been correlated with breathing abnormalities during sleep, faulty chemical control of breathing, and constricted airways, among other factors.

8. Children are vulnerable to many diseases, because they have few immunities. Early signs of fatal adult diseases—heart disease, stroke, cancer—have been found among large numbers of children. Diseases are the greatest killers of children in their first year of life, but accidents kill the greatest number of children over 1 year old. At any time, 10 to 20 percent of children under 18 have chronic physical problems, and if mental retardation, sensory impairments, and behavior disorders are included, then the figure climbs to 30 to 40 percent of children under 18.

9. Some children suffer from sleep disorders, most of which are benign.

10. Hyperactive children are so active, distractible, and excitable that they disrupt their environment, cause others to react negatively, and incur many social, cognitive, and emotional problems in development. Stimulant medications, like Ritalin, are effective treatments for significant numbers of hyperactive children.

11. Autism is a childhood disorder that is characterized by early onset, profound uncommunicativeness, and impaired social and emotional ties.

12. Accidents and injuries of many sorts injure and kill hundreds of thousands of children every year. Fires and car accidents kill the most children, but the types of accidents that are most common

change with age. Boys of every age have more accidents than girls. Less obvious causes of developmental problems are environmental toxins, especially those that are present in small amounts over long periods.

13. Child abuse is another peril to children. Abusive parents may claim that they love their children, but they injure or kill them when the children seem too demanding, when the level of stress in the family gets too high, when the family is isolated and without resources, when a child is unwanted, and when the parents themselves were abused as children. Many factors have been found to correlate with child abuse; there is not yet a single "explanation" for this kind of deadly violence.

14. Adolescents face a special set of health problems: alcohol and drug abuse, eating disorders that result from a concern with appearance, and pregnancy and sexually transmitted diseases.

15. Laws and education have proved helpful in preventing and treating many of the health hazards to children.

KEY TERMS

Catch-up growth	Glial cells	Menarche	Apnea
Restraining effect	Nissl substance	Secular trend	Otitis media
Asynchrony	Ribosomes	Critical body weight	Scoliosis
Neuroglia	Dendrites	Colostrum	Parasomnias
Neurons	Axons	Marasmus	Sleep terrors
Growth curve	Neurotransmitters	Kwashiorkor	Sleep enuresis
Epiphyses	Synapses	Failure to thrive	Hyperactivity
Fontanels	Corpus callosum	Hypopituitary dwarfism	Amphetamines
Adipocytes	Brain hemisphere	Small for gestational	Ritalin
Adipocyte hypothesis	Lateralization	age	Autism
Metabolism	Broca's area	Small for dates	Child abuse
Cerebral cortex	Wernicke's area	Sudden Infant Death	Bulimia
Cerebellum	Growth spurt	Syndrome (SIDS)	Anorexia nervosa
Myelination	Secondary sex		
	characteristics		

SUGGESTED READINGS

Bruch, Hilde. *Eating Disorders.* New York: Basic Books, 1973. Anorexia nervosa, obesity, and other eating disorders explained by a woman who has done extensive research in this field. She pays particular attention to the developmental roots of these disorders.

Caplan, Frank. *The First 12 Months of Life.* New York: Grosset & Dunlap, 1973. *The Second 12 Months of Life.* New York: Grosset & Dunlap, 1977. The territory of the first two years—the expected behavior, physical growth, and emotional changes—described and illustrated clearly for parents.

Eden, Alvin N., and Heilman, Joan Rattner. *Growing Up Thin.* New York: David McKay, 1975. A "fat proofing" prevention program for each stage of a child's growth, to be instituted by parents.

Kempe, Ruth, and Kempe, C. Henry. *Child Abuse.* Cambridge: Harvard University Press, 1978. Presents a medical (pediatric and psychiatric) approach to the problem of child abuse and neglect. The focus is on understanding the causes and consequences of child abuse and methods of treating the parent and the child.

Levenkron, Stephen. *Treating and Overcoming Anorexia Nervosa.* New York: Charles Scribner's, 1982. A description of the "nurturant-authoritative" treatment in which the therapist acts as a helping, caring person and assumes control while teaching the anorexic to trust herself or himself.

Lowrey, George H. *Growth and Development of Children* (7th ed.). Chicago: Year Book Medical Publishers, 1978. A detailed and readable analysis of the physical growth of each system of the body, with a section on the behavior predicted at each level of development.

Tanner, James M. *Foetus into Man: Physical Growth from Conception to Maturity.* London: Open Books, 1978. An interesting and comprehensive discussion of physical development by the leading authority. A number of useful graphs and statistics are given.

Whalen, Carol K., and Henker, Barbara (Eds.). *Hyperactive Children: the Social Ecology of Identification and Treatment.* New York: Academic Press, 1980. A diverse collection of theoretical and empirical articles on hyperactivity, including an examination of contextual factors likely to influence the diagnosis and treatment of hyperactive children.

CHAPTER 7

Emotions

WHAT ARE EMOTIONS?

Emotions: everybody feels them; everybody reacts to them. The infant gurgles happily as his father throws him into the air. The toddler scowls in anger as a playmate grabs her crayon. The 5-year-old grows frightened on the first morning of kindergarten. The teenager rejected by his steady date crumples into depression. The examples of how emotions color everyday experience are legion. But what exactly *are* emotions? Although people within a culture may agree readily on what "sadness" or "joy" or "anger" mean, those words do not refer to fixed, tangible things in the way that "bicycle" or "mouse" do. Words for emotions are conveniently shared but, nevertheless, imprecise constructs (Shields and Stern, 1979).

A definition of emotion is hard to formulate for several reasons. First, emotions are diverse and varied. There is no consensus among behavioral scientists on what the emotions are. Some investigators, for example, have identified 10 basic emotions: interest-excitement, joy, surprise-startle, distress-anguish, anger, disgust-revulsion, contempt-scorn, fear, shame, and guilt (Darwin, 1872; Ekman, Friesen, and Ellsworth, 1972; Izard, 1971, 1977; Tomkins, 1962, 1963). Others have described mixtures of emotions: joy + acceptance = love + friendliness; fear + surprise = alarm + awe; joy + fear = guilt (Plutchik, 1980).

A second reason that emotions are hard to define is that they have many different aspects. Emotions involve: (1) elicitors, which are the triggering situations or events; (2) receptors, which are the actions of the central nervous system; (3) states, which are specific changes in physiology; (4) expressions, which are the observable changes in face, body, voice, or action that accompany emotional states; and (5) experiences, which are a person's perception and interpretation of his or her emotional state and expression (Lewis and Rosenblum, 1978). Any comprehensive definition of emotion would have to include the subjective, or felt, experience of emotion—"I felt glad to see you" or "I was scared to death." It would have to account for the biological processes in the brain and nervous system, and it would have to account for observable expressions of emotion, particularly facial expressions.

A third difficulty in defining emotions is that they affect the whole person, not just a single biological system, and they tend to occur in clusters or combinations. It is rare for people to feel a single, pure emotion before another emotion seeps in to change the mixture.

Finally, it is hard to define emotions because the aspects of emotional experience vary not only from one individual to another, but also from one culture to another. The Western psychologist's list of basic emotions would seem woefully lacking to people from other cultures. To the contemporary citizen of Japan, *amae*—feeling mutually dependent on another person—is a basic emotion (Kato, 1979). To the Utku Eskimo, *naklik*—wanting to care for and protect another—is a basic emotion (Briggs, 1970). Any comprehensive definition of emotion would have to transcend such cultural differences.

Just as we consider the term "weather" as a broad term for various relations among humidity, temperature, wind speed, and the like, Jerome Kagan (1978) has suggested that we consider "emotions" as a broad term for various relations among external elicitors, thoughts, and changes in feeling.

MEASURING EMOTIONS

In the last decade, as their methods of measuring emotional expressions have improved, psychologists have grown increasingly interested in studying emotions. To measure emotional expressions, psychologists may observe individuals' faces or body postures or listen to their voices. One system for measuring emotion is Carroll Izard's (1979) **Maximally Discriminative Facial Movement (MAX)** system. With this system, observers identify patterns of facial expressions that have been linked to various emotions. Each facial expression is defined as a certain set of movements. MAX classifies 27 different expressions of the brows, forehead, eyes, nose, cheeks, and mouth. Thus for sadness an observer might note raised inner corners of the brows, squinted eyes, and corners of the mouth drawn downward. MAX identifies patterns that include anger-rage, interest-excitement, enjoyment-joy, fear-terror, sadness-dejection, discomfort-pain, and disgust (see photos **page 269**).

Paul Ekman and Wallace Friesen (1978), of San Francisco's University of California Medical School,

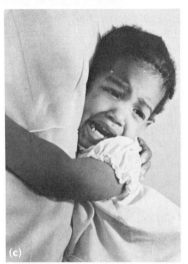
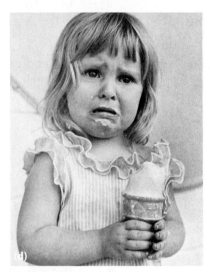
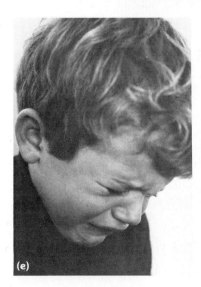
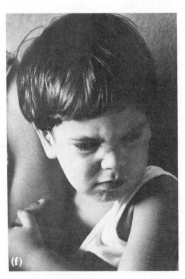

Facial expressions of emotions are common across ages, sexes, and cultural groups. Here we see (a) interest, (b) joy, (c) fear, (d) distress, (e) grief and (f) disgust.

have devised another system for reading facial expressions of emotion. In their system, each of the 80 facial muscles that a person tenses is numbered. Even contradictory expressions—smiles that mask anger for example—can be specified in this system. When this technique is combined with computer analyses of brain activity and nervous system arousal, psychologists can identify specific emotions with great accuracy. Each emotion creates a unique pattern of both brain and nervous system activity and tensing of facial muscles. Although the distinct brain pathways for each emotion have yet to be mapped, psychologists already know that negative emotions activate the right half of the cortex and positive emotions, the left half. Richard Davidson (1984) has speculated that some of the defense mechanisms described by psychoanalysts may eventually be explained by specific forms of brain activation. For example, among people who repress their feelings and report feeling calm even though instruments show that they are anxious, Davidson has found a communications gap between the right-hemisphere center for processing negative emotion and the left-hemisphere center for processing language.

But measuring emotions through facial expressions is not yet an exact science. With infants and children especially, behavioral scientists face problems of accuracy. The criterion for accuracy is usually a match between the intent of the person expressing an emotion and the judgment of an observer; clearly this criterion cannot be applied to infants or young children. Another problem is that infants may respond to a single elicitor with more than a single expression of emotion. Infants' and children's emotional responses are not all the same either. One child may show anxiety with a rise in heart rate, another with stomach contractions, a third by talking rapidly. One child may also show the same emotion in different ways, perhaps showing active interest first with an increase in heart rate, later with a decrease in heart rate (Kagan, in press).

Body movements and properties of voice can also give clues about a speaker's emotional state. The voice can convey pleasure, anger, fear, joy, and surprise. Researchers have been inventive in their methods of measuring the emotional properties of voices. Some have had subjects sing notes of music or read alphabet letters or sets or identical sentences to convey certain emotions. Investigators

have shown that pitch level can differentiate happiness from sadness (Skinner, 1935) and grief from anger (Fairbanks and Pronovost, 1938). Stress, intonation, loudness, and pauses all help to convey emotion.

INNATE OR LEARNED?

Are emotions innate? Yes. Are they learned? Yes. First, evidence that aspects of emotions are innate comes from a variety of sources: emotional expressions have been demonstrated to be recognizable cross culturally; emotions have clear evolutionary antecedents in nonhuman primates; and emotions are found in human infants.

Cross-cultural studies of people from both literate and preliterate societies have shown a biologically based universality in some, though not all, emotional expressions. When subjects from two preliterate cultures were asked both to demonstrate and to identify pictures of emotional expressions appropriate to certain events—the death of a child was one such event—they were identical in their expressions and in their identifications of happiness, sadness, disgust, and anger (Ekman and Friesen, 1972; Ekman, Sorenson, and Friesen, 1969). Not only facial expressions, but crying, screaming, and laughing have also been shown to be universal expressions of distress, fear, and joy (Scherer, 1979).

Evidence suggesting the biologically adaptive value of certain facial expressions provides further support for the position that emotions are innate. Many observers, from Charles Darwin (1872/1975) to ethologist Niko Tinbergen (1951), have argued that facial expressions of emotion evolved from those once associated in animals with fighting, threatening, courting, and other acts. According to evolutionary theories, certain facial expressions have been naturally selected because they increase a species' chances for survival. In expressions of anger, for example, the eyebrows are lowered, the eyelids are tensed and narrowed, the nostrils flare, and the mouth is either open and squarish or tightly closed. Originally, perhaps the lowered eyebrows and tensed eyelids improved vision by cutting down on glare. Flared nostrils may have increased oxygen consumption. The open mouth may have bared the teeth for biting. All of these features

Photograph Judged						
Judgment	Happiness	Disgust	Surprise	Sadness	Anger	Fear
Culture			**Percent Who Agreed with Judgment**			
99 Americans	97	92	95	84	67	85
40 Brazilians	95	97	87	59	90	67
119 Chileans	95	92	93	88	94	68
168 Argentinians	98	92	95	78	90	54
29 Japanese	100	90	100	62	90	66

As this table indicates, there is a great deal of agreement—and some lack of agreement—among the members of different cultures about the meaning of facial expressions. This suggests that we are biologically programmed to recognize and produce the emotions conveyed by certain facial expressions but that learning also plays a role.

would have had adaptive value and might therefore have been preserved as facial expressions of anger.

Work with primates also has suggested an innate basis for certain emotions. In one study by Gene Sackett (1966), for instance, rhesus monkeys were raised in isolation for their first 9 months. Twice a week from the time they were 2 weeks old, these monkeys were shown slides of other monkeys' activities, and their responses were observed. Rather abruptly at 2½ months of age and until 4 months of age, slides of other monkeys threatening increased the isolated monkeys' incidence of rocking, huddling, withdrawing, and vocalizing. Even without direct experience of actual threats, these monkeys responded appropriately to signals of emotional expression and expressed their reaction in ways that convey fear in both animals and humans.

Human infants' expressions of emotion may have survival value as well. Infants' cries and smiles influence their caregivers to feed and tend them in ways essential to the infants' survival and do so

even before the infants can have had any feedback about how they are influencing others. The early and apparently meaningless smiles of infants—many happen during sleep—tend to evoke positive reactions from the infants' mothers (Emde, Gaensbauer, and Harmon, 1976). Infants' grimaces of disgust as they spew unpleasant objects from their mouths serve to signal a caregiver to help remove the intolerable thing. Cries bring a caregiver running with help or food. Not only do infants' emotional expressions have survival value, but some of them are remarkably similar to the emotional expressions of older children and adults—further evidence that some aspects of emotions are innate. One comprehensive study of infants' facial expressions was conducted Susan Hiatt, Joseph Campos, and Robert Emde (1979). When these researchers observed and recorded infants' facial expressions within a given period of time after the infants were presented with certain elicitors of emotions, they found that 10- to 12-month-old infants' faces reg-

Even infants express a variety of emotions, facially and vocally.

istered adult-like patternings for joy and surprise, but not for fear. In a study by Craig Stenberg, Joseph Campos, and Robert Emde (1983) of 7-month-olds whose teething biscuit was removed just as they began to mouth it, the investigators found strong evidence for the infants' facial patterning of anger. Likewise, investigators have found that infants of 1, 4, and 7 months of age show angry faces in response to having their arms restrained and that infants between 8 and 19 months show anger when they receive an inoculation (Izard, Hembree, Dougherty, and Coss, in press; Stenberg, 1982). Even 2-hour-old infants' facial reactions to different tastes have shown distinctly different positive and negative reactions (Rosenstein and Oster, 1981).

To learn more about universals of human emotions, Emde (1980) used ratings by adults of in-fants' expressions. Photographs of 10 normal, 3½-month-old infants were taken as the infants played with their mothers, met a stranger, or looked at a pattern. When the infants were 12 months old, more photographs of their emotional reactions were taken. In one procedure, 25 adults were asked to sort into piles that "seem to belong together," pictures of infants and cards showing mothers' responses to their own infant's picture. In another procedure, after examining the pictures, adults were asked to give a single word or phrase for "the strongest and clearest feeling that the baby is expressing." Results from the two procedures were consistent. The adults categorized over 99 percent of the photos as belonging to one of the eight basic emotions identified in adults by Izard (1971), plus the category "bored-sleepy." Interest, joy, and distress were common expressions of infants in these situations at 3½ months. Fear, surprise, and anger—emotions whose expression might require more experience and cognition—were common only in the second half of the infants' first year (Emde, Kligman, Reich, and Wade, 1978). Thus, emotions include both the innate and the learned.

Blind babies provide another source of evidence that emotions are partly innate and partly learned. Congenitally blind babies, it was found (Eibl-Eibesfeldt, 1973), express emotions in just the ways sighted babies do. Over time, however, the blind babies' expressions deteriorate, especially those around the eyes.

Also over time, people learn how to modulate and control the expression of their emotions. In effect, they learn their own culture's norms, or display rules, for expressing emotion (Ekman, 1980). People learn when to exaggerate, to mask, to pretend, or to neutralize certain emotions. Thus just as cultural universals for some emotional expressions support the notion that emotions are innate, cultural variations support the notion that emotions are learned as well. Learning these cultural norms

RESEARCH FOCUS

INFANTS' ABILITIES TO EXPRESS EMOTIONS

In a series of five studies, Carroll Izard and several colleagues at the University of Delaware (Izard, Huebner, Risser, McGinnes, and Dougherty, 1980) investigated whether infants would show facial expressions for discrete emotions and whether the facial expressions could be reliably classified. College undergraduates from introductory psychology courses served as subjects. They saw videotapes of mothers and experimenters trying to elicit from infants smiling, interest, and surprise; inoculations and blood tests being given to the infants; nurses approaching and trying to take the infants before and after the medical procedures; infants being shown a surprise toy and being given something that tasted sour. The facial expressions recorded were of 50 infants, both black and white, between 1 and 9 months old. Two judges familiar with an anatomically based coding system for facial expressions chose pictures of each infant's discrete emotions. They found examples of interest, joy, surprise, sadness, anger, disgust, fear, and contempt, all of which (except contempt, which was judged coincidental) were judged to be appropriate responses to the situation.

Some of the student subjects were asked to label with a word or phrase the emotion they saw "most strongly and clearly expressed on the baby's face." Others were asked to choose from a list of nine emotions the category that "best describes the expression on the baby's face." Still others were asked to choose which of 10 adults' facial expressions "best matches the baby's expression." Even without any special training, the students were far more accurate than could be accounted for by chance in identifying the babies' expressions. Chance would call for 12.5 percent correct, but the percentage of facial expressions correctly identified was 81 percent for joy, 72 percent for sadness, 69 percent for surprise, 67 percent for interest, 52 percent for fear, 44 percent for contempt, 41 percent for anger, and 37 percent for disgust. The experimenters' first hypothesis—that untrained subjects could reliably identify infants' facial expressions—was supported. Similar results were obtained from untrained subjects who were nurses rather than students.

Coders then applied MAX—the system for classifying facial expressions of emotion—to short segments of the videotapes of the babies. These results were then compared to the patterns theoretically expected in another classification system, Izard's Facial Expression Scoring Manual (FESM) system. Nearly 90 percent of the emotional expressions were found to correspond, a finding that led the investigators to conclude that infants can produce 8 reliably identifiable facial expressions and several blends. Subjects had been the least accurate in identifying negative emotional expressions, perhaps because they are inherently more difficult to distinguish or perhaps because the subjects did not want to attribute negative emotions to babies. Brief training was found to increase significantly the subjects' accuracy of identification.

Gradually children learn to modulate and control their expressions of emotion. They hold back the tears, even though the pain is great.

for emotional expression begins early in life. In their investigation of the socialization of emotions, Michael Lewis and Linda Michalson (1982) noted that children learn how to express emotions and that this learning begins early in infancy during interactions with adults. Children learn when, and in which situations, emotions can be expressed. They learn how to modify or suppress socially unacceptable emotions, and evidence suggests that even 10-month-olds do so as they interact with people whom they know well (Feinman and Lewis, 1981). Children also learn the labels for emotions. Of course, children may have some limited understanding of emotional experiences before they have learned specific labels for those emotions. An 18-month-old may pat a grief-stricken parent in sympathetic understanding, without knowing the words for the parent's feeling (Borke, 1971). But learning the culturally approved label for an emotion does affect its expression and, presumably, the way it is experienced. In Tahiti, for instance, grief is forbidden, and the Tahitian language contains no word for this feeling. When a Tahitian encounters a situation that would evoke grief in one of us—after the death of a loved one, say—the Tahitian does experience grief. But the grief is considered a form of illness, because it violates the social rules for emotional expression (Levy, 1973).

Children probably learn most about emotions from their parents. Parents tend to attribute emotions to their infants—"Don't be afraid, baby," "I know you love Mommy," "Oh, you're embarrassed"—even before the infants can actually experience these emotions (Pannabecker, Emde, Johnson, Stenberg, and Davis, 1980). It is likely that children learn about emotions from their parents' labels as well as from their parents' reactions to emotional expressions. A 1-year-old may cry after a tower of blocks falls down. Her mother says, "You're frustrated" and helps her to rebuild the tower. The mother has labeled the feeling of frustration. Another 1-year-old may cry after hurting his leg. His mother says, "You hurt yourself" and holds him. She has labeled his response to pain. Two quite different emotional and socialization experiences will have followed from crying, a single emotional state (Lewis and Michalson, 1982).

In a study of how parents label emotions, Lewis and Michalson (1981) investigated how mothers labeled the emotions of their 1-year-old infants when they were reunited after a brief separation. When the mothers returned to their crying infants, only one-fourth gave emotional labels to the infants' responses. These mothers used four different emotional labels that were appropriate to the situation; they said that the children were "tired/sad," "angry/mad," "scared/upset," or "missed me." The mothers' labels corresponded to the eliciting situation and to aspects of the infants' behavior—"an-

Children learn about expressing emotions from their parents' reactions when they are angry or hurt themselves.

gry/mad'' children had thrown toys around; "tired/sad'' children seemed depressed. Although few differences appeared between mothers who labeled and mothers who did not, Lewis and Michalson wondered whether the labelers were more sensitive to negative than to positive emotions. They also speculated that mothers who use more numerous and more differentiated words for feelings may produce children whose experiences of feelings are in turn more differentiated.

In another study of how parents teach their preschoolers about emotions, Esther Greif, and her colleagues (Grief, Alvarez, and Ulman, 1981) found that as parents read a picture book to their children, nearly three-quarters of them mentioned emotions. They most often mentioned anger, joy, and distress. Mothers mentioned feelings to sons and daughters equally, but fathers mentioned feelings twice as often to daughters as to sons. This sex differentiated socialization of emotions was reflected in the children's behavior, too. When the children's own, spontaneous mentions of feelings were tallied, it was found that daughters had produced 17 out of the 20 mentions.

In a third study, Virginia Demos (1982) observed and filmed emotionally expressive behavior in infants between 6 months and 2 years of age. Consistent with other studies, she found that the infants' facial expressions corresponded to those described for adults as signaling discrete emotions, such as distress or enjoyment. Although the infants' facial expressions were patterned in these universal ways, they varied in subtleties of intensity, length, and other blended elements. Thus, although enjoyment always involved a smile, for example, there were variations in the width of the smile, representing, Demos suggested, individual differences. Despite the fact that children were learning some of the cultural rules for displaying emotions—like smiling often—no child under 1 year of age tried to control or mute an expression of feeling, and no parent tried to suppress a child's feelings. The older children attempted to control expressions of distress by pressing, sucking, or funneling their lips. Learning appropriate display rules and labels to modify innate emotional expressions, it seems, is a slow and gradual process. But both innate and learned components are clearly present in the finished product: the grin of the adolescent who has mastered a new skill, the tender expression of the mother with her new baby, the tears of the man who has lost his wife of many years.

HEAD AND HEART

Just as emotions are both innate and learned, they also involve both head and heart—both cognition and physiology. But does the thought come first and the physical feeling follow, or is it just the reverse? Several psychologists have addressed this question, and they have reached quite different conclusions. Sylvan Tomkins (1962) holds that the neurons firing automatically in the brain activate feelings. No thought or appraisal is necessary, and feelings may be activated by an image, another feeling, a drive, or an **innate releaser.** Like Tomkins, Izard, too, believes that feeling is primary. Izard (1981) calls attention to the **hippocampus,** which is located in the brain's **limbic system** ("emotional brain"). He suggests that before infants develop short-term cognitive memory, they process information in this emotion system. The social smile of the 1½- to 5-month-old infant, for example, emerges reflexively and automatically in response to a high-pitched human voice or a nodding face. Even after cognition has begun to develop, Izard maintains, it is unlikely to exist independently of feeling. Instead, as emotion and cognition interact in conscious thought, "affective-cognitive" brain structures develop. According to Izard's (1977) **differential emotions theory,** emotions are distinct patterns of actions. They consist of three components: facial and bodily expressions, visceral and hormonal reactions, and the consciousness of emotions themselves. Facial and bodily expressions send neural signals to the cortex of the brain where they are "felt" as an emotion. Thus, in Izard's view, emotion comes before cognition both developmentally and temporally.

Robert Zajonc (1980) also holds that feeling and cognition are controlled by separate systems and that feelings are primary. They are encoded in the viscera or the muscles and not necessarily in words. Zajonc notes, for example, how little trouble we have identifying the emotions expressed by people who speak a foreign language. Perception is virtually always colored by feeling: we immediately feel attraction or repulsion when we are introduced to someone; we immediately like or dislike the book we are reading or the house we are visiting. These emotional judgments tend to be irrevocable because they "feel" valid to us. We remember the emotional quality of a memory before the particulars emerge in consciousness. To Zajonc, feelings are basic and inescapable; although people may control the expression of an emotion, they cannot control the experience of it.

As evidence for the primacy of emotions, these theorists cite an experiment by Campos, Emde, and colleagues (Meng, Henderson, Campos, and Emde, 1983). The subjects were two groups of 16-month-olds. One group was twice briefly separated from their mothers; the other played happily with puppets. After a brief interval, children in both groups were given a problem in which they had to turn a bar away from themselves to draw a toy toward them. It was found that up to a certain point, the happier the babies had been as they played with the puppets, the better was their (cognitive) performance on the bar-turning problem. Above a certain level of happiness, however, their performance decreased. In contrast, the more unhappy the babies had been, the worse their performance on the problem. A second study that supports the position of emotional primacy is provided by Stanford's Gordon Bower (1981). In this experiment, adult subjects learned lists of material while they were in each of four emotional states—joyfulness, sadness, anger, or fear—as induced hypnotically. They later returned to the laboratory to test their recall of the lists while they were in either the same or a different emotional state from the original one. Recall was highest when the subjects were in the same emotional state as during original learning and lowest when they were in the opposite one. Bower concluded that feelings organize and give access to memories. In a third experiment, Soviet actors who had received training in the Stanislavsky method—creating genuine emotion in themselves and bringing it to their dramatic roles—were asked first to feel and to express an emotion; then to feel the emotion but to try and appear impassive; finally to show an emotion by facial expression without feeling the emotion (Rusalova, Izard, and Simonov, 1975). The experimenters recorded heart rate and reaction of facial muscles. They found the greatest change in heart rate in the condition where the actors felt and expressed emotion naturally. The lowest heart rates occurred

during the third condition, and some subjects said that they could not prevent themselves from feeling when their faces registered emotions. All three of these studies demonstrate that emotions are primary: they affect subsequent cognition, and they occur in situations that are not realistically (i.e., cognitively) evocative.

To psychologists Stanley Schachter and Jerome Singer or George Mandler, however, it is not emotion but cognition that is primary. Cognitive appraisal is necessary for interpreting physiological arousal as an emotion. Theirs are **cognition-arousal theories** of emotion. In a classic experiment, whose unwitting subjects were told that they were participating in an "experiment in vision," Schachter and Singer (1962) injected adults with epinephrine, a powerful stimulant. Subjects who had been informed that the injection would cause an adrenaline rush showed little arousal. But subjects who had been misinformed about the injection and therefore could not readily interpret their physical arousal tended to adopt the feelings—either anger or happiness—of a confederate of the investigators who was in the room with the subject. Schachter and Singer's experiment has been cited as an example of how people attribute emotions on the basis of their physiological sensations. Mandler (1962, 1975), too, has asserted that feelings are inextricably tied to attributions or meanings. He has described a "jukebox" theory of emotions: physical arousal is the coin that sets up the emotional experience, and puzzlement about the source of the arousal is the button that selects the emotion to be played. In cognition-arousal theories, visceral arousal does not clearly define an emotional state or experience. It motivates an individual to search for an antecedent or cause for the visceral feelings and to identify that cause as an emotion.

To some psychologists, neither of these views—that emotion precedes or is primary to cognition, or vice versa—is adequate. Some have suggested other ways of reconciling the head-first or heart-first positions. Richard Dienstbier (in press), for example, suggests that the relevance of facial or autonomic nervous system feedback varies with the particular emotion being expressed. Disgust, he speculates, would rely heavily on feedback from the mouth, throat, and esophagus, and sexual arousal would rely on feedback from the genitals—that is, heart first. In contrast, an emotion like anxiety that is characterized by hormonal and sympathetic nervous system responses may depend more on prior cognitive appraisal. Others have presented alternative explanations that include both head and heart. One alternative account has been suggested by Campos and his colleagues (Campos, Barrett, Lamb, Goldsmith, and Stenberg, 1983). Their account incorporates the notion of a goal as a necessary component in the elicitation of emotions. Joy, for example, is elicited when a person appreciates that his goal—a wished-for event or object—is likely to be reached. Sadness results when the wished-for object is unobtainable. Interest is elicited when the wished-for object is obtained.

Another suggestion for integrating head and heart is presented by Howard Leventhal (1979). Leventhal's **perceptual motor processing theory** of emotion proposes that emotion is created by three different mechanisms: an innate facial-motor mechanism, a memory for emotion, and a conceptual system containing rules for emotional experience. Leventhal agrees with Izard that facial muscles are responsible for states of feeling, and out of them memories are formed. The face is structured to provide excellent feedback about feelings. But feedback does not explain *all* emotional experience. In fact, argues Leventhal, feelings also arise when the spontaneous motor system feeds *forward* into the voluntary motor system, a process that may occur before activity even begins in the facial muscles. The second mechanism for processing emotion involves cognitive structures. Feelings are evoked by the process of classifying mental representations of particular experiences. Leventhal believes that this process explains why infants smile when they recognize familiar objects or why people who have lost an arm or leg may feel phantom pain and distress in the lost limb. Only a central memory structure for emotions can account for the experience of phantom pain, Leventhal argues. Third, emotions are processed in an abstract conceptual system that contains memories and cognitions *about* feelings. In this system, feelings are given causes and consequences, and they are evaluated as good or bad. It is here that attitudes and evaluations are generated out of specific emotional experiences.

Whichever position is taken—emotions are primary, cognition is primary, or both directions exist—the clear consensus is that emotional experi-

ences include elements from both cognition and physiology, both head and heart.

THEORIES OF EMOTIONAL DEVELOPMENT

We are interested not only in the underlying bases of emotional experiences, but also in how those experiences change with age. Several quite different theories of emotional development have been proposed by observers of human behavior. Cognitive theorists like Jean Piaget have discussed how emotions develop as infants interact with their physical environments. Psychoanalytic theorists like Sigmund Freud and René Spitz have discussed how emotions arise from social relationships. Contemporary theorists like Alan Sroufe have tried to integrate the psychoanalytic and cognitive approaches by connecting emotions that arise in social contexts with those that arise in response to the physical environment.

For Piaget, emotions were inseparable from cognition. Together they form symbolic schemes, the basic building blocks of intelligence. Emotions supply the scheme's energy in the form of interest or lack of it and the tendency to approach or avoid. Emotions can delay or accelerate cognition. Cognition supplies the structure for development, the goal or desire, and the rules by which specific content is rendered meaningful. As Piaget wrote:

> There is no behavioral pattern, however intellectual, which does not involve affective factors as motives. Behavior, therefore, has a unity even if the structure (cognitive) does not explain its energetics (affective) and if, vice versa, its energetics do not account for its structures. The two aspects, affective and cognitive, are at the same time inseparable and irreducible. (Piaget and Inhelder, 1969, p. 158)

Piaget compared emotion to the gasoline that fuels a car and cognition to the engine that harnesses it. Emotional energy, Piaget believed, does not itself change with age, but emotions develop as their cognitive components develop through stages. Earlier feelings are transformed as development proceeds.

For Freud (1900, 1915), infants at first possess neither cognition nor emotion, just arousal and the reduction of arousal or tension and its reduction. Emotion is a form of energy that denotes disorganization or disequilibrium; the ego works to discharge this disorganizing energy and to attain a state of equilibrium. The first real emotions appear after the first 2 or 3 months of life as the infant begins to develop ego functions like memory. Later, ego functions like self-control and symbolizing develop, and emotions like guilt, pride, and shame emerge. In short, the undifferentiated tension of infancy turns into increasingly differentiated and complex forms of psychological experience and behavior.

Both Piaget and Freud offered only limited accounts of emotional development. Sroufe (1979) has tried to go beyond their accounts and to provide more detail, more empirical data, and a developmental timetable. Like Freud, he suggests that tension is the key to the emotions of early infancy. He cites research (e.g., Berlyne, 1969; Cicchetti and Sroufe, 1976; Emde et al., 1976) showing that newborns smile and infants laugh when the level of neurological excitation, or tension, first rises and then quickly falls below a certain threshold. How much tension can an infant tolerate? That limit depends on how the infant evaluates any given situation. Being thrown in the air by his father may thrill an infant, but being thrown in the air by a stranger may frighten him (Sroufe, Waters, and Matas, 1974). Too high a level of tension creates negative emotion.

During the first 2 years of life, Sroufe theorizes, as the infant's brain and muscles grow more organized and effective, successive reorganizations of behavior occur. In the first stage, emotions are based on changes in the level of physiological tension, as we have described. In the third or fourth month of life, the infant begins to react to specific familiar or unfamiliar events, and emotions like wariness become possible. In the fifth month, infants develop intentionality, the motivation to complete an action, and they will cry if they are frustrated. Joy and fear develop after the ninth month of life, once the infant can interpret events as meaningful—a stranger as frightening or Mother as wonderful, for example. By the end of the first year, elation, anxiety, and anger appear. At 18 months, shame, affection, and defiance appear, and pride, love, and guilt appear at about 3 years of age along with cognitive advances. Thus as cognitive devel-

opment proceeds, it interacts reciprocally with emotional development.

Campos and his colleagues (Campos et al., 1983) have given one of the most complete accounts of emotional development to date. They have proposed seven postulates of emotional development:

1. A set of differentiated, core, emotions—for example, fear, surprise, joy—exists from birth to death. Each emotion is a "family," in that its expression changes in the course of development, although it retains crucial features of feeling tone, expression, and relationship to goals.

2. As children develop cognitively, such complex and coordinated emotions as guilt, shame, depression, and envy appear.

3. As the individual develops, different circumstances become effective in eliciting emotional responses. The infant smiles at a bull's-eye target; the 2-year-old does not.

4. The relationship between the expression and experience of emotion changes over the course of development. By adulthood, for example, most people seldom express the emotions they are experiencing directly and freely.

5. The way an individual copes in response to emotions also changes with cognitive and motor development. The baby who can crawl away from a frightening stranger may then enjoy playing with that stranger.

6. The expression of emotions is socialized into acceptable forms.

7. Receptiveness to emotional expression changes in the course of development.

As these postulates demonstrate, emotional development proceeds simultaneously along several fronts. A complete and adequate theory of emotional development will have to account for changes on all of these fronts. In the 1980s, great strides are likely in the understanding of emotional development.

BASIC EMOTIONS

Now that we have described some theories of how emotions develop, we will take a look at a few specific emotions. Joy, anger, fear, and sadness are perhaps the most basic human emotions.

JOY

People of every age, from the infant to the very old, know the pleasurable feeling called joy. Yet joy is an elusive emotion; try to catch it or to corner it, and it disappears. Joy is a feeling that visits when the conditions are right, but no one can manufacture those conditions. Joy seems just to happen. When it does happen, joy makes people feel loved, lovable, and confident. Joy is often a side effect of some perception, thought, or act, a feeling that follows creative work, discovery, triumph, or the reduction of stress (Izard, 1977). Joy may be the result of a sharp decline in the density of neural firing. When a baby is tossed into the air and then lands safely in her father's arms, first she is hugely excited, then securely joyous (Izard, 1977). The expresson of joy—lips pulled back and curving gently upward, eyes twinkling—is universally recognized, even by very young infants. When 4- and 6-month-old infants were shown slides of joyous,

angry, and neutral facial expressions, the infants fixed their gaze far longer on the joyous faces than the others (LaBarbera, Izard, Parisi, and Vietze, 1976).

Joy may cement the bonds of intimacy between friends or loved ones. The joyous smile of the infant cements its ties to its parents and thereby increases its chances of survival. Izard (1977) has suggested that individuals differ in their biologically based capacity for joy, a capacity that strongly influences how people feel about themselves and how they think others feel about them—their "social self-concept" (Fitts, 1971). Evidence for the biological foundation of joy comes from studies of infants and toddlers. In one study of Soviet toddlers who had been institutionalized since birth and who were tended equally by a group of caregivers, marked individual differences in the toddlers' frequency of smiling and laughing showed up (Izard, Izard, and Makarenko, 1977).

As we saw in Chapter 5, it is generally accepted that smiling is an innate and universal response in infancy. Newborns smile spontaneously and reflexively within a few hours after birth, usually when they are sleeping or drowsy (Wolff, 1963). This

People of all ages know and express joy in playful interactions.

smiling is consistent with feelings of pleasure, but these very early smiles are responses to internal, not external, states. By the age of 4 weeks, infants will smile at a high-pitched human voice, in what may be the first manifestation of social smiling. Later, social smiles are responses to people. Between the ages of 2½ and 5 months, infants smile at any smiling face that comes toward them and seem to experience something like enjoyment. At 4 months, they discriminate between unfamiliar and familiar faces and smile differently at familiar people. These true social smiles are extremely helpful in cementing the emotional bond between mother and infant. Between 9 and 12 months, infants laugh when a familiar face disappears and then quickly reappears, as in a game of peekaboo. Thus, as Izard points out, as the infant advances cognitively—from the earliest reflexive smiling, to smiling at any approaching human face, to smiling differentially at familiar and unfamiliar faces, to holding an image in mind while anticipating the joy of reunion—the experience of joy also changes.

When infants cry, they pull back and away from the stimulus. But when they laugh, they stay oriented toward the stimulus, reaching out to try and maintain or reproduce the situation. Laughter, like smiling, is a sign of joy. The infant begins to laugh when about 3 or 4 months old. Laughing occurs immediately after stimulation, reflecting a sharp tension swing or arousal jag (Berlyne, 1969), a rapid increase in excitation followed quickly by relaxation. More vigorous stimulation is required to produce a laugh than a smile—bouncing, tickling, blowing on the baby's stomach—stimulation that earlier would have been too exciting and arousing to assimilate and would have caused distress. If tension is to be maintained and the baby's laughing to continue, the stimulation movements, vocalization, and expressions must be varied or intensified.

In one experiment, Alan Sroufe and Jane Wunsch (1972) used a considerable variety of ploys to get babies of different ages up to 12 months to laugh (Figure 7.1). At 5 months babies would laugh at jiggling, at tickling under the chin, and when their mother covered her face. At 7 and 8 months, they laughed at their mother shaking her hair, at their mother with a cloth in her mouth, and at "coochy coo" and horsey sounds. Still older infants laughed at more subtle visual and social complexities. By 12 months of age, infants chortled

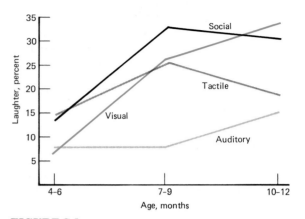

FIGURE 7.1

Laughter of infants in the first year of life in response to four different kinds of stimuli: social (mother), visual (cloth over mother's face), tactile (jiggling, tickling), auditory (horsey sounds) (Sroufe and Wunsch, 1972).

at their mother's walking like a penguin, sticking out her tongue, or sucking on the baby's bottle. At this age, a combination of ploys and the baby's mental effort to interpret an **incongruity** produced laughs. Infants of this age also began to laugh in anticipation of a familiar stimulus—such as blowing on the tummy—or when they actively participated in the situation. Now they laughed not at the cloth in front of Mother's face but at the fact that they could pull the cloth and unveil Mother. Still later, infants laughed when they created the spectacle themselves. They might stuff the cloth in Mother's mouth and then laugh. Developmental psychologists suggest that smiling and laughing follow a common course: at first the smile or laugh is produced directly by a stimulus; later by interpreting, anticipating, or producing a stimulus (Sroufe, 1979).

ANGER

Anger occurs when people are prevented, frustrated, or restrained from doing what they wish; when they are insulted, interrupted, taken advantage of, or forced to act against their wishes; when they are in pain or prolonged distress. Anger makes people want to attack the "enemy"; it makes them feel powerful and impulsive; the muscles tighten, and the face warms. Angry people feel tense and more self-confident than they do for any other negative emotion (Bartlett and Izard, 1972). The facial expression of anger consists of a frown, a hard stare at the object of the anger, dilated nostrils, lips pulled back to reveal clenched teeth, and often a red flush to the skin. As mentioned earlier, Stenberg and colleagues (1983) observed how 7-month-olds reacted to having a teething biscuit pulled out of their mouths after they'd begun to suck on it for a few seconds. By viewing the infants' facial expressions just before and just after the biscuits were snatched away, the investigators found that the infants' faces clearly registered an angry expression in response to having the biscuit removed. When the biscuit was taken away more than once, the infants' expressions grew increasingly angry, and their faces flushed. The investigators noted that infants grew especially angry when their mothers stood by letting this happen and then started pulling the biscuit out of the infants' mouths themselves. The babies may have expected their mothers to protect and comfort them. They did not react so strongly to frustration by a stranger.

Like other emotions, anger changes with development. Infants first deal with frustrations by distressed crying. When they are between 4 and 6 months old, they make angry cries, which signal their determination to remove the source of offense. In a study of how infants between 2 and 19 months reacted to the pain of an injection, Izard and his associates (Izard, Hembree, Dougherty, and Spizzirri, 1983) found that babies under 8 months old showed physical distress in their facial expressions immediately after the injection (Figure 7.2). Only two babies under 8 months old did not show physical distress. The facial expression of one of these babies was angry; the other was sad. But among the 19-month-olds, only one-third showed physical distress first, although most showed physical distress within 10 seconds after their injection. The majority looked angry. As the babies got older, they expressed physical distress for shorter periods of time. Babies who were slow soothers expressed anger more of the time than the babies who were more quickly soothed. The investigators did not find, as John Bowlby (1973) had hypothesized, that pain caused fear.

Children often are taught to control or conceal parts of this angry expression. Adaptive over the course of human evolution, anger helped people to mobilize their energies and to defend themselves

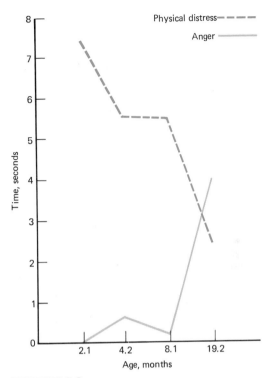

FIGURE 7.2

Duration of physical distress and anger expressions in the first 10-seconds after an inoculation. As babies get older they show less distress and more anger. (Izard, Hembree, Dougherty, and Spizzirri, 1983.)

forcefully. But in nearly all cases today, cultural rules and laws prevent the full expression of anger. Because anger is so proscribed by social conventions, humans have adapted by learning to express anger in words rather than physical attacks.

Studies of children's angry expressions, several of them done in the 1930s, have been based on observations and reports of children's behavior at home and in nursery school (Bridges, 1931; Goodenough, 1931; Green, 1933; Jersild and Markey, 1935; Muste and Sharpe, 1947; Walters, Pearce, and Dahms, 1957). Angry outbursts were found to peak at 2 years, especially undirected temper tantrums. Thereafter children did less angry crying and hitting. Beginning at 3 years of age, children became more retaliatory, seeking revenge for injury and giving vent to their anger verbally, by scolding, insulting, and threatening others. At all ages, boys were more likely to express their anger physically, girls verbally. For 2-year-olds, the most common irritants were the attempts of their parents to establish routines of eating, sleeping, playing, bathing, and going to the bathroom. Children aged 3 to 5 became angry because of difficulties with playmates (Feshbach, 1956, 1970; Goodenough, 1931).

Control of anger is a fundamental problem for children in this period and later. They must learn to hold back their rage and decide when it is appropriate to act out, to give vent to it, and how far they can go. They must modulate their reactions to match the provocation. Gradually children find socially acceptable ways to express anger. Some expression of anger in the preschool period is acceptable and even desirable because it is considered part of mature social behavior. By the end of the preschool period, whether or not children are consistently able to control their fears and anger, they know that some masking of feelings is important, and they begin to do so to avoid embarrassment and derision (Saarni, 1979).

FEAR AND SADNESS

Fear is the most dangerous of the emotions, for people may die of it. Fear evolved as a warning signal and a way of remobilizing thought and actions. It is a response to psychological or physical dangers. What do people do when they are afraid? Typically they open their eyes wide, watch warily, stop moving, tremble, cry out, hide, flee, or cling to someone else for safety. Frightened people may experience perceptual changes that focus and narrow their vision, slow their thinking, and freeze their movements. People differ noticeably in their individual reactions to fear, in accordance with their temperament (Kagan, 1974), and level of maturity (Bowlby, 1973; Izard, 1971).

But some causes of fear seem to affect us all. Jeffrey Gray (1971) has classified the innate causes of fear as: *intensity*—a loud noise or severe pain, for example; *novelty*—strange places and people; special *evolutionary dangers*—heights and darkness; and *social interaction*—threatening or angry exchanges with others. Bowlby (1973) suggested that people innately fear being alone or being approached suddenly. He further suggested that many day-to-day fears are extensions of biological reactions to these innate fears. Thus, for example, fear of ghosts and burglars may be extensions of the natural fear of darkness.

But these are just hypotheses. In the last two decades, researchers have empirically studied the

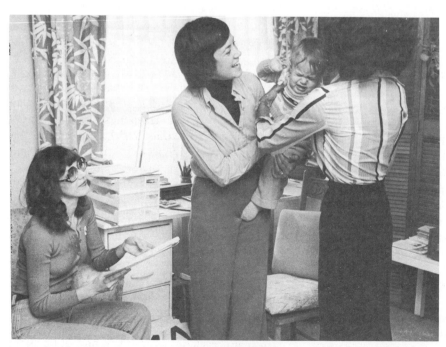

It does not happen all the time, with every baby, or with each unfamiliar adult, but this baby is clearly demonstrating "stranger anxiety" as she turns away from the unfamiliar women.

emergence and prevalence of specific fears in infancy and childhood. One of the earliest fears studied is infants' so-called *fear of strangers* or *stranger anxiety.*

At some time between 4 and 6 months of age, babies become wary of unfamiliar people. Gordon Bronson (1972) has observed wariness in experiments: the infant inspects a stranger's immobile, sober face for a prolonged period, some 15 to 30 seconds, then frowns, breathes heavily, and finally starts to cry. The wariness reaction is considered to be the first real negative emotion of the human infant. It is thought to be a reaction to what is unfamiliar and cannot be assimilated. A face is attractive to look at, and the infant's first reaction is curiosity and interest. He looks and smiles and ceases other activity. But then tension builds up as he refrains from doing anything else and works mentally to figure out who the person is. When tension is high and sustained and the infant cannot assimilate the face of the stranger, he may become distressed and look away. If the infant can assimilate the face, tension relaxes; the infant keeps looking, smiles, and may reach out to the person. Infants at this age will also be wary of Mother and other familiar persons who behave strangely (Brazelton, Tronick, Adamson, Als, and Wise, 1975). They will not be wary of unfamiliar objects. A physical object can be completely novel, but a strange face or the face of Mother with an incongruous expression is a variant on something familiar. This incongruity causes the greatest confusion and wariness (Bronson, 1972).

By the time the infant is 7 to 9 months old, he or she may be even more wary of strangers. The percentage of infants who were wary of strangers in experimental studies is 10 percent at 5 months; 20 percent at 6 to 7 months; 25 percent at 8 months; 35 percent at 9 months; 60 percent at 10 months (Waters, Matas, and Sroufe, 1975); and 69 percent at 11 months (Skarin, 1977). The reaction peaks in intensity at the end of the first year (Décarie, 1974).

A variety of theoretical explanations for the phenomenon of stranger anxiety has been offered. Psychoanalytic writers, such as Spitz (1965), have suggested that it reflects a child's love for Mother and fear of losing her. Ethologically oriented writers (Freedman, 1965) claim it to be an instinctual "flight reaction" to any strange stimulus. The theories that seem the most plausible and well worked out at the present time, however, give a cognitive explanation. According to them, by 7 to 9 months the infant's response is more than a simple reaction to an unfamiliar person. Experiments show that by this age infants are strongly influenced by two things, their situation when they see the stranger and their own past experience with strangers (Bronson, 1978; Brooks and Lewis, 1976; Emde et al., 1976; Skarin, 1977; Sroufe, 1977). If the mother is holding the baby when a stranger appears, the infant rarely cries and is usually inclined to smile. But if the infant is alone, looking up from a crib or playpen; or if the baby is being held by a stranger; or if the stranger puts his or her face too close to that of the baby or looks solemn, or behaves in an otherwise scary manner; or if the baby is already distressed or in an unfamiliar place, the reaction to a stranger is more likely to be fearful. The fear expressed by babies, however, even at the peak of its intensity, is not likely to be full-blown. Unless the stranger continues to intrude, babies usually frown, pucker up their faces, and avert their gaze; their heart rate accelerates, but they do not cry.

In the second half of their first year, infants are also fearful of looming objects, the visual cliff (see Research Focus: Infants' Fear of Heights), a person who approaches wearing a mask, and Mother without her glasses if they are accustomed to seeing her with glasses. Infants are not afraid of novel objects or unfamiliar children or midgets—for they do not loom or behave incongruously—unless the infants associate them with frightening past experiences. At this age babies have already had time to develop negative categories, such as "noisy stranger" or "scary outsider." In experiments, babies who were distressed by one stranger were more distressed by a second. In fact, most infants reserve real fear for strangers who remind them of past frights—a stranger in white lab coat who is seen after the baby has been to the doctor's office for shots or the arrival of a baby-sitter signaling impending separation from the mother.

Over the preschool period, fears prevalent in infancy, fears of the uncontrollable, unfamiliar, unassimilable—such as loud noises, sudden movements, flashes of light, shadows, strange people and situations—decrease, but fears of animals and imaginary creatures, of the dark and of being left alone, and of bodily injury increase (Jersild and

Holmes, 1935). Interviewing children about their fears, David Bauer (1976) found that 47 percent of 4- to 6-year-olds were afraid of animals, 74 percent of frightening dreams, 74 percent of ghosts and monsters. One recent study (Schwarz, 1979) assessed the fear of 3- to 5½-year-old children experimentally. Children in an unfamiliar room were suddenly confronted by a toy gorilla, which walked out of a box, stopped, and pounded its chest. Only children who had a realistic knowledge of toy gorillas or who were allowed by the experimenter to control the toy were not afraid of it. Between 15 months and 4 years, children increasingly fear death, robbers, imaginary creatures, and being alone (Macfarlane, Allen, and Honzik, 1954); children of toilet-training age may fear the toilet; 3-

year-olds are afraid of dogs; 4-year-olds are afraid of the dark (Miller, 1983).

By second grade, children, Bauer (1976) found, were less likely to imagine monsters, though bedtime fears and nightmares were still common. But now they had a new worry. Children over 8 were more likely to fear the possible aggression of others: "He would have killed me" or "Those guys wanted to cut my head off." At about 8 years of age, children are beginning to master the concept of causality (Piaget 1926, 1951). The second-graders knew what circumstances were dangerous or could cause physical injury. Their fears and anxieties change to reflect their new perception of reality. By sixth grade a boy no longer imagined a dragon lurking in his room or worried about a boogyman

RESEARCH FOCUS

INFANTS' FEAR OF HEIGHTS

Is the fear of heights innate or learned? Joseph Campos, Susan Hiatt, Douglas Ramsay, Charlotte Henderson, and Marilyn Svejda (1978) wanted to find out. After interviewing over 60 mothers by phone, they found that every one reported that her infant first took no notice of heights but then, after a fall, developed caution about them. Campos and his associates devised a study to test whether infants go through a developmental shift in their behavior on that indicator of depth perception, the visual cliff (see p. 185). For some of the 6- to 9-month-old infants, the test was to crawl across the deep side of the cliff to the beckoning mother; for others, it was to be lowered slowly onto the visual cliff and to see if they exhibited increased heart rate or the **placing response,** a rapid extension of the arms and fanning of the fingers just as the infant comes in contact with a solid surface.

Much as they had expected, the researchers found that the 9-month-olds, who had an average of two months' crawling experience, refused to cross the deep side of the visual cliff (Figure 7.3). The 7-month-olds had enough depth perception to affect their placing responses; they demonstrated the placing response to the shallow side of the visual cliff but, with few exceptions, not to the deep side. But they did not refuse to cross the deep side. Thus by 7 months of age, the infants did perceive

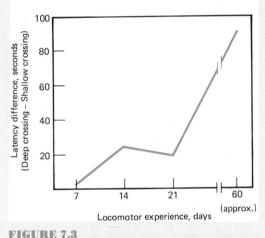

FIGURE 7.3

How reluctant babies are to cross the deep and the shallow sides of the visual cliff as a function of how long they have been crawling. (Campos, Hiatt, Ramsay, Henderson, and Svejda, 1978.)

depth, as demonstrated by their placing response, but showed little if any fear of the height. Only among infants who could crawl, the researchers found, did heart rates speed up significantly as the infants were lowered toward the deep side of the visual cliff. They concluded that motor experience, or learning, could fully account for the infants' fearful reactions to the visual cliff and, thus, to heights.

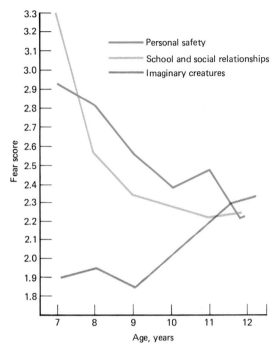

FIGURE 7.4

Variation in children's fears with age for imaginary creatures, school and social relationships, and personal safety. (Barnett, 1969.)

coming to get him, but he feared instead bodily injury in his soccer games or physical injury in a car accident or an airplane crash (Figure 7.4).

Children at this age are also beset by another fear that did not preoccupy them earlier, fear of an unpleasant social situation. Being sent to the principal's office is as much a concern as being hit by a car or truck. In another study (Scherer and Nakamura, 1968), school anxieties were the most common fears expressed by a group of 9- to 11-year-olds, who cited among their worries getting poor grades, failing a test, and being sent to the principal's office. At 12 years old, children fear sexuality, abortion, suicide, and handicapped children (Miller, 1983).

Children's understanding of death also changes from the imaginary to the more realistic during middle childhood; 5- and 6-year-olds tend to anthropomorphize death, perceiving it as a monster; 7- to 10-year-olds are more likely to associate death with separation and bodily injury (Grollman, 1967). And 6- to 8-year-olds in Bauer's (1976) study were likely to say that a scary dream was one in which they themselves or a loved one was killed. Younger children rarely conceived of being killed and did not dream of situations in which a loved one died. By 9 or 10 children begin to comprehend that death is universal, that all living things die (Childers and Wimmer, 1971).

Throughout early childhood, youngsters tend to express fear by crying and looking sad. Only in middle childhood do children cry little or not at all when they are afraid (Izard, 1977). In their first 14 years of life, fully 90 percent of children fear some specific thing (Macfarlane et al., 1954). Only about 5 percent of them have extreme fears or phobias, however (Miller, 1983). Fears often are set off by such cognitive processes as remembering or anticipating. By first identifying someone or something as fearful, then anticipating feeling fear, and finally actually meeting the dreaded person or thing, children may cognitively construct fears for themselves. Parents also may create fears in their children. Some parents minimize their children's experience of fear and try not to communicate their own fears to their children. They apologize for frightening their children and teach them to tolerate and counteract fear. Other parents do not minimize fears and, in fact, use fear as a disciplinary force. They communicate their fears to their children without apology, disregard their children's signs of fear, and teach their children neither to tolerate nor to counteract the source of fear (Izard, 1977).

Throughout life, people feel sadness when they are separated from others, especially those for whom they care. Feeling isolated, left out, rejected, or uncared for makes people sad. In infants, the major source of sadness is separation from their mothers or fathers (see p. 458). Sadness usually makes people feel a sense of loss and misery. In a full facial expression of sadness, the eyebrows arch up and inward, the upper eyelids are drawn up, the corners of the mouth are drawn down, the chin pushes up the center of the lower lip, and the person may cry. As they do with anger, children learn to change and minimize the facial expression and cry of sadness. Late in childhood, youngsters learn to shorten and mute their crying and to shift their facial expression quickly. Parents may help children to modify expressions of sadness in several different ways: by punishing them for crying, rewarding them for not crying, or by comforting them and attempting to help them cope effectively with the source of distress.

RESPONDING TO EMOTIONS IN OTHERS

Just as we express emotions, we also respond to emotions. In this section, we will look at the development of the infant's and child's abilities to respond to others' expression of emotions.

INTERACTION

In the interaction of mother and child, each affects the other's emotions. When this ongoing social interaction functions well, each partner responds appropriately to the other's emotional behavior. Jeffrey Cohn and Edward Tronick (1983) of the University of Massachusetts tested the ability of 3-month-old babies to respond to the emotional cues of their mothers. Some mothers were asked to act as they normally would, some to act depressed—to slow their speech, keep their face impassive, and to minimize touching their infant or moving their own body. The babies responded quite differently to normal and "depressed" mothers. Babies of "depressed" mothers spent fully half of the time protesting, reacting warily, or giving but fleeting smiles. Babies of normally acting mothers showed

much more variety in their play, protested or acted wary only rarely, and when they smiled, did so for significant periods of time. They behaved in well organized fashion—playing, looking at the mother, and smiling at her. But infants of the "depressed" mothers behaved in poorly organized fashion—protesting, showing wariness, looking away from the mother—and this negativity was likely to carry over into later interactions. Cohn and Tronick concluded that babies do read their mothers' emotional signals and modify their own behavior accordingly.

In a study of 6-month-old infants, Dale Hay, Alison Nash, and Jan Pedersen (1981) observed same-sex pairs interacting. They particularly wanted to see how babies reacted to another baby's distress. Out of 22 babies, 19 showed distress at least once. At any given moment, one baby's distress was independent of its partner's, but 16 of the 19 children whose partner grew distressed looked at him or her for nearly the whole episode of distress. Some also leaned, gestured, or touched the other. Thus, although they did not act as if they were themselves distressed, the babies did not ignore the other's distress; their behavior was affected by their partner's emotional expression. Moreover, the peer's distress had a cumulative effect on the baby; if there were no toys present and

Glee is expressed in excited interaction with peers, and children who are most gleeful tend also to be best liked.

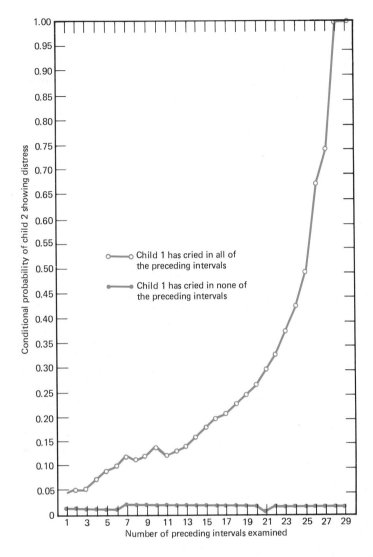

FIGURE 7.5

The likelihood that an infant will cry increases the longer an infant companion cries. (Hay, Nash, Pederson, 1981.)

the peer went on crying, it was likely that the baby eventually would become distressed (Figure 7.5).

A further example of how children respond to their peers' emotions comes from a study by Sroufe and his colleagues (Sroufe, Schork, Motti, Lawroski, and LaFreniere, 1984). They believed that a child's capacity for joy and pleasure, as shown by smiling, expressions of enthusiasm, and the like, would strongly color other children's reactions. They hypothesized that children who know how to have fun and who help others to have fun are likely to be popular with their peers. Their observations showed a strongly positive relationship between the frequency of a child's emotionally positive interactions and being well liked. In the scene described, the children were free to play as they wished:

With great positive affect Howard says, "Let's go to the movies!" Howard, John, Tracy, and Linda move off excitedly to a back corner of the room, while Jerry and Eddie watch them go. The four, with much shared excitement, set up a cardboard "screen" and line chairs in front of it to "watch." Jerry moves his chair to the front (very carefully so as not to hit anyone). As he is sitting, he notices that he is blocking Tracy's view, so he moves his chair to the side. Led by Howard's improvised fantasies, all enjoy the "movie." Then, at one point in response to the "movie," Howard stands up and begins to dance. His enthusiasm spreads to the others and, at his suggestion, they all move joyously to a larger play area and begin to dance. A teacher responds to their mood by providing a record player. All four children eagerly anticipate the music with broad smiles on their faces. A scene of uproarious glee follows (Sroufe et al., 1984, p. 22).

The four central characters in this gleeful group—Howard, John, Tracy, and Linda—were ranked as competent and popular. Eddie and Jerry, their audience, were not so competent or popular. Clearly, the expression of emotion has immediate and dramatic effects on social interaction—between mother and infant, between infant and infant, and between children, classmates, and teachers. But how does this happen? Do children just respond to the overt behavior of their partners, or do they recognize others' emotional expressions and respond to that message?

RECOGNITION

Investigations of whether infants recognize others' emotions have their difficulties. For one, just what does "recognition" consist of in the early months? Is it a higher cortical function or a more primitive response triggered perhaps by specific emotional expressions? Maria Barrera and Daphne Maurer (1979) reported that 3-month-olds who saw a frowning face cried more than infants who saw a smiling face. But were the infants crying because, as the investigators suggested, they recognized that a frown meant sadness or because they found the frowning face uninteresting? Do infants look longer at a face with a toothy grin because they read the pattern as a smile or because the teeth make the face more salient? In an experiment with 4-month-old infants, Harriet Oster (Oster and Ewy, 1980) showed infants in one group a sad face and a closed-mouth smile and infants in another group a sad face and a toothy, open-mouth smile. A third group of infants saw the sad face and toothy grin upside down. The investigators found that the infants looked longer at the right-side-up toothy grin than the sad face but did not look longer at the upside-down toothy grin. This study suggests that infants do respond to differences in facial pattern rather than differences in contrast, contour, or the like, but because they did not look longer at the closed-mouth smile than at the sad face, it is pos-

sible that 4-month-olds cannot yet read smiles from the position of the mouth alone without seeing teeth. In another study (Caron, Caron, Caldwell, and Weiss, 1973), involving hundreds of infants, only beginning at about 5 months of age did infants discriminate patterns of facial communication, especially those involving the mouth or the whole face. Oster (1981) has speculated that infants between 3 and 6 months old may not be able to distinguish physical subtleties of facial or vocal expressions of emotion, may be especially insensitive to negative expressions, and may have a built-in predisposition to smile at human faces or voices, a reaction that is adaptive for the development of secure social relations.

Even with older children, there are difficulties in studying recognition of emotions. In one of the few investigations of 2- to 3-year-olds, Patricia Smiley and Janellen Huttenlocher (in preparation) found that children could usually attach the correct emotional label (out of two choices) to a facial expression. Similar work with older children by Linda Camras (1977) showed that 4-year-olds, too, could label facial expressions of emotion. By 3 to 4 years of age, it seems, children recognize facial expressions universally interpreted to signal happiness, sadness, anger, and fear. As they get older, they more accurately recognize a wider range of emotions, and they can predict how a person will feel in emotional situations. Helene Borke (1971) (see Fig. 7.6) asked children to identify drawings of happy, sad, fearful, and angry faces. Then the children heard short stories about a child who ate a favorite snack, lost a toy, got lost in the woods, and was made to go to bed. The children were asked to choose the picture of the face that best expressed how the child in the story felt. Borke found that accuracy increased over the ages studied, 3 to 8 years old. The youngest children could identify the emotions on the four faces and the emotions of the children in the happy stories. Of the 4-year-olds, 60 percent correctly recognized which stories were about fear, as did all the 6-year-olds. Only at 5½ were children substantially correct about the sad stories; only later did children recognize the emotion in stories about anger.

In a more recent study of 3-year-olds' understanding of emotions (Trabasso, Stein, and Johnson, 1981), the children were asked to look at a picture of a child and explain either the cause—

FIGURE 7.6
In Borke's (1971) study children were asked to identify drawings of happy, sad, afraid, and angry faces and then to point to the one that best expressed how children felt in short stories they were told.

"What do you think made Jenny angry?"—or the consequences—"What does Jenny do when she gets angry?"—of six different emotions (sadness, anger, happiness, fear, surprise, excitement). All the children knew the difference between cause and effect. Almost all the children explained sadness as the result of some loss: "Jenny was sad because her mom and dad left her." Happiness was usually explained as the result of a new possession, like a birthday present, or as the absence of unhappiness: "He was happy because he didn't go to bed hungry." In a similar study of 6- to 12-year-olds, Demos (1974) asked the children to explain the causes and consequences of positive and negative emotions. Like the 3-year-olds, the 6-year-olds ascribed anger to attack or abuse by another person; fear to strange beings like ghosts or monsters; and sadness to rejection by parents or peers or to the loss of a valued possession. Also like 3-year-olds, 6-year-olds imagined responding to anger with destructive acts.

Susan Harter (1979) interviewed children from 3 to 12 years of age to determine how well they understood emotions. She found that all the children interviewed could name and give examples of being happy, sad, angry, and scared, although the youngest needed to be reminded of the emotion "scared" and could not name it spontaneously. The older children could name more of the different emotions. Preschoolers, however, could not imagine how someone might feel *two* emotions together or in close succession. "Can you feel good about going to visit Grandma but grouchy about having to pack?" They responded: "No way!" or "It's hard to think of this feeling and that feeling because you have one mind," or "I've never done that, you know; I've only lived 6 years."

After the age of 5 or 6, children's abilities to recognize mixed emotions advance. In a study by Daphne Bugental (Bugental, Kaswan, and Love, 1970), 5- to 12-year-old children and adults responded to videotapes of adults who gave mixed messages. The mixed messages consisted of words, tone of voice, or facial expression that were a mixture of positive and negative and therefore emotionally inconsistent. When the speaker smiled while saying something negative, adults thought that the speaker was joking. But children rated the message as negative—particularly when the speaker was a woman—when even one of the three elements was negative. Said the investigators, "Children, when confronted with a conflicting message, resolve the ambiguity by assuming the worst" (Bugental et al., 1970, p. 655).

REFERENCE

Who hasn't seen a toddler fall down in a heap, only to look at his mother's reaction to decide whether he should cry or not? A mother's laughter can assuage a child's fear; a mother's fear can turn her child's worry into panic. Psychologists are learning how infants and children refer to another person's facial expression or tone of voice for clues about the action they are expected to take.

In an unfamiliar situation, infants tend to orient themselves so that they can see their mother's face (Carr, Dabbs, and Carr, 1975). Perhaps they do so because they can get important cues about how to act in the unfamiliar situation from the mother's face and gestures. If the mother is out of sight, infants will rely on cues from her voice (Campos and Stenberg, 1981). In one study of this **social referencing** in 1-year-olds (Sorce, Emde, Campos, and Klinnert, 1981), one group of infants who had to cross a visual cliff with an apparent drop-off of 4 feet, refused to cross the glass. A second group, who faced no apparent drop-off, crossed immediately without checking their mothers' faces. But a third group, confronting a drop-off of 2 feet, looked at their mothers for cues before they did anything. When the mother looked afraid, not a single infant crossed the glass. When she looked happy, 80 percent of the infants crossed; when she looked interested, 75 percent crossed; and when she looked angry, 11 percent crossed. When mothers looked sad—an inappropriate response—one-third of the infants crossed but vacillated before doing so. In short, the results of this investigation showed not only that infants referred to their mothers' expressions for cues in an unfamiliar situation, but also that they behaved dramatically differently depending on the sort of emotional messages they received from their mothers' faces.

As many researchers have noted, beginning at about 5 months of age, infants respond to the arrival of a stranger by repeatedly looking now at the stranger and then at their mother. To test empirically whether emotional communication from the mother influences infants' reactions to strangers, Maria Boccia and Joseph Campos (1983) asked mothers of 8½-month-olds to respond to a stranger's arrival either by uttering an abrupt, unfriendly hello and frowning or by smiling at the baby and stranger and saying hello cheerfully.

When the mother acted wary, the infants' heart rate sped up, they smiled less, and they showed more distress. When the mother greeted the stranger cheerfully, the heart rate of infants slowed down.

As they continue to develop sensorimotor skills and, later, to learn language, children come to depend less on social referencing and more on their own, internal strategies for evaluating the unfamiliar. But it is likely that people never completely outgrow referring to others when they need to evaluate ambiguous situations (Campos and Stenberg, 1981).

EMPATHY

Psychologists generally agree that **empathy** is a vicarious emotional response in which the emotions of the observer match to some extent the emotions of the person being observed. An empathic response is one in which someone responds *as if* he or she were feeling what another person is feeling. Not all emotional responses to another's discomfort are empathic by any means, and people react with pleasure, surprise, or self-interest to others' signs of discomfort. Few children under 2 respond at all to another's distress, and some actually taunt or hit a

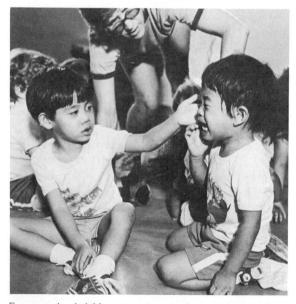

Even preschool children express sympathy and try to comfort someone who is hurt. This young boy tries to pat away the pain felt by his twin brother.

crying playmate. By the age of 2, however, most children respond empathically at least part of the time (Zahn-Waxler, 1983).

Martin Hoffman (1978, 1982) describes how the degree of emotional matching as well as the range of emotions to which one responds empathically increase in the course of perceptual and cognitive development. He suggests that there are several possible mechanisms by which empathy may develop. One is conditioning. Empathy may appear by the process of association, as when one child's cry of pain makes another child cry because he associates the sound with his own past pain (Humphrey, 1922). A second possibility is that empathy is an unlearned motor response that mimics another person's emotional expression (Lipps, 1906). As people observe others, they automatically mimic their facial and bodily expression and thereby create cues for themselves of the other person's feelings. A third possibility is that some empathic responses are reflexive, as when newborns cry at the sound of other babies crying or when they hear a tape recording of themselves crying (Sagi and Hoffman, 1976). Finally, empathy may arise when one person imagines how it would feel to be in another person's place. In each form of empathy, an observer is subject to different cognitive and perceptual demands. At one extreme of development, reflexive crying makes no such demands; at the other extreme, imagining oneself in another's place relies entirely on internal symbolization, an advanced cognitive skill. The forms of empathy also vary in the degree to which they are involuntary or voluntary. Reflexive crying, conditioning, and mimicry are largely involuntary. Symbolically mediated conditioning and imagining another's plight are largely under voluntary control.

Carolyn Zahn-Waxler and Marian Radke-Yarrow (Zahn-Waxler and Radke-Yarrow, 1979; Zahn-Waxler, Radke-Yarrow, and Brady-Smith, 1977) have found that the earliest emotional reaction children show to others' distress is crying or sadness. At around 18 months, children begin to *act* by offering to help, share, protect, defend, comfort, or console. They may try to comfort people who are crying or hurt by snuggling, patting, hugging, helping, or feeding them or by giving them their own teddy bear. One young boy's mother bumped her elbow and cried out, "Ouch!" Her son at once screwed up his face and rubbed his *own* elbow and only then began to rub his mother's elbow. Another child, seeing a sad look on his father's face, looked sad, sucked his thumb, and pulled on his father's ear, the means by which he usually comforted himself (Hoffman, 1978). Young children give another person what they themselves would find comforting—a bottle, a doll, a cookie, their own mother's hand. These young children are clearly sympathetic but do not know how to help. Zahn-Waxler and Radke-Yarrow had mothers keep diaries in which they recorded their children's responses to others' distress and then tested children with simulated incidents in the laboratory, such as spilling papers or having a mother "accidentally" bump her elbow. They found that at both 2 and 7 years of age, children had about the same intensity of distress. The children did, however, behave differently according to their natures. The child who at 2 plugged her ears or fled the scene when she heard cries or witnessed anger, at 7 complained impatiently, "I can't take much more of this crying." The compassionate child, who at 2 fled to her mother and buried her head in the mother's lap when her friend got hurt, later comforted a crying infant, lips quivering; still later, she gave her sandals to her younger friend so that her friend's bare feet would not burn as they walked together on the hot pavement. Finally, there was the detached intellectualizer. At 2 she exclaimed, "Annie's crying. She's sad. See her tears," as she peered intently into the victim's face and wiped away the tears. At 7 this child asked solicitously, and curiously, "Where does it hurt? How much does it hurt? Why does it hurt?"

In a later study of school age children, Zahn-Waxler, with Sarah Friedman and Mark Cummings (1983), first played to the children the sounds of a baby in another room crying. Then each child saw a mother appear and look around for a bottle to give her hungry baby. The mother sat down to feed the baby and talked with the child. Later, a tester played babies' cries on a tape recorder and asked the children about their feelings and observed the behavior the cries evoked. Videotapes of the children were coded as either positive—smiles and laughter—or negative—grimaces of distress or anxiety, body movements of restlessness or tension. It was found that the babies' cries elicited negative emotion in 40 percent of the children and smiles in 18 percent. Compared to anger and fear, empathy was the most frequent response in all age groups. Children who had infant brothers or sisters were somewhat less empathic and reported marginally more anger in the laboratory than children who did not have siblings.

Another, perhaps less valid, way of assessing children's empathy has been to ask children how they feel after hearing an emotional story. For example, children are told a story about a girl who loses her pet dog and are asked to describe the emotions they are feeling. The older the children are, studies using this technique suggest, the more often and more exactly they match their emotions to those felt by the person in the story (Feshbach, 1973; Feshbach and Roe, 1968). Being the same sex, race, and age as the subject in the story also make children respond more empathically. For example, a white girl of 5, hearing the story of a white girl who lost her dog, would feel more sadness and loss than had the story been about a Chinese teenage boy (Feshbach, 1973; Feshbach and Roe, 1968; Stotland, 1969).

EMOTIONS AND PROSOCIAL BEHAVIOR

Our emotions affect not only how others act towards us, but also how we act towards them. A feeling of empathy, for example, may motivate people to help others they see in distress. Young children, as we have just seen, respond to distress not only with negative feeling, but with active attempts to comfort or help (Zahn-Waxler and Radke-Yarrow, 1979; Zahn-Waxler et al., 1977). Older children also respond empathically and with even more appropriate gestures of aid (Zahn-Waxler et al., 1983), and those who are more empathic are more inclined to help. Children respond more quickly if a person's signs of distress are intense, and they feel less empathic after they have offered help (Hoffman, 1982).

For children to behave empathically toward a person in distress, certain conditions must prevail.

RESEARCH FOCUS

EMPATHY IN PRESCHOOLERS

Janet Strayer (1980), of Simon Fraser University in Burnaby, British Columbia, wanted to learn about how and when preschoolers respond empathically to their playmates. She was especially interested in watching their real-life reactions, as opposed to those engineered in a laboratory or other artificial setting. She therefore observed 14 children at a university day-care center as they played freely over a period of some 30 hours. She sampled the children's interactions at 5-minute intervals and rated their empathic responses to other children's expressions of happiness, sadness, anger, or hurt.

In the 30 hours of observation, Strayer found 423 opportunities for empathic reactions. Children responded empathically to 39 percent of these opportunities. They were more empathic toward happy behavior and least empathic toward anger.

Children most often responded to happiness with signs of happiness of their own—smiles, laughter, approving comments like "That's a good one." They responded to sadness by offering to share toys or coming near, hugging, or saying comforting things like "That's a nice hat you've got." They responded to anger as if it were a request and, for example, moved aside if someone angrily called, "I can't see it." They responded to others' hurt with attempts at comfort or with anger at the responsible person or object.

All of the children reacted empathically at some point. But which children were most empathic? The happy children were. The saddest children were the least empathic. Most of the empathic responses were spontaneous, not the result of requests. Strayer concluded that young children know that others feel differently from themselves and that they can respond effectively to them. Above all, children's own emotional states have a real bearing on their demonstrations of unselfish behavior.

The person in distress must engage the child's attention, and the child must be in the "right" mood (Hoffman, 1982). They "right" mood changes with age, however. As a general rule, children behave altruistically—for another person's benefit without expectation of extrinsic reward—most often when they are in a positive mood, less often when they are in a neutral mood, and least often when they are in a negative mood (Cialdini, Kenrick, and Baumann, 1982). The findings on the relation between positive mood and **altruism** or prosocial behavior are quite consistent. The memory of happy events, an unexpected gift or sum of money, humor, success on a task, and even good weather have been demonstrated to enhance unselfish behavior in children and adults (Cunningham, 1979; Isen, Clark, and Schwartz, 1976; Isen and Levin, 1972; Kazdin and Bryan, 1971; Kidd and Berkowitz, 1976; Rosenhan, Underwood, and Moore, 1974).

But the relation between negative mood and prosocial acts is less straightforward. Some studies have found that young children in a negative mood act *more* altruistically than those in a neutral mood.

For example, one group of children volunteered to make coloring books for children in the hospital after they had talked about a sad incident involving someone else. Children in a control group that had not talked about the sad incident were not so likely to volunteer (Barnett, Howard, Melton, and Dino, 1980). In another study to investigate the relation between distress or concern for others and helping behavior, the subjects were 4- to 6-year-old children in the Soviet Union (Nevrovich, 1974). In one condition, children were brought into a room strewn with toys and asked to put them away "so your friends can play with them later; if you do not put the toys in order your friends will not be able to play with them and they will be sad." After 20 minutes, the children were offered the choice of continuing to straighten up the room or of taking a walk. Only one-third of the 4- to 5-year-olds and one-half the 5- to 6-year-olds chose to stay and straighten up. In another condition, the children got the same instructions but were also shown pictures of children looking sadly at the strewn-about toys that they could not play with. In this condition, over

How altruistically children behave depends on their own mood as well as on the need of the other person.

half the younger children and all but one of the older children chose to stay and straighten up the toys. In a third condition, in which the children saw pictures of a sick child who was sad about not being able to play with the messy toys, nearly all the children chose to stay and clean up the room.

In contrast, some studies have shown that children in a negative mood act *less* altruistically than those in a neutral or positive mood. In one study, fourth-graders who thought that they had performed badly in bowling chose to donate less to charity than did a control group (Isen, Horn, and Rosenhan, 1973). In another study, second- and third-graders who thought about sad memories gave less to charity than children in a neutral mood (Moore, Underwood, and Rosenhan, 1973). In a third study, Robert Cialdini and Douglas Kenrick (1976) tested three groups of students: 6- to 8-year-olds, 10- to 12-year-olds, and 15- to 18-year-olds. In each group, some subjects were told to think about sad past experiences and some, neutral past experiences. When the students were later given the chance to donate coupons for prizes to other students, of the youngest children, those in a negative mood donated less than those in a neutral mood. In the middle age group, those in a negative mood donated slightly more than those in a neutral mood. The high schoolers in the negative mood donated substantially more than those in the neutral mood. They had reached the characteristically adult pattern for altruistic behavior, to help more when in a negative mood. Similarly, in a study of second- through sixth-graders (Barnett, King, and Howard, 1979), students were asked to think about sad events that had befallen either themselves or another person and then had the chance to act generously. The younger children were not generous. Only the older, more socialized sixth-graders acted generously. Age then seems to be one factor that helps to explain the inconsistent results from research on the relation between emotions and prosocial behavior.

RESEARCH FOCUS

HOW SADNESS AFFECTS ALTRUISM

A group of researchers from Kansas State University, Mark Barnett, Jeffrey Howard, Elaine Melton, and Geri Dino (1982), wanted to study how feelings of sadness about oneself and others might affect the behavior of children judged to be highly empathic versus those judged to be slightly empathic. Accordingly, they chose as subjects white sixth-graders from three middle-class Kansas communities. First, the researchers asked teachers to rate each child's degree of empathy on statements such as, "This child seems sad when he/she sees someone else who is sad." Children also rated their peers. The combined ratings were used to establish which children were highly empathic and which were not at all empathic.

Next, when they were alone together in a room, an experimenter asked each student to recall and talk about either sad incidents he or she had experienced or those another child had experienced. The experimenter encouraged the children to dwell on the associated sad feelings for a full minute. In another condition, the experimenter encouraged a child to discuss and think about neutral information, such as when he or she had started school. The experimenter then told each child that she had to leave the room but that her assistant would arrive in a few minutes. Each child was reminded that he or she could make some booklets for needy children or look at some pamphlets. The experimenter also reminded the children to keep thinking about what they had discussed together.

Barnett and his associates found that the children who had thought about sad events felt significantly sadder than the other children, although there was no difference between those who had thought sad things about themselves and those who had thought sad things about another child. The investigators also found that children rated highly empathic made many more booklets for the needy children than the less empathic children did. The children who had thought sadly about another child made more booklets than any of the other groups of children. The investigators concluded that their study showed a complex relationship among a child's tendencies toward empathy, feelings of the moment, and focus of attention in affecting their prosocial behavior.

Strayer (1980) has suggested that laboratory findings on altruism are of questionable ecological validity, for acts in a laboratory hardly resemble those in naturalistic, real-life settings and children's altruism in real-life situations does not correlate with their performance in laboratory tasks. This may be another explanation of the inconsistencies in research findings. Hoffman (1982) offers other possible explanations. For one thing, people are more likely to respond altruistically to those who seem like them, whether in sex, race, or qualities of personality. Altruism is most likely to flourish when people are not so preoccupied with their own needs that they cannot respond to another's. People who are concerned about failing, who are dependent on others' approval, or who are experiencing the physical discomfort of a loud or aversive noise are less likely to respond altruistically. Hoffman suggests that the kindergartners in one study (Kameya,

1976) who did not act altruistically toward children in distress were themselves in such distress that they could not respond to others. Thus there may a middle range of arousal within which people are most likely to respond altruistically. If they are too distressed themselves or, at the other extreme, too little engaged, they are not likely to act altruistically. In fact, Hoffman suggests that if people feel too uncomfortable at another's distress, they may not only avoid interacting with the other but even derogate or blame the other: "If you hadn't been so careless (foolish, weak, silly, etc.), you wouldn't be in such a predicament." How we interpret the reason for another person's distress is quite likely to influence whether we respond altruistically, indifferently, or abusively. Once again, we see the familiar theme of the interdependence of emotion and cognition.

SUMMARY

1. Emotions are hard to define, because they are diverse and varied, have many different aspects, affect the whole person rather than a single biological system, and tend to occur in mixtures. The term "emotion" might be considered a label for various relations among external elicitors, thoughts, and changes in feeling. Emotion may also be defined as a subjective feeling, the evaluation of that feeling, and associated changes in physiology and observable expression.

2. Psychologists may observe facial or bodily expressions or listen to tone of voice to measure emotion. MAX is one system for classifying the presence or absence of various expressions of the forehead, eyes, nose, cheeks, and mouth that have been linked theoretically to discrete emotions.

3. Emotions are both innate and learned. The biological universality of emotions has become evident through cross-cultural studies and work with nonhuman primates and with blind and sighted infants. Learned components are apparent in studies of how children pick up from their parents their culture's rules for expressing, controlling, exaggerating, masking, neutralizing, and interpreting emotions.

4. Psychologists generally agree that emotions have both a physiological and a cognitive component, but they disagree on which is primary and on how the two interact. Some believe that cognitive appraisal is necessary for interpreting physiological arousal; others disagree, believing that physiology alone can produce emotion.

5. Piaget focused on how emotions develop as infants and children interact with their physical environments. Freud and Spitz focused on emotional development within social relationships. In contemporary developmental psychology, Sroufe and Campos have tried to integrate these two sides of emotions.

6. Infants and children, like adults, respond to other people's emotions. Infants respond to the emotional tone of their mothers. Six-month-olds notice other babies' emotional expressions. Preschoolers who are happy, have a capacity for fun, and can express negative emotions without losing control are better liked by their peers and cope better with frustration than those who are sad and less socially competent.

7. Children grow increasingly skilled at understanding others' emotions, at labeling pictures of faces with the appropriate emotion, and at understanding the causes and consequences of emotions.

8. Infants use their mothers' facial expressions for cues about how to behave in uncertain situations.

9. Empathy develops along with cognitive and perceptual skills. It may develop through conditioning, motor mimicry, reflex, or imagining oneself in another's place. Infants sometimes react to others' distress with crying or sad looks; at around 18 months, they begin to act helpful.

10. Children in a positive mood are likely to behave altruistically. The findings on the relation between negative mood and altruism are less consistent. It has been suggested that as children learn over time to take pleasure from altruism, their altruistic behavior increases following a negative mood. There may also be an optimal range of arousal in which altruistic behavior is most likely to occur; arousal that is too intense or too weak may inhibit altruism.

KEY TERMS

Maximally
  Discriminative Facial
  Movement (MAX)
Innate releaser
Hippocampus

Limbic system
Differential emotions
  theory
Cognition-arousal
  theories

Perceptual-motor
  processing theory
Incongruity
Fear of strangers
Stranger anxiety

Placing response
Social referencing
Empathy
Altruism

SUGGESTED READINGS

Cicchetti, Dante, and Hesse, Petra (Eds.). *Emotional Development.* San Francisco: Jossey-Bass, 1982. Part of the New Directions for Child Development Series, this paperback contains four chapters that reflect the cutting edge of thinking about emotional development.

Dunn, Judith. *Distress and Comfort.* Cambridge: Harvard University Press, 1977. A developmental psychologist discusses what scientists know about what upsets babies, how they can be comforted, and how the parent-child relationship affects an infant's emotions.

Izard, Carroll E. *Human Emotions.* New York: Plenum, 1977. A comprehensive presentation of Izard's theory of discrete emotions, including discussion of fear, shame, shyness, joy, surprise, interest, and guilt.

Izard, Carroll (Ed.). *Measuring Emotions in Infants and Children* (2 vols.). New York: Cambridge University Press, Vol. 1, 1982; Vol. 2, in press. These two volumes present contemporary work on the measurement of emotions in chapters by researchers who include Jerome Kagan, Michael Lewis, Martin Hoffman, George Mandler, and Linda Camras.

Lewis, Michael, and Michalson, Linda. *Children's Emotions and Moods.* New York: Plenum, 1983. An analysis of the term "emotion" and a new theory of emotional development in childhood, plus an original system for assessing children's emotions.

Lewis, Michael, and Rosenblum, Leonard A. (Eds.). *The Development of Affect.* New York: Plenum, 1978. An extensive collection of chapters by the major developmental researchers in early emotional development, including Robert Emde, Joseph Campos, Harriet Oster, Jerome Kagan, Martin Hoffman, Carroll Izard, and Alan Sroufe.

PART IV

COGNITION

STRUCTURE

The newborn's palm accidentally brushes against the thin handle of a rattle in his crib, and he reflexively grasps it. At 3 months, he studies and reaches for the rattle voluntarily. Between 4 and 6 months, he becomes able to grasp the rattle and bring it to his mouth. By 8 months, he looks briefly for the rattle when it disappears from sight. By 9 months, he can reach behind himself for the rattle without seeing it. He can search behind a screen for the rattle if he sees it hidden there. By 1 year of age, assuming he is still interested in the rattle, he will search for it, even if he has not seen it hidden. He has a mental picture of the rattle, and his mental picture does not depend on his immediate sensory perceptions.

The journey from early reflexive behavior to the later ability to guide behavior by images or structures retained in the mind is one of the most fascinating journeys in human development. No one has charted this journey and its consequences more carefully than Jean Piaget.

PIAGET'S THEORY

Jean Piaget was a trained observer. At the age of 10, he published a scientific note on an albino sparrow he had seen in a park. His writings on mollusks were known to specialists in other countries soon after he was 15. He also had graduate training in biology. Piaget constructed his theory from his knowledge of biology and from his systematic observations of children, primarily his own three, Jacqueline, Lucienne, and Laurent. Piaget watched the children's actions, occasionally intervening and experimentally altering circumstances to try to arrive at causes of their behavior. In the excerpt that follows, Piaget observes a newborn crying, notes surrounding circumstances, records the effects of his own behavior on the newborn, and compares the reaction of the newborn to human crying and to another sound.

Obs. 1: On the very night after his birth, T was wakened by the babies in the nearby cots and began to cry in chorus with them. At 0;0 (3)[1] he

---

[1] In Piaget's shorthand, this represents the age 0 years, 0 months, and 3 days.

was drowsy, but not actually asleep, when one of the other babies began to wail; he himself thereupon began to cry. At 0;0 (4) and 0;0 (6) he again began to whimper, and started to cry in earnest when I tried to imitate his interrupted whimpering. A mere whistle failed to produce any reaction (Piaget, 1962, p. 7).

When working with older children, Piaget probed their thinking through questions and problem-solving experiments as well as by observing them. From the careful recordings of his observations and experiments, Piaget wove hypotheses, tested the hypotheses again and again, and then put them together. Piaget has bequeathed to us both the most comprehensive of all theories of cognitive development and some of the most accurate observations of children's cognitive behavior at carefully identified stages from infancy to adolescence.

As he observed his own three children and others, Piaget remained remarkably open to the children's every activity and to the smallest changes in their manner of dealing with the world. In Piaget's view, children are active participants in the learning process, even in infancy.

THE SENSORIMOTOR PERIOD

Infants, as they gain more control over their muscles, elaborate early reflexes and random movements into voluntary actions. Their reflexes are their basic building blocks. Sucking, for example, is a reflexive prepackaged set of actions. Infants, feeling a nipple in their mouth, will reflexively suck. In Piaget's lexicon, the infant's prepackaged sucking is a **scheme**. A scheme is a basic unit of knowledge, a mental structure. It may be an observable pattern of action, such as sucking, looking at Mother's face, or stroking a cat; it may be an image of an object, such as the infant's mental picture of the rattle that has been hidden from him; it may be a complex idea, such as an expectation, a belief, or a plan; or it may be a logical operation, such as addition or subtraction. For the infant, schemes are at first all of the action type. Because the baby's early mental activity is confined to direct sensory and motor experiences, Piaget has called the period from birth to about 2 years the **sensorimotor**

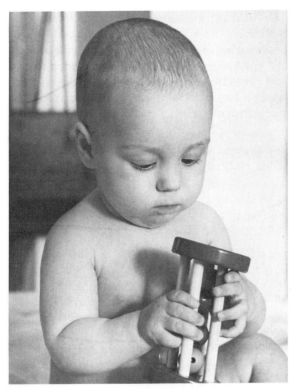

During the sensorimotor period, the infant's schemes revolve around actions such as grasping, shaking, patting, and looking at objects.

period. During this period, babies show their intelligence through their interesting and ingenious actions and the ways in which they handle physical objects. They do not at this age know or think in the sense of understanding and reflecting about their world. Their schemes, however, are many, complex, and varied.

How do their schemes grow and change during this period? For one thing, advances in perceptual and motor development offer infants new schemes as they grow older. At first a baby is limited to motor reflexes, such as grasping what is in his hand, and primitive perceptual abilities, such as looking. But soon he is able to hit, shake, wave, slide, swing, and tear objects as well. Given a block and cup, a 5-month-old will first apply his hitting, patting, and shaking schemes; a little later he will examine the block and cup and turn them around. At 10 months, he may slide the block and cup along the floor, rub them together, or try to put the block inside the cup and take it out. Later, he may practice "letting go" with the block, dropping it repeat-

edly on purpose. At 13 months, he may use a building scheme, turning the cup over and putting the block on top of it, or he may "drink" from the cup. Still later, he may give the cup to his mother or father or hold it to their lips.

Perceptual development and motor development are not solely responsible for changes in the infant's schemes. Two mental processes guide development throughout this period and throughout life, **organization** and **adaptation.** The organizing process is how the infant combines and integrates separate schemes. For example, the 3-month-old staring at, and then reaching for, the rattle has combined the looking and reaching schemes; the 5-month-old holding the rattle to his or her mouth has combined the schemes of looking, grasping, and mouthing. The adapting process is how people extend and modify schemes. They do so through two complementary processes, **assimilation** and **accommodation.** In assimilation, new information is added to what individuals already know. Assimilation is a taking-in process; people incorporate a new object or experience into their existing set of schemes. By this process, very young infants put most new objects in their mouths as they try out their sucking scheme on every available object. The infant who already has a fluffy stuffed duck that he hugs will quickly apply the same cuddling scheme to a new fluffy stuffed bunny. Fortunately, individuals are not limited to assimilation, or we would all be sucking on the corner of this book. People also accommodate their schemes to new objects and experiences that do not fit them. Breast-fed babies who are given a bottle for the first time change their sucking scheme, moving the head to a slightly different position, adjusting the mouth to the nipple, and modifying their jaw and tongue movements as necessary. The infant who is given a real, live puppy soon realizes that the old hugging scheme that worked so well with duck and bunny needs to be modified to accommodate the bouncy behavior of this new pet.

Finally, schemes change over the sensorimotor period as infants develop the ability to remember and their memory span increases. Infants eventually form internal mental representations of persons and objects, so that they do not have to be looking at them to know or to remember that these persons and objects exist.

SENSORIMOTOR STAGES

In Piaget's theory, the sequence of development is invariant. Each advance is based on the previous level of mastery. The sensorimotor period has six stages, each building on the preceding one.

Stage 1: Practice and Repetition of Reflexes (Birth to 1 Month).

The first of the six stages in the sensorimotor period, from birth to 4 weeks, is taken up with the practice and repetition of reflexes, specifically with sucking, grasping, looking, and listening. Anything that touches the infant's lips she will suck. She will start to suck when she is hungry, and she will make sucking movements in her sleep. If her finger happens into her mouth, she will suck on it and perhaps other fingers as well. By the end of her first month, the infant has had some experience with the suckables and graspables of this world as they have touched her mouth and her hands. She spends her days trying to fit the world into her limited repertoire of reflexes.

Stage 2: the First Acquired Adaptations (1 to 4 Months).

At about 1 month of age, the infant begins to repeat reflexes and random actions for pleasure. She moves her hand at random before her eyes or she sucks it by chance, but now she finds the sight or taste of the hand intriguing, and she repeats her actions. She will also kick her legs with much glee over and over again.

Piaget called such repetition of an initially random or reflexive action a **circular reaction.** The infant's initial action causes a reaction; she repeats it because it is pleasurable. A circular reaction is, in a sense, the first step toward all accommodations, because it is the willful altering of a behavior pattern by repeating it (Piaget, in Gruber and Voneche, 1977, p. 202). The earliest circular reactions, which prolong, refine, and modify the infant's simple motor acts and reflexes, are called **primary circular reactions**—primary because they involve only the infant's own body.

Another significant step in cognitive development is taken in this stage. In the first month of life, the infant recognized no boundary between herself and objects. In the second sensorimotor stage, she gets her first inkling that an object is a separate entity. When the infant drops the rattle she has been holding, she stares at where it last was, her hand. But if nothing reappears within a few seconds, she gives up. The rattle still has no permanence for her. It does not exist if it is not in her immediate experience. Thus she quickly "forgets" that she even held it. For her, out of sight is truly out of mind.

Stage 3: Procedures for Making Interesting Sights Last (4 to 8 Months).

When Piaget's daughter, Lucienne, was 3 months old, she began to understand that her leg shaking, undertaken for sheer pleasure, was making the dolls that her father had attached to her bassinet swing back and forth.

At 0;3 (5) Lucienne shakes her bassinet by moving her legs violently (bending and unbending them, etc.) which makes the cloth dolls swing from the hood. Lucienne looks at them, smiling, and recommences at once. These movements appear simply to be the concomitants of joy. . . . The next day . . . I present the dolls: Lucienne immediately moves, shakes her legs, but this time without smiling. Her interest is intense and sustained. . . .

0;3 (8) . . . a chance movement disturbs the dolls: Lucienne . . . looks at them . . . and shakes herself with regularity. She stares at the dolls, barely smiles and moves her leg vigorously and thoroughly. . . .

At 0;3 (16) as soon as I suspended the dolls she immediately shakes them, without smiling, with precise and rhythmical movements with quite an interval between shakes, as though she were studying the phenomenon. Success gradually causes her to smile (Piaget, 1952, pp. 157–158).

Lucienne's leg shakings were now **secondary circular reactions**—repeating an action because something or someone has made a response to the action. Lucienne began to notice that the dolls moved when she shook her legs, so she repeated her movements and watched intently for them to move again too. Her attention was no longer directed only at her own body but to other objects and events, the dolls and their movements. She repeated her action to prolong the interesting sight.

Intelligent behavior at this point is motivated by a desire to make interesting things last. But sometimes the child becomes confused about which activity will achieve this goal. After Laurent, Piaget's son, produced a rattling noise from the top of his cradle by pulling the rope hanging from it, he pulled the same rope to make his mother stay in the room (Piaget, 1952). Laurent apparently believed that what made an interesting noise would also make his mother stay. Piaget called this notion of causality **magico-phenomenistic,** because the link between the child's action and the result seems to the child to be magical. Laurent did not understand the difference between means and ends and thus could not evaluate when a particular action was appropriate for a desired end. He got started pulling the rope for its effects largely through chance, not by figuring out how pulling the rope might affect the world. Yet secondary circular reactions are the first signs that infants have any inkling of causality; they link actions giving them pleasurable sensations with what they perceive to be happening in the world.

Infants' conceptions of objects also make some progress in this stage. If an infant's ball is near her toy chest, partially covered by a cloth, she may remove the cloth. She recognizes the object as her ball, even if she can see only part of it. This "reconstruction of the whole from the part" is evidence that the infant has some primitive mental representation of the toy. This is, however, just the beginning of the concept of **object permanence.** If the toy is entirely covered with the cloth, the infant's reaction will be the same as in sensorimotor stage 2. She will show no interest in the ball, apparently forgetting about its existence. She will not look for the ball, even if she has watched the cloth being put over it.

Stage 4: Coordination of Means and Ends (8 to 12 Months).

Very soon, however, an infant will search briefly for her ball after she sees it being put away. Her search is at first short and helter-skelter. Even so, she has a goal—to find her ball—and she goes through a sequence of actions to try to accomplish her goal. She has in mind an actual purpose, and she attempts to find appropriate actions to carry it out. After Mother closes the cookie jar, which the infant cannot open, she will suggestively place her mother's hand on the jar and wait. She is beginning to see that objects and other people can have an effect on the world. But her notion of causality is still limited. She considers herself the cause or initiator of all activity.

The infant becomes able to make more distinctions among objects. She will look at a toy and decide what to do with it before taking action. She hugs Raggedy Ann instead of tasting her red-yarn hair, and she rolls her ball instead of shaking it. The infant is beginning to make general distinctions about where things are in space. If she sees a ball hidden *behind* a screen, she will now retrieve it and bring it *in front of* the screen. At this stage, the infant loves games in which things and people disappear and reappear. Her mother often plays peekaboo with her, vanishing behind the foot of the crib or covering her face with her hands. With this primitive grasp of behind and in front of, the infant also begins to develop a notion of *before* and *after*, the beginning of a concept of time.

When her ball is moved from one hiding place to another, however, the infant cannot follow the sequence of visual displacements. For example, when her ball is hidden beneath cloth A, then taken out and hidden beneath cloth B, all in full view of the infant, she will watch attentively. But the moment the ball disappears the second time, the infant will look for it under cloth A! This has been called the **A, not B, phenomenon.**

The A, not B, phenomenon reveals some important advances in the infant's concept of object permanence. At this time she can search for the ball that is entirely hidden from sight. Earlier, she had to see a piece of it. Now she can retain a mental representation of the object without actually seeing it. But this representation is still tied to the *act* of searching for the object and the specific place at which the infant saw the ball being hid. The infant only removes the cloth when it is placed over the ball *just* as she begins her search. Thus she still has no complete representation of the object as an entity separate from other entities and separate from herself.

Stage 5: Experiments in Order to See (12 to 18 Months).

At about 1 year of age, an infant begins to experiment with and vary her actions to see their effects. Now she will not simply place her mother's hand on the cookie jar; she may also tug the jar toward her mother's hand and look at her mother, expecting the jar to be opened. Her intelligence is now indicated by **tertiary circular reactions,** repeating actions but modifying them slightly each time to test the effect of the modification. The toddler performs "experiments in order to see." Now that she can move around on her legs, leaving her hands free, she has great curiosity and becomes a tiny scientist, exploring the effects her varied actions have on the world and, accordingly, changing her actions.

The toddler picks up a jar of grape jelly and seems to be thinking, "What new things can I do with this? I've already sniffed, touched, and tasted jelly. How about pouring some on the floor or dabbing jelly on the doggy? And then maybe just drop the jar?" These actions may not seem to represent progress for the parents who clean up the consequences, but by just such experiments, she will learn the relationship between cause and effect, between her actions and the results—jelly stains on the floor, broken jar, and disgruntled dog and Mom. And in the future she will gradually

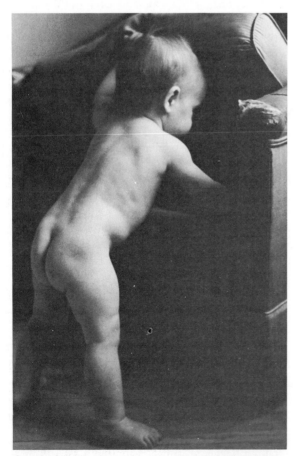

At around 1 year of age, object permanence develops to the point at which the infant can search for an object entirely hidden from view.

modify her actions so that she puts the jar down carefully, takes the jelly out with a spoon, and offers the dog a lick.

Experiments to test effects of actions on objects in this period advance children's notion of causality to the extent that they infer cause simply from seeing effects. Laurent can suspect that when his carriage moves, Papa Piaget is causing the movement.

At 1;1 (4) Laurent is seated in his carriage and I am on a chair beside him. While reading and without seeming to pay any attention to him, I put my foot under the carriage and move it slowly. Without hesitation Laurent leans over the edge and looks for the cause in the direction of the wheels. As soon as he perceives the position of my foot he is satisfied and smiles (Piaget, 1954, p. 335).

A child can now take into account a visible displacement of her ball from under cloth *A* to under cloth *B* and will retrieve it from under cloth *B*. She looks for the ball where she has seen it last. She has begun to understand space as something her ball can move through and still remain the same ball. A change of location does not affect the toddler's representation of the object. She comprehends space as something separate from objects and an object as one and the same thing, wherever it is. She cannot follow invisible displacements, hiding that goes on out of her sight, however. If her father hides a coin in his hand and then puts his hand under the sofa cushion, leaving the coin there, the toddler looks in his hand for the coin. She does not consider under-the-sofa-cushion as a hiding place because she has not seen the coin openly being put there. Her concept of the object is still tied to her last perception of it.

Stage 6: Invention of New Means Through Mental Combinations: the Beginnings of Thought (18 to 24 Months).
In the sixth and final stage of the sensorimotor period, children have a mental representation of causality, which is a step beyond the perception of causality.

At 1;4 (12) Jacqueline has just been wrested from a game she wants to continue and placed in her playpen from which she wants to get out. She calls, but in vain. Then she clearly expresses a certain need, although the events of the last ten minutes prove that she no longer experiences it. No sooner has she left the playpen than she indicates the game she wishes to resume!

Thus we see how Jacqueline, knowing that a mere appeal would not free her from confinement, has imagined a more efficacious means, foreseeing more or less clearly the sequence of actions that would result from it (Piaget, 1954, pp. 336–337).

The toddler can picture and follow a series of events in her mind. She solves a problem by making **mental combinations** before she acts. She no longer has to go through the process of trial and error, for she imagines and invents solutions, as Jacqueline did to get out of her playpen. She can, for example, imagine what will happen when she pulls the door toward her. So she moves her little chair out of the way first, without opening the door and knocking over the chair, as she might have done earlier.

She now figures out sequential displacements of an object, even if she has not seen these displacements. She uses her imagination and looks under the sofa cushion for the coin surreptitiously hidden there. If she sees her ball roll under the sofa and disappear, she does not have to bend down and look for it immediately. She looks instead at the sofa for a moment and realizes that the ball must have rolled under it and out the other side. She goes around the table beside the sofa, a path quite different from that taken by the ball, and finds the ball over by the bookcase, a short distance behind the sofa.

The toddler's ability to figure out invisible displacements is evidence that she has a mental representation of the object completely divorced from her immediate perceptions. She can look for the

---

RESEARCH FOCUS

INFANTS' UNDERSTANDING OF CAUSE AND EFFECT

Piaget described six stages in infants' understanding of causality. During the first three stages of the sensorimotor period, infants act as if events were extensions of their own actions. During the fourth stage, they recognize that touching can make things happen. During the fifth stage, they understand that other people can make things happen, and, in the sixth stage, they learn that causes for actions may be out of their direct perceptual field. Miriam Sexton (1983), of the University of Massachusetts Medical School, wanted to test how infants at the fourth, fifth, and sixth stages behaved towards people whom they considered agents of causality. Sexton hypothesized that infants in the fourth stage would not treat others as agents of causality, because infants do not yet believe that anyone besides themselves can make things happen. Infants in the fifth stage might attribute independent agency to a few familiar people, like their mother. Infants in the sixth stage would understand better how others might act as agents of causality.

The subjects were 54 infants from 11 to 23 months old. In the first part of the experiment, infants watched events caused by their mother, the examiner, and then apparently by no one. The episodes included such actions as raising a ball by pulling a thread suspended from the ceiling; activating a battery-operated toy bird, fire engine, drumming bear; and moving a Slinky. Sexton counted how often a baby approached either its mother or the examiner for help with a toy as an indicator of the baby's use of agents. She found that the infants' number of approaches increased with age, precisely what one would expect from Piaget's theory. Older infants turned more toward the mother when she had activated the toy than when it had been activated without any apparent cause, and they turned more toward the examiner when she had activated a toy. The 23-month-olds turned to either the examiner or to their mother, according to which they had seen activate a toy. The youngest infants, in contrast, rarely turned to either adult for help. They tried to solve the problem by themselves; when they did not succeed, they quickly turned to some other activity. The older infants not only turned to the adults for help, but many also protested quite noisily if their requests were refused. This study documents infants' increasing understanding of causality with increasing age and development.

coin and ball in places other than where she saw them last or ever saw them. Her concept of object permanence is now fully developed.

The concept of object permanence has important real-life implications for both the child and her parents. Since a child can now retain the image of an object, she may also experience a keener sense of loss when a particular object or person is missing. She begins to make more specific demands. If her parents take her on a trip and forget her favorite stuffed animal, she will soon be looking for it and probably crying for it. When her mother disappears into the bathroom and closes the door, she is likely to find her child waiting—impatiently—outside the door when she reopens it.

Mental representation is a culminating achievement of the sensorimotor period.

IMITATION

In Piaget's theory, imitation develops in stages, as the other aspects of cognition do. The physical act of copying is a way of internalizing what is seen or heard. Over the course of the sensorimotor period, the child develops—along with mental representations of objects and causes—mental images of actions, indirect copies that can be used long after the child has seen the action happen.

Early on, in her first circular reactions, the infant prolonged her reflexive behavior and her looking for the pleasure of it. Early imitation, too, stems from the desire to prolong a sensation, to extend a pleasurable or interesting action. The 4-month-old pats her hand on her high chair several times, after which her mother pats the high chair. The infant will then pat again *as if* in imitation. At this age, however, if her mother had been the first to pat, the infant would not have responded this way. The mother is only feeding into her daughter's circular reactions. Piaget called this **pseudoimitation,** because the infant is limited to imitating actions already in her repertoire and ones she herself has just performed. An infant will be capable of true imitation only when she can imitate another person's novel behavior.

During the third stage of the sensorimotor period, the infant's ability to imitate advances. Pseudo-imitations become quicker and more accurate. The infant now will copy the novel actions of another person, although she is limited to the parts of her

As the infant develops mental images of actions, he or she can imitate other people's actions. The ability to imitate grows surer and more accurate. This infant is waving goodbye, a pseudoimitation (limited to familiar actions and to visible parts of the body), clearly pleases the mother.

body immediately visible to her, her hands and feet. The actions she copies must also be in her repertoire, that is, she must be able to make the motions necessary. Waving bye-bye is a typical early imitation given hearty encouragement by parents.

In the fourth stage of the sensorimotor period, the infant can imitate actions that are new to her and that involve parts of her body she cannot see, such as her face. She can blow out a candle, open and close her mouth exaggeratedly, and wrinkle her nose after watching her father make these faces while playing with her. Imitation becomes more accurate in the fifth sensorimotor stage. By the sixth stage, the child can even imitate the movement of objects, such as the opening of a box by opening her mouth. Even more important, by this stage she can imitate actions she saw sometime earlier, what Piaget called **deferred imitation.** She will imitate a friend's behavior that she witnessed the day before or she will say "Onceuponatime . . ." in the same intonation mother uses to begin bedtime stories.

Piaget described an early deferred imitation by Jacqueline:

At 1;4, J. had a visit from a little boy of 1;6 whom she used to see from time to time, and who, in the course of the afternoon, got into a terrible temper. He screamed as he tried to get out of his play-pen and pushed it backwards, stamping his feet. J. stood watching him in amazement, never having witnessed such a scene before. The next day, she herself screamed in her play-pen and tried to move it, stamping her foot lightly several times in succession. The imitation of the whole scene was most striking. Had it been immediate, [the imitation] would naturally not have involved representation, but coming as it did after an interval of more than twelve hours, it must have involved some representative or pre-representative element (Piaget, 1962, p. 63).

To imitate her playmate of yesterday, Jacqueline must have some memory of his actions. According to Piaget, the ability to remember and imitate actions is of the same order as the realization that objects have permanence. Both are attained at about the same time.

THE PREOPERATIONAL PERIOD

Two-year-old children are about to enter a new phase of growing up. They will soon be able to count and play and imagine things in a very different way from that of their baby days. They will no longer be bound by what they can see and taste and touch. They will learn to pretend. They will be able to apply what they have mastered in one setting to another. They have already begun to move into what Piaget called the **preoperational period** (Table 8.1). They are gathering the mental images that will eventually be integrated into a logical system of understanding the world.

Piaget compared early intelligence to a slow-motion film that is made up of one static frame after another and does not convey continuity. During the sensorimotor period, the infant can only "look at" or retain one picture at a time. By the

end of the preoperational period, the mind works like a movie projector, possessing many pictures and moving from one to another quickly. But the child still focuses on successive states and does not understand the transformations that have taken place between the beginning of the film and the end of it. During the school-age period of concrete operations, the child's mind is more like a movie projector with the child in control of the projection. The child runs the mental pictures back and forth, reversing them, recognizing connections between the sequences, retaining the individual representations, but also remembering how the pictures are transformed and what part each frame plays in the whole plan of the film.

SYMBOLIC FUNCTION

Children begin to break out of the boundaries of the here and now sometime around 18 months to 2 years of age, while they are still in the sensorimotor period. Having acquired sensorimotor schemes for manipulating objects during this period, they are now able to hold mental representations of these objects and actions in their heads. They evoke mental images of the objects and actions without seeing them. Then they begin to understand, create, and use *symbols* to represent these objects and actions, people and places that are not present. This ability to symbolize is called the **symbolic function,** and it opens up vast new domains for children from 2 to 4 years old. Pretend play, drawing, and, most important, language are all modes of symbolic representation, on which children in this age period elaborate and expand. They use all these strategies for representing objects and actions, for remembering events that have happened, and imagining those that never will—unhindered for the most part by the rules of logic. When she was 2, a toddler could hear her cat's meows in her head, point to a picture of a cat, and call it a cat. At 3 she could draw a picture with two circles and ears and call it "Frisky." She could pretend that she was holding and petting Frisky, or that she was chasing a bird and meowing. She could even joke and make up stories about a giant cat named "Frosky."

A symbolic representation, in Piaget's terms, is a **signifier,** which stands for the signified object or an action. A signifier may be mental or concrete.

TABLE 8.1
PIAGET'S PERIODS OF COGNITIVE DEVELOPMENT

Period	Activities and Achievements
Sensorimotor Birth to 2 years	Infants discover aspects of the world through their sensory impressions, motor activities, and coordination of the two.
	They learn to differentiate themselves from the external world. They learn that objects exist even when they are not visible and are independent of the infant's own actions. They gain some appreciation of cause and effect.
	They make detours and retrace their steps to reach a goal.
Preoperational 2 to 7 years	Children cannot yet think by operations, by manipulating and transforming information in basic and logical ways.
Symbolic Function 2 to 4 years	Children can think in images and symbols and elaborate on them. They become able to represent something with something else. They acquire language, play games of pretend, and mix reality and imagination.
	They can draw or describe their path to a goal.
Intuitive Thought 4 to 7 years	Intelligence is said to be intuitive because children cannot make general statements. Egocentrism declines as children become able to take other peoples' perspectives into account. They begin to think in classes and see relationships, but they can cope with only one classification at a time.
	They can make guesses about cause and effect.
Concrete Operational 7 to 11 years	Children can understand logical principles that apply to concrete external objects.
	They can think of an object in the process of being transformed rather than thinking of it just in its present state. They can take in more than one aspect of a situation, appreciate that certain properties of an object remain the same despite changes in appearance, and sort objects into categories.
	They can make or interpret a simple map, appreciate the perspective of another viewer.
	They can handle two concepts, such as longer and shorter, at the same time.
Formal Operational Over 11 years	Adolescents and adults can think abstractly. Their thinking is no longer constrained by the "givens" of the immediate situation but can work in probabilities and possibilities. They regard reality as only one aspect of what might be. Adolescents can imagine other worlds, especially ideal ones.
	They can reason about purely verbal or logical statements. They can relate any element or statement to any other, manipulate variables in a scientific experiment, and deal with proportions, and analogies. They become actively engaged in the world of ideas and reflect on their own activity of thinking.
	They can prove a geometric theorem, explain the trajectory of a rebounding ball; they can construct whole systems of belief.

At age 1 year, 3 months, Jacqueline used a concrete symbol, her own finger.

J. was playing with a clown with long feet and happened to catch the feet in the low neck of her dress. She had difficulty in getting them out, but as soon as she had done so, she tried to put them back in the same position. There can be no doubt that this was an effort to understand what had happened: otherwise the child's behavior would be pointless. As she did not succeed, she put out her hand in front of her, bent her forefinger at a right angle to reproduce the shape of the clown's feet, described exactly the same trajectory as the clown and thus succeeded in putting her finger into the neck of her dress. She looked at the motionless finger for a moment, then pulled at her dress, without of course being able to see what she was doing. Then, satisfied, she removed her finger and went on to something else (Piaget, 1962, p. 65).

In this brief incident, Jacqueline used her finger, the signifier, to stand for the clown's foot, the signified. Jacqueline offered her father additional examples when she was 2 years of age.

At 2;0 she moved her fingers along the table and said: "Finger walking . . . horse trotting." Similarly, at 2;1, she slid a postcard along the table and said "car." At 2;3 she made a quick circular movement with her fingers and said: "Bicycle spoilt." Then she began again: "Bicycle mended" (Piaget, 1962, p. 124).

Jacqueline's walking fingers, the postcard, and the circular finger movement are the signifiers that stand for the signified, the actual horse, car, and bicycle respectively.

As indicated earlier, Piaget divided signifiers into two categories, those that are idiosyncratic or personal and those that are conventional or social. He called personal signifiers *symbols* and conventional signifiers *signs*. The most important signs are words. They are accepted and understood by others to represent certain specific actions or objects. For example, most English-speaking people agree that the word "bicycle" refers to a two-wheeled object that one may balance, pedal, and ride. Thus the word conveys specific and also generally accepted information, even though the person using the word may have a special kind of bicycle in mind

or associate a special feeling with the word. Piaget proposed that children think first in symbols and that these pave the way for the use of signs. Personal signifiers eventually enable children to acquire conventionally shared signifiers.

Symbolic Play

Piaget considered the pretending of toddlers to be very early evidence of their symbolic thinking. Pretending to be a bird through gestures is one kind of **symbolic play.** Children also pretend that one object is another, as Jacqueline did when she slid a postcard along the table and said "car." Even earlier, at 1 year and 3 months, Jacqueline played a pretending game with a piece of cloth, which she then extended from one object to another.

J. saw a cloth whose fringed edges vaguely recalled those of her pillow, she seized it, held a fold of it in her right hand, sucked the thumb of the same hand and lay down on her side, laughing hard. She kept her eyes open, but blinked from time to time as if she were alluding to closed eyes. Finally, laughing more and more she cried "Nene" (nono) pillow. The same cloth started the same game on the following days. At 1;3 she treated the collar of her mother's coat in the same way. At 1;3 it was the tail of her rubber donkey which represented the pillow! And from 1;5 onwards she made her animals, a bear and a plush dog also do "nono" (Piaget, 1962, p. 96).

Sometimes children interject symbolic play into their other play. Imagine a 2½-year-old putting together an animal puzzle. After placing the dog beside the bone, the cat by the bowl of milk, and the bird in its tree, he grabs the horse, stands it on its feet in front of the puzzle and says, "Ride, horsey, ride" as he hops it across the floor. Children may pretend to be Mama or Daddy or Grandma and identify themselves as such. They may also have an imaginary playmate who has a definite appearance and character and is a constant companion.

During the sensorimotor period, children engage in activities for the sheer pleasure of making something happen. They pull a string to make a mobile swing or splash their hands in bath water to make a commotion. Piaget called this practice play. In the preoperational period, play takes on the fun of pretend and make believe. But this pretending can

As the toddler's repertoire of language and motor skills enlarges, she begins to play symbolically. Now she can pretend in her play.

be utterly serious business. The child may not completely separate fantasy from reality. Piaget's daughter stood beside him making at the top of her lungs the sounds of bells. When asked to move and be quiet, she refused angrily and stated, "Don't. I'm a church." And woe be to anyone who tries to sit where an imaginary playmate has already settled himself.

Children as they become older elaborate on their symbolic play so that it covers many intricate details. A little girl pretending to be a teacher may ring a bell to call the children to order, carefully go through the phases of instructing the class, give the children blackboard drill, correct papers at her desk, scold a student, and so on. Children may also use symbolic play in an attempt to deal with unconscious conflicts, fears, disappointments, and aggression. They may "correct" reality or satisfy their egos by carrying out some forbidden act. They may, for example, pretend to cook at a stove after being admonished for going near the stove in the kitchen. Children also enact scenes to relive unpleasant events and thus free themselves of their own fears and anxieties. Piaget cites the example of his daughter guiding her doll through a reenactment of a real scene from the previous day when she fell and cut her lip. The child instructed her doll

not to be upset or worry because her lip would be all right. And Erik Erikson (1950) gives an example of a little boy who was angry with his mother over her brief departure. With toys, the boy re-created a situation in which he made his mother go away, threw her away, and made her come back at will. He also created a situation with a mirror, in which he played "going away" from himself. Through symbolic play, children may work at readying themselves for reality and "cure" their ills.

Drawing

Drawing is another realm of symbolic function. Nursery school walls, mother's and father's workplaces, and the preschooler's room are often adorned by the child's "artwork." Eventually, drawing is similar to symbolic play, in that it is done for pleasure, and it is like imitation, in that it is also the child's effort to imitate the real world. At first, however, drawings or scribblings merely reflect the child's pleasure at putting crayon to paper and creating some configurations at will. Children begin by covering all or part of the paper with random and repetitive marks, usually straight lines at first, then curves and spirals. In the second stage, around age 3, scribblers draw simple forms, such as circles and squares and *X*'s. At age 3½, they combine forms into designs, lining up strings of circles or crosses or putting a square within a rectangle (Kellogg, 1970).

Although scribblers are still mastering their shapes, the drawing may be accompanied by explanations that give the scribblers an actual relation to reality. "This is a house and a Mommy and a Daddy going for a walk" was the way a 3-year-old explained his drawing, which consisted primarily of large and small lines begun at various points on the paper. The drawings themselves provide proof that the child has a mental image of reality and wishes to communicate it. Drawings past the mere scribble-for-fun stage begin to reveal children's pride in their work and their serious attempts to bring their art into line with their perception of reality and their own personal experiences.

The average 3-year-old child has obvious artistic limitations. A round object represents both a person and a tree, or a straight line serves in one instance as a cat, in the next as a bicycle. The child's drawing of people may range anywhere from a mere straight line, to a circle with appendages, to three circles, to stick figures. All, according to the preschool artist, are people. Yet young children's drawings rather consistently omit certain parts of the body and include others. Children's drawings of people usually include the head, eyes, legs, arms, hair, and even hands and feet before they show the torso. Researchers have asked why and offer various theories as explanations.

Piaget explained the sparseness of children's drawings, specifically the omission of body parts and lack of resemblance to reality, by the child's mental image. That image, according to Piaget, is incomplete and global and lacks the detail and specificity of that of the older child or adult. Piaget cited the "tadpole" drawings as a clear example. The "tadpole" drawing (Figure 8.1) is a representation of a person commonly drawn by a 4-year-old. Attached to a circular form—the person's body, which looks more like a big face—are two vertical lines and two horizontal lines representing legs and arms.

Preschoolers sometimes draw with what is called **intellectual realism,** putting in everything that exists instead of drawing everything that is seen. The child adds parts of the body that are visually out of perspective. For example, a man's hand held behind his back may show through his body or the top of his head may show through his hat; his profile may have two eyes. The distortions of children's drawings during the preoperational period may lend them a certain freshness and charm, even a similarity to the great modern paintings of Pablo Picasso and Paul Klee (Gardner, 1980).

Language

The most important means of symbolic representation is language, the true cornerstone of symbolic function. Children have usually acquired their first recognizable words by their first birthday and then add a few new ones each month. By 19 months they usually have vocabularies of about 50 words. From then on, as children become more accustomed to the symbolic representation of things,

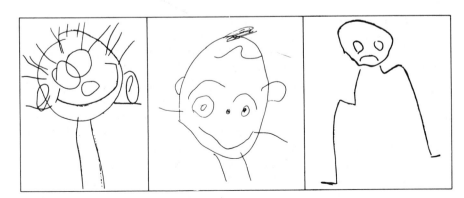

FIGURE 8.1

Four-year-old children's drawings of people usually consist of a large head or face, to which they attach sticks or other thin lines for arms and legs. The question is why do they leave out the body (Golomb, 1974).

they acquire words at a very rapid rate. Their speech may at first contain private symbols, single words that mean much more to the child than their conventional definitions. "Baby" may mean that the child wants something and is said to any adult on hand, with appropriate gestures, to make what is wanted clearer. Children may also make up words that they expect other people to understand. But, gradually, children's words become restricted to conventional signifiers, or signs, accurately matched to their accepted meanings. Children represent phenomena with these conventional signs, and these signs or words are an important aspect of the later development of concepts. By the words they learn, children are put in closer communication with members of their family, their neighbors and peers, and ultimately with the knowledge of present and past generations. The importance of language in the child's development merits detailed discussion and is the subject of Chapter 11.

INTUITIVE THOUGHT

The period of **intuitive thought** extends from about 4 years to about 6 or 7 years of age. The thinking of children in these years is considered preconceptual or prelogical. The period ends when the child possesses real concepts and can think by logical operations. Children in the period of intuitive thought know many things about people, animals, toys, and food. They apply themselves to tasks and try to reason about progressively more complex problems. But their reasoning and the solutions they propose are, nevertheless, often wrong when judged by adult standards. There are several ways of demonstrating the limitations and the stretching of children's intuitive thought.

Dreams

Children's intuitive thought is evident in their explanation of dreams. Piaget suggested that there are three stages in the development of an accurate understanding of dreams. In the first stage, children focus on the appearance of things. The way they see it, dreams are real, live actions. They assume that dreams originate and take place outside of themselves. As one little girl commented on waking up one morning, "Mommy, I didn't sleep last night; we had a circus in my room." Thus the 4- to 5-year-old child gives responses like the following.

When do you dream? *At night.* Where is the dream when you are dreaming? *In the sky.* Can you touch the dream? *No, you can't see and besides you're asleep.* When you are asleep, could another person see your dream? *No, because you're asleep.* Why can't one see it? *Because it is night.* Where do dreams come from? *From the sky (Piaget, 1975, pp. 93–94).*

Between 5 and 6, children vacillate, guessing that dreams originate in the head but take place outside of them.

What is a dream? *You dream at night. You are thinking of something.* Where does it come from? *I don't know.* What do you think? *That we make them ourselves.* Where is the dream while you are dreaming? *Outside.* Where? *There (pointing to the street, through the window) (Piaget, 1975, p. 107).*

Seven-year-old children understand that dreams take place inside themselves and are produced by their own thoughts and imagination.

In children's dreams, as in our own, mental images represent familiar objects, experiences, and sometimes conflicts. Children in the period of intuitive thought may awaken in fright or feel anxious about their dreams because they believe that what they have dreamed is real. Piaget gives several examples.

At 3;7, when [the child] was trying to overcome a tendency to bite her nails, she said when she woke, but was still half asleep: "When I was little, a dog bit my fingers," and showed the finger she most often put in her mouth, as she had probably been doing in her sleep. . . . At 5;4 [the child], who had been wanting cats instead of guinea pigs for pets . . . "dreamt that a cat had eaten the baby guinea-pigs"; and at 5;8: "All the guinea-pigs were dead and there were lots of cats in the hen-house (where the guinea-pigs were). They ran away when we came, like the guinea-pigs when we give them dandelions. One of the cats was ginger. It was mine" (Piaget, 1962, p. 178).

Intuitive thought is characterized by this inability to distinguish fantasy clearly, especially dreams, from reality. The intellectual realism that causes children to depict in their drawing a hand that was actually hidden from view also prevents them from making clear distinctions between what they have "seen" in their sleep and what actually happens.

Identity Constancy

Preschool children may at times be confused by superficial changes in physical appearance—even of members of their own family.

At 2;7, seeing Lucienne, her sister, in a new bathing suit, with a cap, Jacqueline asked: What's the baby's name? Her mother explained that it was a bathing costume, but Jacqueline pointed to Lucienne herself and said: But what's the name of that? (indicating Lucienne's face) and repeated the question several times. But as soon as Lucienne had her dress on again, Jacqueline exclaimed very seriously: "It's Lucienne again," as if her sister had changed her identity in changing her clothes (Piaget, 1962, p. 224).

Apparently the intuitive mode of thought keeps children from seeing the identity of living things when outward appearance is altered, for Jacqueline could not recognize her sister Lucienne in her new bathing suit and cap.

Rheta DeVries (1969) conducted a study to investigate whether the young child recognizes the **identity constancy** of living beings. Children between the ages of 3 and 6 were introduced individually to a very docile cat named Maynard. After they had petted the cat, they were told that Maynard was about to look different. The experimenter told the children to keep an eye on the animal's tail during the transformation to verify that it was the same animal. Then, while screening Maynard's front end from their view, she placed a ferocious-looking dog mask on Maynard and turned him around. The children were then asked a series of questions about the animal's identity, the change in its appearance, what had happened and why, what food the animal would now prefer, what was its inclination to bite, and some questions about their own emotional response to the transformed animal. Then each child observed the removal of Maynard's mask. The youngsters were then questioned about their belief in magic and its ability to make the changes just seen.

DeVries's results supported Piaget's view that preschool children only gradually understand identity constancy. The children's appreciation for the identity of Maynard increased with age. The young-

est children, 3 years old, assumed that Maynard had run away or disappeared and that the masked animal was a dog. Children with the next level of understanding expected Maynard to remain a cat when the mask was put on him, but once it was in place, they thought he was a dog. At the third level of understanding, physical, perceptible aspects of Maynard were considered constant, but with the mask on he was a dog. Children at the fourth level denied that the animal had changed, but they changed the name of the masked animal. At the fifth level, children asserted the constancy of Maynard but entertained the possibility that magic could change a cat into a dog. The 6-year-old children believed that Maynard had remained a cat. They clearly recognized and understood identity constancy.

Perspective Taking

Preoperational children are in many ways **egocentric,** for they find it difficult to imagine that any life goes on when they are not around to see it. They cannot understand that the perceptions of other people differ from their own. What they see, hear, feel, and pretend, they assume others do as well. When their eyes are closed, no one can see them. Indeed, the very sun and moon follow them when they walk. Preoperational children have never heard of the Copernican revolution. They think that

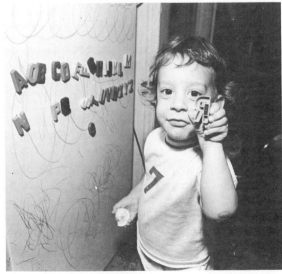

This 2-year-old gives away his egocentric thinking as he shows the photographer his "R."

the world revolves around them. Although not necessarily selfish, they are self-centered in their thinking.

Piaget was the first researcher to study the egocentric perspective of preschool children. His "three mountains" experiment was his demonstration that these children are physically rooted and unable to take the perspective of another person. In this experiment, a three-dimensional model of three mountains of varying heights and colors (Figure 8.2) is placed on a table surrounded by four chairs. Each of the children is asked to walk around

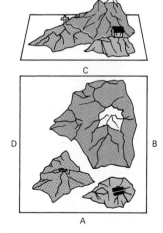

FIGURE 8.2

In Piaget's three-mountain task, an experimenter asks the child how the scene appears to the doll, which the experimenter seats in different positions (B, C, and D) around the table. The experimenter may ask the child to describe the scene seen by the doll, to construct it from cardboard models, or to pick the correct picture from a collection of ten (Piaget and Inhelder, 1967).

the table and view the model from all sides. Then, the child sits in a chair and a wooden doll is placed in one of the other chairs. The child is given a series of 10 photographs showing different views of the mountains and asked which one shows the scene as it would look to the doll.

The youngest children hold up pictures at random, indicating that any picture is representative. Somewhat older children choose the picture that represents their own view, not the doll's. By age 6 or 7 the child realizes that the view of the mountains is affected by position but cannot reliably choose the correct picture. He guesses. He changes his mind. He tries another picture. He goes back to the first. Only at ages 9, 10, and 11 is the child always able to pick the correct perspective.

John Flavell and his associates (Flavell, Botkin, Fry, Wright, and Jarvis, 1968; Flavell, Everett, Croft, and Flavell, 1981; Flavell, Shipstead, and Croft, 1978) have been especially active in studying the child's social knowledge or awareness of what others think or know. On the basis of parental reports and a series of ingenious experiments, they and others have shown that early in the preschool period, children are quite limited to their own perspective. For example, when asked to show someone their fingernails, they hold up their hands with palms out. They will hold a book up to their face and say, "What is this picture?" When "showing" a picture to an examiner, children will position it so that they themselves can see it, not the examiner. Children of 2 or 3 will think that Mommy knows a "secret" or a piece of information if they do (Marvin, Mossler, and Greenberg, 1975; Mossler, Marvin, and Greenberg 1976). They will ask, "What's this?" from the next room or from the solitude of the bathroom exclaim exasperatedly, "You *know* I need the toilet paper!" They will choose a toy fire engine for their father's birthday present or a new tricycle for their mother.

Concatenative Thinking

Much of the thinking of preoperational children is concatenative. They link together a series of separate, unconnected ideas. **Concatenative thinking** reveals the child's failure to analyze parts and integrate them into a coherent whole. Thus the child focuses on superficial attributes and links thoughts that have no logical or conceptual relation to one another.

Yet children are trying to put things together. Even their faulty logic—as illustrated in these answers—reveals a wish to make connections.

The sun does not fall down. Why? *Because it is hot. The sun stops there.* How? *Because it is yellow. And the moon, how does it stop there? The same as the sun, because it is lying down on the sky. Because it is very high up, because there is [no more] sun, because it is very high up (Piaget, 1926, p. 229).*

This child has attempted to account for the positions of the sun and moon by relating some of their attributes, but the sentences are nonsensical. This particular form of concatenative thinking is called **syncretism.** The child attempts to find an explanation at any cost by connecting unrelated ideas into a whole.

In **juxtaposition,** a second form of concatenative thinking, the child places one idea or event next to the other without concern for cause and effect. For example, when asked why something has happened, the child may state the effect as the cause:

The man fell from his bicycle because he broke his arm.

I had a bath because afterwards I was clean.

I've lost my pen because I'm not writing.
(Piaget, 1924, pp. 17–18.)

This little boy has some sense that the people, objects, and events "go together," but he has no understanding of what that relationship is.

Animism, Finalism, Artificialism

As anyone who has spent an afternoon with a chatty preschooler knows, the conversation is peppered with frequent and trying whys. Why is it raining? Why do I have to put on my boots? Why is that lady's nose so short? Why is the grass green? Why? Why? Why?

"Why is it rolling?" the little boy of 5 asks about his marble, which he has just dropped and which is now rolling gently down toward his father at the bottom of a small slope. He is told, "Because it is on an incline." The response is physically accurate, indeed, but completely unsatisfying to the child, who asks his father another question, "It knows you are down there?" The same boy wonders why two mountains, a big one and a little one, are next to each other. The kind of answer he expects would not entail a complicated discussion of geological principles. He wants to hear that the big mountain is for long drives and big people and that the little one is for short walks and children.

According to Piaget, children look for reasons that confirm their prelogical and egocentric beliefs in **animism, finalism,** and **artificialism.** Animism is the belief that all things are living and endowed with intentions, consciousness, and feelings. Marbles, the moon, and clouds all move of their own free will, and the moon may feel cold.

The moon moves; it moves because it's alive.

The clouds go very slowly because they haven't any paws or legs; they stretch out like worms and caterpillars; that's why they go slowly.

The moon's hiding in the clouds again. It's cold.
(Piaget, 1962, p. 251.)

Children believe that Daddy's car hurts itself when it bumps along the stony dirt road in the country. The trees and houses sleep at night because the children do. The wind is a voice and so even are the thoughts in their heads. The oven is alive because "it cooks the dinner and the tea and the supper" (Piaget, 1965, p. 196). Intuitive-thinking children egocentrically believe that everything is alive because they are.

Finalism is the belief that all movement is meant to accomplish some end: the marble rolls down the slope in order to get to Father; the clouds move because they are bringing rain; the sun sinks down to go to bed early, at twilight; and the chicken crosses the road to get to the other side. According to Piaget, children believe that the movements of objects are directed toward a goal because their own movements are.

Artificialism is the child's belief that everything in the world and in the sky has been built by people or by a divine being who fabricates things in human fashion. The mountains, big or small, "grew" because stones were manufactured and then planted. Lakes have been hollowed out and then filled with water. In fact, cities are built first, then the rivers and lakes are added to make them pretty and to provide places for swimming. This creationism, divine or human, reflects in yet another way the egocentricity of childish explanations. The adult, trying to answer a 4-year-old's incessant whys, would do well to keep in mind how the child thinks and spare himself trips to the encyclopedia.

Concepts

One of the most important cognitive achievements of childhood, according to Piaget, is building up stable and permanent concepts, which children hold in mind to guide them through surroundings that are always changing. A concept is a way of organizing information into a generalization. Let us take the concept "dog" as an example. The concept is an *abstraction,* in that it captures the essence of the commonalities of dogs—they bark, are furry, have four legs and a tail, and are generally friendly to little children. Dogs maintain their identity despite superficial changes, such as wearing a sweater to keep warm or dressing up with ribbons in their fur. The concept identifies a particular animal based on its appearance and actions. Yet it is a generalization because it applies to *all* dogs, not just a particular one. It is also a **classification** because it groups all dogs on the basis of their similarity and excludes other animals, such as cats, birds, horses, and pigs, because they are different.

Children at the stage of intuitive thought are in the process of acquiring concepts about many things in their world. Concepts of objects—dog, car, and tree, for example—are acquired relatively early. The child's progress toward more abstract concepts, such as number and age, is slower.

Number. Many 2- to 3-year-olds can count from 1 to 2. The number 3, if known at this young age, usually refers to anything above 2. Between ages 3 and 4, children have a fairly stable idea of the number 3 and can use it appropriately. In most nursery schools, children go daily through the process of practicing their numbers. We hear the rhythmic, unsure blend of preschool voices as they count: "1, 2, 3, 4, 5," and so on. If we ask one of the new learners to count independently, we will probably hear number 5 or 6 or 8 missed altogether or interjected out of place. Between 4 and 5 years of age, children can count with relative ease from 1 to 10 and many of them beyond. Yet children understand far less about number than it appears, despite the fact that they may memorize a string of

numerals. They have not yet formed the concept of number.

When children 4 to 5 years old are confronted with two rows of objects varying in number, such as 6 bottles and 12 glasses, and are asked to match an equal number of bottles with glasses, they are unable to do it. Instead of placing 1 bottle in front of 1 glass, the children lengthen the row of bottles so that the two sets of objects cover equal spaces and thus appear to correspond 1 glass to 1 bottle (Figure 8.3). If the row of 6 bottles is already longer than the row of 12 glasses—because the bottles are farther apart than the glasses—children think there are more bottles than glasses.

During the second stage in the development of the concept of number, when children are 5 and 6 years of age, they vacillate in their understanding of the one-to-one correspondence of objects and thus of the concept of number. Children arrange the bottles and glasses so that there are 6 of each, 1 bottle corresponding to each glass. If the corre-

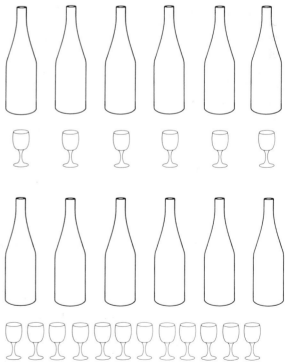

FIGURE 8.3

The preoperational child will agree that bottles and glasses lined up in one-to-one correspondence are the same in number. When the glasses are put close together and the bottles are spread out, the child thinks that there are more bottles than glasses.

spondence is altered in length by the experimenter, however, so that 6 bottles make a row longer than 12 glasses, children revert to the thinking of the first stage.

"Look, imagine that these are bottles in a café. You are the waiter, and you have to take some glasses out of the cupboard. Each bottle must have a glass." He put one glass opposite each bottle and ignored the other glasses. *"Is there the same number?—Yes.—(The bottles were then grouped together.)—Is there the same number of glasses and bottles?—No.—Where are there more?—There are more glasses."* The bottles were put back, one opposite each glass, and the glasses were then grouped together. *"Is there the same number of glasses and bottles?—No.— Where are there more?—More bottles.—Why are there more bottles?—Just because"* (Piaget, 1965, p. 44).

Finally, at age 6 or 7, the child will be able to match glasses to bottles and will not be confused by lengths of rows. The first- or second-grader carefully dispenses his bag full of candy or gum to friends, making sure that he has more than enough left for himself.

Other researchers have conducted numerous studies with children in an attempt to probe the child's concept of number. One of the most outstanding of these studies was one devised by Rochel Gelman (1972). She gave 3- to 5-year-old children sets of three cards with different numbers and spacing of dots on them. In one set, for example, two of the cards had two dots on them that were spaced at different intervals. The third card had three dots on it, but with the same spacing as one of the cards with two dots (Figure 8.4). When asked which cards had the same number of dots, children made correct choices as long as the numbers were ones that they could count. Once the number of dots exceeded that of their counting ability, however, they made errors. Then the length of the row of dots became the determining factor.

Age. The concept of age is a special case of the concept of number. Many 2- and 3-year-old children can tell you how old they are. The proud occasion of a birthday and a party helps them to remember their ages and to hold up a few fingers. Children have no clear understanding of what 2, 3, and 4 years mean, however. At this age they do not know how long a year lasts or understand the relationship of their age to that of other people.

Rom, 4;6, does not know her birthday. She has a small sister called Erica: How old is she? *Don't know.* Is she a baby? *No, she can walk.* Who is the older of you two? *Me.* Why? *Because I'm the bigger one.* Who will be older when she starts going to school? *Don't know.* When you are grown up, will one of you be older than the other? *Yes.* Which one? *Don't know.* Is your mother older than you? *Yes.* Is your granny

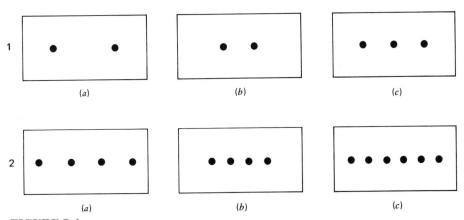

FIGURE 8.4
Gelman (1972) gave children sets of three cards and asked them which two cards had the same number of dots. (1) When the number of dots was small enough that the children could count them, they answered correctly, choosing *a* and *b*. (2) When there were more dots than they could count, they went by the length of the line formed by the dots, choosing *a* and *c*.

older than your mother? *No. Are they the same age? I think so. Isn't she older than your mother? Oh, no.* Does your granny grow older every year? *She stays the same.* And your mother? *She stays the same as well.* And you? *No, I get older.* And your little sister? *Yes! (categorically) (Piaget, 1969, p. 203).*

The child has equated size with age and thus decides that her mother is older than she. But, because Granny and Mother are similar in size, their ages must be the same. Grandmother and Mother do not get older every year, even though she does. Thus, as "time" goes on, age differences can be annulled or reversed if growth continues. The same thinking is applied to animals and to the inanimate. A child states that dogs do not grow older because they stay the same size and stones do not grow older for the same reason. Aging, rather than being a continuous process, is to the child a matter of arriving at a particular state and then remaining the same.

Children do not understand that the order of birth is related to the person's age. One child, when asked whether he or his father was born first, proudly stated that he was born first and would continue to grow older and that his father would remain the same age as would his mother because they were old already. The child's reasoning at nearly 8, however, shows a partial understanding of age.

Vet, 7;10: I have a little sister, Liliane, and a nine-month-old brother, Florian. Are you the same age? *No. First of all there's my brother, then my sister, then me, then Mama and then Papa.* Who was born first? *Me, then my sister and then my brother.* When you are old, will Florian still be younger than you? *No, not always.* Does your father grow older every year? *No, he remains the same.* And you? *Me, I keep growing bigger.* When people are grown-up, do they get older? *People grow bigger and then for a long time they remain the same, and then quite suddenly they become old (Piaget, 1969, p. 207).*

Vet understands that she was born before her brother and sister, but she still has the notion of age as a process that is determined by size and that proceeds to an end state. The period of nongrowth for her parents extends for a long time, and then rapidly old age takes over.

Dour, a few months younger, has grasped the fact that age differences persist but fails to understand the order of births.

Dour, 7;5: How old are you? *Seven and a half.* Have you any brothers or sisters? *No.* Any friends? *Yes, Gerald.* Is he older or younger than you? *A little older; he's twelve years old.* How much older is he than you? *Five years.* Was he born before or after you? *I don't know.* But think about it. Haven't you just told me his age? Was he born before or after you? *He didn't tell me.* But is there no way of finding out whether he was born before or after you? *I could ask him.* But couldn't you tell without asking? *No.* When Gerald will be a father, will he be older or younger than you? *Older.* By how much? *Five years.* Are you getting old as quickly as each other? *Yes.* When you will be an old man what will he be? *A grandfather.* Will he be the same age as you? *No. I'll be five years less.* And when you will be very, very old, will there still be the same difference? *Yes, always (Piaget, 1969, p. 209).*

Even though he knows that his friend is 5 years older than he, Dour does not understand that the friend's advanced age would mean he was born 5 years earlier. To understand age, the child must coordinate the order of births and the permanence of age differences, which is difficult to do when thought is still only intuitive.

Classification

The way children arrange cutouts—say of a number of rectangles, triangles, and arcs that are red, blue, and yellow—when asked to "put together things that look alike" reveals their ability to classify objects. Piaget found that children of 2 and 3 years can arrange the cutouts in a line or a big circle, or they may make what they consider to be a house or a wagon with a few cutouts. They pay no attention whatsoever to the shapes and colors of the cutouts. Then, from 4 to 6, they begin to pair cutouts, sometimes by shape, putting two rectangles together, and sometimes by color, putting a yellow arc with a yellow triangle. When they arrange the cutouts in a line now, the first few may be blue rectangles followed by a yellow one, then a few yellow triangles followed by two yellow arcs, with arcs of red and blue bringing up the rear (Figure 8.5). Children begin to learn to sort the

FIGURE 8.5
When 4- to 6-year-old children are asked to put together cutouts that look alike, they may choose several with the same shape and color, then one of another shape but the same color, then a cutout of the second shape but a second color, and so on. They make successive pairings of cutouts that have shape or color or both in common, but they have no overall plan or organization (Piaget and Inhelder, 1956).

cutouts, but they are distracted from one property to another as they juxtapose them. According to Piaget, only at about age 7 are children able to classify by plan, arranging all the cutouts by shape or by color or by both.

Another way of exploring children's developing ability to classify is to listen to their attempts to reason things out. **Transductive reasoning** is the name given to preoperational children's logic.

A child on the afternoon when she had not had her nap says, "I haven't had my nap, so it isn't afternoon" (Piaget, 1962, p. 232).

To this child's way of thinking, a nap is a particular characteristic of the afternoon and therefore defines it. She reasons from the particular to the particular. Adults reason either from the general to the particular, which is deductive logic, or from the particular to the general, which is inductive logic. The little girl did not understand that although afternoon *activities* include naps, neither a nap nor any other activity makes up an afternoon. Here is an example of Jacqueline's transductive reasoning.

J. had a temperature and wanted oranges. It was too early in the season for oranges to be in the shops and we tried to explain to her that they were not yet ripe. "They're still green. We can't eat them. They haven't yet got their lovely yellow color." J. seemed to accept this, but a moment later, as she was drinking her camomile tea, she said: "Camomile isn't green; it's yellow already. Give me some oranges" (Piaget, 1962, p. 23).

The child reasons that because the tea had turned yellow, the oranges had, too. Jacqueline apprehends something of the notion of green things turning yellow, but she mistakenly groups oranges, which must ripen, with tea leaves, which change the color of the water. She reasons as though their quality of green-turning-to-yellow makes oranges

and camomile tea of the same class. She needs to understand that all the things turning from green to yellow do not do so at the same time or with the same consequences.

THE CONCRETE OPERATIONAL PERIOD

During the period of middle childhood, children develop the ability to reason about objects and to carry out logical operations on objects. This usually begins around age 7, although the time is by no means set. Children may apply some rudimentary logical reasoning as early as 4 or 5 but do not master other logical reasoning until later on, during the teen years. Individual children acquire these abilities at slightly different rates.

Unlike preoperational thought, which is intuitive, impulsive, and relies heavily on immediate perception, **concrete operational thinking** is logical, rule bound, and integrated. An **operation** is a mental activity that transforms or manipulates information for some purpose; it is also an integral part of an organized network of related thinking. Examples of operations are adding, subtracting, multiplying, and dividing. The child who has developed concrete operational thinking can count and measure, add and subtract. She also understands that the contents in a tall, thin glass could be poured into a short, fat one and not be changed. Her thinking is not dominated by visual impressions. She knows by principle that milk and cookies are not changed in amount by their container or by how they are spread out. She recognizes that multiplication is related to division, that subtraction is the opposite of addition, that equals, greater than, less than, and union and intersection of sets are all interrelated. When a child can manipulate information mentally and her thinking is organized into an integrated system, it is what Piaget called operational (Piaget and Inhelder, 1969). The term "concrete" refers to the fact that the child can reason only about tangible objects, such as milk and cookies.

Recognition that certain manipulations of objects are **reversible** is a major advance of concrete operational thinking. Realizing that milk poured from one glass to another can be poured back again is one example of this. The child who recognizes that the effects of one manipulation can be reversed by applying the opposite is able to perform **inversion.**

A second important aspect of concrete operation is the child's ability to **decenter.** Decentering is focusing on and coordinating two or more dimensions—height *and* width for example—at once. The child at this stage recognizes **reciprocity**—that one dimension, such as the narrowness of the glass, may make up for or compensate for its other dimension, height. For this reason, a shorter but wider glass may hold the same amount as a taller but narrower glass.

A third advance that separates operational thinking from preoperational is the child's ability to put manipulations of objects in symbolic form. Piaget maintains that preoperational children's mental representations are like pictures or images of what they see. These are called **iconic representations.** In contrast, in the period of concrete operations, children are able mentally to represent and remember events and objects in symbolic form. Symbols can be manipulated mentally more easily than iconic representations. Symbols can condense a great amount of information, such as a long series of actions, into a single word, which is easier to remember. Preoperational children are biased in favor of present states, as opposed to past states, a form of temporal **centration** (Flavell, 1977; Piaget and Inhelder, 1969). But once children can

A psychologist tests a boy's understanding of the conservation of liquid quantity. When the liquid is poured into the tall, thin beaker, it looks to the boy as though it is more than the liquid in the short jar. The psychologist then encourages the boy to pour the liquid into the other jar. But until he understands conservation, the boy continues to think that the liquid has changed amounts.

mentally symbolize, they are able to imagine series of events, such as the planting of a seed, the sprouting of a bud, and then the blossoming of a flower. They can also think much more clearly about past events.

CONSERVATION EXPERIMENTS

A number of tasks were devised by Piaget to investigate the development of concrete operations in school-aged children. One important set of these tasks concerns the phenomenon of conservation. **Conservation** is the recognition that the number, length, quantity, mass, area, weight, and volume of objects and substances are not changed by transformations in their appearance (Figure 8.6). The child has the ability to conserve liquid quantity, because she recognizes that when milk is poured from one container into a differently shaped one, the quantity of milk is not changed. She also has the ability to conserve number; she knows that bunching five cookies together on a small plate or spreading them out on a large one does not change their number.

Piaget's experiments on conservation demonstrate how children think in the preoperational period and how their thinking progresses from intuitive thought to operational in three stages. In an experiment to determine their ability to conserve the amount or mass of a substance—to see the substance as the same amount however its shape is changed—children are shown two balls of clay. They are asked to add clay to either ball until they are both equal in amount. After children agree that both balls have the same amount of clay, the experimenter rolls out one ball into a snake. He then asks the children, "Now, do both these pieces have the same amount of clay?"

At Stage 1, at about 4 to 5 years of age, children state that the snake has more clay because it is longer. At Stage 2, the transitional stage, 5- to 6-years-old children vacillate in their answers. They are indecisive about which is greater. They may be able to see the amount of clay as the same when the transformation in shape is small, when the ball of clay is not rolled out too much, but they fail when the change is great. They may guess correctly when asked to predict the result of a transformation, saying that the amount of clay will still be the same when rolled out, but then change their minds when they see the longer piece of clay. They seem to remember that the balls of clay were originally identical in size, but they are swayed by seeing the longer length. They are still centered on length without being able to take skinniness into account. They may even imagine that some clay has magically been added. Children in Stage 2 still cannot reverse or invert their mental images. They do not realize that rolling out the clay can be reversed and the clay snake transformed back into a ball. They are dependent on their immediate perception of objects; to them the snake *looks* bigger.

Children in Stage 3, however, at age 6 to 7, are finally able to follow and remember the transformation of the clay; thus they realize that both the ball and the snake are equal in amount, despite the difference in shape. They will say that the snake can be rolled into a ball again or that the snake is longer but that it is also skinnier. When children have this insight into the identity of substances and can state a reason why the amounts of clay in the ball and snake are the same, they are said to be able to conserve substance.

Kenneth O'Bryan and Frederic Boersma (1971) sought to prove that children do not decenter until the period of concrete operational thinking. They recorded the eye-movement patterns of children who were participating in experiments on conservation of length, area, and liquid quantity. The children were independently judged by traditional Piagetian definitions to be at Stage 1, 2, or 3 of conservation. The Stage 1 nonconservers spent most of their viewing time looking at only one dimension, the "dominant" one; the Stage 2 transitional children shifted focus from one dimension to the other, but the shifts were infrequent. The Stage 3 conservers, however, shifted focus rapidly and often, indicating decentration.

According to Piaget's experiments (e.g., Piaget and Inhelder, 1969), children go through the same stages in mastering conservation of all the different quantities, number, length, weight, and so on. But even though the underlying principles and the reasoning required are the same, children do not conserve all quantities or on all tasks at the same time, mastering number, length, liquid quantity, mass, weight, and volume in that order. Piaget called this phenomenon **horizontal décalage**—from the French *décaler*, to unwedge or displace—meaning

Type of Conservation	Child sees	Experimenter then transforms display	Child is asked conservation question
Length	Two sticks of equal length and agrees that they are of equal length	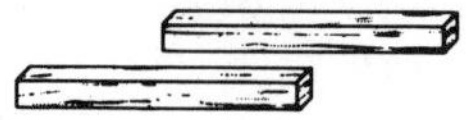 Moves stick over.	*Which stick is longer?* *Preconserving* child will say that one of the sticks is longer. *Conserving* child will say that they are both the same length.
Liquid quantity	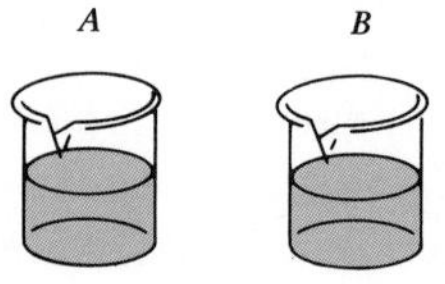 *A* *B* Two beakers filled with water and says that they both contain the same amount of water.	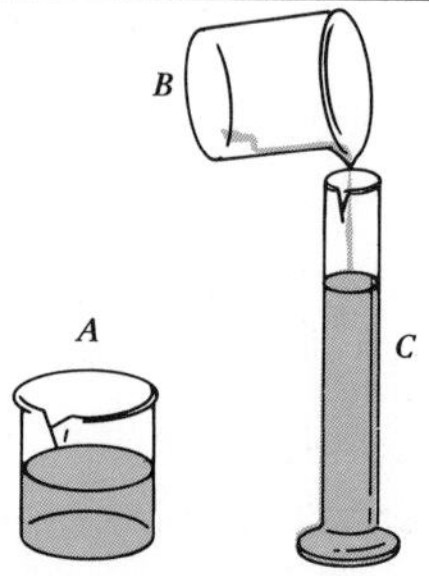 *B* *A* *C* Pours water from *B* into a tall, thin beaker *C*, so that water level in *C* is higher than in *A*.	*Which beaker has more water?* *Preconserving* child will say that *C* has more water: "See, it's higher" *Conserving* child will say that they have the same amount of water: "You only poured it!"
Substance amount	 Two identical clay balls and acknowledges that the two have equal amounts of clay.	 Rolls out one of the balls.	*Do the two pieces have the same amount of clay?* *Preconserving* child will say that the long piece has more clay. *Conserving* child will say that the two pieces have the same amount of clay.
Area	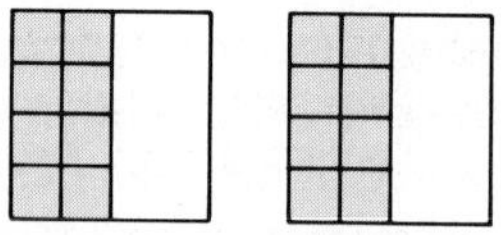 Two identical sheets of cardboard with wooden blocks placed on them in identical positions. The child acknowledges that the same amount of space is left open on each piece of cardboard.	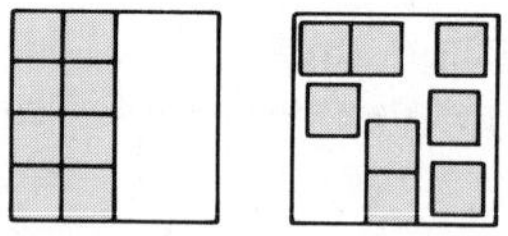 Scatters the blocks on one piece of cardboard.	*Do the two pieces of cardboard have the same amount of open space?* *Preconserving* child will say that the cardboard with scattered blocks has less open space. *Conserving* child will say that both pieces have the same amount of open space.
Volume	 Two balls of clay in two identical glasses with an equal amount of water. The child acknowledges that they displace equal amounts of water.	 Changes the shape of one of the balls.	*Do the two pieces of clay displace the same amount of water?* *Preconserving* child will say that the longer piece displaces more water. *Conserving* child will say that both pieces displace the same amount of water.

FIGURE 8.6

These procedures are traditional methods of testing children's abilities to conserve length, liquid quantity, substance amount, area, and volume.

that the similar abilities to conserve the different quantities are not in alignment; they do not all come at the same time. For example, the 7-year-olds who know that the snakelike piece of clay can be rolled back into a ball do not realize that the ball and snake have the same weight. By about age 9, they will say that the weight of clay is not changed by rolling it out. Finally, at 11 or 12, they will recognize that the volume of the clay is not changed by reshaping it. Conservation is not *fully* mastered until the child recognizes that the weight and volume of a piece of clay as well as its amount remain the same, despite physical transformations. In acquiring the ability to conserve, children first master the tasks that are simplest, then those that are more complex—first those in which the dimensions are salient and visible, then those in which the dimensions are not visually apparent.

SERIATION

Simple **seriation** consists of arranging a number of similar objects in a series according to the one quantified way in which they vary. Ordering a number of sticks from shortest to longest is the commonest example of simple seriation. According to Piaget, the child, as in learning conservation, goes through three stages in becoming able to seriate. Children of 4 to 5 separate the sticks into two or three groups, short, medium, and long, and then seriate the sticks within each smaller group. But they cannot coordinate the separate groups into one series. If they are shown that sticks arranged in order of length make a staircase at the top, they will arrange sticks so that their tops show this progression. But the bottoms of the sticks, ignored, will have a ragged alignment. In the second stage, 5- to 6-year-olds seriate the entire set by making a great number of comparisons and shifts of sticks until they get the order correct. Finally, in the third stage, 6- to 7-year-olds and older children attack the problem systematically, searching through the pile of sticks first for the shortest (or the longest), then for the next in the series, and so on, ordering them without error (Piaget and Inhelder, 1969). The systematic approach, requiring formulated, planful thinking, indicates that the child's reasoning is fully operational.

A child is shown two cookies, a chocolate chip cookie and a molasses cookie. The chocolate chip cookie is smaller than the molasses. She is told that the box of gingersnaps in the cupboard contains cookies smaller than the chocolate chip cookie. She does not have to see a gingersnap to know that it is smaller than the molasses cookie and, in fact, is the smallest cookie of the three. This kind of thinking is called **transitive inference.** When a child is shown that B is smaller than C and told that A is smaller than B, the child is able to infer, without being shown A and C together, that A is smaller

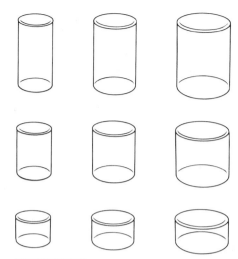

FIGURE 8.7
When children can put glasses varing in height and width in matrix order, they understand multiple seriation.

than C. Piaget maintained that children are successful in thinking through such transitivity problems when they are able to formulate some sort of mental representation of the logical relationship of seriation, $A < B < C$.

Multiple seriation is arranging a number of similar objects in a series according to the two, or more, quantified ways in which they vary. For example, children may be given a set of nine glasses that vary in height and width and asked to form a matrix, arranging the glasses in columns by increasing height and in rows by increasing width (Figure 8.7). Children 5 to 7 years old are able to form such a matrix if they have already seen one and can simply copy it from memory. But only older children can put together a correct matrix from the one they are told to construct when the model they have seen is backward (Bruner and Kenney, 1966). Children who are 5 and most 6-year-olds do not have the ability to create a multiple-seriation matrix on their own.

CLASSIFICATION

To be able to classify objects, children must notice that certain ones are alike in one way, others in a second way, and then sort them into groups depending on their similarities. For example, suppose a child is shown a drum, a harp, a flute, a screwdriver, a hammer, a saw, a peach, a pear, and an

At the level of concrete operations, the child can sort objects into simple, but not yet multiple classifications.

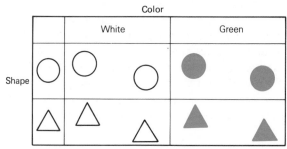

FIGURE 8.8
When children can sort cutouts of two shapes and two colors into mutually exclusive piles, arranged in color columns and shape rows, they understand multiple classification.

Are there more tulips or more flowers?

FIGURE 8.9
Given this class inclusion problem, children will say, "More tulips." Because they are unable to grasp the concepts of general class, flowers, and of subclass, tulips, they interpret the question as asking, "Are there more tulips or more daisies?"

apple and is told to put together the things that go together. A concrete operational child would successfully sort the objects into three groups, musical instruments, tools, and fruit. This is a *simple-classification* problem. A *multiple classification* problem requires simultaneous sorting of objects on the basis of two or more similarities. For example, given cardboard cutouts in two shapes and two colors—two white triangles, two white circles, two green triangles, and two green circles—concrete operational children are able to put the triangles together and circles together in rows and also sort the cutouts into columns by color. They lay out a four-cell, color-by-shape matrix (Figure 8.8).

The most interesting and frequently studied of the classification skills is **class inclusion.** Children who master class inclusion recognize that if a general class of objects can be broken down into two or more subclasses, the number of objects in the general class must be larger than the number of objects in any subclass.

Preoperational children have a rather vague notion of general classes. If they are shown nine tulips

and five daisies (Figure 8.9) and asked to point to the flowers, they will point to all of them. They will point only to the tulips when asked where the tulips are. But when they are asked, "Are there more tulips or more flowers?" they will answer "More tulips." With a limited understanding of the general class of flowers and an even more limited ability to coordinate the classes of flowers and tulips, they seem unable to think beyond the fact that there are more tulips than daisies.

Concrete operational children are able to keep in mind the fact that daisies and tulips are both flowers and answer that there are more flowers than tulips. They understand that something can be both larger and smaller at the same time, that although the number of tulips is larger than the number of daisies, they are fewer in number than all flowers. As with many of the other concrete operational skills, class inclusion seems to be grasped by children when they are 7 or 8, according to Piaget.

TIME, DISTANCE, AND SPEED

Whether or not they can express it in a mathematical formula, most adults realize that speed is the distance traveled per unit of time. Piaget was curious about what children understood of this relationship. He set up pairs of toy train tracks and asked children to watch two trains move and then say which train went faster. Four- to five-year-olds talked about the stopping points of the two trains, which train passed the other, and which one was ahead. If one train started much farther back on the track and ended up slightly behind the other train, these children would insist that the train that ended up slightly ahead had traveled faster and gone farther, completely ignoring the starting points of the two trains. Only when the train came from behind and passed the other train before the children's eyes would they correctly answer that it was traveling faster. Not until children are well into the period of concrete operations are they able to understand concepts of time, distance, and speed and to coordinate all three of them.

HUMOR

Children of 5 or 6 may realize that older brothers and sisters and adults pose riddles and tell jokes, but they do not really understand how the riddles and jokes are constructed. They may think that a riddle is a question with an arbitrary answer. "Why does the elephant flap his ears?" "Because his skin is gray." They may think that a real answer will do. "To shoo away the flies." But through operational thinking, especially reversibility, which allows them to hold past and present situations in mind, they soon realize that words and phrases may have more than one meaning and that many riddles and jokes are based on incongruities of words and re-

lations. Once they understand the point of jokes, they love to tell them. Children can now appreciate puns, for example:

Hey, did you take a bath?
Why, is one missing?

The mastery of conservation makes this joke enjoyable for children in the early grades of school:

Waitress Should I cut the pizza in eight pieces for you?

Fat woman Oh no, make it six. I could never eat eight.

And understanding class inclusion makes this one great fun:

Butcher What kind of meat will it be?

Customer I don't want any meat. Just give me a hamburger.

Going back and forth in thought between different ideas, meanings, and relations, as Paul McGhee (1979) points out, is essential to humor.

Children 7 and 8 years old will laugh themselves silly over corny jokes such as these (Shultz and Horibe, 1974, p. 14.):

Order! Order in the court!
Ham and cheese on rye, please, Your Honor.

Waiter, what's this?
That's bean soup, ma'am.
I'm not interested in what it's been. I'm asking what is it now.

I saw a man-eating shark in the aquarium.
That's nothing, I saw a man eating herring in the restaurant.

Call me a cab.
You're a cab.

Doctor, come at once! Our baby swallowed a fountain pen!
I'll be right over. What are you doing in the meantime?
Using a pencil.

We may not find these jokes hilarious for the simple reason that their absurdities and puns are all too familiar. Humor depends on resolution of a cognitive challenge and is not funny to those who are beyond the cognitive level of the joke. A joke must be congruent with the cognitive resources of an individual to evoke real merriment. Researchers (Prentice and Fathman, 1975; Zigler, Levine, and Gould, 1967) have found that children show the greatest preference for humor that provides a moderate level of difficulty for their cognitive capacities. They are amused by jokes that are understandable yet challenging enough to surprise them.

THE FORMAL OPERATIONAL PERIOD

Whereas earlier thinking was concrete and earth-bound, formal operations allow for greater abstraction and speculation. Children with concrete operational thinking are able to discuss the world as it *is;* formal operational thought allows adolescents and adults to discuss the world as it *might become.* At this stage, people are comfortable with hypothetical thinking and have a greater ability to imagine the logical consequences of existing states. They consider subjects of great moment and seriousness—love, morality, and work; politics, religion, and philosophy.

Having formal operational thinking is a necessary, but not sufficient, condition for achieving identity, formulating ideological goals, and selecting an occupation. Adolescents will want to choose a job or career, a political candidate, a spiritual or religious mentor. Without the flexibility of formal thought that allows them to place their lives in a personal and societal perspective, they are not able to figure out their "place" in the world.

Adolescents discuss endlessly self, sex, love, friendship, society, religion, justice, and the meaning of life. With their formal operational thinking, they are better able to form general concepts and to understand the impact of the past on the present and the present on the future. The capacity to think about how one thing relates to another allows them to question social institutions and examine the limits and possibilities of personal and collective action. Their new thinking is full of challenges and daring, but it also gives them a greater capacity to evaluate the immediate and long-range costs and benefits of actions and events. Finally, with greater complexity of thinking, adolescents are able to envision the world not only as it might be, but also as it ought to be.

When do adolescents begin to have this new way of thinking that will allow them to plan for the future, to be morally responsible for their actions, to be committed to certain political or religious ideals? At about 11 or 12, children are able to think about the future, but their abstracting cognitive skills are still new and unpracticed. Their ability to apply these new skills to practical and personal problems remains limited.

As Piaget saw it, adolescents' suddenly expanding powers of thought blur the boundaries between self and society. Young adolescents may fail to distinguish "between the ego's new and unpredicted capacities and the social or cosmic universe to which they are applied" (Inhelder and Piaget, 1958, p. 345). The lines between thought and action and between their own thoughts and those of others become blurred so that young adolescents may at one moment believe that everyone thinks as they do and the next moment that their feelings and thoughts are absolutely unique (Peterson and Offer, 1980). They believe that other people are thinking about them more than is true. But gradually, they are able to consider others and society as well as themselves. Young adolescents' egocentrism diminishes, their sense of unlimited power dissipates, and they are able to grasp reality. This, according to Piaget, is the "true beginning of adulthood" (Inhelder and Piaget, 1958, p.346).

LOGICAL ABILITIES

Formal operations consist of four overlapping logical abilities:

1. Hypothetico-deductive thinking.
2. Inductive thinking.
3. Reflective thinking.
4. Interpropositional logic.

Hypothetico-deductive thinking and **inductive thinking** are the abilities to generate hypotheses and to think logically about abstractions, such as symbols and propositions, as well as about available information. These two processes constitute what we more commonly refer to as the scientific method, whereby factors are systematically controlled and observed in order to test particular hypotheses.

Reflective thinking, which is also called re-

Formal operational thinking allows adolescents to form broad concepts and hypotheses, and these skills make for long conversations about themselves, society, love and sex, and the meaning of religion, justice, and life.

cursive thinking, is the ability to think about thought—to reflect on one's own mental processes. In Piagetian terms, this is the ability to perform operations on operations. It is the ability to think about one's own thoughts from the perspective of another person, to analyze one's thoughts and cognitive strategies objectively, and to evaluate whether they are appropriate to the task at hand. For example, the high schooler can now frame an argument for or against a proposition—that the drinking age should or should not be lowered, that nuclear arms should or should not be banned— and understand whether the argument is strong or weak. In earlier stages of thought, adaptation was a process of interacting with the environment. In the formal operational period, adaptation is a process of abstracting from one's thoughts, of representing to oneself ideas about symbols, words, and concepts. Words learned during early childhood— *love, country, parent*—change in meaning as they resonate within a new conceptual system (Neimark, 1982).

Interpropositional logic is the ability to judge the truth of logical relations among propositions. The concrete operational child is able to test the empirical truth of a single proposition. With formal operations, the adolescent or adult is able to test the logical truth that connects propositions. For example, suppose an 8-year-old and a 13-year-old are each told that the following two propositions are true and asked to judge the truth of the conclusion.

Proposition 1: All elephants are animals.
Proposition 2: All animals are green.
Conclusion: All elephants are green.

A concrete operational child will judge the truth of each proposition in isolation, will recognize the empirical falsity of the second proposition and of the conclusion, and will judge the conclusion false. Thinking in the concrete operational period is dominated by, and therefore limited by, what is known to be true about the world from experience. Thinking, although not limited by immediate perceptions, is nevertheless tied to what is concrete and active. Elephants are not actually green; the conclusion is false.

In contrast, a formal operational person will *logically connect* the statements. *If* all elephants are animals, and *if* all animals are green, *logically* all elephants must be green. In other words, the *logic* of the propositions can be manipulated without

With the ability to perform formal operations, adolescents can test the logical truth of propositions and conclusions—and carry out scientific experiments.

regard to their *content*. Formal operational thought focuses on the *structure* of a chain of reasoning rather than in whether the content of thought conforms to reality. According to Piaget, mature reasoning rests on a base of what he called formal propositional logic, on this ability to combine, evaluate, negate, and reverse propositions and their implications objectively.

Piaget devised a number of tests of formal operations. In one, the person is shown a pendulum consisting of a set of weights, which can be changed, and a string, which can be shortened or lengthened. The subject is then shown how to change the weights, change the string length, vary the height from which the pendulum weight is released, and vary the amount of initial push given the weight. He or she is asked which of these factors or a combination of them determines how fast the pendulum swings. To solve the problem, the subject must begin by holding all factors but one constant at a time and vary each systematically. If the answer is not yet evident, the subject must

then vary two factors at a time, and so on. Actually, one factor alone, the length of the string, determines the speed at which the pendulum travels in its arc. A similar test of formal operations, the flexibility of rods, is illustrated in Figure 8.10.

In another test, the subject is asked to suppose that six people of a district are running for town council and that the top three vote getters will be elected. Then, he or she is asked how many different combinations of three people could be elected. Obtaining the answer, 20, depends on the ability to think and work systematically, say by combining symbols standing for the candidates in a methodical way. Altogether, Piaget devised 15 such tests of formal operations.

Recently, psychologists have begun to test formal operations empirically to learn when and how people develop these abilities. One longitudinal study of the development of formal operations has shown that once children begin to acquire formal operations, they do so quite rapidly. The transitional stage is usually short, and regressions almost never happen (Neimark, 1975). No matter what the task or the expectation of the researcher, nearly all studies have shown that between the ages of 11 and 15 adolescents' thought undergoes a change in quality and power.

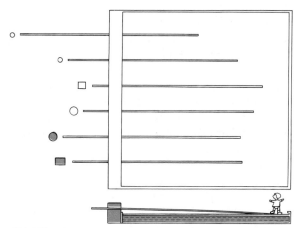

FIGURE 8.10

In the experiment on the flexibility of rods, the rods can be shortened or lengthened by varying the point at which they are clamped. Their cross sections are indicated on the left; colored forms indicate that the rods are made of brass, white forms that they are made of other metals. Dolls of different weights are placed on the ends of the rods. The maximum flexibility desired of a rod is that its end touch the water (Inhelder and Piaget, 1958).

In one series of experiments that tested several thousand 12-, 13-, and 14-year-olds' abilities on the pendulum task, investigators found that 14 percent, 18 percent, and 22 percent respectively of English school children were capable of formal operations (Shayer, Kucheman, and Wylam, 1976; Shayer and Wylam, 1978). When students were selected from schools that admitted only those in the top 20 percent of the ability range, the respective percentages were 40, 43, and 64. When students were selected from the top 8 percent of the ability range, the percentages were even higher: 61, 80, and 85 percent respectively. These experiments showed the increase in incidence of formal operational abilities with age predicted by Piaget and also suggested that formal operational abilities are tied closely to conventional measures of intelligence. With traditional experimental measures and instructions ("How does this work?"), the incidence of formal operations in the general population appears to be quite low (in this study, 22 percent). Another way of increasing the incidence of formal operations is by simplifying the tasks or by using more familiar objects (Neimark, 1982).

Researchers interested in the development of formal operations also have studied developmental changes in how people interpret works of art, poetry, and literature (Cometa and Eson, 1978; Gallagher, 1978; Hardy-Brown, 1979; Kenney and Nodine, 1979; Seefeldt, 1979). They have found that people at the stage of concrete operations interpret art and metaphors literally and focus on their content rather than their form. At the stage of formal operations, individuals are more likely to focus on the artist's intentions and on the form of the work. This refocusing on form rather than content is characteristic of the shift from concrete-operational to formal-operational thought.

Although the theory that Piaget used to explain children's cognitive development is only hypothetical and is, in part, already being replaced by other theories, Piaget's careful and systematic observations have provided the most vivid and detailed picture so far of the developing cognitive capabilities of the child. And the theoretical notions he proposed offer important insights into children's thinking. His notion of symbolic function is a useful way of thinking about differences between the thinking of a 1-year-old and of a 3-year-old. The notion of intuitive thought remains a good way to

describe how a 4-year-old child will attack a new problem; and Piaget's term "egocentric" conveys an important limitation in the mental capacity of young children. The ideas about object permanence and conservation Piaget suggested have been widely accepted. His formulation of constructs like accommodation, equilibrium, and assimilation has reshaped how people think about intellectual development, about the *interactive* nature of cognition and the environment within which it develops, and the active way that children approach learning. Although, as we will see later, experience and special training may change the specific ages at which cognitive milestones are reached, Piaget's overarching distinctions among sensorimotor, preoperational, and operational abilities continue to be useful for describing children's thinking from infancy through childhood. Piaget was a brilliant observer of children, and his work was instrumental in showing adults how to take children's mental life into account on *children's* terms. He delved into a broad range of topics, and there is no question that Piaget's work changed the way that people think about thinking.

CRITICISMS OF PIAGET'S THEORY

Not all behavioral scientists are persuaded by all aspects of Piaget's theory, however; some have raised strong objections to his intepretations. Although he remains a theorist of towering stature, new evidence has begun to suggest that parts of Piaget's theory are imprecise or incorrect.

OBJECT PERMANENCE

Several psychologists have questioned Piaget's explanation of how infants develop object permanence. They have questioned both the patterns by which infants search for hidden objects and Piaget's assumptions about why they search for hidden objects. Piaget's test of object permanence, you will recall, gives infants a choice of two locations in which they can search for the hidden object, and many infants continue to search where they earlier had found the object—point *A*—rather than at the location where the object was hidden—point *B*. Researchers since Piaget's experiments have suggested that such "*AB* errors" may be artifacts of the particular test, rather than a milestone in cognitive development. In one series of studies, for example, five locations for hiding objects were lined up horizontally, with the points *A* and *B* at either end. Infants 9 months old (Bjork and Cummings, 1979) or 12 to 14 months old (Cummings and Bjork, 1981) first had five attempts to look for the object when it was hidden at point *A*. Most of them looked at point *A* or very near it. Then, in plain view, the experimenter moved the object and hid it at point *B*. But the infants did not make *AB* errors, as Piaget would have predicted. Instead, they searched at or near point *B*.

In a second series of experiments, researchers showed that infants make *AB* errors even when the object is not hidden but remains in full view and is visually tracked by the infant at all times. In one study, for example, 10-month-old infants searched at a point at which an object earlier had been hidden even while the object was visible somewhere else (Harris, 1974). Could it be that in Piaget's test, infants were **perseverating** because they had succeeded at point *A* before, rather than that they lacked the awareness that a permanent object had been moved?

A third source of evidence that throws doubt on Piaget's interpretation is the research that demonstrates that infants tend not to make *AB* errors if they can begin searching for an object immediately after it has been hidden rather than waiting for one or more seconds. Infants 9 months old who were allowed to search immediately after an object was hidden found it on the first try. But those who had to wait 1, 3, or 7 seconds were more likely to search at point *A*. Both the infants' attentiveness and direction of gaze affected where they searched (Gratch, Appel, Evans, Le Compte, and Wright, 1974). In yet another study to demonstrate complexities in infants' search for hidden objects, infants watched an experimenter hide an object at point *A* and then move it to a second place, point *B*, when point *A* was either clearly marked or unmarked (Lucas and Uzgiris, 1977). Only when point *A* was clearly marked did the infants search there after the object had been moved. In a second procedure in this same study, infants searched at point *A* more often when there was a marker at point *A* that looked like the object being hidden, suggesting that they were using the marker as a cue for searching. Likewise, when infants could link the object in its new hiding place with an easily identifiable object there, they were less likely to search in the old hiding place (Freeman, Lloyd, and Sinha, 1980). Thus how and where objects are hidden, for how long, the movements of adults in hiding them, and the attentiveness of infant subjects all have been found to affect infants' patterns of searching.

Piaget claimed that infants cannot form mental representations of objects that are out of sight until after they are some 6 months old. Several recent studies contradict this claim also. In one ingenious experiment by Thomas Bower and Jennifer Wishart (1972), 5-month-olds accurately and invariably reached for an object in front of them after that object had disappeared because the lights were suddenly turned off. Five-month-olds also have been found to be more likely to pull off a small, easily manipulated cover from an object than the large, cumbersome covers often used in Piaget's tests (Rader, Spiro, and Firestone, 1979). Experiments like these suggest that Piaget's tasks for testing object permanence may include quite irrelevant cognitive and motor skills. They suggest that infants get better at knowing how to search, not that they begin to hold a mental image of the hidden object and proceed to look for it.

Paul Harris (1983) points out that finding a hidden object requires two things: (1) mentally representing the hidden object and (2) figuring out where it might be. Piaget did not allow for the possibility that an infant might be capable of the first but not the second operation: that an infant might know that an object exists without being able to find it. Recent research suggests that development may consist of ever improving search strategies rather than the dawning realization of the permanence of objects proposed by Piaget.

SYMBOLIC FUNCTION

The notion that children in the preoperational period are only beginning to use and understand symbols is undoubtedly correct. But contemporary researchers have questioned Piaget's evidence for the development of symbolic function, too. One thing they have questioned is Piaget's interpretation of children's drawing as evidence that they have limited or incomplete mental images.

The problem, they contend, is in children's motoric limitations and inability to represent a mental image graphically (Golomb, 1974) or in their memory, which is not yet efficient at retrieving information on body parts (Freeman, 1980). Others suggest that children's representation of a person is spatial in nature, that they tend to focus on the ends of the body. Thus 3½-year-olds start with the head and end immediately with the legs. According to Jacqueline Goodnow (1977), the problem lies in children's lack of strategy in executing their drawings. She found that children understood what people looked like but often needed help in expressing their mental image. One study (Brown, 1981) illustrates this point. Kindergarten children in a public school were asked specifically what they would include in a drawing of themselves that would appear on their work folders for identification. Teacher and class started at the top of the head, the teacher asking questions and the children responding about hair, eyebrows, eyes, ears, neck, shoulders, arms, and so on. The children obviously knew what people looked like and could identify parts of the body. After this discussion, the children were asked to make drawings of themselves. The drawings were executed with the greatest of detail. The teacher was astounded because all previous attempts of the children to draw persons, including themselves, had ended up quite global and barren. Thus, with a little help, the children were able to create more realistic representations of themselves.

EGOCENTRISM

According to Piaget, in the preoperational period, children's reasoning is bound by the limits of their own perceptions; they cannot take the perspective of another person. But several studies have shown that even very young children are not always egocentric in their perspective or misled by perceptual cues. In one investigation (Masangkay et al., 1974), 2- and 3-year-olds were shown a card held vertically. The card had a different picture on each side, and the children were asked, "What do *you* see?" and "What do *I* see?" Every 3-year-old and half of the 2-year-olds in the study answered correctly. In a similar study, children between 1 and 3 years old were asked to show a hollow cube, with a picture of a familiar object pasted in the bottom, to someone sitting across from them (Lempers, Flav-

ell, and Flavell, 1977). Every child over 2 years could do so. These studies suggest that young children are able to infer another person's perspective.

At 2 to 3 years, many children can hide an object from another person by placing it behind a screen, even though placed there it still remains visible to the child (Flavell et al., 1978), and they can understand that a white card will look pink to an experimenter wearing rose-colored glasses (Liben, 1978). Martin Hoffman (1979) describes a degree of social awareness in an even younger child, 20-month-old Marcy.

Marcy wanted the toy her sister Sara was playing with. She asked Sara for it but Sara refused vehemently. Marcy paused as if reflecting, then ran to Sara's rocking horse (which Sara never allowed anyone to touch), climbed up on it and began yelling "Nice horsey! Nice horsey!" keeping an eye on Sara all the time. Sara came running angrily, whereupon Marcy immediately climbed down, ran to the toy and grabbed it (Hoffman, 1979, p. 13).

This child, undoubtedly precocious, showed an awareness of her sister's inner state and thoughts, at an age when she may not have been able to understand the instructions that would have to be given in a test to determine her perspective-taking ability. The age at which children take another's perspective depends to a large extent on the circumstances.

It takes longer for children to learn just how things look to another person, and this ability depends heavily on the nature of the task assigned and the kind of response required. In one investigation of perspective taking, Helene Borke (1975) showed young children three displays and asked them to turn replicas of the displays so that a doll could see them. Two of the displays were of familiar objects—a toy sailboat on a lake, for example—and one was Piaget's three mountains task. Borke found that 3- and 4-year-olds correctly predicted the doll's perspective in the vast majority of trials with the familiar objects. But on Piaget's three mountains task, only 40 percent of the 3-year-olds and 67 percent of the 4-year-olds responded correctly. In variations of the three-mountains experiment, researchers have found that it is easier for children to give the right answer if they are able to rotate the model so that it looks like what the doll sees rather than choosing the right picture (Hutten-locher and Presson, 1973). Researchers have also found that children do better if they are rotated or moved to a new position while the model is covered. Once seated in the new position and asked what the model under the cover looks like, the children are able to imagine the new view; they are not distracted by looking at the mountains while trying to imagine them from another view (Hard-wick, McIntyre, and Pick, 1976). Other studies have used simple, symmetrical objects and avoided left-right discrimination to make the task easier. Taken together, these investigations demonstrate that preschoolers are less egocentric than Piaget had theorized, especially when the tasks they are given are appropriate to their age.

In one recent experiment, Flavell tested the hypothesis that children go from a less advanced level of understanding of other people's perspective to a more advanced level (Flavell et al., 1981). At the first level, children understand that they may see an object that others do not see, and vice versa. At the second level, they understand that, in addition, the object they see may look different from another person's point of view. Fifteen 3-year-olds from a suburban nursery school were given four tasks, two for each level of development. The first-level tasks were: (1) to look at a card with a picture of a dog on one side and a cat on the other side and to tell, when the card was held vertically in front of him,

which animal the experimenter, seated opposite, saw; (2) to look at a picture of a turtle that lay flat on a table and was bisected vertically by a plain card so that its feet but not its back were visible from one side and its back but not its feet was visible from the other side and for the child to say what part of the turtle the experimenter saw. All of the children answered the first-level questions correctly. The second-level tasks were: (1) to look at the same turtle picture as in the Level 1 test and to answer whether it looked right side up or upside down to the experimenter; (2) to look at a picture of a worm lying between a red and a blue blanket and to answer whether the worm looked to the experimenter to be lying on the red or blue blanket. About half of the children reported what they themselves, not the experimenter, saw on the Level 2 tasks. No child showed Level 2 understanding of the turtle picture, and only four showed Level 2 understanding of the worm picture. The experimenters concluded that children proceed from more to less egocentric cognition. But clearly, this progression begins earlier and is more complicated than the simple shift in the concrete operational stage indicated by Piaget.

CONSERVATION

Piaget suggested that young children do not understand conservation of mass, liquid, number, and

RESEARCH FOCUS

"OWN VIEW" OR "GOOD VIEW"

According to Piaget, preoperational children fixate on their own points of view. Given a choice between their own and another person's view of an object or scene, children egocentrically choose their own view. Paul Light and Carolyn Nix (1983) of England's University of Southampton wanted to test the conditions under which children respond egocentrically. They hypothesized that children prefer their own view of a display only when their view is especially good, that is, when it offers them the clearest view of the objects. They tested this hypothesis with 4- to 6-year-old schoolchildren. The objects displayed in the middle of a square table were familiar: a jar of instant coffee and a bottle of

orange soda. Around the table were four chairs, designated by the researchers as North, South, East, and West. From two chairs, one could see the two objects clearly and side by side. From two other chairs, one of the objects hid the other. The view from each chair was photographed. Children were asked first to choose the photograph that matched what a doll sitting in the East chair could see. Then the children sat at East and chose the photograph that matched what a doll sitting at North could see.

Light and Nix found that for both tasks, the children most often chose a picture showing the best view of the objects, i.e., with both objects visible (65 percent in the first condition; 75 percent in the second condition). Children's apparently egocentric behavior may actually reflect something else: in this case, a more informative or perhaps esthetic choice.

the like, because they are **centered,** that is, they focus on one dimension of an object and ignore the other. They may see height but ignore width in a task of conservation of liquid, for example. Could this phenomenon, too, be affected by the nature of Piaget's testing procedures?

Contemporary investigators have suggested that sometimes the very wording of questions designed to ferret out children's conservation abilities actually obscures them. When children look at two collections, each with the same number of objects, they may answer yes to both "Are there the same number in each?" and "Does one have more?" (Rothenberg, 1969). Why? "More" may describe the amount of space occupied; "the same" may mean "looks the same." The children's apparently illogical answers may not refer to number at all. "Bigger" may also mean "taller" to children (Maratsos, 1974), and so they may answer questions about conservation of mass, area, or liquid apparently illogically. Even asking a child questions just before and just after a transformation may suggest to the child that the first answer was incorrect (Rose and Blank, 1974). Children are found to answer questions about conservation correctly far more often when they are asked just once to judge how many objects there are, for when children declare the rows equal, they think that the request for a second judgment means that they are supposed to change their answer. When they only have to judge the arrays once, they are likelier to focus on judging number. In an attempt to test for conservation among third graders, Bruce Pennington and his associates (Pennington, Wallach, and Wallach, 1980) gave them standard Piagetian tasks of numerical equivalence and identity. They then tried

to rule out the possibility that some children's misunderstanding of the wording of questions would make them seem not to understand conservation. When the investigators asked the children, "Are there still 13?" rather than "Are there the same number as before?" the number of children who failed to understand conservation dropped from 19 to 8. In short, Piaget's standard tasks for appraising conservation abilities may cause so much semantic confusion in children that they are poor tests of actual ability.

Young children sometimes can conserve also when they are given a better chance of overcoming distraction. Jerome Bruner (1964) selected children 4 to 7 years old who had failed in an earlier testing of their ability to conserve liquid quantity. He tried a new way of presenting the problem. In the second experiment, the children were shown two identical narrow beakers of water and one wide, empty one. A screen was placed in front of the beakers so that the children could not see the deceptive perceptual difference in height when the water from one of the tall, narrow beakers was poured into the wide one. They were simply told what the experimenter was doing and then asked which beaker contained more water (Figure 8.11). In the second assessment of conservation, correct answers were given by 50 percent of the 4-year-olds, an increase from 0 percent; by 90 percent of the 5-year-olds, an increase from 20 percent; and by all the 6- and 7-year-olds, an increase from 50 percent.

The children who answered correctly usually justified their responses by saying, "It's still the same water" or "The water was only poured." Then the screen was removed, and the children were asked again which beaker held more water. All the 4 year-

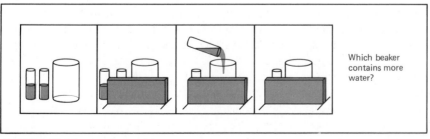

FIGURE 8.11

In this procedure for testing children's conservation of liquid quantity, a screen prevents them from seeing the level of the liquid in the wide beaker. When this procedure is followed, children answer correctly at earlier ages that the beakers contain equal amounts of water (Bruner, 1964).

olds reverted to their earlier nonconserving responses. But most of the 5-, 6-, and 7-year-olds who had answered correctly when the screen was in place stuck by their answers. In another test given some minutes later—the original standard Piagetian version without screen—significantly more 5-, 6-, and 7-year-olds gave correct conservation responses than had the first time (Table 8.2). The conserving children, according to Bruner, had an "internal verbal formula that shielded them from the overpowering [visual] appearances" (1964, p. 7).

CLASSIFICATION

Piaget had found that young children cannot sort objects into classes. But recent studies have cast doubt on this finding, too. Nancy Denney (1972) suggests that, in the United States, the current stress on preschool education, children's experiences in nursery school, and their hours of "Sesame Street" have made them more aware of classifications. She found that half of a group of 36 children 2 years old in Buffalo, New York, could sort 32 cardboard cutouts—in four shapes, two sizes, and four colors—into collections with some similarity. Of 36 children 4 years old, 23 sorted the cutouts into a completely similar group or groups by one or two of the three properties. Eleanor Rosch and her associates (Rosch, Mervis, Gray, Johnson, and Boyes-Braem, 1976) hypothesized that young children can sort objects according to basic, sensorimotor criteria. They assigned children from kindergarten, first, third, and fifth grades to sort color pictures of familiar pieces of clothing, furniture, vehicles, and people's faces into either basic or superordinate categories. Basic categories included "things people put on their bodies"; superordinate categories included "clothing." In a second experiment, 3- and 4-year-olds were given similar tasks. Children at every age could sort the pictures into

RESEARCH FOCUS

CONSERVATION OF LENGTH

Like others who have looked for more accurate tests of conservation abilities than Piaget's standard tasks, William Schiff (1983) gave a second chance to children who had failed Piaget's task for conservation of length. Schiff tested 3½- to 5½-year-old children on several different tasks. One task was a conservation of length task, using sticks with their ends aligned or not, administered in the traditional, Piagetian manner. Children were asked whether in each pair sticks were "the same length" or "one is longer than the other." In the other tasks, conservation of length was assessed nonverbally. The child was shown two same-length sticks, placed parallel on the table in front of him, about 4 inches apart, with their ends aligned, and he was shown a selection of wooden boxes of different lengths. He was asked to put each stick into the box where it "fits just right." After he had placed each stick in a box, the same pair of sticks was placed again on the table in front of him, but this time their ends were not aligned. The child again was asked to put each in the box where it "fits just right." Finally, two sticks of unequal length were placed on the table, and the question was repeated. This kind of task was repeated several times with small variations such as having the child touch the boxes rather than putting the sticks inside. Schiff found that preoperational children did *not* fail to conserve length because they centered on only one dimension, or because they were misled by their perceptions, or because they misunderstood the invariant properties of quantities. Instead, these children seemed to fail such tasks because of the way they interpreted the words "same length" or "longer than" and applied them to the pairs of sticks. The very same children who failed to perceive identical length when they had to solve problems verbally presented could perceive the similarity when the problems were presented nonverbally. It is very likely, Schiff concluded, that immature language, not immature perception, interferes with children's performance on word problems about conservation. Unlike adults, to whom individual words convey many different properties, children may understand only one or two properties for a given word. Any cognitive task that taps children's language rather than their perception will therefore erroneously imply a misunderstanding of conservation.

TABLE 8.2
CHILDREN GIVING CORRECT RESPONSES IN TESTS
OF CONSERVATION OF LIQUID QUANTITY

Age	Pretest: Standard Piagetian, Percent	Screen, Percent	No Screen, Percent	Posttest: Standard Piagetian, Percent
4	0	50	0	0
5	20	90	80	70
6, 7	50	100	100	90

basic categories. But only half of the kindergartners and first-graders could sort items according to superordinate categories. Thus, contrary to Piaget's descriptions, even 3-year-olds can sort objects into classes if they are simple enough.

Piaget also had found that before children were 9 or 10 they could not compare the size of a subordinate class to that of a superordinate class—tulips to flowers, for instance. Researchers have wondered whether Piaget's manner of presenting these problems may have overemphasized the subclass within the class as a whole. Thus if tulips are stressed more than flowers, the child may not consider them flowers. But if flowers are pointed out as a general category, more important than a specific type of flower, the child will focus on the whole class instead of on the tulips. Using this strategy, researchers (Markman and Siebert, 1976; McGarrigle, Grieve, and Hughes, 1978) have been able to get children to succeed on class-inclusion problems earlier than Piaget had found. Linda Siegel and her colleagues (Siegel, McCabe, Brand, and Matthews 1978) guided children 3 and 4 years old by using the word "all." When asked, "Are there more Smarties [Canadian M & Ms] or more of *all* the candies?" the children answered correctly. Ellen Markman (1973) used the word "family" to emphasize the general class. She showed children who had failed earlier on the standard class-inclusion problem a picture of two large dogs and four small ones. Over half of the 7-year-olds in her study answered correctly when asked, "Who would have more pets, someone who owned the baby dogs or someone who owned the *family?*" Markman (Markman and Siebert 1976) also asked kindergartners and first-graders "Who would have more toys to play with, someone who owned the [10]

blue blocks or someone who owned the *pile* of [10 blue plus 5 red] blocks?" They found that children were more likely to answer this question correctly than the Piagetian one: "Who would have more toys to play with, someone who owned the [10] blue blocks or someone who owned the [10 blue plus 5 red] blocks?" Phrasing questions so that children hear "collection" terms—"family," "group," "pile"—that emphasize the general class as much as the subclass improves their performance on tasks of classifying objects. In yet another study, Paul Ahr and James Youniss (1970) found that children's class inclusion improved when the original question, "Are there more dogs or animals?" was replaced so that each subclass was named and the word "more" preceded each subclass and the general class as well: "Are there more dogs or more cats, or more animals?" As Barbara Hodkin (1981) stresses, class inclusion is a function of language as well as logical ability.

VELOCITY

Friedrich Wilkening (1981) has pointed out that Piaget's velocity tasks test children's understanding of the relations among time, speed, and distance by having them choose which vehicle went farthest or fastest. This choice tests children's ability to *ignore* dimensions, Wilkening holds, but fails to show their ability to integrate information from two dimensions. Wilkening therefore tested 5- and 10-year-olds' and adults' abilities to integrate speed, distance, and time. He showed them a display of a dog sitting near its house. A bridge led from the doghouse across a lake. When the dog barked, a turtle, guinea pig, or a cat got frightened and ran from the dog. The subjects were to listen to the dog barking for 2, 5, or 8 seconds and to point to the spot on the bridge reached by one of the fleeing animals. Wilkening found that subjects of every age could integrate information about the length of the barking with the speed of the fleeing animal. The children followed the imaginary path with their eyes and then pointed to the spot on the bridge where the animal would have stopped. They had followed a rule requiring the multiplication of speed by time. Thus even the 5-year-olds could, under certain conditions, make judgments about velocity. What they could not do was to integrate distance and speed to estimate time, a task requiring division, a more complex operation than multiplication.

FORMAL OPERATIONS AND BEYOND

Piaget proposed that formal operations are unusual in children younger than 11 or 12 and common among late adolescents and adults. Some have questioned this proposal, however, because most studies show that only 40 to 60 percent of the adolescents and adults tested can perform at the level required by Piaget's tasks (Keating, 1980; Neimark, 1982). Common sense suggests that most adults do engage in formal operations quite routinely. They plan for the future, knowing that their plans are contingent on possible unforeseen events, and they commonly evaluate the logic of what they are told. This casts doubt on Piaget's tasks. His logic, too, has been questioned. Piaget has been roundly criticized for presenting explanations of formal-operational logic that are either mistaken, paradoxical, incomplete, or ambiguous (Braine and Rumain, 1983). Finally, he has been criticized for not going far enough, when he suggested that formal operations are the highest level of cognition people achieve.

Michael Commons, Francis Richards, and Deanna Kuhn (1982) of Harvard University studied college undergraduates and graduate students to see whether they could engage in forms of reasoning more advanced (i.e., more complex and powerful) than formal operational reasoning. The investigators describe formal operational thought as "second-order reasoning," for it is concerned with the interrelations of classes. They then hypothesized the existence of a "third-order" form of reasoning, called **systematic operations,** in which relations among classes or among relations are re-

flected on to form systems, and "fourth-order reasoning," or **metasystematic operations,** which are mental operations performed on systems. The researchers found a few undergraduates and many graduate students capable of third- and fourth-order reasoning, a finding that tended to support their belief that the stage of formal operations is not the most advanced stage of logical thought.

STAGES

Perhaps the aspect of Piaget's theory to have received the most critical examination has been his notion that development occurs in universal, developmentally sequenced, and irreversible stages. This notion has a number of implications that have been tested by researchers. One such implication is that all components of a given stage appear in an individual at the same time. For example, if the concrete operational period is a stage, a child should acquire conservation of weight and volume, class inclusion, seriation, and perspective taking all at about the same time. Another implication is that if the stages Piaget described are indeed universal, they should occur in the same order in many different cultures. Yet another implication of Piaget's stage concept is that the operations characterizing developmental stages cannot be taught to a child who is in an earlier stage; the child must construct these operations at his own pace out of his interactions with the environment. We will briefly examine the evidence for and against these three implications.

Stage Coherence

Most of the empirical studies that have focused on the first implication have shown that the various components of a stage are not correlated. That is, an individual child does not necessarily have the same level of understanding for each operation in a given stage (Gelman and Baillargeon, 1983). Research shows that particular concrete operations are acquired at different ages and not necessarily even in the same order that Piaget proposed (e.g., Brainerd, 1978; Osherson, 1974). The finding that the kinds of errors the children make on these different tasks are not parallel also calls into question Piaget's contention that all the abilities that characterize a stage emerge from the same cognitive structures. In general, psychologists have not been able to confirm Piaget's hypothesis that several abilities derive from an integrated and reversible structure. Instead, they have found low correlations between children's abilities on presumably related tasks (Acredolo and Acredolo, 1979; Tuddenham, 1971).

Cross-cultural Universality

A substantial amount of research has been done in other countries to test the universality of Piagetian stages. Because cognitive development is supposedly logical and inevitable, whatever the individual and cultural differences in rates of development, children in Europe, Africa, China, and Australia should all go through the same sequence. Piaget maintained that only the *rate* of acquisition might be influenced by the cultural surroundings, not the *order* of acquisition.

In general, cross-cultural studies show that although the rate of acquisition of various concepts is influenced somewhat by environment, the sequence is only rarely and minimally affected. No children in any culture can, for example, grasp the notions of time and the future before they acquire an understanding of the present and the past. The same organizing mental operations emerge in all children, although children may become more skilled at using those that are valued and practical in their culture (Cole, Gay, Glick, and Sharp, 1971).

One study, for example, conducted in Africa, showed that the stages of sensorimotor intelligence for African babies were the same as those observed in Europe and the United States, but that the rate and content of cognitive development were affected by environmental factors (Dasen, Inhelder, Lavallée, and Retschitzki, 1978). African babies were found to proceed through the stages of sensorimotor intelligence earlier than their European counterparts, although moderately malnourished African babies' development was somewhat slower. African babies also imitated what they saw in their culture. They would carry a doll on their back, whereas a French baby would put a doll in its carriage, for instance.

More advanced abilities that are important for survival within a culture are likely to be acquired, but those that are unimportant may not be (Dasen, 1977). Thus members of nomadic, hunting groups develop advanced spatial abilities, and members of farming groups develop sophisticated conservation abilities. Yet with training, individuals in both cultures can readily acquire the missing abilities. This brings us to the third implication.

Training

According to Piaget, at the center of the process of cognitive growth are children's self-initiated and self-motivated interactions with their physical surroundings. It is in their everyday activities that children acquire an understanding of the properties of objects and the physical workings of the world. Piaget did not promote deliberate training or teaching as a way of encouraging children's development of concrete operations. At his most generous, Piaget allowed that transitional children, children in Stage 2 of mastering an operation, might benefit from training. But the training would be useful only if it were tailored to fit the child's existing mental capacities and offered information about concepts at the next higher stage. He did not believe that short-term training could create new mental capacities or structures.

As soon as Piaget's work became popular in the United States during the 1960s, however, American psychologists undertook studies to find out whether children could be trained to understand concepts earlier than Piaget had suggested that they develop. The first training studies were generally not successful, but later ones have been.

In one training study, Gelman (1969) demonstrated that 5-year-olds could be taught to conserve number and length and that later many could generalize from their training and conserve liquid quantity and mass. Gelman hypothesized that young children are distracted by irrelevant cues. If this hypothesis were correct, children trained to attend to the relevant relations would be able to conserve. She first tested the 5-year-olds to determine that they could not conserve number, length, liquid quantity, and mass and then exposed them to one of three situations.

1. The control group of children were shown a set of three toys, two identical and one different. The children were asked to point either to two toys that were the same or two that were different. They were given a prize whenever they chose correctly. The purpose of including this group was to ensure that children do not fail to conserve simply because they do not know the meanings of the words "same" and "different."

2. Children in the second group were shown sets of three items having to do with number and length. Two of them were always identical, and the third was different. For example, there might be two rows of five chips and one row of three, with the first row of five chips spread apart, the next row of five placed close together, the last row of three spread out to the length of the first row of five (Figure 8.12). The children were asked to point to two rows of chips that had the same, or different, numbers of chips. Again, the children were rewarded for all correct choices, but they were not told why their answers were correct.

3. The children in the third group were shown exactly the same items and asked the same questions as those in the second group, but they were given no rewards and had no way of knowing whether they had made the correct discriminations.

Children in the first group picked the same or different toys almost perfectly from the start, eliminating misunderstanding of these words as a factor in the study. The children in the second group quickly began to learn to discriminate between number and length. But the children in the third group, who did not know whether their answers were correct, learned very little.

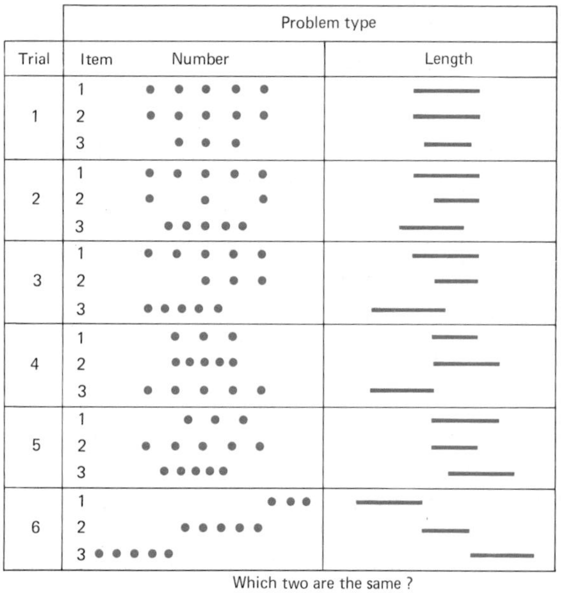

Children in all three groups were given tests on number, length, liquid quantity, and mass conservation the day after training and again 2 to 3 weeks later. The children in the first group, who had received no training in number and length discrimination, had, as expected, picked up no ability to conserve. Choices of the children in the third group, whose attention had not been guided by rewards, were at the end of training at chance levels of accuracy, as they had been at the beginning. Mere exposure to materials illustrating conservation principles had not provoked self-discovery. As for the children in the second group, the probability of their answering correctly on the tests for which they had been trained, for conservation of number and length, had at the end of training risen from chance levels to 95 percent. Their rate of success on those for which they had not been trained, tests for conservation of liquid and mass, was 57 percent immediately after training and rose to 68 percent on the later test. These results strongly suggested that by receiving feedback that helped them focus on the relevant relations, preoperational children quickly became concrete operational in conservation of quantities for which they were trained and were at least in a transitional stage for conservation of other quantities. Moreover, even though they had been told only that their earlier choices were right or wrong, not why, they now gave explanations for their answers that showed they understood conservation principles. The results cast some serious doubts on Piaget's views about training.

Most of the training studies of concrete operations have been attempts to teach children conservation, class inclusion, or transitive inference. Some of these studies have simply paired the child with another, more advanced youngster, because Piaget had suggested that children's conversations with their peers are of some help to them in learning about the world. In one study (Silverman and Stone, 1972), 14 pairs of third-grade children—one child in each pair understood conservation, the other did not—discussed or argued about conservation of area. In 11 of the 14 pairs, the conserving child brought the other child around. These children who learned from their peers were still able to conserve area when tested a month later.

In other studies, an adult has told or shown the children principles that are believed essential for understanding the operation, such as reversibility and reciprocity. Piaget did not originally believe that

| | | Problem type | |
Trial	Item	Number	Length
1	1	• • • • •	————
	2	• • • • •	————
	3	• • •	——
2	1	• • • • •	————
	2	• • •	——
	3	• • • • •	————
3	1	• • • • •	————
	2	• • •	——
	3	• • • • •	———
4	1	• • •	——
	2	• • • • •	——
	3	• • • • •	———
5	1	• • •	———
	2	• • • • •	——
	3	• • • • •	——
6	1	• • •	————
	2	• • • • •	———
	3	• • • • •	———

Which two are the same ?

FIGURE 8.12

These sets of chips and sticks are examples of the groups of items that Rochel Gelman (1969) used in training children to discriminate number and length.

language helped children to conserve. Researchers have disagreed, however, and have devised verbal rules about the effects of transformations. Children do learn to conserve when taught these rules and when informed about their correct and incorrect responses.

Children have also been trained to make transitive inferences, that is, to answer questions about relative length—$A > B > C > D$; and height—Mary is taller than Jane. Jane is taller than Nancy. Nancy is taller than Robin. Once children have been taught to memorize the premise that $A > B$ and so on, it has been found that their ability to make the inference that $A > D$ or that Mary is taller than Robin does not depend on age (Harris and Bassett, 1975; Stetson, 1974). Even 4- and 5-year-olds, children much younger than Piaget's age of concrete operations, have been trained to make transitive inferences.

Finally, children can be taught formal operational thinking. Robbie Case (1974) tested 52 6- and 8-year-olds on the flexibility-of-rods experiment (Figure 8.10). In this experiment to test formal operational thinking, subjects must isolate variables in order to determine which of them—type of metal, length of rod, cross-sectional shape of rod, or mass of the object placed at the end of the rod—contribute to the amount of rod bends. In the pretest, both the 6- and the 8-year-olds were unable to do the task. In each of the next 4 days the children were given "analogy training." They were taught how to isolate variables and to test and keep track of possibilities in several similar, but not identical, problems. After training, the children were again tested. There was no change in the 6-year-olds' performance, but approximately 75 percent of the 8-year-olds did significantly better on the task. Many solved the problem perfectly. Thus, although there are limits to the effectiveness of the training, it was successful with 8-year-olds who were, presumably, squarely in the middle of concrete operational thinking.

Training studies have not generally supported Piaget's claim that only transitional children, those in between stages, can benefit from training. In fact, the gains of lower stage and transitional children have been virtually identical (Brainerd, 1978). In addition, studies have found training to be more effective than self-discovery; Piaget, of course, believed the opposite, that self-discovery is superior. Although for most normal children who do not have the advantages of training provided in these experiments, cognitive development may very well proceed at the rate, in the order, and through the processes Piaget suggested, according to the bulk of evidence from numerous training studies, cognitive development is likely to be incremental and affected by many factors rather than proceeding in set stages determined only by interactions with the physical environment.

NEO-PIAGETIAN ALTERNATIVES

Because all these criticisms have been made of Piaget's theory, many contemporary developmental psychologists have moved away from a strictly Piagetian approach to understanding children's thought and knowledge. Robbie Case (Case, 1974, 1978; Case and Khanna, 1981) and Juan Pascual-Leone (1970, 1980) are among the people who have tried to keep the valuable parts of Piaget's theory as they construct alternative theories of cognitive development. They have proposed a theory of intellectual development that revolves around the strategies children use for solving problems. In one such problem, children are shown two pitchers. The experimenter says that he will pour several glasses of orange juice and several glasses of water into each pitcher. The children have to say which pitcher's contents tastes more strongly of orange juice. They may count the glasses, but they may not pour them out. Children between 3 and 4½, who are at the earliest stage of *isolated centration,* notice only the presence or absence of juice. Children between 4½ and 6, who are at the stage of *unidimensional comparison,* notice the quantity of juice. Children of 7 to 8, who are in the stage of *bidimensional comparison,* notice the number of water glasses as well as the number of juice glasses and compare the numbers near each pitcher. By the age of 9 to 10, when children are in the stage of *bidimensional comparison with quantification,* they notice how many more or fewer glasses are next to the pitchers. At each stage, the strategy used is more powerful and works for a greater number of problems. Each higher stage requires a child to store more items in short-term, or working, memory. Case has suggested that children's working memory increases in capacity and that they move from one cognitive stage to another only when the capacity of their working memory is large enough. Children's cognitive abilities also grow more automatic with practice. They therefore expend less effort in executing familiar problem-solving strategies. As cognition grows more automatic, more space in working memory is freed for further cognitive growth.

Kurt Fischer (1980) has proposed a **skill theory** of cognitive development that also builds on Piaget's. This theory is designed to describe the structure of cognitive skills at any point in development, how skills change and develop, and why cognitive development often is so uneven. In brief, Fischer proposes that skills develop in three tiers: first, sensorimotor skills; second, representational skills; and third, abstract skills. All thought begins with actions—the infant feels, mouths, and grasps a blanket. Representational thoughts are built on such sensorimotor actions. Actions always involve both the thinker and the environment, and the thinker must always adapt actions or skills to specific objects in the environment. Each tier can be broken down into 10 increasingly complex levels of skills. As children master specific skills, they build upon and transfer skills from one domain to another. Development is gradual, and people attain relatively different degrees of proficiency within levels. Only in those skills they are called on by factors in the environment to perfect most consistently will people reach their highest possible level. The rule, not the exception, thus is for people to achieve unevenly within levels and to be at different levels for different skills.

These neo-Piagetian alternatives illustrate in a cursory way what may become a new wave of theory building in cognitive developmental psychology in the 1980s and 1990s, as psychologists go beyond Piaget's theorizing—elaborating, modifying, building on, but not abandoning the enormous and valuable body of that great man's thought and observation.

SUMMARY

1. During the sensorimotor period, infants perform and modify reflex actions. They develop the awareness that objects are permanent and that actions have consequences.

2. During the preoperational stage of development, young children begin to symbolize and to represent objects and actions mentally. Pretend play, language, and drawing reflect this developmental advance.

3. The thinking of children between about 4 and 6 years of age is intuitive, concatenative, egocentric, animistic, and finalistic.

4. Concept formation requires the ability to think about classes of items. Children form concepts in ways that, with time, grow increasingly like that of adults.

5. During the concrete operational period, children develop the abilities that allow them to reason according to rules, count and perform arithmetic functions, understand certain aspects of the conservation of matter, focus on more than one dimension of a task at a time, make and appreciate jokes.

6. The adolescent or adult in the formal operational stage can think abstractly, speculatively, and hypothetically. Formal operational thought is characterized by deductive and hypothetical logic, by the ability to manipulate one variable while holding others constant, and by the ability to understand the relationships between parts and wholes. For the first time, in this stage one can think about thinking.

7. Some researchers have postulated the existence of forms of thought beyond formal operations called "systematic" and "metasystematic" operations.

8. Piaget's theory of cognitive development has drawn heavy criticism from many quarters, although he is still respected as an important, seminal, and original thinker. Psychologists have taken issue with Piaget's descriptions of how infants develop object permanence, of their egocentric thought and inability to take another person's point of view, of their tendency to focus on only one dimension of mass or the relations among time, speed, and distance. In several cases, investigators have found that the tasks devised by Piaget for testing cognitive development are flawed. When the tasks are modified—familiar objects substituted for unfamiliar, wording revised, and the like—many more children appear to be at more advanced stages of cognition than Piaget's tasks had suggested.

9. Alternatives to Piaget's theory have been proposed by several psychologists. Pascual-Leone and Case have theorized about the increasingly complex strategies children between 3 and 11 use for solving problems and about the corresponding increases in their capacity to store things in working memory. Kurt Fischer has proposed a skill theory of cognitive development that stresses individual differences in learning.

KEY TERMS

Scheme
Sensorimotor period
Organization
Adaptation
Assimilation
Accommodation
Circular reaction
  (primary, secondary,
  tertiary)
Magico-phenomenistic
  thinking
Object permanence
A, not B, phenomenon
Mental combinations
Pseudoimitation

Deferred imitation
Preoperational period
Symbolic function
Signifier
Symbolic play
Intellectual realism
Intuitive thought
Identity constancy
Egocentric
Concatenative thinking
Syncretism
Juxtaposition
Animism
Finalism
Artificialism

Classification
Transductive reasoning
Concrete operational
  thinking
Operation
Reversible
Inversion
Decenter
Reciprocity
Iconic representations
Centration
Conservation
Horizontal décalage
Seriation
Transitive inference

Class inclusion
Hypothetico-deductive
  thinking
Inductive thinking
Reflective thinking
Interpropositional logic
Perseverating
Centered
Systematic operations
Metasystematic
  operations
Skill theory

SUGGESTED READINGS

Cole, Michael, and Scribner, Sylvia. *Culture and Thought: a Psychological Introduction.* New York: Wiley, 1974. The question whether there are important cultural differences in thought processes, examined by reviewing research on culture and cognition, perception, language, memory, and problem solving.

Commons, Michael L., Richards, Francis A., and Armon, Cheryl. *Beyond Formal Operations: Late Adolescent and Adult Cognitive Development.* New York: Praeger, 1983. A collection of articles representing much of the most important research on cognitive development beyond what Piaget called formal operations.

Evans, Richard I. *Jean Piaget: the Man and His Ideas.* New York: Dutton, 1973. This book includes an autobiography and an interesting interview in which Piaget discusses his theory.

Ginsburg, Herbert, and Opper, Sylvia. *Piaget's Theory of Intellectual Development* (2nd ed.). Englewood Cliffs, N.J.: Prentice-Hall, 1979. An elucidation of Piaget's theory and helpful examples of each stage of cognitive development, in words any undergraduate can understand.

Goodnow, Jacqueline. *Children's Drawings.* Cambridge: Harvard University Press, 1977. Analysis of children's drawings as a medium of expressing their thought processes and social development. Gives answers to probing questions about what children are doing when they draw and many examples of drawings by children.

McGhee, Paul. *Humor: Its Origins and Development.* San Francisco: Freeman, 1979. An excellent and highly readable review of research on humor as it relates to child development. McGhee indicates how cognitive development and sex differences influence the appreciation and creation of humor.

Piaget, Jean. *Play, Dreams, and Imitation in Childhood.* New York: Norton, 1962. One of the major classics written by Piaget, weaving together his theoretical framework with wonderful examples of children's play, dreams, and imitation.

Piaget, Jean. *Six Psychological Studies.* New York: Random House, 1967. A brief overview of Piaget's theory, giving the chronology of cognitive and affective development.

CHAPTER 9

Process

Psychologists have long been interested in answering when and how learning begins and develops. How does the learning of the infant differ from that of the older child? Are there universal principles of human and animal learning? What processes are involved in the acquisition of new habits and new knowledge? How can these processes be studied? What are the most effective strategies for learning or remembering?

In Chapter 8, we discussed cognitive structures and the forms that ideas and mental representations take. We paid particular attention to Jean Piaget's theory of cognitive development. In this chapter, we will look at the *processes* of cognitive development. Our focus here will be on distinctly American approaches to cognitive development: the schools of learning theory and information processing.

LEARNING PROCESSES

Early in this century, when psychology was a young science, many psychologists both here and abroad were interested in isolating and describing the processes and laws of learning. To do so, they filled their laboratories with dogs and rats, birds and cats, pigeons playing ping-pong, and horses who could count. Based on their experiments, these behaviorists described two basic learning processes: classical conditioning and operant conditioning.

CONDITIONING: CLASSICAL, OPERANT

Ivan Pavlov, the Russian psychologist, was one of the first to demonstrate **classical conditioning.** He showed that a stimulus, which alone did not elicit a response, would elicit a response after it was repeatedly paired with a second stimulus that had such an effect. In a classic experiment, Pavlov rang a bell just before food was put in a dog's mouth. The dog's response to the food was to salivate. After repeated pairings of the bell and the food, the dog began to salivate when it heard the bell alone. In the terminology of classical conditioning, the food was the **unconditioned stimulus,** the salivation it elicited the **unconditioned response;** the bell, the **conditioned stimulus;** and the sali-

vation it elicited, the **conditioned response.** Generally, the conditioned response was similar to, but somewhat weaker than, the unconditioned response.

In the United States John Watson applied Pavlov's methods to a human infant (Watson and Rayner, 1920) and popularized classical conditioning as a method of child rearing (Watson, 1928). In a famous demonstration, Watson chose a 9-month-old named Albert as his subject and set out to make Albert afraid of a white rat. First, he demonstrated that Albert was not afraid of a white rat, a rabbit, cotton batting, or other white items. He then demonstrated that when Albert heard a steel bar out of sight loudly rapped, he jumped. Two months later, Watson began to condition Albert. Whenever Albert saw the white rat, he heard the steel bar rapped. After seven repetitions, Albert drew back at the sight of the rat, cried and tried to crawl away. Five days later and at two other sessions, Albert reacted similarly to the white rat and to some extent to the other white items, too. He had been conditioned to fear previously positive stimuli. Classical conditioning takes place in everyday situations, too: the child whose doctor comes to be associated in the child's mind with painful injections or the aunt who comes to be associated with painful, cheek-pinching greetings make the child recoil in fear, just as Albert recoiled from the white rat.

Operant conditioning bears a family resemblance to classical conditioning, for it, too, involves an association between a response and a stimulus. In operant conditioning, a subject makes a spontaneous or operant response, which is followed by a stimulus that increases the likelihood that the response will be repeated. Such a stimulus is called a **reinforcer.** A laboratory pigeon pecks at a bar on the side of its cage. Its peck releases a pellet of food into the cage. The pigeon pecks again at the bar and receives another food pellet. The rate of operant bar pushing is increased by the presentation of reinforcing food pellets. As long as food is presented, the bar will be pressed at a high rate. If reinforcement is discontinued, bar pushing will decline. Under B. F. Skinner's influence, the study of animals pecking for food pellets in their cages was extended to the investigation and modification of the behavior of humans in schools, hospitals, and homes. Researchers investigated which responses could be changed, which stimuli were effective rein-

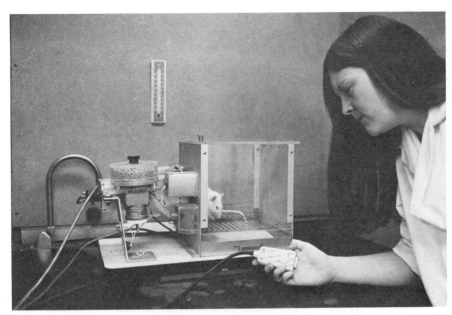

In operant conditioning the desired response from the animal is reinforced by food pellets. The principles of operant conditioning have been applied to the shaping of human behavior.

forcers, and which schedules of reinforcement were most effective.

In the last 30 years, operant conditioning has been used to modify many kinds of responses in children and adults. In one study of verbal behavior, for example, children in third, sixth, and tenth grades were asked to choose a pronoun from a list and to use it in a sentence (Baer and Goldfarb, 1962). When a student used a sentence that began with the pronoun "I," the experimenter commented supportively—and reinforcingly. Consequently, the frequency of "I" sentences increased. In a similar experiment with 9- and 12-year-olds (Rowley and Keller, 1962), the frequency of "I" sentences for children in a control group that received no reinforcement did not change, but children who received a smile and a nod or supportive comments used more "I"s.

In perhaps more important applications, operant conditioning has been used to change undesirable behavior. Habitual thumb sucking is one instance. One boy with this problem was allowed to watch cartoons on television, but as soon as he sucked his thumb, the screen went blank. He soon stopped sucking his thumb (Baer, 1962). Similar methods of behavior modification have been used with children who mutilate themselves (Lovaas, Freitag,

Gold, and Kassorla, 1965). Usually, when an adult sees a child mutilating himself, the adult responds by trying to intervene. But by doing so, the adult unwittingly reinforces the child's behavior. If adults ignore the self-mutilation, chances are that it will grow less frequent. Ignoring a young child's bedtime tantrums has the same effect. In extreme cases, when positive reinforcement does not work, aversive stimuli have been used to modify the behavior. Experimenters have trained autistic children to approach adults, for example, by administering painful electric shocks that cease when the child moves toward the adult (Lovaas, Schaeffer, and Simmons, 1965). Using operant conditioning procedures, researchers have made children more sociable, less aggressive, less phobic, better at reading, and less likely to wet their beds (Stevenson, 1970).

What do children find reinforcing? In one investigation of this question (Witryol, Tyrrel, and Snowden, 1964), girls and boys 10 years old were shown five objects, each of which was consistently paired with one of five incentives: a piece of bubble gum, a penny, a toy charm, supportive words from the experimenter, or nothing at all. They chose the object paired with the penny most often and the object paired with nothing least often. They chose the other three objects equally often. Boys increasingly often chose the object paired with the penny; girls increasingly often chose that paired with supportive words from an experimenter. Thus a variety of stimuli can be reinforcing; how reinforcing depends on the individual. In another study (Terrell, 1958), children did not differ in giving correct responses that were reinforced by signal lights, candy, or moving a bean from one jar to another in hopes of later trading the beans for candy. All of these conditions were reinforcing. Children who were promised candy after they had made the signal light glow a certain number of times did worse, however. Vague promises, it seems, do not provide effective reinforcement.

PRINCIPLES OF OPERANT LEARNING

Once they had discovered operant conditioning, American behaviorists began to identify its laws and principles. We will briefly discuss some of the most important of these principles here.

Schedule of Reinforcement

The speed with which an animal or human being can be conditioned and the strength of the learned response depend on the **schedule of reinforcement** (the percentage of responses that are followed by reward). Reinforcement can follow the response every time it occurs—a **continuous reinforcement schedule**—or just some of the time—a **partial reinforcement schedule.** In one series of experiments that varied the schedule of reinforcement (Ryan, 1966; Ryan and Voorhoeve, 1966; Ryan and Watson, 1966), investigators found that as the schedule of reinforcement decreased from 100 to 50 percent, children moved more rapidly or pulled more levers—the desired responses. But with a reinforcement schedule below 50 percent, the children slowed down their responding. Thus rewarding the majority of the occurrences of a desired response on a partial reinforcement schedule was more effective than rewarding all of the occurrences or a minority of them. This is generally the finding for responses that are simple and obvious. When the operant response to be conditioned is not so simple or initially strong or when another competing re-

sponse is also possible and can interfere with learning of the right one, then partial reinforcement is not as efficient as continuous reinforcement (Stevenson, 1970).

Delay of Reward

When the rewards following an operant response are delayed, animals' learning of the response is slower. The pigeon who pecks at the bar in its cage and then has to wait several minutes for a food pellet may not associate the reward with the pecking response and so will not increase its rate of pecking. Evidence about the effects of delayed reinforcement on children's learning is less consistent. Five- and six-year-olds who were given problems in discriminating size and shape lost interest in the problems when reinforcement was delayed (Terrell and Ware, 1961; Ware and Terrell, 1961). In other experiments, too, young children often lose interest if they feel bored and frustrated by delayed reinforcement. But these effects can be overcome if children are told to look at the reward they will be getting (Fagan and Witryol, 1966) or if they can tell themselves about the rewards to come (Terrell, 1965).

Satiation and Deprivation

Stimuli can lose their power as incentives or reinforcers if subjects have been exposed to them to the point of **satiation.** Stimuli can grow in power if subjects first have been deprived of them. In one demonstration of this principle, preschoolers were praised every fifth time they dropped marbles into one of two holes in a jar (Gewirtz and Baer, 1958a, 1958b). Before they began the conditioning task, one group of children, the deprived group, spent 20 minutes alone in an empty room; a second group of children, the satiated group, were given praise as they did a simple task for 20 minutes. The deprived children increased the most in the number of marbles they dropped into the hole during the conditioning task; the satiated children increased the least. As they did in this case, **deprivation** and satiation can make stimuli more or less salient to subjects.

Generalization

When people can see familiar features in a learning situation, their learning is more efficient, for they do not have to learn every element anew. One way to see familiar features is to generalize from a familiar to a new stimulus—as little Albert did in responding to other white objects as he had to the white rat. If people generalize too broadly, they risk responding inappropriately. Thus the child who generalizes from the furry, four-legged neighborhood dog and tries to pet a furry, four-legged skunk risks a smelly attack. But if people generalize too narrowly, they do not apply what they already know to new situations. In general, the more a familiar stimulus—the furry, four-legged dog—resembles an unfamiliar stimulus—the furry, four-legged skunk—the likelier a subject will respond similarly to them. The **gradient of generalization** is this degree of likelihood. Generally, the gradient of generalization is smaller for older than for younger children; more mature children generalize less broadly than younger children do. Generalizing from one stimulus to another is more likely if the training has been extensive, if the two stimuli both can be described by the same word, and if the training has included several stimuli rather than a single stimulus (Stevenson, 1970).

Children may generalize from one stimulus to another—as in the case of the dog and skunk—and they may generalize their responses as well. Thus the child who is afraid of the neighborhood dog may cry when it approaches, or he may scream, cringe, or run away. A child who speaks aggressively when angry or frustrated may, instead, act aggressively, punching and hitting (Slaby, 1974).

Extinction

When reinforcement of a particular response stops, the frequency of the responses to it gradually declines, and the conditioned response is said to be extinguished. Parents who once catered to their toddler's demands when he or she threw a tantrum and who then scrupulously ignore those tantrums should see them extinguished after a few noisy episodes. How quickly this happens depends in part on how often and how consistently the toddler had been reinforced by his parents' acquiescence to his furious demands in the past. **Extinction** occurs most slowly if parents have given in on a partial reinforcement schedule, if there have not been many such reinforced tantrums in the past, and if the incentives for the tantrum are high—the

child gets a new toy or a whole chocolate cake. Researchers have identified these conditions affecting extinction through painstaking laboratory experiments (see Stevenson, 1970). In one such experiment (Kass, 1962), children 4, 6, 8, and 10 years old were told how to operate a slot machine. They then tried the machine 30 times to win pennies for buying a prize. The likelihood of their winning pennies ranged from 0 to 100 percent on one of six reinforcement schedules. Finally, the children were placed on an extinction schedule; they got no more pennies. The number of responses the children made after the reinforcement stopped was directly related to their schedule of prior reinforcement; children who made the most responses during extinction were those who had received the least reinforcement. Children who had received 100 percent reinforcement stopped working the slot machine almost as soon as the pennies stopped coming. An indication of the persistence of the effects of partial reinforcement appears in the fact that after only three reinforcement trials, children in this study made an average of 240 responses during extinction. The parallel of adult gambling at the slot machines in Las Vegas is obvious. In another study using slot machines (Kass and Wilson, 1966), 6- and 7-year-olds went through 3, 9, 21, 45, or 60 training trials before extinction started. Their responses during extinction decreased significantly as the number of training trials increased. Harold Stevenson (1970) has suggested that the powerful effects of partial reinforcement and limited training can be explained by the fact that children are more likely to continue making a conditioned response if they cannot tell the difference between the training trials and the extinction trials. If they have gone through many trials in which their response invariably was followed by reinforcement, they will immediately realize that things have changed when reinforcement stops, and they will stop too.

VERBAL MEDIATION

Human beings have one special ability that distinguishes them from lower animals: they can talk. Does this ability change the ways that human beings learn, or do the principles of pigeons' pecking apply to human habits? One classic set of studies by Tracy and Howard Kendler explored the way that people's language affects their learning. The Kendlers used an experimental task that involved what they called **reversal** and **nonreversal shifts.** The subject would be presented with sets of four stimuli, say squares, that differed in color and size. At first, two stimuli would be selected as correct, say the large blue square and the large red square. Once the subject had learned that the correct stimulus quality was largeness, the experimenter would shift the problem so that either smallness would be the correct quality (a reversal shift within the same dimension) or redness (a nonreversal shift) would be correct. The ability to use language should make reversal shifts easier because the subject already would have labeled the correct dimension—size—and would just have to shift to the other end of the size continuum. Thus language could mediate the learning of the new correct response. If there were no verbal mediation, nonreversal shifts would be easier, because one of the stimuli (the large red square in this case) already had been correct before the shift. Experiments on human and animal subjects were used to test the so-called verbal mediation hypothesis—with some success. Animal subjects did learn nonreversal shifts more quickly; adult humans learned reversal shifts more quickly. The focus of interest then turned to children as the critical test of the verbal mediation hypothesis.

Experiments that followed did suggest that the use of verbal labels made a crucial difference to whether the child found reversal or nonreversal shifts more difficult. In one experiment, for example, 5- and 6-year-old subjects who had attached verbal labels to the stimuli performed better on reversal shifts; those who had not attached labels did better on nonreversal shifts (Kendler and Kendler, 1959). In another experiment, 3- to 5-year-olds, who did not use verbal labels, learned nonreversal shifts faster than reversal shifts (Kendler, Kendler, and Wells, 1960). In a third experiment, the proportion of kindergarten children demonstrating reversal shifts was higher among those who were required to say aloud during training why they were choosing particular squares—at least when the correct dimension was color (Kendler, 1964). These studies were interpreted as demonstrating the critical importance of verbal mediation in human learning.

OBSERVATIONAL LEARNING

Experience tells us that learning is not restricted to choosing red or blue squares, or pressing bars in the laboratory, or getting the right answer on a test. We learn vast quantities of information incidentally, casually, as we observe everyday events, and we need no pellets of food, pennies, or kind words to motivate us. The absurdity of trying to achieve operant conditioning in the everyday but complex task of driving a car is captured in Albert Bandura's acerbic description:

As a first step our trainer, who has been carefully programmed to produce head nods, resonant hm-hms, and other verbal reinforcers, loads up with an ample supply of candy, chewing gum, and filter-tip cigarettes. A semi-willing subject, who has never observed a person driving an automobile, and a parked car complete the picture. Our trainer might have to wait a long time before the subject emits an orienting response toward the vehicle. At the moment the subject does look even in the general direction of the car, this response is immediately reinforced, and gradually he begins to gaze longingly at the stationary automobile. Similarly, approach responses in the desired direction are promptly reinforced in order to bring the subject in proximity to the car. Eventually, through skillful use of reinforcement, the trainer will teach the subject to open and close the car door. With perseverance he will move the subject from the back seat or any other inappropriate location chosen in this trial-and-error ramble until at length the subject is shaped up behind the steering wheel. It is unnecessary to depict the remainder of the training procedure beyond noting that it will likely prove an exceedingly tedious, not to mention an expensive and hazardous, enterprise (Bandura, 1962, pp. 212–213).

Bandura, as we mentioned in Chapter 1, has demonstrated that children learn many things from watching other children and adults. **Observational learning** is especially rich in social situations, and Bandura (Bandura and Walters, 1963) has suggested that principles of learning derived from laboratory studies must be modified to extend to social situations. In one controlled study of observational learning (Bandura and Huston, 1961), over 90 percent of the 4-year-olds imitated a model's incidentally knocking a doll from one of the stimuli in a learning task, and 45 percent marched around the room in the same bizarre way as the model had. Or, in an incident closer to home, when one of the authors of this book took an aspirin (to quell a headache brought on by writing this chapter), her 2½-year-old son turned around to watch her just as she had popped the aspirin into her mouth and began to drink some water. All the child saw was her hand cover her mouth; he did not see the aspirin. For the rest of the day, he drank by first tapping his mouth and then drinking—a home-grown example of observational learning.

In a demonstration of **incidental learning** (Stevenson, 1954), children between the ages of 3 and 7 made their way through a maze at the end of which were a locked and an unlocked box. The children were instructed to go to the unlocked box, find a key in it, unlock the locked box, and get a prize from it. The unlocked box contained various items, including a matchbox and a purse, and, for different groups of children, the key was in, on, or under the matchbox or the purse. Later, the children were instructed to find the matchbox or the purse. The older the children, the greater was their incidental learning of the location of these items. Presumably, this was because young children are less efficient at categorizing, coding, and labeling objects than older children are. But there must be a limit to incidental learning, or we would be flooded with useless information. A person eventually must grow selective in attending to relevant rather than irrelevant stimuli. Several studies (e.g., Hagen and Hale, 1973; Maccoby and Hagen, 1965; Siegel and Stevenson, 1966) have demonstrated that incidental learning increases between grades 1 and 5 and decreases between grades 5 and 7. Incidental learning in the Stevenson (1954) study was also highest when the key had been inside the purse or matchbox and the child had had to open the container to find it, and it was lowest when the key had been on the container and the child had merely to pick it up. Clearly, manipulating an object increases its salience, and it will be noticed and remembered.

RECENT CHANGES IN LEARNING THEORY

Within the last 10 years, the psychology of learning has veered away from the strict dogma of classical and operant conditioning. As Stevenson put it:

What we have experienced in the past decade is a change as great as that which occurred early in the century in the shift from the psychology of introspection to that of behaviorism. Moreover, the change has been rapid, and psychologists trained in the tradition of the behaviorists have been forced either to modify their positions or to be regarded as atavistic remnants of an earlier time in the history of psychology (Stevenson, 1983a, p. 215).

For one thing, old findings have been reevaluated. Some investigators (Harris, 1979; Samelson, 1980) have scrutinized Watson's reliance on a single subject—baby Albert—and a single study to establish the validity of his evidence on classical conditioning in human beings. They suggest that Watson's attempts to condition Albert to fear a white rat were neither as successful nor as clear as Watson maintained. Old films of the experiment show that the infant's conditioned response only slightly resembled the unconditioned response.

Another change has been in the increased awareness that children are different from both animals and adults. Classic learning theorists assumed that children learn in the same incremental units as pigeons, are affected by the same laws of reinforcement as adults, and behave as predictably and compliantly in the laboratory as any of these subjects; basic learning processes are the same for people of all ages. Only in the last 10 to 15 years have psychologists begun to appreciate the uniqueness of learning in childhood and begun to explore developmental changes in speed and efficiency of learning, generalization, reinforcement, incentives, and drives.

Perhaps as a result of these concerns or perhaps because of the seductiveness of newer approaches to understanding cognitive development, laboratory experiments on children's learning, which were prominent and influential in American psychology for nearly half a century, had nearly stopped by the middle of the 1970s. Those conditioning experiments that were done in the late 1970s and early 1980s were attempts to answer questions raised long ago rather than attempts to break new ground. Today, many developmental psychologists believe that behaviorism has lost the power to generate useful, new, testable hypotheses. It has failed to deliver consistent results or predictions about children, and it has not been used too successfully with infants. The verbal mediation hypothesis also has been abandoned. Many investigations since the Kendlers' have shown that children and adults may know words quite well but still not use them as guides in remembering, learning, or directing their actions (Stevenson, 1983a).

Another change in the last decade has been the incorporation of more cognitive elements in the explanation of observational learning. According to Bandura, the dean of social learning, learning reflects a "continuous, reciprocal interaction between cognitive, behavioral, and environmental determinants" (1977, p. vii). As children observe others, they cognitively encode their observations in words or images, which they later retrieve and act upon; they form mental representations of what they see. Then, in *some* instances, depending on their interpretation of what is wanted or needed or will be rewarded, children imitate what they have observed. Whereas the behaviorists considered every organism a "black box" whose inner workings were beyond the bounds of proper psychological inquiry—only *observable* behavior was to be investigated—social learning theorists today try to understand the mental representations and events that are part of the learning process. In one study to test whether observational learning depends on such mental images, Bandura and his associates (Bandura, Grusec, and Menlove, 1966) asked one group of 6- to 8-year-olds to describe in words how

RESEARCH FOCUS

PRESCHOOLERS LEARN BY IMITATING THEIR PEERS

A recent study of how preschoolers learn by imitating their peers shows the attention developmental psychologists now give to cognitive processes. Helen Morrison and Deanna Kuhn (1983) studied observational learning in a group of 4- to 6-year-olds, specifically to test the proposition that children learn by attending to and assimilating models of behavior that are slightly more advanced or complex than their own. Too great a mismatch between their level of competence and that of a model is less likely to aid their learning. The researchers therefore studied the kinds of attention children paid to a model, their subsequent imitation, and cognitive changes.

They chose a construction activity called a Multiway Rollway, a set of ramps, chutes, angles, couplers, base units, and marbles. The pieces can be put together to form a ramp or a roadway on which marbles will roll, and the toy draws on children's knowledge of angles, gravity, rotations, paths, and trajectories. By watching children play with the toy, the researchers established seven levels of performance, ranging from no ostensible understanding of the toy's possibilities, through simple to complex constructions, and finally to the successful construction of an incline and an angle. To find a baseline of performance for each subject in the study, they observed each of the children playing alone with the toy. Later, observations were conducted with one focal child in a play group of four children. In each group, the focal child could observe play that was on the same level as, a level or two above, and a level or two below his or her own performance level. The children played together for three sessions. Children who advanced to higher levels of play for at least 1 minute were classified as having made a temporary gain. If the gain showed up in the final session, when the child played alone, it was considered a stable gain.

The results of the study showed that some children made no gains, but no children declined. The gainers spent more time playing with the toy than did the nongainers and more time watching their peers. Stable gainers spent significantly more time watching the other children in the group playing than did temporary gainers, and temporary gainers spent more time watching the other children play than did nongainers. The children the gainers watched most were those who were one level more advanced than they were. Gains in level of performance were directly linked to observing more advanced children (particularly children advanced by just one level). Older children were more observant than younger children and imitated the advanced model more often.

a model was playing; asked a second group to count as they watched the model (an activity that presumably interfered with their formation of mental images); and asked a third group simply to watch passively. The children who had described the model's behavior later were more likely than the others to imitate the model.

Bandura's shift from focusing on the child as social learner to the child as social thinker reflects a broader shift among developmental psychologists. Beginning in the early 1970s, psychologists from several disparate schools of thought—the behaviorists, the information processors, and the traditional developmentalists—shifted into a closer alliance in their investigation of what goes on inside the "black box." Information processors began to investigate the characteristic gaps in children's memories. Cognitive psychologists investigated children's learning strategies. Learning theorists allowed the existence of thought. And all three joined developmental psychologists in their concern with age-related changes in learning and knowledge. Whereas traditional behaviorists had asked children to learn nonsense syllables, to view isolated words and pictures, and to respond to stimuli that varied in color and form, psychologists in the 1970s began

to investigate principles of organization as children learned sequences of pictures, sentences, and stories in richly meaningful domains, like chess, history, and physics. Whereas once the focus had been on learning as an accumulation of facts and habits, controlled by reinforcement, the focus became how children as active learners organize, reorganize, and make sense out of information.

Learning theory was the most dynamic and exciting field in American psychology from the 1930s to the 1960s. It led to many interesting experiments and fresh insights about what makes people act as they do, and it led to many useful applications for teaching and managing children and for eliminating behavior problems. But learning theory has turned out to be limited in its ability to explain human cognitive development. Thus the current emphasis in the field of developmental psychology (and in this chapter) is on the newer approach to cognition provided by information processing.

INFORMATION PROCESSING

The information-processing approach dominates the fields of cognitive psychology and cognitive

The information processing approach focuses on how peoples' ability to handle information is limited by memory, the number of symbols to be manipulated, the speed with which they can manipulate symbols, and their ability to resist interference.

development today. It depicts people as symbol manipulators with specific, limited capacities to organize information into sets and subjects. Psychologists who take an information-processing approach investigate patterns of errors, verbal statements, eye movements, and people's representations of information in their efforts to produce and test models of cognitive activity. They study how people's ability to handle information is limited by their memory span, by the absolute number of symbols to be organized, by the speed with which they can manipulate those symbols, and by their ability to resist interference. They study how people rehearse and organize, how they memorize information, and how they use information to solve problems.

THE INFORMATION-PROCESSING SYSTEM

One of the earliest models of the information-processing system was a theory of attention proposed by Donald Broadbent (1958). This theory was made up to explain what happens in **dichotic listening tasks.** In such tasks, people are given information in one ear over a headphone that is different from the information that is given in their other ear. Then they must repeat back the information. They might hear "2" in the left ear and "5" in the right ear, followed by "4" in the left ear and "1" in the right ear, followed by "8" in the left and "7" in the right ear, and so on. This task is

quite easy if the person can repeat all the numbers heard by one ear and then all the numbers heard by the other (2, 4, 8 / 5, 1, 7). A person finds it much more difficult to integrate the sets of numbers heard by both ears in the order they were heard (2, 5 / 4, 1 / 8, 7). In explaining why people find the latter task more difficult, Broadbent theorized that the numbers, like any information, pass through the senses to a short-term memory store, where they remain for several seconds (see Figure 9.1). From the short-term store, the numbers pass through a filter that selects some information for further attention, according to its physical characteristics—such as which ear received the information. The numbers attended to then go to a limited capacity perceptual system where their meaning is extracted; then they go on to long-term memory where responses are framed. Broadbent suggested that because the selective filter can switch a person's attention from one ear to the other only so quickly, the person first attends to information entering one ear and retains the other ear's information in the short-term store, then switches attention to the unattended ear's information.

All other information-processing theorists following Broadbent have postulated that information flows through a sensory apparatus to a long-term storage system filtered by a limited capacity to attend to new information. One direct descendant of Broadbent's theory of attention is Richard Atkinson and Richard Shiffrin's (1968) theory of memory.

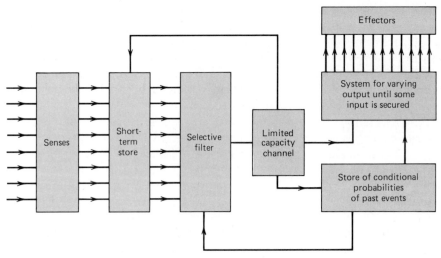

FIGURE 9.1
Broadbent's (1958) model of the information processing system.

Atkinson and Shiffrin postulated that the memory system consists of a sensory register for each of the senses (auditory, visual, and so on), a short-term store, and a long-term store. The rate at which information can be transferred into each store is limited, and the sensory and short-term stores are further limited in their capacity to register and hold information. Part of the evidence for Atkinson and Shiffrin's model came from an elegant experiment by George Sperling (1960). College students were shown a 3 by 4 matrix of letters for $\frac{1}{20}$ of a second. When the students had to name as many letters as they could recall right after they had seen the matrix, they usually remembered 4 or 5, or about 40 percent. But when they were asked immediately after seeing the matrix to recall the letters in just one row, they could remember 80 percent of the letters in the row. When the experimenter waited for 1 second after the students had seen the matrix before telling them which row he wanted them to recall, their rate of remembering fell back to 40 percent. Sperling's interpretation was that the visual image formed during exposure to the matrix (and held in the sensory register) lasted for only a limited period of time and had dissipated by the time either 4 or 5 letters had been recalled or 1 second had passed. Another experiment that lent support to Atkinson and Shiffrin's model was one showing that when a bright light was presented at the same time as a matrix of letters, it interfered with the formation of mental images in the sensory register (Eriksen, 1966).

In the short-term store, according to Atkinson and Shiffrin's model, information that has been processed by the sensory register is combined with information from long-term memory to perform whatever calculations are necessary. Because the short-term store is part of the conscious mind, people are aware of its workings, as they are not aware of the workings of the sensory register or long-term memory. This short-term store has only a limited capacity to retain meaningful chunks of material. Ordinarily, information disappears from short-term memory within 15 to 30 seconds, but rehearsal can retain it for longer periods and improve the chances of its moving into long-term memory.

These information-processing models of attention and memory, proposed by Broadbent and by Atkinson and Shiffrin, inspired cognitive and developmental psychologists to a flurry of experiments during the 1960s and 1970s. Researchers searched for the answers to specific questions: Which components of the information-processing system change with age? What is the size of memory stores? How fast can information be processed? How long can information be retained? By using a variety of techniques, they tried to answer these questions.

METHODS OF ASSESSING INFORMATION PROCESSING

One technique was **chronometric analysis.** Chronometric analyses are based on the simple premise that thinking takes time. Although that premise is simple, it is not always accepted. Many people find it hard to believe that it takes more time to add 4 + 3 than 4 + 2 (Groen and Parkman, 1972). Chronometric analyses may include measuring the time it takes for someone to react to a stimulus, measuring the time from the presentation of one stimulus to the quickest possible reaction to a second stimulus, measuring the errors that are made when thinking time is limited, and measuring the time it takes for a person to solve two tasks that differ in one or more ways. In one chronometric analysis, for example, college students were shown pairs of three-dimensional objects, one standing upright, the other rotated (Shepard and Metzler, 1971). As quickly as possible, the students answered whether the objects were the same. The greater the degree of rotation, the longer it took the students to answer. Similar findings have emerged from studies of how quickly children and adults mentally rotate items that they see (Kail, Pellegrino, and Carter, 1980). It takes third- and fourth-graders about $\frac{1}{150}$ of a second per degree to rotate figures mentally, but adults take only $\frac{1}{250}$ of a second per degree.

A second method that was used to study information processing is **protocol analysis.** In protocol analyses, the researcher gives a subject a problem and tells him or her to say out loud everything that comes to mind as he or she solves the problem. The subject's words and unspoken actions are recorded. From this record, the researcher details a graph of the subject's thought processes and writes a flow chart and computer program to describe them. When people describe their thoughts to the researcher at the same time as they are thinking them, these protocols agree with other indications of what is going on in the subject's head. Only when the descriptions are given after the fact, or when they are about very brief thought processes is there a problem with their reliability. But useful protocols are long and complex, and interpreting them is difficult and depends heavily on the skill of the individual investigator.

A more economical and objective method that was used to study information processing is the analysis of eye movements. Analyses of eye movements can tell where the eye focuses and for how long, and the assumption is that the mind's focus follows that of the eye. In one study, 4- to 8-year-olds were shown pairs of houses, each with six

In the information processing model, reading is less a series of smooth glides of the eyes than a series of bursts and pauses for clarification and interpretation.

FIGURE 9.2
A sample of the stimuli used in research by Eliane Vurpillot: a pair of different houses and a pair of identical houses (Vurpillot, 1968).

windows, and were asked whether and how the houses were different (Vurpillot, 1968) (see Figure 9.2). The most efficient way to solve the problem is systematically to compare pairs of corresponding windows on the two houses from one row to the next. Recordings of eye movements showed that older children used this strategy and scanned more efficiently and thoroughly than younger children.

In another experiment, Marcel Just and Patricia Carpenter (1980) studied people's eye movements while they were reading. They found that the eye remains on connectives like "and" or "but" only one-sixth as long as it remains on words with content, especially those that are unfamiliar. The assumption is that these words take longer to process. A person looks at the word "automobile" for less time than the word "Ferrari" (unless he or she owns a Ferrari) and, presumably, because he or she looks longer, takes longer to process the phrase "myriad attenuated ontological concerns" than "many worries about final causes." Words that occur in central clauses are looked at longer than are words in peripheral clauses, which expand or embellish the main point. People also fix their eyes longer at the ends of sentences, as they integrate information and make sense out of the sentence they have just read. Grammatical errors or ambiguities can stop the reader's eyes dead in their tracks; it takes quite a while to figure out such gems as, "The hand of God stepped in" or "Are there more square blocks that are not red than there are

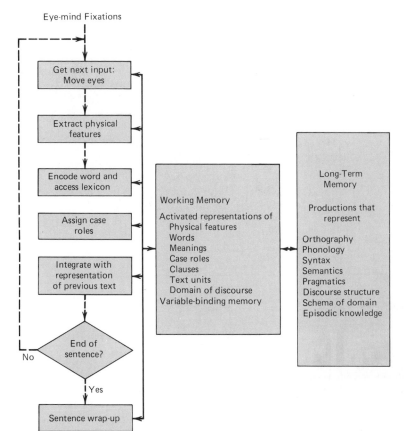

Eye-mind Fixations

Get next input:
Move eyes

Extract physical
features

Encode word and
access lexicon

Assign case
roles

Integrate with
representation
of previous text

End of
sentence?

No

Yes

Sentence wrap-up

Working Memory

Activated representations of
Physical features
Words
Meanings
Case roles
Clauses
Text units
Domain of discourse
Variable-binding memory

Long-Term
Memory

Productions that
represent

Orthography
Phonology
Syntax
Semantics
Pragmatics
Discourse structure
Schema of domain
Episodic knowledge

FIGURE 9.3
Just and Carpenter's (1980) model of reading.

red blocks that are not square?'' Just and Carpenter's study clearly demonstrated that reading is less a smooth glide than a series of stops and starts for clarification and interpretation. Findings from the research were put together by Just and Carpenter into the information-processing model pictured in Figure 9.3.

Finally, much as Sherlock Holmes hunted down criminals by analyzing their cigarette ashes, psychologists have tried to understand how people process information by analyzing the errors that they make. One example of error analysis focuses on the rules children use to solve problems. Robert Siegler (1976) showed children a balance with four pegs on each side of the fulcrum. By putting metal weights on the pegs, the children could tilt the balance to one side or the other. The children were asked to predict which side of the balance would go down when they put on the weights. By analyzing the patterns of the children's predictive errors, Siegler discovered that children typically used

one of four rules to solve the problem (see Figure 9.4). The first rule took into account only the number of weights on each side of the fulcrum. If one side had more weights, the children using this rule predicted that it would go down; if the weights were equally distributed on the two sides, they predicted that the scale would not go down. The second rule took weight into account if the sides were unequal; if the weights were equal, it took into account how far the weights were from the fulcrum. The third rule took into account distance from the fulcrum as well as weight, and children using it could predict correctly when one or both distance and weight were equal; if they were unequal, however, the children were at a loss to solve the problem. The fourth rule was the correct one, that the way to predict whether the balance would tip was to calculate the product of weight times distance. Children using this rule always made the correct prediction.

With all of these methods, psychologists in the

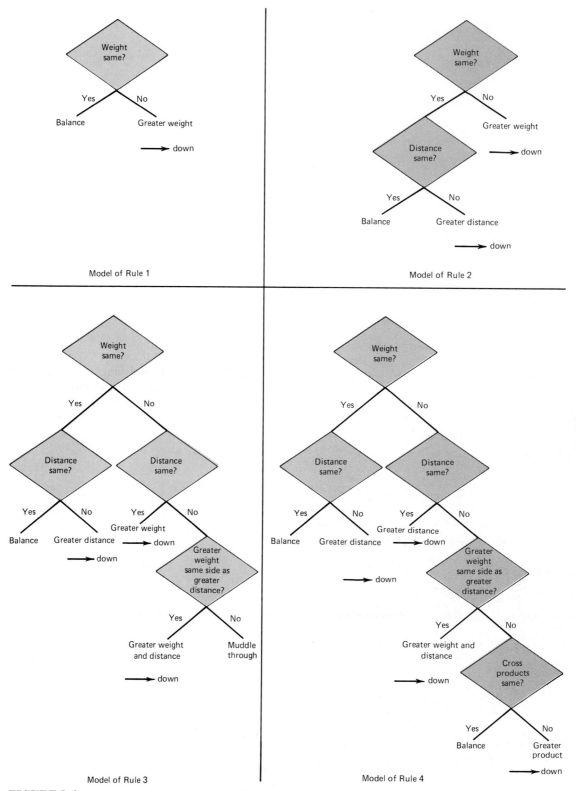

FIGURE 9.4
Models of rules for performing the balance-scale task (Siegler, 1983).

last decade have gained substantial knowledge of the information-processing system. Some of this knowledge is discussed in the following sections.

BASIC CAPACITIES

Attention, perception, and memory are three basic human capacities. They are present from birth and form part of every act of information processing throughout life.

Attention

The first step in processing information is to attend to the environment, exploring its features, focusing on some object or action out of the incalculably vast array available, and thereby bringing it into the information-processing system. Very young infants can attend to the environment for only short periods. Most of their time is spent drowsing, sleeping, or feeding. As they mature, their periods of attentiveness lengthen. Toddlers have shorter attention spans than older children, and they are

As children get older, they focus their attention more intently and can shut out competing stimuli.

easily distracted, whether they are watching a television program, playing, or performing a task for an experimenter. But the preschooler who moves quickly from one activity to another eventually becomes the school-age child who can sit for long periods working or listening to others. These older children are far better at shifting their attention, too, as when someone yells "Look over here" or "Hey, get the ball." Adults can attend so intensely and can shut out all competing stimuli so effectively that they are nearly impervious to interruption. One Chicago surgeon was so intent on his work that when part of the operating room ceiling caved in, he did not even notice (Csikszentmihalyi, 1976).

Exploration. From birth, infants begin to explore actively with eyes and ears, touch, smell, and taste. This exploration is an essential part of the attention process. The ability to explore one's surroundings improves with brain maturation and with practice. It grows more swift, economical, systematic, and focused in direction, but from the beginning, it is purposeful and directed. As we saw in Chapter 5, newborns do not scan randomly: they scan the edges of objects or single features, often the most informative parts of objects, such as the vertex or sides of a triangle. Later, they scan the internal features of stimuli, like the eyes in a face. Young children scan stimuli extensively but are not as systematic in their visual exploration as older children. We mentioned one study of developmental changes in visual exploration when we were describing the use of eye movement recordings in information-processing research (Vurpillot, 1968; see p. 354). As the experiment with six-windowed housefronts showed, 5-year-old children did not scan systematically or exhaustively. They did not compare the two housefronts window by window; they did not start at one corner and work their way to the other; they did not even look at every window on the house. Older children (8 to 9 years old) did follow these scanning strategies, and when they had found a difference between two windows, they efficiently stopped scanning. In another study, all ages of children were found to scan patterns in a downward direction, but older children scanned from the top of the pattern, whereas 5-year-olds and younger children scanned from the point in the pattern that first caught their interest (Day, 1975). In a third study of developmental changes in visual exploring (Elkind, 1977), children were asked to name the pictures they saw pasted onto a card—hat, parrot, chair, and the like. Five-year-olds left out some pictures and named others twice as they jumped from one picture to another. Eight-year-olds imposed an order on the pictures, naming them systematically from left to right and top to bottom and made no errors. When the pictures were pasted in a triangular pattern, however, the 5- and 8-year-olds were equally accurate.

Vision is not the only sense used to explore the environment. Infants explore by mouthing for their first year of life, and even at the age of 8 or 9 months prefer mouthing to exploring with their hands. At about 1 year of age, they begin to explore more with their hands, banging and squeezing things (Gibson and Walker, 1982). Developmental changes occur in scanning by touch as well as in visual scanning. This coincidence suggests that central processes direct all of the sensory registers.

Selectivity. A second aspect of the attention process is being selective about which part of a stimulus to focus on. Virtually from birth, infants are selective in what they pay attention to. We discussed their preferences among visual stimuli in Chapter 5. These early visual preferences, we saw, are largely determined by cortical and visual capacities rather than by the properties of the stimuli. Beginning at the age of 3 or 4 months and thereafter, however, the properties of the stimuli affect children's attention. Some children attend to color more than size; others attend to shape more than color (Odom, 1978). A child may attend first to color, then to shape, then to size, and so on. But whatever the differences among individual children, all children grow increasingly selective as they get older. This has been demonstrated in a study by John Wright and Alice Vlietstra (1975). Nursery school children shown a model of a house with several covered windows on it took far longer than older children to find an object hidden behind one of the window screens because they did not attend to clues, like the size of the window. They simply opened and shut all the windows—and went on doing so even after they had found the hidden object!

Because young children are so easily distracted, have short attention spans, and limited selectivity, it is a challenge to study their attention. The challenge is illustrated in the results of one investigation of young children's attention (Zinchenko, Chzhi-Tsin, and Tarakanov, 1977). Children were shown an irregularly shaped object, and their eye movements were recorded. Later, they were asked to pick out a shape that matched the one they had seen. Six-year-olds attended to the entire outline of the stimulus object and later could match it quite well. But younger children attended to the center of the object—where they could see the camera recording their eye movements—and later could not match the shape very well. Their inadequate performance may reflect less mature selective attention, but it may just as well reflect limited understanding of the task or willingness to perform it.

Researchers have relied on children's television programs to get around the problems of enlisting young children's cooperation in research on selective attention. In studies using this method, 2-year-olds watching television with their mothers have been found to be more easily distracted, to talk more to other people, to play more with toys, and to look around the room more than 4-year-olds (Anderson and Levin, 1976). Both 2- and 4-year-olds' attention has been observed to be drawn to the television by women's, children's, and odd-sounding voices; by laughter and applause; by changes in sound; and by sound effects (Anderson, 1979). Young children, it seems, attend most to what they understand best.

As they get older, children get increasingly skilled at knowing which stimuli should be attended to (Gibson and Rader, 1979). They get better at focusing their attention at will. They get better at responding to others' requests that they compare two objects, attend to one event but not another, or find one object within a clutter. In one series of studies to demonstrate this improvement with age (Pick, Christy, and Frankel, 1972; Pick and Frankel, 1974), second- and sixth-graders were asked to compare pairs of wooden animals that differed in shape, color, and size. Sixth-graders were more effectively guided by suggestions from the experimenter about which aspects they would be expected to compare, and they were more flexible in varying their strategies from one trial to another. In another study, John Hagen and Gordon Hale (1973) told 7- to 13-year-olds that they would see some cards, each containing a picture of a common household object and an animal, and that they

CHILDREN'S TELEVISION VIEWING

Watching television requires that viewers both watch and listen and that they coordinate the information from both senses. Kathy Pezdek and Eileen Hartman (1983) studied how children process visual and aural information as they watch television and play with toys or listen to a record at the same time. Anecdotal evidence suggests that even very young children can monitor the TV sound track while they play with toys—swiveling their heads and attention back to the screen when lively music, a change in voice, sound effects, and other sounds signal important content. The researchers wanted to probe this complex processing feat in young children more systematically.

They first presented 5-year-olds with a 20 minute episode of "Sesame Street" in which they heard the sound track only, saw the visual track only, or heard and saw both tracks. An auditory segment might be two puppets talking to each other, a visual segment might be a nonverbal demonstration of how to grow beans, and an audiovisual segment might be a conversation about and demonstration of fixing a radio. Right after the children had watched the program, their comprehension was tested. Not surprisingly, for auditory segments, children who had heard only the sound track understood more than those who had seen only the video track; they also understood as well as the children who had seen and heard the audio and visual tracks. For visual segments, children who had seen but not heard the episode understood more than those who had only heard it and understood as well as the children who had both seen and heard the episode. For mixed segments, children who had both seen and heard the episode understood most.

With these results before them, the researchers showed the "Sesame Street" episode to another group of 5-year-olds. Some of the children had toys available to play with, for visual distraction. For some children, a record of *Peter and the Wolf* played slightly more softly than the television in the background, for auditory distraction. Other children had neither toys nor record. The children were allowed to play with the toys or listen to the record, if either was present, or to watch television "just as they would if they were in their own home." Observers noted when the children watched television and when they did something else.

All of the children watched the visual and mixed segments more than they watched the auditory segments. But the children who had toys available watched the television less than the other children did. These children understood the auditory material as well as the undistracted children, but they understood less about the visual content. Children who had heard the record playing in the background understood less about the television program's auditory segments, but they did fine with the visual segments.

This study demonstrates that even young children modify their visual and auditory attention appropriately and learn quickly to attend selectively to stimuli in the environment. The tape segments in this study were each only a few minutes long, and yet 5-year-olds were able to evaluate quickly their mode of presentation and spontaneously adjust their visual attention. Even when they were not looking at the screen, they processed the auditory information. Only when an auditory recording interfered with this process did they miss information.

Children can do two things at once—for example, watch television and do their homework—by deploying their attention efficiently.

would be asked to remember the location of some of them. After a child saw the cards, the cards were placed face down and the experimenter showed the child a cue card with a picture of one of the objects or animals on it. The child then pointed to the face-down card depicting the same object or animal as the cue card. Later, the child was asked which objects and animals had been on the same cards. The 12- and 13-year-olds did not do as well as the younger children on this incidental learning task, because the older children had focused their attention on only the relevant part of the pictures.

With age, children also grew better at listening to one voice or message and ignoring another. Selective listening has been demonstrated in many studies in which children are instructed to attend to and report about one of two tape-recorded messages. In one of the earliest of these, Eleanor Maccoby (1967) found that children as young as 5 could pay attention to one voice when two short messages were presented to different ears, but older children were better at ignoring one message. In more recent experiments, children between 7 and 11 were told that they would hear two words at once and should press a key if they heard a target word (Geffen and Sexton, 1978; Sexton and Geffen, 1979). The pairs of words were played to different ears or spoken by different voices. The older the children, the better their "hit rate" at perceiving the target words, and the fewer intruding stimuli they attended to.

Perception

Another basic capacity involved in processing information is **perception.** Perception is the obtaining of information about the world through the senses. It is an active process. We do not just passively hear or see; we deliberately listen and look. The pupils of our eyes open and close, our eyes move and focus, our heads and bodies shift. And we integrate the stimuli that activate our various senses so that we do not perceive separate visual, auditory, and tactile worlds.

According to one important theory of perception—that of James and Eleanor Gibson (see Gibson and Spelke, 1983)—we perceive events, objects, and places by seeking out and detecting invariants in what we see and hear. Our ability to perceive these invariants, research suggests, im-

proves with physical maturation and with practice. Only with experience, for instance, do we perceive the boundaries between objects and their surroundings, a perception that adults take for granted. Infants do not know where one object ends and another begins or where one object ends and its background begins. They come to perceive an object when they see connected surfaces that remain connected while in motion (Spelke, 1982), and they perceive the difference between object and background as the object moves and the texture of the background is added to and subtracted from along the moving object's edges. By perceiving the invariants in these connected movements— of a caterpillar crawling along a leaf, a ball rolling along a sidewalk, or Mother entering the room— children perceive caterpillar, ball, and Mother as objects.

Maturation and experience also affect our perception of the properties of objects, properties like flexibility, texture, and shape. When do infants be-

This toddler is manipulating objects of different shapes and textures. Maturation and experience affect people's perception of objects' properties. Visual perception of shapes develops throughout childhood and grows increasingly differentiated.

gin to perceive rigidity or flexibility, strength, elasticity, fuzziness, rubberiness, furriness, woodenness? How does their perception change as they get older? Even at 1 month, infants appear to differentiate between rigid and flexible substances in their mouths, like teething rings and nipples, for example (Gibson and Walker, 1982). As early as 3½ months, infants can see the difference between rigid and flexible motion—between a ball being rolled and a ball being squeezed, for instance (Gibson, Owsley, and Johnston, 1978; Gibson, Owsley, Walker, and Megaw-Nyce, 1979). At 6 months, they can feel the difference between rough and smooth textures (Steel and Pederson, 1977) and will continue to respond to an object's texture even if it changes color (Ruff, 1980). One-year-olds distinguish between rigid and elastic substances by handling them differently. They bang the hard objects and squeeze, press, and wipe the spongy ones (Gibson and Walker, 1982). Very young infants also can see the difference between flat and solid objects (Cook, Field, and Griffiths, 1978) and between objects of different simple shapes like spheres and cubes (Ruff, 1980). Infants as young as 2 months perceive that the shape of an object remains constant when it is rotated (Bower, 1966; Caron, Caron, and Carlson, 1979). By 10 months of age, children can recognize visually or by touch simple shapes they have manipulated (Gottfried, Rose, and Bridger, 1977; Soroka, Corter, and Abramovitch, 1979). Visual perception of shapes continues to develop throughout childhood. Children come to perceive shapes that are more and more complex and embedded in complex backgrounds and to perceive the subtle relationships among the shapes of solid objects.

In addition to perceiving the properties of flexibility, shape, and texture, people perceive the color, temperature, scent, size, and animacy of the objects around them. In infants and children, the development of the perception of all of these properties follows the same few general principles that are illustrated by the studies we have already described on the perception of objects' flexibility, shape, and texture (Gibson and Spelke, 1983). First, very young infants have rudimentary abilities to perceive the properties of objects. Second, as they get older and develop strategies of exploration and manipulation, children's perception of objects becomes increasingly differentiated. Third, objects are first perceived and best perceived when they participate in events—when they move, fulfill a function, or mean something.

Memory

To an investigator working with an information-processing model, memory consists of the temporary or permanent holding of information within the cognitive system. "Remembering" really refers to several different kinds of mental operations and kinds of storage.

Basic Memory Storage. In the "store" model of memory, information enters the system as a sensory trace in one of the sensory registers. This trace decays within a few seconds or even less. If a line of print were flashed at you very quickly, all the letters that you could visualize for a brief moment after that presentation would form the sensory trace of that stimulus. Once information is recorded in the sensory register and selected by attentional processes, it goes into short-term memory. Here it lasts for some brief period, between a few seconds and a minute. Information in short-term memory is used for working on the tasks at hand. It is used to remember a telephone number from the directory while you dial it, the spelling of a word while you look it up in the dictionary, the number of a theatre seat until you sit down, and a remark by the professor until you write it down. The amount of information short-term memory can hold is limited to a small number of **chunks.** Chunks may contain different amounts of information, but there is a limit to how many chunks can be stored. George Miller (1956) suggested that this number was 7 plus or minus 2. After short-term memory, selected information goes into long-term memory, where it lasts for minutes, weeks, or years. Long-term memories include the name of your first love, the multiplication tables, the chemical symbols for water, and what happened at your graduation prom.

Much evidence consistent with this model of memory stores has been collected. In one important study, Fergus Craik (1970) demonstrated the separation between short- and long-term memory. He first presented college students with 10 lists of 10 words each. After each list, the students were asked to recall its 10 words. When all 10 lists had been gone through, Craik unexpectedly asked the students to recall all 100 words. The task had changed: instead of using short-term memory, the students now had to draw from long-term memory. On the short-term task, the students had been quite successful at remembering words at the beginning of the lists, a phenomenon known as the **primacy effect,** and extremely good at remembering words from the end of each list, the so-called **recency effect.** But on the long-term memory task, the recency effect disappeared. This finding strongly suggested that primacy effects reflect long-term memory processes and that recency effects reflect short-term memory; in so doing, this finding documented the distinction between short-term and long-term memory stores.

Despite such evidence, some investigators have questioned the stores model of memory. For one reason, the measurements of various sensory registers vary elusively from one experiment to another. Thus one researcher (Efron, 1970) found that traces remained in the auditory register for about ⅛ of a second; others (Glucksberg and Cowan, 1970) found that traces remained for 5 seconds. Similar variations have been found for the visual register—from ¼ of a second to 25 seconds. For another thing, estimates of the capacity of the short-term store have ranged from 2 chunks (Glanzer, 1972) to 20 chunks (Hunt and Love, 1972). Finally, estimates of how long information is stored in short-term memory have varied from 15 seconds (Peterson and Peterson, 1959) to far longer.

Information processors have reacted to these discrepancies in several ways. Some investigators have modified the stores model slightly—distinguishing between primary (sensory and short-term) memory and secondary (long-term) memory or between a sensory store and the rest of memory, for instance. Others have moved away from the stores model in favor of models that involve the depth of processing (Craik and Lockhart, 1972) or the specificity of encoding (Thomson and Tulving, 1970)—models that emphasize the way in which information is processed and the intended purpose of processing rather than the limits imposed by fixed stores. All in all, however, the stores model remains dominant among researchers, for it is straightforward, makes useful distinctions about memory phenomena, and has yet to be replaced by a better model (Siegler, 1983).

Two Forms of Memory. The toddler smiles as her mother's face comes into view and she recognizes the familiar image. This kind of memory, **recognition,** takes place in the presence of the remembered object or person. Later that day as she works in her office, the toddler's mother steals a moment to recall that lovely smile of recognition. **Recall** is memory that takes place when the remembered object or person is not present.

Recognition. Recognizing an object or an image that one has seen before is the simplest kind of remembering. Without the ability to recognize, every object and every experience would seem new, and there would be no cognition as we know it. In recognition, information about an object is retrieved in the object's presence: the baby recognizes Grandpa or a stuffed bear by matching the sensory trace with an image in its long-term memory (Perlmutter and Lange, 1978). Although it seems simple, recognition has several parts: the initial sensory encoding and then the retention of

The simplest kind of remembering is recognizing an object or an image that one has seen before.

the encoded information (Anderson and Bower, 1974; Cohen and Gelber, 1975).

The capacity to recognize appears early. Even newborn premature infants can recognize a simple stimulus as one they have just seen and so habituate to it (Werner and Siqueland, 1978). Two-month-old infants can recognize a stimulus they saw the day before (Martin, 1975). With development, infants grow more accurate at recognition, because they require less time to register visual images and because they can scan stimuli more thoroughly, and so they are able to encode more and more complex images. Individual infants as well as infants of different ages vary in how efficiently and well they encode visual information, although once they have encoded the information, individual differences do not seem to influence how long it is retained (Werner and Perlmutter, 1980).

Children old enough to talk can tell an experimenter whether they recognize objects they have seen before. In one study of recognition memory, Nancy Myers and Marion Perlmutter (1978) showed 2- and 4-year-olds 18 small, attractive objects. Later, they showed them 36 objects, the original 18 plus another 18. The 2-year-olds recognized 81 percent of the original objects; the 4-year-olds recognized 92 percent. Both groups were extremely accurate at realizing which objects they had never seen. Thus with age, there was some improvement in recognition, but even the 2-year-olds were amazingly accurate. Recognition among school-age children is close to perfect for simple objects but less accurate for complex objects that require more extensive encoding (Perlmutter, 1980). School-age children are a match for adults in recognizing labeled, realistic pictures (e.g., "a woman with a long neck"), but adults excel at recognizing abstract forms (e.g., "black and brown stripes") (Nelson and Kosslyn, 1976). Again, this suggests that with age, recognition skill improves in the process of encoding rather than in retention.

Recall. Recall is a more difficult process than recognition, because information must be retrieved from memory with no prompts from the environment. There is no object present to trigger the memory. How well people recall information depends, for one thing, on how much practice they have had in doing so. Unlike recognition memory, which is similar in all cultures (Cole and Scribner, 1977), recall varies widely from one culture to an-

other. In our society, we rely heavily on written material to help us remember: the student takes notes in class and reads textbooks; the actor learns written lines and may use cue cards; and children are not expected to memorize much more than their ABCs. But in societies with a strong oral tradition, people develop their powers of recall to great heights. The poet Homer, for example, sang the entire *Iliad* and *Odyssey* from memory—a staggering feat of recall. In our society, it is the unusual individual who can recite a simple sonnet, unless he or she is preparing for an exam in English literature. Now that computers are growing so popular, we will rely less and less on recall for phone numbers, multiplication tables, and mathematical formulas, although we will still call on memory for past experiences and events.

Even infants, it seems, can do the latter. Asked by her father to find her doll, an 11-month-old left the room she was in, found her doll, returned to the room, and began playing with the doll. To do so, she had had to retrieve from memory the mental image of her doll at her father's mention of the word "doll" and recall where she had left it and how to get there and back—no mean feat. When Daniel Ashmead and Marion Perlmutter (1980) asked parents to keep diaries of their infants' recall, they found that infants between 7 and 11 months old could recall games like peekaboo and pattycake, bath and meal routines, and where to find familiar household objects and toys. These are simple and routine events, of course. Recall memory in infants and young children is not nearly as accurate, consistent, or extensive as recognition memory. By the age of 3 or 4, however, children's recall organizes itself into conceptual categories. Perlmutter and Myers (1979) showed preschool children nine small objects one at a time from nine different conceptual categories, such as animals, utensils, vehicles, and the like, labeled them, and put them in a box. Even though they were told that they could keep the objects they remembered, the 3-year-olds remembered only about two objects, the 4-year-olds three or four objects. Most of the children recalled the last object they had seen. When the nine objects were from just three categories, the children remembered more of them. When the experimenter prompted the children with a clue—"Do you remember any other animals?"— they recalled even more. Perlmutter (1980) suggests that preschoolers recall poorly because they lack the language necessary for processing information, strategies for remembering, and because they tend to retrieve information inefficiently. Out of the laboratory and in familiar surroundings, preschoolers can recall better. They recall social interactions and cartoon characters (though only rarely objects—the usual target of laboratory research), and their recall extends back for several months (Todd and Perlmutter, 1980). By school age, recall improves further as children learn strategies for remembering.

Factors that Influence Memory.

What kind of information is remembered best? Developmental psychologists know that the mode in which information is presented—written words, spoken words, or pictures—affects how well it is remembered. Many studies support the adage that a picture is worth a thousand words. In one recent study (Dempster and Rohwer, 1983), pictures were recalled better than spoken words, and spoken words were recalled better than printed words by third-, sixth-, and ninth-graders (see Figure 9.5). Children were presented with 21-item lists of printed words, spoken words, and pictures and

asked to recall as many of the items as they could immediately after each list had been presented. They were given 2 minutes to recall the items. Pictures improved recall, especially for items in the middle of lists. In another study of the effects of the mode in which information is presented, Zolinda Stoneman and Gene Brody (1983) tested 3- to 5-year-olds for the immediate and long-term recognition of material that was presented orally, visually, or both. They found that children recognized advertised products better when they had seen or had seen and heard rather than when they had just heard the advertisements. In a somewhat similar study, Donald Hayes and Dana Birnbaum (1980) showed cartoons to adults and to preschoolers and later asked them questions about what they had seen and heard. Information in the cartoons was presented visually, orally, both visually and orally, or orally but on a sound track that was not matched with the visual image. The children recognized what they had seen far more accurately than what they had heard; the adults recognized both equally well. Few of the preschoolers had even realized when the sound track was inappropriate. Apparently, they had simply ignored it. A subsequent study of 5-year-olds' memory of the images and sound from

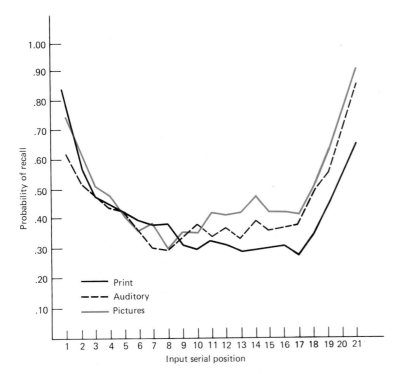

FIGURE 9.5
The probability of immediate recall is related to the item's serial position and mode of presentation (Dempster and Rohwer, 1983).

a "Sesame Street" episode also suggested that visual images are more salient and memorable than sounds (Pezdek and Stevens, 1984).

Not only the kind of information, but a person's feelings and motives affect what he or she will remember. In a study of 5-year-olds, for example, children heard 18 key words worked into either three happy stories or three unhappy stories (Bartlett and Santrock, 1979). To reinforce the mood of the stories, each was appropriately illustrated by drawings, and after the story was read to the child by an experimenter who acted either happy or sad, the child was asked to point to a happy or sad face to indicate how the story made him or her feel. Immediately after the three stories had been read, the first experimenter left the room, and a second experimenter came in. This person acted either happy or sad, showed the child six happy or sad pictures, and then asked the child to recall the stories he or she had heard from the first experimenter. Recall of the 18 key words was greatest when the children were in the same mood as they had been when they heard the stories. Emotions clearly affected recall.

In a study of how motives affect memory, Michael Moore, Jerome Kagan, and Marshall Haith (1978) first asked teachers to rate 8-year-olds on the following motives: dominance, affiliation, hostility to their peers, and academic mastery. The students who were rated highest and lowest acted as subjects. They were asked to listen to 20 sentences and, on the next day, to choose from pairs of sentences those that they had heard the day before. Unbeknownst to the children, none of the sentence pairs had actually appeared the day before but had been constructed to reflect the motives on which the students originally had been rated. One sentence in each pair reflected a strong motive in the student, and the other reflected a weak motive. For example, hostility to peers was reflected in the sentence, "The child was mad at his friend for not sharing his Coca-Cola," and dominance was reflected in, "The child could drink Coca-Cola faster than anyone." Asked whether they had seen either of these sentences, in 70 percent of the cases the children claimed to remember those that reflected their own strong motive, a finding that suggests that motives do affect memory.

How meaningful information is also affects people's ability to remember it. Some information-processing theorists (Craik and Lockhart, 1972) think that information processing occurs at different levels, from a shallow perceptual level, to deeper and more meaningful levels. Information that receives scant and superficial analysis is soon forgotten; information processed at deeper levels is remembered better and longer. Development seems to improve children's abilities to process information at the deepest levels (Naus, Ornstein, and Hoving, 1978). In one recent study to explore how this aspect of children's memories develops, Elizabeth Ghatala (1984) tested second- and sixth-graders' recall of words under two conditions. In one condition, children were asked to give rhymes for the words; in the other condition, they were asked to define the words. The words they were given were either very meaningful or not very meaningful (judging by how many associated words children of the same age could generate.) Recall was greatest for meaningful words that were defined by the children. Older children did better than younger, because more words were meaningful for them. In brief, mode, mood, motives, and meaning can all affect the remembrance of information.

COGNITIVE STRATEGIES

"Thirty days hath September, April, June, and November. . . ." "Red sky at morning; sailors take warning. Red sky at night; sailors' delight." Those two chestnuts are mnemonic devices, tricks to help people remember information. Such strategies can help people to enter information into their memories or to get it out again. The most common strategies that people use to enter (encode) information are **rehearsal, organization, imagery, elaboration,** and studying. Retrieval strategies include **visualization, persevering,** drawing inferences, and using external cues.

Rehearsal

Rehearsal is simply repeating information until it is fixed in memory. Just like an actor rehearsing lines in a play, someone might rehearse a telephone number, a list of irregular verbs, or the laws of physical motion. It has been thought that children younger than 5 do not rehearse information (Perlmutter and Myers, 1979). But even preschoolers, as long as they understand the goal of an activity and are not distracted by unfamiliar surroundings, have been shown to plan—if not strictly to rehearse—how to remember material (Meacham, 1972; Wellman, 1977a). A Soviet psychologist, Z. M. Istomina (1975), found that when children were asked to remember a short shopping list, they remembered many of the items because the task itself made sense to them. Even 5-year-olds made attempts at rehearsal, but the attempts children made grew more deliberate and effective with age.

Alik (4 years, 3 months) listened to the instructions to the end, nodding his head after each word, and saying, "Uhuh." He recalled correctly two items on the list and when asked, "What else do you have to buy?" he answered calmly: "Nothing else; we have everything."

Serezha (5 years, 4 months) listened attentively to the list and repeated each of the experimenter's words in a whisper. He recalled four items, but could not recall the fifth. He looked confusedly at the experimenter and repeated the same words one more time. "There's something else I have to buy, but I've forgotten it."

Dima (6 years, 6 months) listened to the list, muttering silently, and then repeated it almost as if to himself. He quickly recalled three items, then paused, screwed up his eyes, and said, with concern: "Oh! What else was there? Nope, I can't remember what else I have to buy" (Istomina, 1975, pp. 24–26).

When young children do rehearse information, they do so differently from older children. Pre-schoolers try to remember information by pointing to it, staring at it, or naming it. In a study by Henry Wellman, Kenneth Ritter, and John Flavell (1975), 2- and 3-year-olds were shown a toy dog hidden under a container and asked either to wait with the dog or to remember where it was hidden while the experimenter left the room for a moment. The results were charming. The 2-year-olds refused to wait; they marched out of the room. But the 3-year-olds stared at the container, or stared at the container and nodded "yes" and looked at the other containers and nodded "no," or rested their hand on the correct container. At about the age of 5, children begin naming the objects to remember. Third-graders in rehearsing a list repeat a single word many times in rote fashion; older children refine their rehearsal strategies, rehearsing the whole list systematically (Ornstein, Naus, and Liberty, 1975) (see Table 9.1). They also spend more time rehearsing and testing themselves than younger children do (Hagen and Stanovich, 1977). By high school age, systematic, complex rehearsal plans typically appear (Ornstein and Naus, 1978). By college age, students spontaneously rehearse according to the particular demands of a given task (Butterfield and Belmont, 1977).

Five-year-olds can be trained to rehearse, and rehearsal improves their recall, but they rarely do so spontaneously. In one series of studies (Flavell, Beach, and Chinsky, 1966; Keeney, Canizzo, and Flavell, 1967), when 5- and 10-year-olds were asked to memorize objects, few of the 5-year-olds rehearsed spontaneously—assessed by their lip movements while their eyes were hidden by a

TABLE 9.1
LIST TO REMEMBER: YARD, CAT, MAN, DESK

Word presented	Third-grader's rehearsal	Eighth-grader's rehearsal
Yard	yard, yard, yard, yard	yard, yard, yard
Cat	cat, cat, cat, yard	cat, yard, yard, cat
Man	man, man, man, man	man, cat, yard, man, yard, cat
Desk	desk, desk, desk, desk	desk, man, yard, cat, man, desk, cat, yard

Source: Ornstein, Naus, and Liberty, 1975.

space helmet! Nearly all of the 10-year-olds did; for them and for the few 5-year-olds who moved their lips, recall was greater. When the 5-year-olds were instructed by the experimenter to whisper the names of the objects they were to remember, their recall improved. But when the children were later given another memorization task, the 5-year-olds again did not rehearse the items, and their recall declined. Training can be very effective; it can make young children perform as well as older children and, conversely, if older children are prevented from rehearsing, their memories are as spotty as those of young nonrehearsers. But these effects are not permanent. Rehearsal is clearly one aspect of cognitive processing that needs time, and rehearsal, to develop. Children must develop some knowledge of how their memories work before they can make full use of their abilities.

Organization

Another way people can increase their recall is by grouping items into classes, clusters, or chunks. Ordinarily, people can store only about seven chunks of information—precisely the number of digits in a local telephone number. But by increasing the number of items in each chunk, people can remember longer strings of digits. For long distance numbers, for example, one chunk is for access to long distance (1-), one chunk is for the area code (-714-), one chunk is for the local exchange (-555-), and then the other four digits are four separate chunks (-1-2-1-2), for a total of 7. A few chunks can also make grocery shopping easier: remembering the chunk ''desserts'' can shake loose the items chocolate cookies, peaches and pears, and ice cream.

Even 2-year-olds remember related items more quickly than those that are unrelated; big and tall is easier to recall than big and sad, say (Goldberg, Perlmutter, and Myers, 1974). But their categories often shift. The ability to organize items according to concepts improves with age. Young children may organize words by rhyming or by similar sounds— ''big'' and ''pig,'' ''bat'' and ''pat,'' whereas older children and adults more consistently organize words by their meanings (Bach and Underwood, 1970; Hasher and Clifton, 1974). Younger children also organize more according to things that go together (bat and ball); older children organize more according to things that belong to the same class (bat and racquet) (Flavell, 1970). It is difficult, though, to be sure that this change is a developmental one. Sandra Smiley and Ann Brown (1979) asked kindergartners, grade-school children, college students, and elderly adults to say which two pictures out of three were alike. Subjects could pair the pictures either thematically (things that go together, like horse with saddle or needle with thread) or taxonomically (things that belong to the same class, like horse with cow or needle with pin). Younger subjects paired the pictures thematically; older ones, taxonomically. But when the subjects were asked for an alternative choice, and to justify it, they did so easily. The subjects had chosen according to personal preference, not ability, a preference that affected both their rate of learning and recall (Overcast, Murphy, Smiley, and Brown, 1975; Smiley and Brown, 1979).

Imagery

Young children of 4 or 5 can be trained to use organizational strategies, as they can be trained to rehearse, but the effects are weaker and less durable than the effects of training in older children (Moely, Olson, Halwes, and Flavell, 1969; Williams and Goulet, 1975). Imagery is the strategy of visually associating items to be remembered. Imagery can help people to remember names, for example: a sand-covered cat for ''Sandra Katz.'' Children who do not discover this mnemonic technique on their own can be trained to use it. Joel Levin (1980) has used imagery to help fourth- and fifth-graders learn the 50 capital cities of the United States. After providing the students with concrete ''keywords'' for each place name: ''apple'' for ''Annapolis,'' ''marry'' for ''Maryland,'' and showing them illustrations in which the keywords for each state and its capital were combined pictorially (e.g., a judge ''marrying'' two apples), the experimenter found that the children could recall the names of the states and capitals better than a group of children who had been allowed to study the names on their own. Watching educational television programs like ''Sesame Street,'' in which words and numbers often are taught through images, may improve children's ability to use this cognitive strategy (Reese, 1977).

Why does imagery strengthen recall? Perhaps it underscores associations between items to be remembered. Perhaps it provides two forms—words and pictures—in which information can be recalled. Perhaps it subjects the information to deeper and thus better remembered levels of cognitive processing. Perhaps it does all of these things.

Elaboration

When people link together two or more unrelated items in order to remember them, they are using a strategy called elaboration. Elaboration is at work in the mnemonic, "In fourteen hundred ninety-two, Columbus sailed the ocean blue." Children recall better when their elaborative sentences are active— "The lady flew on a broom"—rather than static— "The lady had a broom" (Buckhalt, Mahoney, and Paris, 1976). Older children elaborate more than younger children do (Paris and Lindauer, 1976), use more active elaborations, and remember better when they generate the elaborations than when an experimenter does (Reese, 1977). Younger children benefit more from an experimenter's elaborations, perhaps because the adult's are of better quality (Turnure, Buium, and Thurlow, 1976).

Studying

As they get older, children spend more time studying, and this, too, improves their recall. They also learn strategies for studying. They do more note-taking, underlining, outlining, using of study aids (Brown, Bransford, Ferrara, and Campione, 1983). Study strategies, like other cognitive strategies, change quantitatively and qualitatively over the course of development. In a study of 7- and 9-year-olds and adults, the youngest children spent the least time focusing on the items they had forgotten during a test; only the adults studied items they had missed (Masur, McIntyre, and Flavell, 1973). Similarly, when 4-, 6- and 8-year-olds were told that they would be asked to recall 40 pictures in either a few minutes, a day, or a week, only the 8-year-olds studied longer when they expected a long delay (Rogoff, Newcombe, and Kagan, 1974). Eleven-year-olds but not 5-year-olds used different memory strategies when they thought they would be asked to recall rather than recognize objects (Horowitz and Horowitz, 1975).

Students must use strategies to attend to the

RESEARCH FOCUS

USING STORIES TO REMEMBER INFORMATION

When adults hear a scrambled or incomplete version of a story, they know enough about how stories are structured to be able to retell the story in good, sensible order. Very young children do not know enough about narrative structure to set right a scrambled story. At what point do children begin to apply the principles of a "good" story that allow them to order a story, and can young children be trained to apply these principles? These two questions were the focus of an investigation by Ray Buss, Steven Yussen, Samuel Mathews, Gloria Miller, and Karen Rembold (1983).

Students from second and sixth grade and from college heard a tape of a story about a fish named Albert. Some got a straightforward version of the story, and others got one of two scrambled versions of the story. In the scrambled versions, sentences that logically followed one another were rearranged. Some of the subjects were then told to

recall the stories as they had seen or heard them, and others were told to rearrange the stories so that they made sense. In general, as the researchers had predicted, subjects recalled less of the scrambled stories than of the straightforward stories. Even after they had been told to make "good stories," the younger two groups did not recall the stories any better. The college students did; they apparently benefited from imposing a logical order on their scrambled stories.

In a second part of the study, the researchers had some of the younger children listen to scrambled stories and then gave them training in how to order sentences into a proper story sequence (first the name of the character, then what made the story begin, then what the character did after the story began, and, finally, how the story ended) and then retell the stories in the right order. The instruction proved very effective, for the children could accurately retrieve and reorder information according to a typical story form. Thus story form is one useful retrieval strategy that older children and adults use spontaneously and that younger children can be taught.

Studying improves recall. By high school age, individuals can take notes and use other sophisticated cognitive strategies to learn and remember important material.

most important material if they are to understand it and perform well on tests. Grade-school children typically have trouble picking out the centrally important material in a lesson, and so their studying is less effective than that of high school students. With age, grade-school children improve in their abilities to predict and identify what is important (Brown and Smiley, 1977). The major strategies they use for focusing their attention are to delete trivia and repetitions, to substitute superordinate terms for subordinate examples or episodes, and to use topic sentences. Even fifth-graders can use the simplest of these strategies—deletion, for example—but only older students can accurately identify topic sentences (Brown and Day, in press).

Retrieval Strategies

People also use various strategies for retrieving information that is already stored in memory. One strategy is *visualization*. If a pair of glasses has been misplaced, it sometimes helps to retrace one's steps mentally and to imagine *every* place the glasses might be. Drawing logical *inferences* between events also helps people remember them. If people can go through the logical connections between chunks of information, they often can retrieve a forgotten chunk. *Persevering,* or simply concentrating, on forgotten information can sometimes

bring it to mind. So can going back to trying to remember it after a break. Finally, using external cues can improve recall as well. Thus seeing the string tied around one's finger brings the necessary information to mind: return the library books, call home, or turn off the lights. Young children cannot use external cues very well in remembering. In one study, 25 percent of the 3-year-old children and 75 percent of the 5-year-olds spontaneously turned over pictures lying face down on the floor to remind themselves of toys earlier paired with the pictures (Ritter, Kaprove, Fitch, and Flavell, 1973). But even with coaching, 30 percent of the 3-year-olds could not use the pictures to retrieve information. Using external cues is difficult even for 6-year-olds (Kobasigawa, 1974). When 6-year-olds were allowed to use cue cards to help them recall pictures on cards they had seen earlier, only one-third of the children did so, and inefficiently at that, using the cue card to remember only one out of three possible pictures before taking the next cue card. Eleven-year-olds, in contrast, used the cue cards to remember as many pictures as they could. When the younger children were prompted to recall all three pictures, however, their recall was equal to that of the older group.

METACOGNITION

Metacognition is what people understand and know of their own cognitive processes. It is what they think about thinking, know about knowing, and remember about remembering. One reason young children do not use the cognitive strategies we have just discussed may be that they lack this kind of awareness. In the information-processing model, metacognition is the operation of the central processor or the supervising executive system that intelligently evaluates its own operations (Brown, et al., 1983). "Metacognition" is an umbrella term for various different, but related, cognitive skills: predicting how accurate one's memory will be, controlling one's thought processes, planning and evaluating the efficiency of one's plans, and evaluating the effectiveness of one's attempts to solve problems (Sternberg and Powell, 1983). It is manifested in predicting, checking, monitoring, reality testing, and problem solving (Brown, 1978). Educator John Holt was describing metacognition when he distinguished between good and poor students:

Part of being a good student is learning to be aware of one's own mind and the degree of one's own understanding. The good student may be one who often says that he does not understand, simply because he keeps a constant check on his understanding. The poor student who does not, so to speak, watch himself trying to understand, does not know most of the time whether he understands or not. Thus the problem is not to get students to ask us what they don't know; the problem is to make them aware of the difference between what they know and what they don't (Holt, 1964, pp. 28–29).

Good students, who have some degree of meta-cognitive awareness, read differently when they are reading for detail, for general impressions, for fun, for making up a title, or for finding an item as quickly as possible, but poor students do not adjust for these different goals (Forrest and Waller, 1981; Smith, 1967). Because they often do not monitor their own comprehension, school-age children tend to gloss over ambiguities, inconsistencies, and un-truths in material they hear or read, even when they are told ahead of time that these problems may appear (Garner, in press; Markman, 1979). Younger children, told to listen to taped instructions for building houses out of blocks, appeared puzzled when the tapes gave them inaccurate information, but they were unlikely to reply, when asked, that the instructions had been faulty (Flavell, Speer, Green, and August, 1981).

One domain under the umbrella of metacognition is **metamemory.** Metamemory includes children's sensitivity to which situations call for conscious efforts at memorization and knowledge of which factors affect memory. It includes, for example, knowing that faces are easier to remember than names, that everybody forgets things sometimes, that poorly organized material is more difficult to recall, and that repeating a fact will help in memorization. A number of empirical investigations have been made to find out what children understand of their own memories' limitations. Asked, "Do you forget?" school age children said that they forgot at times; preschool children denied forgetting (Kreutzer, Leonard, and Flavell, 1975). Asked how many of 10 pictures they thought they could remember, school-age children realized that they would not be able to remember all of them, but preschoolers said that they could remember all of

them (Flavell, Friedrichs, and Hoyt, 1970). Pre-schoolers do understand some things about memory. They know that some things about people—their clothing, their physical build—do not affect memory. They know that noise interferes with memory; and they know that it is harder to remember many than a few items (Wellman, 1977b). They know what remembering, forgetting, and learning are. They know that it is hard to remember long-ago events and easier to relearn information than to learn it fresh. They also know that studying for some time makes it easier to remember information (Kreutzer et al., 1975). But beyond knowing these things, preschool children are limited in their meta-memories. Third- and fifth-graders know that time affects memory, that pairs of antonyms are easier to remember than unrelated words, and that they would be likelier to remember a short list studied for a short time than a long list studied for a long time. They also know about ways to improve memory—tying strings around fingers, reading notes, listening to tape recordings, and asking for information from other people (Kreutzer et al., 1975). When Mary Anne Kreutzer and her colleagues (Kreutzer et al., 1975) asked children how they might remember a telephone number, nearly all third- and fifth-graders, but only 40 percent of the kindergartners interviewed, said that they should phone right away. Most of the older children, but only 60 percent of the kindergartners, said that they would write down the number and rehearse it or use some other mnemonic strategy. In another study (Yussen and Levy, 1977), when children between third and ninth grades were quizzed about how they might try to recall a forgotten idea or a lost item, the youngest children gave one or two suggestions and then stopped. But students of junior-high age offered many plausible suggestions.

Just knowing about memory is not the same thing as remembering, however: metamemory does not directly predict a person's performance on a memory task (Siegler, 1983). The accuracy of children's reports about how memory works and their actual memorization often bear only a moderate relation (Brown et al., 1983). Knowing about how to solve problems, another aspect of meta-cognition, may be more closely related to a better performance. Adults who are good at solving problems spend more time identifying their behavior, thinking out loud, stating rules, and judging their efficiency. Adults who explicitly state rules improve their abilities to solve standard laboratory puzzles and story problems (Gagne and Smith, 1962; Gick and Holyoak, 1980). Children who have been told to state out loud a sequence of goals for solving math problems dramatically improve their rate of solutions (Pellegrino and Schadler, 1974).

Some psychologists (e.g., Cavanaugh and Perlmutter, 1982) have commented that the concept of metacognition has not yet contributed much to the understanding of how cognition works. Others have questioned how accurately children can report on their own thinking and how accurate such uncorroborated data can be. Investigations of metacognition have been limited because young children cannot solve a problem and describe their thinking at the same time, and because even older subjects find it difficult when they are asked to predict or imagine what people would do in hypothetical situations. Further research is necessary to specify how thinking about thinking affects thinking itself.

THE KNOWLEDGE BASE

Another component in the information-processing system is the knowledge that a person has accumulated. The obvious fact that what a person knows must influence what he or she can learn or remember has only recently received attention by researchers. Only now are information processors beginning to suggest that age changes once ascribed to the development of cognitive strategies and capacities may actually derive from changes in children's knowledge. One kind of knowledge people acquire is knowledge of familiar routines—eating in a restaurant, having a birthday party, and so on. When Judith Hudson and Katherine Nelson (1983) investigated preschoolers' and first-graders' knowledge of these familiar routines, they found, not surprisingly, that the children could remember more about the most familiar events. Another kind of knowledge is conceptual. A semantic network is a way of representing a person's knowledge of a set of interrelated concepts. The network of a more knowledgeable person is more extensive and complicated than that of a novice. For example, the hacker's semantic network for "computers" is far more complex, dense, and fraught with internal connections than that of either the child just learning to interact with a computer or the adult who

has only read about computers in *Newsweek* (Figure 9.6). A study by Michelene Chi of a 4½-year-old expert on dinosaurs illuminates the importance of the semantic network for learning, thinking, and remembering (Chi and Koeske, 1983). First, the boy was asked to name all the dinosaurs he knew. In seven sessions, he named 46 different kinds of dinosaur, of which the investigators chose 20 as better known (the boy had mentioned them each an average of 4.5 times) and another 20 as less well known (each mentioned only once). The investigators also identified the properties of dinosaurs that the boy could recognize and generate (habitat, locomotion, appearance, size, diet, and so on). On the basis of these data, the investigators drew up semantic networks for the two sets of more and less familiar dinosaurs. The semantic network for the better known dinosaurs was, as expected, more complex, dense, and highly interrelated.

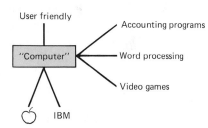

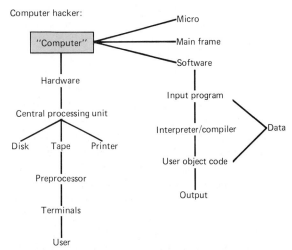

FIGURE 9.6
Two imaginary semantic networks illustrating the difference between a computer hacker's concept of "computer" and that of a casual reader of *Newsweek*.

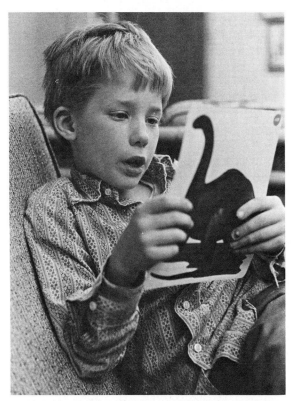

By mapping the semantic network of this 4½-year-old expert on dinosaurs, researchers demonstrated how his knowledge of interrelated concepts influenced his learning, thinking, and remembering.

Later, the investigators read the two lists of dinosaur names to the boy and asked him to recall the names. He recalled 10 from the list of well known dinosaurs and only 5 from the less well known list, showing that knowledge significantly affects memory. In a study of how students' prior knowledge of baseball affected their learning (Spilich, Vesonder, Chiesi, and Voss, 1979), investigators found that more knowledgeable college students recalled more facts from a prose passage about a baseball game. They also recalled more abstract items and made errors that reflected confusions of abstract principles of the game and its organization. The least knowledgeable students made the lowest-level errors—confusing the order and content of actions.

The powerful effect of the knowledge base on memory was further demonstrated in a study of child experts and adult novices at chess (Chi, 1978). For 10 seconds, the subjects were shown a chessboard with pieces on it and then were asked

to reproduce the arrangement they had seen. The children reproduced the arrangement much more accurately than the adults, a finding that could not be ascribed to their superior intelligence or memory abilities but to their superior knowledge of chess. Similarly, in a cross-cultural study of Moroccan rug sellers and Koranic scholars (Wagner, 1978), the knowledge base proved crucial. The scholars were highly educated and had long training in memorization; the rug sellers were not well educated but knew about rugs in intimate detail. The rug sellers proved superior at recognizing rugs that they had seen before; the scholars excelled at remembering verbal material.

But what is the process by which knowledge affects memory? For one thing, a larger and more solid knowledge base allows a person to draw more inferences and to integrate incoming information into a more complete network. When people are asked to retell a story, they typically leave out some parts, make explicit parts that were only implicit, and embellish other parts. Adults cannot distinguish between sentences they have heard before and those they have inferred (Bransford and McCarrell, 1974). Children are the same way. Toby Landis (1982) tested school-age children on their recognition of a sentence from a story read to them a week earlier, which was supposedly about either a famous person or a fictitious character. Children who had heard the famous-person story thought that well-known facts about the character, which had *not* been included in the story, were in fact in it. Because they were familiar with the subject, they had integrated the new information into their existing network of knowledge so that later on they could not tell what they had heard in the story and what they already had known about the person.

As children's knowledge grows, they become increasingly adept at drawing inferences and at integrating new information with old. When second-, fourth-, and sixth-graders were asked to recall a story (Brown, Smiley, Day, Townsend, and Lawton, 1977), all the children embellished equally on the story's details, but the oldest children's embellishments were more relevant to the story's theme, probably because they already knew more about the topics of the stories (life among Eskimos and desert Indians). Remembering is not just a parroting back of random facts; it is a process of constructing, of adding within an existing framework, of checking for plausibility against existing knowledge, and of increasing inferences about new information (Siegler, 1983). Clearly, the knowledge base is an essential part of the cognitive process.

EVERYDAY COGNITION

Common sense tells us that children do not behave the same way at home or at school as they do in a laboratory—where much of the research on cognitive processing has taken place. The laboratory is unfamiliar, devoid of social stimulation, and as carefully controlled for outside influences as the investigator can arrange. But natural settings like home or school are rich in social stimulation, and the kinds of learning and remembering that children demonstrate there—their "everyday" cognition—can be quite different from what they demonstrate in more sterile and objective assessments. Children demonstrate complex cognitive skills earlier when the problems are meaningful and familiar (DeLoache and Brown, 1979) and in familiar, relaxed surroundings. As we saw in the study by Istomina (1975), for instance, children also better remember items when they appear in familiar forms, like shopping lists. As Judy DeLoache (1980) points out, developmental psychologists tend to view young children as cognitively inept. Parents, who watch their children learn and remember every day, tend to think that their children have impressive powers of memory. The records parents keep when their infants make "any behavior that utilizes past experience" (Ashmead and Perlmutter, 1980) are much richer and more complex than those collected by unfamiliar observers. Incidents like the following would never have occurred in the laboratory: the bottle an 11-month-old was playing with rolled partly under a refrigerator; the baby left the room, played for 20 minutes or so, returned and retrieved the bottle from under the refrigerator, and then took up playing where she had left off. Social situations seem to provide infants with cues to jog their memories. Toddlers between 18 and 30 months have performed extremely well on a hide-and-seek game at home (DeLoache, 1980; DeLoache and Brown, 1983). Their parents teach them that Big Bird is going to hide and that they should remember where Big Bird is hidden so that they can find him later. They watch their parents hide Big Bird somewhere in the house and then,

when a kitchen timer rings in 3 to 5 minutes—a very long time for such young children—they usually jump up and find the toy without mistakes. Even when they have to wait for much longer times, the children are accurate in remembering where Big Bird is hidden. Children over 2 years of age are better than younger children at finding Big Bird when he is hidden in one of a set of unmarked boxes, for they effectively use a nearby piece of furniture as a marker. The younger children make fewer errors when Big Bird is hidden in a natural spot at home—in the toy chest, on a shelf—than when he is hidden in an unmarked box.

For older children, everyday cognition includes reading, writing, and arithmetic. All these processes require many coordinated skills and more complex coordination than is required in most laboratory assessments of information processing. Reading, for instance, includes perceptual discrimination of letters, integration of the letters into meaningful units, and integration of smaller into larger units of meaning. Even the most basic of these skills, per-

The counting ability of a preschooler typically depends on her memory, logical ability, and confidence.

ceiving the differences between letters, is no mean feat. Our alphabet offers many chances for confusion: *d* for *b,* *m* for *n,* or *u* for *n.*

Counting is another everyday cognitive domain in which even toddlers demonstrate knowledge. A 2-year-old might count, "1, 2, 3, 8, tree!" A 4-year-old might count accurately from 1 to 39 and then jump immediately to 60. Preschoolers' count-

ing strategies depend not only on memory and logical ability, but also on their confidence. The child who loudly recites the numbers from 1 to 5 may shift strategies and begin counting on her fingers for 6 to 10 and fall into a tentative whisper for anything over 10. To study how preschoolers count, Robert Siegler and Mitchell Robinson (1982) formulated information-processing models

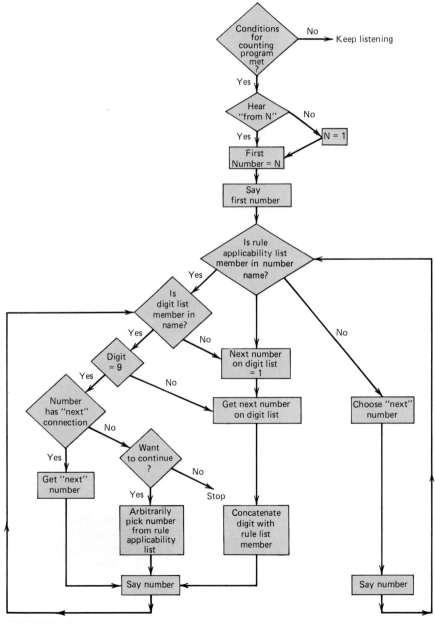

FIGURE 9.7
An information-processing model of counting (Siegler, 1983).

of the development of counting, comparing magnitude, adding, and several conservation skills. Their model of the counting process in 4-year-olds, for instance, predicts at what point the child will stop, repeat, omit, invent numbers, and count on from an arbitrary starting point. Children first tag the numbers 1 through 9 as the digit repetition list and then tag the decade names, 20 through 90, as the rule applicability list. Given a number from which to start counting by 1's, children use the "next" connection until they reach a number requiring the application of a rule. This model of an everyday cognitive activity as seen through the eyes of an information processor is diagrammed in Figure 9.7. It demonstrates the cognitive complexity of even the simplest activity of an average 4-year-old.

MECHANISMS OF DEVELOPMENT

Clearly, the information-processing system of adults is superior to that of children, and the information processing of children is more efficient and complex than that of infants. What is it about the ability to process information that improves with age? Is it basic capacities, encoding processes, retrieval processes, cognitive strategies, depth of processing, size of the knowledge base—or all of these? By what mechanisms do any of these factors change? Unfortunately, final answers to these essential questions have not yet been established. Controversy remains about how the information-processing system develops.

Some people (e.g., Pascual-Leone, 1970) have suggested that it is the capacity of short-term memory that changes with age. Preschoolers can hold only two or three chunks of information in short-term memory, 5-year-olds only four, and 7-year-olds only five chunks (Morrison, Holmes, and Haith, 1974), but thereafter the capacity remains at a constant seven chunks. Other information processors (e.g., Siegler, 1983) have concluded that the basic storage capacities of the sensory register and short-term memory do not change greatly with age; a preschooler seems to have as large a capacity as an adult. Another suggestion has been that until the age of 5, children's capacity to encode information into the sensory register increases. (After that age, their capacity is the same as adults'.) Children also, it has been noted, transfer informa-

tion more efficiently from the sensory register into short-term memory after about age 4 or 5. Some data suggest, however, that the improvement of encoding processes, like learning to group information into chunks, or other cognitive strategies, like rehearsal, changes that affect how much children can remember, is what develops during childhood. In a recent study of 8- to 21-year-olds by Robert Kail and Marilyn Nippold (1984), for example, older subjects remembered more information (names of animals and furniture) than younger ones, but the information was organized into the same number of clusters, judging by the bursts and pauses in the subjects' recital of names. Efficiency in allocating attention is another aspect of information processing that increases with age (Manis, Keating, and Morrison, 1980). This increased efficiency and speed of information processing may then free in memory storage operating space previously needed for performance (Case, Kurland, and Goldberg, 1982). At the same time, increases in one's accumulated knowledge occur with increasing age, and these increases have been suggested as the basis for improved information processing in older children and adults (e.g., Chi, 1976). Finally, other psychologists have suggested that it is not processing capacity that changes but the interaction among an increasing knowledge base, improved use of strategies, and increasingly efficient basic processes (Brown et al., 1983).

Although many questions about what changes in information processing remain open, several suggestions have been offered to account for how these changes come about. Self-modification is one such suggestion, yet how the child actually regulates himself or herself has never been specified adequately. Piaget's notions of accommodation and equilibration are examples of self-modification, yet

For 40 years now we have had assimilation and accommodation, the mysterious and shadowy forces of equilibration, the Batman and Robin of the developmental processes. What are they? How do they do their thing? Why is it after all this time, we know no more about them than when they first sprang on the scene? What we need is a way to get beyond vague verbal statements of the nature of the developmental process (Klahr, 1982, p. 80).

Accordingly, Klahr and Wallace (1976) tried to specify how self-modifications might operate, suggesting that people preserve their cognitive goals, contents of working memory, and the outcomes of their cognitive operations along a time line. As they move along that time line, people try to eliminate redundancies, to find processing shortcuts, and to detect consistencies. For example, a child may have seen two robins and two cardinals. Her time line contains all of her cognitive productions from scanning the birds with her eyes. These productions might overlap enough to form a "robin" node that corresponds to a visual concept. Eventually, the "robin" concept might overlap enough with the "cardinal" concept to allow for the category, "birds."

Automatization is another mechanism that may account for developmental changes in cognition (Case, 1978). Although the underlying capacity of working memory is constant from a very early age, functional capacity grows as operations are executed more automatically and thereby free more working memory space for other operations. Automaticity increases as a person has more experience with a particular stimulus and gains general experience and maturity. A third mechanism of change is encoding (Siegler, 1983). Children must acquire many diverse encodings. They must segment and abstract what they see and hear into a useful level of abstraction and a complete representation of reality. If such information is inadequately encoded, further progress in information processing is hampered.

AN INTERACTIVE MODEL OF COGNITIVE PROCESSING

We close the chapter with a description of one model of cognitive processing that represents an attempt to integrate the components of learning and information processing—to put together all the sections in this chapter. The tetrahedral model of Ann Brown, John Bransford, Roberta Ferrara, and Joseph Campione (1983) makes central the interaction and compatibility between the problem solver and the problem to be solved. These developmental psychologists consider the interaction among four properties: activities of the learner, characteristics of the learner, nature of the materials

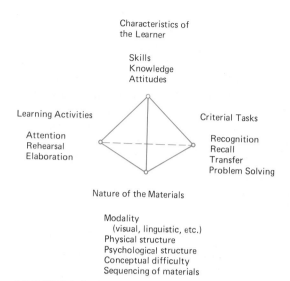

FIGURE 9.8
An organizational framework for expanding questions about learning (Brown, Bransford, Ferrara, and Campione, 1983. Adapted from Jenkins, 1979, and Bransford, 1979).

to be learned, and qualities of the task by which learning is assessed (see Figure 9.8). The form and function of each of these factors, they suggest, are strongly shaped by the other three corners of the tetrahedron. As we pointed out earlier, some controversy surrounds the question: What develops? Whether the answer is basic capacity, or efficient use of that capacity, or the amount of knowledge, and so on, is debatable. But Brown and her colleagues take the position that there is no simple either/or answer to this question. The answer is not, "It's all strategies," or "It's all knowledge," or "It's all storage or operating space." The system is an interactive one, to which all of these components— each affected by the others—contribute.

To begin with, consider the activities of the learner—activities like rehearsing, exploring, organizing, elaborating, studying. These activities are closely tied to the person's knowledge of the material to be learned. Even rehearsal, the most content-free of all of these activities, is shaped by the learner's knowledge of the information to be rehearsed (Ornstein and Naus, 1978). The nature of the task on which the learner is being tested also determines whether and which activity the learner will engage in. For example, adults do not rehearse material if it is in either a very long or very short list, and young children spontaneously perform learning activities only when they understand the goal (like finding a toy). They do not try actively to learn just for learning's sake.

Next, consider what the learner brings to the situation. What is the importance of the learner's own characteristics—memory capacity, knowledge base, self-awareness about cognition? These factors also contribute to the learning process. So, too, does the nature of the materials to be learned—their physical and psychological structure, conceptual difficulty, sequence, and perceptual form. The research on recognition memory in young children shows the importance of considering the nature of materials to be learned. In their review of this research, Perlmutter and Myers (1979) found that when materials are familiar and the items distinct, even very young children recognize them readily. But when materials are complex or require sustained, systematic scanning and comparisons, young children do poorly at recognizing them.

Finally, the task by which learning is assessed contributes to the learning process. Learning is not undertaken in a vacuum; there is always an end product in mind. Effective learners are aware of this end product and tailor their learning activities ac-

cordingly. Quite different strategies would be involved in learning facts in order to understand them and in order to remember them. Concentrating only on rote memorizing of facts may blind a learner to internal connections—whether logical or illogical, plausible or implausible. Learning the significance of material requires something of the questioning attitude of the detective (Bransford, Stein, Shelton, and Owings, 1981). Comprehension also requires the revision of hypotheses in the face of conflicting information, a kind of flexibility and reality testing that often differentiates successful from unsuccessful students.

In sum, to understand fully the learning process, it is necessary to consider each of the four corners of the tetrahedron. This is necessary for psychologists interested in cognitive development, and, as Brown and her colleagues (1983) suggest, it may be useful for learners themselves. To learn effectively, children may be helped if they know something of their own abilities, something of which learning activities are possible and appropriate, something of the end product of their efforts, and something about the nature of the materials they are learning.

SUMMARY

1. Behaviorists study and apply the principles of classical and operant conditioning. In classical conditioning, a stimulus, which causes no response, is paired with a second stimulus, which does cause a response, until the subject makes the same or similar response to the first stimulus alone. In operant conditioning, positive reinforcement is given (or not) immediately following a subject's spontaneous (operant) response until the rate of that response increases (or decreases). The speed of operant conditioning is affected by the schedule of reinforcement and the subject's prior satiation or deprivation. Conditioned responses generalize from one stimulus or task to another. Extinction of a response occurs when reinforcement is stopped. Observational learning occurs without reinforcement when people watch and imitate others.

2. Recently, stimulus-response theories of learning have been replaced by more cognitive models of learning. Whereas behaviorally oriented devel-

opmental psychologists confined their investigations to observable behavior, many psychologists today investigate the mental events that underlie or correspond to observable behavior.

3. Information processing, the dominant approach to cognitive psychology today, depicts the individual as a manipulator of symbols with specific, limited abilities to organize information. Like computers, people are depicted as encoding information, processing and storing it, and retrieving it. They also monitor their own cognitive processes with a collection of mental activities called "metacognition." Information-processing theories hold that information enters a perceptual, sensory store, then short-term (working) memory, and finally long-term memory.

4. To test how people process information, psychologists may use chronometric or protocol analyses or analyze eye movements or patterns of errors.

5. Attention is a basic cognitive capacity and operates according to principles of selectivity and exploration.

6. Perception, another basic process, is the active obtaining of information through the senses.

7. Two forms of remembering are recognition of a familiar image in its presence and recall of an image from memory. The mode in which information enters memory—in words, symbols, sounds—as well as a person's feelings and motives and the meaningfulness of the information all affect the process of remembering.

8. Cognitive strategies for encoding information include rehearsal, organization, and elaboration. Strategies for retrieving information include using external cues, drawing inferences, and persevering. Children's strategies for studying, like their strategies for remembering, change qualitatively over time. Older children do more organizing of material, ask more questions, take more notes, underline and outline more, and they know how to focus on more important material and to tune out trivia and redundancies.

9. What people already know—their knowledge base—affects how they learn and remember, although it is difficult for psychologists to separate the effects of cognitive strategies and operations from those of the knowledge base. Differences in the knowledge base also explain age changes and individual differences in cognition.

10. Young children whose cognitive skills are still fragile and emerging show greater feats of remembering, organizing, and learning when they are in familiar surroundings and when they understand the nature of a task than when they are in strange surroundings and do not understand the task.

11. Theories of how cognition changes with development must take into account not only characteristics of the learner, but also of the task and the test.

KEY TERMS

Classical conditioning
Unconditioned stimulus
Unconditioned response
Conditioned stimulus
Conditioned response
Operant conditioning
Reinforcer
Schedule of reinforcement

Continuous reinforcement schedule
Partial reinforcement schedule
Satiation
Deprivation
Gradient of generalization
Extinction

Reversal and nonreversal shifts
Observational learning
Incidental learning
Dichotic listening tasks
Chronometric analysis
Perception
Chunks
Primacy effect
Recency effect

Recognition
Recall
Rehearsal
Organization
Imagery
Elaboration
Visualization
Persevering
Metacognition
Metamemory

SUGGESTED READINGS

Bisanz, Jeffrey, Bisanz, Gay L., and Kail, Robert (Eds.). *Learning in Children*. New York: Springer-Verlag, 1983. A number of recent studies examining the social, motivational, and cognitive aspects of learning in young children.

Brainerd, Charles J. (Ed.). *Recent Advances in Cognitive-Developmental Theory*. New York: Springer-Verlag, 1983. Several post-Piagetian frameworks for understanding cognitive development, including social learning, ethological, genetic, and information-processing approaches. This is the "new wave" in cognitive development.

Brown, Ann L., Bransford, John D., Ferrara, Roberta A., and Campione, Joseph C. Learning, Remembering, and Understanding. In P. H. Mussen (Ed.), *Handbook of Child Psychology* (vol. 3) (4th ed.). New York: Wiley, 1983. A comprehensive overview of recent research on learning and memory with emphasis on the interactive and dynamic nature of these processes.

Kail, Robert. *The Development of Memory in Children*. San Francisco: W. H. Freeman, 1979. A comprehensive yet simply written book presenting the current state of knowledge about children's abilities to memorize and remember.

Perlmutter, Marion (Ed.). *Children's Memory*. San Francisco: Jossey-Bass, 1980. The studies reported in this volume of *New Directions for Child Development* focus on infants' and young children's cognition and memory as they are demonstrated in their everyday lives.

Siegler, Robert S. (Ed.). *Children's Thinking: What Develops?* Hillsdale, N.J.: Lawrence Erlbaum Associates, 1978. An impressive collection of articles covering memory development, problem solving, and the development of representational processes in children.

Stevenson, Harold. How Children Learn—The Quest for a Theory. In P. H. Mussen (Ed.), *Handbook of Child Psychology* (vol. 1) (4th ed.). New York: Wiley, 1983. This chapter traces the development of theories of children's learning and the impact of these approaches on learning research and teaching strategies over the past couple of decades.

CHAPTER 10

Intelligence

DEFINING INTELLIGENCE

The beaming grandmother held her 6-month-old granddaughter on her lap and watched the baby explore a vivid orange rattle with her mouth. Baby and rattle, in constant motion, were covered with drool. Still the grandmother watched, transfixed by the infant. After several minutes she sighed deeply and announced, "This child is brilliant! A regular scientist already."

What did the grandmother see in the infant that led her to make such a statement? What *is* intelligence? This question has fascinated philosophers, theologians, and scientists for 3000 years. In attempts to formulate a universal definition, they have suggested that intelligence is "moral uprightness," "the ability to reason well," "learning thoroughly and quickly," "perseverence," "creative imagination," and "the ability to make fine sensory or esthetic discriminations." Modern psychologists, too, implicitly or explicitly have presented a variety of definitions of intelligence. In 1924, the psychologist Edward Thorndike wrote that intelligence was the quality of mind that distinguished great minds from idiots. To this associative-learning theorist, intelligence consisted of connections between stimulus and response: greater intelligence consists of more connections, lower intelligence of fewer connections. For Jean Piaget, the function of intelligence, like that of all biological abilities, was adaptation to the environment. As children advance through stages of development and adapt to their environments, old cognitive structures are reorganized and extended and intelligence increases. In Piaget's view, children are actively involved in constructing their own intelligence. Like Piaget, Reid Tuddenham (1964) and Roger Webb (1974) have suggested that the key to intelligence is adaptation. Intelligence, Tuddenham holds, is not a trait but how adaptive a person's behavior is. The virtue of this view is that it centers on performance and is less culture bound than some other definitions. In such a view, the hunting skills of a Bushman and the fishing skills of a Polynesian are highly intelligent. Webb has expanded the definition of intelligence to encompass *power, structure,* and *style.* Power is a measure of the neurological speed with which a person learns. It grows less important with age. In grade school, power is most important. But

Albert Einstein's intelligence led him to perceive unities in the physical world that forever changed the way others see. His piercing intelligence allowed him to master logic, mathematics, and physics and to approach them from a starkly original vantage point.

two college graduates faced with the problem of designing a better computer or two parents faced with the problem of weaning their infant arrive at solutions by putting together what they already know and not by learning something brand new. Thus, with age, the speed of acquiring new information becomes less important than integrating and applying old information. Structure is a specific mental capacity, such as recognition memory or creative thinking. Style is the culturally learned aspect of cognition—the scientific rationalism of the West or the contemplative mysticism of the East.

Clearly, psychologists hold diverse ideas about what intelligence is. What does the average person think intelligence is? We all have an idea of what intelligence is, and we call a person intelligent who resembles this idea. We may consider two people with quite different qualities to be intelligent, two people who resemble our idea of "intelligent person" along different dimensions (Neisser, 1979). People's everyday conceptions of intelligence and intelligent behavior strongly accord with the definitions of the experts. Like the experts' definitions, laypeople's definitions are diverse. Robert Sternberg and his colleagues (Sternberg, Conway, Ketron, and Bernstein, 1981) found that people in a college library defined intelligent behavior as what experts would consider academically intelligent; business commuters at a train station and housewives in a supermarket defined as intelligent behavior that experts would consider everyday intelligence. With age, too, people's ideas about intelligence change. The definitions of intelligence given by children and adults are quite different. In interviews by Steven Yussen and Patrick Kane (in press), it was clear that among first-, third-, and sixth-graders, the oldest children had the most differentiated and least global ideas about intelligence and were most likely to think of intelligence as an internal quality rather than an overt behavior. Not only do children at different ages have different notions of intelligence, but also people have different notions of what intelligence means for children at different ages. Robert Siegler and Dean Richards (1983) asked college students what they thought intelligence was for 6-month-olds, 2-year-olds, 10-year-olds, and adults. The students thought that for 6-month-olds, intelligence consisted of recognizing people, motor coordination, alertness, awareness of the environment, and verbalizing. For 2-year-olds, the students mentioned language and learning ability, awareness of people and surroundings, motor coordination, and curiosity as signs of intelligence. For 10-year-olds and adults they mentioned language, learning, problem solving, reasoning ability, and creativity.

Because the definitions of intelligence are so diverse, many people who have tried to define intelligence have thrown up their hands and decided that intelligence is whatever intelligence tests measure. **Psychometrics** is the field of standardized testing of intelligence and achievement. Psychometricians define intelligence as the ability to respond correctly to intelligence test questions. They search for patterns of individual differences across tests and presume that they derive from individual mental abilities. Psychometrics has probably been the most influential approach to defining intelligence in this century. The psychometric definition has not been accepted universally, however. An alternative definition is that intelligence is the ability

to perceive relationships through the processes of induction and deduction. The information-processing definition of intelligence, as the ability to solve problems and to adapt effectively to the environment, is based on these abilities to perceive relationships, to discriminate, and to draw conclusions. In cultures like ours, with a heavy bias in favor of the rational, the ability to manipulate abstract symbols is also an important defining characteristic of intelligence.

MEASURING INTELLIGENCE

HISTORY OF INTELLIGENCE TESTING

Sir Francis Galton (1822–1911) was the first person to attempt to define and measure systematically individual differences in intelligence. Believing that people inherited different intellectual capacities, Galton established a laboratory in London and developed the technique of statistical correlation to study intelligence. He expected that intelligence would be correlated with the ability to make subtle sensory discriminations. Therefore he measured people's abilities to discriminate among blocks that differed only slightly in size or weight. Galton's tests were not designed to measure intelligence per se but to identify intelligent people.

James Cattell introduced some of Galton's ideas to the United States. He devised 50 psychophysical tests of intelligence, including how strongly a hand could squeeze, how quickly an arm could move, and the like (Cattell, 1890). Physical energy, Cattell believed, was inseparable from mental energy.

Alfred Binet in 1896 criticized the Galton laboratory for its narrow focus on simple sensory and cognitive processes and for neglecting "higher mental abilities." His criticism and subsequent test designs changed the direction of mental testing. In 1905 Binet and Théophile Simon constructed their objective test identifying mentally defective children who would be unable to profit from traditional classroom instruction (see p. 6). The test that they developed for the French Ministry of Public Education has since served as a model for almost all mental tests.

Binet and Simon (1916) believed that the core of intelligence was judgment—"good sense"—and knowledge. They suggested that the brighter the child, the earlier he or she would be able to answer items on the test correctly. The test items were at progressive levels of difficulty and could be answered correctly by the majority of children at each chronological age. For example, a 3-year-old was expected to be able to name the objects in a picture, repeat a sentence of six syllables, and repeat two digits. A 12-year-old was expected to interpret the meaning of a picture, repeat a sentence of 26 syllables, and repeat seven digits (see Table 10.1). Binet and Simon, like those who study learning and cognition today, believed that intelligent thought consists of direction (knowing what to do and how to do it), adaptation (selecting and monitoring a strategy), and criticism of one's thought or actions.

Binet and Simon administered their test items to many, many children and thus established a "normative" age at which most children could answer the item correctly. By comparing a child's actual answers to this norm, the administrator of the test could determine a child's mental age (MA). One problem with an MA score, however, is the difficulty in comparing the relative intelligence of children of different ages. For example, who is more intelligent, a 6-year-old with an MA of 9 or a 10-year-old with an MA of 13? The second child certainly "knows more," but is he or she an intelligent person who knows more or can do more *at an earlier age* than the other child? In 1912, William Stern (1871–1938) developed the concept of the **intelligence quotient (IQ)** to resolve this issue. An individual's IQ was defined as mental age divided by chronological age multiplied by 100. Thus a child of average intelligence, performing at the normal level for his or her chronological age would receive an IQ of 100. For example, the 6-year-old just described has an IQ of $\%$ × 100, or 150. The 10-year-old has an IQ of $^{13}/_{10}$ × 100, or 130. Thus, although the 10-year-old definitely knows more, the 6-year-old is comparatively more intelligent. To make comparisons of ages even more consistent, today IQ is computed so that the mean score for each age is adjusted to IQ = 100 with a **standard deviation** of 15 points. This means that two thirds of all people fall within the "normal" range of IQ between 85 and 115, and 95 percent fall within the range of IQ between 70 and 130 (Figure 10.1).

In 1916, Lewis M. Terman (1877–1956) defined

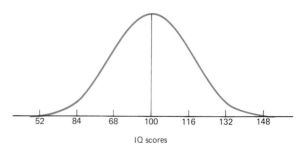

52   84   68   100   116   132   148

IQ scores

FIGURE 10.1

The distribution of IQ scores of the general population follows a normal curve.

intelligence as the ability to think abstractly and to use abstract symbols, especially verbal symbols. He added 36 items to the Binet-Simon test. These modified it to reflect his theory and extended its use to children aged 2 to 16. Since revised, Terman's Stanford-Binet test is the instrument by which the validity of all subsequent mental tests has been measured.

Writing at approximately the same time as Galton and Binet, Charles Spearman (1863–1945) was the first psychologist to articulate a coherent theory of the nature of intelligence and to develop the statistical methods by which to test his theory empirically. Spearman (1904) proposed that intelligence was a unitary trait rather than a collection of separate abilities. In Spearman's theory, intelligence consists of *conceptualization,* the ability to induce general laws and relationships from particular instances, and *abstraction,* the ability to deduce particular relationships from general laws. Intelligence operated according to the psychological mechanism of mental energy and consisted of two factors, *g* and *s*. **Factor g** represents the true and general intellectual ability applied in all intellectual tasks; **factor s** represents the several specific or idiosyncratic abilities required for particular cognitive tasks. Spearman claimed that the correlation between any two mental tests depends on the degree to which they measure *g*. The goal in designing a mental test is to measure as much *g* as possible. The measurement of *g* and *s* is based on factor analysis of all possible correlations among all possible pairs of tasks. A smaller number of factors is thus obtained to account for individual variations in test performance.

A widely used series of intelligence tests has been developed since 1938 by David Wechsler,

TABLE 10.1
ITEMS FROM THE 1908 BINET SCALE

Age 3 years

1. Points to nose, eyes, mouth.
2. Repeats sentences of six syllables.
3. Repeats two digits.
4. Enumerates objects in a picture.
5. Gives family name.

Age 4 years

1. Knows own sex.
2. Names certain familiar objects shown to him or her: key, pocketknife, and a penny.
3. Repeats three digits.
4. Indicates the longer of two lines 5 and 6 centimeters in length.

Age 5 years

1. Indicates the heavier of two cubes (of 3 and 12 grams and also of 6 and 15 grams).
2. Copies a square, using pen and ink.
3. Constructs a rectangle from two pieces of cardboard, having a model to look at.
4. Counts four pennies.

Age 6 years

1. Knows right from left as shown by indicating right hand and left ear.
2. Repeats sentence of sixteen syllables.
3. Chooses the prettier in each of three pair of faces.
4. Defines familiar objects in terms of use.
5. Executes an order that contains three instructions.
6. Knows own age.
7. Knows morning and afternoon.

Age 7 years

1. Tells what is missing in unfinished pictures.
2. Knows number of fingers on each hand and on both hands without consulting them.
3. Copies the "Little Paul" with pen and ink.
4. Copies a diamond, using pen and ink.
5. Repeats five digits.
6. Describes pictures as scenes.
7. Counts thirteen pennies.
8. Knows names of four common coins.

Age 8 years

1. Reads a passage and remembers two items.
2. Counts up the value of three simple and two double sous (or 1¢ and 2¢ stamps in American scales).
3. Names four colors—red, yellow, blue, and green.
4. Counts backward from 20 to 0.
5. Writes short sentence from dictation, using pen and ink.
6. Gives differences between two objects from memory.

Age 9 years

1. Knows date—day of week and of month, also month and year.
2. Recites days of the week.
3. Makes change on 4¢ out of 20¢ in simple play-store transactions.
4. Gives definitions of familiar objects.
5. Reads a passage and remembers six items.
6. Arranges five blocks in order of weight.

Age 10 years

1. Names, in order, the months of the year.
2. Recognizes all of nine pieces of money.
3. Constructs a sentence to include three given words—Paris, fortune, gutter. Two unified sentences are acceptable.
4. Answers easy comprehension questions.
5. Answers difficult comprehension questions.

Age 11 years

1. Points out absurdities in contradictory statements.
2. Names sixty words in 3 minutes.
3. Defines abstract terms—charity, justice, kindness.
4. Puts words, arranged in a random order, into a sentence.

Age 12 years

1. Repeats seven digits.
2. Finds in 1 minute three rhymes for a given word—obedience.
3. Repeats a sentence of twenty-six syllables.
4. Answers problem questions—a test of common sense.
5. Gives interpretation of pictures.

Age 13 years

1. Draws the design that would be made by cutting a triangular piece from the once-folded edge of a quarto-folded paper.
2. Rearranges in imagination the relationship of two triangles and draws the results as they would appear.
3. Gives the differences between pairs of abstract terms, such as pride and pretension.

who has described intelligence as "the overall capacity of an individual to cope with the world" (Wechsler, 1974, p. 5) rather than an ability like memory or reasoning. Wechsler constructed the first modern intelligence test suitable for administration to adults, the Wechsler-Bellevue (1944). In 1955, this test was revised and standardized; it is the widely used Wechsler Adult Intelligence Scale (WAIS). Wechsler also devised the Wechsler Intelligence Scale for Children (WISC), revised in 1974.

Wechsler's idea of intelligence was broad. He believed that intelligent behavior may call for

> one or more of a host of aptitudes (factors) which are more in the nature of conative and personality traits than cognitive capabilities. These involve not so much skills and know-how as drives and attitudes, and often what may be described as sensitivity to social, moral, or aesthetic values. They include such traits as persistence, zest, impulse control, and goal awareness—traits which, for the most part, are independent of any particular ability. Wechsler (1974, pp. 5–6).

Both Wechsler's and Binet's ideas of intelligence were broader than the range of abilities for which their IQ scales actually test.

IQ TESTS

Individual Tests

Both the Wechsler and the Stanford-Binet tests are administered by an experienced tester to an individual child or adult. The tester has to be trained to administer, score, and interpret the results of each test and to issue instructions neutrally and in a form that effectively does not vary from one subject to the next. A skilled tester can establish rapport with the subject and can detect when a subject is confused, sick, or overly nervous.

The types of questions on the children's and adults' Wechsler scales are nearly identical, but the children's questions are easier. For children between 4 and 6½, there is a Wechsler Preschool and Primary Intelligence Scale (WPPSI). The WISC-R (a revised form of the WISC) is used for children between 5 and 15 years old. Both children's and adults' scales are divided into *verbal* and *perfor-*

mance subtests. The former tap an individual's knowledge and information, vocabulary, comprehension of everyday skills, mathematical skills, recall, and interpretation. The latter tap intelligence through a subject's abilities to code numbers into symbols, copy designs made with blocks, put pictures in a logical sequence, complete a picture, and assemble a cut-up picture of an object (see Table 10.2). The tester begins with problems the subject can answer easily and ends with those difficult enough to foil repeated attempts at solution. Out of the many subtests, which cluster around different abilities, a subject receives a score for general intelligence.

Whereas the Wechsler scales assess separate clusters of abilities, the Binet test provides a variety of items for different age levels. In its present form, the Stanford-Binet scale tests children as young as 2 with such tasks as inserting a circle, square, and triangle into the appropriate holes in a board; identifying body parts on a doll; building a tower out of four blocks; and identifying pictures of common objects. Tests for 8-year-olds tap vocabulary, through word definitions; recognition of verbal absurdities and objects' similarities and differences; solutions of everyday problems; and naming the days of the week. Tests for 14-year-olds assess vocabulary, ingenuity, inductive and spatial reasoning, solutions of math word problems, and reconciliation of opposites. The most advanced test measures vocabulary, interpretations of proverbs, orientation, reasoning, identifying central ideas in a story, and solving analogies.

Group Tests

Some intelligence tests are administered to groups of people rather than to individuals. Two common group tests are the Otis-Lennon Mental Ability Test and the California Test of Mental Maturity. Individual and group tests are different enough so that often one cannot effectively substitute for the other. Group tests do not allow for the ready detection of subjects who are ill or nervous or for any individual's especially good or poor performance. In their favor, however, the tests require little special training of the test administrator, can be given economically to large numbers of people at once, produce objective scores, and have been standardized on more people than have individual tests.

TABLE 10.2
SAMPLE ITEMS SIMILAR TO THOSE ON THE WECHSLER INTELLIGENCE TESTS

Verbal Subtests

1. *Information and Knowledge*
   How many wings does a bird have?
   Who wrote *Tom Sawyer*?
   What is steam made of?

2. *Comprehension*
   What should you do if you see someone forget his book when he leaves a restaurant?
   What is the advantage of keeping money in a bank?

3. *Arithmetic and Numerical Reasoning*
   Sam had three pieces of candy and Joe gave him four more. How many pieces of candy did Sam have altogether?

4. *Verbal Similarities*
   In what way are a lion and a tiger alike?
   In what way are an hour and a week alike?

5. *Digit Span and Memory*
   Repeat these numbers: 9 3 4 8 7 1

6. *Vocabulary*
   What does _____ mean or what is a _____?
   The words given cover a wide range of familiarity and difficulty.

Performance Subtests

1. *Digit Symbol*

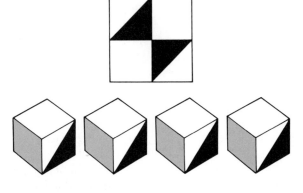

2. *Block Design*

3. *Picture Arrangement*

4. *Picture Completion*

5. *Object Assembly*

One intelligence test for young children is the Peabody Picture Vocabulary Test. A child is asked to point to various pictures. Testing the child individually allows an examiner to establish rapport and to detect special circumstances—sleepiness, nervousness, and the like—that might affect performance.

Vocabulary Tests

Although psychologists usually avoid using the sub-tests in isolation, the verbal subtest (especially vocabulary) of the Wechsler scales is a better predictor of children's success in school and their general intelligence than the performance subtests (Saddler, 1974). On the Stanford-Binet, too, the vocabulary tests are often good predictors of children's general intelligence. Tests that measure only verbal abilities have, therefore, been devised and have proved quite useful. The best known of these, the Peabody Picture Vocabulary Test (PPVT) measures intelligence by having a child point to a picture (see Figure 10.2). Because this test does not rely on a child's spoken responses, it was once thought to be a fairer test of the abilities of children from minority groups than other IQ tests, which require children to speak standard English. However, research showed that

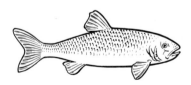

FIGURE 10.2

An illustration of the kind of item that appears in the Peabody Picture Vocabulary Test (PPVT); the child is asked to point to the fish.

minority-group children's scores on the PPVT were actually lower than on other IQ tests (Cundick, 1970), and so it was no solution after all. Although it measures the size of a child's vocabulary, it does not assess how children use or remember language. But the PPVT has its advantages: the main one is that it takes only 15 minutes to administer.

Culture-Free and Culture-Fair Tests

Intelligence test results are relative and describe an individual's position—average, above average, below average—in relation to the positions of other members of a group. In establishing norms for intelligence tests against which individuals are to be measured, age has long been accepted as an important criterion. But is it fair to measure a 10-year-old from a hunter-gatherer society who has never had formal schooling against the same norms as a 10-year-old from middle-class America? Is it fair to measure a poor, disadvantaged black, or Chicano, or native American 10-year-old by those norms? Some people have answered those questions with a resounding "no." Because some intelligence tests

have been criticized as being biased in favor of Western and middle-class norms and, therefore, as unfairly penalizing subjects from other cultural backgrounds, attempts have been made to construct **culture-fair tests** of intelligence. One such test is the Raven Progressive Matrices Test. The Raven test relies on 60 different designs, each with a missing piece (see Figure 10.3). The subject tries to supply the missing piece from several possible alternatives. Thus instead of relying on language or pictures, which ordinarily are culture bound, the Raven test relies on designs. However, the Raven test has itself been criticized (Anastasi, 1976) as culture bound because better educated subjects score higher on it than those who are less well educated.

To solve the problem of intelligence tests that are biased against nonmiddle-class blacks, attempts have been made to construct **culture-free tests**. Adrian Dove (1968), a black sociologist, composed the Dove Counterbalance General Intelligence Test, also known as the "Chitling Test." The test is meant as a tongue-in-cheek reminder that a person's vocabulary is strongly affected by social fac-

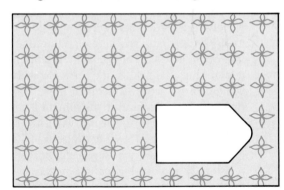

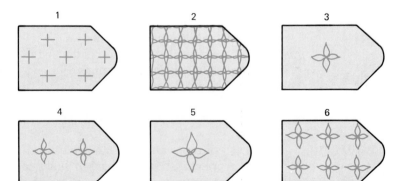

FIGURE 10.3
Sample item from the Raven Progressive Matrices Test. The person must pick out the piece below that is missing from the matrix above.

tors. The middle-class white is not likely to score well on a test of intelligence with questions like:

A *"gas head" is a person who has a*

    a. *fast-moving car*
    b. *stable of "lace"*
    c. *"process"*
    d. *habit of stealing cars*
    e. *long jail record for arson*

or

Cheap chitlings (not the kind you purchase at a frozen-food counter) will taste rubbery unless they are cooked long enough. How soon can you quit cooking them to eat and enjoy them?

    a. 45 minutes
    b. 2 hours
    c. 24 hours
    d. 1 week (on a low flame)
    e. 1 hour

(The correct answers both are c.)

HOW USEFUL ARE INTELLIGENCE TESTS?

At this point we should have a better idea of what intelligence might be and of how psychologists attempt to identify and measure it. But we still have not addressed the matter of performance versus competence.

Intelligence tests are measures of performance, and performance is determined by a complex interaction of aptitude, achievement, and motivation. Performance on any test is influenced by at least the following five factors:

1. Native ability.

2. Miscellaneous information picked up at home, at school, from television, and elsewhere.

3. The ability to read, understand, and make logical inferences from written material.

4. Skill at taking tests and the ability to work fast under pressure.

5. The desire to cooperate and to apply oneself.

William Crano and his colleagues (Crano, 1974; Crano, Kenny, and Campbell, 1972) did a longitudinal study to determine whether IQ was a better predictor of academic achievement or academic achievement a better predictor of future IQ scores. They obtained IQ scores and achievement test scores from children in the fourth and sixth grades. For middle-class children, the strongest correlation was between IQ scores in the fourth grade and achievement in the sixth grade. For lower-class children, the strongest correlation was between achievement in the fourth grade and IQ scores in the sixth grade. The researchers interpreted these correlations to mean that middle-class children with high IQs can be expected to do increasingly well in school but that poor achievement will lower the IQ scores of lower-class children, perhaps because the children tune out or fail to take the test seriously. At least for lower-class children, IQ tests seem to be a decreasingly valid indication of intellectual potential.

A mental test must have three properties if it is to be considered a good test of intelligence, **reliability, validity,** and **stability**. If the test items all do a good job of predicting the total score, the test is reliable. But if the items themselves have nothing to do with intelligence or measure it incompletely, the test, though reliable, is not valid. Stability refers to how consistent a person's score is over time, that is, to how similar a score obtained on one test is to that obtained on an equivalent test administered at a later time. Stability is one form of reliability. The validity of IQ scores is a much more complicated matter. The validity of an instrument is a measure of how accurately it measures what it is supposed to measure. If a thermometer registers 212°F when it is placed in a pot of boiling water at sea level and registers 32°F when the water is frozen, we can feel pretty confident that the thermometer is a valid instrument for measuring temperature. The measurement of intelligence is more elusive. Four types of validity are possible: construct validity, content validity, criterion validity, and concurrent validity.

Construct validity indicates how well a test conforms to the best scientific notion of the underlying trait or construct being measured. But construct validity is a theoretical, not an empirically measurable, concept; thus the other forms of validity have been devised to approximate construct validity.

A test has **content validity** if the items it contains fairly represent a clearly specified body of knowledge. For example, the content validity of a math test is high if the items have to do with arithmetic, algebra, geometry, and the like. The content validity is suspect if the questions concern the mating behavior of killer bees. Because intelligence is not defined by reference to any specific body of knowledge, the content validity of IQ tests is difficult to determine.

Criterion validity refers to a test's ability to predict success on a second variable that is supposed to be related to the ability being tested. For example, if academic success and economic success are believed to depend on intelligence, we would expect IQ scores to correlate positively with school grades, school achievement scores, and eventually with personal income. And we expect people who get good grades and who succeed in society to score higher on IQ tests. In fact, the correlation between IQ and school achievement is about .50 (Brody and Brody, 1976; Matarazzo, 1972), and the correlation between IQ and later economic success the same (Jencks et al., 1972). These are clearly significant but not perfect correlations. These figures for criterion validity do not therefore conclusively establish whether IQ tests are measuring intelligence, but they do indicate that the tests measure with a fair degree of accuracy something that society values; they are good predictors of an individual's ability to succeed in our present society.

Concurrent validity is a measure of how well one test correlates with another established test, one alleged to measure the identical construct and already considered valid. The concurrent validity of any newly devised intelligence test is usually determined by how highly individuals' scores correlate with their scores on the Stanford-Binet or the WAIS. This process, of course, begs the real question. Concurrent validity can establish that a new test measures the *same* thing as the established test but not that it is measuring the *right* thing. In fact, a new test that is a *better*, more valid, measure of intelligence will get the same poor correlation with the standard as will a new test that is a *bad* test of intelligence.

TESTS OF INFANTS

The infant's pace of development is rapid and continuous, as brain and body grow in size and as

The Bayley Scales of Infant Development are often used to test infants' powers of perception, sensation, and other cognitive skills.

behavior grows more complex. Because their cognitive and physical growth are enmeshed, and because cognitive abilities at this time must be inferred from physical abilities, measuring infants' intelligence poses special challenges. By observing how infants at different ages behave when they are presented with particular stimuli—looking at, holding, or grasping a cube; responding to or ignoring a bell ringing; building a tower of blocks or throwing the blocks on the floor—adults can measure the infants' development against established norms for infants of that age. Accurate measurement of infants' rapidly developing mental abilities depends not only on the adequacy of the test, but also on the skill of the examiner and, perhaps most important, on the state of the infant (Honzik, 1976). The ideal time to test an infant is when the infant is quietly alert, interested, and responsive. The ideal time is elusive, however, and many a subject does his or her share of dozing off, crying, squirming, protesting, and ignoring. The examiner must monitor the infant's constant changes during a single test session, for the typical infant is a study in perpetual motion. As Arnold Gesell described a typical moment:

At 28 weeks the baby sees a cube; he grasps it, senses surface and edge as he clutches it, brings it to his mouth, where he feels its qualities anew, withdraws it, looks at it on withdrawal, rotates it while he looks, looks while he rotates it, restores it to his mouth, withdraws it again for inspection, restores it again for mouthing, transfers it to the other hand, bangs it, contacts it with the free hand, transfers, mouths it again, drops it, resecures it, mouths it yet again, repeating the cycle with variations—all in the time it takes to read this sentence (Gesell and Amatruda, 1941).

It was Gesell, the pioneer of the measurement of infant intelligence, whose work influenced the content of all existing infant intelligence tests. To Gesell, the measurement of the infant was a **developmental diagnosis** to appraise the maturity of the nervous system with the aid of behavioral norms. Gesell and his colleagues therefore conducted many precise observations of infants' behavior at various ages, from which they extracted **norms** (milestones) of infants' behavior (see page 10). For example, they observed how infants responded to a 1-inch cube: at 4 weeks of age, the majority of the infants tested grasped the cube when it was placed in their hands; at 16 weeks, they stared at it when it was put on a table in front of them; at 28 weeks, when shown the cube, they grasped it in the palm of their hands; at 40 weeks, they grasped it with their fingers. Gesell divided his observations into four categories of behavior: adaptive, motor, language, and personal-social. Adaptive behavior was exemplified by the infant's response to the cube, as described above. Gesell

TABLE 10.3
SOME ITEMS FROM THE BAYLEY SCALE OF INFANT MENTAL DEVELOPMENT

Item No.	Age Placement and Range (Months)	Item Title	Score Pass	Fail	Other
1	0.1	Responds to sound of bell			
2	0.1	Quiets when picked up			
3	0.1 (.1-3)	Responds to sound of rattle			
4	0.1 (.1-4)	Responds to sharp sound: click of light switch			
5	0.1 (.1-1)	Momentary regard of red ring			
6	0.2 (.1-1)	Regards person momentarily			
7	0.4 (.1-2)	Prolonged regard of red ring			
8	0.5 (.1-2)	Horizontal eye coordination: red ring			
9	0.7 (.3-3)	Horizontal eye coordination: light			
10	0.7 (.3-2)	Eyes follow moving person			
11	0.7 (.3-2)	Responds to voice			
12	0.8 (.3-3)	Vertical eye coordination: light			
13	0.9 (.5-3)	Vocalizes once or twice			
14	1.0 (.5-3)	Vertical eye coordination: red ring			
15	1.2 (.5-3)	Circular eye coordination: light			
16	1.2 (.5-3)	Circular eye coordination: red ring			
17	1.3 (.5-3)	Free inspection of surroundings			
18	1.5 (.5-4)	Social smile: when adult talks and smiles			
19	1.6 (.7-4)	Turns eyes to red ring			
20	1.6 (.5-4)	Turns eyes to light			
21	1.6 (.5-5)	Vocalizes at least 4 times			
22	1.7 (1-4)	Anticipatory excitement			
23	1.7 (.5-5)	Reacts to paper on face			
24	1.9 (1-4)	Blinks at shadow of hand			
25	2.0 (1-5)	Visually recognizes mother			

tested hand-eye coordination with objects, like red 1-inch cubes, a red ring and a string, a pellet of sugar, and a small bell. Motor skills included the fine hand skills of building with blocks or picking up small objects and the gross motor skills of sitting up and walking. Language included both understanding and uttering. Personal-social behavior consisted of an infant's responses to others and its efforts to help itself.

Today, among the most widely used tests of infant intelligence are the Gesell Developmental Schedules (Gesell et al., 1940; Gesell and Amatruda, 1941; Gesell and Thompson, 1934), the Griffiths Scale of Mental Development (Griffiths, 1954), the Cattell Infant Intelligence Scale (Cattell, 1940), and the Bayley Scales of Infant Development (Bayley, 1933, 1969). In addition, many pe-

diatricians use a short screening test, the Denver Developmental Screening Test. All these tests are tuned to age-related changes in motor skills, hand-eye coordination, speech and hearing, and personal-social actions. These tests, widely used by researchers and clinicians, have proved generally reliable.

The Bayley Scales of Infant Development have been especially widely used. Originally devised by Nancy Bayley to test children in the Berkeley Growth Study, the scales were revised and restandardized in 1969. The revised scales assess the sharpness and discriminatory power of infants' sensory-perceptual capacities and responses, their acquisition of object constancy, memory, learning, problem solving, vocalizing, classifying, and generalizing (see Table 10.3).

TABLE 10.3
CONTINUED

Item No.	Age Placement and Range (Months)	Item Title	Score		
			Pass	Fail	Other
142	22.4 *(16-30+)*	Blue form board: places 6 blocks			
143	23.0 *(17-30+)*	Builds tower of 6 cubes			
144	23.4 *(16-30+)*	Discriminates 2: cup, plate, box			
145	23.8 *(17-30+)*	Names watch, 4th picture			
146	24.0 *(17-30+)*	Names 3 objects			
147	24.4 *(19-30+)*	Imitates strokes: vertical and horizontal			
148	24.7 *(19-30+)*	Points to 7 pictures			
149	25.0 *(19-30+)*	Names 5 pictures			
150	25.2 *(18-30+)*	Names watch, 2nd picture			
151	25.4 *(18-30+)*	Pink form board: reversed			
152	25.6 *(18-30+)*	Discriminates 3: cup, plate, box			
153	26.1 *(16-30+)*	Broken doll: mends exactly			
154	26.1 *(19-30+)*	Makes train of cubes			
155	26.3 *(19-30+)*	Blue form board: completes in 150 seconds			
156	26.6 *(19-30+)*	Pegs placed in pegboard in 22 seconds			
157	27.9 *(22-30+)*	Folds paper			
158	28.2 *(22-30+)*	Understands 2 prepositions			
159	30.0 *(22-30+)*	Blue form board: completes in 90 seconds			
160	30+ *(22-30+)*	Blue form board: completes in 60 seconds			
161	30+ *(22-30+)*	Builds tower of 8 cubes			
162	30+ *(21-30+)*	Has concept of one			
163	30+ *(23-30+)*	Understands 3 prepositions			

To score: Check P (Pass) or F (Fail). If "Other," mark O (Omit), R (Refused), or RPT (Reported by mother).

Source: The Psychological Corporation, 1969

STABILITY AND CHANGE IN IQ SCORES

In looking at what happens to intelligence for a whole group of people, we see a general onward and upward trend, as we saw for physical growth. When Bayley (1966, 1968) plotted mental growth between infancy and 36 years in the Berkeley Growth Study, she found that intelligence increased rapidly until early adolescence, increased more slowly until midadolescence, and then tapered off by late adolescence. Raymond Cattell (1963, 1971) and John Horn (Horn, 1968; Horn and Cattell, 1966) have proposed that even during adulthood, some kinds of intelligence continue to increase. **Fluid intelligence**, the ability to manipulate abstract symbols, to solve analogies and classification problems, and to complete logical series, increases until the late 20s and then slowly decreases. **Crystallized intelligence**, knowledge of one's culture, vocabulary, general level of information, and reading comprehension, increases throughout adulthood.

But as with physical growth, when we look at paths of individual development rather than averages, the story changes. Only one-fifth of the children from the Berkeley Growth Study retained the same status relative to their peers for the first 9 years (see Figure 10.4). Some of the individual test

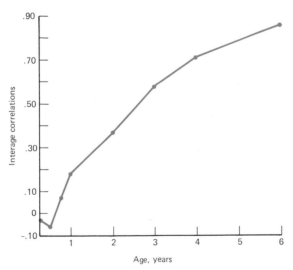

FIGURE 10.4
Prediction of IQ scores on the Stanford-Binet at 8 years from earlier scores on the California Infant and Preschool scales in the Berkeley Growth Study (Honzik, 1976).

scores shifted radically. One girl's went from 133 to 77; one boy's went from the middle 90s to 160, then to 135. Over time, 13 children varied by 30 or more points, one-third of the group varied by 20 points, and nearly two-thirds varied 15 or more points. Although the averages showed continuity, individual cases were far from stable. In less stable families than the white middle-class sample in the Berkeley study, the stability of children's IQ scores could be even lower.

The Bayley, Gesell, Cattell, and Griffiths tests all have been used to try to predict later IQ scores of individual infants. Although it would be convenient if infant and childhood tests meshed closely, the reality is that they do not, and predictions made from infant tests have not proved accurate. How stable is intelligence over time? Comparisons of scores from intelligence tests conducted in infancy, childhood, adolescence, and adulthood suggest, first, that there is no meaningful correlation between intelligence scores obtained during infancy and those obtained later. When meaningful correlations between infant and childhood test scores have been found, it is probably because children with extremely low scores have been included (Honzik, 1976). Only after children reach 4 years of age do IQ test scores start to predict later IQ test scores. Then, as children get older, their IQ test scores vary less and less and predict scores in adulthood better and better.

Why do test scores from the earliest months of life rarely agree with the scores later on? For one thing, infants vary greatly in their rates of mental development. Some develop rapidly, some slowly; as with other forms of development, children go through periods of rapid growth interspersed with plateaus of slower consolidation. For another thing, it has been difficult to identify the precursors in infancy of the abilities we consider intelligence in adulthood. Infants' intelligence centers on perceptual and sensorimotor abilities; older children's intelligence centers on quite different ways of organizing experience. Robert Sternberg and Janet Powell (1983) suggest that as children get older, intelligence consists of increasingly differentiated and more numerous abilities and that the relative importance of various abilities shifts. Peter Hofstaetter (1954) factor analyzed the data from the Berkeley Growth Study and found that until 20 months of age, most of the differences in infants'

Intelligence in 2-year-olds is characterized by persistence.

Intelligence in 4-year-olds is characterized by symbol manipulation.

intelligence could best be termed "sensorimotor alertness." From the age of 3½ years, however, sensorimotor alertness intelligence accounted for virtually no individual differences in intelligence. Between 20 months and 3½ years, the factor that best accounted for intelligence was persistence; from 4 years onward, the factor was manipula-

tion of symbols (abstraction). Thus "intelligence" means something quite different for children of different ages and reflects a dynamic succession of abilities. Bayley (1933b) also described the different factors that accounted for intelligence at different points in development: in the first 10 months, visual following, perceptual interest, manual dexterity, and social responsiveness; near the 10-month mark, vocal communication; from 10 months to 2½ years, perceptual interest, perceptual discrimination, dexterity, and vocal interest, with memory of forms and verbal knowledge growing important toward the end of the period. From 2½ to 4 years, dexterity, memory for forms, and verbal knowledge were important. From 4 to 6 years, memory for forms, verbal knowledge, vocabulary, and spatial relations were important; for 6 to 8 years, verbal knowledge, complex spatial relations, and vocabulary were the important factors. Over time, more complex factors came to substitute for earlier, simpler, perceptual factors.

A third explanation for the lack of predictability from infant tests might involve individual differences in temperament. One comparison of Swedish children (Brucefors et al., 1974) showed that those who gained the most in IQ between 3 months and 8 years started out at an average level of 84 and ended up at 114, whereas the group who lost the most started out at 111 and ended up at 84. The investigators attributed these shifts to differences in activity level at 3 months. Less active 3-month-olds, they suggested, may respond less to test objects and tasks and therefore score lower than their more active counterparts, but the quiet babies may be learning in ways that allow them to consolidate their gains when they are older.

Given the discrepancy between the composition of infants' and older children's intelligence, Robert McCall (1976) has suggested that it might be useful to abandon the search for stability of IQ and refocus on the nature of developmental changes in infant intelligence. Accordingly, he and his colleagues (McCall, Hogarty, and Hurlburt, 1972) looked for patterns within the responses of 6-, 12-, and 24-month-olds to the Gesell scales. For 6-month-olds, the principal component of intelligent behavior was visually guided exploration of perceptual contingencies—splashing in the bathtub, banging a spoon on a table, or reaching for a dangling ring. For 12-month-olds, the principal components were a mixture of sensorimotor skills, social imitation, and the beginnings of utterances. For 18-month-olds, verbal and motor imitation (repeating words, scribbling in imitation) and understanding speech (pointing to parts of the body, or pointing to pictures of objects) were added to the 12-month behaviors. For 24-month-olds, intelligence was more strongly verbal, now including labeling objects and pictures as well as understanding and imitating words.

An alternative approach to McCall's is to search for one or two components of intelligence that will be stable in infancy and through childhood. Joseph Fagan and Lynn Singer (1983) hypothesized that early individual differences among infants in recognizing a previously seen stimulus reflect the same perceptual encoding differences—in discriminating, identifying, and recalling—that later recognition tests and intelligence tests tap. They tested this hypothesis with a number of samples of children and found that, indeed, infants' abilities to recognize visual stimuli were significantly correlated with how they did on later tests of verbal intelligence. The 12 correlations they found between infant recognition and childhood intelligence averaged .44. This relation held for samples of children with normal intelligence and those with Down's syndrome; it held for all socioeconomic groups; and it held for males and females.

This last finding is somewhat unusual in the annals of intelligence tests: a consistent finding has been that the stability of IQ scores is greater for females than for males. For example, the age at which girls but not boys first vocalize eagerness and displeasure, say "da da" or an equivalent, and say two words correlates moderately with intelligence scores into adulthood (Bayley, 1968). Other measures of infant girls' "speech quotient" have also proved moderately predictive of later intelligence (Kagan, 1971; Moore, 1968;). In addition, 6-month-old girls' scores, but not boys', on the Gesell scales predicted their Stanford-Binet IQ scores at age 3½ (McCall et al., 1972); 8-month-old girls' scores on the Bayley scales also were better predictors of WISC IQs at age 7 (Goffeney, Henderson, and Butler, 1971).

Pediatricians often want tests of infants' abilities that will help them to diagnose handicaps as early as possible. In this effort, infant intelligence tests have proved to have some useful predictive power. In an extensive study of the prenatal and postnatal development of all children born on the Hawaiian island of Kauai between 1954 and 1955 (Bierman, Connor, Vaage, and Honzik, 1964; Werner and Bayley, 1966; Werner, Bierman, and French, 1971), pediatricians categorized the children at 20 months as being of retarded, low normal, normal, or superior intelligence. The children were administered the Cattell IQ test as well, but the test scores and the pediatricians' ratings did not agree strongly. In the years that followed, children judged by pediatricians as below normal but who had normal IQ test scores were likely to develop below average speech, motor abilities, and general physical robustness. Those children pediatricians judged normal and whose IQ scores were below 80 did poorly in grade school. Children who did poorly both in the pediatricians' judgments and on the infant intelligence tests scored poorly on IQ and achievement tests at 10 years. Tests of infants' intelligence can be helpful for diagnosing and predicting behavior when the scores are very low, but they are less helpful when the scores fall within the normal range (McCall et al., 1972).

CRITICISM OF IQ TESTS

Tests of infants' intelligence are not the only tests to have been roundly criticized. All tests of intelligence have been criticized for their bias against minority groups and for their failure to predict adaptive behavior beyond the confines of the schoolroom. The tests, according to one critic (David McClelland, quoted in Fincher, 1976, p. 205) are successful only "if one judges by the usual American criteria of size, influence, and profitability." Some argue that the tests measure nothing of value; others hold that they measure something far narrower than intelligence. Standardized tests measure particular skills, like reading and writing. They test previous achievement and the kind of one-right-answer convergent thinking rewarded nowhere so reliably as in the classroom, and they predict school performance—for which reason, critics insist, they should stay in school "where they belong" (Fincher, 1976). It is not uncommon for tests of the worth of metals or of engines to last for years, yet tests of human ability last a tiny fraction of that time. Furthermore, IQ tests may penalize late bloomers, shatter self-esteem, and stunt motivation. The tests generally penalize creativity or even the seeing of two right answers to a single question, and they make no allowances for mood or temperament, headaches or anxiety, boredom or sleepiness.

Most of the tests have been standardized on groups of children who are white and middle class, children whose rearing and culture endow them with norms and skills quite different from those of children who are poor or black, brown, yellow, or red. The tests assume children's familiarity with standard English and with the objects and routines of middle-class life. Where is the justice, critics ask, in labeling a minority child "retarded" for scoring poorly on a test that bears little relation to the realities of his or her life? On the Binet test, for example, children are asked the correct response to, "What's the thing for you to do if another boy hits you without meaning to do it?" The correct response is to assume it was an accident and to walk away—a suicidal response in some black communities (Williams, 1970). Presumably, a girl is supposed to answer this question about "another boy" hitting her by automatically accommodating to and overlooking its inherent illogic.

Although the intelligence tests may be biased, they do reflect certain social realities. In our society, intelligence tests are designed to measure success in schools that by and large operate on middle-class values. These tests predict success, because the children who learn and observe middle-class norms are the children who achieve in school and in the working world.

Out of a concern for the effects on minority-group members of being labeled retarded—with its implications for classroom placement, others' attitudes and expectations, and occasionally even institutionalization—Jane Mercer (1971) studied the difference between individuals' scores on standard intelligence tests and their successfully adaptive everyday behavior. For the latter, she measured such things as young children's abilities to dress and feed themselves, older people's abilities to shop, hold a job, travel, and the like. Her subjects were over 600 blacks, Chicanos, and whites. She found that of the people labeled retarded—those who had scored between 75 and 84 on standard tests—virtually all could shop and travel alone, and most had finished eighth grade and held a job. Those who scored below 70, however, did not cope

well in everyday life, and Mercer suggested that 70 be the mark at which the "lethal" label of **retarded** be applied. Even so, 90 percent of the black children and 60 percent of the Chicano children who scored under 70 passed the test of adaptive behavior. This finding suggests that poor or minority-group children are likeliest to suffer unfair consequences of being labeled retarded on the sole basis of IQ test scores. Perhaps the lethal label should be set even lower than an IQ of 70 for people in these minority groups.

Many of the psychologists who administer standard IQ tests are white, and black children may feel too suspicious of them to perform well (Labov, 1970). When the test is given under relaxed conditions, however, black children sometimes perform better with white than black testers (Bucky and Banta, 1972). When the test is given under stressful conditions, and black children are anxious about

When conditions for testing are relaxed, black children do as well or better with white testers than black testers. But when conditions are stressful, black children do better with black testers.

their performance, they do better with a black tester (Katz, Roberts, and Robinson, 1965). In general, all children perform best on IQ tests when they are given a chance to grow familiar with the test and testing situation and when the atmosphere is friendly and relaxed.

CORRELATES OF INTELLIGENCE

If a test is valid, its results bear a meaningful and significant relation to real-world behavior. Are IQ tests valid? Yes and no. As we have seen, they are highly correlated with children's performance in school—school grades correlate with IQ scores about .70 (McClelland, 1973)—and with performance on tasks that reward knowledge of information, convergent thinking, and middle-class norms. They predict performance better in grade and high school than in college or graduate school. They help educators identify and educate the exceptional students at both ends of the distribution curve, and on occasion they may actually eliminate class barriers by identifying bright minority-group children (Tyler, 1976). But school achievement is just one domain. What about others?

Terman, who made up the earliest version of the Stanford-Binet Intelligence Scales, also conducted a long-term study of gifted children (Terman, 1925; Terman and Oden, 1959). The mean IQ of these gifted children was 151. In adult life, many of the men—the women had become house wives, to whom recognition for achievement is not customarily awarded—had achieved greatly and illustriously in either their business or professional careers. In the 1920s, Terman fully expected that the results of his longitudinal study of gifted children would show a strongly positive relation between their individual IQ scores and their success later in life. As children, these gifted subjects were bigger, stronger, earlier to reach puberty, better students, and even more morally advanced than their less gifted peers. As adults, not only were the men illustrious, but they suffered less alcoholism, delinquency, mental illness, criminal convictions, or early deaths. Terman's study established conclusively that his gifted subjects were, as a group, effective and successful in their lives. But it did not bear out his expectations about the predictability of IQ at

the individual level in this homogeneous group, which excluded the poor, the rural, and the nonwhite. Terman had judges independently compare the records of 150 of the most successful men—the A group—with those of 150 of the least successful—the C group. The differences between the two groups were dramatic: the A's held better jobs and earned twice what the C's did; the A's were healthier, happier, more happily married to better educated wives. The C's suffered unemployment, had fewer hobbies, narrower interests, more divorces. But the average IQ of *both* groups was 150!

If IQ correlated so imperfectly with social success, what does it correlate with? What about success at work? IQ test scores predict success for those in jobs that require abstraction and symbol manipulation—selling stocks or teaching undergraduates, for example—better than they predict success in other kinds of jobs—police work, for example (Ghiselli, 1966). If tests are to predict job performance accurately, they must specify the criteria for performing each job. A test for police or fire-fighting work should not, as some civil service tests now do, plumb an applicant's comprehension of obscure nouns. It would be far more useful if it assessed the applicant's abilities to do what police or fire fighters actually do. Some occupations require a certain level of intelligence, but once above that minimum level, more intelligent people do not necessarily achieve or succeed more. In one study, for example, the mathematicians with the greatest professional success did not have IQs any higher than those of their less successful colleagues (Helson and Crutchfield, 1970). Christopher Jencks and Mary Jo Bane (Bane and Jencks, 1973) conclude that IQ accounts for 10 percent of the difference between individuals' job performance and for less than 5 percent of their income. They explain that special skills account for some kinds of economic success: the ball player should be able to hit a ball, and the business executive should be good at directing subordinates. The ability to inspire confidence is always helpful, but finally, they say, there is the matter of . . . luck.

The relation between IQ and creativity is not straightforward either. Intelligence tests may actually penalize creative thinking, and so some creative people may perform poorly on them. Creativity in the verbal area is more likely to be reflected in intelligence tests than is musical or artistic talent.

PREDICTORS OF INTELLIGENCE

The environment and heredity both play their part in shaping an individual's intelligence. As we saw in Chapters 2 and 3, heredity influences intellectual capacity, and environment shapes the actual expression of that capacity. Both heredity and environment are involved, too, in IQ differences related to race and social class.

RACE AND ARTHUR JENSEN

A major controversy surrounding IQ testing concerns its use to support alleged differences in the intelligence of members of the white and black races. At one extreme are those who maintain that group differences in intelligence reflect genetic differences. At the other extreme are those who maintain that the differences in IQ either are invalid because of defects in the test itself or reflect the many social, economic, and cultural differences between groups. The finding that whites as a group outperform blacks as a group on IQ tests by approximately 15 points is not disputed by anyone (Brody and Brody, 1976; Jencks et al., 1972; Jensen, 1980). There is, however, considerable disagreement over how to interpret this finding. According to Arthur Jensen (1980), even when blacks and whites of equivalent socioeconomic status are compared, whites still outperform blacks by 12 points. This difference, Jensen maintains, is too large to be explained by environmental factors alone.

The IQ debate, which polarized psychologists in the 1970s, actually heated up in the late 1960s when the results of a massive study by the Department of Health, Education, and Welfare revealed a marked difference in the performances of black and white children (Health Examination Survey of 1963–1965). White children scored substantially higher on the WISC administered to a sample of over 7000 children selected to represent the 1 million noninstitutionalized children in the United States between the ages of 6 and 11. The racial difference in scores existed for every region of the country, although the scores of both white and black children living in the South were significantly lower than those of children living in other regions of the country. Although the intellectual development of children was found to have a stronger association with the socioeconomic status (SES) of their family than with race, the racial difference in intelligence appeared consistently.

In an extensive analysis of the results of this study, Jensen (1969) distinguished between lower-level intelligence, or **associative intelligence** and higher-level intelligence, or **conceptual intelligence** (see Table 10.4). Jensen presented evidence that he claimed proved that blacks score lower on IQ tests because they cannot learn as well as whites at the higher level of conceptual thinking. He maintained that blacks and whites are equal only at the level of associative thinking and memory. In a later study, Jensen (1973) administered IQ tests to 2000 whites, blacks, and Mexican-American pupils in grades 4, 5, and 6. Again, he claimed to find proof for racial differences in conceptual thinking.

Associative, or Level I learning, is stimulus-response learning. Conceptual learning, or Level II learning, is the active, cognitive transformation of stimuli. Jensen is not alone in these ideas; they were commonly debated by property owners in the 18th century. Here is a comparison of blacks and whites first published in 1794:

Comparing them by their faculties of memory, reason, and imagination, it appears to me that in memory [blacks] are equal to whites; in reason much inferior, as I think one could scarcely be found capable of tracing and comprehending the investigations of Euclid [that is, geometry]; and that in imagination they are dull, tasteless, and anomalous (cited in Rose, 1976, p. 71).

It was written by Thomas Jefferson.

A thorough understanding of the issues involved in this controversy requires a statistical sophistication beyond the scope of this book. One key to the debate, however, is the degree to which intelligence is determined by genetic factors. To measure the influence of genes on intelligence, we would have to hold environment constant, that is, raise a group of children from birth, some say from conception, under identical conditions. Beyond the humanitarian and practical problems that make such a project impossible, environment cannot be held constant because, in many respects, the individual controls and influences his or her own environment.

TABLE 10.4
JENSEN'S LEVELS OF INTELLIGENCE

Level I Associative: Memory and Knowledge
When did Columbus discover America?
Pick out the word that does not belong:
   door   kitchen   painted   garage   porch
Underline the word that goes with the set:
   arm, hand, foot, neck: body/man/knee/take

Level II Conceptual: Abstraction and Analogy
What does this mean: "Fight fire with fire."
"Cat" is to "kitten" as "dog" is to _____.
"Before" is to "behind" as "future" is to _____.

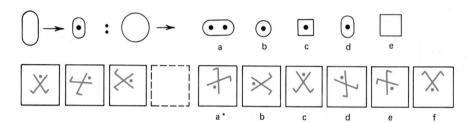

Source: Illustrations taken from the Culture Fair Intelligence Test, Scale 3, Form B. Copyright © 1950, 1961, by the Institute for Personality and Ability Testing, Inc. All rights reserved. Reproduced by permission of the copyright owner.

From the results of available studies of similarities in the intelligence of twins, siblings, natural and adopted offspring—the next best thing for estimating a genetic contribution—Jensen (1973) estimated the heritability of intelligence to be 80 percent. Because adults tend to treat identical twins as "more alike" than fraternal twins, and because adoption agencies try both to place children in homes with the same religious and cultural backgrounds as those of their natural parents and to place all children in "good" homes, the impact of environment in twin and adoption studies may be muted. Therefore Jensen's estimate of the heritability of intelligence as 80 percent is likely to be inflated. Using a different set of studies, Jencks (Jencks et al., 1972) estimated the purely genetic component to be only 45 percent.

Some researchers have attempted to defuse the racial overtones of this IQ debate by pointing to differences in the early circumstances and upbringing of blacks and whites, such as prenatal health care, adequacy of nutrition, child care, and parents' education. Other psychologists maintain that intelligence tests are culturally biased and that statistical manipulations of the effects of income, schooling,

and other variables cannot eliminate the pervasive and cumulative discriminations faced by blacks. It is certainly true, as we have seen, that all intelligence tests contain some material reflecting culture; otherwise they would have no value for society. The objective of a test designer is to eliminate items that discriminate against groups for reasons that have nothing to do with the purposes of the test. Jensen (1980) maintains that blacks do even less well than whites on so-called "culture-reduced" test items, for example, the nonverbal analogies in Table 10.4, than they do on so-called "culture-loaded" test items, the verbal analogies.

Even the staunchest supporters of the heritability of IQ would not deny that the environment has some influence on intellectual development. Jensen himself (1977) has claimed that there are cumulative effects of deprivation on IQ and that the gap between disadvantaged and advantaged children widens as the children become older. Studies of black children reared in white families further substantiate the importance of environmental factors in intelligence. As we saw in Chapter 2, for example, Sandra Scarr and Richard Weinberg (1976; 1983) studied 176 children, most of whom were black and all of whom had been adopted into white, upper-middle-class families. The adoptive families were all well educated and held professional jobs. The natural parents of the adopted children had high school degrees. The mean IQ score of the adopted children was 106, above average. Although lower than the mean IQ score, 116, of the natural children of these adoptive parents, it was higher than would have been expected had the children remained with their biological parents, who had IQ scores of less than 100. Children who had been adopted in infancy scored an average IQ of 111; children adopted later scored an average of 97.5. The study did not refute the importance of heredity, but it indicated that IQ scores could be increased by 10 to 20 points by better circumstances, and the earlier the better.

Finally, data indicate that young black children have higher IQs than their older siblings did at the same age. This difference has been attributed to the improved schooling and other social advantages of the younger siblings (Kamin, 1978).

Often forgotten in the emotion of the IQ debate is that the outcome is of little practical application. First, even if IQ tests are assumed to be valid, the variation in IQ scores within a race is three times larger than the difference in IQ scores of blacks and whites. Knowing a person's race is therefore virtually useless as a predictor of that person's intelligence. Second, if people's IQ scores are within the normal range, they do not by themselves indicate how well individuals would do when they apply intelligence to everyday matters. If the goal is to eliminate social and economic injustice, many more practical steps can be taken than to debate endlessly the validity or bias of mental tests. To go beyond the racial debate about differences in IQ scores, a first step is to look to factors in the immediate family environment of the individual. It is to this kind of analysis that we now turn.

FAMILY FACTORS

What are the environmental factors within families that affect the expression of intelligence? From several longitudinal studies of the relation between intelligence and factors within children's home environments in Seattle, Los Angeles, Little Rock, Toronto, and Houston, Allen Gottfried (1984) has extracted a number of predictive environmental factors. The common measurement of the actual environment in the home among all the studies was Bettye Caldwell's Home Observation for Measurement of the Environment (HOME) (see p. 85). In this combination of observation and interview, investigators noted mothers' responsiveness, involvement, and restrictiveness; the organization of the child's time and the physical environment; the materials with which the child played; and the child's everyday opportunities for variety and stimulation.

Books, pictures, signs, and a variety of toys, all in well-arranged space, provide a stimulating environment within which a young child's intellect can flourish.

The most pervasive finding in all these studies was the strong association between the HOME scales and the family's SES. Children from homes in which parents' income, education, and occupation were higher had a more advantageous home environment. Their mothers were more responsive and involved, provided more materials for play, and there were more opportunities for daily stimulation. This finding held for white, black, and Hispanic children. Two of the studies (Beckwith and Cohen, 1984; Bradley and Caldwell, 1984) showed, moreover, that racial or ethnic differences in home stimulation were a function of socioeconomic factors, not race itself. Mothers of relatively higher intelligence also provided more enriched environments for their children.

The studies also consistently reported strong and positive relations between the HOME scores and children's intelligence. Robert Bradley and Bettye Caldwell (1984), for example, found significant correlations (averaging .58) between HOME scales when a child was 1 year old and IQ scores at 3 years old, the highest correlations being for appropriate play materials and mothers' involvement. The HOME scales for 2-year-olds also correlated positively (.63) with children's IQ scores at age 4½, and again mothers' involvement and appropriate play materials were the most highly predictive of HOME scales. The other studies reported similar patterns of correlations, although in some, the degree of organization and variety of stimulation were more important than the mothers' involvement. The availability of play materials was reported as one of the most important factors in four of the five studies. The other factors were not significantly correlated so consistently.

A meta-analysis done by Gottfried of data from all the studies taken together confirmed the relative importance of maternal involvement, play materials, and variety (see Table 10.5). The less crowded a child's personal space and the more organized the child's home and play materials and the more involved and responsive the mother, the greater the quantity and quality of intellectual stimulation in the home and the higher the child was likely to score on tests of intelligence. These patterns of connection between home environment and children's intelligence applied to both boys and girls in families of either high or low degrees of formal education. When SES and mothers' intelligence were statistically controlled in these studies, social and physical factors in the child's home environment still were consistently found to correlate with children's intelligence.

Keith Owen Yeates and his colleagues, in a separate longitudinal study in North Carolina (Yeates, MacPhee, Campbell, and Ramey, 1983), found that when the effects of mothers' IQ were removed,

TABLE 10.5

CORRELATIONS BETWEEN *HOME* ENVIRONMENT AND CHILDREN'S IQ

HOME Scale	Mean Correlation with IQ					
	Bayley Scale at 1 year[a]	Bayley Scale at 2 years[a]	Stanford-Binet at 3 years[a]	Stanford-Binet at 4 years		Grand mean[a]
Responsivity	.12	.17	.23	.19[a]	.38[b]	.7
Restriction-punishment	.02	.16	.11	.19	.29	.12
Organization	.10	.17	.13	.16	.21	.14
Play materials	.18	.23	.24	.29	.37	.23
Involvement	.14	.25	.33	.26	.38	.24
Variety	.10	.24	.24	.28	.28	.21
Total	.17	.32	.34	.38	.50	.30
N	(626)	(455)	(365)	(404)	(344)	(1850)

Notes: [a] HOME assessed at 1 year. [b] HOME assessed at 2 years.
Source: Adapted from Gottfried, 1984.

the association between children's IQs and their home environment was not significant at ages 2 or 3, but it was significant at age 4. In Gottfried's analysis, too, preschool measures of children's intelligence were more consistently and highly associated with HOME variables than were infant measures of intelligence (see Table 10.5). However, it is noteworthy that in an investigation of older children (Longstreth et al., 1981), whose average age was 12, the home environment measure did not add to the predictability of children's IQ beyond what could be predicted from knowing the mother's IQ. Taken together, these findings suggest that the home environment may be a greater influence

RESEARCH FOCUS

MOTHER-CHILD INTERACTION AND COGNITIVE DEVELOPMENT

What characteristics of mother and child best predict the child's competence in language and other forms of intelligence at age 2? That was the central question asked by Sheryl Olson, John Bates, and Kathryn Bayles (1984). To answer it, they chose 168 pairs of normal mothers and infants from working-class to upper-middle-class backgrounds and observed them and their homes at three different times. They took HOME inventories when the children were 6 months old and administered the Bayley Intelligence Scales to the infants. When the children were 13 months old and again at 24 months, the mothers and babies were assessed and given more IQ tests. The researchers assessed not only the infants' test competence, but also their sociability with both their mothers and the examiners.

When the children were 6 months old, the behavior of mothers and children essentially did not correlate, and the infants' IQ scores were not related to measurements of their interaction with their mothers. At 13 months, the correlations between mothers' behavior and infants' competence were stronger, and several were statistically significant. By 24 months, major categories of mother and child behavior, especially the frequency of verbal interaction and conflicts, were highly intercorrelated and were significantly correlated with the child's IQ. Mothers who talked to their children and did relatively little restricting or punishing tended to have the most intelligent 2-year-olds.

But what about prediction of IQ at age 2 from earlier mother-infant interaction? The best predictors of IQ at age 2 were: close contact with the mother and stimulating objects at home; a mother who was highly involved with her infant, was emotionally and verbally responsive, and provided appropriate materials for play at 6 months; and at 13 months, the same variables plus a mother who was not restrictive or punitive and, to some degree, had a higher SES. These factors all were incorporated into a single statistical analysis showing the probable causal links between mother-infant interaction and the 2-year-old's IQ. The results of this statistical analysis, pictured in Figure 10.5, showed that a few environmental factors could explain 40 percent (a relatively large proportion) of the 2-year-olds' IQ scores.

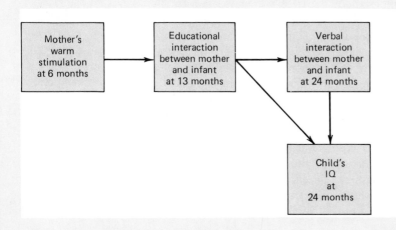

FIGURE 10.5
Path analysis showing environmental antecedents of child's IQ at 2 years of age. Arrows indicate causal direction (Olson, Bates, and Bayles, 1984).

on children's intellectual growth during the pre-school years than it is either earlier (when biological factors are more important) or later (when the child has established his or her niche in the environments of home, school, and peers).

Theodore Wachs and Gerald Gruen (1982) reviewed all of the literature on elements within the family environment that predict children's IQ in the first 5 years and sketched a scenario for promoting high intelligence during these years. During the first 6 months, they suggest, infants do best who have a variety of stimulating materials available when they want to look at them and a mother (or other caretaker) who spends a substantial amount of time in physical contact with them. Physical contact increases the infant's attention, and the stimulating materials—mobile, pictures, toys—give the infant

something to which to attend. During the second 6 months, infants' intelligence continues to develop if one or two warm and sensitive adults care for them and provide them with a rich variety of experiences. Now that they are creeping about on their own, infants should be given enough room to explore but not so much room that they endanger their safety. They need things to look at and things to reach for, things that are colorful and have interesting shapes and sizes, and things that respond in some way to their actions. Once infants start walking, they continue to need these interesting and responsive toys, freedom to explore, the teaching of skills—when they are receptive—and different sorts of interactions with parents who are sensitive and warm. During the second year of life, toddlers increasingly need adults to respond to their

RESEARCH FOCUS

COGNITIVE DEVELOPMENT OF CHICANO CHILDREN

Like the intellectual development of other children, that of Mexican-American children is influenced by environmental factors. Yet little research is available on the factors that contribute to the development of intelligence in Mexican-American families. To address this problem, Ronald McGowan and Dale Johnson (1984) studied the home environments, the background and attitudes of Mexican-American mothers, and the intellectual development of their first-, second-, or third-grade children. All of the children were from Houston; some were participants in a two-year intervention program designed to make mothers more effective teachers of their children. The investigators gathered information on the number of years and where the mothers had attended school. They also measured mothers' attitudes toward traditional versus modern family behavior and toward success and achievement. Mothers' encouragement of the children's vocalizations, their use of reasoning, and the level of interaction with their children were assessed. Children's IQs were tested at age 3 and again at age 6 or 8. Also noted were 3-year-olds' preference for English or Spanish and a score of HOME variables—factors constituting the quality and quantity of social, emo-

tional, and cognitive support available in children's homes.

The investigators found that a child's IQ score at age 3 was related to the number of years his or her mother had gone to school, the mother's encouragement of her child's independence, and reciprocal interaction between mother and child. The more educated the mother, the less likely she was to demonstrate traditional attitudes, the more likely she was to stimulate her child intellectually, and the higher the child's IQ score was likely to be at age 3. But the investigators were puzzled to find that at the age of 8, children of mothers with more traditional attitudes scored higher on tests of nonverbal ability than children of less traditional mothers. They speculated that mothers who are traditional yet affectionate produce children who are "quietly competent." Another puzzle was the modest correlation between the mothers' intellectual stimulation and the children's intelligence scores. HOME scores of mothers' stimulation predicted only children's performance in tests of verbal comprehension. Why were correlations lower in this study than in others? The investigators suggested that this might be because their measures failed to capture the richness of the relationship between the mothers and children in this study or because standard intelligence tests may not be valid for assessing the abilities of Mexican-American children.

social signals and needs, to read and talk to them, and to actively help them explore. They should not be coerced or restricted. Girls at this stage, the research suggests, need a variety of different new toys; boys do not need so many new things. Boys need an environment that is highly regular, where everything has its time and its place. Boys are also especially sensitive to the harmful effects of noise and crowding. They do best with several toys in a space where they can be alone with an adult and perhaps one or two other children. Between age 2 and 3, many of the other factors that were previously important continue to be so: exploratory freedom, a physically and socially responsive environment, warm interaction with adults, verbal stimulation, training in specific skills, and the avoidance of restriction and coercion. Adults now also need to respond appropriately to their child's attempts at talking. The same factors will remain important to children's intelligence when they are 3, at which age it becomes important for them to interact with a variety of people. After the age of 4, children still need many of the same things— varied experiences with people, adults who are warm and responsive, instruction in skills, room to explore. Boys still need time out from noise and confusion, and they need a relationship with a nurturant adult. But the relevance of avoiding restriction and coercion becomes less and less salient after this age.

MODIFYING INTELLIGENCE

As Wachs and Gruen's (1982) scenario for promoting high intelligence in children suggests, a stimulating and nurturant environment can enhance children's intelligence. In the past 20 years, many attempts have been made to provide such enriched environments for children from poor families. These **interventions** have demonstrated just how much intelligence can be modified by the environment. One exemplary intervention is the Abcedarian Project at the Frank Parker Graham Center in Durham, North Carolina. As Craig Ramey, Dale Farran, and Frances Campbell (1979) point out, for the poor, black children who attended that program for a good part of the day, the correlations usually found (and found in their control group) between children's and their mothers' IQ scores

A model day-care center can successfully intervene to modify preschoolers' intelligence. Many investigators have reported IQ increases of from 5 to 15 points in children who attend educational programs.

were not significant (−.05 versus .43 for the control group), even though the two groups of mothers did not differ fundamentally in attitudes, behavior, or intelligence. The intervention had successfully modified children's intelligence scores. It had overcome some of the effects of their unstimulating family circumstances and allowed these children to realize more of their intellectual potential. Children in the program scored higher than the control group on IQ tests at ages 2 and 3 (by 10 and 15 points) (Ramey and Campbell, 1979). In a follow-up when the children were 4 and 5 years old, children in the program still scored higher than the control children (by 12 and 7 IQ points) (Ramey and Haskins, 1981). This study is exemplary because it used an experimental design, assigning infants at random to the control group or to the day-care program; it presented a comprehensive, full-day, infancy-to-school-age educational experience; and it included extensive observations and assessments of the children and the program.

Many other investigators have also shown IQ gains of 5 to 15 points for children attending their educational programs (e.g., those that collaborated in the Consortium for Longitudinal Studies summarized by Lazar, Darlington, Murray, Royce, and Snipper, 1982). A dramatic demonstration of the extent to which IQ scores can be modified comes from a program in Milwaukee offered to children at risk for retardation because their mothers had IQs under 80 (Garber and Heber, 1973). This program, too, was comprehensive, beginning when the children were 3 months old and lasting, full days, for 6 years. Mothers were helped to develop job, homemaking, and child-rearing skills. Children were given sensorimotor stimulation and, later, training in language, reading, arithmetic, and problem solving. Although the IQ scores of the children in the program and those of a control group who received no extra stimulation or support were comparable for the first 1½ years, by the age of 5½, the children in the program were scoring an average of 30 points higher on IQ tests. Unfortunately, some questions have been raised about this "miracle in Milwaukee" because its investigators have not made public their data records, but for now it holds the record for the most substantial modification of IQ scores that has been accomplished through an educational intervention program.

Not only do the IQ scores of children in such intervention programs surpass those of their peers who did not attend an early education program, but also their self-confidence and their performance in, and attitudes toward, school are better. They are less likely to stay back a grade in school or to need special education. Even their brothers and sisters benefit indirectly from the effects of their participation in an early intervention program (Klaus and Gray, 1968). The benefits are most marked for children from disadvantaged homes, but middle-class children also have been found to benefit from educational enrichment (Caldwell, 1973).

Not all interventions have been aimed directly at the child; some have approached the child indirectly by modifying the mother's behavior. In one such study, of Chicago mothers and children from low-income housing, Diana Slaughter (1983) compared mothers who had participated in one of two parent-education programs with those who had not, over the period when their children were 2 to 4 years old. Mothers who had participated in discussion groups where they shared their experiences of child rearing and social life scored higher than mothers in the control group on measures of ego development, expressed social values, openness and flexibility of attitudes toward child rearing, and their style of teaching their children. They interacted more and played more elaborately with their children. Their children in turn tested higher on IQ tests (especially in verbal intelligence) and talked more often than children in the control group. This study is one of many to document the effects of intervention through mothers' involvement in their children's education.

One important question raised by childhood intervention programs, however, is how long their effects last. A longitudinal study by Susan Gray and her colleagues (Gray, Ramsey, and Klaus, 1982) showed that girls seemed to profit more than boys

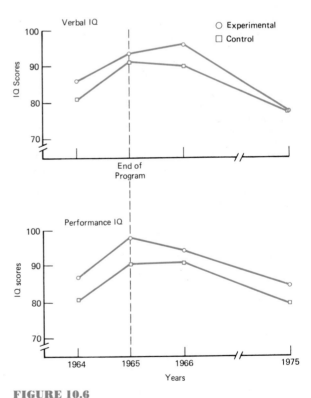

FIGURE 10.6

IQ (WISC) Verbal and Performance scores for children in the Early Training Project taken during the program and after it ended (Gray, Ramsey, and Klaus, 1982).

from being in a preschool intervention program and that the effects were quite long lasting, with a correlation of .67 between IQ scores at ages 5 and 17. Nevertheless, the IQ scores of the children began falling a year or so after the program ended and 10 years later were nearly the same as the IQs of control groups (see Figure 10.6). This pattern is typical of these studies. IQ gains from an intervention during the preschool period usually last a year or two and then begin to diminish. If no further intervention occurs, the gains have disappeared by the time children are 10 to 17 years old (Lazar et al., 1982). Indirect benefits like improved self-esteem and feelings about school may be enduring, but children need continued support and stimulation if the gain in IQ points is to endure.

These intervention programs begun in the 1960s and 1970s have generally focused on children from low-income families. In the 1980s, it seems that middle-class parents are trying to increase their infants' IQ scores by enriching their environments and giving them deliberate training and stimulation. Whether the immediate IQ gains observed for these "superbabies" persist will likely depend as well on the continued support and stimulation they receive at home and in school.

NEW APPROACHES TO INTELLIGENCE

Dissatisfied with the psychometric approach, psychologists from several schools of thought recently have taken new tacks in studying intelligence. The familiar IQ test is being supplanted by other techniques for assessing intelligence, and our definition of intelligence as what IQ tests measure is being replaced by broader conceptions.

INFORMATION-PROCESSING COMPONENTS

Information processors have proposed one alternative view of intelligence. They suggest that individual differences in processing speed, in choice of cognitive strategies, and in the content of long-term memory reflect differences in intelligence. At some point in the future, research in information processing may tell us about individual differences in

metacognition—in people's accuracy and speed in choosing cognitive strategies—and how these relate to intelligence (Sternberg, 1979).

Some information processors have attempted to learn whether individual children differ reliably in cognitive processing and whether these differences relate systematically to ability. One study by Dan Keating and Bruce Bobbitt (1978) used as subjects 9-, 13-, and 17-year-olds with high and average IQ scores on the Raven Progressive Matrices and drilled them in three kinds of information processing. On tasks of simple reaction time (pressing a button as soon as a red light appeared) and more complex reaction time (pressing a green button when a green light appeared and a red button when a red light appeared), the older and brighter children performed best. But the difference between the two reaction times, which reflects cognitive processing, was greater for the younger and less bright children. On tasks requiring sorting cards and matching pairs of letters, the older and brighter children again did best and were less adversely affected by additional, complex demands than younger, less able children. On memory scanning, too, the same patterns held. When the results of the various procedures were integrated, it was found that the difference between complex and simple reaction times, the difference between simple and complex matching, and the duration of memory scanning comparisons accounted for 62 percent of the individual differences in IQ scores. Age accounted for 47 percent of this variation among individuals and central processing for 15 percent. Central processing is thus not the same as IQ. Its usefulness as a predictor of success in school or in life remains to be seen.

Another information processing technique for studying individual differences in intelligence has focused on children's verbal abilities. Children are presented with sentences that substitute a made-up word for a real word: "John fell into a *contavish* in the road," where "contavish" substitutes for "hole," for instance. In the first study to use this technique, Heinz Werner and Edith Kaplan (1952) tested children between 8 and 13 years old on their ability to guess the real word, and they found that performance increased gradually with age. More recently, M. M. van Daalen-Kapteijns and M. Elshout-Mohr (1981) used a similar task to investigate individual differences in verbal comprehension.

Subjects with high ability, they found, applied and transformed a known word's meaning in a different way from subjects with low verbal ability. Those with high ability tended to process words more analytically, could flexibly pick and choose elements among familiar models for unknown words, and could combine these elements into coherent wholes. Those with lower ability were less skillful in choosing elements or in combining them into a whole. In another study of verbal comprehension, Powell and Sternberg (1981) gave high-school students brief passages to read in which unknown words appeared. They found that the students' abilities to acquire, retain, and transfer the meaning of the words correlated about .60 with their verbal IQ scores. This approach, then, also offers an alternative measurement of verbal intelligence.

These two approaches, measuring mechanistic processes like the speed of access to words and measuring processes involved in understanding words, are just two examples of how information processors are breaking down the concept of intelligence into measurable components and exploring individual differences in both the speed and the adequacy of processing information. This approach to intelligence will no doubt continue to be explored and refined in the 1980s.

COMMON PRINCIPLES

Another contemporary approach is to look for commonalities rather than components in various definitions of intelligence. According to Sternberg and Powell (1983), certain principles are common to various approaches to intelligence and transcend particular schools or paradigms. Virtually every theory and definition of intelligence, for example, posits the existence of a central, executive, control function or strategy. Some people call this faculty "intellectual judgment" (Spearman, 1927), and some call it the ability to make good decisions or to plan ahead (Sternberg et al., 1981), but this "rose by any other name" is always considered critical to intellectual development. A second common principle centers on the thoroughness with which people process information. Intelligence requires a thorough encoding of stimuli that need to be combined, and more intelligent people use all, not just some, available information, and they use

it to greatest advantage. Third is the ability to understand increasingly higher orders of abstraction and complexity. Less intelligent people are more shallow and more concrete in their thinking. Fourth is greater flexibility in choosing strategies and using information. Intellectual immaturity is characterized by ignorance of when or how to shift strategies or to transfer information. These four principles, being common to all definitions of intelligence, may be thought to constitute its core.

MULTIPLE INTELLIGENCES

The last new approach to studying intelligence is to look not for commonalities but for differences. Howard Gardner (1983) has proposed that in their richly various thoughts and deeds, people display many different kinds of intelligence. He questions the very existence of broadly horizontal abilities, such as perception and memory, and suggests that we explore not "intelligence" but "intelligences."

The poet searching for the felicitous expression, the child generating fresh utterances, the fiery preacher, the machinist who explains the operation of a complicated lathe, and the politician who moves masses all show their *linguistic intelligence*. In choosing words sensitively and accurately, in analyzing what they read, in remembering, in explaining, and in convincing, people use aspects of linguistic intelligence. Linguistic intelligence may manifest itself also in mimicry and in memory for experiences. Of all forms of intelligence, the linguistic is the most widely shared—the most democratic—and, as we have seen in this chapter, the most extensively studied and understood by psychologists. The complexity and originality of a 4-year-old child's utterances would put any computer to shame, and the 5-year-old's implicit understanding of linguistic rules defies the explanations of experts. But the differences among individuals in linguistic intelligence are enormous. Albert Einstein, we are told, did not talk until he was 3; Jean-Paul Sartre wrote books by the time he was 7.

The earliest form of intelligence to emerge is musical: the appreciation of melody, rhythm, timbre, and the quality of tones. How does *musical intelligence* develop? In the normal course of development, the infant can produce individual sounds and patterns of sounds and can imitate tones and melodies. Two-month-olds have been observed to match the pitch, loudness, and melody of their mothers' songs, and 4-month-olds can match rhythm as well. At about the age of $1\frac{1}{2}$, children begin to sound out their own patterns of tones—seconds, minor and major thirds, and fourths—and they sing spontaneous little songs. Soon they can imitate bits of familiar songs, and by the age of 3 or 4, the sounds they hear around them have overcome their spontaneous sound play. Even more than with linguistic intelligence, individual children differ in their abilities to match pitch, parts of songs, and melody. Except in those with exceptional ability, children's musical intelligence rarely develops significantly beyond the early school years.

Unlike linguistic or musical intelligence, *logical-mathematical intelligence* originates in the mind's confrontation with objects. As children order, reorder, and assess quantity, they begin to develop their logical and mathematical abilities. Soon they have moved away from concrete objects to the operations one can perform on objects and, later, the relations among these operations. From sensorimotor skills, they progress to abstraction.

Spatial intelligence draws on the abilities to recognize differences between nearly identical forms or similarities between forms when they are rotated or incomplete. Spatial intelligence allows one to play chess (and to win!), to make paper airplanes that fly, and to follow the assembly instructions that come with Junior's new model space shuttle. Without spatial intelligence, we could not accurately perceive with our eyes or create mental pictures. Spatial intelligence allows you to answer the following questions. On a horse, which point is higher, the top of the tail or the lowest part of its head? Which takes longer to bring into focus, the eyelashes of an elephant or of a mouse? Which faucet on your bathroom sink controls the hot water?

Have you ever seen a great pantomimist at work? Then you have seen *bodily (kinesthetic) intelligence* at work. This is the intelligence that allows people to use their bodies in highly differentiated and skilled ways and to work skillfully with objects that require both fine and gross motor skills. The football player and the boxer tend to use gross motor skills, the typist or the pianist or the sharpshooter to use fine motor skills. Dancers and swimmers have bodily intelligence. Our culture distinguishes sharply between mind and body, and so to

some people, the idea of bodily intelligence may at first seem contradictory or jarring. But the timing, calibration, sense of direction, smoothness of performance, and mastery of alternatives necessary to competent physical action certainly manifest intelligence.

Gardner also describes something he calls *personal intelligence,* a set of capacities that allow one to know oneself and one's feelings, to discriminate among one's feelings, and to label them, encode them symbolically, and to use them in guiding one's behavior. It is highly developed in the novelist who can write introspectively about feelings, in the therapy patients who deeply understand their feelings, and in the wise old person who advises others out of long experience. Personal intelligence is also intelligence about others' feelings—the child who can read the moods of the people she or he knows, the adult who can read even the hidden intentions and wishes of others, the therapist who gives skilled and sensitive advice.

Beyond these domains of intelligence, Gardner describes several higher level capacities that elude categorization. Common sense, for example, seems to apply to people who can plan ahead, exploit opportunities, and act prudently. Common sense is not so much a manifestation of highly developed social or mechanical abilities as it is the ability to integrate information from a wide field and to incorporate it into a generally effective plan of action. Originality, the ability to make up a new and worthy story or dance or other item, is another higher level capacity, one Gardner maintains rarely extends beyond a single domain. Few people are strikingly original in more than a single field; the Leonardo da Vincis are rare in human history. Metaphorical capacity—the ability to create metaphors, to understand analogies, and to cut across intellectual domains in the process—is another higher cognitive ability. To Aristotle, this capacity signified genius.

These three new approaches to intelligence—breaking the concept down into more basic, information-processing components, sifting through various definitions of the concept for core principles, and dividing intelligence into separate domains—suggest that the notion of a single quantitative IQ score to sum up a person's intelligence may eventually be a thing of the past. Our concept of intelligence is being enriched and expanded by continuing work in this field.

SUMMARY

1. The definition of intelligence has interested people for several thousand years. Piaget considered the function of intelligence to be adaptation to the environment. Others have considered intelligence to consist of neurological speed, specific mental capacities, and styles of cognition that are culturally transmitted. One useful definition is that intelligence is the ability to perceive relationships, through processes of both induction and deduction. Some theorists have considered intelligence to be one general ability; others have considered it a collection of many abilities.

2. Early intelligence tests focused on simple sensory and cognitive processes. Binet and Simon took into account the relation between chronological and mental age. Like other widely used IQ tests, the Binet test was standardized on large groups of children of different ages. The Binet and Wechsler scales are the most common individually administered IQ tests today.

3. An ideal test of intelligence is reliable, valid, and its scores stable over time.

4. Tests of infants' intelligence, such as the Gesell, Bayley, Griffiths, and Cattell scales, tap sensorimotor and perceptual skills in the earliest months. Later they tap social and language abilities. It is generally agreed that intelligence in infancy is more a question of perceptual and motor skills and that more verbal, abstract, social, and personal skills comprise intelligence in older children.

5. The IQ test scores of infants bear essentially no relation to their later scores. Only after the age of 4 or 5 do IQ scores begin to stabilize. However, when investigators isolate components common to infant and childhood intelligence—visual recognition and encoding of stimuli—they find moderate correlations between scores on infant and childhood IQ tests.

6. IQ tests have been criticized for their bias against minority groups and for their irrelevance to behavior other than classroom performance. IQ does not strongly correlate with success in life, income, creativity, or drive. It does correlate with success in school and in tasks that require knowledge of information, convergent thinking, and middle-class norms.

7. Arthur Jensen suggests that blacks as a group score several points lower on IQ tests than whites because they inherit less higher-level (conceptual) intelligence. His suggestion has been met with sharp criticism from those who maintain that differences in test scores reflect environmental, not biological, factors.

8. Intelligence is the product of inheritance, biology (prenatal environment, nutrition, and the like), and environmental stimulation. Evidence from many studies suggests that children of any social class or race who live in homes with more responsive parents, more varied and stimulating materials, less crowding, and better organization of time and space get the highest scores on IQ tests. For preschool children especially, the home environment is an important predictor of IQ.

9. Early childhood intervention programs can increase children's performance on IQ tests, but without continued support and enrichment, the children's gains diminish over time.

10. Several new approaches to the study of intelligence recently have emerged: the measurement of information-processing components, the search for common principles, and the theory of multiple intelligences (linguistic, musical, mathematical, spatial, bodily, and interpersonal). These are likely to increase our understanding of intelligence in the future.

KEY TERMS

Psychometrics	Culture-fair tests	Content validity	Fluid intelligence
Intelligence quotient (IQ)	Culture-free tests	Criterion validity	Crystallized intelligence
	Reliability	Concurrent validity	
Standard deviation	Validity	Developmental diagnosis	Retarded
Factor *g*	Stability		Associative intelligence
Factor *s*	Construct valididty	Norms	Conceptual intelligence
			Interventions

SUGGESTED READINGS

Brody, Erness Bright, and Brody, Nathan (Eds.). *Intelligence: Nature, Determinants, and Consequences.* New York; Academic Press, 1976. Excellent historical background on intelligence testing from the earliest IQ tests to the present, plus a balanced presentation of both sides of the Jensen controversy.

Fincher, Jack. *Human Intelligence.* New York: C. P. Putnam's Sons, 1976. A discussion of conventional notions of intelligence and their inadequancies, written in a provocative journalistic style.

Gardner, Howard. *Frames of Mind.* New York: Basic Books, 1983. A new view of human intelligence in which IQ, or verbal intelligence, is just one of several "intelligences." These include musical accomplishment, spatial reasoning, bodily mastery, and the ability to understand ourselves and others.

Gottfried, Allen W. (Ed.). *Home Environment and Early Cognitive Development.* Orlando, Fl.: Academic Press, 1984. A collection of recent longitudinal studies of young children's home environments demonstrating how the stimulation in early environments is related to children's intelligence.

Gray, Susan, W., Ramsey, Barbara K., and Klaus, Rupert A. *From 3 to 20: The Early Training Project.* Baltimore: University Park Press, 1982. A detailed report of the Early Training Project, a unique longitudinal study of the enduring effects of a preschool intervention program on later educational performance.

Lewis, Michael (Ed.). *Origins of Intelligence.* New York: Plenum, 1976. An examination of infant intelligence from a variety of perspectives, including social, biological, cognitive, affective, historical, and socio-political.

Resnick, Lauren B. (Ed.). *The Nature of Intelligence.* Hillsdale, N.J.: Lawrence Erlbaum Associates, 1976. A critical examination of the cognitive and adaptive processes involved in intellectual functioning and an assessment of their relations to tested IQ.

CHAPTER 11

Language

All normal children learn language: moving inexorably from their infant wails for food and attention, to babbling sounds that seem meaningless, to an association of sounds with actions and objects, and, finally, to an understanding of the specific rules of their language and the many exceptions to these rules. The ages at which words, two-word sentences, and then longer ones first appear may vary from child to child, yet most children go through the same sequence in the acquisition of language. Considering the vast number of words and the many complex grammatical rules of a language, children absorb them with a remarkable rapidity.

How do children master language? Do they imitate what they hear and receive reinforcement from parents, or are they physiologically predisposed to communicate by using language? Is the mind inherently equipped to learn the rules of language, or are the rules "out there," requiring effort for their absorption?

THE BEGINNING OF PSYCHOLINGUISTICS

SKINNER VERSUS CHOMSKY

B. F. Skinner claimed that adults through their systematic reinforcement of the behavior of children cause them to acquire all new skills, including language. In 1957, Skinner published *Verbal Behavior,* in which he attempted to explain how children are conditioned to talk by their parents. When babies babble "babababa," as Skinner's argument goes, their parents are delighted and talk back; the babies, so rewarded and pleased, make the same sounds again. When they say "mama," mothers give them even more excited attention. Later, parents hand cookies to toddlers who manage "kuh." And later still, they help their children with grammatical constructions by understanding and responding to their attempts at sentences and by repeating their words in the correct form and order. Through this process, children's words and sentences gradually converge with adult forms of speech.

Very soon after Skinner's book appeared, Noam Chomsky, a linguist, took issue with him in a review written a short distance away from Skinner's office on the Harvard campus. Chomsky argued that no theory of language learning could be practically based on operant conditioning principles: parents simply did not go to such ends to correct their children's uses of language. Chomsky also argued that the language of adults heard by children is so degenerate, so riddled with "false starts" and structural errors, that it would be surprising indeed were children to acquire language merely by listening to this speech.

Chomsky admitted that reinforcement as well as imitation and motivation played important roles in the child's acquisition of language, but he did not consider reinforcement sufficient to explain the child's propensity for learning language. He called attention to the "remarkable capacity of the child to generalize, hypothesize, and 'process information' in a variety of very special and apparently highly complex ways which we cannot yet describe, or begin to understand, and which may be largely innate" (N. Chomsky, 1957, p. 158). Chomsky described this innate capacity of the human brain as a sort of "black box" for understanding regularities of speech and the fundamental relationship of words. He called it a **language acquisition device (LAD),** to emphasize its automatic nature. The speech heard by the child enters the LAD, and by the processing that goes on there, the child unconsciously gathers ideas about language rules. Through this generative neural capacity, children acquire rules for understanding and constructing their native language.

Chomsky offered an explanation of the nature of language in keeping with his interpretation of the processes by which children acquire it. Following the writings of 17th-century philosophers of language, he proposed that language has two levels, a **surface structure** and a **deep structure.** The surface structure of the sentence consists of the actual words in it and the order in which they occur. The deep structure has to do with fundamental syntactical relationships underlying these words— for example, those between nouns and verbs—and also with the intended meaning—the thought to be conveyed. The following sentences will help to illustrate the difference between these two levels:

(1) Arnold kicked the ball.
(2) The ball was kicked by Arnold.

The two sentences clearly have different surface structures, yet they have, in Chomsky's view, the

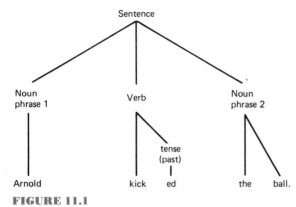

FIGURE 11.1

This diagram of a sentence shows its deep structure.

same deep structure. Sentence 1 is an active, direct statement; sentence 2 is in the passive voice. The sentences have two different syntactic forms, yet as children acquire language they seem to recognize that these sentences have the same meaning. They also know the meanings of sentences that they have never heard before. After hearing a thought expressed in the passive voice, they will recognize the same thought expressed in the active voice. Such recognition is possible, in Chomsky's opinion, because the deep structure is identical for both active and passive forms of a sentence. This deep structure can be represented by the tree diagram in Figure 11.1. Both sentences have certain basic constituents, the noun phrases "Arnold" and "the ball" and the verb "kick." Through a set of transformations, which are the several possible syntactical ways of arranging these constituents, children can take the basic or deep structure depicted in the diagram and put it into different surface structures.

The transformation given in the example is passivization. In it, "Arnold" (NP1) and "the ball" (NP2) are reversed. A passive marker, "by," is added to "Arnold," and the tense is corrected. A child who had never before heard the sentence, "The ball was kicked by Arnold," would still recognize its deep structure and be able to transform the constituents and understand the new surface structure. In a similar way, adults recognize the sentences in this book, though they are encountering them for the first time. The syntaxes of all known human languages are strikingly similar. From this fact, Chomsky derived his idea that deep structures are somehow innate to

the processes of the human brain and give us our special capacity to learn language.

CONTEMPORARY APPROACHES

Children often make mistakes when they are learning to speak. They may say things like "When they should go?" or "Drive car man?" Some linguists have suggested that errors like these derive from children's attempts to apply to their speech the transformational rules described by Chomsky. Other linguists claim that mistaken applications of transformational rules cannot easily account for children's errors. Some errors that might be expected if children were misapplying transformational rules turn out to be rare or nonexistent, and other explanations for the errors that do occur are more satisfactory (Bresnan, 1978; 1982). An alternative to Chomsky's transformational grammar is **nontransformational grammar.** As we have suggested, transformational rules imply that there is a uniform deep grammar underlying grammatically related utterances. In nontransformational grammar, underlying functions are expressed directly in different surface forms. According to this approach, what you hear is what you get: the elements a person hears *are* as they *seem.* For example, in a transformational description of *John liked Mary,* one would point out that its deep structure is the same as that for *Mary is liked by John* and that the latter is produced by a transformation of the former. But in a nontransformational description, the underlying functional representation of both *John liked Mary* and *Mary is liked by John* would be: *like* (subject=*John;* object=*Mary*). If the speaker chooses to make the logical subject the grammatical subject of the sentence, the sentence will come out in the active voice: *John likes Mary.* If the speaker chooses to make the logical object the grammatical subject and the logical subject the object of a phrase beginning with *by,* then the sentence will come out in the passive voice: *Mary is liked by John.* The virtue of nontransformational grammar is that it does not suggest that a child analyzes fixed, uniform underlying structures in order to speak. There is little evidence that children engage in such analyses, despite claims of transformational grammarians to the contrary (Maratsos, 1983).

THE LANGUAGE OF LANGUAGE

Some of the terms used in studies of language and of how children learn language are familiar; others have resulted from the interweaving of psychology and linguistics.

Linguistics is the study of human speech in its various aspects. Linguists have been especially interested in how language is structured. In the early 1950s, George Miller, Charles Osgood, and other psychologists introduced linguistics into the field of psychological study. Thereafter, the term **psycholinguistics,** itself a new word, was applied to the issues and research interests shared by linguists and psychologists, and a distinct discipline was established. Psycholinguistics asks how language relates to other aspects of human behavior. Even newer fields are developmental psycholinguistics, which is the study of the child's acquisition of language, and **sociolinguistics,** the study of the language of particular social groups—of people who are of the same social class, race, or sex.

Phonology is the study of the sound system of a language and how it develops. A **phoneme** is the smallest unit of sound that distinguishes one utterance from another by signaling a difference in meaning. Languages differ in the number and kinds of phonemes they contain. English has about 45 phonemes; some languages use as many as 60, others as few as 20. English speakers observe the difference between /hat/ and /rat/ and between /r/ and /l/. But to Chinese speakers, /r/ and /l/ can vary freely; they are not phonemes. As we will see later, when children begin to apply themselves to the task of learning to speak their own language, they appear to have only a limited number of sounds at their disposal. But the sounds they do use are related to the larger adult sound system in a regular and predictable way.

The sounds of language are designated by the way they are produced in the mouth and throat. All languages are divided into vowels, sounds in which air flows freely after passing the vocal chords, and consonants, sounds in which air flow is blocked in some particular way. For example, when it is blocked or stopped completely, the consonant is called a **stop consonant.** The phoneme /p/ is such a consonant. If you say the words "sto*p*" and "ro*p*e," you will be able to feel the obstruction of the air flow yourself. A lesser blocking of the flow is called a **fricative.** Fricatives allow more air to pass through the mouth. The phoneme /s/ is such a consonant, as in the word "peace."

A consonant may also be voiced or unvoiced. If only air is forced through the mouth and the vocal chords are not used to produce the consonant, it is unvoiced. If the vocal chords are used, it is a **voiced consonant.** By placing your hand on your throat while you utter a consonant, you can distinguish between the two kinds. A vibration in the throat indicates voicing. In the words "peat" and "peace," /t/ and /s/ are **unvoiced consonants.** Their voiced counterparts are /d/ for /t/ and /z/ for /s/, as in "hee*d*" and "pay*s*." All these sounds are made in roughly the same part of the mouth but differ in whether they are stop or voiced consonants.

Morphology is the study of the units of meaning in a language. A **morpheme** is the smallest unit of a language that by itself has a recognizable meaning. It is a word or a part of a word. For example, "word" is one morpheme because it cannot be broken down into any smaller units of meaning. "Words," however, is two morphemes, because it can be broken down into "word" and "-s," the latter indicating plurality or more than one (Figure 11.2). Many prefixes and suffixes are morphemes—*post*war, war*like;* as are verb endings that signal tense—"-ed" (patt*ed*) or "-ing" (patt*ing*).

Syntax consists of the rules by which words and morphemes are combined to form larger units, such as clauses and sentences. Standard word order in English is subject-verb-object (SVO): "She painted the picture." Some languages, however, are not so strict and allow word order to vary or require some other order, such as SOV, as in German.

Semantics is the study of meanings, of how the sounds of language are related to the real world and our own experiences. Although we as adults are quite in accord about the relationship between the sound "dog" and the object it identifies, children are not always in agreement. For them "dog" may indicate a host of four-legged furry creatures that includes not only dogs, but also horses, cows, kitties, and teddy bears.

Pragmatics is the study of how language is used in a social context. Language can perform many functions—asking questions, ordering, com-

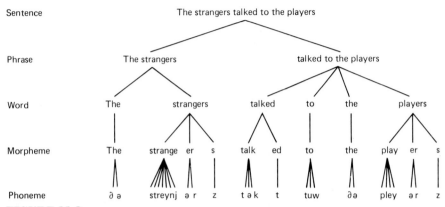

FIGURE 11.2

The sentence diagram indicates several levels of analysis. The sentence is composed of phrases, which are composed of words, which are composed of morphemes, which are composed of phonemes.

manding, soothing, ridiculing, and so on. An utterance may have the syntax of a question—as in "Can you shut the window?"—yet perform the function of a request. The speaker of this sentence is not interested in hearing whether or not the listener is capable of shutting the window. He assumes that the listener can, and is, in fact, telling him to do so.

WHEN AND HOW DOES LANGUAGE BEGIN?

BEFORE CHILDREN'S FIRST WORDS

It is generally agreed that children begin to use language between approximately 12 and 18 months. Long before they utter their first understandable words, however, they arduously apply themselves to the task of analyzing the complex phenomenon called language.

Mothers have often claimed that their child "doesn't talk, but she understands everything." In a study of the extent to which "everything" is understood, Janellen Huttenlocher (1974) found that children as young as 10 months do indeed comprehend many language expressions but that mothers have been guilty of a common parental error—they read more into the child's behavior than was probably intended by the child. The children studied understood a great deal more than

they could say, but they used cues other than words to determine Mother's meaning. Mother might point to the ball at the same time that she said, "Where is the ball?" Or the ball itself would serve as a cue when Mother said, "Roll the ball to me." What else would the baby do with a ball? By asking children to locate certain objects—"Where is the ball?"—or to perform certain actions—"Give the ball to Mommy"—without giving them gestural cues and in contexts that were essentially ambiguous, Huttenlocher was able to trace the beginning of language understanding. She found that proper names and object words were the first responded to and that the very first word understood was often a pet's name. She also found that children have, to some degree, an understanding of the meaning of words, the semantic component of language, before they begin to use words.

Babblings are the first sounds of infants that resemble speech. We have already indicated in Chapter 5 that these repetitions of syllables are a source of delight to parents, although the string of sounds has no meaning. By repeating syllables, infants experiment with and practice many of the sounds that will eventually be put together into meaningful words. But some of them are sounds that they have not heard and will not use later. The fact that during the first year the babblings of infants the world over are the same—whether or not particular sounds will find their way into later speech—has been taken as evidence that each human infant possesses the potential to master any language (Jakobson, 1968). At about 9 months, the babblings

This mother is making her point perfectly clear by gestures; her words are superfluous.

of babies whose language will be English start to lose their German gutturals and French nasals. In this same period, infants begin to shorten some of their utterances, to "duh," "da," and "ma." Although these new sounds, soon to replace babblings, bear little or no relation to any words we may know as speakers of adult language, they seem very much like language. The shortened quality of these utterances, their languagelike intonation, and their appropriateness to context make them sound as though they should be understood.

John Dore (1978a) has found that before the end of the first year, in this period between babbling and words, infants use the same short speech sounds repeatedly in specific contexts. That is, sounds are chosen and uttered for a particular purpose. Children's *affect expressions,* the accepting "ooh wow" and the protesting grunts "uh-uh-uh," convey joy and anger. They do not appear to be addressed to anyone. Children also use speech sounds when they gaze toward an object or adult, with the apparent intention of obtaining an object or getting the adult to help in some way. For example, a toddler wants Raggedy Andy, who sits on the shelf, and, after struggling for some moments

The gesture of this 1-year-old infant is a physical cue that precedes language.

to reach him, realizes that she is too short. The toddler may then pull Mother toward the shelf and point or reach toward the doll while making short, urgent, or whining sounds and glancing back and forth between Mother and Raggedy Andy. This has been called an *instrumental expression,* because the child appears to use vocalization as a tool to obtain a particular goal.

Children may choose one sound, such as "dah" or "duh," as an *indicating expression.* They make the sound to get the adult's attention and usually point at the same time, but the sound does not convey dissatisfaction when adults do not act. Finally, a particular sound may be made when children look at any one of a group of objects, such as their fluffy toy animals. Or they may choose a sound to designate different objects that they feel the same way about. These sounds are called *grouping expressions.*

THE FIRST WORDS: 1 TO 2 YEARS

Making the Most of What You Have

All of language development for the child can be regarded as a gradual decrease in dependence on context for communication and a gradual increase in reliance on the tools that an abstract language system provides. This movement away from context does not happen all at once. Children's first clearly intelligible words, said near the end of their first year, are usually uttered in conjunction with some action. "Hot," which may come out "ah," is said while touching bath water, or the child may notice the front door swinging open and say "ohpn" (Greenfield and Smith, 1976; Rodgon, 1978). The first words usually name an entity that has, in some way, changed. Things that have appeared, disappeared, opened, or closed in the immediate surroundings are commented on first— "Daddy" when the child's father appears at the door, "Mama" when Mother is leaving.

First words, such as "mih" for milk, "bah" for ball, and "puh" for apple, may bear only a vague resemblance to adult speech. But children use them in a context that helps their parents understand. They continue to make the motions—pointing, reaching, and other physical cues—that helped them communicate before they could utter words.

They may point to the refrigerator or to the chocolate syrup as they say "mih," thereby requesting that milk be poured and chocolate be put in it. Even though children have very few words and say only one of them at a time, with word and gesture and actions and facial expressions working together, they possess a much greater ability to communicate. They can name objects or persons, make requests and demands, describe actions, and with intonation express emotional states of joy, displeasure, and surprise at encountering something unusual. These single-word utterances have been called **holophrases.** In the light of the accompanying gesture or intonation or both, they seem to do the work of a whole sentence.

Which Sounds?

The first recognizable words are not perfect renditions of those children have heard from adults around them because children are limited in their speech sounds and combinations. The very first words spoken by babies the world over are likely to contain the consonants *p, b, t, d, m,* and *n,* for which the tongue is in the front of the mouth, and the vowel sounds *a* and *e,* which come from the back of a relaxed mouth. These are the sounds most easily formed. Babies still keep playing with many of the sounds that they have acquired through their babblings, until they can utter *k* and *g* correctly in their vocal gymnastics. But when they are putting the main effort into saying a word, they are restricted to easily formed sounds.

The first words often take the consonant-vowel form, which means that they are "reduced" (de Villiers and de Villiers, 1979): duck becomes "duh," bed "beh." Vowel-consonant and consonant-vowel-consonant combinations are also heard in this early period, as in "up" and "cup." Only later do children produce sound clusters beginning with a vowel, "itty" for kitty and "appuh" for apple. Consonant clusters, groups of two or more consonants, pose a particular problem for the novice and are reduced to a more manageable form: spoon becomes "poon," stop "top" (Greenfield and Smith, 1976; Waterson, 1978). Children also have a tendency to use voiced consonants at the beginning of a word and unvoiced at the end, no matter what the adult pronunciation. So they may say "bie" for pie and "dok" for dog.

When children try to say a two-syllable word, they often repeat one of the syllables twice (de Villiers and de Villiers, 1979), as in the familiar "baba" for bottle and the less familiar "beebee" for airplane. They have difficulty handling two different syllables at the same time, but they are aware that the word is multisyllabic. They may also make all vowels or consonants of a word identical so that doggy becomes "goggy" or "doddy." At this stage of acquiring language, children repeat and combine familiar speech sounds in order to lengthen their utterances (Waterson, 1978).

Which Words?

The first words children learn include names of objects. These are quite similar from child to child. They cover the same general categories, such as foods, animals, and toys. Katherine Nelson (1973) conducted a longitudinal study of 18 toddlers, using mothers' reports of children's vocabularies and tape recordings of their speech. She found that between 15 and 24 months, when children have obtained a vocabulary of 50 words or more, the following words appeared:

RESEARCH FOCUS

CATEGORY DEVELOPMENT

How do young children group the words they are learning into larger categories? Do they use common principles, or does each child categorize idiosyncratically? Leslie Rescorla (1981), of Yale University, studied six children, participants in a longitudinal study of language development, as they learned vocabulary words and formed rudimentary categories. The children were followed from the time they were about 1 year old for at least 6 months. Rescorla relied on mothers' diaries of their children's new words, discussions with the mothers, and visits with the children at home. She focused on three categories of words used by adults: animals, fruit, and vehicles. When she visited the children, she brought toys that belonged in these categories as well as some that did not. She recorded the names the children gave the toys and the names they understood to see how the children categorized these objects.

Children's language and category development varied significantly from one child to another. Daniel, for example, had 13 labels for vehicles, whereas Erica had only 4. The children generally had the most names for animals, the fewest for fruit, and an intermediate number for vehicles. Many of them overextended vehicle words, subsuming helicopter under plane and tricycle or motorcycle under bike. All of the children organized vehicles around the word car. For about a month, cars were just cars, but thereafter the children overextended car to de-

note trucks, buses, trains, strollers, and other vehicles. After the period of overextension, the children's concept of car narrowed, and they acquired the words bike, truck, and bus, with few overextensions. Several children showed that they could understand finer distinctions among vehicle words than they could actually say.

As Rescorla analyzed the data on animal categories, she found that the children who had had the most differentiated vehicle categories were the same ones who had the most differentiated animal and fruit categories as well. The three children with the greatest number of animal names did not apply a single dominating concept, and they rarely made labeling mistakes. The other three children operated quite differently. All heavily overextended either dog or cat, and all indicated better comprehension of different animal labels than they could produce by themselves.

Rescorla concluded that the children did perceive meanings to cluster around concepts for aircraft, large commercial vehicles, large four-legged animals, and round fruit and that they used these concepts as exemplars in forming categories. Once past a period of overextension, the children learned new, more specific words in each category. The number and type of the children's words corresponded roughly to the range and structure of adult English. Rescorla also concluded that the children had a rudimentary and intuitive grasp of superordinate categories, even though they had learned only one term for superordination (fruit).

It will be no surprise should one of this child's early word's be "nose." Such a prominent and responsive object! You tweak it and you hear its name.

Many early words accompany actions. This infant *seems* to be saying "sock."

Among the infant's first words are basic nouns like "flower." It is unusual for first words to be either more specific—"geranium"—or less specific—"plant."

"juice," "milk," "cookie" (foods)

"dog," "cat," "duck" (animals)

"ball," "block" (toys)

"ear," "eye," "nose" (body parts)

"shoe," "hat," "sock" (clothing)

"car," "boat," "truck" (vehicles)

"momma," "dadda" (people)

Nouns for basic categories are acquired first rather than nouns at a higher level of generality or nouns that are specific. So, for example, "flower" is much more likely to be in the child's early vocabulary than either "plant" (general) or "rose" (specific); "dog" more likely than either "animal" or "collie" (Brown, 1958; Rosch, Mervis, Gray, Johnson, and Boyes-Braem, 1976). Mothers usually choose nouns at the basic level when naming things for their toddlers (Mervis and Mervis, 1982).

Other early words are closely tied to actions, actions that involve first the children themselves and later other things and then people (Greenfield and Smith, 1976). The first action words are rarely full-fledged verbs but rather the prepositions that appear with verbs, for example, "up" as in "pick me up," "down" as in "put me down" or "I get down," "on" as in "put on me." Next, children use intransitive verbs—verbs with no object of the action—such as "dance" or "go." Later, they add transitive verbs—verbs that do have an object—such as "eat" and "take." And even later children talk about unchanging states (or nonactions) with words such as "dirty" or "green" (Greenfield and Smith, 1976).

Children often use their early words to cover much more than the conventional adult meaning. The larger meanings that children have for words have been called **overextensions.** They are usually based on perceptual properties of the object or action, such as shape, movement, size, sound, and texture. Thus, for the child, "fly" may mean all very small objects, including raisins as well as insects; "bowwow" can signify all furry animals (Figure 11.3), "ball" all objects that are round, and "dance" any kind of turning around (Brown, 1958; Clark and Clark, 1977; Rosch, 1975). Overextensions may be based on objects' categorical properties as well (See Research Focus: Category Development). Children seem to overextend words because their vocabularies are limited and not because they fail to understand differences between

objects. Children can, for example, pick out pictures of a dog and a cat, even if they can only call both a "cat" (Fremgen and Fay, 1980).

Jeremy Anglin (1975) has documented children's **underextensions** of words. They may think that "dog" applies only to their family's dog and not to dogs on the street, or dogs on television, or dogs in picture books.

The one-word stage lasts from about 12 to 18 months. During this period, children are gradually building up a vocabulary, one word at a time. Their words, as indicated, name objects—"ball," "car," "cat"—and make requests—"More," "Up," "Down"—and they also perform social rituals—"Bye-bye," "Hi," "Go." Through enthusiasm for communication on the child's part and willingness on the mother's, conversations can also be held, one word at a time. For example, (Scollen, 1974):

Child Fan.

Mother Fan, yeah.

Child Cool.

Mother Cool, yeah. Fan makes you cool.

Stanford University's Eve Clark (1983) has proposed that children acquire language according to two principles, **contrast** and **conventionality.** Children proceed, Clark suggests, by contrasting the meanings of pairs of words and by learning which words are conventionally used by experienced speakers of their language. Children perceive a gap in their ability to talk about something and search for the words to fill it. When they hear a new word, they assume that it is different from, and contrasts with, the words they already know. At first, children look for words to label members of categories that are salient to them. One child may be interested in cars and trucks and will attend more to words in this category than the child who is more interested in animals, for example. Later, the child who is interested in trucks may set up several categories for trucks—moving trucks, delivery trucks, mail trucks, vans, big trucks, noisy trucks, dump trucks, and so on—and listen for new words for truck categories. Hearing new words applied to trucks, he may also start looking for the kinds of trucks they name. In the meantime, he fills gaps in his vocabulary in one of three different ways: by overextending the words he has; by relying on general-purpose words like *that*; and by coining new words whose meanings stand in con-

FIGURE 11.3
What does mother mean when she says, "Bow wow"? This is the challenge confronting the little boy when he first hears the word. He attempts to find out by saying a few bowwows himself (Gleitman, 1981).

trast to those of words he already knows. Children often coin new words for actions—*"Mommy nippled Anna"* or *"I'm going to gun you,"* or *"It's not pepping"* (nothing is coming out of the pepper shaker) or *"Can I sprink the lawn?"*—and for instruments—*a chop* for an axe or *a knock-thing* for something to knock with. They also coin words for agents: *"a smile-person"* for someone who smiles at people or *"a hitter man"* for someone who hits things.

After the child has acquired some 50 words, at around 18 to 24 months, language undergoes an explosion, propelling the child to the next stage of language development, two-word combinations (Table 11.1).

TWO-WORD SENTENCES: 2 TO 3 YEARS

Although two-word sentences prevail in children's language from 2 to 3, children continue to use one-word and begin to use three-word utterances. During the two-word phase, children use their small but growing vocabularies with remarkable ingenuity.

Remarks of the 2-Year-Old

Children's utterances continue to be limited to the here and now. As in the one-word stage, they comment on actions and name objects; they also remark now on possession, location, recurrence of an action or object, and nonexistence: "Doggy bark," "Milk fell," "Go car," "Molly room," "My truck," "Daddy home," "More car," "Sock again," "Allgone kitties," "Cookie gone." They rarely, even at this stage, however, comment on the state of something, such as "Door shut."

The form of two-word sentences is more elaborate, less ambiguous, and slightly less tied to context than one-word expressions. Calling Mother's attention to an object, once an act of pointing and naming, now is spoken: "See doggy," "That

TABLE 11.1
LANGUAGE DEVELOPMENT MILESTONES

3 months	Markedly less crying than at 8 weeks; when talked to and nodded at, smiles, followed by squealing-gurgling sounds, usually called cooing, which is vowel-like in character and pitch-modulated; sustains cooing for 15 to 20 seconds.	18 months	Has a definite repertoire of words—more than 3, but fewer than 50; still much babbling but now of several syllables with intricate intonation patterns; no attempt at communicating information and no frustration for not being understood; words may include items such as "thank you" or "come here," but there is little ability to join any of the lexical items into spontaneous two-item phrases; understanding is progressing rapidly.
4 months	Responds to human sounds more definitely; turns head; eyes seem to search for speaker, occasionally some chuckling sounds.		
5 months	The vowel-like cooing sounds begin to be interspersed with more consonantal sounds; acoustically, all vocalizations are very different from the sounds of the mature language of the environment.	24 months	Vocabulary of more than 50 items (some children seem to be able to name everything in the environment); begins spontaneously to join vocabulary items into two-word phrases; all phrases appear to be own creations; definite increase in communicative behavior and interest in language.
6 months	Cooing changes into babbling resembling one-syllable utterances; neither vowels nor consonants have very fixed recurrences; most common utterances sound somewhat like *ma, mu, da, di.*		
8 months	Reduplication (or more continuous repetition) becomes frequent; intonation patterns become distinct; utterances can signal emphasis and emotions.	30 months	Fastest increase in vocabulary with many new additions every day; no babbling at all; utterances have communicative intent; frustrated if not understood by adults; utterances consist of at least two words, and many have three or even five words; sentences and phrases have characteristic child grammar, that is, they are rarely verbatim repetitions of an adult utterance; intelligibility is not very good yet, though there is great variation among children; seem to understand everything that is said.
10 months	Vocalizations are mixed with sound-play, such as gurgling or bubble blowing: appears to wish to imitate sounds, but the imitations are never quite successful; beginning to differentiate between words heard by making differential adjustments.		
12 months	Identical sound sequences are replicated with higher relative frequency of occurrence, and words (*mamma* or *dadda*) are emerging; definite signs of understanding some words and simple commands ("Show me your eyes").		

Source: Adapted from Lenneberg, 1967, pp. 128–130.

doggy." To indicate proximity, the child says, "Bottle here." Two nouns indicate object and its location—"Towel bed" to mean the towel is on the bed, or the child may choose a sound, such as "uh," as an all-purpose marker for "in," "on," "on top of," and so on (E. Clark, 1978).

Children's two-word utterances are examples of **telegraphic speech.** When Mother says to her daughter, "Oh, your poor kitty got wet in the rain," the 2-year-old will exclaim, "Kitty wet." When her

father says to her, "Let's go to the grocery store," she will say excitedly, "Go store." She will give evidence of understanding all aspects of a situation. If she wants her mother to give her a picture book, she may say first, "Give book," and then "Mommy give" if her mother does not hand it to her immediately. Her third request may be "Mommy book." She has expressed agent, action, and object. She actually understands more than comes to the surface and is uttered in each two-word sentence. But most of the connecting words—auxiliary verbs; copula verbs, such as *is, are,* and *looks;* articles; prepositions; conjunctions; and pronouns—are omitted from her utterances. They are left out because at this age children can remember and express only a limited number of units of information at one time; thus they express the most important ones, agent, action, and object.

Children may ask for an action, an object, or for information by saying "Go swim," "Give ball," "Want cookie," "Where Daddy?" Rising intonation can also make their words a request, for example: "Go óut?" or "No móre?" (Clark and Clark, 1977). Another **prosodic** (voice modulation) device used by children to elaborate their limited, but developing, system is word stress. Leslie Weiman (1976) found that the word stressed in two-word utterances bears a relation to the word's semantic role. A child who says "Play park" with the word "park" emphasized wants to go to the park. The stress makes clear that the child wants to play in a special place. Weiman observed that in verb-location expressions, locations were always stressed. In modifier-noun expressions, such as "Big car," the modifier was stressed; in verb-object pairs, such as "Hit ball," the object received the stress; and in agent-verb combinations, such as "Mama dance," the verb was stressed. The stressed word seemed to be new information introduced to the listener and the unstressed word already given information, which suggests that children have not only some notion of semantic relations, but also a developing competence in conversational skills.

Grammars for Children's Word Combinations

Taken with the systematic nature of these first word combinations, psycholinguists in the early 1960s tried to figure out the strategies that children were using in their speech patterns. They offered a set of rules by which children might be governing their language. According to this grammar, children's words are divided into a **pivot class** and an **open class.** For a word to be designated as a pivot word, its position has to be fixed. That is, it must appear *only* in first position in a two-word combination or *only* in second position, but not in both; it has to occur with great frequency, never appear alone, and never in combination with another pivot. Pivot words as a class are small in number and are rather

slowly added to children's vocabularies, compared to words of the open class. The open class contains a fairly large number of words, words are added to it rapidly, and its constituents occur alone at times. Some examples are (Bowerman, 1973):

Pivot-open order: *More* milk
                  More cookie
                  All-gone cookie
                  All-gone milk
                  Kimmy come
                  Kimmy swim

Open-*pivot* order: Mess *here*
                  Pillow *here*
                  Pig *tail*
                  Cow *tail*
                  Daddy *tail* . . . nope

It became evident, however, that the pivot-open classification failed to capture completely the system in children's early language. Although some words fit the pattern and always appear to be either pivot or open words, many others do not do so consistently. The pivot-open description, pointing out only form consistencies, also took no account of meaning. It did not distinguish between "Christy room," meaning Christy's room, a possessive relation, and "Christy room," meaning Christy is in the room, a locative relation. In addition, it bore no relation to adult grammar and thus had no value for describing utterances longer than three words.

Other grammars that considered the meaning of word combinations used by children were suggested to take the place of pivot-open grammar. One such grammar was **case grammar,** proposed by Charles Fillmore (1968). Case grammar is based on case *relations,* which are the universal concepts or deep structures that identify such matters as who did what to whom. Fillmore found that words in an utterance fit into categories depending on their relation to one another. In Fillmore's system, an *agent* is the initiator of an action: "Kimmy" in "Kimmy sit," "Kimmy come," "Kimmy swim." An *instrument* is the object by which an action is carried out: "spoon" in "Eat spoon," "bike" in "Ride bike." The *experiencer* is the receiver of an action: "Kimmy" in "Kimmy hurt," "Kimmy hot." And the *locative* indicates where the action or state is occurring: "home" in "Doggy home." "Kimmy home." Case grammar's categories—agent, instrument, experiencer, locative, action—seem to explain the patterns in children's early language better than the simple pivot-open distinction. Although 2-year-olds' observations about the world have certain commonalities, any individual child may, because of a particular cognitive style or learning pattern, put words in a different order. Case grammar accommodates these variations better than the conventional adult subject-verb-object (SVO) order or the simple designation of pivot words. An additional advantage of case grammar is that unlike some systems, which are limited to describing the early simple constructions, it provides a means of specifying children's language from its early stages to its final complexity.

LANGUAGE COMPLEXITIES: 2 TO 5 YEARS

Children's three-word sentences are still by necessity telegraphic, but they are more nearly complete. The child will now ask for her picture book by saying, "Mommy give book." She is able to speak in sentences that have the usual SVO form of adult sentences. The other elements to be added—inflections; definite pronouns, such as I, me, you, and we; prepositions; articles; and auxiliary verbs—begin appearing, too.

GRAMMATICAL MORPHEMES

Word order is only one of the ways of indicating meaning in English; **inflections,** a particular type of morpheme, are another. In English, inflections are generally suffixes and provide additional information, such as plurality (-s), tense (-ed), and possession ('s). At first they are almost entirely absent from children's language. Between the ages of 2 and 3, as children switch from predominantly two-word to longer utterances, they do begin to acquire the inflections of adult speech (Dale, 1976). Dan Slobin (1973) has argued that we may expect inflections on the *ends* of words to appear first in the child's speech, say before auxiliary verbs, because they are more perceptually salient, that is, they are easier for the child to notice. So, in attempting to convey "The cat is drinking," the child, who until now has said simply "Cat drink," is more likely to say "Cat drinking" to indicate an ongoing action rather than "Cat is drink" or "The cat drink."

Roger Brown (1973) conducted a thorough study of the order in which three children—Adam, Eve, and Sarah—acquired inflections (Figure 11.4). At least 2 hours of each child's spontaneous speech, in conversation with Mother, were recorded each month. In his analysis, Brown also noted the use of prepositions, articles, and auxiliary verbs, which make their appearance during the same period. These small words and the inflections are called **grammatical morphemes.** The children added 14 grammatical morphemes to their speech in nearly the same order (Table 11.2). The first of the morphemes to be acquired was the present progressive verb form—"I walking," "You talking"—which marks ongoing actions. Next to appear were the prepositions "in" and "on" as the children noted the location of things. Then Adam, Eve, and Sarah acquired the plural marker -s. Number is a concrete and conceptually relevant

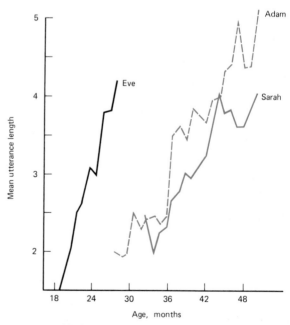

FIGURE 11.4

Roger Brown believes that the best index of children's early language is the average number of morphemes in their utterances. He, Courtney Cazden, and Ursula Bellugi-Kilma (1969) began studying the speech of Adam, the son of a minister, Eve, the daughter of a graduate student, and Sarah, the daughter of a clerk, when they first started stringing words together. Eve, who was studied for only 10 months because her family moved away, combined words when younger than Adam and Sarah and progressed at almost twice their rate.

TABLE 11.2
GRAMMATICAL MORPHEMES IN CUSTOMARY ORDER OF ACQUISITION

Morpheme	Meanings expressed or presupposed	Example
Present progressive	Temporary duration	I walk*ing*.
In	Containment	*In* basket.
On	Support	*On* floor.
Plural	Number	Two balls.
Past irregular[a]	Earlierness[b]	It *broke*.
Possessive inflection	Possession	Adam*'s* ball.
Uncontractible copula[c]	Number; earlierness	There it *is*.
Articles	Specific-nonspecific	That *a* book. That *the* dog.
Past regular	Earlierness	Adam walk*ed*.
Third person regular	Number; earlierness	He walk*s*.
Third person irregular	Number; earlierness	He *does*. She *has*.
Uncontractible progressive auxiliary	Temporary duration; number; earlierness	This *is going*.
Contractible copula[d]	Number; earlierness	That *'s* book.
Contractible progressive auxiliary	Temporary duration; number; earlierness	I*'m* walk*ing*.

[a] Formation of past tense by means other than *-ed*.
[b] Denotes understanding that an action or state may occur before the time of utterance.
[c] Use of the verb *to be* as a main verb without contraction.
[d] Use of the verb *to be* as a main verb with contraction.

Source: Brown, 1973.

Children may learn grammatical rules but not apply them. They may know how to say "Daddy drive car," a complete sentence, but still use a sentence fragment like "Daddy car." They also may know how to inflect verbs—to add *-ed* or *-ing,* for example—but not do so. Why would children alternate in this fashion between more and less primitive utterances? Michael Maratsos (1983) has suggested that children may not assume that a grammatical form that is expressed *sometimes* has to be expressed *every* time. Verb inflections, for example, are omitted habitually in many different languages and dialects. In Black English and Chinese, to name just two cases, verb endings are usually unnecessary. They may be unnecessary in children's English as well, and what is obligatory to the adult, experienced speaker may well be optional to the child.

NEGATIVES

In this period, children extend the meaning of one of their favorite words, "no" (Figure 11.5). In Lois Bloom's (1970) examination of negation, she found that children first use the word "no" to indicate *nonexistence,* as in "No milk" when a cup is empty; next, they use it for *rejection* of an offer, as in "No ball" when the child is pushing a ball away, and "No down" when they do not want to

notion for the child at this time. Receiving two cookies rather than one may be the most important event of the day. Following the addition of the plural came some irregular past tenses and then the possessive 's, a relation that children have clearly expressed by word order and the use of "my" since they began using two words. In a study of a large number of children, Jill and Peter de Villiers (1973) found them adding grammatical morphemes in the same order.

This 2-year-old says an emphatic "NO!" to the prospects of leaving with Mother and indicates that she already has urgent plans of her own.

FIGURE 11.5

The two-word utterances of young children are often ambiguous, as illustrated in Maurice Sendak's story *Higglety Pigglety Pop*. An adventurous dog takes a job as nurse to Baby. He must persuade Baby to eat, or he will be fed to the lion in the basement. (*a*) Baby at first refuses the food, saying "No eat!"—I will not eat. (*b*) The dog then eats up the refused food, to which Baby objects vehemently, crying out "No eat!"—Don't eat my food. (*c*) Baby angrily pushes the button, making the dog-nurse fall down to the waiting lion, but Baby accidentally falls down too. Baby cries out "No eat!"—Don't eat me. (Sendak, 1979; Gleitman, 1982).

be put down; and third, they use it for *denial* of a statement, as in "No bottle" after the child has been given a cup and told it is a bottle.

"No" and "not" are the first forms used for all three meanings. When children begin to speak in sentences longer than three words, they still put negatives first—"No want to go home," "No put shoes on"—but then they put negatives within them, inserting them properly between subjects and verbs: "I no want milk," "He not good boy." Children will also use the auxiliaries "won't," "can't," and "don't": "He won't stop," "I can't put it on—too little," "Don't leave me." Children say "won't" before they say "will" and "can't" before they say "can." Such words are probably learned as whole units and are not initially understood as being made up of "can" and "not" or "will" and "not" (Bloom, 1970; Clark and Clark, 1977; de Villiers and de Villiers, 1979; Klima and Bellugi, 1966).

OVERREGULARIZATION

When children first learn the past tenses of verbs, they learn them by rote. Although only a small number of English verbs are irregular in forming the past tense, many of the basic verbs used around children do have irregular past tenses—ate, broke, brought, came, drank, fell, flew, gave, hit, ran, saw,

thought, took. Children learn many of these verb forms before they learn past tense verbs ending with the regular inflection -ed, such as jumped, walked. Once children have acquired a past tense form of a verb, they do not immediately use it every time context indicates that they should. Only gradually does the proportion of instances in which they apply the past tense increase. By the time that they are applying regularly formed past tenses correctly about half the time, children begin to **overregularize** and overapply the rule for making past tenses. They extend the rule to irregular verbs and say breaked or broked, comed or camed, flied, goed or wented, hitted, helded or holded, runned. These young scientists, looking for order and simplicity in the world, consider English to be more systematic than it is and overgeneralize the rules that they have discovered. They are certain that they are now using the correct forms. In fact, for a time, they may not even hear the forms that they once used, as in this example (from Gleason, 1967):

Child My teacher *holded* the baby rabbits and we *patted* them.

Adult Did you say your teacher *held* the baby rabbits?

Child Yes.

Adult What did you say she did?

Child She *holded* the baby rabbits and we *patted* them .

Adult Did you say she *held* them tightly?

Child No, she *holded* them loosely.

Children have the same sort of trouble with nouns that have irregular plurals. They will start talking about their foots, the mouses in the cellar, the mans in the street, and the sheeps in the field. By the time children are ready for school, they usually have their irregular past tenses and noun plurals back in their vocabularies. Some errors may persist, however, into elementary school.

SPECIFICATION: ADJECTIVES AND PREPOSITIONS

The more difficult the concept expressed by a word, the later it is acquired. Children first learn the most general, global adjectives, such as "big," "little," "good," "bad." In the period in which they start putting together three-word sentences, however, they learn adjectives with more specific dimensional meanings, such as "long" and "short," "tall" and "short," "high" and "low," "wide" and "narrow." At the same time, they learn more specific prepositions for location than "in" and "on," such as "behind," "in front of," "under," and "over." They learn positive adjectives before negative ones—for example, they know "more" in their two-word stage and may use it incessantly, but "few" and "less" do not appear until later. In fact, 3-year-old youngsters have trouble with antonyms. After they have learned "more–few" for number, "tall–short" for height, and "wide-narrow" for breadth, they sense that the adjectives apply to the same dimension, but they do not always get the directions straight for the meanings of the adjectives. Margaret Donaldson and George Balfour (1968) showed 3-to-5-year-old children two toy apple trees, one having more apples on its branches than the other. They asked the children first which tree had more apples, then which tree had fewer. To answer *both* questions, the majority of the children pointed to the tree with more apples. Indeed, children as old as 7 years may still treat "less" as though it meant "more," a fact that is especially noteworthy considering that this is the

age when subtraction is taught. Teachers are quite aware of the difficulty children have with this concept (Palermo, 1973).

QUESTION WORDS

Questions have a prolonged history in children's acquisition of language because of the variety of ways in which they may be formed. Initially, questions are simply signaled by rising intonation on an essentially declarative sentence, "Doggy eat?" Later, an auxiliary verb is introduced, "Doggie can eat?"; then the auxiliary and subject are reversed by the child, "Can doggie eat?"

Wh-questions, those beginning with what, who, where, and so on, have the following order of acquisition, as might be expected from the level of complexity of the questioning word: first, where, what, whose, and who, in that order; later, why, how, and when. The first of these questions acquired ask about locations (where), objects (what), and agents (who). Causation (why), manner (how), and time (when) appear to be more difficult concepts (de Villiers and de Villiers, 1979; Ervin-Tripp, 1970). Children continue to interpret "when" as "where" as late as 3 years of age (Ervin Tripp, 1970):

Mother When are you having lunch?

Child In the kitchen.

Children's ordering of words in wh-questions follows a progression similar to that used for questions in general. Before the subject and verb are reversed to form a question, the form is declarative: "What Mommy will do?" "Where we can go?" And consistent with other patterns of acquisition, wh-questions may often appear as unanalyzed wholes, such as "Whatsat?" In fact, "whatsat" is often among a child's first "words."

RELATIVE CLAUSES AND CONJUNCTIONS

During the age period when language is increasing in complexity, children become able to coordinate two or more ideas in a single utterance. One of the ways they do so is with **relative clauses** (Clark and Clark, 1977). The first relative clauses have no markers at all: "Here's the thing *I need.*" Later they are marked by the all-purpose "that": "Here's the thing *that I need.*" "Who" and "which" are not used in relative clauses until some months later.

What children choose to modify with relative clauses follows a specific order. Initially, they elaborate "empty" nouns, such as "thing" or "kind," as in "Here's the thing that I need for this." Then children put the relative clause next to a common noun: "Here's the ball that I need for this." But rarely does a child place such a clause in the middle of the main clause, as in "The ball that I need is over there." Interrupting a main clause with a relative one, called **embedding,** is a more complex procedure than linking two ideas sequentially (E. Clark, 1977; Clark and Clark, 1977) and so comes later.

Children discover that they may also link two ideas together with "and" to form a **coordinate sentence:** "Mommy took me to the store, and I bought some candy." Other coordinators or conjunctions used very often by 3-year-olds are "if," "when," and "because": "I want to draw, if Jimmy does." "I have dinner, when it gets dark." "I want this truck, because it is red." "Before," "after," and "until" are not as frequent. Until about 5 years of age, children describe two events in the temporal order in which they actually occurred: "We went to the zoo, and then we had ice cream." "We brushed our teeth, and then we went to bed." Coordinate constructions are easier for children to comprehend if the order expressed mirrors the real order of events and is a logical or irreversible one— "Feed the baby before you put her to bed" versus "Feed the baby before you pick up the pencil" (E. Clark, 1971; Kavanaugh, 1979). Mothers should remember this when they are giving their children directions. Some sequences they consider irreversible are not so to children. If children are told, "Before you come to the table, go comb your hair," they think that they can tend to their hair later.

THE FINISHING TOUCHES: 5 TO 10 YEARS

Although the larger part of the English language system is acquired by age 5, subtle forms of syntax pose a problem for the child for several years to come. In the sentences:

John wanted to draw a picture.
John told Bill to shovel the driveway.

no subject is stated explicitly for the dependent infinitive clauses "to draw a picture" and "to shovel the driveway." According to Carol Chomsky (1969), children follow what has been called the **minimum distance principle (MDP)** in interpreting such constructions. They correctly choose John as the subject of the first infinitive and Bill as the subject of the second. They will, however, misinterpret the sentence:

John promised Bill to shovel the driveway.

because it is not Bill who will shovel the driveway but John. Thus children frequently take the verbs "ask" and "promise" to mean "tell":

John promised Bill to shovel the driveway.

This is understood as:

John told Bill to shovel the driveway.

for children make Bill the subject of "to shovel." Similarly:

John asked Bill what to do.

This is understood as:

John told Bill what to do.

Carol Chomsky also tested children on whether the construction "easy to see" is subject to misinterpretation. First, she showed children ages 5 to 10 a big doll and asked each, "Is the doll easy to see or hard to see?" Even the youngest said that the doll was easy to see. When she put a blindfold on the doll and asked the same question, 78 percent of the 5-year-olds and 57 percent of the 6-year-olds said that the doll was "hard to see" and took off her blindfold to help her out of her difficulty. Most of the 7-year-olds and all the 9- and 10-year-olds continued to answer correctly—that the doll was "easy to see." Interestingly, children do not misunderstand the sentence "The book is hard to read," for a book is clearly inanimate and not expected to read. The MDP continues to influence children's language use and understanding until some time between 9 and 10 years.

In the early 1970s, psychologists recognized that they might be able to figure out something about children's thinking from the language they used when they were asked to understand and retell a story. Like Noam Chomsky, psychologists have looked for deep structure, in this instance that lurking beneath the surface structure of a story. In Table 11.3, the story "Melvin, the Skinny Mouse" is analyzed according to the psychologists' proposed deep-structure categories. Theorists believe that children have some mental representation of these categories and use them in understanding, retelling, and making up stories (Johnson and Mandler, 1979; Stein and Glenn, 1979).

TABLE 11.3
STRUCTURE OF A SIMPLE STORY EPISODE

Categories	"Melvin, the Skinny Mouse"
Setting	1. Once upon a time, there was a skinny little mouse named Melvin
	2. who lived in a big red barn.
Initiating event	3. One day, Melvin found a box of Rice Krispies underneath a stack of hay.
	4. Then he saw a small hole in the side of the box.
Internal response	5. Melvin knew how good the cereal tasted
	6. and wanted to eat just a little bit of cereal.
Internal plan	7. He decided to get some sugar first
	8. so that he could sweeten his cereal.
Attempt	9. Then Melvin slipped through the hole in the box
	10. and quickly filled his cereal bowl.
Direct consequence	11. Soon Melvin had eaten every bit of the Rice Krispies
	12. and had become very fat.
Reaction	13. Melvin knew he had eaten too much
	14. and felt very sad.

Source: Stein and Glenn, 1982.

The episodes in a story are regarded by children as a sequence of events that is set in motion by a principal character who wishes to fulfill a goal. Studies have shown that what children remember best about a story are the settings, initiating events, and consequences. Because these categories are also the ones found in stories made up by them, researchers assume that they are the most salient to schoolchildren. The story of Melvin as recalled by first-graders and fifth-graders was accurate in terms of temporal organization of events. Both groups remembered that Melvin the mouse found a box of Rice Krispies first, then found sugar, then slipped right into the box, then ate all the cereal and got fat. First-graders, Nancy Stein and Christine Glenn (1979) concluded, do have a set of expectations about how a story is formed. They noticed a marked difference between the elements in a story made up by a kindergartner and those in one told by a fifth-grader, however.

Kindergartner There's a boy. He's walking. He's catching a fish.

Fifth grader There's a boy who wants to catch a fish. He went to the lake and got a big one.

Whereas the story told by the kindergartner is just a series of actions, which are not integrated, the fifth-grader adds motivation by explaining, at the very beginning, the goal of the boy's actions. In the fifth-grader's tale, actions become more explicitly instrumental in obtaining an end or goal. The categories that explain the structure of stories made up and remembered by children are still very much in debate (Black and Wilensky, 1979; Mandler and Johnson, 1980).

Understanding or telling a story also involves knowing the relations between events in the story and those *implied* by social or cultural convention. Integrating this implied information into the text is called **inferencing.** One kind of inferencing is lexical, for example, knowing that when the story says "John cut the paper," John was probably using scissors, even though it is not explicitly stated. Another kind of inferencing is logical, for example, knowing that:

If the bird is in the cage
and if the cage is under the table,
then the bird is under the table.

Between first and fifth grades, children become more adept at making these inferences. Hearing and making up new stories become a source of enjoyment and learning in their lives.

CHILDREN'S CONVERSATIONS: THE SOCIAL FUNCTION OF LANGUAGE

A speaker may convey a command either directly, "Close the window," or in an indirect form, "Would you mind closing the window?" or "It's awfully drafty in here." Marilyn Shatz (1974, 1978) provides evidence from analyses of children's responses to their mothers' requests for action that they understand indirect commands as early as at 19 months of age. Although they have no sophisticated insight into the particular working of the request, children simply identify an action in the adult's utterance and carry out this action. They follow the common interaction pattern: adult speaks, child does something. Mother says, "Why don't we play ball?" Evan gets his ball, having understood "play" and "ball." Father says, "Do you want to give Daddy your coat?" Evan understands only the words "coat" and "Daddy," but he knows action is required of him. If he is either wearing or holding his coat, he will probably respond appropriately. Responding to adult speech with an action may be considered the first step in acquiring a full social conversational ability (Dore, 1978b).

In addition to taking action, children imitate and repeat in order to respond to their parents' words and continue the turn-taking sequence (Slobin, 1968, p. 438):

Mother It fits in the puzzle somewhere.
Adam Puzzle? Puzzle someplace?
Mother Turn it around.
Adam Turn it around?
Mother No, the other way.
Adam Other way?
Mother I guess you have to turn it around.
Adam Guess turn it around. Turn round.

Children "keep the conversation going" by acknowledging the words, by agreeing with or questioning them, or by asking for more information. They indicate the function of the imitated utterances with their intonations (Keenan, 1977):

Adult We are going out.
Child Out?

The child uses imitation here to express a question. In the following, the child uses imitation to acknowledge the adult's comment:

Adult And this is a big man.
Child Big man.

The young child tends to respond in some way, whether through speech or action, every time the adult speaks. When the adult makes a request, the child carries out the act requested. When the adult asks a question, the child answers. And when the adult makes a statement, the child responds by imitating the utterance (Folger and Chapman, 1978).

At later ages, children apply what they have learned about repeating the adult's words. They elaborate on them in order to take turns in a conversation. Sometime during the third year, children are able to carry on a conversation centered on a common topic for at least one turn:

Adult Let's get ready for the park.
Child The park has the big slide. I'm going on the big slide.

In an early work, Jean Piaget (1926) suggested that "dialogues" of preschoolers with their peers, as opposed to their talks with adults, were more accurately termed **collective monologues**, because neither the preschooler nor his peer really listens to, or responds to, the words of the other. Young children do engage in "private speech," talk about what they are doing, repeat themselves, and play with words to a greater extent than older children and adults. But more recent research suggests that conversations of preschoolers are focused more than half the time (Garvey and Hogan, 1973) and that children do respond appropriately to each other's questions and replies (Spilton and Lee, 1977; Wellman and Lempers, 1977). Moreover, preschoolers are more likely than older children to clarify any misunderstandings and to express reciprocation of feelings (Gottman and Parkhurst, 1977).

Young children often engage in what Piaget called "collective monologues," talking vaguely about the same things but without much connection in their exchanges and without much listening either. But, with increasing age and experience, there are fewer collective monologues and more connected dialogues.

Language can also express politeness and deference. At around 6 years of age, children understand that they should speak politely. When they request something, they are able to use forms like, "Can I swing?" or "Please, may I swing?" instead of a command, "Let me swing" (Bates, 1976; Garvey, 1975). In many European languages, the pronoun system expresses politeness. For example, a French "you" can be expressed by the familiar form, *tu*, or the polite, formal *vous*. *Tu* not only means "the person to whom I am speaking" but also indicates familiarity and closeness between the speaker and listener. Children and people of low status are addressed with *tu*, and *vous* is used to convey respect and formal distance. European children develop an awareness for these social differences in pronouns at about the same age that American children begin to make polite requests (Hollos, 1977). Children 6 years old can learn the linguistic expressions for social conventions because they know that other people have perspectives different from their own. Even younger children, of 3 and 4, indicate such an awareness when they modify the complexity of their speech and use baby talk when speaking to babies, dolls, and stuffed animals (Gleason and Weintraub, 1978; Shatz and Gelman, 1973).

THE CONTROL FUNCTION OF LANGUAGE

The Russian linguist, Alexander Luria (1961, 1969), has described children's growing responsiveness to the control function of language. When they are about 2, he suggests, children may obey a simple command from another person, or they may not. At this age a child may obey her mother's "No!" and stop hitting her playmate. But she just as well may not obey. A command called to a child in mid-action—"Don't spill that juice!"—may actually goad the child into continuing even more vigorously than before. Luria suggests that only when they are about 5 years old can children regularly stop or inhibit their response when they are asked to do so.

Why do children obey some commands but not others? Why does the control function of language seem to improve with age? These were the questions asked by two research teams. Eli Saltz, Sarah Campbell, and David Skotko (1983) studied a group of middle-class, midwestern children enrolled in a summer daycamp. For purposes of analysis, they divided the children into a younger group—3½ to 4½ years old—and an older group—4½ to 6½ years old. After telling the children that they would be playing a game to see how well they could follow instructions, an experimenter played for the children a tape recording of 30 different commands. Half were positive—"Clap your hands"—and half were negative—"Don't touch your toes." The experimenter modeled each behavior, even for negative commands. The loudness of the commands was varied from soft (below normal speech but clearly audible) to a loud shout. Saltz and his colleagues found that most of the children's errors were impulsive commissions rather than inhibited omissions. That is, the children were likely to touch their toes when told, "Don't touch your toes," rather than not to clap their hands when told, "Clap your hands." Overall, younger children made significantly more errors than older children. However, when a command was spoken softly, younger children could respond appropriately. It

was when a command was spoken loudly that they were not likely to obey it. Saltz's research team concluded that Luria was right to suggest that children younger than 5 often respond to the physical energy of an instruction—the loudness of a command or modeled behavior—even when the instruction is to inhibit their behavior. In other words, shouting "Don't do that!" is likely to cause the 2- or 3-year-old to do just the opposite.

Virginia Tinsley and Harriet S. Waters (1982) tested another aspect of Luria's theory of verbal control, this time with commands given by the children themselves rather than by adults. Children 2 years old were given a toy hammering board with one colored peg and a wooden hammer. First, the children were asked to hammer the peg as the experimenter had just done while they were watching. Then, one group of children was told to say "one" as they hammered the peg. A second group of children was told to say "one" and then to hit the peg. Tinsley and Waters found that children performed better when they said "one" at the same time as they acted; they performed worse if they said "one" and then acted. The researchers concluded that their results confirmed Luria's suggestion that young children can modify their actions best when they say something aloud at the same time, even when the word spoken ("one") is irrelevant to their actions. But saying something before they act seems only to confuse them.

HOW IS LANGUAGE ACQUIRED?

Children learn language rapidly and with surprising regularities. Researchers trying to determine how they do so concentrate on several possible answers—the language that children hear, innate mental processes, or a combination of the two.

SPEECH TO CHILDREN BY MOTHERS

Mother and child often share the same experiences. During play they share toys, during meals they share food, and in many other contexts they focus on the same objects and are affected by the same events—and Mother talks about them. The stage is set for a basic understanding of reference, the recognition that words refer to things and events. The child may also learn to distinguish parts of the interactive situation, such as the agent, the action, the experiencer, and the object acted upon from these conversations. In sharing an action that Mother comments on, the child may glean something about the order of words.

It is unlikely, however, that she receives specific grammatical instruction; most parents do not directly teach their children syntax. Intuitively, parents forgo correcting the grammar of their small children. They seem to know that children are speaking as well as they can and that eventually their grammar will improve. They monitor instead the *content* of what is said (Brown and Hanlon, 1970; Hirsch-Pasek, Treiman, and Schneiderman, 1984; Slobin, 1975). For example, when the child with chocolate crumbs on his lips says, "I not eat cookie," mother is more likely to respond, "Yes, you did eat it," than to request that the child say "No, I did not eat the cookie." Parents may offer the child a correct version of his or her incorrect sentence (Hirsch-Pasek et al., 1984). But they do not reprove the child. For instance:

Child Where we should go?

Mother Where should we go? To the store, I think.

not

Child Where should we go?

Mother Don't say "where we should go?" It's "Where should we go?"

Although adults are not giving lessons on grammar, they do greatly modify their speech when talking to children (Slobin, 1975); the younger the child, the greater the modification (Snow, 1972). As indicated earlier, adults speak to babies in what has been called baby talk or *motherese,* using first sounds that the infant babbles and later concrete nouns in short, simple sentences, which they repeat for emphasis. These sentences, compared to adult–adult speech, contain more commands and questions, fewer pronouns, verbs, modifiers, and conjunctions, fewer past tenses and fewer false starts. In talking to children, parents are given to whisperings and exaggerated intonations as well as to redundancy. There is little variation in wording. Par-

ents enunciate clearly, and they stick to the "here and now." Motherese contains fewer broken sentences, grammatical errors, or complex syntactical arrangements than adult speech. It also contains more repetitions of both the mother's speech and the child's speech as well as more pauses between utterances and major clauses (Furrow, Nelson, and Benedict, 1979; Garnica, 1977; Slobin, 1975). In motherese, pronouns may be avoided altogether when it would normally be appropriate to use them (Wills, 1974):

Mother Where are *Mommy's* eyes?
Did *Adam* eat it?

"We" may be used instead of "I":

Mother *We* don't want any more on the floor.

Mothers also use simplified, more basic words when talking to children, the same words that the children understand. For example, when the child has just learned the word "kitty," Mother will call all felines—cougars, tigers, lions, and panthers—"kitty cats," overextending her use of the term, just

Motherese is an attempt to talk so that the young child can understand. Sentences are short, simplified, and repetitive.

as the child is likely to do (Blewitt, 1983; Mervis and Mervis, 1982).

From the beginning, mothers' speech is also to some extent "tuned" to their babies' behavior. Mothers are more likely to comfort, reassure, and praise their babies when the babies look at them rather than at a toy or elsewhere (Penman, Cross, Milgrom-Friedman, and Meares, 1983). The speech of mothers and other people gradually changes as a child's language advances (Fraser and Roberts, 1975; Furrow et al., 1979; Kavanaugh and Jirkovsky, 1982; Slobin, 1975). As children get older, mothers' sentences get longer, and declarative sentences replace questions or commands (Maratsos, 1983; Newport, 1976). But there is no *simple* correspondence between the mothers' syntactic levels and length of sentences and those of their children (Chesnick, Menyuk, Liebergott, Ferrier, and Strand, 1983; Kavanaugh and Jirkovsky, 1982; Nelson, Denninger, Bonvillian, Kaplan, and Baker, 1983).

Motherese may be part of a general communication strategy that takes into account children's level of understanding as well as their level of speaking. Motherese is not a set of language lessons, except in the sense that it provides examples

RESEARCH FOCUS

HOW MOTHERS TALK TO THEIR CHILDREN

Psychologists long have been interested in the relation between mothers' and children's speech. Certainly children learn principles of syntax and vocabulary from the speech they hear around them, but how, specifically, do they do so? Keith Nelson, Marilyn Denninger, John Bonvillian, Barbara Kaplan, and Nancy Baker (1983) observed 25 children who were between 22 and 27 months old. Their mothers were well educated, middle-class Americans who held widely disparate views about how to talk to children. The researchers recorded the children's and their mothers' speech. Then they measured the level of syntactic complexity in children's speech at 27 months; the change in their syntactic complexity between 22 and 27 months; the mothers' mean utterance length; the number of auxiliaries mothers used in forming verbs; the total number of elements in the mothers' verbs; and how often the mothers replied contingently to the children's verbalizations. One kind of contingent reply was a simple recast, which referred to and clarified one central aspect of the meaning of the child's previous utterance. A child who said "broke" might hear it recast as, "The truck broke." Complex recasts referred to and changed more than one aspect of meaning in the child's utterance. For example, the child might say, "It fell," to which the mother might reply, "The barrel fell off the wagon and rolled down the hill."

Mothers' imitations of children's utterances were also considered contingent replies, and, finally, continuations were contingent replies that continued a child's topic but neither recast nor imitated it.

Nelson and his team found a positive relation between mothers' use of many simple recasts and continuations and children's language growth. But they found a negative relation between mothers' more frequent complex recasts and changes in topics and children's language growth. Mothers who want to help their children to learn vocabulary words and syntax would thus be advised to pick up their children's topics of conversation with simple recasts or new sentences that continue the conversation and avoid changing the topic, recasting it in a complex structure, or imitating the child's utterances. Nelson and his colleagues suggest that mothers' replies that depart to a *moderate* degree from children's utterances hold the children's attention and thereby may help them to learn syntax. They also note that children hear many more elements of language than they can immediately profit from and that not all mothers adjust their speech to their children's. Sometimes, just a few examples—properly timed, properly adjusted to the child's current structural and strategic levels, and embedded in the conversation so that they hold a child's attention—can advance a child's language development. Although a mother's contingent replies seem to affect the rate of her child's language growth between 22 and 27 months, the researchers note, even the slow learners end up as linguistically competent 4½-year-olds.

for a child. Mostly, it seems that motherese is a mother's attempt to speak so that a child can understand her. In one study, for example, adults told stories to a 2-year-old boy. Whenever he said "What?" or "Hum?" the adults shortened their next sentence considerably (Bohannon and Marquis, 1977). But even though mothers do not use motherese deliberately to teach their children to speak, motherese contains elements that do make it easier for children to learn than adult speech does. According to the **motherese hypothesis,** the short sentences, clear enunciation, grammatical correctness, and concreteness of a caretaker's speech help a child to acquire language.

What is the evidence for this hypothesis? Do children benefit in any way from the motherese modifications of the speech they hear? Shorter utterances very likely ease comprehension, because the memories of young children are limited. Simpler sentences probably help children to pick out the most important words. Although some simplifications probably do help, it does not follow that the simpler the language, the better. A study by Alison Clarke-Stewart (Clarke-Stewart and Hevey, 1981) determined that within the normal range for motherese—in this study, mothers' sentences to their 30-month-olds ranged from two and one-half to six words long—the longer the mother's sentences were than the child's, the more advanced was the child's spoken language. Apparently children are not encouraged to advance linguistically if the language they hear is reduced to their level; it should be somewhat more complex. A number of other investigators have also looked for links between mothers' and children's language levels. Lila Gleitman, Elissa Newport, and Henry Gleitman (1984), of the University of Pennsylvania, studied the relation between mothers' speech and the length of their children's utterances. Paralleling Clarke-Stewart's (Clarke-Stewart and Hevey, 1981) results, they found that for 1½-year-olds, the longer and more complex the mother's sentences, the more rapid the child's increase in language complexity (use of auxiliaries). Mothers' use of **expansions** (corrected repetitions of the child's utterances) and interjections such as "mhmm" were also positively related to children's use of auxiliaries. Gleitman and her colleagues suggest that children are helped to learn language when their caretaker uses moderately complex sentences, for these

stimulate learning in a way that very simple sentences do not. Having found that mothers' speech styles do not change much during the period when their children are acquiring language, the researchers suggest that it is the child who plays the major role in actively selecting the language he or she finds salient (See Research Focus: the Motherese Hypothesis, for details of the Gleitman study.)

Simplifying, shortening, repeating, and emphasizing their own speech is only one thing mothers do when talking to children. They may also extend the child's speech:

Child Doggy out?
Mother Doggy wants to go out?

Expansions with a falling intonation serve to confirm what the child has said; those with a rising intonation check for comprehension (Slobin, 1975). When a toddler wants her mother to get the picture book on top of the table and says, "Get book," mother may extend her words to "Mother get the book" or "Will Mother get the book, please?" to indicate a better way of asking for assistance. When the toddler comes in carrying her bottle and the unscrewed nipple and says, "Mommy fix," mother may expand the statement to "Mommy fix the bottle," giving a more complete description of the action requested.

Courtney Cazden (1972) has tried to determine whether some expansions or extensions of children's words are more helpful than others. At an overcrowded day-care center, one which would be considered "linguistically deprived," she tested the effects of two kinds of verbal extension programs. In one, adults simply expanded children's spontaneous speech, for example:

Child Get book.
Adult You get book.

In the other, adults gave well-formed responses to the children's speech:

Child Get book.
Adult Okay, I'll get the book.

Children who were not in one of the two programs formed a control group. Cazden found that responding well to the child's use of language brought more improvement than simply expanding the child's statement.

In another study designed to determine what type of adult response helps children learn language, Keith Nelson (1980) found that some mothers, when their children were 22 to 27 months old, made simple *recasts* of their children's sentences. They changed only one component in the child's utterance, subject or verb or object:

Child Doggy jump.
Adult (simple recast) Doggy is jumping.

Other mothers made complex recasts, changing or adding two or three components:

Adult (complex recast) "The dog is jumping over the fence."

Comparing the language growth of the children in the two groups, Nelson found that a large proportion of the children hearing simple recasts of their words increased the length of their utterances and used more auxiliary verbs. Children hearing complex recasts of their words did not advance as fast on either of these measures. In fact, giving complex responses actually seemed to hinder children's language growth. In the simple recast, Nelson con-

RESEARCH FOCUS

THE MOTHERESE HYPOTHESIS

The motherese hypothesis holds that the more a mother (or other caretaker) simplifies and restricts her speech to the child, the more quickly and correctly the child will learn language. Accordingly, her sentences should be short, clearly spoken, grammatical, and directed to the here-and-now. Lila Gleitman, Elissa Newport, and Henry Gleitman (1984) measured several aspects of mothers' and children's speech to test this hypothesis. The researchers computed correlations between mothers' speech at one time and children's language growth from that time to a later one, controlling statistically for the children's initial language level at the time of first assessment. Their subjects were six children who ranged in age from 18 to 21 months and another six children who were between 24 and 25 months at the first assessment. All of the subjects were girls from upper-middle-class, academic families. The children and mothers were observed once at home as they chatted and played and again 6 months later.

The mothers' utterances were analyzed for intelligibility; quality of form, length, structural and psycholinguistic (relationship of deep to surface structure) complexity; sentence type; and frequency of repetition and expansion. Children's utterances were analyzed for syntactic complexity, length, noun and verb phrase length and frequency, plurals and possessives, and auxiliaries. Each child's growth score consisted of the difference between these child-language measurements at the two home visits 6 months apart. Most of the

significant correlations, the investigators found, occurred between mothers' speech and the language abilities of the younger children. Mothers' use of expansions, their sentence complexity, and the length of their utterances were positively related to the younger children's use of auxiliaries. In most cases, no significant correlations were found between aspects of mothers' and older children's speech. The one exception to this was that mothers' use of questions answerable by "yes" or "no" was related to the older children's use of auxiliaries. A negative relation appeared between mothers' repetitions and children's language growth.

On the basis of these results, Gleitman and her colleagues suggest that mothers have their strongest effect in the early stages of children's language development. At this stage, children tend to focus on stressed syllables and search for a simple, central sentence form—usually the declarative—which they can use for communicating. Once children progress to structurally more complex language, they seem to be less affected by input from their mothers.

Is the motherese hypothesis borne out in predicting that children learn best from the simplest language? No, conclude the Gleitmans and Newport, children learn best from language that is more complex than their own. What is more, only items like inflections, markers of case and aspect, certain pronouns and prepositions—items of which there are a limited number and that do not map directly onto objects or actions in the environment—are linked to the mother's input. Nouns and verbs are not. Children pick and choose what, when, and how they learn from their mothers' speech.

cludes, children can notice and analyze a new grammatical structure more effectively.

Nelson (1981) tested this hypothesis experimentally by having adults deliberately give recasts of children's sentences, either by fixing the verb:

Child Where it go?
Adult It will go there.

or by recasting a statement as a question:

Child The fox ran.
Adult The fox ran, didn't he?

After five 1-hour sessions with the recaster, children's language was assessed. Children who had heard recast verbs advanced in their use of verbs, but not of questions; children who heard recast questions advanced in them, but not in verbs. It does appear that children notice extensions of their language.

Other deliberate attempts to accelerate children's development of language have also been successful. Froma Roth (1984), of the University of Maryland, worked on syntax with a group of children between 3½ and 4½ years of age. She found that after they heard sentences like "The dog chases the pig that sits on the duck," watched them enacted, and then enacted them themselves, the children could learn several kinds of relative clauses that at first were beyond their developmental grasp.

Although deliberate attempts to teach children language, like Cazden's (1972), Nelson's (1980b), and Roth's (1984) can succeed, it is important to realize that this does not mean that mothers talk to their children as they do *to teach* them language or that such modifications of speech are necessary for linguistic development. Elena Lieven (1978), for example, found a mother-child pair in which the mother virtually never linked her utterances to her child's. Yet the child learned to speak. No matter how extensively adult speech is simplified, articulated, responsive, or repeated for a child, input cannot solve the problem of acquisition. The child still must analyze for himself or herself the underlying patterns in the welter of examples he or she hears.

IMITATION

Soon after children begin to combine words, they frequently echo spontaneously the speech addressed to them. As is true of much in the course

Some language lessons between mother and child are structured and deliberate, as when this mother shows her 2-year-old son a counting book. But other language "lessons" are unstructured, spontaneous, and hardly lessons at all.

of language development, children vary considerably in the degree to which they imitate the speech of others. Some children may not echo at all. Others, much to a parent's chagrin, are quite amazing in their ability to parrot back an exact repetition of an adult's utterance, even days after they originally heard it.

B. F. Skinner proposed that imitation is the sole mechanism by which children acquire language. The evidence against this position is now overwhelming. On the one hand, children use constructions found nowhere in adult speech—"foots," "runned," "breaked," and "Allgone wet." On the other hand, children with Down's syndrome and autistic children, who do learn language only through imitation, do not have normal speech. Clearly, children do not learn language through imitation alone; the issue is more complex.

It is possible that imitation is *one* strategy by which children learn language, though not the only one. They probably learn all their vocabulary through imitation, for instance. But in learning syntax, Grover Whitehurst and Ross Vasta (1975) suggest, children probably go through a three-step process, with imitation the middle step. First, they comprehend the grammatical form of an adult's words. Then, they selectively imitate the form. Later, they use the form in their own sentences. Children imitate neither totally novel nor totally familiar constructions; they seem to concentrate on those just entering their repertoire (Bloom, Hood, and Lightbown, 1974). Children, in fact, appear to be incapable of imitating constructions that they have not yet mastered themselves.

Adult Adam, say what I say: Where can I put them?

Adam Where I can put them (Slobin, 1971, p. 52).

Adult This one is the giant, but this one is little.

Child Dis one little, annat one big (Slobin and Welsh, 1973, p. 490).

OTHER FACTORS IN THE ENVIRONMENT

Correlational studies indicate that children have greater language ability the higher the level of their parents' education. Being exposed to adult speakers other than members of the immediate family relates positively to acquiring a vocabulary of 50 words at an earlier age. The number of peers with whom the child comes in contact appears to have no effect on learning language, but spending too much time with these other children rather than with an adult does slow down the process (Nelson, 1973). Firstborn children, who interact primarily with parents, acquire language faster than later-born children, who spend more time speaking to other children.

Children who spend considerable time watching television acquire language later than those who do not (Nelson, 1973). Hearing children of deaf parents will not acquire spoken language if they only watch television (Sachs and Johnson, 1976). The same is true for acquisition of a second language. Dutch children who are exposed to German only through television cannot speak it. A child must interact with a speaker of the language to acquire it, even if the interaction with a live speaker is only 4 percent of the child's total experience of the language (Friedlander, Jacobs, David, and Wetstone, 1972).

THE PHYSIOLOGICAL ELEMENT

Of course, the most scientific method of examining how the environment affects a child's linguistic development would be to deprive the child of all contact with any language. Humane and practical reasons make such an experiment impossible. Yet certain unfortunate children have been subjected to conditions in which they are isolated from language.

The language information that deaf children are able to acquire from their surroundings may be minimal. Some parents choose that their deaf children be given only *oral* training and not learn sign language. Oral schools give instruction in speaking, in lip reading, and in discriminating sounds, for very few individuals are entirely deaf. Susan Goldin-Meadow and Heidi Feldman (1977) analyzed the spontaneous gestures that deaf children so trained create for communication. The gestural systems, which they make up on their own, have a number of properties of natural spoken language. The deaf children develop a vocabulary of signs referring to actions, objects, and people as well as an order for

The gesture systems that deaf children see and use have the properties of spoken language. The similarities suggest that some components of language, such as the urge to communicate, may be inborn.

the signs in an "utterance." These findings suggest that there is a strong tendency for children to communicate and to communicate systematically. They also point to the possibility of an innate set of language components that will be expressed—in gestures should words not be available.

The deprivation of some children has been so extreme that they have virtually no access to language. One of these was Genie, whom we described in Chapter 3. This unfortunate creature, you will recall, was discovered and rescued at the age of 13½, unable to speak or understand language and unable to stand up. She had spent the first 20 months of her life grossly malnourished and ignored most of the time. Then, her father began his real abuse. By day, she was confined in a small bedroom and harnessed to an infant's potty seat. At night, when Genie was not forgotten, her father

put her into a sleeping bag, which constrained her arms, and then into an infant's crib with wire mesh sides and a wire mesh cover overhead. He growled and bared his teeth at Genie and beat her if she made a sound. Caged by night, harnessed by day, Genie was left somehow to endure the hours and years of her life (Curtiss, 1977).

After an emaciated and severely retarded Genie was discovered, she spent some time in a hospital and then went to live in a foster home. She was given special therapy and language training. After 6 years, she had learned to speak in sentences, to take a bus to school, and to express normal emotions.

Certain aspects of language have not been acquired by Genie, however. She does not use **proforms** "what," "which," "that," and the like; passive sentences such as "John was hit by a ball;" or questions with subject-auxiliary-verb inversion, such as "Are you sleeping?" Auxiliary verbs are rarely heard in her speech. She says, "John gone home," not "John has gone home" or "John will have gone home." Although she has access to a storehouse of words, which she can combine to express simple ideas—"No more take wax," "No want to eat breakfast," she cannot yet combine more than one idea into a single sentence. Even with a number of years of extensive therapy and language training and even though she has made remarkable progress socially, Genie remains at the telegraphic-speech stage of a 2- or 3-year-old. To acquire complex features of language, it may be that the individual must be exposed to speech before a certain age, at least before 13 if not earlier, or for a relatively long period, more than the 6 years of training Genie has received.

Many people believe that language cannot be acquired past a critical period, spanning the time from infancy to puberty and ending at about 13 years of age. Eric Lenneberg (1967) suggested that the preschool years are especially important and that at this stage the brain is maturationally primed for acquiring language. Children who have suffered damage to the part of the brain primarily involved in language, the left hemisphere for most people, learn to speak again much better than do adults who have suffered the same damage. The argument is that beyond the critical period, brain physiology is no longer auspicious for acquiring language. The fact that Genie has learned to speak at all suggests that no strong claim for an absolute critical period ending at 13 years can be made. But her present language problems leave open the possibility that some aspects of language must be learned before children reach 13 if their language is to reach the usual adult level of complexity.

BILINGUALISM

LEARNING TWO LANGUAGES

Some children grow up hearing, and eventually speaking, two languages. Does this hinder them in learning language or interfere with their cognitive development? Before we can answer these questions, there are several points to be understood.

First, children rarely have perfectly equal proficiency in both languages because the amount of time they are exposed to each varies. In addition, children learn the two languages in different contexts. Generally the primary language is learned at home and the secondary language from playmates and at school. The mother, however, may speak only the primary language to the child, the father the secondary.

Much of the research on bilingualism has been an attempt to determine whether learning two languages affects intelligence and reasoning. Does it hinder children to expose them to a second language before they have fully mastered the first? Because, as we have seen, children do not completely master a language until they are 9 or 10 years of age, and they stand a much better chance

RESEARCH FOCUS

GENETIC FACTORS IN LANGUAGE ACQUISITION

Listen to a group of parents talking, and you'll hear about the little girl who spoke her first sentence at 10 months and about the little boy, now a famous musician, who barely spoke until kindergarten. How many of these great individual differences in language acquisition are hereditary, and how many are the result of environmental factors? Karen Hardy-Brown, Robert Plomin, and John DeFries (1981), of the University of Colorado, studied 50 adopted 1-year-olds and their biological and adoptive parents in order to answer that question. They visited the 1-year-olds at home and reexamined them at 2, 3, and 4 years of age. (Future visits are planned). Most of the parents are white; the education and socioeconomic status of the biological parents are generally lower than those of the adoptive parents (but not disadvantaged). The researchers recorded the language between adoptive mothers and 1-year-olds as they played, as the children ate, and as the parents taught the children a pegboard task. The parents' cognitive abilities and vocabularies were tested; the children's vocalizations, communicative gestures, imitations of adult speech and questioning intonation, and vocabulary were also tested. Some of the data came from video-

tapes, some from mothers' reports, some from standardized tests. The investigators coded the following aspects of the mothers' behavior: vocalizing, gesturing, sentence types, imitating, teaching, utterance length, and repetitions.

For the infants, Hardy-Brown and her colleagues found a cluster of interrelated measures that indexed general language competence: size of vocabulary; imitation of adult speech; frequency of true words, vocal signals, and vocalizations directed to another person; questioning intonation; syllable structure; and level of gestures. Only two measures of the adoptive mothers' speech were found to be related to the infants' competence in communicating (and these might have been due to chance): imitations of, and contingent vocal responses to, the infants' vocalizations. Socioeconomic status and educational level, cognitive ability, and vocabulary level of the adoptive parents did not relate to the infants' language competence. Neither did adoptive mothers' overall frequency of speaking or reading to their 1-year-olds, the syntactic complexity of their speech to their children, or the presence of an older sibling in the home. In contrast, the cognitive ability, especially memory, of the biological mothers did relate to the 1-year-olds' language competence, suggesting that language development in the first year of life is in large part genetically governed.

Learning two languages during childhood does not interfere with cognitive development or fluency of expression, although it may slow down the acquisition of vocabulary.

of achieving near native proficiency when they start younger than this, the question is an important one.

Until the 1960s, most studies reported that bilingualism had detrimental effects on intelligence (e.g., Jones, 1960). But later reexamination of these studies indicated that factors other than bilingualism had probably influenced the results. Socioeconomic status was rarely controlled for—bilingual children may come from families with lower income and less education—and in at least one study, children were declared bilingual simply on the basis of their names! When socioeconomic status has been controlled, and therefore did not significantly influence the results of the observations and experiments, bilinguals have done as well as, if not better than, monolinguals on both verbal and nonverbal tests (Bain, 1976; Lambert, 1972). Bilinguals have also expressed more ideas in a test of storytelling (Doyle, Champagne, and Segalowitz, 1978).

Being bilingual appears to have no detrimental effect on cognitive development or verbal fluency; if anything, bilingual children may have an advantage compared to monolinguals. There is still some question about how fast bilingual children acquire vocabulary words, however. Scores of preschool bilingual children in naming picture objects in their dominant language, as measured by the Peabody Picture Vocabulary Test, have been found to be significantly lower than those of preschool mono-

linguals (Doyle et al., 1978). The fact that children are exposed to two languages in their early life does not appear to affect the reported age of the first word, however.

It has often been said that to help children acquire both languages simultaneously, the language contexts should be kept completely separate. For example, children should speak only Spanish in the home, or the mother should speak to the child only in Spanish, the father only in English. Some researchers have questioned this belief. A study by Anna-Beth Doyle, Mireille Champagne, and Norman Segalowitz (1978) showed that hearing two languages from the same person did not affect children's vocabularies. The most significant predictor of the number of words these children knew was their mother's education.

The language-learning task for bilingual children is a challenging one. They must learn to distinguish two systems of rules instead of one. In spite of this complexity, if two languages are spoken in the home, by the time children are 3, they are usually able to speak both languages with relatively little confusion. Mix-ups do occur, though, particularly early on. The most common one is "lexical borrowing," the use of a word from the primary language while speaking the secondary language—because the child has not yet learned that particular word (Ben-Zeev, 1977; Lindholm and Padilla,

1978). Virginia Volterra and Traute Taeschner (1978) have proposed three stages through which the bilingual child passes before achieving a comfortable balance between the two languages, at about 4 years of age. First, a word is acquired in one language or the other, but not both. Second, one set of syntactic rules is applied to both lexicons. And third, each language is strongly associated with the person who uses it or the context in which it is generally heard, such as at nursery school or at home. The child may become quite upset if, for example, the father, who has always spoken German, suddenly speaks French.

Some children in the United States come to school unable to speak English, which presents another kind of problem. Most of their parents agree that it is important for these children to learn English. Several means of instruction have been tried in the schools. Children may be put into classes in which only English is spoken, "total immersion" style, and left to sink or swim. They may be taught in their native language for the first months or years and then gradually eased into English, or they may be taught in both languages from the beginning. Any of these methods can work. What seems to be most important is that the school not demean the children or their native language while it is teaching them English.

The fact that children are able to acquire *two* languages is *even* more remarkable than the fact that they acquire *one*. And the findings that show for the most part positive, or at worst neutral, effects of bilingualism on cognitive development and language use suggest that, in a multicultural society such as ours, the one drawback, a slower rate of vocabulary growth for a limited period of time, may be a rather small price to pay for greater ultimate facility in languages and greater communicative ability.

BLACK ENGLISH

Some linguists who have analyzed the language typically spoken in black ghetto homes have concluded that this version of English should be understood as an entirely different dialect of nonstandard English with rules of its own and its own ways of indicating a speaker's competence and ability. They have named this dialect **Black English** (Labv, 1970). They also contend that giving *standard* language tests to black ghetto children makes them appear to be more verbally deprived and inferior than they are. Similar arguments are raised by those who favor bilingual education for children from Spanish-speaking homes. Children who use Black English as well as those who actually speak a different language tend to be treated as though they have no language of their own. They are unable to compete on tests with children who speak standard English, and their low scores on such tests may be used as a sign of genetic inferiority.

William Labov, one of the foremost proponents of recognizing Black English as a distinct dialect, claims that regarding blacks as verbally deprived is a myth. Lower-class blacks are "bathed in verbal stimulation from morning till night" (1970, p. 163). But schoolroom standards for the effectiveness of speech tend to be entirely different from standards that prevail in street culture. Labov (1970) gives as an example the language of Larry, a speaker of Black English and a 15-year-old gang member put back from the 11th grade to the 9th grade and threatened with further action by the school authorities. The interviewer's name is John Lewis:

JL What happens to you after you die? Do you know?

Larry Yeah, I know.

JL What?

Larry After they put you in the ground, your body turns into—ah—bones, an' shit.

JL What happens to your spirit?

Larry Your spirit—soon as you die, your spirit leaves you.

JL And where does the spirit go?

Larry Well, it all depends.

JL On what?

Larry You know, like some people say if you're good an' shit, your spirit goin' t'heaven . . . 'n' if you bad, your spirit goin' to hell. Well, bullshit! Your spirit going to hell anyway, good or bad.

JL Why?

Larry Why? I'll tell you why. 'Cause, you see, doesn't nobody really know that it's a God, y'know, 'cause I mean I have seen black gods, pink gods, white gods, all color gods, and don't nobody know it's really a God. An' when they be sayin' if you good, you goin' t'heaven, that's bullshit, 'cause you ain't goin' to no heaven, 'cause it ain't no heaven for you to go to.

JL *Well, if there's no heaven, how could there be a hell?*

Larry *I mean—ye-aah. Well, let me tell you, it ain't no hell, 'cause this is hell right here, y'know!*

JL *This is hell?*

Larry *Yeah, this is hell right here! (Labov, 1970, pp. 164–166).*

Labov points out the Black English elements of Larry's speech, such as negative inversion—"don't nobody know"; negative concord—"you ain't goin' to no heaven"; modified copula—"when they be sayin' "; optional copula deletion—"if you're good . . . if you bad"; "it" substituted for standard "there"—"it ain't no heaven . . . it ain't no hell"; full forms of auxiliaries—"I have seen." Black English also has stylistic qualities, such as summing up a complex argument in a few words and avoiding qualifications or reservations in stating opinions. Labov stresses the logic Larry uses, his directness. He emphasizes the fact that speakers of Black English take "great delight in exercising their wit and logic," even if the subject is improbable. Here is the logical argument Larry presented, translated into acceptable standard English. Which would receive a better grade, this or Larry's Black English version?

After you die, your spirit leaves your body, but I don't believe one's spirit goes to heaven. In fact, nobody knows whether there is definitely a heaven, or even a God. Just look at all the many versions of God people have. We have no proof that there is a God or a heaven, but if you look at this world, at these mean streets where murder, rape, and mugging are the rule, we have proof of a hell. So after you die your spirit would like to get away, but there's only one place for it, the hell that's right here.

A number of other studies support the contention that black ghetto children are in effect bilingual. In one study of groups of children—one black, one white—who had been matched for social class and nonverbal intelligence, both groups did equally well at understanding standard English sentences, but the whites were significantly worse in understanding sentences in black dialect (Genshaft and Hirt, 1974). A review of studies of children in kindergarten and the primary grades concludes that "no acceptable, replicable research has found that the dialect spoken by black children presents a unique problem in comprehending standard English" (Hall and Turner, 1974).

As the foregoing suggests, it is important to control for social class and intelligence when giving black and white children language tasks. The race and class of the experimenter may also be a factor to control. When experimenters are white and middle class, lower-class black children may be inhibited and hindered during a test or interview (Edwards, 1979). In a study conducted by Labov (1970), a congenial white interviewer attempted to speak with two black ghetto boys. He received at best one-word answers. When a black interviewer spoke to the same boys in Black English, he was able to evoke detailed responses, which gave no hint of verbal deprivation.

THE LANGUAGE AND THOUGHT ISSUE

A long-standing theoretical issue concerns the relation of language and thought. Communication is of course a principal reason for speaking—we have already seen that language emerges in an interactive context and is not spoken spontaneously in isolation—but language is also intimately connected with thought. Within the time frame of the child's development, the growth of language and thought overlap. Whether acquiring or using language, children certainly are thinking. They are remembering words and associating them with meanings. They are figuring out rules about putting words together. And they are using words and sentences to express their thoughts. But the question is do children first have a *thought* and then try to express it in words, or does the *language* they have first shape their thoughts?

According to one theoretical point of view, acquiring language is, to some degree, a problem-solving task to which children apply the analytic tools and knowledge that they have developed thus far. The language of children reflects their current cognitive abilities. Children will not use a morpheme expressing a tense or plurality before they understand these concepts (Nelson, 1974; Siegel, 1978). But does language itself help in the development of these concepts? Would children have these concepts if they did not know any words and were not exposed to language?

The cognitive abilities of deaf children, who have limited or no access to the language used by those around them, suggest that the answer to this question is yes. Although the intellectual development of deaf children proceeds more slowly, it goes through the same stages and ends up at the same level as that of hearing individuals (Furth, 1966).

Three major theorists, Jean Piaget, Benjamin Whorf, and Lev Vygotsky—among others—have written on the relation of language and thought.

JEAN PIAGET

That language is not entirely necessary for cognitive development has been suggested by Piaget. His research on sensorimotor intelligence in the first 18 months of life clearly demonstrated that children have thoughts about objects before they can name them. Children need a firm mental representation of an object before they can connect a word to it. In Piaget's view thought can affect language, but not having language does not prevent the individual from thinking.

But can learning words help children to think? Piagetian researchers have examined the possibility that, through language training, children can advance more rapidly to the next level of cognitive development. In one of these studies, children were taught the verbal expressions used by youngsters who had been able to describe how two pencils, two balls of clay, and two quantities of beads differed. The training sessions, which exposed the children to comparatives, such as long and thin, short and fat, and more and less, proved largely unsuccessful (Sinclair-de Zwart, 1967). Although children appeared to understand the language instructions and how to use the words, it was concluded that their level of mental maturity prevented them from solving the Piagetian tasks, such as conservation, correctly. Piaget himself and other Piagetian researchers have proposed, however, that language *interaction* with other youngsters may help children to advance intellectually, even though verbal training does not. They consider that children's attempts to convince their peers of their own ar-

guments or points of view, the ensuing disputes, and the conflicts generated by being made aware of contradictions are necessary steps in cognitive growth (Inhelder and Karmiloff-Smith, 1978).

BENJAMIN WHORF

Even more strongly than Piaget, Benjamin Whorf (1897–1941) believed that language affects thought. From his observations of Western languages and of American Indian languages, he developed two related hypotheses about the relation between language and thought, **linguistic determinism** and **linguistic relativity.** The hypothesis of linguistic determinism holds that the structure of language determines the structure of all higher levels of thinking—language determines thought. According to the hypothesis of linguistic relativity, the forms of the particular language affect the individual's perception of the world. A strong version of Whorf's hypotheses, then, claims that language determines both our perceptions and thoughts about the world. For example, the Innuit (Eskimo) language has a number of terms to indicate the texture, recency, and fall of *snow*. Whorf would claim that not only does this multiplicity of words reflect the Eskimos' greater dependence on snow in their surroundings and their subsequent need to make finer distinctions than we, but it also enables speakers of the Innuit language *better to see* these distinctions.

It is true that languages differ in terms of what is expressed and how it is expressed. Edward Sapir (1884–1929), a scientist of extraordinary breadth, wrote musingly of these differences.

In German and in French we are compelled to assign "stone" to a gender category—perhaps the Freudians can tell us why this object is masculine in the one language, feminine in the other; in Chippewa we cannot express ourselves without bringing in the apparently irrelevant fact that a stone is an inanimate object. If we find gender beside the point, the Russians may wonder why we consider it necessary to specify in every case whether a stone, or any other object for that matter, is conceived in a definite or an indefinite manner, why the difference between "the stone" and "a stone" matters. "Stone falls" is good enough for Lenin, as it was good enough for Cicero (Sapir, 1958, pp. 158–159).

The Innuit language has a number of terms to indicate different kinds of snow, a life-and-death aspect of life in the Arctic. Do Eskimo people see snow in ways different from our own, or do they just talk about it more?

Different languages also vary in the way they divide the color spectrum. Languages may have many words for the colors of the spectrum, as English does. Other languages, for example, Bassa, spoken in Liberia, or the language of the Dani in New Guinea, use only two words for the entire spectrum, light and dark. Does this mean that speakers of Bassa *perceive* only two colors in the world around them and see no other distinctions, as a staunch Whorfian might claim? A number of studies have shown that this is not so. Certain colors of the spectrum, called focal colors, are more salient, that is, more easily distinguished and more often chosen as exemplars of a category, by both adults and children, whether or not there is a specific term for them in a language (Berlin and Kay, 1969; Heider, 1971a).

Slobin, a psychologist, has addressed the issue of linguistic relativity.

Heat, in Indo-European languages, is a noun. A large number of nouns designate concrete things. Perhaps this is why so much effort was expended in the history of Western science in the search for a heat substance, like "phlogiston" and "caloric." Perhaps if Western scientists had spoken a language like Hopi, where heat is a verb, they may have started out with the more appropriate kinetic theory of heat at which they finally arrived. (But note that in spite of the language—if it was a determiner—Western scientists did eventually free themselves from the notion of a heat substance when this notion proved itself inadequate on empirical and rational grounds.) (Slobin, 1971, p. 129).

Although languages have different words and constructions and can express certain notions with varying degrees of flexibility, it is generally the case that the intentions expressed in one language can be translated into another. Ease and variability of expression will probably be determined by how important any particular concept or relation is to the culture and speakers of the language. In this sense, language may be more a reflection than a determiner of cultural perceptions and individual thought, encoding information that is socially important.

Just as distinct languages have been examined to find out about their influence on the thought patterns of the people speaking them, so have dialects in the United States and Great Britain been investigated. Studies have examined whether the simpler speech patterns of working-class people hinder their thinking. Although speech patterns are a reflection of social class, do they actually help create class differences and lock people within them?

Basil Bernstein, an English sociologist, has identified two speech patterns, the **elaborated code** of the middle class and the **restricted code** of working-class speakers of English. Middle-class speakers use longer sentences, which are more grammatically complex and precise. The sentences may communicate feelings and emotions and intentions, but they are also more independent of immediate context in their wording and interpretation. Working class speakers use short, grammatically uncomplicated sentences referring primarily to concrete objects and immediate events. Their sentences are less flexible and more dependent on the assumption that the listener shares the same knowledge and background information as the speaker. Starting a conversation with the sentence, "He gave me this," when the listener does not know for certain who and what "he" and "this" are, is one example of a restricted use of language. A person using an elaborated code would begin the same conversation with "My friend Harry gave me this car." Bernstein (1966) has suggested that a restricted code of expression does restrict thinking. Evidence supporting this position, however, is equivocal.

Some researchers have found that lower-class children in the United States, compared to middle-class children, have less grammatical ability and do not communicate as effectively with a listener (Anastasiow and Hanes, 1976; Bruck and Tucker, 1974). But such findings are often confounded by the type of English spoken in inner cities and rural areas, which may have different, but also systematic, rules that deviate from those of accepted standard American English.

LEV SEMENOVICH VYGOTSKY

According to Russian psychologist Lev Semenovich Vygotsky, thought and speech have separate roots but later coincide. "Thought and word are not connected by a primary bond. A connection originates, changes, and grows in the course of the evolution of thinking and speech" (Vygotsky, 1934, p. 119). The "preintellectual" roots of speech are emotional expressions—children's crying and babbling and possibly even their very first words. Vygotsky proposed an early period when thought is not touched by speech or speech by thought. When children are approximately 2 years of age, these two lines of development, thought and speech, meet; speech begins to serve the intellect, becoming rational, and thoughts become verbal. The child seems to have discovered the symbolic function of language. The union of thought and speech is marked by the child's curiosity about words and requests for names and by a rapid increase in vocabulary. Thereafter, children talk more and more to themselves. At first they may describe what they have just done. Angie may take off her mittens and then say, "Take off mittens." Then she will describe what she is doing as she does it: "Put kitty in the doll cradle. Pull up the blanket. Rock the cradle." Eventually, at about 4, language will help her form ideas, and she will say aloud or to herself what she is going to do.

According to Vygotsky, private speech branches off from social speech, becoming more and more abbreviated and internalized, and is referred to then as **inner speech.** Inner speech is critical to the organization of thought. Words children have acquired and their associated meanings, for example, influence how children classify unfamiliar items. They know that a hat is "clothing" because it is placed on the body or that a celery stalk is a "vegetable" because it is green and not sweet to taste. Intellectual growth in Vygotsky's theory depends on the development of both inner speech and **social speech.** In Vygotsky's view children retain a certain amount of nonlinguistic thought and nonintellectual speech: nonlinguistic thought being used initially in solving problems and only later becoming embodied in words; nonintellectual speech being used, for example, in memory, when only language forms need be retained. But in most intellectual activities, speech and thought, once developing along separate pathways, are inextricably bound together.

Does thought precede language, as Piaget believed or do thought and speech develop along parallel paths that eventually meet and produce language, as Vygotsky proposed? (See Figure 11.6.) Children are not perplexed by such questions. When they are 2, they cannot think about thinking. But their two and three-word utterances

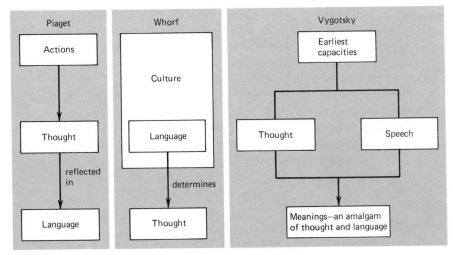

FIGURE 11.6

Jean Piaget, Benjamin Whorf, and Lev Semenovich Vygotsky each had a different idea about the relation between language and thought, an age-old question (Gardner, 1978).

will continue to provide adults with questions and theories about the way language is related to thought. Since people first began to document and pay serious attention to the language of children, a great deal of progress has been made. So far we have been limited for the most part to *descriptions* of their language use, however, and have difficulty explaining *why* their language is not only different from that of adults but also systematic and governed by rules. We do not know how the child acquires these rules and on what bases they are gradually modified to approach the rules of adult language. We do know, however, that children have a tremendous desire to communicate with those around them, to share observations, to make their needs known.

We also surmise that their tendency to structure and systematize their communications may be innate. This tendency to make behavior and the events of the world systematic, predictable, and understandable may apply to more than the domain of language. Far from being passive recipients of the knowledge provided by family and culture, children are active participants, constructing the world anew for themselves from relatively small clues and a great deal of rather sophisticated creative energy.

SUMMARY

1. B. F. Skinner, the outspoken advocate of learning theory, maintains that children acquire language in the same way that they learn other behavior, through systematic reinforcement. Linguist Noam Chomsky claims that parents do not pay this amount of close attention to their children's speech, that children have an innate ability to gather notions about the rules of language.

2. Language in Chomsky's view has a surface structure, which consists of the actual words spoken or written and their order; and a deep structure, which has to do with the underlying meaning of the words and their syntactical relationships. Some linguists now suggest that a nontransformational grammar better describes how children learn language than Chomsky's transformational rules do.

3. Infants first babble to practice moving their mouth, lips, tongue, and throat. Eventually, they shorten some of their syllables and combine particular ones with gestures and intonation to get the attention and assistance of adults.

4. A child's first clearly intelligible word near the

end of the first year usually exclaims on something that is especially noticeable or changing in the immediate surroundings. Between 12 and 18 months, children acquire a vocabulary of nearly 50 words, many of them being names of objects; others are connected with actions. Children are able to extend the meaning of their single words with gestures and intonation so that a word acts as a whole sentence.

5. Between 18 and 24 months, children begin putting two words together in regular "telegraphic" ways of their own creation that make combinations unlike those in adult speech. They fill gaps in their vocabularies according to the principles of contrast and conventionality. They can now remark on possession, location, recurrence of an action or an object, and nonexistence. They may be able to communicate without gestures.

6. From 2 to 5 years of age, children add grammatical morphemes to their speech, in much the same order; expand their negatives; lose their irregular past tenses and plurals, and then regain them; learn more specific adjectives and prepositions, question words, and word order; and add relative and coordinate clauses.

7. Luria has suggested that language has a control function as well as a communicative one.

8. From 5 to 10 years of age, children add finishing touches to their language; they become able to determine the subjects of infinitives, for example, and understand the implied, but not stated, meaning of phrases.

9. Conversations with adults help children acquire language. Adults tend to adapt their utterances to the age of the child, but children actively select those features of their caretakers' language that they find most salient.

10. Eric Lenneberg suggested that children learn language so rapidly in the preschool years that during this period the brain must be maturationally primed for it. He and others think that the critical period for acquiring langue ends at age 13. It may, indeed, be difficult to learn certain complexities of language beyond this age.

11. Bilingualism appears not to be detrimental to young children's cognitive development and verbal fluency, and it will ultimately be of great cultural advantage to them. Black English has its own phonological and grammatical rules, making children who speak it, in effect, bilingual. When schools teach non-English-speaking children standard English it is important not to demean them or their primary language.

12. The relation between language and thought is one of the great issues of the ages. Piaget believed that in infancy thought certainly precedes language. Later, however, children's conversations with their peers are a way of advancing their thinking. Benjamin Whorf believed that language determines our perceptions and thoughts about the world. Lev Vygotsky held that thought and speech have separate roots, but that at 2 years of age, children discover the symbolic function of language. Thereafter, their words help them to think.

KEY TERMS

Language
  acquisition
  device (LAD)
Surface structure
Deep structure
Nontransformational
  grammar
Linguistics
Psycholinguistics
Sociolinguistics
Phonology
Phoneme

Stop consonant
Fricative
Voiced consonant
Unvoiced consonant
Morphology
Morpheme
Syntax
Semantics
Pragmatics
Holophrase
Overextension
Underextension

Contrast
Conventionality
Telegraphic speech
Prosodic
Pivot class
Open class
Case grammar
Inflection
Overregularize
Relative clause
Embedding
Coordinate sentence

Minimum distance
  principle (MDP)
Inferencing
Collective monologue
Motherese hypothesis
Expansions
Proform
Black English
Linguistic determinism
Linguistic relativity
Elaborated code
Restricted code
Inner speech
Social speech

SUGGESTED READINGS

Clark, Herbert, and Clark, Eve. *Psychology and Language: an Introduction to Psycholinguistics.* New York: Harcourt Brace Jovanovich, 1977. A comprehensive, yet readable, review of the general field of psycholinguistics that covers findings on both adults and children.

de Villiers, Peter A., and de Villiers, Jill G. *Early Language.* Cambridge: Harvard University Press, 1979. A concise guide to the major advances as children learn language between birth and 6 years of age. Includes recent findings in developmental psycholinguistics and engaging examples from the speech of children.

Greenfield, Patricia M., and Smith, James A. *The Structure of Communication in Early Language Development.* New York: Academic Press, 1976. A review that includes material from the authors' longitudinal diary study of the language acquired by two children between 1 and 2 years of age.

Nelson, Keith E. (Ed.). *Children's Language* (2 vols.). New York: Halsted Press, 1978. A good collection of articles treating a number of topics in developmental psycholinguistics, including bilingualism, the language of apes, and the relation of language and thought.

Slobin, Dan I. *Psycholinguistics* (2nd ed.) Glenview, Ill.: Scott, Foresman, 1979. A critical review of the research studies on children's language and the theories on which they are based.

Wanner, Eric and Gleitman, Lila. *Language Acquisition: the State of the Art.* Cambridge: Cambridge University Press, 1982. A collection of chapters by outstanding researchers in the area of language development—including Lila Gleitman, Dan Slobin, Elissa Newport, and Eve Clark—that presents a sophisticated and up-to-date overview of the field.

Weir, Ruth H. *Language in the Crib.* The Hague: Mouton, 1970. An in-depth analysis of a child's very early speech.

PART V

RELATIONSHIPS

CHAPTER 12

Family

The social bonds that begin to form in the first weeks and months of life are no less important to an infant's physical and psychological health than food and shelter. From the infant's earliest gazes, smiles, and cries, its caregivers take cues about how to meet the infant's needs for physical contact, for play, for emotional warmth and closeness, and for consistent, responsive care. The social bonds that an infant forms to parents and siblings provide a foundation for later social relationships, and the quality of the infant's attachment to its mother colors how the infant approaches the wider world. The coordinated "dance" of mother and child is repeated in the child's interactions with others. It is within the family, no matter what shape that family happens to take, that children first learn about social relationships.

ATTACHMENT TO MOTHER IN INFANCY

In the first year of life, infants become increasingly skilled at communicating, and they use this skill in forming a deep, enduring tie with the person they interact with most frequently and fondly, most often the mother. It is the infant's first love affair—with all the joys of togetherness and pains of separation

During their first year of life, infants form abiding attachments to their mothers. This bond is an infant's first love.

or rejection that love affairs bring at any age. The term applied to this first love relation is **attachment.** John Bowlby (1969) has described this attachment as an affectional tie the infant forms to another specific person that binds the two together in space and endures over time. It develops in phases (Ainsworth, 1973):

1. *The initial preattachment phase: undiscriminating social responsiveness.* At first the newborn infant looks at anyone, all faces seeming beautiful, and can be comforted by anyone, all arms being welcome. This phase lasts only a few weeks or months and comes to an end when the infant is capable of discriminating among people and picking out his or her mother from the crowd. Because infants discriminate with some of their senses earlier than with others—olfactory, then tactile, then auditory—it is difficult to say when the first phase ends. It is usually considered to last until the infant fairly consistently discriminates visually, at 2 to 3 months of age.

2. *The attachment-in-the-making phase: discriminating social responsiveness.* In the second phase of social responsiveness, infants discriminate between familiar people, usually family members, and unfamiliar ones, and they respond differently to them. At first, they smile and vocalize more with these familiar people. Then, they greet familiar people and cry when these people leave the room. Certain familiar people may now be better able to stop the infant's crying. This phase ends at about 6 or 7 months, when the infant actively seeks proximity with one particular familiar person.

3. *The clear-cut attachment phase: proximity seeking.* Only in the third phase can infants be said to possess a true attachment to a specific person. After the bond is formed, infants will actively seek physical contact with this person by crawling after her or him, calling, embracing, or clambering up on her or his lap. When that person leaves their sight, infants will very likely follow or protest, immediately or after a short time. Although for *most* American infants, the first "object of their affection" is Mom—who began her own attachment to the infant some months earlier—sometimes the first object of attachment is Daddy, a grandparent, an older sibling, even a frequently visited neighbor. Infants can become attached to more than one person by the end of their first year, but not to many persons. This phase continues through the second and third years.

THEORIES OF ATTACHMENT

Both psychoanalysts and learning theorists have appreciated and extolled the significance of the infant's primary attachment to its mother. Sigmund Freud identified the infant's relation with its mother as "unique, without parallel, established unalterably for a whole lifetime as the first and strongest love-object" and as "the prototype of all later love relations" (1938, p. 85). He, however, did not attempt a complete account of its development. Later, his followers, notably Anna Freud, Margaret Mahler, and René Spitz, fleshed out the notion of this primary "object" relation with mother. They tended to emphasize the pleasure of feeding as the basis for its development. Social-learning theorists, such as Robert Sears, also emphasized feeding. They claimed that the infant's desire for physical contact with its mother was simply a secondary drive stemming from the association of mother with satisfaction of a primary drive, hunger. Operant learning theorists, such as Jacob Gewirtz, on the other hand, viewed attachment as nothing special, merely one more example of behavior maintained by mutual reinforcements between mother and infant.

Drawing first on ethology and also on psychoanalysis, control-systems theory (cybernetics), and Jean Piaget's theory of cognitive development, Bowlby (1969) provided a more complete and, to many, a convincing account of the course and nature of attachment. According to Bowlby's comprehensive theory, attachment originates in inherited species-characteristic behavior. By sucking and clinging, crying and smiling, vocalizing and following, the infant brings or keeps the caregiver close. Throughout past eons of evolution, proximity was necessary for sheer physical survival. The baby is born with behavior that will ensure proximity of a caregiver.

All infants are genetically predisposed to seek proximity, but the amount and kind they need depend on their experience and on the situations in which they find themselves. The degree of proximity required by a particular child is his or her **set goal**, which operates much like a thermostat.

When heat falls below the temperature at which the thermostat is set, the furnace turns on. Infants have different set goals, depending on the experience each has had with his or her particular caregiver. An infant whose mother has been absent, aloof, or unresponsive is likely to need more proximity than one whose mother has been accessible and responsive. Infants who are ill or tired may also require more proximity. Some infants will seek to be near their mother primarily when she gets up and moves away. The baby may then crawl after her or call to her. For other babies, just the threat of their mother's departure or distance may activate the baby's nearness-seeking behavior. If the infant's efforts to gain proximity are not successful, or if the threat of departure has already caused too much anxiety, the baby may cry—another means of ensuring or sustaining proximity (Table 12.1).

Since Bowlby first articulated his theory, it has been supplemented by Mary Ainsworth and Alan Sroufe in particular. Ainsworth (1973) emphasizes a second set goal, which must be balanced with proximity seeking—the urge of infants to explore their surroundings. Sroufe (e.g., Sroufe and Waters, 1977) has added an affective or emotional dimension to the theory, suggesting that the appropriate set goal is not just physical proximity, but also a feeling of security.

TABLE 12.1
SOCIAL MILESTONES

Birth to 3 months: *the dance begins* . . .

- visually fixes on mother's eyes and holds gaze
- smiles at nodding head, high voice
- first social smile—smiles at mother's face
- cries when mother does not interact normally
- discriminates between sight of mother and others

3 to 6 months: *emotions appear* . . .

- gives first laugh
- expresses wariness when confronted by stranger
- responds differentially to mother

6 to 12 months: *focused relationships develop* . . .

- babbles vowels and consonants
- laughs at incongruity
- expresses fear at stranger in threatening context
- becomes real partner in social interaction
- deliberately seeks and maintains proximity to mother or father

DIFFICULTIES IN ASSESSING ATTACHMENT

The attachment bond, once formed, is always there. But, however fundamental, attachment is an internal feeling and must be inferred, by psychological researchers, from observable behavior. This necessity has made the assessment of attachment challenging.

One way to infer attachment is to determine the infant's response to separation from his or her mother. This cannot be the sole criterion, however, for children who protest their mother's departure in one situation may not mind it in another. Distress at separation, in fact, can reflect both strong attachment and ambivalent attachment (Ainsworth, Blehar, Waters, and Wall, 1978). Mere physical proximity itself does not convey the subtle emotion that is an important part of attachment. Common acts, such as smiling or crawling after mother, cannot be counted up; the meaning depends on their context. A little girl may turn her face away when her mother picks her up, which is quite different from turning it away when her nose is being wiped. One study (Tracy, Lamb, and Ainsworth, 1976) demonstrated the importance of context: although infants approached both mother and an unfamiliar visitor equally often when they wanted to play, they went only to mother when they wanted to be picked up.

Given the difficulty of assessing attachment, what solutions have been offered? A major study of attachment by Ainsworth (Ainsworth and Wittig, 1969; Ainsworth et al., 1978) offered a research method that has become standard for assessing attachment of 12- to 18-month-olds, the so-called **strange situation**. An infant is brought to a laboratory playroom and observed from behind one-way windows. The infant, accompanied by the mother, is introduced to the unfamiliar but otherwise unalarming playroom, which is equipped with an assortment of attractive toys. Mother puts baby on the floor at some distance from the toys and sits down in her assigned chair. Mother has earlier been instructed about roles in this drama; the observer taps on the glass when it is time to go to the next step. A stranger enters and sits in her assigned chair. She is first silent, then talks to the mother, then tries to play with the baby. Next, the mother leaves the baby alone with this stranger for 3 minutes.

Mother returns to the room and is reunited with the infant. Then both she and the stranger go out—leaving the baby alone. The stranger returns before the mother and tries again to play with, or soothe, the baby. Finally, the mother returns, talks to, and picks up her baby.

How do children react to separation and reunion with their mother in this "strange situation"? In Ainsworth's study, most accepted being put down by their mother in the unfamiliar room; 78 percent approached the toys within 1 minute. Only a few found this situation mildly distressing; most started exploring right away. They kept visual tabs on their mother—smiling and vocalizing to her from across the room—but they paid more attention to the toys than to their mothers. When their mothers left the room for the first time, however, one-fifth of the children immediately burst into tears, and half cried during her 3-minute absence. Some children searched for their mothers by going to the door, looking at the door, or going to her chair. At the end of this episode, when the mothers returned, 78 percent greeted her by approaching, reaching, smiling, touching, or speaking to her; one-third cried.

When the mothers left the room the second time, the infants were even more likely to become distressed: 78 percent cried, and the mothers of half the children had to come back before the 3 minutes were up. Hardly any children played with the toys. The stranger, who returned before the mother, had little success in reassuring the children who were already crying; 71 percent continued to weep. Then, the mother returned, and in this second reunion, more children than before indicated their attachment. Their most common response was to continue crying (50 percent) and to cling tightly to mother or climb into her arms (78 percent vs. 33 percent in the first reunion).

This situation reveals the enormous difference in the way 1-year-olds react to their mother and to a stranger. Children gave the stranger visual attention and wary smiles, but they spoke to and touched and stayed close to mother (Figure 12.1). Even the children who did approach the stranger—only 9 percent of the group—were also likely to retreat from her and move closer to mother. Although they appeared somewhat wary, the children did not avoid the stranger after their mothers had left the room the first time. When their mothers left the

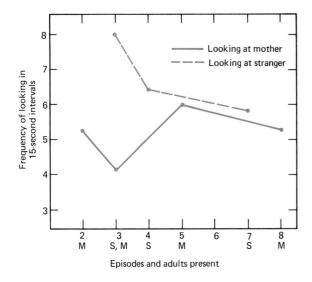

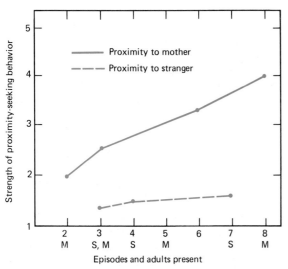

FIGURE 12.1

Children in the strange situation show more interest in the stranger (S) but stay closer to mother (M) during all episodes (Ainsworth, Blehar, Waters, and Wall, 1978).

second time, accompanied by the stranger, the children were more distressed by her absence. When the stranger returned, the majority refused her offer of a toy or sympathy. While mother was gone the first time, half had accepted a toy from the stranger.

PATTERNS OF ATTACHMENT

From these infants' reactions to being reunited with their mother after separation in the strange situa-

tion, Ainsworth discovered that most children exhibit one of three qualitatively different patterns of attachment. Avoidant children, 22 percent of the sample, either ignored the returning mother outright or diluted their welcome by turning or looking away from her. They did *not* seek proximity or contact, treating their mother much as they had the stranger. They rarely cried when their mother left the room, and if they did not like being all alone, the stranger's return alleviated their loneliness.

Securely attached children, the normal and largest group, 66 percent, actively sought and maintained contact with their mothers. They may or may not have been distressed by being separated from their mother, but they were clearly more interested in her than in the stranger. Before the separations, her presence in the room gave the infants a secure base from which they could venture forth to explore the toys and surroundings. But after the separations, they greeted their mother enthusiastically on her return, and they stayed close to her while they played.

The third and smallest group, the ambivalent children, 12 percent, became extremely upset as their mother was leaving the room. They might go to her when she returned, but when lifted up, they took no comfort from her and squirmed angrily to get down.

ATTACHMENT BEHAVIOR AT HOME

The strange situation is, admittedly, an artificial one, valuable for its experimental control rather than its natural validity. Ainsworth had the opportunity to compare her 1-year-old subjects' behavior in the strange situation with what she had observed in their homes during the previous year. One behavior at home that related to behavior in the laboratory was the infant's attitude toward physical contact. The avoidant children who did not like being picked up in the laboratory did not like it at home either. But children who responded positively to physical contact in the laboratory, the securely attached children, had at home often raised their arms to be picked up. They were happy to be in their mother's arms and when put down were content, shifting to their own independent activities. Crying when left alone at home, however, was not related to crying when left alone in the laboratory.

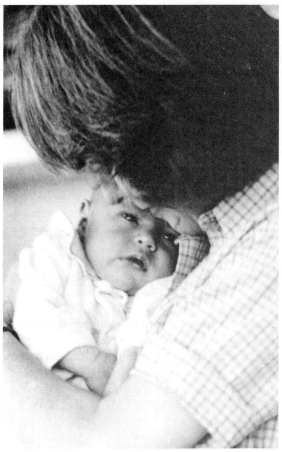

A loving relationship with mother, or another caregiver, is essential for the baby's social and emotional development.

FORMING A SECURE ATTACHMENT

Most children form a close relationship with their mother and a secure attachment to her. What qualities of a mother are most likely to foster a secure attachment? From studies of children in institutions, psychologists know that no close relationship forms with a caregiver if a baby in its first year does not interact with one adult regularly (DuPan and Roth, 1955; Provence and Lipton, 1962; Tizard and Tizard, 1970; Wolins, 1969). For a close relationship to form, some amount of contact and interaction is necessary. What kind of contact, and how much interaction are necessary? According to Bowlby (1951), the following are necessary for the development of attachment: a loving relationship with one person in the infant's family, usually the

mother, from the beginning and continuing unbroken beyond infancy and through childhood. Some of these suggestions have received empirical support.

A Loving Relationship. Adequate physical care, a good feeding schedule, appropriate discipline, and the physical presence of a mother do not in and of themselves ensure a secure attachment. A loving relationship is a necessary ingredient. Although some interaction is necessary to the formation of any attachment, the quality or intensity of that interaction is more important than its mere quantity (Figure 12.2). An infant comes to love as it feels warmth and affection, frequent and sustained cuddling, other tender physical contact, smiling and laughing in play, and the sense of enjoyment parents convey as they feed, talk about, and do things for their infant (Ainsworth, 1973; Rutter, 1974). Compared to mothers of insecurely attached children, mothers of securely attached children have been observed to be more supportive and helpful to their children and to issue commands more affectionately (Arend, Grove, and Sroufe, 1979; Pastor, 1981).

As Rudolph Schaffer (e.g., Schaffer and Crook, 1978) points out, love is the heightening of *all*

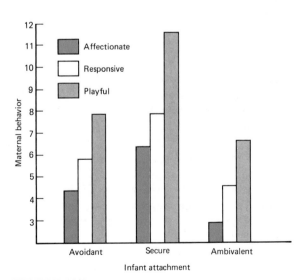

FIGURE 12.2

Mothers whose year-old infants are securely attached to them are very affectionate, responsive, and playful. Those of avoidant children are less so, and mothers of ambivalent children are least likely to show these qualities (Clarke-Stewart, 1973).

emotions, positive *and* negative. The most affectionate mother is capable of intense anger. Barbara and Jack Tizard (1974), comparing mothers and nurses in a residential institution, found that mothers not only provided more affection but were more frequently cross and upset. Nurses were not emotionally involved. The proportion of warmth to coolness and affection to anger affects the infant's social development. The attachment of children to mothers who are often critical, rejecting, and interfering is of poor quality. They are likely to become avoidant infants (Ainsworth, 1973; Beckwith, 1972). Children's attachments to mothers who are abusive, unresponsive, and neglectful are also insecure and anxious. Byron Egeland and Alan Sroufe (1981) studied attachment and quality of mothering in two groups of mothers and their children. One group consisted of 33 mothers who gave excellent care to their children: in feeding, health care, protecting their children from danger at home, providing competent baby-sitters, and generally encouraging their children's growth and development. Another group of 31 mothers neglected or seriously abused their children: they were unresponsive or violent, offered poor physical care, exposed their children to danger, and often left their children without adequate supervision. The investigators tested the quality of attachment of the children in the two groups at 12 and 18 months. There were significant differences between the two groups: 75 percent of the children whose mothers gave them excellent care were securely attached, compared to only 38 percent in the inadequate-care group. The earlier an infant's maltreatment had begun, the more likely the infant was to form an insecure attachment to the mother.

As investigations of unresponsive mothers suggest, a particularly important part of the loving relationship is **empathy**. Love brings with it sensitivity to the needs of the other, and this is particularly true of maternal love. The loving caregiver sees things from the baby's point of view, is vigilant and on the alert to the baby's signals, interprets them correctly, and responds promptly and appropriately. Empathy suffuses every aspect of mother-infant interaction. Mothers who are sensitive are more likely to have securely attached, happy, and sociable children (Ainsworth, 1973; Clarke-Stewart, 1973; Schaffer and Emerson, 1964).

Another important part of the loving relationship is physical contact. We cannot manipulate the rearing of human infants just to satisfy our curiosity about how varying the environment affects social development. But within reasonable limits, we can ethically manipulate the rearing of animals. Animal studies have yielded important information about human social development. One of the outstanding investigations has been the work done at the Wisconsin Primate Laboratory by Harry Harlow and his associates. Beginning in the 1950s, Harlow's group separated rhesus monkeys from their mothers 6 to 12 hours after birth and raised them in social isolation. Some of these monkeys died, and the others were extremely tense and withdrawn. Harlow then provided monkeys with **surrogate mothers**; later, he experimented with giving monkeys isolated from their mothers play periods with their peers. Other monkeys were raised with their own mothers but deprived of contact with peers.

Perhaps the most famous of the now classic studies compared the infant monkeys' reactions to two surrogate mothers: one made of wire mesh, the other of the same wire mesh wrapped in terry cloth (Harlow and Zimmerman, 1959). Each infant was raised individually in a cage with both of these artificial mothers. In half the cages, the nursing bottle was attached to the bare-wire form, in the other half to the terry mother. Results were dramatic (Figure 12.3): regardless of which surrogate mother provided food, the baby monkey spent most of the day cleaving and chattering to the soft terry cloth mother. Contact comfort, not lactation, was essential for learning to love. When a large wooden spider was placed in the cage, only the cloth mother offered a haven of safety. The attachment to the cloth mother persisted as long as the infants were kept with her. They even ran to embrace her after being separated from her for a year. In later experiments, the temperatures, texture, and movements of the surrogate mothers were varied. Infants clearly preferred surrogates who were the most like real mothers—warm, soft, smooth, and rocking (Harlow and Mears, 1979).

Although the infants were attached to the terry surrogate mother, she still was not as good as a real live mother. Infants exposed only to the stolid passivity of wire and cloth did not learn communication, trust, or how to deal with fear. They did not learn how to mate or nurture. Monkeys who were raised with agemates and no mother, real or sur-

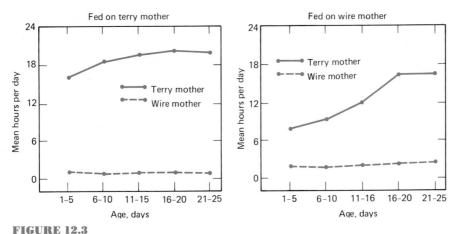

FIGURE 12.3
Whether young monkeys are fed by a terry surrogate mother or one made of wire mesh, they spend much more time on the comfortable terry mother (Harlow and Mears, 1979).

rogate, did not learn to play or explore or feel secure. They spent their time clinging to one another. Monkeys who were raised by their mothers but kept away from peers did poorly in social and sexual relations (Harlow and Mears, 1979).

A Relationship with One Person. When infants are raised in institutions, they are likely to have many caretakers, but these people may be less affectionate, cuddle for shorter periods, and play less stimulating games with their charges. When there are few caretakers, the baby's attachment to any one of them is stronger, and early exchanges are smoother (Caldwell et al., 1963; Miller, 1969; Schaffer and Emerson, 1964).

A Relationship in the Infant's Own Family. The loving relationship necessary for optimal attachment is easier to provide in a family than in an institution or even in a communal arrangement such as a kibbutz (Gerwirtz, 1965). But it is important that the home provide adequate loving care, not that it be given necessarily by the child's *biological* parents (Tizard and Rees, 1974).

A Continuing Unbroken Relationship Beyond Infancy and Throughout Childhood. Infants are distressed by separation from their mothers and families. When infants or their mothers must undergo the unavoidable separation of a hospital stay, they go through certain stages similar to those in the loss of a loved one. Infants who are over 6 months of age and

have formed an attachment to their mother at first scream and cry and reject all efforts to comfort them. If their mother reappears, they are ambivalent to her. This active protest of the separation lasts only a few days for most children. Then, they become increasingly miserable, apathetic, and hopeless. This is a period of mourning or despair. Finally, the child becomes contented and seems to lose interest in the missing parent. If the mother visits, the child may ignore her, avoid her, or cry (Robertson and Robertson, 1971).

Certain steps will reduce pain of separation and alleviate its effects (Robertson and Robertson, 1971). The mother can arrange to visit the child frequently, or the child can be prepared ahead of time for the separation. Another familiar person, loving and responsive to the child, can be with him or her during the separation and be ready to deal with the change in mood that the separation may cause. Finally, the mother, when she returns, can try to be especially sensitive and accepting of the child's behavior.

Day care for infants tends to challenge some of the assumptions about the conditions necessary for optimal social development. Most of the studies of infant day care find that it has no apparent negative effects on the child's attachment (Brookhart and Hock, 1976; Caldwell, Wright, Honig, and Tannenbaum, 1970; Doyle, 1975; Hock, 1976; Kagan, Kearsley, and Zelazo, 1978; Ricciuti, 1974). These studies tend to focus on exceptionally good day-care arrangements, however, and the measures they have employed are not necessarily the most probing. Moreover, in most cases the infants observed did have the benefit of a continuous loving relationship in their own home and family in addition to day care. In two studies (Schwartz, 1979; Vaughn, Joffe, Egeland, Dienard, and Waters, 1979) of less than optimal day care, a greater number of infants attending in the first year of life were observed in the strange situation to be avoidant. Because there were some confounding factors in these two studies, we cannot accept their findings as definitive evidence either. As more and more working mothers rely on day care for their infants, effects on attachment should be monitored closely.

SIGNIFICANCE OF A SECURE ATTACHMENT

The quality of children's attachment to their mothers depends in part on the temperamental style of the children—difficult and unresponsive versus easy and outgoing, for example—and in part on the quality of mothering they receive. In general, infants who are securely attached to their mothers seem more socially and emotionally competent than infants who are insecurely attached, and these advantages seem to persist well into childhood (Arend et al., 1979; Londerville and Main, 1981; Main, 1977; Pastor, 1981; Waters, Wippman, and Sroufe, 1979). In one study, securely attached 23-month-olds were more sociable than insecurely attached children when playing with children their own age (Pastor, 1981). In other studies, 2-year-olds who were insecurely attached to their mothers were less cooperative, enthusiastic, persistent, and less competent at problem solving than securely attached children. Securely attached children also were more compliant and likelier to have internalized controls (Londerville and Main, 1981; Matas, Arend, and Sroufe, 1978). When the children in the Matas et al. (1978) study were reassessed at the age of 4½, those earlier classified as securely attached were more flexible, persistent, resourceful, and curious. On measures of ego resiliency, those classified as anxious and ambivalent were impulsive; those classified as avoidant were restrained; and those classified as securely attached were in between, or moderate in ego control (Arend et al., 1979). Securely attached children scored signifi-

cantly higher on measures of initiative and skill in interactions with peers than did children who were insecurely attached at this age (Waters et al., 1979). In that the mothers were absent from this measurement, the results suggest that continuities in children's behavior exist independently of the mothers' presence.

Michael Lewis, Candice Feiring, Carolyn McGuffog, and John Jaskir (1984) evaluated a group of over 100 children when they were 1 and 6 years old, to examine the relation between early attachment and later psychopathology. They found that for boys, insecure attachment at 1 year of age related significantly to psychopathology at 6 years of age. No such relationship was found for girls, however. Boys who had had an avoidant attachment later showed more schizoid tendencies; boys who had had an ambivalent attachment later showed more depressive and withdrawn tendencies. But even among the boys, attachment was only one factor—stressful life events and changes in family life being others—that affected the development of psychopathology. The investigators concluded that although attachment is important in a child's psychological development, secure attachment does not prevent the later development of pathology and insecure attachment does not ensure it.

DEVELOPING AUTONOMY

At 1 year old, the child is on the brink of a great adventure, one that will change the infant who clings tightly to Mama's skirts to an autonomous child, ready to leave hearth and home for an independent life at school. During a four-year period, children "hatch" from their dependent relation with their mother (Mahler, Pine, and Bergman, 1975) and become self-reliant individuals.

The distress of children at being separated from their mother declines in intensity, and they are able to tolerate being a greater distance from her. As we have just seen, in a number of studies, a mother is asked to leave the child alone or with a stranger for a few minutes (Feldman and Ingham, 1975; Maccoby and Feldman, 1972); in others, naturally occurring separations have been observed (Clarke-Stewart, 1973; Clarke-Stewart and Hevey, 1981). During the period from 1 to 4 years of age, children show less and less distress at brief separations from their mother; from 2 to 4 years, they also seek less and less proximity and physical contact with her. Harriet Rheingold and Carol Eckerman (1971) found an impressive mathematical regularity in the distance children would venture from their mother: for each additional month of age, children went about a foot farther during 15 minutes of free play outdoors (Figure 12.4). When playing outdoors, such as in a park, children seem to establish their own physical boundaries and keep within them without being retrieved. They move in brief bouts, move and stop and look and return, as long as mother is within view and facing them. Children in other cultures (Barry and Paxson, 1971) and young monkeys (Suomi, 1974) have also been observed to seek less physical contact with their mother and to move farther away from her as they grow older.

If a stranger is present or the situation is otherwise stressful, children 3 years of age may still be upset at separation from their mother. Lois Murphy (1962) found that one-third of the 3-year-olds she studied still had trouble separating from their moth-

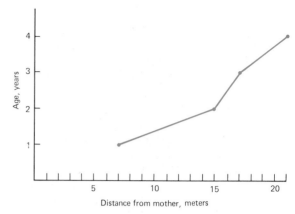

FIGURE 12.4

The distance a child is willing to venture from mother's side increases systematically with age (Rheingold and Eckerman, 1971).

ers to leave home or to go upstairs with an examiner. Even at this age, it seems, children want physical comfort and reassurance from mother in times of mild stress. Not until the child is 4 years old is distress at a brief separation really rare (Marvin, 1977).

The fact that older children need not be as near their mother does not mean that they care less for her than at the "peak" of manifesting attachment to her. Although *physical* contact diminishes, the *relationship* remains strong and is evident in other patterns of behavior. Children more frequently smile, talk, and show their mother an object from a distance (Clarke-Stewart and Hevey, 1981; Maccoby and Feldman, 1972). Children can and do leave their mother's side, but they continue to check back and are not disturbed as long as they can see or hear her (Carr, Dabbs, and Carr, 1975; Mahler et al., 1975; Rheingold, 1973). Roderick Adams and Richard Passman (1979) found that 3-year-olds, accompanied into an unfamiliar playroom by their mother's voice or her televised image, played and explored more and were more comfortable than when they were alone or with a stranger.

At the same time that the child is seeking independence and autonomy from mother, she is actively encouraging the child's independence. She does this by first being less physically close to her child, then by relaxing her constant attention and surveillance, and finally by starting fewer interactions. When the child is 3, mother and child are

Between the ages of 2 and 4, children comfortably play and explore farther and farther away from their mothers and need less physical contact than they do in their earliest years.

approximately equal partners in the initiation of social exchanges (Clarke-Stewart and Hevey, 1981).

After mother and child are able to communicate verbally rather than just physically, the mother begins to try to mesh her plans with those of the child. The child-master–mother-slave pattern of infancy no longer prevails. The child is now able to wait until mother finishes what she is doing before having his or her demands satisfied. If mother says she has to leave the child alone so that she can go make a phone call—and the child agrees—he or she is not disturbed by a brief separation (Marvin, 1977).

This developing partnership has its rocky moments. Toddlers assert their independence, lessening their physical dependence on their mother and striking out farther and longer on their own. At the first stirrings of independence, children turn their back on mother, both literally and figuratively. They want to use their developing muscles to do everything themselves; they want to see everything for themselves as well, a wish that often gets them into trouble. When thwarted, they give explicit demonstrations of their anger, throwing food on the floor, refusing to budge, and holding their breath. Over and over, they say "no!" to their mother's requests. The negativism of the **terrible twos**, well known to parents and friends, is the child's bid for autonomy raised to an exaggerated degree. In secure mother-child relationships, this period is relatively short-lived. After a year or so, most children progress to a balance between the satisfaction of their wishes and those of their mothers.

THE FATHER'S SPECIAL ROLE

Until recently, the father's relationship with his infant was almost totally ignored by child development researchers. As Margaret Mead is reputed to have said, "Fathers are a biological necessity but a social accident." There were many reasons for this exclusion. Researchers had studied breast feeding and the importance of hormones in making mothers nurturant. Moreover, the major psychological theories had concentrated on the mother's role during infancy and paid no attention to the father's. Indeed, in the period when these theories were formulated, fathers in our society were spending little time with their infants. At least partly because of the women's movement, psychological theory now emphasizes the child's entire social network (Weinraub, Brooks, and Lewis, 1977). Researchers are taking a new look at adult-infant interaction. Now we have some, though still not much, information about how fathers care for, play with, and think about their infants.

Despite the expressed interest of fathers in sharing child care, the actual amount of father-infant interaction in most American families is still surprisingly limited. In most homes today, the mother is still more available to her infant and naturally spends more time with the infant. The nature of her contact is also different; she expends more effort in physical care, in feeding, bathing, and dressing her infant. In one sample of middle-class families in Boston, Milton Kotelchuck (1976) found that mothers spent 9 hours a day with the child, fathers 3 hours. Most of the fathers (75 percent) took no routine responsibility for physical care; in fact, 43 percent of them had never changed a diaper. When fathers picked up their babies, they spent more time playing with them—38 percent of the time they were with the baby versus 26 percent of the time for mothers. This finding has been confirmed in other studies of middle-class New England families in which fathers worked and mothers stayed home (Clarke-Stewart, 1978a, 1980; Lamb, 1977).

These studies of fathers had their limitations: parental reports may be inflated, or an interaction may be exaggerated when an observer is present. Yet another study tried to find out what happened throughout the day, how much the father actually interacted with his infant in the privacy of his own home (Rebelsky and Hanks, 1971). Microphones were attached to the infant, and all verbalizations directed toward the child were recorded. Fathers in this small sample interacted with their infants an average of only 37 seconds a day!

New fathers do report that they are absorbed, preoccupied, and engrossed with their newborn infants (Greenberg and Morris, 1974). They are elated and proud after the delivery. They think that their infant is beautiful and unique and want to hold and touch their baby, and they do just that. In observations made while mother and baby were still in the hospital (Parke and O'Leary, 1976), new fathers looked and smiled at their baby, talked to it, and felt and touched it just as much as mothers did. They actually held and rocked the baby more. Mothers did more feeding of the infants, more wiping, and more caretaking. But this did not mean that fathers were less competent or less willing to care for their babies. Ross Parke and Douglas Sawin (1975) found that the father's sensitivity to his baby's cries, coughs, and sneezes during feeding was equal to that of the mother. Like the mother, the father stopped feeding the infant and looked more closely at it, then made soothing sounds. Infants consumed as much milk when their fathers fed them as when their mothers did. Fathers were also responsive to the infant's babblings and mouth movements (Parke and Sawin, 1975) and to their infant's smiles and cries (Frodi, Lamb, Leavitt, and Donovan, 1978).

Parke and Sawin (1975) also studied how mothers and fathers played with their infants in the first 3 months. Fathers were rougher and more physical than mothers. In a detailed examination of video-taped face-to-face play, Michael Yogman (1977) found that fathers tap their infants rhythmically and play poking games 44 percent of the time, mothers only 28 percent of the time. Mothers, on the other hand, use the soft, repetitive, imitative burst-pause talking style (described earlier) for 47 percent of their playtime with baby, fathers for 20 percent of their playtime. Mother chimes and rhymes; father tosses the infant into the air or plays "horsey." Father's play at home with older infants is also rough-and-tumble and stimulating, especially his play with sons (Clarke-Stewart, 1978a, 1980; Kotelchuck, 1976; Lamb, 1977). With 8-month-old babies, Thomas Power and Ross Parke (1983) found no differences in the length of time mothers and fathers played. So long as the infants played contentedly with their toys, few differences were observed between mothers' and fathers' behavior. But mothers and fathers played differently when their babies' attention and interest were waning.

RESEARCH FOCUS

CHILDCARE IN NONTRADITIONAL FAMILIES

Michael Lamb and his associates (Lamb et al., 1982) wondered whether mothers and fathers who assumed nontraditional gender roles act differently with their infants from those who assume traditional gender roles. To find out, they first located Swedish families in which the fathers had been serving as primary caretakers of their firstborn 8-month-old infants while the mothers went out to work. Swedish national policy allows every parent 9 months paid leave following the birth of a child. Couples are free to divide the 9 months between them, and about 10 percent of Swedish fathers take some paid leave. The researchers' major question was whether these caretaking fathers would act more like traditional fathers (same sex, different gender role) or traditional mothers (different sex, same gender role). In observations lasting over an hour, of parents acting "as naturally as possible" at home with their infants, the research team noted when either parent picked up or held the infant in the course of disciplining, playing, kissing, soothing, or responding to the infant's request to be picked up. They also noted when the parents acted affectionately, smiled, vocalized, or actively tended to the infant's needs. Different styles of play—reciprocal, parallel, gently stimulating, vigorously physical, conventional, or idiosyncratic—were recorded as well.

The researchers admitted to being surprised by their results. In every case, mothers did more disciplining, kissing, soothing, vocalizing, holding, and tending to the infant's needs than fathers did, regardless of their gender role. There was no difference in the parents' styles of play with the infants. Thus, contrary to their expectations, the researchers found that sex had a stronger effect on parents' behavior than gender role. The nontraditional Swedish parents acted much like their traditional American counterparts. Mothers and fathers acted differently, regardless of their roles in caretaking, a finding that suggests that differences in parents' behavior are not simply artifacts of their current gender roles. Such differences may be deeply rooted in individuals' childhood socialization, or they may have biological roots. Only further research on these questions will tell.

Mothers tended to take cues from their baby, following the baby's gaze toward a particular toy and then playing with that toy. They spent more time watching or holding toys when the baby's interest flagged. Fathers, however, did not follow the baby's gaze and often tried unsuccessfully to get the baby to play with a toy in which he or she was not interested. Fathers also spent more time playing physically with the baby when the baby's interest flagged.

How do babies respond to such differences between their parents? Yogman (1977) finds that by 2 months their infants frown more often at father, 7.7 percent of the time, versus 2.2 percent of the time at their mother. Kotelchuck (1976) finds that by 12 months, 55 percent of the infants are more attached to mother than to father. Michael Lamb (1976a, 1976b) also found more attachment to mother in the strange situation; so did Leslie Cohen and Joseph Campos (1974). Still, either parent is vastly preferred to a stranger; 30 percent of the infants frowned at a stranger. Infants protest the departure of either parent, cling to either after reunion. They spend more time close to their mothers; but they laugh, smile, and look, clearly enjoying themselves, during physically stimulating play with father (Clarke-Stewart, 1978a; Lamb, 1977).

Tiffany Field (1978) compared the behavior of fathers who were primary caregivers with that of fathers who were the traditional secondary caregivers. Primary caregivers, whether fathers or mothers, did less smiling, laughing, imitating, and baby talking. But fathers, regardless of their caregiving role, still engaged in more physical playing and poking. So fathers play rambunctiously with infants not simply because they have had less experience with them. They are probably both physiologically and culturally predisposed to engage in physical play. Male monkeys, too, tend to play with offspring rather than holding and protecting them (Suomi, 1977). In Sweden, where more fathers are primary caretakers for their infants, Michael Lamb, Ann Frodi, Carl-Philip Hwang, Majt Frodi, and Jamie Steinberg (1982) investigated the differences in parents' behavior between such nontraditional families and those in which the mother was primary caretaker. Several hours of observation of each family at home showed that parents played similarly with their infants. But all of the mothers held, picked up, and tended to their infant's needs more

than the fathers did, no matter whether the parents' gender roles were traditional or not. Nontraditional fathers showed more affection to their infants than traditional fathers did, the reverse of the pattern found among mothers. To their surprise, the researchers found that the parents' sex had more bearing on behavior than did traditional or nontraditional gender role.

In studies of traditional families in the United States, it has been observed that by the end of the first year children are as attached to their father as to their mother. But after infancy, as the mother's caretaking role declines, the father's role becomes more prominent. He is preferred playmate and taskmaster, especially with his sons (Clarke-Stewart, 1980; Lamb, 1977; Lynn and Cross, 1974). Fathers in other cultures, too, become increasingly involved with their children in the postinfancy period (Barry and Paxson, 1971); so do fathers in lower species such as monkeys (Suomi, 1979). The more the father assumes the role of playmate and plays with his child, the more likely the father-child relationship is to be joyful and the more likely the mother is to talk and play with the child (Clarke-Stewart, 1980).

According to the sociologist Talcott Parsons (e.g., Parsons and Bales, 1955), writing three decades ago, the particular function of fathers is to bring society's norms into the family and through discipline, demands, and love pry their children loose from dependency on their mothers. Mothers,

Fathers may involve themselves in children's hobbies, their quiet play, their routine care, and perhaps most typically rough-and-tumble play.

on the other hand, are supposed to keep the family functioning smoothly by being emotionally expressive and supportive and by giving children and husband unconditional love. Theirs is the **expressive role**, whereas fathers' is the **instrumental role**. Even today, with so many mothers working, some of these divisions in the roles of mothers and fathers endure, at least in the minds of parents and children.

Fathers perceive themselves as disciplinarians and teachers. They are concerned about their children's education and safety, and they regard socialization that takes place outside the family as useful. Fathers are more likely to approve of physical punishment and to use it; they introduce their sons to, and train them in, sports. With both sons and daughters, they are generally less nurturant and more restrictive than mothers (Baumrind, 1979; Lynn, 1974; Lytton, 1976). But the issue of discipline is not a simple *either* (mother)/*or* (father) one. In a recent observational study of 32-month-old boys and their interactions with parents, Hugh Lytton (1980) found that, in line with previous research, most of the boys turned to their mothers for comfort and nurturance and to their fathers for play. But contrary to previous research and theory, mothers were the primary disciplinarians, even when fathers were present, and more of them disciplined their sons physically than fathers did.

One final difference between mothers and fathers is their encouragement of children's traditional masculine and feminine behavior. In one study of families in the 1970s, Mavis Hetherington, Martha Cox, and Roger Cox (1978) found that boys with fathers who were warm, dominating, and demanding tended to be more masculine. The son's masculine behavior was encouraged both by his father's warmth and by seeing him decide, dominate, discipline, and act in other ways that the son perceived as masculine. Girls whose fathers were warm and restrictive, liked women, and made distinctions between masculine and feminine behavior tended to behave in a traditionally feminine manner. (Older studies, too, have found that fathers encourage traditional sex roles in these ways.) But fathers do not have to foster traditional sex roles in their children. The father who raises a more assertive and independent daughter tends to be warm but encourages early independence and achievement rather than feminine qualities. In addition, he behaves in a more positive, egalitarian way toward his wife. The father who raises a more nurturant and socially responsible son tends to be warm and dominating toward him but emotionally expressive and supportive toward his wife. In short, the father models the nontraditional sex role himself (Hetherington et al., 1978).

PERCEPTIONS OF PARENTS IN MIDDLE CHILDHOOD

Parents are central in the lives of most children, at least until the children reach adolescence. But children who told their parents everything about nursery school and kindergarten may be more guarded about the events of second grade. When grade-school friends come to visit, parents tend to hear a lot of whisperings, for the children now have secrets. Children may defend their friends when their parents criticize their language or table manners. Parents now must ask more questions of their children, and many begin to wonder, "What are they really feeling?" To judge from Jella Lepman's collection of children's views in *How Children See Our World* (1971), school-age children are still intensely involved with their parents, though they are not always willing to admit it.

My mamma is the best. I'd like to tell her that, but I never can! All the trying comes to nothing, and then I do something that makes her sad and she knows it. I lie in bed at night and think about it. Suddenly the door opens and my mommy comes in to see if I'm asleep. I quickly close my eyes. She gives me a kiss and then I think that maybe she knows anyway how much I love her (Suzanne, 6, Germany, Lepman, 1971, p. 6).

But children of this age understand that parents have special privileges; some of them resent the inequality between adults and children.

Mothers nibble before meals and tell you not to. That's what a mother is (Mary Claire, 7, United States, Lepman, 1971, p. 6).

A mother doesn't do anything except she wants to. Nobody makes her take baths and naps or takes away her frog (Gary, 6, United States, Lepman, 1971, p. 9).

Despite their occasional reticence and resentment, children of this age are capable of appreciating their parents, perceiving their burdens, worrying about them, and valuing them as they were unable to do in early childhood.

> *Mommy*
> *Mommy, I see you*
> *With your blue apron*
> *And your pale face,*
> *Mommy, I see you,*
> *I always see you.*
> *When you have a minute,*
> *You sit by the fire,*
> *Mending our clothes.*
> *Mommy, I see you*
> *Cooking the steaming soup*
> *For all of us.*
> *Poor Mommy, you work*
> *To help your children.*
> *Mommy, I see you*
> *When you're very tired*
> *You close your blue eyes.*
> *(Claude, 8, France,*
> *Lepman, 1971, p. 9)*

As children move into the wider world of school, sports, lessons, and excursions with friends, parents' rules remain important. Parents must find a balance between restrictiveness and permissiveness. Children at this age understand that rules are necessary. In one study (Appel, 1977), kindergarten children evaluated a permissive mother positively, but third-graders evaluated their mother's permissiveness negatively. The older children seemed to recognize that rules at home were necessary and useful. In a series of investigations by Michael Siegal and Jackie Rablin (1982), 4- to 8-year-old children were told stories in which a child refused to return a toy, threw sand, knocked over some blocks, hurt a puppy, and acted rudely to a grandmother. In each story, the child's mother told the child to stop misbehaving. The subjects were asked whether the mother was good or not good. In response, 70 to 90 percent of the children thought the mother was good. They preferred the mother who intervened, considered misbehavior naughty whether the mother intervened or not, and considered a child naughtier whose mother allowed misbehavior than a child whose mother did not.

REDEFINING PARENT-CHILD RELATIONSHIPS IN ADOLESCENCE

In the ordinary course of events, adolescents do not leave their families abruptly or completely. It would be more accurate to say that adolescents, with the help of their families, redefine their relationships to family members. For some young people, this process of redefinition may be continuous and relatively tranquil. For others, it may come in jumps—two forward and one back. For still others, the process of redefinition is fraught with anger, anxiety, depression, and guilt. Daniel Offer has suggested the terms "continuous growth," "surgent growth," and "tumultuous growth" for these three patterns of change in adolescence (Offer and Offer, 1975).

Adolescents continue to express strong feelings of attachment to their parents, but their new strivings for independence force them to loosen these ties. The middle-class boys interviewed and tested by Offer considered their mothers to be "sources of solace, comfort, instruction" (1969, p. 115) and reported warm and close feelings for them. As Offer writes, they regard their mothers as

> *more understanding and interested than fathers, who are more pragmatic and practical and who are good models for the future. . . . While respectful toward their fathers, even when they are mildly rebellious, these boys are quite am-*

Adolescents feel strongly attached to their parents, but at the same time they cherish their autonomy. Many adolescents consider their mothers to be the most important influence in their lives.

bivalent about their mothers. They cherish and deplore their dependency, and though eager to move out on their own, they are reluctant to move away from their mother's care (Offer, 1969, p. 115).

BOYS' PROBLEMS, GIRLS' PROBLEMS

The change in their relationship to parents may cause adolescents to feel conflict, ambivalence, even despair. John Coleman's 1974 cross-sectional study of 800 English boys and girls of ages 11, 13, 15, and 17 documents the changing and sometimes stressful nature of adolescents' relationships to their parents. Only at the end of adolescence, at ages 17 and 18, are these unsettled feelings resolved. Coleman found that the rocky path to a new level of independence differs for boys and girls.

The boys in Coleman's group sought freedom from constraint and felt "chained, cribbed, cabined, and confined" when with parents. The girls, however, sought autonomy *within* the family unit. Their desire for independence and identity was more likely to take the form of wanting to have independent thoughts and feelings while remaining part of the family. Asked to complete the sentence, "When a girl is with her parents, . . ." the girls in Coleman's group said: "she is not herself. They think they know her but they don't. She becomes like them and cannot find her identity" (Coleman, 1974, p. 33). Elizabeth Douvan and Joseph Adelson (1966) have observed similar differences in the attitudes of male and female American teenagers.

Parents treat males and females somewhat differently from birth onward; they continue to do so when their children reach adolescence. A comparison of parent-child relations for male and female high-school students documents these differences (Stinnett, Farris, and Walters, 1974). Using questionnaire replies from 499 11th- and 12th-graders, researchers found twice as many boys as girls reporting that their fathers had been the primary source of discipline when they were children. Twice as many girls as boys reported being praised often during childhood. Girls indicated that they received equal amounts of affection from their mothers and fathers, but boys identified their mothers as the

principal source of affection. Nevertheless, both boys and girls identified their mother as the greatest influence in their lives.

At adolescence, the young son wants to assert himself as a member of the family who no longer simply takes orders from his father or mother. Laurence Steinberg (1979) observed middle-class boys with their parents during the initial, middle, and late stages of puberty. Watching them and making tapes of their exchanges, Steinberg found that before puberty fathers and mothers appeared to have an equally strong influence over their sons. At the onset of puberty, boys acted more assertively toward their mothers. During middle adolescence, tension was high between mother and son; neither would defer to the other, and they tended to be distant. At the end of this period, father stepped in and insisted that the teenager restrain his assertiveness. Even with an easing of tension in the period after puberty, the adolescent boy is more assertive toward his parents than he was before puberty, especially toward his mother. By this time, the mature adolescent boy has become more influential in family decision making.

Parents may grant their adolescent sons greater freedom, but they seem to be anxious and have fears about letting go of their daughters. A daughter's adolescence appears to be a greater cause of tension and dissatisfaction within families than a son's adolescence. Parents worry about their daughter's safety and her sexual behavior, especially the possibility of pregnancy (Hoffman and Manis, 1977).

Graham Kinloch (1970), using the self-reports of 100 first-year students at a large midwestern university, found significant differences in girls' and boys' conflicts at home. Girls had more of them, and they concerned emotional issues, such as "arguing" and "going around with certain boys and girls." Boys' conflict were on more objective issues, such as "getting to use the car," "church attendance," and "responsibility at home." Girls were also more likely to report scoldings, emotional flare-ups, threats, and cussing by their parents.

Girls may feel more ambivalent about autonomy than boys. They are not encouraged, as boys are, to make the break with their parents, yet they fear that they will lose their new sense of self if they continue to be compliant daughters. In the self-reports of 1000 adolescent girls collected by Gisela

Konopka (1976), only 25 percent did not feel close to their mothers, and even this minority regretted their distance from their mothers. One 15-year-old runaway revealed her ambivalence poignantly, claiming to feel old yet obviously needing her mother: "I feel really old for fifteen; there just isn't any place to go. Mama, I miss you—and I just spent my last dollar for cigarettes" (Konopka, 1976, p. 67). When adolescent girls were at odds with their parents, they attributed the problem not to strictures but to their parents' lack of respect for their maturity. The girls, according to Konopka, very much wanted their parents to acknowledge the fact that they were no longer children. As one 17-year-old expressed it, "My mother and I are in complete conflict because she tries to baby me because I am her only child . . . I'm trying to grow up and she's not letting me" (Konopka, 1976, p. 67).

PARENTS' PRACTICES

Although most adolescents are not militantly at odds with the values of the parent generation, adolescence is a time when limits are tested. In this "intergenerational dialectic," as Douvan and Adelson (1966) put it, the child stands for freedom and the parent for control. Limits must be established, but not in the same way as for children. With children, parents can usually just assert their power and expect compliance. But with adolescents, power is no longer sufficient justification of parental authority. "Because the adolescent can imagine viable alternatives to parental directives, the parent must be ready to defend his or her directives on rational grounds" (Baumrind, 1975, p. 125). Parents of adolescents must expect a fair amount of arguing and resistance, and they must be prepared to explain, defend, and argue their reasons for setting limits.

Even a rational explanation of limits may be resisted by adolescents. But the parents' use of reasoning encourages adolescents to explain and defend their own positions. Adolescents learn that neither complete withdrawal nor antisocial aggression is the way to exercise independence, that dissent can be expressed constructively and may, in certain instances, accomplish change. They develop confidence in peaceable self-assertion.

Adolescents may initially resist all limits, particularly in the more stressful early years of adoles-

cence, between the ages of about 12 and 14. They are acutely attuned to the possibility of parental repression. The movement away from family may begin, as Donald Cohen and Richard Frank (1975) have observed, with a deliberate devaluation of the parent. Young adolescents of about 11 or 12 are extremely sensitive to the exercise of adult power. At this prickly age, the young adolescent is

embarrassed to submit to adult good manners or to accept adult help openly, revolted by praise or punishment perceived as infantilizing. In spite of his continuing need and desire for support and guidance, he may hesitate or altogether cease to play with or to communicate feelings to adults (Cohen and Frank, 1975, p. 138).

Especially at this early stage, adolescents need continued parental guidance—parental authority but not parental oppression. As teenagers mature, parents should give them more and more opportunities to make decisions about their lives. In fact, giving adolescent girls responsibility seems especially important for fostering their independence.

Parents who shelter and protect their daughters encourage them to be affiliative, empathic, and compliant in their relations with their parents. For girls who are preparing exclusively for marriage and motherhood, these qualities may be entirely suitable. But the majority of them will also work outside the home. To compete in the job market, girls need to develop some of what Judith Bardwick and Elizabeth Douvan (1971) call "independent sources of self-esteem," or what Diana Baumrind (1975) would designate as "social agency"—the ability to be an agent or instrument of one's own destiny, a "social agent" rather than a "social victim." For girls, too much protectiveness, warmth, and support may make them overly dependent on the affection and approval of others. It is important for a girl to discover that she can stand up to parental disapproval, pursue a course of action not supported by them, and be willing to gamble with the threat of loss of love (Baumrind, 1975).

THE DUAL IDENTITY CRISIS: ADOLESCENCE AND MIDOLESCENCE

In the best of all worlds, adolescents will have parents who remain stalwart and firm, providing an example of commitment and a standard against which the adolescents can forge their own identities (Lidz, 1969). But the timetable of aging in many families is such that adolescents have parents just entering their 40s, and two crises often concur: "the crisis of adolescence in the child and reactivated adolescent crisis in his parents" (Anthony, 1969, p. 59). At a time when parents are relinquishing authority and worrying about the safety and success of their adolescent children as they embark on independent paths, and at a time when the children themselves feel life opening up before them, parents must come to terms with the limits of their own lives, the frustrations of their ambitions and ideals. "The youth's idealism," notes psychiatrist Theodore Lidz, may "irritate the cynicism of middle-age disappointment" (1969, pp. 108–109). Parents' responses to their children's behavior always bear a relationship to the events of the parents' own point in the life cycle. But parents trying to deal with a midlife crisis can find their own adjustment greatly complicated by a teenage child. For example, the child's transition to adolescence may trigger or aggravate marital conflict between a father and mother who are in their own **midolescence**, who are facing, perhaps for the first time, their own broken dreams and unfulfilled lives.

In a study comparing college graduates who became full-time homemakers with those who were professionally employed, the well-educated, full-time homemaker was likely to greet her children's adolescence with ambivalence and regret, whereas the mothers who had a profession were more comfortable with the prospect of their children's independence (Birnbaum, 1971). A mother or father who has used a child as "a substitute source of emotional gratification" (Lidz, 1969, p. 109) may have an unusually difficult time allowing that child the independence necessary for adolescent development. The adolescent's interest in the opposite sex may become freighted with parents' wishes to continue to hold on to the child. The major conflict between fathers and daughters in the Konopka (1976) study was the fathers' suspicious protectiveness over their daughters' sex drive. One of Konopka's subjects, a white, 16-year-old, rural girl, expressed the issue this way: "He expects me to be his 'little girl' all my life, and I think he is just not realizing that he can't have that; and that, I think,

is what he expected out of me for a long time" (Konopka, 1976, p. 69). In a traditional family, the conjunction of a father's midlife frustrations, a mother's discovery of unfulfilled aspirations, and an adolescent's striving for greater autonomy can cause severe strife.

Catherine Cooper, Harold Grotevant, and Sherri Condon (1983) observed patterns of family communication to find out what promotes adolescents' sense of identity. They found that adolescents' abilities to explore their identity related to their fathers' willingness to disagree openly and to initiate compromises and to their mothers' assertiveness and initiation of compromises. Thus, in a family in which all of the members are clearly individuated and interact humorously, candidly, spontaneously, and vulnerably, the adolescent engages in a great deal of identity exploration and role taking. In a family in which family members rarely disagree and the level of individuation is low, adolescents do not explore identity issues. As one such adolescent put it "I'm having a hard time deciding what to do. It would be easier if they would tell me what to do, but of course I don't want that" (Cooper et al., 1983, p. 55).

SIBLING RELATIONSHPS

If either of my sisters left the family I would go crazy because I'm so used to fighting with my 9-year-old sister and arguing about dumb things. I love my 7-month-old sister, holding her and feeding her. That's why I wouldn't like to be an only child (David, 11, in Lepman, 1971, p. 20).

Like David's family, 87 percent of American families have more than one child (Falbo, 1979), and how siblings get along with each other has become of interest to researchers in the last few years. Although this body of work has begun to show meaningful results, in her review of many of the studies of sibling interaction, Judy Dunn (1983) cautions that most of the studies focus on only two siblings, even when families contain more than two children. Most studies also focus on the interaction between the firstborn and secondborn siblings. Dunn suggests that these tendencies limit the applicability of the studies' findings to large families or to nonwestern cultures. Even so, Dunn sees several trends clearly emerging from the studies of young siblings' interactions.

As many studies have shown, babies are clearly interested in other children (e.g., Brooks and Lewis, 1976; McCall and Kennedy, 1980). Once they are 6 months old, babies begin to interact more and more often with their older siblings, as evidence from diary studies in Canada, Britain, the United States, and many other cultures shows (Abramovitch, Pepler, and Corter, 1982; Dale, 1983; Dunn and Kendrick, 1982a). A diary study of 54 London families with two children, for example, showed that by the time they are 1 year old, secondborn babies spend almost as much time with their older siblings as with their mothers—and much more time than with their fathers (Lawson and Ingleby, 1974). Similarly, Stephen Bank and Michael Kahn (1975) found that 4- to 6-year-old siblings spent twice as much time alone together as they spent with their parents. Brenda Bryant (1982) found that about one-third of laterborn children shared a room with a sibling.

Siblings show their mutual interest not only in the frequency of their interaction, but also in the frequency with which they imitate one another. In the United States, laboratory observations by Lamb (1978a, 1978b) demonstrated that babies watched and imitated older siblings. Observations of Canadian toddlers showed that imitation characterized nearly one-third of the interactions between 20-month-olds and their older siblings (Pepler, Corter, and Abramovitch, 1982). Imitation was equally common among British 14-month-olds and their older siblings (Dunn and Kendrick, 1982a). Younger siblings imitated their older siblings far more than the reverse, but older siblings often imitate their younger siblings as well—a tendency that highlights the reciprocal nature of the sibling relationship. Several researchers have noted with what excitement and pleasure siblings do things in tandem (Buhler, 1939; Dunn and Kendrick, 1982a; Greenwood, 1983). One pair of 2-year-old twins was observed by their mother to hold long conversations early in the morning as they lay in their beds (Keenan, 1974). They exchanged noises and words, listened carefully to each other, and carried on extensive dialogues.

Just as sibling relationships are marked by imitativeness, they are marked by strong positive and negative emotions.

He loves being with her and her friends—he's very fond of one of her friends. He trails after Laura. . . . They play in the sand a lot . . . making pies. She organizes it, and swipes away things that are dangerous and gives him something else. They go upstairs and bounce on the bed. Then he'll lie there while she sings to him, and reads books to him. And he'll go off in a trance with his hanky [comfort object]. The important thing is there are becoming games that they'll play together. He'll start something by laughing and running towards some toy, turning round to see if she's following. He'll go upstairs and race into one bedroom and shriek, and she joins him. . . .

It's worse now he's on the go. He annoys her. They fight a lot—more than four or five big fights a day, and every day. They're very bad tempered with each other. He makes her cry such a lot (Dunn and Kendrick, 1982a, p. 39).

In these descriptions of two sibling pairs from Judy Dunn and Carol Kendrick's longitudinal study of sibling pairs in 40 British families, a younger brother of 14 months and an older sister of almost 3, two quite different relationships are portrayed. But as Dunn has suggested, it is more accurate to say that siblings often feel ambivalent toward one another than to try to characterize their relationships along a continuum of warm to cold. Not only do siblings act competitively, but they also act cooperatively; not only do siblings hit each other, but they also help each other; not only do siblings fight over toys, but they also share their treasures.

As they grow older, there is a tendency for younger siblings to behave more positively to their older siblings. By the time the laterborn is 3 years old, siblings often cooperate in games and play, show physical affection and concern, and try actively to help and comfort (Dunn, 1983; Dunn and Kendrick, 1982a). Dunn suggests that the ability to take the sibling's perspective, which these activities imply, comes from the children's close familiarity with each other's worlds and the reciprocal nature of their relationship. Because siblings share so much and understand each other so well, they are particularly well placed to understand the other's

Siblings interact often and with intense feeling. Some of the feelings are kind and positive, and some are competitive and harsh.

distress—or to cause it. Older children often serve as interpreters of their younger siblings' wishes or feelings: "Kenny wants cakey Mum" or "Jo-Jo likes monkeys." They clearly understand the younger child's point of view. As one older brother said as he watched his younger brother playing with a balloon, "He going pop in a minute. And he going cry. And he going be frightened of me too. I *like* the pop" (Dunn and Kendrick, 1982a, p. 46). Siblings can annoy, tease, and compete with devastating accuracy. Nearly one-third of the interactions among siblings observed by researchers have been found to be antagonistic, with elder siblings more likely to antagonize younger siblings than the reverse (Dale, 1983; Dunn and Kendrick, 1982a; Pepler et al., 1982). Yet, with age, the laterborns themselves increased not only in positive actions toward their siblings but in antagonistic and aggressive actions as well. By their second year, laterborns could tease their older siblings quite perspicaciously.

In general, Dunn and Kendrick (1982a) were impressed with the wide range of individual differences they saw in several hours of watching sibling pairs playing at home: in firstborns, positive behavior ranged from 0 to 94 percent of their social behavior (with a mean of 55 percent); in secondborns it ranged from 35 to 100 percent (with a mean of 70 percent). But no matter how positive peer interactions are, it is unlikely that they are as positive as interactions with parents. When Bryant (1979) asked 7- and 10-year-olds to compare their parents and siblings, on all dimensions except physical punishment the children thought that their parents were more active, nurturant, demanding of achievement, and inclined to do things with the child; siblings were more punitive (see Figure 12.5). A study of 4- to 8-year-olds at home by Linda Musun Baskett and Stephen Johnson (1982), showed similarly that children interacted more often and more positively with parents than with siblings.

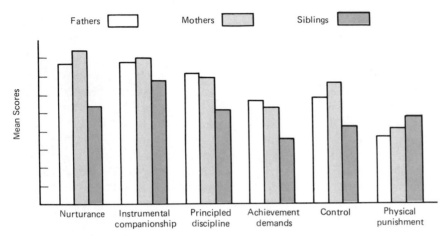

FIGURE 12.5
Children describe their parents as more active than their siblings on five out of six caretaking dimensions (Bryant, 1979).

The higher observed incidence of hostile acts by older to younger siblings is an example of mismatched behavior. As behavior geneticists have noted, many siblings differ markedly in personality, intellectual development, and psychopathology, despite the fact that they share genes and a family environment. Siblings differ as much as they do because their genes, though shared, are not identical, and neither is their family environment. Parents inevitably treat individual children differently, and siblings create different environments for each other.

As we have seen, the reciprocity of sibling interactions is expressed in frequent imitation and excited play and talk. But the sibling relationship also includes complementary aspects, especially in the areas of caretaking, teaching, and the formation of attachments (Dunn, 1983). Children in many cultures around the world are expected to take care of their younger brothers and sisters. In a review of 186 societies, Herbert Barry and Leonora Paxon (1971) found that in 40 percent of them, infants were cared for by people besides their mothers, and in more than 80 percent young children were cared for by their older siblings. A study of three particular African societies showed that older siblings scolded, helped, fed, and supervised their younger siblings much as adults would, but they also played with and acted aggressive towards them more than adults would (Whiting and Pope-Edwards, 1977). Most older siblings in the United

States and Britain also show interest in a newborn sibling, worry when it cries, and try to help entertain and care for it (Dunn, Kendrick, and MacNamee, 1981; Legg, Sherick, and Wadland, 1974; Trause et al., 1981). When 54 pairs of siblings found themselves in an unfamiliar laboratory setting, more than half of the 4-year-olds promptly and effectively comforted and reassured younger siblings who were distressed at their mother's absence (Stewart, 1983).

Most siblings are friendly and cooperative with each other, but is this bond a form of attachment, such as one observes between children and their mothers? Can siblings provide security and comfort for each other? Two early studies (Ainsworth, 1967; Schaffer and Emerson, 1964a) indicate that many babies grow attached to older siblings, act distressed in their absence, greet them joyously, and prefer them as playmates. Rudolph Schaffer and Peggy Emerson (1964a) suggested that attachment to the mother appears at about the same time as attachment to a sibling. Dunn and Kendrick (1982b) similarly found that half the 14-month-olds in their sample missed an absent older sibling, and one-third went to the older sibling when they felt distressed. In Beatrice Whiting and Carolyn Pope-Edwards' (1977) cross-cultural study, 2-year-olds turned to their siblings for comfort, food, and help. In a strange situation, older siblings can comfort younger siblings and serve as a secure base when a stranger approaches (Stewart, 1983). When 16-

to 22-month-olds played in a yard with their older siblings, they went farther and for longer periods from their mothers than when they played alone (Samuels, 1980), and twins, observed in a laboratory playroom when they were between 8 and 24 months old, served the same functions for each other (Clark and Krige, 1979). Children who were admitted to a residential nursery were far less distressed if they were accompanied by a sibling (Heinicke and Westheimer, 1966). Thus for the younger child at least, the relationship to an older sibling may be characterized as an attachment.

If older siblings act like parents in providing security to younger siblings, they also speak in some ways as mothers do to young children. Like adults speaking motherese, older siblings may repeat, explain, and help a younger child to practice speech. Here a 31-month-old tries to dissuade his younger brother from eating a candy that fell on the floor. Telling him that the family dog, Scottie, will eat it, he urges the baby into the kitchen with ever shorter sentences:

> *No don't you eat it. Scottie will eat it. Scottie will eat it. No not you. Scottie will eat it. Not you. Scottie. Not you. Shall we go in door? Right. Come on. Come on. In door. In door Robin. In door (Dunn and Kendrick, 1982a, p. 50).*

Mothers tended to ask more questions and to issue fewer statements than older siblings, in Sara Harkness's (1977) study of Kenyan families and Dunn and Kendrick's (1982a) study of British families. In structured settings, children of 6 and 7 have shown that they can teach younger siblings quite effectively, more effectively in fact than unrelated teachers (Cicirelli, 1972, 1977, 1978). Robert Stewart (1983) also found that preschoolers could teach younger siblings quite well, drawing their attention and suiting their instructions to the younger siblings' actions. But he notes that their mothers were supervising these proceedings quite closely. In a study of children explicitly teaching their siblings at home, Debra Pepler (1981) found that older children often taught—physical skills, games, how to use toys, labels, words, and numbers—but younger children rarely did so.

Dunn and Kendrick (1982b) found few sex differences in siblings' cooperative, caregiving, and helping behavior, although firstborn girls did more caring for their infant siblings—no doubt because

their mothers encouraged them—and younger siblings were less often negative toward their older sisters than their older brothers. As for teaching, Victor Cicirelli found that in a structured teaching task, older sisters taught more effectively than older brothers (1972) and were more likely to offer help to their younger siblings (1973). Ann Minnett, Deborah Lowe Vandell, and John Santrock (1983) videotaped 7- and 8-year-olds as they wrapped a package with their younger siblings and saw who could toss the most cards into a wastebasket. Again, older sisters were more likely than older brothers to praise and teach a younger sibling.

At home, siblings are part of a family constellation that includes their parents. The relationships of mothers and children are interconnected over both the short and long term. Dunn and Kendrick (1982a) found that when a mother and an older daughter had shared an intense, playful relationship before the birth of a second child, the older daughter greeted the baby with hostility; by 14 months of age, the baby was returning that hostility. Furthermore, when mothers were warm and playful with the baby, both siblings later were quite hostile to each other. One possible interpretation of these patterns is that the mother played with a younger child to compensate for the older daughter's hostility; a more likely explanation is that the daughter's hostility was a reaction to the mother's warmth toward the new baby. In any case, the relationships within the mother-and-siblings triangle markedly and immediately affect one another. When a mother feeds or tends her baby, her interaction with her older child changes, and confrontations increase (Kendrick and Dunn, 1980). Siblings' quarrels are also likely to draw in their mother, and her responses correlate with the frequency of subsequent hostility between the siblings (Kendrick and Dunn, 1983).

FAMILY VARIATION

DIVORCE

In earlier decades, fathers were away from their children principally because of work or war. Now the greatest single cause of fathers' absence is divorce. There are well over a million divorces in this country every year, and 70 percent of these families have children. The divorce rate for parents of pre-school children has risen from 8 percent in 1950 to 20 percent in 1980. At the present rate, 50 percent of the children born in the 1980s will spend some time in a single-parent family, usually with the mother. It is not just the child who suffers from the separation but the noncustodial parent as well. To make matters worse, the custodial parent is usually stripped of the economic, emotional, and labor support of the spouse. Hetherington et al., (1976, 1978, 1982) studied 96 families with children in nursery school, half of them divorced families. Through interviews, personal records, and psychological tests and observations at home, in the laboratory, and in nursery school, the researchers evaluated the families at 2 months, 1 year, and 2 years after the divorce. In all families, the mother retained custody of the child or children. In the year after the divorce, mothers grew more authoritarian and less affectionate with their youngsters. Family routine grew more chaotic. Children grew more unruly. For fathers, the first year after the divorce marked the beginning of a growing emotional detachment from their children: the emotional bond deteriorated and the number of contacts diminished. By 2 years after the divorce, fewer than one-half the fathers saw their children as often as once a week, although all lived nearby. If the father did have frequent contact with the family, however, this was helpful for the mother and for the son's development. Two years after the divorce, fathers were again growing stricter, mothers more patient, children more cooperative. Family routine grew more stable.

But the evidence gathered in this and other studies (e.g., Biller, 1976; Hetherington et al., 1978) indicates that there may be long-lasting adverse effects on boys whose parents divorce. In the first year after a divorce, sons are more aggressive and ornery and lack control at home and in nursery school. Two years after the divorce, most of them are more feminine and less mature. The aggression, which had been physical the first year, has been transformed into a more feminine form, verbal aggression. Many preschool sons become "sissies." But if the divorced father continues to see his young son frequently, the boy is likely to be more masculine in behavior. If the child has an older brother, a stepfather, an uncle, or a grandfather who cares for him, or if his mother makes a deliberate effort to support and encourage independence and mature masculine behavior and if she has a positive attitude toward men and her ex-husband, the little boy becomes as masculine as his peers.

Preschool children may find divorce incomprehensible because they lack a firm sense of the continuity of family relationships. They tend to think that a family consists of people living in the same house. If the father moves out, it seems to the child that he is no longer a part of the family. The egocentrism of children causes them to attribute the actions of their parents to something they have done—in the case of divorce, something that they have done wrong. Children of 60 middle-class families were interviewed at the time of the divorce and one year later by Judith Wallerstein and Joan Kelly (1980). Between the ages 3½ and 6, children's predominant feeling concerning the divorce was self-blame. They saw the difficulty in their parents' marriage not as an issue between mother and father but as something that had gone wrong between themselves and their parents. At the same time, parents often are preoccupied with their own differences, and the quality of parenting deteriorates. Divorce itself *creates* stress within families.

A divorce when children are between 6 and 12 may interfere with their developing sense of industry, with the broadening of their thinking, and with their growth in social understanding, which paves the way for good relations with their peers. School-age children are better able to cope with divorce than preschoolers because they are more aware of their own feelings and more open about admitting their sadness, but, still they may keep up a courageous front, suffering inside. They no longer are likely to blame themselves for the divorce, as they might have at a younger age, but they still fear abandonment and are angry at their parents' breakup. They are often torn between feelings of family loyalty and shame at their parents' behavior (Wallerstein and Kelly, 1980).

School-age boys whose fathers are absent after the divorce are more likely to have trouble with mathematics (Shinn, 1978) and with their masculinity (Biller and Bahm, 1971). They have fewer such difficulties if the divorce comes later in their childhood and they have a father substitute or an older male sibling (Drake and McDougall, 1977).

Divorce may aggravate the tensions of parent and adolescent child struggling for identity. Divorce is likely to pose a special problem if the divorced parent regresses to adolescent behavior and becomes a competitor on the dating scene, flaunts his or her own sexuality, or describes the sexual inadequacies of the former mate. Meeting the single parent's date or temporary roommate may cause some adolescents to withdraw in consternation, others to feel morally indignant (Wallerstein and Kelly, 1974). A parent may also force the adolescent child into serving as an emotional surrogate for the absent mate or as a parent for younger sisters and brothers.

RESEARCH FOCUS

STRESS AND THE SINGLE PARENT

Marsha Weinraub and Barbara Wolf (1983), of Temple University, posed several questions about what it is like for children to grow up in a family with only one parent, their mother. They wondered whether single mothers face more life changes and stresses and fewer social supports or community ties than married mothers. They wondered whether single mothers have more difficulty coping with their stresses and responsibilities than married mothers. They wondered also whether interaction between parents and children is influenced by social supports and whether the relationship among stresses, support, and mother-child interactions differs in single- and two-parent families. Their subjects were 14 single mothers and their children and 14 married mothers and their children, matched for child's age and mother's education and income. The single mothers worked substantially more hours a week than the married mothers. Half of the single women had been divorced; half chose to raise a child alone from the beginning. Only women who were older than 22 and who had raised their child alone from birth or shortly thereafter were included as subjects.

Single mothers, the researchers found, had experienced significantly more stressful life changes in the previous year than married mothers had, and the nature of the changes differed as well. Single women faced changes in jobs, living arrangements, or personal goals; married women faced pregnancy, birth, and home mortgages. Single mothers had fewer social contacts and were less likely to confide in people they saw often than married mothers were. Single mothers also considered their friends, relatives, and people in social or church groups less supportive than married mothers did and were less satisfied with the support that they did receive. Their social networks changed more often than those of the married mothers. Single mothers used twice the amount of day care as married mothers did. Although single mothers had to cope on their own with finances, child care, and household responsibilities, they reported no more difficulty coping than married mothers. Only in the area of household responsibilities did single mothers have more trouble coping.

The relations between mothers and children did not differ appreciably in the one- and two-parent families. Single mothers did no better or worse at controlling, nurturing, or communicating with their children, and the children seemed equally compliant and mature. Yet in both kinds of families, mothers who were more stressed were less nurturant. Unexpectedly, Weinraub and Wolf found that single mothers who had the most social contacts tended to be less nurturant and to have less control over their children. These single mothers generally were of two types: young divorced women who had moved in with their parents and whose social contacts included critical relatives; and mothers who lived alone with their children and who sought social contacts through work or dating. The latter faced a dilemma that was unusual among married mothers: having to chose between spending time with children or adults, that is, having to choose between her children and her own needs for intimacy and social support.

In short, Weinraub and Wolf found substantial differences in the lives of single and married mothers. Single mothers are under more stress from life changes and from the longer hours they work. Their social networks offer them less support for their role as parent. Married mothers can more easily integrate their roles as mother, worker, and adult woman. Despite the increased pressures they operate under, however, single mothers are much like married mothers in their ability to handle their children.

Their parents' divorce may make adolescents anxious about their own potential as marriage partners. Having seen their parents, important models for their own behavior, fail in marriage (sometimes abysmally), adolescents may worry that they will prove equally inept. On the positive side, adolescents who watch their parents divorce are forced to see them as human beings. Although that change may be painful, it may also be realistic and healthy—as one 17-year-old put it, "I'm also seeing him more as a person than as my important daddy" (Wallerstein and Kelly, 1974, p. 491). At an age when they are readying themselves to act autonomously, adolescents whose parents divorce may cope fairly well with the forced autonomy that divorce entails for them. Younger children, far less ready to rely on themselves and far more needy of a strong, bolstering family, fare less well than adolescents when their parents divorce.

The effects of divorce are likely to be the most severe in the year or two following it (Hetherington et al., 1978). Whether or not children are affected adversely over a long period of time seems to depend on the way the parents handle the divorce and on their relationships with their children afterward (Wallerstein and Kelly, 1980). Some fathers maintain meaningful contact with their children after a divorce. Others, as indicated earlier, virtually disappear from the children's world. Robert Hess and Kathleen Camera (1979) explained how children ages 9 to 11 were faring in 16 intact families and 16 divorced families. Parental harmony and good parent-child relations were found to be more important to the well-being of these children than an intact marriage, as determined by the stress they felt, their aggressiveness, how well they did their schoolwork, and their social relations. The negative effects of divorce can be greatly mitigated, according to this study, if positive relationships with both parents can be maintained, and if the father's relationship with the child is deep and he remains involved in the day-to-day life of the child. More fathers are now gaining custody of their children after a divorce (Figure 12.6). In a study of a small group of middle-class children, ages 6 to 11, whose parents had been divorced, Richard Warshak and John Santrock (1979) found that it was better for the self-esteem and social relations of the boys to be in the father's custody. The girls fared better with their mothers. These custody decisons had

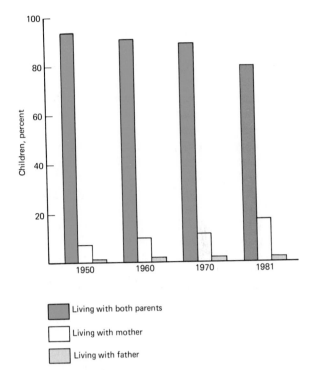

FIGURE 12.6
Although the vast majority of children still live with both parents, the proportion of those living with either mother or father is rising quickly. The 20.1 percent of children living with one parent in 1981 was an increase of 53.9 percent since 1970 (Bureau of the Census).

been worked out, not through court battles but by mutual agreement of the parents, the best assurance for a favorable outcome.

MOTHERS' EMPLOYMENT

Sometimes I wish my mother didn't work, because when it is my birthday, I can't have it on the real day. But otherwise I like my mother to work because we can get more money to go for a holiday every year and also to be rich (Diana, 8, Canada, in Lepman, 1971, p. 10).

When there were comparatively few families in which mothers with young children worked outside their homes, psychologists knew little about the patterns of interaction in such families. But in 1982, 48 percent of married mothers of preschoolers and 60 percent of single mothers of preschoolers were in the labor force (Hoffman, 1984). As this family pattern has grown more common, psychologists have begun to investigate how such parents and children get along, how mothers' work affects family life, and other important questions. In a review of the relevant literature, Lois Wladis Hoffman (1984) of the University of Michigan has noted that working mothers spend less time taking care of their children than mothers who are housewives do, although this difference varies by social class. College-educated working mothers with preschool children spend one-quarter less time in child care than housewives do; they also spend less time sleeping and watching television (Hill and Stafford, 1978). But a study of middle-class nursery school children showed no differences in the amount of time working mothers and housewives spent *alone* with their children (Goldberg, 1977). The working mothers, however, had less time in which they were within calling distance or in the same room but doing something without their children. Several investigators have suggested that the time working mothers spend playing and talking with their children is especially intense and that they set aside uninterrupted chunks of time to spend with their children (Hoffman, 1980; Pedersen, Cain, Zaslow, and Anderson, 1983). Fathers in families with working mothers spend more time taking care of their children and doing housework (Pleck and Rustad, 1980).

Observations of working mothers and their children have produced conflicting results. In comparisons of working mothers' and housewives' interactions with their infants, the mothers' employment status seems to make little difference in the quality of interaction. The differences that do appear suggest that working mothers pay more attention and talk more to their young children (Hoffman, 1984). Some researchers have hypothesized that a job that improves a mother's morale will improve her relationship with her child and that a job that strains her will diminish her relationship with her child, and the data bear out this hypothesis (Hock, 1980; Schubert, Bradley-Johnson, and Nuttal, 1980; Stuckey, McGhee, and Bell, 1982). The cause, however, is not yet clear. It may be either that happier workers make happier mothers or that happier mothers make happier workers.

In one exploratory study, Lindsay Chase-Lansdale (1981) investigated how mothers' employment affects the attachment of first-born children to their parents in 110 intact middle-class families. In all these families, the mothers had returned to work before their infant was 3 months old—therefore before a true attachment had formed. Chase-Lansdale found no relation between the mother's working and the security of her child's attachment. Neither did she find any relation between mothers' working and the attachment of daughters to their fathers. But one result proved unexpectedly significant: the attachment between fathers and sons in two-worker families was less secure than in one-worker families. This finding probably reflects the familiar theme in research on environmental effects: boys are more vulnerable to environmental stresses than girls are. Although many studies have shown no differences in the effects of mothers' employment on sons and daughters, those that have found differences generally have found positive effects on daughters and negative effects on sons. Daughters of working mothers are more independent and outgoing; they are socially and personally better adjusted; they achieve more; and they admire their mothers and women in general more than do daughters of housewives (Hoffman, 1984). In contrast, middle- and working-class sons of working mothers do less well in school and score lower on intelligence tests than sons of housewives. Only among lower-class boys do academic differences tend to favor the sons of working mothers. But in two-worker, lower-class families, the relationship between father and son may be strained (Hoffman, 1979, 1980). Hoffman suggests that daughters of working mothers have a model for social competence and high status within the family; they get training in independence, self-confidence, and high self-esteem. But the story is different for the sons of working mothers. In working-class families, mothers' work may carry negative connotations: it can mean that fathers have failed to provide financially for their families, and it often is seen as a violation of mothers' gender role. As for why middle-class sons of working mothers perform worse academically than sons of housewives, Hoffman (1972) suggests that housewives intensely socialize their sons so that they perform well in school.

Could the increased training in independence that children of working mothers get be too much or too early for sons but not for daughters? Some psychologists (e.g., Chase-Lansdale, 1981) have suggested this as an explanation for why fathers in two-income families, who encourage their sons' independence, have less secure relationships with them. Another explanation comes from a study of 2- to 6-year-old children of working parents (Stuckey, McGhee, and Bell, 1982). It was found that in two-income families, daughters got more attention than sons. But in traditional families, it was the sons who got more attention. An observational study of 1-year-olds showed the same patterns (Zaslow, Pedersen, Suwalsky, and Rabinovich, 1983). Similarly, in a study of 150 white 3-year-olds and their two parents, mothers who worked full time described their daughters the most positively and their sons the least positively (Bronfenbrenner, Alvarez, and Henderson, 1983: Bronfenbrenner and Crouter, 1982). Fathers also described their daughters in the most flattering terms, sons in the least. Said one mother who taught full time at a university about her daughter:

Great, incredibly lovable, bright, creative. At times she can be a pain in the neck with her strong will. But that can carry into positive as well as negative. She's very opinionated—about books, clothes, where she wants to go and when. But I think it's good that she has confidence and can assert herself (Bronfenbrenner et al., 1983, p. 9)

But another mother who worked full time said this about her son:

He really is an ornery child. He's very difficult to manage. He fights us on just about everything. I think that's our biggest problem right now, trying to have him control his actions (Bronfenbrenner et al., 1982, p. 10).

Why would parents react so differently to their sons and daughters? Perhaps sons actually are more active and less compliant than girls (Block, in press) and present more of a strain to their working, overburdened mothers and fathers. Perhaps families in which the wife has a more egalitarian role do not subscribe to the traditional pattern of favoring sons (Hoffman, 1979) and interacting more with them than with daughters (Block, in press). Only further research will sort out the reasons that daughters more often flourish and sons flounder in families with employed mothers.

DISTRESS

Distress in a family can come in many different forms: mental illness, physical handicaps, financial strain, divorce, emotional crisis, and on and on. It is impossible to be comprehensive in discussing the effects of all such sources of distress on children's development or family relationships. Therefore we have chosen only a sampling of studies to illustrate the effects of distress on family interactions and relationships.

Parents with Mental Illness

When a parent is mentally ill, the effects on the family can be profound. What happens to the children in these families? Arnold Sameroff, Ronald Seifer, and Melvin Zax (1982) followed from pregnancy until their children were 2½ years old 260 women with varying degrees of mental illness. They found that although all of these children tended to do worse on tests than children from comparable families with no mental illness, of the mentally ill mothers, those diagnosed as schizophrenic had the least severe effects on their children's development. Children whose mothers were diagnosed as neurotic and depressed were worse off, but it was the length and severity of the illness that best predicted adverse effects. In other studies, too, when teachers and peers have been asked to rate the competence of children in their classes, their ratings have not been related to the diagnostic category of the mothers' mental illness but have been related to whether the mother was mentally ill at all and how seriously (Fisher, Kokes, Harder, and Jones, 1980; Weintraub, Neale, and Liebert, 1975). But as Sameroff and his colleagues (1982) note, no single biological or environmental cause explains the difficulties in these families. Poverty, chronic and severe illness, poor coping skills, and many other factors all contribute to problems for children and parents. Offspring of schizophrenic parents, for example, are 10 to 15 times likelier than offspring of normal parents to develop schizophrenia themselves. This incidence seems to reflect both environmental and genetic conditions. But investigators cannot isolate any single condition in the family environment. They find instead a welter of problems—prolonged emotional disturbance, unstable family organization, poverty, and low social status—all of which seem to put a child at high risk for serious developmental problems.

Problem Children

A child with a serious handicap requires accommodations and adjustments from parents and other family members. Family members must attune their behavior and their expectations to the handicapped child. Babies who are blind and deaf, for example, have been observed to interact less predictably with their parents than normal babies, and their parents repeat simple acts more often with these babies than parents of normal babies do (Walker and Kershman, 1981). Many blind children have severe social problems (Fraiberg, 1974, 1975, 1977). Their mothers often feel anxious about how to deal with them, even when the babies seem to be forming attachments normally.

Children who are physically handicapped or who have severe behavior problems present their families with frequent and frustrating aversive episodes. In these families, the mother can be considered the victim of the child's aversive behavior, for she must deal with it day in and day out. Even experienced, skillful parents have trouble avoiding aversive behavior when they must cope with a chronically ill or handicapped child, and mothers tend to bear the brunt of the problems. Questionnaires and self-reports show that mothers of handicapped children are more troubled psychologically than either their husbands or parents of normal children (Tavormina, Boll, Dunn, Luscomb, and Taylor, 1975).

Although a child originally may be diagnosed as "the problem," families are dynamic, and the reactions of family members can easily exacerbate the problem. The child's actions plus the family's reactions can add up to a vicious circle. Thus although it can be shown (e.g., Johnson, Wahl, Martin, and Johanssen, 1973) that coercive boys have coercive mothers, it is not easy to tell whether sons first react against demanding mothers or mothers first react against negative sons. Whichever it is, the net effect within a family is disruption, aggression, despair, and low self-esteem (Patterson, 1980). Poverty, marital problems, and the absence of a father all can affect how well a mother manages a problem child (Hetherington et al., 1976; Horne and Reinker, 1978; Johnson et al., 1973). As Gerald Patterson (1980) observed in his study of "mothers as victims," in the normal family mothers are caretakers who share with fathers the routine problems in child management. But in families with a problem child, the mother becomes a lone crisis manager. She often engages in prolonged coercive exchanges with the problem child, in which the child attacks her and quickly escalates the battle, even though she did nothing to provoke the attack, escalates but moderately, and withdraws as quickly as possible.

Patterson (Patterson, 1980; Patterson and Cobb, 1973) carried out a longitudinal study of families referred by schools, courts, mental health clinics, or professionals in private practice as having a child (usually a son) between 3 and 13 who was out of control. The problems of the children tended to be chronic and serious: stealing, truancy, arson, or social aggression in the form of hitting, teasing, whining, and the like. Researchers observed these families interacting and coded many of their behaviors. When data from 27 problem families and 27 matched control families were compared (Patterson and Cobb, 1973), few differences in the fathers' behavior were found. In distressed families, fathers tended to act as resident "guests" and "good guys" who abdicated their responsibilities for serious child-management problems to their "bad-guy" wives. Mothers were the primary targets of their children's dependency, disapproval, destructiveness, and whining. These mothers ended up feeling stressed, depressed, psychologically troubled, and lacking in self-esteem—ideal victims for further attacks.

As social psychologist Robert Bales (1953) once noted, families seem to behave more aversively than most other groups. Mothers are five times more negative with their own preschool children than with other children the same age (Halverson and Waldrop, 1970). Spouses are more negative with each other than with strangers (Birchler, Weiss, and Vincent, 1975). Even with normal children, the mother's role typically confronts a woman with more unpleasantness than the father's role does. Mothers must respond often and intimately, but they receive little positive feedback for doing so. Mothers with preschool children report feeling maximally stressed (Campbell, 1975). They must constantly monitor their preschoolers, issuing commands and prohibitions every few minutes (Minton, Kagan, and Levine, 1971; Patterson, 1976). Punishment works much more quickly than positive reinforcement does—and it offers a furious parent an outlet for his or her anger—reasons that families may fall, willy-nilly, into negative patterns of interaction. Not only do parents of aggressive or deviant children tend to be poor models of social skill and to find it difficult to set or to enforce limits for their children (Goldin, 1969), but they also issue many more commands than do parents of normal children (Delfini, Bernal, and Rosen, 1976).

James Garbarino, Janet Sebes, and Cynthia Schellenbach (1984) studied 62 two-parent families that contained a 10- to 16-year-old who had been referred by schools, churches, or social agencies for help with the adolescent's adjustment problems. The families were all visited at home, interviewed, and tested. The investigators assessed what the parents considered appropriate or inappropriate behavior in their adolescent children and how they would respond to such behavior. They also assessed whether parents sexually or physically, verbally or psychologically abused or neglected their children. They noted the problems and competencies of the children, conflicts between parents, and how the families operated as social systems. Families were assigned to two risk categories according to how likely they were to engage in destructive behavior.

Highly destructive and nondestructive families did not differ in socioeconomic characteristics or parents' age. The destructive families had more children, however, implying that their resources may have been stretched further than those in nondestructive families. Destructive families presented a picture of group and individual problems and stress. They were more chaotic and ''enmeshed'' rather than ''connected'' and flexible. The adolescents in these destructive families showed more developmental dysfunctions—immaturity, somatic complaints, uncommunicativeness, delinquency, aggression, hyperactivity—and more substance abuse. The stress of divorce had damaged some of them; all of the families with stepparents were classified as destructive. The parents in nondestructive families, in contrast, coped better with the stresses of their youngsters' adolescence and adjustment problems by disavowing coercion, offering greater supportiveness and administering less punishment.

All of these studies of distressed families illustrate one thing, whether the original source of distress is the external environment, a parent's mental illness, a child's physical handicap, or a child's behavior problems: distressed families find themselves with many different and interrelated problems for both the individual family members and the family group as a whole.

PARENT-CHILD INTERACTION

Patterns of interaction in normal families as well as in these distressed families can be traced to characteristics of child, of parent, and of the external environment. Families low in conflict tend to be relatively free from external sources of stress; to have children old enough to understand the requirements of cooperation or compliance; to have resolved earlier conflicts satisfactorily; and to engage often in activities where all family members contribute to a goal (Maccoby and Martin, 1983).

No family operates in total isolation from its environment, and this environment may have either positive or negative effects. External events serve as strong sources of stress and support to families. Stress preoccupies parents, and parents who are preoccupied play less with their young children and stimulate, support, and help them less. With very young children, parents do not interact less, but their interactions are more peremptory, critical, and interfering (Zussman, 1980). Stress causes some mothers to act irritably and aversively to their children and to keep on acting aversively; it causes other mothers to withdraw from interaction (Forgatch and Wieder, cited in Patterson, 1982).

Within the family, children influence what their parents do and vice versa: interactions and relationships are two-way streets. Even infants, as we saw in Chapter 5, are skillful in drawing their parents to them when they wish. Older children constantly initiate interactions with their parents and help to determine how often they will be disciplined for breaking rules. But parents not only react to what their children do, they react according to how they interpret the child's actions. Mothers of hyperactive boys who are put on medication to control the hyperactivity, for example, typically need time to adjust their perceptions and their behavior toward their now more manageable sons (Bell, 1977). One psychological variable that affects parents' perceptions of their children's action is the parents' locus of control—or how much the parent feels that he or she is in control of the environment rather than the reverse. In one series of investigations by Daphne Bugenthal (Bugenthal, Caporael, and Shennum, 1980; Bugenthal and Shennum, 1981), experimental confederates, who were children aged 7 to 9, were instructed to act uncooperatively toward an adult in a staged construction task. Adults with an internal locus of control responded with negative comments and a more assertive tone of voice; adults who did not have this sense of control over the environment did not grow more assertive, but let the children go on acting unruly.

Children's temperaments also influence the nature of parent-child interactions. Mothers of difficult children do more controlling, warning, prohibiting, removing of objects, and asserting of their power than mothers of children with easy dispositions. Difficult children in turn tend to persist in their troublesome behavior longer than other children do and to ignore, protest, or to fuss at their mother's attempts to control them (Bates, 1980). In a longitudinal study of infants between 12 and 18 months old, Eleanor Maccoby and Carol Jacklin (in press) found that mothers of difficult babies tended to hold and comfort them more than did mothers of easier children. But mothers of difficult sons tended to teach them less and to withdraw from socializing them. This tendency to withdraw has also shown up in a study of older boys (Olweus, 1980) whose mothers were more permissive toward aggression than other mothers were. David Buss (1981) found that parents of especially active children tended to get into power struggles with them and that their mothers had trouble establishing good working relationships with them. Fathers had less trouble dealing with active sons than mothers, Buss found, tending to dramatize their activity and joke about their pranks, whereas mothers tended to act hostilely.

Parents' requests and demands of children form strings of interactions that depend in great part on how the children respond. If a child complies with mild pressure from the mother, the interaction may end there. But a child who does not comply is often met with a mother's redoubled efforts at control. If families are to avoid excessive conflict, children must learn to comply with mild pressure from parents. As children approach their second birthday, parents tend to perceive them as increasingly competent and assertive. They refuse more of their children's demands and expect from them a minimal degree of compliance and cooperation. During the second year, children can more effectively convey their wishes to their mothers, and mothers grow more responsive in turn (Bronson, 1974). Gradually, mothers and children engage in more and more attempts to influence one another. Which partner originates these attempts, of course, varies

Authoritative parents set firm limits on their children's behavior but treat the youngsters with respect, explaining carefully and emphatically the reasons for restrictions. Authoritarian parents simply apply force to shape their children's behavior.

according to the situation. Only with increasing maturity does the child even begin to understand the notions of cooperation and compliance. When children generally comply with other people's requests, they show that they have begun to understand how social rules operate (Maccoby and Martin, 1983). How soon and how consistently children comply with their mothers' requests depend on the rela-

LONG-TERM CONSEQUENCES OF MOTHER-INFANT INTERACTION

Do mothers and infants who get along well continue to get along well as they grow older? Do mothers and infants who get along poorly continue on their course as well? These were two of the questions John Martin (1981) raised in a longitudinal study that started with 49 10-month-olds and their middle-class mothers. For each pair, Martin focused on the balance of power, style of physical contact, the mother's teaching style, and the child's trust in the mother.

One of the first things Martin measured was the intensity of interaction in each pair. After each mother and infant entered a room, the infant was placed amid some toys on the floor and later in a high chair. The mother was given two long questionnaires to fill out. Through a one-way mirror, observers monitored the infants' touching, vocalizing, smiling, looking, fussing, and crying. When the children were 22 months old, they returned with their mothers for another assessment in the laboratory. First, mothers were asked to try to get their toddlers to laugh as much as possible during a 2-minute period, then, to quiet their toddlers, and, finally, to get them to talk. They were also asked to teach the children how to put away blocks, how to use a toy mailbox, and how to play a toy xylophone. The mothers again filled out a questionnaire as their children looked on, and the children finally were tempted by a moving toy to leave their mothers' view. From all of these tasks with the 22-month-olds, Martin derived measures of children's compliance, coerciveness, and willingness to explore and of mothers' teaching style and closeness of physical contact. Finally, when the children were 42 months old, they and their mothers went through another battery of tasks: measuring the child's height, cooperating in a game of marbles, feeding the child a cookie, leaving the child alone in the room for 1 minute, and so on. From the mother and child's behavior in these tasks, Martin derived more measures: child compliance and ability to sit and wait, child's degree of trust, mother's teaching style and firmness.

Martin had made several related hypotheses about the mutual influence of mothers and children. First, he hypothesized that children's compliance with their mothers' demands would depend on temperamental characteristics of the children and the mothers' trustworthiness and cooperativeness. In support of the hypothesis, he found that for boys, compliance at 22 months was predicted by responsive mothering and a low level of infant demands at 10 months. By 42 months, however, compliance bore less relation to the boys' temperamental level of demandingness than to the boys' history of interaction with their mothers. For girls, greater compliance at 22 months was predicted by greater involvement by the mother and a less demanding infant at 10 months.

Second, Martin hypothesized that children grow coercive when they feel that their mothers have not cooperated with them or provided what they want and need. This hypothesis was supported for boys but not for girls. Mothers who were responsive to their 10-month-old sons tended to have less coercive 42-month-olds. Third, Martin hypothesized that cycles of uncooperative, coercive behavior develop between some mothers and children. Supporting this hypothesis, he found that mothers' firmness caused sons to grow more coercive, and children's noncompliance and demandingness caused their mothers to be more manipulative.

Finally, Martin hypothesized that children's trust in their mothers is a function of the children's temperamental characteristics as well as of their mothers' behavior. Willingness to explore (using the mother as a secure base) was the measure of trust Martin used. It turned out to be predicted by infants' demandingness at 10 months as well as their mothers' responsiveness and involvement.

Thus Martin's study illustrates the complex interplay of characteristics in interactions between mothers and children and the complex accommodations each must make as their relationship develops.

tionship mother and child have established and on the mother's skill. In the toddler period, securely attached children are more compliant than insecurely attached children (Matas et al., 1978), and mothers who closely monitor the child's attention and adapt their demands to it—first by capturing the child's attention and then by narrowing down their demands to the task at hand—procure more compliance (Schaffer and Crook, 1980). At later ages, too, the most cooperative and least disobedient children are those whose mothers are highly involved, positive, and affectionate (Hatfield, Ferguson, and Alpert, 1967). In general, observations of parents and children suggest that compliance and cooperation flourish where they are given mutually and that parents who respect their child's individuality and competence, who explain and reason rather than physically punish or coerce, engender cooperativeness and compliance (Baumrind and Black, 1967; Lytton, 1979; Minton et al., 1971). It may be more accurate to describe family interaction not as someone doing something *to* someone else, but as people interacting *with* people. Parents and children regulate one another and themselves, even as external events impinge on all of them.

SUMMARY

1. The first, focused love relation the infant forms is called an attachment. This relationship, most often formed first with the mother, develops over time and may be secure, avoidant, or ambivalent. Psychologists can test the nature of children's attachment by placing them in an unfamiliar room and watching their reactions to their mother's leaving and return.

2. To foster the development of a secure attachment in her infant, it is important that the mother be loving and warm, give tender physical care, smile and laugh, and enjoy feeding, talking about, and tending the infant. When mothers are abusive, unresponsive, or neglectful, their children are likely to develop insecure attachments. The quality of attachment depends in part on children's temperamental characteristics and in part on the quality of mothering.

3. From the time they are about 1 year old, children begin to separate themselves from their mothers, show increasingly less distress at brief separations, seek less physical contact, and grow into increasingly autonomous, self-reliant individuals.

4. In general, fathers spend less time than mothers taking care of their children. When they are with their children, however, fathers play more and do more roughhousing than mothers. Fathers are likely to become more involved with their children once they are past infancy.

5. As adolescents strive for independence, the nature of their relationship with parents changes. This change may cause the adolescent to feel conflict, ambivalence, or unhappiness. Parents may grant their adolescent sons more freedom than they grant their daughters.

6. Children ordinarily are interested in their siblings, tend to imitate them, and invest strong emotions in their relationship. Often this relationship is an ambivalent one. Siblings may differ because their parents treat them differently and because the children create different environments for each other.

7. Divorce is a source of stress for parents and children. In its wake, family relations and routines break down, parenting deteriorates, and children—sons especially—seem difficult and unruly. By 2 years after a divorce, parents may have reestablished more balanced relations with their children, and children may have accommodated themselves to their new family situation. Boys seem still to suffer, however; they are more likely to have problems with school, relationships, and self-esteem.

8. Working mothers spend less time in childcare than housewives do, but the time they spend with their children may be especially intensely focused. Working mothers seem to talk more and pay more attention to their young children. Daughters of working mothers tend to see them as models for independence, self-confidence, and social competence; but sons in two-income families tend to be less securely attached to their fathers, to do less well in school, and to score lower on intelligence tests than sons in traditional families.

9. Distress can visit families in many forms: chronic physical or mental illness, divorce, financial problems, handicaps, children who are out of control. Stress in any form tends to make parents less emotionally available to their children, and children may suffer in a variety of ways from this neglect. Although a problem may originate in one member of a family, it rarely fails to spread throughout the entire family. Most distressed families have many problems, and it is exceedingly difficult for investigators to separate out any single "cause" from this welter of problems. Prolonged emotional disturbance, unstable family organization, poverty, and low social status all put children at high risk for developmental problems. Mothers tend to bear the brunt of family distress. It is they who act as crisis managers; it is they who spend the most time responding to family members' needs and demands.

Mothers and children can enter into destructive chains of interaction that neither can break.

10. Parents and children profoundly affect how the other behaves both in the short and the long run. Parents' perceptions and responsiveness, the temperamental characteristics of children, and the external environment all contribute to the nature and quality of family interactions. Families low in conflict tend to be relatively free from external sources of stress, to have children old enough to understand the requirements of cooperation and compliance, to have resolved earlier conflicts satisfactorily, and to engage in activities where all contribute to a goal.

KEY TERMS

Attachment	Empathy	Terrible twos	Instrumental role
Set goal	Surrogate mother	Expressive role	Midolescence
Strange situation			

SUGGESTED READINGS

Ainsworth, Mary D. S., Blehar, Mary C., Waters, Everett, and Wall, Sally. *Patterns of Attachment: A Psychological Study of the Strange Situation.* Hillsdale, N.J.: Lawrence Erlbaum Associates, 1978. Details Ainsworth's assessment procedure for studying qualitative differences in infant-mother attachment and reviews the results of research using the strange situation assessment procedure.

Bowlby, John. *Attachment and Loss,* vol. 1, *Attachment.* New York: Basic Books, 1969. The first of Bowlby's influential trilogy on the theory of attachment; a seminal book that inspired a whole line of research on children's early social relations with their mother.

Kamerman, Sheila B., and Hayes, Cheryl D. (Eds.). *Families That Work: Children in a Changing World.* Washington, D.C.: National Academy Press, 1982. An excellent review of research on changing patterns of parents' work and family structure and their effects on child development.

Lamb, Michael (Ed.). *The Role of the Father in Child Development* (2nd ed.). New York: Wiley, 1981. A diverse collection of articles that describe how fathers affect their children's development.

Lewis, Michael, and Rosenblum, Leonard A. (Eds.). *The Child and Its Family.* New York:

Plenum, 1979. One of a series of books, each consisting of the collected papers presented at an annual conference in child development. The papers, which reflect current thinking of the foremost researchers on each topic, are rather technical but worth reading selectively.

Parke, Ross D. *Fathers.* Cambridge: Harvard University Press, 1977. A comprehensive but quite readable presentation that reviews the research on the roles of the father, how they differ from those of the mother, and what effects they have on children's development.

Rutter, Michael. *The Qualities of Mothering: Maternal Deprivation Reassessed.* New York: Aronson, 1974. Excellent review of research on important questions about mothering: How many caregivers should a baby have? Does the mother have to be there all the time? How significant is the presence of the father?

Wallerstein, Judith S., and Kelly, Joan B. *Surviving the Breakup: How Children and Parents Cope with Divorce.* New York: Basic Books, 1980. A detailed account of the results of the California Children of Divorce Project, which shows how children of different ages cope with this stressful life event.

CHAPTER 13

FRIENDS

As children develop, they deal ever more often and with ever greater sophistication with those who make up their social world. They form relationships with adults beyond their immediate family, among them, babysitters, teachers, and neighbors, relationships that are profoundly important in shaping their lives. They play and, later, cooperate with other children. They progress from the more solitary and immature actions, forms of communication, and social understanding of early childhood and learn more about the social roles that they and other people take. They come to understand the complexities of social interaction, to understand how others affect them, and how they affect others. The 2-year-old who cries, grabs at toys, and communicates in the most rudimentary way somehow turns into the sensitive, resourceful, and sociable 12-year-old, as the child both actively gathers and passively absorbs social information.

FRIENDLY ADULTS

STRANGERS

We have already discussed in Chapter 5 the fearful and wary reactions of infants to strangers. But what if the stranger tries to make friends with the infant? Can the stranger succeed? If the stranger just sits and says or does nothing but smiles responsively, children look with curiosity and interest and tend to smile at the stranger, which is their way of exploring the social situation (Eckerman and Whatley, 1975; Rheingold and Eckerman, 1973). Inge Bretherton (1978) found that when Mother was nearby, children welcomed the attention of an unfamiliar woman who sat down and invited them to play. They spoke to the stranger, laughed in play, and spontaneously offered her toys. They became increasingly and significantly more active and cooperative in their play as the exchanges proceeded. And they were more likely to initiate some activity with the stranger if she was paying attention to them and not talking with the mother. Hildy Ross and Barbara Goldman (1977b) found that when the stranger played actively with the child—gesturing, talking, and offering toys—the child spent more time near her, looked at her, touched her, played with the toys, and initiated games with her. One way for a stranger to approach a year-old infant

who has been afraid or puzzled earlier is to copy some bit of activity, such as a game, in which the mother usually engages with the baby (Rafman, 1974).

When the stranger can spend more time with the child, she can also improve her relations with the infant and even earn his or her affection. Donald Fleener (1973) had a research assistant spend 2½ hours a day for 3 days feeding, playing, and talking to each infant in a sample of 10- to 14-month-olds. At the end of the time, the infants drew close to the former "stranger," touched her, and cried when they were apart—though indications of attachment were not as intense as those for their mothers. Henry Ricciuti (1974) observed infants after they had spent several months in an experimental, half-day day-care program. When they were 7 months of age, their day caregiver left them briefly. The reaction of the infants was similar to that when the mother departed. They had formed a relationship with the caregiver. Finally, Wendy Roedell and Ronald Slaby (1977) gave 3-month-olds 3 weeks of relating to a "proximal" stranger, who rocked and patted the infant; a "neutral" stranger, who made no response at all; and a "distal" stranger, who smiled, talked, played, and stayed close but did not touch the infant. By the end of 3 weeks, the infants were spending most of their time with the distal stranger. When given the opportunity to choose a partner—by rolling over to her on a specially devised wheeled scooter—they chose the distal stranger over the neutral stranger and the neutral stranger over the proximal one. The researchers suggest that the toucher was least preferred because she violated the infant's expectations about interaction, was more difficult to control, and was not as responsive as the distal player.

Thus, interactions with strangers are rich and varied, and positive reactions can be promoted with care and a little good sense. A stranger is not inevitably feared. Without considerable earlier experience, the infant's exchanges with a stranger will not be as complex, smooth, or synchronous as those with Mother (Fafouti-Milenković and Užgiris, 1979). But given time, infants can clearly develop significant relations with adults other than Mother and Father.

Toddlers, too, given the chance, form such relationships with other adults, though their affection for them seldom competes with what they feel for their parents. From ages 1 to 3, children usually interact with strangers only when Mother is present. About the age of 3, children begin to socialize with unfamiliar adults even when Mother is not around (Maccoby and Feldman, 1972). When strangers first appear, children look at them and recognize them as young or old, male or female, tall or short, and so on. The child usually indicates interest and some excitement. Then the stranger does something—approaches, smiles, speaks, invites the child to come over. This is interpreted by the child in the context of whether he or she regards the person as normal and natural or peculiar and potentially scary. The child either approaches or avoids the stranger accordingly.

If the stranger is attentive and friendly, the child is likely to respond in kind (Connolly and Smith, 1972). If he or she touches the child, the child's reaction, either positive or negative, is heightened. The child will probably fear the vigorous and gruff male stranger (Clarke-Stewart, 1978b; Lemly and Schwarz, 1979; Weisberg, 1975). Younger children prefer calm, cuddly physical contact to tickling or bouncing. Older ones like to be tickled (Weisberg, 1975). But whatever the form of contact, it is important that it be "natural," something familiar to the child and comfortable for the adult. A child whose relationship with Mother is secure and who has had pleasant experiences with strangers is likely to approach with interest and to become friendly and cooperative during succeeding encounters with a warm and responsive new acquaintance.

Individual children vary, of course, in their friendliness toward strangers. One factor that predicts their friendliness is how warm and friendly their mothers are to a stranger (Babad, Alexander, and Babad, 1983; Feiring, Lewis, and Starr, 1984). Another predictor is a child's own experiences in day care or at home. A study by Alison Clarke-Stewart (1984) showed that preschool children who were in day care and who had had more and positive experiences with adults outside of their immediate families were more sociable and competent with unfamiliar adults and were better liked by them in return than were children who had been cared for by their parents alone. Children's reactions to strangers depend also on the context within which they meet the stranger. Young children are likelier to feel friendly when they are in a familiar

setting, like home, than when they are in an unfamiliar setting, like a university laboratory or "playroom." Children are also likelier to be friendly when their mother is available (Campos, Emde, Gaensbauer, and Sorce, 1973; Greenberg and Marvin, 1982) and when she communicates positively to them about the stranger (Feinman and Lewis, 1983).

TEACHERS

School-age children may find an adult friend in a teacher. But teachers present new challenges, for they do not feel the same way about all of their students, no matter how even-handed they try to be. Teachers' feelings affect how they act toward their students, of course. By interviewing teachers at a school with white, middle-class students, Melvin Silberman (1971) found four distinct attitudes teachers have toward their students.

1. *Attachment.* Teachers feel attachment toward students who are sources of pleasure to them, students who fulfill their personal needs and make few demands on their energies. When these students come up with ideas, the teacher is likely to give them credit and public praise: "Class, Robbie just told me an excellent idea for making a three-dimensional poster. Robbie, would you tell the class your idea?"

2. *Concern.* Teachers feel concerned about students who are demanding yet receptive and appreciative. "She can see what you're trying to show her and really take off." Believing that these students are truly worthy of their professional attention, teachers respond to them openly and frequently in the classroom.

3. *Indifference.* Students who do not make a vivid impression on the teacher for their ability, responsiveness, needs, or misbehavior tend to be nearly forgotten, existing on the "periphery of the teacher's vision." As one teacher told Silberman, "I really tend to forget she's in the room. She's neither a goody-goody nor a baddy-baddy." When such a student reminded her teacher that the class was late for gym, she was brushed off; then, a moment later, the teacher hurriedly organized the class so that the children were able to leave immediately for gym.

4. *Rejection.* Some students are very demanding, so much so that their claims on the teacher's atten-

Teachers almost always have favorite pupils to whom they give more attention and help than they do others.

tion, often coupled with disruptive behavior, are perceived as illegitimate and overwhelming. "He has problems that are beyond the scope of the classroom teacher. I've given up." "His arrogance makes him impossible to deal with." Rejected students, Silberman reported after observing teacher dealings with them, could do no right. They were under continual surveillance, and most of the teacher's interactions with them consisted of efforts to control them, reprimands, prohibitions, or blaming them in front of the class. Even when the rejected student asked for help—"What can I write about?"—the teacher's reaction was negative and unhelpful—"Oh, you'll think of something, or is that asking too much?" Silberman's interviews and observations make it clear that students in the same classroom do not share a common experience, simply because the teacher does not feel the same way about them.

Various investigators have attempted to discover what qualities of children make teachers have different attitudes toward them. Sex and sex-related behavior are one major source of disapproval and approval. Boys, being more aggressive, tend to incur the disapproval of the teacher, who is likely to be a woman. The behavior of girls is usually more in keeping with the teacher's standards of good classroom behavior, but girls have fewer contacts with their teachers in the classroom (Meyer and Thompson, 1956). Teachers spend much of their time actively trying to socialize boys by controlling them and tempering their aggressive behavior. In terms of Silberman's four attitudes, boys seem more likely to be rejected or arouse concern; teachers become attached to girls or treat them with indifference.

Children's physical attractiveness, especially their facial appeal (Adams and Cohen, 1974; Delefes and Jackson, 1972) as well as where they sit in the classroom (Adams and Biddle, 1967) affects the number and type of interactions between child and teacher. The bright, well-adjusted, high-achieving, attractive student who sits closer to the teacher seems to receive the most attention and praise.

The traits that favorably impress most teachers—activity, behavior that is not disruptive or overly hostile, responsibility toward the group—tend to be more typical of middle-class children. In their review of research on classroom socialization, John Glidewell and his associates (Glidewell, Kantor,

Smith, and Stringer, 1966) concluded that middle-class behavior is more important than middle-class status as such. Teachers give as much attention to the lower-class as the middle-class pupil, but much of the attention is paid to controlling behavior and to speech patterns that cause communication problems.

PEER INTERACTION

Interactions with adults have the potential for being intense, instructional, and stable. Adults do not usually set conditions on interactions—"If you give me some candy, I'll play with you." Their interactions are both physical and verbal, full of care and concern. The chains of adult-child interactions tend to be smooth and relatively long. And because the adult still carries the primary responsibility for the exchanges, they are relatively predictable and controllable. Interactions with peers, in contrast, are more often physical and playful, spontaneous and unpredictable, casual and transitory. Children do many different things together: play, teach, cooperate, help; punch, hit and kick. What they do together depends on their age, sex, and individual quirks, on the time of day, the time of year, the place and space.

PLAY

Even infants interact with other children and accept unfamiliar children more readily than unfamiliar adults. Other children's small size and interesting behavior may make them less threatening and

Infants do not really play "together" because their social skills are still poor. But they do come together over attractive objects.

more attractive to infants (Lewis and Brooks, 1974). Observers in the 1930s noted many expressions of infants' friendliness, such as touching, cooing, exchanging toys, and cooperating in play (Bühler, 1933; Maudry and Nekula, 1939). M. Margaret Shirley (1933) described the activities of twins Freddie and Winnie:

At 21 weeks Freddie turned and reached for Winnie, who was lying beside him on the bed. Accidentally he stuck two fingers in her mouth, and she chewed on them, much to his amusement. In their 51st week, according to the mother's report, Freddie was sitting on the bed playing with two safety pins clasped together. He held them out to Winnie, who was sitting beside him. Just as she reached and touched them he jerked them away, and both babies laughed; they continued this for some time (Shirley, 1933, pp. 83–84).

After the studies done in the 1930s, researchers neglected the peer relations of infants until the mid-1970s. Their recent studies suggest that infants are fascinated by others like themselves and that those who have contact become more friendly as the months go by. When toys are involved, infants may engage in a give-and-take game or a struggle (Eckerman, 1973; Mueller and Lucas, 1975; Vandell, Wilson, and Buchanan, 1979). Infants usually have more to do with their peers after they are 12 months old.

Patterns of Peer Play

Toddler Play: From 1 to 2. Although babies 12 months old smile and laugh at each other, in most of their play they are emotionally neutral. During their second year, babies begin to act less neutral. Expressions of both positive and negative feelings grow increasingly frequent in the second year (Ross and Goldman, 1977a), although up to 70 percent of toddlers' play is still serious in tone (Mueller and Brenner, 1977; Rubenstein and Howes, 1976).

Ross and Goldman (Goldman and Ross, 1978; Ross and Goldman, 1977a) videotaped the meetings of unacquainted pairs of 1- and 2-year-olds. Despite the fact that the children had never played with each other before, in just 13 hours of tape, over 2000 explicitly positive social overtures were observed. These were mostly positive vocalizations and attempts to give or receive a toy. The positive overtures were more common than withdrawing, hitting, fighting, crying, or swiping. Even at this early age, the children initiated 36 spontaneous peer games. These games required a considerable degree of sustained mutual attention, smiling and laughing, repetition, and alternation of turns: 12 were reciprocal ball games, 9 imitative games, and in 15 of the games, the youngsters took complementary roles—tickler-ticklee, toucher-touchee, giver-taker, actor-laugher.

Carol Eckerman, Judith Whatley, and Stuart Kutz (1975) also found that pairs of children of this age range who were brought into a laboratory playroom interacted with each other frequently, positively, and in preference to interacting with their mothers, who were also present in the playroom. The children exchanged toys, imitated each other, and coordinated their play.

A third study of peer interaction, by Wanda Bronson (1975), brought toddlers together in play groups of three or four. As in the other studies, the children's positive interactions were more frequent than negative ones. But even though they were members of a group, the children still played together in pairs. The pairs in these larger groups of children had more frequent peevish or aggressive exchanges than the pairs of children observed by Ross and Goldman and by Eckerman and her colleagues. The presence of additional children may have caused additional stress.

The toddlers in all three studies had more positive than negative interactions, but the play of the older toddlers was more intentional and lasted longer and was also more varied, intense, coordinated, and complex. Play consisted of more games with a greater number of turns.

These three studies examined the play of children who were strangers. Edward Mueller and Thomas Lucas (1975) followed the play of five firstborn boys—Bernie, Larry, Noah, Jacob, and Don—who met together two mornings a week for 3 months when they were about 13 to 18 months old. The researchers identified three stages of peer contact as these boys became older and better acquainted. In the first stage, one child's curious examination of an object attracted the attention of the other boys. But there was no interaction. If one child acted, the others watched; if one boy gestured or vocalized to another, he was ignored. In the second stage, these social bids were responded to. Often, in the beginning, a second boy imitated the first; later there were longer and longer interaction chains. In the third stage, the little boys tried to elicit not imitation but the appropriate complementary response—a take to a give, a catch to a throw, a run to a chase (Table 13.1).

Physical objects seem central to the smooth functioning of early peer interaction. This attention to objects was noted by Charlotte Bühler before 1933 in one of the earliest observational studies:

> In the majority of cases, infants in the second half year of life will come into contact. They will touch each other, smile, squeal, and utter sounds, and perhaps they will begin to play with each other's clothes or feet, or make movements in front of each other. They may forget each other after a while. Persistent contact, however, will be formed only on another basis, that is, the presence of a material in which both children are equally interested (Bühler, 1933, p. 399).

Since then the importance of objects in peer interaction has been stressed by Mueller and his associates. Some social behaviors, such as give and take, *require* the presence of an object. But even beyond this, Mueller has suggested, toys may act as either a carrot, attracting a peer, or a stick, forcing the child to notice the peer who takes away his toy (Mueller and Vandell, 1979). As Bronson (1975) notes, the object of toddler sociability seems to be to *do* together rather than to *be* together. Activity with things was the predominant mode of play for the acquainted boys observed by Mueller, and 88 percent of their activity involved an object. Toys are the prime currency of social exchange for toddlers, allowing them to show, give, retrieve, and appropriate. At first, the toy is the focal point of the interaction. Later, it is used to mediate the social interaction, and the peer becomes the focus. The toy remains essential as the instigator or facilitator, however. For example:

> Initially drawn to the train Larry was pulling, Russell began to follow Larry and then to imitate the course and direction of Larry's movements. At this point Larry became interested in Russell's running. Alternating rounds of lead and follow, with happy sounding cries and screams, grew out of Russell's initial pursuit of the object (Mueller, 1979, p. 89).

TABLE 13.1
THREE STAGES OF EARLY PEER PLAY

	Stage 1: Object-centered contacts	
Time, seconds	**Noah, 14½ months**	**Larry, 16 months**
0	At engine alone, toots horn once.[a]	Approaches. Hits engine with toy.
	Toots horn once.	Grasps steering handle. Looks at Jacob's face. Steps backward.
17	Toots horn, 4 times.	Grasps steering handle. Steps back again.
	Grasps steering handle.	Grasps steering handle.
34	Reaches for horn, withdraws Bernie's hand.	VOCALIZES AT NOAH'S FACE.
66	Looks at Bernie's face.	Departs.
84	Toots horn, 12 times, then departs.	

	Stage 2: Contingent interactions	
Time, seconds	**Bernie, 13 months**	**Larry, 15 months**
34	VOCALIZES "DA," LOOKING AT LARRY.	LAUGHS, LOOKING AT BERNIE.
40	VOCALIZES "DA," LOOKING AT LARRY.	LAUGHS, LOOKING AT BERNIE.
43	VOCALIZES "DA," LOOKING AT LARRY.	LAUGHS, LOOKING AT BERNIE.
47½	VOCALIZES "DA," LOOKING AT LARRY.	LAUGHS, LOOKING AT BERNIE.
50	VOCALIZES "DA," LOOKING AT LARRY.	LAUGHS, LOOKING AT BERNIE. LAUGHS (IN FORCED WAY) 3 MORE TIMES, LOOKING AT BERNIE.
54	VOCALIZES "DA," LOOKING AT LARRY.	LAUGHS, LOOKING AT BERNIE.
59	VOCALIZES "DA," LOOKING AT LARRY.	LAUGHS, LOOKING AT BERNIE.
62½	VOCALIZES "DA," LOOKING AT LARRY.	LAUGHS, LOOKING AT BERNIE.
66	VOCALIZES "DA," LOOKING AT LARRY.	LAUGHS, LOOKING AT BERNIE.
69	Turns and walks away.	LAUGHS, (IN FORCED WAY), LOOKING AT BERNIE AND WATCHES HIM LEAVE ROOM.

	Stage 3: Complementary exchanges	
Time, seconds	**Bernie, 16 months**	**Larry, 18 months**
32	LOOKS AT LARRY AND PICKS UP PAPER. Puts paper to wall. Releases paper. Picks up paper from floor. OFFERS PAPER AND VOCALIZES TO LARRY.	
51		RECEIVES PAPER FROM BERNIE. Puts paper to wall. Releases paper. BACKS AWAY AND LOOKS AT BERNIE.
65	POINTS AT PAPER AND LOOKS AT LARRY.	LOOKS AT BERNIE AND PICKS UP PAPER. Puts paper to wall. Releases paper. BACKS AWAY AND LOOKS AT BERNIE.
72	Departs.	
81		LOOKS AT BERNIE AND PICKS UP PAPER. Puts paper to wall. Releases paper and departs, following Bernie.

Note: [a] Simultaneous events appear on the same line; socially directed behavior is in capital letters.

Source: Adapted from Mueller and Lucas, 1975, pp. 232–231, 243, 250–251.

Preschool Play: 2 to 5 Years. As children get older, their social contacts grow increasingly frequent, and they pair off or form groups (Charlesworth and Hartup, 1967; Lougee, Grueneich, and Hartup, 1977). Their play continues to be more positive than negative; one group of researchers found the ratio of positive to negative interactions among preschool children to be about 8:1 (Walters, Pearce, and Dahms, 1957). A classic study of peer interaction in the preschool period was done by Mildred Parten in the 1920s. She observed 34 children 2 to 5 years old in free-play periods in nursery school and identified five ways children play in the company of others (Parten, 1932, 1933).

1. *Solitary play.* The child plays alone with toys other than those used by the nearby children. He or she takes no notice and makes no effort to be close to them.

2. *Onlooker play.* The child spends most of his or her time watching other children play. The child often talks to them, asking questions and giving suggestions, but the child does not participate.

3. *Parallel play.* The child plays independently with toys like those of the child next to him or her, but their activities are unrelated. The child plays beside another child but not with him or her.

4. *Associative play.* The child plays with another child. They converse about their common, if not identical, activity and borrow and loan toys. But each child acts on his or her own. The children do not have a shared goal.

5. *Cooperative play.* The children play together and help one another in an activity that engages both of them. There is a division of roles and a sharing of goals.

Parten found that as children grow older they engage in more **associative play** and **cooperative play.** Her hierarchy has held up reasonably well in similar recent studies (e.g., Rubin, Watson, and Jambor, 1978; Smith, 1978). There is definitely an increase in associative and cooperative play and a decrease in solitary play as children grow older and become more sociable and socially skilled. **Parallel play** *predominates* only with 2-year-olds or young 3-year-olds, but older 3- and 4-year-olds may still play this way. Between the ages of 2 and 4, children also gradually stop staring, crying, sucking, and running away from encounters with their peers, and they engage in more conversation (Smith, 1978).

Catherine Garvey (1974) has studied the details of peer interaction in the preschool period with the benefit of modern technology. She videotaped and

These preschoolers are playing cooperatively with wooden blocks. As they play together, they share goals and divide their roles.

then analyzed 20-minute play sessions of pairs of children 3½ to 5½ years old. About 66 percent of each session was spent in mutual engagement. Much of the children's play was physical and object related, but there were several other kinds.

1. *Ritual play.* Repetitive, rhythmic exchanges or turns, with exaggerated intonation, distorted rhythms, broad gestures.

Amy (4 years old) I can see this.
Ben (4 years old) I can't see Amy.
Amy I can see Ben.
Ben I can't see Amy.
Amy I can see Ben.
Ben I can't see Amy.
Amy I can see Ben (slight pause).
Ben Can't see Amy.
Amy Can't see Ben.
Ben Can't see Amy. Trashcan! (Garvey, 1974, p. 177).

Such activity is clearly play—enjoyable, spontaneous, and engaged in for its own sake. *All* children had at least one episode of **ritual play,** but the rituals of the older children were shorter.

2. *Language play.* Rhyming, nonsense words, work play, beginning in casual conversation. Only the older preschool children engaged in **language play.**

Boy (5 years old) Hey.
Girl (5 years old) Mother mear (laugh) mother smear.
Boy (laugh).
Girl I said mother smear mother near mother tear mother dear (laugh).
Boy Peer.
Girl Fear.
Boy Pooper.
Girl What?
Boy Pooper. Now that's a . . . that's a good name (Garvey, 1974, p. 69).

3. *Pretend play.* Playing out roles—house, school, doctor's office, and so on. Children 3 years old had simpler versions of **pretend play,** usually playing house with a mother, a father, and a baby.

Girl (3 years old) Say, "Go to sleep now."
Boy (3 years old) Go to sleep now.
Girl Why? (whining).
Boy Baby . . .
Girl Why?
Boy Because.
Girl No say "Because" (emphatically).
Boy Because! (emphatically).
Girl Why? Because why?
Boy Not good. You bad.
Girl Why?
Boy 'Cause you spill your milk.
Girl No, 'cause I bit somebody.
Boy Yes, you did.
Girl Say, "Go to sleep. Put your head down" (sternly).
Boy Put your head down (sternly).
Girl No.
Boy Yes.
Girl No.
Boy Yes. Okay, I will spank you. Bad boy (spanks her).
Girl My head's up (giggles). I want my teddy bear (petulant voice).
Boy No, your teddy bear go away (sternly).
Girl Why?
Boy 'Cause he does (walks off with teddy bear) (Garvey, 1974, p. 83).

Older children added grandparents, siblings, and other elaborations and subtleties. All the young pairs of unacquainted children who seem to "hit it off" in another study (Gottman and Parkhurst, 1980) engaged in well-developed domestic pretend play.

Factors Influencing Peer Play

Sex. Whether the play group or pair is made up of boys, girls, or both makes a significant difference in the nature of peer play. Even as early as the preschool period, children tend to select same-sex playmates (Parten, 1933) and to be more sociable to them (Jacklin and Maccoby, 1978; Langlois, Gottfried, and Seay, 1973). Investigators have consistently observed that at this age all-boy

One measure of a child's social skills and, in consequence, popularity with other children, is how the child attempts to join ongoing interactions. The entering child always risks rejection from the others, but rejection is far more likely if the entrant is too quick to take center stage. The boy in this picture seems to be making the cautious, sensitive approach most likely to gain him access to the girls' reading group.

groups or pairs are more vigorous in their play. Their play consists of more rough and tumble, wrestling, fights, and tugs-of-war over toys as well as more frequent independent, assertive, and autonomous movement. Girls, by contrast, are more orderly when they play together, more sedentary, quiet, and cooperative; they play in smaller groups and stay closer to teachers and equipment. But when children are put together in mixed-sex groups in nursery school, girls become more independent and boys become less destructive (DiPietro, 1981; Greenberg and Peck, 1974; Smith and Connolly, 1972).

Setting and Materials. In their own homes, children initiate more positive as well as more aggressive social interactions than they do at another child's house (Jeffers and Lore, 1979). Outdoors, there is more running, jumping, laughing, smiling—and less aggression (Smith and Connolly, 1972). Indoors, materials like sand, clay, paper, and paints encourage parallel play; dolls and a playhouse promote cooperation (Parten, 1933).

Toy guns bring out aggressive play (Turner and Goldsmith, 1976), and large equipment encourages social interaction (Mueller, 1979). If only one toy is available, conflicts are more likely (Bühler, 1933; Maudry and Nekula, 1939), but if there are no toys, there is more contacting, smiling, gesturing, and imitating (Eckerman and Whatley, 1977).

Whether adults are present or not also affects play. In other primate species, the young are less vigorous and suppress aggression and sex play in the presence of adults (Rosenblum and Plimpton, 1979; Suomi, 1979). Informal observation suggests that human adults have the same effect on their children. Adults, when they are present, can also deliberately encourage more cooperative play by regarding the child as a member of the group rather than as a competitive individual (Bryan, 1975; Kagan and Madsen, 1971).

The size of the play group affects peer interaction. No matter how big the group is, children younger than 4 or 5 can play only with one other partner at a time (Bronson, 1975; Parten, 1933). Their activities when they are with one companion

are more positive, sustained, and coordinated than when they are in a large group (Bronson, 1975; Mueller, 1979; Vandell, 1975).

Experience. Finally, the amount of experience children have had playing with one another and with other children affects their play. When first introduced to a new child or a new group, preschool-aged children may be shy, cling to their mother, and ignore or even avoid the other child or children. As they spend time together, preschoolers increasingly approach, touch, and stay close to one another (Roopnarine and Field, 1983). After a few play sessions together, most overcome their initial shyness and interact more skillfully, playfully, and vigorously, becoming fully integrated into the group within a few months (McGrew, 1972; Mueller and Brenner, 1977; Smith and Connolly, 1972).

As 3- to 5-year-olds become acquainted, they go through the following steps: (1) show and tell, recounting their special experiences; (2) me tooing, establishing common ground; (3) talking about activities; (4) resolving disagreements; (5) stereotyped pretend play; and (6) idiosyncratic pretend play (Gottman and Parkhurst, 1980). Experience with one peer may also transfer to the first encounter with another peer. Children are more cooperative and competent in play during their first meeting if they have a previous history of being with peers (Lewis, Young, Books, and Michalson, 1975; Lieberman, 1977).

GAMES

In the early grades, most children's out-of-school activities with their peers consist of games, formal and informal. The child who had some difficulty piling up his blocks at 3 is busy practicing for a baseball game at 8. The girl who could just about make it around the nursery school circle for duck-duck-goose is trying in fourth grade to play tennis like Tracy Austin. In between their formal lessons and team games, schoolchildren are playing tag, jacks, king of the mountain, Simon Says, hopscotch, jump rope, ring-a-lievo. Their new mastery of motor skills and their growing interest in peers bring a burst of game activity.

Children still play some of the games Grandma and Grandpa did when they were young. A great many games have enormous antiquity. Jacks have

been found in prehistoric caves in Kiev, and the game is pictured on jars from ancient Greece. Sometimes only the names change. "Walking to Jerusalem" has become "musical chairs." A survey of game preferences for American children over 60 years (Sutton-Smith and Rosenberg, 1971) indicates that in general games have become more informal and that increased adult supervision has made them less rough. But the most significant changes over the years reflect role changes in our culture. The game survey reveals that girls in fourth, fifth, and sixth grades today are more like boys in their game and activity choices than 60 years ago. Girls now often swim and play marbles, fox and hounds, and baseball. They choose more active games at an earlier age, games that used to be the province of boys.

Boys in turn have taken up with increasing fervor even more clearly "masculine" sports and vigorous games, such as football and wrestling. Girls continue to jump rope and play hopscotch and jacks, when they are not showing their skills on the baseball diamond or the basketball court. Girls do not, even now, engage in the warriorlike fantasy games of boys, such as soldiers, cops 'n' robbers, cowboys and Indians. They dress up and imitate the glamor of famous models and stars. They do not imitate domestic activities as much as they used to. They also take more interest in leadership games, such as Simon Says, statues, and follow the leader. With this feminine encroachment on leadership games, the boys' interest has waned. If "Simone" says, Simon won't follow.

Erik Erikson (1977) suggested that in early childhood the small world of manageable toys is a harbor that children establish to return to when they need to overhaul their egos. Children of school age have already moved from this little world, this microsphere, to the macrosphere, the world shared by others. Games are instrumental in this transition. According to Jean Piaget playing games gives children practice with rules and brings them closer to the world of work. Of his three forms of play, sensorimotor, symbolic, and games with rules, only the third sort persists into adulthood. The competitive and cooperative team games of children help them to prepare for later cooperative and competitive activities. The kissing games, which precede actual dating, bridge the typical sex segregation of middle childhood and pave the way for the boy-girl activities that will become significant during adolescence.

Rivka Eifermann (1971) suggests another important function of games, challenge. Children must have the skill and understanding required by the game, yet not be overqualified so that the game is too easy to play. The challenge alters for different games. In competitive games, such as marbles, children vie for the recognition and even envy of other players. In group games, such as soccer, the challenge is to act in effective coordination with others. Success reinforces the child's new and special feelings—"I am growing up."

TEACHING

Although adults most often serve as children's teachers, children can and do teach each other. Educators in the United States have considered peer teaching to confer benefits—better motivation and achievement—on both tutor and tutee. But, as Willard Hartup (1983) has noted in a review of the relevant literature, evidence for the actual rewards of peer teaching is inconsistent. Tutors are most likely to reap rewards in increased self-esteem and positive feelings about school if they tutor for an extended period, are underachievers who are several years older than their tutees, and are carefully trained and supervised. When tutoring does not benefit the tutor, a possible reason is that the tutoring was not pleasurable. The tutoring role confers social status, adults' attention, and children's deference. On the other side of the school desk, tutees stand to improve their knowledge of the subjects covered and their performance on standardized tests (Cloward, 1976; Paoni, 1971; Willis, Morris, and Crowder, 1972). Reading skills are especially likely to improve after sustained individualized instruction, although brief tutoring can also be helpful (East, 1976).

In general children like to teach younger children and to learn from older children. They like tutors of their own sex, although the sex of the tutor is not related to the success of the tutoring. They are somewhat likelier to make advances in achievement with an older tutor, but tutors of their own age can also be effective (Guarnaccia, 1973; Hamblin and Hamblin, 1972; Linton, 1972; Thomas, 1970). In some cases, children are carefully chosen

Children generally like to teach those who are younger and learn from those who are older than they. In tutoring situations like the one pictured here, child tutors seem able to adjust their teaching to the abilities of their young tutees.

and trained as tutors, but in other cases, they spontaneously teach one another. Kindergartners and second-graders, for example, have been observed to approach a classmate for just such spontaneous teaching. In about one-third of these instances, the peer-teacher approached a classmate to offer help (Cooper, Ayers-Lopez, and Marquis, 1982). Children also seem to adjust their teaching to meet their tutees' abilities. Observations of 9- and 10-year-olds, for example, showed that when they tutored children 4 years younger than themselves, they did more in the way of focusing the young tutees' attention, suggesting strategies for learning, giving redundant information, and praising, helping, and assessing the tutees' progress than they did when they tutored children only 2 years younger than they (Ludeke, 1978).

In one recent study of how children compare to adults as teachers of other children, Shari Ellis and Barbara Rogoff (1982), observed middle-class 7-year-olds being taught by either a 9-year-old or an adult. In a room designed to look like a kitchen, the younger children were taught to put groceries on shelves and to sort photographs of common objects into compartments on a tray. Children who had been taught by an adult were better at remembering and generalizing than those who had been taught by an older child. Children taught by the adults correctly placed 68 percent of the items on which they were tested; children taught by older children placed only 45 percent correctly. Adult teachers provided three times as much spoken information as child teachers, although the two groups did not differ in the amounts of nonverbal information they provided. The adult teachers also provided more categorical than item-specific information, and they elicited more participation from the children they were teaching. The child teachers seemed to imitate their own school teachers on the photo-sorting task, using teacherly strategies and language—"That's correct!"—but without their teachers' effectiveness.

COOPERATING, HELPING, AND SHARING

Children who are 1 or 1½ years old may try to comfort people who are crying or hurt, by snuggling, patting, hugging, helping, or feeding them. They offer what they themselves would find comforting—a bottle, a doll, a cookie, their own mother's hand. These young children are clearly sympathetic but do not know how to help. During their second year, children's attempts to offer comfort grow more elaborated and differentiated than their first expressions of affection or offerings of objects. Children directly help, give suggestions, try to rescue, express sympathetic words, referee fights, and protect victims (Zahn-Waxler, Iannotti, and Chapman, 1982). Over the preschool period, the intensity of children's sympathy for distress and their inclination to help do not increase (Zahn-Waxler and Radke-Yarrow, 1979; Zahn-Waxler, Radke-Yarrow, and Brady Smith, 1977).

In the school years, children's increasing sensitivity to the wider social world brings with it new possibilities for prosocial behavior, for cooperation and generosity, for helping and sharing and caring actions that benefit others and are carried out without expectation of benefit to the self. But the values of the society, at least the values of people in the United States, give children a number of expectations about how they should behave; some of these values may conflict with children's prosocial inclinations. On the one hand, children get the message that they should cooperate and share with others and try to help them. But society also stresses the values of competition, acquisition of property, the pitting of one individual against another, the importance of winning. These often militate against prosocial behavior.

In our culture, childhood does not represent a straight, upward rise in prosocial behavior. Observations in both laboratories (Hartup and Coates, 1967) and at nursery schools (Hartup and Keller, 1960; Strayer, Wareing, and Rushton, 1979; Walters et al., 1957) have shown that preschoolers seldom are altruistic, although they share more often than they offer to help. Studies of older children indicate a ceiling on their prosocial behavior and even a decline in it toward the end of middle childhood. Children who are trained in competition or exposed to a relatively competitive culture, who live in small families and have few responsibilities around home, are less inclined to cooperate, less inclined to help another in need, less inclined to compassion.

Research by Ervin Staub (1975) indicates that children are usually more willing to donate a possession, such as a candy bar, as they grow older. Sharing such possessions as pencils and candy with peers also seems to increase. But in a laboratory experiment, sixth-grade children, who were alone in a room and heard a bookcase crash in the next room and a child cry for help, were less likely to try to go to the rescue than fourth-graders in the same situation. When two youngsters were together and heard these sounds of distress, even children in the fourth grade did not try to help. Prosocial behavior in younger children, those in first and second grade, is encouraged by the presence of another. But for children in the fourth to sixth grades, concern about the evaluations of their peers seems to inhibit prosocial behavior.

Competitiveness, the desire to do something better than others do, does increase linearly with age. As we have seen, school children like playing competitive games. These games may be one way of asserting and confirming their developing identities (Staub, 1979).

What happens when children have a choice of

cooperating or competing? This question was studied by Millard Madsen and his associates (Madsen, Kagan, and Madsen, 1971), using various board games. The Madsen Cooperation Board (Figure 13.1) is 18 inches square and has an eyelet in each of the four corners. A metal cylinder sitting in the center of the board has four strings attached to it, and each string passes through an eyelet. The cylinder holds a ballpoint pen that records the cylinder's movements on a piece of paper covering the board. Four children sit around the board, one in each corner and each holding a string. The paper on the board has a numbered circle on each of the four sides. The players must cooperate in order to draw lines through circles; they are given 1 minute to do so, and by doing so, they win prizes. If children oppose one another, one child can prevent the others from drawing a line through any of the circles. Instructions can be modified to stress group rewards: "If the pen draws a line through each of the four circles twice, everyone will get two prizes instead of one." Individual rewards also can be stressed. The children are told to write their names in the circle near them. "When the pen draws a line across one of the circles, only the child whose name is in the circle gets a prize." Obviously, it is still in the children's interest to cooperate and help one another win in turn.

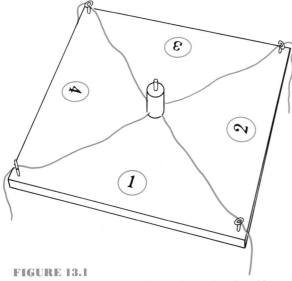

FIGURE 13.1
The object of the cooperation board, designed and used by Millard Madsen and Spencer Kagan, is for children to draw lines through the target circles. To do this, they must cooperate in pulling their strings (Raven and Rubin, 1983).

When there are group rewards to be shared by all, children of all cultures cooperate. When the instructions are changed to provide individual rewards, cultural differences appear. Kibbutz-reared children cooperate and urge cooperation on others. "Let's help each other, c'mon." But American children as well as urban Israeli youngsters choose to compete when cooperation is still their best policy. Urban Americans are particularly prone to being irrationally competitive. Americans 4 to 5 years old are more cooperative than those 7 to 9, but Mexican children do not become more irrationally competitive with age. In a comparision of retarded and nonretarded children at 6 and 7 and at 11 and 12, the retarded group was more cooperative than the normal group. But even the retarded group became less cooperative with age (Madsen and Connor, 1973).

Predicting and Promoting Prosocial Actions

Which factors make it more likely that children will cooperate, help, or share?

Personal Qualities. Children's tendencies to help and share seem to be unrelated to their socioeconomic status (SES), according to the majority of studies. Social standing and the money available to the family have no bearing on compassion. The majority of researchers find also that boys and girls are equally generous, even though in our culture, girls receive more rewards for being helpful and cooperative, boys for being competitive (Mussen and Eisenberg-Berg, 1977).

Children who are generous and helpful usually have strong egos and self-control and are competent and well adjusted. Paul Mussen and Nancy Eisenberg-Berg (1977), however, suggest that children who are the *most* generous are not necessarily the *best* adjusted. They did a study in which fourth-grade boys could donate some of the prizes they earned to others. The stingiest boys scored lower than others in tests of self-control, perseverance, and vigorousness. The most generous also showed signs of instability, for they were naive and prone to feeling guilty. The best adjusted boys gave moderately.

Children who are helpful and generous are also likely to be more astute, more expressive, and more active, which includes being gregarious and assertive. David Barrett and Marian Radke-Yarrow

(1977) observed a group of 5- to 8-year-old boys and girls at summer camp. Those who were adept at inferring what emotions were behind changes in behavior, seen in a videotaped playlet, were generous to others and were also more assertive. Those who were not adept at inferring emotions were selfish and unassertive. In general, studies indicate that having considerable empathy and being able to put oneself in another's place are associated with generosity and helpfulness. But this is not always the case. Nancy Eisenberg-Berg and Randy Lennon (1980) investigated empathy, social understanding, and prosocial behavior in younger children, 4 and 5 years old. To assess empathy and social understanding, they told the children stories. In one story, for example, a child gets many presents at a birthday party; in another, a child wins an art contest and gets toys and recognition; in another, a child has a bicycle accident and cannot go to the circus with friends. When each story was finished, the children were asked, individually, how they felt and how the character in the story felt. Childrens' reactions were considered empathic if they matched the emotion of the child in the story. Their social comprehension was the number of correct answers they gave when asked how the story characters felt. The researchers also observed how often over a 10-week period the children shared, helped, or offered another child comfort in their preschool classes. How generous, kind, and sympathetic children were in these observations, they found, was not related to how empathic or socially understanding they appeared in response to the stories. Being sensitive to, and knowledgeable about, others may not always be enough to make very young children want to help them. Whether they feel that helping is appropriate may depend on lessons learned from their parents and their culture.

Influence of Models. The probable influence of parents on children's generosity and compassion has been probed in two ways. One way is through experimental studies in which children watch an adult performing a prosocial act. The model may have won pennies, candies, or coupons that she can redeem for toys that will go to needy children. For some children the model is stingy and selfish and does not give; for others the model generously donates her pennies, candies, or cou-

pons. Watching models demonstrate generosity does tend to increase children's willingness to help and share (Mussen and Eisenberg-Berg, 1977).

Do these effects last? Children 6 to 10 years old watched a model donate generously and were given the opportunity to rehearse donating behavior. The prosocial effects lasted for 7 days. Three weeks later these children behaved generously in a different situation. Even 2 to 4 months later, the effects of the modeling were evident. Because of the many examples of proved greater generosity and its durability, these experimental studies are believed to indicate that watching their parents be generous, sensitive, and compassionate helps children to be so too.

Results of experiments suggest that a model is more likely to be imitated by youngsters in middle childhood if she or he combines prosocial behavior with warmth and interest and with the exercise of power. In these studies, the model is to some children aloof, giving them only minimal help, ignoring their requests and their achievements. To other children, the model is friendly and sympathetic, praises them for their accomplishments, and offers help and support regularly. Simply describing the model as powerful, does not increase the children's tendencies to imitate the model. Instead, the model must, as parents do, actually demonstrate direct control (Bryan, 1975).

Parental Discipline. The second way of studying the influence of parents on children's prosocial actions has been to look for correlations between parental discipline and children's prosociality. Studies following this strategy suggest that parents are most likely to promote children's prosocial behavior when they are warm and loving, when they themselves behave in a prosocial manner, and when they use inductive disciplinary practices, reasoning with their children rather than asserting power through physical punishment or threats. They ask their children to consider the work that lies ahead for Grandma's arthritic hands after the children have run through her petunia bed or they ask the children to realize that Uncle Harry, upstairs in bed with a cold, needs rest and that their racket is disturbing him. Mothers who use **inductive discipline** have children who are more likely to share candy with their schoolmates and give generously to UNICEF.

Preaching at the child has a positive effect, at least for a while, especially if it is consistent with the parents' own behavior. But we know that the "Do as I say, not as I do" injunction does not work. Children's behavior is influenced more by the parent's *behavior* than by what the parent *says* (Bryan, 1975). In instructing the child, parents can beneficially emphasize do's, not don'ts, and appeal to person, not position. They can say, "Do it because it will make me feel happy," not "Do it because I said to and I'm your mother." They can be helpful to others themselves and offer affection to the child. In their naturalistic study of development of prosocial behavior in young children, Carolyn Zahn-Waxler and Marian Radke-Yarrow (Zahn-Waxler, Radke-Yarrow, and King, 1979) found that the most powerful factor predicting sympathetic behavior when a child saw someone in distress was the intensity with which the mother conveyed the message, "Children must not hurt others." She did this by forceful prohibitions, accompanied by explanations, when the child hurt someone. "*Look* what you did! You must *never* poke anyone's eye!" The mother's sympathy—hugging, kissing, and soothing her child when he or she was hurt—also encouraged the child to be sympathetic.

Parents who stress reparations—encouraging their children to make up for slights or damage by apologizing—seem to rear boys and girls who are more considerate. Taking on responsibility also makes children more generous. For example, children who had to teach another child how to make puzzles for hospitalized youngsters were more likely than children in a control group, who just made puzzles, to donate to a charity a few days later, to work in the interests of orphans a few weeks later, and to make more puzzles for hospitalized children still later (Krebs and Sturrup, 1974).

Fifth-grade pupils who had good reputations for being considerate and sensitive toward others, helpful to their peers, and charitable and sharing— as judged by sociometric ratings—had parents who ranked altruism high in their hierarchy of values. But at this age, when children are identifying strongly with the parent of the same sex, it is interesting to find that their relationship with Father was the most important one for considerate boys, their relationship with Mother the most important one for considerate girls (Hoffman, 1975).

In sum, by being warm and reasoning with their children about their treatment of others, by giving them responsibilities, and by being themselves both their brother's and humankind's keeper, parents can dispose their children to compassion and generosity.

Influence of Peers. Children readily and naturally provide other children with opportunities for prosocial behavior that differ from those provided by adults. After children play roughly, for instance, they have the opportunity to make up and to repair bruised feelings as well as bruised knees. Children's frequent crying or expressions of pain provide opportunities for others to give comfort and help. Children also offer their peers either encouragement or discouragement for acting prosocially. How others in a group react to a child's distress affects the would-be helper's motivation; if someone in a group has just called out, "He's crying because he's a selfish sissy. Let him cry," a child is unlikely to break ranks and offer comfort.

Studies of children in nursery school (Strayer et al., 1979) and kindergarten (Stith and Conner, 1962) show that about 60 percent of children's sharing, helping, cooperating, and comforting are directed toward peers and only about 40 percent toward teachers. In one laboratory study by Carolyn Zahn-Waxler, Ronald Iannotti, and Michael Chapman, (1982) groups of children between 4 and 11 years old were shown an adult who hurt her back while demonstrating a physical exercise, a baby crying from hunger, and a peer who had been hurt on a ladder. The investigators noted the children's expressions of sympathy, indirect efforts to help (telling someone else to help) and direct offers of help. They found that the younger children were much more likely to help the infant than to help the adult, although they expressed more sympathy to the adult than the infant. Only the oldest children were equally likely to help infant, peer, and adult. Other investigators have observed that in mixed-age kindergartens, the older children help the younger children (Bizman, Yinon, Mivtzari, and Shavit, 1978). In cultures where children are charged with caring for younger brothers and sisters, they show more altruism than children from age-segregated cultures (Whiting and Whiting, 1973).

HITTING AND HURTING

Two mothers of 2-year-olds ruminated about their very different toddlers. ''I worry about Sarah,'' said the first. ''If someone takes a toy away from her, she just looks lost and never even tries to get it back. Maybe nursery school will toughen her up.'' ''I wish some of Sarah would rub off on David,'' said the second mother. ''When he wants something, he bulldozes it away from whoever is holding it. I am black and blue from his aggression.'' The parents of 2-year-olds do not, of course, have a corner on aggressive children. At one time or another, virtually every parent worries about a child's aggressive behavior—or lack of it. Where does children's aggression come from, when does it express itself, and how does it change over time?

The Development of Aggression

When psychologists observe children 1 or 1½ years old, they find that nearly half of their interchanges are disruptive or conflicting. Dale Hay and Hildy Ross (1982) observed pairs of 21-month-old children and found that 87 percent of them engaged in at least one conflict, although the conflicts were short lived. Most of the conflicts were struggles for possession, and children who tugged or actively resisted tended to hold sway over those who merely gestured or asked for an object. But these conflicts had a truly social flavor. Even when a duplicate was available, children still quarreled over a single object, for one child's possession often seemed to whet another child's appetite.

Between the ages of 2 and 4, children first grow more and then less aggressive (Hartup, 1974; Blurton Jones, 1972; Walters et al., 1957). After the third year, physical aggression like hitting and stamping decreases, and verbal aggression increases (Goodenough, 1931; Jersild and Markey, 1935). Older preschoolers tend to quarrel longer but less often than younger preschoolers (Garvey, 1974). Most quarrels are still over playthings and possessions. Sex differences in quarreling grow more pronounced. Ways of expressing hostility also change, as screaming, weeping, hitting, and physical attacks give way to verbal abuse. Whereas the infant raged at physical discomfort and the 2- or 3-year-old raged against having to train her actions

to others' wishes, the 4-year-old's main object of anger is his peers (Goodenough, 1931).

Hartup (1974) has distinguished between the 4- to 6-year-old's **instrumental aggression,** directed at retrieving an object, space, or privilege from a peer, and the 6- to 7-year-old's person-oriented **hostile aggression.** Both age groups, he found, were equally likely to respond aggressively to having their space, movements, or possessions blocked. But the older children were more likely than the younger to react aggressively if another child insulted, criticized, or tattled on them.

Older children have lost their babyish expressions of aggression—the whining, crying, and grabbing of toys. In the school years, fighting in the playground, disrupting class, hurting animals, attacking teachers, destroying school property, and running away from home can be the new and serious forms that aggression takes. In adolescence,

Children are likely to respond with aggression to incursions into their space, possessions, or movements. Older children are likelier than younger ones to react aggressively to people who insult, criticize, or tattle on them.

These scenes from films of Bandura's research demonstrate how children imitate exactly the attacks of an adult model on a Bobo doll.

although overt antisocial behavior, such as fighting and disobedience, declines, covert antisocial behavior, such as stealing or using drugs, increases (Loeber, 1982).

Determinants of Aggression

The determinants of aggression are many and complex (see Figure 13.2). Frustration has been regarded as a major cause of aggression ever since John Dollard and his colleagues (Dollard, Doob, Miller, Mowrer, and Sears, 1939) made this connection. At home, children are frustrated by punishment and by not being given constant love and attention by their parents. In nursery school, they may become frustrated when they are left out of a playground game, fail to understand what a teacher wants, or are not able to play immediately with the toys they find the most appealing.

Children learn aggressive behavior patterns through imitation of models, primarily parents but also teachers, other children, and characters on television. Two important studies of aggression in the laboratory had children, ages 3 to 5 years, watch an adult punch, throw, kick, and sit on a 3-foot inflated, rubber Bobo doll, either before their eyes or on film (Bandura, Ross, and Ross, 1961, 1963). Another group of children watched a film of a cartoon character hitting the Bobo doll, and still others saw an adult sitting quietly near the doll, paying no attention to it. Each of the children was then allowed to play briefly with toys before they were stopped and led to a room containing other toys and a Bobo doll. The children who had watched a pummeling of Bobo often copied the attack, blow for blow. At home, the researchers suggested, parents who are hostile and punitive serve as models of aggression and are imitated by their children.

Children also learn aggression through selective reinforcement. Parents may not respond to a child's prosocial behavior. Perhaps they pay attention only to the child when he or she does something naughty, such as hitting another child or a sibling. In this way parents reinforce aggressive behavior.

An important longitudinal study of aggression

DETERMINANTS OF AGGRESSION

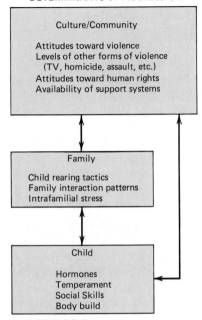

FIGURE 13.2

An ecological model of aggression (Adapted from Parke, 1982).

during middle childhood was conducted by Leonard Eron, Leopold Walder, and Monroe Lefkowitz (Eron, Walder, and Lefkowitz, 1971; Lefkowitz, Eron, Walder and Huesmann, 1977). Using all the third-graders in the semirural area of Columbia County, New York, these researchers tested 2600 children and interviewed 1800 parents. Most of their attention was directed to a smaller sample of boys and girls, whom they then followed from age 9 to 19. They found that home life and certain kinds of parental behavior can frustrate youngsters and instigate aggressive acts on their part. Rejection, lack of loving attention from each parent, and disharmony between parents make children aggressive. Their parents have not rewarded aggressive children for prosocial behavior and view their job as correcting the child rather than "catching the child being good." Their own disharmony has prevented them from paying proper attention to their sons and daughters, making the children anxious about losing their parents' love and support. Children who identified with their parents were not aggressive, because they feared punishment. But children who did not identify with parents became more aggressive the more they were punished. When parents were aggressive themselves, children

did not internalize the self-restraining values and rules professed by their parents. But they did imitate their parents, doing what they did, not what they said.

Most aggressive children are unwanted and rejected, a review by Norma and Seymour Feshbach (1972) suggests. They have been given little affection and attention and have not been taught to conform to social conventions. Their parents may impose restrictions and punish aggressive behavior, but they have not fostered alternative outlets for the anger children inevitably feel, such as expressing it verbally. They have failed to provide positive encouragement that would serve to replace aggression with other behavior. Children may know what they cannot do but not what they *should* do. Physical punishment can both stimulate anger and provide a model of aggressive behavior. Its long-term effect on children is very likely increased aggressiveness. On the other hand, if parents permit aggression, especially that of boys and do not attempt to control it, these children, too, are likely to have aggressive outbursts. Having one permissive parent and one punitive parent in a family is especially detrimental to children. They are more likely to learn to control anger and aggression when discipline is consistent and mixed with love and reasoning and when parents are not often angry with them or each other. Not only do family dynamics, like child rearing and disciplinary practices, levels of stress, and patterns of interaction among parents and children contribute to a child's aggressiveness, however, but so do the child's hormones, temperament, physical appearance, muscularity, and social skills.

Hormones play important roles during prenatal and later development and may modify behavior. Experimental work on animals shows that the presence of male sex hormones during certain critical periods can increase the aggressive behavior of genetic females. If these hormones are absent or if female sex hormones are present, aggressiveness is diminished (Tieger, 1980). But in human beings, hormones seem to act indirectly on aggressive behavior. One study of males and females who had been prenatally exposed to synthetic progestins showed that these individuals were more aggressive than their same-sex siblings who had not been exposed to progestin (Reinisch, 1981). But the evidence is inconsistent on the connection between testosterone, another sex hormone, and aggression. Some researchers (Kreuz and Rose, 1972) have found a positive relation between blood levels of testosterone and males' aggressive and antisocial behavior, but others have not found this relation (Olweus, Mattsson, Schalling, and Low, 1980). Only certain kinds of aggression (aggressive responses to threats and provocations and intolerance of frustration) were linked to higher testosterone levels in the latter study. A similar but weaker relation between testosterone and aggression has been reported in women during part of the menstrual cycle (Persky, 1974).

As far as physical appearance goes, a kind of self-fulfilling prophecy may work to make some unattractive children more aggressive than their attractive peers. Thus, although the aggressiveness of attractive and unattractive 3-year-olds is not different, unattractive 5-year-olds tend to be more aggressive and boisterous than attractive 5-year-olds (Langlois and Downs, 1980). As for temperament, children who develop aggressive behavior problems are more likely to have been "difficult" infants—more active, irregular, sensitive, nonadaptive, intense, persistent, and distractible (Thomas, Chess, and Birch, 1968).

RESEARCH FOCUS

SOCIAL UNDERSTANDING IN AGGRESSIVE BOYS

Do aggressive children see the world as a more hostile place, or do they just act more aggressively because they are unable to inhibit their actions? Kenneth Dodge and Cynthia Frame (1982) conducted several studies of aggressive children to try to answer this question. Their subjects were elementary school boys, chosen on the basis of teachers' and peers' ratings as being aggressive or nonaggressive. The boys were privately and confidentially interviewed about how they would react to several incidents that might involve them or another child: getting hit in the back with a ball, getting milk spilled on their back, losing a pencil and a lunch bag and later seeing another boy with them. In each story, the protagonist was a boy the subject actually knew, who was, according to the teachers' and peers' ratings, aggressive or nonaggressive. Dodge and Frame found that all the subjects attributed more hostility to the aggressive than to the nonaggressive protagonists, especially when the events had negative rather than ambiguous effects. All subjects were also equally likely to attribute malice to the protagonist when another child was the target. But when they themselves were the victims of aggression, the aggressive subjects said that they would retaliate with more aggression than the nonaggressive subjects said they would.

In a second procedure, aggressive and nonaggressive boys watched short films of a boy actor describing to a woman how he acted with his classmates. They were then asked to recall as much as they could of what the boy had said. Some of his descriptions were of hostile acts, and some were of benevolent or neutral acts. To some of the subjects, the actor was described as a popular boy, to some as aggressive, and to some he was not described at all. When the boy had been labeled as popular, all the subjects recalled more benevolent statements. When the boy had been labeled as aggressive, they recalled more hostile statements. Contrary to the researchers' predictions, the aggressive boys did not recall more hostile statements than the nonaggressive boys. Both groups were biased toward recalling more aggressive than benevolent statements, and both groups were biased toward recalling statements consistent with the label assigned the boy actor.

In a third procedure, the researchers observed the aggressive boys in play groups. They found that aggressive acts were provoked when a boy was the target of aggression, but the aggressive boys instigated many more acts of aggression than they received.

In sum, this research showed that aggressive boys are more likely than nonaggressive boys to attribute hostility to ambiguous actions but only when an action is directed at the aggressive boy himself. Aggressive boys do not indiscriminately misattribute or selectively recall hostility. The investigators suggest that the cause for the heightened aggression in some boys is neither a lack of discrimination nor a lag in cognitive maturity but rather a paranoic interpretation of potentially aggressive actions.

Family members are important in the early socialization of aggression, but later peers are important in the development, maintenance, and modification of children's aggression. Peers act to reinforce, to elicit, to model, and to absorb hostility. In an experiment by William Hall (1974), pairs of 6- to 7-year-old boys played together. One child in each pair had been trained by the researchers to act either aggressively or passively. When that child acted aggressively, the probability of the other child's acting aggressively was .75. Passive children who are victimized by aggressive peers fight back either immediately, as in this study, or eventually (Patterson, Littman, and Bricker, 1967). Children are especially likely to imitate the filmed aggression of a model if that model is a boy (Hicks, 1965).

Another possible determining factor in children's aggressiveness is their misunderstanding of social situations. Kenneth Dodge (1980) has suggested that children who persist in responding aggressively to others who are innocent may be misreading others' intentions. Dodge exposed aggressive and nonaggressive boys in the second, fourth, and sixth grades to frustration meted out by an unfamiliar peer whose intent was hostile, benign, or ambiguous. Boys of every age reacted more aggressively to the peer who acted hostilely than to the peer who acted benignly. But when the peer's intent had been ambiguous, the aggressive boys reacted as if the peer had acted hostilely, and the nonaggressive boys reacted as if he had acted benignly.

Finally, individuals and families operate within the broader culture, where their levels of aggression are mediated by the availability of support systems, attitudes toward violence, children's and parents' rights, and exposure to violence in the mass media (see pp. 105–106) and in real life. The causes of aggression are indeed complex.

How can parents reduce their children's aggressiveness? One tack is to change children's perceptions of those who frustrate them. In one study (McCandless, 1966), third-graders were prevented from finishing a task and winning a cash prize by a frustrator. If the children were told that the frustrator was sleepy or upset, they attacked less, both verbally and physically. Parents can encourage children to excuse their classmates' slights or shoves and promote their children's cooperative ventures. In experiments by Muzafer and Carolyn Sherif (Sherif and Sherif, 1964; Sherif, Harvey, White,

Hood, and Sherif, 1961), shifting to a cooperative goal changed the way campers perceived "the others." Instead of frustrators and rivals, they became friends and confidants. Much more research needs to be done to find alternatives to aggression—whether in teachers, parents, or children—and to find how the painful and destructive consequences of aggression can be replaced by a healthy assertiveness that helps children to cope with pressures and to persist in spite of frustration.

THE PEER GROUP

ORGANIZATION

From their first days in company with other preschoolers, whether at a nursery school, day-care center, or play group, children soon learn that interactions with their peers are fragile, beginning or ending at any time. They learn, too, that they are likely to meet resistance as they try to enter ongoing interactions between other children, for nursery-school children try to protect their own interactions from the potentially disruptive intrusions of others. William Corsaro (1981) has suggested that the structure of young children's peer groups reflects their understanding of this social fragility and resistance to disruption. Peer groups of four to seven children allow children readier access to ongoing play than groups limited to just one or two playmates. And this is just what Corsaro observed in the nursery schools he visited.

In the school years, the size of boys' and girls' play groups differ. So common is the sex segregation of children's peer groups that many adults—who would protest racial or ethnic segregation among children—take the phenomenon for granted. From the beginning of school until adolescence, boys play with boys, and girls play with girls. After reviewing many studies of sex segregation, Carol Dweck (1981) suggests that this alienation begins when girls grow rather rigid and absolute about following and setting social rules. When boys refuse to follow these rules of obedience, cleanliness, and orderliness, girls reject them. The boys meanwhile have begun to develop their own culture, and they soon vociferously reject girls. Girls form smaller groups, play in smaller spaces,

Sex differences in the peer groups of preschoolers and school-age children show up repeatedly. The pattern for girls tends to be an intimate, intensive, fairly quiet twosome. Boys engage in more active, extensive, heirarchical, and team activities.

and play at refining social rules and roles. They learn about personal relationships, about how to read subtle cues, and about unarticulated rules of social contact. Boys in their larger groups play more physical games in larger spaces. Boys' games tend to be competitive and to contain extensive, explicit rules for achieving a stated goal. Boys' groups teach about long-range goals rather than about the subtle cues to emotional states.

One longitudinal study conducted by Mary Waldrop and Charles Halverson (1975) compared peer relations of boys and girls at 2½ and again at 7½. The children were observed for a month at a research nursery school when they were 2½, and later, when they were 7½, their mothers kept detailed diaries of the children's informal, naturally occurring peer-group activities. Two patterns of peer interaction were evident. One was an **intensive peer interaction** style, typical of the sociable 7½-year old girl. She played with only one other girl. At the height of her involvement with her playmate, she expressed intense feelings about her and shared many experiences and fantasies with her. **Extensive peer interaction** was typical of the social schoolboy. He played with three or more other boys, engaging in noisy activity, which was usually focused on a game such as baseball or soccer.

These investigators also asked the question, "Does the sociable child of 2½ become the sociable child of 7½?" In this longitudinal study, children who were friendly and smiling, who were involved with their peers and tried to help them, and who were able to cope with aggressive peers at 2½ were also likely at 7½ to spend many hours outside school with peers, to be socially at ease, and to be the ones who decided what and with whom they would play.

Because they need to test their wings, experiment with new aspects of their identity, and determine whether they are socially acceptable and desirable to the opposite sex, adolescents spend far greater amounts of time with peers than younger children do. Not only do they spend more time with their peers, but they value these contacts far more than younger children ordinarily value theirs. Using a method called "experiential sampling," Mihalyi Csikszentmihalyi and Reid Larson (Csikszentmihalyi, Larson, and Prescott, 1977; Larson, Mayers, and Csikszentmihalyi, 1977) measured the time adolescents aged 13 to 18 spent with friends, family members, and alone; they also measured the way adolescents felt in these different situations. The researchers used beepers to contact their subjects at random times during the day and evening. Whenever the subject was "beeped," he or she filled out a self-report form and answered such questions as, "Who were you with?" "What were you doing?" "Do you wish you were doing something else?" The investigators found that talking with peers compared to time at school, with family, or alone was the commonest social activity and the one during which the adolescents reported feeling the best. When the logs were broken down by sex, it was found that boys felt freer, more open, and more involved with friends than with family. They also felt more powerful, stronger, and more active with their friends. Girls also preferred to spend time with friends rather than with family, although the preference was less marked than for boys.

During adolescence a peer group typically shifts from the single-sex group of childhood to a mixed group. "Ugh, boys! I *hate* boys," says the typical 8-year-old girl. "You're having a party? Any boys going to be there?" she begs 5 or 6 years later. In one study, Australian researcher Dexter Dunphy (1963) used observation, questionnaires, interviews, and diaries of 300 boys and girls between the ages of 13 and 21. Dunphy found that for the younger adolescents the peer group was a single-sex **clique** consisting of half a dozen or fewer members (Figure 13.3). Later, but still during early adolescence, the single-sex cliques began to interact. They tended to banter, tease, and try to embarrass members of the opposite-sex groups, as anyone who listens to junior high schoolers tormenting one another between classes can attest. By high school, adolescents may belong to both a single-sex clique and to a mixed group. Thus 3 "best girlfriends" may be friendly with 3 or 4 boys. Gradually a larger group forms, as two to four cliques merge into a fairly cohesive group of 20 or

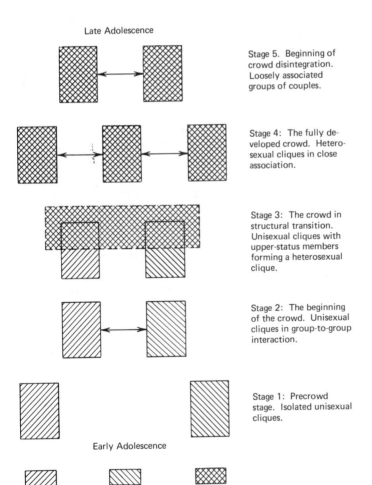

Late Adolescence

Stage 5. Beginning of crowd disintegration. Loosely associated groups of couples.

Stage 4: The fully developed crowd. Heterosexual cliques in close association.

Stage 3: The crowd in structural transition. Unisexual cliques with upper-status members forming a heterosexual clique.

Stage 2: The beginning of the crowd. Unisexual cliques in group-to-group interaction.

Stage 1: Precrowd stage. Isolated unisexual cliques.

Early Adolescence

Boys   Girls   Boys and girls

FIGURE 13.3
The social structure of peer groups passes through five identifiable stages during the course of adolescence (Dunphy, 1963).

so. These progressive changes in the structure of peer groups reflect progressive needs among adolescents. The crowd of 20, for example, can help its members learn what to do and say with members of the opposite sex before they actually start dating.

Peer groups in adolescence have **dominance hierarchies.** These hierarchies show adolescents their place among their peers and may exert a strong influence on them as they consolidate their identities. As the adolescent matures, sources of status on which these hierarchies are based change. In a study of 500 adolescents at a summer camp, conducted by Rich Savin-Williams (1977), younger adolescent boys 12 to 14 attributed status to physical maturity, athletic ability, and physical fitness. The tall fellow who had started shaving, who swam fastest and belted the ball hardest, rose to the top of the heap. In contrast, the 14- to 17-year-old boys grouped together on the basis of intelligence, creativity, craft skills, cabin spirit, peer popularity, and camp experience.

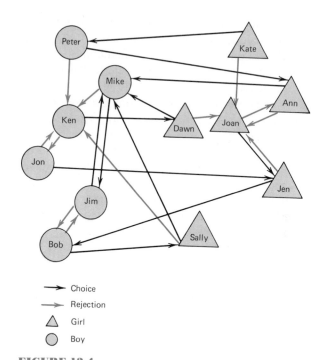

FIGURE 13.4
This sociogram indicates the child liked and the child disliked by each youngster in a small social group.

POPULARITY

Watch a group of schoolchildren choosing up sides for a game of Red Rover, and the process may seem at first glance a random one. Yet a wealth of research indicates that children prefer peers who have a number of specific qualities.

One of the oldest and most popular ways of studying social relations and peer status is called **sociometry.** Researchers determine the patterns of attraction and rejection among the members of a group through questioning. Children are asked, "Who are your three best friends?" "Which of your classmates do you like least?" "Which three children do you like to play with?" ". . . to walk home with after school?" ". . . to have on your basketball team?" The answers given can be charted graphically in a **sociogram** (Figure 13.4). Another way of studying peer status is ethological. Researchers observe children in a natural setting to determine which ones are often alone, sat near, sought out for help and advice. These observations of children are often supplemented by tests for particular social skills.

Children tend to choose friends who look good to them (Kleck, Richardson, and Ronald, 1974),

and teachers and other adults also prefer good-looking children (Lerner and Lerner, 1977), attributing friendliness and other positive qualities to those who are more attractive. Although children also prefer peers of their own ethnic group, physical attractiveness appears to override this concern. Judith Langlois and Cookie Stephan (1977) showed photographs of attractive and unattractive children of three ethnic groups—black, Anglo, Mexican-American—to children of these groups. Children of all three ethnic groups perceived the attractive children as smarter and friendlier and more sharing, more likeable and less mean, whether or not the children belonged to their own ethnic group.

Children between 6 and 12 also strongly prefer peers of their own sex. In fifth grade, at least, a girl can still be popular with the girls, though not popular with boys. Girls accept boys who are favored by other boys (Reese, 1962). And girls who are least accepted by boys are also least accepted by girls. During middle childhood, boys and girls are not attracted by members of the opposite sex who act particularly masculine or feminine. William Ickes and Richard Earnes (1978) found the least interaction and attraction in pairs of boys and girls who conformed to masculine and feminine stereotypes. If at least one child in the pair had both masculine and feminine qualities, there was more sociability and attraction.

Children favor peers who are academic achievers and those with moderate levels of aspiration; the overreachers and the underreachers are less fully accepted (Hartup, 1970). Children also select friends who have higher status in the group. Which is more important, similarity or status? Sociometric studies reviewed by Maureen Hallinan (1981) suggest that status plays a more important role in the formation of a friendship and similarity of sex, race, and achievement in the continuation or stability of the friendship.

Another unchangeable legacy influencing popularity is the child's first name. John McDavid and Herbert Harari (1966) had boys and girls between 10 and 12 rate attractiveness of names. A month later the children chose the most popular and least popular in their own group. The children with the more attractive names were also the most popular. Attractive names, in the opinion of schoolchildren, are ordinary names—not Percival or Hildegarde, but Jenny and Mike. Even when separate groups of children rated youngsters for the appeal of their names and for their popularity, those judged to have attractive names by one group were those considered popular by the other. Whether parents who choose unusual names for their children also have some faults as parents or whether the name by itself is the road to rejection is not known.

In trying to answer why some children are popular, some rejected, and some neglected, Thomas Berndt (1983) reviewed the research on individual children's social skills and behavior and their status in a sociogram. Children who rarely interact with other children, he concluded, are not likely to be popular and are likely to be neglected. Shy children, in other words, are likely to be ignored. Rejected children do try to play with others, but they are aggressive and disruptive. Popular children interact often with their peers and when they do are cooperative and friendly.

In one study of social skills and status, Dodge (1983) watched how previously unacquainted second-grade boys found their status within a newly formed peer group. Unpopular boys (according to a sociogram) acted inappropriately (e.g., standing

on tables), disrupted ongoing play, and spent a good deal of time playing alone because their frequent approaches to other boys produced only brief interaction. They were inept or aggressive and engaged in little cooperative play or social conversation. Even when they acted like more popular boys, they were less well received. Popular boys were physically attractive, often cooperative, rarely aggressive or inappropriate in their actions. When they approached others, they were usually well received and interacted for relatively long periods of time. Other boys considered them good leaders and good sharers. "Controversial" boys—who were liked by some children and disliked by others—acted more cooperatively and engaged in more social talk than the popular boys; they were socially skilled; but often they were also hostile or aggressive.

John Coie and Janis Kupersmidt (1983) observed fourth-grade, poor, black boys, some of whom knew each other, some of whom did not, as they played and worked together. Consistent with Dodge's observations of white, mostly middle-class boys, Coie and Kupersmidt found that distinctive behavior patterns quickly emerged for boys of popular, rejected, and neglected status. Popular boys were rarely aggressive and almost exclusively set the rules and provided suggestions in difficult or ambiguous situations. They were seldom targets of others' aggression and were therefore less likely to be provoked to act aggressively or inappropriately. Neglected boys were the least interactive and aggressive. Rejected boys were talkative, active, and aggressive, and they were less likely than others to keep working or playing with the group during structured activities.

Other researchers have confirmed the idea that certain traits in children make them consistently popular or unpopular as they develop and move into various peer groups. Martha Putallaz (1983) found that children's acceptance into existing groups depended largely on how well they understood and adapted to the group's own mores (see Research Focus: Entering a New Peer Group). Kenneth Rubin and Tina Daniels-Beirness (1983) assessed the sociometric status of kindergartners and measured their intelligence, problem-solving strategies, and popularity. A year later they repeated these assessments and asked the children's first-grade teachers to rate their social competence.

They found that a child's sociometric status was relatively stable over time (correlation = .48) and that popularity in both years correlated positively with using prosocial strategies for solving problems, engaging in positive rather than aggressive social interaction, engaging in parallel and constructive play, and having a high IQ. Unpopular children were aggressive, distractible, hyperactive, and less verbally mature on IQ tests.

To explore the relation between popularity and social skills, in yet another study John Gottman, Jonni Gonso, and Brian Rasmussen (1975) gave third- and fourth-graders in a middle- and low-income school tasks to test their ability in recognizing the emotions of facial expressions and their knowledge of how to make friends, to give help, and to take another person's point of view. Unpopular children did not know how to make friends. In the test for this skill, the experimenter asked the child to pretend that the experimenter was a newcomer with whom the child wanted to be friendly. Children who gave the newcomer information and extended an invitation to visit, after a period of

finding out about the person, received high ratings on the test and turned out to be the more popular children in the class. Observations of classroom behavior indicated that popular children gave and received more praise than unpopular children and spent less time daydreaming.

Unpopular children also tend to be less adept at managing conflict, as Steven Asher and Peter Renshaw point out in their profile of "children without friends" (1981). When asked what they would do if a child took away their game, unpopular children were more likely to say "punch him" or "beat her up." Popular children have the ability to maintain friendships by helping their friends, conversing, and playing cooperatively. Unpopular children may act aggressive, silly, babyish, or they may show off. They are usually less resourceful than popular children, and they may be anxious and quite uncertain about their self-worth.

A number of experiments have attempted to change the behavior of unpopular children through coaching and other means. Sherri Oden and Steven Asher (1977) coached isolates in a third and a

RESEARCH FOCUS

ENTERING A NEW PEER GROUP

Children tend to acquire the same social status in whatever peer groups they join. Popular children are popular, and unpopular children are unpopular in essentially every peer group they participate in. Martha Putallaz (1983) was interested in identifying the differences in the behavior of popular and unpopular children as they tried to enter ongoing peer groups. Unpopular children, she predicted, would be likelier to disagree, to ask questions, to talk about themselves, to state their personal opinions and feelings, and to try to control and divert the group's attention to themselves. Popular children would tend to try to integrate themselves into the ongoing interactions in the group.

To test her hypothesis, Putallaz asked two boys to act as confederates while a naive subject came and joined in their play. The two confederates were asked to play a board game and not to say anything except in response to the subject. At a signal from Putallaz, the two boys shifted into a rhyming game.

They then played a question and answer game, a game that called for the subject to supply a needed clue, involved the subject in a mild dispute over a toy, and said that they wanted to play the board game by themselves. The behavior of the subjects, 22 boys who were about to enter first grade, was coded for agreement, disagreement, statements of feeling and self-reference, and requests for information. It was also coded for relevance to the two other boys' discussions and for conformity and interference. To make sure that the latter two factors were not functions of differences in the boys' intelligence, Putallaz had them take intelligence tests.

Four months later, sociometric ratings were made of the subjects, now in first grade. Sociometric status did not relate to whether the children's reactions to the two confederates had been prosocial, negative, or neutral, but there was a relationship with the relevance and perceptual acuity of their behavior. As Putallaz had predicted, those children who had most accurately sized up the ongoing situation and had adapted themselves to it proved to be the most popular boys in their first-grade classes.

fourth grade about how to play with others, pay attention, cooperate, take turns, share, communicate, and give support and encouragement to their peers. Several days after the six coaching sessions had been completed, all third- and fourth-grade children were asked how they enjoyed playing with each of their classmates. The sociometric rating for the coached children had increased significantly, and their improvement was still evident one year later. Another successful coaching program (Ladd, 1981) taught children to use positive and supportive statements, guided them in making useful suggestions to playmates, and also gave them practice in self-evaluation. Some children do not realize that what they do affects whether classmates like them. Recognizing the impact one has on others is an important step to peer acceptance.

Although many different observers have found that children tend to be equally popular or unpopular within their various peer groups during childhood, the qualities that make for popularity in childhood may not be the same as those that make for popularity in adolescence or adulthood (Asher and Renshaw, 1981). Even though helpfulness, sharing, and cooperation are desirable in people of any age, if they are to be popular, older children and adolescents need more subtle psychological skills than younger children. They need to be able to identify shared interests, disclose thoughts and feelings, and maintain an atmosphere of trust. They may also have to apply different skills within different peer groups, for the qualities prized in one peer group may be reviled in another.

CLOSENESS AND CONFORMITY

Beginning at age 5 or 6, if not earlier, children exist in two worlds, the world of home and family and the world of community and friends. They continue to do so throughout childhood and into adolescence. During the school years, peaceful existence in the two worlds of family and friends is still possible. By the end of middle childhood, these two worlds are much more likely to be in opposition because adolescents are willing to engage in unconventional behavior with their peers and because parents are on guard and try to dissuade them.

In a study pitting advice offered by peers against conflicting advice offered by parents, David Utech and Kenneth Hoving (1969) found that between the third and eleventh grades, children become less and less inclined to follow the advice of their parents. Several other studies (Bixenstine, DeCorte, and Bixenstine, 1976; Bowerman and Kinch, 1956; Devereaux, 1970) also demonstrate that children between the ages of 10 and 13 are more and more willing to go along with peers. Moreover, children's judgments yield much more to the conflicting judgment of a majority of their classmates than to that of their teacher (Berenda, 1950).

Berndt (1978b) studied four age groups: third, sixth, ninth, and eleventh-graders. Between third and sixth grade, children became more susceptible to the persuasion of their peers to engage in antisocial activities that went against their own inclinations. Between sixth grade and ninth, they became even more susceptible, especially boys. In this age range, children preferred to be with their peers rather than to go for walks with their parents or to do some prosocial act suggested by parents, such as helping at the library.

Another study, of fourth, seventh, tenth-graders, and college undergraduates, confirmed this decline in children's closeness in their relationships with their parents (Hunter and Youniss, 1982). At fourth grade, children were more intimate with their parents than with their friends. They claimed that parents knew how they felt, talked things over with them, did things with them, and were more enjoyable to talk to. But by tenth grade, friends were more intimate. Parents were perceived as more nurturant than friends, helping their children to solve problems, doing things they need, and the like, until adolescence, when friends were perceived as being just as nurturant as parents. But although peers' influence increased as children got older, parents exerted more control over their children's behavior than friends did—told them what to do and disagreed with them—at *all* ages.

One standard technique by which social psychologists measure conformity to group pressure is to show a subject lines of varying lengths in a laboratory. A panel of lights tells the subject whether their peers agree or disagree with their judgment of relative line lengths. Philip Costanzo and M. E. Shaw (1966) studied subjects in four age groups, 7 to 9, 11 to 13, 15 to 17, and 19 to 21, using this technique. The experimenters manipulated the lights so that subjects believed that peers disagreed with their own accurate appraisal of line length. The question was, "Will the subject say that a short line is a longer line because peers say so?" Costanzo and Shaw found that conforming to peers' judgments of line lengths peaked in subjects 11 to 13 years old, then dropped off sharply (Figure 13.5).

The decline in conformity is less marked when the norms are not those of peers but those of a group with higher prestige (Patel and Gordon, 1960). Sophomores may be more influenced by the dress and behavior of seniors, for example. In another study of conformity, Michael Siman (1977) used responses to questionnaires from 41 adolescent cliques, in sixth through twelfth grades. He assessed the values of a particular group, determined a group norm, and then measured individuals' deviations from it. He found peer-group values a better prediction of adolescents' behavior than individuals' values, particularly for antisocial behavior, such as smoking, playing hooky, hurting someone, or doing something illegal. In a more recent study of how peers and parents influence adolescents, Jon Krosnick and Charles Judd (1982) also found that smoking is one area in which peers are more influential than parents. Until late adolescence, young people will engage in these activities simply because their peers do so (Condry and Si-

man, 1974). Siman also found, however, that often parent norms and peer norms were congruent. He suggested that the peer group acts as a filter through which parents' norms must pass so that they grow meaningful to the individual.

The transformation from dependent child to relatively independent young adult is not a simple transfer of allegiance from parents to peers, even though adolescents' uniform hairstyles, club jackets, and choice of words may sometimes make it seem so. Adolescents will turn to parents or peers according to the particular issue in question. Faced with hypothetical dilemmas, the ninth-grade girls in one study (Brittain, 1963, 1966) indicated that they would ask parents or peers for advice, depending on who could best handle the dilemma. In deciding which part-time job to take, whether to enter a beauty contest, or which boy to date, girls tended to choose parents for advice. But when deciding how to dress for a football game, what course to take in school, or which dress to buy, they turned to their peers for advice.

Conforming to peers does level off at about tenth grade (Floyd and South, 1972). The influence of both parents and peers continues throughout adolescence, but at about age 15 the adolescent shows more autonomy from both friends and family. Berndt (1978b) notes what he calls "a true growth in autonomy" by the end of high school. By the ages of 18 and 19, adolescents are making many of their own decisions.

As they mature, adolescents are less concerned with being part of the leading crowd. James Coleman (1961) found that at 13 and 14 years of age 21 percent of the boys and 25 percent of the girls not in the leading crowd expressed a strong desire to be part of it. But by ages 17 and 18, only 12 percent of the boys and 11 percent of the girls still wanted to be part of the "in" crowd.

John Coleman (1974) asked adolescents to complete the sentence, "If someone is not part of the group . . ." After age 13 girls more often have positive feelings toward an outsider; boys do so after they are 15. Throughout adolescence, but especially in early adolescence, the attitude of boys toward the outsider is rather harsh, perhaps because, Coleman suggests, ridicule of an outsider makes boys feel that their own group is closer and more solid than it actually is. By late adolescence boys stop ridiculing the outsider.

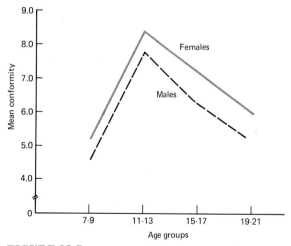

FIGURE 13.5
Young people in early adolescence have great susceptibility to peer pressures; girls are more conforming than boys (Costanzo and Shaw, 1966).

RELATIONSHIPS WITH PEERS

FRIENDSHIPS

Even in their preschool years children, after repeated exposure to particular playmates, begin to form rudimentary friendships with a select few. They choose to spend time with and be close to these particular peers, not just any peer, and may express sadness when separated from them (Isaacs, 1933). The friends they choose are likely to be of the same age, sex, and energy and activity level as themselves (Gamer, Thomas, and Kendall, 1975). If they do not have real friends at this age, they are likely to create an imaginary friend (Manosevitz, Prentice, and Wilson, 1973) who can serve as a companion in play and sometimes as a scapegoat when the child is accused of a misdeed. "No! I not do it! Burdette doed it." Compared to their exchanges with peer strangers, preschool children engage in more pretend play when with their friends, have more connected dialogues, and are more likely to talk about what they have in common than how they are different. They are more agreeable with their friends and comply more often with what their friends want to do. They offer sympathy and assistance to their friends and ask about their feelings (Table 13.2).

During preschool years, though, friendships are

TABLE 13.2
LOVERS' QUARREL BETWEEN TWO 4-YEAR-OLDS

Eric	Naomi
Where's that mask? Well . . .	
	I already took it away so I don't wanted it.
Well, I want to show it to your mother.	
	(Running out of room) But I don't want it. I'm throwing it away.
Hey Naomi, that's your best mask (hurt).	
	But I don't like it.
Well, I like it. Don't throw it away (hurt).	
	I don't like it. I'm putted it back (angry).
Oh no you're not! (angry)	
	Yes, you don't put it . . .
If you . . . if you're going to . . . if you put it back there I'll never speak to you again.	
	But . . . still I'm going to be your friend. I'll marry you.
Well, If . . . if you promise not to throw this away I'll marry you.	
	Yes.
OK. I want to show it to your mother.	
	All right.
Yeah. (Goes out of room and talks to mothers.) (When Eric returns they play exuberantly with balloons.) Hey could you get up there and get my balloon?	
	That's the best one.
Don't you know, I love you, and I'm going to marry you, Naomi?	
	I love you too, and I'm going to marry you. (Voice breaking with emotion) I hope you'll give me a ring.

Source: Gottman and Parkhurst (1980).

Even preschoolers can and do form friendships with those whom they see and play with repeatedly. They are agreeable, affectionate, sympathetic, and caring to their friends.

fleeting things. Robert Selman (Selman, 1981; Selman and Selman, 1979) called this the period of *momentary playmateship*. Friends are valued for their material possessions and for living close by. As one little boy said in an interview with Selman, "He's my friend because he has a giant Superman doll and a real swing set." A little girl explained, "She's my friend—she lives on my street." By the end of the preschool period, the child enters a stage Selman calls *one-way assistance*. At this point, the friendship may be based on more than Superman dolls; children begin to understand that feelings and intentions, not just things, keep friends together. But they take into account only their own needs and satisfaction. Said one child: "She's not my friend anymore because she wouldn't go with me when I wanted her to." And another: "You trust a friend if he does what you want." This is the highest level reached in the preschool period; only later do friendships become reciprocal and intimate.

As they progress through their elementary school years, friends become more and more important. Agemates, once simply the people who happened to be on the other end of the seesaw, become central to the life of a school-age child. The early, one-way quality of peer relationships, when a friend was "someone who does what I want when I want it," changes now to a more cooperative and sympathetic mutual exchange. Children's joy in learning and doing is heightened by the presence of buddies, pals, and teammates. In middle childhood, girls and boys are old enough to form rather intense friendships and to feel strong affection for their few close friends. They may even have a best friend. They empathize with this friend as well as having long talks and good times. They will grieve if the friend moves away, but making a new one is exciting. James Youniss and Jacqueline Volpe (1978) asked children in middle childhood how they would indicate that they liked someone or were friends with someone. They found that children of 6 and 7 were likely to think of friendship as a sharing of goods, toys, or "fun." Children 9 to 10 years old considered friendship to be a sharing of inner thoughts and feelings. They understood that friendship does not develop between just any two people who live near each other and that friends give each other mutual respect and affection. These children realized that acts of friendship could change a person's feelings from lonely and sad to happy.

Berndt (1978a) investigated what children think about friendship by showing children brief cartoons; in one, for example, two boys begin to quarrel over a silver box. An earlier picture described the boys as "best friends" to half the children, as "acquaintances" to the other half. The viewers, kindergartners, third-graders, and sixth-graders, were asked how they expected the interaction to turn out. Children of all three ages expected friends to share more and quarrel less than "kids who simply go to the same school but don't know each other well." In a second step, Berndt asked the children questions, such as, "How do you know someone is your best friend?" Only 2 percent of the kindergartners and third-graders cited intimacy and trust as a condition of friendship. But 38 percent of the sixth-graders found trust crucial: "I can tell him secrets and he won't tell anybody else"; "I tell her everything that happens to me." These older children also felt loyalty was important and disloyalty could cause a friendship to break up.

Selman (Selman, 1981; Selman and Selman, 1979) described the friendships of children 6 to 9 years of age as *two-way, fair-weather cooperation.* Children have the notion of reciprocity in thinking and in friendship. A friend is a person who can adjust to another's specific likes and dislikes. At this age, there is simple give and take between friends, but the commitment is not yet sufficiently strong to weather serious conflict. One of Selman's 9-year-old subjects said, "Trust means if you want to do things for him he will want to do things for you." Children now understand that a child will feel upset and jealous when a friend chooses another youngster to go with on an outing, not just because of

missing out on the event but because of being left out, rejected, regarded as something other than number one by his or her friend.

Children of ages 9 to 15 have *intimate, mutually shared relationships.* Friendships are important for sharing problems and for mutual support; they are based on a commitment and an underlying loyalty that can transcend minor disputes. Friendship is also an exclusive bond, which often involves possessiveness. Selman quotes a 12-year-old on the subject: "Trust is everything in a friendship. You tell each other things that you don't tell anyone else, how you really feel about personal things. It takes a long time to make a close friend, so you really feel bad if you find out that he is trying to make other close friends, too" (Selman and Sel-

RESEARCH FOCUS

HOW CHILDREN BECOME FRIENDS

By what social processes do children become friends? John Gottman (1983) observed children between 3 and 6 years old at home as they talked and played with another child their age. In some cases, the visiting child was unfamiliar, and in some cases, a best friend. From tape recordings made by the host child's parent, Gottman coded the content of the children's play: demands ("Gimme that," "Let's play house"), social rules ("You have to take turns"), statements of emotion ("I made this for you"), exchanges of information ("White and red makes pink"), and the like. Out of these, he investigated the clarity and connectedness of communication between the children; speech was considered unconnected when it was a series of collective monologues. He noted the children's exchange of information, which often took the form of summons and answer: "Hey, you know what?" "What?" "You're a nut." Establishing common ground was coded when the children found something to do together—"How about drawing now?"—or when they explored their similarities and differences. He looked at the ways children resolved disputes, their statements of self-disclosure, their responsiveness, and their positive exchanges.

Gottman then correlated these variables with whether the children were friends or not. He found that children who were friends both agreed and

disagreed more than previously unacquainted children did. The frequency of the guest child's agreement with the host child was the best measure of the difference between friends and strangers and the best predictor of how much progress toward friendship the previously unacquainted pair was making according to their mothers. When two unfamiliar children first met, those who hit it off best interacted in a connected fashion and with little conflict; they exchanged information successfully and established common activities. In later visits, the clarity of their communication, their information exchange, their exploration of both similarities and differences, their resolution of conflicts, and their self-disclosure all were important. Mutual responsiveness and positive exchanges, however, which at the beginning were important for managing conflicts and for establishing pretend play, grew less important over time. The older children were more skillful than the younger children at exchanging information, establishing common activities, and exploring differences. They were also more skillful at resolving conflicts, tended to disagree less, and, late in the relationship, engaged in more self-disclosure.

In a nutshell, how did children make friends? Those who hit it off and progressed toward friendship could exchange information; establish common activities; explore their similarities and differences; resolve conflicts; joke, gossip, and fantasize and tell things about themselves.

man, 1979, p. 74). Cognitive advances enable the preadolescent to step outside of a relationship, seeing both his or her own perspective and that of the friend, and gaining a third perspective, one which recognizes friendship as an entity to be enjoyed and treasured.

In a study of how intimately school-age children know their best friend, Rafael Diaz and Thomas Berndt (1982) asked fourth- and eighth-graders questions like what their best friend worried about, what their friend considered a favorite sport, and when the friend's birthday was. They also looked into how often friends got together and how long they had been friends. Eighth-graders knew more about their friends' personal characteristics and preferences and presumably were more intimate with their best friends than fourth-graders. There were no age differences in how much children knew about external information like the friend's birthday; the extent of this knowledge was greater if the children were cognitively advanced, had been friends for a long time, and saw each other often. Children who got together most often also knew the most personal things about their best friends.

According to Berndt (1982), friendships grow markedly more intimate between middle childhood and early adolescence. In situations that call for cooperation and competition, young adolescents are more cooperative with their friends than are younger children. Young adolescents tend to share their friends' attitudes toward school and elements of peer culture, such as music and clothes, in part because they look for friends who are like themselves and in part because they influence one another.

In late adolescence friendships mature into fuller and more steadfast appreciation of the other person, despite differences in interests and personality. Selman (1979) described adolescent friendship as both "autonomous" and "independent," a paradox explained by the fact that a friendship must satisfy the adolescent's needs for both independence and dependence. "If you are really close friends and trust each other, you can't hold onto everything. You gotta let go once in a while," said one teenager. Adolescents have begun to understand that people can communicate on various levels, that they may share information and interests and may also communicate deeper, even unverbalized, feelings. Friends are understood to support

each other and to share a certain intimacy, but they must also, as one of Selman's subjects put it, "give each other a chance to breathe."

In a major study of the friendships of girls between 11 and 18 years old, Elizabeth Douvan and Joseph Adelson (1966) saw that the actual quality of friendships changed over time. Among 11- to 13-year-olds, friendships centered on shared activities, such as going shopping, and lacked depth and mutuality. Among 14- to 16-year-olds, however, security and loyalty were prime considerations in friendship. These girls needed a friend with whom to identify and share anxieties; a loyal friend was reassuring to a girl worrying about who she is and whether boys will like her. In this new, uncertain realm of boy-and-girl interaction, girls needed to know that they had a friend who would not desert them, even if one of them began to date. As girls become more secure in dating, their friendships become more relaxed. This less possessive sort of friendship approximates the tolerance, sharing, and true intimacy that develop in the heterosexual relationships of young adults.

DATING

The young adolescent, negotiating the uncharted seas of relationships with the opposite sex, leaves the relative security of family norms and single-sex cliques to confront a confusing mixture of prudery and promiscuity. Because of its sexual overtones, dating may be fraught with tension for young adolescents, pulled in one direction by parents' prohibitions and in the other direction by peers' exhortations and bravado.

In the United States, girls begin to date at 14 or 15, boys at 15 or 16. There are, of course, wide variations according to individual, even geographical, exigencies. Some adolescent girls and boys continue to feel more comfortable with same-sex friends until later adolescence. Girls in the Douvan and Adelson (1966) study sample found more mutuality and stability in their same-sex friendships than in their relationships with the boys they dated. Girls of 14 to 16 tend to turn to a girlfriend over "boy troubles," often collaborating on dating strategies. One study has found that girls who go steady very early in adolescence appear to fear or to lack goals of personal and academic achievement (Douvan and Gold, 1966). On the other hand, those

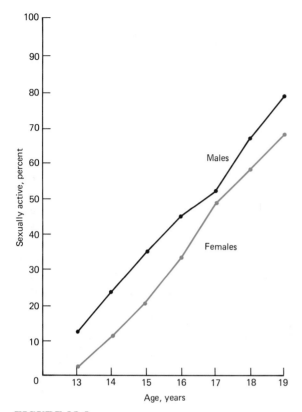

FIGURE 13.6
Current statistics indicate that by age 16, among boys 45 percent and among girls 33 percent are sexually active. By age 19 the percentages are 79 for boys and 68 for girls (Alan Guttmacher Institute, 1981).

who do not date at all face other social problems. Adolescent girls of 16 or older who do not date have only superficial notions of what makes a girl attractive to a boy. Douvan and Adelson (1966) found that these "nondaters" were very dependent on their families, insecure, and self-absorbed. They were aware of being out of step with their classmates—and they were worried about it.

Dating serves adolescents in several important ways. It helps them to find and test their identities. It helps them to make sexual experiments and discoveries. It helps them chart their popularity and success. And it is a means of practicing intimacy with members of the opposite sex and of learning the social skills that will eventually be brought to bear in choosing and keeping a mate.

Although accurate figures are virtually impossible to come by and although popular notions of a modern sexual revolution may be greatly exagger-

ated, findings from a recent investigation suggest that dating has undergone several qualitative changes in the last decade or so. If dating was once an activity that extended over a period of several years in which boys and girls spent time together but did not fully exchange sexual or emotional intimacies, it is not so "innocent" any longer. Patricia Miller and William Simon (1980) have enumerated three significant changes.

First, adolescents now see the adult social world as sexually active and as preoccupied with sex. Second, because society seems less bent on prescribing proper behavior than it used to be, adolescents are more likely to make a personal choice about whether to engage in sexual activity. Miller and Simon found that although adolescents do still tend to date for some time without having sexual intercourse, eventually they are likely to do so with their steady dating partner (Figure 13.6). Third, the distinction between what is acceptable behavior for the two sexes is blurring; the old double standard is disappearing.

Despite the diminishing of the double standard (Table 13.3), however, there are still substantial differences in the sexual experiences of boys and girls. Adolescent girls younger than 16 do not usually have sexual intercourse, although they may engage in heavy petting (Zelnik and Kantner, 1977). Young adolescent boys are likely to consider sex a game of "getting" as much as possible.

The boy's strategy is to try and "get" as much as he can with the girl's permission, or at least without violent protest. A usual strategy for the boy is to test the limits nonverbally with the aid of slowly moving arms and crawling fingers. The girl communicates equally nonverbally by either moving toward or away from the boy and by accepting or pushing away the troublesome hands (Coleman, 1980, p. 439).

By middle and late adolescence, dating tends to imply an emotional commitment and what John Gagnon (1972) has called the "rhetoric of love." But girls, it has been found (Miller and Simon, 1980), are more likely to invest their sexual activity with love than boys. Among Miller and Simon's college students, 23 percent of women said that they had been in love with, and 59 percent said that they were planning to marry, their first sexual partner. Only 5 percent of the women reported no

TABLE 13.3
SEXUAL INTERCOURSE BEFORE AGE 20

Studies	Women (%)	Men (%)
Kinsey, Pomeroy, and Martin, 1948; Kinsey, Pomeroy, Martin, and Gebhard, 1953	20	45
Sorensen, 1973	45	59
Zelnik and Kantner, 1977, 1979	55	—
Alan Guttmacher Institute, 1981	68	79

emotional involvement with their first sexual partner, but 45 percent of the young men reported no emotional involvement.

An important longitudinal study by Richard and Shirley Jessor (1975) focused on the beginnings of sexual experience in two groups of young people, one in high school, the other in college. The Jessors found that those who had already had sex and those who would have sex in the next year were less conventional than their peers in values and outlook. Their parents and especially their peers were less controlling and provided more support and opportunity for sexual exploration. The students were less involved with conventional institutions. They were more likely to have used marijuana more than once—61 percent of high school nonvirgins versus 24 percent of virgins. The correlation with drinking was even higher; among high-school students, 96 percent of the male nonvirgins and 87 percent of the female had engaged in drinking.

But what brings adolescents together in the first place? Physical attraction, as you would expect. In the early stages of adolescence, young people "package" themselves to be attractive—there is almost nothing so homogeneous in appearance as a group of 13-year-old girls ready for a social event. They may later be less conformist about their dress and hairstyle, but physical attractiveness continues to be a major incentive for dating someone new, even at the ages of 19 or 20 (Walster, Aronson, Abraham, and Roltman, 1966). Besides physical attractiveness, friendliness, popularity, personality, and academic and athletic abilities figure in dating choices. Shared attitudes are another source of attraction. Studies of popularity have tended to concentrate on the most and least popular in a group (Cavior and Dokecki, 1973). A young person might have to be exceptionally attractive or accomplished to have the most dates in the class, but the middle range of moderately attractive, moderately intelligent, and moderately athletic teenagers do manage to find others with similar qualities and enjoy a moderate amount of popularity and dating.

Besides the cosmetic packaging that is part of the dating process, social packaging may camouflage the self rather than revealing it. For young men there is the problem of striking a balance between a macho ideal and the sense of vulnerability or inadequacy they may actually feel as they begin to date. Sex-role stereotyping can create conflicts for young women who wish to be appealingly feminine yet who also need to express their increasing maturity and independence. Adolescent girls today may be less likely to play dumb in order to appeal to dates (Komarovsky, 1973; see Table 13.4). Self-image concerning intellectual ability and sexuality is also higher, according to a questionnaire answered by a group of adolescent girls in 1980 (Offer, 1981) and compared to a similar questioning of girls in 1970. This change may bring more spontaneity and honesty in high-school dating. But during these early years of dating, the burden of trying to be attractive and yet controlling sexual impulses can still lead to some strained relations. **Sexual identity** is an important part of the overall sense of individual identity that develops during the teenage years, being shaped by the experience of socializing with the opposite sex and feeling desirable or undesirable, the events that surround sexual arousal, and the combination of guilt, anxiety, and satisfaction that accompanies such feelings.

TABLE 13.4
READINESS IN YOUNG WOMEN TO PLAY DOWN INTELLECTUAL ABILITIES

Question	1950 (%)	1970 (%)
When on dates, have you ever pretended to be intellectually inferior to the man?		
Yes	32	17
No	68	83
Do you have any hesitation about revealing your equality or superiority to men in intellectual competence?		
Yes	35	16
No	65	84

Source: Adapted from Komarovsky, 1973.

HOMOSEXUAL RELATIONSHIPS

Homosexuals became a much more visible segment of our society during the 1970s, but homosexual activity prior to adulthood is relatively rare. In one survey by Robert Sorensen (1973), only 11 percent of all adolescent boys and 6 percent of adolescent girls reported having had a homosexual experience, and they did not report homosexual behavior on a continuous basis or a clear acknowledgment of themselves as homosexuals.

Homosexual experience tends to increase with age for boys but not for girls. Boys are also more likely to report that their homosexual experience was with an older adolescent or adult, whereas the majority of girls report same-sex contact with someone their own age. Moreover, the first homosexual experiences reported by girls occur largely between the ages of 6 and 10, for boys at 11 or 12. A substantial number of adolescents in the Sorensen survey were tolerant of homosexuality for members of their own sex: 41 percent of the boys and 40 percent of the girls agreed, "If two boys and two girls want to have sex together, it's all right so long as they both want to do it" (Sorensen, 1973, p. 294). But three fourths of all boys and girls claimed that they had never had sex with a same-sex partner and that, "I'm sure I'd never want to" (p. 294).

Some young boys do not act as expected for their sex. Persistent playing with dolls or other "girls' toys" or wanting to dress in girls' clothes despite pressure from peers and adults to do otherwise may suggest the possibility of a homosexual predisposition.

Sex research by Alfred Kinsey and others reveals that many people who are heterosexual have experimented with, or been aroused by, a person of the same sex, especially in their youth. Many homosexuals also report experimenting with heterosexual activities (Bell, Weinberg, and Hammersmith, 1981; Kinsey, Pomeroy, Martin, and Gebhard, 1953; Kinsey, Pomeroy, and Martin, 1948). Although fewer than 4 percent of the men and 3 percent of the women in the United States have made the exclusive choice of same-sex partners, over one-third of all men and about 13 percent of all women have a single homosexual experience; many more report homosexual fantasies.

Adolescents, being especially anxious about having sexually appropriate feelings and behavior, may feel a deep sense of guilt and shame over homosexual impulses. They may repress their anxieties, only to have them surface later as sexual fears or dysfunctions (Masters and Johnson, 1970). Adolescents and adults have been concerned whether there is a difference between a decided same-sex preference and a transient homosexual impulse or experience. According to an authoritative study of homosexuality by Alan Bell, Martin Weinberg, and Sue Hammersmith (1981), a strong inclination to be either heterosexual or homosexual appears to exist *before* sexual activity actually begins. Sexual orientation is "a pattern of feelings and reactions" that is ingrained in the individual before he or she becomes sexually active. A complex web of psychological, social, and probably physiological tendencies combines and emerges in childhood and early adolescence as the preference for a homosexual or heterosexual partner.

Bell, Weinberg and Hammersmith also found that in the past, the importance of the role of parents in a son's **sexual preference** has been "grossly exaggerated." And even though many homosexual boys do not act as expected for their gender and are isolated from their peers, peer rejection in itself does not cause homosexuality or figure in the homosexual's "unmasculine" behavior. They suggest that children who grow up to be homosexual do not conform to stereotypical notions of gender roles and may actually influence members of their family to reinforce their homosexual tendency. Thus a young boy who is constitutionally predisposed to be less "masculine" than his father would like may cause his father to withdraw emotionally or to act

hostilely, in consequence of which, the son may feel bitter and fail to identify with his father. These researchers favor an explanation of homosexuality as proceeding from very early hormonal events, although they note that the nature-nurture debate over the origins of homosexual behavior continues strong in both the scholarly and the popular press. As they cautiously state, their "findings are not inconsistent with what one would expect to find if, indeed, there were a biological basis for sexual preference" (Bell, Weinberg, and Hammersmith, 1981, p. 216).

This conclusion receives further support from a recent study by Richard Green (1985). In a unique longitudinal study of young boys who were referred to a clinic because their parents were worried about their preference for wearing girls' clothes, playing with girls' toys, and engaging in girls' activities, Green found that of the 43 boys he was able to follow to the present, 29 are now, as young adults, avowed homosexuals or bisexuals. In a matched comparison group of 34 boys, there are no homosexuals or transsexuals. Of the many factors that Green assessed in the boys' home environments—their relations with their mothers and fathers, and so on—only one was related to whether a boy became overtly homosexual: the presence of the boy's natural father in the home. The most likely, though admittedly speculative explanation for these findings, is that a predisposition toward homosexuality is biologically based, but the expression of that predisposition may be inhibited by a strong father figure.

SOCIAL UNDERSTANDING

Understanding the people who make up their social world, interpreting others' emotions and intentions, communicating with friends and acquaintances, and negotiating social rules and norms are important aspects of **social cognition** that develop during childhood.

INTERPRETATION

To function in the social world, children must learn to read and interpret social situations. One kind of cue they read is others' expressions of emotion. As we saw in Chapter 7, children learn the meanings of various facial and vocal expressions of emotion and infer others' emotional states in particular situations. Researchers have probed what aspect of an emotion children respond to—the facial expression or the situation causing it—by presenting stories and pictures with mixed or incongruous messages. Francine Deutsch (1974) showed 3- to 5-year-old girls several video clips. In some, a positive act—a woman is working at a desk when a second woman enters and gives her coffee, for example—was followed by a positive (congruous) emotion: the woman smiles. In others, the positive act was followed by a negative (incongruous) response: the woman scowls. In still others, negative acts brought negative or positive emotions.

The preschool girls were significantly more accurate in describing what happened in the film when the emotion expressed was congruous with the situation. But when the two were incongruous, the children were more accurate in describing the situation than the facial expression. The offer of a cup of coffee was easier to discern than the emotion implied by a scowling face. Neal Burns and Lorna Cavey (1957) also found that preschool children answered how a character in an illustrated story was feeling on the basis of the situation. Children saw a boy and a doctor with a hypodermic needle. They easily identified the boy's feeling: "He feels scared." They used the situation to identify feeling, even if the boy had a smile on his face. By 6 years of age, however, the children recognized the boy's emotional state from his facial expressions.

Unfortunately, in these studies, the situational cue was often more salient than the facial one, because it was conveyed in both pictures and narrative. In a more recent study, Jackie Gnepp (1983) presented preschool, first-grade, and sixth-grade children with both situational and facial cues in a single medium: pictures. In this study, there was no difference in how well facial expression and situational cues were understood when each was presented alone. When the two, presented together, were conflicting, kindergarten children tended to make inferences consistent with the facial expression, whereas sixth-graders used facial expressions about half the time and situational cues the other half. Children at all three ages perceived, attended to, and remembered *both* facial and situational cues. But their interpretation of a story was influenced by whether the cues conflicted, and the chil-

dren's ability to come up with an interpretation that reconciled the conflict improved with age. The average child succeeded in integrating the conflicting cues 46 percent of the time in kindergarten, 65 percent in first grade, and 80 percent in sixth grade. When asked to make up a story to reconcile conflicting cues, some children elaborated on the information they saw, some created alternate situations, some invented an idiosyncrasy for a story character, some masked the expression of emotion, and some reinterpreted the facial cues.

In another study of how children interpret facial and contextual cues to other children's emotions, Lisa Reichenbach and John Masters (1983) found that third-graders were more accurate than preschoolers only when they were given multiple cues. As in Gnepp's (1983) study, when the cues conflicted, the younger children relied more heavily on facial expressions, and the older children relied more on contextual cues. In this study, the researchers also noted that, compared to children from intact families, children from divorced families were less accurate in judging their peers' emotions and tended to overinterpret anger and to underinterpret happiness.

In a study by Jackie Gnepp, Joshua Klayman, and Tom Trabasso (1983), three emotions—happiness, sadness, and a combination of sad and angry (called upset)—were studied by telling the subjects stories that gave them three sources of information from which to infer the protagonist's emotion: *situational* information about the person's social or physical circumstances, such as "She has just won a prize"; *normative* information about the usual behavior of the group to which the person belongs, such as "The teens in her town hate disco music"; and *personal* information about the attitudes of this particular person, such as "This teenage girl really hates disco music." Children as young as 4½ were more likely to use personal information than normative, and normative information than situational. The use of personal information is, of course, regarded as the highest level of inference, for it requires the listener to consider the protagonist's unique personal attitudes.

By preschool age, children clearly have some sophistication in interpreting emotional expressions and social situations. But how are they at inferring others' thoughts and intentions? Thomas and Emily Berndt (1975) found that half of children just under

5 years old correctly judged a character's actions as intentional or accidental in a filmed story. But these children and a group of 8-year-olds were only half as accurate in judging intentions as a group of 11-year-olds. Children, and young children especially, tended to guess more accurately about intended than accidental actions. Michael Smith (1978) showed children short films of voluntary movements (walking, chewing), involuntary movements (sneezing, yawning), and mechanical movements (being pushed by an object or having an arm moved by an umbrella hook). The 4-year-olds assumed that all of the actions they saw were intended. This finding is consistent with Piaget's (1929) notion that young children indiscriminately ascribe intent to other people's behavior as well as to the behavior of objects. The 5-year-olds, however, not only differentiated between intentional and unintentional actions, but they had begun to interpret intentionality in terms of the effects of actions as well. They tended to infer that positive effects were intended and that negative effects were unintended. The 6-year-olds were much like adults in their abilities to distinguish among intentional and unintentional acts and effects.

When children of 5 or 6 years are allowed to comment freely on films of people's behavior, they tend to describe obvious actions, events, and expressions. As they get older, they infer more about people's intentions, feelings, and motives. John Livesley and Dennis Bromley (1973) found that even 4- and 5-year-olds draw inferences about a filmed character's inner states. They are not very adept at identifying and describing the more subtle and specific inner feelings of persons in a complex and realistic film, however. Dorothy Flapan (1968) showed 6-, 9-, and 12-year-olds a film portraying a variety of feelings, motivations, family relationships, and social situations. In one episode, for example, a young girl is punished by her father for not sharing her new roller skates; later, the father tries to make up for punishing her by taking her to the circus. In another episode, the girl accidentally kills a squirrel. In a third episode her father gives the girl a calf, which the mother calls her "pretend" calf, but then, seeing the daughter's disappointment, decides that the calf really does belong to the girl. Children reported on the film by describing, explaining, and interpreting what they had seen.

Differences between the 6-year-olds and chil-

dren in the two older groups were quite apparent. All three age groups reported when anger, hurt, or happiness was being expressed, but when asked about the intentions of the adults in the film, the 6-year-olds often said, "I don't know." The 9- and 12-year-olds were able to respond, and they recognized that the protagonist was actively thinking and planning actions with definite goals in mind.

This study indicated that as children grow older, they are able to explain causes and infer thoughts and intentions not obviously expressed or specifically mentioned. The younger children were able to describe a situation or report an overt action; the older children could explain what had taken place; and the oldest children were able to infer thoughts, intentions, and feelings not openly expressed. Only at the most advanced age were children able to infer what an actor was thinking about another actor's feelings.

CONCEPTS OF OTHER PEOPLE

As they develop, children acquire concepts about people: what makes them act as they do, what makes one different from another, what a "person" is. Generally speaking, young children tend to define people in terms of environmental circumstances and visible actions; older children define people in terms of personality constants; adolescents and adults define people in terms of their actions, personal qualities, and situations.

Age is one aspect of a person to which even infants respond. Infants 6 or 7 months old have been observed to distinguish between pictures of the faces of adults, children, and infants and to look longer and smile at those of infants (Fagan, 1972; Lewis and Brooks-Gunn, 1979). They also respond more positively to the approach of an unfamiliar child than that of an unfamiliar adult (Brooks and Lewis, 1976; Lewis and Brooks, 1974), and when an adult woman midget—with an adult face and a body as tall as that of a child—approaches, the children respond with surprise (Brooks and Lewis, 1976). Thus even infants use the relationship between face and height to read a person's age. This recognition is mirrored in their earliest words, which distinguish between "baby," referring to self and peers, and "mommy" and "daddy," referring to adults. Later, words for older children appear (Konner, 1975). When 3-year-olds were asked to sort pictures of people from 1 to 70 years old into the categories of small children and older children, parents, and grandparents, they could sort the pictures, even though they could not state the people's ages in years (Edwards and Lewis, 1979). They had the most trouble categorizing pictures of people, 5, 11, and 40 years old, precisely those ages that adults consider transitions from early childhood, middle childhood, and early adulthood.

Infants are also sensitive to the difference of sex. By using such physical cues as height, face, and voice, infants as young as 6 months of age differentiate men from women (Fagan, 1972; Lewis and Brooks, 1974). Later, children use culturally dependent cues like dress and hairstyle to distinguish males from females, boys from girls. Eighteen-month-olds can label adults' sex correctly 90 percent of the time, calling women "mommy" or "lady," calling men "daddy" or "man" (Lewis and Brooks-Gunn, 1979).

But what of more subtle concepts than those of age and sex, those conveyed by height and dress? What concepts do children have of how people think and feel? R. Selman (1980) used fictional dilemmas to probe this question in children aged 4 to 10. In one example, children are told that:

> Eight-year-old Tom is trying to decide what to buy his friend, Mike, for a birthday party. By chance, he meets Mike on the street and learns that Mike is extremely upset because his dog, Pepper, has been lost for two weeks. In fact, Mike is so upset that he tells Tom, "I miss Pepper so much that I never want to look at another dog again." Tom goes off, only to pass a store with a sale on puppies. Only two are left, and these will soon be gone (Selman, 1980, p. 94).

To find out what children understand of inner thoughts and feelings, the interviewer then asks the children whether Tom should buy a puppy for Mike's birthday, and why. Children's responses to these dilemmas seem to form three levels of social awareness. The first level, Selman says, is characterized by physicalist conceptions of persons. Children at this level, who are usually younger than 6, do not distinguish between inner, mental events and outer, physical events and observable actions. They typically reply to the dilemma as if a person's

feelings and statements were inextricable: "If he says that he doesn't want to see a puppy ever again, then he really won't ever want to." At the next level of understanding, at around age 6, children distinguish between subjective and objective experience, but they still think that the subjective and objective are invariably consistent. By age 8, children understand that inner thoughts and outward expressions may be inconsistent or contradictory. In response to the dilemma, they might say that although Mike *says* he does not want another puppy, inside he really does want one. With the knowledge that people's facades may differ from their inner experiences, children reach a level of reflective, psychological understanding.

Another shift toward greater psychological understanding that occurs during this age period was documented by William Rholes and Diane Ruble (1984). Children between 5 and 10 years old were read vignettes about children who had either positive or negative characteristics. For example, some children were portrayed as generously sharing a lunch, some as ungenerously refusing to share lunch with a hungry child. The subjects then rated the children in the vignettes as "nice and kind," "brave," "mean," and so on, and were asked about how the children might act in other, comparable circumstances. Although children at all these ages rated the story characters as equally generous, stingy, and so on, the older children far more often than the younger children predicted that the fictional characters would behave consistently from one situation another. The younger children did not believe, as most adults do, that a person's behavior in different situations can be predicted by abiding personal dispositions.

Psychological understanding of others deepens as children continue to develop. Carl Barenboim (1981) found that at around the age of 10, children made a rapid and pronounced shift from describing other people in terms of their behavior to describing them in terms of inferred, stable, psychological attributes. The younger children would say something like: "Billy runs a lot faster than Jason" or "Penny draws the best in our whole class," when they were asked to describe a child they knew. The older ones would describe a classmate with: "He's really conceited; he thinks he's great" or "Linda is real sensitive, a lot more than most people" (see Figure 13.7).

Selman's and Barenboim's findings are consistent with earlier data collected by Livesley and Bromley (1973) in England. When Livesley and Bromley recorded how children between 7 and 16 years old perceived others, they found the same progression from physical and behavioral to psychological descriptions. Younger children described their acquaintances in terms of appearance, name, age, sex, routine habits, possessions, and social roles:

> Max sits next to me; his eyes are hazel and he is tall. He hasn't got a very big head; he's got a big pointed nose [age 7 years, 6 months] (Livesley and Bromley, 1973, p. 213).

Older children's descriptions focused on more inferential psychological aspects like personality traits, general habits, motives, values, and attitudes:

> Andy is very modest. He is even shyer than I am when near strangers and yet is very talkative with people he knows and likes. He always seems good tempered and I have never seen him in a bad temper. He tends to degrade other

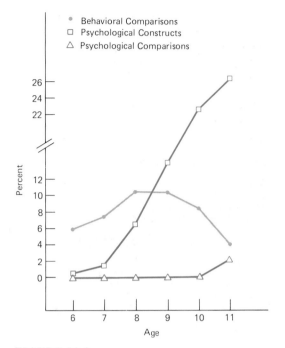

FIGURE 13.7

The percentage of psychological constructs and psychological comparisons in children's descriptions of other people increases with age (Barenboim, 1981).

RESEARCH FOCUS

CHILDREN'S PERCEPTIONS OF THEIR PEERS

Children, like adults, use information about their peers' appearance, background, interests, and psychological characteristics to classify them and guide interactions with them. Christian Gruber (1984) compiled over 70 descriptive phrases and asked 4- to 6-year-old children to name which of their classmates fit each phrase. The phrases described behavior ("noisy," "doesn't talk much"), interests ("plays cars and trucks," "likes to draw and paint"), academic interests ("is not very good at writing," "likes to read books"), and sociometric judgments ("I like," "I don't like"). Gruber also asked adults to rate the descriptions as neutral or evaluative, specific or general, positive or negative, and boy-typed or girl-typed.

He found that the older children agreed more strongly than the younger on which children were most active, noisy, likable, and so forth. The terms about which they agreed most were the ones that were sex typed and positive or negative. Six-year-old boys strongly agreed on who was boy-typed (e.g., "plays cars and trucks," "plays sports," "plays outside") and described by negative terms (e.g., "breaks things," "hits") and less strongly on who was described by girl-typed or positive terms. Six-year-old girls agreed most on which classmates fit girl-typed (e.g., "plays house and dolls") and positive terms (e.g., "is good at learning numbers"). The children were also sensitive to how effective their peers were in their environment, as indexed by clusters of descriptions of immaturity ("acts like a baby," "cries," "is small and weak") and independence ("doesn't ask for help," "works hard"). Boys liked other boys who had high levels of activity—which adults dislike—but disliked those who had girl-typed interests. Girls had just the opposite preferences. In sum, children as young as 6 may perceive of their peers in rich and psychologically complex ways that take into account their peers' social competence and social roles.

people's achievements and yet never praises his own. He does not seem to voice his opinions to anyone. He easily gets nervous [age 15 years, 8 months] (Livesley and Bromley, 1973, p. 221).

Adolescents can also appreciate that although individuals have enduring dispositions, a person's behavior depends on the particular situation. The statement, "She acts very quiet and serious in school, but she's really crazy when she's with her friends," implies that personality may have many aspects, each of which may be revealed under varying social circumstances. Barbara Peevers (1979) has found gains up to the age of 17 in the use of dispositional terms to describe others. As they mature, adolescents develop abilities to distill fundamental aspects of personality from their many observations of a person's behavior, and they begin to extrapolate from what is revealed in ordinary circumstances how a person might react in extraordinary circumstances. They come to understand, that is, what is enduring in a person's actions from one situation to another and to see how the environment might constrain behavior but not change underlying characteristics. Formulating an implicit theory of personality, one that will serve to guide their own behavior, is one of the significant accomplishments of adolescents' social development (Barenboim, 1977; Hill and Palmquist, 1978).

In fact, some of the emotional pain of adolescence comes from discovering the real personality traits, warts and all, of their own parents. The girl who has idealized her father is crushed to learn that he has a tendency to brag, to cheat at cards, or to be unfaithful. The pain of such discoveries is beautifully depicted in Arthur Miller's *Death of a Salesman,* when Willie Loman's teenage son, who had idolized his father, finds Willie in a hotel room with another woman. Fortunately for most adolescents, the discoveries they make about personalities around them are tolerable. In time, they adjust their idealized versions of their parents to their new perceptions of social behavior. By the end of adolescence, their expectations of themselves and others are more realistic.

COMMUNICATION

An important part of learning about the social world is learning how to communicate with the people in

Children often provide inadequate, uninformative communications, failing to notice or to mention important points. Yet even when they are not understood, children rarely get feedback from their confused—"Huh?"—listeners.

it. Communication involves skills in both sending and receiving messages. As listeners, children must learn that messages are sources of information and must learn to evaluate the quality of those messages. As speakers, children must learn many basics: how to identify and label what is important; how to limit the contents of their messages; how to order the elements in the message; and how to change the message when they discover they are not being understood.

In a study of 4- to 6-year-olds, Ralph Roberts and Charlotte Patterson (1983) found that 86 percent of the children even at this age understood that a listener did not know in advance what they were going to tell him or her and that the purpose of a message was to inform the listener. Thus the basic rationale for communication is known quite early. Nevertheless, errors in implementation are frequent. Children often provide inadequate, uninformative statements, in part because they may fail to single out relevant stimuli or to make necessary comparisons (Glucksberg, Krauss, and Higgins, 1975). Even when children know how to make necessary comparisons, they may not know when to do so; even when they notice things, they may forget to mention them. If the conditions are quite simple, even 4- and 5-year-olds can give a listener extra information when asked (Cosgrove and Patterson, 1979). But listeners do not often ask. Young children rarely get feedback on the adequacy of their communications. Although young children may respond correctly to crisp, informative messages, they are less likely than older children to notice or to request clarification when a message is ambiguous (Markman, 1981). If someone points out that a message was confused or inadequate, even 5- or 6-year-old children are likely to realize then that the message was ambiguous (Robinson, 1981; Robinson and Robinson, 1977; Singer and Flavell, 1981). But they seem to require this prompting in order to detect failures in communication—failures that they usually blame on the speaker. Explicit feedback about their mistakes in communication, rare as it may be in ordinary conversation, seems to improve children's abilities both to speak and listen (Patterson and Massad, 1980; Sonnenschein and Whitehurst, 1983).

Susan Sonnenschein (1984) wanted to know what kinds of mistakes young listeners make and what kinds of feedback improve their communications. She showed kindergartners three triangles that differed in color, pattern, or size. The children were told that they were playing a communication game with two dolls, Bugs Bunny and Daffy Duck. Bugs, the speaker, knew above which triangle a star was hidden; Daffy did not. Bugs was to "tell Daffy something about the triangle with the star above it so that Daffy can pick it out. If Bugs does a good job, Daffy will be able to pick the triangle with the star above it." The children listened to Bugs's description and stated whether Bugs had done a good job. In every case, Bugs's message was ambiguous; it applied to two triangles, not just one. For example, Bugs would say "the red triangle" when the display included two red triangles. With some children, Daffy picked the correct triangle; with others, he picked the wrong one of the two triangles Bugs had described; with others, he picked the triangle not described at all. In a fourth group, Daffy did not choose a triangle and instead told Bugs what was wrong with his clue and asked him to clarify his ambiguous message. A week later, the children repeated the game, but this time the child and the experimenter took the place of Bugs and Daffy. Children who were most adequate communicators (speakers) in this test were those who had heard Daffy ask Bugs to clarify his message. Those who had seen Daffy pick the wrong one of

the two ambiguously described triangles also realized that Bugs had given an inadequate, ambiguous message, but this did not help them make their own message clear. Thus feedback can show a child that a message is ambiguous either explicitly, through asking for clarification, or implicitly, by watching a listener flounder and make a plausible but incorrect response. But to improve the child's ability to speak, it seems, feedback must be explicit.

Young children, then, have limited skills in communicating. As they get older, children grow more effective at speaking and listening, and they can apply their skills in a broader and more complex range of circumstances. As their abilities to understand others' points of view improve, and as they learn how to make effective comparisons, children progressively extend their communication skills.

RULES AND NORMS

As they develop, children also learn the rules and norms that govern social interactions and society at large.

Children want to know about the regularities in their world, about what is invariable and what is not. They construct social rules out of information that they gather in their social interactions, and they also passively receive information about how they and others are expected to behave. One child came home from her first day in second grade:

Child Mom, guess what? Two and three is five in Mrs. McIntyre's [second-grade teacher] room, too!

Mother What do you mean?

Child It's the *same* as first grade—two and three is five. Is it the same in *every* room? . . . Everywhere? . . . In China, too?

Mother Yes, it is.

Child (musing) It's a rule everywhere. . . . Can't anybody make it be something else?

Older sister No, it's a rule. It's always five. And you better not say anything else or Mrs. McIntyre will say you're wrong. You can't fool around with rules about numbers (Shantz, 1982, p. 167).

By school age, children are quite familiar with

the culturally defined and arbitrary rules establishing dress codes, forms of address, and table manners, the so-called **social conventions**. William Damon (1977) and Elliot Turiel (1975, 1977) have tried to determine just when children acquire these social rules by interviewing them intensively. In one study the children were told a story about Melissa:

Melissa is a new girl at school. She comes from a country in the Far East. In her country there are different eating habits, and the people there eat many kinds of food with their fingers. One day a teacher saw her eating some spaghetti with her fingers and got upset (Damon, 1977, p. 243).

At the youngest age interviewed, children seemed to think that Melissa's behavior was fine. They did not feel bound by the rules of American table etiquette and said that whatever people wanted to do, they could:

Interviewer Do you think it is okay for Melissa to eat with her fingers?

Karen (4 years, 2 months) Yes.

Interviewer It is? How come that is okay?

Karen Because different people eat different ways (Damon, 1977, p. 250).

At the next age children no longer confused rules with personal habits, but they thought rules should be respected to avoid the displeasure of authority figures.

Interviewer Was it wrong for Melissa to eat with her fingers in school?

Andrea (5 years, 1 month) Yes. . . . Because she can't use her fingers.

Interviewer Why not?

Andrea The mother will hit her (Damon, 1977, p. 255).

A year or so later children recognized that rules could have exceptions.

Interviewer Do you think it was wrong for Melissa to eat with her fingers?

Tom (6 years, 2 months) No, she didn't learn how to eat with other stuff.

Interviewer Do you think it was wrong?

Tom No, because she was new to this country anyway.

Interviewer Why do you think the teacher got really upset when she saw her doing that?

Tom She may not know that she was new to the country (Damon, 1977, p. 261).

Finally, children in middle childhood come to respect rules because they understand their social function. They realize that social conventions are necessary for maintaining order.

Interviewer What if there was a rule about eating with a fork at Melissa's school?

Heather (8 years, 8 months) If there is a rule then she would have to eat that way.

Interviewer Why is that?

Heather Because then everyone would have to do the same thing no matter how they were taught at home or it wouldn't be fair.

Interviewer Couldn't Melissa just ignore the rule?

Heather No. Because then everybody would start looking at her and start doing it . . . what a mess! Then if only one person didn't do it they would make fun of him, and they might not think it's fair (Damon, 1977, p. 271).

Even very young children know many of these rules. Nancy Much and Richard Shweder (1978) have classified cultural rules into regulations, conventions, moral truths, and instructions, and have found that even children between 2 and 6 years old can recognize when these rules have been broken. To recognize that a rule has been broken, of course, means that a child recognizes the rule itself. Larry Nucci and Elliot Turiel (1978) found that preschoolers distinguished between social transgressions—playing in the wrong place or playing at the wrong time—and moral transgressions—hitting another child or stealing—just as adults do. Similarly, school-age children did not believe that all school rules are necessarily right. Many thought that even if no official policy existed, a teacher should scold a child for hitting another child (Weston and Turiel, 1979).

Young children's appreciation of this distinction between social conventions, which are arbitrary, and moral rules, which are absolute, has been questioned by other researchers, however. In one study, first- and second-graders were interviewed about rules and heard stories about social transgressions—a boy who gets up in the morning and washes his face but does not comb his hair—and moral transgressions—children refusing to share or hitting (Shantz and Shantz, 1977). The children were then asked to point to the face that best represented what they thought about the naughty child—from a broadly smiling "very good" to a frowning "very bad" face. Although, on the *average*, children ranked the moral transgressions as worse than the social transgressions, all children did not rank all moral transgressions as more serious than all social transgressions. They thought that some of the social transgressions, like not combing your hair, were as serious as the moral transgressions, whereas others, like a boy playing with dolls, were not as bad.

Although there seems to be some question about how early children make the distinction between social and moral rules, there is no question that they are quite aware of the importance of rules from an early age. Development brings with it increasing awareness of subtle distinctions between types of rules and greater flexibility in complying with arbitrary rules. This flexibility may peak when adolescents deliberately reject the rules established by a person in authority.

Social norms, which are another kind of rule, are used by adolescents to guide behavior and expectations. Norms at this age define peer groups.

In one Minnesota high school in the mid-1970s, for instance, *sporties* were adolescents of both sexes who engaged in sports, went to sports activities, and drank beer. *Workers* held jobs, saved money, owned cars, and had social lives that revolved around their cars. *Crispies* used drugs, excelled at football, and did not work hard in school. *Musicians* spent time in the music room and at performances and drank liquor. *Debaters* read a lot, got good marks, joined intellectual clubs, and drank Pepsi-Cola at their parties (Hartup, 1983). In a Connecticut high school, students were divided into "the zero squad," those in special education classes, and "root eaters," the intellectuals. Labels like these are shorthand descriptions of the social norms that dictate acceptable behavior in the cliques and gangs that are important in the social world of adolescence. The awareness and self-conscious labeling in such norms is another indication of advanced social understanding.

SCRIPTS AND ROLES

The final indication of developing social understanding that we will discuss is children's growing repertoire of scripts and roles. Early on, children learn "scripts" for familiar events and routines like

An important part of social understanding is learning the "script" for familiar events like a birthday party. Children have to learn about the ceremony of cake and candles, giving and receiving presents, singing "Happy Birthday," and all the other customary facets of a birthday party in our culture.

going shopping, taking a bath, going to school, or having a party. Roger Schank and Robert Abelson (1977) have suggested that the script is the most basic level of knowledge of events. The script includes roles, props, and expected actions. For example, the script for having a meal in a restaurant includes the roles of customer, server, cook, and cashier; the props of menu, food, bill, and tip; and the expected actions of entering the restaurant, being seated, ordering, eating, paying, and leaving. Children learn about scripts for repeated events in their lives at the same time as they learn about the people in it—mommy, daddy, teachers, doctor, bus driver. They take roles, and they play at roles as they learn about the social world. Here are two 4-year-olds playing out the script of parents planning tonight's dinner in a pretended telephone conversation:

Gay Hi.

Daniel Hi.

Gay How are you?

Daniel Fine.

Gay Who am I speaking to?

Daniel Daniel. This is your daddy. I need to speak to you.

Gay All right.

Daniel When I come tonight, we're gonna have . . . peanut butter and jelly sandwich, uh, at dinner time.

Gay Uhmmmm. Where're we going at dinner time?

Daniel Nowhere. But we're just gonna have dinner at 11 o'clock.

Gay Well, I made a plan of going out tonight.

Daniel Well, that's what we're gonna do.

Gay We're going out.

Daniel The plan, it's gonna be, that's gonna be, we're going to McDonald's.

Gay Yeah, we're going to McDonald's. And, ah, ah, ah, what they have for dinner tonight is hamburger.

Daniel Hamburger is coming. Okay, well, goodbye.

Gay Bye (Nelson and Gruendel, 1979, p. 76).

Katherine Nelson and Janice Gruendel (1979) have interviewed children between 3 and 8 years old about "what happens" when you have a birthday party, plant a garden, and other familiar situations. The youngest children's scripts are sketchy and general—"You cook a cake and eat it." As they get older, the children include social aspects in their scripts, such as children arriving at a birthday party and playing games, and they describe them with more complex details. Scripts are representations of conventional events—what usually happens—rather than descriptions of specific instances—what happened last week. Their value lies in telling people how to act in familiar situations. Without scripts, every action, sign, and signal would strike people as new, and all of their energies would go into decoding their social world.

A social role is a cluster of expected behaviors for a particular category of people. Knowledge of roles, like scripts, develops gradually throughout childhood. The toddler first pretends to perform some act or has a doll perform some act but is not aware that the acts are part of a social role. Later the child understands that certain actions are part of social roles, that mothers buy things, make phone calls, and clean house; that doctors wear white coats, ask to look at your tongue, and give injections. At age 4, the child understands how two or three roles fit together and can play "family." By age 6, most children understand how whole networks of roles work together—teachers, students, principal, janitors. At each step of this sequence, children understand more complexities and variations about social roles (Watson, 1981).

SOCIAL COMPETENCE

As children grow older their social behavior matures. They acquire more social skills, and they replace aggression with cooperation. Observations of children between 2 and 5 years old made in preschools and play groups, for example, show that as children get older, they stare, cry, point, suck, and flee less and talk, play socially, smile, and laugh more (Mueller, 1972; Blurton Jones, 1972; Smith and Connolly, 1972). As they make eye contact and vocalize more, their communication becomes more effective (Savitsky and Watson, 1975). They become more successful in their collaborative attempts (Cooper, 1977), and they play together more (Tieszen, 1979).

By school age, children spend more time with other children and grow more adept at understanding their perspectives. Communication skills grow more effective and sensitive too, (Levine and Sutton-Smith, 1973). Children more reliably use feedback from their listeners, and they can more reliably infer other people's motivations. They understand how to interpret and follow social rules, something that younger children have trouble doing. In groups, they act more synchronized and harmonious than younger children, who act more like collections of independent individuals. They share more and are more altruistic; they are less aggressive and quarrelsome. All of these skills combine to make the school-age child increasingly socially competent (Hartup, 1983).

Is there a connection between the level of social understanding children demonstrate as they reflect about hypothetical situations and this developing social competence? Robert Selman, Mira Schorin, Carolyn Stone, and Erin Phelps (1983) interviewed and observed girls in the second, third, fourth, and fifth grades to investigate this question. They found that the answers girls gave to a dilemma about what a girl should do when her wishes and a friend's feelings conflicted were related to their social interaction strategies in real groups. Immature strategies in these groups included grabbing and insults; commands and tattling were more mature; suggestions and compromising were higher still; and joking and making way for minority rights were at the highest level. Girls with the lowest levels of reasoning in the social-understanding dilemma used the fewest advanced interaction strategies in their groups. Girls who reasoned at a high level of social understanding about hypothetical friendships also used relatively advanced interaction strategies when they were in a group with other girls.

Connections between social understanding and social skills have also been demonstrated in adolescence. Adolescents who effectively meet social challenges are also those who consider it important to help others, to be socially involved, and to get along with their parents and friends (Ford, 1982). They describe themselves as competent to meet those goals, and they are likelier than their peers to want to set and meet their own goals rather than just "going with the flow." They are more empathic and more resourceful in dealing with social and personal problems and in thinking of the possible consequences of their actions on others.

Children become better able to infer intentions and inner feelings and to recognize social rules during the same age period as they develop concrete logical operations. Piaget (1970) considered the development of these social abilities to be a consequence of the development of logical operations. Is there a connection between social understanding and logical operations?

Marida Hollos (1975) tested children 7 through 9 years of age from three social settings on the plains of Hungary—dispersed farms, a village, and a medium-sized town—on conservation and classification tasks and on their ability to understand another person's point of view. The children were all from working-class, two-parent families. Those living on isolated farms spent most of their days playing alone or watching and helping their mother do chores. They had few conversations with their parents or brothers and sisters. If they attended school, they came home immediately after school ended to care for the farm animals and had no opportunity to play with their peers. Children living in the village, by contrast, played with their peers all day or after school, or they grazed the family animals together. At the midday meal their families discussed the day's activities. The town in the study was a major marketing, administrative, cultural, and educational center. The children living there spent much of their time with their peers, participated regularly in family discussions, and were used to a variety of activities and to strangers of all sorts and ages.

The children were given four tasks to test their ability to adopt another's point of view. The first was a visual perspective test similar to Piaget's three-mountain task (see p. 314), consisting of a doll with a camera, a group of miniature buildings mounted on a square piece of wood, and photographs to represent the four perspectives from which the doll could have taken pictures of them. For the second task, the child was told a story with many proper names and asked to repeat it to a second experimenter. In the third task, an experimenter showed the child a seven-picture cartoon sequence suggesting an obvious story, which the child told. A second experimenter entered the room. Three pictures were removed from the sequence, changing the story. The child was asked to pretend to take the second experimenter's place, telling the story as the experimenter would tell it. The fourth task tested the children's knowledge of personal pronouns, which in Hungarian are complex and indicate personal relationships.

The farm children were better than village and town children in conserving and classifying but much poorer in taking another person's point of view (Figure 13.8). The two realms of logical operations and social understanding, judging from this investigation, are quite separate. The ability to think logically is more likely to develop out of interactions with physical objects, but social understanding is almost certainly influenced by the social milieu.

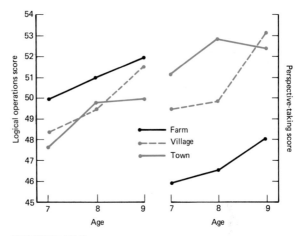

FIGURE 13.8
Hungarian children living on farms are ahead of village and town children in thinking logically but behind them in taking another person's point of view (Hollos, 1975).

SUMMARY

1. Strangers can make friends with infants by playing with them, imitating their mothers, and not violating their expectations about interaction. Individual preschoolers vary in their friendliness toward unfamiliar adults, but they are rarely as attached to unrelated adults as they are to their parents. Teachers feel differently toward children according to such characteristics as the children's sex, demandingness, physical attractiveness, and responsiveness.

2. From the time they are just a few months old, babies like to look at and be with other babies and small children. The earliest peer interactions tend to be short lived and more a matter of individuals doing things near each other than true cooperation. Preschoolers' play grows increasingly more positive than negative, more truly interactive, more complex, sustained, and cooperative.

3. Children who teach other children may reap rewards in self-esteem, positive feelings toward school, and school achievement. Their tutees are especially like to benefit from tutoring in reading skills. Children generally like to learn from older children and to teach younger children. Children use more physical demonstrations and modeling of tasks than adult teachers; adults state more rules and directions.

4. Children show marked individual differences in cooperativeness, competitiveness, and prosociability. These qualities tend to increase over time. The attitudes of parents, other children, and society at large also influence children's prosocial behavior.

5. Physical aggressiveness peaks between 2 and 4 years and then tends to diminish as children mature and develop social skills. Preschoolers often express instrumental aggression, directed at retrieving an object or privilege; 6- and 7-year-olds' aggression is more often aimed directly at people. The occurrence of aggression is influenced by social factors like frustration, stress, child rearing, disciplinary practices, and patterns of family interaction; biological factors, such as hormones, appearance, and sex; and cultural factors, such as exposure to violence in the mass media and real life, the availability of support systems, and attitudes towards individual rights.

6. Groups of children try to resist disruption from intruders, even as solitary children try to join ongoing interactions. As early as the age of 3, girls and boys gravitate toward different kinds of group activities. Children who are sociable as preschoolers are usually sociable in middle childhood. Popular children tend to be popular in any peer group they enter, because they have valued social skills:

adapting to ongoing group activities rather than disrupting them, offering suggestions and leadership in ambiguous situations, rarely acting aggressive or inappropriate. Likewise, unpopular and neglected children tend to act in ways that make them unpopular or neglected in any peer group they enter.

7. From the time they enter school, children begin to feel the influence of peers as well as parents. Over time, their conformity to peers increases, peaking early in adolescence. Adolescent peer groups may act as filters though which parents' values must pass.

8. Preschoolers choose special playmates as friends, although their friendships are fleeting. In elementary school, friends grow more important, and friendships are more cooperative and reciprocal. After about the age of 9, children enter into intimate, mutual relationships with their friends. Girls' friendships tend to be more intimate than boys'. Dating and sexual relations bring males and females together in a new form of friendship, itself usually the outgrowth of physical attraction. Homosexual relations for girls tend to start between the ages of 6 and 10 and to be with someone their own age: for boys, they begin between the ages of 11 and 12, often with someone older. But for both boys and girls, homosexual experiences are rare.

9. To function well in their social world, children must learn to read and interpret others' feelings and intentions. Young children tend to rely on external cues; older children infer internal psychological states and motives and can differentiate intentional from unintentional actions. By early adolescence, children realize that people may say one thing and mean another.

10. Children form their concepts of other people on the basis of characteristics like age and sex, social roles, habits, personality traits, physical and, after the age of 8 or 10, psychological dispositions. Older children understand the predictability of an individual's behavior from one situation to another better than young children do.

11. To communicate effectively, children must understand that messages are sources of information and must be able to judge their quality. As speakers, they must identify and label the principal features of things, choose the contents of and the order of messages, and repair breakdowns in communication. Perspective taking and making meaningful distinctions are two skills that aid communication.

12. Children develop an understanding of social conventions, moral rules, and social norms. They come to distinguish between moral and social rules and to use norms to define social groups. They also come to understand social roles and scripts with increasing sophistication as they grow older.

13. As they develop, children grow increasingly socially competent overall. They are increasingly efficient, mature, and empathic, in getting along with others. They are better at solving interpersonal problems, communicating, and becoming socially involved. Their competence is reflected in their thoughtful responses to hypothetical dilemmas designed to probe their social understanding as well as their patterns of social behavior.

KEY TERMS

Associative play
Cooperative play
Parallel play
Ritual play
Language play
Pretend play

Inductive discipline
Instrumental aggression
Hostile aggression
Intensive peer interaction

Extensive peer interaction
Clique
Dominance hierarchy

Sociometry
Sociogram
Sexual identity
Sex preference
Social cognition
Social conventions

SUGGESTED READINGS

Alan Guttmacher Institute. *Eleven Million Teenagers.* New York: 1976; and *Teenage Pregnancy: the Problem That Hasn't Gone Away.* New York: Alan Guttmacher Institute, 1981. Excellent charts, statistics, and studies concerning the ongoing problems of teenage pregnancy, prenatal care, and parenting.

Asher, Steven R., and Gottman, John M. (Eds.). *The Development of Children's Friendships.* Cambridge: Cambridge University Press, 1981. A broad sampling of the relatively new area of research into peer relations and their impact on a child's development. The chapters on children without friends, and how training can improve their social standing, and Robert Selman's chapter on children's capacities for friendship are of special interest.

Bell, Alan F., Weinberg, Martin S., and Hammersmith, Sue K. *Sexual Preference.* Bloomington: Indiana University Press, 1981. A perspective stressing the deep-rooted, multifaceted nature of our choice to be either heterosexual or homosexual in the context of an in-depth survey of San Francisco homosexuals and lesbians.

Damon, William. *The Social World of the Child.* San Francisco: Jossey-Bass, 1977. A discussion of how children reorganize their ways of understanding social reality and deal with the principal social relations and regulations of their lives. The book is liberally sprinkled with actual conversations between children and adults.

Eisenberg, Nancy (Ed.). *The Development of Prosocial Behavior.* New York: Academic Press, 1982. A presentation of different studies on the development of prosocial behaviors in childhood, examining the roots and determinants of prosocial thought and behavior.

Higgins, E. Tony, Ruble, Diane N., and Hartup, Willard W. (Eds.). *Social Cognition and Social Development.* New York: Cambridge University Press, 1983. An overview of current research and theory concerning social cognition and social behavior in children, with a focus on the developmental roots of social cognitive abilities.

Rubin, Kenneth H., and Ross, Hildy S. (Eds.). *Peer Relationships and Social Skills in Childhood.* New York: Springer-Verlag, 1982. A collection of articles by many of the most eminent researchers in the field, which examines the development of peer relationships and social skills from infancy through early adolescence.

PART VI

PERSONALITY

CHAPTER 14

Moral Development

When psychologists study moral development, they want to find out how children learn the difference between truth and falsehood; how they learn to be trustworthy, even when no one is looking; and how they learn to overcome the temptation to cheat. They want to know how children come to behave "morally," how they reason out moral problems. And how does this moral behavior and reasoning change as they develop? Psychologists also want to know whether children who lie and cheat experience guilt and if not, why not.

To chart moral development, people have had to solve many problems of definition and method. Unlike physical development, for example, moral development poses risks of cultural bias. It is one thing to study morality in middle-class Minnesotans by asking them about cheating on school tests. It is quite another to put the same question to Thai refugees who have never been to school or heard of tests. To assume that the principles of moral judgment and moral behavior prevailing in the United States are also those of the Union of Soviet Socialist Republics would be even worse.

Three theoretical approaches have dominated the research into moral development, the cognitive, the affective, and the social learning. Each has its own method of defining what morality is and how it may be studied.

MORAL REASONING

Cognitive developmentalists studying morality focus largely on the thought processes behind moral concepts—on the patterns of moral reasoning in children and adolescents. They are interested in finding the links between children's developing cognitive abilities and their advances in moral reasoning. They take as their broad theoretical framework Jean Piaget's ideas about cognitive stages. As children proceed from one cognitive stage to another, not only can they grasp and coordinate more facets, say of time and space, but they can also grasp more complex moral ideas.

During the preoperational period young children revel in and explore the meaning and boundaries of their newfound selfhood. Their world revolves around this self. Egocentric, even tyrannical, they are largely concerned with their own interests and wants. Even as they fight against sharing a favorite toy with anyone else, even as they grumble when their will is frustrated, they are, ideally, learning to love and respect their new self. Only then can love and respect turn outward. During the concrete operational period, children can see beyond themselves. They learn about their world, and they learn to love their family and their community. They understand that when two people take turns in a game or when they lend each other something, they are acting and reacting, giving and taking. Children reason about morality in this period in two-dimensional forms of give and take. They can take turns at a board game or skipping rope; they can lend a jacket or a ball.

Gradually, during the concrete operational period, children learn to coordinate more than two dimensions. They begin to comprehend the multitude of roles and attitudes and values that people have. They become capable of reciprocity, of mutual cooperation in groups of three or more. The child who once refused to share her tricycle can now enjoy playing softball on a team, and the child who once punched his playmate for usurping the sandbox can now comfort the "new kid" who never gets picked for soccer games. Finally, during the period of formal operations, adolescents become able to reason about abstract concepts, such as truth, rules, and fairness. With this reasoning incorporated into their moral judgments, adolescents are able to appreciate justice and embrace causes.

Following Piaget's lead, psychologists studying moral reasoning believe that children's morality advances through their interactions with other people. Interaction serves the important functions of exposing people to others' dissimilar thinking and of providing the essential, external arena in which people try out their moral judgments. When children are confronted by reasoning more advanced than their own and when they are ready to perceive it as more advanced, they resolve this difference by adopting the higher reasoning, thus advancing to the next stage of moral development. Interestingly enough, exposure to less advanced reasoning does not necessarily hinder moral development because children reject such reasoning.

PIAGET'S THEORY OF MORAL DEVELOPMENT

THE RULES OF THE GAME

Piaget based much of his theory of moral development on careful observation and skilled questioning of children playing games of marbles. He noticed that as children became older and more cognitively advanced, their marble games changed. The nature of the rules they followed in these games altered, and so did how willing they were to keep the rules. For Piaget, the essence of morality lay in the person's respect for rules. Did children apply rules; if so, how; and did they have a consciousness of rules; if so, what kind? Did they consider the rules of a game obligatory and sacred or subject to choice and alterable?

Piaget believed that by studying how children thought about and followed game rules, he would discover principles of early moral development, because within the structure of a game children must cooperate and resolve certain issues. Within a game of marbles, Piaget reasoned, children must deal with fairness—who goes first; reciprocity—turn taking; and justice—conceding a marble if they lose. And they do so in the company of their peers, not under the supervision of adults.

Piaget analyzed his observations of children playing marbles in terms of his general stage of cognitive development. Playing by rules and playing to win first appear at the beginning of the concrete operational period. Children are concerned about who controls the game and that all the players adopt the same rules. In this period, between the ages of 5 and 10, children operate within a system of **external morality,** according to Piaget. In the external-morality system, rules are perceived as sacred and unalterable and as absolute extensions of authority figures. When Piaget asked children who made up the rules to marbles, they answered that God or their Daddy had. At this stage, children may change the rules in practice as they go along but deny verbally that rules can be

These two fellows are playing chess with leaves for chessmen. It is likely that they are at the stage Piaget called "moral realism," when conforming to rules is considered good and breaking rules is considered bad.

changed. Take Ben, for example, whom Piaget (1932) interviewed about the rules for playing marbles.

> Invent a rule. *I couldn't invent one straight away like that.* Yes you could. I can see that you are cleverer than you make yourself out to be. *Well, let's say that you're not caught when you are in the square.* Good. Would that come off with the others? *Oh, yes, they'd like to do that.* Then people could play that way? *Oh, no, because it would be cheating.* But all your pals would like to, wouldn't they? *Yes, they all would.* Then why would it be cheating? *Because I invented it: it isn't a rule! It's a wrong rule because it's outside of the rules. A fair rule is one that is in the game* (Piaget, 1932, pp. 54–55).

Ben, who is 10 years old, believes that although he might invent a rule, it would be invalid, a "wrong rule." Only an external authority can invent a "fair rule." Although he thinks that all his friends would like to play the game his way—his rule makes it easier to win—he believes that it would not be fair for them to do so.

When Piaget asked another child if a rule could be changed, the child replied that God would punish him by having him miss in a game of marbles if the rule were changed. Piaget described the 5- to 10-year-old child as having a sense of "moral realism." Any act that conforms to a rule is perceived as good; any act not conforming is bad. In moral realism rules are taken literally, and "the good" is viewed only in terms of obedience. Moral actions are evaluated in terms of their exact conformity to established rules. Their thinking constrained by a rather rigid respect for authority figures, children at this stage follow what Piaget called "morality of constraint."

By the end of the concrete operational period, at around age 11, children's ideas about rules are no longer constrained. These older children operate by **internal (autonomous) morality,** which develops with formal operational thinking. They know that rules may be changed if everybody con-

FIGURE 14.1

"Who is naughtier, John or Henry?" According to Piaget's research, younger children, focusing on the consequences, say John. Older children, appreciating the intentions of the two, say Henry.

sents, that rules can be formulated through reasoning and discussion among equals.

INTENTIONS AND CONSEQUENCES

A second method that Piaget used to find out about children's moral development was to ask them questions about moralistic stories. A version of one of these stories follows:

A little boy who is called John is in his room. He is called to dinner. He goes into the dining room. But behind the door there is a chair, and on the chair there is a tray with fifteen cups on it. John couldn't have known that there was all this behind the door. He goes in, the door knocks against the tray, bang go the fifteen cups and they all get broken!

Once there was a little boy whose name was Henry. One day when his mother was out he tried to get some jam out of the cupboard. He climbed up on to a chair and stretched out his arm. But the jam was too high up and he couldn't reach it and have any. But while he was trying to get it he knocked over a cup. The cup fell down and broke.

Then the children were asked who was naughtier, John or Henry, and who should get punished more. Piaget found that children from 5 to 10 said John was naughtier because he broke more cups (Figure 14.1). They based their judgment on the consequences of the act. From age 11 on, children claimed that Henry was naughtier because he was trying to sneak jam. They based their judgment on the intentions of the actor. This change in moral judgment parallels the shift found in children's attitudes toward the rules for marbles, from attention to the external—a heap of broken glass—to reasoning about the internal—the intentional "crime."

Other stories told by Piaget to concrete operational children of different ages revealed additional parallel changes. Children shift from thinking that moral judgments are absolute to realizing that they are relative, that different people have their own perspectives on a situation. They shift from believing that punishment always and inevitably follows wrongdoing to realizing that punishment is meted out by fallible human beings and that the wrong-

doer may or may not be punished. And they shift from thinking that punishment is always of the same severity, no matter what the misdeed, to realizing that "the punishment may fit the crime." When these children are told a story about a little boy who accidentally breaks a pot of flowers while playing ball where he should not be, the older ones appreciate the appropriateness of having the boy replant the flowers, instead of spanking him, sending him to his room, or taking away his toys (Table 14.1).

In the later stages of moral development, which extend through adolescence and adulthood, children recognize the reciprocity between individuals and the intentionality of actions. Children acquire this more sophisticated morality as they gain mutual respect for their peers and learn to take reciprocal roles in their relations with them and as their relationships with adults become more egalitarian and they share in making decisions and rules.

Although Piaget describes his two levels of external constraint versus internal autonomy as "stages," they are not as tightly organized as his stages of cognitive development. They are more like the beginning and end points of moral reasoning than a structured system of successive transformations.

KOHLBERG'S STAGES OF MORAL DEVELOPMENT

Lawrence Kohlberg, like Piaget, emphasizes the cognitive nature of moral judgments. Taking Piaget's two stages as a point of departure, he has postulated six stages of increasingly mature moral reasoning. Both Piaget and Kohlberg consider moral development to be the emergence of more and more mature notions of justice and believe that these notions will create ever greater social harmony and reciprocity. Like Piaget, Kohlberg has interviewed his subjects by presenting them with stories about moral dilemmas.

In 1957, Kohlberg began longitudinal testing of a group of 72 middle-class boys in Chicago, ages 10 through 16. The interviews he gave them originally consisted of 10 of these hypothetical moral dilemmas. For example, the Heinz dilemma places the issues of life and law in conflict. The following is one version of this dilemma.

TABLE 14.1
PIAGETIAN PROGRESS

Age	Moral milestones	Cognitive milestones
5 to 6	Children will feel rage or anger when punished unjustly. Children first become conscious of rules, know that stealing is bad, fear punishment for breaking rules. Rules are sacred and cannot be changed. Children categorize "good" and "bad." Good is rewarded, bad punished. Children think that if they do something good, something good will happen to them; if they do something bad, something bad will happen. Children do not realize that if no one is looking, they will not be caught for wrongdoing.	Children can classify, count, and compare objects. Children begin to see the consequences of actions and can understand that actions produce changes. Children can conserve only through repeated trial and error.
7 to 8	Children judge an act by its consequences not by the actor's intentions. Children can take into account someone else's needs besides their own.	Children can conserve liquid without trial and error but not weight or volume. They can take into account two things at the same time (height and width), but not three (height, width, and weight).
8 to 9	Children try to win games. All adopt the same inflexible rules. They judge it unfair to change rules, even by mutual consent. They cannot understand group compromise.	Children can conserve weight but not volume.
9 to 10	Children consider intentions. He broke my toy, but it was an accident; he tripped and fell on it. Children believe that they can change rules, but they prefer "standardized rules" to their own.	Children can imagine the conservation of liquid. Transitive inference, even with the objects in front of them, is difficult.
10 to 11	Children know that others have feelings that can get hurt. Children can cooperate in games. They can decide who is to go first and how many turns each person should take.	Children can add, subtract, multiply, and divide with pencil and paper but less well in their heads or without their fingers. Children can conserve weight or volume with the help of physical objects. They can perform transitive inference when objects are present.
11 to 12	Children believe that any rule adopted by mutual consent is as good as an established rule; they know rules and values to be relative, not absolute. Children can cooperate with others to formulate and change rules for mutual amusement or interest.	Children think abstractly and perform mental operations, such as conservation, transitive inference, addition, and subtraction in their heads.

In Europe, a woman was near death from a special kind of cancer. There was one drug that the doctors thought might save her. It was a form of radium that a druggist in the same town had recently discovered. The drug was expensive to make, but the druggist was charging ten times what the drug cost him to make. He paid $200 for the radium and charged $2000 for a small *dose of the drug. The sick woman's husband, Heinz, went to everyone he knew to borrow the money, but could only get together about $1000, which was half of what it cost. He told the druggist that his wife was dying and asked him to sell it cheaper or let him pay later. But the druggist said, "No, I discovered the drug and I'm going to make money from it." So Heinz got desperate and considered breaking into the man's store to steal the drug for his wife. Should Heinz steal the radium? (Kohlberg and Gilligan, 1971, pp. 1072–1073).*

In interviewing the boys in his study, Kohlberg was not interested in whether they said that Heinz should or should not steal the radium but in the reasons they gave for their judgments. These reasons, he believed, reflected the "structures" of their moral thought. Kohlberg found three general levels or moral reasoning in the responses the boys gave as they grew older—preconventional, conventional, and postconventional—and two stages at each of these levels. Thus there are six stages altogether.

Children using **preconventional moral reasoning** try to avoid punishment and receive rewards. Moral action is considered to be determined from outside the self, usually by authority figures. Most children younger than 9 and some older than 9 reason at this level. In the first stage of preconventional reasoning, children argue that "might makes right." We behave morally, they say, to avoid punishment and out of an unquestioning deference to superior power. A child in Stage 1 might feel that Heinz should not steal the drug because he will be punished or that Heinz should steal the drug because his wife is so important and powerful in Heinz's life.

In Stage 2 of preconventional reasoning, a "marketplace morality" prevails. Moral action involves making deals for a fair exchange. For example, a child in Stage 2 might feel that Heinz should not steal the drug because it would not be worth the risk of going to jail. At this stage, the child recognizes that jail is not an inevitable consequence of the act of stealing, which is a Stage 1 notion. The child now weighs the possibility of Heinz's getting caught against his desire to restore his wife's health. Many children at the second stage of preconventional reasoning advocate stealing a drug to save a stranger's life if the stranger would

later repay them by saving their life. This they regard as a fair exchange. The goal at this stage is to "look out for number one." Both stages of preconventional morality are basically selfish.

At the level of **conventional moral reasoning,** behaving correctly is viewed as following society's rules and conventions. Most adolescents and adults reason on this level. They are concerned with conforming to, and justifying, the mores of society, with "being a dutiful husband or wife" and "maintaining social order." Moral action involves living up to family obligations and showing concern for others.

During Stage 3, the first conventional stage, people decide how to act by judging how others will feel about their actions. They want to please others and to have their approval, so they do the "good" thing. This stage of moral reasoning has been called that of the "good boy-nice girl." Many Stage 3 children feel that Heinz should steal the drug for his wife because he loves her and cares about her and that she and the rest of the family will approve of his action. They regard the family as more important than individuals and institutions outside the family.

In Stage 4, rules and social order are respected for their own sake. This is the so-called "law-and-order" stage of moral reasoning. Moral action is viewed as doing one's duty for the benefit of the social majority. A Stage 4 response to the Heinz dilemma might focus on the fact that the husband, even if he did not love his wife, should steal the drug to save her life because he has made a marriage vow to take care of her. The sacredness of his vow and his duty as a husband would compel him to steal the drug. Another Stage 4 response makes the opposite case.

No, Heinz should not steal the drug. It is quite understandable why he might do so, knowing the drug could save his wife's life. However, there are laws in this society and whether or not they are fair, there is something to be said for obeying them while they are still laws. Stealing is against the law. Although two wrongs don't make a right is an old cliché, I feel it is a valid one. The druggist was certainly wrong—he was putting the value of money higher than the value of life. Heinz was wrong for breaking the law that was made for everyone's good (Kohlberg, Colby, Gibbs, and Speicher-Dubin, 1978).

Most adolescents and adults reason that moral actions consist of following social rules and conventions. When social rules are obeyed for their own sake, the stage of "law and order" morality has been reached.

Here the subject's concern for the common good goes beyond the Stage 3 concern for the good of the family. In Stage 4, people see society as protecting the rights of the individual.

Kohlberg's level of **postconventional moral reasoning** is acquired by only about 20 percent of the adult population, usually after the age of 20. People behave morally because of their own personal standards rather than because of authority figures or society. People think about moral issues on their own and base their thinking on principles of social reciprocity and justice.

To reason about moral dilemmas at the postconventional level, individuals must be able to think abstractly, weighing a number of courses of action and making decisions about right and wrong. They must understand relativism, that is, that any particular culture's definition of right and wrong, however logical, is only one among many possibilities. No longer constrained by social conventions, people at this stage reason that the rights of the individual must be respected, even if they conflict with the interests of the majority (Kohlberg and Gilligan, 1971).

In the first postconventional stage, Stage 5 individuals recognize that laws are established by mutual agreement and can be changed through the democratic process. They view rules as arbitrary but respect them because they protect human welfare. They believe that by being a member of society one is under a contractual obligation to obey societal laws, but individual rights can sometimes supersede these laws if the laws become destructive. The following response to the Heinz dilemma

was given by a 24-year-old named Joe:

It is the husband's duty to save his wife. The fact that her life is in danger transcends every other standard you might use to judge his action. Life is more important than property.

Suppose it were a friend, not his wife?

I don't think that would be much different from a moral point of view. It's still a human being in danger.

Suppose it were a stranger?

To be consistent, yes, from a moral standpoint.

What is this moral standpoint?

I think every individual has a right to live and if there is a way of saving an individual, he should be saved (Kohlberg, 1976, p. 38).

Notice that Joe favors stealing the drug for wife, friend, and stranger alike. For him, human life is more important than any other standard, legal or otherwise.

In Stage 6, the highest in Kohlberg's scheme for moral reasoning, individuals make their judgments on the basis of universal ethical principles. These principles are logically consistent and based on the highest ethical values: justice, reciprocity, equality, and respect for human life and rights. They are established through individual reflection, not laid down by society. Thus moral action is prescribed by inner conscience and may or may not be in accord with public opinion or societal laws (Table 14.2). The morality of Martin Luther King, Jr., Ma-

TABLE 14.2
KOHLBERG'S STAGES OF MORAL DEVELOPMENT

Moral reasoning	What is right?	How people answer the Heinz dilemma	
		Pro	Con
Preconventional Level Stage 1: Punishment-obedience orientation	To obey the rules of others in order to avoid punishment. Obedience for its own sake, and avoiding physical damage to persons and property.	He should steal the drug. It is not really bad to take it. It is not like he did not ask to pay for it first. The drug he would take is only worth $200; he is not really taking a $2000 drug.	Heinz shouldn't steal; he should buy the drug. If he steals the drug, he might get put in jail and have to put the drug back anyway.
Stage 2: Instrumental-exchange orientation	Following rules only when it is to your advantage; acting to meet your own interests and needs and letting others do the same. Right is also what is fair, what is an equal exchange, a deal, an agreement.	Heinz should steal the drug to save his wife's life. He might get sent to jail, but he'd still have his wife.	He should not steal it. The druggist is not wrong or bad; he just wants to make a profit. That is what you are in business for, to make money.
Conventional Level Stage 3: Good-boy–nice-girl orientation	Living up to what is expected by people close to you or what people generally expect of people in your role as son, brother, friend, and so on. Being "good" is important and means having good motives, showing concern for others. It also means having mutual relationships based on trust, loyalty, respect, and gratitude.	If I were Heinz, I would have stolen the drug for my wife. You can't put a price on love; no amount of gifts makes love. You can't put a price on life either.	He should not steal. If his wife dies, he cannot be blamed. It is not because he is heartless or that he does not love her enough to do everything that he legally can. The druggist is the selfish or heartless one.
Stage 4: System-maintaining orientation	Carrying out the duties that are your obligation. Laws are to be upheld except in the extreme case when they conflict with other fixed social duties. Right is also contributing to society, the group, or institution.	When you get married, you take a vow to love and cherish your wife. Marriage is not only love; it's an obligation like a legal contract.	It is a natural thing for Heinz to want to save his wife, but it is still always wrong to steal. He still knows he is stealing and taking a valuable drug from the man who made it.

TABLE 14.2
(continued)

Moral reasoning	What is right?	How people answer the Heinz dilemma	
		Pro	Con
Postconventional Level			
Stage 5: Social-contract orientation	Being aware that people hold a variety of values and opinions, that most values and rules are relative to the group. These relative rules should usually be upheld, however, in the interest of impartiality and because they are a social contract. Some values and rights, such as *life* and *liberty*, however, must be upheld in any society, regardless of majority opinion.	The law was not set up for these circumstances. Taking the drug in this situation is not really right, but it is justified to do it.	You cannot completely blame someone for stealing, but extreme circumstances do not really justify taking the law in your own hands. You cannot have everyone stealing whenever they get desperate. The end may be good, but the ends do not justify the means.
Stage 6: Universal-ethical-principles orientation	Following self-chosen ethical principles. Particular laws or social agreements are usually valid because they rest on such principles. When laws violate these principles, you must act in accordance with the principles, which are universal: giving equal rights to all and respecting the dignity of human beings as individuals.	This is a situation which forces him to choose between stealing and letting his wife die. In a situation where the choice must be made, it is morally right to steal. He has to act in terms of the principle of preserving and respecting life.	Heinz is faced with the decision of whether to consider the other people who need the drug just as badly as his wife. Heinz ought to act not according to his particular feelings toward his wife but considering the value of all the lives involved.

Source: Kohlberg, 1969, pp. 379–380.

hatma Gandhi, and Mother Teresa exemplifies the kind of principled moral reasoning attained in this stage.

Kohlberg and his associates now have completed a 20-year, longitudinal study of the original sample of Chicago boys (Colby, Kohlberg, Gibbs, and Lieberman, 1983). The boys were interviewed every 3 to 4 years, and their responses were recorded. The investigators found that the boys did proceed through the developmental stages in the hypothesized order, the same order as showed up in cross-sectional comparisons of boys of different ages at the beginning of the study. No subject skipped a stage; only rarely did a subject seem to "regress," or move down a stage. Factor analyses showed that the subjects' answers to the various moral dilemmas were interrelated. Most important, the subjects' moral reasoning continued to advance for the duration of the study, by which time the subjects were men in their thirties (see Figure 14.2).

CRITICISMS OF KOHLBERG'S STAGES

Kohlberg's work has been criticized on several grounds. First, when any two people have analyzed a child's responses to moral dilemmas, they have agreed on the child's stage of moral reasoning only three-quarters of the time or less. Second, Kohlberg and his colleagues have revised their conceptions of Stages 4, 5, and 6 several times, leading some people to criticize the theory as artificial (Kurtines and Grief, 1974). People also have criticized Kohlberg for postulating a hierarchy that is politically liberal in outlook. Conservatism seems to be Stage 4, law-and-order reasoning.

Over the last two decades, Kohlberg and several colleagues—most notably Anne Colby and John Gibbs (Kohlberg et al., 1978)—have refined their scoring system and altered some of Kohlberg's original theoretical assumptions. The notion that human life is more important than individual property rights, for example, was originally believed by Kohlberg to be a Stage 6 notion, but it has now been redefined as more characteristic of Stage 5. The researchers have failed to uncover any Stage 6 reasoning in the responses of their ordinary subjects and considerably less Stage 5 thinking than Kohlberg originally reported. Consequently, Kohlberg and his colleagues (Kohlberg et al., 1978) have suggested that Stage 6 is for the most part a the-

Kohlberg's highest stage of moral reasoning was inspired by the truly exceptional lives of a handful of individuals, such as Mother Teresa of Calcutta, who seem to make moral decisions according to principles that go beyond the interests of self, family, and nation.

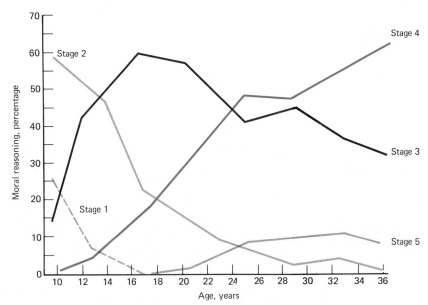

FIGURE 14.2
Percentage of boys and men at different ages giving moral reasoning at each of Kohlberg's five stages.
Source: Colby, Kohlberg, Gibbs, and Lieberman, 1983.

oretical construct suggested to Kohlberg by the lives and writings of extraordinary individuals and not empirically verifiable.

Others have criticized Kohlberg's scheme of moral development for reflecting culture-bound rather than universal values. To test whether his stages were universal, Kohlberg extended his study to middle-class and lower-class urban, tribal, and rural village boys between 10 to 21 years old in several different cultures, including Taiwan, Turkey, and Mexico's Yucatán Peninsula . In all groups, Kohlberg found that Stage 1 through Stage 4 reasoning appeared in sequence as the subjects matured. In most of the groups, some subjects attained Stage 5 reasoning. But the age at which they did so varied according to the subject's intelligence and the group's social and cultural characteristics. People in the poorer tribes and villages were less likely to reach Stage 5 reasoning. If they did reach Stage 5, they did so later, a lag that Kohlberg attributed to two factors. First, people in these groups often did not reason at the level of formal operations. Second, their opportunities for participating in formal social institutions were limited. Elizabeth Simpson (1974) contends, however, that Kohlberg has not found postconventional thinking in these groups because his theory is biased. She argues that the moral dilemmas do not represent real life and that they are culture bound.

Barbara Reid (1984) has tried to incorporate

RESEARCH FOCUS

MORAL JUDGMENT IN TURKEY

Lawrence Kohlberg and an Israeli associate, Mordecai Nisan (Nisan and Kohlberg, 1982), wanted to test the proposition that the stages of moral reasoning that Kohlberg had described and tested in the United States are universal and culturally invariant. Accordingly, they chose to study subjects from Turkey, a nation with a strong nonwestern culture. Some of the subjects were male students, young workers, and young soldiers from a small rural village in Turkey with a traditional culture. Other subjects were students and workers from the Turkish capital, a large city. The researchers conducted interviews in 1964, 1966, 1970, and 1976. All subjects were included in a cross-sectional investigation, and those who were interviewed twice or more were included in a longitudinal investigation. Each subject was presented with the same six hypothetical moral dilemmas during each interview. The dilemmas had been revised for the Turkish setting. For example, the dilemma of Heinz and the drug was changed to:

A man and wife have just migrated from the high mountains. They started to farm, but there was no rain and no crops grew. No one had enough food. The wife became sick from having little food and could only sleep. Finally, she was close to dying from having no food. The husband could not get any work and the wife could not move to another town. There was only one grocery store in the village, and the storekeeper charged a very high price for food because there was no other store and people had no place else to go to buy food. The husband asked the storekeeper for some food for his wife and said he would pay for it later. The storekeeper said, "No, I won't give you any food unless you pay first." The husband went to all the people in the village to ask for food, but no one had food to spare. So he got desperate and broke into the store to steal food for his wife (Nisan and Kohlberg, 1982, p. 868).

The subjects' responses to questions about the dilemmas were scored by raters who did not know the subjects' identity, age, or social group. The investigators calculated scores for the subjects' use of all five stages of moral reasoning and assigned each individual a moral maturity score.

Findings on the Turkish subjects showed clear advances in moral judgment. The subjects' moral reasoning advanced with age and continued beyond 18 years in both the rural and urban subjects. But the rate of development was found to be slower among the rural subjects. Some of the rural men reached Stage 3 reasoning, but only 12 percent of the oldest of them used any Stage 4 reasoning—what Nisan and Kohlberg call a "satisfactory level in the moral functioning of traditional communities." The investigators suggested that men use higher levels of moral reasoning on issues that resemble their personal experience. Although they had not investigated native Turkish moral values, Nisan and Kohlberg concluded that their work had confirmed both the cultural invariability and the stage sequence of Kohlberg's theory of moral development.

social and cultural factors into an analysis of moral development. She analyzes, for example, the extent of regulation or constraint imposed on a person—a measure called "grid"—and the person's commitment to given group—the "group" measure. By combining "grid" and "group" measures for a person, Reid can predict that person's level of moral reasoning. For example, in a study of British scientists, the ambitious high achievers scored low on both grid and group measures. These individuals worked independently and did not participate in the hierarchy of their surrounding work groups. A second group of scientists, who scored high on grid and low on group measures, tended to be passive conformists. A third group of scientists (high grid and high group) participated in their professional hierarchy and tended to be ritualists with a mechanistic view of nature. Finally, a fourth group of scientists (low grid, high group) consisted of small factions in disagreement with the larger society. These grid-group combinations were significantly related to individuals' levels of moral reasoning. Stage 3 reasoning was used by people who worked in situations over which they had little control and in which no group could argue for their rights (high grid, low group). Stage 4 reasoning was used by people who were in, and committed to, professional hierarchies (high grid, high group). Stage 5 reasoning was common among individuals in environments of little social control and little commitment to a group, especially as contrasted to commitment to oneself (low grid, low group). Reid suggests that people reason at various levels strategically and because others find the reasoning appropriate. They change their moral reasoning not because their logic advances—as Kohlberg holds—but because they move to a new grid and group.

Not only may Kohlberg's stages of moral judgment be related to cultural or social-environmental differences, but they may also be affected by historical events.

Historical circumstances, particularly compelling and dramatic events such as wars are likely to affect individuals' moral reasoning and actions significantly.

Consider the subjects tested in Kohlberg's 20-year longitudinal study, initiated in the mid-1950s. Over the period in which these subjects have been assessed for moral judgment, Americans have experienced the civil rights struggle, student protests, the Vietnam War, Watergate, and the women's movement. All of these events have raised issues of justice and have focused attention on moral concerns. It seems highly likely that these social events have had an impact generally on people's concepts of fairness. Changes in moral judgment scores over the past 20 years, therefore, may reflect cultural change as well as individual ontogenesis (Rest, Davison, and Robbins, 1978, p. 272).

Yet another criticism has been raised by Elliot Turiel (1978a). He has argued that Kohlberg has failed to make a necessary distinction between social rules, such as etiquette and the rules for a game, and moral rules, such as "Do not steal." Turiel believes that these rules are distinct and develop independently. He contends that morality is defined by principles of justice that prescribe behavior, whereas social rules and conventions are part of, and are defined by, social organizations. Furthermore, conventional rules can be altered arbitrarily, but moral rules cannot. In one study Turiel (1978) asked American children from 6 to 17 years old the question, "If a country had no rule against stealing, would it be right for a person to steal in that country?" Most children believed that it would still be wrong to steal. When asked whether it would be right for youngsters in another country to play a game by differing rules, the children said

that if the players agreed, the rules could be changed.

Kohlberg views moral judgment and social understanding as one and the same and calls it "sociomoral perspective." Research suggests, however, that people may be relatively sophisticated socially and advanced at seeing things from another's perspective but be less advanced in their moral reasoning. Joseph Hickey (1972), for example, found that delinquent and nondelinquent youths had the same levels of social understanding but that the delinquents reasoned morally at significantly lower stages.

Most recently, Carol Gilligan (1982) has aroused wide interest with her criticism of Kohlberg's theory as sexist. Gilligan opposes Kohlberg's analysis because it is based on and biased toward male responses. She suggests that women and men differ psychologically in ways that directly impinge on

RESEARCH FOCUS

MORAL AND SOCIAL RULES

Larry Nucci and Maria Santiago Nucci (1982), of the University of Illinois, decided to investigate how children playing freely and without adult supervision would react to violations of either moral or social rules. They also wanted to see whether boys and girls would react differently. Children, they thought, might construe spitting or chewing grass as violations of social rules, and throwing sand at a smaller child or taking away a younger child's sled as violations of moral rules—and respond differently to the two kinds of violations. The Nuccis defined moral rules as "those that involved acts having intrinsic effects upon the welfare and rights of individuals or groups" and social rules as "existing consensual norms" (p. 1339). They visited 10 suburban Chicago playgrounds and watched children as they played without adult supervision. They focused on play among groups of five or more children who were either 7 to 10 years old or 11 to 14, and they observed 4 hours of play for each age group. Observations consisted of describing transgressions against moral and social rules and noting children's responses to the transgressions. These responses included: statements of in-

jury or loss, retaliation, statements of disorder or deviation, declarations of rules, ridicule, threats, and commands.

In all, the Nuccis witnessed 900 transgressions and found that children in both age groups responded more often to moral than social transgressions. Children retaliated and made statements about injury, loss, and unfairness more often in response to moral than social transgressions. In contrast, they ridiculed or made statements about disorder and deviation more often in response to violations of social rules. The investigators also found significant differences between boys' and girls' reactions, in that boys were likelier than girls to retaliate for moral trangressions. As others had found when they observed children in supervised, school settings, the Nuccis found that for moral transgression children focused on the *intrinsic* features of the violation but for transgressions of social rules they focused on the *external* social organization that had been disrupted. Unlike children who were supervised, children without adult supervision responded to violations of seemingly arbitrary social conventions—for example, calling two boys riding a sled "faggots" or ridiculing two children who were tying their shoes with, "Bobby and Allison sittin' in a tree, K-I-S-S-I-N-G."

their moral reasoning. Women are more attuned to the relationships and connections among people; men are more attuned to individual achievement, to the separateness and distinctiveness of each person. Women take much of their personal identities from their personal relationships; men take theirs from their work. From these psychological underpinnings, women are likely to be morally concerned with how people are connected, obligated to one another, and generally interrelated and interdependent. Men are likely to be morally concerned with justice, individual rights and obligations, and equitable solutions to each separate person's conflicting and competing claims. Says Gilligan, women's is a morality of caring, and men's is a morality of justice.

Given their different orientations to moral reasoning, it is not surprising that when men and women or boys and girls respond to one of Kohlberg's hypothetical moral dilemmas, they respond quite differently. Gilligan contends that women are automatically disadvantaged by Kohlberg's ratings of moral maturity. Kohlberg's moral dilemmas pose conflicts of individual rights and social justice, precisely those areas in which men are trained to reason analytically. These dilemmas draw on men's powers of logical deduction and rational thought. But women, who see the dilemmas more as problems in the web of human relationships, score lower on Kohlberg's ratings of moral maturity. Gilligan criticizes Kohlberg's system for rating all responses centering on caring for others or personal responsibility as Stage 3 reasoning—a low normal score for adults and one that places women below men.

Gilligan describes the responses of two 11-year-olds, a boy and a girl, to the dilemma about Heinz, his sick wife, and the greedy druggist. Both children were bright and not obviously given to sex-role stereotyping. Jake feels quite sure that Heinz should steal the drug to save his wife. After analyzing the dilemma as a conflict between life and property, Jake argues logically that life takes priority:

For one thing, a human life is worth more than money, and if the druggist only makes $1,000, he is still going to live, but if Heinz doesn't steal the drug, his wife is going to die. (Why is life worth more than money?) Because the druggist can get $1,000 later from rich people with cancer, but Heinz can't get his wife again. (Why not?) Because people are all different and so

you couldn't get Heinz's wife again (Gilligan, 1982, p. 26).

As Jake says, the judge should give Heinz a light sentence for stealing; Jake believes that rational people can recognize and agree on "the right thing to do." Jake sees the dilemma as "sort of like a math problem with humans," a problem in logic, in other words, to be solved rationally.

But Amy responds to the same moral dilemma in quite a different way. As Gilligan points out, Amy's answers convey a surface impression of stunted logical development and an inability to think for herself. But Amy is actually answering the question of *how* Heinz should act, not the question of *whether* he should act. Should Heinz steal the drug, Amy is asked:

Well, I don't think so. I think there might be other ways besides stealing it, like if he could borrow the money or make a loan or something, but he really shouldn't steal the drug—but his wife shouldn't die either (Gilligan, 1982, p. 28).

Why shouldn't Heinz steal the drug, Amy is then asked:

If he stole the drug, he might save his wife then, but if he did, he might have to go to jail, and then his wife might get sicker again, and he couldn't get more of the drug, and it might not be good. So, they should really just talk it out and find some other way to make the money (Gilligan, 1982, p. 28).

In Amy's eyes, the problem is one of enduring relationships and human needs. The wife's survival is based on the preservation of relationships, Gilligan notes, and her life is valued in terms of relationships as well: "If she died, it hurts a lot of people and it hurts her." The druggist's failure to respond to another's need thus becomes a central problem. Amy has answered a question the interviewer has failed to imagine. Gilligan points out that because Amy does not see the dilemma as a problem in moral logic, Kohlberg's ideas elude her. To Amy, the problem is one of impressing the druggist with the dying wife's needs or of appealing to others who might help. The problem is not one of rules that prevail in a world of people standing alone—as it was for Jake and for Kohlberg. Whereas Jake saw the need for agreement mediated through logic and law, Amy sees the need for agreement mediated through the communication among interrelated people. In Kohlberg's analysis, Amy's responses appear a full stage lower in maturity than those of Jake. This impression is misleading, Gilligan contends, because Amy has perceived the central truths in a morality of caring, a central tenet in nonviolent resolutions of conflicts.

When Jake and Amy are asked, "When responsibility to oneself and responsibility to others conflict, how should one choose?" Jake answers again as if he were dealing with a problem of human mathematics. Says Jake:

You go about one-fourth to the others and three-fourths to yourself (Gilligan, 1982, p. 35).

But Amy characteristically answers in terms of relationships and caring:

Well, it really depends on the situation. If you have a responsibility with someone else, then you should keep it to a certain extent, but to the extent that it is really going to hurt you or stop you from doing something that you really, really want, then I think maybe you should put yourself first. But if it is your responsibility to somebody really close to you, you've just got to decide in that situation which is more important,

yourself or that person, and like I said, it really depends on what kind of person you are and how you feel about the other person or persons involved (Gilligan, 1982, p. 36).

Jake takes his responsibility to himself for granted and asserts that responsibility consists of *not doing* what he wants out of deference to others. But Amy considers responsibility to consist of *doing* what other people expect her to do, regardless of her personal wishes. Both children want to avoid hurt, but their analyses of the solution are quite different.

Gilligan suggests that real-life moral dilemmas, such as that presented by an unwanted pregnancy, be used to measure women's moral maturity. When she questioned 21 women who had to decide whether to have an abortion, Gilligan found that they analyzed their dilemma with a steady eye on "caring."

Gilligan's criticisms of Kohlberg in turn have been met with criticism of her work. Anne Colby and William Damon (1983) have argued that Gilligan's study of women's thoughts about abortion lacked controls rigorous enough to support her contention of Kohlberg's bias against women. Furthermore, they argue that Kohlberg's system can be said to discriminate against women only if women actually score lower than men do—as Gil-

Carol Gillgian has suggested that in the real-life moral dilemma that an unwanted pregnancy presents, women's morality is one of caring about people's interdependence. Men, she suggests, subscribe to a morality of justice, individual rights, and equitable solutions to all.

ligan maintains. But when subjects' educational and work backgrounds are controlled, women do *not* score lower than men in moral reasoning (Rest, in press; Walker, in press). Colby and Damon grant that Kohlberg's early scoring measures did tend to confound form and content but point out that his most recent measures separate them and that measures of trust, caring, relationships, affiliation, and social harmony appear in his scoring for *every stage* of moral reasoning.

Damon himself, however, has taken exception to Kohlberg's approach for presenting children with moral dilemmas filled with the unfamiliar and unusual. He suggests that a better test than Heinz and the druggist for studying young children's moral reasoning might be something like the following:

> *Here are four little children just about your age. Well, actually, George here is a couple of years younger than the other three. Let's pretend that they were at school one day when their teacher, Miss Townsend, asked them to go outside with a couple of men. The men told the four kids that they really liked bracelets made by little children, and they asked the kids if they would make some bracelets for them. The kids spent about fifteen or twenty minutes making lots of bracelets for the men. Michelle here made a whole lot of bracelets, more than anyone else, and hers were the prettiest ones, too. John and Ellen made some nice bracelets, too; and, as you can see, John is the biggest boy there. George, the younger kid, didn't do so well. He only made half of a bracelet, and it was not very pretty.*
>
> *Well, one of the men thanked them all for making bracelets, and put before them ten candy bars, which he said was their reward for making the bracelets. But he said that the kids would have to decide what the best way was to split up the candy bars between themselves. Let's pretend that these are the ten candy bars [represented with poker chips]. How do you think the kids should split them up between themselves? (Damon, 1977, pp. 64–65).*

Damon (1977) classifies children's responses to this problem into six different levels:

- At Level 0–A, children confuse desire with justice. They see no need for objective justifications.

- At Level 0–B, children cite some objective but arbitrary reason for their decision, but they do not think in terms of the principle of rewarding special work or good deeds. They might say, "We should get more candy because we're boys."

- At Level 1–A, children insist on equal treatment for everyone as the best way of settling claims. "Everybody gets the same number of candy bars," they argue.

- At Level 1–B, children see justice as the reward for goodness. They see that although everyone claims a reward, some people are more deserving than others. They might argue that Michelle should get the most candy because she made the most and prettiest bracelets.

- At Level 2–A, children recognize that people have their own claims and that some compromise must be reached in settling those claims. They might argue, "Michelle should get more candy because she made more bracelets, but little George shouldn't be penalized for being young."

- At Level 2–B, children not only recognize competing claims but also envision justice as serving larger purposes and the social good. They might rule out some claims as irrelevant and argue that a reward system be worked out to affirm production, group cohesion, caring, or some other broad principle.

Damon suggests that moral development is a series of confusions in a child's mind. At the earliest level, children confuse justice with their own desires; at the most advanced level, justice is confused with a situational ethic. Although Damon does not explain how children resolve their confusions and move to other levels, his original theory probes important cognitive processes in moral development and demonstrates how developmental psychologists are now extending, refining, and extrapolating from— as well as criticizing—Kohlberg's theory of moral reasoning.

TRANSITIONS IN MORAL REASONING

Cognitive developmentalists maintain that when individuals are confronted often enough with reasoning one stage higher than their dominant mode, they are thrown off balance and resolve it by advancing to the next stage. James Rest, Elliot Turiel, and Lawrence Kohlberg (1969) measured children's reactions to reasoning at stages different from their own. They had children read a series of moral dilemmas in a booklet. After each dilemma, subjects wrote in their own responses and then read "advice" given by other children on what the story character should do. This advice was at varying stages from the subjects' own stage—one or two stages above or one stage below that of the subjects. The subjects were asked to choose which advice was the best, the worst, the smartest, and the most reasonable. Children were also asked to restate the advice in their own words. Children were considered to understand the advice if their restatement was at the same stage of moral reasoning as that of the original. In this study, children were most likely to understand thinking that was a stage below their own moral reasoning; however, they rejected thinking at that stage as inadequate,

calling it the "worst" advice. They found reasoning one and two levels above their own level more difficult to comprehend, but they preferred it to reasoning at their own level and below.

But does this preference for thinking one stage higher affect the individual's own subsequent moral reasoning? Turiel (1966) tested children by giving them brief training sessions in one stage below, one stage above, or two stages above their own. The group presented with reasoning at the stage just one above their own were found to show the most positive change in their thinking when they were tested again. The other children did not shift significantly.

A number of similar studies reviewed by Rest (1983) did not report such results, however, and some researchers have questioned the appropriateness of short-term training. They have argued that, aside from many methodological problems—for example, that training sessions may be too short and too specific, that stage assessments are crude—actual moral growth is a slow process. Longitudinal

---

RESEARCH FOCUS

TRAINING IN MORAL REASONING

Can children be taught moral reasoning so that they can skip forward through Kohlberg's sequence of stages faster than their ages would lead one to predict? Lawrence Walker (1982), of the University of British Columbia, wanted to find out. He therefore chose 100 fifth- through seventh-grade, middle-class, parochial-school students. He first assessed the subjects' cognitive development. Word problems and tests of logic were used to assess formal operations; class-inclusion and conservation-of-weight problems were used to assess concrete operations. He also tested the children's perspective-taking abilities and administered three of Kohlberg's moral dilemmas. Only the 50 children— or half of the original number—whose cognitive and perspective-taking test results were higher than their moral reasoning, (suggesting that they were capable of further moral development) were included in the training procedures. These children were exposed to moral reasoning that was behind or ahead of their own levels.

Training consisted of hearing a man and woman present reasoning about six moral dilemmas. Children were randomly assigned to hear *conflicting* opinions supported by reasoning one stage below their own; one stage above their own or two stages above their own; or to hear *agreeing* opinions at their own level (the neutral condition); or to hear no reasoning (the control condition). Walker tested the children after 1 week and again at 7 weeks after treatment. No children, he found, regressed or skipped a stage. Children exposed to reasoning one and two levels above their own advanced one stage in moral reasoning and were still reasoning about one-half of a stage above their original levels on the follow-up tests. Children exposed to other reasoning or to none did not advance. Although he conceded that he could investigate only the lower levels of development because his subjects were relatively young, Walker concluded that his findings supported Kohlberg's contention that order of stages of moral development is invariant. At the same time, he suggested that the timetable for reaching moral stages can be accelerated by training.

studies have found that changing a full stage takes 4 years or more.

EMOTIONS AND MORALITY

GUILT AND EMPATHY

What is the role of the emotions in children's moral development? The general hypothesis from psychoanalytic theory is that morality develops in early childhood out of fear and anxiety at the thought of losing a parent's love and from guilt over incestuous fantasies about the opposite-sex parent (Freud, 1930). **Guilt** encompasses feelings of having committed a sin, done something evil, subjected someone to an unjustice, and of being generally in the wrong and deserving punishment. When the child has developed a sense of guilt, moral sanctions emanate from within.

In psychoanalytic theory, the child's ability to identify with the parent is necessary for the formation of conscience. It is *the* essential relationship for fostering moral growth, one that cannot be replaced by other identifications with teachers, peers, or siblings. Taking the role of the parent leads the child to internalize parental standards wholly and unquestioningly.

Empirical research does not support the contention that conscience is formed only through identification with parents however. Studies comparing the moral development of kibbutz-reared and family-reared Israeli children (reviewed by Kohlberg, 1964), for example, have shown no differences in the guilt felt by the two groups of children and in their morality, even though kibbutz-reared children received their moral socialization primarily from caregivers and teachers in the Children's House where they lived. Nevertheless, identification with some adult authority and acceptance of that authority's standards probably are necessary for children to feel guilt and behave morally.

Guilt and morality may be induced in another way, through empathy. When children can distinguish themselves from others, when they understand that someone else's distress is not their own, they can experience pain or **sympathetic distress** *for* the victim. According to Martin Hoffman (1976), who has studied both children's empathy

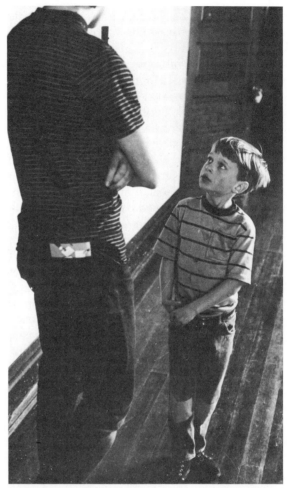

According to psychoanalytic theory, the young boy develops his conscience by identifying with his father and adopting his standards. The youngster feels guilty when he does not live up to his father's expectations.

and moral development extensively, sympathetic distress is at first accompanied by guilt only when children feel responsible for the plight of the victim. Later, guilt accompanies sympathetic distress even when children are not directly responsible for the victim's plight, if they perceive that they could have done something to prevent the painful situation. Failure to act on behalf of someone stirs guilt in older children and adults.

DISCIPLINARY METHODS AND MORAL ACTION

How likely children are to feel empathy and guilt and to behave morally may be related to their parents' methods of discipline. Parents may simply assert their power with physical punishment, by taking away the child's toys or privileges, by applying force, or by threatening any of these. Parents rely on their child's fear of punishment to deter the child from transgressing. The moral responses of children disciplined consistently in this way are at the lowest level. For example, several studies have measured children's moral orientation by having them provide endings or answer questions about stories in which the protagonist commits a crime or an act of aggression against another person (Aronfreed, 1961; Hoffman and Saltzstein, 1967). Children's responses are taken to reflect "internal" moral orientation if they mention reparation for wrongdoing, acceptance of blame or responsibility, or if they stress emotional and ethical issues. Responses that focus on physical calamity or punishment imposed by others as a result of the transgression indicate "external" moral orientation. Children whose parents use power-assertive discipline are more likely to have an external moral orientation (Hoffman, 1970). Hoffman suggests that power-assertive discipline, with its threat of severe punishment, arouses so much emotion in children that they are unable to concentrate on moral issues, such as the effect of a transgression. These children are also more likely to cheat, less likely to experience guilt or to accept blame after a moral transgression.

Another disciplinary practice of parents is to withdraw love when their children misbehave, acting angry or disapproving; ignoring their children, refusing to speak to, or listen to them; stating a dislike for them; isolating them or threatening abandonment. This disciplinary method does not have clear or consistent effects on moral development. Children whose parents withdraw love may respond morally or not. But if this method arouses a great deal of emotion—because children feel seriously threatened with loss of their parents' love—they, too, like the children threatened with punishment by their parents, are probably unable to concentrate on moral issues.

The most effective disciplinary method for advancing moral development is to create an atmosphere of warm approval, praise, and acceptance for the child and then explain why the child should act in particular ways. This method, less punitive than either assertion or love withdrawal, is persua-

sive in appealing to children's pride, competence, self-esteem, and concern for others. Parents may point out how the child's actions will affect someone else: "If you throw snow on their walk, they will have to clean it up all over again"; or explain someone's motives to the child: "Don't hit him. He didn't mean to push you. He tripped"; or explain someone's needs: "He's afraid of dogs, so don't let Spot get too close to him." Parents commonly focus on the consequences to others of their very young children's behavior. By middle childhood, they stress the effects of the children's behavior on themselves, the parents. This kind of discipline helps children integrate their capacity for empathy with knowledge of how their behavior affects others. This, Hoffman suggests, may be the essential contribution of discipline to the child's moral development.

LEARNING MORAL BEHAVIOR

Social-learning theory assumes that parents and others in a position to socialize children shape their moral behavior through modeling and that moral beliefs center around social "virtues," such as truthfulness, cleanliness, punctuality, and other good behavior. Children acquire moral behavior and values as they are socialized into specific cultures.

RESISTANCE TO TEMPTATION

Early social-learning research conducted by Hugh Hartshorne and Mark May (1928–1930) focused on children's "moral character." In their experiments—testing some 11,000 children ranging in age from 8 to 16—Hartshorne and May gave children the opportunity to cheat, lie, or steal. Each test tempted the child to do something for personal gain that he or she would not want others to find out about. In each situation, children were not aware that their behavior was being observed. Children were tempted to copy somebody else's answers during a test or to cheat in party games, in sports contests, or when doing duties at home. They were tested in a number of settings: at home, at school, at clubs, on playgrounds, and at church.

Hartshorne and May concluded that honest behavior was influenced by the situation and such factors as punishment, reward, and pressures for conformity rather than by a guilt-motivated conscience. They based this conclusion on the fact that children could not be divided into clear-cut groups of cheaters and noncheaters. If honesty were a personality trait, they reasoned, children with the trait would resist temptation to lie both at home and at school. But honesty, they found, depended on the circumstances. Nearly all children were dishonest on some occasions. They were the most likely to be honest when there was risk of detection and it took effort to cheat. Not cheating was motivated by caution rather than by honesty. When entire classes were studied and compared, it was found that in some classes many children cheated, in other classes almost none cheated. Hartshorne and May attributed this difference to group pressures to conform rather than to children's individual decisions about honesty.

Roger Burton (1963) used techniques of data analysis not available at the time Hartshorne and May performed their study to reanalyze some of their data. He chose six cheating situations that were the most reliable of Hartshorne and May's situations, and he did find some evidence for an "honesty factor." Some of the children tended to be more consistently honest, some more consistently dishonest. Even so, children's honesty varied in different settings.

Subsequent research on **resistance to temptation** has partially confirmed Hartshorne and May's findings (Burton, 1976), but it has partitioned their vast research area into smaller, more manageable parts. For example, Mavis Hetherington and Solomon Feldman (1964) studied cheating by college students on three course examinations: 59 percent of the students cheated on at least one of the three examinations; 64 percent of these cheated on two of the three exams; 22 percent cheated on all three. The most honest of the cheaters, 6 percent of them, cheated on one portion of one exam. Thus cheating varied both with the individual and in amount. Keep in mind, however, that in these studies the researchers did not take into account what level of proficiency students had in the subject areas of the tests. It may be that the students who cheated less or not at all did not need to because they knew the subject matter. The fact that individual differences in ability were not controlled for may explain the observed variability in cheating.

Rather than being a definite and fixed personality trait, children's honesty seems to depend on the situation, such as the likelihood of being caught in a misdeed.

MODELING MORALITY

Social-learning researchers have looked at the effects of adult and peer models on children's resistance to temptation. In one study (Stein, 1967), it was hypothesized that children who watched an adult either yield to, or resist, temptation would imitate the adult's behavior. The 84 fourth-grade boys in the study, which was done in Minneapolis, were divided into three groups and assigned one by one to do a boring job while an interesting movie taken on the school playground was run just outside the boy's field of vision. Each boy was instructed to remain in his chair in order to perform the assigned task. To see the movie he had to leave his chair. Boys were scored as resisting temptation if they stayed put. Just before they began their task, the boys in the first group saw an adult get up from his chair and boring work and go peek at the movie. Boys in the second group saw an adult stay seated and keep at his task. Those in the third group did not see a model. Boys who had watched an adult give in to temptation yielded more readily than subjects who saw no model or a resisting model. But the boys who saw a resisting model had no greater resistance to temptation than children who saw no model. Thus seeing "honest" behavior does not necessarily produce greater "honesty," but seeing "dishonest" behavior may induce greater "dishonesty"—or so this experiment suggests.

PUNISHMENT

Studies of how punishment affects children's moral behavior have focused on a combination of punishment and reasoning. These studies have shown that simply telling children that cheating is bad does not by itself effectively decrease cheating. For very young children such statements have no effect at all, unless they increase their fear of discovery. With adolescents, however, they can inhibit cheating to some degree (Burton, 1976).

Although punishment has been proved the most effective when it comes immediately after a transgression, this condition is difficult to fulfill as children grow older. Parents may not find out that their teenager played hooky from school until a day or two later. Parents must re-create the situation for children before punishing them in order to reinforce the connection between the transgression and the punishment. In a study by David Andres and Richard Walters (1970), children watched themselves transgressing on videotape while their actions were described or they were told to commit their act again and were then punished. These methods were better at preventing future transgressions than giving children delayed punishment without recreating the situation.

WHAT IS MORAL MATURITY?

The three theories of moral development that have been discussed do not agree about the state of children as they enter the world and how they change in their moral reasoning and behavior. Those who subscribe to a cognitive developmental view see children as potentially moral; given contact with progressively higher levels of moral reasoning, their own moral reasoning advances, much as their cognitive abilities advance. Psychoanalysts find the child to be initially immoral, a slave to antisocial, uncontrollable impulses. Social-learning theorists see the child as initially amoral and then as learning to behave in a way consistent with how the child's culture defines morality.

Each theory also has a different concept of mature morality. For cognitive developmentalists, moral maturity is the ability to make autonomous moral decisions. The morally mature individual has passed through a series of successive stages and gradually acquired notions of reciprocity, fairness, equality, and a sense of justice. These thoughts provide a basis for moral action. Psychoanalysts see moral maturity as control of impulses. The morally mature individual is held in check by strong emotions of guilt. The intensity of guilt lets the person accept blame for transgressions and try to make reparations for wrongdoing. Moral standards are internalizations of the codes of parents. For social-learning theorists, the most important indicator of moral maturity is moral action, which varies from culture to culture. Social-learning theorists would call self-control, honesty, and resistance to temptation mature moral behavior.

Proponents of all three theories, despite their differences, agree that the onset of adolescence signals an important change in moral development.

Although the foundation for morality is laid before adolescence, behavior is not morally mature until then. Only then do young people achieve the cognitive sophistication to reflect on their thoughts and values and compare them to those of others. These abilities pave the way for a more autonomous view of rules, of laws, and of obedience to authority. Adolescent rebellion against parents and other authority figures is not in and of itself a moral phenomenon, but it is a necessary forerunner to autonomy in judgment, moral and otherwise. The adolescent's autonomy means increasing ego strength, self-awareness, and self-control. By the time young people reach adolescence, they have become consistently more honest or dishonest than they were as children. Adolescents also have a greater grasp of the motives and implications of their actions than children do, having developed a

Many adolescents feel sympathetic distress and social guilt. These feelings compel them to embrace social causes and to worry about the future of humanity.

sense of sympathetic distress and a sense of personal as well as social guilt. Their sense of justice and fair play may motivate adolescents to redress an immoral act, an unfair public policy, an unjust rule.

MORAL REASONING AND MORAL ACTION

Theories of moral development may separate moral reasoning; moral emotions, such as empathy and guilt; and moral actions. But when we use the term "moral," we usually assume that it means all three. Can an action be considered moral if it is not performed in the service of an underlying moral principle? Is a person moral if he or she makes mature moral judgments but acts like a criminal? Researchers have studied how moral judgments and emotions are linked to the actions of individuals.

One way of studying the question has been to look at the moral reasoning of children who do or do not behave honestly. In a study by Richard Krebs and Lawrence Kohlberg (1973), four of Hartshorne and May's experimental tests of cheating were given to 120 junior high-school students, and they were interviewed about their judgments concerning Kohlberg's moral dilemmas. Of the children whose moral reasoning was preconventional, 75 percent cheated on one or more of the tasks, 66 percent of those whose reasoning was at the conventional level, and only 20 percent of the postconventional subjects cheated. These results suggest that there is indeed a relation between moral reasoning and moral behavior.

In another study, however, Krebs (1967) found a positive relation between higher Kohlberg stages of reasoning and honesty only if the children were given the dilemmas *before* they were tempted to cheat. If they were interviewed *after* the temptation tests, higher moral reasoning seemed to be associated with *less* resistance to temptation. It may be that by interviewing children about their moral judgments before a temptation test, those who had higher moral reasoning were made suspicious about the situation that followed the interview. Because advanced stages of moral development are associated with more advanced reasoning of other kinds, the children may have inferred from the interview that any cheating on their part would be detected. The moral-dilemmas interview may have brought the subjects' higher moral judgments into consciousness so that they were more likely to act on them. The relation between moral reasoning and moral action, at least as measured by moral dilemmas and opportunities to cheat, is not as clear as we might expect. Other studies trying to document the link between moral thought and action have run into the same difficulty.

Norma Haan, Brewster Smith, and Jeanne Block (1968) tested a number of college students involved in political activism at the University of California at Berkeley to determine their level of moral reasoning. They expected students who were involved in protest against the established system to be more likely to reason on the postconventional level. The results indicated that 75 percent of the subjects whose moral reasoning was scored at Kohlberg's Stage 6 and 41 percent of those at Stage 5 participated in a campus free-speech sit-in. Only 6 percent of the Stage-4 (law and order) and 18 percent of Stage-3 (good boy-nice girl) reasoners participated. So far so good; moral reasoning predicts moral action. Surprisingly, however, 60 percent of the preconventional Stage-2 (instrumental exchange) reasoners, who base their moral judgments on self-interest, also participated in the sit-

RESEARCH FOCUS

MORAL REASONING AND DECISION MAKING

To most people, it makes intuitive sense that people might offer moral reasons for how someone else should act that would differ quite markedly from those they might offer for their own actions. Richard Weiss (1982) tested this assumption on a group of 16- to 18-year-old, middle-class, public high school students in California. In their first session with Weiss, half of the students were presented with one of two moral dilemmas. One dilemma depicted a teenager who holds a party when her parents are away. The other depicted a teenager who leaves the home of vacationing neighbors to join friends, despite the fact that he has been given responsibility for the house. Subjects in the "self" perspective were told to imagine themselves in the dilemma. Subjects in the "other" perspective were told to imagine that the dilemma applied to a hypothetical "someone else." All the subjects were asked to decide whether to tell the parents or neighbors what has happened in their absence and to decide, "In this situation, for everybody concerned, what's the best or wisest thing to do, and why?" All the subjects also answered seven questions designed to probe their moral reasoning. In a second interview about 3 weeks after the first, Weiss administered the vacation dilemma to the students who previously had evaluated the party dilemma, and vice versa. He also had the students who pre-viously had been in the "self" condition imagine that the dilemma applied to the hypothetical "someone else," and vice versa.

Did the students apply the same moral standards to others as to themselves? Much as Weiss had predicted, he found that the students applied a higher moral standard to others than to themselves. Although the students more often than not decided that the adults in the dilemmas should be told about the unwise acts of the teenagers, they opted for disclosure *less* often when they imagined themselves in the dilemmas. When they had to imagine themselves in a dilemma, students showed much more concern for getting caught or getting in trouble—what Weiss called "prudential concerns"—than they did when they had to imagine someone else in the dilemma. The teenagers tended to segregate moral reasoning from decision making and, in dilemmas about others, applied standards that did not "count" for themselves. Only when students imagined themselves in the dilemmas did their level of moral reasoning seem integrated with their decisions.

Weiss found evidence of four levels of moral reasoning; with each succeeding level, he suggests, the students' awareness of bias in decision making increased. At all four levels, Weiss found evidence of prudential concerns, but the teenagers who showed some evidence of the highest level of reasoning were less likely than those at lower levels to make self-serving decisions in either the self or the fictitious-other dilemma.

in. The activism of the morally immature, Stage-2 reasoners and the morally mature, Stage-6 reasoners was indistinguishable. Haan, Smith, and Block suggest that the postconventional activists perceived themselves as protecting the civil rights of all individuals within the community, whereas the preconventional activists were demonstrating for their own personal rights. Thus we cannot always judge individual morality solely by actions. We must also know the reasons for the actions.

Rest (1983) has proposed a four-component model for integrating moral beliefs with moral actions. The first component consists of interpreting a situation and surmising how one's actions might affect others. Many people, Rest notes, find it difficult to interpret even simple situations. People also differ enormously in their sensitivity to others' needs and welfare, a sensitivity that tends to develop with age. Not only must people interpret the situation, but they must also interpret their own feelings in that situation. Even imperfectly understood situations arouse feelings of alarm, empathy, anger, envy, exhilaration. Once people have thought about alternative possibilities and how these might affect others as well as themselves, they judge and integrate these alternatives.

Rest's second component is the determination of a moral ideal, of what *ought* to be done in a particular situation. Kohlberg's and Piaget's levels of moral reasoning contribute mainly to this second component. Rest's third component is deciding what one actually is going to do in the specific situation, determining a real course of action. Often, other sorts of values besides moral values weigh heavily in a person's choice of action. Religious values, ambition, and self-interest are just three such possibilities. As Rest points out, when Damon (1977) presented real children with his moral dilemma about dividing candy bars among a group, there was a discrepancy between the moral values some of the children espoused and their actual distribution of real candy bars: Despite their reasoning about fairness and equal rewards, the children gave themselves a disproportionate share of the candy bars. There is often a gap, notes Rest, between what people think they *should* do and what they *will* do.

The final component in Rest's scheme is executing and carrying out a plan of action, a process that involves planning a sequence of actions; surmounting obstacles, fatigue, and disappointment; resisting distractions and other temptations; and keeping the goal in mind. Acts both moral and immoral—preparing for a track meet, robbing a bank, rehearsing for a play, or murdering someone—all require skills in regulating oneself and in mobilizing oneself to action.

SUMMARY

1. Cognitive developmentalists are interested in the thought processes children use in determining right and wrong. They believe that children's morality advances through exchanges with others, which expose them to thinking that is different from their own. As their thinking becomes more sophisticated, so does their moral reasoning.

2. Piaget initially studied the morality of children by observing them at games of marbles and questioning them about the rules they followed. From ages 5 to 10, children have external morality; they believe that rules are proclaimed from on high and are unalterable. At about age 11 children begin to operate by autonomous morality and know that rules are formulated through reasoning and discussion.

3. Piaget also told children stories about youngsters who have done something wrong. Children at first judge others in these stories by the consequences of their acts, later by their intentions.

4. Lawrence Kohlberg presented children with moral dilemmas and found three levels of moral reasoning. At the preconventional level, children first try not to break rules because they do not want to be punished. They regard as moral actions that serve their own immediate interests and earn fair exchange from others.

5. At the conventional level of moral reasoning, children are concerned about following society's rules and conventions. Their concerns are for the family and for being good boys and good girls. They develop a law-and-order attitude, respecting rules for their own sake and for their protection of the rights of the individual.

6. Only one in five people reason morally at the postconventional level. They regard rules as arbitrary but respect them because they protect human welfare. A very few people go on to form their moral judgments through inner reflection and meditation about universal ethical principles. They achieve a universal world view of morality.

7. Carol Gilligan has critized Kohlberg's theory as being biased against women. She argues that women see morality in terms of relationships and caring for others, whereas men see morality in terms of justice for single individuals and their competing claims.

8. William Damon has characterized moral developments as a series of unfolding confusions in children's minds. He believes that more realistic moral dilemmas than Kohlberg's will elicit better indications of children's moral reasoning.

9. In the affective view of morality, children develop a conscience and the capacity for guilt through identification with an adult authority. Then, moral sanctions emanate from within. Children may also acquire morality through feeling sympathetic distress for people in trouble.

10. Parents' discipline affects moral development. Physical punishment and withdrawing love may upset children so much emotionally that they are unable to concentrate on moral issues. Parents should be warm and loving and explain to children why they must act in particular ways. This kind of discipline helps children integrate their capacity for empathy with knowledge of how their behavior affects others.

11. Social-learning theory focuses on moral actions and assumes that parents and others in a position to socialize children shape their course of action to the morality of the culture. Children's ability to resist temptation is a crucial test of whether they have learned to be moral. Hugh Hartshorne and Mark May found in an extensive study that nearly all children were dishonest on some occasions.

12. Although foundations for morality are laid earlier, behavior is not morally mature until adolescence, when young people have the sophistication to reflect on their values and have a better grasp of the motives and implications of their actions.

13. As James Rest and others point out, moral thinking and moral actions are not identical. Rest proposes that interpreting a situation, determining a moral ideal; deciding what one is actually going to do; and carrying out one's intentions are the ties between thoughts about moral issues and actions.

KEY TERMS

External morality
Internal (autonomous) morality

Preconventional moral reasoning
Conventional moral reasoning

Postconventional moral reasoning
Guilt

Sympathetic distress
Resistance to temptation

SUGGESTED READINGS

Damon, William (Ed.). *Moral Development.* San Francisco: Jossey-Bass, 1978. A collection of provocative essays on how the culture transmits its standards and values to the young child.

Erikson, Erik. *Gandhi's Truth: on the Origins of Militant Nonviolence.* New York: W. W. Norton, 1969. A biography of the man who led India to independence through great leadership and passive resistance, written by one of the outstanding theorists in the field of child development.

Gilligan, Carol. *In a Different Voice: Psychological Theory and Women's Development.* Cambridge: Harvard University Press, 1982. An original theory of moral development in women, contrasting their moral and psychological orientation to those of men and supported by data gathered in extensive interviews with women at various ages.

Kurtines, William M., and Gewirtz, Jacob L. (Eds.). *Morality, Moral Behavior, and Moral Development.* New York: Wiley-Interscience, 1984. A comprehensive collection of writings by scholars and researchers in the area of moral development (including Rest, Kohlberg, Damon, Turiel, and Hoffman). The volume includes representatives of each of the major theoretical approaches to moral development—cognitive-developmental, structural, learning-behavioral, and social-personality—as well as philosophical and historical perspectives.

Lickona, Thomas (Ed.). *Moral Development and Behavior.* New York: Holt, Rinehart & Winston, 1976. Critical issues in the study of moral development examined by the most significant contributors in the field, including Lawrence Kohlberg, James Rest, Martin Hoffman, and Robert Selman.

Piers, Maria W. *Infanticide: Past and Present.* New York: W. W. Norton, 1978. The origins and motives for the deliberate killing of infants, explored by a specialist in child development and early education. The mothers, or mother figures, who become private murderers have always themselves been the victims of emotional starvation and social oppression.

Zassenhaus, Hiltgunt. *Walls: Resisting the Third Reich—One Woman's Story.* Boston: Beacon Press, 1974. A stirring personal account of moral courage. The rescue of 1200 Scandinavian political prisoners through her efforts is one of the best modern examples of the difference a person's moral determination can make.

CHAPTER 15

Becoming an Individual

A month after their "graduation," the former Lamaze classmates reunited. The new parents compared notes on their new babies' lengths and weights, their sleep schedules, and their earliest smiles. Soon the talk had taken a new tack. "Andy's been placid and easygoing since the first minutes in the delivery room. He sleeps, eats, and looks around. We got lucky." Another new father chimed in, "Jenny certainly knows her own mind. She'll cry until we figure out what she wants, even if that takes all night, every night." The childbirth class instructor, an experienced pediatric nurse, said, "You find out early in the game just how different every newborn's style really is." These babies had begun to show the temperamental styles that would color their development for years to come. With age, as their personalities took on greater complexity, these children would continue to differ in the ways that they handled novelty, anxiety, and the routines of school and family life. As their lives broadened from the nursery to the neighborhood, these children—like all children—would continue to develop as unique individuals.

INFANT TEMPERAMENT

Dr. Alexander Thomas and Dr. Stella Chess, working with infants and children during the 1950s, were struck by the temperamental differences reported by parents during the first few weeks of life. They were aware of the prevailing emphasis on environmental influences and of the inclination to blame Mother for all childhood psychopathology. But how, they asked, could such early evidence of behavioral traits be attributed entirely to the mother? In 1956, they initiated the 20-year New York Longitudinal Study (NYLS) to trace the development of temperament from the newborn period and on through childhood and into adolescence. Much of the information on infancy and early childhood obtained through this study was gathered on the original group of 141 children born in 1956 and followed closely through 1962. This was a middle- and upper-middle-class group of children, a high percentage of whose parents were college educated. In 1961, 95 children of Puerto Rican working-class parents were added to the study. Other special groups were also added, including a number of low-birth-weight infants, many

of whom had suffered neurological impairments, and a group of mildly retarded children. After the 1964–1965 rubella epidemic, 243 children with congenital rubella defects joined the others.

Most of Thomas and Chess's findings, reported in a number of articles and finally in the book *Temperament and Development* (1977), were obtained through carefully constructed questionnaires, which parents filled out. The investigators tried to limit interpretation by asking parents specific questions—how their children reacted to their first bath, to wet diapers, to their first taste of cereal—within several weeks of the 2-month, 6-month, and 1-year ages they chose as checkpoints. Every effort was made to obtain objective descriptions of specific aspects of behavior, but the parents were still the primary source of information on the children's behavior in infancy, raising the problem of parental bias. As the children grew, therefore, the researchers obtained other data by questioning teachers in nursery and elementary schools and by observing and testing the children. When the children were 16, each youngster and his or her parents were interviewed separately. The information collected from these other sources corroborated the parents' reports and suggested that patterns of activity and behavior evident in infancy could be traced through adolesence and into adulthood (Thomas and Chess, 1981).

Individual infants had differed in nine aspects of temperament, according to responses parents had made to questionnaires during the infancy period:

1. *Activity level.* Some infants splash in the tub, wriggle when their diapers are changed, and thrash their arms and legs. They move often during sleep. Later they are always reaching for toys, crawling after the cat, and trying hard to walk. Other infants lie quiet and still much of the time.

2. *Rhythmicity or regularity.* Some infants settle into a 4-hour feeding schedule almost from birth, have regular bowel movements, and sleep at predictable intervals. Other babies eat varying amounts, awake at a different hour each morning, and move their bowels at almost any time.

3. *Approach or withdrawal.* Some infants smack their lips when given new food, and others spit it out; some reach for a new toy, and others push it away; some smile and make noises at the sight of a new face, and others grimace and fuss.

4. *Adaptability.* Some babies are apprehensive during the first bath but later enjoy bathing. If they are at first afraid of toy animals, they later play happily with them. Other babies never do get used to sudden sharp noises, to having their diapers changed, or to a babysitter.

5. *Threshold of responsiveness.* Some babies are aware of every sight and sound. They even notice when vitamins have been added to their applesauce and refuse to eat it. Others are oblivious to loud noises, to wet diapers, and to what they are eating.

6. *Intensity of reaction.* Some babies merely whimper when they are hungry and do not fuss when clothing is pulled over their heads. Others chortle loudly when Father plays rough-and-tumble with them; knock the spoon of baby food out of Mother's hand; scream and kick when their temperature is taken; and make dressing a daily battle.

7. *Quality of mood.* Some babies wake up happy and smile much of the day. Other fuss even when they are nursing and cry even when they are being rocked.

8. *Distractibility.* Some babies forget that they are hungry if they are rocked, that their clothes are being changed if they are given a toy. Others cry until they are fed and until the dressing is finished.

9. *Attention span and persistence.* Some babies watch their mobiles intently and coo for long periods. Other spit out a pacifier after only a few minutes.

Thomas and Chess (1977) found that these behavioral traits tended to cluster into a small number of temperament patterns or constellations. They were able to identify three groups of babies:

1. *The easy baby.* The easy baby gets hungry and sleepy at predictable times. He or she is almost always cheerful, reaches out for a new stuffed rabbit, eagerly accepts new foods, makes little fuss about ordinary frustrations, and smiles at everyone. Of the NYLS sample, 40 percent were easy babies.

2. *The difficult baby.* The difficult baby does not establish regular eating and sleeping patterns, requires a long time to adjust to new routines, and cries a great deal and quite loudly. Difficult babies are unhappy and unfriendly; they spit out new food

and are likely to throw tantrums at the slightest frustration. Of the NYLS sample, 10 percent were difficult babies.

3. *The slow-to-warm-up baby.* The slow-to-warm-up baby does not take to most new offerings—the first bath, the taste of new food, the first meeting with a stuffed rabbit. But given time, the child will become interested in, and even enjoy, these additions to his or her life. These infants are mild in their reactions, letting new food dribble down their chins, and they are somewhat irregular in their habits. Of the babies of the NYLS, 15 percent were slow-to-warm-up babies.

Thomas and Chess found these temperaments in the working-class, predominantly Puerto Rican sample as well as in the original middle-class sample, which included a large proportion of Jewish families. Differences in child-rearing practices of the two groups did not seem to make for marked temperamental differences. Thomas and Chess also found no decisive sex differences in temperamental traits. They concluded that "Temperamental individuality is well established by the time the infant is two to three months old" (1977, p. 153).

But these temperamental traits are not immutable. The degree to which they are distorted into psychopathology or enhanced to emerge as productive behavior depends on what has been called **goodness of fit.** This concept was first described in 1913 by a biochemist, Lawrence Henderson, and it has since been applied in different ways by psychologists (e.g., Kagan, 1971). Goodness of fit as applied to children suggests that at any time during development they may be consonant (in harmony with) their surroundings or they may be at odds or dissonant with them. If the fit between the earliest behavior of infants and the values and expectations of their parents is a good one, infants are likely to have optimal development. If the fit is poor, development may be less than optimal (Thomas and Chess, 1977).

Thomas and Chess found that parents were deeply affected by whether a child was easy or difficult in infancy. When the mother believed that she was responsible for her infant's behavior, an easy child tended to reassure her that she was indeed an adequate mother. But when the parent was looking for early signs of assertiveness, perhaps because of a personal history of being easily victim-

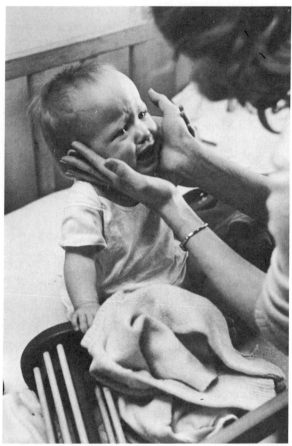

The infant's easy or difficult temperament makes a profound difference in the parents' "quality of life" for the first months of a baby's life.

ized or being too compliant, a difficult child might prove welcome. The manner in which the infant's temperamental traits mesh with parental needs and expectations determines whether these initial traits will be perpetuated or modified. For example, a slow-to-warm-up child may make an anxious and impatient mother feel resentful, as though the child's indifference were a deliberate attack on her tranquility. Instead of patiently and gradually exposing the infant to new situations, which might eventually modify the infant's temperament, the tense and willful mother may pressure, punish, and generally communicate negative feelings, making things even more trying for the child.

Parents' expectations may also change as the child becomes older. A good fit in infancy may not predict a good fit later on. Parents who were pleased by their child's quietness during infancy may become anxious and impatient with inactivity as the child matures, fearing some connection with low intellect. Parents who were delighted that their infant was easily dissuaded from crying or fussing by a colorful toy may be disappointed later when their child is easily distracted at school. Distractible boys were particularly frowned on by parents in the NYLS sample. Thus, although initial temperamental traits did not vary according to sex, parental reactions did when the question of achievement was raised. Thomas and Chess found that the nature of parents' responses to the child's temperament generally depended on whether it was consonant with their goals, standards, and values rather than whether it was similar to their own personality characteristics. In assessing goodness of fit, we must look to parental values, not just parental traits.

Evidence from a number of other studies in which unbiased observers directly examined early infant behavior tends to support the Thomas and Chess findings. Babies, from the first week of life, have an individual style of responding to stimuli, which affects the parent-child relationship, the way the infant experiences the world, and the child's development (Benjamin, 1961; Bergman and Escalona, 1949; Escalona, 1963; Escalona and Leitch, 1952; Korner and Grobstein, 1966, 1967; Korner and Thoman, 1970).

Anneliese Korner (1973) observed normal infants during two feeding cycles at 2 to 4 days of age, before handling by their mothers had had a chance to shape their responses. She found that some of these infants were more easily soothed and remained comforted longer. The infants who were not easily soothed tended to make mothers, particularly inexperienced mothers, feel less competent.

Cuddliness, the degree to which the infants nestled in the arms of persons holding them and were calmed by or sought contact, also affected their mothers' feelings of relatedness and competence. A clustering of traits showed up in the Korner sample and persisted as the newborns became older infants. Cuddlers were more placid and needed more sleep; they formed attachments to their caregivers early and intensely, and they were more likely to suck their thumbs and to become attached to fuzzy blankets or comforting, pliable toys. As in an earlier study (Schaffer and Emerson, 1964b), the noncuddlers were restless, easily aroused, quick-moving, active babies. They did not like to cuddle, even when tired or ill, and they did not easily tolerate physical restraint. The cuddlers needed physical contact and comfort for satisfactory progress. A mother who could not provide them might be particularly detrimental to a cuddler but better able to handle a noncuddler. On the other hand, a mother who herself required physical closeness and reassurance from her infant would receive little from a restless noncuddler.

Some babies were able to comfort themselves with thumb sucking and other hand–mouth contacts. Others, from the very beginning, needed their mothers to reduce their tensions. Self-comforting thus appears to be another temperamental trait of infancy. Activity level is also a major distinction in the early behavior of infants. Highly active infants can discharge emotions by making noise, crying, and grimacing. These infants enjoy novelty, change, and strong excitation. Inactive infants need to sift, diminish, manage, or avoid stimuli. They tend to be analytic and reflective, to look around them and to make small movements.

A longitudinal study of twins in the massive Collaborative Perinatal Project by Hill Goldsmith and Irving Gottesman (1981) also provided evidence for several of Chess and Thomas's temperament dimensions. It demonstrated the heritability (co-twin similarity) of activity level in infancy and persistence at a task, irritability, active adjustment, and fearfulness in childhood. Support for Chess and Thomas's dimensions was also provided by research showing that extreme inhibition or fearfulness in the face of the unfamiliar are stable qualities (Kagan, 1982).

Even so, some researchers (e.g., Bates, 1980) have suggested that the concept of temperament be recast as a social perception—an intellectual construction by parents—rather than as a characteristic intrinsic to the individual child. This suggestion has sparked some debate (Carey, 1983; Plomin, 1982; Rothbart, 1982; Thomas, Chess, and Korn, 1982). In support of the social perception view is the finding that parents' ratings of children's temperaments often do not agree with those of objective observers (Bates, 1980). But in support of the intrinsic trait view, in one exemplary study, Judy Dunn and Carol Kendrick (1980) found a strong correlation between mothers' descriptions of their 1½- to 3½-year-old children's behavior and systematic observations of the children's spontaneous actions, made by familiar observers at the child's home, over periods of at least an hour. This study suggests that when parents feel at ease, and when observations are conducted in natural settings for substantial periods of time, observers get a slice of life that is reasonably similar to what parents report. Under these circumstances, observers' and parents' reports are quite likely to jibe. Even under more limited conditions, there is some overlap between what parents report about their infants' reactions and what observers see in the laboratory (see Research Focus: Measuring Infants' Temperaments). High correlations also have been reported between the mother's and father's descriptions of their infant, even when the two parents are quite different from each other and have reacted differently to their infant (Thomas et al., 1982). Of course, parents are not perfect reporters, and the available scales for assessing temperament are not perfect instruments. No child or adult behaves exactly the same way in every situation—feeding, napping, toileting, going to a party—or on every occasion. Everyone has good days and bad days. People change as they develop and as the environment exerts its effects on them. Despite all of these qualifications, the evidence for the existence of some temperamental qualities, such as the "difficult" baby syndrome, seems solid. As anyone who has lived with an infant will have to agree, individual infants really do have individual temperaments.

PERSONALITY DIMENSIONS

What happens to differences in temperament after infancy? The seeds of differences sown in the early years grow and blossom in childhood as each youngster develops his or her own unique style. As we will see, children differ in many ways, among

---

RESEARCH FOCUS

MEASURING INFANTS' TEMPERAMENTS

In the ordinary course of social life, we all make impressionistic judgments about people. "She's a real go getter," we say, or "He's a sourpuss." Carol Malatesta and Jeannette Haviland (in press) were interested in rendering such impressionistic judgments about people in scientific terms and seeing if the judgments could be applied to infants. To describe the infants' temperaments, they used a questionnaire that measured anger, fear, activity level, responsiveness to soothing, and attention span. This questionnaire was based on the assumption that two broad categories of behavior, reactivity and self-regulation, make up what people commonly call "temperament." Reactivity includes individual reactions to external change. Self-regulation includes behavior patterns of approach and avoidance, among others, that modulate reactivity. In addition to this questionnaire of infant behavior, they applied the maximally discriminative facial movement (MAX) system (see p. 266) to code the infants' facial expressions of emotion.

In the study, 60 middle-class mothers and their 3- or 6-month-old infants participated. They came to the laboratory, and their interaction was videotaped. Mothers were asked to play with their infants as they would at home for 15 minutes. The mother then left the room briefly and returned to comfort her fretting infant as the cameras recorded the reunion for one minute. At the end of the session, the mother completed questionnaires about her infant's temperament and her own personality. The middle 5 minutes of the play session and the 1-minute reunion were coded according to the MAX system.

Malatesta and Haviland predicted that they would find some overlap between their measures of temperament and emotion. In fact, they did, on three of the nine comparisons they made. The more the mother claimed that her infant smiled and laughed at home, the less likely was the infant to look angry, hurt, or sad in the coded videotaped interaction in the laboratory. The more active the baby was as home, the more interested he or she appeared during the videotaped interaction. And the more difficulty the mother had soothing the baby at home, the more emotionally labile he or she was in the laboratory. To their surprise, the researchers found a negative relation between the mothers' reports of infants' distress at imposed limitations at home and the infants' facial expressions of anger in the laboratory. They suggest that perhaps the temperament measure of distress at limitations in fact measures not anger but persistence or stubbornness. On other measures, they found no significant correlations.

The researchers concluded that parents do form impressions of their children's temperaments and that these are substantially related to the children's expressive behavior as recorded in a brief laboratory session. Given the briefness of this laboratory assessment, the correspondence is encouraging and suggests that there may be emotion-dominant patterns of reactivity and self-regulation, which parents can discern reliably, in infants as young as 3 months.

them their perceptual-cognitive style, their views about academic success, and their sociability.

COGNITIVE STYLE

Cognitive style is a term that covers the manner of perceiving and responding to the environment, and it is one way in which individuals differ. Children who make comparable scores on IQ tests and have similar socioeconomic backgrounds can vary markedly when it comes to actual school performance. They may take in new subject matter immediately or slowly, be distracted by birds on the windowsill or not hear or see them at all, do better or less well in their schoolwork than their ''raw'' ability would predict, act with confidence in their own ability or with uncertainty.

Reflection and Impulsiveness

Recognizing that IQ and verbal ability did not always account for how children attacked problems in the classroom, Jerome Kagan (Kagan, 1965; Kagan, Rosman, Day, Albert, and Phillips, 1964) considered whether some children might be more reflective, others impulsive. He devised the Matching Familiar Figures Test in which the child is given a standard picture of a common object (Figure 15.1) and six variants, one identical and each of the other five differing in a minute detail that is not easily identified. The child who responds to the test quickly, barely scanning the figures, commits numerous errors; Kagan called this style ''impulsive.'' The child with a ''reflective'' style responds slowly, comparing specific parts of the figures, and tends to make fewer errors. Children's **reflection** and **impulsiveness** become evident at age 5 or 6 and then show up in the way they handle a number of school tasks. These qualities do not change too much over time (Messer, 1976).

Impulsive children blurt out the first answer that comes to mind and take no time to consider other possibilities. When the teacher calls on them to read aloud, they have trouble. They mispronounce words, substitute wrong words, omit some words but add others, and sometimes skip entire lines in their hurried progress through the passage (Kagan, 1965). Reflective children analyze visual stimuli into components and pay attention to details of a problem, whereas impulsive children focus on the total

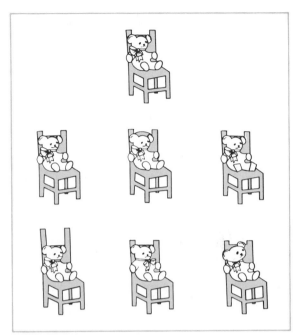

FIGURE 15.1

In the Matching Familiar Figures Test, the child must pay close attention to details, a challenge that separates out the reflective children from the impulsive. The impulsive child sees that all these bears are similar and, having no inclination for close scrutiny, chooses any one of them for the matching figure (Kagan, 1965).

stimulus and on the total problem (Zelniker and Jeffrey, 1976; Figure 15.2). Reflective children not only spend more time evaluating their hypotheses, but they also gather more information on which to base their decisions, and they gather it more systematically than impulsive children (Messer, 1976).

Impulsive children can be taught to be more deliberate (Egeland, 1974). Scanning strategies, training children to look at all the alternatives and each component of the alternatives, are more effective in decreasing errors than are asking the children to wait before they respond or increasing their motivation to do well (Heider, 1971b).

Hyperactive children, children who have severe learning disabilities, and those who fail in school are more likely to be impulsive (Messer, 1976). Kagan believes that anxiety about making a mistake goads reflective children to their deliberations (Kagan and Kogan, 1970). They seem very concerned about being correct on tests of intellectual ability (Messer, 1970). Impulsive children are more

FIGURE 15.2

When asked to study and then immediately recall this picture, a reflective boy gave this account: "Flowers, trees, a girl, a baby carriage, grass, a frog, two birds, trees, leaves, a baby carriage, a rose leaf, on the water, the frog is on top of the leaf, sky, some earth, and that's it." He scored themes, 0; details, 12. An impulsive boy said, "A girl sailed a doll on the water and the doll ran away and she told the dog to go and save her doll. The dog took hold of the boat and brought it to the bank. There was also a grove and two birds." He scored themes, 5; details, 9 (Zelniker and Jeffrey, 1976).

anxious about their overall competence (Block, Block, and Harrington, 1974). Reflective children also appear to be more attentive (Campbell, 1973), less aggressive (Thomas, 1971), and perhaps quicker to arrive at more advanced stages of moral development (Schleifer and Douglas, 1973). One study of humor (Brodzinsky, 1975) found that impulsive children were spontaneous in their mirth, but reflective children understood better the humor of the situation.

Field Dependence and Independence

Another well researched aspect of cognitive style has to do with **field dependence** and **indepen-dence.** This quality can be defined as the individual's ability to separate a part from the whole. Put more technically, it is the capacity "to overcome embedding contexts in perception" (Kogan, 1976). Herman Witkin and his associates (Witkin, Dyk, Paterson, Goodenough, and Karp, 1962), the principal investigators of this ability, began their research with adults and later extended it to children. The first test that they devised was the rod and frame test. The subject sits in a tilted seat in total darkness, facing a luminous rod surrounded by a luminous frame. The rod and frame can be rotated independently by the experimenter; the subject tries to give the experimenter directions that will bring the rod to a vertical position. The frame is always tilted so that when the rod is vertical with respect to gravity, it will not be vertical within the frame. Field-independent individuals use internal cues to spatial orientation and ignore the misleading cues suggested by the frame. Field-dependent individuals depend on the frame for their orientation. Another test for field dependence requires the subject to find a geometrical figure embedded within a larger picture or pattern designed to mask it (Figure 15.3). Field dependent children have trouble locating the embedded figure.

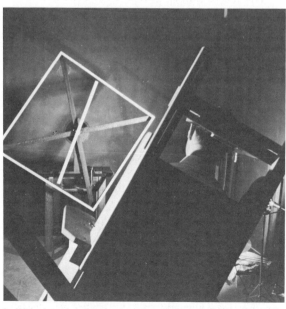

In Witkin's rod and frame test the subject must adjust the rod so that it is vertical, ignoring the misleading cues of the angle of his chair and the orientation of the frame around the rod.

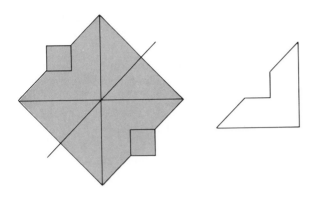

Can you locate the V—shaped figures in the green design?

FIGURE 15.3
People who are field-dependent have difficulty finding the hidden figure in items on the Embedded Figures Test.

The Witkin group found that field-dependent children looked to other children and adults whom they respected for cues about how to act in social situations that confused them. Field-independent children decided how to act on their own. When social situations were not confusing or when the other person present had no more information than the child, both field-dependent and field-independent children acted on their own.

There is reason to believe that field dependence and other related traits depend on a predisposition to perceive and act in these particular ways rather than on factors in the environment. A study in which the same children were observed at 1 and at 3½ years (Moskowitz, Dreyer, and Kronsberg, 1981) showed that at both ages children who would be tested later and prove to be field-dependent sought more emotional reassurance from their mothers than did those who would later test as field-independent. But the mother's behavior, whether she touched, talked to, and smiled at her child a great deal, had no relation to whether her reassurance was sought or to whether her child would later be found field-dependent.

Creativity

Creativity can be considered a style of thinking in which a person uses what is known to speculate on the unknown and thus generates new associations and new theories, new artifacts and new creations. There are two kinds of thinking that provide new information. In **convergent thinking,** the person seeks one correct answer to a recognized problem. In **divergent thinking,** the person thinks in different directions, sometimes searching, sometimes posing a question, sometimes seeking variety. The creative abilities of fluency, flexibility, and originality depend on divergent thinking (Guilford, 1962).

Earlier in this century, giftedness was considered to refer only to intellectual talent. As such, it was measured by intelligence tests. But in the 1960s, James P. Guilford and others became convinced that the gift of creativity was not being disclosed by these tests. They realized that IQ was an inadequate measure of creativity. Jacob Getzels and Philip Jackson (1962) pointed out that the conventional IQ test measures knowledge of the usual and expected, the so-called convergent or "safe" thinking, not creative or divergent thinking, thinking that is innovative and discovers what is not yet known. In their sample of 245 boys and 204 girls from a private high school in the Midwest, Getzels and Jackson found that the top 20 percent in creativity were below the top 20 percent in IQ and vice versa.

Since the 1960s, researchers have attempted to pinpoint the cognitive processes that make up creative thinking. Kenneth O'Bryan and Russell MacArthur (1969) found that creative 9-year-olds were able to switch back and forth between hindsight and foresight in handling ideas. Roberta Milgram and her colleagues (Milgram, Milgram, Rosenblum, and Rabkin, 1978) looked at the quantity of responses and the unusual quality of responses of sixth-graders and high-school seniors. They found that giving a large number of conventional responses was a prerequisite for making unusual responses. Fluency or sheer quantity was important.

Is there a single creative personality? We need think only of the personalities of Emily Dickinson and D. H. Lawrence, Lillian Hellman and Tennessee Williams, to realize that many personality "types" are creative. But certain behavior traits do complement creative thinking.

Creative individuals are free to see the world in unconventional ways. Whatever their outward appearance may be, they are nonconformist in their thinking, and they are often so in their behavior. They are quite likely to disregard social rituals, and they would rather spend their time in creating something than in playing social games. They are sometimes regarded as outsiders. To tolerate this status, creative individuals have what Carl Rogers (1959) calls "an internal locus of evaluation." The value of what they create is for them established not by the praise or criticism of others but by whether it satisfies and expresses oneself.

The creative adolescents in the Getzels and Jackson (1962) study, whose drawings often mocked conformity and convention (Figure 15.4), received less approval from their peers and teachers than did students with high IQs. Teachers liked the stu-

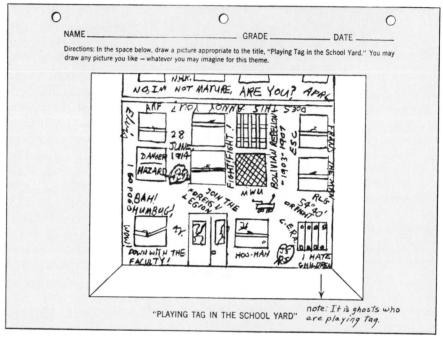

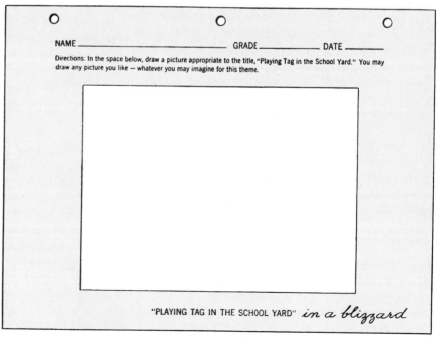

dents with high IQs better than they did the highly creative students, even though the creative adolescents were achieving beyond what their IQ scores would predict.

But creative individuals also seem to require less approval. The students in the study were given the Outstanding Traits Test, which is divided into three sections: "How much would you like to have this trait?" "How much does this trait predict success in adult life?" "How important does the teacher think this trait is?" Both the high-IQ and the exceptionally creative students agreed completely on

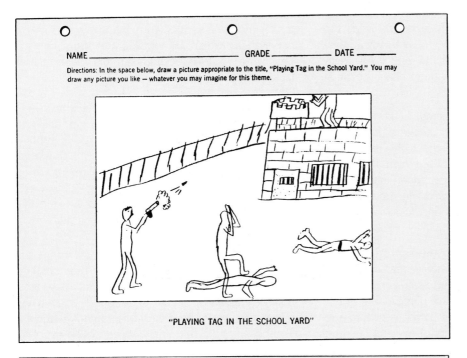

"PLAYING TAG IN THE SCHOOL YARD"

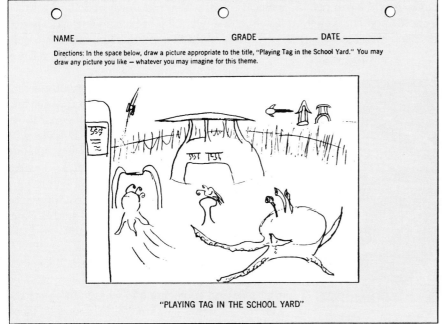

"PLAYING TAG IN THE SCHOOL YARD"

FIGURE 15.4

Creative children, when asked to draw a picture of an incident are not literal about it at all, mocking convention, sometimes depicting violence, fashioning new creatures, and almost always employing humor (Getzels and Jackson, 1962).

what constitutes success; they both indicated that the traits of successful people and those that they regarded as important to the teacher were very nearly the same. But the high-IQ students then claimed that these were the traits they wanted for themselves. The creative adolescents wanted different traits. They agreed with the high-IQ group that a sense of humor would be tenth in importance for success in adult life, but they ranked it third in importance for themselves. The high-IQ adolescents chose high marks, high IQ, and goal-directedness as more important for themselves. As Getzels and Jackson comment:

In effect, the high IQ is saying: "I know what makes for success and what teachers like, and I want these qualities, too"; the high creative is saying, "I know as well as the high IQ what makes for conventional success and what teachers like, but these are not necessarily the qualities I want for myself" (Getzels and Jackson, 1962, p. 36).

Creative children tend to come from families that are more egalitarian and permissive and encourage free expression of opinion and feelings. The father is likely to be self-employed (Dryer and Wells, 1966; Ellinger, 1964; Nichols, 1964; Weisberg and Springer, 1961). The mothers of high-IQ children in the Getzels and Jackson (1962) study were more likely to be home all the time than were the parents of highly creative students. These mothers were vigilant and had conventional standards. Mothers

Creativity requires that a person persevere in developing necessary skills and a unique vision, regardless of whether other people approve.

of creative children had greater freedom, encouraged individual divergence and risk taking, and were less preoccupied with financial security.

Another trait of creative individuals is their openness and naivete. They seem better able than others to remain open to experience and unusual possibilities. Rogers (1959) called this openness **extentionality:** "The individual is alive to the existential moment as it is, thus being alive to many experiences which fall outside the usual categories . . ." (p. 75). Associated with this openness and lack of rigidity is an ability

to play with ideas, colors, shapes, relationships, to juggle elements into impossible juxtapositions, to shape hypotheses, to make the given problematic, to express the ridiculous, to translate from one form to another, to transform into improbable equivalents. It is from this spontaneous toying and exploration that there arises the hunch, the creative seeing of life in a new and significant way (Rogers, 1959, pp. 75–76).

We are often struck by the simplicity of creative ideas. They seem not so much entirely new as a new arrangement or use for existing or even familiar and therefore taken-for-granted elements. The observation that girls who had been exposed to cowpox did not contract smallpox, and the observation that, when in a trolley moving next to a faster vehicle, we seem to be standing still, are two naive perceptions that led to major creative breakthroughs: the use of vaccination to cure smallpox and the theory of relativity.

Creativity is, by popular expression, 10 percent inspiration and 90 percent perspiration. As Silvano Arieti (1976) has pointed out, even Leonardo da Vinci, Sigmund Freud, and Albert Einstein had teachers and submitted to discipline. The creative individual must be persistent enough to develop necessary skills and then persistent enough to pursue a unique vision, regardless of the approval or disapproval of others. A number of studies have associated creativity with humor (Getzels and Jackson, 1962; Lieberman, 1965; Torrance, 1962; Weisberg and Springer, 1961). Yvonne Treadwell (1970) asked 83 junior and senior undergraduates in science and engineering to write humorous captions for a series of cartoons. She then tested these subjects on creativity and asked them about their appreciation of humor and their use of it in their daily lives. She found that creativity was related to how novel the students' cartoon captions were and how much they claimed to appreciate humor, but not to how often they claimed to use it. Creative persons may find more things funny but are not necessarily jokesters themselves. All these traits, nonconformity, self-direction, openness to unusual possibilities, simplicity, persistence at tasks, and appreciation of humor, seem to contribute to the capacity for creativity.

ACADEMIC ACHIEVEMENT

Equally able children differ in their expectations about what they will achieve and in attributing their successes and failures. Children who in school usually expect a moderate amount of success and attribute their successes and failures to themselves are "most likely to succeed." Children who expect failure and attribute their successes and failures to factors beyond their control usually achieve less, even though they may have the same intellectual ability. Two kinds of research contribute to our current view of children's academic success and failure, studies of personal control and investigations into the way children learn to feel helpless or in control.

Locus of Control

Studies of personal control or **locus of control** try to determine how children commonly ascribe responsibility for their experiences. They pose a fundamental question human beings have asked in one form or another for centuries: Is our destiny in our own hands or is it essentially controlled by fate, by powers beyond us? People who perceive a causal relation between personal behavior and the events of their lives are identified as having an internal locus of control. Those who attribute events of their lives to forces beyond their control have an external locus of control (Lefcourt, 1976). The Intellectual Achievement Responsibility (IAR) questionnaire is an important tool for assessing locus of control in school-age children and for determining whether children take responsibility for success and failure. It includes questions such as "When you get a high grade on a test, is it (a) because you studied hard?" (internal locus of control) "or (b) because the test was easy?" (external locus of control).

In several studies using this questionnaire, it was found that the children who believe themselves personally responsible for their successes achieved the most (Chance, 1965). They did well in reading, math, and language (Crandall, Katkovsky, and Crandall, 1965). Whatever their socioeconomic status (SES), high-school students with a sense of personal control spent the most time doing homework (Franklin, 1963) and persisted in attempts to solve complex logical puzzles (Janus, 1965). They also had the highest report card grades (McGhee, and Crandall, 1968) and grade point averages, in eighth to eleventh grades (Lessing, 1969).

Careful analysis of the IAR scores revealed, however, that they varied by the test-taker's sex and grade in school. Girls took greater responsibility for failure than boys, and this difference in sense of responsibility increased in adolescence. Girls seem to become more anxious and concerned about failure as they progress through the school years (Stein and Bailey, 1973). Subsequent studies showed that a sense of responsibility for success was a good predictor of achievement for boys, but for girls a sense of responsibility for failure was the most significant predictor of achievement (Messer, 1972). According to one interpretation, these differences are culturally conditioned. Girls who do well in school may consider it too assertive and thus too masculine to take credit for their success or to blame others for their failure. Boys who do well do not have to explain away their superiority because it is consonant with the masculine gender role to take credit for success.

The IAR is actually better at predicting grades than standardized achievement test scores (McGhee and Crandall, 1968). Teachers appear to be influenced in their grading by the student's motivation. An eager student is more likely to receive high grades than an apathetic one. Children who believe that they do not control the events of their lives tend to have more painful relations with their teachers than children who take responsibility. And children who believe in fate attribute more negative qualities to their teachers *and* themselves than do children who believe in personal control (Bryant, 1974).

An unanswered question plagues one's attempts to interpret these findings, however. Do success and cultural conditions, including the teacher's behavior, determine the individual's locus of control, or does locus of control determine success?

Learned Helplessness

Some children, after repeated failures, come to believe that they simply cannot surmount failure. Their attitude, which tends to perpetuate failure, is known as **learned helplessness.** In one study by Carol Dweck (1976), a person present when children were given an impossible task and necessarily failed was called a "failure experimenter." Then the children were given other tasks, and the same person was present. For children who believed that their efforts had little to do with their achievement, the mere presence of the failure experimenter caused them to fail on tasks they were entirely capable of accomplishing. When these chidlren were trained to attribute success to their own efforts however, their successes increased. The very concept of learned helplessness indicates that certain attitudes about control and success are learned and therefore can change. When they do change, the children are more successful. "Helpless" children have also been found to ruminate about the reasons for their failures, whereas mastery-oriented children, after a failure, want to move on to another opportunity for success (Diener and Dweck, 1978). Reinforcing a connection in children's minds between success and individual effort and helping them to move on when they do fail, should, according to these findings, increase feelings of control and reduce feelings of helplessness.

TYPE A BEHAVIOR

We all recognize them. They are the people who read while they are driving, who chomp their food so quickly they seem to inhale it, who fly off the handle, who rush through the day. They are Type A people. Compared to their slower paced Type B fellows, Type A people act, think, and feel more quickly and intensely. Compared to a Type B person with the same intelligence score, a Type A person gets higher grades and is involved in more activities. Type A behavior seems to enhance professional achievement and productivity—a great advantage in a competitive, industrialized society like our own. But Type A behavior has its dangers as well. Type A people often feel hostile, angry, urgently rushed, and anxious (Brody, 1984). Those qualities, uncomfortable enough in their own right, have been linked to heart disease in adult men. In

fact, it was two San Francisco cardiologists, Meyer Friedman and Ray Rosenman (1974), who first described Type A behavior. Although Type A and Type B adults differ on certain neurological, hormonal, and physiological measures (Friedman, 1978), the specific mechanisms by which Type A behavior is translated into heart disease have not yet been uncovered. The connection between Type A behavior and factors associated with heart disease has shown up in studies of young people as well as adults, however. In an investigation of children between 10 and 17 years old, it was found that the Type A personality traits of eagerness and energy correlated with blood levels of cholesterol and triglycerides (Hunter, Wolf, Sklov, Webber, and Berenson, 1981).

Because it is widely accepted that Type A behavior can contribute to the development of heart disease, researchers have tried to uncover the psychological and social factors that foster Type A behavior. Some have observed how parents encourage their children's competitiveness, aggression, and impatience. For example, one mother encouraged her blindfolded son as he tried to pick up a pile of blocks. When time was up, she said, "Next time try for six blocks." Said another mother to her son, after the same task, "Next time go a little faster." Both sons had been classified as Type A (Brody, 1984).

Thomas Wolf, Monny Sklov, Paula Wenzl, Saundra Hunter, and Gerald Berenson (1982), of Louisiana State University, investigated how 160 fifth- and sixth-graders reacted to a variety of tasks in order to explore the differences between Type A and Type B children. They hypothesized that Type A children would perform the assigned tasks more hurriedly and intensely than Type B children and that Type B children would perform hurriedly and intensely only if they were so instructed. First, the researchers asked the children to rate themselves on scales describing their own behavior. From the children's ratings on scales like "I am easygoing—I am hard driving," "It does matter if I am late—It doesn't matter if I am late," "I walk fast—I walk slowly" the investigators classified them as Type A or B. Then, the children were given a number of tasks, which included: reading an emotionally charged passage, eating two graham crackers, delivering an envelope to a box, playing marbles, estimating when 1 minute had passed, and crossing out numbers on a page. The Type A children read more loudly than Type B children, ate their graham crackers and delivered the envelope faster, were more competitive in playing marbles, crossed out more numbers, and estimated that 1 minute had passed more quickly than Type B children did. All of the findings supported the hypothesis that Type A children would act more hurriedly, intensely, aggressively, and competitively than Type B children. The research team concluded that Type A people try harder to exert and maintain control over environmental demands and challenges.

SOCIABILITY

Every child has a social style, a set of personal traits affecting his or her relations with others. A child may be outgoing and friendly or shy and retiring. Social style may vary somewhat over the course of the child's development. The value others place on particular traits may also vary as the child matures. Outgoingness, for example, tends to be linked to academic success in primary school, but a more introverted style is associated with academic success at the university level (Entwistle, 1972). The difficult child who did not seek much physical contact in infancy and was unhappy and unfriendly may, with strong support from parents and other positive experiences, become an outgoing adult (Thomas and Chess, 1977). Yet there is considerable evidence suggesting that a child's sociability is to some degree inherited (Buss, Plomin, and Willerman, 1973; Plomin, 1974; Scarr, 1969b); sociability is moderately stable over time (Kagan and Moss, 1962) and is later an important personality trait in adulthood (Buss and Plomin, 1975). Of individual traits that have been studied longitudinally, sociability is one of the most pervasive and enduring (Beckwith, 1979).

Sociability has been defined as the "tendency to seek out and remain with others" (Buss and Plomin, 1975, p. 91). The infant's preference for cuddling is one of the earliest manifestations of sociability. All infants need soothing, but sociable infants prefer social soothing. They want touching and close contact with their mothers and soft talk from them. Active noncuddlers also need soothing, but they are more likely to be comforted by blankets, toys, rocking, and other means that do not

A few children are very sociable creatures, and a few are very private. Most children fall between these two extremes, and all children have a distinct social style.

require the presence of another person. As the infant becomes more comfortable in his or her surroundings, the need for soothing abates and the desire for stimulation increases. Both types of infants require arousal, but sociable infants want stimulation from people. They enjoy the banter of peekaboo and pat-a-cake. The unsociable child is more likely to be aroused by objects and events, such as toys, watching television, listening to records, and playing solitary games that can be exciting in themselves.

The tendency to be sociable is played out through relationships and is modified somewhat by them. As indicated earlier, the infant who smiles and responds to parents sets up a positive feedback cycle. The unsociable child, needing less attention and soon made restless by the restraints of being held, tends to be cool and rejecting of nurturance. With certain parents this seeming rejection of themselves may set up a negative feedback cycle. If affection is forced on unsociable children, the consequences may be rebellion and hostility. Sociable children, on the other hand, run the risk of remaining too dependent (Buss and Plomin, 1975).

Sociable children are more interested in their peers and in group activities. Their friendships are marked by greater attention and affection, more give and take. Unsociable children are more likely to pursue goals independently, needing their peers less and responding to them with less warmth. Because group academic and athletic activities are part of childhood in this culture and because adults are more responsive to sociable children, the unsociable youngster is likely to find childhood more difficult.

PERSISTENT PATTERNS

Which of the dramatic differences in babies, apparent from the first days of life, are persistent and which transient? Can we trace forward the consequences of the individual temperaments of infants? Or can we trace specific strengths and vulnerabilities backward to identifiable predispositions in infancy? A major issue in the study of differences of individuals is the stability or continuity of these differences over time. Thomas and Chess (1977) suggest that some traits may appear stable because the surroundings of the children are stable and they

continue to express these traits in the same manner. On the other hand, often the context of children's behavior does change and new forms of behavior emerge at different ages.

Activity level, adaptability, and intensity, three temperamental traits studied by Thomas and Chess (1977), were generally stable for children of both sexes up to 5 years. They tended to be quite stable from one year to the next, though not necessarily over the entire first 7 years. The easy, slow-to-warm-up, and difficult temperament patterns often shifted because of the experiences of the children.

Carl, a most difficult infant who did not handle new situations and persons well, grew up to have relatively untroubled school years. His surroundings remained pretty much the same, and he faced few new situations. He lived in the same house and had the same friends until he graduated from high school. When he went away to college, however, where he had no friends, he was thrown into a depression and was unable to study or to make new friends. Another of the difficult children in the NYLS sample could not live up to his parents' standards and became even more difficult. Unable to concentrate on any goal, he found himself continually drifting and shifting direction. Circumstances contradictory to his nature had intensified and exaggerated a temperamental trait into a behavior disturbance. Yet a third difficult child, Nancy, who had received little support from her parents and teachers in early childhood, gained favorable

 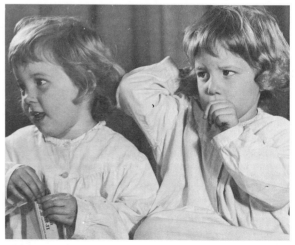

The different temperaments of these identical twins, one "easy going," the other "difficult," persisted from infancy through childhood.

attention at age 9 when her musical and dramatic ability became obvious. Suddenly her difficult temperament was viewed as an "artistic temperament." She was able to recover from her 6-year-old spell of explosive outbursts, hair pulling, fear of the dark, and poor relations with her peers. A new developmental stage signaled the emergence of new skills, which in turn triggered a much more positive attitude and more positive experiences. Thus, in some instances, the temperamental factors that were influential in the past continue to be so. In other instances, different aspects of temperament come to the fore.

The new emphasis on lifespan development makes the question of traits' stability of even greater concern to developmental psychologists. Some psychologists who previously stressed developmental continuity (e.g., Kagan, 1971) have now demonstrated discontinuity in their own views by swinging to a position emphasizing discontinuities in development (Kagan, Klein, Finley, Rogoff, and Nolan, 1979). They now express doubt that adult temperament can be predicted simply on the basis of the temperament of the newborn or the experiences the infant has in the first few years of life. Generally, our assumptions about enduring personal styles are stronger than our data. In longitudinal studies, of which there have been few, psychologists have not been notably successful in picking out behavior or patterns to follow that demonstrate compelling stability or continuity. They may have chosen poorly the traits to look at, measured them inadequately, or defined them too narrowly and specifically. Or it may be that in our world of shifting contexts and unstable environments, individual styles are not as consistent and predictable from age to age as we like to believe. The evidence is definitely not all in on just how stable individual dispositions are.

Despite changes and discontinuities, children do have personal traits that distinguish them as unique, however. Individuals have varying degrees and different combination of traits; they are not collections of polarities—impulsive rather than reflective, sociable rather than unsociable, and so on. Certain traits tend to cluster together. One study, for example, found that quickness of response was related to extroversion (Bentler and McClain, 1976). Field dependence is often associated with sociability. Reflection many times goes hand in hand with

an internal locus of control. But the combinations are not always the same, and they may vary over time. Each person is truly unique.

Psychologists have used the term "personality" to refer to such clustered traits in a person. But the word may imply that these traits are more consistent, continuous, and stable than they actually are. Psychologists now know that people adapt their behavior to specific situations and that behavior changes, often markedly so, as people age. Many psychologists therefore prefer to talk about "individual differences," rather than invoking the strong connotations of "personality."

GROUP VARIATION

We have been discussing temperaments and dispositions of individual children. Children have other patterns of behavior that are associated with their membership in particular groups. One kind of group that is important is the ethnic or racial group to which a child belongs.

ETHNIC DIFFERENCES

An ethnic group consists of people who share a common national origin, speak the same language, observe the same religious faith, have the same general child-rearing practices, and enjoy the same foods, music, and manner of dress. Historically, in the United States, immigrants from the same towns and country banded together for companionship and help and to keep, in their pilgrimage from peasant village to industrial metropolis, some of the modes of behavior to which they were accustomed. The ethnic group became a source of values and support, providing the intimacy of communal life for strangers in an impersonal, urban society (Greeley, 1969).

Beginning in the middle of the 19th century, the pressing need to orient and educate millions of immigrants to the United States resulted in attempts to level barriers between one culture and another, to downplay and often denigrate languages, foods, and habits that were not "American," not part of the white, Anglo-Saxon, Protestant culture. But denying cultural differences only served to distort history and deplete the self-esteem of individuals who belonged to these groups. Millions of Americans—blacks, Chinese, Japanese, Jews, Italians, Poles, Irish, Germans, Puerto Ricans, Mexicans, Ukrainians, Greeks, American Indians—were excluded from history books, plays, films, and other expressions of American life. Or they were depicted in demeaning stereotypes, the bad Italian, the dumb Mexican, the conniving Jew, the ignorant Pole, the step-an-fetchit black. Two books, *Beyond the Melting Pot,* by Nathan Glazer and Daniel Patrick Moynihan (1963), and *The Decline of the WASP,* by Peter Schrag (1971), chronicled the growing awareness in the 1960s that cultural differences do exist in our pluralistic society. It has now become apparent that the solidarity of the nation depends on recognizing the many cultures that comprise it. Studies have been undertaken to examine authentic differences of ethnic groups.

These studies clearly demonstrate that ethnicity is a critical factor in an individual's development. It is a significant source and modifier of values, attitudes, perceptions, needs, and models of expression (Seelig, 1975). Evidence suggests that some observable ethnic differences are inherited. But ethnic differences represent a complex cultural patterning in which inherited traits are only a few of many, many strands. We have only begun to identify these strands.

Causes of Ethnic Difference

The role played by genes in the behavior and intelligence of any member of an ethnic group is difficult to assess, because so many other factors in the culture and in the physiological makeup of groups may influence the individual. Cultural values and child-rearing attitudes, the circumstances facing the children as they grow up, their perceptual and educational experiences—all these have bearing on the behavior of children at any given time.

Take Chinese children, for example. In the first days of life, Chinese-American babies are much like European-American infants in their sensory capacities, central nervous system maturation, motor activities, and social responsiveness. They are however calmer, less changeable, less perturbable, and more easily consoled when upset (Freedman, 1974; Kuchner, 1980). So there may be, as Kagan (Kagan, Kearsley, and Zelazo, 1979) puts it, an

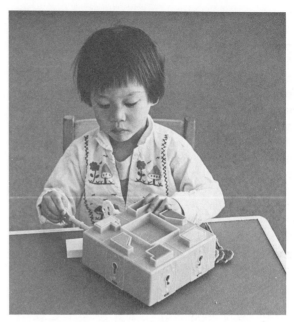

Ethnic background shapes people's development. Chinese children may well be socialized to be quiet, studious, and controlled, like this 2½-year-old who is persisting at solving a puzzle.

inherited "disposition toward inhibition" in Chinese children.

Any inherited tendency toward inhibition is powerfully reinforced in Chinese culture. Kagan and his colleagues (Kagan, Kearsley, and Zelazo, 1979) observed Chinese-American children from 4 to 29 months of age. They reported that Chinese parents are less likely to reward and stimulate babbling and smiling in infants than are Caucasian parents. In another sample of 105 mothers—35 Chinese mothers matched for age, education level, and SES with 35 Protestant and 35 Jewish mothers—the Chinese mothers were significantly more in favor in maintaining close control of their children (Kriger and Kroes, 1972).

Chinese-American children in Chicago nursery schools were more emotionally controlled than Caucasian children (Green, 1969). In the Kagan study (Kagan, Kearsley, and Zelazo, 1979), Chinese and Caucasian children enrolled in day-care centers as well as those spending their days at home were observed in a number of situations. The Chinese children were less vocal, less active, and less likely to smile and were more apprehensive when their mothers left them for a brief period or when an unfamiliar person entered the room. They were quieter, stayed closer to the mother, and played less. Although speculating that a disposition toward inhibition may be inherited, Kagan points out that in his study most of the differences observed did not show up until the last half of the first year of life and were more pronounced in children of working-class parents than in middle-class children. Familial experiences, he concludes, also make a significant contribution to the differences in behavior of ethnic groups.

Older children from different ethnic backgrounds may behave differently in test situations because of their life circumstances. Urban crime statistics reveal that the victims of crime are usually poor and black and that the criminal is likely to be a young man. So it is not surprising that in one study a young male stranger confronting a group of poor black children was not immediately welcomed. In this study, 880 schoolchildren were put in a situation in which they could choose to aid or not aid a young male experimenter who was a stranger to them. Girls were less likely to trust the experimenter than boys. Blacks were less likely to trust a white experimenter than were white children. But blacks were even less likely to trust a black experimenter (Wubberhorst, Gradford, and Willis, 1971). Trusting, especially aiding, a black male stranger would have been contrary to their survival training.

Finally, elements of a test may hinder one ethnic group more than another. Blacks and whites have been found to do equally well on the standard block design test used in intelligence testing when red and white blocks are used. But certain physi-

RESEARCH FOCUS

CHINESE-AMERICAN AND EUROPEAN-AMERICAN FAMILIES

Do mothers and children from different ethnic groups have characteristic styles of interacting? Sheila Smith and Daniel Freedman (1983) decided to investigate this question with 16 Chinese-American and European-American mothers and their 2-year-olds in Chicago. The European-American mothers were born in America, had high-school educations, and had husbands in nonprofessional occupations. The Chinese-American mothers had been born in Canton, China, gone to school for about 10 years, spoke Chinese at home, had lived in America for an average of 7 years, and had husbands who were waiters or cooks.

Smith and Freedman videotaped the mothers playing with their children at home and also teaching their children how to put blocks of various shapes into the matching holes in a toy turtle. On the shapes task, they coded all of the mother's promptings or efforts to help her child. From these observations, Smith and Freedman derived measurements of the mother's overall rate of such "control" behaviors; the number of trials when the mother helped the child; the number of trials when a child independently tried to put the blocks in; and the number of trials when the child was not paying attention. During the play session, the researchers coded self-directed play, mother-directed play, and passive watching.

Smith and Freedman found that during the play sessions, the Chinese children spent less time in self-directed play and more time watching passively than the Caucasian children. All of the Chinese children and only half of the Caucasian children had at least one period of passive watching. No group differences in mother-directed play showed up. The Chinese children's self-directed play, in other words, gave way to passive watching rather than to playing with their mothers. On the shape-sorting task, children from both groups were quite attentive to putting in the shapes, but during the first half of the session, the Chinese mothers were more likely to control their children's behavior by prompting them to respond. In general, the Caucasian children played and worked more independently, watched less, and demonstrated their autonomy more dramatically than the Chinese children did. Thus the Caucasian children got experience in self-assertion and in actively structuring their environments from mothers who allowed them considerable room to act independently and autonomously. The Chinese children, in contrast, accepted—or perhaps needed—relatively strong control from their mothers that, compared to the Caucasian children, seemed to limit their independence and activity.

ological factors of darkly pigmented people affecting their perception of blue cause them to have difficulty perceiving the contours of blue-yellow block designs (Mitchell and Pollack, 1974).

Patterns of Abilities

Research has suggested that ethnic groups have different patterns of abilities (Anastasi, 1958), one group having better mathematical skills than verbal, another having better verbal skills than mathematical. A major study conducted in 1965 sought to determine the ethnic patterns for verbal, reasoning, mathematical, and spatial abilities (Lesser, Fifer, and Clark, 1965). Middle-class and lower-class children from four ethnic groups—Chinese, Jews, blacks, and Puerto Ricans—were selected. The researchers attempted to devise tests of these abilities that were free of specific cultural content but still measured these intellectual traits. They also tried to structure the testing situation to reduce any bias on the part of the testers. The results of this study indicated that Chinese children had better reasoning and spatial abilities and moderate mathematical and verbal abilities, whereas Jewish children had greater verbal and mathematical skills but did less well on questions testing reasoning and spatial abilities (Figure 15.5).

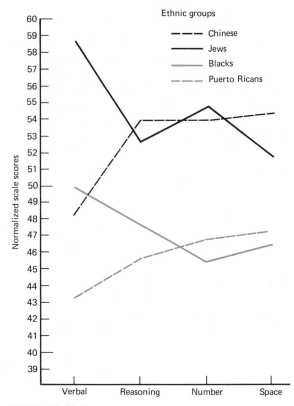

FIGURE 15.5

Research studies indicate distinctive patterns of mental abilities for different ethnic groups (Lesser, Fifer, and Clark, 1965).

School Motivation

A number of tests have been devised to determine the achievement motivation of various ethnic groups. For example, children see a series of pictures meant to evoke fantasies about achievement, or children are given topic sentences, and the stories they then write are analyzed for evidence of achievement motivation. Most of these tests rely heavily on the use of words, however, and ethnic groups vary in verbal facility. Moreover, young children, lacking the necessary verbal skills, tend to withdraw when confronted by such tests.

To overcome these problems, one test developed for preschool children uses imaginary figures called "gumpgookies." In each item on the test, two gumpgookies, as depicted in words and pictures, indicate different motivations. One gumpgookie might be working, the other one watching, one planning a future goal, one concentrating on an immediate goal (Adkins, Payne, and Ballif,

1972). The child is asked to choose the gumpgookie who behaves and feels as he or she does. A total of 1588 children from 10 ethnic groups were given the gumpgookie motivation test. Their ages ranged from 3 to 6, and most of them were drawn from Head Start programs. The black, WASP, and Puerto Rican children indicated higher degrees of achievement motivation than the Mexican-American, Oriental, American Indian, and Hawaiian children.

In a study of 263 high-school students in a southwestern community, James Anderson and William Johnson (1971) attempted to identify factors in the Mexican-Americans' homes that might explain why these children have little academic motivation and do poorly in school. The Mexican-American families differed from the other families studied in several ways: Spanish was the language spoken at home, even if the families had been in the United States for three generations. The students' mastery of English as taught in the schools was definitely influenced by the language spoken at home. The Mexican-American parents also had a lower educational and occupational standing. The educational level of the father was linked to the child's mastery of English. Mexican-American children in this study had less confidence in their ability to succeed than did their classmates. Their grades in both English and mathematics were lower because they did not have confidence.

A longitudinal study of Mexican-American and American children, who in the beginning were in their first, fourth, and seventh years and were watched over a 6-year period, sheds further light on aspects of Mexican-American life that affect school performance. When the scores of each American child were paired with those of a Mexican-American child of the same sex, school grade, and SES, the Mexican-American children appeared to be less active than the American children, less verbal, less externally oriented, more cooperative, more fatalistic, and more pessimistic in outlook (Holtzman, Diaz-Guerrero, and Swartz, 1975).

Cooperation and Competition

The cooperativeness revealed in this study appears to be a hallmark of Mexican culture. One observational study of a Mexican village found almost no competitiveness and aggression (Romney and Romney, 1963). Mexicans living in the United States also tend to encourage cooperation and to control competitiveness (Madsen, 1964). Americanization tends to increase the competitive tendencies of Mexican children, making them more competitive than their peers living in a small Mexican town but less competitive than Afro-Americans or Anglo-Americans (Kagan and Madsen, 1971).

American children are often rewarded for competitive behavior. They strive for grades, class rank, and other honors that pit them against their classmates. But children can achieve at school through cooperation. In Communist countries, children have a sense both of cooperating and of achieving individually when they contribute to the common good (Bronfenbrenner, 1970; Kessen, 1975). The competitiveness held up in the United States as the most direct path to success catches Mexican-American children, raised to value cooperation, in a par-

alyzing cultural conflict, which undermines their confidence and their abilities.

Beginning with the earliest years of school, parents and children of minority ethnic groups feel themselves caught between the values of the home and those espoused by professional educators. This is a major unresolved problem in American education. The challenge of the future is education for pluralism. Schools and other cultural institutions need to support the values of the many ethnic groups in which children grow up rather than attempting to socialize these children into the conformity advocated in the mid-19th century. It is unlikely that ethnic group differences will ever disappear from American society (Glazer and Moynihan, 1963). Such a leveling of differences would cost inestimably in group pride and individual self-esteem. If we can understand and celebrate cultural and individual differences rather than attempting to eliminate them, we have a better chance of preparing all the nation's children for the complex, changing, multiethnic society that is contemporary America.

SEX DIFFERENCES

Psychologists have amassed a vast literature on the differences between males and females. From birth onward, physical differences distinguish boys from girls, and these differences may affect how men and women feel, think, and behave (Wesley and Wesley, 1977). As newborns, girls have skeletal systems that are several weeks more mature than those of boys; by adolescence, girls' skeletal systems are an average of 3 years more mature than boys'. For the first 7 years of life, boys and girls are equal in height. At 7 years, girls begin to grow taller than boys; boys catch up and grow taller than girls by age 10. As adults, men are on average 6 percent taller and 20 percent heavier than women. At puberty, boys begin to metabolize more quickly and to produce more physical energy than girls. As a consequence, they need about 25 percent more protein and calories than girls, except when females are pregnant and lactating (Shepherd-Look, 1982). Physical differences like these are clear-cut and indisputable.

Another physical dimension on which males and females are clearly different is their vulnerability to physical assaults. From conception, males are more vulnerable than females to a host of assaults. More males are miscarried and stillborn than females. More boys die in childhood, and boys are more vulnerable to many childhood diseases than girls are. More boys than girls, for example, contract pneumonia and die from it; boys are also more vulnerable to malnutrition (Stott, 1966). Among the Japanese children afflicted with slowed growth and other problems after the atomic bombing of Hiroshima and Nagasaki, boys fared worse than girls (Bayley, 1966). In the grade school years, boys more often than girls suffer from speech, learning, and behavior problems such as stuttering and reading problems. More boys than girls suffer from mental retardation, emotional problems, and sleep disorders (Bentzen, 1963; Knopf, 1979). For children and adolescents, the problems in which the incidence among females exceeds that among males are rare indeed (Shepherd-Look, 1982).

Differences in physical development, strength, and vulnerability, then, are fairly consistent and straightforward. But what about differences in the psychological domain? The most comprehensive attempt to summarize research on psychological sex differences to date is *The Psychology of Sex Differences* (1974), in which Eleanor Maccoby and Carol Jacklin reviewed some 1400 studies. Reservations expressed about this survey by other scholars (e.g., Block, 1976; Fairweather, 1976; Tieger, 1980) reveal the challenging problems that bedevil all researchers and reviewers seeking to differentiate between physiological and sociocultural contributions to sex differences. Many studies are based on self-reports and reports from parents and teachers, who are less than objective observers. Other studies are not sufficiently sensitive to age and age-related shifts. Many report undirected and accidental findings of sex differences. Younger age groups have been overrepresented in the research, despite the fact that differences increase with age. Moreover, the sex of the experimenter or observer, which also plays a part in the outcome of a study, has not always been controlled. Many of the studies do not control for the special circumstances of the social situation, the nature of the interaction, whom the child is interacting with—a man, a woman—and who else is present.

Despite the varying quality of the studies surveyed and the many problems with this area of research, the general conclusions in this volume still provide a useful overview of the study of sex differences. Maccoby and Jacklin divide the research findings into three categories: fairly well established sex differences, unfounded beliefs about sex differences, and sex differences still open to question because evidence is scant or because findings are ambiguous.

Fairly Well Established Sex Differences

Verbal versus Visual-Spatial Abilities. Girls consistently have been found to have greater verbal ability than boys. Their greater language fluency and comprehension are most obvious at about age 11 and after. But indications of greater sensitivity to sounds and language appear much earlier. In infancy, girls are more easily startled by loud noises and are more responsive to tones, speech patterns, and subtle vocal cues (e.g., Friedman and Jacobs, 1981; Gunnar and Donahue, 1980). They begin to speak earlier and sing in tune earlier. They begin to read earlier than boys.

Male infants seem to attend to different cues. They are more likely to ignore their mothers and babble to a blinking light or stare at a geometric figure. As soon as they have greater motor ability, they are more likely to manipulate objects and attempt to take them apart. In preschool, boys are better at manipulations in three-dimensional space, such as folding paper or rotating an object, and later, during the school years, in imagining such manipulations. Girls at this age more frequently give elaborate verbal descriptions that are less appropriate to the task. In this age period, boys' visual ability also shows to advantage on embedded-figures tests. Beginning at ages 12 and 13, boys gain mathematical skills faster than girls, but the difference is not as great as the difference in spatial ability. Research seems to indicate that when problems can be solved by either a verbal or a spatial process, girls and boys may be equal. But when problems demand a spatial solution, girls are at a disadvantage; when they require a verbal solution, boys have the disadvantage.

Differences in the verbal and visual abilities of males and females, though fairly well established, should not be overestimated. Many studies have not documented sex differences (Boles, 1980; Plomin and Foch, 1981). Even those that have done so document only statistical differences between groups of males and females. These differences may not be very large in real terms, and they only apply on the average, not to the individual. The studies indicate that even consistent differences are not immutable. Spatial and verbal abilities are not genetically conferred in the same ways as color blindness or blond hair. Their expression is far likelier to depend on the attitudes and expectations of parents (Harris, 1975).

Aggression. Behavior intended to anger, hurt, harm, or irritate another is engaged in more by boys than girls. In all cultures, boys are more aggressive toward their peers, both physically and verbally. They also mock-fight and have more aggressive fantasies than girls. These differences are found as early as 2 years, when boys are more likely to become angry and strike an obstacle or another toddler to get a toy they want. Reviewing 32 observational studies of children 6 years and younger, Maccoby and Jacklin (1980) found that 24 of them indicated more aggression in boys, 8 of them no difference in the aggression in boys and girls, and none of them greater female aggression. The aggressiveness of both sexes tends to decline after the preschool years, but boys and men remain more aggressive through the college years.

Although they may be less inclined to hit another child, girls of 6 and 7 may be more unfriendly and rejecting toward a newcomer than boys are (Feshbach, 1969). Longitudinal studies indicate that the aggression of girls is more likely to be verbal and therefore more socially acceptable than the physical aggression of boys. In one study (Mallick and McCandless, 1966), girls of 8 and 9, compared to boys of this age, expressed less dislike of a frustrating sixth-grade child. But given the chance to deliver an electric shock to the frustrating child or to interfere with the child's successful completion of a task, when they were assured that their behavior would not be seen or reprimanded, girls behaved just as aggressively as boys. Such findings as these suggest that girls have just as many hostile feelings as boys but are more likely to express them in verbal slights and antisocial acts than with physical force.

Aggressive behavior of males is fairly stable, according to Jerome Kagan and Howard Moss's (1962) longitudinal study. The physical aggression of boys was found to be related to adult competitiveness but not necessarily to later overt aggression. Girls who were physically aggressive to peers before they were 6, however, were unlikely to become competitive women. Their aggression often became a source of anxiety.

Unfounded Beliefs about Sex Differences

A good number of popular notions about sex differences, among them the following four misconceptions, have been proved false by recent research.

Girls Have Less Self-Esteem. In one study of self-esteem that supports this notion, Deborah Fein and her colleagues (Fein, O'Neill, Frank, and Velit, 1975) interviewed 307 boys and girls in grades 2 through 6. When asked the question, "Do you get upset easily when you are scolded?" 50 percent of the boys said no, but only 25 percent of the girls said no. To the question, "Can you make up your mind and stick to it?" 70 percent of the boys said yes; only 53 percent of the girls said yes. Being able to withstand scolding and being decisive both relate to self-esteem. Apparently the social pressures on girls to comply and obey can lower their self-esteem. A study by Dweck and her associates (Dweck, Davidson, Nelson, and Enna, 1978) showed that compared to girls boys feel more confident about their abilities to solve problems and less often feel helpless. Nevertheless, in general, overall self-satisfaction and self-confidence of boys and girls are similar throughout childhood and adolescence (Maccoby and Jacklin, 1974).

It is the domains from which they derive their self-esteem that separate the boys from the girls. Girls consider themselves more socially competent and boys view themselves as stronger, more powerful, dominant, and potent (Maccoby and Jacklin, 1974). Boys are more concerned than girls about controlling or manipulating external events—even if they have to lie—and exerting such control figures more prominently in boys' self-images than in girls'. Asked to describe themselves, males point to qualities like power, ambition, energy, agency, instrumentality, initiative, and control over external events (Gunnar-Von Gnechten, 1978). In contrast, females describe themselves as more generous, sensitive, nurturing, considerate, and concerned for others (Bakan, 1966; Bem, 1974; Block, 1973, 1983; Carlson, 1971; Gough, 1968; Parsons and Bales, 1955; Spence and Helmreich, 1978; Spence, Helmreich, and Stapp, 1975). Girls of 15 and older are more self-conscious and concerned about how others regard them than boys are (Rosenberg and Simmons, 1971), and men between 18 and 22 tend to feel more in control of their fate (Maccoby and Jackin, 1974). In sum, males take pride in being powerful and masterful; females take pride in human relationships, expressiveness, and communion.

Girls Are More Suggestible Than Boys.

Studies reviewed by Maccoby and Jacklin indicate that boys are as likely as girls to imitate others spontaneously. Girls are somewhat more likely to adapt their own judgments to those of their peer group in general, but boys are more likely to accept peer-group values when these conflict with their own.

Girls Are Better at Rote Learning and Simple, Repetitive Tasks; Boys Excel at Tasks That Require Higher-Level Thinking and Are More Analytic.

Both sexes are equally proficient at all kinds of learning tasks—rote learning, discrimination learning, learning to shift to opposite solutions, and learning to figure out probabilities. There is no difference between boys and girls in analyzing only the elements needed for a task; boys do not excel at disembedding information, except when the task is visual-spatial.

Girls Are Not Motivated to Achieve.

Observational studies of strivings for achievement have found either that boys and girls are the same or that girls are more motivated to achieve. Boys have to be challenged by appeals to their ego and by competition to tell stories that reveal as much ambition as those told by girls. A review done by Althea Stein and Margaret Bailey (1973) generally supports the view that a striving for achievement is no more likely in boys than it is in girls. These reviewers suggest that for girls, mastering social skills has been an area of achievement, not an alternative to achievement. But there is an inherent conflict between the traits needed for intellectual and occupational achievement—independence, assertiveness, competitiveness, belief in one's competence—and the social skills girls are expected to acquire: dependence, compliance, cooperativeness, and diffidence.

Open Questions about Sex Differences

Some research findings about sex differences are ambiguous. The evidence is too meager to demonstrate either physiological or cultural causes or to establish with certainty that the differences really exist.

Girls Are More Sociable and Nurturing than Boys.

Maccoby and Jacklin contend that the two sexes are equally sociable. They use as evidence the following research findings. Boys and girls are equally likely to imitate another person, to depend on adults and seek their help or attention, to stay in a room alone. Girls do not spend more time with playmates, although they do tend to prefer one other companion or small groups, whereas boys prefer large peer groups. Nevertheless, there are several reasons to consider the sociability issue still open to question.

From the first few months of life, girls have certain sensitivities that might dispose them to social cues, ultimately making them more social than boys. They have greater skin sensitivity, and they are more attentive to social contexts, including faces, speech patterns, and subtle vocal cues. They are more likely to cry when they hear another baby wailing. They can distinguish between their mother's face and a dangling toy earlier. The fact that girls speak earlier and more frequently is likely to mean that they are more sociable, more able to initiate and participate in social exchanges. Girls have also been observed to be relatively more responsive to the social advances of others (Hoffman, 1977; Restak, 1979). In social relationships, females are more affiliative and cooperative, and their relationships tend to be more intimate and intense than males' (Caldwell and Peplau, 1982; Hoffman, 1977). Girls gravitate toward playing in small groups (Lever, 1976), and whereas boys in their peer groups tend to emphasize solidarity, loyalty, and doing things together, girls emphasize intimacy, mutual support, and the sharing of confidences (Rubin, 1980). Females also stay physically closer and make more eye contact with other people than males do (Ashear and Snortum, 1971; Tennis and Dabbs, 1975). When Ladd Wheeler and John Nezlek (1977) studied students' diaries of socializing at the beginning and end of the first year of college, they found that compared to the men, women socialized more intensively and relied on their close women friends to help them through anxious social moments.

Both sexes appear to be equally able to understand the emotional reactions of others. When encountering an emotional situation, such as seeing pictures of a child who has lost a pet dog, boys and girls are equally adept at assessing how the child feels. But one survey of the research on empathy finds that girls are more likely to respond vicariously to another's feelings. Their faces, posture, and words of sympathy are more likely to reflect the distress of the person they watch. And adult women are more distressed than men when watching a person receive a shock (Hoffman, 1977). Studies of other cultures also indicate that young girls consistently behave in a caring fashion. Boys may try to solve the other person's problem when they see him or her in an emotional situation, but girls tend to imagine themselves in the other's situation.

Certainly boys are socialized for the role of active mastery, girls for responding to the needs and feelings of others. In one study that hinted at the importance of socialization, Carol Shigetomi, Donald Hartman, and Donna Gelfand (1981) studied sex differences in altruistic behavior. From teachers' ratings and the results of a classroom task, the researchers assembled an altruism score for each of the subjects, several hundred fifth- and sixth-graders. The students also performed several tasks in which they could help other children. In this study, it was found that girls were *perceived* by teachers as much more altruistic than boys, but the *actual* differences in girls' and boys' behavior were far less pronounced. The tendency of girls to be more responsive and empathic cannot yet be attributed to social conditioning alone, however. There may be a physiological basis for this socialization. In lower animals, female hormones play a role in nurturant behavior. More evidence is needed before psychologists can determine whether the same holds true for human beings.

Boys Are More Active. Infant boys and girls do not differ in overall levels of activity. Among preschoolers, however, boys seem more active than girls. But boys are only more active in certain situations, such as when other boys are present. Whether boys stimulate other boys to great bursts of activity out of fear, anger, curiosity, or simple animal high spirits we do not know. Boys and men describe themselves as more daring and adventurous than girls or women describe themselves (Longstreth, 1970), and researchers consistently find them to be so (Block, 1983). As we saw in Chapter 6, throughout childhood and adolescence, boys have far more accidents and require more emergency medical attention than girls do (Manheimer, Dewey, Mellinger, and Corsa, 1966; Manheimer and Mellinger, 1967).

Girls Are More Compliant and Passive. Boys make more attempts to dominate one another than girls do. They also attempt to dominate adults more often than girls do. Girls tend to be more compliant with adults, but not with agemates. In mixed-sex groups there is no clear-cut pattern, but it is likely that males comply more to a male peer group than females to a female group. Girls are as willing as boys to explore novel surroundings. They are no more likely than boys to withdraw from social interaction; neither are they more likely to yield or withdraw in the face of aggression (Maccoby and Jacklin, 1974).

Androgyny

Some men conform to the masculine stereotype of being competitive, active, and independent. Some women conform to the feminine stereotype of being emotional, sensitive, and concerned with others. But there are many individuals of both sexes who have a range of good qualities, both masculine and feminine. They are called **androgynous.**

According to studies conducted in high school and college, these flexible individuals, who are able to combine desirable qualities that by tradition are possessed separately by the two sexes, have greater self-esteem and are more socially competent, more achievement oriented, and less conformist than individuals who are strongly masculine or feminine or than individuals who have no strong masculine or feminine traits whatsoever (Spence and Helmreich, 1978). Androgynous people of both sexes tend to be more nurturing; in one study, they were more responsive to a baby and to a kitten and more empathic to a lonely peer (Bem, Martyna, and Watson, 1976). They may also be more creative. A longitudinal study that followed creative artists from enrollment in professional art school to adulthood (Getzels and Csikszentmihalyi, 1976) showed that individuals who choose art as a career were more likely to be androgynous. Recognition that individuals of both sexes have a range of feminine and masculine qualities may help us to separate further legitimate sexual differences from myths.

Whence Sex Differences?

Although we cannot yet mark the precise boundaries of differences between the sexes, psychologists often have speculated about the origins of such differences. One hypothesis they have offered is that differences between the sexes originate in the X chromosome. They suggest that certain traits are sex-linked, or X-linked (Shepherd-Look, 1982). Males, you will recall, inherit only one X chromosome and one Y chromosome, but females inherit two X chromosomes. Because recessive genes are expressed only when they are present on both chromosomes of a pair, it is reasonable to use that fact to test whether certain sex-differentiated characteristics are located on the X chromosome. So far, this strategy has not uncovered the sought-after distributions of characteristics in the population. Studies of spatial ability, for example, in girls with only one X-chromosome (Turner's Syndrome) or in chromosomally normal subjects have not shown inheritance patterns consistent with the sex-linked hypothesis (Polani, Lessof, and Bishop, 1956; Vandenberg and Kuse, 1979).

If the sex chromosomes do not adequately explain sex differences, perhaps brain structure does. The consistent verbal superiority of girls and the visual-spatial advantage of boys have led some researchers to investigate possible differences in boys' and girls' brains. Electroencephalograms show that when boys are involved in a spatial task, such as figuring out mentally which of three folded shapes can be made from a flat irregular piece of paper, the right hemisphere of their brain is activated. Girls use both hemispheres for this kind of task (Restak, 1979). Are differences in thinking related to differences in the development and use of the two hemispheres of the brain? This question has produced some fascinating findings.

As we discussed in Chapter 6, the two hemispheres of the brain are not completely alike in functions. The left hemisphere appears to control verbal skills. It apparently picks out relevant details and processes such details sequentially. The right hemisphere processes overall configurations, organizing and processing information in terms of gestalts (wholes). Research on males and females who have undergone brain surgery and strokes; tests determining the spatial abilities of normal males and females; and techniques that direct stimuli through one ear or the other and determine whether there is ear advantage, which is thought to reflect asymmetry in the functioning of the cerebral hemispheres, suggest that males generally have a more clear-cut division, with spatial ability in the right hemisphere and verbal ability in the left. In boys, the right hemisphere appears to have the dominant role in processing visual-spatial information as early as age 6 (Witelson, 1976). Tackling spatial problems with both hemispheres, as girls do, may be less efficient than using the right one alone. This female "flexibility" may actually interfere with spatial processing (Levy, 1969). On the other hand, the fact that boys have less flexibility in using their hemispheres may account for the greater incidence in males of disorders in which language deficits are a predominant symptom.

But the data on brain lateralization contain puzzles. Although most right-handed children show a right-ear advantage when listening to words and a left-sided advantage for spatial stimuli, no consistent differences appear between the sexes (Flannery and Balling, 1977; Leehey, 1977). Deborah Waber (1976) suggests that the timing of maturation, not sex, is the key factor in determining brain lateralization. She found that early-maturing adolescents, whichever their sex, did better on tests of verbal ability than on tests of spatial ability. Late-maturing adolescents showed the opposite pattern. Nora Newcombe and Mary Bandura (1983), who studied 11-year-old girls, supported Waber's findings by showing that spatial ability was highest in those who matured later, who showed masculine personality traits and intellectual interests, and who wanted to be boys. The girls who scored highest in measures of femininity matured earliest and performed less well on tests of spatial ability.

Do hormones, those powerful chemicals secreted by the ductless glands of the endocrine system, cause sex differences in behavior? It is well established that hormones circulating in the bloodstream affect the development of physical characteristics of females and males. In prenatal development, the presence of the hormone androgen is necessary for the development of male sexual characteristics. But research into how exactly hormones influence behavior faces serious problems. For one thing, hormone levels are anything but constant during prenatal or postnatal development; they are produced cyclically and respond sensitively to environmental factors. For another, researchers face the problem of trying to separate the effects of genes from those of hormones, because many hormonal programs are written right into the genetic code. In one recent study, Melissa Hines and Carl Shipley (1984) looked at the possible influence of prenatal exposure to hormones on girls' development. They compared girls whose mothers had taken a synthetic estrogen during pregnancy with their sisters who had not been exposed to the estrogen. Because they knew that males' brain lateralization is greater than females', Hines and Shipley tested the two groups of daughters and found that the girls exposed to estrogen had a more masculine pattern of brain lateralization. But they found no differences between the two groups in verbal or spatial abilities.

The area of sex differences in which the role of hormones has been studied most extensively is aggression. Researchers have found a relationship between aggression and the presence of the male sex hormones in studies of animals. But the relationship is not a unidirectional one. In studies of primates, not only do hormone levels affect social behavior but, conversely, the social situation can affect hormone levels. When a rhesus monkey is number one in his colony, his testosterone level is higher than that of the other male monkeys. But when this top monkey is put in a colony where he is unknown and where he must reestablish himself, his hormone level plummets. Furthermore, when a low-status male is put in a cage with a female over whom he is dominant and with whom he can have sex, his testosterone level rises (Rose and Bernstein, 1972). In studies of humans, the findings have been contradictory. It is likely that stress, for example, which affects circulating hormone levels,

anxiety, and depression, mediates the link between hormones and behavior. In human beings, moreover, not only is the evidence for a direct hormonal connection not conclusive, but there is also some evidence that boys may learn their aggressiveness. The perception of sex differences does seem to affect how parents treat their sons and daughters from birth. Even neutral behavior, such as greater physical activity of infants, tends to be interpreted by parents of boys as aggression. Although boys apparently receive no more direct, positive reinforcement for aggression from their parents than girls do, subtle differences in the treatment of boys and girls may encourage them to be aggressive. Studies of the possible causes of aggression show that a boy becomes markedly aggressive when he begins with an aggressive temperament and is raised by a punitive father or a negative mother (Eron, Walder, and Lefkowitz, 1971; Olweus, 1980).

A major longitudinal study that followed children from 8 to 18 years of age (Eron et al., 1971) showed, as did other studies, marked and continuing greater aggression in boys. It was attributed to constitutional differences in muscle structure and hormone levels and to social attitudes condoning, if not rewarding, aggressive behavior in males. Extensive interviews with parents and children revealed that the aggression of boys and girls could be traced to different situations. Punitive fathers with good occupations but little education, even if they were not regularly at home, were likely to raise aggressive boys. Upper-class boys who were severely punished for aggression were more aggressive than others of their status; the more they were punished, the more aggressive they became. Girls' aggression was related to mothers' and fathers' attitudes toward them, not to occupation or education. Mothers who were punitive and fathers who were rejecting or paid them little loving attention were the most likely to have aggressive daughters. Nevertheless, although these girls were aggressive compared to other girls, they were less inclined to retaliate than boys, failing to strike back as highly aggressive boys do when given opportunity.

Prescribed social roles so reinforce the tendency toward spatial superiority and physical aggressiveness in males and verbal skill and nurturance in females that biological predisposition is difficult to separate from social conditioning. Gaining experience may be mediated from within; boys may on their own seek out opportunities to sharpen spatial or combative skills and girls ways to sharpen verbal or caretaking skills. But in a culture prepared to hand blocks and guns to boys and dolls to girls, even the slightest inherited predisposition could be built into a major psychological difference.

In the next section, we turn our attention directly to the socialization of these social roles and gender-appropriate behavior.

GENDER ROLES

Gender roles and manifest sex differences are not the same. Whereas sex differences include characteristics that are biologically based, gender roles are thoroughly social constructions. Gender roles are those ways of behaving that are socially prescribed for males and females in a particular culture. They are encouraged, or socialized, in children by parents, peers, teachers, and the community at large.

Socialization of Gender Roles

From the moment of birth, boys and girls are perceived by parents as different. Girls are seen as smaller, weaker, prettier; boys as firmer, better coordinated, stronger, and more alert (Rubin, Provenzano, and Luria, 1974). Parents have these biased perceptions, even though newborn boys and girls are not measurably different. With their young children, parents generally encourage sons and daughters to behave differently in every area of activity. They provide vehicles, educational materials, sports equipment, machines, toy or real animals, and military toys for their sons, and they decorate their rooms with pictures of animals. They provide dolls, dollhouses, and housekeeping toys such as rolling pins, dishes, and stoves, for their daughters, and they decorate their rooms with lace, ruffles, fringe, and floral designs. They give sons toys that encourage inventiveness, manipulation, and feedback about the physical world and daughters toys that encourage imitation, are used near a caretaker, and provide less opportunity for variation or innovation (Fagot, 1978; Fein, Johnson, Kosson, Stork, and Wasserman, 1975; Rheingold and Cook, 1978; Rosenfeld, 1975). And they expect children to play with toys appropriate to their gen-

der (Schau, Kahn, Diepold, and Cherry, 1980).

In a review of studies conducted in the 1960s and 1970s of differences in parents' socialization of sons and daughters, Jeanne Block (1983) found evidence for differences in socialization according to both parents' and children's sex. She noted that these differences intensify as the children grow older and that they remain quite consistent across various social, educational, and cultural backgrounds. Parents described themselves as encouraging sons more than daughters to achieve, compete, control their feelings, act independently, and assume personal responsibility. They claimed to punish sons more often than they punish daughters. Fathers especially are more authoritarian with their sons; they are stricter, firmer, less tolerant of aggression directed toward themselves or of behavior that diverges from the traditional masculine stereotype. Fathers encourage instrumentality, mastery, and orientation to tasks with their sons; with their daughters, they encourage expressiveness and dependence. In raising daughters, parents are less punitive, warmer, physically closer, more confident of the child's trustworthiness and truthfulness, expect more "ladylike" behavior, and expect more reflectiveness than they expect from their sons. Mothers supervise their daughters more strictly than they do their sons. Even across cultural boundaries, such differences appear (Barry, Bacon, and Child, 1957). Girls are pressured to be nurturant, obedient, responsible, unselfish, kind, well mannered, and, later, to marry well and to raise children; boys to be self-reliant and successful, ambitious and strong willed (Hoffman, 1977; Tudiver, 1979).

Observational studies of parents' actual behavior show differences in their interactions with sons and daughters, too. While feeding their infants, for example, mothers are more responsive and stimulating to sons than to daughters, and both fathers and mothers have been shown to respond more readily to sons' vocalizations than to daughters' (Murphy and Moriarty, 1976; Parke and Sawin, 1976). Such differences persist beyond infancy. Studies have shown that boys receive both more positive and more negative responses from their parents than girls do. Boys generally are given more room to explore than girls are (Lewis and Weinraub, 1974). The chores they are assigned more often take them outside the house and away from the direct supervision of a caretaker. Girls often are assigned chores

Child rearing takes some special effort if parents do not want their children to develop stereotyped sex roles. Providing toys and materials that are not traditionally sex-typed and encouraging their use can help.

as "helpers"; for girls, these homebound chores reinforce the importance of the family (Duncan, Schuman, and Duncan, 1973; Whiting and Edwards, 1975).

In another review of the research on socialization of gender roles, Dee Shepherd-Look (1982) noted that parents have been reported to respond more often to boys' large movements than to those of girls; boys are handled and played with more roughly than girls, and girls are treated as if they were more fragile. In matters of autonomy—dressing, bathing, keeping their rooms neat, or staying close to home—mothers have been found to hold similar expectations of sons and daughters. But beginning at school age, girls tend to be more closely monitored and protected than boys.

In the area of aggression, the findings are not entirely consistent, but there is certainly no evidence that the greater aggressiveness that has been observed for boys is the result of deliberate parental encouragement. Some researchers have found no differences in the socialization of boys and girls as far as displaying or returning aggression or settling fights goes (e.g., Newson and Newson, 1968; Sears, Rau, and Alpert, 1965). Other researchers have found that boys are punished more severely for acting aggressively to other people (Serbin, O'Leary, Kent, and Tronick, 1973). Although parents do not want their children to be taken advantage of, they do not consider aggression an acceptable way for boys or girls to solve problems (Shepherd-Look, 1982).

Fundamental changes in values could alter the divergence in parents' socialization of boys and girls. So far research on children's development in families in which mother and father have nontraditional values and share caretaking has for the most part examined only a few, atypical families. But even in traditional families, parents can socialize their children in less gender-stereotyped ways. In a study by Diana Baumrind (1979), some boys were prosocial in the typically feminine way—communal and friendly. They had mothers who were particularly responsive to their needs and wishes. Some girls were unusually independent and assertive for their sex. They had parents who pushed them by being less warm and nurturing and by making strong demands for independent behavior. A recent study of children in the Stanford area suggests that in the last decade, rigid gender socialization by parents may have diminished. After observing and questioning children at home, at school, and in the laboratory, over the first 6 years of life, Jacklin and Maccoby (reported in Turkington, 1984) found that these parents did *not* stereotype their children. They treated little boys and little girls similarly, giving them equal amounts of warmth and nurturance, acceptance and restriction. The one exception to this pattern was that fathers offered more gender-stereotyped toys to their children and tended to play more roughly with their sons than their daughters. The boys and girls in the study were not notably different in muscle strength, moodiness, tactile sensitivity, sleep patterns, age of first walking or toileting, intelligence, irritability, or level of activity. Overall, girls seemed slightly more timid than boys, and boys were somewhat readier to show anger and aggression. But the investigators found that individual boys and girls varied as much from their same-sex as from their other-sex peers. Jacklin and Maccoby suggest that teachers, neighbors, relatives, the mass media, and even chance encounters may influence children's development of stereotyped gender roles more than parents do.

Parents who do not want their children to develop the traditional, stereotyped gender roles will still have to make special efforts in the 1980s. Despite the growing opportunities for women to work at jobs not open to them in the past, these traditional gender roles remain firmly entrenched in society. The forces combining to perpetuate them are formidable: physiological predispositions, a society that continues to place most child-rearing responsiblity with women, both obvious and subtle cultural reinforcements, and the fact that most of the people who are rearing children had traditional upbringings. With or without an Equal Rights Amendment, socialization of boys is likely to remain different from that of girls.

Even strangers act differently to boys and girls.

In an attempt to assess the effects of labeling on the observer, 204 college men and women were shown a film of a 9-month-old infant playing with four unfamiliar toys (Condry and Condry, 1976). Half of the subjects were told that they were observing "David," the other half a girl named "Dana." The infant in the film was seen as having different emotions and significantly different levels of emotional intensity, depending on the sex attributed to the infant and the sex of the observer. The students who watched David found him expressing considerable pleasure and little fear as he played. Those who watched Dana saw less pleasure and more fear in her reactions. When the infant in the film made some sort of negative response to a jack-in-the-box, students watching David thought that he was angry, while those watching Dana thought that she was afraid. Male students made especially sharp distinctions in describing the emotions of David and Dana.

In another study, Carol Seavey, Phyllis Katz, and Sue Zalk (1975) tested adults' reactions to a 3-month-old girl dressed in a yellow jumpsuit. Most of the adults were graduate students in their 20s who had no children. When these young adults, who generally considered themselves free of sex bias, were told the baby was a girl or boy and asked to play with her, both the men and the women were likely to use gender-stereotyped toys. On hand were a Raggedy Ann doll, a small rubber football, and a flexible plastic ring. Those who believed the baby was a girl chose Raggedy Ann; those who believed her to be a boy chose the football. When the child was called simply "baby" to some of the adults, men used the flexible plastic ring and handled the child the least; women used the gender-stereotyped toys and handled the child the most. All these adults attempted to guess whether the infant was a girl or boy, referring to the infant as soft and fragile if they guessed girl or commenting on the baby's strong grasp and lack of hair if they guessed boy.

In a third study, by Hannah Frisch (1977), adults were given the opportunity to play with 15-month-old infants they did not know. There were 24 infants in the study, half boys, half girls, and each was introduced once as a girl and once to a different adult, as a boy. The adults encouraged the infants they thought were boys to play actively and usually picked a ball for the two of them to play with. They chose a doll or bottle for their play with girls, and they talked more to them. The infants played very much the same no matter what their true sex was or how they were treated by the adults.

At school, teachers, like these strangers, often reinforce gender differences. Evidence from several studies suggests that teachers pay more positive and negative attention to boys than to girls (Meyer and Thompson, 1956; Serbin et al., 1973) and respond to them with more ideas about solving problems and with specific information (Golden and Birns, 1975). For example, among fifth-graders who were assigned tutors, girls with the lowest academic abilities received the least support, praise, and encouragement and the most criticism (Frey, 1979). This pattern of relative inattention and criticism toward girls has been found even on the university level (Carnegie Commission on Higher Education, 1973; Hochschild, 1975). Compared to boys, girls more often have been found to feel helpless in the face of a task, seeing failure as an inevitable result of their lack of ability. Boys tend to externalize failure and blame it on bad luck or lack of effort. These differences may follow from the kinds of feedback that teachers give children. Girls are most often criticized for work that is inaccurate or poorly thought out, but boys are criticized for their behavior or nonintellectual aspects of their work, such as messiness or nonconformity to rules. In short, girls who are criticized on the grounds of their abilities feel helpless in the face of failure. Boys, who consider teachers' criticisms extrinsic to themselves, do not interpret failure as a reflection of their abilities (Dweck and Bush, 1976; Dweck et al., 1978; Dweck and Goetz, 1977). Textbooks reinforce these biases. Many portray girls as less important than boys (Taylor, 1973). Even achievement tests portray all professors, doctors, and team members as males; school teachers are female; and some professions are implied to be closed to females (Saario, Jacklin, and Tittle, 1973).

Children's books and television programs also contribute to the different socialization of the sexes, as the findings from many studies show (e.g., Weitzman, Eifler, Hokada, and Ross, 1972). Both commercial and educational television show more male than female characters. Even "Sesame Street," public television's award-winning children's show,

has more male than female characters. Big Bird is told that he is "a boy bird and will have to help with men's work, important work" and "should get a girl bird to help Susan with her work of flower arranging" (Gardner, 1970). Children who watch a lot of television have more traditional ideas about gender roles than children who do not (Freuh and McGhee, 1975).

Gender-Stereotyped Activities

Unfortunately, with stereotyped messages so prevalent—at home, at school, in the street, on television—it is nearly impossible to assess their effects. One study (Fischer and Torney, 1976) showed that some 5-year-old children were affected by hearing stories in which the main character was either independent—he or she worked on a puzzle alone until it was finished and was reinforced for his or her independence—or dependent—he or she asked for help with the puzzle and got help. Girls who heard the story in which the main character asked for help were more likely to do so themselves later when given a block-design task. This study suggests that socialization can reinforce sex differences in children and affect their activities and behavior. Studies of preschoolers have indeed shown clear sex differences in their toy preferences and play. Girls are likelier to paint, help teachers, look at books, and listen to stories; boys are likelier to hammer or play with cars and trucks. Girls like stuffed animals, dolls, cooking tools, and dressing up; boys like to manipulate objects, play with blocks and carpentry tools (Sears et al., 1965). By middle childhood, boys prefer games that involve competition, body contact, and tests of strength; girls like games that involve taking turns, word play, and choral activities (Sutton-Smith and Sovasta, 1972).

In one study that tested a large sample of children, Lorraine Nadelman (1974) found that girls preferred pictures of dolls and other gender-stereotyped objects, boys liked pictures of footballs and the like. Boys had stronger gender-stereotyped preferences. Girls were more open in their preferences. Although girls did not choose decidedly masculine activities, they did make more neutral choices. Boys may be more rigid in their preferences because parents and teachers allow them less flexibility in their activities. "Sissy" is a more serious charge than "tomboy" in our culture. For American

 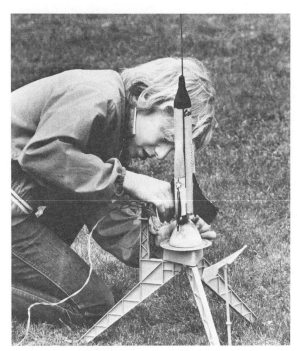

Self-adornment is one quality traditionally associated with girls' activities in our culture. Manipulating objects and competing (to see how far and fast a rocket can fly) are traditionally associated with boys' activities.

children, the need to prove masculinity may be greater than the need to prove femininity.

Knowledge of Gender Roles

An adult might mistake a 6- or 7-year-old girl with short hair for a boy. But the physical similarity of children during most of childhood masks a growing distinction between the sexes in what is going on under that short hair. Between the ages of 4 and 8, children learn much about what it *means* to be male or female. They not only act in the gender-stereotyped ways we have just described, but they come to *recognize* gender stereotypes, the bold outlines of masculine and feminine, the games, occupations, clothing, and behavior usually associated with being boy or girl, man or woman. Although a boy of 2 or 3 might be able to tell you that he is a boy, he believes that he could be a girl or a mommy if he wanted to be. All he would have to do is play girls' games or wear dresses and grow his hair long. "Boy" may mean no more to him than the names Tom, Dick, and Harry. Children at this age lack a sense of the constancy of sex (Kohlberg, 1966). They do not understand that it is anatomical and that it cannot be changed.

Development of **sex constancy** has been tested by asking children to select pictures, drawings, or dolls of a boy, a girl, a man, a woman (Emmerich, Goldman, Kirsh, and Sharabany, 1977; Thompson, 1975; Thompson and Bentler, 1971). The 2-year-olds could select which of the pictures was the same sex as they, but they were not sure whether it was a boy or a girl. The 3-year-olds selected correctly *and* knew the picture was of a boy or a girl. Children between 4 and 6 could choose appropriate clothes for Mommy and Daddy, but they made their choice according to hair length, not body build or genitals. Few children thought that a girl remained a girl if she changed her haircut, clothing, and activities. The immutability of sex is not an *easy* notion for preschool children to grasp, for it must be distinguished from other personal attributes that *do* change, such as age and size. Children may easily perceive themselves to have more in common with an opposite-sex agemate than with the same-sex adult, if they do not yet understand the significance of sex. Learning this takes considerable experience and a degree of cognitive maturity not achieved until age 6 or even older.

Even at 3, however, although children do not know that sex is immutable, they do have **gender identity.** They are likely to get upset if someone makes a mistake about their gender. Research with very young children whose genitals have both male and female characteristics (and for whom corrective surgery is often considered) suggests that by the age of 3 a child has a sense of gender identity that is difficult to alter later on (Money, Hampson, and Hampson, 1957).

Young children also have some rudimentary knowledge of gender roles—of what is appropriate behavior for boys and girls, men and women. Nancy Eisenberg, Edward Murray, and Tina Hite (1982) questioned 3- and 4-year-olds about which sex-typed toys they thought that they themselves, another boy, or another girl would like to play with and why. The children often justified their choices for other children on the grounds of gender roles and stereotypes (though when it came to choosing toys for real play, they rarely resorted to such justifications). Knowledge of gender roles increases in middle childhood. Deborah Best and her colleagues (Best et al., 1977) conducted a cross-cultural study of gender-role stereotyping in young children in three countries: the United States, Ireland, and England. In her study, 5- and 8-year-olds heard about or saw conventional gender stereotypes, as defined by university students, in brief stories and in silhouettes of human figures. In all three countries, recognition by children of sex traits increased from 5 to 8 years of age. Children knew more male traits than female traits at both ages, and knowledge of male stereotypes developed earlier. Children have a strong tendency to identify with adults of their own sex between ages 7 and 10, which sometimes serves to counteract the stereotypes. Fred Rothbaum (1977) asked boys and girls aged 7, 10, and 14 to make up stories about adults who take charge and tell others what to do, adults who are kind to those in need, adults whom everybody obeys, and adults who try to cheer up a friend by being kind. He found that both boys and girls were more likely to invent male characters to take charge and be obeyed, using a gender stereotype, but that they created characters of their own gender to be kind and cheerful, supposedly feminine traits.

At first, children may subscribe to gender stereotypes with considerable rigidity and oversimplification. For example, 6-year-old Michael may think that only men can be doctors, all cooks are women, and only boys can play ball, despite the fact that his mother is a surgeon, his father is a chef, and his sister is captain of the girls' softball team. Gradually, as experience modifies their views, children allow for more variations. It may be that during this modifying phase parents, siblings, peers, teachers, television, and textbooks are able to reduce stereotypes significantly. Sonia Marantz and Annick Mansfield (1977) examined the effects of the job or profession of their mothers on children's sex-role stereotyping. They found stereotypes to be the most rigid at 5 to 6 years; influenced the most by mother's work status at 7 to 8; the least stereotyped, regardless of mother's work status, at 9 to 11.

Dale Marcus and Willis Overton (1978) asked 96 kindergartners, first-graders, and second-graders about their preferences in games, television programs, and future vocations. Second-graders did not indicate any greater preference for gender-stereotyped activities than the younger children. Marcus and Overton speculate that preferences that are neutral or associated with the opposite sex may be easier to state once children have sure knowledge that their sex will not be altered by anything they do. Dorothy Ullian (1976) found that 6-year-olds felt they must conform to gender-role expectations to maintain their sex identity. But at 8, with sex constancy firmly established, children understood that playing a boyish game would not change a girl, that putting on an apron would not change a boy.

Theories of Gender-Role Development

Psychoanalytic Theory. Sigmund Freud (1938) proposed that children develop sex-appropriate social behavior through identification with the parent of the same sex. His theory of gender-role development in boys has been widely accepted by psychoanalysts. In infancy and early childhood, a boy develops a uniquely strong attachment to his mother. He loves her and wants to possess her, but the father stands in the way. The boy hates and fears his father (the father is seen as punitive and the boy fears the father may cut off his [the boy's] penis if the father finds out how the boy feels). Plagued with guilt, too, the boy faces an emotional crisis that must be resolved. He resolves it in the phallic stage of psychosexual development, between 3 and 5 years. Freud saw an analogy to the boy's plight in the myth of the Greek king Oedipus, who was as an infant abandoned on a mountain top by his father, rescued by a kind shepherd, and raised in nearby Corinth. Returning to Thebes as a young man, he unknowingly encountered and killed his father and married his own mother. The young boy has secret fantasies of being rid of his father so that he can marry his mother, thereby changing himself from the threatened to the threatener. Freud called the boy's plight the Oedipal conflict. His real-life compromise is to repress his fantasies and to identify with his father, to try to resemble him in as many ways as possible and thus experience his mother's sexual love vicariously. For this reason, according to psychoanalytic theory, boys adopt the values and behavior of their fathers.

Freud's explanation of how girls come to identify with their mothers is more controversial. The simplest theory, put forward by some of Freud's followers, is that in the second and third year, girls develop an **anaclitic identification,** one that is based on earlier dependency. Up to this point, the daughter, too, has developed an intense attachment to her mother. But in the anal period, toilet training and other disciplinary actions begin; Mother then starts withdrawing or withholding her love, making it uncertain and conditional. The daughter, fearing the loss of her relationship with the mother, identifies with her, **introjecting** (taking into herself) Mother's wishes, standards, attitudes, and values. She makes her mother's behavior part of her own, all to guarantee that she will never lose mother's love.

But Freud's own explanation, the Electra complex, parallels the boy's Oedipus complex. According to this explanation, when the mother starts withdrawing her unconditional love, the girl becomes increasingly devoted to her father. She wants to have him, for one reason because she loves him, for another because she finds out he has a penis and she wishes that she had one too. She fears her mother, believing her to have been responsible for her own penisless state, and she is angry at her mother for withdrawing her affection. But her rebellious thoughts bring intense feelings of fear and guilt that cannot continue. The compromise the little girl makes in the phallic stage, according to Freud, is first to decide that she will settle for a baby from her father, instead of a penis, and second (like

the boy) to realize that she can accomplish this only vicariously, by identifying with her mother. Thus, through identification with the same-sex parent, both boys and girls acquire a sense of strength, a conscience and control over their emotions and impulses, empathy and moral values, and identities as males and females.

Explaining so many social outcomes by a single mechanism is an appealing aspect of psychoanalytic theory. Unfortunately, the theory falls short in many respects. A major problem is the difficulty of testing it. Other problems are encountered when we try to make sweeping applications of psychoanalytic theory. Evidence from cross-cultural research indicates that boys do not always have rivalrous relations with their fathers. Moreover, children identify with and imitate people other than parents, such as sports heroes whom they have never met. "Like father like son" is not a statistically sound statement. And changing the incentives for a certain behavior can totally alter the likelihood of its occurrence (Bandura, 1969b; Lynn, 1974; Zigler and Child, 1973).

Social-Learning Theory. According to early social-learning theorists and current operant-learning theorists, children behave as they do because they are rewarded for these kinds of behavior by parental attention and punished or ignored for other kinds of behavior. Usually they are rewarded by affection, approval, praise, and tangible gifts and punished by scolding and spanking. Sometimes even scolding is rewarding if the children would otherwise be completely ignored.

This theory, too, has some appeal, but making behavior more frequent by rewarding it has been easier to demonstrate in the laboratory than in the complexity of real-life parent–child relations. There is no strong evidence that all social behavior is reinforced. Learning often seems to occur without any obvious reinforcement.

Observational-learning theory holds that children learn social behavior through their eyes and ears, by observing and imitating people and events. Observational learning, too, has been demonstrated for the most part in the laboratory with relatively inconsequential and artificial kinds of behavior, such as hitting a Bobo doll or donating a cheap toy to another child. In real life, many models—parents, siblings, relatives, neighbors, teachers, television personalities—often act in contradictory ways. If children choose to imitate the behavior of the persons who are more lenient with them or the behavior that stands to benefit them the most or the behavior of the model most recently observed, imitations are likely to be short-lived and difficult to trace to particular models.

Carolyn Waxler and Marian Radke-Yarrow (1975) attempted to test observational learning in the real world by watching mothers with their children. During half an hour of free play with a set of toys, *all* children, at least once, imitated the way their mother played with the toys. The number of times they imitated their mother was related to her pacing and style. They followed more of her suggestions when she was enthusiastic and demonstrated only a few ways of playing with the toys. But this investigation did not uncover a simple link between modeling and imitation. Instead, imitation seemed to reflect ongoing mother-child relationships, which differed from pair to pair. Children may learn through observation in the laboratory and in real life, but this seems at best only part of the picture. Even social-learning theorist Bandura does not claim that observational learning accounts for all a child's socialization and recognizes reinforcement and cognition as important too.

Cognitive Theory of Gender-Role Development.

The cognitive theory of gender-role development is derived from Jean Piaget's theory and interpreted primarily by Lawrence Kohlberg (1969). He suggests that children imitate other people only if it makes sense to them, if they think that is what they are supposed to do, if they perceive the people as competent and similar to themselves. Children imitate what they regard as competent behavior because they like to feel competent too.

Kohlberg (1966), has paid particular attention to explaining how he believes cognition figures in the development of gender roles. The formation of gender identity is in large part the child's comprehension and acceptance of a physical reality. Children first make a cognitive judgment, "I am a boy"

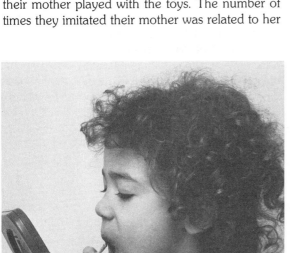

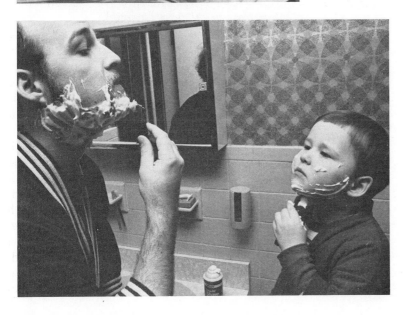

Children like to imitate the adults they see around them, particularly adults of the same sex.

or "I am a girl." Only after they have identified and labeled themselves as boy or girl do they value and assume masculine and feminine ways (Figure 15.6). In social-learning theory, the sequence would be as follows: boy wants rewards; he is rewarded for masculine actions; therefore he wants to be a boy. In the cognitive view, the boy asserts that he is a boy, then wants to do masculine things; therefore the opportunity to do masculine things is rewarding. He prefers Father because of his perception of Father as male and similar to himself.

Kohlberg finds evidence in the studies of others that imitation of, and preference for, the same-sex parent increase with age, which tends to support his theory that children imitate their same-sex parent only after they have come to realize that they have a stable gender identity. Ronald Slaby and Karin Frey (1975) found that only when individual children had developed a sense of sex constancy,

around 5 or 6 years of age, did they prefer watching the same-sex model. In another study by James Bryan and Zella Luria (1978), 5- and 6-year-olds preferred and recalled a same-sex model, even though they had paid as much attention to an opposite-sex one.

Nevertheless, the learning of gender roles remains a chicken-and-egg problem. The cognitive explanation adds an important and essential dimension to our theorizing about social development, for it presents children as thinking, interpreting, and knowing, not simply as copying and reacting automatically. But it downplays physiological proclivities for masculine and feminine behavior and is less useful for explaining behavior in the first 3 to 4 years. The cognitive theory of development does not explain, for example, the finding that gender identity cannot usually be reassigned after age 3 without seriously confusing a child.

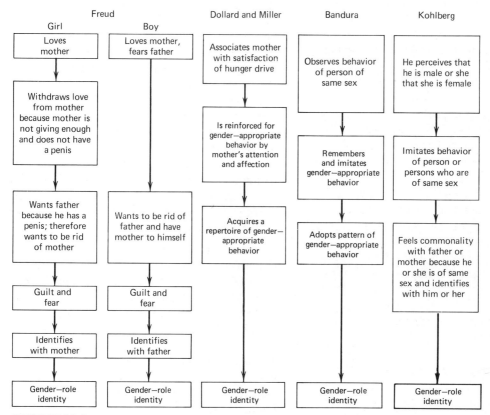

FIGURE 15.6

Four theories have very different explanations of how children develop gender roles and form gender-role identities as they move through early childhood.

SELF-CONCEPT AND IDENTITY

SELF-RECOGNITION IN INFANCY

One of the most important psychological developments of infancy is the infant's recognition that she or he is a separate being who exists independently of others. Michael Lewis and Jeanne Brooks-Gunn (1979) have studied infants between 5 and 24 months old to see how and when the recognition of self emerges. They have found that between 5 and 8 months of age, infants smile at their image in a mirror or on videotape, gaze intently at themselves, touch themselves, and bounce, wave, or clap. But at this early age, there is no evidence that infants distinguish their image from that of another person whose action is contingent on the infant's. Between 9 and 12 months, infants use their mirror image to guide reaching and begin to understand that mirrors show reflections. Between 15 and 18 months, infants will touch their own nose when they observe a spot of rouge on it; and some infants can point to and label pictures of themselves. By 21 to 24 months, infants can reliably differentiate between themselves and others, using their own name and personal pronouns for themselves and others.

Bennett Bertenthal and Kurt Fischer (Bertenthal and Fischer, 1978; Fischer, 1980) have also studied the stages in which infants acquire a sense of self, and their observations agree with those of Lewis and Brooks-Gunn. First, infants look at and touch some part of their mirror image. Next, infants reach for a hat hanging over their head after seeing it reflected in a mirror. Later, they turn to see a real toy behind them after watching it first appear in the mirror. Infants respond in this way after they have acquired object permanence. Still later, at about 18 months of age, infants touch noses after a dot of rouge is placed on them. By the age of 2, children answer appropriately when their mothers point to the children's mirror image and asks, "Who's that?"

From these investigations, a developmental sequence emerges (Harter, 1983). In the first stage, infants are interested in their mirror image but give no sign that they perceive themselves as independent or as causal agents. In the second stage, infants understand how their actions affect reflected images. In the third stage, they understand the difference between mirror images that reflect their own and other people's actions. In the fourth stage, infants recognize that they are objects and can distinguish between themselves and others. They have an internal image of their own face that they can compare with an external image. Finally, infants understand that they have unique features that can be named and labeled with words.

DEVELOPING A CONCEPT OF SELF

Thus by the age of 2, children realize that they are distinct from other people. A little boy now may grab a toy and insist, "Mine"; he may see his photograph and pipe, "Me." He begins to tell people, "I am a boy" or "I am a baby." But children of this age still cannot see themselves as others see them. Their **self-concept** is based on fleeting, sometimes inaccurate, perceptions. When they are asked to describe themselves, they often do so in terms of some favorite behavior: "sits and watches television," "is a helper who does the dishes," "can pick things up" (Keller, Ford, and Meacham, 1978). They do not describe themselves in terms of more stable attributes like "smart" or "pretty." Only at school age do intelligence or attractiveness form part of the child's self-concept. Then, a dramatic change takes place in the way children see themselves. At a time when physical changes are gradual and distinctions between male and female are more a matter of dress and hairstyle than body proportion, children begin to recognize that they have unique and defining personal qualities. They gain a strong sense of their gender and what role they will play as men or women. They also judge their personal traits and worthiness.

My name is Bruce C. I have brown eyes. I have brown hair. I have brown eyebrows. I'm 9 years old. I LOVE! sports. I have seven people in my family. I have great! eye site. I have lots! of friends. I live on 1923 Pinecrest Dr. I'm going on 10 in September. I'm a boy. I have a uncle that is almost 7 feet tall. My school is Pinecrest. My teacher is Mrs. V. I play Hockey! I'am almost the smartest boy in the class. I LOVE! food. I love freash air. I LOVE School (Montemayor and Eisen, 1977, p. 317).

To determine how the concept of the self changes in the school years, Raymond Montemayor and Marvin Eisen (1977) asked 262 boys and girls from a suburban midwestern university community to give 20 different answers to the question, "Who am I?" Not every child loves school, fresh air, and sports, but most children of 9 or 10 identified themselves as Bruce did, by the concrete facts of their existence. The 9- and 10-year-olds were likely to refer to their sex, age, name, territory, likes, dislikes, and physical self. But by age 11 many children especially girls, began to emphasize their personality and relations with others. A sixth-grade girl of 11½ gave this answer to "Who am I?"

My name is A. I'm a human being. I'm a girl. I'm a truthful person. I'm not pretty. I do so-so in my studies. I'm a very good cellist. I'm a very good pianist. I'm a little bit tall for my age. I like several boys. I like several girls. I'm old-fashioned. I play tennis. I am a very good swimmer. I try to be helpful. I'm always ready to be friends with anybody. Mostly I'm good, but I lose my temper. I'm not well-liked by some girls. I don't know if I'm liked by boys or not (Montemayor and Eisen, 1977, pp. 317–318).

Most children start middle school with a relatively shallow self-concept and do not yet differentiate themselves from others or from their surroundings. They may love sports, but they do not think of themselves as athletes. Gradually, by selecting and integrating new discoveries about themselves and by using new cognitive powers, they bring into focus a picture of the self that is sharp and unique.

Personeity is the word that has been applied to a growing sense of self-identity that develops during middle childhood and erupts in adolescence. Personeity is awareness of being in the past, now, and in the future a "human person separate from and entirely like no other" (Guardo and Bohan, 1971, p. 1911). When asked, "Why can't you be a boy?" an 8-year-old girl did not cite hair length, energy, clothing, as a younger child might have. "I'm me and he's him. Well that I can't change in any way cause I've got to stay like this myself."

Younger children are likely to use the continuity of their name as the reason they will remain the same person through time, but by the age of 8 they begin to realize that their names are simply arbitrary designations. As one girl expressed it: "My name isn't what I am. It's just my name!" A girl of nearly 9, when asked what would be the same if her name

were changed, answered, "My per-son-al-it-y."

John Broughton (1978) and Robert Selman (1980) interviewed a number of children about their knowledge of themselves. Broughton used direct questions, like "What is the self?" and "What is the mind?" Selman used more indirect means, presenting the children with hypothetical dilemmas and then asking them questions about the stories. Both investigators showed that young children conceive of themselves in physical terms. They locate their "self" within their body, usually within their head, and therefore conflate self, mind, and body. As one child at this stage of understanding replied: "I am the boss of myself . . . [because] my mouth told my arm and my arm does what my mouth tells it to do" (Selman, 1980, p. 95). A body, many children say, can have a self and a mind. Even plants, animals, and dead people have selves and bodies. Because children conceive of themselves in physical terms, they also differentiate themselves from others in those terms: "I am different from my brother because I am bigger, different from that tree because I am smaller." At about the age of 8, children begin to understand the difference between mind and body, especially between self and body. In adolescence, this distinction grows sharper. In middle childhood comes the understanding that one is unique not solely for physical reasons but also for what one thinks and feels. As one 10-year-old put it:

I am one of a kind. . . . There could be a person who looks like me or talks like me, but no one who has every single detail I have. Never a person who thinks exactly like me (Broughton, 1978, p. 86).

In a study of 3- to 5-year-olds, Ann Keller, LeRoy Ford, and John Meacham (1978) found that the children conceived of themselves in terms of what they did. The researchers asked the children to say spontaneously up to ten things about themselves and to complete these sentences: "I am a _____" and "I am a boy/girl who _____." Over half of the children's responses referred to actions: "I play ball" or "I walk to school." Responses that referred to body parts were relatively uncommon (less than 10 percent). Only about 5 percent of the children's responses referred to their likes and dislikes, psychological facets of the self concept. Like Broughton (1978) and Selman (1980), these investigators found that young children define themselves in physical terms—actions and material possessions—before they define themselves in psychological terms. Actions remain an organizing feature of children's self-concept for several years, although in a fashion that changes slightly over time. Kindergartners say, "I ride a bike," but third-graders say, "I ride a bike better than my brother does." The older children still describe themselves largely in terms of what they do, but they also describe how well they do it compared to other children (Secord and Peevers, 1974).

In adolescence, the concept of self is further colored by psychological and social relations. Young adolescents are aware of their self-awareness and know that people can think about their own experiences. With this awareness typically come both increased self-consciousness and a sense of control (Broughton, 1978; Secord and Peevers, 1974; Selman, 1980). Later in adolescence, people come to understand that some mental events are beyond conscious control. Thus adolescence begins with a conception of the self as capable of reflecting upon and controlling experience. It ends with a conception of conscious and nonconscious thought and the boundaries within the self of self-awareness and self-control.

Robert Bernstein (1980) found that 10-year-olds sum up descriptions of themselves by reiterating what they have said before and are not troubled by seeming inconsistencies. But by mid-adolescence, young people recognize self-described inconsistencies, although they do not yet integrate them into a consistent whole. At this age, someone might say, "Well, when I am around my friends, I am really talkative and animated, but just around my family, I sort of keep to myself. It's sort of like I am two different people; I don't know why." By late adolescence young people reconcile the discrepancies in their descriptions, and their images, of themselves. They begin to think of themselves in terms of stable, abstract, and unifying characteristics. When this conception of a stable personality combines with a conception of stable beliefs, the mature adolescent has a complex, self-aware, and systematic understanding of self (Damon and Hart, 1982).

SELF-ESTEEM

As the notion of who I am solidifies during childhood and adolescence, so, too, does the judgment of how worthy I am. The personal judgment of worthiness, the individual's good opinion of himself or herself, is called **self-esteem.** Children's notions of self-worth are formed from their private reactions to themselves and the reactions of others who play a significant role in their lives. Their mastery of developmental tasks and their competence in dealing with life situations also affect their self-esteem.

Self-esteem develops gradually, but the middle years of childhood are crucial. As children move from a vague, simple concept of self and their own uniqueness, they also judge the self, sometimes overlooking or underestimating certain attitudes, inflating or overemphasizing others. Two children with similar intelligence, health and physique, and social and economic backgrounds may vary considerably in their self-esteem.

Self-esteem tends to be fairly resistant to change once it is established. Individuals who have little self-esteem are afraid to let down their guard. Convinced that they are inadequate, they fear exposing that inadequacy and risking rejection. Individuals with *very* little self-esteem are likely to be maladjusted. Those with good self-esteem have a capacity that will affect their adult lives, the capacity to give and receive love.

Stanley Coopersmith (1967) and his colleagues conducted an extensive investigation of the self-esteem of 85 fifth- and sixth-grade boys. They interviewed mothers first alone and then with their sons, and they gave the boys self-image questionnaires and the Thematic Apperception Test (TAT), a series of cards depicting dramatic but ambiguous situations for which subjects are asked to make up stories. The researchers found that certain parental attitudes and traits tended to predict children's self-esteem. Parents of boys who had high self-esteem were concerned and attentive. They established clear limits that helped their sons know what was expected of them and gave them a sense that social norms are real and significant. These parents were not overly harsh in punishing their sons and did not exert undue pressure on them to do well in school. They had definite ideas and values and were able and willing to present and enforce their beliefs. The limits they established were reasonable and appropriate, not arbitrary and inflexible. They loved their sons and sought and respected their opinions. The parents themselves were poised and relatively self-assured individuals who took child rearing seriously and believed that they could cope with it. The husband and wife were on good terms with each other and had clearly established lines of authority and responsibility. Both mother and father led active lives outside the family.

The boys with high esteem tended to be more independent and creative than those with little esteem. They were more likely to be socially accepted as peers and leaders, more capable of expressing opinions and accepting criticism, more assertive and even outspoken.

Diana Slaughter (1977) studied a group of children who had attended a Head Start program. They were now in middle school, grades 6 to 8. She found that positive teacher evaluations in Head Start had increased the motivational levels of the children when they were in kindergarten through third grade. By sixth grade, children's self-esteem was related to their academic grades. A review (Lang, 1969) of 13 studies of black high and low achievers between ages 4 and 16 singled out self-esteem as an important factor separating the high achievers from the low. A sense of confidence and personal control may help minority students to do well in school.

A review of studies in which connections were traced between self-esteem and achievement in middle-class students (Wylie, 1979) shows that the two are only modestly related, however (with correlations in the .30 and .40 range). What is more, the direction of influence seems to be from high achievement to high self-esteem rather than the reverse. In one study, for example, Jerald Bachman and Patrick O'Malley (1977) traced the connections between high-school boys' self-esteem and their later school and work success. Although their findings suggest that academic achievement influences self-esteem, they found no evidence that self-esteem causes later success. Other studies of the relationship between achievement and self-esteem suggest that achievement affects a student's perceptions of his or her own abilities and others' perceptions of those abilities as well (Calsyn and Kenny, 1977; Connell, 1981; Harter and Connell, 1982). Among third- through ninth-graders, achievement in school was found to influence students' estimations of their competence. This estimation of their competence in turn influenced their motivation to achieve. The higher the students' opinion of their academic abilities, the greater was their motivation to do well in school (Connell, 1981; Harter and Connell, 1982). Other investigators also have found this causal relationship between students' self-esteem and their desire to do well in school (Shiffler, Lynch-Sauer, and Nadelman, 1977). Overall, school achievement seems to influence students' feelings about their competence in school and their opinions of themselves *academically;* it does not seem to spill over significantly into students' opinions of themselves in other spheres of their lives.

ADOLESCENCE AND IDENTITY

Transitions

The voyage of adolescence has two phases. In the first, the child's body takes on definite sexual characteristics, and he or she faces the awesome, at first only dimly perceived, fact—I am becoming capable of reproducing. For the first time, cognitive powers allow young people to consider themselves equal to rather than inferior or subordinate to adults. This first phase, during which they become aware of themselves as entities who will live separate from and be different from parents, is the transition to adolescence, or **early adolescence.**

In the second phase of adolescence, young people have grown accustomed to some of the physical changes of puberty and, although still under the wing of their parents, are no longer totally controlled by them. Now they begin to plan in fairly specific terms for adulthood and the future. This second phase, **later adolescence,** serves as a transition to early adulthood.

Although people use the terms ''adolescent,'' ''teenager,'' and ''high schooler'' interchangeably, adolescence does not always begin in the teens or coincide with high school. For girls adolescence is likely to begin between the ages of 11 and 14 during junior high school or the upper grades of grammar school. Adolescent boys mature approximately two years later than girls. Early adolescence typically spans the years from 11 or 12 to 16 or so.

Pressures of Early Adolescence

The early years of adolescence are often the most trying. This seems to be a period when the child's personality shifts or loosens up. The kaleidoscope is shaken, but the pieces have not yet fallen into place as a pattern of identity. Even an easygoing child may become moody and irritable. Young adolescents typically suffer from confusion, conflict, moodiness, outbursts of anger, and, in some cases, reversion to infantile fears. According to the ideas expressed by adolescent specialist Fritz Redl (1969), this is the way a girl going through this phase might behave:

Jan has become restless lately. She cannot seem to stick with any one activity but jumps from one thing to another. She seems to have lost her common sense, arriving at home with farfetched notions of what she is going to do, complaining about teachers she does not like. She makes totally unreasonable plans for what she will be when she grows up. She is irritable with her parents, barely talking to them, and bickers with her sister and brother. She seems to be building a barrior between herself and the rest of the family by continually emphasizing how different she is. Music played at peak volume, slovenly dress, and general inconsiderateness underline that barrier. She resents meeting family obligations, especially if they involve even the slightest sacrifice of time spent away from her friends. She enjoys shocking her family and their grown-up visitors with her tough language and disrespectful ways. She is very secretive, shutting herself in her room to talk to her friends on the phone (Redl, 1969, p. 123).

Young adolescents of 11 or 12 may be relatively uninterested in school or in acquiring knowledge. The great industriousness of middle childhood seems to have broken down as sexual interest begins to stir (Cohen and Frank, 1975). In early adolescence, young people feel enormous stress at the same time as their ability to cope with stress and change is at a low ebb. They are exceptionally vulnerable people. Although they still live at home, still go to school, and are still relatively free of work pressures, these comforting continuities with the past can provide preadolescents only small protection against formidably disruptive challenges. The first disruption is biological: the whole body configuration is changing. Young adolescents must cope with this disruption with relatively little information about the wide range of normality. They must also cope with baffling mood swings that are partially related to physiological changes. To young adoles-

cents, these are most stressful (Hamburg, 1974).

In addition to physical and physiological changes, young adolescents are under intense psychological stress. Daniel Offer (1969), in a study of 70 adolescent boys in a middle-class community, reported that the disruptions between teenagers and parents occurred the most often during early adolescent years and frequently disappeared by the time the teenager entered high school. Rebellion manifested itself most clearly at ages 12 and 13, when the preadolescents described themselves as getting into fights with their parents over seemingly small and insignificant issues. They bickered over taking out the garbage, what to wear, what time to be home, about not going to church, and about going to the movies with their friends.

It is no surprise that the stress the young adolescent feels should reverberate through the entire family. The young adolescent is new at this game, struggling mightily to take on a whole new set of suddenly desirable teenage behavior and values. Uninitiated, unpracticed, the fledgling may take on the most conspicuous and stereotyped aspects of the new role. The young adolescent exaggerates independence and emancipation, becoming derisive and rebellious toward parents. The parents, too, may be new at this game, but new or not, they may react to this hostility and moodiness in what Beatrix Hamburg (1974) calls a "counterpunitive style." A downward spiral of negative exchanges ends in explosive outbursts and stalled communication on both sides. Parents may also interpret their adolescent's behavior as a signal for them to step aside and withdraw their guidance. The effect of their withdrawal is to thrust the young adolescent even further toward the peer group. A group of young adolescents, no matter how attractive, no matter how comforting, is rarely flexible or resourceful enough to afford anyone a rich medium in which to grow and develop. Worse, when the peer group indulges in drugs or forms of acting out, the young adolescent can be in for a great deal of trouble.

Problems of Self-Esteem

Despite the rebellious protests to the contrary, adolescents need and secretly want the support of their parents. The adolescents who have little self-esteem also have uninterested and uninvolved parents. Even punitive parents who are interested and involved have children with fewer self-esteem problems than indifferent parents (Rosenberg, 1965). Girls in particular may be thwarted by unresponsive, unsupportive parents or teachers.

Our understanding of adolescence is based largely on research in high schools. Yet by the time girls enter high school, they are well beyond their difficult and stressful early adolescence. In one study of junior high students of both sexes, 12-year-old girls were found to suffer most from self-consciousness, unstable self-image, low self-esteem, and unhappiness. Although the subjects as a group tended to suffer from these problems, the girls suffered more. In sixth and seventh grades girls appeared more vulnerable and had lower self-esteem than boys. The hardest-hit girls were those going through several changes at once. They had reached puberty, had begun dating, and had shifted to junior high school (Figure 15.7). The shift to junior high school appeared to cause self-esteem to drop, self-image to founder, and self-consciousness to increase (Simmons, Rosenberg, and Rosenberg, 1973). J. P. Connell and Susan Harter have found similarly that in the first year of junior high school, children's estimations of their own competence plummet (Connell, 1981; Harter and Connell, 1982). Young adolescents may be able to cope with any single stress, but the multiplication of stresses may overwhelm them.

Social psychologist Kurt Lewin has aptly depicted the young adolescent's predicament as acute disorientation. The adolescent is like an astronaut landing on an unfamiliar planet. As Lewin has pointed out, everything is new, even one's once-familiar body: "the predictable reliable face, arms, legs, thighs, chest, genitals, hair now alter and become strange and unknown" (1951, p. 143). Just as their body has grown strange, their primary allegiance is shifting from one social group, the family, to another, their peers. Young adolescents have a sense of standing at the boundary of two groups but not squarely within any known territory. Physical and social changes make the young adolescent, to use Lewin's analogy, "a marginal man." The 12- or 13-year-old wants to identify with the teenage group but is still regarded as an outsider by teenagers and as a child by parents.

Adolescent Asynchronies

In all my recent interviews with adolescents of ages twelve to sixteen—really, they are long dis-

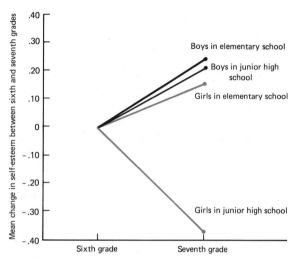

FIGURE 15.7

Boys gain some self-esteem between sixth and seventh grades; girls attending seventh grade in an elementary school do too, although not as much. The self-esteem of girls attending seventh grade in a junior high school plummets (Simmons, Van Cleave, Blyth, and Bush, 1979).

cussions or what the kids call "rap sessions"—the notion of connection or integrity returns again and again. How are these new young people connecting with themselves and, as metaphorical as it sounds, with their lives? . . . they have invented phrases like, "getting it together" and "we couldn't connect" (Cottle, 1971, p. 315).

"Making connections," "getting it together" are no mere slang phrases. Making connections is the serious business of adolescence. It is the adolescent girl who must live with breasts that have sprouted while still feeling the profound need to hide in the maternal bosom and draw nourishment from a loving protector. It is the adolescent boy who must deal with choices that could affect his career, his whole future, while secretly longing to forget about it all and hunch down in front of the Saturday morning cartoons. It is adolescents who question, "Am I normal?" while too young to have a clue to the answer from personal experience, yet old enough to pose the question for the first time in a conscious way. As Thomas Cottle puts it, how do they know

whether others masturbate or have wet dreams or fear the darkness, even at age fifteen, or peek through keyholes at girls? How does [the ado-

lescent] know the parameters of the perverse even as he walks upon them or falls, finally, over to the other side (1971, p. 328)?

Adolescents must put it all together—the sexual stirrings, the social demands, the new awareness, the fear of being different, the need to be someone unique yet not alien. No wonder they feel disconnected, disorganized. Nor do the physical changes in adolescence proceed harmoniously or smoothly or all take place at the same time. The unevenness in the rates of growth is commonly referred to as *asynchrony* (Eichorn, 1975; Tanner, 1970). Within each individual, different systems grow at different rates. Feet and hands undergo a growth spurt before legs and arms lengthen, and they grow before the trunk does; the nose achieves its adult length before the jaw thickens. And so it goes with the rest of the body in what seems to be at times erratic, even chaotic progress (Tanner, 1970). Asynchrony is also the hallmark of growth within a group of adolescents. Following the physical development of 67 adolescent boys, Herbert and Lois Meek Stolz (1951) identified 51 different patterns in timing of height and growth of legs, hips, shoulders, and other body parts.

But it is probably the asynchrony of physical and psychosocial changes that most perplexes adolescents. They feel the discrepancy between the early development of adult physical and sexual characteristics and the late development of many adult psychological traits and social skills. Some cultures impose a clear demarcation between childhood and adulthood, thereby forcing the effects of these asynchronies of adolescence into an ordered pattern. The passage from childhood to adulthood, which in our society is a long and complex journey, is abbreviated. The advent of puberty is marked by public events, ordeals or celebrations referred to as "rites of passage." Once the physically mature youngster has completed the rite, be it a circumcision, a ritual offering, a betrothal, an elaborate ceremony, he or she is considered part of the adult world.

In our culture, the gulf between puberty (physical maturity) and an adult role (social maturity) yawns wider than ever. The period between puberty and social maturity is almost as great as the period between birth and puberty. Puberty occurs long before marriage, parenting, or economic independence. For those seeking professional careers and advanced education, 20 years may elapse between puberty and true economic independence. For others who are not college bound, there is likely to be a period of uncertain employment, apprenticeship, and often bleak opportunities. The American adolescent, as Baumrind (1975) puts it, is omnipotent in imagination yet relatively impotent in action.

Psychological Effects of Physical Change

What effects do the hormonal changes of puberty have on the psychological states of adolescent boys and girls? For example, does the tenfold increase of the hormone testosterone at puberty lower frustration thresholds so that the adolescent male is more easily provoked than girls or younger boys? Some experiments indicate that adolescents became more aggressive when they were administered a mild form of androgen (Wolstenholme and O'Connor, 1967).

As for females, to what extent are the discomforts of menstruation psychosocial—brought about by negative attitudes of parents and society—and to what extent are they caused by the hormonal changes, particularly variations in estrogen levels, over the menstrual cycle? Melville Ivey and Judith Bardwick (1968) tested 26 normal college students aged 19 to 22 for variations in anxiety during the menstrual cycle. The young women were asked to talk for 5 minutes on any memorable life experiences. In the 2 to 3 days preceding menstruation, when estrogen levels are low, they spoke more often of death, mutilation, and separation from loved ones. They feared damage to the body, yearned for love, and felt helpless. By contrast, at ovulation, when the estrogen level is highest, the students talked of success and the ability to cope well with a situation. The young woman who said before menstruation:

They had to teach me how to water ski. I was clumsy. It was really embarrassing 'cause it was kind of like saying to yourself you can't do it and the people were about to lose patience with me (Bardwick, 1971, p. 31),

during ovulation described a very different situation:

So I was elected chairman. I had to establish with them the fact that I knew what I was doing.

I remember one particular problematic meeting and afterwards L. came up to me and said, "You really handled the meeting well." In the end it came out the sort of thing that really bolstered my confidence in myself (Bardwick, 1971, p. 31).

Ivey and Bardwick concluded from this pattern of mood swings that hormonal changes significantly affect psychological behavior. They even went so far as to say that the menstrual cycle has as much influence on women's behavior as individual psychological differences.

That females may cope or not cope, test anxious, hostile, or depressive, appear healthy or neurotic on psychological tests, is due as much to menstrual cycle as to core psychological characteristics (Ivey and Bardwick, 1968, p. 344).

Other researchers (Dalton, 1964; Mandell and Mandell, 1967) have connected suicides, acts of violence, and psychiatric admissions to periods when levels of estrogen and progesterone are fluctuating.

Alice Dan (1976) has studied the patterns of mood variation in married women and has a different view. She believes that mood changes that have been attributed to the menstrual cycle stem from normal human variability. Although Dan found clear cyclical changes in women, their husbands also showed variability in mood and behavior. Dan's study raises questions about the role of hormones and the assumption that men are more stable than women. She suggests that cyclical variations in behavior are typical of both sexes. The cycles of women's behavior and moods may approximate the lunar month, but they are not necessarily synchronized with estrogen levels. Dan's research suggests that the monthly cycle may be a natural way of organizing energy patterns over time, not a source of additional or "special" behavior change. The mutual influence of hormones and physiological factors is an open and intriguing question.

How a young woman reacts to the onset of menstruation and whether she has physical pain tend to depend on the culture. Some cultures confine the menstruating woman, placing taboos on anything she touches, uses, or even looks at. Others glorify her, believing she has supernatural

powers that can increase fertility and cure disease. The Apache line up to be blessed by her, but the Carrier Indians of British Columbia symbolically bury her alive, forcing her to live totally alone for 3 or 4 days, believing her a threat to anyone who sees her (Benedict, 1934). Margaret Mead (1928) decribed in great detail the Samoan calmness and stress on continuity in reacting to change. Menarche for the Samoan girl was marked by no ceremony, no sense of crisis, and little if any physical pain.

Our own culture is ambivalent about menarche. On the one hand, we fail to celebrate it. On the other, as Margaret Mead commented in 1930, we have great anxiety about it:

We prescribe no ritual; the girl continues on a round of school or work, but she is constantly confronted by a mysterious apprehensiveness in her parents and guardians. Her society has all the tensity of a roomful of people who expect the latest arrival to throw a bomb (Mead, 1971, p. 180).

Despite greater openness today about sex and reproduction, this negative attitude prevails. A 1977 study of 350 American adolescent girls revealed that most believed that menstruation brings physical discomforts, greater emotionality, and changes in mood as well as disrupting activities and social relations (Ruble and Brooks, 1977; and see Research Focus: The Experience of Menarche for a more recent survey). Menarche is the signal for many girls to change their attitudes and behavior (Figure 15.8).

In a study of 35 white, middle-class girls before and after menarche, psychiatrists Lynn Whisnant and Leonard Zegans (1975) gave a picture of personal and cultural reactions to menstruation. Although most of their subjects had seen commercially prepared films on menstruation, read pamphlets, and perhaps discussed the event briefly with their mothers as part of a facts of life talk, they

had little conception of what the inside of the body was like or how it functioned. Clitoris, labia, and vulva were unfamiliar words to them, and their external genitalia were most likely to be referred to as "it," "down there," or "the hole" (Whisnant and Zegans, 1975, p. 811).

FIGURE 15.8

The drawing on the left was done by a young girl at the age of 12 years, 1 month, before her menarche. She saw herself quite differently just 6 months later, after her first menstrual period (Gardner, 1982, from Koff, Rierdan, and Silverstone, 1978).

The girls were well informed about the hygiene of menstruation—how often to shower and change their pads—but they had only the vaguest ideas about why women menstruated. The premenarcheal girls were looking forward to announcing the event to their family and friends, but when menstruation began, they tended to be secretive and private, telling only their mothers. They also became more concerned about their relations with other people, especially with their fathers, and some reported feeling closer to their mothers, even if they had not felt particularly close before.

Esther Blank Greif and Kathleen Ulman (1982) of Boston University have found that the onset of menstruation is memorable for most girls. Although many perceive it negatively and try to keep their menstruating a secret, factors like a girl's age at the time of menarche, her knowledge and expectations, her own personality, and the support she gets from her family all can influence how she interprets menstruation. Girls who are well prepared both physically and psychologically and who begin menstruating at about the same time as most of their peers tend to feel that menstruation is a normal event. These investigators suggest that to classify girls' reactions to menarche as merely positive or negative is simplistic because reactions to menarche are complex results of many different factors.

RESEARCH FOCUS

THE EXPERIENCE OF MENARCHE

The onset of menstruation (menarche) is a momentous event in a young woman's life. It requires her to react to profound physical and emotional changes. Diane Ruble and Jeanne Brooks-Gunn (1982) administered anonymous questionnaires to 600 girls, fifth- through twelfth-grade, and interviewed privately 120 girls in the fifth- and sixth-grades. The questionnaires probed the girls' reactions to menstruation and menarche, whether they had felt prepared, whether they had felt any physical symptoms, and whether they or others in their families had felt embarrassed, frightened, upset, surprised, proud, or excited.

Ruble and Brooks-Gunn found that most girls had mixed feelings about menarche. They were neither strongly negative nor strongly positive. Although there is a widely held belief that the first period is not accompanied by cramps, many girls reported feeling cramps with their first period. Yet few attached much importance or felt restricted by these physical symptoms. Menstruation seemed less painful than most girls had feared, as their reports of relief and pleasant surprise implied. Girls also were not secretive about their menstrual periods, discussing them first with their mothers and later with friends. Much of the discussion centered on physical and emotional symptoms accompanying their periods; little centered on menstruation as a rite of passage or an episode in self-definition. Given these findings, Ruble and Brooks-Gunn have questioned whether menarche is the trauma it sometimes is reported to be. They found also that girls who had felt unprepared or begun to menstruate early reported generally more symptoms, more negative reactions, and (as seventh-graders) a more negative self-image. But they did not find that early maturing girls felt more surprised or less prepared than other girls. In short, although menarche can be disruptive for a limited time for unprepared and early maturing girls, it is a memorable event that does not exert long-lasting negative effects on self-image.

Body Image

Each physical change in adolescence is greeted with an emotional reaction, although the reactions vary of course from one adolescent to the next. One important reaction is the new value the adolescent's body acquires, a value referred to as the individual's **body image.** Body image is a concept of physical appearance and feelings about it that are based on the individual's current and past experiences of his or her own body, real and fantasized (Schonfeld, 1969). Many adolescents are at least temporarily dissatisfied with the changes in their bodies. Opinion polls have shown that as many as 52 percent of adolescents report dissatisfaction with their weight—girls wanting to lose it, boys wanting to gain it. One national survey of 12- to 17-year-olds found that 48.4 percent of the girls wanted to be thinner and 49.8 percent of the boys wanted to be taller. At 12 years of age, 36 percent of the girls and 21 percent of the boys reported having **acne.** At 17 years of age 68 percent of the boys and 53 percent of the girls had this complaint (Scanlon, 1975). Dissatisfaction with their posture has also ranked high on adolescents' lists of self-criticisms (Hamburg, 1974).

A concern with one's physical appearance—and usually some dissatisfaction with it—is typical of the young person going through adolescence.

A fear that the physical characteristics they suddenly find themselves with are not up to par, a fear of departing from some vague norm, is widespread among adolescents. They most fear being different from what is appropriate for their sex but have few guidelines about what is normal and suitable. At an age when to be like one's peers is the greatest good, adolescent boys will compare height, strength, and muscles to those of their peers. If testes and penis are not growing like a locker-mate's, if they do not have hair on their face or chest when their friends do, boys may question their virility. Girls compare breasts and the advent of menstruation to mark their progress through the no-gender land of early adolescence to the goal of puberty.

In a memorable essay, "A Few Words About Breasts" (1975) Nora Ephron amuses us with one of the body-image problems of a young woman in the 1950s:

Even though I was outwardly a girl and had many of the trappings generally associated with girldom—a girl's name, for example, and dresses, my own telephone, an autograph book—I spent the early years of my adolescence absolutely certain that I might at any point gum it up. I did not feel at all like a girl. I was boyish. I was athletic, ambitious, outspoken, competitive, noisy, rambunctious. I had scabs on my knees and my socks slid into my loafers and I could throw a football. I wanted desperately not to be that way, not to be a mixture of both things, but instead just one, a girl, a definite, indisputable girl. As soft and pink as a nursery. And nothing would do that for me, I felt, but breasts (Ephron, 1975, pp. 1–2).

Adolescents want desperately to be attractive, and their self-concepts will depend in large degree on whether they consider themselves favorably endowed. In fact, if they do so judge themselves, they will be happier and have higher esteem well into their 40s than those who consider themselves plain or homely during their teens (Berscheid, Walster, and Bohrnstedt, 1973).

Although adolescents are more objective than children about their bodies, they are still not completely accurate in their appraisals. A boy's perception of his body and its physical capabilities or attractiveness may be quite different from the image his peers or teachers have of him. Adolescents draw their body image to some extent from psychological factors that have become internalized over many of years of development. Although the body may have changed radically during adolescence, young people are influenced by their old body image. Once a chubette, always a chubette. Whether they achieve a positive picture of their new, adolescent self depends to a large extent on the quality of the early self-image. The psychological filter that adolescents apply to their development is composed of self-esteem, the ability to judge themselves realistically, and a host of other psychological factors from their childhoods, which they carry into adolescence.

The opinion of parents, teachers, and peers also affects the adolescent's body image. In early adolescence, the assessments of others are particularly crucial because the sense of what is normal fluctuates as the body undergoes dramatic changes. Unfortunately for some adolescents, school principals and teachers are almost as strongly influenced by body stereotypes as adolescents are themselves. Harrison and David Clarke (1961) found that adolescents and adults have more regard for the larger, more muscular, and physically fit boy than for his weaker and less athletic counterpart. In their study, school principals and teachers chose 69 percent of the very fit boys as those they would most like to have for sons and 69 percent of the less fit as those they would least like to have for sons.

Early and Late Maturation

We know that individuals vary in the times at which their bodies change during adolescence, but what, if any, are the effects of these variations on young people? Does earliness or lateness of development affect the adolescent and the reactions of others to him or her? Mary Cover Jones and Nancy Bayley (1950) studied the effects of early and late maturation during adolescence by choosing 16 of the most physically mature individuals and 16 of the most physically immature out of 90 boys in the Berkeley Growth Study. They followed the boys from the time they were 14 until they were about

18½ as they participated in sports, waited for physical examinations, talked with girls at a dance, and interacted with classmates. Their peers said the **late maturers** were restless, less grown-up, and bossy. Adults said the late maturers were tense, eager, peppy, and restless. The late maturers were self-conscious and immature in their behavior. A fair proportion of them tried to counteract their physical disadvantage by greater activity and striving for attention, although some withdrew. The poised and relaxed boys who had been **early maturers** physically were, on the other hand, usually accepted and treated by both adults and peers as being mature. They appeared to have relatively little need to strive for status. From their ranks came the student leaders in senior high school.

Paul Mussen and Mary Cover Jones (1957) gave these same young men the TAT pictures. After analyzing their stories, they concluded that the early maturers were self-confident, independent, and capable of adult social behavior. The late maturers, they found, were rebellious against their parents and thought little of themselves, considering themselves to be rejected, dominated, and dependent.

These studies made clear that early maturation carried with it definite social advantages, and that late maturation had the *potential* for producing anxiety and feelings of inadequacy. Not all the late maturers felt anxious however and individuals dif-

The early-maturing boy has social advantages in high school and is likely to be a leader and greatly admired.

fered widely in how they dealt with their delayed development.

The early and late maturers were studied again when they were 33. The early developers were still socially advantaged; they were poised, cooperative, responsible, held good positions at work, and were leaders in their social organizations. The late developers were impulsive, touchy, and nonconforming; they were not as well adapted or as successful, and some still felt rejected and inferior. But they were more flexible, perceptive, and assertive (Jones, 1957)

Harvey Peskin (1967) looked at the same information collected on these men but came to different conclusions. He pointed out that the late maturers were not, as Mussen, Bayley, and Jones had implied, psychologically disturbed, unless greater expressiveness, eagerness, and lack of inhibition are taken as signs of disturbance. In fact, he saw the early maturers as suffering definite developmental handicaps. He compared the early maturers' rigidity and control of impulses with the late maturers' insightfulness and playfulness. Peskin suggested that the early maturer pays a psychological price for his social prominence by clinging rigidly to patterns that brought early success. Whichever interpretation is accepted, these studies of early versus late maturing support the notion that the timing of the onset of puberty affects the emotional development of the individual.

Most of the studies on how the timing of adolescence affects the individual have been of boys. But there are several studies (e.g., Faust, 1960; Greif and Ulman, 1982; Harper and Collins, 1972; Weatherly, 1964) that suggest that the effects are comparable for boys and girls, with an average rate of maturing being most advantageous for both. In a study of 96 seventh-grade girls, for example, those who felt that they had matured early or late were likely to interpret their development negatively. Girls who felt that they had matured on time tended to interpret their development positively (Wilen and Peterson, 1980).

A group of investigators at Stanford University (Duke, Jennings, Dornbusch, and Siegel-Gorelick, 1982) classified nearly 6000 adolescents according to when they reached puberty. They then asked the adolescents, their parents, and their teachers to answer an array of questions about the adolescents' school performance, intelligence, and related matters. The research group found no significant differences among early-maturing, midmaturing, and late-maturing girls. But for late-maturing boys, at every age beyond 12, disadvantages in development showed up. Compared to midmaturing boys, late-maturing boys were less likely to intend to finish college and were less likely to be expected by their parents to do so. Their teachers less often considered late-maturing boys to have above-average intelligence or to rank them in the top third of their class in academic achievement. Clearly, the actual and perceived timing of puberty exert complex psychological influences on adolescents.

The Identity Crisis

The pivotal task of putting together the various aspects of the self—sexual, ideological, personal, achievement goals, and feelings of confidence or doubt, recognition or isolation—that Erik Erikson (1968) called the identity crisis is really part of a developmental process that has been going on since infancy. But the individual does not realize until adolescence how many developmental pieces have been accumulating.

There is the piece from the earliest encounter of mother and infant. If that encounter was one of mutual trustworthiness and recognition, Erikson suggests adolescents will observe in their newly discovered self an element of trust. They believe that they will find sources of love and admiration as they grow into adulthood, just as they found them in that original encounter. They can have faith in the promise of the future. On the other hand, the remnant from the first encounter may be a dark suggestion that isolation is the only way to deal with a world that cannot be trusted. Time must be made to stand still. The future is dangerous.

Second, in Erikson's scheme, there is the piece left over from the parents' attempts to regulate the child. If these early confrontations brought children self-control without loss of self-esteem, adolescents looking in on themselves will recognize an element of independence and self-certainty. But perhaps that primitive crisis left a remnant of shame and doubt. If so, adolescents are more likely to alternate between self-consciousness and self-doubt, on the one hand, and defiant dirtiness, messiness, or total rejection of society on the other hand.

From the next developmental crisis of early

childhood, when the youngster wishes to explore new territories and master new skills, adolescents may retain the proud sense of initiative—"I am what I can imagine I will be" (Erikson, 1968, p. 122). But if the first inklings of what actions are permissible, which dreams possible, were too grandiose or too constricted, adolescents are left with a prevailing sense of guilt. If their young ideals met with disillusioningly grim reality, a cycle of guilt and violence is unleashed. The adolescent may be unwilling to experiment with roles and willing to follow any leader who glorifies and impersonalizes conflict.

Finally, newly self-aware adolescents take stock of their most recently acquired assets, those of their school years. If the first 5 years of school have netted them a sense of capability, adolescents are convinced that their industry will be rewarded. If their efforts at school and at home, on the ball field, in the swimming pool, on the skating rink, at the piano, before an easel, on the stage, in the workshop—have made something work, adolescents have the conviction, "I am what I can learn to make work" (Erikson, 1968, p. 127).

In Erikson's theory, all these pieces come together in adolescence as young people create their own identities.

Out of Erikson's ideas about identity formation have come intriguing findings about college students' feelings of commitment and crisis in regard to religion, politics, and work (Marcia, 1964, 1966). College students tend to resolve their identity crisis in one of four ways. One group comes through its identity crisis with a sense of identity and commitment to an occupation or political ideology. Another group does not commit itself and experiences **identity diffusion.** A third group of college students is actively engaged in a critical search for an occupation or an ideology. Theirs is a state of **moratorium.** A fourth group forecloses its search for identity and, with a strong sense of commitment but no sense of crisis, accepts the identity prescribed by parents. Over the course of an undergraduate career, many students achieve a sense of identity. Students in the state of moratorium are especially likely to move to a position of identity resolution or diffusion (Waterman, Geary, and Waterman, 1974). After college as well, people continue to achieve identity and to move away from positions of moratorium or diffuse identity

(Waterman and Goldman, 1976). In general, although many college students successfully consolidate their sense of identity before, during, or after their college years, the differences between individuals are strong in both the rate of development and its culmination. Not all students, by any means, successfully navigate the shoals of the identity crisis.

But not all adolescents go through a massive reevaluation of their identities, either, as research by Jerome Dusek and John Flaherty (1981) has shown. These researchers were interested in studying the many sources from which adolescents draw their self-concepts and in learning whether self-concepts develop continuously or discontinuously. For three years, Dusek and Flaherty followed adolescents between the ages of 11 and 18, an age range that encompasses the beginning of puberty and the intensification of the sex drive, changing relations between the sexes, choosing careers, the emergence of idealistic thinking as well as changes in intellectual performance and self-esteem. For the most part, they found that even important environmental events did not cause adolescents to remake their self-images. Individuals' self-concepts tended to form slowly, gradually, and in a pattern of stable change. The investigators believe that their findings refute the theories—offered by Freud (1958), Hall (1904, 1907), and others—that depict adolescence as a period of storm and stress, of upheaval, and abrupt discontinuties. Changes in adolescents' relations with their parents and friends emerge slowly and gradually. The individual who enters adolescence is basically the same as the one who leaves it. But it is worth noting that the data were collected during the mid-1970s, a time of relative political and cultural calm. In contrast, data collected in activist, tumultuous early 1970s (Nesselroade and Baltes, 1974) had shown stronger effects on development from broad cultural trends. Many cultural and social factors can, of course, influence the course of individual development. Going to a new school, graduating, planning for work or college, and forging new relationships with parents and friends all challenge the adolescent's self-concept. But most adolescents meet these challenges squarely. Out of the many personal, social, cultural, and even historical strands from which they must weave a coherent self-image, the vast majority of young adults develop soundly, adequately, and successfully.

SUMMARY

1. Temperament styles—difficult, easy, and slow-to-warm-up—are evident in infancy and remain stable through adolescence and adulthood. These styles manifest themselves in activity levels, rhythmicity, tendencies to approach or avoid, adaptability, responsiveness, intensity of reactions, moods, distractibility, and attention span.

2. Some psychologists believe that infant temperament is better understood as a social construct formed by parents, but there is some evidence for temperament as biological.

3. Children's unique personalities reflect individual differences on such dimensions as cognitive style (reflectiveness or impulsiveness, field dependence and independence), perceptual style, views about academic success, creativity, and sociability.

4. People can be divided into Type A's and Type B's. Type A's are more hostile, angry, urgently rushed, competitive, and anxious than their slower paced, more relaxed Type B counterparts. Parents may encourage Type A behavior by exhorting their children to succeed and compete.

5. Certain personality traits are stable over time and interrelated. Activity level, adaptability, and intensity are stable for the first five years of life.

6. Ethnicity is a source and modifier of children's values, attitudes, perceptions, needs, and modes of expression. Some observed ethnic differences are inherited. Differences in verbal, mathematical, and spatial abilities seem to form patterns among certain ethnic groups. Members of various ethnic groups also hold different attitudes toward academic achievement, cooperation, and competition.

7. Sex differences occur in certain behavior patterns and personality traits. Empirical evidence suggests that girls excel in verbal ability, boys excel in spatial ability and are more aggressive. The evidence is missing or questionable in the case of other purported sex differences: females do not have lower self-esteem, are not more suggestible or better at repetitive tasks, and are not less motivated to achieve than males. Still open are questions about whether females are more sociable and nurturant or less active and dominating than males.

8. Aggregate sex differences should not mask the fact that individual differences among males and females are often greater than the differences between the sexes. Furthermore, many males and females do not conform to gender-appropriate stereotypes and tend to be androgynous. With varying degrees of success, researchers have tried to explain sex differences on the basis of sex chromosomes, brain structure, sex hormones, and socialization.

9. Gender roles are taught to children by other children, by parents and other family members, teachers and textbooks, television programs, and other mass media. Some researchers have found that parents differentially socialize their children according to the children's sex and in some cases the parents' sex. Others have found no appreciable differences in parents' socialization of the sexes but great differences in the reactions of other children and adults.

10. Children know which sex they are by about age 3, and this sense of sex identity is relatively impervious to change. Various theories—psychoanalytic, social learning, cognitive—have been proposed to account for how children learn the behaviors considered appropriate to their sex.

11. Infants gradually learn to distinguish themselves from others. From early childhood through adolescence, the sense of self is progressively refined from a concept that is largely based on physical attributes to an integrated, complex concept of uniquely personal inner and outer experiences.

12. Self-esteem gradually develops out of success and others' reactions to oneself; it is correlated with academic achievement.

13. Adolescence begins with physical changes but ultimately changes social understanding and relations. Relationships with family members and friends are redefined. The same-sex peer groups of early adolescence eventually form into heterosexual groups in which adolescents can learn mature behavior appropriate to their gender.

14. The physical changes of adolescence heighten young people's self-consciousness and concerns with body image. Adolescents who mature at roughly the same time as their friends do tend to feel most comfortable with themselves. Boys who mature late especially may suffer social and academic disadvantages.

15. Most adolescents emerge from their period of personal and social experimentation with stronger senses of their own identities. Although some theorists have proposed that adolescence is a stormy period, full of abrupt and painful change, more recent evidence suggests that the changes of adolescence are more gradual and more successful.

KEY TERMS

Goodness of fit
Cognitive style
Reflection
Impulsiveness
Field dependence
Field independence
Convergent thinking

Divergent thinking
Extentionality
Locus of control
Learned helplessness
Androgynous
Sex constancy
Gender identity

Anaclitic identification
Introjection
Self-concept
Personeity
Self-esteem
Early adolescence
Later adolescence

Body image
Acne
Late maturers
Early maturers
Identity diffusion
Moratorium

SUGGESTED READINGS

Bronfenbrenner, Urie. *Two Worlds of Childhood: U.S. and U.S.S.R.* New York: Russell Sage Foundation, 1970. A book that manages to convey a picture of real children while examining the family-centered early-child care and socialization of the United States and the nursery-collective system of the Soviet Union.

Chess, Stella, and Thomas, Alexander. *Your Child Is a Person.* New York: Viking Press, 1965. An excellent book integrating the notion of temperamental differences in children with practical advice on child rearing.

Cottle, Thomas J. *Time's Children: Impressions of Youth.* Boston: Little, Brown, 1971. A series of impressionistic essays on adolescents' experiences, feelings, and needs, written from a social scientist's frame of reference and with a journalist's flair.

Erikson, Erik. *Identity, Youth, and Crisis.* New York: W. W. Norton, 1968, An elucidation of his theory of adolescence as a crucial stage in the life cycle, demanding resolution of earlier crises.

Getzels, Jacob, and Csikszentmihalyi, Mihalyi. *The Creative Vision: A Longitudinal Study of Problem Finding in Art.* New York: Wiley, 1976. An examination of the personalities, values, and special aptitudes of a group of young artists. They are followed several years after graduation to determine how the ability to find problems is related to the creative vision.

Lipsitz, Joan. *Growing Up Forgotten.* Lexington, Mass.: D. C. Heath, 1977. A review of research on early adolescence, showing the extent to which we have neglected this age group. Schools, service agencies, and the juvenile justice system are examined and all found wanting.

Tavris, Carol, and Offir, Carole. *The Longest War: Sex Differences in Perspective.* New York: Harcourt Brace Jovanovich, 1977. An entertaining and comprehensive review of research on sex and gender differences, discussed from the perspectives of psychologists, biologists, sociologists, psychoanalysts, and anthropologists.

GLOSSARY

A, not B, phenomenon The inability of the child, until 12 months of age, to follow the movements of an object when it is first hidden under A, then put, while the child watches, under B. The child looks for the object under A.

accommodation In Piaget's theory, the process of adjusting existing ways of thinking, of reworking schemes, to encompass new information, ideas, or objects. In the visual system, the adjustment of the lens of the eye to shifting planes of focus.

achondroplasia Failure in the normal development of cartilage, causing dwarfism in many animals. In human beings, the most common type of congenital abnormal bone development; individuals have unusually large heads, long trunks, and short limbs.

acne An inflammatory disease involving the oil glands and hair follicles of the skin and causing pustular eruptions.

adaptation In Piaget's theory, the mental processes by which people extend and modify their thinking. They do so in two ways, by assimilation and by accommodation.

adipocyte A fat cell.

adipocyte hypothesis The theory that there may be a critical period in the first year or two of the baby's life during which nutrition affects the number of fat cells formed.

afterbirth The placenta and the parts of the fetal membranes that are delivered after the birth of the baby, in the third and final stage of labor.

altruism Action performed for another's benefit without expectations of extrinsic reward.

alveolvi Tiny air sacs of the lungs walled by a very thin epithelial membrane; they are surrounded by capillaries and are the site of respiration.

amniocentesis A prenatal medical procedure for diagnosing genetic abnormalities. A small amount of amniotic fluid is withdrawn from the pregnant woman by hollow needle. The chemical contents of the fluid reveal some diseases directly; cells from the fetus are cultured and studied for chromosomal anomalies. See sonogram.

amnion A thin, membranous, fluid-filled sac surrounding the developing embryo and fetus.

amphetamines Central nervous system stimulants that induce euphoria and have proven effective in the treatment of narcolepsy in adults and hyperactivity in children.

anaclitic identification In psychoanalytic theory, girls' identification with their mothers. In the second or third year a girl, fearing the loss of her mother's love, identifies with her, taking into herself mother's wishes, standards, attitudes, and values.

analgesics Agents that bring insensibility to pain, or relieve it, without loss of consciousness.

anal stage In Freud's theory, the psychosexual stage of toddlerhood, from 12 to 36 months, during which the child receives pleasure through stimulation of the anus and pays much attention to elimination.

androgyny The quality or state of possessing both masculine and feminine characteristics.

androsperm A sperm carrying the Y chromosome; if this particular sperm penetrates the ovum, a male child will be conceived.

anesthesia Loss of sensation and usually consciousness, without loss of vital functions, through administration of an agent that blocks the passage of pain impulses to the brain.

anesthetics Substances that produce anesthesia.

animism The belief that all things are living and endowed with intentions, consciousness, and feelings.

anorexia nervosa A severe disorder in which the person, usually an adolescent girl, eats very little and loses 25 percent or more of original weight. The girl has an intense fear of becoming obese, feeling fat even when emaciated.

anoxia Oxygen deprivation of the tissues, especially of such severity and duration that the brain or other part is damaged permanently.

antiseptic A substance used in the process of destroying the microorganisms that invade tissues and cause infection.

Apgar score A rating of the neonate's physical well-being, ranging from 0 to 10, determined by grading the infant's heart rate, breathing effort, muscle tone, reflex irritability, and color at 0, 1, and 2 points—poor, fair, or good.

apnea An interruption of breathing.

artificial embryonation A surgical procedure in which the embryo is retrieved from the surrogate mother and transferred to the womb of the adopting mother.

artificial insemination A procedure in which either the husband's sperm or a donor's are introduced via syringe rather than through sexual intercourse.

artificialism The belief that everything in the world and in the sky has been built either by people or by a divine being who fabricates things in human fashion.

asepsis The process of denying microorganisms access to tissues in a medical treatment, such as sterilizing instruments, gowns, and dressings and washing hands before a surgical operation.

assimilation In Piaget's theory, the process of adjusting new information and objects to make them fit existing ways of thinking or schemes.

associative intelligence A lower order of intelligence applied in acquiring knowledge by memorizing.

associative play A form of social play in which two children talk and play together, but each has his or her own goals; they do not cooperate with each other.

asynchrony Want of coincidence in time; the condition of two or more events not happening together.

astigmatism A defect of vision owing to corneal irregularity.

attachment An affectionate, close, and enduring relationship between two persons who have shared many experiences; the tie to their parents felt by children 6 months and older.

auditory evoked response (AER) The electrical response made by the brain to an auditory stimulus.

authoritarian parent A parent who rears the child to believe that his or her often arbitrary rules are law, that misconduct by the child will be punished. The authoritarian parent is detached and seldom praises the child.

authoritative parent A parent who sets firm limits and provides direction for the child but at the same time is willing to listen to the child's objections and make compromises.

autism A rare but devastating childhood psychosis characterized by profound withdrawal and inability to communicate or form social relationships.

autosomal dominant Pattern of inheritance in which only one of a pair of genes will cause the individual to possess a characteristic; the gene is dominant over the other gene of the pair.

autosomal recessive Pattern of inheritance in which the individual possesses a characteristic only if he or she has two genes for it, one from each parent; the gene is recessive and is expressed only if it has a like partner.

autosome A chromosome other than a sex chromosome. In the human being, one chromosome of the 22 pairs that carry most of the genetic code for physical size, eye color, hair color, nose structure, chin structure, intelligence, and so on.

autostimulation The notion that active, irregular sleep, sleep with rapid eye movements, provides practice or exercise for higher parts of the baby's brain.

axons Long thin fibers that may extend a considerable distance from the nerve cell body and that conduct impulses away from it.

babbling Extending repetitions of consonant-vowel combinations beginning when babies are about 4 months old; vocal play that exercises the speech musculature and gives babies practice in making sounds.

behaviorism A school of psychology that originated with John Watson and his proposal that only observable behavior should be studied, without reference to consciousness or mental processes.

Black English A name for the language usually spoken in black ghetto homes, which William Labov believes should be understood as a dialect of nonstandard English that has rules of its own and its own ways of indicating a speaker's competence and ability.

blastocyst A hollow, fluid-filled sphere whose wall is one cell thick except for the heap of large cells at one side forming the embryonic disk.

blastula A hollow, fluid-filled sphere made up of more than 100 cells; its wall is uniformly one cell thick, but the cells on one side are larger.

body image A subjective picture of personal physical appearance established by past and present self-observations and by noticing the reactions of others.

bonding The formation of an enduring attachment, such as to one's child, especially in the period immediately following birth.

brain hemispheres The two halves of the brain, each with its characteristic functions.

breech position Position of the fetus during childbirth in which its buttocks or legs come through the birth canal before the head.

Broca's area Part of the brain's motor cortex that primarily controls muscles for speech.

bulimia A disorder in which the individual indulges in secret and episodic eating binges, which often end in self-induced vomiting.

canalized Relatively invulnerable to environmental effects.

case grammar A set of rules describing children's early speech, based on case relations—universal concepts or deep structures that identify such matter as who did what to whom. Proposed by Charles Fillmore.

catch-up growth Rapid physical growth during the first 5 months by an infant whose size was restricted by a small womb or by maternal malnutrition; or by a child who has been restored to health after illness or malnutrition.

central social structure A group of people in which most members select the same few individuals as liked.

centration The cognitive property of focusing on one dimension of an object while ignoring another dimension. Piaget suggested that young children cannot understand principles of conservation because they are centered.

cephalocaudal (development) A pattern of physical growth and motor development progressing from head to foot; in human beings, followed prenatally and throughout childhood.

cerebellum The region of the brain that coordinates movement and sensory input.

cerebral cortex The outer layer of gray matter covering the brain; responsible for complex information and conscious thoughts.

cerebral lateralization The division of functions between the left and right hemispheres of the brain. The left hemisphere appears to control verbal skills, the right hemisphere visual skills and imagery.

cervix The very small outer or lower opening of the uterus; opens to the vagina.

cesarean section A surgical procedure in which the newborn is delivered through incisions in the abdominal and uterine walls. See sonogram.

child abuse The flagrant mistreatment or neglect of children, which federal and state laws now require doctors, clinic and hospital personnel, teachers, social workers, police officers, coroners, and other professionals to report. Defined by federal law as "the physical or mental injury, sexual abuse, negligent treatment or maltreatment of a child under the age of 18 by a person who is responsible for the child's welfare."

childbed fever An abnormal condition that results from infection of the placental site following delivery.

chorion The outermost of the membranes surrounding the developing embryo and fetus; villi from the chorion become part of the placenta.

chorionic villi biopsy A test of chromosomes in which a sample of fetal tissue, from the membrane that eventually forms part of the placenta, is taken through the mother's cervix and submitted to analysis.

chromosomes Microscopic threadlike structures, consisting of a linear string of genes; chromosomes are the transmitters of inheritance and are present in the nucleus of every cell.

chronometric analysis A method of assessing information processing by measuring the time it takes to solve problems.

chunks Groups or constellations of bits of information encoded together in memory to make meaningful units of information. For example, the numbers 5-14-81 are "chunked" together to form a date.

circular reaction In Piaget's theory, an action that is repeated because it pleases; the initial action causes a reaction.

classical conditioning A basic form of learning in which a neutral stimulus, through association with a physiologically significant stimulus, eventually comes to evoke the response made spontaneously to the significant stimulus.

classification The process of sorting objects into mutually exclusive groups.

class inclusion In Piaget's theory, the ability to consider an object as belonging simultaneously to a number of categories, each successive one of greater breadth; a concrete operation.

clique A closely knit, small circle of persons who tend to exclude others.

cochlea In the inner ear, a bony, fluid-filled canal, coiled like a snail, containing within it a smaller, membranous, fluid-filled spiral passage wherein lie the nerve endings essential for hearing.

cognitive-arousal theories (of emotion) Theories of emotion, such as that proposed by Schachter and Singer, suggesting that for the experience of an emotion, cognitive appraisal of physiological arousal is necessary.

cognitive style The way an individual conceptualizes or approaches tasks; a distinctive way of perceiving, feeling, and solving problems that constitutes part of an individual's personality.

cohort A group of individuals born at the same time or during the same historical period.

collective monologue Piaget's term for the conversation of two preschoolers who talk in turn but are not really listening or responding to each other's words.

colostrum A yellowish protein-rich fluid that is secreted from the breasts a few days before the baby's birth and 2 to 4 days after.

concatenative thinking Linking together of a series of separate, unconnected ideas.

concept A general notion or idea; a mental image abstracted from particular perceptions.

conception The formation of a viable zygote through the union of ovum and sperm, being the first step in the development of a new human being. The act of becoming pregnant.

conceptual intelligence A higher order of intelligence applied in abstraction and analogy.

concordance In genetic studies of twins, their similarity in one or more traits or in a diagnosis.

concrete operational thinking In Piaget's theory, the mental ability of children from ages 7 to 11 by which they can think logically about physical objects and their relations. Concrete operations include conservation, reversibility, seriation, and classification.

concurrent validity A measure of how well one test correlates with another established test; a test alleged to measure the identical construct and already considered valid.

conditioned response In classical conditioning, the response (e.g., salivation) of a subject elicited after exposure to a conditioned stimulus (e.g., a bell).

conditioned stimulus In classical conditioning, the stimulus (e.g., a bell) manipulated to elicit a conditioned response (e.g., salivation).

confluence theory A theory of the child's intellectual development that considers it to depend on the overall intellectual quality of the home—made up of the combined intellectual levels of siblings and parents.

congenital Existing at or dating from birth.

consanguinity The condition of being related by blood or descended from a common ancestor. Consanguinity studies examine the degree of relationship between family members who have the same trait or disorder.

conservation In Piaget's theory, the ability to recognize that important properties of a given quantity of matter, such as number, volume, and weight, remain constant despite changes in shape, length, or position.

construct validity A test's ability to conform to the best scientific notion of the underlying trait or construct being measured.

content validity A test's ability to represent a clearly specified body of knowledge.

continuous reinforcement schedule In learning theory, the rewarding of a response every time it occurs.

contrast In language learning, a principle by which children assume that the meanings of the new words they hear are different from those they already know.

contrast sensitivity The smallest degree of contrast between light and dark that a person can see. Contrast sensitivity is quite limited at birth and soon improves.

conventionality In language learning, a principle by which children learn how words are used by experienced speakers.

conventional moral reasoning Kohlberg's intermediate level of moral reasoning, in which conforming to social standards, such as pleasing others by being a "nice guy" and maintaining "law and order" for its own sake, are the primary moral values.

convergent thinking Thinking that has as its goal the selection of a single, acceptable, conventional solution to a problem.

cooperative play Play in which two or more children share goals and divide roles while playing. This form of play is difficult for many preschoolers.

coordinate sentence A sentence with two clauses of the same rank connected by and, or, or but.

corpus callosum The band of myelinated tissue that connects the two hemispheres of the brain.

correlation The degree and direction of relationship between two variables, which may be positive, with both increasing or decreasing at the same time, or negative, with one increasing and the other decreasing.

couvade A ritual of cultures in many parts of the world in which the father takes to his bed when his child is born and complains that he has suffered the pains of childbirth.

couvade syndrome Empathic reactions of men to their wife's pregnancy; they suffer nausea, backaches, and other physical distresses of pregnancy.

cretinism Condition beginning in prenatal or early life in which physical and mental development is stunted; caused by a severe deficiency in the secretion of thyroid hormone.

criterion validity A test's ability to predict success on a second variable that is supposed to be related to the ability being tested.

critical body weight The weight of a young girl, about 100 pounds, at which according to theory, her metabolism initiates the changes of puberty.

critical period An interval of time during which certain physical or psychological growth must occur if development is to proceed normally and during which the individual is vulnerable to pertinent harmful events and open to beneficial effects.

cross-cultural study A study comparing children or adults from different cultures, which may contribute to understanding how the sociocultural environment affects development.

cross-fostering The exposure through adoptive parents to conditions very different from those that would have been provided by natural parents.

crossing-over The exchange of portions from strands of homologous chromosomes that have broken at the same level during meiosis.

cross-sectional study A development research method in which groups of children of different ages but similar in other important ways—educational level, socioeconomic status, proportion of males to females—are compared at some specific point in time, usually for a specific aspect of behavior. The groups represent different age levels.

crowning During delivery, the first appearance of the newborn's head, usually with the face toward the mother's back.

crystallized intelligence A person's knowledge of his or her culture and general level of information, vocabulary, and reading skill.

culture-fair tests Tests of ability that do not (even inadvertently) penalize members of minority groups for ignorance of middle-class values and norms.

culture-free tests Tests that are not biased against nonmiddle-class subjects because they do not depend on culturally transmitted information.

day care A custodial arrangement for the everyday, daytime care of infants and children whose parents are working or otherwise unavailable. Day care may take place in private homes or in public buildings; groups may be small or large, separated into distinct age groups or not.

day-care center An institutional setting in which preschool children are cared for when their parents are working or otherwise unavailable. Day-care centers usually are open 5 days a week, all day, all year round.

decentration In Piaget's theory, the ability or process of focusing on more than one dimension, such as length and height, simultaneously; a concrete operation.

deep structure The fundamental syntactical relationships and the basic meaning underlying the actual words of a sentence; identified by Noam Chomsky.

deferred imitation The child's ability, beginning between 18 and 24 months of age, to mimic a person's actions witnessed sometime earlier. A term used by Piaget.

dendrites Any of the usually short and branched extensions of a nerve cell that conduct impulses toward the cell body.

deoxyribonucleic acid (DNA) A complex chemical substance whose molecules vary in constituting genes and are able to replicate themselves.

deprivation The withdrawal or absence of stimulation or of a particular stimulus.

depth of focus The distance that an object can be moved without a viewer perceiving a change in sharpness.

developmental diagnosis Assessment of the present state of an infant's or child's maturity relative to others of the same age, which suggests whether the individual is developing at a normal rate.

dialectical view A conception of human development—and especially such processes as communication, language, and problem solving—as a constant process of thesis, antithesis, and synthesis.

dichotic listening tasks The presentation of different information in the two ears simultaneously.

diethylstilbestrol (DES) A hormone formerly prescribed to pregnant women to prevent miscarriages. It was found to cause abnormalities and disease in the sex organs of their children when they reached their teens.

differential-emotions theory Izard's theory that each emotion is a discrete pattern within the nervous system and is exhibited in distinct, discriminable facial and bodily expressions.

differential-environment theory A theory that considers a child's intellectual development to be contingent on the amount of parental attention received, which depends inversely on the number of children in the family.

diffuse social structure A group of people in which many individuals rather than a small number of "leaders" are liked by the other members of the group.

divergent thinking Thinking that goes in different direction and searches for new ideas and a number of solutions to a problem.

dizygotic (DZ) Birth partners who have developed from two ova fertilized at the same time by two sperm. The genotypes of these twins are as different as those of any siblings.

dominance hierarchy The status order of a group whereby one individual dominates all, the next one down all below him or her, and so on to the person dominated by all.

double-blind study Research in which neither subjects nor reseachers know which subjects are in a treatment group and which are in a control group. Double-blind studies may prevent bias from coloring research results.

Down's syndrome A disorder caused by an extra chromosome 21; the affected child is mentally retarded and has a number of distinctive physical signs.

drive An incitement to action having its origins in an internal physiological tension.

dyslexia A pattern of difficulties in reading and spelling that appears in people of normal intelligence who have no known emotional or neurological problems. Dyslexia is characterized by the perceptual reversal of letters (e.g., b appears as d).

early adolescence The first phase of adolescence during which young people become aware that their bodies are no longer childlike and that they will eventually live apart from their parents.

early maturer A young person who undergoes the physical changes of adolescence a year or two before the majority of his or her agemates.

ecological approach A view of human behavior that looks at how people are affected throughout their lives by the changing environments within which they live and grow.

ectoderm The outermost of the three primary germ layers of the embryo from which develop the skin, sensory organs, and nervous system.

ego In Freud's theory, the predominantly conscious part of the personality that acts on the reality principle and makes decisions while restraining the id and taking the strictures of the superego into account.

egocentric One's inability to take another person's point of view; this imbues and colors one's thinking in early childhood.

elaborated code Speech that is complex and detailed, a pattern that is hypothesized to prevail among middle-class speakers. See restricted code.

elaboration A strategy for memorizing in which the individual relates an item to be remembered to other items with which it can be linked.

Electra conflict The female counterpart of the Oedipal conflict in psychoanalytic theory. In the phallic stage, at about age 4, little girls have an erotic attachment for father and are antagonistic toward mother. These feelings are usually repressed in some way.

electrocardiograph (EKG) An instrument that records the changes of electric potential occurring during the heartbeat.

electroencephalogram A tracing that shows the changes in electric potential produced by the brain.

electroencephalograph (EEG) An instrument that records the electrical activity of the brain.

embedding In speech, putting a relative clause within a main clause.

emboîtment The supposed encasement in the gamete of a minute preformed baby. Also, the theory that the germs of succeeding generations are enclosed, one within the other, in the germ cell of one of the parents.

embryo In the human being, the developing individual from 2 to 8 weeks following conception during which time basic body structures and organ systems are forming.

embryology The study of the development of the individual from the fertilized egg to birth.

embryonic disk The larger cell heaped at one side of the blastocyst that will become the embryo and subsequently the fetus.

embryonic stage The period extending from the 2nd to the 8th week after conception during which the organs of the conceptus are differentiated and rudimentary anatomy becomes evident.

empathy The capacity to experience vicariously another person's emotional state.

encoding Putting impressions into short-term memory by reviewing them in the mind.

endoderm The innermost of the three primary germ layers of the embryo from which develop the lining of the digestive tract, the salivary glands, pancreas, and liver, and the respiratory system.

endogenous smiles Spontaneous smiles made by the sleeping or drowsy infant during the first 2 weeks of life; it comes when the baby relaxes after an internal neurophysiological arousal.

epidural anesthesia Medication injected under the mother's skin at the bottom of the spine to relieve the pain of childbirth; it numbs the body between chest and knees. Epidural anesthesia may slow the contractions of labor and the newborn's motor abilities.

epiphyses Parts of the bone, usually near the end, that ossify separately and later unite with the main part through further ossification; a secondary center of ossification.

episiotomy A small incision in the vulva to allow sufficient clearance for birth.

equilibration In Piaget's theory, the process of restoring harmony between the world and the individual's view of the world; the principal motive responsible for cognitive development.

ethology The observational study of how animals behave in their natural surroundings.

exogenous smiles Smiles made by an infant, beginning at about one month of age, to something in the external world, such as a nodding head speaking with a high voice.

expansions The more elaborate and complex echoings of a young child's speech that adults offer in attempts to teach the child language.

experiment A research technique for testing a hypothesis and determining causal relationships. An independent variable, or situation, is manipulated to determine its effect on the dependent variable, which is usually some reacton of the individuals in the experimental group. A control group is not exposed to the special

situation. Subjects are assigned randomly to the two groups.

expression The display of genetic characteristics in an individual's phenotype.

expressive role According to sociologist Talcott Parsons, the role of mother within the social network of the family; she keeps the family functioning smoothly by being emotionally expressive and supportive and by giving children and husband unconditional love.

extensive friendship pattern A sociable schoolboy's way of making friends; he distributes his attentions to a number of boys, not just to a single, close buddy. See intensive friendships pattern.

extensive peer interaction See extensive friendship pattern.

extentionality The ability to remain open to experiences and to unusual possibilities. A term used by Carl Rogers.

external morality In Piaget's theory, the code of ethics of schoolchildren that has its origin outside of them. The children obey rules in the belief that the rules have been laid down by authority figures and that they will be punished if they do not obey them.

extinction In learning theory, the decline in frequency and ultimately the cessation of a conditioned response after reinforcement is discontinued.

extroverted The inclination of a person to be friendly, uninhibited, and outgoing.

factor g In Charles Spearman's concept of intelligence, the true and general intellectual ability applied in all intellectual tasks.

factor s In Charles Spearman's concept of intelligence, one of the several specific or idiosyncratic abilities required for particular cognitive tasks.

failure to thrive Want of attaining expected height, weight, and behavior by a baby for no evident organic reason; usually caused by emotional neglect and inattention of parents.

fallopian tubes The pair of tubes that conduct the egg from the ovary to the uterus, having at its upper end a funnel-shaped expansion to capture the egg; fertilization occurs in the fallopian tubes.

fear of strangers (stranger anxiety) A fear of unfamiliar people that may develop during the first year of life as the infant comes to recognize the difference between familiar and unfamiliar people.

fertility The capacity to reproduce.

fetal alcohol syndrome A congenital condition of infants whose mothers drink excessively during pregnancy. The infants have a small head, widely spaced eyes, a flat nose, and underdeveloped upper jaw, and are retarded in mental and motor development.

fetal stage The period, extending from the 9th week after conception until delivery, during which the conceptus grows large and its organs and muscles begin to function.

fetology A new field of medicine that treats problems of the fetus before birth.

fetus The developing unborn child from approximately 8 weeks after conception until birth.

field dependence A cognitive style in which the individual is unable to ignore misleading perceptual cues when doing certain cognitive tasks and tends to respond to influences in the immediate surroundings.

field independence A cognitive style in which the individual is able to maintain his or her spatial orientation and to ignore misleading perceptual cues.

finalism The belief that all movement is meant to accomplish some end.

fluid intelligence The ability to manipulate abstract symbols.

fontanel One of the six spaces, covered by membrane, between the bones of the fetal or young skull.

formal operation In Piaget's theory, the mental ability, supposedly attained in adolescence, by which the individual can think logically about abstractions, can speculate, and can consider the future, that is, what might and what ought to be. Formal operations include hypothetico-deductive, inductive, and reflective thinking and interpropositional logic.

fovea The central part of the retina in which visual images are formed. The fovea is not distinct in infants.

fricative A speech sound in which the expired voiced or voiceless breath has a frictional passage against a narrowing at some point in the breath channel.

full-term baby An infant born in the normal range of 259 to 293 days after the first day of mother's last menstrual period.

galvanic skin response (GSR) The lowered resistance of the skin to the passage of an electric current, caused by increased activity in the sweat glands when the sympathetic nervous system is active because the individual is anxious.

gamete A mature germ cell of either sex, sperm or ovum, possessing a single chromosome of each pair through meiosis and capable of uniting with a gamete of the opposite sex to form a new individual.

gender roles Those behaviors and attitudes a society considers acceptable for males and females.

gender (sex) constancy The understanding that one cannot change gender or sex at will or over time. Children gradually acquire a notion of gender constancy.

gender (sex) identity The deeply ingrained sense of being a boy or girl, man or woman. After age 3, gender identity resists change. In adolescence, the feelings that develop in response to sexual fantasies and overt sexual experiences.

gene The basic unit for the transmission of hereditary characteristics; a portion of DNA in a fixed linear position on a chromosome.

generalization In learning theory, the production of similar responses to stimuli that are similar to ones that have already been learned.

genital stage In Freud's theory, the last stage of psychosexual development in which the individual has mature sexual relations with the opposite sex.

genotype The individual's genetic makeup, the totality of the genes inherited from the parent cells. The genes are present in each cell of the developing individual, beginning with the fertilized egg.

gentle birth A method of childbirth to give the newborn a welcoming introduction to the world, advocated by Frederick Leboyer. Lights are dimmed, sounds muffled; the baby is put immediately on the mother's stomach and then into a warm bath.

germinal stage The period from conception until about 14 days later when the many-celled conceptus has become firmly implanted in the wall of the uterus.

gestation The total period of prenatal development as calculated from the first day of the mother's last menstrual period; the average is 280 days, or 40 weeks, or 9 calendar months.

glial cells Brain cells that help nourish neurons and provide their myelin sheaths.

goodness of fit The mesh or harmony between an individual and a setting or a model and data; more specifically here, between an infant's temperament and the expectations, goals, and values of his or her parents.

gradient of generalization In learning theory, the likelihood that a subject will respond in the same way to a new stimulus as to a similar, familiar one.

grammatical morpheme One of the inflections or a small word such as an article, a preposition, or an auxiliary verb.

growth curve A graphic representation of the relative growth of an individual or population during successive periods similar in length.

growth spurt In adolescence, the sharp and rapid increase in height and other physical growth that continues for about 3 years.

guilt A feeling of responsibility or remorse for having violated some ethical, moral, or religious principle.

gynosperm A sperm carrying an X chromosome; if this sperm penetrates the ovum, a female child will be conceived.

habituate To make used to; to accustom a person to something by frequent repetition or prolonged exposure.

Head Start A national preschool program designed to provide children from poor families with the advantages usually afforded middle-class children including nutrition, health care, and educational experiences.

hemophilia A hereditary blood defect of males, inherited through the mother, in which clotting is delayed and hemorrhage from even minor injuries is difficult to control.

heterozygous With respect to a trait, having a gene pair made up of one dominant gene and one recessive gene.

hippocampus The part of the brain responsible for memory.

holophrase Single-word utterance that 12- to 18-month-old children combine with gesture and intonation to accomplish the work of a whole sentence.

homologous (chromosomes) A pair of chromosomes that are generally similar in size and shape, one having come from the male parent, one from the female parent.

homologue One of a pair of homologous chromosomes.

homozygous With respect to a trait, having a gene pair made up either of two dominant genes or of two recessive genes.

horizontal décalage In Piaget's theory, the notion that the similar abilities to conserve the different quantities of matter are not in alignment in cognitive development; children do not acquire these abilities all at the same time.

hostile aggression Children's negative acts aimed at hurting another person.

hydrocephaly An abnormal increase in the amount of cerebrospinal fluid within the cranium, especially in infancy, that causes the cerebral ventricles to expand; the skull, in particular the forehead, to enlarge; and the brain to atrophy.

hyperactivity A disorder in which the child cannot remain still or pay attention in situations that demand it. Other symptoms are distractibility, little tolerance for frustration, readily aroused emotions, and problems in learning, listening, completing tasks, and getting along with peers.

hypopituitary dwarfism The condition in which the pituitary gland is unable to produce enough growth hormone and the individual's bone and sexual development are immature. Other symptoms are lethargy and shyness.

hypothetico-deductive thinking In Piaget's theory, the ability to consider "what might be" and "what would happen if . . ."; a formal operation.

iconic representation In Jerome Bruner's theory, the preschooler's mental picture or image of what he or she sees. Children think by forming images and manipulating them.

id In Freud's theory, the unconscious aspect of the personality, which is made up of impulses and is governed by the pleasure principle. The id, present at birth, wants whatever satifies and gratifies and wants it immediately.

identity constancy The child's ability to recognize that the identity of an animal or a person does not change, even if aspects of physical appearance do; gradually achieved between ages 3 to 6.

identity crisis In Erikson's life-cycle theory, the core crisis of adolescence; the urgent need for greater self-understanding and self-definition.

identity diffusion In Erikson's terms, the kind of resolution of the identity crisis of individuals who do not commit themselves to a cause or life course.

imagery A cognitive strategy for remembering in which visual images are associated with items to be memorized.

implant The process by which the trophoblast grows into the uterine wall.

imprinting The rapid, innate learning of very young birds and perhaps other animals, within the limited critical period of time, to follow and form a continuing filial attachment to the first large moving object seen.

impulsiveness A style of learning in which a child quickly selects a mode of action or an answer to a question and thereby often makes mistakes; identified by Jerome Kagan.

incongruity The quality of being inharmonious, inconsistent, or out of character. Causes mental effort and laughter in infants; serves as a basis for riddles and jokes of middle childhood.

incubator An apparatus for the housing of premature or sick babies.

index case An individual who in a study of possible inheritance bears the traits or the disorder in which the investigator is interested.

induced labor Uterine contractions started by the administration of drugs or by the breaking of the membranes surrounding the fetus and placenta.

inductive discipline A method of managing children's behavior through reasoning with them about their actions, particularly their misbehavior, rather than asserting authority or withholding love.

inductive thinking The ability to reason from a part to a whole, from particulars to generals, from the individual to the universal; a formal operation.

inferencing In understanding stories and logical statements, becoming aware of what is implied.

inflection The variation or change of form that words undergo to make distinctions of number, case, gender, person, tense, mood, voice, or comparison.

information processing A theory that describes the flow of information into and out of memory; stresses quantitative mental capacities rather than qualitative advances.

innate releaser A stimulus that automatically, without the necessity for thought or appraisal, activates part of the brain.

inner speech In Lev Vygotsky's theory, the private speech that branches off from social speech, becoming abbreviated and internalized; critical to the organization of thoughts.

instrumental aggression Children's attempts to retrieve an object, space, or privilege from a peer through negative means.

instrumental role According to sociologist Talcott Parsons, the particular role of father within the social network of the family; father brings society's norms into the family and through discipline, demands, and love pries his children loose from dependency on their mother.

intellectual realism A preschooler's method of drawing in which the child puts in everything that exists rather than just what is seen from a certain perspective.

intelligence quotient (IQ) Originally, an individual's intelligence defined as mental age, as determined by a standard test, divided by chronological age and multiplied by 100. Now a deviation IQ, determined by the standard deviation of the distribution of MA scores at a given age level and the deviation of the individual's score from the mean of this distribution.

intensive friendship pattern The way a sociable schoolgirl generally makes friends, with one other little girl; at the height of their friendship, they express intense feelings and share many experiences and fantasies. See extensive friendship pattern.

intensive peer interaction See intensive friendship pattern.

interactionist The theory that development is an interplay between the individual's predisposition, consisting of genetic factors, past history, and present state, and surrounding forces, such as other individuals, social institutions, and cultural traditions.

internal (autonomous) morality In Piaget's theory, the more advanced and mature form of moral reasoning in which the individual recognizes that rules are formulated through reasoning and discussion among equals.

interpropositional logic The ability to judge the truth of the logical relationship of propositions; a formal operation.

introjection The psychological assimilation of another person's values and traits into one's own ego system.

introversed The inclination to be shy, anxious, and withdrawn.

intuitive thought In Piaget's theory, the preconceptual or prelogical thought of children from about 4 to 6 or 7 years of age.

inversion In Piaget's theory, the ability to think an object, whose physical appearance has been changed by some action, back to its original state and thereby check its sameness; a concrete operation.

juxtaposition A form of concatenative thinking in which the preschool child places one idea or event next to the other without concern for cause and effect.

Klinefelter's syndrome A disorder of males in which an extra X chromosome keeps the testes small at puberty, disrupts hormonal balance, and is likely to cause sterility and some breast development.

kwashiorkor Severe malnutrition of children 2 to 4 years old whose diet consists mostly of carbohydrates with very little protein. Symptoms are generalized swelling of the stomach, face, and legs; anemia; thinning hair, which changes color; and skin lesions.

language acquisition device (LAD) In Noam Chomsky's view, the child's inborn brain capacity to absorb the regularities of speech, to understand the fundamental relationships of words, and unconsciously to gather notions about language rules.

lanugo A soft, fine hair that covers the fetus's body during the 5th and 6th months of prenatal development; some may persist on parts of the newborn's body for a few weeks after birth.

laparoscopy Examination of the interior of the abdomen through a very small incision, now usually by a fiber optic.

late maturers Young people who undergo the physical changes of adolescence one or more years after the majority of their agemates.

latency period In Freud's theory of psychosexual development, the years from age 7 to 11 during which the child has few sexual interests.

later adolescence The second phase of adolescence during which young people achieve some independence, become more comfortable with the physical changes of puberty, and begin to plan in fairly specific ways for adulthood and the future.

lateral geniculate nucleus (LGN) The part of the vision system that relays impressions from the retina to the cortex of the brain.

lateralization See cerebral lateralization.

learned drive A motive that becomes so through its association with the satisfaction of a primary drive.

learned helplessness An attitude of individuals that they simply cannot surmount failure, which tends to perpetuate it.

limbic system The part of the brain responsible for emotions.

linear systems analysis A method for analyzing infants' visual perceptions of patterns according to the sine waves of a pattern's light frequencies.

linguistic determinism Benjamin Whorf's theory that the structure of language determines the structure of all higher levels of thinking—that is, language determines thought.

linguistic relativity Benjamin Whorf's hypothesis that the forms of the particular language affect the individual's perception of the world.

linguistics The study of human speech in its various aspects, including phonetics, phonology, morphology, syntax, and semantics.

locus of control The way in which individuals commonly ascribe responsibility for their experiences, positing it within themselves or on external forces beyond their control.

longitudinal study A development research method in which the same group of children is studied over an extended period of time to determine how they change with age.

macrosystem In the ecological view of development, the broad institutional patterns in a person's culture that affect his or her development.

magico-phenomenistic thinking In Piaget's theory, the infant's faulty linking of an inappropriate action and a desired end, which seems magical to the child because he or she does not really understand means and ends.

marasmus Severe malnutrition of infants under one year of age who are deprived of necessary proteins and calories. They gain no weight, hardly grow, lose their muscles, and become emaciated.

maturation The developmental acquiring of skills by normal children through physiological growth, probably chiefly neural growth, rather than through learning.

Maximally Discriminative Facial Movement (MAX) A system for measuring emotions that breaks down facial expressions into sets of specific muscle movements.

meiosis A process of cell division unique to the gamete cells, leaving each sperm or ovum with 23 single chromosomes instead of 23 pairs.

menarche The first menstrual period; the establishment of menstruation.

mental combinations In Piaget's theory, the imagining and inventing of courses of action in the mind before carrying them out; an ability acquired between 18 and 24 months of age.

mesoderm The middle of the three primary germ layers of the embryo from which the skeleton muscles, kidneys, and circulatory system develop.

mesosystem In the ecological view of development, the network of ties among major settings in a person's life, such as family, school, friends, church, and camp, which affect the person's development.

metabolism The chemical processes by which nutrients and other substances are broken down, used, and eliminated from the body.

metacognition A person's understanding and knowledge of his or her own cognitive processes.

metamemory The awareness of the phenomenon of memory and an understanding of how it works and how to aid it.

metasystematic operations Mental operations performed on systems.

microanalytic technique In studies of social communications, a method that allows very close examination, such as stopping frames of films and videotapes or running them in slow motion.

microcephaly Abnormal smallness of head and brain area, usually causing mental retardation.

microsystem In the ecological view of development, the network of ties between a person and his or her immediate setting, such as a school or office.

midlife transition A period beginning about age 40 that usually involves both an intense reexamination of past choices and facing up to and resolving the psychological issues of embarking on the final half of life; an emotionally upsetting time.

midolescence A period in midlife when adults come face to face with the unfulfilled aspects of their lives.

minimum distance principle (MDP) According to Carol Chomsky, children's tendency to choose as the subject of an infinitive the noun closest to it—for example, the choice of Andrea instead of Martha in the sentence "Martha promised Andrea to weed the garden."

mitosis The usual process of cell division in which the chromosomes split and duplicate within the nucleus, then separate, with one member of each duplicate going to one of the two daughter cells formed through division of the cytoplasm.

mnemonic A special device aiding memory, such as a rhyme; a sentence in which first letters of words serve as a code, a diagram, a graph.

monozygotic (MZ) Birth partners who have developed from a single fertilized egg and thus have the same genotype.

Montessori nursery schools Schools devoted to a philosophy of education that draws on children's natural curiosity and where children engage in age-graded activities that systematically train their muscles, minds, and senses.

Moro's reflex The newborn's normal reflexive response to a loud sound or a sudden drop of head and neck: the infant flings arms and legs out, fans its hands, and then convulsively brings arms toward the middle of the body.

morpheme The smallest unit of a language that by itself has a recognizable meaning and cannot be broken down any further.

morphology The study of the units of meaning in a language.

morula A solid ball of 12 to 16 cells formed 60 hours after fertilization through several cell divisions; resembles a mulberry.

motherese Another word for baby talk; the special language form used by adults when speaking to infants. The voice is usually high in register but has an exaggerated range of pitch and loudness. The adult chooses simple phrases and nonsense syllables and repeats them in a singsong fashion.

motherese hypothesis The suggestion that the short sentences, clear enunciation, grammatical correctness, and concreteness of a mother's speech help a child to acquire language.

motor milestone One of the succession of motor abilities acquired by human babies during the first two years of life as they gain control of their head and limb movements.

myelination The accretion of myelin, a soft, white, somewhat fatty substance that coats the axon of a nerve cell and insulates it and increases the speed of impulses traveling along it.

natural childbirth A system to lessen pain during labor and birth that avoids general anesthesia and prepares parents for the birth of their child. They are given instructions on the mechanics of labor and birth as well as exercises to strengthen the mother's abdominal muscles and to encourage her proper breathing during labor.

natural experiment A research technique that compares one group of subjects exposed to a particular real-life situation to another group of subjects, similar in every other way, but who have not been exposed to that particular situation.

nature In developmental psychology, the genetic and physiological factors that can affect development of the individual.

neonatology A specialization in medicine directed to the medical care of the infant during the newborn period.

neuroglia Delicate, branching connective tissue that fills the spaces between neurons, supporting and binding them together.

neuron action potentials A brief change in the electrical charge of an axon that is the physical basis of a nervous impulse.

neurons Nerve cells.

neurotransmitters Chemicals in the brain that carry or inhibit electrical charges across the synapses between neurons.

Nissl substance Material surrounding neurons that often appears just when a new function emerges.

nontransformational grammar A theory proposing that ideas are expressed directly in different surface forms rather than through grammatical transformations of deep structures.

norm A single value or a range of values constituting the empirically established average or standard performance on a test under specified conditions.

nursery school A preschool program that prepares children for kindergarten, usually with periods of group activities and shorter hours than day care. See day care.

nurture In developmental psychology, the factors in the environment that can affect development of the individual.

object permanence The understanding that objects continue to exist, even though they are out of sight or disappear from view; develops gradually between 6 and 18 months of age. A term used by Piaget.

observational learning The learning that occurs from watching other people without any apparent external reinforcement.

Oedipal conflict In Freud's theory, the erotic attachment little boys in the phallic stage have for mother and their fear that father will find them out. These feelings are usually repressed in some way.

oocytes Immature egg cells.

open class A classroom in which both use of space and choice of activities are flexible and decisions about where to be and what to do are often made by children, individually and in small groups, rather than by the teacher.

open word One of a class of words in one of the grammars for children's early two-word sentences. Words in the open class can take either position, are sometimes used alone, are numerous, and are added rapidly to children's vocabularies.

operant conditioning A learning process described by B. F. Skinner in which the individual responds again in a way rewarded in the past or refrains from activity earlier punished.

operation In Piaget's theory, a basic and logical mental manipulation and transformation of information.

oral stage In Freud's theory, the psychosexual stage from birth to 12 months during which the mouth of the infant is the source of sustenance and pleasure, and his or her interest is in feeding.

organization In Piaget's theory, the process of combining and integrating perceptions and thoughts that continues throughout a lifetime. A cognitive strategy for memorizing, grouping items into more general classes, clusters, or chunks.

organogenesis The origin and development of organs in animals and plants.

ossification The process of bone formation in which, beginning in the center of each prospective bone, cartilage cells are replaced by bone cells.

ovary The typically paired female reproductive organ that releases ova and in vertebrates female sex hormones; in the adult human female an oval, flattened body suspended from a ligament.

overextension Children's generalized use of a given word for several objects that share a particular characteristic but have others that are dissimilar, such as "fly" for flies, specks of dust, all small insects, crumbs of bread.

overregularize To extend the rules for the inflections denoting past tense and plural to verbs with irregular past tenses and nouns with irregular plurals.

ovulation Release of a maturing ovum from the ovary into a fallopian tube; it occurs once about every 28 days from puberty until menopause.

ovum transfer A procedure for treating infertility whereby an ovum is surgically removed from a woman's ovary, fertilized in vitro, and then reintroduced into her own or a surrogate mother's uterus for gestation.

oxytoxin A hormone secreted together with vasopressin by the posterior lobe of the pituitary; stimulates both the uterine muscles to contract, initiating the birth process, and the breasts to eject milk. Also synthesized and used in obstetrics to induce labor and control postnatal hemorrhage.

paired comparison A method of testing infant memory by showing the baby a new stimulus either to the right or left and then an old stimulus on the opposite side.

palmar grasp A newborn's normal reflexive response when a finger or thin object is pressed into the palm; the muscles in the hand flex so tightly that those in the upper arm and forearm flex too, and the infant can briefly suspend his or her weight.

parallel play Play in which two children are side by side using similar toys in similar ways, but their activities are not related.

parasomnias Sleep disorders.

parity The number of children previously borne by a mother; can affect the course of a child's prenatal development, birth, and infancy.

partial reinforcement schedule In learning theory, the rewarding of a response less than every time it occurs.

pedigree An ancestral line. The pedigree technique studies heredity by looking for evidence of a particular trait or disorder in earlier and present members of a family.

perception The obtaining and interpreting of information about the world through the senses.

perceptual-motor processing theory of emotion Leventhal's theory that emotion is created by an innate facial-motor mechanism, a memory for emotion, and a conceptual system with rules for emotional experience.

permissive parent A parent who gives children as much freedom as possible and allows them to do virtually what they want. The permissive parent does not state or enforce rules and gives children few responsibilities.

perseverating In cognitive theory, the tendency of infants to continue to search for an object where they once found it rather than where it was hidden.

persevering A cognitive strategy for retrieving information from memory in which one concentrates on trying to recall forgotten material.

personality The unique and consistent way in which an individual behaves and approaches the world. The complex of traits distinguishing one person from all others.

personeity The awareness of being in the past, now, and in the future a human person separate from and entirely like no other.

phallic stage In Freud's theory of psychosexual development, the period in which the genital area gives physiological pleasure and is of interest to the preschool child.

phenotype All the observable characteristics of the individual that depend on how the environment has affected expression of the genotype.

phenylketonuria (PKU) An inherited inability to produce a liver enzyme that metabolizes phenylalanine, which is contained in most protein foods; the buildup of phenylalanine and phenylpyruvic acid in body fluids damages the brain and causes restlessness and agitation. A special diet until 6 years of age will prevent much of the retardation.

phocomelia The condition of having extremely short limbs so that feet and hands arise close to the trunk; the principal deformity of children whose mothers took the tranquilizer thalidomide in 1960.

phoneme The smallest unit of sound that signals a difference in meaning in a particular language.

phonology The study of the sound system of a language and how it develops.

phylogeny The evolution of a race or genetically related group as distinguished from the development of the individual.

pivot class One of a class of words in one of the grammars for children's early two-word combinations. Words in the pivot class appear only in the first position or the second, not in both, occur with great frequency but never alone or with another pivot word, are small in number, and are added rather slowly to children's vocabularies.

placebo An inert substance given to a naive subject who believes it to be medication; used to distinguish effects with a physiological cause from those with a psychological cause.

placenta The disk-shaped structure rich in blood vessels by which the circulation of the embryo and then the fetus interlocks with that of the mother, allowing food and oxygen to diffuse into the conceptus and carrying away its body wastes.

placing response In infants, the reaction to crawling onto a solid surface that consists of a rapid frontwise extension of arms and a fanning of the fingers.

pneumograph A device for recording chest movements during respiration.

polygenic trait A characteristic that is produced by the equal and cumulative effects of several genes, for example, skin color, body shape, intelligence, and memory.

postconventional moral reasoning Kohlberg's highest level of moral reasoning in which the person chooses and follows universal principles, realizing that some of the rules of society can be broken.

postterm babies Infants born later than normal, more than 293 days after the first day of mother's last menstrual period.

pragmatics The study of how language is used in a social context.

preconventional moral reasoning Kohlberg's first level of moral reasoning in which the child obeys rules to avoid punishment and to secure a fair exchange with others.

preoperational period In Piaget's theory, the second stage in the development of logical thinking, lasting from approximately 2 to 7 years of age, in which the child begins to employ mental symbols, to engage in symbolic play, and to use words. Thought remains egocentric in nature, and the child focuses on the striking states and conditions of objects and events, ignoring others. The child cannot think by operations, cannot logically manipulate information.

preterm babies Infants born earlier than normal, in fewer than 259 days after the first day of mother's last menstrual period.

primacy effect The memory phenomenon in which information from the beginnings of lists is retained better than information from the middles of lists.

primapara The mother of a firstborn.

primary drive A physiological need of the individual, such as for food or sleep.

primitive drive A physiological need of the individual, such as for food or sleep.

primitive streak A thickening caused by the growth of ectodermal cells; gives rise to the mesoderm and ultimately to the brain, the spinal cord, all the nerves and sensory organs, and the skin.

proform One of the aspects of language learned rather late, such as use of what, which, that, passive sentences, questions with subject–auxiliary verb inversion.

prosodic Pertaining to voice modulation.

protocol analysis A method of assessing information processing in which a subject's words and actions are recorded as the subject says aloud everything that comes to mind while he or she is solving a problem.

proximodistal (development) A pattern of physical growth and motor development progressing from the spine toward the extremities; in human beings, followed prenatally and throughout childhood.

pseudodialogue A conversation between mother and infant in which the mother pauses for an imagined response from her baby, thus teaching her child the turn-taking nature of conversation.

pseudoimitation Repetition of another's action by infants of 4 months, who are limited to movements in their repertoire that they have made only shortly before. A term used by Piaget.

psychoanalysis Freud's method of treating psychiatric patients; helps the disturbed individual to bring unconscious conflict and repressed past experiences to awareness through free association and analysis of dreams.

psycholinguistics The psychological study of language, its rules, and acquisition.

psychometrics A branch of psychology measuring mental abilities, traits, and processes; the study of mental testing.

psychoprophylactic method A method of childbirth based on Ivan Pavlov's theory of conditioned reflexes. Through intensive training the expectant mother prepares herself to concentrate on control of her breathing and relaxation of her muscles so that they will not act against the natural muscular contractions of labor. The expectant father is her helpmate.

psychosocial moratorium In Erikson's life-cycle theory, a period of time set aside in adolescence for establishing identity, for finding a role, the work, the attitude, and the sense of social connectedness that will allow a person to assume a place in adult society.

puberty The period when the reproductive system matures and the secondary sex characteristics develop.

pyloric stenosis A condition of newborns, usually males, in which the opening from the stomach to the intestines closes, preventing digestion of food. Pyloric stenosis is corrected surgically.

quickening The first motion of a fetus in the uterus felt by the mother, usually between the 4th and 5th month.

rapid eye movements (REM) The fast movements of the eye under the closed eyelid during the baby's irregular sleep. REM sleep is the stage of sleep during which adults dream.

reaction range In Irving Gottesman's theory, the extent to which the same genotype may vary in phenotypes and dissimilar genotypes may translate into similar phenotypes through reaction with the environment.

reactivation In learning theory, the reinstatement of a learned response through reexposure to a stimulus.

recall A form of memory in which one must retrieve information seen or heard before without prompts from the external environment.

recency effect The short-term memory phenomenon in which information from the ends of lists is retained better than information from the middles of lists.

reciprocity In Piaget's theory, the recognition that one dimension, such as width, may make up for another, such as shortness; a concrete operation.

recognition Recognizing an object, item or image as one that has been seen or heard before; the simplest form of memory.

reflection A way of learning by weighing all possible alternatives before choosing an answer to a question; identified by Jerome Kagan.

reflex An unlearned, involuntary response of a part of the body to an external stimulus.

rehearsal A cognitive strategy for remembering that consists of repeating information until it is fixed in memory.

reinforcement In operant conditioning, an instance in which a response is followed by favorable consequence, increasing the likelihood that the response will be made again.

reinforcement contingencies Past and present rewards for actions, making it likely that the individual will behave the same way in the future.

reinforcer The favorable consequence that follows reinforcement. See reinforcement.

relative clause An adjective clause modifying an antecedent and usually introduced by a relative pronoun or relative adverb.

reliability In psychometrics, the consistency of a test as a measuring device; for example, if all the items on a test do a good job of predicting the total score.

resistance to temptation The ability to refrain from a misdeed in a provoking situation; tested extensively by Hugh Hartshorne and Mark May.

restraining effect The contrivance of maternal influences to keep a fetus with a genotype for large size small enough to develop in and be born from the uterus of a small mother.

restricted code Speech that is simple and not detailed, a pattern that is hypothesized to prevail among speakers from lower social classes. See elaborated code.

retarded (mentally) A label applied to individuals who score below some cutoff point on IQ tests.

retina The part of the eye that transforms light into nerve signals to the brain.

reversal and nonreversal shifts Changes in the right (reinforced) response that are either (reversal shift) within the same dimension (e.g., large to small, black to white) or (nonreversal shift) across different dimensions (e.g., large to black, small to white).

reversible In Piaget's theory, the realization that one manipulation of an object can be reversed by applying the opposite; a concrete operation.

Rh incompatibility A condition that exists when the fetus of an Rh-negative mother has inherited Rh factor from the father. The Rh factor in the baby's red blood cells, through hemorrhaging, can trigger the mother's immunogenic system to produce antibodies, which will cross the placenta and destroy red blood cells of the fetus. Laterborns are at greater risk than the first born. The buildup of the mother's antibodies can now be prevented.

ribonucleic acid (RNA) A complex chemical substance that is able to use the information in DNA molecules to assemble proteins.

ribosomes The part of cells containing RNA and producing proteins necessary for the growth and survival of cells.

Ritalin Methylphenidate, a stimulant that is administered to hyperactive children and enables them to focus longer on tasks.

rooting reflex A newborn's normal reflexive response to the mother's breast on its cheek; the infant turns its head and starts to suck.

rubella (German measles) A mild form of measles; if contracted by a woman during the embryonic period of her pregnancy, may cause blindness, deafness, heart malformations, and mental retardation in her child.

saccadic eye movements (saccades) Small sideways movements of the eyes from one point of fixation to another. Saccadic eye movements move the eyes to objects of focus during visual scanning and reading.

satiation The state following repeated presentation of a stimulus.

schedule of reinforcement In learning theory, the percentage of responses that are followed by reinforcement (positive or negative).

scheme In Piaget's theory, a basic unit of knowledge, which may be an observable pattern of action, an image of an object, or a complex idea.

schizophrenia The most common and severe psychosis, which may show itself in adolescence. The symptoms are jumbled thoughts and speech, flat or inappropriate emotions, hallucinations and delusions, loss of contact with reality.

scientific method A method for generating hypotheses and empirically testing them; extraneous factors are systematically eliminated and factors under study are rigorously controlled by the investigator.

scoliosis Lateral curvature of the spine.

secondary sex characteristics Bodily and physiological signs of maleness and femaleness, other than the sex organs, which emerge during pubescence and indicate physical maturity—breast development, pubic and facial hair, voice changes.

secular trend The pattern of physical maturation happening earlier, with people growing taller and heavier over successive generations.

self-concept The individual's sense of his or her identity as a person, beginning with the infant's discovery of parts of the body and then between 1 and 2 years of age the child's recognition of selfhood, of differentiation from others. Children's later self-concepts include the qualities and traits that they think are characteristic of themselves.

self-esteem One's high or low estimation and opinion of oneself.

self-righting tendency A regulative mechanism promoting normal prenatal development, overcoming all but the most adverse circumstances.

semantics The study of meanings, of how the sounds of language are related to the real world and our own experiences.

seminal vesicle A pouch on either side of the male reproductive tract that is connected with the seminal duct and that secretes a whitish fluid that mixes with the sperm to form semen.

sensitive period An interval of time during which a very young animal is supposedly predisposed to learn particular behavior according to ethologists.

sensorimotor period In Piaget's theory, the period of cognitive growth from birth to approximately 2 years of age during which knowledge is acquired through sensory perceptions and motor skills. Babies show their intelligence through ingenious actions and ways of handling objects.

seriation In cognitive theory, simple seriation is the process of arranging similar objects in a series according to the one quantified way in which they vary (e.g., arranging sticks from long to short). Multiple seriation is the process of arranging similar objects in a series according to the two or more quantified ways in which they vary (e.g., arranging glasses in columns from short to tall and in rows from narrow to wide).

set goal The degree of proximity to mother required by a particular child. The child's natural predisposition to seek proximity is modified by what his or her past experiences with mother have been.

set-point theory A theory of obesity that suggests that everyone's weight settles around a given point and diverges from the point only under extreme conditions.

sex (gender) constancy The understanding that one cannot change gender at will or over time. Children only gradually acquire a notion of sex constancy that is based on their immutable anatomy.

sex (gender) identity The deeply ingrained sense of being a little boy or little girl, a man or woman. After age 3, gender identity is difficult to alter. In adolescence, the feelings that develop about having experiences as a sexual person.

sex preference Inclination to choose either males or females as sexual partners, a pattern of feelings and reactions apparently ingrained in the individual before sexual activity begins.

sickle cell anemia An inherited blood abnormality in which the defective hemoglobin molecules crystallize and stick together to form elongated bundles of rods when oxygen level is low. The red blood cells sickle, causing blockage in capillary beds and bringing fever and pain to chest, abdomen, and joints.

signifier In Piaget's theory, a symbolic representation that stands for the signified object or the signified action; it may be mental or an object.

skill theory Fischer's theory of cognitive development in which it is proposed that children's skills develop unevenly—from simple to complex sensorimotor, then representational, and finally abstract skills.

sleep enuresis Bed wetting.

sleep terrors A sleep disturbance among children that involves loud crying, racing pulse, but little memory for the episode.

small for dates Babies who are born at full term but who have low birth weights.

small for gestational age Full-term babies who have a low birth weight.

social cognition What children know and understand about the social world: social rules and norms and social expressions, intentions, and actions.

social conventions Rules of conduct, attitude, or behavior in a society, culture, or subculture, such as table manners, a style of dress, a form of address.

socialization The process by which children acquire the habits, attitudes, skills, and standards that their families and social group value for adulthood.

social referencing The act of seeking cues from others about how to behave in unfamiliar situations.

social speech The speech of a toddler that is meant to communicate; earliest speech is not social.

socialization agents Parents, other relatives, teachers, books, television figures, and all the others in a child's environment who try to influence the child to become a mature, productive, and responsible member of society.

sociobiology The school of thought that posits a genetic basis to social behavior.

sociogram The graphic representation of the relationships, positive or negative, or the exchanges, frequent or infrequent, among the members of a group. Individuals are customarily represented as circles or squares connected by lines, short or long, depending on the social closeness of the two individuals.

sociolinguistics The study of the language of particular social groups, of people who are of the same social class, race, or sex.

sociometry The study of the patterns of attraction and rejection, or popularity and leadership, among members of a group, usually through questioning. Psychodrama and sociodrama are other methods.

sonogram A picture of the conceptus obtained through high-frequency sound waves that indicates its size and position. Useful in amniocentesis and in deciding whether cesarean section is necessary.

speeded labor Uterine contractions that are sped up by the administration of drugs.

spermatozoon A male gamete or sperm cell.

stabilimeter An instrument for recording the amplitude and frequency of the movements of infants.

stability In psychometrics, the consistency of a person's test scores over time.

standard deviation A statistical index of the variability within a distribution. It is the square root of the average of the squared deviation from the mean.

statistical significance The magnitude of difference that has little probability, less than .05, of occurring by chance alone and therefore should be accepted as real.

stereopsis The perception of depth that occurs when two pictures of the same scene, taken at slightly different angles, are viewed side by side.

stimulation-stress factor (SSF) A comprehensive measure of all sensory input, proposed to account for the decreasing age of menarche.

stop consonant A speech sound in which the expired voiced or voiceless breath is blocked or stopped completely at some point in the breath channel.

storm and stress Translation of the German phrase, *Sturm und Drang,* used by early psychologists to characterize the presumed disruptions and extremism of adolescence. Now widely regarded as a stereotyped view, it survives nevertheless.

stranger anxiety The baby's wariness of unfamiliar people, beginning when he or she is 4 to 6 months old and peaking at the end of the first year.

strange situation A standard laboratory method for assessing the attachment of children 12 to 18 months old to their mother. The child is observed in a playroom with mother and a stranger, alone with the stranger, reunited with mother, alone in the room, then with the stranger again, then reunited with mother.

structuralist view The theory of Piaget that knowledge is gained as the child's predisposition of the mind to order things takes in information from the environment.

structured class A traditional class in which children spend most of their time on lessons, usually in the "basics," the three R's. They are generally in their seats at desks or tables arranged in neat rows, receiving instruction from the teacher. Subject matter is from a set curriculum established for the class as a whole.

sucking reflex A newborn's reflexive response to anything that touches its lips; the infant immediately starts to suck.

sudden infant death syndrome (SIDS) The sudden and unexplained death of apparently healthy babies who are usually between 2 and 4 months old. They stop breathing during sleep.

superego In Freud's theory, the conscience that develops through identification with the parent. The imposition of civilization and culture as filtered through parents' rules and the regulations of adult society.

surface structure The actual words of a sentence and the order in which they occur; identified by Noam Chomsky.

surrogate mother In Harry Harlow's experiments, an artificial mother made of wire or cloth to test the infant monkey's reactions to having only some of its needs of mother fulfilled. In human beings, a woman who agrees by contract to bear a child for a biological father and an adoptive mother and to give them the infant after birth.

symbol A sound, written word, object, action, or drawing that stands for or signifies something else.

symbolic function In Piaget's theory, the ability of 2- to 4-year-old children to understand, create, and use symbols to represent objects and actions, people and places, that are not present; expressed in language, pretend play, and drawings.

symbolic play Piaget's term for the pretending and make-believe of young children.

sympathetic distress The feeling of distress for others who are hurt, angered, or crying, Failure to act to help those in distress stirs guilt in older children and adults.

synapse The point of contact between adjacent neurons where nerve impulses are transmitted from one to the other.

syncretism A form of concatenative thinking in which the preschool child attempts to find an explanation at any cost by connecting unrelated ideas into a whole.

syntax Rules of a specific language by which words, and morphemes, are combined to form larger units such as clauses and sentences.

systematic operations Proposed stage of cognition beyond formal operations in which people reflect on and form systems out of relations among classes.

Tay-Sachs disease A recessive-gene disorder of fat metabolism causing severe mental retardation, muscular weakness, eventual blindness, and death, usually in the 3rd year. Found for the most part in Jewish families of northeastern European ancestry.

telegraphic speech The two-word sentences of young children, which contain only the most necessary words.

temperament A basic and apparently largely inherited behavior pattern of an infant or older person; the natural disposition of an individual.

template A pattern or mold used in making something of similar dimensions and contours.

teratogenic (agent) An external agent that may cross the barrier of the placenta and interfere with the development of the embryo or fetus.

teratogens Teratogenic agents.

teratology The study of serious malformations and deviations from the normal in animals and plants. Now applied to human beings with the goal of understanding the causes of abnormalities and anticipating risks in prenatal development.

terrible twos An age at which children test their autonomy in the world; their bad behavior consists of negativism and temper tantrums, their good of growing independence and mastery of their surroundings.

testes The typically paired male reproductive organ, which is located in the scrotum and in which sperm develop after puberty.

thalidomide A mild tranquilizer prescribed to women in 1960 to relieve the nausea and vomiting of morning sickness. The children of those who took it on critical days in the embryonic period were born without ears or with the stunted limbs of phocomelia.

thermogenesis theory A theory of obesity, well-documented in animal research, that suggests how efficiently individuals burn calories is more important in determining obesity than the number of calories consumed.

tonic neck reflex The newborn's normal reflexive response when placed on its back; the infant turns its head to one side and assumes a fencing position, extends arm and leg on this side, bends opposite limbs, and arches body away from the direction faced.

totipotent Referring to the ability of a cell formed during the first 60 hours of cell division after fertilization to develop into a complete person if separated from the zygote.

toxemia (of pregnancy) A disorder that usually has its onset in the last trimester; symptoms are persistent nausea and vomiting or, in preeclampsia, hypertension, sudden and rapid increase in weight through retention of water in the tissues, and albumin in the urine.

transcript (of RNA) A copy, reproduction, or rendering from one form into another.

transductive reasoning In Piaget's theory, preoperational children's logic in which they reason from the particular to the particular without generalization.

transitive inference The mathematical notion that if A equals (or is greater than) B and B equals (or is greater than) C, it follows that A equals (or is greater than) C. Children begin to be able to make transitive inferences toward the end of the concrete operational period if they have visual aids. An abstract transitive inference is a formal operation.

trimester One of the three, 3-month periods into which the term of pregnancy is divided.

trophoblast The outer layer of small cells of the blastocyst from which the chorion and the amnion and the nonmaternal parts of the placenta develop.

Turner's syndrome A disorder of females in which absence of an X chromosome keeps stature short, ovaries rudimentary, and prevents secondary sexual characteristics from developing.

tympanum The eardrum.

ultrasound A wave phenomenon of the same physical nature as sound but with frequencies above the range of human hearing. Can be used to picture a fairly detailed outline of the conceptus.

unconditioned response In classical conditioning, a subject's automatic response (e.g., salivation) to a stimulus (e.g., food).

unconditioned stimulus In classical conditioning, the object (e.g., food) that automatically and without conditioning elicits a response (e.g., salivation).

underextension Children's tendency to use a word too narrowly, such as applying the word "cat" only to the family cat and not to cats in the alley, on television, or in picture books.

unvoiced consonant A consonant in which air is forced only through the mouth and not over the vocal cords.

uterus An organ in female mammals, resembling, when not pregnant, a flattened pear in size and shape; contains and nourishes the young during development previous to birth.

validity In psychometrics, the ability of a test to measure what it is supposed to measure.

vas deferens The paired spermatic duct in male mammals through which the spermatozoa travel from the testes to the seminal vesicles on sexual climax. The vas deferens joins the duct of the seminal vesicle to form an ejaculatory duct.

vasectomy An operation that removes a small section of each vas deferens through small scrotal incisions and thus prevents transfer of sperm to the seminal vesicles. Makes males sterile; sometimes used as a means of birth control.

vernix A white, pasty substance made up of the fetus's shed dead-skin cells and fatty substances from oil glands; serves as a protective coating.

villus On the surface of the chorion, a rootlike extension that may grow into the lining of the uterine wall during implantation and rupture the small blood vessels it meets.

visual acuity The smallest distance between two lines that a person can detect. Visual acuity is poor in early infancy and improves dramatically in the first year of life.

visual cliff A laboratory structure for testing infants' depth perception; it consists of a glass-topped table with a middle runway on one side of which there appears to be a drop.

visualization A cognitive strategy for retrieving information from memory by which one replays one's experience in mental images.

voiced consonant A consonant in which air is forced over the vocal cords.

Wernicke's area The part of the brain that coordinates hearing.

Wet nurses Women who care for and suckle babies who are not their own.

XYY syndrome A condition of males in which an extra Y chromosome causes unusual tallness, facial acne at adolescence, and mental dullness. The syndrome has sometimes been associated with antisocial behavior.

zone of proximal development As described by Vygotsky, the difference between what a child is capable of doing on his or her own and what he or she can accomplish with help from a person who is more advanced.

zygote A single cell formed through the union of two gametes, a sperm and an ovum; in time the human zygote will develop into a human being.

REFERENCES

Abikoff, H., Gittelman-Klein, R., and Klein, D. F. Classroom observation code for hyperactive children: A replication of validity. *Journal of Consulting and Clinical Psychology*, 1980, *48*, 555–565.

Abramovitch, R., Pepler, D., and Corter, C. Patterns of sibling interaction among preschool-age children. In M. Lamb and B. Sutton-Smith (Eds.), *Sibling relationships: Their nature and significance across the lifespan*. Hillsdale, N.J.: Lawrence Erlbaum Associates, 1982.

Acredolo, C., and Acredolo, L.P. Identity, compensation and conservation. *Child Development*, 1979, *50*, 524–535.

Acredolo, L. P., and Hake, J. L. Infant perception. In B. B. Wolman and G. Strickler (Eds.), *Handbook of developmental psychology*. Englewood Cliffs, N.J.: Prentice-Hall, 1982.

Adams, G., and Cohen, A. Children's physical and interpersonal characteristics that affect student-teacher interaction. *Journal of Experimental Education*, 1974, *43*, 1–5.

Adams, J. F. Earlier menarche, greater height and weight: A stimulation-stress factor hypothesis. *Genetic Psychology Monographs*, 1981, *104*, 3–22.

Adams, R. E., and Passman, R. H. Effects of visual and auditory aspects of mothers and strangers on the play and exploration of children. *Developmental Psychology*, 1979, *15*, 269–274.

Adams, R. L., and Phillips, B. N. Motivation and achievement differences among children of various ordinal birth positions. *Child Development*, 1972, *43*, 155–164.

Adams, R. S., and Biddle, B. J. *An analysis of classroom activities: A final report* (ERIC Document EDO 15537). Columbia: University of Missouri, 1967.

Adkins, D. C., Payne, F. D., and Ballif, B. Motivation factor scores and response set scores for ten ethnic-cultural groups of preschool children. *American Educational Research Journal*, 1972, *9*, 557–572.

Ahr, P. R., and Youniss, J. Reasons for failure on the class inclusion problem. *Child Development*, 1970, *41*, 131–143.

Ahrentzen, S. The environmental and social context of distraction in the classroom. In A. E. Osterberg, C. P. Tiernan, and R. A. Findlay (Eds.), *Design research interactions*. Ames, Iowa: Environmental Design Research Association, Inc., 1981.

Aiello, J. R., Nicosia, G., and Thompson, D. E. Physiological, social, and behavioral consequences of crowding on children and adolescents. *Child Development*, 1979, *50*, 195–202.

Ainsworth, M. D. S. *Infancy in Uganda: Infant care and the growth of love*. Baltimore: Johns Hopkins University Press, 1967.

Ainsworth, M. D. S. The development of infant-mother attachment. In B. M. Caldwell and H. N. Ricciuti (Eds.), *Review of child development research*, Volume 3. Chicago: University of Chicago Press, 1973.

Ainsworth, M. D. S., and Bell, S. M. Infant crying and maternal responsiveness: A rejoinder to Gewirtz and Boyd. *Child Development*, 1977, *48*, 1208–1216.

Ainsworth, M. D. S., Blehar, M., Waters, E., and Wall, S. *Patterns of attachment: Observations in the strange situation and at home*. Hillsdale, N.J.: Lawrence Erlbaum Associates, 1978.

Ainsworth, M. D. S., and Wittig, B. A. Attachment and exploratory behavior of one-year-olds in a strange situation. In B. M. Foss (Ed.), *Determinants of infant behaviour*, Volume 4. London: Methuen, 1969.

Alan Guttmacher Institute. *Eleven million teenagers*. New York: Alan Guttmacher Institute, 1976.

Alan Guttmacher Institute, *Teenage pregnancy: The problem that hasn't gone away*. New York: Alan Guttmacher Institute, 1981.

Aleksandrowicz, M. K., and Aleksandrowicz, D. R. Obstetrical pain-relieving drugs as predictors of infant behavior variability. *Child Development*, 1974, *45*, 935–945.

Allen, J. *Visual acuity development in human infants up to 6 months of age*. Unpublished doctoral dissertation, University of Washington, 1978.

Altus, W. D. Birth order and its sequelae. *Science*, 1966, *151*, 44–49.

Ambrose, J. A. The development of the smiling response in early infancy. In B. M. Foss (Ed.), *Determinants of infant behavior*. New York: Wiley, 1961.

Ament, A. Treatment of hyperactive children: Letter to the editor. *Journal of the American Medical Association*, 1974, *230*, 372.

Anastasi, A. *Differential psychology*, New York: Macmillan, 1958.

Anastasi, A. *Psychological testing* (2nd ed.). New York: Macmillan, 1976.

Anastasio, N. J., and Hanes, M. L. *Language pattern of poverty children*. Springfield, Ill.: Charles C. Thomas, 1976.

Anderson, D. R. Active and passive processes in children's television viewing. Paper presented at the annual meeting of the American Psychological Association, New York, September 1979.

Anderson, D. R., and Levin, S. R. Young children's attention to Sesame Street. *Child Development*, 1976, *47*, 806–811.

Anderson, J. G., and Johnson, W. H. Stability and change among three generations of Mexican-Americans: Factors affecting achievement. *American Educational Research Journal*, 1971, *8*, 285–309.

Anderson, J. R., and Bower, G. H. A propositional theory of recognition memory. *Memory and Cognition*, 1974, *26*, 530–541.

Andres, D., and Walters, R. H. Modification of delay of punishment effects through cognitive restructuring. In *Proceedings of the 78th annual convention of the American Psychological Association*, 1970.

Andrews, S. R., Blumenthal, J. B., Johnson, D. L., Kahn, A. J., Ferguson, C. J., Lasater, T. M., Malone, P. E. and Wallace, D. B. The skills of mothering: A study of Parent Child Development Centers. *Monographs of the Society for Research in Child Development*, 1982, *47*(6, Serial No. 198).

Angle, C. R., and McIntire, M. S. Paper presented at the International Conference on Heavy Metals in the Environment, Toronto, 1975.

Angle, C. R., McIntire, M. S., and Vest, G. Blood lead of Omaha school children—topographic correlation with industry, traffic and housing. *Nebraska Medical Journal,* 1975, *60,* 97–102.

Anglin, J. M. The child's first terms of reference. In S. Ehrlich and E. Tulving (Eds.), Bulletin de Psychologie (Special Issue on Semantic Memory), 1975.

Annis, L. F. *The child before birth.* Ithaca, N.Y.: Cornell University Press, 1978.

Anthony, E. J. The reactions of adults to adolescents and their behavior. In H. Caplan and F. Lebovici (Eds.), *Adolescence: Psychosocial perspectives.* New York: Basic Books, 1969.

Apgar, V., and Beck, J. *Is my baby all right?* New York: Pocket Books, 1974.

Appel, Y. H. Developmental differences in children's perception of maternal socialization behavior. *Child Development,* 1977, *48,* 1689–1693.

Appleton, T., Clifton, R., and Goldberg, S. The development of behavioral competence in infancy. In F. D. Horowitz (Ed.), *Review of child development research,* Volume 4. Chicago: University of Chicago Press, 1975.

Arend, R., Gove, F. L., and Sroufe, L. A. Continuity of individual adaptation from infancy to kindergarten: A predictive study of ego-resiliency and curiosity in preschoolers. *Child Development,* 1979, *50,* 950–959.

Aries, P. *Centuries of childhood.* New York: Random House, 1962.

Arieti, S. *Creativity: The magic synthesis.* New York: Basic Books, 1976.

Armitage, S. E., Baldwin, B. A., and Vince, N. A. The fetal sound environment of sheep. *Science,* 1980, *208,* 1173–1174.

Aronfreed, J. The nature, variety and social patterning of moral responses to transgression. *Journal of Abnormal and Social Psychology,* 1961, *163,* 223–240.

Ashear, V., and Snortum, J. R. Eye contact in children as a function of age, sex, social and intellectual variables. *Developmental Psychology,* 1971, *4,* 479.

Asher, S., and Renshaw, P. Children without friends: Social knowledge and social skill training. In S. R. Asher and J. M. Gottman (Eds.), *The development of children's friendships.* New York: Cambridge University Press, 1981.

Ashmead, D. H., and Perlmutter, M. Infant memory in everday life. In. M. Perlmutter (Ed.), *New directions in child development, children's memory.* San Francisco: Jossey-Bass, 1980.

Aslin, R. N. Experiential influences and sensitive periods in perceptual development: A unified model. In R. N. Aslin, J. R. Alberts, and M. R. Petersen (Eds.), *Development of perception: Psychobiological perspectives,* Volume 2, *The visual system.* New York: Academic Press, 1981.

Atkinson, R. C., and Shiffrin, R. M. Human memory: A proposed system and its control processes. In K. W. Spence and J. T. Spence (Eds.), *Advances in the psychology of learning and motivation,* Volume 2. New York: Academic Press, 1968.

Axelrod, J. Neurotransmitters. *Scientific American,* 1974, June, *230,* 59–71.

Babad, Y. E., Alexander, I. E., and Babad, E. Y. Returning the smile of the stranger: Developmental patterns and socialization factors. *Monographs of the Society for Research in Child Development,* 1983, *48*(5, Serial No. 203).

Babson, S. G., and Benson, R. C. *Management of high-risk pregnancy and intensive care of the neonate.* St. Louis: C. V. Mosby, 1971.

Bach, M. J., and Underwood, B. J. Developmental changes in memory attributes. *Journal of Educational Psychology,* 1970, *61,* 292–296.

Bachman, J. G., and O'Malley, P. M. Self-esteem in young men: A longitudinal analysis of the impact of educational and occupational attainment. *Journal of Personality and Social Psychology,* 1977, *35,* 365–380.

Baer, D. M. Laboratory control of thumbsucking by withdrawal and re-presentation of reinforcement. *Journal of Experimental Analysis of Behavior,* 1962, *5,* 525–528.

Baer, P. E., and Goldfarb, G. E. A developmental study of verbal conditioning in children. *Psychological Reports,* 1962, *10,* 175–181.

Bain, B. Verbal regulation of cognitive processes. A replication of Luria's procedures with bilingual and unilingual infants. *Child Development,* 1976, *47,* 543–546.

Baird, D. The epidemiology of prematurity. *Journal of Pediatrics,* 1964, *65,* 909–924.

Bakan, D. *The duality of human existence.* Chicago: Rand McNally, 1966.

Baker, S. P. Motor vehicle occupant deaths in young children. *Pediatrics,* 1979, *64,* 860–861.

Bakwin, H. Sleep-walking in twins. *Lancet,* 1970, *2,* 446–447.

Bakwin, H. Car-sickness in twins. *Developmental Medicine and Child Neurology,* 1971, *13,* 310–312. (a)

Bakwin, H. Constipation in twins. *American Journal of Diseases of Children,* 1971, *121,* 179–181. (b)

Bakwin, H. Nail-biting in twins. *Developmental Medicine and Child Neurology,* 1971, *13,* 304–307. (c)

Bakwin, H. Enuresis in twins. *American Journal of Diseases of Children,* 1971, *121,* 222–225. (d)

Baldwin, A. L. The effect of home environment on nursery school behavior. *Child Development,* 1949, *20,* 49–61.

Baldwin, A. L., Cole, R. E., and Baldwin, C. P. (Eds.). Parental pathology, family interaction, and the competence of the child in school. *Monographs of the Society for Research in Child Development,* 1982, *47*(5, Serial No. 197).

Baldwin, A. L., Kalhorn, J., and Breese, F. H. Patterns of parent behavior. *Psychological Monographs,* 1945, *58*(3, Whole No. 268).

Bales, R. F. The equilibrium problem in small groups. In T. Parsons, R. Bales, and E. Shils (Eds.), *Working papers on the theory of action.* New York: Free Press, 1953.

Ballou, J. The significance of reconciliative themes in the psychology of pregnancy. *Bulletin of the Menninger Clinic,* 1978, *42,* 383–413.

Baltes, P. B. (Ed.). *Life-span development and behavior,* Volume 1. New York: Academic Press, 1978.

Baltes, P. B., and Schaie, K. W. (Eds.). *Life-span developmental psychology: Personality and socialization.* New York: Academic Press, 1973.

Bandura, A. Social learning through imitation. In M. R. Jones (Ed.), *Nebraska Symposium on Motivation: 1962.* Lincoln: University of Nebraska Press, 1962, 211–269.

Bandura, A. *Principles of behavior modification.* New York: Holt, Rinehart & Winston, 1969. (a)

Bandura, A. Social-learning theory of identificatory process. In D. A. Goslin (Ed.), *Handbook of socialization theory and research.* Chicago: Rand McNally, 1969. (b)

Bandura, A. *Social learning theory.* Englewood Cliffs, N.J.: Prentice-Hall, 1977.

Bandura, A., Grusec, J. E., and Menlove, F. L. Vicarious extinction of avoidance behavior. *Journal of Personality and Social Psychology,* 1967, *5,* 16–23.

Bandura, A., and Huston, A. C. Identification as a process of incidental learning. *Journal of Abnormal and Social Psychology,* 1961, *63,* 311–318.

Bandura, A., Ross, D. M., and Ross, S. A. Transmission of aggression through imitation of aggressive models. *Journal of Abnormal and Social Psychology,* 1961, *63,* 575–582.

Bandura, A., Ross, D. M., and Ross, S. A. Imitation of film-mediated aggressive models. *Journal of Abnormal and Social Psychology,* 1963, *66,* 3–11.

Bandura, A., and Walters, R. H. *Social learning and personality development.* New York: Holt, Rinehart & Winston, 1963.

Bane, M. J., and Jencks, C. Five myths about your I.Q. *Harper's Magazine,* February 1973, 28–40.

Bank, S., and Kahn, M. D. Sisterhood-brotherhood is powerful: Sibling subsystems and family therapy. *Family Process,* 1975, *14,* 311–337.

Banks, M. S., and Salapatek, P. Infant pattern vision: A new approach based on the contrast sensitivity function. *Journal of Experimental Child Psychology,* 1981, *31,* 1–45.

Banks, M. S., and Salapatek, P. Infant visual perception. In P. H. Mussen (Ed.), *Handbook of Child Psychology,* Volume 2. New York: Wiley, 1983.

Barash, D. P. *Sociobiology and behavior.* New York: Elsevier, 1977.

Bardwick, J. M. *Psychology of women: A study of biocultural conflicts.* New York: Harper & Row, 1971.

Bardwick, J. M., and Douvan, E. Ambivalence: The socialization of women. In V. Gornick and B. K. Moran (Eds.), *Women in sexist society.* New York: Basic Books, 1971.

Barenboim, C. Developmental changes in the interpersonal cognitive system from middle childhood to adolescence. *Child Development,* 1977, *48,* 1467–1474.

Barenboim, C. The development of person perception in childhood and adolescence: From behavioral comparisons to psychological constructs to psychological comparisons. *Child Development,* 1981, *52,* 129–144.

Barnet, A. B., Lodge, A., and Armington, J. C. Electroretinogram in newborn human infants. *Science,* 1965, *148,* 651–654.

Barnett, M. A., Howard, J. A., Melton, E. M., and Dino, G. A. Effect of inducing sadness about self or other on helping behavior in high- and low-empathic children. *Child Development,* 1982, *53,* 920–923.

Barnett, M. A., King, L. M., and Howard, J. A. Inducing affect about self or other: Effects on generosity in children. *Developmental Psychology,* 1979, *15,* 164–167.

Barnett, R. C. Parental child-rearing values: Today and yesterday. Paper presented at the annual meeting of the Eastern Psychological Association, Washington, D.C., 1978.

Barrera, M. E., and Mauer, D. *The perception of facial expressions by the three-month-old.* Paper presented at the biennial meeting of the Society for Research in Child Development, San Francisco, March 1979.

Barrett, D. E., and Radke-Yarrow, M. Prosocial behavior, social inferential ability, and assertiveness in children. *Child Development,* 1977, *48,* 475–481.

Barry, H., Bacon, M. K., and Child, I. L. A cross-cultural survey of some sex differences in socialization. *Journal of Abnormal and Social Psychology,* 1975, *55,* 327–332.

Barry, H., and Paxson, L. M. Infancy and early childhood: Cross-cultural codes. *Ethnology,* 1971, *10,* 467–508.

Bartlett, E. S., and Izard, C. E. A dimensional and discrete emotions investigation of the subjective experience of emotion. In C. E. Izard (Ed.), *Patterns of emotions: A new analysis of anxiety and depression.* New York: Academic Press, 1972.

Bartlett, J. C., and Santrock, J. W. Affect-dependent episodic memory in young children. *Child Development,* 1979, *50,* 513–518.

Baskett, L. M., and Johnson, S. M. The young child's interactions with parents versus siblings: A behavioral analysis. *Child Development,* 1982, *53,* 649–650.

Bates, E. *Language and context: The acquisition of pragmatics.* New York: Academic Press, 1976.

Bates, J. E. Detailed progress report on "Difficult infants and their mothers." Unpublished report, Indiana University, 1980. (a)

Bates, J. E. The concept of difficult temperament. *Merrill-Palmer Quarterly,* 1980, *25,* 299–319. (b)

Battle, E. S., and Lacey, B. A. A context for hyperactivity in children. *Child Development,* 1972, *43,* 757–773.

Bauer, D. H. An exploratory study of developmental changes in children's fears. *Journal of Child Psychology and Psychiatry,* 1976, *17,* 69–74.

Baumrind, D. Current patterns of parental authority. *Developmental Psychology Monographs,* 1971, 4(1, Part 2).

Baumrind, D. Early socialization and adolescent competence. In S. E. Dragastin and G. H. Elder (Eds.), *Adolescence in the life cycle.* New York: Wiley, 1975.

Baumrind, D. Sex related socialization effects. Paper presented at the biennial meeting of the Society for Research in Child Development, San Francisco, March 1979.

Baumrind, D., and Black, A. E. Socialization practices associated with dimensions of competence in preschool boys and girls. *Child Development,* 1967, *38,* 291–327.

Bayer, L. M., and Bayley, N. *Growth diagnosis* (2nd ed.). Chicago: University of Chicago Press, 1976. (First edition 1959).

Bayley, N. *The California First Year Mental Scale.* Berkeley: University of California Press, 1933. (a)

Bayley, N. Mental growth during the first three years: A developmental study of 61 children by repeated tests. *Genetic Psychology Monographs,* 1933, *14,* 1–92. (b)

Bayley, N. Learning in adulthood: The role of intelligence. In H. J. Klausmeier and C. W. Harris (Eds.), *Analysis of concept learning.* New York: Academic Press, 1966. (a)

Bayley, N. Developmental problems of the mentally retarded child. In I. Phillips (Ed.), *Prevention and treatment of mental retardation.* New York: Basic Books, 1966. (b)

Bayley, N. Behavioral correlates of mental growth: Birth to thirty-six years. *American Psychologist,* 1968, *23,* 1–17.

Bayley, N. *Bayley Scales of Infant Development.* New York: Psychological Corporation, 1969.

Bayley, N. The development of motor abilities during the first three years. In M. C. Jones, N. Bayley, J. W. McFarlane, and M. P. Honzik (Eds.), *The course of human development.* Waltham, Mass.: Xerox College Publishing, 1971. (a)

Bayley, N. Some increasing parent-child similarities during the growth of children. In M. C. Jones, N. Bayley, J. W. McFarlane, and M. P. Honzik (Eds.), *The course of human development.* Waltham, Mass: Xerox College Publishing, 1971. (b)

Becker, M. H. The health belief model and sick role behavior. In M. H. Becker (Ed.), *The health belief model and personal health behavior.* Thorofare, N.J.: Charles B. Slack, 1974.

Becker, M. H., Drachman, R. H., and Kirscht, J. P. Predicting mothers' compliance with pediatric medical regimens. *Journal of Pediatrics,* 1972, *81,* 843–854.

Becker, M. H., Nathanson, C. A., Drachman, R. H., and Kirscht, J. P. Mothers' health beliefs and children's clinic visits: A prospective study. *Journal of Community Health,* 1977, *3,* 125–135.

Becker, W. C. Consequences of different kinds of parental discipline. In M. L. Hoffman and L. W. Hoffman (Eds.), *Review of child development research,* Volume 1. New York: Russell Sage Foundation, 1964.

Beckwith, L. Relationships between infants' social behavior and their mothers' behavior. *Child Development,* 1972, *43,* 397–411.

Beckwith, L. Prediction of emotional and social behavior. In J. D. Osofsky (Ed.), *Handbook of infant development.* New York: Wiley, 1979.

Beckwith, L., and Cohen, S. E. Home environment and cognitive competence in preterm children during the first 5 years. In A. W. Gottfried (Ed.), *Home environment and early cognitive development.* San Francisco: Academic Press, 1984.

Bell, A., Weinberg, M., and Hammersmith, S. K. *Sexual preference.* Indianapolis: Indiana University Press (Alfred C. Kinsey Institute for Sex Research Publication), 1981.

Bell, R. Q. Research strategies. In R. Q. Bell and L. V. Harper (Eds.), *Child effects on adults.* Hillsdale, N.J.: Lawrence Erlbaum Associates, 1977.

Bell, R. Q., and Harper, L. V. *Child effects on adults.* Hillsdale, N.J.: Lawrence Erlbaum Associates, 1977.

Bell, S. M., and Ainsworth, M. D. S., Infant crying and maternal responsiveness. *Child Development,* 1972, *43,* 1171–1190.

Belsky, J., Goode, M. K., and Most, R. K. Maternal stimulation and infant exploratory competence: Cross-sectional, correlational and experimental analyses. *Child Development,* 1980, *51,* 1168–1178.

Bem, S. L. The measurement of psychological androgyny. *Journal of Consulting and Clinical Psychology,* 1974, *42,* 155–162.

Bem, S. L., Martyne, W., and Watson, C. Sex typing and androgyny: Further explorations of the expressive domain. *Journal of Personality and Social Psychology,* 1976, *34,* 1016–1023.

Benedict, R. *Patterns of culture.* Boston: Houghton Mifflin, 1934.

Benjamin, J. The innate and the experiential in development. In H. Brosin (Ed.), *Lectures on experimental psychiatry.* Pittsburgh: University of Pittsburgh Press, 1961.

Bennett, N. *Teaching styles and pupil progress.* London: Open Books, 1976.

Bennett, W., and Gurin, J. *The dieter's dilemma: Eating less and weighing more.* New York: Basic Books, 1982.

Bentler, P. M., and McClain, J. A multitrait-multimethod analysis of reflection-impulsivity. *Child Development,* 1976, *47,* 218–226.

Bentzen, F. Sex ratios in learning and behavior disorders. *American Journal of Orthopsychiatry,* 1963, *33,* 92–98.

Ben-Zeev, S. The influence of bilingualism on cognitive strategy and cognitive development. *Child Development,* 1977, *48,* 1009–1018.

Bereiter, C., and Engelmann, S. *Teaching disadvantaged children in the preschool.* Englewood Cliffs, N.J.: Prentice-Hall, 1966.

Berenda, R. W. *The influence of the group on the judgments of children.* New York: King's Crown Press, 1950.

Bergman, P., and Escalona, S. Unusual sensitivities in very young children. In P. Greenacre (Ed.), *The psychoanalytic study of the child,* Volume 314. New York: International Universities Press, 1949.

Bergman, T., Haith, M., and Mann, L. Development of eye contact and facial scanning in infants. Paper presented at the meeting of the Society for Research in Child Development, Minneapolis, March 1971.

Berlin, B., and Kay, P. *Basic color terms: Their universality and evolution.* Berkeley: University of California Press, 1969.

Berlyne, D. E. Laughter, humor and play. In G. Lindzey and E. Aronson (Eds.), *Handbook of social psychology,* Volume 3. Boston: Addison-Wesley, 1969.

Berman, J. L., and Ford, R. Intelligence quotients and intelligence loss in patients with phenylketonuria and some variant states. *Journal of Pediatrics,* 1970, *77,* 764–770.

Bernal, J. Crying during the first 10 days of life and maternal responses. *Developmental Medicine and Child Neurology,* 1972, *14,* 362–372.

Bernal, J., and Richards, M. P. M. The effects of bottle and breast feeding on infant development. Paper presented at the annual conference of the Society for Psychosomatic Research, London, November 1969.

Bernard, S., and Sontag, L. W. Fetal reactivity to tonal stimulation: A preliminary report. *Journal of Genetic Psychology,* 1947, *70,* 205–210.

Berndt, T. J. Children's conceptions of friendship and the behavior expected of friends. Paper presented at the annual meeting of the American Psychological Association, Toronto, August 1978. (a)

Berndt, T. J. Developmental changes on conformity to parents and peers. Paper presented at the annual meeting of the American Psychological Association, Toronto, August 1978. (b)

Berndt, T. J. The features and effects of friendship in early adolescence. *Child Development,* 1982, *53,* 1447–1460.

Berndt, T. J. Correlates and causes of sociometric status in childhood: A commentary on six current studies of popular, rejected, and neglected children. *Merrill-Palmer Quarterly,* 1983, *29,* 439–448.

Berndt, T. J., and Berndt, E. G. Children's use of motives and intentionality in person perception and moral judgment. *Child Development,* 1975, *46,* 904–912.

Bernstein, B. Elaborated and restricted codes: Their social origins and some consequences. In A. G. Smith (Ed.), *Communication and culture.* New York: Holt, Rinehart & Winston, 1966.

Bernstein, R. M. The development of self-system during adolescence. *Journal of Genetic Psychology,* 1980, *136,* 231–245.

Berry, M. Development of the cerebral neocortex of the rat. In G. Gottlieb (Ed.), *Studies on the development of behavior and nervous system: Aspects of neurogenesis,* Volume 2. New York: Academic Press, 1974.

Berscheid, E., Walster, E., and Bohrnstedt, G. Body image: The happy American body. *Psychology Today,* 1973, November, 119–131.

Bertenthal, B. I., and Fischer, K. W. Development of self-recognition in the infant. *Developmental Psychology,* 1978, *14,* 44–50.

Bertoncini, J., and Mehler, J. Syllables as units in infant speech perception. *Infant Behavior and Development,* 1981, *4,* 247–260.

Best, D. L., Williams, J. E., Cloud, J. M., Davis, S. W., Robertson, L. S., Edwards, J. R., Giles, H., and Fowles, J. Development of sex-trait stereotypes among young children in the United States, England, and Ireland. *Child Development,* 1977, *48,* 1375–1384.

Bhatia, V. P., Katiyar, G. P., and Agarwal, K. N. Effect of intrauterine nutritional deprivation on neuromotor behavior of the newborn. *Acta Paediatrica Scandinavica,* 1979, *68,* 561–566.

Bibring, G. L., Dwyer, T. F., Huntington, D. S., and Valenstein, A. F. A Study of the psychological processes in pregnancy and of the earliest mother-child relationship. *Psychoanalytic Study of the Child,* 1961, *16,* 9–24.

Bierman, J. M., Connor, A., Vaage, M., and Honzik, M. P. Pediatricians' assessments of the intelligence of two-year-olds and their mental test scores. *Pediatrics,* 1964, *34,* 680.

Biller, H. B. The father and personality development: Paternal deprivation and sex-role development. In M. E. Lamb (Ed.), *The role of the father in child development.* New York: Wiley, 1976.

Biller, H. B., and Bahm, R. M. Father absence, perceived maternal behaviors, and masculinity of self-concept among junior high school boys. *Developmental Psychology,* 1971, *4,* 178–181.

Binet, A., and Simon, T., *The intelligence of the feeble-minded* (Trans. E. S. Kite). Baltimore: Williams & Wilkins, 1916.

Birchler, G. R., Weiss, R. L., and Vincent, J. P. Multimethod analysis of social reinforcement exchange between maritally distressed and nondistressed spouse and stranger dyads. *Journal of Personality and Social Psychology,* 1975, *31,* 349–360.

Birnbaum, J. A. Life patterns, personality style and self esteem in gifted family oriented and career committed women. Unpublished doctoral dissertation, University of Michigan, 1971.

Birren, J. E., and Klaus, F. Riegel: Man, scholar and scientist. *Human Development,* 1978, *21,* 348–351.

Bixenstine, V. E., De Corte, M. S., and Bixenstine, B. A. Conformity to peer-sponsored misconduct at four age levels. *Developmental Psychology,* 1976, *12,* 226–236.

Bizman, A., Yinon, Y., Mivtzari, E., and Shavit, R. Effects of the age structure of the kindergarten on altruistic behavior. *Journal of School Psychology,* 1978, 16, 154–160.

Bjork, E. L., and Cummings, E. M. The "A, not B" search error in Piaget's theory of object permanence: Fact or artifact? Paper presented at the meeting of the Psychonomic Society, Phoenix, November 1979.

Bjorksten, J. The limitation of creative years. *Scientific Monthly,* 1946, *62,* 94.

Black, J., and Wilensky, R. An evaluation of story grammars. *Cognitive Science,* 1979, *3,* 213–230.

Blackstock, E. G. Cerebral asymmetry and the development of infantile autism. *Journal of Autism and Childhood Schizophrenia,* 1978, *8,* 339–353.

Block, J., Block, J. H., and Harrington, D. M. Some misgivings about the matching familiar figures test as a measure of reflection-impulsivity. *Developmental Psychology,* 1974, *10,* 611–632.

Block, J. H. Conceptions of sex role: Some cross-cultural and longitudinal perspectives. *American Psychologist,* 1973, *28,* 512–529.

Block, J. H. Issues, problems, and pitfalls in assessing sex differences: A critical review of *The psychology of sex differences. Merrill–Palmer Quarterly,* 1976, *22,* 283–308.

Block, J. H. Differential premises arising from differential socialization of the sexes: Some conjectures. *Child Development,* 1983, *54,* 1335–1354.

Block, J. H. Personality development in males and females: The influence of differential socialization. *Child Development,* in press.

Bloom, L. *Language development: Form and function in emerging grammars.* Cambridge; MIT Press, 1970.

Bloom, L., Hood, L., and Lightbown, P. Imitation in language development: If, when, and why. *Cognitive Psychology,* 1974, *6,* 380–428.

Blos, P. *The young adolescent: Clinical studies.* New York: Free Press, 1974.

Blurton Jones, N. Categories of child-child interaction. In N. Blurton Jones (Ed.), *Ethological studies of child behavior.* Cambridge: Cambridge University Press, 1972.

Boccia, M., and Campos, J. Maternal emotional signalling: Its effect on infants' reaction to strangers. Paper presented at the meeting of the Society for Research in Child Development, Detroit, April 1983.

Bogatz, G. A., and Ball, S. *The second year of Sesame Street: A continuing evaluation.* Princeton, N.J.: Educational Testing Service, 1971.

Bohannon, J. N., III, and Marquis, A. L. Children's control of adult speech. *Child Development,* 1977, *48,* 1002–1008.

Boles, D. B. X-linkage of spatial ability: A critical review. *Child Development,* 1980, *51,* 625–635.

Borke, H. Interpersonal perception of young children: Egocentrism or empathy? *Development Psychology,* 1971, *5,* 263–269.

Borke, H. Piaget's mountains revisited: Changes in the egocentric landscape. *Developmental Psychology,* 1975, *11,* 240–243.

Bornstein, M. H. Qualities of color vision in infancy. *Journal of Experimental Child Psychology,* 1975, *19,* 401–419.

Bornstein, M. H. Infant's recognition memory for hue. *Developmental Psychology,* 1976, *12,* 185–191.

Boskind-Lodahl, M. Cinderella's stepsisters: A feminist perspective on anorexia nervosa and bulimia. *Signs,* 1976, *2,* 315–320.

Bower, G. Mood and memory. *American Psychologist,* 1981, *36,* 128–148.

Bower, T. G. R. The visual world of infants. *Scientific American,* 1966, *215,* 80–92.

Bower, T. G. R. The object in the world of the infant. *Scientific American,* 1971, *225,* 30–38.

Bower, T. G. R. Object perception in infants. *Perception,* 1972, *1,* 15–30.

Bower, T. G. R., Broughton, J. M., and Moore, M. K. Infant responses to approaching objects: An indicator of response to distal variables. *Perception and Psychophysics,* 1970, *9,* 193–196.

Bower, T. G. R., and Wishart, J. G. The effects of motor skill on object permanence. *Cognition,* 1972, *1,* 165–172.

Bowerman, C. E., and Kinch, J. W. Changes in family and peer orientation of children between the fourth and tenth grades. *Social Forces, 1956, 37,* 206–211.

Bowlby, J. *Maternal care and mental health.* World Health Organization Monograph 2. Geneva: World Health Organization, 1951.

Bowlby, J. *Attachment and loss,* Volume 1, *Attachment.* New York: Basic Books, 1969.

Bowlby, J. *Attachment and loss,* Volume 2, *Separation.* New York: Basic Books, 1973.

Brackbill, Y. Extinction of the smiling reponse in infants as a function of reinforcement schedule. *Child Development,* 1958, *29,* 115–124.

Brackbill Y. Long-term effects of obstetrical anesthesia on infant autonomic function. *Developmental Psychobiology,* 1977, *10,* 529–535.

Brackbill, Y. Obstetrical medication and infant behavior. In J. D. Osofsky (Ed.), *Handbook of infant development.* New York: Wiley, 1979.

Brackbill, Y., and Nichols, P. L. A test of the confluence model of intellectual development. *Developmental Psychology,* 1982, *18,* 192–198.

Bradley, R. H., and Caldwell, B. M. 174 Children: A study of the relationship between home environment and cognitive development during the first 5 years. In A. W. Gottfried (Ed.), *Home environment and early cognitive development.* San Francisco: Academic Press, 1984.

Bradley, R. H., Caldwell, B. M., and Elardo, R. Home environment, social status, and mental test performance. *Journal of Educational Psychology,* 1977, *69,* 697–701.

Braine, M. D. S., Heimer, C. B., Wortis, H., and Freedman, A. M. Factors associated with impairment of the early development of prematures. *Monographs of the Society for Research in Child Development,* 1966, *31*(4, Serial No. 106).

Braine, M. D. S., and Rumain, B. Logical Reasoning. In P. H. Mussen (Ed.), *Handbook of child psychology,* Volume. 3. New York: Wiley, 1983.

Brainerd, C. J. *Piaget's theory of intelligence.* Englewood Cliffs, N.J.: Prentice-Hall, 1978.

Bransford, J. D., and McCarrell, N. S. A sketch of a cognitive approach to comprehension: Some thoughts about what it means to comprehend. In W. B. Weimer and D. S. Palermo (Eds.), *Cognition and symbolic processes.* Hillsdale, N.J.: Lawrence Erlbaum Associates, 1974.

Bransford, J. D., Stein, B. S., Shelton, T. S., and Owings, R. A. Cognition and adaptation: The importance of learning to learn. In J. Harvey (Ed.), *Cognition, social behavior, and the environment.* Hillsdale, N.J.: Lawrence Erlbaum Associates, 1981.

Brask, B. H. The need for hospital beds for psychotic children. *Ugesberift for Laeger,* 1967, *129,* 1559–1570.

Brazelton, T. B. Psychophysiologic reactions in the neonate: II. Effects of maternal medication on the neonate and his behavior. *Journal of Pediatrics,* 1961, *58,* 513–518.

Brazelton, T. B. *Infants and mothers.* New York: Delacorte Press/Seymour Lawrence, 1969.

Brazelton, T. B., Tronick, E., Adamson, L., Als, H., and Wise, S. Early mother-infant reciprocity. In *Parent-infant interaction.* Ciba Foundation Symposium 33. Amsterdam: Associated Scientific Publishers, 1975.

Breland, H. M. Birth order, family configuration and verbal achievement. *Research Bulletin.* Princeton, N.J.: Educational Testing Service, 1972.

Brennan, W. M., Ames, E. W., and Moore, R. W. Age differences in infants' attention to patterns of different complexities. *Science,* 1965, *151,* 1354–1356.

Brent, L. Radiations and other physical agents. In J. G. Wilson and F. C. Fraser (Eds.), *Handbook of teratology.* New York: Plenum, 1977.

Bresnan, J. A realistic transformational grammar. In M. Halle, J. Bresnan, and G. A. Miller (Eds.), *Linguistic theory and psychological reality.* Cambridge: MIT Press, 1978.

Bresnan, J. The passive in lexical-functional grammar. In J. Bresnan (Ed.), *The mental representation of grammatical relations.* Cambridge: MIT Press, 1982.

Bretherton, I. Making friends with one-year-olds: An experimental study of infant-stranger interaction. *Merrill-Palmer Quarterly,* 1978, *24,* 29–52.

Bridges, K. M. B. *The social and emotional development of the pre-school child.* London: Routledge, 1931.

Briggs, J. L. *Never in anger.* Cambridge: Harvard University Press, 1970.

Brittain, C. Adolescent choices and parent-peer cross-pressures. *American Sociological Review,* 1963, *28,* 385–391.

Brittain, C. Age and sex of siblings and conformity toward parents versus peers in adolescence. *Child Development,* 1966, *37,* 709–714.

Broadbent, D. E. *Perception and communication.* London: Pergamon Press, 1958.

Brody, E. B., and Brody, N. *Intelligence: Nature, determinants and consequences.* New York: Academic Press, 1976.

Brody, J. E. TV violence cited as bad influence. *New York Times,* December 7, 1975, p. 20.

Brody, J. E. Therapy helps teen-age girls having anorexia nervosa. *New York Times,* July 14, 1982, Section 4, p. 20.

Brody, J. E. Heart attacks and behavior: Early signs are found. *New York Times,* February 14, 1984, Section C, p. 1.

Brodzinsky, D. M. The role of conceptual tempo and stimulus characteristics in children's humor development. *Developmental Psychology,* 1975, *2,* 843–850.

Broman, S. H., Nichols, P. L., and Kennedy, W. A. *Preschool IQ: Prenatal and early developmental correlates.* Hillsdale, N.J.: Lawrence Erlbaum Associates, 1975.

Bronfenbrenner, U. *Two worlds of childhood: U.S. and U.S.S.R.* New York: Russell Sage Foundation, 1970.

Bronfenbrenner, U. Toward an experimental ecology of human development. *American Psychologist,* 1977, *32,* 513–531.

Bronfenbrenner, U., Alvarez, W. F., and Henderson, C. R., Jr. Working and watching: Maternal employment status and parents' perceptions of their three-year old children. Unpublished manuscript, Cornell University, 1983.

Bronfenbrenner, U., and Crouter, A. C. Work and family through time and space. In S. Kamerman and C. D. Hayes (Eds.), *Families that work: Children in a changing world.* Washington, D.C.: National Academy Press, 1982.

Bronson, G. W. Infants' reactions to unfamiliar persons and novel objects. *Monographs of the Society for Research in Child Development,* 1972, *37*(3, Serial No. 148).

Bronson, G. W. Aversive reactions to strangers: A dual process interpretation. *Child Development,* 1978, *49,* 495–499.

Bronson, W. C. Mother-toddler interaction: A perspective on studying the development of competence. *Merrill-Palmer Quarterly,* 1974, *20,* 275–301.

Bronson, W. C. Developments in behavior with age-mates during the second year of life. In M. Lewis and L. A. Rosenblum (Eds.), *Friendship and peer relations:* New York: Wiley-Interscience, 1975.

Brookhart, J., and Hock, E. The effects of experimental context and experiential background on infants' behavior toward their mothers and a stranger. *Child Development,* 1976, *47,* 333–340.

Brooks, J., and Lewis, M. Infants' responses to strangers: Midget, adult, and child. *Child Development,* 1976, *47,* 323–332.

Brophy, J. E., and Evertson, C. M. Process-product correlations in the Texas Teacher Effectiveness Study: Final report (Research Report 74–4). Austin, Tex.: Research and Development Center for Teacher Education, 1974.

Brophy, J. E., and Evertson, C. M. *Learning from teaching: A developmental perspective*. Boston: Allyn & Bacon, 1976.

Brophy, J. E., and Good, T. L. *Teacher-student relationships: Causes and consequences*. New York: Holt, Rinehart & Winston, 1974.

Brossard, M., and Decarie, T. The effects of 3 kinds of perceptual-social stimulation on the development of institutionalized infants. *Early Child Development and Care*, 1971, *1*, 111–130.

Broughton, J. Development of concepts of self, mind, reality, and knowledge. *New Directions for Child Development*, 1978, *1*, 75–100.

Broughton, R. Sleep disorders: Disorders of arousal. *Science*, 1968, *159*, 1070–1078.

Broughton, R., and Gaustaut, H. Recent sleep research in enuresis nocturia, sleep walking, sleep terrors, and confusional arousals. In P. Levin and W. Loella (Eds.), *Sleep 1974*. Basel: Karger, 1975.

Brown, A. L. Knowing when, where, and how to remember: A problem of metacognition. In R. Glaser (Ed.), *Advances in instructional psychology*, Volume 1. Hillsdale, N.J.: Lawrence Erlbaum Associates, 1978.

Brown, A. L., Bransford, J. D., Ferrara, R. A., and Campione, J. C. Learning, remembering, and understanding. In P. H. Mussen (Ed.), *Handbook of Child Psychology*, Volume 3. New York: Wiley, 1983.

Brown, A. L., and Day, J. D. Macrorules for summarizing texts: The development of expertise. *Journal of Verbal Learning and Verbal Behavior*, in press.

Brown, A. L., and Smiley, S. S. Rating the importance of structural units of prose passages: A problem of metacognitive development. *Child Development*, 1977, *48*, 1–8.

Brown, A. L., Smiley, S. S., Day, J. D., Townsend, M. A., and Lawton, S. C. Intrusion of a thematic idea in children's comprehension and retention of stories. *Child Development*, 1977, *48*, 1454–1466.

Brown, E. Personal communication, University of Chicago, 1981.

Brown, H., Adams, R. G., and Kellam, S. G. A longitudinal study of teenage motherhood and symptoms of distress: Woodlawn Community Epidemiological Project. In R. Simmons (Ed.), *Research in community and mental health*, Volume 2, Greenwich, Conn.: JAI Press, 1981.

Brown, J., Bakeman, R., Snyder, P., Fredrickson, W., Morgan, S., and Hepler, R. Interactions of black inner-city mothers with their newborn infants. *Child Development*, 1975, *46*, 677–686.

Brown, R. How shall a thing be called? *Psychological Review*, 1958, *65*, 14–21.

Brown, R. *A first language: The early stages*. Cambridge: Harvard University Press, 1973.

Brown, R., and Hanlon, C. Derivational complexity and order of acquisition in child speech. In J. R. Hayes (Ed.), *Cognition and the development of language*. New York: Wiley, 1970.

Brozek, J. Nutrition, malnutrition, and behavior. In M. R. Rosenzweig and L. W. Porter (Eds.). *Annual Review of Psychology*, 1978, *29*, 157–177.

Brucefors, A., Johannesson, I., Karlberg, P., Klackenberg-Larsson, I., Lichenstein, H., and Svenberg, I. Trends in development of abilities related to somatic growth. *Human Development*, 1974, *17*, 152–159.

Bruch, H. Obesity in adolescence. In H. Caplan and F. Lebovici (Eds.), *Adolescence: Psychosocial perspectives*. New York: Basic Books, 1969.

Bruck, M., and Tucker, G. R. Social class differences in the acquisition of school language. *Merrill-Palmer Quarterly*, 1974, *20*, 205–220.

Bruner, J. S. The course of cognitive growth. *American Psychologist*, 1964, *19*, 1–15.

Bruner, J. S. From communication to language: A psychological perspective. In I. Markova (Ed.), *The social context of language*. New York: Wiley, 1978.

Bruner, J. S., and Kenney, H. The development of the concepts of order and proportion in children. In J. S. Bruner, R. R. Olver, and P. M. Greenfield (Eds.), *Studies in cognitive growth*. New York: Wiley, 1966.

Bryan, J. H. Children's cooperation and helping behaviors. In E. M. Hetherington (Ed.), *Review of child development research*, Volume 5. Chicago: University of Chicago Press, 1975.

Bryan, J. H., and Luria, Z. Sex-role learning: A test of the selective attention hypothesis. *Child Development*, 1978, *49*, 13–23.

Bryant, B. K. Locus of control related to teacher-child interperceptual experiences. *Child Development*, 1974, *45*, 157–164.

Bryant, B. K. Siblings as caretakers. Paper presented at the annual meeting of the American Psychological Association. New York, September 1979.

Bryant, B. K. Sibling relationships in middle childhood. In M. Lamb and B. Sutton-Smith (Eds.), *Sibling relationships: Their nature and significance across the lifespan*. Hillsdale, N.J.: Lawrence Erlbaum Associates, 1982.

Buckhalt, J. A., Mahoney, G. J., and Paris, S. C. Efficiency at self-generated elaborations by EMR and nonretarded children. *American Journal of Mental Deficiency*, 1976, *81*, 93–96.

Bucky, S. F., and Banta, T. J. Racial factors in test performance. *Developmental Psychology*, 1972, *6*, 7–13.

Bugental, D., Kaswan, J. W., and Love, L. R. Perception of contradictory meanings conveyed by verbal and nonverbal channels. *Journal of Personality and Social Psychology*, 1970, *16*, 647–655.

Bugenthal, D. B., and Shennum, W. A. Adult attributions as moderators of the effects of shy vs. assertive children. Paper presented at the meeting of the Society for Research in Child Development, Boston, April 1981.

Bühler, C. The social behavior of children. In C. A. Murchison (Ed.), *A handbook of child psychology*. New York: Russell & Russell, 1933.

Bühler, C. *The child and his family*. London: Harper & Bros., 1939.

Bullough, V. L. Age at menarche: A misunderstanding. *Science*, 1981, *213*, 365–366.

Burns, N., and Cavey, L. Age differences in empathic ability among children. *Canadian Journal of Psychology*, 1957, *11*, 227–230.

Burton, R. V. Generality of honesty reconsidered. *Psychological Review*, 1963, *70*, 481–499.

Burton, R. V. Honesty and dishonesty. In T. Lickona (Ed.), *Moral development and behavior: Theory, research and social issues*. New York: Holt, Rinehart & Winston, 1976.

Burton, W. *Helps to Education*. Boston: Crosby and Nichols, 1863.

Buss, A. H., and Plomin, R. *A temperament theory of personality development*. New York: Wiley, 1975.

Buss, A. H., Plomin, R., and Willerman, L. The inheritance of temperaments. *Journal of Personality,* 1973, *41,* 513–524.

Buss, D. M. Predicting parent-child interactions from children's activity level. *Developmental Psychology,* 1981, *17,* 59–65.

Buss, R. R., Yussen, S. R., Mathews, S. R., II, Miller, G. E., and Rembold, K. L. Development of children's use of a story schema to retrieve information. *Developmental Psychology,* 1983, *19,* 22–28.

Buster, J. E., Bustillo, M., Thorneycroft, I. H., Simon, J. A., Boyers, S. P., Marshall, J. R., Louw, J. A., Seed, R. W., and Seed, R. G. Nonsurgical transfer of in vivo fertilized donated ova to five infertile women: Report of two pregnancies. *Lancet,* 1983, *2,* 223–224.

Butler, N. R., and Goldstein, H. Smoking in pregnancy and subsequent child development. *British Medical Journal,* 1973, *4,* 573–575.

Butler, N. R., Goldstein, H., and Ross, E. M. Cigarette smoking in pregnancy: Its influence on birth weight and perinatal mortality. *British Medical Journal,* 1972, *2,* 127–130.

Butterfield, E. C., and Belmont, J. M. Assessing and improving the executive cognitive functions of mentally retarded people. In I. Bialer and M. Sternlicht (Eds.), *Psychological issues in mentally retarded people.* Chicago: Aldine, 1977.

Caldwell, B. M. The rationale for early intervention. *Exceptional Children,* 1970, *36,* 717–726.

Caldwell, B. M. Infant daycare—the outcast gains respectability. In P. Robey (Ed.), *Child care—who cares?: Foreign and domestic infant and early child development policies.* New York: Basic Books, 1973.

Caldwell, B. M., Hersher, L., Lipton, E. L., Richmond, J. B., Stern, G. A., Eddy, E., Drachman, R., and Rothman, A. Mother-infant interaction in monomatric and polymatric families. *American Journal of Orthopsychiatry,* 1963, *33,* 653–664.

Caldwell, B. M., Wright, B., Honig, A., and Tannenbaum, G. Infant day care and attachment. *American Journal of Orthopsychiatry,* 1970, *40,* 397–412.

Caldwell, M. A., and Peplau, L. A. Sex differences in same-sex friendship. *Sex Roles,* 1982, *8,* 721–732.

Calsyn, R. J., and Kenny, D. A. Self-concept of ability and perceived evaluation of others: Cause or effect of academic achievements? *Journal of Educational Psychology,* 1977, *69,* 136–145.

Campbell, A. The American way of mating. *Psychology Today,* 1975, 37–43.

Campbell, S. B. Cognitive styles in reflective, impulsive and hyperactive boys and their mothers. *Perceptual and Motor Skills,* 1973, *36,* 747–775.

Campbell, S. B., and Paulaukas, S. Peer relations in hyperactive children. *Journal of Child Psychology and Psychiatry,* 1979, *20,* 233–246.

Campos, J. J., Barrett, K. C., Lamb, M. E., Goldsmith, H. H., and Stenberg, C. Socioemotional development. In P. H. Mussen (Ed.), *Handbook of child psychology,* Volume 2. New York: Wiley, 1983.

Campos, J., Emde, R., Gaensbauer, T., and Sorce, J. Cardiac and behavioral responses in human infants to strangers: Effects of mother's absence and of experimental sequence. *Developmental psychology,* 1973, *11,* 589–601.

Campos, J. J., Hiatt, S., Ramsay, D., Henderson, C., and Svejda, M. The emergence of fear on the visual cliff. In M. Lewis and L. A. Rosenblum (Eds.), *The development of affect.* New York: Plenum, 1978.

Campos, J. J., Langer, A., and Krowitz, A. Cardiac responses on the visual cliff in prelocomotor human infants. *Science,* 1970, *170,* 196–197.

Campos, J. J., and Stenberg, C. R. Perception, appraisal and emotion: The onset of social referencing. In M. E. Lamb and L. R. Sherrod (Eds.), *Infant social cognition.* Hillsdale, N.J.: Lawrence Erlbaum Associates, 1981.

Camras, L. A. Facial expressions used by children in a conflict situation. *Child Development,* 1977, *48,* 1431–1435.

Canning, H., and Mayer, J., Obesity: Its possible effect on college acceptance. *New England Journal of Medicine,* 1966, *275,* 1172–1174.

Card, J., and Wise, L. Teenage mothers and teenage fathers: The impact of early childbearing on the parents' personal and professional lives. *Family Planning Perspectives,* 1978, *10.*

Carew, J. Experience and the development of intelligence in young children. *Monographs of the Society for Research in Child Development,* 1980, *45*(1–2, Serial No. 183).

Carey, W. B. Some pitfalls in infant temperament research. *Infant Behavior and Development,* 1983, *6,* 247–254.

Carlson, R. Sex differences in ego functioning. *Journal of Consulting and Clinical Psychology,* 1971, *37,* 267–277.

Carmichael, L. Manual of Child Psychology (2nd ed.). New York: Wiley, 1954.

Carnegie Commission on Higher Education. *Opportunties for women in higher education.* New York: McGraw-Hill, 1973.

Caron, A., Caron, R., Caldwell, R., and Weiss, S. Infant perception of the structural properties of the face. *Developmental Psychology,* 1973, *9,* 385–399.

Caron, A. J., Caron, R. F., and Carlson, V. R. Infant perception of the invariant shape of an object varying in slant. *Child Development,* 1979, *50,* 716–721.

Carr, S. J., Dabbs, J. M., Jr., and Carr, T. S. Mother-infant attachment: The importance of the mother's visual field. *Child Development,* 1975, *46,* 331–338.

Carter, G. L., and Kinsbourne, M. The ontogeny of right cerebral lateralization of spatial mental set. *Developmental Psychology,* 1979, *15,* 241–245.

Case, R. Structures and strictures: Some functional limitations on the course of cognitive growth. *Cognitive Psychology,* 1974, *6,* 544–573.

Case, R. Intellectual development from birth to adulthood: A neo-Piagetian interpretation. In R. S. Siegler (Ed.), *Children's thinking: What develops?* Hillsdale, N.J.: Lawrence Erlbaum Associates, 1978.

Case, R., and Khanna, F. The missing links: Stages in children's progression from sensorimotor to logical thought. In K. W. Fischer (Ed.), *New directions for child development: cognitive development.* San Francisco: Jossey-Bass, 1981.

Case, R., Kurland, D. M., and Goldberg, J. Operational efficiency and the growth of short-term memory span. *Journal of Experimental Child Psychology,* 1982, *33,* 386–404.

Cattell, J. M. Mental tests and measurements. *Mind,* 1890, *15,* 373.

Cattell, P. *The measurement of intelligence in infants and young children.* New York: Science Press, 1940.

Cattell, R. B. Theory of fluid and crystallized intelligence: An initial experiment. *Journal of Educational Psychology,* 1963, *54,* 105–111.

Cattell, R. B. *Abilities: Their structure, growth, and action.* Boston: Houghton Mifflin, 1971.

Cavanaugh, J. C., and Perlmutter, M. Metamemory: A critical examination. *Child Development,* 1982, *53,* 11–28.

Cavanaugh, P. J., and Davidson, M. L. The secondary circular reaction and response elicitation in the operant learning of six-month-old infants. *Developmental Psychology,* 1977, *13,* 371–376.

Cazden, C. *Child language and education.* New York: Holt, Rinehart & Winston, 1972.

Cedarbaum, S. Personal communication, 1976. Cited by C. B. Kopp and A. H. Parmelee, Prenatal and perinatal influences on infant behavior. In J. D. Osofsky (Ed.), *Handbook of infant development.* New York: Wiley, 1979.

Cermak, L. S., and Craik, F. I. M. (Eds.). *Levels of processing in human memory.* Hillsdale, N.J.: Lawrence Erlbaum Associates, 1979.

Chafetz, M. E. Alcoholism: Drug dependency problem No. 1. *Journal of Drug Issues,* 1974, *4,* 64–68.

Chance, J. E. Internal control of reinforcements and the school learning process. Paper presented at the meeting of the Society for Research in Child Development, Minneapolis, March 1965.

Charlesworth, R., and Hartup, W. W. Positive social reinforcement in the nursery school peer group. *Child Development,* 1967, *38,* 993–1002.

Charlesworth, W. R., and Kreutzer, M. Facial expressions of infants and children. In P. Ekman (Ed.), *Darwin and facial expression.* New York: Academic Press, 1973.

Charters, W. W., Jr. The social background of teaching. In H. L. Gage (Ed.), *Handbood of research on teaching.* Chicago: Rand McNally, 1963.

Chase-Lansdale, P. L. Effects of maternal employment on mother-infant and father-infant attachment. Unpublished doctoral dissertation, University of Michigan, 1981. Dissertation Abstracts International, 198, *42,* 2562.

Chen, E. Twins reared apart: A living lab. *New York Times Magazine,* December 9, 1979, p. 110.

Chesnick, M., Menyuk, P., Liebergott, J., Ferrier, L., and Strand, K. Who leads whom? Paper presented at the meeting of the Society for Research in Child Development, Detroit, April 1983.

Chi, M. T. Short-term memory limitations in children: Capacity or processing deficits? *Memory and Cognition,* 1976, *4,* 559–572.

Chi, M. T. Knowledge structures and memory development. In R. S. Siegler (Ed.), *Children's thinking: What develops?* Hillsdale, N.J.: Lawrence Erlbaum Associates, 1978.

Chi, M. T., and Koeske, R. D. Network representation of a child's dinosaur knowledge. *Developmental Psychology,* 1983, *19,* 29–39.

Childers, P., and Wimmer, M. The concept of death in early childhood. *Child Development,* 1971, *42,* 1299–1301.

Chomsky, C. *The acquisition of syntax in children from 5 to 10.* Research Monograph 57. Cambridge: MIT Press, 1969.

Chomsky, N. *Syntactic structures.* The Hague: Mouton, 1957.

Chomsky, N. *Reflections of language.* New York: Pantheon, 1975.

Cialdini, R. B., and Kenrick, D. T. Altruism as hedonism: A social development perspective on the relationship of negative mood state and helping. *Journal of Personality and Social Psychology,* 1976, *34,* 907–914.

Cialdini, R. B., Kenrick, D. T., and Baumann, D. J. Effects of mood on prosocial behavior in children and adults. In N. Eisenberg (Ed.), *The development of prosocial behavior.* New York: Academic Press, 1982.

Cicchetti, D., and Sroufe, L. A. The relationship between affec-tive and cognitive development in Down's syndrome infants. *Child Development,* 1976, *47,* 920–929.

Cicirelli, V. G. Concept learning of young children as a function of sibling relationships to the teacher. *Child Development,* 1972, *43,* 282–287.

Cicirelli, V. G. Effects of sibling structure and interaction on children's categorization style. *Developmental Psychology,* 1973, *9,* 132–139.

Cicirelli, V. G. Sibling structure and intellectual ability. *Developmental Psychology,* 1976, *12,* 369–370.

Cicirelli, V. G. Children's school grades and sibling structure. *Psychological Reports,* 1977, *41,* 1055–1058.

Cicirelli, V. G. Effects of sibling presence on mother-child interaction. *Developmental Psychology,* 1978, *14,* 315–316.

Clark, E. Review of Sesame Street. *Educational Television,* 1970, *2,* 30–31.

Clark, E. On the acquisition of the meaning of before and after. *Journal of Verbal Learning and Verbal Behavior,* 1971, *10,* 266–275.

Clark, E. First language acquisition. In J. Morton and J. C. Marshall (Eds.), *Psycholinguistics Series 1: Developmental and pathological.* London: Paul Elek, 1977.

Clark, E. Strategies for communicating. *Child Development,* 1978, *49,* 953–959.

Clark, E. Meanings and concepts, In P. H. Mussen (Ed.), *Handbook of child psychology,* Volume 3. New York: Wiley, 1983.

Clark, H., and Clark, E. *Psychology and language: An introduction to psycholinguistics.* New York: Harcourt Brace Jovanovich, 1977.

Clark, P. M., and Krige, P. D. A study of interaction between infant peers: An analysis of infant-infant interaction in twins. Paper presented at the second Joint Congress of the South African Psychology Association and the Psychological Institute of South Africa, Potchefstroom, September 1979.

Clarke, A. M., and Clarke, A. D. B. Some continued experiments. In A. M. Clarke and A. D. B. Clarke (Eds.), *Early experience: Myth and evidence.* New York: Free Press, 1976.

Clarke, H. H., and Clarke, D. H. Social status and mental health of boys as related to their maturity, structural, and strength characteristics. *Research Quarterly,* 1961, *32,* 326–334.

Clarke-Stewart, A. *Child care in the family: A review of research and some propositions for policy.* New York: Academic Press, 1977.

Clarke-Stewart, K. A. Interactions between mothers and their young children: Characteristics and consequences. *Monographs of the Society for Research in Child Development,* 1973, *38*(6–7, Serial No. 153).

Clarke-Stewart, K. A. And daddy makes three: The father's impact on mother and young child. *Child Development,* 1978, *49,* 466–478. (a)

Clarke-Stewart, K. A. Recasting the lone stranger. In J. Glick and K. A. Clarke-Stewart (Eds.), *The development of social understanding.* New York: Gardner Press, 1978. (b)

Clarke-Stewart, K. A. The father's contribution to child development. In F. A. Pedersen (Ed.), *The father-infant relationship: Observational studies in a family context.* New York: Praeger Special Studies, 1980.

Clarke-Stewart, K. A. *Daycare.* Cambridge: Harvard University Press, 1982.

Clarke-Stewart, K. A. Daycare: A new context for research and development. In M. Perlmutter (Ed.), *Parent-child interaction and parent-child relations in child development. The Minne-*

sota Symposia on Child Psychology, Volume 17. Hillsdale, N.J.: Lawrence Erlbaum Associates, 1984.

Clarke-Stewart, K. A., and Apfel, N. Evaluating parental effects on child development. In L. S. Shulman (Ed.), *Review of research in education,* Volume 6. Itasca, Ill.: Peacock, 1979.

Clarke-Stewart, K. A., and Fein, G. G. Early childhood programs. In P. H. Mussen (Ed.), *Handbook of child psychology,* Volume 2. New York: Wiley, 1983.

Clarke-Stewart, K. A., and Hevey, C. M. Longitudinal relations in repeated observations of mother-child interaction from 1 to 2½ years. *Developmental Psychology,* 1981, *17,* 127–145.

Clegg, D. J. Teratology. *Annual Review of Pharmacology,* 1971, *11,* 409–423.

Cloward, R. Studies in tutoring. *Journal of Experimental Education,* 1976, *36,* 14–25.

Coates, J. Pot more perilous than we thought: U.S. Report from National Institute on Drug Abuse, Marijuana and Health. *Chicago Tribune,* March 26, 1980, Section 1, pp. 1, 14.

Cohen, D., and Frank, R. Preadolescence: A critical phase of biological and psychological development. In D. V. Silva (Ed.), *Mental health in children.* Westbury, N.Y.: PJD Publications, 1975.

Cohen, L. B. and Gelber, E. R. Infant visual memory. In L. B. Cohen and P. Salapatek (Eds.), *Infant perception: From sensation to cognition: Basic visual processes,* Volume 1. New York: Academic Press, 1975.

Cohen, L. J., and Campos, J. J. Father, mother, and stranger as elicitors of attachment behaviors in infancy. *Developmental Psychology,* 1974, 10, 146–154.

Cohen, S., Evans, G. W., Krantz, D. S., and Stokols, D. Physiological, motivational, and cognitive effects of aircraft noise in children. *American Psychologist,* 1980, *35,* 231–243.

Cohen, S., Glass, D. C., and Singer, J. E. Apartment noise, auditory discrimination, and reading ability in children. *Journal of Experimental Social Psychology,* 1973, *9,* 407–422.

Cohen, S,, Krantz, D. S., Evans, G. W., Stokols, D., and Kelly, S. Aircraft noise and children: Longitudinal and cross-sectional evidence on adaptation to noise and the effectiveness of noise abatement. *Journal of Personality and Social Psychology,* 1981, *40,* 331–345.

Cohen, S., and Weinstein, N. D. Nonauditory effects of noise. In G. W. Evans (Ed.), *Environmental stress.* New York: Cambridge University Press, 1982.

Cohn, J. F., and Tronick, E. Z. Three-month-old infants' reaction to simulated maternal depression. *Child Development,* 1983, *54,* 185–193.

Coie, J. D., and Kupersmidt, J. B. A behavioral analysis of emerging social status in boys' groups. *Child Development,* 1983, *54,* 1400–1416.

Colby, A., and Damon, W. Listening to a different voice: A review of Gilligan's In a Different Voice. *Merrill-Palmer Quarterly,* 1983, *29,* 473–481.

Colby, A., Kohlberg, L., Gibbs, J., and Lieberman, M. A longitudinal study of moral judgment. *Monographs of the Society for Research in Child Development,* 1983, *48*(1, Serial No. 200).

Cole, M., Gay, J., Glick, J. A., and Sharp, D. D. *The cultural context of learning and thinking: An exploration in experimental anthropology.* New York: Basic Books, 1971.

Cole, M., and Scribner, S. Cross-cultural studies of memory and cognition. In R. V. Kail, Jr., and J. W. Hagen (Eds.), *Perspectives on the development of memory and cognition.* Hillsdale, N.J.: Lawrence Erlbaum Associates, 1977.

Coleman, J. C. *The adolescent society.* Glencoe, Ill.: Free Press, 1961.

Coleman, J. C. *Relationships in adolescence.* London: Routledge & Kegan Paul, 1974.

Coleman, J. C. Friendship and the peer group in adolescence. In J. Adelson (Ed.), *Handbook of adolescent psychology.* New York: Wiley, 1980.

Coleman, M. A report on the autistic syndromes. In M. Rutter and E. Schopler (Eds.), *Autism: A reappraisal of concepts and treatment.* New York: Plenum, 1978.

Colton, R. H., and Steinschneider, A. The cry characteristics of an infant who died of the sudden infant death syndrome. *Journal of Speech and Hearing Disorders,* 1981, *46,* 359–363.

Cometa, N. S., and Eson, M. E. Logical operations and metaphor interpretation: A Piagetian model. *Developmental Psychology,* 1978, *49,* 649–659.

Commons, M. L., Richards, F. A., and Kuhn, D. Systematic and metasystematic reasoning: A case for levels of reasoning beyond Piaget's stage of formal operations. *Child Development,* 1982, *53,* 1058–1069.

Concerns (Midwest Family Planning Association), 1980, 5.

Condry, J., and Condry, S. Sex differences: A study of the eye of the beholder. *Child Development,* 1976, *46,* 812–819.

Condry, J., and Siman, M. L. Characteristics of peer adult-oriented children. *Journal of Marriage and the Family,* 1974, *36,* 543–554.

Conel, J. L. *The postnatal development of the human cerebral cortex* (8 vols.) Cambridge: Harvard University Press, 1939–1967.

Connell, J. P. A model of the relationship among children's self-rated cognitions, affects and academic achievement. Unpublished doctoral dissertation. University of Denver, 1981.

Conners, C. K. *Food additives and hyperactive children.* New York: Plenum, 1980.

Connolly, K., and Smith, P. K. Reactions of pre-school children to a strange observer. In N. Blurton Jones (Ed.), *Ethological studies of child behaviour.* Cambridge: Cambridge University Press, 1972.

Connor, J. M., and Serbin, L. A. Behaviorally based masculine- and feminine-activity-preference scales for preschoolers: Correlates with other classroom behaviors and cognitive tests. *Child Development,* 1977, *48,* 1411–1416.

Cook, M., Field, J., and Griffiths, K. The perception of solid form in early infancy. *Child Development,* 1978, *49,* 866–869.

Cook, T. D., Appleton, H., Conner, R. F., Shaffer, A., Tamkin, G., and Weber, S. J. *Sesame Street revisited.* New York: Russell Sage Foundation, 1975.

Cooper, C. R. Collaboration in children: Dyadic interaction skills in problem solving. Paper presented at the meeting of the Society for Research in Child Development, New Orleans, March 1977.

Cooper, C. R., Ayers-Lopez, S., and Marquis, A. Children's discourse during peer learning in experimental and naturalistic situations. *Discourse Processes,* 1982, *5,* 177–191.

Cooper, C. R., Grotevant, H. D., and Condon, S. M. Individuality and connectedness in the family as a context for adolescent identity formation and role-taking skill. *New Directions for Child Development,* 1983, *22,* 43–59.

Cooper, H. M., Baron, R. M., and Lowe, C. A. The importance of race and social class information in the formation of expectancies about academic performance. *Journal of Educational Psychology,* 1975, *67,* 312–319.

Coopersmith, S. *The antecedents of self-esteem.* San Francisco: W. H. Freeman, 1967.

Cornell, E. H. Infants' recognition memory, forgetting, and savings. *Journal of Experimental Child Psychology,* 1979, *28,* 359–374.

Corner, G. W. *Ourselves unborn, an embryologist's essay on man.* New Haven, Conn: Yale University Press, 1944.

Corsaro, W. A. Friendship in the nursery school: Social organization in a peer environment. In S. R. Asher and J. M. Gottman (Eds.), *The development of children's friendships.* New York: Cambridge University Press, 1981.

Corter, C., Trehub, S., Boukydis, C., Ford, L., Celhoffer, L., and Minde, K. Nurses' judgments of the attractiveness of premature infants. *Infant Behavior and Development,* 1978, *1,* 373–380.

Cory, C. Newsline: Report on project on human sexual development. *Psychology Today,* 1979, January, p. 14.

Cosgrove, B. B., and Henderson, B. E. Male genitourinary abnormalities and maternal diethylstilbestrol. *Journal of Urology,* 1977, *117,* 220–222.

Cosgrove, J. M., and Patterson, C. J. Adequacy of young speakers' encoding in response to listener feedback. *Psychological Reports,* 1979, *45,* 15–18.

Costanzo, P. R., and Shaw, M. E. Conformity as a function of age level. *Child Development,* 1966, *37,* 967–975.

Cottle, T. The connections of adolescence. In J. Kagan and R. Coles (Eds.), *Sixteen: Early adolescence.* New York: Basic Books, 1971.

Craik, F. I. M. The fate of primary items in free recall. *Journal of Verbal Learning and Verbal Behavior* 1970, *9,* 143–148.

Craik, F. I. M., and Lockhart, R. S. Levels of processing: A framework for memory research. *Journal of Verbal Learning and Verbal Behavior,* 1972, *11,* 671–684.

Crandall, V. C., Katkovsky, W., and Crandall, V. J. Children's beliefs in their control of reinforcements in intellectual academic achievement behaviors. *Child Development,* 1965, *36,* 91–109.

Crano, W. D. Causal analyses of the effects of the socioeconomic status and initial intellectual endowment on patterns of cognitive development and academic achievemnt. In D. R. Green (Ed.), *The aptitude-achievement distinction.* Monterey: California Test Bureau, 1974.

Crano, W. D., Kenny, J., and Campbell, D. T. Does intelligence cause achievement? A cross-lagged panel analysis. *Journal of Educational Psychology,* 1972, *63,* 258–275.

Cravioto, J., Birch, H. G., DeLicardie, E., Rosales, L., and Vega, L. The ecology of growth and development in a Mexican preindustrial community. Report I: Method and findings from birth to one month of age. *Monographs of the Society for Research in Child Development,* 1969, *34*(5, Serial No. 129).

Crockenberg, S. Early mother and infant antecedents of Bayley scale performance at 21 months. *Developmental Psychology,* 1983, *19,* 727–730.

Crockenberg, S. B., Bryant, B. K., and Wilce, L. S. The effects of cooperatively and competitively structured learning environments on inter- and intrapersonal behavior. *Child Development,* 1976, *47,* 386–396.

Csikszentmihalyi, M. *Beyond boredom and anxiety.* San Francisco: Jossey-Bass, 1976.

Csikszentmihalyi, M., Larson, R., and Prescott, S. The ecology

of adolescent activity and experience. *Journal of Youth and Adolescence,* 1977, *6,* 281–294.

Cummings, E. M., and Bjork, E. L. The search behavior of 12 to 14 month-old infants on a five-choice invisible displacement hiding task. *Infant Behavior and Development,* 1981, *4,* 47–60.

Cunningham, M. R. Weather, mood, and helping behavior: The sunshine Samaritan. *Journal of Personality and Social Psychology,* 1979, *37,* 1947–1956.

Cundick, B. P. Measures of intelligence on Southwest Indian students. *Journal of Social Psychology,* 1970, *81,* 319–337.

Cunningham, S. Bulimia's cycle shames patient, tests therapists. *APA Monitor,* January 1984, p. 16.

Curtiss, S. *Genie: A psycholinguistic study of a modern-day wild child.* New York: Academic Press, 1977.

Daalen-Kapteijns, M. M. van, and Elshout-Mohr, M. The acquisition of word meanings as a cognitive learning process. *Journal of Verbal Learning and Verbal Behavior,* 1981, *20,* 386–399.

Dale, N. Early pretend play in the family. Unpublished doctoral thesis, University of Cambridge, 1983.

Dale, P. *Language development: Structure and function* (2nd ed.). New York: Holt, Rinehart & Winston, 1976.

Dalton, K. *The premenstrual syndrome.* Springfield, Ill.: Charles C. Thomas, 1964.

Damon, W. *The social world of the child.* San Francisco: Jossey-Bass, 1977.

Damon, W., and Hart, D. The development of self-understanding from infancy through adolescence. *Child Development,* 1982, *53,* 841–864.

Dan, A. J. Patterns of behavioral and mood variation in men and women: Variability and the menstrual cycle. Unpublished doctoral dissertation, University of Chicago (Committee on Human Development), 1976.

Daniels, P., and Weingarten, K. *Sooner or later: The timing of parenthood in adult lives.* New York: W. W. Norton, 1982.

Darwin, C. On the origin of species by means of natural selection. New York: D. Appleton & Co., 1859.

Darwin, C. R. *The expression of the emotions in man and animals.* London: John Murray,, 1872.

Dasen, P. Are cognitive processes universal? A contribution to cross-cultural Piagetian psychology. In N. Warren (Ed.), *Studies in cross-cultural psychology,* Volume, 1. London: Academic Press, 1977.

Dasen, P., Inhelder, B., Lavallée, M., and Retschitzki, J. Naissance de l'intelligence chez l'enfant Baoulé de Côte d'Ivoire. Berne: Hans Huber, 1978.

Davids, A., and Holden, R. H. Consistency of maternal attitudes and personality from pregnancy to 8 months following childbirth. *Developmental Psychology,* 1970, *2,* 364–366.

Davidson, J. R. Post-partum mood change in Jamaican women: A description and discussion on its significance. *British Journal of Psychiatry,* 1972, *121,* 659–663.

Davidson, R. *Emotion, cognition, and behavior.* Cambridge: Cambridge University Press, 1984.

Dawson, C. D. Cerebral lateralization in individuals diagnosed as autistic in early childhood. *Brain and Language,* 1982, *15,* 353–368.

Day, B., and Brice, R. Academic achievement, self-concept development, and behavior patterns of six-year-old children in open classrooms. *Elementary School Journal,* 1977, *78,* 132–139.

Day, M. C. Developmental trends in visual scanning. In H. W. Reese (Ed.), *Advances in child development and behavior,* Volume 10, New York: Academic Press, 1975.

Dayton, G. O., Jr., Jones, M. H., Aiu, P., Rawson, R. A., Steele, B., and Rose, M. Developmental study of coordinated eye movements in the human infant: I. Visual acuity in the newborn human: A study based on induced optokinetic mystagmus recorded by electro-oculography. *Archieves of Ophthalmology,* 1964, *71,* 865–870.

Décarie, T. G. *The infant's reaction to strangers.* New York: International Universities Press, 1974.

DeCasper, A. J., and Fifer, W. P. Of human bonding: Newborns prefer their mother's voices. *Science,* 1980, *208,* 1174–1176.

Decker, S. N., and DeFries, J. C. Cognitive ability profiles in families of reading disabled children. *Developmental Medicine and Child Neurology,* 1981, *23,* 217–227.

Deeths, T. M., and Breeden, J. T. Poisoning in children—a statistical study of 1,057 cases. *Journal of Pediatrics,* 1971, *78,* 299.

DeFleur, M. L., and DeFleur, L. The relative contribution of television as a learning source for children's occupational knowledge. *American Sociological Review,* 1967, *32,* 777–789.

DeFries, J. C., and Baker, L. A. Parental contributions to longitudinal stability of cognitive measures in the Colorado Family Reading Study. *Child Development,* 1983, *54,* 388–395.

Delefes, P., and Jackson, B. Teacher-pupil interaction as a function of location in the classroom. *Psychology in the Schools,* 1972, *9,* 119–123.

Delfini, L., Bernal, M., and Rosen, P. Comparison of deviant and normal boys in home settings. In E. J. Mash, L. A. Hamerlynck, and L. C. Handy (Eds.), *Behavior modification and families,* Volume I, *Theory and research.* New York: Brunner/Mazel, 1976.

DeLoache, J. S. Naturalistic studies of memory for object location in very young children. *New directions for child development: Children's memory,* San Francisco: Jossey-Bass, 1980.

DeLoache, J. S., and Brown, A. L. Looking for Big Bird: Studies of memory in very young children. *Quarterly Newsletter of the Laboratory of Comparative Human Cognition,* 1979, *1,* 53–57.

DeLoache, J. S., and Brown, A. L. Very young children's memory for the location of objects in a large-scale environment. *Child Development,* 1983, *54,* 888–897.

Demos, E. V. Children's understanding and use of affect terms. Unpublished doctoral dissertation, Harvard University, 1974.

Demos, E. V. Facial expressions of infants and toddlers: A descriptive analysis. In T. Field and A. Fogel, (Eds.), *Emotion and early interaction.* Hillsdale, N.J.: Lawrence Erlbaum Associates, 1982.

Demos, J., and Demos, V. Adolescence in historical perspective. *Journal of Marriage and the Family,* 1969, *31,* 632–638.

DeMyer, M. K., Barton, S., Alpern, G. D., Kimberlin, C., Allen, J., Yang, E., and Steele, R. The measured intelligence of autistic children: A follow-up study. *Journal of Autism and Childhood Schizophrenia,* 1974, *4,* 42–60.

Denney, N. W. A developmental study of free classification in children. *Child Development,* 1972, *43,* 1161–1170.

Dennis, W. Causes of retardation among institutional children: Iran. *Journal of Genetic Psychology,* 1960, *96,* 47–59.

Dennis, W. Creative productivity between the ages of 20 and 80 years. *Journal of Gerontology,* 1966, *21,* 1–8.

Dennis, W. *Children of the crèche.* New York: Appleton-Century-Crofts, 1973.

Deutsch, F. Female preschoolers' perceptions of affective responses and interpersonal behavior in videotaped episodes. *Developmental Psychology,* 1974, *10,* 733–740.

Devereaux, E. C. The role of the peer group experience in moral development. In J. P. Hill (Ed.), *Minnesota Symposia on Child Psychology,* Volume 4. Minneapolis: University of Minnesota Press, 1970.

deVilliers, J. G., and deVilliers, P. A. A cross-sectional study of the development of grammatical morphemes in child speech. *Journal of Psycholinguistic Research,* 1973, *2,* 267–278.

deVilliers, P. A., and deVilliers, J. G. *Early language.* Cambridge: Harvard University Press, 1979.

DeVries, R. Constancy of generic identity in the years three to six. *Monographs of the Society for Research in Child Development.* 1969, *34*(3, Serial No. 127).

Diaz, R. M., and Berndt, T. J. Children's knowledge of a best friend: Fact or fancy? *Developmental Psychology,* 1982, *18,* 787–794.

Dibble, U., and Straus, M. Some social structure determinants of inconsistency between attitudes and behavior: The case of family violence. *Journal of Marriage and the Family,* 1980, *42,* 71–80.

Diener, C. I., and Dweck, C. S. An analysis of learned helplessness: Continuous changes in performance, strategy and achievement cognitions following failure. *Journal of Personality and Social Psychology,* 1978, *36,* 451–462.

Dienstbier, R. A. The role of emotion in moral socialization. In C. E. Izard, J. Kagan, and R. B. Zajonc (Eds.), *Emotions, cognition and behavior.* Cambridge: Cambridge University Press, in press.

DiPietro, J. A. Rough and tumble play: A function of gender. *Developmental Psychology,* 1981, *17,* 50–58.

Dmowski, W. P., Gaynor, L., Rao, R., Lawrence, M., and Scommegna, A. Use of albumin gradients for X and Y sperm separation and clinical experience with male preselection. *Fertility and Sterility,* 1979, *31,* 52–57.

Dodge, K. A. Social cognition and children's aggressive behavior. *Child Development,* 1980, *51,* 162–170.

Dodge, K. A. Behavioral antecedents of peer social status. *Child Development,* 1983, *54,* 1386–1399.

Dodge, K. A., and Frame, C. L. Social cognitive biases and deficits in aggressive boys. *Child Development.* 1982, *53,* 620–635.

Dodson, J. C., Kushida, E., Williamson, M., and Friedman, E. G. Intellectual performance of 36 phenylketonuria patients and their nonaffected siblings. *Pediatrics,* 1976, *58,* 53–58.

Dodwell, P. C., Muir, D., and DiFranco, D. Responses of infants to visually presented objects. *Science,* 1976, *194,* 209–211.

Dollard, J., Dobb, L., Miller, N. E., Mowrer, O. H., and Sears, R. R. *Frustration and aggression.* New Haven, Conn.: Yale University Press, 1939.

Dollard, J., and Miller, N. E. *Personality and psychotherapy: An analysis of learning, thinking, and culture.* New York: McGraw-Hill, 1950.

Donaldson, M., and Balfour, G. Less is more: A study of language comprehension in children. *British Journal of Psychology,* 1968, *59,* 461–472.

Donovan, B. *The cesarean birth experience: A practical, comprehensive, and reassuring guide for parents and professionals.* Boston: Beacon Press, 1977.

Donovan, W. L., Leavitt, L. A., and Balling, J. D. Maternal

physiological response to infant signals. *Psychophysiology*, 1978, *15*, 68–74.

Dore, J. Conditions for the acquisition of speech acts. In I. Markova (Ed.), *The social context of language.* New York: Wiley, 1978. (a)

Dore, J. Variation in preschool children's conversational performances. In K. E. Nelson (Ed.), *Children's language*, Volume 1. New York: Gardner Press, 1978. (b)

Dorr, A. Children's reports of what they learn from daily viewing. Paper presented at the biennial meeting of the Society for Research in Child Development, San Francisco, March 1979.

Douglas, V. I. Stop, look, and listen: The problem of sustained attention and impulse control in hyperactive and normal children. *Canadian Journal of Behavioral Science*, 1972, *4*, 259–282.

Douglas, V. I. Higher mental processes in hyperactive children. In R. M. Knights and D. J. Bakker (Eds.), *Treatment of hyperactive and learning disordered children.* Baltimore: University Park Press, 1980.

Douvan, E., and Adelson, J. *The adolescent experience.* New York: Wiley, 1966.

Douvan, E., and Gold, M. Modal patterns in American adolescence. In L. W. Hoffman and M. L. Hoffman (Eds.), *Review of child development research*, Volume 2. New York: Russell Sage Foundation, 1966.

Dove, A. Taking the chitling test. *Newsweek*, July 15, 1968, pp. 51–52.

Doyle, A-B. Infant development in day care. *Developmental Psychology*, 1975, *11*, 655–656.

Doyle, A-B., Champagne, M., and Segalowitz, N. Some issues on the assessment of linguistic consequences of early bilingualism. In M. Paradis (Ed.), *Aspects of bilingualism.* Columbia, S.C.: Hornbeam Press, 1978.

Doyle, W., Hancock, G., and Kifer, E. Teachers' perceptions: Do they make a difference? Paper presented at the annual meeting of the American Educational Research Association, New York, April 1971.

Drake, C. T., and McDougall, D. Effects of the absence of a father and other male models on the development of boys' sex roles. *Developmental Psychology*, 1977, *13*, 537–538.

Dreyfus-Brisac, C. Neurophysiological studies in human premature and full-term newborns. *Biological Psychiatry*, 1975, *10*, 485–496.

Duffty, P., and Bryan, M. H. Home apnea monitoring in 'near-miss' sudden infant death syndrome (SIDS) and in siblings of SIDS victims. *Pediatrics*, 1982, *70*, 69–75.

Dugdale, R. (1877) *The Jukes: A study in crime, pauperism, disease, and heredity.* New York: G. P. Putnam's Sons, 1910.

Duke, P. M., Carlsmith, J. M., Jennings, D., Martin, J. A., Dornbusch, S. M., Gross, R. T., and Siegel-Gorelick, B. Educational correlates of early and late sexual maturation in adolescence. *Journal of Pediatrics*, 1982, *100*, 633–637.

Duncan, D., Schuman, H., and Duncan, B. *Social change in a metropolitan community.* New York: Russell Sage Foundation, 1973.

Dunn, J. Sibling relationships in early childhood. *Child Development*, 1983, *54*, 787–811.

Dunn, J., and Kendrick, C. Studying temperament and parent-child interaction: Comparison of interview and direct observation. *Developmental Medicine and Child Neurology*, 1980, *22*, 484–496.

Dunn, J., and Kendrick, C. The speech of two- and three-year-olds to infant siblings: "Baby Talk" and the context of com-

munication. *Journal of Child Language*, 1982, *9*, 579–595. (a)

Dunn, J., and Kendrick, C. *Siblings: Love, envy, and understanding.* Cambridge: Harvard University Press, 1982. (b)

Dunn, J., Kendrick, C., and MacNamee, R. The reaction of first-born children to the birth of a sibling: Mothers' reports. *Journal of Child Psychology and Psychiatry*, 1981, *22*, 1–18.

Dunphy, D. C. The social structure of urban adolescent peer groups. *Sociometry*, 1963, *26*, 230–246.

DuPan, R. M., and Roth, S. The psychologic development of a group of children brought up in a hospital-type residential nursery. *Journal of Pediatrics*, 1955, *47*, 124–129.

Dusek, J. B., and Flaherty, J. F. The development of the self-concept during the adolescent years. *Monographs of the Society for Research in Child Development*, 1981, *46*(4, Serial No. 191).

Dweck, C. S. Children's intepretation and evaluative feedback: The effect of social cues on learned helplessness. *Merrill-Palmer Quarterly*, 1976, *22*, 105–109.

Dweck, C. S. Social-cognitive processes in children's friendships. In S. R. Asher and J. M. Gottman (Eds.), *The development of children's friendships.* New York: Cambridge University Press, 1981.

Dweck, C. S., and Bush, E. S. Sex differences in learned helplessness: I. Differential debilitation with peer and adult evaluators. *Developmental Psychology*, 1976, *12*, 147–156.

Dweck, C. S., Davidson, W., Nelson, S., and Enna, B. Sex differences in learned helplessness. II: The contingencies of evaluation feedback in the classroom. III: An experimental analysis. *Developmental Psychology*, 1978, *14*, 268–276.

Dweck, C. S., and Goetz, F. E. Attributions and learned helplessness. In J. H. Harvey, W. Ickes, and R. F. Kidd (Eds.), *New directions in attribution research*, Volume 2. Hillsdale: N.J.: Lawrence Erlbaum Associates, 1977.

East, B. A. Cross-age tutoring in the elementary school. *Graduate Research in Education and Related Disciplines*, 1976, *8*, 88–111.

Ebbs, J. H., Brown, A., Tisdall, F. F., Moyle, W. J., and Bell, M. The influence of improved prenatal nutrition upon the infant. *Journal of the Canadian Medical Association*, 1942, *46*, 6–8.

Eckerman, C. O. Competence in early social relations. Paper presented at the American Psychological Association Convention, Montreal, August 1973.

Eckerman, C. O., and Whatley, J. Toys and social interaction between infant peers. *Child Development*, 1977, *48*, 1645–1656.

Eckerman, C. O., Whatley, J. L., and Kutz, S. L. Growth of social play with peers during the second year of life. *Developmental Psychology*, 1975, *11*, 42–49.

Eckerman, C. O., Whatley, J. L., and McGehee, L. J. Approaching and contacting the object another manipulates: A social skill of the one-year-old. *Developmental Psychology*, 1979, *15*, 585–593.

Edelman, R. Cell-mediated immune function in malnutrition. In R. M. Suskind (Ed.), *Malnutrition and the immune response.* New York: Raven Press, 1977.

Edelman, R., Suskind, R., Sirisinha, S., and Olson, R. E. Mechanisms of defective cutaneous hypersensitivity in children with protein-calorie malnutrition. *Lancet*, 1973, *1*, 506–508.

Edwards, C. P., and Lewis, M. Young children's concepts of social relations: Social functions and social objects. In M.

Lewis and L. A. Rosenblum (Eds.), *The child and its family.* New York: Plenum, 1979.

Edwards, J. R. Social class differences and the identity of sex in children's speech. *Journal of Child Language,* 1979, *6,* 121–127.

Effron, R. The relationship between the duration of a stimulus and the duration of a perception. *Neuropsychologia,* 1970, *8,* 37–55.

Egeland, B. Training impulsive children in the use of more efficient scanning techniques. *Child Development,* 1974, *45,* 165–171.

Egeland, B., and Sroufe, L. A. Attachment and early maltreatment. *Child Development,* 1981. *52,* 44–52.

Eibl-Eibesfeldt, I. *Ethology: The biology of behavior.* New York: Holt, Rinehart & Winston, 1970.

Eibl-Eibesfeldt, I. The expressive behavior of the deaf- and blind-born. In M. von Cranach and I. Vine (Eds.), *Social communication and movement.* New York: Academic Press, 1973.

Eichorn, D. H. Physiological development. In P. H. Mussen (Ed.), *Carmichael's manual of child psychology, Volume 1.* New York: Wiley,, 1970.

Eichorn, D. H. Asynchronizations in adolescent development. In S. E. Dragastin and G. H. Elder (Eds.), *Adolescence in the life cycle.* New York: Wiley, 1975.

Eichorn, D. H. Physical development: Current foci of research. In J. D. Osofsky (Ed.), *Handbook of infant development.* New York: Wiley, 1979.

Eifermann, R. R. *Determinants of children's game styles.* Jerusalem: Israel Academy of Sciences and Humanities, 1971.

Eimas, P. D., Siqueland, E. R., Juzczyk, P., and Vigorito, J. Speech perception in early infancy. *Science,* 1971, *171,* 303–306.

Eisenberg, L. The fathers of autistic children. *American Journal of Orthopsychiatry,* 1957, *27,* 715–724.

Eisenberg, L., and Kanner, L. Early infantile autism. *American Journal of Orthopsychiatry,* 1956, *26,* 556–566.

Eisenberg, N., Murray, E., and Hite, T. Children's reasoning regarding sex-typed toy choices. *Child Development,* 1982, *53,* 81–86.

Eisenberg, R. B. Auditory behavior in the human neonate: I. Methodologic problems and the logical design of research procedures. *Journal of Auditory Research,* 1965, *5,* 159–177.

Eisenberg, R. B. *Auditory competence in early life: The roots of communicative behavior.* Baltimore: University Park Press, 1976.

Eisenberg, R. B. Stimulus significance as a determinant of infant responses to sound. In E. B. Thoman (Ed.), *Origins of the infant's social responses.* Hillsdale, N.J.: Lawrence Erlbaum Associates, 1979.

Eisenberg-Berg, N., and Lennon, R. Altruism and the assessment of empathy in the preschool years. *Child Development,* 1980, *51,* 552–557.

Ekman, P. Biological and cultural contributions to body and facial movement in the expression of emotions. In A. Rorty (Ed.), *Explaining emotions.* Berkeley: University of California Press, 1980.

Ekman, P., and Friesen, W. Constants across cultures in the face and emotion. *Journal of Personality and Social Psychology,* 1972, *17,* 124–129.

Ekman, P., and Friesen, W. V. *Unmasking the face.* Englewood Cliffs, N.J.: Prentice-Hall, 1975.

Ekman, P., and Friesen, W. V. The facial action coding system (FACS). Palo Alto, Calif.: Consulting Psychologists Press, 1978.

Ekman, P., Friesen, W. V., and Ellsworth, P. *Emotion in the human face: Guidelines for research and an integration of findings.* New York: Pergamon, 1972.

Ekman, P., Sorenson, E., and Friesen, W. Pancultural elements in the facial expression of emotion. *Science,* 1969, *164,* 86–88.

Elashoff, J. D., and Snow, R. E. A case study in statistical inference: Reconsideration of the Rosenthal-Jacobson data on teacher expectancy. Technical Report 15, School of Education, Stanford University, 1970.

Elkind, D. Perceptual development in children. In I. L. Janis (Ed.), *Current trends in psychology.* Los Altos, Calif.: Kaufmann, 1977.

El'Konin, D. B. Symbolics and its functions in the play of children. *Soviet Education,* 1966, *8,* 35–41.

Ellinger, B. D. The home environment and the creative-thinking ability of children. Unpublished doctoral dissertation, Ohio State University, 1964.

Elliott, J. Risk of cancer, dysplasia for DES daughters found "very low." *Journal of American Medical Association,* 1979, *241,* 1555.

Ellis, A. C., and Hall, G. S. A study of dolls. *Pedagogical Seminary,* 1896, *4,* 129–175. Abridged and reprinted in G. S. Hall et al., *Aspects of child life and education.* New York: D. Appleton & Co., 1907, 157–204.

Ellis, S., and Rogoff, B. The strategies and efficacy of child versus adult teachers. *Child Development,* 1982, *53,* 730–735.

Elmer, E. *Children in jeopardy: A study of abused minors and their families.* Pittsburgh: University of Pittsburgh Press, 1967.

Elmer, E., and Gregg, C. D. Developmental characteristics of the abused child. *Pediatrics,* 1967, *40,* 596–602.

Emde, R. N. Levels of meaning for infant emotions: A biosocial view. In W. A. Collins (Ed.), *Development of cognition, affect, and social relations. The Minnesota Symposia on Child Psychology,* Volume 13. Hillsdale, N.J: Lawrence Erlbaum Associates, 1980.

Emde, R. N., Gaensbauer, T., and Harmon, R. Emotional expression in infancy: A biobehavioral study. In *Psychological issues,* Monograph 37. New York: International Universities Press, 1976.

Emde, R. N., Kligman, D. H., Reich, J. H., and Wade, T. D. Emotional expression in infancy: I. Initial studies of social signaling and an emergent model. In M. Lewis and L. A. Rosenblum (Eds.), *The development of affect.* New York: Plenum, 1978.

Emmerich, W., Goldman, K. S., Kirsh, B., and Sharabany, R. Evidence for a transitional phase in the development of gender constancy. *Child Development,* 1977, *48,* 930–936.

Entwisle, D. R., and Doering, S. G. The first birth: A family turning point. Baltimore: Johns Hopkins University Press, 1981.

Entwistle, N. J. Personality and academic attainment. *British Journal of Educational Psychology,* 1972, *42,* 137–151.

Ephron, N. A few words about breasts. *Crazy Salad.* New York: Knopf, 1975.

Ericson, A., Kallén, B., and Westerholm, P. Cigarette smoking as an etiologic factor in cleft lip and palate. *American Journal of Obstetrics and Gynecology,* 1979, *35,* 348–351.

Eriksen, C. W. Temporal luminance summation effects in backward and forward masking. *Perception and Psychophysics,* 1966, *1,* 87–92.

Erikson, E. H. *Childhood and society* (1st ed., 1950). New York: W. W. Norton, 1963.

Erikson, E. H. *Identity: Youth and crisis.* New York: W. W. Norton, 1968.

Erikson, E. H. *Toys and reasons.* New York: W. W. Norton, 1977.

Erlenmeyer-Kimling, L., and Jarvik, L. F. Genetics and intelligence: A review. *Science,* 1963, *142,* 1477–1479.

Eron, L. D., Walder, L. O., and Lefkowitz, M. M. *Learning of aggression in children.* Boston: Little, Brown, 1971.

Ervin-Tripp, S. Discourse agreement: How children answer questions. In J. R. Hayes (Ed.), *Cognition and the development of language.* New York: Wiley, 1970.

Escalona, S. Patterns of infantile experience and the developmental process. In R. Eissler (Ed.), *The psychoanalytic study of the child,* Volume 18. New York: International Universities Press, 1963.

Escalona, S., and Leitch, M. Early phases of personality development: A non-normative study of infant behavior. *Monographs of the Society for Research in Child Development,* 1952, *17*(1, Serial No. 54).

Espenschade, A. S., and Meleney, H. E. Motor performances of adolescent boys and girls today in comparison with those of twenty years ago. *Research Quarterly,* 1961, *32,* 186–189.

Etzel, B. C., and Gewirtz, J. L. Experimental modification of caretaker-maintained high rate operant crying in a 6- and a 20-week-old infant: Extinction of crying with reinforcement of eye contact and smiling. *Journal of Experimental Child Psychology,* 1967, *5,* 303–317.

Evans, D. R., Newcombe, R. G., and Campbell, H. Maternal smoking habits and congenital malformations: A population study. *British Medical Journal,* 1979, *2,* 171–173.

Evans, G., and Hall, J. The older the sperm. *Ms.,* January 1975.

Fafouti-Milenković, M., and Uzgiris, I.C. The mother-infant communication system. In I. C. Uzgiris (Ed.), *New directions for child development: Social interaction and communication during infancy.* San Francisco: Jossey-Bass, 1979.

Fagan, J. F. Infants' recognition memory for faces. *Journal of Experimental Child Psychology,* 1972, *14,* 453–476.

Fagan, J. F. Infants' delayed recognition memory and forgetting. *Journal of Experimental Child Psychology,* 1973, *16,* 424–450.

Fagan, J. F., and Singer, L. T. Infant recognition memory as a measure of intelligence. In L. P. Lipsitt and C. K. Rovee-Collier (Eds.), *Advances in infancy research,* Volume 2. Norwood, N.J.: Ablex, 1983.

Fagan, J. R., and Witryol, S. L. The effects of instructional set and delay of reward on children's learning in a simultaneous discrimination task. *Child Development,* 1966, *37,* 433–438.

Fagot, B. I. The influence of sex of child on parental reactions to toddler children. *Child Development,* 1978, *49,* 459–465.

Fairbanks, G., and Pronovost, W. Vocal pitch during simulated emotion. *Science,* 1938, *88,* 383–386.

Fairweather, H. Sex differences in cognition: A function of maturation rate? *Science,* 1976, *192,* 572–573.

Falbo, T. Only children, stereotypes, and research. In M. Lewis and L. A. Rosenblum (Eds.), *The child and its family.* New York: Plenum, 1979.

Fantz, R. L. The origins of form perception. *Scientific American,* 1961, *204,* 66–72.

Fantz, R. L. Pattern vision in newborn infants. *Science,* 1963, *140,* 296–297.

Fantz, R. L. Visual perception from birth as shown by pattern selectivity. *Annals of the New York Academy of Science,* 1965, *118,* 793–814.

Farkas-Bargeton, E., and Diebler, M. F. A topographical study of enzyme maturation in human cerebral neocortex: A histochemical and biochemical study. In M. A. B. Brazier and H. Petsche (Eds.), *Architectonics of the cerebral cortex.* New York: Raven Press, 1978.

Faust, M. S. Developmental maturity as a determinant in prestige of adolescent girls. *Child Development,* 1960, *31,* 173–184.

Faust, M. S. Somatic development of adolescent girls. *Monographs of the Society for Research in Child Development,* 1977, *42*(1, Serial No. 169).

Federation CECOS, Schwartz, D., and Mayaux, M. J. Female fecundity as a function of age: Results of artificial insemination in 2193 nulliparous women with azoospermic husbands. *New England Journal of Medicine,* 1982, *306,* 404–406.

Fein, D., O'Neill, S., Frank, C., and Velit, K. M. Sex differences in preadolescent self-esteem. *Journal of Psychology,* 1975, *90,* 179–183.

Fein, G., Johnson, D., Kosson, N., Stork, L. and Wasserman, L. Sex stereotypes and preferences in the toy choices of 20 month-old boys and girls. *Developmental Psychology,* 1975, *11,* 527–528.

Fein, G., Schwartz, P., Jacobson, S., and Jacobson, J. Environmental toxins and behavioral development. *American Psychologist,* 1983, *38,* 1188–1197.

Feingold, B. F. *Why your child is hyperactive.* New York: Random House, 1975.

Feinman, S., and Lewis, M. Social referencing and second-order effects in ten-month-old infants. Paper presented at the meeting of the Society for Research in Child Development, Boston, April 1981.

Feinman, S., and Lewis, M. Social referencing and second-order effects in ten-month-old infants. *Child Development,* 1983, *54,* 878–887.

Feiring, C., Lewis, M., and Starr, M. D. Indirect effects and infants' reaction to strangers. *Developmental Psychology,* 1984, *20,* 485–491.

Feldman, S. S., and Ingham, M. E. Attachment behavior: A validation study in two age groups. *Child Development,* 1975, *46,* 319–330.

Ferguson, C. A. Baby talk in six languages. *American Anthropologist,* 1964, *66,* 103–114.

Fernald, A. *Four-month-olds prefer to listen to "motherese."* Paper presented at the meeting of the Society for Research in Child Development, Boston, April 1981.

Feshbach, N. Sex differences in children's modes of aggressive responses toward outsiders. *Merrill-Palmer Quarterly,* 1969, *15,* 249–258.

Feshbach, N. Empathy: An interpersonal process. Paper presented at the annual meeting of the American Psychological Association, Montreal, September 1973.

Feshbach, N., and Feshbach, S. Children's aggression. In W. W. Hartup (Ed.), *The young child: Reviews of research,* Volume 2. Washington, D.C.: National Association for the Education of Young Children, 1972.

Feshbach, N., and Roe, K. Empathy in six and seven year olds. *Child Development,* 1968, *39,* 133–145.

Feshbach, S. The catharsis hypothesis and some consequences of interaction with aggressive and neutral play objects. *Journal of Personality,* 1956, *24,* 449–462.

Feshbach, S. Aggression. In P. H. Mussen (Ed.), *Carmichael's manual of child psychology.* New York: Wiley, 1970.

Field, T. Interaction behaviors of primary versus secondary caretaker fathers. *Developmental Psychology*, 1978, *14*, 183–184.

Field, T. M., and Walden, T. A. Production and discrimination of facial expressions by preschool children. *Child Development*, 1982, *53*, 1299–1311.

Field, T. M., Woodson, R., Greenberg, R., and Cohen, D. Discrimination and imitation of facial expression by neonates. *Science*, 1982, *218*, 179–181.

Fillmore, C. J. The case for case. In E. Bach and R. T. Harms (Eds.), *Universals of linguistic theory.* New York: Holt, Rinehart & Winston, 1968.

Fincher, J. *Human Intelligence.* New York: G. P. Putnam's Sons, 1976.

Fine, P. R., and Dobin, D. D. *International Symposium on Recent Advances in the Assessment of the Health Effects of Environmental Pollution.* Paris: C.E.C., 1974.

Fine, P., Thomas, C. W., Subs, R. H., Cohnberg, R. E., and Flashner, B. A. Pediatric Blood Lead Levels. *Journal of the American Medical Association*, 1972, *221*, 1475–1479.

Fischer, K. W. A theory of cognitive development: The control and construction of hierarchies of skills. *Psychological Review.* 1980, *87*, 447–531.

Fischer, L., Kokes, R. F., Harder, D. W., and Jones, J. E. Child competence and psychiatric risk: VI. Summary and integration of findings. *Journal of Nervous and Mental Disease*, 1980, *168*, 353–355.

Fischer, P. L., and Torney, J. V. Influence of children's stories on dependency, a sex-typed behavior. *Developmental Psychology*, 1976, *12*, 489–490.

Fitts, W. H. The self-concept and self-actualization: Studies on the self-concept and rehabilitation. Dede Wallace Center, Nashville, 1971.

Flanagan, G. L. *The first nine months of life.* New York: Simon & Schuster, 1962.

Flannery, R., and Balling, J. D. Hemispheric specialization of spatial ability in children. Paper presented at the meeting of the Society for Research in Child Development, New Orleans, March 1977.

Flannery, R. C., and Balling, J. D. Developmental changes in hemispherical specialization for tactile spatial ability. *Developmental Psychology*, 1979, *15*, 364–372.

Flapan, D. *Children's understanding of social interaction.* New York: Teachers College Press, Columbia University, 1968.

Flavell, J. H. Developmental Studies of mediated memory. In H. W. Reese and L. P. Lipsitt (Eds.), *Advances in child development and behavior,* Volume 5. New York: Academic Press, 1970.

Flavell, J. H. *Cognitive development.* Englewood Cliffs, N.J.: Prentice-Hall, 1977.

Flavell, J. H. Stage-related properties of cognitive development. *Cognitive Psychology*, 1978, *2*, 421–453.

Flavell, J. H., Beach, D. H., and Chinsky, J. M. Spontaneous verbal rehearsal in memory tasks as a function of age. *Child Development*, 1966, *37*, 283–299.

Flavell, J. H., Botkin, P. T., Fry, C. L., Wright, J. W., and Jarvis, P. E. *The development of role-taking and communication skills in children.* New York: Wiley, 1968.

Flavell, J. H., Everett, B. A., Croft, K., and Flavell, E. R. Young children's knowledge about visual perception: Further evidence for the Level 1-Level 2 distinction. *Developmental Psychology*, 1981, *17*, 99–103.

Flavell, J. H., Friedrichs, A. G., and Hoyt, J. D. Developmental changes in memorization processes. *Cognitive Psychology*, 1970, *1*, 324–340.

Flavell, J. H., Shipstead, S. G., and Croft, K. Young children's knowledge about visual perception: Hiding objects from others. *Child Development*, 1978, *49*, 1208–1211.

Flavell, J. H., Speer, J. R., Green, F. L., and August, D. L. The development of comprehension monitoring and knowledge about communication. *Monographs of the Society for Research in Child Development*, 1981, *46*(5, Serial No. 192).

Fleener, D. E. Experimental production of infant-maternal attachment behaviors. Unpublished manuscript, Indiana University-Purdue University, 1973.

Fleming. A. T. New frontiers in conception. *New York Times Magazine*, July 20, 1980.

Floyd, H. H., and South, D. R. Dilemma of youth: The choice of parents or peers as a frame of reference for behavior. *Journal of Marriage and the Family*, 1972, *34*, 627–634.

Fogel, A. Temporal organization in mother-infant face-to-face interaction. In H. R. Schaffer (Ed.), *Studies in mother-infant interaction.* London: Academic Press, 1977.

Fogelman, K. Smoking in pregnancy and subsequent development of the child. *Child: Care, Health and Development*, 1980, *6*, 233–249.

Folger, J. P., and Chapman, R. S. A pragmatic analysis of spontaneous imitations. *Journal of Child Language*, 1978, *5*, 25–38.

Folstein, S., and Rutter, M. Genetic influences and infantile autism. *Nature*, 1977, *265*, 726–728.

Ford, M. E. Social cognition and social competence in adolescence. *Developmental Psychology*, 1982, *18*, 323–340.

Forehand, G., Ragosta, M., and Rock, D. Conditions and processes of effective school designation. Final report, U.S. Office of Education, Department of Health, Education, and Welfare. Princeton, N.J.: Educational Testing Service, 1976.

Forman, G. E., and Hill, F. *Constructive play applying Piaget in the preschool.* Monterey, Calif.: Brooks/Cole, 1980.

Forrest, D. L., and Waller, T. G. Meta-memory and meta-cognitive aspects of decoding in reading. Paper presented at the meeting of the American Educational Research Association, Los Angeles, April 1981.

Fourcin, A. J. Acoustic patterns and speech acquisition. In N. Waterson and C. E. Snow (Eds.), *The development of communication.* New York: Wiley, 1978.

Fox, H. E., Steinbrecher, M., Pessel, D., Inglis, J., Medvid, L., and Angel, E. Maternal ethanol ingestion and the occurrence of human fetal breathing movements. *American Journal of Obstetrics and Gynecology*, 1978, *132*, 354–358.

Fraiberg, S. Blind infants and their mothers: An examination of the sign system. In M. Lewis and L. A. Rosenblum (Eds.), *The effect of the infant on its caregiver.* New York: Wiley, 1974.

Fraiberg, S. The development of human attachments in infants blind from birth. *Merrill-Palmer Quarterly*, 1975, *21*, 315–334.

Fraiberg, S. *Every child's birthright. In defense of mothering.* New York: Basic Books, 1977. (a)

Fraiberg, S. *Insights from the blind.* New York: Basic Books, 1977. (b)

Frankenberg, W. K., and Dodds, J. B. The Denver Developmental Screening Test. *Journal of Pediatrics*, 1967, *71*, 181–191.

Franklin, R. D. Youth's expectancies about internal versus external control of reinforcement. *Dissertation Abstracts,* 1963, *24,* 1684.

Fraser, C., and Roberts, N. Mothers' speech to children of four different ages. *Journal of Psycholinguistic Research,* 1975, *4,* 9–16.

Frazier, T. M., Davis, G. H., Goldstein, H., and Goldberg, I. Cigarette smoking: A prospective study. *American Journal of Obstetrics and Gynecology,* 1961, *81,* 988–996,

Freedman, D. G. Hereditary control of early social behavior. In B. M. Foss (Ed.), *Determinants of infant behavior,* Volume 3. New York: Wiley, 1965.

Freedman, D. G. *Human infancy: An evolutionary perspective.* Hillsdale, N.J.: Lawrence Erlbaum Associates, 1974.

Freedman, D. G. *Human sociobiology: A holistic approach.* New York: Free Press, 1979.

Freeman, N. H. *Strategies of representation in young children: Analysis of spatial skill and drawing processes.* London: Academic Press, 1980.

Freeman, N. H., Lloyd, S., and Sinha, C. G. Infant search tasks reveal early concepts of containment and canonical usage of objects. *Cognition,* 1980, *8,* 243–262.

Fremgen, A., and Fay, D. Overextensions in production and comprehension: A methodological clarification. *Journal of Child Language,* 1980, *7,* 205–211.

Freud, A. Adolescence. *Psychoanalytic Study of the Child,* 1958, *13,* 255–278.

Freud, S. Three contributions to the sexual theory (Trans. A. A. Brill). *Nervous and Mental Disease Monograph Series, 7,* 1910.

Freud, S. *Three contributions to the theory of sex.* New York: Nervous and Mental Disease Publishing Co., 1930.

Freud, S. *An autobiographical study* (Trans. J. Strachey). London: Hogarth Press, 1935.

Freud, S. *An outline of psychoanalysis.* London: Hogarth Press, 1938. (a)

Freud, S. *The interpretation of dreams* (The Basic Writings). New York: Modern Library, 1938. (Originally published, 1900). (b)

Freud, S. *Instincts and their vicissitudes,* (Vol. 14 of the Standard Edition). London: Hogarth, 1968. (Originally published, 1915).

Freudenberg, R. P., Driscoll, J. W., and Stern, G. S. Reactions of adult humans to cries of normal and abnormal infants. *Infant Behavior and Development,* 1978, *1,* 224–227.

Freuh, T., and McGhee, P. E. Traditional sex role development and amount of time spent watching television. *Developmental Psychology,* 1975, *11,* 109.

Frey, K. S. Differential teaching methods used with girls and boys of moderate and high achievement levels. Paper presented at the meeting of the Society for Research in Child Development, San Francisco, March 1979.

Friedlander, B. Z., Jacobs, A. C., David, B. B., and Wetstone, H. S. Time sampling analysis of infant's natural language environments—the home. *Child Development,* 1972, *43,* 730–740.

Friedman, M. Type A behavior: Its possible relationship to pathogenic processes responsible for coronary heart disease. In T. Dembroski, S. Weiss, J. Shields, S. Haynes, and M. Feinleib (Eds.), *Coronary-prone behavior.* New York: Springer-Verlag, 1978.

Friedman, M., and Rosenman, R. *Type A behavior and your heart.* New York: Knopf, 1974.

Friedman, S. L., and Jacobs, B. S. Sex differences in neonates'

behavioral responsiveness to repeated auditory stimulation. *Infant Behavior and Development,* 1981, *4,* 175–183.

Friedrich, L. K., and Stein, A. H. Aggressive and prosocial television programs and the natural behavior of preschool children. *Monographs of the Society for Research in Child Development,* 1973, *38*(4, Serial No. 151).

Frisch, H. L. Sex stereotypes in adult-infant play. *Child Development,* 1977, *48,* 1671–1675.

Frisch, R. E., and Revelle, R. Height and weight at menarche and a hypothesis of critical body weights and adolescent events. *Science,* 1970, *169,* 397–399.

Frodi, A. M., and Lamb, M. E. Sex differences in responsiveness to infants: A developmental study of psychophysiological and behavioral responses. *Child Development.* 1978, *49,* 1182–1188.

Frodi, A. M., Lamb, M. E., Leavitt, L. A., and Donovan, W. L. Fathers' and mothers' responses to infant smiles and cries. *Infant Behavior and Development,* 1978, *1,* 187–198.

Fullard, W., and Reiling, A. M. An investigation of Lorenz's babyness. *Child Development,* 1976, *47,* 1191–1193.

Furrow, D., Nelson, K., and Benedict, H. Mother's speech to children and syntactic development: Some simple relationships. *Journal of Child Language,* 1979, *6,* 423–442.

Furth, H. G. *Thinking without language: Psychological implications of deafness.* Englewood Cliffs, N.J.: Prentice-Hall, 1966.

Gaffar, M., and Corbier, J. Contribution a l'étude de l'influence socio-économique sur la croissance et le développement de l'enfant. *Courrier,* 1966, *16,* 1–25.

Gagné, R. M., and Smith, E. C. A study for the effects of verbalization on problem-solving. *Journal of Experimental Psychology,* 1962, *63,* 12–18.

Gagnon, J. H. The creation of the sexual in early adolescence. In J. Kagan and R. Coles (Eds.), *Twelve to sixteen.* New York: W. W. Norton, 1972.

Galdston, R. Dysfunction of parenting: The battered child, the neglected child, the emotional child. In J. G. Howells (Ed.), *Modern perspectives in international child psychiatry.* New York: Brunner/Mazel, 1971.

Gallagher, J. M. Reflexive abstraction and education. In J. M. Gallagher and J. Easley (Eds.), *Knowledge and development,* Volume 2, *Piaget and education.* New York: Plenum, 1978.

Galton, F. *Hereditary genius* (1st ed., 1869). Cleveland: World Publishing, 1962.

Gamer, E., Thomas, J., and Kendall, D. Determinants of friendship across the life span. In M. F. Rebelsky (Ed.), *Life: The continuous process.* New York: Knopf, 1975.

Ganchrow, J. R., Steiner, J. E., and Daher, M. Neonatal facial expressions in response to different qualities and intensities of gustatory stimuli. *Infant Behavior and Development,* 1983, *6,* 189–200.

Ganon, E. C., and Swartz, K. B. Perception of internal elements of compound figures by one-month-old infants. *Journal of Experimental Child Psychology,* 1980, *30,* 159–170.

Garbarino, J., Sebes, J., and Schellenbach, C. Families at risk for destructive parent-child relations in adolescence. *Child Development,* 1984, *55,* 174–183.

Garber, H., and Heber, R. The Milwaukee project: Early intervention as a technique to prevent mental retardation. University of Connecticut Technical Paper, March 1973.

Gardner, H. *Artful scribbles: The significance of children's drawings.* New York: Basic Books, 1980.

Gardner, H. *Frames of mind: The theory of multiple intelligences.* New York: Basic Books, 1983.

Gardner, J. A. Sesame Street and sex role stereotypes. *Women,* 1970, *1,* 42.

Garn, S. M. Body size and its implications. In L. W. Hoffman and M. L. Hoffman (Eds.), *Review of child development research,* Volume 2. New York: Russell Sage Foundation, 1966.

Garner, R. Monitoring of passage inconsistency among poor comprehenders: A preliminary test of the "piecemeal processing" explanation. *Journal of Educational Research,* in press.

Garnica, O. K. Some prosodic and paralinguistic features of speech directed to young children. In C. E. Snow and C. A. Ferguson (Eds.), *Talking to children: Language input and acquisition.* Cambridge: Cambridge University Press, 1977.

Garvey, C. Some properties of social play. *Merrill-Palmer Quarterly,* 1974, *20,* 163–180.

Garvey, C. Requests and responses in children's speech. *Journal of Child Language,* 1975, *2,* 41–63.

Garvey, C., and Hogan, R. Social speech and social interaction: Egocentrism revisited. *Child Development,* 1973, *44,* 562–568.

Gayl, I. E., Roberts, J. O., and Warner, J. S. Linear systems analysis of infant visual pattern preferences. *Journal of Experimental Child Psychology,* 1983, *35,* 30–45.

Geffen, G., and Sexton, M. A. The development of auditory strategies of attention. *Developmental Psychology,* 1978, *14,* 11–17.

Gelman, R. Conservation acquisition: A problem of learning to attend to relevant attributes. *Journal of Experimental Child Psychology,* 1969, *7,* 167–187.

Gelman, R. The nature and development of early number concepts. In H. W. Reese (Ed.), *Advances in child development and behavior,* Volume 7. New York: Academic Press, 1972.

Gelman, R., and Baillargeon, R. A review of some Piagetian concepts. In P. H. Mussen (Ed.), *Handbook of child psychology,* Volume 3. New York: Wiley, 1983.

Genshaft, J. L, and Hirt, M. Language differences between black and white children. *Developmental Psychology,* 1974, *10,* 451–456.

Gerbner, G. Violence in television drama: Trends and symbolic functions. In G. A. Comstock and E. A. Rubenstein (Eds.), *Television and social behavior,* Volume, 1, *Media content and control.* Washington, D.C.: U. S. Government Printing Office, 1972.

Geschwind, N. Specialization of the human brain. *Scientific American,* 1979, *241,* 180–201.

Gesell, A. L. *Infancy and human growth.* New York: Macmillan, 1928.

Gessell, A., and Amatruda, C. *Developmental diagnosis.* New York: Paul B. Hoeber, 1941.

Gessell, A., Halverson, H. M., Ilg, F. L., Thompson, H., Castner, B. M., Ames, L. B., and Amatruda, C. S. *The first five years of life.* New York: Harper, 1940.

Gesell, A., and Thompson, H. *Infant behavior: Its geneis and growth.* New York: McGraw-Hill, 1934.

Getts, A. G., and Hill, H. F. Sudden infant death syndrome: Incidence at various altitudes. *Developmental Medicine and Child Neurology,* 1982, *24,* 61–68.

Getzels, J. W., and Csikszentmihalyi, M. *The creative vision: A longitudinal study of problem finding in art.* New York: Wiley, 1976.

Getzels, J. W., and Jackson, P. W. *Creativity and intelligence.* New York: Wiley, 1962.

Gerwirtz, J. L. The course of infant smiling in four childrearing environments in Israel. In B. M. Foss (Ed.), *Determinants of infant behavior,* Volume 3. New York: Wiley, 1965.

Gewirtz, J. L., and Baer, D. M. The effect of brief social deprivation on behaviors for a social reinforcer. *Journal of Abnormal Social Psychology,* 1958, *56,* 49–56. (a)

Gewirtz, J. L., and Baer, D. M. Deprivation and satiation of social reinforcers as drive conditions. *Journal of Abnormal Social Psychology,* 1958, *57,* 165–172. (b)

Gewirtz, J. L., and Boyd, E. F. Does maternal responding imply reduced infant crying? A critique of the 1972 Bell and Ainsworth report. *Child Development,* 1977, *48,* 1200–1207. (a)

Gewirtz, J. L., and Boyd, E. F. Experiments on mother-infant interaction underlying mutual attachment acquisition: The infant conditions the mother. In T. Alloway, P. Pliner, and L. Krames (Eds.), *Attachment behavior: Advances in the study of communication and affect,* Volume 3. New York: Plenum, 1977. (b)

Ghatala, E. S. Developmental changes in incidental memory as a function of meaningfulness and encoding condition. *Developmental Psychology,* 1984, *20,* 208–211.

Ghiselli, E. E. *The validity of occupational aptitude tests.* New York: Wiley, 1966.

Gibson, E. J., Owsley, C. J., and Johnson, J. Perception of invariants by five-month-old infants: Differentiation of two types of motion. *Developmental Psychology,* 1978, *14,* 407–415.

Gibson, E. J., Owsley, C. J., Walker, A., and Megaw-Nyce, J. Development of the perception of invariants: Substance and shape. *Perception,* 1979, *8,* 609–619.

Gibson, E. J., and Rader, N. Attention: The perceiver as performer. In G. A. Hale and M. Lewis (Eds.), *Attention and cognitive development.* New York: Plenum, 1979.

Gibson, E. J., and Spelke, E. S. The development of perception. In P. H Mussen (Ed.), *Handbook of child psychology,* Volume 3. New York: Wiley, 1983.

Gibson, E. J., and Walk, R. D. The "visual cliff." *Scientific American,* 1960, *202,* 64–71.

Gibson, E. J., and Walker, A. Intermodal perception of substance. Paper presented at the meeting of the International Conference on Infant Studies, Austin, Texas, March 1982.

Gick, M. L., and Holyoak, K. J. Analogical problem solving. *Cognitive Psychology,* 1980, *12,* 306–355.

Gilligan, C. *In a different voice: Psychological theory and women's development.* Cambridge: Harvard University Press, 1982.

Glanzer, M. Storage mechanisms in free recall. In G. H. Bower (Ed.), *The psychology of learning and motivation: Advances in research and theory,* Volume 5. New York: Academic Press, 1972.

Glazer, N., and Moynihan, D. P. *Beyond the melting pot.* Cambridge: MIT Press, 1963.

Gleason, J. B., and Weintraub, S. Input language and the acquisition of communication competence. In K. E. Nelson (Ed.), *Children's language,* Volume 1. New York: Gardner Press, 1978.

Gleitman, L. R., Newport, E. L., and Gleitman, H. The current status of the motherese hypothesis. *Journal of Child Language,* 1984, *11,* 43–79.

Glenn, S. M., and Cunningham, C. C. What do babies listen to most? A developmental study of auditory preferences in non-handicapped infants and infants with Down's syndrome. *Developmental Psychology*, 1983, *19*, 332–337.

Glick, P. C. Social change and the American family. In *The Social Welfare Forum, 1977*. Official proceedings, 104th annual forum, National Conference in Social Welfare, Chicago, May 1977, pp. 43–62.

Glick, P. C., and Norton, A. J. Marrying, divorcing, and living together in the United States today. *Population Bulletin, 1977, 32,* 3–38.

Glidewell, J. C., Kantor, M. B., Smith, L. M., and Stringer, L. A. Socialization and social structure in the classroom. In L. W. Hoffman and M. L. Hoffman (Eds.), *Review of child development research,* Volume 2. New York: Russell Sage Foundation, 1966.

Gloger-Tippelt, G. A process model of the pregnancy course. *Human Development*, 1983, *26*, 134–148.

Glucksberg, S., and Cowan, G. N. Memory for nonattended auditory material. *Cognitive Psychology*, 1970, *1*, 149–156.

Glucksberg, S., Krauss, R. M., and Higgins, E. T. The development of referential communication skills. In F. D. Horowitz (Ed.), *Review of child development research,* Volume 4. Chicago: University of Chicago Press, 1975.

Gnepp, J. Children's social sensitivity: Inferring emotions from conflicting cues. *Developmental Psychology*, 1983. *19*, 805–814.

Gnepp, J., Klayman, J., and Trabasso, T. A hierarchy of information sources for inferring emotional reactions. *Journal of Experimental Child Psychology*, 1982, *33*, 111–123.

Goddard, H. H. *The Kallikak family: A study in the heredity of feeble-mindedness.* New York: Macmillan, 1912.

Goertzel, V., and Goertzel, M. G. *Cradles of eminence.* Boston: Little, Brown, 1962.

Goffeney, B., Henderson, N. B., and Butler, B. V. Negro-white, male-female 8-month developmental scores compared with 7-year WISC and Bender test scores. *Child Development,* 1971, *42,* 595–604.

Gold, M., and Reimer, D. J. Changing patterns of delinquent behavior among Americans 13 through 16 years old: 1967–72. *Crime and Delinquency Literature,* 1975, *7,* 483–517.

Goldberg, R. J. Maternal time use and preschool performance. Paper presented at the meeting of the Society for Research in Child Development, New Orleans, March 1977.

Goldberg, S., and DiVitto, B. A. *Born too soon: Preterm birth and early development.* San Francisco: W. H. Freeman, 1983.

Goldberg, S., Perlmutter, M., and Myers, N. Recall of related and unrelated lists by two-year-olds. *Journal of Experimental Child Psychology,* 1974, *18,* 1–8.

Golden, M., and Birns, B. Social class and infant intelligence. In M. Lewis (Ed.), *Origins of intelligence.* New York: Plenum, 1976.

Goldfarb, W. Effects of psychological deprivation in infancy and subsequent stimulation. *American Journal of Psychiatry,* 1945, *102,* 18–33.

Goldin, P. C. A review of children's reports of parent behaviors. *Psychological Bulletin,* 1969, *71,* 222–236.

Goldin-Meadow, S., and Feldman, H. The development of a language-like communication without a language model. *Science,* 1977, *197,* 401–403.

Goldman, B. D., and Ross, H. S. Social skills in action: An analysis of early peer games. In J. Glick and K. A. Clarke-Stewart (Eds.), *The development of social understanding.* New York: Gardner Press, 1978.

Goldman, P. S. Maturation of the mammalian nervous system and the ontogeny of behavior. In J. S. Rosenblatt, R. A. Hinde, E. Shaw, and C. Beer (Eds.), *Advances in the study of behavior,* Volume 7. New York: Academic Press, 1976.

Goldsmith, H. H. Genetic influences on personality from infancy to adulthood. *Child Development,* 1983, *54,* 331–355.

Goldsmith, H. H., and Gottesman, I. I. Origins of variation in behavior style: A longitudinal study of temperament in young twins. *Child Development,* 1981, *52,* 91–103.

Goldstein, H. Factors influencing the height of seven-year-old children: Results from the National Child Development Study. *Human Biology,* 1971, *43,* 92–111.

Golomb, C. *Young children's sculpture and drawing: A study in representation development.* Cambridge: Harvard University Press, 1974.

Golub, H. L., and Corwin, M. J. Infant cry: A clue to diagnosis. *Pediatrics,* 1982, *69,*197–201.

Goodenough, F. L. *Anger in young children.* Minneapolis: University of Minnesota Press, 1931.

Goodnow, J. *Children's drawings.* Cambridge: Harvard University Press, 1977.

Gordon, R. E., and Gordon, K. K. Social factors in prevention of postpartum emotional problems. *Obstetrics and Gynecology,* 1960, *15,* 433–438.

Gordon, R. E., Kapostins, E. E., and Gordon, K. K. Factors in postpartum emotional adjustment. *Obstetrics and Gynecology,* 1965, *25,* 158–166.

Goren, C., Sarty, M., and Wu, P. Visual following and pattern discrimination of face-like stimuli by newborn infants. *Pediatrics,* 1975, *56,* 544–549.

Gottesman, I. I. Heritability of personality: A demonstration. *Psychology Monographs,* 1963, *77,* No. 572.

Gottesman, I. I. Personality and natural selection. In S. G. Vandenberg (Ed.), *Methods and goals in human behavior genetics.* New York: Academic Press, 1965.

Gottesman, I. I., and Shields, J. Schizophrenia in twins: 16 years' consecutive admissions to a psychiatric clinic. *Diseases of the Nervous System,* 1966, *27,* 11–19.

Gottfried, A. W. Home environment and early cognitive development: Integration, meta-analyses, and conclusions. In A. W. Gottfried (Ed.), *Home environment and early cognitive development.* San Francisco: Academic Press, 1984.

Gottfried, A. W., Rose, S. A., and Bridger, W. H. Crossmodal transfer in human infants. *Child Development,* 1977, *48,* 118–123.

Gottman, J. M. How children become friends. *Monographs of the Society for Research in Child Development,* 1983, *48*(2, Serial No. 201).

Gottman, J. M., Gonso, J., and Rasmussen, B. Social interaction, social competence and friendship in children. *Child Development,* 1975, *46,* 709–718.

Gottman, J. M., and Parkhurst, J. T. Developing may not always be improving: A developmental study of children's best friendships. Paper presented at the meeting of the Society for Research in Child Development, New Orleans, March 1977.

Gottman, J. M., and Parkhurst, J. T. A developmental theory of friendship and acquaintanceship processes. In W. A. Collins (Ed.), *Development of cognition, affect, and social relations. The Minnesota Symposia on Child Psychology,* Volume 13. Hillsdale, N.J.: Lawrence Erlbaum Associates, 1980.

Gough, H. E. College attendance among high aptitude students as predicted from the California Psychological Inventory. *Journal of Counseling Psychology,* 1968, *15,* 269–276.

Gratch, G., Appel, K. J., Evans, W. F., LeCompte, G. K., and Wright, N. A. Piaget's Stage IV object concept error: Evidence of forgetting or object conception? *Child Development*, 1974, *15*, 71–77.

Gray, J. A. *The psychology of fear and stress*. New York: McGraw-Hill, 1971.

Gray, S. W., Ramsey, B. K., and Klaus, R. A. *From 3 to 20: The Early Training Project*. Baltimore: University Park Press, 1982.

Greeley, A. M. *Why can't they be like us?* New York: Institute of Human Relations Press, 1969.

Green, E. H. Group play and quarrelling among preschool children. *Child Development*, 1933, *4*, 302–307.

Green, R. *Sissy boys to gay men: A 15-year prospective study*. New Haven, Conn.: Yale University Press, in press.

Greenberg, B. S. Children's reaction to TV blacks. *Journalism Quarterly*, 1972, *49*, 5–14.

Greenberg, D. J. Accelerating visual complexity levels in the human infant. *Child Development*, 1971, *42*, 905–918.

Greenberg, M., and Morris, N. Engrossment: The newborn's impact upon the father. *American Journal of Orthopsychiatry*, 1974, *44*, 520–531.

Greenberg, M., Rosenberg, L., and Lind, J. First mothers rooming-in with their newborns: Its impact upon the mother. *American Journal of Orthopsychiatry*, 1973, *43*, 783–788.

Greenberg, M. T., and Marvin, R. S. Reactions of preschool children to an adult stranger: A behavioral system approach. *Child Development*, 1982, *53*, 481–490.

Greenberg, S. B., and Peck, L. F. A study of pre-schoolers' spontaneous social interaction patterns in three settings: All female, all male and coed. Paper presented at the annual convention of the American Educational Research Association, Chicago, 1974.

Greenfield, P. M., and Smith, J. H. *The structure of communication in early language development*. New York: Academic Press, 1976.

Greenwood, K. The development of communication with mother, father, and sibling. Unpublished doctoral thesis, Cambridge University, 1983.

Greif, E. B., Alvarez, M., and Ulman, K. J. Recognizing emotions in other people: Sex differences in socialization. Paper presented at the biennial meeting of the Society for Research in Child Development, Boston, April 1981.

Greif, E. B., and Ulman, K. J. The psychological impact of menarche on early adolescent females: A review of the literature. *Child Development*, 1982, *53*, 1413–1430.

Griffiths, R. *The abilities of babies*. New York: McGraw-Hill, 1954.

Grobstein, C. External human fertilization. *Scientific American*, 1979, *240*, 57–68.

Groen, G. J., and Parkman, J. M. A chronometric analysis of simple addition. *Psychological Review*, 1972, *79*, 329–343.

Grollman, E. A. *Explaining death to children*. Boston: Beacon Press, 1967.

Grossmann, K., Thane, K., and Grossmann, K. E. Maternal tactual contact of the newborn after various postpartum conditions of mother-infant contact. *Developmental Psychology*, 1981, *17*, 159–169.

Gruber, C. P. Social attributions and children's early peer perceptions. Unpublished doctoral dissertation, University of Chicago, 1984.

Gruber, H. E., and Vonecke, J. J. (Eds.), *The essential Piaget*. New York: Basic Books, 1977.

Guarnaccia, V. J. Pupil tutoring in elementary math instruction. Unpublished doctoral dissertation, Columbia University, 1973.

Guilleminault, C., and Anders, T. Sleep disorders in children, Part II. *Advances in Pediatrics*, 1976, *22*, 151–174.

Guardo, C. J., and Bohan, J. B. Development of a sense of sex-identity in children. *Child Development*, 1971, *42*, 1909–1921.

Guilford, J. P. Creativity: Its measurement and development. In M. Parnes and P. Harding (Eds.), *A source book for creative thinking*. New York: Charles Scribner's Sons, 1962.

Gunnar, M. R., and Donahue, M. Sex differences in social responsiveness between six months and twelve months. *Child Development*, 1980, *51*, 262–265.

Gunnar-Von Gnechten, M. R. Changing a frightening toy into a pleasant toy by allowing the infant to control its actions. *Developmental Psychology*, 1978, *14*, 157–162.

Gupta, S., Dhingra, D. C., Singh, M. V., and Anand, K. Impact of nutrition on intelligence. *Indian Pediatrika*, 1975, *12*, 1079–1082.

Haan, N., Smith, M. B., and Block, J. Moral reasoning of young adults: Political-social behavior, family background, and personality correlates. *Journal of Personality and Social Psychology*, 1968, *10*, 183–201.

Haddad, G. G., Walsh, E. M., Leistner, H. L., Grodin, W. K., and Mellins, R. B. Abnormal maturation of sleep states in infants with aborted sudden infant death syndrome. *Pediatric Research*, 1981, *15*, 1055–1057.

Hagen, J. W., and Hale, G. H. The development of attention in children. In A. D. Pick (Ed.), *Minnesota Symposia on Child Psychology*, Volume 7. Minneapolis: University of Minnesota Press, 1973.

Haith, M. M. The response of the human newborn to visual movement. *Journal of Experimental Child Psychology*, 1966, *3*, 112–117.

Haith, M. M. *Rules that babies look by: The organization of newborn visual acuity*. Hillsdale, N.J.: Lawrence Erlbaum Associates, 1980.

Haith, M. M., Bergman, T., and Rook, M. J. Eye contact and face scanning in early infancy. *Science*, 1977, *198*, 853–855.

Hales, D. J., Lozoff, B., Sosa, R., and Kennell, M. H. Defining the limits of the maternal sensitive period. *Developmental Medicine and Child Neurology*, 1977, *19*, 454–461.

Hall, G. S. The contents of children's minds. *Princeton Review*, 1883, *59*, 38–43.

Hall, G. S. *Adolescence*, Volume 1. New York: D. Appleton & Co., 1904.

Hall, G. S. *Adolescence*, Volume 2. New York: D. Appleton & Co., 1907.

Hall, V. C., and Turner, R. R. The validity of the "different language explanation" for poor scholastic performance by black students. *Review of Educational Research*, 1974, *44*, 69–81.

Hall, W. M. Observational and interactive determinants of aggressive behavior in boys. Unpublished doctoral dissertation, Indiana University, 1974.

Hallgren, B. Enuresis: A clinical and genetic study. *Neurologica Scandinavica et Acta Psychiatrica Neurologica*, 1957, 1–159.

Hallinan, M. T. Recent advances in sociometry. In S. R. Asher and J. M. Gottman (Eds.), *The development of children's friendships*. New York: Cambridge University Press, 1981.

Halverson, C. T., and Waldrop, M. F. Maternal behavior toward own and other preschool children: The problem of "owness." *Child Development*, 1970, *41*, 839–845.

Hamblin, J. A., and Hamblin, R. L. On teaching disadvantaged preschoolers to read: A successful experiment. *American Educational Research Journal*, 1972, *9*, 2209–2216.

Hamburg, B. Early adolescence: A specific and stressful stage of the life cycle. In G. V. Coelho, D. A. Hamburg, and J. E. Adams (Eds.), *Coping and adaptation*. New York: Basic Books, 1974.

Hanson, J. W. Unpublished paper, 1977.

Harding, P. G. R. The metabolism of brown and white adipose tissue in the fetus and newborn. *Clinical Obstetrics and Gynecology*, 1971, *14*, 685–709.

Hardwick, D., McIntyre, A., and Pick, A. The content and manipulation of cognitive maps in children and adults. *Monographs of the Society for Research in Child Development*, 1976, *41*(3, Serial No. 166).

Hardy, J. B., and Mellits, E. D. Does maternal smoking during pregnancy have a long-term effect on the child? *Lancet*, 1972, *2*, 1332–1336.

Hardy-Brown, K. Formal operations and the issue of generality: The analysis of poetry by college students. *Human Development*, 1979, *22*, 127–136.

Hardy-Brown, K., Plomin, R., and DeFries, J. C. Genetic and environmental influences on the rate of communicative development in the first year of life. *Developmental Psychology*, 1981, *17*, 704–717.

Harkness, S. Aspects of social environment and first language acquisition in rural Africa. In C. E. Snow and C. A. Ferguson (Eds.), *Talking to children: Language input and acquisition*. Cambridge: Cambridge University Press, 1977.

Harlow, H. F., and Griffin, G. Induced mental and social deficits in rhesus monkeys. In S. F. Osler and R. E. Cooke (Eds.), *The biosocial bases of mental retardation*. Baltimore: Johns Hopkins University Press, 1965.

Harlow, H. F., and Mears, C. *The human model: Primate perspectives*. New York: Wiley, 1979.

Harlow, H. F., and Zimmerman, R. R. Affectional responses in the infant monkey. *Science*, 1959, *130*, 431–432.

Harper, J. F., and Collins, J. K. The effects of early or late maturation on the prestige of the adolescent girl. *Australian and New Zealand Journal of Sociology*, 1972, *8*, 83–88.

Harris, B. Whatever happened to little Albert? *American Psychologist*, 1979, *34*, 151–160.

Harris, L. J. Sex differences in spatial ability: Possible environmental, genetic and neurological factors. In M. Kinsbourne (Ed.), *Hemispheric asymmetrics of function*. Cambridge: Cambridge University Press, 1975.

Harris, P. L. Perseverative search at a visibly empty place by young infants. *Journal of Experimental Child Psychology*, 1974, *18*, 535–542.

Harris, P. L. Infant cognition. In P. H. Mussen (Ed.), *Handbook of child psychology*, Volume 2. New York: Wiley, 1983.

Harris, P. L., and Bassett, E. Transitive inference by four year old children. *Developmental Psychology*, 1975, *11*, 875–876.

Harter, S. *Children's understanding of multiple emotions: A cognitive-developmental approach*. Address given at the Ninth Annual Piaget Society Meeting, Philadelphia, 1979.

Harter, S. Developmental perspectives on the self-system. In P. H. Mussen (Ed.), *Handbook of child psychology*, Volume 4. New York: Wiley, 1983.

Harter, S., and Connell, J. P. A comparison of alternative models of the relationships between academic achievement, and chil-

dren's perceptions of competence, control, and motivational orientation. In J. Nicholls (Ed.), *The development of achievement–related cognitions and behaviors*. Greenwich, Conn.: JAI Press, 1982.

Hartshorne, H., and May, M. A., *Studies in the nature of character*, Volume, 1, *Studies in deceit*. New York: Macmillan, 1928.

Hartshorne, H., May, M. A., and Maller, J. B. *Studies in the nature of character*, Volume 2, *Studies in self-control*. New York: Macmillan, 1929.

Hartshorne, H., May, M. A., and Shuttleworth, F. K. *Studies in the nature of character*, Volume, 3, *Studies in the organization of character*. New York: Macmillan, 1930.

Hartup, W. W. Peer interaction and social organization. In P. H. Mussen (Ed.), *Carmichael's manual of child psychology*, Volume 2. New York: Wiley, 1970.

Hartup, W. W. Aggression in childhood: Developmental perspectives. *American Psychologist*, 1974, *29*, 336–341.

Hartup, W. W. Peer relations. In P. H. Mussen (Ed.), *Handbook of child psychology*, Volume 4. New York: Wiley, 1983.

Hartup, W. W., and Coates, B. Imitation of a peer as a function of reinforcement from the peer group and rewardingness of the model. *Child Development*, 1967, *38*, 1003–1016.

Hartup, W. W., and Keller, E. D. Nurturance in preschool children and its relation to dependency. *Child Development*, 1960, *31*, 681–690.

Harvey, D., Prince, J., Bunton, J., Parkinson, C., and Campbell, S. Abilities of children who were small-for-gestational-age babies. *Pediatrics*, 1982, *69*, 296–300.

Hasher, L., and Clifton, D. A. A developmental study of attribute encoding in free recall. *Journal of Experimental Child Psychology*, 1974, *7*, 332–346.

Hatfield, J. S., Ferguson, L. R., and Alpert, R. Mother-child interaction and the socialization process. *Child Development*, 1967, *38*, 365–414.

Hausknecht, R., and Heilman, J. R. *Having a cesarean baby*. New York: Dutton, 1978.

Hay, D. F., Nash, A., and Pedersen, J. Responses of six-month-olds to the distress of their peers. *Child Development*, 1981, *52*, 1071–1075.

Hay, D. F., and Ross, H. S. The social nature of early conflict. *Child Development*, 1982, *53*, 105–113.

Hayes, D. S., and Birnbaum, D. W. Preschoolers' retention of televised events: Is a picture worth a thousand words? *Developmental Psychology*, 1980, *16*, 410–416.

Hayes, L. A., and Watson, J. S. Facial orientation of parents and elicited smiling by infants. *Infant Behavior and Development*, 1981, *4*, 333–3409.

Hebb, D. O. *The organization of behavior*. New York: Wiley, 1949.

Heider, E. R. "Focal" color areas and the development of color names. *Developmental Psychology*, 1971, *4*, 447–455. (a)

Heider, E. R. Information processing and the modification of an "impulsive conceptual tempo." *Child Development*, 1971, *42*, 1276–1281. (b)

Heinicke, C. M., and Westheimer, I. *Brief separations*. New York: International Universities Press, 1966.

Heinonen, O. P., Slone, D., and Shapiro, S. *Birth defects and drugs in pregnancy*. Littleton, Mass.: Publishing Sciences Group, 1976.

Hellman, L. M., and Pritchard, J. A. *Williams' obstetrics* (14th ed.). New York: Appleton-Century-Crofts, 1971.

Helson, R., and Crutchfield, R. S. Mathematicians: The creative researcher and the average PhD. *Journal of Consulting and Clinical Psychology,* 1970, *34,* 250–257.

Henker, B., and Whalen, C. K. The changing faces of hyperactivity: Retrospect and Prospect. In C. K. Whalen, and B. Henker, (Eds.), *Hyperactive children: The social ecology of identification and treatment.* New York: Academic Press, 1980.

Hershenson, M. Visual discrimination in the human newborn. *Journal of Comparative Physiological Psychology,* 1964, *58,* 270–276.

Hess, R., and Camera, K. Post-divorce family relationships as mediating factors in the consequences of divorce for children. *Journal of Social Issues,* 1979, *35,* 333–343.

Heston, L. L. The genetics of schizophrenic and schizoid disease. *Science,* 1970, *167,* 249–256.

Hetherington, E. M., Cox, M., and Cox, R. Aftermath of divorce. Paper presented at the meeting of the American Psychological Association. Washington, D.C., September 1976. (a)

Hetherington, E. M., Cox, M., and Cox, R. Divorced fathers. *Family Coordinator,* 1976, *25,* 417–428. (b)

Hetherington, E. M., Cox, M., and Cox, R. Family interaction and the social emotional, and cognitive development of children following divorce. Paper presented at the Symposium on The family: Setting priorities. Sponsored by the Institute for Pediatric Service of the Johnson and Johnson Baby Company. Washington, D.C., May 17–20, 1978.

Hetherington, E. M., Cox, M., and Cox, R. Effects of divorce on parents and children. In M. Lamb (Ed.), *Nontraditional families.* Hillsdale, N.J.: Lawrence Erlbaum Associates, 1982.

Hetherington, E. M., and Feldman, S. E. College cheating as a function of subject and situational variables. *Journal of Educational Psychology,* 1964, *55,* 212–218.

Hetherington, E. M., and Parke, R. D. *Child psychology: A contemporary viewpoint.* New York: McGraw-Hill, 1975.

Hiatt, S. W., Campos, J. J., and Emde, R. N. Facial patterning and infant emotional expression: Happiness, surprise, and fear. *Child Development,* 1979, *50,* 1020–1035.

Hickey, J. Stimulation of moral reasoning in delinquents. Unpublished doctoral dissertation, Boston University, 1972.

Hicks, D. J. Imitation and retention of film-mediated aggressive peer and adult models. *Journal of Personality and Social Psychology,* 1965, *2,* 97–100.

Hier, D. B., LeMay, M., and Rosenberger, P. B. Autism and unfavorable left-right asymmetrics of the brain. *Journal of Autism and Developmental Disorders,* 1979, *9,* 153–159.

Hill, C. R., and Stafford, F. P. Parental care of children: Time diary estimates of quantity predictability and variety. Working paper series, Institute for Social Research, University of Michigan, Ann Arbor, 1978.

Hill, J. P., and Palmquist, W. J. Social cognition and social relations in early adolescence. *International Journal of Behavioral Development,* 1978, *1,* 1–36.

Hill, R. Drugs ingested by pregnant women. *Clinical Pharmacology Therapeutics,* 1973, *14,* 654–659.

Himes, N. E. *Medical history of conception.* Baltimore: Williams & Wilkins, 1936.

Himmelberger, D. V., Brown, B. W., Jr., and Cohen, E. N. Cigarette smoking during pregnancy and the occurrence of spontaneous abortion and cogenital abnormality. *American Journal of Epidemiology,* 1978, *108,* 470–479.

Hinde, R. A., and Spencer-Booth, Y. Effects of brief separation from mother on rhesus monkeys. *Science,* 1971, *173,* 111–118.

Hines, M., and Shipley, C. Prenatal exposure to diethylstilbesterol (DES) and the development of sexually dimorphic cognitive abilities and cerebral lateralization. *Developmental Psychology,* 1984, *20,* 81–94.

Hirsch, J. Cell number and size as a determinant of subsequent obesity. In M. Winick (Ed.), *Childhood obesity.* New York: Wiley, 1975.

Hirsh-Pasek, K., Treiman, R., and Schneiderman, M. Brown and Hanlon revisited: Mothers' sensitivity to ungrammatical forms. *Journal of Child Language,* 1984, *11,* 81–88.

Hochschild, A. Inside the clockwork of male careers. In F. Howe (Ed.), *Women and the power of change.* New York: McGraw-Hill, 1975.

Hock, E. *Alternative approaches to child rearing and their effects on the mother-infant relationship.* Columbus: Ohio State University Press, 1976.

Hock, E. Working and nonworking mothers and their infants: A comparative study of maternal caregiving characteristics and infant social behavior. *Merrill-Palmer Quarterly,* 1980, *26,* 79–101.

Hodapp, T. V. Children's ability to learn problem-solving strategies from television. *Alberta Journal of Educational Research,* 1977, *23,* 171–177.

Hodkin, B. Language effects in assessment of class-inclusion ability. *Child Development,* 1981, *52,* 470–478.

Hoffman, L. W. Early childhood experiences and women's achievement motives. *Journal of Social Issues,* 1972, *28,* 129–156.

Hoffman, L. W. Changes in family roles, socialization and sex differences. *American Psychologist,* 1977, *32,* 644–657.

Hoffman, L. W. Maternal employment: 1979. *American Psychologist,* 1979, *34,* 859–865.

Hoffman, L. W. The effects of maternal employment on the academic attitudes and performance of school-aged children. *School Psychology Review,* 1980, *9,* 319–336.

Hoffman, L. W. Maternal employment and the young child. In M. Perlmutter (Ed.), *Parent-child interaction and parent-child relations in child development. The Minnesota Symposia on Child Psychology,* Volume 17. Hillsdale, N.J.: Lawrence Erlbaum Associates, 1984.

Hoffman, L. W., and Manis, J. D. Influences of children on marital interaction and parental satisfactions and dissatisfactions. Paper presented at the Conference on Human and Family Development: Contributions of the Child to Marital Quality and Family Interaction Across the Life Span, Pennsylvania State University, University Park, April, 1977.

Hoffman, M. L. Moral development. In P. M. Mussen (Ed.), *Carmichael's manual of child psychology,* Volume 2. New York: Wiley, 1970.

Hoffman, M. L. Altruistic behavior and the parent-child relationship. *Journal of Personality and Social Psychology,* 1975, *31,* 937–943.

Hoffman, M. L. Empathy, role-taking, guilt, and development of altruistic motives. In T. Lickona (Ed.), *Moral development and behavior: Theory, research, and social issues.* New York: Holt, Rinehart & Winston, 1976.

Hoffman, M. L. Sex differences in empathy and related behaviors. *Psychological Bulletin,* 1977, *84,* 712–722.

Hoffman, M. L. Toward a theory of empathic arousal and development. In M. Lewis and L. A. Rosenblum (Eds.), *The development of affect.* New York: Plenum, 1978.

Hoffman, M. L. Empathy, guilt, and social cognition. Paper

presented at the ninth annual symposium of the Jean Piaget Society, Philadelphia, May 31–June 2, 1979.

Hoffman, M. L. Development of prosocial motivation: Empathy and guilt. In N. Eisenberg (Ed.), *The development of prosocial behavior.* New York: Academic Press, 1982.

Hoffman, M. L., and Saltzstein, H. D. Parent discipline and the child's moral development. *Journal of Personality and Social Psychology,* 1967, *5,* 45–47.

Hoffman, R. F. Developmental changes in human infant visual-evoked potentials to patterned stimuli recorded at different scalp locations. *Child Development,* 1978, *49,* 110–118.

Hofstaetter, P. R. The changing composition of intelligence: A study of the t-technique. *Journal of Genetic Psychology,* 1954, *85,* 159–164.

Hogan, D. Family structure affects risk of teen pregnancy. *University of Chicago Chronicle,* 1982, *2*(2), 4.

Hollingshead, A. B., and Redlich, F. C. *Social class and mental illness: A community study.* New York: Wiley, 1958.

Hollos, M. Logical operations and role-taking abilities in two cultures: Norway and Hungary. *Child Development,* 1975, *46,* 638–649.

Hollos, M. Comprehension and use of social rules in pronoun selection by Hungarian children. In S. Ervin-Tripp and C. Mitchell-Kerman (Eds.), *Child discourse.* New York: Academic Press, 1977.

Holt, J. H. *How children fail.* New York: Dell, 1964.

Holtzman, W. H., Diaz-Guerrero, R., and Swartz, J. D. *Personality development in two cultures: A cross-cultural longitudinal study of school children in Mexico and the United States.* Austin: University of Texas Press, 1975.

Honzik, M. P. Value and limitations of infant tests: An overview. In M. Lewis (Ed.), *Origins of intelligence: Infancy and early childhood.* New York: Plenum Press, 1976.

Honzik, M. P., Macfarlane, J. W., and Allen, L. The stability of mental test performance between two and eighteen years. In R. G. Kuhlen (Ed.), *Studies in educational psychology.* Waltham, Mass.: Blaisdell, 1968.

Hoppenbrouwers, T., Calub, M., Arakawa, K., and Hodgman, J. E. SIDS and environmental pollutants. *American Journal of Epidemiology,* 1981, *113,* 623–635.

Horn, J. L. Organization of abilities and the development of intelligence. *Psychological Review,* 1968, *75,* 242–259.

Horn, J. L., and Cattell, R. B. Refinement and test of the theory of fluid and crystallized general intelligence. *Journal of Educational Psychology,* 1966, *51,* 253–270.

Horne, A., and Reinker, P. Father absence as it covaries with out-of-control child behaviors. Unpublished manuscript, University of Indianapolis, Terre Haute, 1978.

Horowitz, A. B., and Horowitz, V. A. The effects of task-specific instructions on the encoding activities of children in recall and recognition tasks. Paper presented at the biennial meeting of the Society for Research in Child Development, Denver, April 1975.

Horsley, S. Psychological management of the pre-natal period. In J. G. Howells (Ed.), *Modern perspectives in psycho-obstetrics.* Edinburgh: Oliver and Boyd, 1972.

Horwitz, R. A. Psychological effects of the "open classroom." *Review of Educational Research,* 1979, *49,* 71–86.

Householder, J., Hatcher, R., Burns, W. J., and Chasnoff, I. Infants born to narcotic-addicted mothers. *Psychological Bulletin,* 1982, *92,* 453–468.

Hoversten, G. H., and Moncur, J. P. Stimuli and intensity factors in testing infants. *Journal of Speech and Hearing Research,* 1969, *12,* 687–702.

How children grow. General Clinical Research Centers Branch, Division of Research Resources. National Institute of Health (DHEW), Bethesda, Md., 1972.

Hudson, J., and Nelson, K. Effects of script structure on children's story recall. *Developmental Psychology,* 1983, *19,* 625–635.

Hughey, M. J., McElin, T. W., and Young, T. Maternal and fetal outcome of Lamaze prepared patients. *Obstetrics and Gynecology,* 1978, *51,* 643–647.

Humphrey, G. The conditioned reflex and the elementary social reaction. *Journal of Abnormal and Social Psychology,* 1922, *17,* 113–119.

Humphrey, T. The development of human fetal activity and its relation to postnatal behavior. In H. W. Reese and L. P. Lipsitt (Eds.), *Advances in child development and behavior,* Volume 5. New York: Academic Press, 1970.

Hunt, C. C. Interveiwed by Peter Gorner, "The sleeping world of quiet mysteries and silent killers." Chicago Tribune, May 3, 1982, Section 3, p. 1.

Hunt, E., and Love, T. How good can memory be? In A. W. Melton and E. Martin (Eds.), *Coding processes in human memory.* Washington, D.C.: Holt, Rinehart & Winston, 1972.

Hunter, F. T., and Youniss, J. Changes in functions of three relations during adolescence. *Developmental Psychology,* 1982, *18,* 806–811.

Hunter, S., Wolf, T., Sklov, M., Webber, L., and Berenson, G. A-B coronary-prone behavior pattern and cardiovascular risk factor variables in children and adolescents: The Bogalusa heart study. Paper presented at the American College of Cardiology, San Francisco, March 1981.

Huttenlocher, J. The origins of language comprehension. In R. L. Solso (Ed.), *Theories in cognitive psychology.* Hillsdale, N.J.: Lawrence Erlbaum Associates, 1974.

Huttenlocher, J., and Presson, C. B. Mental rotation and the perspective problem. *Cognitive Psychology,* 1973, *4,* 277–299.

Huttenlocher, P. Press release, University of Chicago, July 1979.

Huttunen, M. O., and Niskanen, P. Prenatal loss of father and psychiatric disorders. *Archives of General Psychiatry,* 1978, *35,* 429–431.

Ickes, W., and Earnes, R. D. Boys and girls together—and alienated: On enacting stereotyped sex roles in mixed-sex dyads. *Journal of Personality and Social Psychology,* 1978, *36,* 669–683.

Ilg, F. L., and Ames, L. B. *An atlas of infant behavior: A systematic delineation of the forms and early growth of human behavior.* New Haven, Conn.: Yale University Press, 1934.

Ilg, F. L., and Ames, L. B. *Infant and child in the culture of today.* New York: Harper & Row, 1943.

Illsley, R. The sociological study of reproduction and its outcome. In S. A. Richardson and A. F. Guttmacher (Eds.), *Childbearing: Its social and psychological aspects.* Baltimore: Williams & Wilkins, 1967.

Inhelder, B., and Karmiloff-Smith, A. Thought and language. In B. Presseisen, D. Golds, and M. Appel (Eds.), *Topics on cognitive development,* Volume 2, *Language and operational thought.* New York: Plenum, 1978.

Inhelder, B., and Piaget, J. *The growth of logical thinking from childhood to adolescence.* New York: Basic Books, 1958.

Inhelder, B., Sinclair, H., and Bovet, B. *Learning and development of cognition.* Cambridge: Harvard University Press, 1974.

Isaacs, S. *Social development in young children.* New York: Schocken Books, 1972. (Originally published, 1933)

Isen, A. M., Clark M., and Schwartz, M. The duration of the effect of good mood on helping: "Footprints in the sands of time." *Journal of Personality and Social Psychology,* 1976, *34,* 385–393.

Isen, A. M., Horn, N., and Rosenhan, D. L. Effects of success and failure on children's generosity. *Journal of Personality and Social Psychology,* 1973, *27,* 239–247.

Isen, A. M., and Levin, P. F. Effect of feeling good on helping: Cookies and kindness. *Journal of Personality and Social Psychology,* 1972, *21,* 354–358.

Iskrant, A. P., and Joliet, P. Y. *Accidents and homicide.* Vital Health and Statistics Monographs, American Public Health Association. Cambridge, Mass.: Harvard University Press, 1968.

Istomina, Z. M. The development of voluntary memory in preschool-age children. *Soviet Psychology,* 1975, *13,* 5–64.

Iverson, L. L. The chemistry of the grain. *Scientific American,* 1979, *241,* 134–149.

Ivey, M. E., and Bardwick, J. M. Patterns of affective fluctuation in the menstrual cycle. *Psychosomatic Medicine,* 1968, *30,* 336–345.

Izard, C. E. *The face of emotions.* New York: Appleton, 1971.

Izard, C. E. *Human emotions.* New York: Plenum, 1977.

Izard, C. E. *The maximally discriminative facial movement coding system (MAX).* Newark: Instructional Resources Center, University of Delaware, 1979.

Izard, C. E. The primacy of emotion in human development. Paper presented at symposium on emotion and cognition at the biennial meeting of the Society for Research on Child Development, Boston, April 1981.

Izard, C. E., Hembree, E. A., Dougherty, L. M., and Spizzirri, C. C. Changes in facial expressions of 2- to 19-month-old infants following acute pain. *Developmental Psychology,* 1983, *19,* 418–426.

Izard, C. E., Huebner, R. R., Risser, D., McGinnes, G. C., and Dougherty, L. M. The young infant's ability to produce discrete emotion expressions. *Developmental Psychology,* 1980, *16,* 132–141.

Izard, C. E., Izard, C. E., Jr., and Makarenko, Y. A. Observations on a communal group of infants. Unpublished manuscript, University of Delaware, 1977.

Jacklin, C. N., and Maccoby, E. E. Social behavior at thirty-three months in the same-sex and mixed-sex dyads. *Child Development,* 1978, *49,* 557–569.

Jakobson, R. *Child language, aphasia and phonological universals.* The Hague: Mouton, 1968.

JAMA (Journal of the American Medical Association). Editorial: "Obstetrics analgesia and anesthesia," 1957, *165,* 2198.

Jeffers, V. W., and Lore, R. K. Let's play at my house: Effects of the home environment on the social behavior of children. *Child Development,* 1979, *50,* 837–841.

Jelliffe, D. B., and Jelliffe, E. F. P. "Breast-feeding is desirable—and vital for the poor." *Chicago Tribune,* May 5/6, 1982, Section 7, p. 13.

Jencks, C., Smith, M., Acland, H., Bane, M. J., Cohen, D., Gintis, H., Heyns, B., and Michaelson, S. *Inequality: A reassessment of the effect of family and schooling in America.* New York: Harper & Row, 1972.

Jensen, A. R. How much can we boost IQ and scholastic achievement? *Harvard Educational Review,* 1969, *39,* 1–123.

Jensen, A. R. *Educability and group differences.* New York: Harper & Row, 1973.

Jensen, A. R. Cumulative deficit in IQ of blacks in the rural south. *Developmental Psychology,* 1977, *13,* 184–191.

Jensen, A. R. *Bias in mental testing.* New York: Free Press, 1980.

Jensen, K. Differential reactions to taste and temperature stimuli in newborn infants. *Genetic Psychology Monographs,* 1932, *12,* 363–479.

Jersild, A. T., and Holmes, F. B. Children's fears. *Child Development Monograph, 20.* New York: Teachers College Press, Columbia University, 1935.

Jersild, A. T., and Markey, F. V. Conflicts between preschool children. *Child Development Monograph, 21.* New York: Teachers College Press, Columbia University, 1935.

Jessor, R., and Jesor, S. L. The transition from virginity to nonvirginity among youth: A social-psychological study over time. *Developmental Psychology,* 1975, *11,* 473–484.

Joffe, J. M. *Prenatal determinants of behavior.* Oxford: Pergamon, 1969.

Johnson, D. B. Self-recognition in infants. *Infant Behavior and Development,* 1983, *6,* 211–222.

Johnson, N. S., and Mandler, J. M. A tale of two structures: Underlying and surface forms in stories. *Poetics,* 1980, *9,* 51–86.

Johnson, S. M., Wahl, G., Martin, S., and Johanssen, S. How deviant is the normal child: A behavioral analysis of the pre-school child and his family. In R. D. Rubin, J. P. Brady, and J. D. Henderson (Eds.), *Advances in behavior therapy,* Volume 4. New York: Academic Press, 1973.

Johnston, L. D., and Bachman, J. G. *Highlights from student drug use in America, 1975–1980.* National Institute on Drug Abuse. Washington, D.C.: U.S. Government Printing Office, 1981.

Jones, M. C. The later careers of boys who were early or late maturing. *Child Development,* 1957, *28,* 113–128.

Jones, M. C. Personality correlates and antecedents of drinking patterns in adult males. *Journal of Consulting and Clinical Psychology,* 1968, *32,* 2–12.

Jones, M. C., and Bayley, N. Physical maturing among boys as related to behavior. *Journal of Educational Psychology,* 1950, *41,* 129–148.

Jones, K. L., Smith, D. W., Ulleland, C. N., and Streissguth, A. P. Pattern of malformation in offspring of chronic alcoholic mothers. *Lancet,* 1973, *1,* 1267–1271.

Jones, O. H. M. Mother-child communication with pre-linguistic Down's syndrome and normal infants. In H. R. Schaffer (Ed.), *Studies in mother-infant interaction.* New York: Academic Press, 1977.

Jones, S. J., and Moss, H. A. Age, state, and maternal behavior associated with infant vocalizations. *Child Development,* 1971, *42,* 1039–1051.

Jones, W. R. A critical study of bilingualism and nonverbal intelligence. *British Journal of Educational Psychology,* 1960, *30,* 71–76.

Joos, S. K., Pollitt, E., Mueller, W. H., and Albright, D. L. The Bacon Chow Study: Maternal nutritional supplementation and infant behavioral development. *Child Development,* 1983, *54,* 669–676.

Jusczyk, P. W. Perception of syllable-final stop consonants by 2-month-old infants. *Perception and Psychophysics,* 1977, *21,* 450–454.

Jusczyk, P. W., Pisoni, D. B., Walley, A. C., and Murray, J. Discrimination of relative onset time of two-component tones by infants. *Journal of the Acoustical Society of America,* 1980, *67,* 262–270.

Jusczyk, P. W., Rosner, B. S., Cutting, J. E., Foard, F., and Smith, L. B. Categorical perception of non-speech sounds by 2-month-old infants. *Perceptions and Psychophysics,* 1977, *21,* 50–54.

Just, M. A., and Carpenter, P. A. A theory of reading: From eye fixations to comprehension. *Psychological Review,* 1980, *87,* 329–354.

Kagan, J. Impulsive and reflective children: Significance of conceptual tempo. In J. D. Krumboltz (Ed.), *Learning and the educational process.* Chicago: Rand McNally, 1965.

Kagan, J. *Change and continuity in infancy.* New York: Wiley, 1971.

Kagan, J. Discrepancy, temperament and infant distress. In M. Lewis and L. Rosenblum (Eds.), *The origins of fear.* New York: Wiley, 1974.

Kagan, J. On emotion and its development: A working paper. In M. Lewis and L. A. Rosenblum (Eds.), *The development of affect.* New York: Plenum, 1978.

Kagan, J. The construct of difficult temperament: A reply to Thomas, Chess, and Korn. *Merrill-Palmer Quarterly,* 1982, *28,* 21–24. (a)

Kagan, J. The idea of emotion in human development. In C. E. Izard (Ed.), *Measuring emotions in infants and children.* New York: Cambridge University Press, 1982. (b)

Kagan, J., Kearsley, R. B., and Zelazo, P. R. *Infancy: Its place in human development.* Cambridge: Harvard University Press, 1978.

Kagan, J., and Klein, R. E. Cross-cultural perspectives on early development, *American Psychologist,* 1973, *28,* 947–961.

Kagan, J., Klein, R. E., Finley, G. E., Rogoff, B., and Nolan, E. A cross-cultural study of cognitive development. *Monographs of the Society for Research in Child Development,* 1979, *44*(5, Serial No. 180).

Kagan, J., and Kogan, N. Individual variation in cognitive process. In P. H. Mussen (Ed.), *Carmichael's manual of child psychology,* Volume 2. New York: Wiley, 1970.

Kagan, J., and Moss, H. A. *Birth to maturity.* New York: Wiley, 1962.

Kagan, J., Rosman, B. L., Day, D., Alberg, J., and Phillips, W. Information processing in the child: Significance of analytic and reflective attitudes. *Psychological Monographs,* 1964, *78*(1, Whole No. 578).

Kagan, J., and Tulkin, S. R. Social class differences in child rearing during the first year. In H. R. Schaffer (Ed.), *The origins of human social relations.* London: Academic Press, 1971.

Kagan, S., and Madsen, M. C. Cooperation and competition of Mexican, Mexican-American, and Anglo-American children of two ages under four instructional sets. *Developmental Psychology,* 1971, *5,* 32–29.

Kahn, A., and Blum, D. Phenothiazines and Sudden Infant Death Syndrome. *Pediatrics,* 1982, *70,* 75–79.

Kail, R., and Nippold, M. A. Unconstrained retrieval from semantic memory. *Child Development,* 1984, *55,* 944–951.

Kail, R., Pellegrino, J., and Carter, P. Developmental changes in mental rotation. *Journal of Experimental Child Psychology,* 1980, *29,* 102–116.

Kales, A., Jacobson, A., Kun, T., Klein, J., Heuser, G., and Paulson, M. Somnambulism: Further all-night EEG studies.

Electroencephalography and Clinical Neurophysiology, 1966, *21,* 410.

Kales, A., Jacobson, A., Paulson, M., Kales, J., and Walter, R. Somnambulism: Psychophysiological correlates, I. *Archives of General Psychiatry,* 1966, *14,* 586–594.

Kales, J. D., Kales, A., Soldatos, C. R., Chamberlin, K., and Martin, E. D. Sleepwalking and night terrors related to febrile illness. *American Journal of Psychiatry,* 1979, *136,* 1214–1215.

Kalil, K., and Reh, T. Regrowth of severed axons in the neonatal central nervous system: Establishment of normal connections. *Science,* 1979, *205,* 1158–1161.

Kameya, L. I. The effect of empathy level and role-taking training upon prosocial behavior. Unpublished doctoral dissertation, University of Michigan, 1976.

Kamin, L. J. A positive interpretation of apparent "cumulative deficit." *Developmental Psychology,* 1978, *14,* 195–196.

Kanner, L. Problems of nosology and psychodynamics of early infantile autism. *American Journal of Orthopsychiatry,* 1949, *19, 416–426.*

Karnes, M. B., Teska, J. A., and Hodgins, A. S. An approach for working with mothers of disadvantaged preschool children. *Merrill-Palmer Quarterly,* 1968, *14,* 174–184.

Kass, N. Resistance to extinction as a function of age and schedules of reinforcement. *Journal of Experimental Psychology,* 1962, *64,* 249–252.

Kass, N., and Wilson, H. Resistance to extinction as a function of percentage of reinforcement, number of training trials, and conditioned reinforcement. *Journal of Experimental Psychology,* 1966, *71,* 355–357.

Katchadourian, H. Medical perspectives on adulthood. *Daedalus,* Spring 1976.

Kato, S. *A history of Japanese literature.* Tokyo: Kodansha International, 1979.

Katz, I., Roberts, S. O., and Robinson, J. M. Effects of difficulty, race of administrator and instructions on Negro digit-symbol performance. *Journal of Personality and Social Psychology,* 1965, *70,* 53–59.

Kaufman, R., Maland, J., and Yonas, A. Sensitivity of 5- and 7-month-old infants to pictorial depth information. *Journal of Experimental Child Psychology,* 1981, *32,* 162–168.

Kavanaugh, R. D. Observations on the role of logically constrained sentences in the comprehension of "before" and "after." *Journal of Child Language,* 1979, *6,* 353–357.

Kavanaugh, R. D., and Jirkovsky, A. M. Parental speech to young children: A longitudinal analysis. *Merrill-Palmer Quarterly,* 1982, *28,* 297–311.

Kaye, K. Toward the origin of dialogue. In H. R. Schaffer (Ed.), *Studies in mother-infant interaction.* London: Academic Press, 1977.

Kaye, K., and Marcus, J. Imitation over a series of trials without feedback: Age six months. *Infant Behavior and Development,* 1978, *1,* 141–155.

Kazdin, A. E., and Bryan, J. H. Competence and volunteering. *Journal of Experimental Social Psychology,* 1971, *7,* 87–96.

Kearsley, R. The newborn's response to auditory stimulation: A demonstration of orienting and defensive behavior. *Child Development,* 1973, *44,* 582–590.

Keating, D. P. Thinking processes in adolescence. In J. Adelson (Ed.), *Handbook of adolescent psychology.* New York: Wiley, 1980.

Keating, D. P., and Bobbitt, B. L. Individual and developmental differences in cognitive-processing components of mental ability. *Child Development,* 1978, *49,* 155–167.

Keenan, E. Conversational competence in children. *Journal of Child Language,* 1974, *1,* 163–183.

Keenan, E. O. Making it last: Repetition in children's discourse. In S. Ervin-Tripp and C. Mitchell-Kernan (Eds.), *Child discourse.* New York: Academic Press, 1977.

Keeney, T. J., Canizzo, S. R., and Flavell, J. H. Spontaneous and induced verbal rehearsal in a recall task. *Child Development,* 1967, *38,* 953–966.

Keller, A., Ford, L. H., and Meacham, J. A. Dimensions of self-concept in preschool children. *Developmental Psychology,* 1978, *14,* 483–489.

Kellogg, R. *Analyzing children's art.* Palo Alto, Calif.: Mayfield, 1970.

Kempe, H. C., and Helfer, R. E. (Eds.) *Helping the battered child and his family.* Philadelphia: Lippincott, 1972.

Kendler, T. S. Verbalization and optional reversal shifts among kindergarten children. *Journal of Verbal Learning and Verbal Behavior,* 1964, *3,* 428–436.

Kendler, T. S., and Kendler, H. H. Reversal and nonreversal shifts in kindergarten children. *Journal of Experimental Psychology,* 1959, *58,* 56–60.

Kendler, T. S., Kendler, H. H., and Wells, D. Reversal and nonreversal shifts in nursery school children. *Journal of Comparative and Physiological Psychology,* 1960, *53,* 83–88.

Kendrick, C., and Dunn, J. Caring for a second child: Effects on the interaction between mother and first-born. *Developmental Psychology,* 1980, *16,* 303–311.

Kendrick, C., and Dunn, J. Sibling quarrels and maternal responses. *Developmental Psychology,* 1983, *19,* 62–70.

Kennell, J. H., Jerauld, R., Wolfe, H., Chesler, D., Kreger, N. C., McAlpine, W., Steffa, M., and Klaus, M. H. Maternal behavior one year after early and extended postpartum contact. *Developmental Medicine and Child Neurology,* 1974, *16,* 172–179.

Kenney, J. L., and Nodine, C. F. Developmental changes in sensitivity to the content, formal and affective dimensions of painting. *Bulletin of the Psychonomic Society,* 1979, *14,* 463–466.

Kerasotes, D., and Walker, C. E. Hyperactive behavior in children. In C. E. Walker and M. C. Roberts (Eds.), *Handbook of clinical child psychology.* New York: Wiley, 1983.

Kessen, W. Research design in the study of developmental problems. In P. H. Mussen (Ed.), *Handbook of research methods in child development.* New York: Wiley, 1960.

Kessen, W. *The child.* New York: Wiley, 1965.

Kessen, W. (Ed.) *Childhood in China.* New Haven, Conn.: Yale University Press, 1975.

Keye, E. *The family guide to children's television.* New York: Random House, 1974.

Kidd, R. F., and Berkowitz, L. Dissonance, self-concept, and helplessness. *Journal of Personality and Social Psychology,* 1976, *33,* 613–622.

Kimura, D. The asymmetry of the human brain. *Scientific American,* 1975, 70–78.

King, K., Negus, K., and Vance, J. C. Heat stress in motor vehicles: A problem in infancy. *Pediatrics,* 1981, *68,* 579–582.

Kinloch, G. C. Parent-youth conflict at home. An investigation among university freshmen. *Journal of Orthopsychiatry,* 1970, *40,* 658–664.

Kinsbourne, M. Minimal brain dysfunction as a neurodevelopmental lag. *Annals of the New York Academy of Sciences,* 1973, *205,* 268–273.

Kinsey, A. C., Pomeroy, W. B., and Martin, C. E., *Sexual behavior in the human male.* Philadelphia: Saunders, 1948.

Kinsey, A. C., Pomeroy, W. B., Martin, C. E., and Gebhard, P. H. *Sexual behavior in the human female.* Philadelphia: Saunders, 1953.

Kirkwood, S. W. Aspects of fetal environment. In H. Wolff (Ed.), *Mechanisms of congenital malformation.* New York: Association for the Aid of Crippled Children, 1955.

Klahr, D. Nonmonotone assessment of monotone development: An information processing analysis. In S. Strauss and R. Stavy (Eds.), *U-shaped behavior growth.* New York: Academic Press, 1982.

Klahr, D., and Wallace, J. G. *Cognitive development: An information processing view.* Hillsdale, N.J.: Lawrence Erlbaum Associates, 1976.

Klaus, M. H., and Kennell, J. H. *Maternal-infant bonding.* St. Louis: C. V. Mosby, 1976.

Klaus, M. H., Kennell, J. H., Plumb, N., and Zuehlke, S. Human maternal behavior at first contact with her young. *Pediatrics,* 1970, *46,* 187–192.

Klaus, R., and Gray, S. The early training project for disadvantaged children: A report after five years. *Monographs of the Society for Research in Child Development,* 1968, *33*(4, Serial No. 120).

Kleck, R. E., Richardson, S. A., and Ronald, L. Physical appearance cues and interpersonal attraction in children. *Child Development,* 1974, *45,* 305–310.

Klein, R. E., Habicht, J. P., and Yarbrough, C. Effects of protein-calorie malnutrition on mental development. *Advances in Pediatrics,* 1971, *18,* 75–91.

Klima, E., and Bellugi, U. Syntactic regularities—the speech of children. In J. Lyons and R. J. Wales (Eds.), *Psycholinguistic papers.* Edinburgh: Edinburgh University Press, 1966.

Klissouras, V. Heritability of adaptive variation. *Journal of Applied Physiology,* 1971, *31,* 338–344.

Knight, G. P., and Kagan, S. Apparent sex differences in cooperation-competition: A function of individualism. *Developmental Psychology,* 1981, *17,* 783–790.

Knobloch, H., and Pasamanick, B. Prospective studies on the epidemiology of reproductive casualty: Methods, findings and some implications. *Merrill-Palmer Quarterly,* 1966, *12,* 27–43.

Knopf, I. J. *Childhood psychopathology.* Englewood Cliffs, N.J.: Prentice-Hall, 1979.

Kobasigawa, A. Utilization of retrieval cues by children in recall. *Child Development,* 1974, *45,* 127–134.

Koch, H. L. Some personality correlates of sex, sibling position and spacing among five- and six-year-old children. *Genetic Psychological Monographs.* 1955, *52,* 3–50.

Koch, H. L. Some emotional attitudes of the young child in relation to characteristics of his sibling. *Child Development,* 1956, *27,* 393–426.

Koch, J. "When children meet death." *Psychology Today,* August 1977, 64–68.

Koch, L. Dad's great escape. "Family Lib," Chicago Tribune, April 1, 1973.

Koepke, J. E., Hamm, M., Legerstee, M., and Russell, M. Methodological issues in studies of imitation: Reply to Meltzoff and Moore. *Infant Behavior and Development,* 1983, *6,* 113–116. (a)

Koepke, J. E., Hamm, M., Legerstee, M., and Russell, M. Neonatal imitation: Two failures to replicate. *Infant Behavior and Development,* 1983, *6,* 97–102. (b)

Kogan, N. *Cognitive styles in infancy and early childhood*. Hillsdale, N.J.: Lawrence Erlbaum Associates, 1976.

Kohlberg, L. Development of moral character and moral ideology. In L. W. Hoffman and M. L. Hoffman (Eds.), *Review of child development research*, Volume 1. New York: Russell Sage Foundation, 1964.

Kohlberg, L. A cognitive-developmental analysis of children's sex-role concepts and attitudes. In E. E. Maccoby (Ed.), *The development of sex differences*. Stanford: Stanford University Press, 1966.

Kohlberg, L. Stage and sequence: The cognitive-developmental approach to socialization. In D. A. Goslin (Ed.), *Handbook of socialization theory and research*. Chicago: Rand McNally, 1969.

Kohlberg, L. Moral stages and moralization: Cognitive-developmental approach. In T. Lickona (Ed.), *Moral development and behavior: Theory, research, and social issues*. New York: Holt, Rinehart & Winston, 1976.

Kohlberg, L., Colby, A., Gibbs, J., and Speicher-Dubin, B. Standard form scoring manual. Cambridge: Center for Moral Education, Harvard Graduate School of Education, 1978.

Kohlberg, L., and Gilligan, C. The adolescent as a philosopher: The discovery of the self in a postconventional world. *Daedalus*, 1971, *100*, 1051–1086.

Kohn, M. L. *Class and conformity: A study in values* (2nd ed.). Chicago: University of Chicago Press, 1977.

Kolata, G. Studying learning in the womb. *Science*, 1984, *225*, 302–303.

Koluchová, J. Severe deprivation in twins: A case study. *Journal of Child Psychology and Psychiatry*, 1972, *13*, 107–114.

Koluchová, J. A report on the further development of twins after severe and prolonged deprivation. In A. M. Clarke and A. D. B. Clarke (Eds.), *Early experience: Myth and evidence*. New York: Free Press, 1976.

Komarovsky, M. Cultural contradictions and sex roles: The masculine case. *American Journal of Sociology*, 1973, *78*, 873–884.

Konner, M. Relations among infants and juveniles in comparative perspective. In M. Lewis and L. Rosenblum (Eds.), *Friendship and peer relations*. New York: Wiley-Interscience, 1975.

Konopka, G. *Young girls: A portrait of adolescence*. Englewood Cliffs, N.J.: Prentice-Hall, 1976.

Kopp, C. B. Risk factors in development. In P. H. Mussen (Ed.), *Handbook of child psychology*, Volume 2. New York: Wiley, 1983.

Kopp, C. B., and Parmelee, A. H. Prenatal and perinatal influences on infant behavior. In J. D. Osofsky (Ed.), *Handbook of infant development*. New York: Wiley, 1979.

Korner, A. F. Visual alertness in neonates: Individual differences and their correlates. *Perceptual and Motor Skills*, 1970, *31*, 499–509.

Korner, A. F. State as variable, as obstacle and as mediator of stimulation in infant research. *Merrill-Palmer Quarterly*, 1972, *18*, 77–94.

Korner, A. F. Individual differences at birth: Implications of early experience and later development. In J. C. Westman (Ed.), *Individual differences in children*. New York: Wiley, 1973.

Korner, A. F., and Grobstein, R. Visual alertness as related to soothing in neonates: Implications for maternal stimulation and early deprivation. *Child Development*, 1966, *37*, 867–876.

Korner, A. F., and Grobstein, R. Individual differences at birth: Implications for mother-infant relationship and later development. *Journal of the American Academy of Child Psychiatry*, 1967, *6*, 676–690.

Korner, A. F., and Thoman, E. G. Visual alertness in neonates as evoked by maternal care. *Journal of Experimental Child Psychology*, 1970, *10*, 67–78.

Korner, A. F., and Thoman, E. G. Relative efficacy of contact and vestibular stimulation on soothing neonates. *Child Development*, 1972, *10*, 67–78.

Kotelchuck, M. The infant's relationship to the father: Experimental evidence. In M. E. Lamb (Ed.), *The role of the father in child development*. New York: Wiley, 1976.

Kotulak, R. Baby removed from womb, returned in new surgery. *Chicago Tribune*, November 15, 1981, Section 1, pp. 1, 12.

Krebs, D., and Sturrup, B. Role-taking ability and altruistic behavior in elementary school children. *Personality and Social Psychology Bulletin*, 1974, *1*, 407–409.

Krebs, R. L. Some relations between moral judgment, attention, and resistance to temptation. Unpublished doctoral dissertation, University of Chicago, 1967.

Krebs, R. L., and Kohlberg, L. Moral judgment and ego controls as determinants of resistance to cheating. Unpublished manuscript, Center for Moral Education, Harvard University, 1973.

Kreutzer, M. A., Leonard, C., and Flavell, J. H. An interview study of children's knowledge about memory. *Monographs of the Society for Research in Child Development*, 1975, *40*(1, Serial No. 159).

Kreuz, I. E., and Rose, R. M. Assessment of aggressive behavior and plasma testosterone in a young criminal population. *Psychosomatic Medicine*, 1972, *34*, 321–332.

Kriger, S. F., and Kroes, W. H. Child-rearing attitudes of Chinese, Jewish, and Protestant mothers. *Journal of Social Psychology*, 1972, *86*, 205–210.

Kron, R. E., Stein, M., and Goddard, K. E. Newborn sucking behavior affected by obstetric sedation. *Pediatrics*, 1966, *37*, 1012–1016.

Krosnick, J. A., and Judd, C. M. Transitions in social influence at adolescence: Who induces cigarette smoking? *Developmental Psychology*, 1982, *18*, 359–368.

Krugman, S., Ward, R., and Katz, S. *Infectious diseases of children*. St. Louis: C. V. Mosby, 1977.

Kuchner, J. F. R. Chinese-American and European-American: A cross-cultural study of infant and mother. Unpublished doctoral dissertation, University of Chicago, 1980.

Kuhl, P. K. Speech perception in early infancy: Perceptual constancy for spectrally dissimilar vowel categories. *Journal of the Acoustic Society of America*, 1979, *66*, 1668–1679.

Kuhl, P. K. Perceptual constancy for speech-sound categories in early infancy. In G. Yeni-Komshian, J. Kavanagh, and C. Ferguson (Eds.), *Child phonology*, Volume 2, *Perception*. New York: Academic Press, 1980.

Kuhl, P. K. Discrimination of speech by nonhuman animals: Basic auditory sensitivities conducive to the perception of speech-sound categories. *Journal of the Acoustical Society of America*, 1981, *70*, 340–349.

Kuhl, P. K. Perception of auditory equivalence classes for speech in early infancy. *Infant Behavior and Development*, 1983, *6*, 263–285.

Kuhl, P. K., and Hillenbrand, J. Speech perception by young infants: Perceptual constancy for categories based on pitch contour. Paper presented at the meeting of the Society for Research on Child Development, San Francisco, March 1979.

Kurtines, W., and Grief, E. B. The development of moral thought: Review and evaluation of Kohlberg's approach. *Psychological Bulletin,* 1974, *81,* 453–470.

La Barbera, J. D., Izard, C. E., Parisi, S. A., and Vietze, P. Four- and six-month-old infant's visual responses to joy, anger and neutral expression. *Child Development,* 1976, *47,* 535–538.

Labov, W. The logic of nonstandard English. In. F. Williams (Ed.), *Language and poverty: Perspectives on a theme.* Chicago: Markham, 1970.

Ladd, G. W. Effectiveness of a social learning method for enhancing children's social interaction and peer acceptance. *Child Development,* 1981, *52,* 171–178.

Lamb, M. E. Parent-infant interaction in 8-month-olds. *Child Psychiatry and Human Development,* 1976, *7,* 56–63. (a)

Lamb, M. E. Twelve-month-olds and their parents: Interaction in a laboratory playroom. *Development Psychology,* 1976, *12,* 237–244. (b)

Lamb, M. E. Father-infant and mother-infant interaction in the first year of life. *Child Development,* 1977, *48,* 167–181.

Lamb, M. E. Interactions between 18-month-olds and their preschool-aged siblings. *Child Development,* 1978, *49,* 51–59. (a)

Lamb, M. E. The development of sibling relationships in infancy: A short-term longitudinal study. *Child Development,* 1978, *49,* 1189–1196. (b)

Lamb, M. E., Frodi, A. M., Hwang, C. P., Frodi, M., and Steinberg, J. Mother- and father-infant interaction involving play and holding in traditional and nontraditional Swedish families. *Developmental Psychology,* 1982, *18,* 215–221.

Lambert, N., and Sandoval, J. The prevalence of learning disabilities in a sample of children considered hyperactive. *Journal of Abnormal Child Psychology,* 1980, *8,* 33–50.

Lambert, W. The relation of bilingualism to intelligence. In W. Lambert (Ed.), *Language, psychology, and culture.* Stanford: Stanford University Press, 1972.

Landis, T. Y. Interactions between text and prior knowledge in children's memory for prose. *Child Development,* 1982, *53,* 811–814.

Langlois, J. H., and Downs, A. C. Mothers, fathers and peers as socialization agents of sex-typed play behavior in young children. *Child Development,* 1980, *51,* 1227–1247.

Langlois, J. H., Gottfried, N. W., and Seay, B. The influence of sex of peer on the social behavior of preschool children. *Developmental Psychology,* 1973, *8,* 93–98.

Langlois, J. H., and Stephan, C. The effects of physical attractivenesss and ethnicity on children's behavioral attributions and peer preferences. *Child Development,* 1977, *48,* 1694–1698.

Larson. R., Mayers, P., and Csikszentmihalyi, M. Experiential sampling of adolescents' socialization: The contexts of family, friends and being alone. Paper presented at the Conference on Research Perspectives in the Ecology of Human Development, Cornell University, Ithaca, N.Y., August 17–20, 1977.

Lasky, R. E., Syrdal-Lasky, A., and Klein, R. E. VOT discrimination by four-and six-and-a-half-month-old infants from Spanish environments. *Journal of Experimental Child Psychology,* 1975, *20,* 215–225.

Lawson, A., and Ingleby, J. D. Daily routines of preschool children: Effects of age, birth order, sex and social class, and developmental correlates. *Psychological Medicine,* 1974, *4,* 399–415.

Lazar, I., Darlington, R. B., Murray, H., Royce, J., and Snipper, A. Lasting effects of early education. *Monographs of the Society for Research in Child Development,* 1982, 47(2–3, Serial No. 195).

Leboyer, F. *Birth without violence.* New York: Knopf, 1975.

Leehey, S. C. A. A developmental change in right hemisphere specialization. Paper presented at the Society for Research in Child Development, New Orleans, March 1977.

Lefkowitz, M. M. Smoking during pregnancy: Long-term effect on offspring. *Developmental Psychology,* 1981, *17,* 192–194.

Lefkowitz, M. M., Eron, L. D., Walder, L. O., and Huesmann, L. R. *Growing up to be violent: A longitudinal study of the development of aggression.* Elmsford, N.Y.: Pergamon Press, 1977.

Legg, C., Sherick, I., and Wadland, W. Reaction of preschool children to the birth of a sibling. *Child Psychiatry and Human Development,* 1974, *5,* 3–39.

Leifer, M. Psychological changes accompanying pregancy and motherhood. *Genetic Psychology Monographs,* 1977, *95,* 55–96.

Lemly, E. B., and Schwarz, J. C. The reactions of two-year-olds to unfamiliar adults. Report to the Research Foundation (Grant No. 35–497), 1979.

Lemons, J. A., Moye, L., Hall, D., and Simmons, M. Differences in the composition of preterm and term human milk during early lactation. *Pediatric Research,* 1982, *16,* 113–117.

Lempers, J. D., Flavell, E. R., and Flavell, J. H. The development in very young children of tacit knowledge concerning visual perception. *Genetic Psychology Monographs,* 1977, *95,* 3–53.

Lenneberg, E. H. *Biological foundations of language.* New York: Wiley, 1967.

Lenneberg, E. H., Rebelsky, F. G., and Nichols, I. A. The vocalizations of infants born to deaf and hearing parents. *Human Development,* 1965, *8,* 23–37.

Lenz, W. Kindliche Missbildungen Nach Med. Kament Wahrend der Dravidat? *Deutsch. Med. Wochenschr.,* 1961, *86,* 2555–2556.

Lepman, J. (Ed.) *How children see our world.* New York: Avon, 1971.

Lerner, R. M., and Lerner, J. V. Effects of age, sex, and physical attractiveness on child-peer relations, academic performance, and elementary school adjustment. *Developmental Psychology,* 1977, *13,* 585–590.

Lesser, G. S., Fifer, G., and Clark, D. H. Mental abilities of children from different social-class and cultural groups. *Monographs of the Society for Research in Child Development,* 1965, *30*(4, Serial No. 102).

Lessing, E. E. Racial differences in indices of ego functioning relevant to academic achievement. *Journal of Genetic Psychology,* 1969, *115,* 153–167.

Lessler, K., and Fox, R. E. Evaluation of a Head Start program in a low population area. *Journal of Negro Education,* 1969, *38,* 46–54.

Lester, B. M., Heidelise, A., and Brazelton, T. B. Regional obstetric anesthesia and newborn behavior: A reanalysis toward synergistic effects. *Child Development,* 1982, *53,* 687–692.

Levenkron, S. *The best little girl in the world.* Chicago: Contemporary Books, 1978.

Leventhal, H. A perceptual-motor processing model of emotion. In P. Pliner, K. Blankstein, and I. M. Spigel (Eds.), *Advances in the study of communication and affect,* Volume 5, *Perception of emotion in self and others.* New York: Plenum, 1979.

Lever, J. Sex differences in games children play. *Social Problems,* 1976, *23,* 478–487.

Levin, J. R. The mnemonic '80s: Keywords in the classroom. Theoretical paper No. 86, Wisconsin Research and Development Center for Individualized Schooling, Madison, 1980.

Levine, M. H., and Sutton-Smith, B. Effects of age, sex and task on visual behavior during dyadic interaction. *Developmental Psychology,* 1973, *9,* 404–405.

Levine, M. S., Hull, C. D., and Buchwald, N. A. Development of motor activity in kittens. *Developmental Psychobiology,* 1980, *13,* 357–371.

Levitan, M., and Montagu, A. *Textbook of human genetics.* London: Oxford University Press, 1971.

Levy, J. *Nature,* 1969, *224, 614.*

Levy, R. *Tahitians.* Chicago: University of Chicago Press, 1973.

Lewin, K. *Field theory in social science.* New York: Harper & Row, 1951.

Lewis, M. Individual differences in the measurement of early cognitive growth. In J. Hellmuth (Ed.), *Exceptional infant,* Volume 2, *Studies in abnormalities.* New York: Brunner/ Mazel, 1971.

Lewis, M., and Brooks, J. Self, other and fear: Infants' reactions to people. In M. Lewis and L. A. Rosenblum (Eds.), *The origins of fear.* New York: Wiley, 1974.

Lewis, M., and Brooks-Gunn, J. *Social cognition and the acquisition of self.* New York: Plenum, 1979.

Lewis, M., and Craft, S. The epidemiology of childhood diseases. In P. Karoly, J. Steffen, D. O'Grady (Eds.), *Child Health Psychology.* New York: Pergamon Press, 1982.

Lewis, M., and Freedle, R. Mother-infant dyad: The cradle of meaning. In P. Pliner, L. Krames, and T. Alloway (Eds.) *Communication and affect: Language and thought.* New York: Academic Press, 1973.

Lewis, M., and Michalson, L. Affect labelling by mothers during reunion with their one-year-old infants. Unpublished manuscript, Educational Testing Service, 1981.

Lewis, M., and Michalson, L. The socialization of emotions. In T. Field and A. Fogel (Eds.), *Emotion and early interaction.* Hillsdale, N.J.: Lawrence Erlbaum Associates, 1982.

Lewis, M., and Rosenblum, L. A. (Eds.), *The development of affect.* New York: Plenum, 1978.

Lewis, M., and Weinraub, M. Sex of parent × sex of child: Socioemotional development. In R. C. Friedman, R. M. Richart, and R. L. Van de Wiele (Eds.), *Sex differences in behavior.* New York: Wiley, 1974.

Lewis, M., Young, G., Brooks, J., and Michalson, L. The beginning of friendship. In M. Lewis and L. A. Rosenblum (Eds.), *Friendship and peer relations.* New York: Wiley-Interscience, 1975.

Liben, L. S. Perspective-taking skills in young children: Seeing the world through rose-colored glasses. *Developmental Psychology,* 1978, *14,* 87–92.

Liberman, I. Y., Shankweiler, D., Fischer, F. W., and Carter, B. Explicit syllable and phoneme segmentation in the young child. *Journal of Experimental Child Psychology,* 1974, *18,* 201–212.

Lidz, T. The adolescent and his family. In H. Caplan and F. Lebovici (Eds.), *Adolescence: Psychosocial perspectives.* New York: Basic Books, 1969.

Lieberman, A. F. Preschoolers' competence with a peer: Relations with attachment and peer experience. *Child Development,* 1977, *48,* 1277–1287.

Lieberman, J. N. Playfulness and divergent thinking: An investigation of their relationship at the kindergarten level. *Journal of Genetic Psychology,* 1965, *107,* 219–224.

Lieberman, P. *Intonation, perception, and language.* Cambridge: MIT Press, 1967.

Liebert, R. M., and Poulos, R. W. Television and personality development: The socializing effects of an entertainment medium. In A. Davids (Ed.), *Child personality and psychopathology: Current topics,* Volume 2. New York: Wiley, 1975.

Lieven, E. V. M. Turn-taking and pragmatics: Two issues in early child language. In R. N. Campbell and P. T. Smith (Eds.), *Recent advances in the psychology of language: Language development and mother-child interaction, Part 5.* New York: Plenum, 1978.

Light, P., and Nix, C. "Own view" versus "good view" in a perspective-taking task. *Child Development,* 1983, *54,* 480–483.

Lindemann, C. A. *Birth control and unmarried young women.* New York: Springer, 1974.

Lindgren, G. Height, weight and menarche in Swedish urban school children in relation to socioeconomic and regional factors. *Annals of Human Biology,* 1976, *3,* 510–528.

Lindholm, K. J., and Padilla, A. M. Language mixing in bilingual children. *Journal of Child Language,* 1978, *5,* 327–335.

Linton, T. Effects of grade displacement between students tutored and student tutors. Unpublished doctoral dissertation, University of Cincinnati, 1972.

Lipps, T. Das wissen von Fremden ichen. *Psychologische Untersuchnung,* 1906, *1,* 694–722.

Lipsitt, L. P. Personal communication, 1984.

Lipsitt, L. P., Engen, T., and Kaye, H. Developmental changes in the olfactory threshold of the neonate. *Child Development,* 1963, *34,* 371–376.

Lipsitt, L. P., McCullagh, A. A., Reilly, B. M., Smith, J. M., and Sturner, W. Q. Perinatal indicators of sudden infant death syndrome: A study of 34 Rhode Island cases. *Journal of Applied Developmental Psychology,* 1981, *2,* 79–88.

Lipsitt, L. P., Reilly, B. M., Butcher, M. J., and Greenwood, M. M. The stability and interrelationships of newborn sucking and heart rate. *Developmental Psychobiology,* 1976, *9,* 305–310.

Livesley, W. J., and Bromley, D. B. *Person perception in childhood and adolescence.* London: Wiley, 1973.

Locke, J. *An abridgment of Mr. Locke's essay concerning human understanding.* Boston: Manning & Loring, 1794.

Lockyer, L., and Rutter, M. A five to fifteen year follow-up study of infantile psychosis: IV. Patterns of cognitive ability. *British Journal of Social and Clinical Psychology,* 1970, *9,* 152–163.

Loeber, R. The stability of antisocial and delinquent child behavior: A review. *Child Development,* 1982, *53,* 1431–1446.

Londerville, S., and Main, M. Security of attachment, compliance and maternal training methods in the second year of life. *Developmental Psychology,* 1981, *17,* 289–299.

Loney, J. The intellectual functioning of hyperactive elementary school boys: A cross-sectional investigation. *American Journal of Orthopsychiatry,* 1974, *44,* 754–762.

Loney, J., Langhorne, J. E., and Paternite, C. E. An empirical basis for subgrouping the hyperkinetic/minimal brain dysfunction syndrome. *Journal of Abnormal Psychology,* 1978, *87,* 431–441.

Longstreth, L. E. Birth order and avoidance of dangerous activities. *Developmental Psychology,* 1970, *2,* 154.

Longstreth, L. E., Davis, B., Carter, L., Flint, D., Owne, J., Rickert, M., and Taylor, E. Separation of home intellectual environment and maternal IQ as determinants of child IQ. *Developmental Psychology*, 1981, *17*, 532–541.

Lorenz, K. *Studies in animal and human behavior*, Volume 1. Cambridge: Harvard University Press, 1971.

Lougee, M. D., Grueneich, R., and Hartup, W. W. Social interaction in same- and mixed-age dyads of preschool children. *Child Development*, 1977, *48*, 1353–1361.

Lovaas, O. I., Freitag, G., Gold, V. J., and Kassorla, I. C. Experimental studies in childhood schizophrenia: Analysis of self-destructive behavior. *Journal of Experimental Child Psychology*, 1965, *2*, 67–84.

Lovaas, O. I., Schaeffer, B., and Simmons, J. Q. Building social behavior in autistic children by use of electric shock. *Journal of Experimental Research on Personality*, 1965, *1*, 99–109.

Lovibond, S. *Conditioning and enuresis*. New York: Macmillan, 1964.

Lowrey, G. H. *Growth and development of children* (6th ed.). Chicago: Year Book Medical Publishers, 1973.

Lucas, T. C., and Uzgiris, I. C. Spatial factors in the development of the object concept. *Developmental Psychology*, 1977, *13*, 492–500.

Ludeke, R. J. Teaching behaviors of 11-year-old and 9-year-old girls in same-age and mixed-age dyads. Unpublished doctoral dissertation, University of Minnesota, 1978.

Lukasevitch, A., and Gray, R. F. Open space, open education and pupil performance. *Elementary School Journal*, 1978, *79*, 108–114.

Luria, A. R. *The role of speech in the regulation of normal and abnormal behavior*. London: Pergamon Press, 1961.

Luria, A. R. Speech development and the formation of mental processes. In M. Cole and I. Maltzman (Eds.), *Handbook of contemporary Soviet psychology*. New York: Basic Books, 1969.

Lynn, D. B. *The father: His role in child development*. Monterey, Calif.: Brooks/Cole, 1974.

Lynn, D. B., and Cross, A. D. Parent preference of preschool children. *Journal of Marriage and the Family*, 1974, *36*, 555–559.

Lytton, H. The socialization of two-year-old boys: Ecological findings: *Journal of Child Psychology and Psychiatry*, 1976, *17*, 287–304.

Lytton, H. Disciplinary encounters between young boys and their mothers and fathers: Is there a contingency system? *Developmental Psychology*, 1979, *15*, 256–268.

Lytton, H. Parent-child interaction: The socialization process observed in twin and singleton families. New York: Plenum, 1980.

Maccoby, E. E. Selective auditory attention in children. In L. P. Lipsitt and C. C. Spiker (Eds.), *Advances in child development and behavior*, Volume 3. New York: Academic Press, 1967.

Maccoby, E. E., Doering, C. H., Jacklin, C. N., and Kraemer, H. Concentrations of sex hormones in umbilical-cord blood: Their relation to sex and birth order of infants. *Child Development*, 1979, *50*, 632–642.

Maccoby, E. E., and Feldman, S. S. Mother-attachment and stranger-reactions in the third year of life. *Monographs of the Society for Research in Child Development*, 1972, *37*(1, Serial No. 146).

Maccoby, E. E., and Hagen, J. W. Effect of distraction upon central versus incidental recall: Developmental trends. *Journal of experimental child psychology*, 1965, *2*, 280–289.

Maccoby, E. E., and Jacklin, C. N. *The psychology of sex differences*. Stanford: Stanford University Press, 1974.

Maccoby, E. E., and Jacklin, C. N. Sex differences in aggression: A rejoinder and reprise. *Child Development*, 1980, *51*, 964–980.

Maccoby, E. E., and Jacklin, C. N. The "person" characteristics of children and the family as environment. In D. Magnusson and V. Allen (Eds.), *Human development: An interactional perspective*. New York: Academic Press, in press.

Maccoby, E. E., and Martin, J. A. Socialization in the context of the family: Parent-child interaction. In P. H. Mussen (Ed.), *Handbook of child psychology*, Volume 4. New York: Wiley, 1983.

Macfarlane, A. *The psychology of childbirth*. Cambridge: Harvard University Press, 1977.

Macfarlane, J. W., Allen, L., and Honzik, M. P. *A developmental study of the behavior problems of normal children between twenty-one months and fourteen years*. Berkeley: University of California Press, 1954.

Madsen, M. C. Developmental and cross-cultural differences in the cooperative and competitive behavior of young children. *Journal of Cross-Cultural Psychology*, 1971, *2*, 365–371.

Madsen, M. C., and Connor, C. Cooperative and competitive behavior of retarded and nonretarded children at two ages. *Child Development*, 1973, *44*, 175–178.

Madsen, W. *The Mexican Americans of south Texas*. New York: Holt, Rinehart & Winston, 1964.

Magenis, R. E., Overton, K. M., Chamberlin, J., Brady, T., and Lovrien, E. Parental origin of the extra chromosome in Down's syndrome. *Human Genetics*, 1977, *37*, 7–16.

Magnus, E. M. Sources of maternal stress in the postpartum period: A review of the literature and an alternative view. Unpublished paper, the Institute of Gerontology, University of Michigan, 1978.

Magrab, P. R., and Calcagno, P. L. Psychological impact of chronic pediatric conditions. In P. R. Magrab (Ed.), *Psychological management of pediatric problems: Early life conditions and chronic diseases*, Volume 1. Baltimore: University Park Press, 1978.

Mahler, M. S., Pine, F., and Bergman, A. *The psychological birth of the human infant*. New York: Basic Books, 1975.

Main, M. Analysis of a peculiar form of reunion behavior seen in some daycare children: Its history and sequelae in children who are home-reared. In R. A. Webb (Ed.), *Social development in childhood: Day-care programs and research*. Baltimore: Johns Hopkins University Press, 1977.

Malatesta, C. Affective development over the life-span: Involution or growth? *Merrill-Palmer Quarterly*, 1981, *27*, 145–173.

Malatesta, C., and Haviland, J. Measuring change in infant emotional expressivity: Two approaches applied in longitudinal investigation. In C. E. Izard and P. B. Reed (Eds.), *Measuring emotions in infants and children*, Volume 2. Cambridge: Cambridge University Press, in press.

Mallick, S. K., and McCandless, B. R. A study of catharsis of aggression. *Journal of Personality and Social Psychology*, 1966, *4*, 590–596.

Mandell, A. J., and Mandell, M. P. Suicide and the menstrual cycle. *Journal of the American Medical Association*, 1967, *200*, 792–793.

Mandler, G. Emotion. In R. Brown, E. Galanter, E. H. Hess, and G. Mandler (Eds.), *New directions in psychology*. New York: Holt, 1962.

Mandler, G. *Mind and emotions.* New York: Wiley, 1975.

Mandler, G. The generation of emotion: A psychological theory. In R. Plutchik and H. Kellerman (Eds.) *Emotion: Theory, research, and experience,* Volume 1. New York: Academic Press, 1980.

Mandler, J., and Johnson, N. On throwing out the baby with the bathwater: A reply to Black and Wilensky's evaluation of story grammars. *Cognitive Science,* 1980, *1,* 157–168.

Manheimer, D. L., Dewey, J., Mellinger, G. D., and Corsa, L. 50,000 child-years of accident injuries. *Pacific Health Reports,* 1966, *81,* 519–533.

Manheimer, D. L., and Mellinger, G. D. Personality characteristics of the child accident reporter. *Child Development,* 1967, *38,* 491–513.

Manis, F., Keating, D. P., and Morrison, F. J. Developmental differences in the allocation of processing capacity. *Journal of Experimental Child Psychology,* 1980, *29,* 156–169.

Mann, I. *The development of the human eye.* New York: Grune & Stratton, 1964.

Manosevitz, M., Prentice, N. M., and Wilson, F. Individual and family correlates of imaginary companions in preschool children. *Developmental Psychology,* 1973, *8,* 72–79.

Marantz, S. A., and Mansfield, A. F. Maternal employment and the development of sex-role stereotyping in five- to eleven-year-old girls. *Child Development,* 1977, *48,* 668–673.

Maratsos, M. When is a high thing the big one. *Developmental Psychology,* 1974, *10,* 367–375.

Maratsos, M. Some current issues in the study of the acquisition of grammar. In P. H. Mussen (Ed.), *Handbook of child psychology,* Volume 3. New York: Wiley, 1983.

Marcia, J. E. Determination and construct validity of ego identity status. Unpublished doctoral dissertation, Ohio State University, 1964.

Marcia, J. E. Development and validation of ego identity status. *Journal of Personality and Social Psychology,* 1966, 551–558.

Marcus, D. E., and Overton, W. F. The development of cognitive gender constancy and sex role preferences. *Child Development,* 1978, *49,* 434–444.

Marjoribanks, K. Birth order, family environment and mental abilities: A regression surface analysis. *Psychological Reports,* 1976, *39,* 759–765.

Mark, R. *Memory and nerve cell connections.* Oxford: Clarendon Press, 1974.

Markman, E. M. The facilitation of part-whole comparisons by use of the collective noun "family." *Child Development,* 1973, *44,* 837–840.

Markman, E. M. Realizing that you don't understand: Elementary school children's awareness of inconsistencies. *Child Development,* 1979, *50,* 643–655.

Markman E. M. Comprehension monitoring. In W. P. Dickson (Ed.), *Children's oral communication skills.* New York: Academic Press, 1981.

Markman, E. M., and Siebert, J. Classes and collections: internal organization and resulting holistic properties. *Cognitive Psychology,* 1976, *8,* 561–577.

Marshall, W. A., and Tanner, J. M. Puberty. In J. A. Davis and J. Dobbing (Eds,), *Scientific foundations of pediatrics.* Philadelphia: Saunders, 1974.

Martin, J. A. A longitudinal study of the consequences of early mother-infant interaction: A microanalytic approach. *Monographs of the Society for Research in Child Development,* 1981, *46*(3, Serial No. 190).

Martin, R. M. Effects of familiar and complex stimuli on infant attention. *Developmental Psychology,* 1975, *11,* 178–185.

Martinez, C., and Chávez, A. Nutrition and development in infants of poor rural areas. I. Consumption of mother's milk by infants. *Nutrition Reports International,* 1971, *4,* 139–149.

Marvin, R. S. An ethological-cognitive model of the attenuation of mother-child attachment behavior. In T. Alloway, P. Pliner, and L. Krames (Eds.), *Attachment behavior: Advances in the study of communication and affect,* Volume 3. New York: Plenum, 1977.

Marvin, R. S., Mossler, D. G., and Greenberg, M. The development of conceptual perspective-taking in preschool children in a "secret game." Paper presented at the biennial meeting of the Society for Research in Child Development, Denver, March 1975.

Masangkay, Z. S. McCluskey, K. A., McIntyre, C. W., Sims-Knight, J., Vaughn, B. E., and Flavell, J. H. The early development of inferences about the visual percepts of others. *Child Development,* 1974, *45,* 357–366.

Masters, W. H., and Johnson, V. E. *Human sexual inadequacy.* Boston: Little, Brown, 1970.

Masur, E. F., McIntyre, C. W., and Flavell, J. H. Developmental changes in apportionment of study time among items in a multitrial free-recall task. *Journal of Experimental Child Psychology,* 1973, *15,* 237–246.

Matarazzo, J. D. *Wechsler's measurement and appraisal of adult intelligence,* (5th ed.). Baltimore: Williams & Wilkins, 1972.

Matas, L., Arend, R. A., and Sroufe, L. A. Continuity of adaptation in the second year: The relationship between quality of attachment and later competence. *Child Development,* 1978, *49,* 547–556.

Matheny, A. P., Jr., and Dolan, A. B. Persons, situations and time: A genetic view of behavioral change in children. *Journal of Personality and Social Psychology,* 1975, *32,* 1106–1110.

Matsunaga, E., and Shiota, K. Search for maternal factors associated with malformed human embryos: A prospective study. *Teratology,* 1981, *21,* 323–331.

Mattson, A. Long-term physical illness in childhood: A challenge to psychosocial adaptation. *Pediatrics,* 1972, *50,* 801–811.

Maudry, M., and Nekula, M. Social relations between children of the same age during the first two years of life. *Journal of Genetic Psychology,* 1939, *54,* 193–215.

Maurer, D., and Young, R. E. Newborn's following of natural and distorted arrangements of facial features. *Infant Behavior and Development,* 1983, *6,* 127–131.

Mayer, J. Obesity during childhood. In M. Winick (Ed.), *Childhood obesity.* New York: Wiley, 1975.

Maynard, R. Omaha pupils given "behavior" drugs. *Washington Post,* June 29, 1970.

McAnarney, E., and Greydanus, D. Adolescent pregnancy—A multifaceted problem. *Pediatrics in Review,* 1979, *1,* 123–126.

McAnarney, E. R., Pless, I. B., and Satterwhite, B. Psychological problems of children with chronic juvenile arthritis. *Pediatrics,* 1974, *53,* 523–528.

McBride, W. G. Thalidomide and congenital abnormalities. *Lancet,* 1961, *2,* 1358.

McCabe, V. Abstract perceptual information for age level: A risk factor for maltreatment? *Child Development,* 1984, *55,* 267–276.

McCall, R. B. Toward an epigenetic conception of mental development in the first three years of life. In M. Lewis (Ed.), *Origins of intelligence: Infancy and early childhood.* New York: Plenum, 1976.

McCall, R. B. Challenges to a science of developmental psychology. *Child Development,* 1977, *48,* 333–334.

McCall, R. B. Nature-nurture and the two values of development. A proposed integration with respect to mental development. *Child Development,* 1981, *52,* 1–12.

McCall, R. B., Hogarty, P. S., and Hurlburt, N. Transitions in infant sensorimotor development and the prediction of childhood IQ. *American Psychologist,* 1972, *27,* 728–741.

McCall, R., and Kennedy, C. Attention of 4-month-old infants to discrepancy and baby. *Journal of Experimental Child Psychology,* 1980, *29,* 189–201.

McClearn, G. E. Genetic influences on behavior and development. In P. H. Mussen (Ed.), *Carmichael's manual of child psychology,* Volume 1. New York: Wiley, 1970.

McCleary, E. H. *New miracles of childbirth.* New York: David McKay, 1974.

McClelland, D. C. Testing for competence rather than for intelligence. *American Psychologist,* 1973, *28,* 1–14.

McCormick, M. C., Shapiro, S., and Starfield, B. H. Injury and its correlates among 1-year-old children. *American Journal of Disabilities in Children,* 1981, *135,* 159–163.

McDavid, J. W., and Harari, H. Stereotyping in names and popularity in grade school children. *Child Development,* 1966, *37,* 453–459.

McDonald, R. L. The role of emotional factors in obstetric complications: A review. *Psychosomatic Medicine,* 1968, *30,* 223–237.

McGarrigle, J., Grieve, R., and Hughes, M. Interpreting inclusion: A contribution to the study of the child's cognitive and linguistic development. *Journal of Experimental Child Psychology,* 1978, *26,* 528–550.

McGhee, P. E., and Crandall, V. C. Beliefs in internal-external control of reinforcement and academic performance. *Child Development,* 1968, *39,* 91–102.

McGowan, R. J., and Johnson, D. L. The mother-child relationship and other antecedents of childhood intelligence: A causal analysis. *Child Development,* 1984, *55,* 810–820.

McGraw, M. B. Growth: A study of Johnny and Jimmy. New York: Appleton-Century-Crofts, 1935.

McGraw, M. B. Suspension grasp behavior of the human infant. *American Journal of Disabilities in Children,* 1940, *60,* 799–811.

McGrew, W. C. Aspects of social development in nursery school children, with emphasis on introduction to the group. In N. Blurton Jones (Ed.), *Ethological studies of child behaviour.* London: Cambridge University Press, 1972.

McIntire, M. S., and Angle, C. R., *Proceedings of the International Symposium on Environmental Health Aspects of Lead,* Amsterdam, 1972, Luxembourg: C.E.C., 1973.

McKenzie, B., and Over, R. Do neonatal infants imitate?: A reply to Meltzoff and Moore. *Infant Behavior and Development,* 1983, *6,* 109–111. (a)

McKenzie, B., and Over, R. Young infants fail to imitate facial and manual gestures. *Infant Behavior and Development,* 1983, *6,* 85–95. (b)

McLaughlin, B. Child compliance to parental control techniques. *Developmental Psychology,* 1983, *19,* 667–673.

McLoyd, V. C. The effects of the structure of play objects on the pretend play of low-income preschool children. *Child Development,* 1983, *54,* 626–635.

Meacham, J. A. The development of memory abilities in the individual and in society. *Human Development,* 1972, *15,* 205–228.

Mead, M. Coming of age in Samoa. In *From the South Seas: Studies of adolescence and sex in primitive societies.* New York: William Morrow, 1939. (Originally published, 1928)

Mead, M. Adolescence in primitive and modern society. In V. F. Calverton and S. D. Schmalhausen (Eds.), *The new generation.* New York: Arno Press and *The New York Times,* 1971. (Originally published, 1930)

Mead, M., and Newton, N. Cultural patterning of perinatal behavior. In S. A. Richardson and A. F. Guttmacheer (Eds.), *Childbearing: Its social and psychological aspects.* Baltimore: Williams & Wilkins, 1967.

Means, B. M., and Rohwer, W. D., Jr. A developmental study of the effects of adding verbal analogs to pictured paired associates. Unpublished paper, University of California, Berkeley, 1974.

Mechanic, D. The influence of mothers on their children's health attitudes and behavior. *Pediatrics,* 1964, *33,* 444–453.

Mednick, S. A. Breakdown in individuals at high risk for schizophrenia: Possible predispositional perinatal factors. *Mental Hygiene,* 1970, *54,* 50–63.

Mehler, J., Bertoncini, J., Barriere, M., and Jassik-Gerschenfeld, D. Infant recognition of mother's voice. *Perception,* 1978, *7,* 471–497.

Melhuish, E. C. Visual attention to mother's and stranger's faces and facial contrast in 1-month-old infants. *Developmental Psychology,* 1982, *18,* 229–231.

Meltzoff, A. N., and Moore, M. K. Imitation of facial and manual gestures by human neonates. *Science,* 1977, *198,* 75–78.

Meltzoff, A. N., and Moore, M. K. Methodological issues in studies of imitation: Comments on McKenzie and Over and Koepke et al. *Infant Behavior and Development,* 1983, *6,* 103–108. (a)

Meltzoff, A. N., and Moore, M. K. Newborn infants imitate adult facial gestures. *Child Development,* 1983, *54,* 702–709. (b)

Meng, Z., Henderson, C., Campos, J., and Emde, R. N. The effects of background emotional elicitation on subsequent problem solving in the toddler. Unpublished manuscript, University of Denver, 1983.

Mercer, J. R. Socio-cultural factors in labeling mental retardates. *Peabody Journal of Education,* 1971, *48,* 188–203.

Merrick, F. Personal communication to Jean Sorrells-Jones, 1978.

Mervis, C., and Mervis, C. Leopards are kitty-cats: Object labeling by mothers for their thriteen-month-olds. *Child Development,* 1982, *53,* 267–273.

Messer, S. B. The effect of an anxiety over intellectual performance on reflection-impulsivity in children. *Child Development,* 1970, *41,* 723–735.

Messer, S. B. The relation of internal-external control to academic performance. *Child Development,* 1972, *43,* 1456–1461.

Messer, S. B. Reflection-impulsivity: A review. *Psychological Bulletin,* 1976, *83,* 1026–1052.

Meyer, W., and Thompson, G. Sex differences in the distribution of teacher approval and disapproval among sixth-grade children. *Journal of Educational Psychology,* 1956, *47,* 385–396.

Milgram, R. M., Milgram, N. A., Rosenblum, G., and Rabkin, L. Quantity and quality of creative thinking in children and adolescents. *Child Development,* 1978, *49,* 385–388.

Miller, G. A. The magic number seven, plus or minus two. *Psychological Review,* 1956, *63,* 81–97.

Miller, L. B., and Dyer, J. L. Experimental variation of Head Start curricula: A comparison of current approaches. Washington, D.C.: Office of Economic Opportunity, 1970.

Miller, L. C. Fears and anxiety in children. In C. E. Walker and M. C. Roberts, (Eds.), *Handbook of clinical child psychology.* New York: Wiley, 1983.

Miller, P. Y., and Simon, W. The development of sexuality in adolescence. In J. Adelson (Ed.), *Handbook of adolescent psychology.* New York: Wiley, 1980.

Miller, S. Child rearing in the kibbutz. In J. G. Howells (Ed.), *Modern perspectives in international child psychiatry.* Edinburgh: Oliver and Boyd, 1969.

Milner, B. CNS maturation and language acquisition. In H. Whitaker and H. A. Whitaker (Eds.), *Studies in Neurolinguistics,* Volume 1. New York: Academic Press, 1976.

Milstein, R. M. Visual and taste responsiveness in obese-tending infants. Unpublished paper, Yale University, 1978.

Minnett, A. M., Vandell, D. L., and Santrock, J. W. The effects of sibling status on sibling interaction: Influence of birth order, age spacing, sex of child, and sex of sibling. *Child Development,* 1983, *54,* 1064–1072.

Minton, C., Kagan, J., and Levine, J. Maternal control and obedience in the two-year-old. *Child Development,* 1971, *42,* 1873–1894.

Minton, J. H. The impact of Sesame Street on readiness. *Sociology of Education,* 1972, *48,* 141–151.

Minuchin, P. Sex-role concepts and sex typing in childhood as a function of school and home environments. *Child Development,* 1965, *36,* 1033–1048.

Minuchin, P., Biber, B., Shapiro, E., and Zimiles, H. *The psychological impact of school experience.* New York: Basic Books, 1969.

Minuchin, P. P., and Shapiro, E. K. The school as a context for social development. In P. H. Mussen (Ed.), *Handbook of child psychology,* Volume 4. New York: Wiley, 1983.

Mischel, W. *Personality and assessment.* New York: Wiley, 1968.

Mitchell, N. B., and Pollack, R. H. Block-design performance as a function of hue and race. *Journal of Experimental Child Psychology,* 1974, *17,* 377–382.

Mnookin, R. H. Child, family, and state: *Problems and materials on children and the law.* Boston: Little, Brown, 1978.

Moely, B. E., Olson, F. A., Halwes, T. G., and Flavell, J. H. Production deficiency in young children's clustered recall. *Developmental Psychology,* 1969, *1,* 26–34.

Mofenson, H. C., and Greensher, J. Childhood accidents. In R. A. Hoekelman, S. Blatman, P. A. Brunell, S. B. Friedman, and H. H. Seidel (Eds.), *Principles of pediatrics.* New York: McGraw-Hill, 1978.

Molfese, D. L., Freeman, R. B., Jr., and Palermo, D. S. The ontogeny of brain lateralization for speech and nonspeech stimuli. *Brain and Language,* 1975, *2,* 356–368.

Money, J., Hampson, J. G., and Hampson, J. L. Imprinting and the establishment of gender role. *AMA Archives of Neurological Psychiatry,* 1957, *77,* 333–336.

Montagu, A. *Prenatal influences.* Springfield, Ill.: Charles C. Thomas, 1962.

Montemayor, R., and Eisen, M. The development of self-conceptions from childhood to adolescence. *Developmental Psychology,* 1977, *13,* 314–319.

Mood, D., Johnson, J., and Shantz, C. U. Affective and cognitive components of empathy in young children. Paper presented at the southeast regional meeting of the Society for Research in Child Development, Chapel Hill, N.C., 1974.

Moore, B. S., Underwood, B., and Rosenhan, D. L. Affect and altruism. *Developmental Psychology,* 1973, *8,* 99–104.

Moore, M. J., Kagan, J., and Haith, M. M. Memory and motives. *Developmental Psychology,* 1978, *14,* 563–564.

Moore, T. Language and intelligence: A longitudinal study of the first eight years, Part II: Environmental correlates of mental growth. *Human Development,* 1968, *11,* 1–24.

Moore, W. M. The secular trend in physical growth of urban North American negro school children. *Monographs of the Society for Research in Child Development,* 1970, *35*(7, Serial No. 140).

Mora, J. O., Amezquita, A., Castro, L., Christiansen, N., Clement-Murphy, J., Cobos, L. F., Cremer, H. D., Dragastin, S., Elias, M. F., Franklin, D., Herrera, M. G., Ortiz, N., Pardo, F., de Tiansen, B., Wagner, M., and Stare, F. J. Nutrition, health and social factors related to intellectual performance. *World Review of Nutrition and Dietetics,* 1974, *19,* 205–236.

Morrison, F., Holmes, D. L., and Haith, M. M. A developmental study of the effects of familiarity on short term visual memory. *Journal of Experimental Child Psychology,* 1974, 18, 412–425.

Morrison, H., and Kuhn, D. Cognitive aspects of preschoolers' peer imitation in play situation. *Child Development,* 1983, *54,* 1054–1063.

Morrison, J. R., and Stewart, M. A. A family study of the hyperactive child syndrome. *Biological Psychiatry,* 1971, *3,* 189–195.

Morrison, J. R., and Stewart, M. A. The psychiatric status of legal families of adopted hyperactive children. *Archives of General Psychiatry,* 1973, *28,* 888–891.

Morse, C., Sahler, O., and Friedman, S. A three-year follow-up study of abused and neglected children. *American Journal of Diseases of Children,* 1970, *120,* 439–446.

Morse, P. A. The discrimination of speech and nonspeech in early infancy. *Journal of Experimental Child Psychology,* 1972, *14,* 477–492.

Moskowitz, D. S., Dreyer, A. S., and Kronsberg, S. Preschool children's field independence: Prediction from antecedent and concurrent maternal and child behavior. *Perceptual and Motor Skills,* 1981, *52,* 607–616.

Mossler, D. G., Marvin, R. S., and Greenberg, M. Conceptual perspective taking in two- to six-year-old children. *Developmental Psychology,* 1976, *12,* 85–86.

Much, N. C., and Shweder, R. A. Speaking of rules: the analysis of culture in the breach. In W. Damon (Ed.), *New directions for child development: Moral development.* San Francisco: Jossey-Bass, 1978.

Mueller, E. The maintenance of verbal exchanges between young children. *Child Development,* 1972, *43,* 930–938.

Mueller, E. (Toddlers + toys) = (an autonomous social system). In M. Lewis and L. A. Rosenblum (Eds,), *The child in its family.* New York: Plenum, 1979.

Mueller, E., and Brenner, J. The origins of social skills and interaction among playgroup toddlers. *Child Development,* 1977, *48,* 854–861.

Mueller, E., Hollien, H., and Murray, T. Perceptual responses to infant crying: Identification of cry types. *Journal of Child Language,* 1974, *1,* 89–95.

Mueller, E., and Lucas, T. A developmental analysis of peer interaction among toddlers. In M. Lewis and L. A. Rosenblum (Eds.), *Friendship and peer relations.* New York: Wiley-Interscience, 1975.

Mueller, E., and Vandell, D. Infant-infant interaction. In J. D. Osofsky (Ed.), *Handbook of infant development.* New York: Wiley, 1979.

Muir, D., Abraham, W., Forbes, B., and Harris, L. The ontogenesis of an auditory localization response from birth to four months of age. *Canadian Journal of Psychology,* 1979, *33,* 320–333.

Muir, D., and Field, J. Newborn infants' orientation to sound. *Child Development,* 1979, *50,* 431–436.

Murphy, L. B. *The widening world of childhood: Paths toward mastery.* New York: Basic Books, 1962.

Murphy, L. B., and Moriarty, A. E. *Vulnerability, coping and growth.* New Haven, Conn.: Yale University Press, 1976.

Mussen, P. H., and Eisenberg-Berg, N. *Roots of caring, sharing, and helping.* San Francisco: W. H. Freeman, 1977.

Mussen, P. H., and Jones, M. C. Self conceptions, motivations, and interpersonal attitudes of late and early maturing boys. *Child Development,* 1957, *28,* 243–256.

Muste, M., and Sharpe, D. Some influential factors in the determination of aggressive behavior in preschool children. *Child Development,* 1947, *18,* 11–28.

Myers, N. A., and Perlmutter, M. Memory in the years from two to five. In P. A. Ornstein (Ed.), *Memory development in children.* Hillsdale, N.J.: Lawrence Erlbaum Associates, 1978.

Nadelman, L. Sex identity in American children: Memory, knowledge, and preference tests. *Developmental Psychology,* 1974, *10,* 413–417.

Naeye, R. L. Relationship of cigarette smoking to congenital anomalies and perinatal death. *American Journal of Pathology,* 1978, *90,* 289–294.

National Center for Health Statistics. *Anthropometric and clinical findings: Preliminary findings of the first Health and Nutrition Examination Survey. United States, 1971–1972.* Washington, D.C.: DHEW, 1975.

Naus, M. J., Ornstein, P. A., and Hoving, K. L. Developmental implications of multistore and depth-of-processing models of memory. In P. A. Ornstein (Ed.), *Memory development in children.* Hillsdale, N.J.: Lawrence Erlbaum Associates, 1978.

Needleman, H., Gunnoe, C., Leviton, A., Reed, R., Peresie, H., Mather, C., and Barrett, P. Deficits in psychologic and classroom performance of children with elevated dentine lead levels. *New England Journal of Medicine,* 1979, *300,* 689–695.

Neimark, E. D. Longitudinal development of formal operational thought. *Genetic Psychology Monographs,* 1975, *91,* 171–225.

Neimark, E. D. Adolescent thought: Transition to formal operations. In B. B. Wolman and G. Strickler (Eds.), *Handbook of developmental psychology.* Englewood Cliffs, N.J.: Prentice-Hall, 1982.

NEISS Data Highlights, Vol. 4, No. 1. Washington, D.C.: Consumer Product Safety Commission, 1980.

Neisser, V. The concept of intelligence. In R. J. Sternberg and D. K. Detterman (Eds.), *Human intelligence: Perspectives on its theory and measurement.* Norwood, N.J.: Ablex, 1979.

Nelson, K. Structure and strategy in learning to talk. *Monographs of the Society for Research in Child Development,* 1973, *38*(1–2, Serial No. 149).

Nelson, K. Concept, word, and sentence: Interrelations in acquisition and development. *Psychological Review,* 1974, *81,* 267–285.

Nelson, K., and Gruendel, J. At morning it's lunchtime: A scriptal view of children's dialogues. *Discourse Processes,* 1979, *2,* 73–94.

Nelson, K. E. Toward a rare event: Cognitive comparison theory and syntax acquisition. In P. Dale and D. Ingram (Eds.), *Children's language: An international perspective.* Baltimore, Md.: University Park Press, 1980.

Nelson, K. E. Experimental gambits in the service of language acquisition theory. In S. Kuczaj (Ed.), *Language development: Syntax and semantics.* Hillsdale, N.J.: Lawrence Erlbaum Associates, 1981.

Nelson, K. E., Denninger, M. M., Donvillian, J. D., Kaplan, B. J., and Baker, N. Maternal input adjustments and non-adjustments as related to children's linguistic advances and to language acquisition theories. In A. D. Pellegrini and T. D. Yawkey (Eds.), *The development of oral and written languages: Readings in developmental and applied linguistics.* Norwood, N.J.: Ablex, 1983.

Nelson, K. E., and Kosslyn, S. M. Recognition of previously labeled or unlabeled pictures by 5-year-olds and adults. *Journal of Experimental Child Psychology,* 1976, *21,* 40–45.

Nesselroade, J. R., and Baltes, P. B. Adolescent personality development and historical change: 1970–1972. *Monographs of the Society for Research in Child Development,* 1974, *39*(1, Serial No. 154).

Neumann, C. G. Obesity in pediatric practice: Obesity in the preschool and school-age child. *Pediatric Clinics of North America,* 1977, *24,* 117–122.

Neumann, C. G., and Alpaugh, M. Birthweight doubling time: A fresh look. *Courrier du Centre International de l'Enfance,* 1976, *26,* 507.

Nevrovich, A. Institute of Pre-school Education, Moscow, USSR, 1974. Personal communication to C. E. Izard. Cited in C. E. Izard, *Human emotions.* New York: Plenum, 1977.

Newberger, C. M., Newberger, E. H., and Harper, G. P. The social ecology of malnutrition in childhood. In J. D. Lloyd-Still (Ed.), *Malnutrition and intellectual development.* Littleton, Mass.: Publishing Sciences Group, 1976.

Newcombe, N., and Bandura, M. M. Effect of age at puberty on spatial ability in girls: A question of mechanism. *Developmental Psychology,* 1983, *19,* 215–224.

Newport, E. L. Motherese: The speech of mothers to young children. In J. J. Castellan, D. B. Pisoni, and G. R. Potts (Eds.), *Cognitive theory,* Volume 3. Hillsdale, N.J.: Lawrence Erlbaum Associates, 1976.

Newson, J. An intersubjective approach to the systematic description of mother-infant interaction. In H. R. Schaffer (Ed.), *Studies in mother-infant interaction.* London: Academic Press, 1977.

Newson, J., and Newson, E. *Four years old in an urban community.* Harmondsworth, England: Pelican Books, 1968.

Newton, N., and Modahl, C. Pregnancy: The closest human relationship. *Human Nature,* 1978, *1,* March, p. 47.

Newton, N., and Newton, M. Lactation—Its psychological components. In J. G. Howells (Eds.), *Modern perspectives in psycho-obstetrics,* Edinburgh: Oliver and Boyd, 1972.

Nichols, R. C. Parental attitudes of mothers of intelligent adolescents and creativity of their children. *Child Development,* 1964, *35,* 1041–1050.

Nichols, R. C. The inheritance of general and specific ability. In M. Manosevitz, G. Lindzey, and D. D. Thiessen (Eds.), *Behavioral genetics.* New York: Appleton-Century-Crofts, 1969.

Nisan, M., and Kohlberg, L. Universality and variation in moral judgment: A longitudinal and cross-sectional study in Turkey. *Child Development,* 1982, *53,* 865–876.

Niswander, K. R., and Gordon, M. (Eds.) *The collaborative perinatal study of the National Institute of Neurological Dis-*

eases and Stroke: The women and their pregnancies. Washington, D.C.: U.S. Government Printing Office, 1972.

Nizel, A. E. Preventing dental caries: The nutritional factors. *Pediatric Clinics of North America*, 1977, *24*, 141–155.

Northern, J., and Downs, M. *Hearing in children.* Baltimore: Williams & Wilkins, 1974.

Novak, M. A., and Harlow, H. F. Social recovery of monkeys isolated for the first year of life: I. *Developmental Psychology,* 1975, *11*, 453–465.

Nucci, L. P., and Nucci, M. S. Children's responses to moral and social conventional transgressions in free-play settings. *Child Development*, 1982, *53*, 1337–1342.

Nucci, L. P., and Turiel, E. Social interactions and the development of social concepts in pre-school children. *Child Development*, 1978, *49*, 400–408.

Nutrition Committee of the Canadian Paediatric Society and the Committee on Nutrition of the American Academy of Pediatrics. Breast-feeding. *Pediatrics*, 1978, *62*, 591–601.

Nyman, A. J. Problem solving in rats as a function of experience at different ages. *Journal of Genetic Psychology*, 1967, *110*, 31–39.

O'Bryan, K. G., and Boersma, F. J. Eye movements, perceptual activity, and conservation development. *Journal of Experimental Child Psychology*, 1971, *12*, 157–169.

O'Bryan, K. G., and MacArthur, R. S. Reversibility, intelligence, and creativity in nine-year-old boys. *Child Development,* 1969, *40*, 33–45.

Oden, S., and Asher, S. R. Coaching children in social skills for friendship making. *Child Development*, 1977, *48*, 495–506.

Odom, R. D. A perceptual salience account of decalage relations and developmental change. In L. S. Siegel and C. J. Brainers (Eds.), *Alternatives to Piaget: Critical essays on the theory.* New York: Academic Press, 1978.

O'Dougherty, M., Wright, F., Garmezy, N., Loewenson, R., and Torres, F. Later competence and adaptation in infants who survive severe heart defects. *Child Development*, 1983, *54*, 1129–1142.

Offer, D. *The psychological world of the teen-ager: A study of normal adolescent boys.* New York: Basic Books, 1969.

Offer, D. *The adolescent.* New York: Basic Books, 1981.

Offer, D., and Offer, J. B. *From teenage to young manhood.* New York: Basic Books, 1975.

Oliver, C. M., and Oliver, G. M. Gentle birth: Its safety and its effect on neonatal behavior. *Journal of Obstetrical, Gynecological and Neonatal Nursing*, 1978.

Olson, S. L., Bates, J. E., and Bayles, K. Mother-infant interaction and the development of individual differences in children's cognitive competence. *Developmental Psychology*, 1984, *20*, 166–179.

Olweus, D. Familial and temperamental determinants of aggressive behavior in adolescent boys: A casual analysis. *Developmental Psychology*, 1980, *16*, 644–660.

Olweus, D., Mattsson, A., Schalling, D., and Low, H. Testosterone, aggression, physical and personality dimensions on normal adolescent males. *Psychosomatic Medicine*, 1980, *42*, 253–269.

Ornstein, P. A., and Naus, M. J. Rehearsal processes in children's memory. In P. A. Ornstein (Ed.), *Memory development in children.* Hillsdale, N.J.: Lawrence Erlbaum Associates, 1978.

Ornstein, P. A., Naus, M. J., and Liberty, C. Rehearsal and organizational processes in children's memory. *Child Development*, 1975, *26*, 818–830.

Ornstein, R. E. The split and whole brain. *Human Nature*, 1978, *1*, 76–83.

Osherson, D. N. *Logical abilities in children*, Volume 1, *Organization of length and class concepts: Empirical consequences of a Piagetian formalism.* Hillsdale, N.J.: Lawrence Erlbaum Associates, 1974.

Oster, H. "Recognition" of emotional expression in infancy? In M. E. Lamb and L. R. Sherrod (Eds.), *Infant social cognition.* Hillsdale, N.J.: Lawrence Erlbaum Associates, 1981.

Oster, H., and Ewy, R. Discrimination of sad vs. happy faces by 4-month-olds: When is a smile seen as a smile? Unpublished manuscript, University of Pennsylvania, 1980.

Ostrea, E. M., Jr., and Chavez, C. J. Perinatal problems (excluding neonatal withdrawal) in maternal drug addiction: A study of 830 cases. *Journal of Pediatrics*, 1979, *94*, 292–295.

Ounsted, M., Moar, V., and Scott, A. Growth in the first year of life: Effects of sex and weight for gestational age at birth. *Developmental Medicine and Child Neurology*, 1982, *24*, 356–365.

Overcast, T. D., Murphy, M. D., Smiley, S. S., and Brown, A. L. The effects of instruction on recall and recognition of categorized lists in the elderly. *Bulletin of the Psychonomic Society*, 1975, *5*, 339–341.

Palardy, J. N. What teachers believe, what children achieve. *Elementary School Journal*, 1969, *69*, 370–374.

Palermo, D. S. More about less: A study of language comprehension. *Journal of Verbal Learning and Verbal Behavior*, 1973, *12*, 211—221.

Pannabecker, B. J., Emde, R. N., Johnson, W., Stenberg, C., and Davis, M. Maternal perceptions of infant emotions from birth to 18 months: A preliminary report. Paper presented at the International Conference of Infant Studies, New Haven, Conn., April 1980.

Paoni, F. J. Reciprocal effects of sixth-graders tutoring third-graders in reading. Unpublished doctoral dissertation, Oregon State University, 1971.

Papousek, H. A method of studying conditioned food reflexes in young children up to the age of 6 months. *Pavlov Journal of Higher Nervous Activities*, 1959, *9*, 136–140.

Papousek, H. Conditioned head rotation reflexes in infants in the first months of life. *Acta Pediatrica*, 1961, *50*, 565–576.

Papousek, H. Experimental studies of appetitional behavior in human newborns and infants. In H. W. Stevenson, E. H. Press, and H. L. Rheingold (Eds.), *Early behavior.* New York: Wiley, 1967.

Papousek, H., and Papousek, M. Biological aspects of parent-infant communication in man. Invited address at the International conference on Infant Studies, Providence, R.I., March 1978.

Paris, S. C., and Lindauer, B. K. The role of inference in children's comprehension and memory for sentences. *Cognitive Psychology*, 1976, *8*, 217–227.

Parke, R. D. Punishment in children: Effects, side effects, and alternative strategies. In H. Hom and P. Robinson (Eds.), *Psychological processes in early education.* New York: Academic Press, 1977.

Parke, R. D. Children's home environments: Social and cognitive effects. In I. Altman and J. F. Wohlwill (Eds.), *Children and the environment*, Volume 3, *Human behavior and environment.* New York: Plenum, 1978.

Parke, R. D., and O'Leary, S. Family interaction in the newborn period: Some findings, some observations, and some unresolved issues. In K. Riegel and J. Meacham (Eds.), *The developing individual in a changing world*, Volume 2, *Social and environmental issues*. The Hague: Mouton, 1976.

Parke, R. D., and Sawin, D. Infant characteristics and behavior as elicitors of maternal and paternal responsibility in the newborn period. Paper presented at the meeting of the Society for Research in Child Development, Denver, Colo., April 1975.

Parke, R. D., and Sawin, D. B. The father's role in infancy. *Family Coordinator,* 1976, *25,* 265–371.

Parkinson, C., Wallis, S., and Harvey, D. School achievement and behavior of children who were small-for-dates at birth. *Developmental Medicine and Child Neurology,* 1981, *23,* 41–50.

Parsons, T., and Bales, R. F. *Family, socialization, and interaction process*. Glencoe, Ill.: Free Press, 1955.

Parten, M. B. Social participation among preschool children. *Journal of Abnormal and Social Psychology,* 1932, *27,* 243–269.

Parten, M. B. Social play among preschool children. *Journal of Abnormal and Social Psychology,* 1933, *28,* 136–147. Reprinted in R. E. Herron and B. Sutton-Smith (Eds.), *Child's play.* New York: Wiley, 1971.

Pasamanick, B., and Knobloch, H. Retrospective studies on the epidemiology of reproductive casualty: Old and new. *Merrill-Palmer Quarterly,* 1966, *12,* 7–26.

Pascual-Leone, J. A. Mathematical model for the transition role in Piaget's developmental stages. *Acta Psychologica,* 1970, *32,* 301–345.

Pascual-Leone, J. Constructive problems for constructive theories: The current relevance of Piaget's work and a critique of information processing simulation psychology. In H. Spada and R. Kluwe (Eds.), *Developmental models of thinking.* New York: Academic Press, 1980.

Pastor, D. L. The quality of mother-infant attachment and its relationship to toddlers' initial sociability with peers. *Developmental Psychology,* 1981, *17,* 326–335.

Patel, H. S., and Gordon, J. E. Some personal and situational determinants of yielding to influence. *Journal of Abnormal Social Psychology,* 1960, *61,* 411–418.

Paternite, C. E., Loney, J., and Langhorne, J. E. Relationships between symptomatology and SES-related factors in hyperkinetic/MBD boys. *American Journal of Orthopsychiatry,* 1976, *46,* 291–301.

Patterson, C. J., and Massad, C. M. Facilitating referential communication among children; The listener as teacher. *Journal of Experimental Child Psychology,* 1980, *29,* 357–370.

Patterson, G. R. Mothers: The unacknowledged victims. *Monographs of the Society for Research in Child Development,* 1980, *45*(5, Serial No. 186).

Patterson, G. R. *Coercive family process.* Eugene, Ore.: Castalia Press, 1982.

Patterson, G. R., and Cobb, J. A. Stimulus control for classes of noxious behavior. In J. F. Knutson (Ed.), *The control of aggression: Implications from basic research.* Chicago: Aldine, 1973.

Patterson, G. R., Littman, R. A., and Bricker, W. Assertive behavior in children: A step toward a theory of aggression. *Monographs of the Society for Research in Child Development,* 1967, *32*(5, Serial No. 113).

Pedersen, F. A., Cain, R., Zaslow, M., and Anderson, B. Variation in infant experience associated with alternative family role organization. In L. Laesa and I. Sigel (Eds.), *Families as learning environments for children.* New York: Plenum, 1983.

Pedersen, F. A., Zaslow, M. J., Cain R. L. and Anderson, B. J. Cesarean childbirth: Psychological implications for mothers and fathers. *Infant Mental Health Journal,* 1981, *2,* 257–263.

Peery, J. C., and Stern, D. Gaze duration frequency distributions during mother-infant interaction. *Journal of Genetic Psychology,* 1976, *129,* 45–55.

Peevers, B. H. The development of the perception of others: A longitudinal study. Paper presented at the meeting of the American Psychological Association, New York, September 1979.

Peevers, B. H., and Secord, P. F. Developmental changes in attribution of descriptive concepts to persons. *Journal of Personality and Social Psychology,* 1973, *27,* 120–128.

Pellegrino, J. W., and Schadler, M. Maximizing performance in a problem-solving task. Unpublished manuscript, University of Pittsburgh, 1974.

Penman, R., Cross, T., Milgrom-Friedman, J., and Meares, R. Mothers' speech to prelingual infants: A pragmatic analysis. *Journal of Child Language,* 1983, *10,* 17–34.

Pennington, B. R., and Smith, S. D. Genetic influences on learning disabilities and speech and language disorders. *Child Development.* 1983, *54,* 369–387.

Pennington, B. F., Wallach, L., and Wallach, M. A. Nonconservers' use and understanding of number and arithmetic. *Genetic Psychology Monographs,* 1980, *101,* 231–243.

Pepler, D. Naturalistic observations of teaching and modeling between siblings. Paper presented at the biennial meeting of the Society for Research in Child Development, Boston, April 1981.

Papler, D., Corter, C., and Abramovitch, R. Social relations among children: Siblings and peers. In K. Rubin and H. Ross (Eds.) *Peer relationships and social skills in childhood.* New York: Springer-Verlag, 1982.

Perlmutter, M. Development in memory in the preschool years. In R. Greene and T. D. Yawkey (Eds.), *Childhood development.* Westport, Conn.: Technomic Publishing Co., 1980.

Perlmutter, M., and Lange, G. A developmental analysis of recall-recognition distinctions. In P. A. Ornstein (Ed.), *Memory development in children.* Hillsdale, N.J.: Lawrence Erlbaum Associates, 1978.

Perlmutter, M., and Myers, N. A. Development of recall in 2- to 4-year-old children. *Developmental Psychology,* 1979, *15,* 73–83.

Peskin, H. Pubertal onset and ego functioning. *Journal of Abnormal Psychology,* 1967, *72,* 1–15.

Peterson, A. C., and Offer, D. Adolescent development: The years 16 to 19. In J. D. Noshpitz (Ed.), *Basic handbook of child psychiatry.* New York: Basic Books, 1980.

Peterson, L. R., and Petersen, M. J. Short-term retention of individual verbal items. *Journal of Experimental Psychology,* 1959, *58,* 193–198.

Pettersen, L., Yonas, A., and Fisch, R. O. The development of blinking in response to impending collision in preterm, full term, and post term infants. *Infant Behavior and Development,* 1980, *3,* 155–165.

Pezdek, K., and Hartman, E. F. Children's television viewing: Attention and comprehension of auditory versus visual information. *Child Development,* 1983, *54,* 1015–1023.

Pezdek, K., and Stevens, E. Children's memory for auditory and visual information on television. *Developmental Psychology,* 1984, *20,* 212–218.

Piaget, J. *The child's conception of the world.* New York: Harcourt, Brace, 1929.

Piaget, J. *The moral judgment of the child.* Glencoe, Ill.: Free Press, 1932.

Piaget, J. *The origins of intelligence in children.* New York: International Universities Press, 1952.

Piaget, J. *The construction of reality in the child.* New York: Basic Books, 1954.

Piaget, J. *The language and thought of the child.* New York: Meridian Books, 1955. (Originally published, 1926)

Piaget, J. *Play, dreams and imitation.* New York: W. W. Norton, 1962. (Originally published, 1951)

Piaget, J. *The child's conception of number.* New York: W. W. Norton, 1965.

Piaget, J. *The child's conception of time.* New York: Basic Books, 1969.

Piaget, J. Piaget's theory. In P. H. Mussen (Ed.), *Carmichael's manual of child psychology.* New York: Wiley, 1970.

Piaget, J. *The child's conception of the world.* Totowa, N.J.: Littlefield, Adams, 1975. (Originally published, 1929)

Piaget, J., and Inhelder, B. *The psychology of the child.* New York: Basic Books, 1969.

Pick, A. D., Christy, M. D., and Frankel, G. W. A developmental study of visual selective attention. *Journal of Experimental Child Psychology,* 1972, *14,* 165–175.

Pick, A. D., and Frankel, G. W. A developmental study of strategies of visual selectivity. *Child Development,* 1974, *45,* 1162–1165.

Pierce, J. E. *A study of 750 Portland, Oregon, children during the first year.* Papers and Reports on Child Language Development, 8. Stanford: Stanford University Press, 1974.

Piers, M. W. *Infanticide.* New York: W. W. Norton, 1978.

Pitt, B. "Maternity blues." *British Journal of Psychiatry,* 1973, *122,* 431–433.

Pleck, J., and Rustad, M. Husbands' and wives' time in family and paid work in the 1975-1976 study of time use. Unpublished manuscript, 1980. Wellesley College Center for Research on Women.

Pless, I. B., and Roghmann, K. J. Chronic illness and its consequences: Observations based on three epidemiologic surveys. *Journal of Pediatrics,* 1971, *79,* 351–359.

Pless, I. B., and Satterwhite, B. B. Chronic illness. In R. J. Haggerty, K. J. Roghmann, and I. B. Pless (Eds.), *Child health and the community.* New York: Wiley, 1975.

Pless, I. B., and Stulginskas, J. Accidents and violence as a cause of morbidity and mortality in childhood. *Advances in Pediatrics,* 1982, *29,* 471–495.

Plomin, R. A temperament theory of personality development: Parent-child interactions. Unpublished doctoral dissertation, University of Texas, 1974.

Plomin, R. The difficult concept of temperament: A response to Thomas, Chess, and Korn. *Merrill-Palmer Quarterly,* 1982, *28,* 25–33.

Plomin, R. Developmental behavioral genetics. *Child Development,* 1983, *54,* 253–259.

Plomin, R., and Foch, T. T. Sex differences and individual differences. *Child Development,* 1981, *52,* 383–385.

Plutchik, R. *Emotion: A psychoevolutionary synthesis.* New York: Harper & Row, 1980.

Polani, P. E., Lessof, M. H., and Bishop, P. M. F. Colourblindness in "ovarian agenesis" (gonadal dysplasia). *Lancet,* 1956, *2,* 118–119.

Pollin, W., and Stabenau, J. R. Biological, psychological, and historical differences in a series of monozygotic twins discordant for schizophrenia. In D. Rosenthal and S. S. Kety (Eds.), *The transmission of schizophrenia.* Oxford: Pergamon Press, 1968.

Pollitt, E. Behavioral correlates of severe malnutrition in man. In W. Moore, M. Silverberg, and M. Read (Eds.), *Nutrition growth and development of North American Indian children.* Washington, D.C.: DHEW, 1973.

Poulson, C. L. Differential reinforcement of other-than-vocalization as a control procedure in the conditioning of infant vocalization rate. *Journal of Experimental Child Psychology,* 1983, *36,* 471–489.

Powell, G. F., Brasel, J. A. Raiti, S., and Blizzard, R. M. Emotional deprivation and growth retardation stimulating idiopathic hypopituitarism: II. Endocrinologic evaluation of the syndrome. *New England Journal of Medicine,* 1967, *276,* 1279–1283.

Powell, J. S., and Sternberg, R. J. Acquisition of vocabulary from context. Paper presented at the meeting of the American Psychological Association, Los Angeles, August 1981.

Power, T. G., and Parke, R. D. Patterns of mother and father play with their 8-month-old infant: A multiple analyses approach. *Infant Behavior and Development,* 1983, *6,* 453–459.

Pratt, L. Child rearing methods and children's health behavior. *Journal of Health and Social Behavior,* 1973, *14,* 61–69.

Pritchard, J. A., and MacDonald, P. C. *Williams' obstetrics* (16th ed.). New York: Appleton-Century-Crofts, 1980.

Prentice, N., and Fathman, R. Joking riddles: A developmental index of children's humor. *Developmental Psychology,* 1975, *2,* 210–216.

Provence, S., and Lipton, R. C. *Infants in institutions.* New York: International Universities Press, 1962.

Purpura, D. P. Morphogenesis of the visual cortex in preterm infants. In M. A. B. Brazier (Ed.), *Growth and brain development.* New York: Raven Press, 1975.

Putallaz, M. Predicting children's sociometric status from their behavior. *Child Development,* 1983, *54,* 1417–1426.

Queenan, J. T. (Ed.) *A new life: Pregnancy, birth, and your child's first year.* New York: Van Nostrand, 1979.

Querleu, D., and Renard, K. Les perceptions auditives du foetus humain. *Médicine et Hygiéne,* 1981, *39,* 2102–2110.

Quigley, M. E., Sheehan, K. L., Wilkes, M. M., and Yen, S. S. C. Effects of maternal smoking on circulating catecholamine levels and fetal heart rates. *American Journal of Obstetrics and Gynecology,* 1979, *133,* 685–690.

Rader, N., Siro, D. J., and Firestone, P. B. Performance on a stage IV object permanence task with standard and nonstandard covers. *Child Development,* 1979, *50,* 908–910.

Rafman, S. The infant's reaction to imitation of the mother's behavior by a stranger. In T. G. Décarie (Ed.), *The infant's reaction to strangers.* New York: International Universities Press, 1974.

Ramey, C. T., and Campbell, F. A. Compensatory education for disadvantaged children. *School Review,* 1979, *87,* 171–189.

Ramey, C. T., Farran, D. C., and Campbell, F. A. Predicting IQ from mother-infant interactions. *Child Development,* 1979, *50,* 804–814.

Ramey, C. T., and Haskins, R. The modification of intelligence through early experience. *Intelligence,* 1981, *5,* 5–19.

Ramey, C. T., and Mills, P. J. Social and intellectual consequence of day-care for high risk infants. In R. A. Webb (Ed.), *Social development in childhood: Day-care programs and research.* Baltimore: Johns Hopkins University Press, 1977.

Rawat, A. Alcohol harms fetus, study finds. *Chicago Tribune,* April 19, 1982, Section 1, p. 13.

Ray, C. G. Common infectious diseases. In D. W. Smith (Ed.), *Introduction to clinical pediatrics.* Philadelphia: Saunders, 1977.

Rebelsky, F., and Hanks, C. Fathers' verbal interaction with infants in the first three months of life. *Child Development,* 1971, *42,* 63–68.

Redican, W. K. Adult male-infant interactions in nonhuman primates. In M. E. Lamb (Ed.), *The role of the father in child development.* New York: Wiley, 1976.

Redl, F. Adolescents—Just how do they react? In H. Caplan and S. Lebovici (Eds.), *Adolescence: Psychosocial perspectives.* New York: Basic Books, 1969.

Reed, E. Anomalies in development. In F. D. Horowitz (Ed.), *Review of child development research,* Volume 4. Chicago: University of Chicago Press, 1975.

Reese, H. Sociometric choices of the same and opposite sex in late childhood. *Merrill-Palmer Quarterly,* 1962, *8,* 173–174.

Reese, H. W. Imagery and associative memory. In R. V. Kail, Jr., and J. W. Hagen (Eds.), *Perspectives in the development of memory and cognition.* Hillsdale, N.J.: Lawrence Erlbaum Associates, 1977.

Reese, M., Young, J., Buckley, J., Weathers, D., Achiron, M., and Foote, D. Life below the poverty line. *Newsweek,* April 5, 1982, pp. 20–26.

Reichenbach, L., and Masters, J. C. Children's use of expressive and contextual cues in judgments of emotion. *Child Development,* 1983, *54,* 993–1004.

Reid, B. V. An anthropological reinterpretation of Kohlberg's stages of moral development. *Human Development,* 1984, *27,* 57–64.

Reinisch, J. M. Prenatal exposure to synthetic progestins increases potential for aggression in humans. *Science,* 1981, *211,* 1171–1173.

Rescorla, L. A. Category development in early language. *Journal of Child Language,* 1981, *8,* 225–238.

Rest, J. R. Morality. In P. H. Mussen (Ed.), *Handbook of child psychology,* Volume 3. New York: Wiley, 1983.

Rest, J. R. Davison, M. L., and Robbins, S. Age trends in judging moral issues: A review of cross-sectional, longitudinal, and sequential studies of the defining issues test. *Child Development,* 1978, *49,* 263–279.

Rest, J. R., Turiel, E., and Kohlberg, L. Level of moral development as a determinant of preference and comprehension of moral judgments made by others. *Journal of Personality,* 1969, *37,* 225–252.

Restak, R. Male, female brains: Are they different? *Boston Globe,* September 9, 1979, p. A1.

Revill, S. I., and Dodge, J.A. Psychological determinants of infantile pyloric stenosis. *Archives of Disease in Childhood,* 1978, *53,* 66–68.

Rheingold, H. L. Independent behavior of the human infant. In A. D. Pick (Ed.), *Minnesota Symposia on Child Psychology,* Volume 7. Minneapolis: University of Minnesota Press, 1973.

Rheingold, H. L., and Cook, K. V. The contents of boys' and girls' rooms as an index of parents' behavior. *Child Development,* 1975, *46,* 459–463..

Rheingold, H. L., and Eckerman, C. O. Departures from the mother. In H. R. Schaffer (Ed.), *The origins of human social relations.* London: Academic Press, 1971.

Rheingold, H. L., and Eckerman, C. O. Fear of the stranger: A critical examination. In H. W. Reese (Ed.), *Advances in child development and behavior,* Volume 8. New York: Academic Press, 1973.

Rholes, W. S., and Ruble, D. N. Children's understanding of dispositional characteristics of others. *Child Development,* 1984, *55,* 550–560.

Ricciuti, H. N. Fear and the development of social attachments in the first year of life. In M. Lewis and L. A. Rosenblum (Eds.), *The origins of fear.* New York: Wiley, 1974.

Richards, J. E., and Rader, N. Crawling-onset age predicts visual cliff avoidance in infants. *Journal of Experimental Psychology,* 1981, *7,* 382–387.

Richardson, S. A., Goodman, N., and Hastorf, A. H. Cultural uniformity in reaction to physical disabilities. *American Sociological Review,* 1961, *26,* 241–247.

Richman, L., and Harper, D. School adjustment of children with observable disabilities. *Journal of Abnormal Child Psychology,* 1978, *6,* 11–18.

Riegel, K. F. The dialectics of human development. *American Psychologist,* 1976, *31,* 689–699.

Riesen, A. Effects of early deprivation of photic stimulation. In S. F. Osler and R. E. Cooke (Eds.), *The biosocial basis of mental retardation.* Baltimore: Johns Hopkins University Press, 1965.

Ritter, K., Kaprove, B. H., Fitch, J. P., and Flavell, J. H. The development of retrieval strategies in young children. *Cognitive Psychology,* 1973, *5,* 310–321.

Rivara, F. P. Epidemiology of childhood injuries. In *Preventing Childhood Injuries.* Columbus, Ohio: Ross Laboratories, January, 1982.

Rivlin, L., and Rothenberg, M. The use of space in open classrooms. In H. Proshansky, W. Ittelson, and L. Rivlin (Eds.), *Environmental psychology: People and their physical settings* (2nd ed.). New York: Holt, Rinehart & Winston, 1976.

Roberts, C. J., and Lowe, C. R. Where have all the conceptions gone? *Lancet,* 1975, 498–499.

Roberts, R. J., and Patterson, C. J. Perspective taking and referential communication: The question of correspondence reconsidered. *Child Development,* 1983, *54,* 993–1004.

Robertson, J., and Robertson, J. Young children in brief separation: A fresh look. *Psychoanalytic Study of the Child,* 1971, *26,* 264–315.

Robinson, E. J. The child's understanding of inadequate messages and communication failure: A problem of ignorance or egocentrism. In W. P. Dickson (Ed.), *Children's oral communication skills.* New York: Academic Press, 1981.

Robinson, E. J., and Robinson, W. P. Development in the understanding of causes of success and failure in verbal communication. *Cognition,* 1977, *5,* 363–378.

Robson, K. S., and Moss, H. A. Patterns and determinants of maternal attachment. *Journal of Pediatrics,* 1970, *77,* 976.

Roche, A. F. The adipocyte-number hypothesis. *Child Development,* 1981, *52,* 31–43.

Rodgon, M. Overt action and semantic expression of action. In R. N. Campbell and P. T. Smith (Eds.), *Recent advances in the psychology of language: Language development and mother-child interaction, Part A.* New York: Plenum, 1978.

Roedell, W. C., and Slaby, R. G. The role of distal and proximal interaction in infant social preference formation. *Developmental Psychology,* 1977, *13,* 266–273.

Roffwarg, H. P., Muzio, J. N., and Dement, W. C. Ontogenetic development of the human sleep-dream cycle. *Science*, 1966, *152*, 604–619.

Rogers, C. The relationship between the organization of play space and children's behavior. Unpublished masters thesis, Oklahoma State University, 1976.

Rogers, C. M., and Davenport, R. K. Intellectual performance of differentially reared chimpanzees: III. Oddity. *American Journal of Mental Deficiency*, 1971, *75*, 526–530.

Rogers, C. R. Toward a theory of creativity. In H. H. Anderson (Ed.), *Creativity and its cultivation*. New York: Harper, 1959.

Rogoff, B., Newcombe, N., and Kagan, J. Planfulness and recognition memory. *Child Development*, 1974, *45*, 972–977.

Rohe, W. M., and Nuffer, E. L. The effects of density and partitioning on children's behavior. Paper presented at the meeting of the American Psychological Association, San Francisco, 1977.

Romney, K., and Romney, R. The Mixtecans of Juxtlahuache, Mexico. In B. Whiting (Ed.), *Six cultures*. New York: Wiley, 1963.

Roopnarine, J. L., and Field, T. M. Peer-directed behaviors of infants and toddlers during nursery school play. *Infant Behavior and Development*, 1983, *6*, 133–138.

Rosch, E. Cognitive representations of semantic categories. *Journal of Experimental Psychology*, 1975, *104*, 192–233.

Rosch, E., Mervis, C. B., Gray, W. D., Johnson, D. M., and Boyes-Braem, P. Basic objects in natural categories. *Cognitive Psychology*, 1976, *8*, 382–439.

Rose, H., and Bernstein, I. S. Plasma testosterone levels in the male rhesus: Influences of sexual and social stimuli. *Science*, 1972, *216*, 305.

Rose, S. A., and Blank, M. The potency of context in children's cognition: An illustration through conservation. *Child Development*, 1969, *40*, 383–406.

Rose, W. L. *A documentary history of slavery in North America*. Oxford: Oxford University Press, 1976.

Rosenberg, M. *Society and the adolescent self-image*. Princeton, N.J.: Princeton University Press, 1965.

Rosenberg, M., and Simmons, R. G. Black and white self-esteem: The urban school child. Washington, D.C.: American Sociological Association, 1971.

Rosenblatt, P. C., and Cunningham, M. R. Television watching and family tensions. *Journal of Marriage and the Family*, 1976, *38*, 105–110.

Rosenblum, L. A., and Plimpton, E. H. The effects of adults on peer interactions. In M. Lewis and L. A. Rosenblum (Eds.), *The child and its family*. New York: Plenum, 1979.

Rosenfeld, E. F. The relationship of sex-typed toys to the development of competency and sex-role identification in children. Paper presented at the meeting of the Society for Research in Child Development, Denver, Colo., 1975.

Rosenhan, D. L. Effects of success and failure on children's generosity. *Journal of Personality and Social Psychology*, 1973, *27*, 239–247.

Rosenhan, D. L., Underwood, B., and Moore, B. S. Affect moderates self-gratification and altruism. *Journal of Personality and Social Psychology*, 1974, *30*, 546–552.

Rosenstein, D., and Oster, H. *Facial expression as a method for exploring infants' taste responses*. Paper presented at the meeting of the Society for Research in Child Development, Boston, April 1981.

Rosenstock, I. M., and Kirscht, J. P. Practice implications. In M. H. Becker (Ed.), *The health belief model and personal health behavior*. Thorofare, N.J.: Charles B. Slack, 1974.

Rosenthal, D. *Genetic theory and abnormal behavior*. New York: McGraw-Hill, 1970.

Rosenthal, R., and Jacobson, L. Teachers' expectancies: Determinants of pupils' IQ gains. *Psychological Reports*, 1966, *19*, 115–118.

Rosenthal, R. , and Jacobson, L. *Pygmalion in the classroom: Teacher expectation and pupils' intellectual development*. New York: Holt, Rinehart & Winston, 1968.

Rosett, H. L., Weiner, L., Zuckerman, B., McKinlay, S., and Edelin, K. C. Reduction of alcohol consumption during pregnancy with benefits to the newborn. *Alcoholism: Clinical and Experimental Research*, 1980, *4*, 178–184.

Rosner, B. S., and Doherty, N. E. The response of neonates to intra-uterine sounds. *Developmental Medicine and Child Neurology*, 1979, *21*, 723–729.

Ross, D. M., and Ross, S. A. *Hyperactivity: Research, theory, and action* (1st ed.; 2nd ed.). New York: Wiley, 1976; 1982.

Ross, H. S., and Goldman, B. D. Establishing new social relations in infancy. In T. Alloway, P. Pliner, and L. Krames (Eds.), *Attachment behavior: Advances in the study of communication and affect*, Volume 0. New York: Plenum, 1977. (a)

Ross, H. S., and Goldman, B. D. Infants' sociability toward strangers. *Child Development*, 1977, *48*, 638–642. (b)

Roth, F. Accelerating language learning in young children. *Journal of Child Language*, 1984, *11*, 89–107.

Rothbart, M. K. The concept of difficult temperament: A critical analysis of Thomas, Chess, and Korn. *Merrill-Palmer Quarterly*, 1982, *28*, 35–40.

Rothbaum, F. Developmental and gender differences in the sex stereotyping of nurturance and dominance. *Developmental Psychology*, 1977, *13*, 531–532.

Rothenberg, B. A. Conservation of number among four- and five-year-old children: Some methodological considerations. *Child Development*, 169, *40*, 383–406.

Rothenberg, B. B. Children's social sensitivity and the relationship to interpersonal competence, intrapersonal comfort, and intellectual level. *Developmental Psychology*, 1970, *2*, 335–350.

Rousseau, J. J. *Emile* (Trans. B. Foxley). London: Dent, 1911. (Originally published, 1762)

Routh, D. K., Schroeder, C. S., and O'Tuama, L. Development of activity level in children. *Developmental Psychology*, 1974, *10*, 163–168.

Rovee-Collier, C. K. Sullivan, M. W., Enright, M. L., Lucas, D., and Fagen, J. W. Reactivation of infant memory. *Science*, 1980, *208*, 1159–1161.

Rowley, V., and Keller, E. D. Changes in children's verbal behavior as a function of social approval and manifest anxiety. *Journal of Abnormal Social Psychology*, 1962, *65*, 53–57.

Rubenstein, J., and Howes, C. The effects of peers on toddler interaction with mother and toys. *Child Development*, 1976, *47*, 597–605.

Rubin, J. Z., Provenzano, F. J., and Luria, Z. The eye of the beholder: Parents' views on sex of newborns. *American Journal of Orthopsychiatry*, 1974, *44*, 512–519.

Rubin, K. H., and Daniels-Beirness, T. Concurrent and predictive correlates of sociometric status in kindergarten and grade 1 children. *Merrill-Palmer Quarterly*, 1983, *29*, 337–351.

Rubin, K. H., Watson, K. S., and Jambor, T. W. Free-play behaviors in preschool and kindergarten children. *Child Development*, 1978, *49*, 534–536.

Rubin, R. A., Maruyama, G., and Kingsbury, G. G. Self-esteem and educational achievement: A casual-model analysis. Paper presented at the annual meeting of the American Psychological Association, New York, September 1979.

Rubin, Z. *Children's friendships.* Cambridge: Harvard University Press, 1980.

Ruble, D. N., and Brooks, J. Adolescent attitudes about menstruation. Paper presented at the biennial meeting of the Society for Research in Child Development, New Orleans, March 1977.

Ruble, D. N., and Brooks-Gunn, J. The experience of menarche. *Child Development,* 1982, *53,* 1557–1566.

Ruff, H. A. The development of perception and recognition of objects. *Child Development,* 1980, *51,* 981–992.

Ruff, H. A., and Halton, A. Is there directed reaching in the human neonate? *Developmental Psychology,* 1977, *14,* 425–426.

Rugh, R., and Shettles, L. B. *From conception to birth: The drama of life's beginnings.* New York: Harper & Row, 1971.

Ruke-Dravina, V. Modifications of speech addressed to young children in Latvian. In C. E. Snow and C. A. Ferguson (Eds.), *Talking to children: Language input and acquisition.* Cambridge: Cambridge University Press, 1977.

Rusolova, R., Izard, C. E., and Simonov, P. V. Comparative analysis of mimical and autonomic components of man's emotional state. *Aviation, Space and Environmental Medicine,* 1975, *46,* 1132–1134.

Russell, M. J. Human olfactory communication. *Nature,* 1976, *260,* 520–522.

Rutter, M. The development of infantile autism. *Psychological Medicine,* 1974, *4,* 147–163. (a)

Rutter, M. *The qualities of mothering: Maternal deprivation reassessed.* New York: Jason Aronson, 1974. (b)

Rutter, M. On confusion in the diagnosis of autism. *Journal of Autism and Childhood Schizophrenia,* 1978, *8,* 137–161.

Rutter, M., Maughan, B., Mortimore, P., and Ouston, J. *Fifteen thousand hours: Secondary schools and their effects on children.* Cambridge: Harvard University Press, 1979.

Rutter, M., Yule, W., and Graham, P. Enuresis and behavioral deviance: Some epidemiological considerations. In I. Kolvin, R. MacKeith and R. Meadows (Eds.), *Bladder control and enuresis.* Philadelphia: Lippincott, 1973.

Ryan, T. J. Instrumental performance as related to several reward schedules and age. *Journal of Experimental Child Psychology,* 1966, *3,* 398–404.

Ryan, T. J., and Voorhoeve, A. C. A parametric investigation of reinforcement schedule and sex of S as related to acquisition and extinction of an instrumental response. *Journal of Experimental Child Psychology,* 1966, *4,* 189–197.

Ryan, T. J., and Watson, P. Children's response speeds as a function of sex and verbal reinforcement schedule. *Psychonomic Science,* 1966, *6,* 271–272.

Saario, T., Jacklin, C. N., and Tittle, C. K. Sex role stereotyping in the public schools. *Harvard Educational Review,* 1973, *43,* 386–404.

Saarni, C. When not to show what you feel: Children's understanding of relations between emotional experience and expressive behavior. Paper presented at the biennial meeting of the Society for Research in Child Development, San Francisco, March 1979.

Sachs, J. The adaptive significance of linguistic input to prelinguistic infants. In C. E. Snow and C. A. Ferguson (Eds.), *Talking to children: Language input and acquisition.* Cambridge: Cambridge University Press, 1977.

Sachs, J. and Johnson, M. Language development in a hearing child of deaf parents. In W. Von Raffler Engel and Y. Le Brun (Eds.), *Baby talk and infant speech.* Neurolinguistics series, Volume 5. Amsterdam: Swets and Zeitlinger, 1976.

Sackett, G. P. Monkeys reared in isolation with pictures as visual input: Evidence for an innate releasing mechanism. *Science,* 1966, *154,* 1468–1472.

Saddler, J. M. *Assessment of children's intelligence.* Philadelphia: Saunders, 1974.

Safer, D. J. Drugs for problem school children. *Journal of School Health,* 1971, *1,* 491–495.

Sagi, A., and Hoffman, M. L. Empathic distress in newborns. *Developmental Psychology,* 1976. *12,* 175–176.

Salapatek, P. Pattern perception in early infancy. In L. B. Cohen and P. Salapatek (Eds.), *Infant perception: From sensation to cognition: Basic visual processes,* Volume 1. New York: Academic Press, 1975.

Satler, A. Birth without violence: A medical controversy. *Nursing Research,* 1978, *27,* 84–88.

Saltz, E., Campbell, S., and Skotko, D. Verbal control of behavior: The effects of shouting. *Developmental Psychology,* 1983, *19,* 461–464.

Salzman, L. K. Allergy testing, psychological assessment and dietary treatment of the hyperactive child syndrome. *Medical Journal of Australia,* 1976, *2,* 248–251.

Samelson, F. J. B. Watson's little Albert, Cyril Burt's twins, and the need for critical science. *American Psychologist,* 1980, *35,* 619–625.

Sameroff, A. J. Non-nutritive sucking in newborns under visual and auditory stimulation. *Child Development,* 1967, *38,* 443–452.

Sameroff, A. J. The components of sucking in the human newborn. *Journal of Experimental Child Psychology,* 1968, *6,* 607–623.

Sameroff, A. J., and Cavanaugh, P. J. Learning in infancy: A developmental perspective. In J. D. Osofsky (Ed.), *Handbook of infant development.* New York: Wiley, 1979.

Sameroff, A. J., and Chandler, M. J. Reproductive risk and the continuum of caretaking casualty. In F. D. Horowitz (Ed.), *Review of child development research,* Volume 4. Chicago: University of Chicago Press, 1975.

Sameroff, A. J., Seifer, R., and Zax, M. Early development of children at risk for emotional disorder. *Monographs of the Society for Research in Child Development,* 1982, 47(7, Serial No. 199).

Sameroff, A. J., and Zax, M. Perinatal charcteristics of the offspring of schizophrenic women. *Journal of Nervous and Mental Diseases,* 1973, *157,* 191–199.

Samuels, H. R. The effect of an older sibling on infant locomotor exploration of a new environment. *Child Development,* 1980, *51,* 607–609.

Sapir, E. *Language.* New York: Harcourt, Brace, 1921. (Reprinted 1958)

Savin-Williams, R. C. Dominance-submission behaviors and hierarchies in young adolescents at a summer camp: Predictors, styles and sex differences. Unpublished doctoral dissertation, University of Chicago, 1977.

Savitsky, J. C., and Watson, M. J. Patterns of proxemic behavior among preschool children. *Representative Research in Social Psychology,* 1975, *6,* 109–113.

Saxby, L., and Bryden, M. P. Left-ear superiority in children for processing auditory emotional material. *Developmental Psychology*, 1984, *20*, 72–80.

Scanlon, J. *Self-reported health behavior and attitudes of youth 12–17 years*. Vital and Health Statistics, Series 11, 147. Washington, D.C.: U.S. Government Printing Office, 1975.

Scanlon, J. W., Brown, W. V., Weiss, J. B., and Alper, M. H. Neurological responses of newborn infants after maternal epidural anesthesia. *Anesthesiology*, 1974, *40*, 121–128.

Scarf, M. From joy to depression: New insights into the chemistry of moods. *New York Times Magazine*, April 24, 1977, pp. 000–000.

Scarr, S. Genetic factors in activity motivation. *Child Development*, 1966, *37*, 663–673.

Scarr, S. Social introversion-extroversion as a heritable response. *Child Development*, 1969, *40*, 823–832.

Scarr, S., and McCartney, K. How people make their own environments: A theory of genotype—environment effects. *Child Development*, 1983, *54*, 424–435.

Scarr, S., and Weinberg, R. A. The Minnesota Adoption Studies: Genetic differences and malleability. *Child Development*, 1983, *54*, 260–267.

Scarr-Salapatek, S. Genetics and the development of intelligence. In F. D. Horowitz (Ed.), *Review of child development research*, Volume 4. Chicago: University of Chicago Press, 1975.

Schachter, S., and Singer, J. E. Cognitive, social, and physiological determinants of emotional states. *Psychological Review*, 1962, *69*, 379–399.

Schaefer, E. S. Converging conceptual models for maternal behavior and for child behavior. Paper presented at the Conference on Research on Parental Attitudes and Child Behavior, Washington University, St. Louis, March 1960.

Schaefer, E. S., and Bayley, N. Maternal behavior, child behavior and their intercorrelations from infancy through adolescence. *Monographs of the Society for Research in Child Development*, 1963, *28*(3, Serial No. 87).

Schaffer, H. R. Acquiring the concept of the dialogue. In M. H. Bornstein and W. Kessen (Eds.), *Psychological development from infancy: Image to intention*. Hillsdale, N.J.: Lawrence Erlbaum Associates, 1978.

Schaffer, H. R., Collis, G. M., and Parsons, G. Vocal interchange and visual regard in verbal and preverbal children. In H. R. Schaffer (Ed.), *Studies in mother-infant interaction*. London: Academic, 1977.

Schaffer, H. R., and Crook, C. K. The role of the mother in early social development. In H. McGurk (Ed.), *Childhood social development*. London: Methuen, 1978.

Schaffer, H. R., and Crook, C. K. Child compliance and maternal control techniques. *Developmental Psychology*, 1980, *16*, 54–61.

Schaffer, H. R., and Emerson, P. E. The development of social attachments in infancy. *Monographs of the Society for Research in Child Development*, 1964, *29*(3, Serial No. 94). (a)

Schaffer, J. R., and Emerson, P. E. Patterns of response to physical contact in early human development. *Journal of Child Psychology and Psychiatry*, 1964, *5*, 11–13. (b)

Schank, R.C., and Abelson, R. *Scripts, plans, goals and understanding*. Hillsdale, N.J.: Lawrence Erlbaum Associates, 1977.

Schau, C. G., Kahn, L., Diepold, J. H., and Cherry, F. The relationships of parental expectations and preschool children's verbal sex typing to their sex-typed toy play behavior. *Child Development*, 1980, *51*, 266–270.

Scheinfeld, A. *Your heredity and environment*. Philadelphia and New York: Lippincott, 1965.

Scherer, K. Nonlinguistic vocal indicators of emotion and psychopathology. In C. E. Izard (Ed.), *Emotions in personality and psychopathology*. New York: Plenum, 1979.

Scherer, M. W., and Nakamura, C. Y. A peer-survey schedule for children: A factor analytic comparison with manifest anxiety. *Behavior Research and Therapy*, 1968, *6*, 173–182.

Scherz, R. G., Fatal motor vehicle accidents of child passengers from birth through 4 years of age in Washington State. *Pediatrics*, 1981, *68*, 572–576.

Schiff, W. Conservation of length redux: A perceptual-linguistic phenomenon. *Child Development*, 1983. *54*, 1497–1506.

Schleifer, M., and Douglas, V. A. Moral judgments, behavior and cognitive style in young children. *Canadian Journal of Behavioural Science*, 1973, *5*, 133–144.

Schlesinger, H. S., and Meadow, K. P. *Sound and sign: Childhood deafness and mental health*. Berkeley: University of California Press, 1972.

Schmuck, R. A., and Schmuck, P. A. *Group processes in the classroom*. Dubuque, Iowa: William C. Brown, 1975.

Schneck, H. M., Jr. Fetal defects discovered early by new method. *New York Times*, October 18, 1983, p. C1.

Schonfeld, W. A. The body and the body-image in adolescents. In H. Caplan and F. Lebovici (Eds.), *Adolescence: Psychosocial perspectives*. New York: Basic Books, 1969.

Schrag, P. *The decline of the WASP*. New York: Simon & Schuster, 1971.

Schrag, P., and Divoky, D. *The myth of the hyperactive child*. New York: Pantheon, 1975.

Schroeder, C., Teplin, S., and Schroeder, S. An overview of common medical problems encountered in schools. In C. R. Reynolds and T. B. Gutkin (Eds.), *The handbook of school psychology*. New York: Wiley, 1982.

Schubert, J. B., Bradley-Johnson, S., and Nuttal, J. Mother-infant communication and maternal employment. *Childhood Development*, 1980, *51*, 246–249.

Schulman-Galambos, C., and Galambos, R. Brain stem auditory evoked audiometry in newborn hearing screening. *Archives of Otolaryngology*, 1979, *105*, 86–90.

Schwarz, J. C. Young children's fears: Modeling or cognition? Paper presented at the biennial meeting of the Society for Research in Child Development, San Francisco, March 1979.

Sears, R. R. Your ancients revisited: A history of child development. In E. M. Hetherington (Ed.), *Review of child development research*, Volume 5. Chicago: University of Chicago Press, 1975.

Sears, R. R., Rau, L., and Alpert, R. *Identification and child rearing*. Stanford: Stanford University Press, 1965.

Sears, R. R., and Wise, G. W. Relation of cup feeding in infancy to thumb-sucking and the oral drive. *American Journal of Orthopsychiatry*, 1950, *20*, 123–138.

Seavey, C. A., Katz, P. A., and Zalk, S. R. Baby X, the effect of gender labels on adult responses to infants. *Sex Roles*, 1975, *1*, 61–73.

Secord, D., and Peevers, B. The development and attribution of person concepts. In T. Mischel (Ed.), *Understanding other persons*. Oxford: Blackwell, 1974.

Seefeldt, F. M. Formal operations and adolescent painting. *Genetic Epistemologist*, 1979, *5*, 5–6.

Seelig, J. Unpublished paper, Institute for Cultural Pluralism, Chicago, 1975.

Selman, R. L. *The growth of interpersonal understanding: De-

velopmental and clinical analyses. New York: Academic Press, 1980.

Selman, R. L. The child as a friendship philosopher. In S. R. Asher and J. M. Gottman (Eds.), *The development of children's friendships.* New York: Cambridge University Press, 1981.

Selman, R. L., Schorin, M. Z., Stone, C. R., and Phelps, E. A naturalistic study of children's social understanding. *Developmental Psychology,* 1983, *19,* 82–102.

Selman, R. L., and Selman, A. Children's ideas about friendship: A new theory. *Psychology Today,* 1979, October, 70–80.

Serbin, L. A., O'Leary, D. K., Kent, R. N., and Tonick, I. J. A comparison of teacher response to the preacademic and problem behavior of boys and girls. *Child Development,* 1973, *44,* 796–804.

Sexton, M. A., and Geffen, G. Development of three strategies of attention in dichotic monitoring. *Developmental Psychology,* 1979, *15,* 299–310.

Sexton, M. E. The development of the understanding of causality in infancy. *Infant Behavior and Development,* 1983, *6,* 201–210.

Shannon, D., Kelly, D., and O'Connell, K. Abnormal regulation of ventilation in infants at risk for sudden infant death syndrome. *New England Journal of Medicine,* 1977, *297,* 747–784.

Shatz, M. The comprehension of indirect directives: Can you shut the door? Paper presented at the summer meeting of the Linguistic Society of America, Amherst, Mass., July 1974.

Shatz, M. Children's comprehension of their mother's question-directives. *Journal of Child Language,* 1978, *5,* 39–46.

Shatz, M., and Gelman, R. The development of communication skills: Modifications in the speech of young children as a function of the listener. *Monographs of the Society for Research in Child Development,* 1973, *38*(5, Serial No 152).

Shayer, M., Kucheman, D. E., and Wylam, H. The distribution of Piagetian stages of thinking in British middle and secondary school children. *British Journal of Educational Psychology,* 1976, *46,* 164–173.

Shayer, M., and Wylam, H. The distribution of Piagetian stages of thinking in British middle and secondary school children, II: 14 to 16 years old and sex differentials. *British Journal of Educational Psychology,* 1978, *48,* 62–70.

Shenker, R., and Schildkrout, M. Physical and emotional health of youth. In R. J. Havighurst and P. H. Dreyer (Eds.), *Youth—Seventy-fourth yearbook of the National Society for the Study of Education, Part. 1.* Chicago: University of Chicago Press, 1975.

Shepard, R. N., and Metzler, J. Mental rotation of three-dimensional objects. *Science,* 1971, *171,* 701–703.

Sheperd-Look, D. L. Sex differentiation and the development of sex roles. In B. B. Wolman and G. Strickler (Eds.), *Handbook of developmental psychology.* Englewood Cliffs, N.J.: Prentice Hall, 1982.

Shereshefsky, P. M., and Yarrow, L. J. *Psychological aspects of a first pregnancy and early postnatal adaptation.* New York: Raven Press, 1973.

Sherif, M., Harvey, O. J., White, B. J., Hood, W. R., and Sherif, C. W. *Intergroup conflict and cooperation: The robbers' cave experiment.* Norman: University of Oklahoma Press, 1961.

Sherif, M., and Sherif, C. W. *Reference groups.* New York: Harper & Row, 1964.

Sherman, J. A., and Bushell, D. Behavior modification as an educational technique. In F. D. Horowitz (Ed.), *Review of child development research,* Volume 4. Chicago: University of Chicago Press, 1975.

Shields, J. *Monozygotic twins: Brought up apart and brought up together.* London: Oxford University Press, 1962.

Shields, S. A., and Stern, R. M. Emotion: The preception of bodily change. In P. Pliner, K. R. Blankstein, and I. M. Speigel (Eds.), *Perception of emotion in self and others.* New York: Plenum, 1979.

Shiffler, N., Lynch-Sauer, and Nadelman, L. Relationship between self-concept and classroom behavior in two informal elementary classrooms. *Journal of Educational Psychology,* 1977, *69,* 349–359.

Shigetomi, C. C., Hartmann, D. P., and Gelfand, D. M. Sex differences in children's altruistic behavior and reputations for helpfulness. *Developmental Psychology,* 1981, *17,* 434–437.

Shinn, M. Father absence and children's cognitive development. *Psychology Bulletin,* 1978, *85,* 295–324.

Shirley, M. M. *The first two years: A study of twenty-five babies.* Minneapolis: University of Minnesota Press, 1933.

Shovlin, D. W. The effect of the middle school environment and the elementary school environment upon six-grade students. Unpublished doctoral dissertation, University of Washington, 1967.

Shultz, T. R., and Horibe, F. Development of the appreciation of verbal jokes. *Developmental Psychology,* 1974, *10,* 13–20.

Sidman, R. L., and Rakic, P. Neuronal migration, with special reference to developing human brain: A review. *Brain Research,* 1973, *62,* 1–35.

Siegal, M., and Rablin, J. Moral development as reflected by young children's evaluation of maternal discipline. *Merrill-Palmer Quarterly,* 1982, *28,* 499–509.

Siegel, A. W., and Stevenson, H. W. Incidental learning: A developmental study. *Child Development,* 1966, *37,* 811–818.

Siegel, E., Bauman, K., Schaefer, E. Sanders, M., and Ingram, D. Hospital and home support during infancy: Impact on maternal attachment, child abuse and neglect, and health care utilization. *Pediatrics,* 1980, *66,* 183–190.

Siegel, L. S. The relationship of language and thought in the preoperational child: A reconsideration of non-verbal alternatives to Piagetian tasks. In L. S. Siegel and C. J. Brainerd (Eds.), *Alternatives to Piaget: Critical essays on the theory.* New York: Academic Press, 1978.

Siegel, L. S., McCabe, A. E., Brand, J., and Matthews, J. Evidence for the understanding of class inclusion in preschool children: Linguistic factors and training effects. *Child Development,* 1978, *49,* 688–693.

Siegler, R. S. Three aspects of cognitive development. *Cognitive Psychology,* 1976, *8,* 481–520.

Siegler, R. S. Information processing approaches to development. In P. H. Mussen (Ed.), *Handbook of child psychology,* Volume 1. New York: Wiley, 1983.

Siegler, R. S., and Richards, D. D. The development of intelligence. In R. J. Sternberg (Ed.), *Handbook of human intelligence.* New York: Cambridge University Press, 1983.

Siegler, R. S. and Robinson, M. The development of numerical understandings. In H. W. Reese and L. P. Lipsitt (Eds.), *Advances in child development and behavior,* Volume 16. New York: Academic Press, 1982.

Silberman, M. L. Teachers' attitudes and actions toward their students. In M. L. Silberman (Ed.), *The experiment of school-*

ing. New York: Holt, Rinehart & Winston, 1971.

Silverman, I. W., and Stone, J. M. Modifying cognitive functioning through participation in a problem solving group. *Journal of Educational Psychology,* 1972, *63,* 603–608.

Siman, M. L. Application of a new model of peer group influence to naturally existing adolescent friendship groups. *Child Development,* 1977, *48,* 270–274.

Simmons, R. G., Rosenberg, F., and Rosenberg, M. Disturbance in the self-image at adolescence. *American Sociological Review,* 1973, *38,* 553–568.

Simner, M. L. Newborns' response to the cry of another infant. *Developmental Psychology,* 1971, *5,* 136–150.

Simpson, E. Moral development research. A case study of scientific cultural bias. *Human Development,* 1974, *17,* 81–105.

Sinclair-De Zwart, H. *Acquisition du langage et développement de la pensée.* Paris: Dunod, 1967.

Singer, J. B., and Flavell, J. H. Development of knowledge about communication: Children's evaluations of explicitly ambiguous messages. *Child Development,* 1981, *52,* 1211–1215.

Singer, J. L., and Singer, D. G. Fostering imaginative play in preschool children: Television and live model effects. Paper presented at the annual meeting of the American Psychological Association, New Orleans, August 1974.

Singer, J. L., Singer, D. G., and Sherrod, L. R. Prosocial programs in the context of children's total pattern of TV viewing. Paper presented at the biennial meeting of the Society for Research in Child Development, San Francisco, March 1979.

Siqueland, E. R., and Lipsitt, L. P. Conditioned head-turning in human newborns. *Journal of Experimental Child Psychology,* 1966, *3,* 356–376.

Skarin, K. Cognitive and contextual determinants of stranger fear in six- and eleven-month-old infants. *Child Development,* 1977, *48,* 537–544.

Skinner, B. G. *Verbal behavior.* New York: Appleton-Century-Crofts, 1957.

Skinner, R. E. A calibrated recording and analysis of the pitch, force, and quality of vocal tones expressing happiness and sadness and a determination of the pitch and force of the subjective concepts of ordinary soft and loud tones. *Speech Monographs,* 1935, *2,* 81–137.

Skodak, M., and Skeels, H. M. A final follow-up study of one hundred adopted children. *Journal of Genetic Psychology,* 1949, *75,* 85–125.

Slaby, R. G. The effects of aggressive and altruistic verbalizations on aggressive and altruistic behaviors. In J. deWit and W. W. Hartup (Eds.), *Origins and determinants of aggression.* The Hague: Mouton, 1974.

Slaby, R. G., and Frey, K. S. Development of gender constancy and selective attention to same-sex models. *Child Development,* 1975, *46,* 849–856.

Slaughter, D. T. Relation of early parent-teacher socialization influences to achievement orientation and self-esteem in middle childhood among low-income black children. In J. C. Glidewell (Ed.), *The social context of learning and development.* New York: Gardner Press, 1977.

Slaughter, D. T. Early intervention and its effects on maternal and child development. *Monographs of the Society for Research in Child Development,* 1983, *48*(4, Serial No. 202).

Slobin, D. I. Cognitive prerequisites for the development of grammar. In C. A. Ferguson and D. I. Slobin (Eds.), *Studies of child language development.* New York: Holt, Rinehart & Winston, 1973.

Slobin, D. I. On the nature of talk to children. In E. H. Lenneberg, and E. Lenneberg (Eds.), *Foundations of language development,* Volume 1. New York: Academic Press, 1975.

Smiley, P., and Huttenlocher, J. Work in progress, University of Chicago, 1984.

Smiley, S. S., and Brown, A. L. Conceptual preference for thematic and taxonomic relations: A nonmonotonic age trend from preschool to old age. *Journal of Experimental Child Psychology,* 1979, *28,* 249–257.

Smiley, S. S., and Weir, M. W. Role of dimensional dominance in reversal and nonreversal shift behavior. *Journal of Experimental Child Psychology,* 1966, *4,* 296–307.

Smith, C. A. The first breath. *Scientific American,* 1963, *209,* 27–35.

Smith, E. I. The epidemiology of burns: The cause and control of burns in children. *Pediatrics,* 1969, *44,* 821–827.

Smith, H. K. The responses of good and poor readers when asked to read for different purposes. *Reading Research Quarterly,* 1967, *3,* 53–84.

Smith, M. C. Cognizing the behavior stream: The recognition of intentional action. *Child Development,* 1978, *49,* 736–743.

Smith, P. K. A longitudinal study of social participation in preschool children: Solitary and parallel play reexamined. *Developmental Psychology,* 1978, *14,* 517–523.

Smith, P. K., and Connolly, K. Patterns of play and social interaction in preschool children. In N. Blurton Jones (Ed.), *Ethological studies of child behaviour.* Cambridge: Cambridge University, Press, 1972.

Smith, P. K., and Connolly, K. *The behavioural ecology of the preschool.* Cambridge: Cambridge University Press, 1981.

Smith, S., and Freedman, D. G. Mother-toddler interaction and maternal perception of child temperament in two ethnic groups: Chinese-American and European-American. Paper presented at the meeting of the Society for Research in Child Development, Detroit, April 1983.

Snow, C. E. Mother's speech to children learning language. *Child Development,* 1972, *43,* 549–564.

Soar, R. S., and Soar, R. M. An attempt to identify measures of teacher effectiveness from four studies. Paper presented at the meeting of the American Educational Research Association, San Francisco, April 1976.

Soewondo, S., Abednego, B., Pekerti, A., and Karjadi, D. The effect of nutritional status on some aspects of intelligence. *Paediatrica Indonesiana,* 1971, *11,* 28–36.

Sokol, R. J., Miller, S. I., and Reed, O. Alcohol abuse during pregnancy: An epidemiologic study. *Alcoholism,* 1980, *4,* 135–145.

Sonnenschein, S. How feedback from a listener affects children's referential communication skills. *Developmental Psychology,* 1984, *20,* 287–292.

Sonnenschein, S., and Whitehurst, C. J. Training referential communication skills: The limits of success. *Journal of Experimental Child Psychology,* 1983, *35,* 426–436.

Sontag, L. W. Effect of fetal activity on the nutritional state of the infant at birth. *American Journal of Diseases in Children,* 1940, *6,* 621–630.

Sontag, L. W. War and the fetal maternal relationship. *Marriage and Family Living,* 1944, *6,* 1–5.

Sontag, L. W., and Newbery, H. Normal variations of fetal heart rate during pregnancy. *American Journal of Obstetrics and Gynecology,* 1940, *40,* 449–452.

Sorce, J., Emde, R. N., Campos, J. J., and Klinnert, M. Maternal emotional signaling: Its effect on the visual cliff behavior of one-year-olds. Paper presented at the meeting of the Society for Research in Child Development, Boston, April 1981.

Sorensen, R. C. *Adolescent sexuality in contemporary America.* New York: World Publishing, 1973.

Soroka, S. M., Corter, C. M., and Abramovitch, R. Infants' tactual discrimination of novel and familiar tactual stimuli. *Child Development,* 1979, *50,* 1251–1253.

Sorrells-Jones, J. A comparison of the effects of Leboyer delivery and modern "routine" childbirth in a randomized sample. Unpublished doctoral dissertation, University of Chicago, 1983.

Spearman, C. General intelligence, objectively determined and measured. *American Journal of Psychology,* 1904, *15,* 201–293.

Spearman, C. *The abilities of man.* New York: Macmillan, 1927.

Spears, W. C., and Hohle, R. H. Sensory and perceptual processes in infants. In Y. Brackbill (Ed.), *Infancy and early childhood.* New York: Free Press, 1967.

Spelke, E. Infants' intermodal perception of events. *Cognitive Psychology,* 1976, *8,* 553–560.

Spelke, E. Intermodal exploration by 4-month-old infants: Perception and knowledge of auditory-visual events. Unpublished doctoral dissertation, Cornell University, 1978.

Spelke, E. Exploring audible and visible events in infancy. In A. D. Pick (Ed.), *Perception and its development: A tribute to Eleanor J. Gibson.* Hillsdale, N.J.: Lawrence Erlbaum Associates, 1979. (a)

Spelke, E. Perceiving bimodally specified events in infancy. *Developmental Psychology,* 1979, *15,* 626–636. (b)

Spelke, E. S. Perceptual knowledge of objects in infancy. In J. Mehler, M. Garrett, and E. Walker (Eds.), *Perspectives on mental representation.* Hillsdale, N.J.: Lawrence Erlbaum Associates, 1982.

Spelke, E. S., and Owsley, C. J. Intermodal exploration and knowledge in infancy. *Infant Behavior and Development,* 1979, *2,* 13–27.

Spelt, D. K. The conditioning of the human fetus in utero. *Journal of Experimental Psychology,* 1948, *38,* 338–346.

Spence, J. T., and Helmreich, R. L. *Masculinity and femininity: Their psychological dimensions, correlates and antecedents.* Austin: University of Texas Press, 1978.

Spence, J. T., Helmreich, R. L., and Stapp, J. Ratings of self and peers on sex-role attributes and their relation to self-esteem and conceptions of masculinity and feminity. *Journal of Personality and Social Psychology,* 1975, *32,* 29–39.

Spence, M. J., and DeCasper, A. J. Human fetuses perceive maternal speech. Paper presented at the meeting of the International Conference on Infant Studies, Austin, Texas, March 1982.

Sperling, E. Psychological issues in chronic illness and handicap. In E. Gellert (Ed.), *Psychosocial aspects of pediatric care.* New York: Grune & Stratton, 1978.

Sperling, G. The information available in brief visual presentations. *Psychological Monographs,* 1960, *74*(11, Serial No. 498.)

Spilich, G. J., Vesonder, G. T., Chiesi, H. L., and Voss, J. Test processing of domain-related information for individuals with high and low domain knowledge. *Journal of Verbal Learning and Verbal Behavior,* 1979, *18,* 275–290.

Spilton, D., and Lee, L. C. Some determinants of effective communication in four-year-olds. *Child Development,* 1977, *48,* 968–977.

Spinelli, D. N., Jensen, F. E., and Viana Di Prisco, G. Early experience effect on dendritic branching in normally reared kittens. *Experimental Neurology,* 1980, *68,* 1–11.

Spinetta, J. J., and Rigler, D. The child-abusing parent: A psychological review. *Psychological Bulletin,* 1972, *77,* 296–304.

Spitz, R. A. *The first year of life.* New York: International Universities Press, 1965.

Spitz, R. A., and Wolf, K. M. The smiling response: A contribution to the ontogenesis of social relations. *Genetic Psychology Monographs.* 1946, *34,* 57–125.

Sprigle, H. Can poverty children live on Sesame Street? *Young Children,* 1971, *26,* 202–217.

Sprigle, H. Who wants to live on Sesame Street? *Young Children,* 1972, *27,* 91–108.

Sroufe, L. A. Wariness of strangers and the study of infant development. *Child Development,* 1977, *48,* 731–746.

Sroufe, L. A. Socioemotional development. In J. D. Osofsky (Ed.), *Handbook of infant development.* New York: Wiley, 1979.

Sroufe, L. A., Schork, E., Motti, E., Lawroski, N., and La-Freniere, P. The role of affect in emerging social competence. In C. Izard, J. Kagan, and R. Zajonc (Eds.), *Emotion, cognition and behavior.* New York: Plenum, 1984.

Sroufe, L. A., and Stewart, M. A. Treating problem children with stimulant drugs. *New England Journal of Medicine,* 1973, *289,* 407–413.

Sroufe, L. A., and Waters, E. Attachment as an organizational construct. *Child Development,* 1977, *48,* 1184–1199.

Sroufe, L. A., Waters, E., and Matas, L. Contextual determinants of infant affective response. In M. Lewis and L. A. Rosenblum (Eds.), *The origins of fear.* New York: Wiley, 1974.

Sroufe, L. A., and Wunsch, J. P. The development of laughter in the first year of life. *Child Development,* 1972, *43,* 1326–1344.

Starr, A., Amlie, R. N., Martin, W. H., and Saunders, S. Development of auditory function in newborn infants revealed by auditory brainstem potentials. *Pediatrics,* 1977, *60,* 831–839.

Staub, E. A. *The development of prosocial behavior in children.* Morristown, N.J.: General Learning Press, 1975.

Staub, E. A. *Positive social behavior and morality.* New York: Academic Press, 1979.

Stechler, G. Newborn attention as affected by medication during labor. *Science,* 1964, *144,* 315–317.

Steele, B. F., and Pollock, C. B. A psychiatric study of parents who abuse infants and small children. In R. E. Helfer and C. H. Kempe (Eds.), *The battered child.* Chicago: University of Chicago Press, 1968.

Steele D., and Pederson, D. R. Stimulus variables which affect the concordance of visual and manipulative exploration in six-month-old infants. *Child Development,* 1977, *48,* 104–111.

Stein, A. H. Imitation of resistance to temptation. *Child Development,* 1967, *38,* 159–169.

Stein, A. H., and Bailey, M. The socialization of achievement orientation in females. *Psychological Bulletin,* 1973, *80,* 345–366.

Stein, A. H., and Friedrich, L. K. Impact of television on children and youth. In E. M. Hetherington (Ed.), *Review of child development research,* Volume 5. Chicago: University of Chicago Press, 1975.

Stein, N., and Glenn, C. An analysis of story comprehension in elementary school children. In R. O. Freedle (Ed.), *New directions in discourse processing.* Norwood, N.J.: Ablex, 1979.

Steinberg, L. D. Changes in family relations at puberty. Paper presented at the biennial meeting of the Society for Research in Child Development, San Francisco, March 1979.

Steiner, J. E. The gustofacial response: Observation on normal and anencephalic newborn infants. In J. F. Bosma (Ed.), *Fourth symposium on oral sensation and perception*. Bethesda, Md.: U.S. Department HEW, 1973. (CDHEW Publication No. NIH 73–546).

Steinhausen, H.-C. Psychological evaluation of treatment in phenylketonuria: Intellectual, motor and social development. *Neuropaediatrie*, 1974, *5*, 146–156.

Stenberg, C. The development of anger facial expressions in infancy. Unpublished doctoral dissertation, University of Denver, 1982.

Stenberg, C. R., Campos, J. J., and Emde, R. N. The facial expression of anger in seven-month-old infants. *Child Development*, 1983, *54*, 178–184.

Stern, D. N. A micro-analysis of mother-infant interaction—behavior regulating social contact between a mother and her 3½-month-old twins. *Journal of the American Academy of Child Psychiatry*, 1971, *10*, 501–517.

Stern, D. N. Mother and infant at play: The dyadic interaction involving facial, vocal and gaze behaviors. In M. Lewis and L. A. Rosenblum (Eds.), *The effect of the infant on its caregiver*. New York: Wiley, 1974.

Stern, D. N. *The first relationship: Infant and mother*. Cambridge: Harvard University Press, 1977.

Stern, D. N., Jaffe, J., Beebe, B., and Bennett, S. L. Vocalizing in unison and in alternation: Two modes of communication within the mother-infant dyad. *Annals of the New York Academy of Science: Developmental, Psycholinguistics, and Communication Disorders*, 1975, *263*, 89–100.

Sternberg, R. J. Stalking the IQ quark. *Psychology Today*, 1979, September, 42–54.

Sternberg, R. J., Conway, B. E., Ketron, J. L., and Bernstein, M. People's conceptions of intelligence. *Journal of Personality and Social Psychology: Attitudes and Social Cognition*, 1981, *41*, 37–55.

Sternberg, R. J., and Powell, J. S. The development of intelligence. In P. H. Mussen (Ed.), *Handbook of child psychology*, Volume 3. New York: Wiley, 1983.

Sternglanz, S. H., and Serbin, L. A. Sex role stereotyping in children's television programs. *Developmental Psychology*, 1974, *10*, 710–715.

Stetson, P. C. Verbal transitivity in children. Unpublished doctoral dissertation, University of Delaware, 1974.

Stevenson, H. W. Latent learning in children. *Journal of Experimental Psychology*, 1954, *47*, 17–21.

Stevenson, H. W. Learning in children. In P. H. Mussen (Ed.), *Carmichael's manual of child psychology*, Volume 1. New York: Wiley, 1970.

Stevenson, H. W. How children learn—the quest for a theory. In P. H. Mussen (Ed.), *Handbook of child psychology*. New York: Wiley, 1983. (a)

Stevenson, H. W. Making the grade: School achievement in Japan, Taiwan, and the United States. Presentation made at the Center for Advanced Study in the Behavioral Sciences, Stanford, April 1983, and published in its annual report, 1983. (b)

Stewart, M. A. Is hyperactivity normal? and other unanswered questions. *School Review*, 1976, *85*, 31–42.

Stewart, R. B. Sibling attachment relationships: Child-infant interactions in the strange situation. *Developmental Psychology*, 1983, *19*, 192–199.

Stinnett, N., Farris, J., and Walters, J. Parent-child relationships of male and female high school students. *Journal of Genetic Psychology*, 1974, *125*, 99–106.

Stirnimann, F. Uber das Farbempfinden Neugeborener. *Annalen der Paediatrie*, 1944, *163*, 1–25. Cited by W. Kessen, M. Haith, and P. Salapatek, *Human infancy: A bibliography and guide*. In P. H. Mussen (Ed.), *Carmichael's manual of child psychology*, Volume 1. New York: Wiley, 1970.

Stith, M., and Connor, R. Dependency and helpfulness in young children. *Child Development*, 1962, *33*, 15–20.

Stolz, H. R., and Stolz, L. M. *Somatic development of adolescent boys*. New York: Macmillan, 1951.

Stoneman, Z., and Brody, G. H. Immediate and long-term recognition and generalization of advertised products as a function of age and presentation mode. *Developmental Psychology*, 1983, *19*, 56–61.

Stotland, E. Exploratory investigations of empathy. In L. Berkowitz (Ed.), *Advances in experimental social psychology*, Volume 4. New York: Academic Press, 1969.

Stott, D. H. *Studies of troublesome children*. London: Tavistock, 1966.

Stott, D. H. The child's hazards in utero. In J. G. Howells (Ed.), *Modern perspectives in international child psychiatry*. New York: Brunner/Mazel, 1971.

Strauss, M. E., Lessen-Firestone, J., Starr, R., and Ostrea, E. M., Jr. Behavior of narcotics-addicted newborns. *Child Development*, 1975, *46*, 887–893.

Strauss, M. S., Cohen, L. B. Infant immediate and delayed memory for perceptual dimensions. Unpublished manuscript, University of Illinois, 1978.

Strayer, F. F., Wareing, S., and Rushton, J. P. Social constraints on naturally occurring preschool altruism. *Ethology and Sociobiology*, 1979, *1*, 3–11.

Strayer, J. A naturalistic study of empathic behaviors and their relation to affective states and perspective-taking skills in preschool children. *Child Development*, 1980, *51*, 815–822.

Stuckey, M. F., McGhee, P. E., and Bell, N. J. Parent-child interaction: The influence of maternal employment. *Developmental Psychology*, 1982, *18*, 635–644.

Sullivan, J. W., and Horowitz, F. D. The effects of intonation on infant attention: The role of the rising intonation contour. *Journal of Child Language*, 1983, *10*, 521–534.

Suomi, S. J. Social interactions of monkeys reared in a nuclear family environment versus monkeys reared with mothers and peers. *Primates*, 1974, *15*, 311–320.

Suomi, S. J. Adult male-infant interactions among monkeys living in nuclear families. *Child Development*, 1977, *48*, 1255–1270.

Suomi, S. J. Differential development of various social relationships by rhesus monkey infants. In M. Lewis and L. A. Rosenblum (Eds.), *The child and its family*. New York: Plenum, 1979.

Suomi, S. J., Mineka, S., and DeLizio, R. D. Short- and long-term effects of repetitive mother-infant separations on social development in rhesus monkeys. *Developmental Psychology*, 1983, *19*, 770–786.

Super, C. M. Environmental effects on motor development: The case of African infant precocity. *Developmental Medicine and Child Neurology*, 1976, *18*, 561–567.

Suskind, R. M. Characteristics and causation of protein-calorie malnutrition in the infant and preschool child. In L. S. Greene (Ed.), *Malnutrition, behavior and social organization*. New York: Academic Press, 1977.

Susman, E. J. Visual and verbal attributes of television and selective-attention in preschool children. *Developmental Psychology,* 1978, *14,* 565–566.

Sutton-Smith, B., and Rosenberg, B. G. Sixty years of historical change in the game preferences of American children. In R. E. Herron and B. Sutton-Smith (Eds), *Child's play.* New York: Wiley, 1971.

Sutton-Smith, B., and Sovasta, M. Sex differences in play and power. Paper presented at the Eastern Psychological Association, Boston, April 1972.

Svejda, M., Pannabecker, B., and Emde, R. N. Parent-to-infant attachment: A critique of the early "bonding" model. In R. N. Emde and R. J. Harmon (Eds.), *The development of attachment and affiliative systems: Psychological aspects.* New York: Plenum, 1982.

Swanson, J. M., and Kinsbourne, M. Food dyes impair performance of hyperactive children in a laboratory learning test. *Science,* 1980, *207,* 1485–1487.

Sylvester-Bradley, B., and Trevarthen, C. Baby talk as an adaptation to the infant's communication. In N. Waterson and C. E. Snow (Eds.), *The development of communication.* New York: Wiley, 1978.

Takashima, S., Chan, F., Becker, L. E., and Armstrong, D. L. Morphology of the developing visual cortex of the human infant. *Journal of Neuropathology and Experimental Neurology,* 1980, *39,* 487–501.

Tanner, J. M. *Growth at adolescence* (2nd ed.). Oxford: Blackwell Scientific Publications, 1962.

Tanner, J. M. The trend towards earlier physical maturation. In J. E. Meade and A. S. Parkes (Eds.). *Biological aspects of social problems.* Edinburgh: Oliver and Boyd, 1965.

Tanner, J. M. Physical growth. In P. M. Mussen (Ed.), *Carmichael's manual of child psychology.* New York: Wiley, 1970.

Tanner, J. M. Variability of growth and maturity in newborn infants. In M. Lewis and L. A. Rosenblum (Eds.), *The effect of the infant on its caregiver.* New York: Wiley, 1974.

Tanner, J. M. *Foetus into man: Physical growth from conception to maturity.* London: Open Books, 1978.

Tanzer, D., and Block, J. L. *Why natural childbirth?* New York: Schocken Books, 1976.

Tavormina, J. B., Boll, H., Dunn, N. J., Luscomb, R. L., and Taylor J. R. Psychosocial effects of raising a physically handicapped child on parents. Paper presented at the meeting of the American Psychological Association Convention, San Francisco, September, 1975.

Taylor, M. E. Sex role stereotypes in children's readers. *Elementary English,* 1973, *50,* 1061–1064.

Taylor, P. M., Tayler, F. H., Campbell, S. B. G., Maloni, J., and Dickey, D. Effects of extra contact on early maternal attitudes, perceptions, and behaviors. Paper presented at the meetings of the Society for Research in Child Development, San Francisco, March 1979.

Tec, N. Some aspects of high school status and differential involvement with marihuana: A study of suburban teenagers. *Adolescence,* 1972, *6,* 1–28.

Tennes, E. R., Kisley, A., and Metcalf, D. The stimulus barrier in early infancy: An exploration of some formulations of John Benjamin. In R. Holt and E. Peterfreund (Eds.), *Psychoanalysis and contemporary science,* Volume 1. New York: Macmillan, 1972.

Tennis, G. H., and Dabbs, J. M. Sex, setting, and personal space: First grade through college. *Sociometry,* 1975, *38,* 385–394.

Ten-State Nutrition Survey: 1968–1970. IV. Biochemical. Atlanta: U.S. Department of Health, Education, and Welfare, Health Services and Mental Health Administration, Center for Disease Control, 1972. (DHEW Publication No. HSM 72–8132).

Terman, L. M. *Genetic studies of genius,* Volume 1, *Mental and physical traits of a thousand gifted children.* Stanford: Stanford University Press, 1925.

Terman, L. M., and Oden, M. H. *Genetic studies of genus,* Volume 4, *The gifted group at midlife.* Stanford: Stanford University Press, 1959.

Terrell, G. The role of incentive in discrimination learning in children. *Child Development,* 1958, *29,* 231–236.

Terrell, G. Delayed reinforcement effects. In L. P. Lipsitt and C. C. Spiker (Eds.), *Advances in child development and behavior,* Volume 2. New York: Academic Press, 1965.

Terrell, G., and Ware, R. Role of delay of reward in speed and size of form discrimination learning in childhood. *Child Development,* 1961, *32,* 409–415.

Thoman, E. B., Korner, A. F., and Beason-Williams, L. Modification of responsiveness to maternal vocalization in the neonate. *Child Development,* 1977, *48,* 563–569.

Thomas A., and Chess, S. *Temperament and development.* New York: Brunner/Mazel, 1977.

Thomas, A., and Chess, S. Correlation of early temperament with later behavioral functioning. Paper presented at CIBA Foundation temperament conference, London, September 22–24, 1981.

Thomas, A., Chess, S., and Birch, H. G. *Temperament and behavior disorders in children.* New York: New York University Press, 1968.

Thomas, A., Chess, S., and Korn, S. J. The reality of difficult temperament. *Merrill-Palmer Quarterly,* 1982, *28,* 1–20.

Thomas, J. L. Tutoring strategies and effectiveness: A comparison of elementary age tutors and college age tutors. Unpublished doctoral dissertation, University of Texas at Austin, 1970.

Thomas, S. A. W. The role of cognitive style variables in mediating the influence of aggressive television upon elementary school children. Unpublished doctoral dissertation, University of California at Los Angeles, 1971.

Thompson, M. G. Life adjustment of women with anorexia nervosa and anorexic-like behavior. Unpublished doctoral dissertation, University of Chicago, 1979.

Thompson, S. K. Gender labels and early sex role development. *Child Development,* 1975, *46,* 339–347.

Thompson, S. K., and Bentler, P. M. The priority of cues in sex discrimination by children and adults. *Developmental Psychology,* 1971, *5,* 181–185.

Thompson, W. R., and Heron, W. The effects of restricting early experience on the problem-solving capacity of dogs. *Canadian Journal of Psychology,* 1954, *8,* 17–31.

Thomson, C. A., and Pollitt, E. Effects of severe protein-calorie malnutrition on behavior in human populations. In L. S. Greene (Ed.), *Malnutrition, behavior and social organization.* New York: Academic Press, 1977.

Thomson, D. M., and Tulving, E. Associative encoding and retrieval: Weak and strong cues. *Journal of Experimental Psychology,* 1970, *86,* 255–262.

Tieger, T. On the biological basis of sex differences in aggression. *Child Development,* 1980, *51,* 943–963.

Tieszan, H. R. Children's social behavior in a Korean preschool.

Journal of Korean Home Economics Association, 1979, *17,* 71–84.

Tilden J. T., and Chacon, M. Associated Press report on sudden infant death syndrome. *Chicago Tribune,* November 6, 1981, Section 1, p. 14.

Tinbergen, N. *The study of instinct.* Oxford: Oxford University Press, 1951.

Tinsley, V. S., and Waters, H. S. The development of verbal control over motor behavior: A replication and extension of Luria's findings. *Child Development,* 1982, *53,* 746–753.

Tizard, B., and Rees, J. A comparison of the effects of adoption, restoration to the natural mother, and continued institutionalization on the cognitive development of four-year-old children. *Child Development,* 1974, *45,* 92–99.

Tizard, B., and Tizard, J. A. The cognitive development of young children in residential care. *Journal of Child Psychology and Psychiatry,* 1970, *11,* 177–186.

Tizard, J., and Tizard, B. The social development of two-year-old children in residential nurseries. In H. R. Schaffer (Ed.), *The origins of human social relations.* London: Academic Press, 1971.

Todd, C. M., and Perlmutter, M. Reality recalled by preschool children. In M. Perlmutter (Ed.), *New directions in child development: Children's memory.* San Francisco: Jossey-Bass, 1980.

Tompkins, S. S. *Affect, imagery, consciousness,* Volume 1, *The positive affects.* New York: Springer, 1962.

Tompkins, S. S. *Affect, imagery, consciousness,* Volume 2, *The negative affects.* New York: Springer, 1963.

Torrance, E. P. *Guiding creative talent.* Englewood Cliffs, N.J.: Prentice-Hall, 1962.

Trabasso, T. On the making of inferences during reading and their assessment. In J. T. Guthrie (Ed.), *Reading comprehension and education.* Newark, Del.: International Reading Association, in press.

Trabasso, T., Stein, N. L., and Johnson, L. R. Children's knowledge of events: A causal analysis of story structure. In G. Bower (Ed.), *Learning and motivation,* Volume 15. New York: Academic Press, 1981.

Tracy, R. L., Lamb, M. E., and Ainsworth, M. D. S. Infant approach behavior as related to attachment. *Child Development,* 1976, *47,* 571–578.

Traub, R. E., Weiss, J., and Fisher, C. W. Studying openness in education: An Ontario example. *Journal of Research and Development in Education,* 1974, *8,* 47–59.

Trause, M. A. Extra postpartum contact: An assessment of the intervention and its effects. In V. L. Smeriglio (Ed.), *Newborns and parents.* Hillsdale, N.J.: Lawrence Erlbaum Associates, 1981.

Trause, M. A., Voos, D., Rudd, C., Klaus, M., Kennell, J., and Boslett, M. Separation for childbirth: The effect on the sibling. *Child Psychiatry and Human Development,* 1981, *12,* 32–39.

Treadwell, Y., Humor and creativity. *Psychological Reports,* 1970, *26,* 55–58.

Trehub, S. E. Infants' sensitivity to vowel and tonal contrasts. *Developmental Psychology,* 1973, *9,* 91–96.

Trehub, S. E., and Curran, S. Habituation of infants' cardiac response to speech stimuli. *Child Development,* 1979, *50,* 1247–1250.

Trethowan, W. H., and Colon, M. F. The couvade syndrome. *British Journal of Psychiatry,* 1965, *111,* 57–66.

Trethowan, W. H., and Dickens, G. Cravings, and aversions of pregnancy. In J. G. Howells (Ed.), *Modern perspectives in psycho-obstetrics.* Edinburgh: Oliver and Boyd, 1972.

Trevarthen, C. Descriptive analyses of infant communicative behavior. In H. R. Schaffer (Ed.), *Studies in mother-infant interaction.* London: Academic Press, 1977.

Trites, R., Ferguson, B., and Tryphonas, H. Food allergies and hyperactivity. Paper delivered at the meeting of the American Psychological Association, Toronto, August 1978.

Tronick, E. Z. (Ed.). Social interchange in infancy: Affect, cognition, and communication. Baltimore: University Park Press, 1982.

Tuaycharoen, P. The babbling of a Thai baby: Echoes and responses to the sounds made by adults. In N. Waterson and C. E. Snow (Eds.), *The development of communication.* New York: Wiley, 1978.

Tuddenham, R. D. The nature and measurement of intelligence. In L. Postman (Ed.), *Psychology in the making.* New York: Knopf, 1964.

Tuddenham, R. D. Theoretical regularities and individual idiosyncracies. In D. R. Green, M. P. Ford, and G. B. Flamer (Eds.), *Measurement and Piaget.* New York: McGraw-Hill, 1971.

Tudiver, J. Parental influences on the sex role development of the preschool child. Unpublished manuscript, University of Western Ontario, London, Ontario, 1979.

Turiel, E. An experimental test of the sequentiality of developmental stages in the child's moral judgments. *Journal of Personality and Social Psychology,* 1966, *3,* 611–618.

Turiel, E. The development of social concepts. In D. DePalma and J. Foley (Eds.), *Moral development.* Hillsdale, N.J.: Lawrence Erlbaum Associates, 1975.

Turiel, E. The development of concepts of social structure. In J. Glick and K. A. Clarke-Stewart (Eds.), *The development of social understanding.* New York: Gardner Press, 1978. (a)

Turiel, E. Social regulations and domains of social concept. *New directions for child development,* 1978, *1,* 45–74. (b)

Turkington, C. Pituitary defect seen in anorexia. *APA Monitor,* January 1984, p. 17.

Turkington, C. Parents found to ignore sex stereotypes. *APA Monitor,* April 1984, p. 12.

Turner, C. W., and Goldsmith, D. Effects of toy guns and airplanes on children's antisocial free play behavior. *Journal of Experimental Child Psychology,* 1976, *21,* 303–315.

Turnure, C. Response to voice of mother and stranger by babies in the first year. *Developmental Psychology,* 1971, *4,* 182–190.

Turnure, J., Buium, N., and Thurlow, M. The effectiveness of interrogatives for promoting verbal elaboration productivity in children. *Child Development,* 1976, *47,* 851–855.

Tyler, L. E. The intelligence we test—An evolving concept. In L. B. Resnick (Ed.), *The nature of intelligence.* Hillsdale, N.J.: Lawrence Erlbaum Associates, 1976.

Ullian, D. Z. The development of conceptions of masculinity and femininity. In B. Lloyd and J. Archer (Eds.), *Exploring sex differences.* London: Academic Press, 1976.

U.S. Department of Health and Human Services. *Health, United States, 1980.* DHHS Publication No. (PHS) 81–1232, 1980, p. 276.

U.S. Department of Health and Human Services. *Health, United States, 1982.* DHHS Publication No. (PHS) 83–1232, 1982.

U.S. Public Health Service. *Alcohol and health: Second special report to the U.S. Congress.* Rockville, Md.: National Institute on Alcohol Abuse and Alcoholism, 1974.

Utech, D. A., and Hoving, K. L. Parents and peers as competing influences in the decisions of children of different ages. *Journal of Social Psychology,* 1969, *78,* 267–274.

Vandell, D. L. Sociability with peer and mother during the first year. Unpublished manuscript, University of Texas at Dallas, 1979.

Vandell, D. L., and Mueller, E. C. The effects of group size on toddlers' social interactions with peers. Paper presented at the biennial meeting of the Society for Research in Child Development, Denver, March, 1977.

Vandell, D. L., Wilson, K. S., and Buchanan, N. R. Peer interaction in the first year: An examination of its structure, content, and sensitivity to toys. Paper presented at the meetings of the Society for Research in Child Development, San Francisco, March 1979.

Vandenberg, S. G. The nature and nurture of intelligence. In D. C. Glass (Ed.), *Genetics.* New York: Rockefeller University Press and Russell Sage Foundation, 1968.

Vandenberg, S. G., and Kuse, A. R., Spatial ability: A critical review of the sex-linked major gene hypothesis. In M. A. Wittig and A. C. Petersen (Eds.), *Sex related differences in cognitive functioning: Developmental issues.* New York: Academic Press, 1979.

Vaughn, B., Joffe, L., Egeland, B., Dienard, A., and Waters, E. Relationships between neonatal behavioral organization and infant-mother attachment in an economically disadvantaged sample. Paper presented at the meeting of the Society for Research in Child Development, San Francisco, March 1979.

Veevers, J. Voluntary childlessness: A review of issues and evidence. *Marriage and Family Review,* 1979, *2,* 1–26.

Volterra, V., and Taeschner, T. The acquisition and development of language by bilingual children. *Journal of Child Language,* 1978, *5,* 311–326.

Vurpillot, E. The development of scanning strategies and their relation to visual differentiation. *Journal of Experimental Child Psychology,* 1968, *6,* 632–650.

Vygotsky, L. *Thought and language.* Cambridge: MIT Press, 1962. (Orginally published, 1934)

Vygotsky, L. S. The genesis of higher mental functions: In J. Wertsch (Ed.), *The concept of activity.* New York: M. E. Sharpe, 1979.

Waber, D. P. Sex differences in cognition: A function of maturation rate? *Science,* 1979, *192,* 572–573.

Wachs, T. D., and Gruen, C. E. *Early experience and human development.* New York: Plenum, 1982.

Wachs, T. D., Uzgiris, I., and Hunt. J. McV. Cognitive development in infants of different age levels and from different environmental backgrounds. *Merrill-Palmer Quarterly,* 1971, *17,* 283–317.

Waddington, C. H. *The strategy of the genes.* London: Allen & Unwin, 1957.

Wagner, D. A. Memories of Morrocco: The influence of age, schooling and environment on memory. *Cognitive Psychology,* 1978, *10,* 1–28.

Waldrop, M. F., and Halverson, C. F., Jr. Intensive and extensive peer behavior: Longitudinal and cross-sectional analyses. *Child Development,* 1975, *46,* 19–26.

Walker, J. A., and Kershman, S. M. The deaf-blind in social interaction. Paper presented at the meeting of the Society for

Research in Child Development, Boston, March 1981.

Walker, L. J. The sequentiality of Kohlberg's stages of moral development. *Child Development,* 1982, *53,* 1330–1336.

Walker, L. J. Sex differences in the development of moral reasoning: A critical review. *Child Development,* 1984, *55,* 677–691.

Wallerstein, J.S., and Kelly, J. B. The effects of parental divorce: The adolescent experience. In E. J. Anthony and C. Koopernick (Eds.), *The child in his family: Children at psychiatric risk,* Volume 3. New York: Wiley, 1974.

Wallerstein, J. S., and Kelly, J. B. *Surviving the breakup.* New York: Basic Books, 1980.

Walsh, T. Premature parenting and child abuse. Paper presented at the workshop on teen parenthood, March 8, 1977, Onondaga Community College, New York.

Walster, E., Aronson, V., Abraham, D., and Roltman, L. Importance of physical attractiveness in dating behavior. *Journal of Personality and Social Psychology,* 1966, *4,* 508–516.

Walters, J., Pearce, D., and Dahms, L. Affectional and aggressive behavior of preschool children. *Child Development,* 1957, *28,* 15–26.

Walters, J., and Stinnett, N. Parent-child relationships: A decade review of research. *Journal of Marriage and the Family,* 1971, *33,* 70–111.

Walters, R. H., and Parke, R. D. The role of the distance receptors in the development of social responsiveness. *Advances in Child Development,* 1965, *2,* 59–96.

Wandersman, L. P. Stylistic differences in mother-child interaction: A review and reevaluation of the social class and socialization research. *Cornell Journal of Social Relations,* 1973, *8,* 197–218.

Ward, I. L. Prenatal stress feminizes and demasculinizes the behavior of males. *Science,* 1972, *176,* 82–84.

Ware, J. C., and Orr, W. C. Sleep disorders in children. In C. E. Walker and M. C. Roberts (Eds.), *Handbook of clinical child psychology.* New York: Wiley, 1983.

Ware, R., and Terrell, G. Effects of delayed reinforcement on associative and incentive factors. *Child Development,* 1961, *32,* 789–793.

Warkany, J., and Kalter, H. Proceedings of the Bi-regional Institute for Maternity Care-Primary Prevention 102, University of California School of Public Health, 1964.

Warshak, R., and Santrock, J. W. The effects of father and mother custody on children's social development. Paper presented at the meetings of the Society for Research in Child Development, San Francisco, March 1979.

Wasz-Hoeckert, O., Lind, J., Vuorenkoski, V., Partanen, T., and Valanne, E. *The infant cry.* London: Heinemann Medical Books, 1968.

Waterhouse, M., and Waterhouse, H. Primate ethology and human social behavior. In R. Michael and J. Crook (Eds.), *Comparative ecology and behavior of primates.* New York: Academic Press, 1973.

Waterman, A. S., and Goldman, J. A. A longitudinal study of changes in ego identity development at a liberal arts college. *Journal of Youth and Adolescence,* 1976, *5,* 361–370.

Waterman, G., Geary, P., and Waterman C. Longitudinal study of changes in ego identity status from the freshman to the senior year at college. *Developmental Psychology,* 1974, *10,* 387–392.

Waters, E. Matas, L., and Sroufe, L. A. Infants' reactions to an approaching stranger: Description, validation, and functional significance of wariness. *Child Development,* 1975, *46,* 348–356.

Waters, E. Wippman, J., and Sroufe, L. A. Attachment, positive affect, and competence in the peer group: Two studies in construct validation. *Child Development.* 1979, *50,* 821–829.

Waterson, N. Growth of complexity in phonological development. In N. Waterson and C. E. Snow (Eds.), *The development of communication.* New York: Wiley, 1978.

Watson, E. H., and Lowrey, G. H. *Growth and development of children* (5th ed.). Chicago: Year Book Medical Publishers, 1967.

Watson, J. B. Psychology as the behaviorist views it. *Psychological Review,* 1913, *20,* 158–177.

Watson, J. B. *Psychological care of infant and child.* New York: W. W. Norton, 1928.

Watson, J. B., and Rayner R. Conditioned emotional reactions. *Journal of Experimental Psychology,* 1920, *3,* 1–4.

Watson, J. S. Smiling, cooing, and "the game." *Merrill-Palmer Quarterly,* 1972, *18,* 323–340.

Watson, M. W. The development of social roles: A sequence of social-cognitive development. *New Directions for Child Development,* 1981, *12,* 33–41.

Waxler, C. Z., and Radke-Yarrow, M. An observational study of maternal models. *Developmental Psychology,* 1975, *11,* 485–494.

Weatherly, D. Self-perceived rate of physical maturation and personality in late adolescence. *Child Development,* 1964, *35,* 1197–1210.

Webb, R. A. Concrete and formal operations in very bright 6 to 11-year-olds. *Human Development,* 1974, *17,* 292–300.

Webster, R. L., Steinhardt, M. H., and Senter, M. G. Changes in infants' vocalizations as a function of differential acoustic stimulation. *Developmental Psychology,* 1972, *7,* 39–43.

Wechsler, D. *Measurement of adult intelligence* (3rd ed.). Baltimore: Williams & Wilkins, 1944.

Wechsler, D. *Manual for the Wechsler Intelligence Scale for children—Revised.* New York: Psychological Corp., 1974.

Weikart, D., Deloria, D., Lawser, S., and Wiegerink, R. Longitudinal results of the Ypsilanti Perry preschool project. *Monographs of the High/Scope Educational Research Foundation,* 1970, (No. 1).

Weil, W. B. Infantile obesity. In M. Winick (Ed.), *Childhood obesity.* New York: Wiley, 1975.

Weiman, L. A. Stress patterns of early child language. *Journal of Child Language,* 1976, *3,* 283–286.

Weinraub, M., Brooks, J., and Lewis, M. The social network: A reconsideration of the concept of attachment. *Human Development,* 1977, *20,* 31–47.

Weinraub, M., and Wolf, B. M. Effects of stress and social supports on mother-child interactions in single- and two-parent families. *Child Development,* 1983, *54,* 1297–1311.

Weintraub, S., Neale, J. M., and Liebert, D. E. Teacher ratings of children vulnerable to psychopathology. *American Journal of Orthopsychiatry,* 1975, *45,* 838–845.

Weisberg, P. Developmental differences in children's preferences for high- and low-arousing forms of contact stimulation. *Child Development,* 1975, *46,* 975–979.

Weisberg, P. S., and Springer, B. J. Environmental factors in creative function. A study of gifted children. *Archives of General Psychiatry,* 1961, *5,* 554–564.

Weiss, R. J. Understanding moral thought: Effects on moral reasoning and decision making. *Developmental Psychology,* 1982, *18,*. 852–861.

Weitzman, L. J., Eifler, D., Hokada, E., and Ross C. Sex role socialization in picture books for pre-school children. *Ameri-can Journal of Sociology,* 1972, *77,* 1125–1150.

Weizmann, F., Cohen, L. B., and Pratt, J. Novelty, familiarity and the development of infant attention. *Developmental Psychology,* 1971, *4,* 149–154.

Wellman, H. M. The early development of intentional memory behavior. *Human Development,* 1977, *20,* 86–101. (a)

Wellman, H. M. Preschoolers' understanding of memory-relevant variables. *Child Development,* 1977, *48,* 1720–1723. (b)

Wellman, H. M. and Lempers, J. The naturalistic communication ability of two-year-olds. *Child Development,* 1977, 48, 1052–1057.

Wellman, H. M., Ritter, K., and Flavell, J. H. Deliberate memory behavior in the delayed reactions of very young children. *Developmental Psychology,* 1975, *11,* 780–787.

Werner, E. E., and Bayley, N. The reliability of Bayley's revised scale of mental and motor development during the first year of life. *Child Development,* 1966, *37,* 39–50.

Werner, E. E., Bierman, J. M., and French, F. E. *The children of Kauai: A longitudinal study from the prenatal period to age 10.* Honolulu: University Press of Hawaii, 1971.

Werner, H., and Kaplan, E. The acquisition of word meanings: A developmental study. *Monographs of the Society for Research in Child Development,* 1952, *15*(1, Serial No. 51).

Werner, J. S., and Perlmutter, M. Development of visual memory in infants. In H. W. Reese and L. P. Lipsitt (Eds.), *Advances in child development and behavior,* Volume 14. New York: Academic Press, 1980.

Werner, J. S., and Siqueland, E. R. Visual recognition memory in the preterm infant. *Infant Behavior and Development,* 1978, *1,* 79–94.

Wertheimer, M. Psychomotor coordination of auditory and visual space at birth. *Science,* 1961, *134,* 1692.

Wesley, F., and Wesley, C. *Sex-role psychology.* New York: Human Sciences, 1977.

Westinghouse and Ohio University. The impact of Head Start: An evaluation of the effects of Head Start on children's cognitive and affective development. In J. L. Frost (Ed.), *Revisiting early childhood education: Readings.* New York: Holt, Rinehart & Winston, 1973.

Weston, D. R., and Turiel, E. Act-role relations: Children's concepts of social roles. Unpublished manuscript, University of California at Berkeley, 1979.

Whalen, C. K., Henker, B., and Dotemoto, S. Teacher response to the methylphenidate (Ritalin) versus placebo status of hyperactive boys in the classroom. *Child Development,* 1981, *52,* 1005–1114.

Wheeler, L., and Nezlek, J. Sex differences in social participation. *Journal of Personality and Social Psychology,* 1977, *35,* 742–754.

Whelan, E. *A baby . . . maybe.* New York: Bobbs-Merrill, 1975.

Whisnant, L., and Zegans, L. A study of attitudes toward menarche among white middle-class American adolescent girls. *American Journal of Psychiatry,* 1975, *132,* 809–814.

White, B. L. An experimental approach to the effects of experience on early human behavior. In J. P. Hill (Ed.), *Minnesota Symposia on Child Psychology,* Volume 1. Minneapolis: University of Minnesota Press, 1967.

White, B. L. *Human infants: Experience and psychological development.* Englewood Cliffs, N.J.: Prentice-Hall, 1971.

White, B. L. *The first three years of life.* Englewood Cliffs, N.J.: Prentice-Hall, 1975.

White, S. H., and Spiker, C. C. The effect of a variable conditioned stimulus upon the generalization of an instrumental response. *Child Development,* 1960, *31,* 313–319.

Whitehurst, G., and Vasta, R. Is language acquired through imitation? *Journal Psycholinguistic Research,* 1975, *4,* 37–59.

Whiten, A. Assessing the effects of perinatal events on the success of the mother-infant relationship. In H. R. Schaffer (Ed.), *Studies in mother-infant interaction.* London: Academic Press, 1977.

Whiting, B. B., and Edwards, C. P. A cross-cultural analysis of sex differences in the behavior of children age three through 11. In S. Chess and H. Thomas, (Eds.), *Annual progress in child psychiatry and child development, 1974.* New York: Brunner/Mazel, 1975.

Whiting, B. B. and Pope-Edwards, C. (Eds.), *The effects of age, sex, and modernity on the behavior of mothers and children.* Report to the Ford Foundation, January 1977.

Whiting, J. W. M., and Whiting, B. B. Altruistic and egoistic behavior in six cultures. In L. Nader and T. W. Maretzek (Eds.), *Cultural illness and health: Essays in human adaptation.* Washington, D.C.: American Anthropological Association, 1973.

Wiener, G. Psychologic correlates of premature birth: A review. *Journal of Nervous and Mental Diseases,* 1962, *134,* 129–144.

Wiesenfeld, A. R., and Klorman, R. The mother's psychophysiological reactions to contrasting affective expressions by her own and an unfamiliar infant. *Developmental Psychology,* 1978, *14,* 294–304.

Wilen, J. B., and Petersen, A. C. Young adolescents' responses to the timing of pubertal changes. Paper presented at the annual meeting of the American Psychological Association, Montreal, September 1980.

Wilkening, F. Integrating velocity, time, and distance information: A developmental study. *Cognitive Psychology,* 1981, *13,* 231–247.

Williams, A. F. Children killed in falls from motor vehicles. *Pediatrics,* 1981, *68,* 576–578.

Williams. C. L., Arnold, C. B., and Wynder, E. L. Primary prevention of chronic disease beginning in childhood. *Preventive Medicine,* 1977, *6,* 344–357.

Williams, K. G., and Goulet, L. R. The effects of cuing and constraint instructions on children's free recall performance. *Journal of Experimental Child Psychology,* 1975, *19,* 464–475.

Williams, R. L. Black pride, academic relevance and individual achievement. *Counseling Psychologist,* 1970, *2,* 321–325.

Williams, T. M. The impact of television: A study of three Canadian communities (ERIC Document ED 171 401), University of British Columbia, 1977.

Williams, T. M. The development of maternal attachment: A longitudinal study. Symposium presented at the meetings of the Society for Research in Child Development, San Francisco, March 1979.

Willis, J., Morris, B., and Crowder, J. A remedial reading technique for disabled readers that employs students as behavioral engineers. *Psychology in the Schools,* 1972, *6,* 67–70.

Wilmore, J. H., and McNamara, J. J. Prevalence of coronary heart disease risk factors in boys 8 to 12 years of age. *Journal of Pediatrics,* 1974, *84,* 527–533.

Wilson, J. G. Current status of teratology. In J. G. Wilson and F. C. Fraser (Eds.), *Handbook of teratology,* New York: Plenum, 1977.

Wilson, J. G., and Fraser, F. C. (Eds.) *Handbook of teratology.* New York: Plenum, 1977.

Wilson, R. S. Synchronies in mental development: An epigentic perspective. *Science,* 1978, *202,* 939–948.

Wilson, R. S. The Louisville Twin Study: Developmental synchronies in behavior. *Child Development,* 1983, *54,* 298–316.

Wilson, R. S., and Harpring, E. B. Mental and motor development in infant twins. *Developmental Psychology,* 1972, *7,* 277–287.

Winick, M. Cellular growth during early malnutrition. *Pediatrics,* 1971, *47,* 969–978.

Winick, M., Brasel, J. A., and Rosso, P. Nutrition and cell growth. In M. Winick (Ed.), *Nutrition and development.* New York: Wiley, 1972.

Witelson, S. F. Sex and the single hemisphere: Specialization of the right hemisphere for spatial processing. *Science,* 1976, *193,* 425–426.

Withers, R. F. J. *Eugenics Review,* 1964, *56,* 81.

Witkin, H. A., Dyk, R. B., Paterson, H. F., Goodenough, D. R., and Karp, S. A. *Psychological differentiation.* New York: Wiley, 1962.

Witkin, H. A., Mednick, S. A., Schulsinger, F., Bakkestrom, E., Christiansen, K. O., Goodenough, D. R., Hirschhorn, K., Lundsteen, C., Owen, D. R., Philip, J., Rubin, D. B., and Stocking, M. Criminality in XYY and XXY men: The elevated crime rate of XYY males is not related to aggression. It may be related to low intelligence. *Science,* 1976, *193,* 547–555.

Witryol, S. L. Tyrrel, D. J., and Snowden, L. M. Five-choice discrimination learning by children under simultaneous incentive conditions. *Child Development,* 1964, *35,* 233–243.

Wolf, T. M., Sklov, M. C., Wenzl, P. A., Hunter, S. M., and Berenson, G. S. Validation of a measure of Type A behavior pattern in children: Bogalusa Heart Study. *Child Development,* 1982, *53,* 126–135.

Wolff, P. H. Observations on the early development of smiling. In B. M. Foss (Ed.), *Determinants of infant behavior,* Volume 2, New York: Wiley, 1963.

Wolff, P. H. The natural history of crying and other vocalizations in early infancy. In B. M. Foss (Ed.), *The determinants of infant behaviour,* Volume 4. London: Methuen, 1969.

Wolins, M. Young children in institutions: Some additonal evidence. *Developmental Psychology,* 1969, *2,* 99–109.

Wolstenholme, G. E. W., and O'Connor, M. *Endocrinology of the testis.* Boston: Little, Brown, 1967.

Wright, J. C. Matching communication pace with children's cognitive styles. In D. D. Hearn (Ed.), *Values, feelings, and morals, I: Research and perspectives.* Washington, D.C.: American Association of Elementary-Kindergarten-Nursery Educators, 1974.

Wright, J. W., and Vlietstra, A. G. The development of selective attention: From perceptual exploration to logical search. In H. W. Reese (Ed.), *Advances in child development and behavior.* New York: Academic Press, Volume 10. 1975.

Wright, L., Schaefer, A. B., and Solomons, G. *Encyclopedia of pediatric psychology.* Baltimore: University Park Press, 1979.

Wubberhorst, J., Gradford, S., and Willis, F. N. Trust in children as a function of race, sex and socio-economic group. *Psychological Reports,* 1971, *29,* 1183–1187.

Wylie, R. C. *The self-concept: Theory and research on selected topics,* Volume 2. Lincoln: University of Nebraska Press, 1979.

Yalom, I. D., Lunde, D. T., Moos, R. H., and Hamburg, D. A. "Postpartum blues" syndrome: A description and related variables. *Archives of General Psychiatry*, 1968, *18*, 16.

Yankelovich, Skelly and White, Inc. *Raising children in a changing society.* General Mills American Family Report 1976–1977. Minneapolis: General Mills, 1977.

Yarrow, L. J., Rubenstein, J. L., and Pedersen, F. A. *Infant and environment: Early cognitive and motivational development.* Washington, D.C.: Hemisphere, 1975.

Yeates, K. O., MacPhee, D., Campbell, F. A., and Ramey, C. T. Maternal IQ and home environment as determinants of early childhood intellectual competence: A developmental analysis. *Developmental Psychology*, 1983, *19*, 731–739.

Yerushalmy, J. The relationship of parents' smoking to outcome of pregnancy: Implications as to the problem of inferring causation from observed effects. *American Journal of Epidemiology*, 1971, *93*, 443–456.

Yerushalmy, J. Infants with low birth weight born before their mothers started to smoke cigarettes. *American Journal of Obstetrics and Gynecology*, 1972, *112*, 277–284.

Yogman, M. W. The goals and structure of face-to-face interaction between infants and fathers. Paper presented at the biennial meeting of the Society for Research in Child Development, New Orleans, March 1977.

Yogman, M. W., Cole, P., Als, H., and Lester, B. M. Behavior of newborns of diabetic mothers. *Infant Behavior and Development*, 1982, *5*, 331–340.

Yonas, A., Cleaves, W., and Pettersen, L. Development of sensitivity to pictorial depth. *Science*, 1978, *200*, 77–79.

Yonas, A., and Pettersen, L. Responsiveness in newborns to optical information for collision. Paper presented at the biennial meeting of the Society for Research in Child Development, San Francisco, March 1979.

Yonas, A., Pettersen, L., and Granrud, C. E. Infants' sensitivity to familiar size as information for distance. *Child Development*, 1982, *53*, 1285–1290.

Young, L. *Wednesday's children: A study of child neglect and abuse.* New York: McGraw-Hill, 1964.

Youniss, J., and Volpe, J. A relational analysis of children's friendship. In W. Damon (Ed.), *New directions in child development: Social cognition.* San Francisco: Jossey-Bass, 1978.

Yussen, S. R., and Kane, P. Children's concept of intelligence. In S. R. Yussen (Ed.), *The growth of insight in the child.* New York: Academic Press, in press.

Yussen, S. R., and Levy, U. Developmental changes in conscious knowledge about different retrieval problems. *Developmental Psychology*, 1977, *13*, 114–120.

Zahn-Waxler, C., Friedman, S. L., and Cummings, E. M. Children's emotions and behaviors in response to infants' cries. *Child Development*, 1983, *54*, 1522–1528.

Zahn-Waxler, C., Iannotti, R., and Chapman, M. Peers and prosocial development. In K. H. Rubin and H. S. Ross (Eds.), *Peer relationships and social skills in childhood.* New York: Springer-Verlag, 1982.

Zahn-Waxler, C., Radke-Yarrow, M. A developmental analysis of children's responses to emotions in others. Paper presented at the biennial meeting of the Society for Research in Child Development, San Francisco, March 1979.

Zahn-Waxler, C., Radke-Yarrow, M., and Brady-Smith, J. Perspective-taking and prosocial behavior. *Developmental Psychology*, 1977, *13*, 87–88.

Zahn-Waxler, C., Radke-Yarrow, M., and King, R. A. Child rearing and children's prosocial initiations toward victims of distress. *Child Development*, 1979, *50*, 319–330.

Zajonc, R. B. Feeling and thinking: Preferences need no inferences. *American Psychologist*, 1980, *35*, 151–175.

Zajonc, R. B., and Markus, G. B. Birth order and intellectual development. *Psychological Review*, 1975, *829*, 74–88.

Zaslow, M., Pederson, F. A., Suwalsky, J., and Rabinovich, B. Maternal employment and parent-infant interaction. Paper presented at the meeting of the Society for Research in Child Development, Detroit, April 1983.

Zelazo, P. R., Zelazo, N. A., and Kolb, S. Walking in the newborn. *Science*, 1972, *176*, 314–315.

Zeller, W. W. Adolescent attitudes and cutaneous health. *Journal of School Health*, March 1970, 115–120.

Zelnik, M., and Kantner, J. F. Sexual and contraceptive experience of young unmarried women in the United States: 1976 and 1971. *Family Planning Perspectives*, 1977, *9*, 55.

Zelniker, T., and Jeffrey, W. E. Reflective and impulsive children: Strategies of information processing underlying differences in problem solving. *Monographs of the Society for Research in Child Development*, 1976, *41*(5, Whole No. 168).

Zigler, E., and Child I. L. *Socialization and personality development.* Reading, Mass.: Addison-Wesley, 1973.

Zigler, E., Levine, J., and Gould, L. Cognitive challenge as a factor in children's human appreciation. *Journal of Personality and Social Psychology*, 1967, *6*, 332–336.

Zinchenko, V. P., Chzhi-Tsin, V., and Tarakanov, V. V. The formation and development of perceptual activity. In M. Cole (Ed.), *Soviet developmental psychology.* White Plains, N.Y.: M. E. Sharpe, 1977.

Zucker, R. A. Sex role identity patterns and drinking behavior in adolescents. Center for Alcohol Studies, Rutgers University, 1967.

Zussman, J. V. Situational determinants of parental behavior: Effects of competing cognitive activity. *Child Development*, 1980, *51*, 792–800.

PHOTO CREDITS

CHAPTER 9

Opener: Eileen Christelow/Jeroboam; *page 345:* Ken Robert Buck/Stock Boston; *page 351:* Elizabeth Hamlin/Stock Boston; *page 354:* Elizabeth Crews; *page 357:* Jill Cannefax/EKM-Nepenthe; *page 359:* Michael Weisbrot & Family; *page 360:* Elizabeth Crews; *page 362:* James Holland/Stock Boston; *page 369:* Peter Southwick/Stock Boston; *page 372:* Susan Ylvisaker/Jeroboam; *page 373:* Elizabeth Crews

CHAPTER 10

Opener: Charles Gatewood/Stock Boston; *page 382:* Philippe Halsman; *page 388:* Cary Wolinsky/Stock Boston; *page 391:* Judith Sedwick/Picture Cube; *page 395:* (top) Janice Fullman/Picture Cube, (bottom) David S. Strickler/The Picture Cube; *page 397:* Bohdan Hrynewych/Southern Light; *page 401:* Ray Ellis/Photo Researchers; *page 405:* Elizabeth Hamlin/Stock Boston

CHAPTER 11

Opener: Elizabeth Crews; *page 418:* (top) Michael Weisbrot & Family, (bottom) Elizabeth Crews; *page 420:* (top left) Peter Vandermark/Stock Boston, (top right) Jean-Claude LeJeune/Stock Boston, (bottom) George Bellrose/Stock Boston; *page 427:* Michael Heron/Woodfin Camp; *page 433:* (top) Guy Gillette/Photo Researchers, (bottom) Patricia Hollander Gross/Stock Boston; *page 435:* Peter Vandermark/Stock Boston; *page 439:* Paul Fortin/Stock Boston; *page 441:* Alan Carey/The Image Works; *page 443:* Elizabeth Crews

CHAPTER 12

Opener: Hazel Hankin; *page 460:* Suzanne Szasz/Photo Researchers; *page 464:* Peter Vandermark/Stock Boston; *page 467:* Jean-Claude LeJeune/Stock Boston; *page 469:* Margaret Thompson/Picture Cube; *page 474:* (left) Erika Stone/Peter Arnold, (right) Mike Mazzaschi/Stock Boston; *page 484:* (left) Bill Stanton/Magnum, (right) Mary Stuart Lang

CHAPTER 13

Opener: Ed Lettau/Photo Researchers; *page 492:* Bohdan Hrynewych/Stock Boston; *page 493:* Elizabeth Crews; *page 496:* Erika Stone; *page 498:* Alan Carey/The Image Works; *page 500:* Elizabeth Crews/Stock Boston; *page 505:* Robert V. Eckert, Jr./Picture Cube; *page 506:* Dr. Bandura; *page 510:* Alan Carey/The Image Works; *page 518:* Alice Kandell/Photo Researchers; *page 523:* Mark Antman/The Image Works; *page 529:* George Bellrose/Stock Boston; *page 532:* James Holland/Stock Boston

CHAPTER 14

Opener: Robin Schwartz/International Stock Photo; *page 543:* Barbara Rios/Photo Researchers; *page 548:* Ed Lettau/Photo Researchers; *page 551:* Raghu Rai/Magnum; *page 553:* (top) Bettye Lane, (bottom) Owen Franken/Stock Boston; *page 556:* Watriss-Baldwin/Woodfin Camp & Associates; *page 559:* Timothy Eagan/Woodfin Camp; *page 563:* Barbara Alper/Stock Boston

CHAPTER 15

Opener: Mike Mazzaschi/Stock Boston; *page 572:* (left) Suzanne Szasz, (right) Wayne Miller/Magnum; *page 576:* David Linton; *page 580:* Peggy McMahon/Picture Group; *page 583:* Abigail Heyman/Archive Pictures; *page 584:* Suzanne Szasz; *page 586:* Elizabeth Crews/Stock Boston; *page 597:* (left) Bettye Lane, (right) David S. Strickler/Picture Cube; *page 600:* (left) David S. Strickler/Picture Cube, (right) David S. Strickler/Monkmeyer; *page 603:* (top) George Malave/Stock Boston, (bottom) David Schaefer/Picture Cube; *page 614:* Stock Boston; *page 615:* Susan Rosenberg/Photo Researchers

PART OPENERS

Part 1 Opener — Marc Chagall: "L'Hommage"/Scala/Art Resource.

Part 2 Opener — Pablo Picasso: "Mother and Child"/The Art Institute of Chicago.

Part 3 Opener — Edvard Munch: "Puberta Oslo"/Art Resource.

Part 4 Opener — W. Dendy Sadler: "The Dame's School" Joslyn Art Museum.

Part 5 Opener — Kate Greenway, Joseph Martin/Scala/Art Resource.

Part 6 Opener — Mary Cassatt - National Gallery of Art, Washington, D.C./Art Resource.

SOURCE NOTES

CHAPTER 2

Page 41, Figure 2.1 I. I. Gottesman. Genetic aspects of intelligent behavior. In N. Ellis (Ed.), *The handbook of mental deficiency: Psychological theory and research.* New York: McGraw-Hill, 1963.

Page 42, Figure 2.3 R. B. McCall. Nature-nurture and the two values of development. *Child Development,* 1981, *52,* 1–12.

Page 44, Figure 2.4 J. D. Watson. *Molecular biology of the gene* (3rd ed.). Menlo Park, Calif.: Benjamin/Cummings Publishing Co., 1976. Reprinted by permission.

Page 49, Figure 2.6 H. H. Goddard. *The Kallikak family.* New York: Macmillan, 1912. Copyright 1940, by Henry H. Goddard.

Page 56, Figure 2.8 Adapted from L. Erlenmeyer-Kimling and L. F. Jarvik. Genetics and intelligence: A review. *Science,* 1963, *142,* 1477–1479. Copyright © 1963, by the American Association for the Advancement of Science.

Page 58, Figure 2.9 R. S. Wilson. Synchronies in mental development: An epigenetic perspective. *Science,* 1978, *202,* 939–948. Copyright © 1978, by the American Associaton for the Advancement of Science.

CHAPTER 3

Page 87, Figure 3.1 Adapted from E. S. Schaefer. A circumflex model for maternal behavior. *Journal of Abnormal and Social Psychology,* 1959, *59,* 232.

Page 108, Figure 3.3 J. Kagan and S. R. Tulkin. Social class differences in child rearing during the first year. In H. R. Schaffer (Ed.), *The origins of human social relations.* London: Academic Press, 1971.

CHAPTER 4

Page 121, Figure 4.1 C. Grobstein. External human fertilization. *Scientific American,* 1979, 240, 6, 60. Copyright © 1979, by Scientific American, Inc. All rights reserved.

Page 126, Figure 4.2 B. M. Patten. *Human embryology* (3rd ed.). New York: McGraw-Hill, 1968.

Page 131, Figure 4.3 C. Grobstein. External human fertilization. *Scientific American,* 1979, *240*(6), 57–68. Copyright © 1979, by Scientific American, Inc. All rights reserved. Neurons: Dr. Dominick P. Purpura, Albert Einstein College of Medicine, 1300 Morris Park Avenue, Bronx, N.Y. 10461.

Page 146, Table 4.1 Adapted from C. L. Blair and E. M. Salerno. *The expanding family: Childbearing.* Boston: Little, Brown, 1976.

Page 148, Figure 4.6 J. G. Wilson. *Environment and birth defects.* New York: Academic Press, 1973. K. L. Moore. *The developing human: Clinically oriented embryology* (2nd ed.). Philadelphia: W. B. Saunders, 1977.

CHAPTER 5

Page 169, 170, Table 5.2 Adapted from E. M. Hetherington and R. D. Parke. *Child psychology: A contemporary viewpoint.* New York: McGraw-Hill, 1975. Used with permission.

Page 172, Figure 5.1 H. P. Roffwarg, J. N. Muzio, and W. C. Dement. Ontogenetic development of the human sleep-dream cycle. *Science,* 1966, *152,* 604–609. Copyright © 1966, by the American Association for the Advancement of Science.

Page 179, Figure 5.3 R. N. Aslin. Experiential influences and sensitive periods in perceptual development. A unified model. In R. N. Aslin, J. R. Alberts, and M. R. Petersen (Eds.), *Development of perception Psychobiological perspectives,* Vol. 2, *The visual system.* New York: Academic Press, 1981.

Page 180, Figure 5.4 R. L. Frantz. Pattern discrimination and selective attention as determinants of perceptual development from birth. In A. H. Kidd and J. L Rivoire (Eds.), *Perceptual development in children.* New York: International Universities Press, 1966.

Page 181, Figure 5.5 C. Goren. Form perception, innate form preferences, and visually mediated head-turning in human neonates. Unpublished doctoral dissertation, Committee on Human Development, University of Chicago, 1970.

Page 182, Figure 5.6 M. S. Banks and P. Salapatek. Infant visual perception. In P. Mussen (Ed.), *Handbook of child psychology,* Vol. 2. New York: Wiley, 1983. Copyright © 1983, by John Wiley & Sons.

Page 184, Figure 5.7A, W. Kessen. Sucking and looking: Two organized congenital patterns in the human newborn. In H. W. Stevenson, E. H. Hess, and H. L. Rheingold (Eds.), *Early behavior: Comparative and developmental approaches.* New York: John Wiley & Sons, 1967. Copyright © 1967, by John Wiley & Sons. *B,* D. Maurer and P. Salapatek. Developmental changes in the scanning of faces by young infants. *Child Development,* 1976, *47,* 523–527.

Page 203, Figure 5.9 L. A. Sroufe. Socioemotional development. In J. D. Osofsky (Ed.), *Handbook of infant development.* New York: John Wiley & Sons, 1979. Copyright © 1979, by John Wiley & Sons.

Page 207, Figure 5.10 A. J. Fourcin. Acoustic patterns and speech acquisition. In N. Waterson and C. Snow (Eds.), *The development of communication.* Chichester, England: John Wiley & Sons Ltd., 1978. Copyright © 1978, by John Wiley & Sons, Ltd. Reprinted by permission.

Page 209, Figure 5.11 C. Trevarthen. Descriptive analysis of infant communicative behavior. In H. R. Schaffer (Ed.), *Studies in mother-infant interaction.* London: Academic Press, 1977.

CHAPTER 6

Page 221, Figure 6.1 G. A. Harrison, J. S. Weiner, J. M. Tanner, and N. A. Barnicot. *Human biology* (1st and 2nd eds.). Oxford: Oxford University Press, 1964, 1977.

Page 222, Figure 6.2 J. M. Tanner. *Foetus into man.* London: Open Books Publishing Ltd., 1978.

Page 223, Figure 6.4 H. V. Meredith. Research between 1960 and 1970 on the standing height of young children in different parts of the world. In H. W. Reese and L. P. Lipsitt (Eds.), *Advances in child development and behavior*, Vol. 12. New York: Academic Press, 1978.

Page 230, Figure 6.8 J. M. Tanner, R. H. Whitehouse, and M. Takaishi. Standards from birth to maturity, for height, weight, height velocity and weight velocity: British children. *Archives of Disease in Childhood*, 1966, *41*, 454–471, 613–635.

Page 232, Figure 6.9 Reprinted with permission from *The CIBA collection of medical illustrations*, Vol. 4, *Endocrine system*, illustrated by Frank H. Netter, M.D., West Caldwell, N.J.: CIBA Pharmaceutical Co., 1974. Copyright © 1965, by CIBA Pharmaceutical Company, Division of CIBA-GEIGY Corp. All rights reserved.

Page 233, Figure 6.10 W. A. Marshall and J. M. Tanner. Variations in the pattern of pubertal changes in boys. *Archives of Disease in Childhood*, 1970, *45*, 13.

Page 241, Figure 6.12 T. Hoppenbrouwers, M. Calub, K. Arakawa, and J. E. Hodgman. SIDS and environmental pollutants. *American Journal of Epidemiology*, 1981, *113*, 623–635.

Page 254, Figure 6.15 Adapted from L. D. Johnston and J. G. Bachman. Highlights from student drug use in America 1975 to 1980. National Institute on Drug Abuse. Washington, D.C.: U.S. Government Printing Office, 1981.

Page 256, Figure 6.16 A. McCreary-Juhasz. A chain of sexual decision-making. *The Family Coordinator*, 1975, *24*, 45.

Page 257, Figure 6.17 Adapted from The Alan Guttmacher Institute. *Teenage pregnancy: The problem that hasn't gone away.* New York, 1981. With permission of the publisher.

Page 258, Figure 6.18 Adapted from The Alan Guttmacher Institute. *Teenage pregnancy: The problem that hasn't gone away.* New York, 1981. With permission of the publisher.

Page 259, Figure 6.19 Adapted from H. Brown, R. G. Adams, and S. G. Kellam. A longitudinal study of teenage motherhood and symptoms of distress. In R. G. Simmons (Ed.), *Research in community and mental health*, Vol. 2. Greenwich, Conn.: JAI Press, 1981.

CHAPTER 7

Page 278, Figure 7.1 Adapted from L. A. Sroufe and J. P. Wunsch. The development of laughter in the first year of life. *Child Development*, 1972, *43*, 1326–1344.

Page 279, Figure 7.2 C. E. Izard, E. A. Hembree, L. M. Dougherty, and C. C. Spizzirri. Changes in facial expressions of 2- to 19-months-old infants following acute pain. *Developmental Psychology*, 1983, *19*, 418–426.

Page 282, Figure 7.3 J. J. Campos, S. Hiatt, D. Ramsey, C. Henderson, and M. Svejda. The emergence of fear on the visual cliff. In M. Lewis and L. A. Rosenblum, *The Development of Affect*. New York: Plenum Press, 1978.

Page 283, Figure 7.4 J. T. Barnett. Development of children's fears: The relationship between three systems of fear measurement. Unpublished M. A. thesis, University of Wisconsin, 1969. In E. M. Hetherington and R. D. Parke. *Child Psychology: A Contemporary Viewpoint* (2nd ed.). New York: McGraw-Hill, 1979.

Page 285, Figure 7.5 D. F. Hay, A. Nash, and J. Pedersen. Responses of six-month-olds to the distress of their peers. *Child Development*, 1981, *52*, 1071–1075.

CHAPTER 8

Page 311, Figure 8.1 C. Golomb. *Young children's sculpture*

and drawing: A study in representation development. Cambridge, Mass.: Harvard University Press, 1974. Reprinted by permission.

Page 314, Figure 8.2 Adapted from J. Piaget and B. Inhelder. *The child's conception of space.* London: Routledge and Kegan Paul, 1956; Atlantic Highlands, N.J.: Humanities Press, 1963.

Page 319, Figure 8.5 J. Piaget and B. Inhelder. *The child's conception of space.* London: Routledge and Kegan Paul, 1956; Atlantic Highlands, N.J.: Humanities Press, 1963.

Page 328, Figure 8.10 B. Inhelder and J. Piaget. *The growth of logical thinking from childhood to adolescence.* New York: Basic Books, 1958.

Page 333, Figure 8.11 Adapted from J. Bruner. The course of cognitive growth. *American Psychologist*, 1964, *19*, 6. Copyright © 1964, by the American Psychological Association. Adapted by permission of the author.

Page 338, Figure 8.12 Adapted from R. Gelman. Conservation acquisition: A problem of learning to attend to relevant attributes. *Journal of Experimental Child Psychology*, 1969, *7*, 174.

CHAPTER 9

Page 354, Figure 9.2 E. Vurpillot. The development of scanning strategies and their relation to visual differentiation. *Journal of Experimental Child Psychology*, 1968, *6*, 632–650.

Page 355, Figure 9.3 M. A. Just and P. A. Carpenter. A theory of reading: From eye fixations to comprehension. *Psychological Review*, 1980, *87*, 329–354.

Page 356, Figure 9.4 R. S. Siegler. Information processing approaches to development. In P. H. Mussen (Ed.), *Handbook of child psychology*, Vol. 3. New York: John Wiley & Sons, 1983. Copyright © 1983, by John Wiley & Sons.

Page 364, Figure 9.5. F. N. Dempster and W. D. Rohwer, Jr. Age differences and modality effects in immediate and final free recall. *Child Development*, 1983, *54*, 30–41.

Page 374, Figure 9.7 R. S. Siegler. Information processing approaches to development. In P. H. Mussen (Ed.), *Handbook of child psychology*, Vol. 3. New York: John Wiley & Sons, 1983. Copyright © 1983, by John Wiley & Sons.

CHAPTER 10

Page 387, Table 10.2 Sample items from the Wechsler Intelligence Scale for Children and the Wechsler Adult Intelligence Scale. Copyright © 1971, by The Psychological Corporation. All rights reserved. Reproduced by permission.

Page 388, Figure 10.2. Sample page from Peabody Picture Vocabulary Test. Copyright © 1959 by L. M. Dunn.

Page 392, Table 10.3 Sample items from Bayley Scales of Infant Development (Mental Scale Record form). Copyright © 1969 by The Psychological Corporation.

Page 400, Table 10.4 Last item Taken from the Culture Fair Intelligence Test, Scale 3, Form B. Copyright © 1950, 1961, by the Institute for Personality and Ability Testing, Inc. All rights reserved. Reproduced by permission of the copyright owner.

Page 402, Table 10.5 Adapted from A. W. Gottfried. Home environment and early cognitive development: Integration, meta-analyses, and conclusions. In A. W. Gottfried (Ed.), *Home environment and early cognitive development.* San Francisco: Academic Press, 1984.

Page 406, Figure 10.6 S. W. Gray, B. K. Ramsey, and R. A. Klaus. *From 3 to 20: The early training project.* Baltimore: University Park Press, 1982.

CHAPTER 11

Page 417, Figure 11.2 H. Gleitman. *Psychology*. New York: W. W. Norton, 1981.

Page 423, Figure 11.3 Adapted from H. Gleitman. *Psychology*. New York, W. W. Norton, 1981.

Page , Table 11.1 E. H. Lenneberg. *Biological foundations of language*. New York: John Wiley & Sons, 1967. Copyright © 1967, by John Wiley & Sons.

Page 424, Figure 11.4 R. Brown, C. Cazden, and U. Bellugi-Klima. The child's grammar from I to III. In J. P. Hill (Ed.), *Minnesota symposia on child psychology,* Vol. 2. Minneapolis: University of Minnesota Press, 1969. Copyright © 1969, by the University of Minnesota.

Page 427, Table 11.2 R. Brown. *A first language: The early stages*. Cambridge, Mass.: Harvard University Press, 1973. Reprinted by permission.

Page 428, Figure 11.5 M. Sendak. *Higglety pigglety pop*. New York: Harper & Row, 1979. H. Gleitman. *Psychology*. New York: W. W. Norton, 1981.

Page 431, Table 11.3 N. L. Stein and C. G. Glenn. Children's concept of time: The development of a story schema. In W. Friedman (Ed.), *Developmental psychology of time*. New York: Academic Press, 1982.

CHAPTER 12

Page 459, Figure 12.1 M. D. S. Ainsworth, M. Blehar, E. Waters, and S. Wall. *Patterns of attachment: Observations in the strange situation and at home*. Hillsdale, N.J.: Lawrence Erlbaum Associates, 1978.

Page 462, Figure 12.3 H. F. Harlow and C. Mears. *The human model: Primate perspectives*. New York: John Wiley & Sons, 1979. Used by permission of V. H. Winston & Sons.

Page 475, Figure 12.5 B. K. Bryant. *Siblings as caretakers*. Paper presented at the annual meeting of The American Psychological Association. New York, September 1979.

CHAPTER 13

Page 495, Table 13.1 E. Mueller and T. Lucas. A developmental analysis of peer interaction among toddlers. In M. Lewis and L. A. Rosenblum (Eds.), *Friendship and peer relations*. New York: John Wiley & Sons. Copyright © 1975, by John Wiley & Sons.

Page 502, Figure 13.1 B. H. Raven and J. Z. Rubin. *Social psychology: People in groups* (2nd ed.). New York: John Wiley & Sons, 1983. Copyright © 1983, by John Wiley & Sons.

Page 507, Figure 13.2 Adapted from R. D. Parke. On prediction of child abuse: Theoretical considerations. In R. Starr (Ed.), *Prediction of abuse*. Philadelphia: Ballinger, 1982.

Page 511, Figure 13.3 D. C. Dunphy. The social structure of urban adolescent peer groups. *Sociometry,* 1963, *26,* 236.

Page 516, Figure 13.5 P. R. Costanzo and M. E. Shaw. Conformity as a function of age level. *Child Development,* 1966, *37,* 967–975.

Page 517, Table 13.2 J. M. Gottman and J. T. Parkhurst. From an early version of A developmental theory of friendship and acquaintanceship processes. In W. A. Collins (Ed.) Development of cognition, affect, and social relations. *The Minnesota Symposia on Child Psychology,* Vol. 13. Hillsdale, N.J.: Lawrence Erlbaum Associates, 1980.

Page 521, Figure 13.6 Adapted from The Alan Guttmacher Institute. *Teenage pregnancy: The problem that hasn't gone away*. New York, 1981. With permission of the publisher.

Page 528, Figure 13.7 M. Hollos. Logical operations and role-taking abilities in two cultures: Norway and Hungary. *Child Development,* 1975, *46,* 645.

Page 535, Figure 13.8 C. Barenboim. The development of person perception in childhood and adolescence: From behavioral comparisons to psychological constructs to psychological comparisons. *Child Development,* 1981, *52,* 129–144.

CHAPTER 14

Pages 549, Table 14.2 L. Kohlberg. Stage and sequence: The cognitive-developmental approach to socialization. In D. A. Goslin (Ed.), *Handbook of socialization theory and research*. Boston: Houghton Mifflin, 1969.

Page 551, Figure 14.2 A. Colby, L. Kohlberg, J. Gibbs, and M. Lieberman. A longitudinal study of moral judgment. *Monographs of the Society for Research in Child Development,* 1983, *48* (1, Serial No. 200).

CHAPTER 15

Page 575, Figure 15.1 J. Kagan. Impulsive and reflective children: Significance of conceptual tempo. In J. D. Krumboltz (Ed.), *Learning and the educational process*. Chicago: Rand-McNally, 1965.

Page 576, Figure 15.2 Reprinted from *La bambola di Guilietta* (Dinah's doll) (Hebrew translation) with permission from Editrice Piccoli S.p.A., Milan, Italy. T. Zelniker and W. E. Jeffrey. Reflective and impulsive children. *Monographs of the Society for Research in Child Development,* 1976, *41,* (5, Whole No. 168).

Pages 578, Figure 15.4 J. W. Getzles and P. W. Jackson. *Creativity and intelligence*. New York: John Wiley & Sons, 1962. Copyright © 1962, by John Wiley & Sons.

Page 588, Figure 15.5 G. S. Lesser, G. Fifer, and Clark, D. H. Mental abilities of children from different social-class and cultural groups. *Monographs of the Society for Research in Child Development,* 1965, *30* (4, Serial No. 102).

Page 610, Figure 15.7 R. G. Simmons, E. F. Van Cleave, D. A. Blyth, and D. M. Bush. Entry into early adolescence: The impact of school structure, puberty, and early dating on self-esteem. *American Sociological Review,* 1979, *44,* 956.

Page 613, Figure 15.8 H. Gardner. *Developmental psychology: An introduction* (2nd ed.). Boston: Little, Brown, 1982. Pictures drawn for the study E. Koff, J. Rierdan, and E. Silverstone. Changes in the representaton of body image as a function of menarcheal status. *Developmental Psychology,* 1978, *14,* 635–642. Used by permission of E. Koff.

AUTHOR INDEX

SUBJECT INDEX

A, not B, phenomenon, 303, 330
Abilities:
  of ethnic groups, 588
  intellectual, see Intelligence; Intelligence quotients (IQs)
  verbal vs. visual-spatial, 590–591
Abstraction, 384
Abuse of children, 252–253
Academic achievement, 581–582
  of ethnic groups, 588–589
  and IQ test scores, 390, 391, 398
  and self-esteem, 608
  see also Schools
Accidents involving children, 250–251
Accommodation, 179, 301
Achievement, academic, see Academic achievement
Achievement motivation, 588–589, 592
Achievement testing, 393. See also Intelligence quotient (IQ) tests
Achondroplasia, 141
Acne in adolescence, 614
Acquired adaptations, 302
Activity levels, sexual differences in, 593
Adaptation phase of pregnancy, 135
Adaptations in Piagetian theory, 301, 302
Adaptive behavior of infants, 392–393
Adipocyte hypothesis, 224
Adipocytes, 224
Adjectives in language development, 429
Adolescence, 230–235
  alcohol in, 253–254
  cliques in, 511
  contraceptives in, 256–258
  crowds in, 511–512
  dating in, 520–523
  development in:
    Erikson on, 14–16
    Freud on, 14, 15
    moral, 562–563
    personality, 28
    Piaget on, 308, 326–329
  drugs in, 254
  early, 608–610
  friendships in, 520
  health problems and hazards of, 253–259
  identity in, 608–617
    sexual, 522
  identity crises in, 471–472, 616–617
  identity diffusion in, 617
  later, 608
  moratorium state in, 617
  parental divorce during, 477–479

parental limits in, testing, 471
parental midolescence crisis in, 471–472
parent-child relationships in, redefining, 469–472
peer groups in, 511–512, 516
physical appearance, concerns about 254–256, 614–615
physical changes in, 611–616. See also Puberty
pregnancy in, 256–259
pressures of, 7, 609–610
as scientific inquiry subject, 7
self-concept in, 607
self-esteem in, 610
sexual activity in, 256–259, 521–524
sexual differences in, problems of, 470–471
sexually transmitted diseases in, 259
social norms in, 532
social understanding and social skill connections in, 534
transitions in, 608–609
Adolescent Adoption Study, 51, 52
Adolescent asynchronies, 610–611
Adopted children, observation studies of, 50–53
Adoptions, interracial, 51–52
Adulthood in Piagetian theory, 308, 326–329
Adults, friendly, effects on children of, 490–493
AERs, see Auditory evoked responses
Afterbirth, 149
Age:
  gestational, infants small for, 238
  in Piagetian theory, 317–318
  at pregnancy, 140–141
  at puberty, 234–235
Aggression:
  Bandura study of, 75, 506
  determinants of, 106, 506–509, 595
  development of, 505–506
  hostile and instrumental, 505
  as peer interaction, 505–509
  sexual differences in, 591, 597
  socialization of, 509
Alcohol:
  in adolescence, 253–254
  during pregnancy, 144–145
  see also Drugs
Altitude in growth, 237
Altruism (prosocial behavior) and emotions, 290–293
Alveoli, 131

Ambivalent children, 459, 463
Amniocentesis, 64, 147
Amnion, 125
Amphetamines for hyperactivity, 245
Anaclitic identification, 602
Analgesics in childbirth, 151, 154, 155
Anal stage of development, 12, 14, 15
Androgyny, 593–594
Androsperm, 45–46
Anesthesia, 150–151, 154, 155
Anger, emotion of, 278–280
Animism in Piagetian theory, 315
Anorexia nervosa, 255–256
Anticipation and preparation phase of pregnancy, 135
Antiseptic procedures, 150
Anxiety, stranger (fear of strangers), 281
Apgar test, 166
Apnea, 241
Appearance, see Physical appearance
Artificial insemination, 123–124
Artificialism in Piagetian theory, 315–316
Asepsis, 150
Assimilation in Piagetian theory, 301
Associative intelligence, 399, 400
Associative play, 496
Astigmatism, 179
Asynchronies:
  adolescent, 610–611
  in growth, 220
Attachment of infants to mothers, 19, 198–200, 456–463
  and employment of mothers, 480
  vs. fathers, 465–467
Attention:
  in information processing, 357–360
  theory of, 352, 353
Auditory evoked responses, 186–187
Authoritarian parents, 87
Authoritative parents, 87, 88
Autism in children, 248–250
Automatization in cognitive development, 376
Autonomous (internal) morality, 544–545
Autonomy, development of, 463–465
Autosomal chromosomes, 46–47, 59–60
Autosomal dominant inheritance, 46
Autosomal recessive inheritance, 46
Autostimulation theory, 172
Avoidant children, 459, 463, 486
Axons, 227–228

Babbling by infants, 206, 417–418

117